Longmans' Economics Series

GENERAL EDITOR
ERNEST L. BOGART
PROFESSOR OF ECONOMICS IN THE
UNIVERSITY OF ILLINOIS

PUBLIC FINANCE. *Edited and Annotated by* ELMER D. FAGAN, *Leland Stanford University; and* C. WARD MACY, *Coe College.*

ECONOMIC HISTORY OF THE AMERICAN PEOPLE. *By* ERNEST L. BOGART.

WORKBOOKS IN ECONOMIC HISTORY OF THE AMERICAN PEOPLE [*Forms A and B*]. *By* ERNEST L. BOGART *and* ROBERT B. BROWNE, *University of Illinois.*

READINGS IN THE ECONOMIC HISTORY OF THE UNITED STATES. *By* ERNEST L. BOGART *and* CHARLES M. THOMPSON, *University of Illinois.*

MODERN INDUSTRY. *By* ERNEST L. BOGART *and* CHARLES E. LANDON, *Duke University.*

BANKING. *By* FREDERICK A. BRADFORD, *Lehigh University.*

WORKBOOK IN BANKING. *By* FREDERICK A. BRADFORD.

MONEY. *By* FREDERICK A. BRADFORD.

MONEY AND BANKING [*in one volume*]. *By* FREDERICK A. BRADFORD.

TAXATION IN THE MODERN STATE. *By* ALZADA COMSTOCK, *Mount Holyoke College.*

INTERPRETIVE ACCOUNTING. *By* F. E. FOLTS, *Harvard University; and* A. B. STILLMAN, *University of Oregon.*

AMERICAN MONETARY AND BANKING POLICIES. *By* GEORGE W. DOWRIE, *Leland Stanford University.*

INDEX NUMBERS ELUCIDATED. *By* WILLFORD I. KING, *New York University.*

OCEAN TRANSPORTATION. *By* ABRAHAM BERGLUND, *University of Virginia.*

IN PREPARATION

MONEY AND BANKING. *By* W. E. SPAHR, *New York University.*

PUBLIC FINANCE

PUBLIC FINANCE

SELECTED READINGS

EDITED AND ANNOTATED BY

ELMER D. FAGAN, Ph.D.

PROFESSOR OF ECONOMICS, STANFORD UNIVERSITY

and

C. WARD MACY, Ph.D.

PROFESSOR OF ECONOMICS, COE COLLEGE

LONGMANS, GREEN AND CO.

LONDON · NEW YORK · TORONTO

1934

LONGMANS, GREEN AND CO.
114 FIFTH AVENUE, NEW YORK
221 EAST 20TH STREET, CHICAGO
88 TREMONT STREET, BOSTON

LONGMANS, GREEN AND CO. Ltd.
39 PATERNOSTER ROW, LONDON, E C 4
6 OLD COURT HOUSE STREET, CALCUTTA
53 NICOL ROAD, BOMBAY
36A MOUNT ROAD, MADRAS

LONGMANS, GREEN AND CO.
480 UNIVERSITY AVENUE, TORONTO

FAGAN & MACY
PUBLIC FINANCE

FIRST EDITION

34 - 39869

PREFACE

MUCH of the best thought which has been given to the problems of public finance has not been easily available to students of this subject. Therefore, it is the purpose of this volume to bring together some results of the mature reflection of many able scholars in this field. This material, together with editorial comments designed to coördinate the selections, offers more extensive and penetrating discussions of important fiscal problems than can be presented in a single general textbook.

A logical sequence has been followed in the arrangement of the subject matter. This feature of the book, together with the editors' efforts to connect this subject matter into a united whole, should insure continuity of thought and make the volume suitable either as a textbook or as a book of collateral readings.

In the selection of material the editors have been guided primarily by the desire to reproduce studies in which emphasis has been placed upon fundamental economic principles in their relation to the problems of public finance. Special attention has been given to the socio-political problems. For example, in the treatment of the inheritance tax, stress has been laid upon its theoretical and social aspects rather than upon description of its operation at a given time and place. This does not mean that descriptive data have been entirely ignored; it does mean, however, that such data, when presented, have been used only for the purpose of giving a proper setting for analytical studies. In other words, the readings have been selected, first of all, for the purpose of stimulating the reader to think in terms of basic economic principles; and, secondly, for the purpose of acquainting him with some outstanding examples of excellent reasoning on fiscal problems.

These being the bases of selection, it is evident that even though some of the factual material will not be current when this book comes off the press, the value of such material will not be diminished for the purpose for which it has been included. Then, too, the bibliographical notes at the end of each chapter should enable the reader to find readily such current data as he might desire.

Unequal emphasis has purposely been given to the different topics treated. Subjects which, in the opinion of the editors, have not received sufficient attention in text books on public finance have been given special prominence in this volume. A case in point is that of the relation between public expenditures and the business cycle.

It was difficult to make a discriminating selection from the abundance of excellent material on fiscal subjects. The exclusion of certain studies was made only after much deliberation. To these and to many other valuable works reference has been made in bibliographical notes.

The editors wish to express their appreciation of the generous coöperation of those authors and publishers who have permitted reproduction of the material in this volume.

ELMER D. FAGAN
C. WARD MACY

CONTENTS

PART II — PUBLIC REVENUES

CONTENTS

PART IV — FINANCIAL ADMINISTRATION

'the dismal science,' and the trail of statistics is over them all.

And yet finance is not lacking in practical or theoretical interest. It is preeminently one of the things that "come home to men's business and bosoms." Consider first the bearing of finance upon the income of the individual citizen. Mr. Robert Luce in an essay[4] upon this subject says: "It can be proved that the average American citizen works one month out of the year for the sake of being governed. In other words, taxation takes one twelfth of his earnings. This average American is the head of a family of five persons, earning a thousand dollars a year. He pays thirty of this into the national treasury, thirty into the state, county, city, or town treasury, and at a moderate estimate twenty-three dollars more for the indirect cost of collection. The total, equal to one month's earnings, does not affect the question of the equitable distribution of the burden, but emphatically shows the importance of the question." We are not here concerned with the exactness of this estimate nor with the data on which it is based. But granting it to be approximately true, it emphasizes the significance of an understanding of public finance for the taxpayer.

M. Leroy-Beaulieu has undertaken an estimate of the part of the income of the nations which is absorbed by taxation in certain countries of Europe. He finds that in Belgium taxes take from six to six and a half per cent. of the public income; in England, seven and three quarters per cent.; in France, eleven per cent.; and in Italy, fifteen or sixteen per cent.[5] * Let the importance of financial legislation and administration be thus brought home more directly to the taxpayer, and the subject will be invested with far greater importance than it now obtains.

THEORETICAL BEARINGS OF PUBLIC FINANCE

NOT alone for the man of affairs does the study of finance have a controlling interest. The historian and the sociologist can ill afford to dispense with its study. This is very commonly recognized in the domain of historical investigation. A fairly definite insight into the life of any period must include some knowledge of the social distinctions in which the financial system was rooted, and which in turn it helped to perpetuate.

The student of constitutional liberty does not need to be

---

* Eds. note: For recent data on the ratio of taxes to national income in various countries, see Chap. II, Tables G, H below.

[4] *Public Opinion*, 1892, p. 51.

[5] *Science des Finances*, I., p. 133.

told of the dominant rôle played by financial issues in modern politics. These issues have been not only the unfailing source of party strife; they have been as well the formative influences in constitutional growth.

But aside from the purely historical import of the subject, finance has for the acute observer of shifting social currents an interest not inferior to that excited by any other social movement. The lines of social cleavage run today substantially parallel with lines of wealth. Those, moreover, who regard the present economic constitution of society as evil are only too apt to look upon the tax power as the readiest implement of reform. The inequalities of the law of competition they would correct by the equity of expropriation. This employment of the tax power may possibly be justified up to a certain limit. The governmental assumption of certain natural monopolies may be warranted upon grounds of public utility.[6] But thoroughgoing Socialism or Collectivism would probably deny that any limit upon the tax power is justifiable which stops short of the proximate realization of their distributive ideal. It is right here that the sociological side of finance becomes of prime importance. The present constitution of private property has been challenged. Whether this institution can or ought to be changed; if so, to what degree; whether the distribution of the social dividend can be effected upon another basis than the present one; — these are the points of contact between Collectivism and the industrial constitution of modern society. In short, the battle-field where Socialism will not improbably assail the conservative forces of society lies within the domain of finance. Thus its study acquires a larger scope and affords a more extended outlook. It remains no longer the mere technique of tax collection and expenditure, but joins the theoretical moral and political sciences, and extends its speculation beyond the world of the Present into the society of the Future.

RELATION TO COGNATE DISCIPLINES

THERE are two roads by which the study of finance may be approached — through the province of Political Economy or through that of Law.[7] The first is the English method; the latter is the method of the typical German publicist. If the former be adopted, finance will be classed as a branch of applied Economics. If the latter alternative be chosen finance will be

---

[6] Cf. Sidgwick, *Principles of Political Economy*, p. 408; also Hadley, *Economics*, p. 397 *sq.*

[7] Cf. Bastable, *Public Finance*, 2nd Ed., p. 7.

viewed as a department of Administration. This divergence in classification illustrates the different historical origin and development of the science in the two countries. Self-government in England involved the necessity of a popularly evolved and approved system of taxation. Hence the necessity of an economic justification of legislation which affected the taxpayer's purse. In Germany, on the contrary, the power of the Crown has imposed from above a financial régime upon the subject; and in consequence the perfecting of administrative machinery was the task of the bureaucracy. Adam Smith typifies the English view, as Stein represents the German conception of the subject. Whichever classification be adopted for the sake of convenience in the logical distribution of the content of knowledge, there can be no essential difference of opinion as to the relation of cognate sciences to the science of Finance. To adapt the abstract formulæ of theory to given conditions the fullest historical knowledge of the concrete conditions is necessary. Statistical data when accessible are as indispensable here as elsewhere in the domain of practical politics. Economics must largely furnish the premises wherever the effect of financial action upon material welfare is involved; and Ethics must not infrequently constitute the court of final appeal where issues of justice and social duty arise.

*   *   *

IN the pages which follow, the principal divisions of public finance will be treated in the following order: Public Expenditures, Public Revenues, Public Credit, and Financial Administration.

QUESTIONS AND PROBLEMS FOR DISCUSSION

1. Of what value is a thorough understanding of the theories and principles of public finance to an office holder? a business man? a public school official? a college student?
2. Is it possible to improve the theory of public finance by a study of actual experiences in financing a government?
3. In 1899, Professor Daniels wrote: "Our chief need . . . is not to equip the financial experts, but to instruct public opinion." To what extent is this true today?
4. Ruskin called government "an apparatus for collecting and spending money." Evaluate this view in light of current activities of governments throughout the world.
5. How do you account for the fact that public finance has a greater attraction for the general public today than it did twenty-five years ago?
6. Collection and expenditure of public revenue are coercive in character. What problems arise because of this fact?

7. How may taxation be used as an agency for effecting a more equal distribution of wealth? Do you believe that it should be so used? Are taxes being levied for this purpose today by the national government? by your own state, county, and city government?

8. Professor Daniels writes that "the battle-field where Socialism will not improbably assail the conservative forces of society lies within the domain of finance." Explain and evaluate.

SUGGESTIONS FOR RESEARCH

1. The functions of the state and the scope of public finance. (See bibliographical note for references.)

2. A comparison and an analysis of the views of Leroy-Beaulieu and Adolph Wagner on the nature and scope of public finance.

3. The relation of public finance to economics, history, political science, and ethics.

4. The character and significance of the differences between public economy and private economy.

BIBLIOGRAPHICAL NOTE

Practically all general works in the field of public finance contain one or more chapters on its nature and scope. A brief but excellent treatment of nature and scope is C. F. Bastable, *Public Finance,* (London, 1917), Introduction, Chap. I. Paul Leroy-Beaulieu in his *Traité de la Science des Finances,* (Paris, 1883), pp. 1-10, is distinctive in that he, unlike Bastable and nearly all other writers on public finance, argues that public expenditure does not fall within the scope of public finance. A profound exposition of the nature of public finance and of its relation to political economy and political science is Adolph Wagner, *Finanzwissenschaft,* (Leipzig, 1883), Vol. I, Introduction, pp. 1-27.

Scholarly discussions of the nature, evolution, and functions of the state may be found in: Adolph Wagner, "Staat in Nationalökonomischer Hinsicht," *Handwörterbuch der Staatswissenschaft,* Siebenter Band, Dritte Auflage, (Jena, 1911), pp. 727-739; Gustav Cohn, *The Science of Finance,* (Chicago, 1895), Bk. I, Chap. I, (Translated by T. B. Veblen); Woodrow Wilson, *The State,* (New York, 1918), Chaps. I-IV; W. W. Willoughby, *The Nature of the State,* (New York, 1896); and S. F. Weston, *Principles of Justice in Taxation,* (New York, 1903), Chaps. I and II.

The differences between public and private economy are discussed in Spahr and others, *Economic Principles and Problems,* (New York, 1932), Chap. XXXI; and in Eheberg, K. T., *Finanzwissenschaft,* (Leipzig, 1921), pp. 3-6.

L. T. Hobhouse in his *Social Evolution and Political Theory,* (New York, 1911), Chaps. VI-IX, discusses the growth of the state and the relationship between the individual and the state. This latter subject is also dealt with in a comprehensive and able manner in W. E. Hocking, *Man and the State,* (New Haven, 1926).

An excellent treatise in political theory is Bernard Bosanquet, *The Philosophical Theory of the State*, (London, 1920). Chap. VIII of this study, "Nature of the End of the State and Consequent Limit of State Action," is of special value to the student of public finance. Other discussions of the basis and ends of political institutions may be found in W. W. Willoughby, *The Ethical Basis of Political Authority*, (New York, 1930), Chaps. XIV-XVI; and L. T. Hobhouse, *The Elements of Social Justice*, (London, 1922), Chap. I.

PUBLIC FINANCE

PART I—PUBLIC EXPENDITURES

CHAPTER II

PUBLIC EXPENDITURES: FACTS AND INTERPRETATIONS

1. THE INCREASE IN PUBLIC EXPENDITURES AND ITS SIGNIFICANCE *

OF ALL the phases of public expenditures, their continuous increase has, whether rightly or wrongly, attracted most attention. Many people see in this increase a cause for great alarm; others, a perfectly natural phenomenon.

The fact of a continuous increase of public expenditures cannot be denied. It is proved by such figures as those in Tables [A] and [B]. The figures show, furthermore, that public expenditures increase more rapidly than population, in other words, that the *per capita* expenditures of government tend to increase. In 1800, the Federal government of the United States was spending, exclusive of debt redemption and post office expenditures, $2 per capita. In 1930, the corresponding figure was $32, or sixteen times as much. The per capita expenditures of the national government of Great Britain and France increased during the same period from 16 shillings and 28 francs respectively to 21 pounds and 1,022 francs.

Wars tend to obscure this tendency of public expenditures to increase continually, for hostilities swell the total expenditures abnormally and the return of peace causes a heavy shrinkage through the rapid drop in direct war expenditures and the gradual reduction in interest charges as the war debt is paid off. The increase of public expenditures leads to increased taxation, and this, in turn, to complaints from taxpayers. Taxpayers are always complaining and always have complained, in ancient as well as in modern times, that governments are spending too much. But, as a matter of fact, the continuous increase in per capita expenditures does not

* Adapted from Walter E. Spahr and others, *Economic Principles and Problems*, (Ray Long and Richard R. Smith, Inc., New York, 1932), Vol. II, Chap. XXXII, pp. 434-460. This chapter was written by Professor Paul Studenski.

necessarily mean correspondingly increased burdens on the taxpayers, because (1) some of the increases in expenditures are only seeming and not real, as will be explained below, (2) public expenditures confer benefits as well as impose burdens, and the benefits may be greater than costs, (3) the increase in the wealth and income of the people, which takes place contemporaneously, offsets in part (and may sometimes offset completely) the increase in public expenditures. Nor does it prove that there is a tendency toward socialism, because the increase in public activity has been accompanied by the expansion of private enterprise.

TABLE [A]

ORDINARY REVENUE OF THE NATIONAL GOVERNMENT OF FRANCE, 1242–1930 [a]

(In millions of francs)

1242	3.7
1364	8.1
1491	44.8
1560	84.0
1683	229.0
1789	475.0
1913	5,171.9
1930	50,398.2

[a] Compiled from F. Nitti's *Principes de Science des Finances* (Marcel Giard, Paris, 1928), Vol. I, pp. 56-57 ; and from the *Memorandum on Public Finance, 1926–1928,* League of Nations Publications, Economic and Financial Section (Geneva, 1929), and the *Statesman's Yearbook* (Macmillan and Co., Ltd., London, 1931). A part of the increase in the 1930 figure over the 1913 one was undoubtedly due to the fact that the franc was worth only 3.92 cents in 1930 as against 19.3 cents in 1913.

DISTINCTION BETWEEN REAL AND SEEMING INCREASES

THE figures of increased governmental expenditures must be taken with certain reservations. If they show a ten-fold increase in the per capita expenditures over a period of a hundred years, this does not mean that the real per capita expenditures of government have increased ten-fold during that period. Certain increases of public expenditures are only nominal. These are increases caused by (a) the substitution of taxation and of payment for service rendered to the government for the older system of requiring specified direct services and goods, (b) more complete accounting and budgeting of expenditures, and (c) depreciation in the value of money.

Furthermore, the figures of expenditures which are compared may not be equally inclusive. The monetary expenditures of governments in feudal and early modern times, and even in the

TABLE [B]

EXPENDITURES OF PRINCIPAL NATIONAL GOVERNMENTS FROM 1800 TO 1930, IN MILLIONS OF DOLLARS

Year	United States (dollars) [a]	Great Britain (pounds) [b]	France (francs) [c]	Germany (marks) [d]	Russia (rubles) [e]	Italy (lira) [f]	Japan (yen) [g]	Canada (dollars) [h]	Belgium (francs; belga) [i]	Sweden (kroner) [j]	Switzerland (francs) [k]
1800	11	60	835		88						
1815	33	112	999		391						
1820	18	55	907		500						
1830	15	49	1,095		428						
1840	24	49	1,364		188				165*		5
1850	40	51	1,473		287				119		9
1860	63	70	2,084		438				159	36	10
1865	1,298	66	2,135	77*	428	1,066			189	45	18
1870	310	69	3,173	362	482	1,022	20	14	217	72	19
1875	275	74	2,936	541	605	1,494	66	24	292	75	22
1880	268	84	3,650	1,111	793	1,468	60	25	383	93	38
1890	318	86	3,288	2,197	1,056	1,880	80	36	418	137	60
1900	521	134	3,747	3,696	1,889	1,743	254	43	574	270	101
1913–14	735	197	5,067*		2,925	3,129	574	127	806		
1918	13,792	2,666	54,537	35,935	47,676*	26,656	735	178	9,350**	1,718*	171
1930	3,946	829	50,398[l]	11,317	11,665[l]	19,746[l]	1,736	358	11,513[l]	811	426

* 1913 figure.
** 1920 figure.

a Annual Report of the Secretary of the Treasury of the United States (1930).
b J. F. Rees, A Short Fiscal and Financial History of England 1815-1918 (Methuen and Co., London, 1921), and Statesman's Yearbook (1931).
c Ch. Nicholas, Les Budgets de la France depuis le Commencement du XIXe siècle (Paris, 1882); M. M. Block, Statistique de la France (Guillaumin et Co. Paris, 1875), 2d ed., Vol. I; Annuaire Statistique de la France (1929), Resumé Retrospective, pp. 171 and 140; Statesman's Yearbook (1931).
* 1913 figure.
d Statesman's Yearbook (1877, 1893, 1903, 1916, 1920, and 1931). * Thaler.
e I. J. Bliock, Finansy Rossii XIX-go Stoletia (St. Petersburgh, 1902), Vol. I, p. 153; Ministerstvo Finansov, 1802-1902 (St. Petersburgh, 1902), 2 vols.; Statesman's Yearbook (1916, 1919, and 1931). * Paper rubles.
f Statesman's Yearbook (1883, 1893, 1903, 1916, 1920, and 1931).
g Financial Annual of Japan, No. 2 (Tokyo, 1902); Statesman's Yearbook (1916, 1920, and 1931).
h The Canada Yearbook (1931).
i Annuaire Statistique de la Belgique (1871, 1891, and 1926); Statesman's Yearbook (1931). * Large expenditures in 1840 for capital outlays.
j Statesman's Yearbook (1866-1901); Statistisk Arsbok (1930-1931), pp. 293 and 316.
k Statistisches Jahrbuch der Schweiz (1930), p. 339.
l This figure is expressed in terms of a devaluated coin.

new countries until recently, constituted but a part of the
real expenditures. Dues were largely paid by the citizens in
services or in kind and not in money, and services likewise
were rendered by the government to the citizens, directly and
without expenditure of money. Thus, the people were required to spend a certain number of days each year in building
roads under the supervision of government officials and they
were not paid by the government for their work; and vassals
were required to maintain armed men and to furnish them in
times of need. A certain proportion of the increase of expenditures in modern times represents, therefore, merely a change
in the form of expenditures, and not a real increase.

Government officials in former times were commonly not
paid salaries but instead were allowed to retain the fees which
they collected. Their fees did not pass through the treasury
and their compensation did not appear as a governmental
expenditure. The figures of expenditures were, therefore, incomplete; and the real difference compared with present
expenditures consequently is smaller than the figures indicate
on their face.

Finally, money does not retain the same value over a period
of years.* Its purchasing power has tended over long periods
of time to decrease because of a more plentiful supply of money
and credit. It has been estimated, for example, that in the time
of Charlemagne a franc was nine times as valuable as in the
nineteenth century. A dollar in the United States in 1800,
when money was scarce and wealth and incomes were measured in small figures, was much more valuable than at present.
On the other hand, in the course of short periods, the opposite
situation frequently obtains and value of money rises for a
time as a result of inflation or other influences. In comparing
public expenditures at different times, therefore, it is necessary
to take into account the different values of money at those
times and adjust the figures to a common base. If this is done,
it may be found that the real increase in expenditures is not

---

* Eds. note: The significance of changes in the value of money upon public
expenditures is illustrated by the following data from *Recent Social Trends in
the United States*, (McGraw-Hill Co., Inc., New York, 1933), Vol. II, p. 1324.

COMBINED GOVERNMENTAL EXPENDITURES, 1915–1929

Government	1929 dollars	Per cent increases 1915 dollars
Federal	289	125
States	299	135
Cities over 30,000	216	85
Other local	205	80
All governments	239	100
All governments (per capita expenditures)	179	65

TABLE [C]

GOVERNMENTAL EXPENDITURES IN CURRENT AND IN 1913 DOLLARS[a]

(Inclusive of current operating expenses, capital outlays, interest and redemption of debt.)

(Total in millions of dollars)

	Federal (Exclusive of post office)		State		Local		Total	
	In current dollars	In 1913 dollars	In current dollars	In 1913 dollars	In current dollars	In 1913 dollars	In current dollars	In 1913 dollars
1890	$291	$361	$77	$96	$487	$605	$855	$1,062
1913	692	692	383	383	1,844	1,844	2,919	2,919
1923	3,885	2,696	1,242	862	5,136	3,564	10,263	7,122
1928	3,970	2,836	1,826	1,304	6,813	4,866	12,609	9,006

Per Capita Expenditures

	Federal (Exclusive of post office)		State		Local		Total	
	In current dollars	In 1913 dollars	In current dollars	In 1913 dollars	In current dollars	In 1913 dollars	In current dollars	In 1913 dollars
1890	$4.61	$5.73	$1.22	$1.52	$7.73	$9.59	$13.56	$16.84
1913	7.17	7.17	3.97	3.97	19.10	19.10	30.24	30.24
1923	34.78	24.13	11.12	7.72	45.98	31.91	91.88	63.76
1928	33.12	23.66	15.24	10.88	56.84	40.60	105.20	75.14

[a] Compiled from Cost of Government, 1928–1929, National Industrial Conference Board (New York, 1930), p. 11.

so great as the nominal increase; or, if comparison is made over a shorter period, the opposite may be true and the real increase may be even greater than the nominal.

We now have fairly reliable index numbers of prices for the past forty or more years and can allow for changes in the purchasing power of money. The present figures of public expenditures compared with even pre-war figures are highly inflated. When the figures are translated into dollars of 1913 purchasing power they shrink considerably and show a much smaller increase than the uncorrected figures. Table [C] shows the difference between the two sets of figures.

BENEFITS AND BURDENS OF PUBLIC EXPENDITURES

AFTER allowing for changes in the price level, it still is true that government expenditures per capita have increased. However, this increase has been accompanied by an increase in the range and quality of public services. As we have already pointed out, public expenditures not only impose burdens; they also confer benefits, and the benefits must be set off against costs. At least from the point of view of the community as a whole, public expenditures are truly burdensome only when the burdens imposed are disproportionate to the social advantage they produce. An increase in public expenditures is, therefore, not necessarily an evil. On the contrary, it is more likely to be a benefit. Whether it is the one or the other depends upon what it secures for the community by comparison with what the same amount would have been used for if left to be spent in private hands. It is true that an increase in expenditures financed by taxation of a particular group may not produce corresponding benefits for that group, but judged by the benefits to the whole community the increase may be advantageous.

Under feudalism and absolutism, governments were spending money mostly for wars and the maintenance of expensive courts. Wars were commonly waged by sovereigns and lords to increase their possessions, settle their private grievances, and, in general, for personal or dynastic reasons. The rank and file of taxpayers had ample reason to object to such expenditures which imposed heavy burdens upon them without conferring commensurate benefits. Capitalism and democracy have tended to give a new direction to public expenditures. They have done away with the expenditures for elaborate courts. While they have retained and further enlarged expenditures for wars and other largely destructive purposes and have led to new forms of wasteful expenditures, they have also resulted in enormous expenditures for constructive social and economic purposes. The increase in per capita expenditures in the modern State reflects the increased activity of government for every member of society in these two directions — the socially destructive one and the socially constructive one. Taxpayers still have reason to complain of certain kinds of increases of public expenditures, but no ground to condemn all increases and no reason to forget that they are the beneficiaries of some of the increases and, in general, beneficiaries of governmental activity as a whole far beyond the amount of their taxes.

The complaints of taxpayers are traceable to the fact that in the public economy, unlike the private one, the benefits and the costs of expenditures are not immediately related in the mind of the taxpayer. When taxpayers demand new services, they think only of the benefits which they will receive as members of the community or as private individuals. On the other hand, when they have to pay taxes, they think only of the costs which public expenditures impose upon them. Just as in one case they tend to exaggerate the advantages to be derived from the expenditures they wish to see made, so in the other case they tend to exaggerate the wastefulness and unproductiveness of the expenditures for which they are taxed.

PUBLIC EXPENDITURES IN RELATION TO WEALTH AND INCOME

THE burdensomeness of taxation can not be judged by any simple formula. It is necessary to take into account the amount of taxes; the community's income (which reflects also its wealth); the share which taxes directly or indirectly take of the people's income; the proportion of taxes put back into the pockets of the taxpayers as interest on bonds and like payments; the utility of the public services produced from taxes in relation to the utility of private expenditures; the distribution of taxes in relation to the distribution of incomes; as well as other factors. Attempts have been made in recent years to measure tax burdens by the ratio of taxes to the national income which may be conceived of as the sum total of the citizen's private incomes. This method of measuring tax burdens is superior to the older methods of measuring them by aggregate or per capita amounts, but it is still a very imperfect method because it fails to take into account the other factors mentioned.

It is difficult to devise a measure of tax burdens which will take account of all the elements involved, inasmuch as some of them are qualitative in character. It is still more difficult to measure changes in the tax burdens, because the elements immediately involved change in the course of time and new elements, such as changes in the price level, enter into the picture. Nevertheless, since taxes are paid out of income and since income is partly a function of wealth, the ratio between taxes and incomes and wealth, or, in short, between taxes and income, is illuminating if the limitations of this method of measuring tax burdens are kept in mind.

While taxes have increased as public expenditures have mounted, wealth and incomes have increased as well; perhaps more rapidly if the comparison is carried back to the days of absolutism. Although pertinent statistical data are missing, it seems probable that the costs of government, whether in the form of taxes or otherwise, were growing progressively heavier towards the end of feudalism and absolutism since the incomes of the people were growing relatively slowly at that time. The advent of capitalism may have actually lightened these burdens. On the one hand, it greatly increased the incomes of the people. On the other hand it relieved them of the feudal dues which were burdensome not only in themselves but also in their restrictive effects on economic progress, while the laissez-faire philosophy tended to check the growth of governmental activity and expenditures. During certain periods in the nineteenth and present centuries, in many countries and localities, incomes have increased more rapidly than taxes because of rapid economic expansion with the result that the ratio of taxes to incomes and the true tax burdens in those times and places have grown lighter. During other periods and in other places, the opposite situation has prevailed as a result of a particularly rapid expansion of governmental functions. But taking the entire period which has elapsed since the time that capitalism had gotten fairly under way, it is probably true that public expenditures and taxes have increased somewhat more rapidly than national income.

Thus in Great Britain the ratio of the expenditures of the national government to the national income seems to have increased from 14.69 per cent in 1818 to 19.45 per cent in 1923, and the ratio of taxes to the national income during the same period from 14.07 per cent to 18.89 per cent. For some years after the Napoleonic War the tax burden continued to be very heavy. "Relief came in the Victorian era," says the Colwyn Committee, "through the unprecedented advance in industry and transportation and in the development of the credit system, accompanied by the rapid growth of the population."[1] Then came the World War and brought on the present rise of the tax burden.

TABLE [D]

GREAT BRITAIN. PER CENT RATIO OF THE EXPENDITURES OF THE NATIONAL GOVERNMENT (*Exclusive of Post Office*) TO THE NATIONAL INCOME IN 1818–1923 [a]

	1818	1913	1923
Interest on internal debt	7.82	0.74	7.14
Payment of internal debt	0.30	0.33	0.75
Interest on external debt	....	....	0.94
Repayment of external debt	....	....	0.30
National defense	3.62	3.36	2.78
War pensions and old age pensions	0.30	0.54	2.45
Other services	1.68	2.36	4.80
Cost of collections	0.97	0.19	0.29
Total expenditures	14.69	7.52	19.46

[a] From report of Colwyn Committee. See footnote 2 of this chapter.

In the United States the ratio of taxes to income has increased over a period of three quarters of a century, although by no means evenly. There have been three distinct periods, each marked by a different level of taxation relative to income : one prior to the Civil War, characterized by a relatively low level of taxation ; one between the Civil War and World War, characterized by a somewhat higher level ; and the present period characterized by a still higher level. Within each there have been fluctuations caused by war, business cycles, and variations in governmental activity. At least in the United States, governmental expenditures have passed through genuine cycles as periods of rapid expansion have been followed by periods of retrenchment.[2] These periods are illustrated by the figures of the ratio of taxes to income in New York State and in the United States, shown in Tables [E] and [F]. It should be

[1] "Report of the Treasury Committee on National Debt and Taxation" (Colwyn Committee), *Parliamentary Papers, Cmd. 2800* (Great Britain, 1927), p. 235. It is interesting to note that, after considering various pertinent factors, the Committee concluded that the tax burden is lighter for the nation as a whole at the present time than it was after the Napoleonic War, despite the present higher ratio of taxes to income. It supported this contention by reference to the fact that the people have now more capacity to bear taxes than they had then, and that taxes are more equitably distributed at the present time and are less oppressive to the poorer classes.

[2] See Paul Studenski, *Public Borrowing* (National Municipal League, New York, 1930), pp. 28-33.

noted, however, that the growth of tax revenues does not completely measure the growth of public expenditures inasmuch as a considerable portion of public expenditures is financed by means of loans and prices for services sold. The ratio of public expenditures to the income of the community or nation will naturally be higher than the ratio of taxes to income.

TABLE [E]

RATIO OF TAXES TO INCOME IN THE STATE OF NEW YORK, 1850–1923 [a]

In per cents

1850	3.8
1860	5.3
1870	10.5
1880	9.1
1890	7.1
1900	8.5
1910	7.4
1921 (post-war depression)	19.5
1923	12.1

[a] Compiled from the *Report on State Expenditures, Tax Burden, and Wealth* by the New York State Special Joint Committee on Taxation and Retrenchment, New York Legislative Document No. 68 (1926), p. 113.

TABLE [F]

RATIO OF TAXES TO NATIONAL INCOME IN THE UNITED STATES 1890–1928 [b]

In per cents

Year	Federal Taxes	State Taxes	Local Taxes	Total Taxes
1890	3.1	0.8	3.3	7.2
1903	2.5	0.8	3.4	6.7
1913	1.9	0.9	3.6	6.4
1919	6.6	0.8	3.5	10.9
1921	9.1	1.4	5.8	16.3
1923	4.3	1.3	4.7	10.3
1928	3.9	1.9	5.7	11.5

[b] Compiled from the *Cost of Government in the United States, 1928–1929.* National Industrial Conference Board (New York, 1930), p. 67.

THE GROWTH OF PUBLIC EXPENDITURES AND THE OUTLOOK FOR SOCIALISM

THE tendency of public expenditures to increase has led some students of public finance to assert that the importance of public economy in the total national economy is constantly increasing and that there exists an historical tendency towards

progressive state socialism. Adolph Wagner, the eminent
German founder of the socio-political school of public finance,
stated this tendency in the form of a law which has come to
be known as Wagner's law of increasing government expenditures. "Comparison of the past and present situation of different countries," says Wagner, "shows that among progressive
people with which we are alone concerned, an increase regularly takes place in the activity of both the central and local
governments. This increase is both extensive and intensive;
the central and local governments constantly undertake new
functions, while performing both old and new functions more
efficiently and completely. In this way more and more of the
economic needs of the people (namely their common needs) are
being satisfied by the State and by the other public agencies
and they are satisfied by them furthermore in a progressively
better manner. The clear proof of this is found in the increasing budgets of the national and local governments. Thus,
functioning as an economic organism serving the needs of the
population with the aid of certain goods which are owned
in common, government becomes, in this fashion, constantly
more and more important both for the entire national economy
and for the individual members thereof. It becomes more
important, not only in the *absolute* sense, but also in the *relative* sense, inasmuch as it takes care of an ever greater and
greater proportion of the aggregate needs of a progressive
people. Public economic activities increase at the expense of
private economic activities, and the collectivistic character of
the whole national economy becomes, in consequence, more
pronounced." [3]
Wagner's law appears to be too sweeping. It does not make
sufficient allowance for the expansion of private economic activity in capitalistic society, the determination and ability of
the dominant groups in that society to check the spread of collectivism, and the irregularity of the social and economic
development generally. The facts are that an expansion has
gone on contemporaneously in the private economy, as reflected in the private expenditures made from private incomes,
and in the public economy as reflected in public expenditures;

[3] Adolph Wagner, *Allgemeine oder theoretische Volkswirthschaftslehre* (C. F.
Winter'sche Verlagshandlung, Leipzig, 1876), Vol. I, Grundlegung, p. 260. The
last phrase in the foregoing translation runs in German as follows: *"so ergiebt
sich . . . eine Zunahme der gesammten zwangsgemeinwirthschaftlichen*, beson-
ders der *staatlichen und communalen, auf Kosten* der übrigen gemein — und
privatwirthschaftlichen Thätigkeit, mithin eine *Steigerung des communistichen
Characters der ganzen Volkswirthschaft."*

and that though the second may have been increasing somewhat faster than the first in progressive countries during the
past half century or so, it is still lagging far behind. Much
of the expansion of government activity has taken the form
of regulation of private enterprise and has been reflected but
little in public expenditures, since regulation generally requires but little expenditure of money. The figures of public
expenditures in most of the capitalistic countries do not show
any marked tendency toward a fundamental change in the
relative position of the two economies and the elevation of
the public economy to a dominant position in them. Such
a change may or may not take place in them eventually. The
figures of public expenditures furnish no proof either way.
Only in the case of a few countries is the tendency toward
such a change unmistakably in evidence.

THE LEVEL OF GOVERNMENTAL EXPENDITURES IN
DIFFERENT COUNTRIES

ONE would expect the per capita governmental expenditures
in this country to be higher than in other countries, because
the wealth and standard of living of the people are so much
higher than elsewhere. Yet the figures sustain this expectation only in part. At least one or two countries have higher
per capita public expenditures than the United States. The
reason lies in the fact that the level of public expenditures of
a country is determined not only by its wealth but also by its
political situation (effects and likelihood of war, for example),
and by its social and political philosophy. The effect of these
factors may be stronger than that of national wealth.

But, regardless of how high the public expenditures in this
country are, the ratio that they bear to the national income of
the people of this country is lower than the ratio of public
expenditures of national income in most of the other progressive countries. This is clearly indicated by the figures given
in Tables [G] and [H]. Since the data on the total national
and local public expenditures are available for only a few
countries it becomes necessary for comprehensive comparisons,
to use the tax data, instead. Since taxes supply approximately
80 per cent of the expenditures in the typical case they afford
a fairly good idea of public expenditures. However, even in
the cases of taxes, only very general comparisons may be made,
for differences in the financial structure of the governments
and their methods of accounting interfere with the complete
comparability of the figures. The estimates of national income with which expenditures and taxes of each country are

compared in these tables vary greatly in their reliability. Some have been derived by means of very careful figuring and great discrimination. Others are rough approximations.

TABLE [G]

Per Capita Public Expenditures in Relation to Per Capita National Income in Various Countries in 1928–1929

	Per capita national income	Per capita public expenditures	Per cent ratio of public expenditures to national income
United States [a]	$700	$107	15
Canada [b]	600	85	14
Great Britain [c]	469	141	30
Germany [d]	283	66	23
France [e]	220	65	30
Italy [f]	120	30	25
Soviet Russia [g]	100	22	22
Japan [h]	101	23	23

[a] *Cost of Government in the United States, 1929–1930,* National Industrial Conference Board (New York, 1932). The national income in 1929 is estimated in this report at 85.2 billion dollars — 5 per cent below the estimates of the National Bureau of Economic Research.

[b] Computed from the figures given in the *Canadian Yearbook* (1930 and 1931).

[c] Computed from the figures given in the *Statistical Abstract for the United Kingdom,* No. 74 ; and the "Budget Supplement," *Economist* (April 18, 1931).

[d] *Statistisches Jahrbuch für das Deutsche Reich* (1931).

[e] Based on figures given in the *Annuaire Statistique de la France* (1929) and by L. D. Bernonville et G. Chevry, "Les Charges Fiscales en France et en Divers Pays," *Bulletin de la Statistique Generale de la France* (Juillet-Septembre, 1931).

[f] Based on the figures given in the *Memorandum on Public Finance, 1926–1928,* Economic and Financial Section, League of Nations (*Geneva,* 1929) ; and by Bernonville et Chevry, *op. cit.*

[g] Compiled from *Kontrolnyie Tzifry, 1928–1929,* Gosplan, U. S. S. R. (1929) and from G. Y. Sokolnikov and Associates, *Soviet Policy in Public Finance, 1917–1928* (Stanford University Press, 1931).

[h] Computed from the figures given in the *Memorandum on Public Finance, 1926–1928,* and the *Resumé Statistique de l'Empire de Japon* (1929).

Three significant facts are clearly brought out by the figures in Tables [G] and [H]: (1) that countries characterized by large per capita incomes, as a rule, are characterized also by large per capita public expenditures and taxes, and that those in which the per capita incomes are small are, as a rule, characterized by the reverse condition; (2) that the variations in per capita expenditures and taxes of the different countries are much greater than the variations in the per cent ratios of the expenditures and taxes to the national income in the different countries. In fact, except for some extreme or special cases, there seems to be considerable similarity in these ratios. Apparently, identity of cultural and political development in the progressive countries of the world and their mutual inter-dependence in the political, commercial and financial spheres, are responsible for the existence of a certain degree of simi-larity in the proportions which public expenditures and charges bear to the incomes of the citizens in these coun-tries; and (3) the per cent ratios of the public expenditures and taxes to the national income have risen in all progressive countries very materially since 1913, in consequence of the World War. The fact that they have risen not only in the belligerent countries but also in those which have not been directly involved in the war further works to illustrate the fact mentioned above, of the interdependence of nations.

TABLE [H]

COMPARATIVE TAX BURDENS IN VARIOUS COUNTRIES IN 1901–1929 [a]

	Per capita taxes			Per cent ratio of taxes to national income		
	1901	1913–1914	1929	1901	1913–1914	1929
United States	$17	$23	$80	7	7	11
Great Britain	20	27	96	10	11	20
Canada	(b)	26	65	(b)	13	11
Australia	(b)	28	79	(b)	10	14-15
Germany	9	16	55	8	9-11	19
France	19	25	51-60	15	14	24-26
Norway	(b)	16	60	(b)	13	20
Sweden	(b)	15	45	(b)	11	15
Denmark	(b)	17	48	(b)	(b)	17
Switzerland	(b)	14	42-44	(b)	6-7	10
Italy	(b)	13	24	(b)	12	21
Soviet Russia	(b)	6	14	(b)	14	14
Japan	(b)	5	14	(b)	14	14

[a] The figures for Great Britain, Germany and France for the year 1900–1901 are taken from E. R. A. Seligman, *Studies in Public Finance* (The Macmillan Co., New York, 1925). Those for the United States are taken in each case from the *Cost of Government in the United States, 1929–1930*, National Industrial Conference Board (New York, 1932). The figures for 1913–1914 and 1928–1929 for the countries other than the United States are based on data given in the official statistical yearbooks of these countries and in the following publications and articles: *Memorandum on Public Finance, 1922–1926*, Economic and Finan-cial Section, League of Nations (Geneva, 1927) and the same *Memorandum for 1926–1928* (Geneva, 1929); L. D. Bernonville et G. Chevry, "Les Charges Fiscales en France at en Divers Pays," *Bulletin de la Statistique Generale de la France* (Juillet-Septembre, 1931); "Budget Supplement," *Economist* (April 18, 1931); G. Y. Sokolnikov and Associates, *Soviet Policy in Public Finance, 1917–1928* (Stanford University Press, 1931); *Kontrolnyie Tzifry, 1928–1929*, Gosplan, U. S. S. R. (1929). The figures of the national income of Sweden, Switzerland and Japan used as a basis for the computation of the per cent ratio of their taxes to national income in 1929, are based on the figures given by H. E. Fisk, "Estimates of National Income," *American Economic Review*, (March, 1930).

[b] Data not available.

As the Tables [G] and [H] show, Great Britain raises in taxes and spends publicly both a larger amount per capita and a larger proportion of the per capita income than does the United States. The other countries raise less taxes and spend less per capita, but these smaller amounts generally represent larger proportions of their national income. In other words, the tax burden in the United States is lighter than in almost any other country. This is due in part to differences in the burden of debts and in part to differences in the prominence of governmental activity in the total national economy here and abroad. The public economy, compared with the private, occupies a less prominent position in this country. Governmental activity relative to private enterprise is less extensive here. It lags farther behind private enterprise partly because of the laissez-faire policy which is more strongly entrenched here than almost anywhere else and partly because private enterprise is more productive here than elsewhere.

DIRECTIONS IN WHICH PUBLIC EXPENDITURES INCREASE AND THEIR PRESENT DISTRIBUTION

THE expenditures of national governments in the leading countries of the world have increased mainly in the direction of expenditures because of war. Year in and year out national legislative chambers have voted larger appropriations for national defense. Every successive war has involved a larger expenditure of money and has bequeathed to posterity a larger national debt, a natural consequence of the increasing magnitude of the conflict waged. Thus, in the United States, the War of 1812 was responsible for a debt of eighty million dollars, the Civil War for one of 2.7 billion dollars (inclusive of treasury notes), and the World War, for a debt of twenty-four billion dollars. The annual payments on account of the World War debt exceed a billion dollars. In most of the large countries, military expenditures, including debt charges, reparations, pensions to veterans, and like items consume from 50 to 75 per cent of the national budget as shown in Table [I]. Payments on account of the debt alone amount to between a quarter and a half of the national budgets.[4]

[4] The interest on and redemption of the public debt, as shown in Table [I], amount to the indicated percentages of the total national budgets in the following countries : Great Britain, 47.2 ; France, 31.1 ; Belgium, 37.7 ; United States, 37.5 ; Italy, 25.9 ; Germany, 29.4 (including reparations ; see note [b] of Table [I]). In the British budget alone, the payments on account of the debt increased from 19 million pounds in 1913–1914, to 369 million pounds in 1928–1929. In Soviet Russia, in consequence of her repudiation of all pre-revolutionary debts, the debt service is almost entirely of a productive origin and amounted in 1928 to only 4.4 per cent of her budget.

TABLE [I]

PURPOSES OF EXPENDITURES OF THE PRINCIPAL NATIONAL GOVERNMENTS [a]

(Per cent of the total expenditures)

	United States 1927	Great Britain 1929	France 1929	Germany 1929–1930	Italy 1928–1929	Russia 1927–1928
General government ..	4.45	5.28	12.82	8.97	16.58	8.40
Military, including war pensions	32.87	22.26	37.66	46.13 [b]	31.48	12.30
Economic services	10.47	5.35	7.26	2.76	9.53	[c]
Social services, including education	1.31	15.60	9.66	8.12	9.76	6.30
Quasi-commercial enterprises [d]	.77	....	.02	.22	4.75	52.80 [e]
Aid to local governments	1.23	2.61	.03	29.66	1.08	14.10
Interest on debt	22.75	39.80	}31.07	.95	24.70	}4.40
Retirement of debt ...	14.76	7.38		3.19	1.19	
Refunds of taxes	4.91	....	1.34	....	.93	....
Miscellaneous	6.48	....	....	....	....	.30
Surplus	....	1.72	.14	....	....	1.40
Total	100.00	100.00	100.00	100.00	100.00	100.00

[a] Compiled from the *Memorandum on Public Finance, 1926–1928*, the Economic and Financial Section of the League of Nations and the same *Memorandum for 1922–1926*, Tables D ; and from G. Y. Sokolnikov and Associates, *Soviet Policy in Public Finance, 1917–1928* (Stanford University Press, 1931), p. 319.

[b] Includes 25.27 per cent for reparations.

[c] The line between economic services and commercial enterprises hardly exists in the case of Russia. Expenditures which in other countries may be apportioned between economic services and quasi-commercial enterprises have been combined under the latter head.

[d] This item includes only expenditures from the general budget for investments in such enterprises or for their deficits. It does not include the expenditures of those enterprises which are covered from their revenues.

[e] This item is the total expenditures for transportation, the communications' service, and financing of the national economy.

The expenditures of these governments for constructive social, cultural, and economic purposes have also increased but they consume everywhere, except in Soviet Russia, less than half, and in most of the large countries less than one-third, of the national or Federal budgets.[5]

As Nitti fittingly puts it, "the statistics of expenditures of our national governments are no credit to our civilization."[6]

[5] The payments for social insurance, old age pensions, unemployment, and other "social services" by the national government of Great Britain increased from 25 million pounds in 1914–1915 to 134 million pounds in 1928–1929, and the grants to local governments for social services during the same period increased from 37 to 101 million pounds. These figures are quoted from Alzada Comstock, *Taxation in the Modern State* (Longmans, Green and Co., New York, 1929), p. 16. The total expenditures and grants for social services by the national government increased from 206 million pounds in 1921 to 342 million pounds in 1929. "Budget Supplement," *Economist* (April 18, 1931).

[6] Nitti, *op. cit.*, p. 185.

The emphasis on war expenditures has been true only of the national- governments. The expenditures of the component state, provincial, or local governments, have increased mainly in the direction of constructive social and economic purposes. Military functions play little or no rôle in these expenditures; and protection (against crime, and so on) — once the primary object of these governments — although still requiring constantly larger outlays has become a distinctly secondary object with them. The combined national, state (or provincial), and local governmental expenditures show a somewhat more hopeful trend than the national expenditures considered above.

The distribution of the combined expenditures of all classes ·of government among the different objects may be recapitulated below. The grouping of the services in this list is somewhat arbitrary, since some of them combine social, economic, and sometimes other aims:

1. *Social and cultural services,* which aim at the improvement of the quality of social life such as (a) cultural improvement (schools, libraries, museums); (b) improvement of public health (child hygiene, milk and food inspection, prevention of communicable and occupational disease); (c) sanitation (sewage, street cleaning, removal of wastes); (d) recreation (parks, playgrounds); (e) social welfare (care of the aged, orphans, mental defectives, sick, and poor; correction of criminals; social insurance for old age, unemployment, industrial accidents, and other contingencies; retirement of public employees).

2. *Constructive economic services,* which seek to facilitate and improve economic activity such as (a) aid to industry, commerce, and agriculture (coining of money and provision for currency; registration of patents and copyrights; tariff protection; conservation and development of natural resources, including reclamation, reforestation, flood prevention; construction and maintenance of highways, bridges, and waterways; subsidization of industries requiring aid; collection and distribution of information; scientific research); (b) regulation of economic activity (regulation of public utilities, railroads, banks, industrial combinations and other business; factory inspection and administration of other labor laws; administration of building and zoning laws).

3. *Services of governmentally-owned enterprises* (post offices, railroads, mines, banks, forests, water supplies, docks, street railways and subways, ferries, toll bridges, toll canals, markets, electric light and gas plants, power plants, municipal housing).

4. *Preparation for war and payment for its consequences* (maintenance of an army and navy, reparations, veterans' pen-

sions, hospitalization and other benefits, and above all, interest on and redemption of the war debt).

5. *Internal protection to life and property* (police and fire protection; militia; administration of justice).

6. *General government and miscellaneous services* (maintenance of the chief executive and the legislature, administration of finance, administration of elections, miscellaneous undistributable items).

The relative importance of these different services varies in different countries. The data for the United States are not available under exactly the heads enumerated in the preceding paragraphs. The available data are shown in Table [J], where they are grouped somewhat differently. The costs of the services of governmentally-owned enterprises are reflected in these figures only in part. Of the costs of the postal service only the deficit is included. If the figures are amplified and are rearranged so as to approximate more closely the foregoing grouping and if the figures of debt redemption and interest are allocated to the different purposes in accordance with the probable origin of the debt, the relative importance of the different services in the United States, combining all classes of government, may be estimated as follows:

(1) Social and cultural services consume between 25 and 30 per cent of the total costs of government (including costs of services furnished for a price), (2) economic services — close to 20 per cent, (3) services of public enterprises — between 10 and 15 per cent, (4) preparation for war and payment for its consequences — more than 25 per cent, (5) internal protection close to 5 per cent, (6) general government and miscellaneous items — 9 per cent.

PUBLIC OWNERSHIP HERE AND ABROAD

IN capitalistic countries only a few enterprises, not essentially governmental in their nature, are operated by the governments. Such fields as industry, transportation, housing, and the like are generally reserved to private enterprise and governments usually step in and undertake operation only when there are special reasons for such actions. Governments may establish and operate an enterprise because it is essential to the performance of some primary function such as national defense. Public ownership and operation may be undertaken to provide an essential service which private capital would not furnish because of the large amount of funds required or the uncertainty of profit. Public ownership and operation may be motivated by a desire to furnish certain services to consumers

TABLE [J]

FUNCTIONAL DISTRIBUTION OF FEDERAL, STATE AND LOCAL EXPENDITURES IN THE UNITED STATES, 1927 [a]

	Amounts in millions of dollars			Percentage Distribution		
	Federal (Exclusive of post office)	State and local	Total	Federal (Exclusive of post office)	State and local	Total
I. General government	333	532	865	8.2	6.5	7.1
II. Protection	1,427	748	2,175	35.0	9.2	17.8
III. Development	268	4,011	4,278	6.6	49.4	35.1
Miscellaneous economic development	159	67	226	3.9	0.8	1.9
a. Highways	94	1,615	1,708	2.3	19.9	14.0
b. Education	15	2,329	2,344	0.4	28.7	19.2
IV. Social welfare	55	1,053	1,108	1.3	13.0	9.1
V. Miscellaneous	2	155	157	0.1	1.9	1.3
VI. Public utilities	56	561	617	1.4	6.9	5.1
VII. Debt redemption	1,133	386	1,519	27.9	4.8	12.5
VIII. Interest	795	675	1,470	19.5	8.3	12.0
	4,069	8,121	12,190	100.0	100.0	100.0

[a] Compiled from *Cost of Government, 1927–1928,* National Industrial Conference Board (New York, 1929), p. 13. The figures are given for 1927 because this is the last year for which data showing detailed functional distribution of the state and local expenditures are available in the reports of this Board. Eds. note: In its study, *Federal Finances, 1923–1932,* p. 22, the Board states that there were no outstanding changes in the distribution of net expenditures from 1927 to 1930.

at a lower price than private enterprise can or will. Governments may be able to furnish them at a lower price either because of certain advantages they possess in operation or because they may raise a part of the funds necessary for operation by general taxation. They may be able to furnish the service on a more equitable basis than private enterprise. They may undertake the operation of some enterprise in competition with a private and otherwise monopolistic organization in order to compel it to furnish services to consumers at a lower price. Public ownership may be motivated by the desire to conserve natural resources for the whole people; or the government may establish a monopolistic enterprise for revenue purposes. Finally, public ownership may be inspired by a desire to introduce socialism in a gradual way.

In the United States there has been relatively little extension of government ownership and operation beyond the strictly governmental functions. Private enterprise has preëmpted here nearly every field of industry and has succeeded in most of them in rendering fairly satisfactory service, that is, if we ignore the periodic crises which characterize it. Public opinion has favored private operation, under a system of public regulation, even in industries which, in foreign countries, are often owned and operated by the government. The industrialists have achieved great political power and cohesion and, generally, have resisted successfully the introduction of public ownership and operation even in cases in which the record of private ownership and operation has been very questionable. The main fields of government ownership and operation are, in the case of the Federal government, the post office, the Panama canal and railroad, the Alaska railroad and, for a time after the World War, merchant vessels. In the case of the states the chief fields are canals, docks, ferries, and toll bridges. In the case of the cities they are water systems, electric light and power plants, gas plants, markets, docks, and, in a few cases, street railways.

The question of public ownership at the present time is an active political issue in the United States only with respect to the electric light and power industries. Great projects for the harnessing of water power must be undertaken very shortly and the question must be decided as to whether public or private enterprise shall execute them, and which of them shall own and operate the works and transmission lines, after the projects are completed. Advocates of public ownership maintain that water power is the only remaining great natural resource not yet alienated to private purposes and that it should be kept in public hands and used for the benefit of all.

In foreign countries government ownership and operation is far more extensive. Railroads, telegraph and telephone systems, and electric light and gas plants are very commonly owned and operated by the public, and the various types of enterprises listed above are also very generally publicly owned. In addition, some governments have also entered the fields of banking, insurance, housing, extraction of coal and metals, and production of building materials. In socialistic Soviet Russia all extractive industries, important manufacturing industries, communication services, foreign trade, banks, and the greater part of the distributive organization are publicly owned; and public ownership has extended even into the field of agriculture where State farms have been organized.

Public ownership is found in its most advanced form, outside of Soviet Russia, in Switzerland, Austria, Germany (particularly since the World War), Holland, the Scandinavian countries, and the newly-established European States. It has made less progress in England where it has been confined mainly to the municipal field, and still less in France and other Latin countries in which government is highly centralized and a vigorous municipal government has failed to develop. "Public ownership," as indicated in a recent German work, "finds its strongest impulses where the labor movement has become a powerful factor and a considerable influence in legislation and administration. It is consequently in the great European industrial centers in the administration of which the labor elements participate in a decisive manner — in 'red' Berlin and 'Vienna,' 'red' Zürich, Copenhagen, Stockholm, Amsterdam and such English industrial cities as Birmingham — that we find the strongholds of the public ownership movement. It is here that the pace for the expansion of the movement is set." [7]

RELATIVE IMPORTANCE OF FEDERAL, STATE AND LOCAL EXPENDITURES

In different countries the shares of the central, state or provincial, and local authorities in the aggregate expenditures vary greatly. In Great Britain the national government is responsible for about 70 per cent of the total governmental expenditures and the local governments for the other 30 per cent.

[7] *Handbuch der Öffentlichen Wirtschaft* (Verlagsanstalt *Courier*, Berlin, 1930), p. 320. In Germany about one-tenth of the strictly industrial workers were engaged in publicly owned industries in 1929. (*Op. cit.*, p. 313.)

In other countries, like France, the importance of national expenditures is still greater. In the United States, on the other hand, because of a more decentralized system of government, the national government accounts for only about 35 per cent of the total government expenditures, the states for about 15 per cent and the local governments approximately 50 per cent.

The expenditures of the different classes of government in the United States have all been increasing but not in the same measure. Eliminating temporary fluctuations caused, for example, by wars, the increase during the past three-quarters of a century has been most rapid in the field of local expenditures, somewhat less rapid in that of Federal expenditures, and least rapid in that of state expenditures. If, however, strictly civil expenditures are considered for recent years it will be found that the increase of Federal expenditures has been less rapid than that of state expenditures since the latter lie almost entirely in the civil sphere.

What is the reason for this more substantial increase of local expenditures as compared with the civil expenditures of either the state or the Federal government? Some persons have ascribed it to the supposedly greater extravagance of municipal governments. But this explanation is inadequate. The reason must be sought in the highly decentralized structure of American government and the highly urban character of American civilization.

Most of the social needs which have required governmental action have been urban rather than rural in character, because urban centers necessarily develop a larger number of needs which can not be satisfied privately; for example, those relating to sanitation and fire and police protection. These urban needs have had to be satisfied, for the most part, by local governments. With the passage of time some of these local functions have been absorbed to some extent by the states as it has appeared that a wide jurisdiction could discharge them more satisfactorily. States have undertaken considerable responsibility for institutions, schools, and highways. In a similar manner, the Federal government has absorbed some functions once discharged by the states such as the regulation of banks, railroads, and industrial combinations, as well as activities like education, highway construction, and control of the consumption of intoxicants which once were preëminently local in nature.

However, this upward diffusion of functions has not stripped the localities or states of their importance. The increase in

Federal expenditures has been due only in a small measure to any assumption by the Federal government of activities formerly performed by the states; and, likewise, the increase in state expenditures has been due only in small part to the assumption by the states of activities formerly performed by local governments. In both cases, the increase has been due mainly to the assumption and extensive development by the government in question of activities formerly performed either not at all, or only to a small degree, by any class of government. The states and municipalities have intensified their activities with respect to certain old functions and have assumed new ones more rapidly than they have relinquished control to governments of wider jurisdiction.

One direction which the expansion of Federal and State activity has taken is the increasing development of Federal and state subsidies to the states and local governments. In the United States, these embrace Federal aid to states for the construction of highways, maintenance of the national guard, vocational education, vocational rehabilitation, agricultural extension work, and forest fire prevention; and state aid to local districts for schools, highways, and other purposes. Similar grants are found in Great Britain, France, and Germany. They are made by the National government to the provincial or local authorities or both for education, housing, health, sanitation, and so on.

The main purpose of these subsidies is two-fold: to equalize the resources of the component governments for the maintenance of essential services, and to secure the enforcement of certain minimum standards throughout the area of the granting authority. The central government, in general, distributes the funds without regard to the area in which they were collected and allocates them according to needs. For example, in the case of state aid for schools, the basis for allocation is predominantly school attendance; in the case of Federal aid for roads, distribution is determined according to area, population, and mileage of postal routes. The effect often is to distribute in the poorer areas funds collected in the richer ones. In making the grants the central authority usually lays down the standards which must be maintained in the aided services or improvements under penalty of withdrawing the grant.

The use of subsidies has been criticized on the ground that it tends toward excessive centralization of control, especially in the Federal government. State subsidies to local districts have been criticized on the ground that they tend to delay such a consolidation of districts as would eliminate needless duplica-

tion of offices and governmental machinery. However, the
fiscal advantages of subsidies recommend them if they are used
in a discriminating manner.

INCREASE IN GOVERNMENT ACTIVITY AS THE PRINCIPAL CAUSE OF THE REAL INCREASE IN PER CAPITA PUBLIC EXPENDITURES

IT IS important to gain some insight into the reasons for the
real increase in per capita public expenditures in view of the
revenue problems which it produces. The outstanding reason
is that the per capita output of public services tends to increase as new services are added and old services are improved
and produced in greater quantity.

The reasons for this increase in the quantity and the improvement in the quality of the per capita output of public
services lie in the growth of wants which press on the government for satisfaction and in the greater responsiveness of governments to the demands made upon them. To trace to their
origins these wants and the greater responsiveness of government to them, is to trace every force in modern civilization.
However, some forces responsible for these developments may
be distinguished as of outstanding importance : (1) The growth
of wealth, which has led to a rise in the scale of living, has
resulted in demands for new and better public services.
(2) The rise of democracy and widespread suffrage has brought
an increased demand for free public education and various
social services. (3) Widespread education, which has raised
the cultural level of the people, has led to the expansion of
wants in every direction, especially for such services as sanitation, recreation, protection, and education itself. (4) The
multiplication of "pressure groups," such as manufacturers' associations, labor unions, farmers' organizations, patriotic soci-
ties, chambers of commerce and like associations, which lobby
for projects beneficial to the interests they represent, is responsible for a large share of the increase in the demands made
upon the government. (5) Nationalism and militarism have
intensified the demands for better military establishments.
(6) Scientific discovery and inventions have brought changes in
industry, commerce, transportation, and modes of living, and
have created new problems calling for government solution,
regulation, and expenditures. (7) The growth of business
activity and particularly industrial development have made necessary increases and improvements in the means of communication furnished by the government — roads, improved waterways,

postal service — as well as other aids to industry. (8) The acquisition of new territory, and the development of old undeveloped areas, usually have led, in the national sphere, to a demand for a greater military establishment, extension of the postal service, and other activities. (9) The concentration of population in cities has brought with it problems and expenses of housing, sanitation, health, police and fire protection, water supply, education, highway construction and maintenance, transportation, recreation, planning, and zoning. (10) The growth of the wage earning and economically insecure class has created problems of protection against exploitation, a demand for regulation of hours and conditions of labor, workmen's compensation, old age pensions, unemployment insurance, public employment bureaus, mothers' pensions, and so on. (11) The ambitions or enthusiasm of administrators and legislators, combined with the growth of humanitarianism and social consciousness, have been responsible for the initiation of expensive services for which there has been no strong demand. (12) The ease with which public loans may be floated has invited and enabled governments to undertake new projects more readily than if they had to be financed by taxation, since legislators and taxpayers are more willing to sanction borrowing than increased taxation.[8]

INFLUENCE OF COST CONDITIONS ON PER CAPITA EXPENDITURES

THE per capita public expenditures are affected not only by the increase and improvement in the output of public services but also by the costs of production of the public services, that is, the conditions under which the services are produced. These conditions may be classified as: (1) favorable conditions tending to decrease the costs of production and hence per capita expenditures and (2) unfavorable conditions tending to increase them. Outstanding among the first is the improvement in the efficiency of the government and also of the industries whose goods and services the government uses. Suffice it only to mention under this class the introduction of greater specialization of labor in government work, the employment of better trained men in it, the use of better materials and equipment, better budgeting and generally the better organization of the work. Some of these improvements and economies have been

---

[8] For a comprehensive discussion of the causes of both the seeming and real increases in public expenditures see G. Jèze, *Cours de Finances Publiques, 1928–1929* (Marcel Giard, Paris, 1929), pp. 80-97.

greatly facilitated by the increase in the output of governmental services and increase in the size of the governmental organization. The superior ability of the larger governmental organization to handle certain services has probably been the prime reason for the occasional transfer of certain governmental functions from town to county governments, from county to state governments, and from state to the Federal government; for the consolidation of school districts; and for the annexation by larger municipalities of smaller ones (a phenomenon analogous to the merger in private industry).

Outstanding among the unfavorable conditions tending to increase the costs of production of governmental services are the exhaustion of natural resources directly or indirectly involved in their production; the unfavorable topography of the districts in which or through which new governmental facilities must be provided; the insufficient density of population in the new districts, which is responsible for an unduly low utilization of the governmental services furnished in them and hence large per capita costs of such services; and the excessive density of population in the old districts which makes the rendering of certain governmental services in them an increasingly difficult matter. On the whole, the favorable cost conditions are probably more powerful than the unfavorable ones, for the per capita output of public services, measured in physical terms, seems to be increasing faster than the per capita public expenditures, measured in the same purchasing power of money. An analysis of the physical output and per capita costs of certain services, such as public education, seems to confirm this hypothesis, particularly if the improvements in the quality of the services rendered are also taken into account.[9]

2. Federal Expenditures Attributable to the Depression *

THE first and most important expenditure due to the depression is $500 million for the capital stock of the Reconstruction Finance Corporation. This expenditure, as has been pointed out, was in the nature of a capital advance. It is theoretically recoverable, but to the extent that losses are incurred, the funds returned to the Treasury will be less than the amount

*From *Federal Finances, 1923–1932* (National Industrial Conference Board, Inc., New York, 1933), Chap. I, pp. 23-25.

[9] For illustrations of costs of municipal services in consolidated and non-consolidated municipal governments and under different topographical conditions and different densities of population, see Paul Studenski's *Government of Metropolitan Areas* (National Municipal League, New York, 1930), Chaps. VII-IX.

advanced for the capital stock. The $125 million subscription to the capital stock of the Federal Land Banks was also directly related to the depression. If it had not been for the depression, there would doubtless have been no occasion for the Federal Government to participate in an increase in the capital stock of these banks.

The inclusion of the net advances on account of the agricultural marketing fund under expenditures attributable to the depression may seem to be unjustified. The legislation providing for the fund was approved on June 15, 1929. It did not owe its existence to the depression, which was then imminent. The principal justification for the inclusion of the net amount advanced in 1932 under the classification mentioned is that the activities financed through the fund were directly related to the depression. As a consequence of the serious effects of the depression and declining price levels on agriculture, the work of the Farm Board and its subsidiary and allied organizations involved essentially a mitigation of the worst effects of the depression. The fostering of coöperative marketing was significant, aside from the depression, but nevertheless the entire range of activities of the Farm Board was influenced by the unusual conditions that prevailed.

Expenditures on account of public works, including advances to the states for road construction, increased from $201 million for 1929 to $507 million for 1932. The principal reason for this increase was legislation enacted for the purpose of alleviating the effects of the depression through the furtherance of construction activities, together with a speeding up of projects for which provision had been made.

The increase in the postal deficit was directly related to the decline in business activity. The deficit charged against ordinary receipts in 1932 was $117 million larger than that for 1929, and it is a fair assumption that all or practically all of the increase resulted from the adverse conditions that existed.

When the expenditures attributable to the depression are considered jointly, it is found that the depression was the cause of an increase for 1932 over 1929 amounting to $1189 million. All other expenditures were actually $31 million less for 1932 than for 1929.[1] Exclusive of refunds of tax receipts, there was an increase in all other expenditures amounting to $81 million.

The principal significance of this analysis is that it clearly indicates that the aggregate expenditures of the Government in 1932 were directly affected by the depression and that, ex-

[1] Debt retirements from surplus in 1929 are excluded in this comparison.

clusive of the expenditures attributable to the depression, there
was very little change between 1929 and 1932.*

QUESTIONS AND PROBLEMS FOR DISCUSSION

1. What were the causes of the increase in public expenditures
   during the last century?
2. Distinguish *real* from *nominal* expenditures.
3. In the recent increase in public expenditures in the United
   States, do you see "a cause for great alarm"? Is this increase
   "a perfectly natural phenomenon"?
4. If public expenditures increase more rapidly than national
   wealth and income does this mean that the burden of public
   expenditures is increasing?
5. Cite examples of distinct social benefits which have resulted
   from increased expenditures during the last two decades.
6. Do mounting costs of government necessarily indicate a
   tendency toward state socialism?
7. In what sense may we regard the recent tremendous increase
   in national government expenditures in the United States as
   an indictment against our economic order? What encouragement, if any, is to be found in the fact that huge sums have
   been spent for civil and public works? for agricultural relief?
   for a large navy?
8. Are expenditures of the Federal government likely to increase
   or decrease relative to state and local expenditures?
9. Increasing governmental activities cause increases in per capita
   public expenditures. In light of general economic and social
   conditions from 1929 to 1933, can the increasing activity on
   the part of our national government since 1933 be justified?
10. Has the growth of political democracy influenced the per capita
    expenditures of governments?

SUGGESTIONS FOR RESEARCH

1. Trends in Federal, state, and local expenditures in the United
   States from 1900 to the present time.
2. The purposes of public expenditures in the United States compared with those in other leading nations.
3. Public expenditures attributable to the depression.
4. A comparison between the recent civil works program of the
   United States and the dole system of England as examples of
   government spending for the purpose of relieving human distress.

* Eds. note: Under Title II of the National Industrial Act of June 16, 1933,
the Federal Government appropriated $3,300,000,000 to cover the cost of an
extensive program of public works. For more recent data relative to expenditures and the depression the reader is referred to the *United States News* and to
annual publications mentioned in the bibliographical note at the close of this
chapter.

5. A comparison between present governmental activities in the United States and England and those of the nineteenth century in these countries.

BIBLIOGRAPHICAL NOTE

An explanation of the growth of public expenditures in principal countries is given in G. D. H. Cole, *The Intelligent Man's Guide through World Chaos,* (London, 1932), Chap. IX, sec. I; Alzada Comstock, *Taxation in the Modern State,* (New York, 1929), Chaps. I, II; and H. W. Guest, *Public Expenditure,* (New York, 1927), Chap. II. Comstock discusses the nature and extent of post-war expenditures in Great Britain, France, and Germany. Guest makes clear the distinction between the real and the unreal elements in the increase of public expenditures.

Professor Bullock in his *Selected Readings in Public Finance,* (Boston, 1924), Chap. III, reproduces studies in which are given interpretations of some significant facts of public expenditures in modern times.

W. F. Willoughby, *Financial Condition and Operations of the National Government, 1921–1930,* (Washington, D. C., 1931), Pt. IV, makes a classification of Federal expenditures based upon character, organization units, functions, and objects. A similar method of treatment can be found in *Federal Finances, 1923–1932,* (New York, 1933), Chap. I, a publication of the National Industrial Conference Board. This chapter, with accompanying tables, presents valuable data relating to Federal aid to states.

A recent and comprehensive treatment of the extent and causes of public expenditures in the United States is *Recent Social Trends in the United States,* (New York, 1933), Vol. II, Chaps. XXV, XXVI.

For a discussion of the financing of the "New Deal" see *An Introduction to Contemporary Economic Problems in the United States,* Vol. II, sec. III, part 20, prepared by Columbia College Associates in Economics, Government and Public Law, History, and Philosophy, (New York, 1934).

Annual publications which present factual information concerning public expenditures are: National Industrial Conference Board, *Cost of Government in the United States,* (New York); *Report of the Secretary of the Treasury of the United States;* United States Census Bureau, *Financial Statistics of States;* also its *Financial Statistics of Cities.* The *Memorandum on Public Finance,* (Economic and Financial Section, League of Nations, Geneva), a serial publication, presents significant facts of public expenditures in many leading countries.

CHAPTER III

SOME ECONOMIC EFFECTS OF PUBLIC EXPENDITURES

THE economic effects of public expenditures are determined primarily by the following factors: (1) magnitude and (2) purpose of public disbursement, (3) source of funds expended, (4) character of public outlay, and (5) phase of the business cycle at the time the expenditure is made. The influence of the first two of these factors was discussed in the preceding chapter. With reference to the first it was pointed out that a statement of the magnitude of an expenditure, without an accompanying distinction between its real and unreal elements, throws little light upon the problem of its economic effects.* Furthermore, it was shown that the economic effects of a public expenditure of given magnitude are dependent in part upon the relationship between the amount of the expenditure and the wealth and income of the community in which it is made.†

The importance of the second factor, purpose, was made clear in the discussion of the range and quality of public service.‡

With regard to the relationship between the third factor, source of funds, and the economic effects of public expenditure, it is evident that an attempt to discuss this problem prior to a comprehensive treatment of public revenue and public credit (the sources of public funds) is illogical. Such treatment constitutes later sections of this volume. Therefore, no attention is here given to this question.

The two remaining factors, character of public outlay and phase of the business cycle, will now be treated.

* See Chap. II, pp. 10-14.
† *Ibid.*, pp. 15-18, 20-22.
‡ *Ibid.*, pp. 14, 23-26.

1. CHARACTER OF PUBLIC EXPENDITURE

(a) Ordinary and Extraordinary Expenditure *

IN discussions of the character of public expenditure, a distinction which is sometimes made is that between ordinary and extraordinary expenditure. According to Bastable, ordinary or "Normal expenditure is that which recurs at stated periods and in a regular manner; it is accordingly capable of being estimated and provided for. Extraordinary expenditure has to be made at indefinite times and for uncertain amounts, and it cannot be reckoned for with any approach to accuracy." †

Between these two types there is, however, no hard and fast line. For example, an expenditure which is extraordinary during the first year of a war may become ordinary if the war is of long duration. Likewise, with an ever increasing scope of State functions, extraordinary expenditure in an early stage of the State's development may become ordinary expenditure in a later and more advanced period. It is evident, therefore, that this classification has significant limitations.

It is in connection with the choice of financing expenditure from current revenue or from borrowing that the distinction between ordinary and extraordinary expenditure most frequently appears. It is generally argued that the extraordinary expenditure of a given year should be transformed into the ordinary one of annual debt charge, if the financing of the extraordinary outlay from current revenue would create an intolerable economic burden.‡

(b) Productive and Unproductive Expenditure §

ANOTHER important distinction relating to the character of public outlay is that between productive and unproductive expenditure. These are very broad terms. Productive expenditures may be defined as those which increase, and unproductive expenditures as those which decrease, economic or social utility.

Professor Lutz divides productive expenditure into the categories of reproductive and non-reproductive.¶ Reproductive

---

* By the editors.
† C. F. Bastable, *Public Finance*, (Macmillan and Co., Ltd., London, 1917), Bk. I, Chap. VIII, p. 130.
‡ See Bastable, *op. cit.*, pp. 133, 134, for discussion of this point; also A. Wagner, *Finanzwissenschaft*, (Leipzig, 1883), Vol. I, pp. 143-148.
§ By the editors.
¶ H. L. Lutz, *Public Finance*, (D. Appleton and Co., New York, 1929), pp. 97-99.

expenditure yields a material or pecuniary income; non-reproductive expenditure results only in immaterial goods. These immaterial goods, e.g., health, education, etc., by increasing physical and mental capacities, may become the means to greater material wealth and income and to greater social welfare.

In connection with the distinction between productive and unproductive expenditure, Professor Lutz asks, What shall be said of expenditure for armament, and for war purposes? His answer is: *

Some expenditure for the national defense, and for the preservation of internal order and security, is undoubtedly proper and justifiable, but it is important to realize that there are limits to this concession. In view of all that has happened since 1914 it would be absurd to contend that the immense expenditure for war purposes by the European Powers during the years preceding the World War was productive in the economic sense, or in any other sense. It has become almost an axiomatic truth that security declines as armament expands. A very large part of the pre-War expenditure on armies, navies and the paraphernalia of warfare, as well as the whole burden of the last senseless conflict, must be put down as utterly wasteful. The economic salvation of Europe, and, indeed of the world, depends upon a prompt and universal realization of the unproductive character of much of the so-called "preparedness" expenditure, and the development of such peaceable means of adjusting international differences as will render war impossible.

(c) Exhaustive Expenditure and Transfer Expenditure

ANOTHER important distinction pertaining to the character of public disbursement is that between exhaustive and transfer expenditure. Professor Pigou's discussion of this point follows.†

AMONG the various ways in which the resources raised by government authority from their subjects are employed a broad threefold distinction may be drawn. First, the government uses its money to secure the production of certain goods and services, whether it sells them to the public for fees (e.g. postal services and gas), or hands them over to the public free (e.g. education), or keeps them in its own hands (e.g. army, navy and civil service). Secondly, it uses its money to make transfers, not as a means of inducing a return in service, to foreigners to whom it is under contractual obligations. Lastly,

* Lutz, op. cit., p. 99.
† Adapted from A. C. Pigou, A Study in Public Finance, (Macmillan and Co., Ltd., London, 1928), Pt. I, Chap. III.

it uses it to make transfers to citizens of its own to whom it is under contractual or other obligations, e.g. to holders of war loans, old age pensioners, insurance contributors, and applicants for Poor Law relief. These three processes, though they can be covered by one general name, are different in substance.

Government expenditures to call out goods or services, whether for the government's own use or for payment to foreign creditors, stand on the same footing. They involve, in the one case directly, in the other indirectly, the actual using-up of a part of the community's resources, so that the community either has to do without these resources itself or has to work harder than it otherwise need have done in order to fill the gap that has for the time been made. These kinds of government expenditure may be called *real* or *exhaustive* expenditure. It need hardly be said that the term exhaustive in no way implies wasteful, or suggests that the community would be better off if the expenditure were not made; for example, expenditure in building a highly remunerative government electricity plant is exhaustive expenditure. On the other hand, government expenditure in interest on war loans, old age pensions, Poor Law services and so on to its own citizens does not involve the actual using-up of anything. Though, of course, those citizens who provide the money have to go without something, those who receive it — and they are probably in part the same people — exercise, apart from costs of collection, an exactly equivalent purchasing power. What is done with this purchasing power is their concern. It may be used to set people to work in exactly the same way as it would have done if it had not been transferred: or it may be used to set people to make capital goods, whereas, apart from the transfer, it would have been used to set them to make consumable goods, or *vice versa;* or to set them to make necessaries for the poor instead of luxuries for the rich, or *vice versa.* These, however, are secondary matters. The essential fact is that, from the point of view of the community as a whole, considered as standing over against the government, there is (apart from the administrative costs involved) no surrender of real resources. This sort of expenditure may be called *transfer* expenditure.[1]

---

[1] It will, of course, be understood that in the above argument we are concerned exclusively with the facts as they exist at a given time, not with the causes of those facts. The cause of the present large internal debt of this country was the Great War; and this cause of our present transfer expenditure obviously itself involved a vast amount of exhaustive expenditure. Again the raising of foreign debt during the war was in part an alternative to engaging in addi-

This distinction is very important, because it enables us to perceive essential differences between things that are verbally the same. Thus, it is widely believed that the real expenditure of a people in waging war is greater or less according as the rate of pay to its soldiers is high or low, and according as a large or small amount of money has to be paid in respect to their dependents. In 1914 many writers argued that Germany could conduct the war more cheaply than we could because her soldiers, being conscripts, received a much lower rate of pay than ours did. Again, it was, and still is, believed by many people that, because married men have dependents, to whom separation allowances must be paid when the men go into the army, whereas, in general, single men have no such dependents, a married soldier involves much more real expenditure to the nation than a single soldier. But the real expenditure involved in the maintenance of the army consists in the services of the soldiers themselves, who are withdrawn by war from civilian employment. Hence, the rate of pay given to them does not directly affect the real expenditure of the community in any degree. If more is paid to them than they would normally earn, a certain transference of resources is made from the rest of the community to them; if less is paid to them than they would normally earn, a certain transference is made from them to the rest of the community. The aggregate real expenditure on the war of them and the rest of the community combined, that is to say, of the country as a whole, is the same in either event; it is equal to the sum of the services which they render.

A second form of the same fallacy often appears in arguments about government extravagance. In many of these arguments every form of alleged extravagance is lumped together under the same head, and it is tacitly assumed that the face value of the extravagance always represents the real expenditure that it involves to the nation. For example, the alleged extravagance of paying £400 a year to Members of Parliament, of paying exorbitant prices to contractors or exorbitant wages to work people, of taking troops to some place at heavy cost and then taking them back to the place from which they came, of making immense quantities of a certain kind of shell which is afterward found to be useless — all these things are supposed to be exactly similar in character and effect. This is incorrect. From the money standpoint of the

tional exhaustive expenditure at home. If, therefore, no foreign debt had been raised, it is highly improbable that we should now be better off to the extent of the payment that has to be made for the service of that debt.

Treasury, it is, of course, true that they stand on the same footing. They all deplete the government balances and make necessary the raising of more money. From the standpoint of the community as a whole, however, they comprise two disparate kinds of extravagance, the effects of which are wholly different. To make masses of shells of a kind that we do not want involves a real using-up of capital and labour : to transport troops from Egypt to the Dardanelles and then to transport them back again, because the ships were not properly packed, also does this. But to pay a man, whether he be a Member of Parliament, or a contractor, or a workman, much more than his services are worth, that, undesirable though it is, does not directly involve any using-up of national resources. In the same way, if the government commandeers — and uses up in war — the services of men or buildings for less than their market worth, or even for nothing at all, this, while lowering the money expenses, does not directly affect at all the real expenses which its action involves.

Yet again, interest on the National Debt is often thought of as a single homogeneous entity. But in practice it includes both interest payable to foreign holders and interest payable to domestic holders. The payment to foreign holders involves the subtraction of so much actual real income — food, textiles and so on — from the use of the people of this country ; whereas the payment to domestic holders involves merely a transfer of control over those things from Englishmen in their capacity of taxpayers to Englishmen in their capacity as fund-holders. If fund-holding and taxpaying were shared out in exactly the same proportions among the people, then, *apart from the cost of administering the taxes and their indirect effects on production,* each individual person would be exactly as well-off as before. A realisation of this fact displays the fallacy of two widely-held opinions about the present European situation. The first of these is that Germany, having wiped out her internal debt by the collapse of the mark, is richer and stronger, as compared with other nations, than before. It is true, of course, that her budgetary problem is simplified, but fundamentally the wiping-out of her internal debt does not affect her aggregate wealth at all. The second opinion, embodied in the Report of the Dawes Committee, is that Germany ought not in fairness to bear less heavy taxation than her former enemies. Since a large part of the taxation of those countries is required to finance internal debt, this is an illicit conclusion. For £100 million of taxation to make foreign reparation payments is much more of a burden on a nation than £100 million of taxation to finance internal debt. In conceivable circumstances a nation might be able to meet internal debt up to the whole amount of its wealth without suffering any direct injury, while at the same time to meet any foreign claim at all would involve some of its members in starvation.

2. Public Expenditure and the Business Cycle

(a) Business Fluctuations and Public Works *

THE main lever with which public authorities can operate on business fluctuations is to be found in their policy of expenditures. Among the expenditures, those regularly recurring cannot be greatly increased or decreased. The amounts disbursed in the form of wages and salaries can scarcely be expanded in times of depression except under quite unusual circumstances. The sums used for the purchase of materials are somewhat more elastic, since the authorities can permit themselves some latitude in determining the quantity of their purchases at any given point of time. This latitude cannot be considerable, however, and the extent of the purchases is not sufficient to exercise an appreciable influence on business conditions. The public expenditures which are both of sufficient magnitude and of sufficient elasticity to warrant the hope that they may be successfully used to counteract changes in business conditions are those destined to provide for the future needs of the community — expenditures for public works. It is on such items, therefore, that the attention of students interested in the problem of alleviating or eliminating business fluctuations has been focused. The purpose of the following investigation is, first, to ascertain whether or not this device — constructing public works with a view to making them dovetail with business conditions — may be considered sound on general principles; further, to determine what its limitations are, on the assumption that it is feasible to distribute public works in such a manner as to give them the greatest possible effectiveness in counteracting business fluctuations; and, finally, to consider the obstacles which stand in the way of this ideal allocation of public works.

The customary practice hitherto has been to construct public works when the need for them arose or became urgent. Since the facilities provided by the public works already in existence have been most severely taxed in periods of business prosperity, and since, moreover, expectations concerning the future trend

* From Georg Bielschowsky, "Business Fluctuations and Public Works," *Quarterly Journal of Economics*, Vol. XLIV, (Feb., 1930), pp. 286–319.

of economic affairs have been most optimistic in these times, the result has been, on the whole, to make expansions and contractions of public works coincide with expansions and contractions of general business activity or follow them with a short lag.[1]   As a rule more public works have been constructed in times of prosperity than in times of depression. The practice has been universally condemned for this very reason.   It has been charged with widening the amplitude of business fluctuations by resulting in a competition for men and materials between public and private undertakings in times of prosperity and in a withholding of government orders during depression.[2]

Though public authorities have shown hitherto little concern about business conditions in the execution of their building programs, they could not well ignore the large increase in unemployment which regularly took place during business depressions.   Their standard device in trying to alleviate this unemployment has consisted in having recourse to so-called relief works, i.e., to set up some kind of public undertaking, the primary object being to furnish the largest amount of work for the unemployed with the smallest possible outlay of capital, the utility of the work undertaken being regarded as a minor consideration.   This practice also has been condemned with a unanimity rare among economists, mainly on the grounds that the works thus improvised are able to absorb only a small percentage of the unemployed, that their cost is very high on account of the inefficiency of workers unaccustomed to their tasks, that in many, even in most cases, they demoralize workers by paying them wages higher than those they have earned and, finally, that the work thus performed is, as a rule, of questionable use to the community.[3]

[1] Statistical investigations on this score are still scarce ; those that have been made confirm our statement.   I mention the following : Paul Bramstedt's investigation on the total expenditures for construction of 43 German cities (including Berlin) during the period 1894-1912 (*Soziale Praxis*, xxii, 387 et seq.) ; the study by Arthur L. Bowley and F. D. Stuart on the total expenditures for public works in England during the period 1906–13 in relation to national unemployment (*Is Unemployment Inevitable ?* [London, 1924], pt. 4) ; finally, F. G. Dickinson, "Public Construction and Cyclical Unemployment," *Annals of the American Academy of Political and Social Science* (cxxxix, 175–209), where a study is made covering the years 1919 to 1925.

[2] Cf. Report of the President's Conference on Unemployment (Washington : Government Printing Office, 1921), pp. 96, 97.

[3] Cf. W. H. Beveridge, *Unemployment. A Problem of Industry*, (London, 1921), pp. 191 et seq.
The validity of these criticisms has been again amply demonstrated by the experience with relief works in England after the war. Cf. Ronald C. Davison, *The Unemployed. Old Policies and New*, (London, 1899), pp. 51 et seq.

OBJECTIONS TO LONG-RANGE PLANNING OF PUBLIC WORKS

WHILE the traditional policy of governments with regard to public works and with regard to unemployment has thus met with universal rejection, the alternative offered for it, which is the long-range planning of public works to assure their flexible distribution, has not been universally accepted as an effective instrument for the promotion of business stability. There are, in the main, three objections which have been raised against this scheme.

The first objection—voiced by Mr. Hawtrey[4]—is to the effect that the best way to overcome depression consists in lowering the bank rate to a level which would make an expansion in the scale of activities attractive to the business public. An expansion of public works is not equally effective for this purpose. The public loans floated for the financing of the new undertakings are likely to do no more than displace private borrowings and thereby reduce private employment. If accompanied by the creation of new credits, expenditures on public works would, indeed, create additional employment, but then a creation of new credits without an increase in public construction would be equally effective in obtaining this result.

Mr. Hawtrey's reasoning holds true in the long run; its weakness lies precisely in disregarding the time element. It may be true that in the end a reduction of interest rates will "melt any depression," but the end is frequently pretty far off. It takes time, and sometimes a considerable period of time, before the volume of business activity responds to the stimulus of a low rate of interest, because it takes time for business men to regain sufficient confidence in their own future to avail themselves of the cheaper credit accommodations. A prompt enlargement in the scale of public construction may do much to shorten the period which elapses before a reduction of interest rates becomes effective and thereby to shorten the period of depression, aside from alleviating its severity. Mr. Hawtrey himself admits this contention by pointing out that an increase in public works would be justified if the bank rate had been reduced to its lowest point without bringing about a revival of trade,[5] and refers to the depression of 1894–96 as an instance of this kind. The same thing, however, has happened to a greater or less extent during every depression. Mr. Hawtrey thinks that the effectiveness of a reduction in the bank rate might be enhanced by having the central bank purchase securi-

---

[4] R. G. Hawtrey, *Trade and Credit*, (London, 1928), chap. 6, pp. 104 et seq.
[5] *Ibid.*, p. 113.

ties in the open market. Such a policy might indeed serve to curtail business stagnation; but would not the same end be better obtained by an increase in corporate profits such as would result from the placing of large government orders? Finally, Mr. Hawtrey is wrong in asserting that an increase of public loans will result in larger displacements of private borrowing. This argument might be correct if advanced against the financing of relief works; it does not apply to the financing of construction executed in accordance with a long-range program which would include only public improvements considered necessary by the government authorities. Since the funds for these works would have to be raised in any event, the volume of credit available for private use would be actually enlarged if their construction and financing were shifted from periods of high to periods of low business activity. This contention is easily proved if we base our reasoning on Mr. Hawtrey's own theory of the trade cycle, which runs in strictly monetary terms. We need only point out that competition for credit accommodations is keener when business is good than when it is bad, and that, consequently, the same amount of public loans will displace a smaller amount of private issues during depression than it would during prosperity.

A different argument against the expansion of public works during periods of bad business has been presented by Professor Cassel.[6] It runs in the following terms. Unemployment is due to the faulty adaptation of the supply of labor to the demand for it. If this adaptation were perfect, there would always be full employment. For this reason a national policy for the prevention of unemployment should be directed towards the elimination of all factors which stand in the way of a perfect adaptability of labor, the most important of these factors being the monopolistic policy of the trade unions. An extension of public works does not alleviate unemployment, because the funds needed for this purpose have to be procured either by taxation or by loans; in either case capital which would have been used by private industry is being claimed by the state and by the increase in public employment will be about offset by the decline of the private demand for labor.

These arguments may be disposed of in pretty much the same fashion as those advanced by Mr. Hawtrey. It may be

---

[6] Gustav Cassel, "Wird die Arbeitslosigkeit durch Notstandsarbeiten verringert?" *Soziale Praxis*, xxxv, 1057–1060. Cf. also the following discussion between Cassel, Lederer, Brentano, Toennies, Wilbrandt, and others in vols. xxxv and xxxvi of the same periodical.

true that a downward adjustment of wage rates in times of depression is frequently inevitable; it may also be admitted that trade unions may lengthen the period of depression by struggling against such an adjustment. The salient point, however, is that even if wage rates were reduced to their "normal" or "natural" level, an increase in employment would not immediately follow. Again, a period of time would have to elapse before business men had satisfied themselves that with these lower labor costs they were able to secure "normal" business profits by enlarging the scale of their operations. Again, a prompt expansion of public works might shorten this waiting period.

Finally we have to consider the arguments of those who hold that business fluctuations are due to fluctuations in the price level, which in turn may be directly traced to changes in the volume of currency and credit; the inference drawn from these premises being that, if price stability could be maintained, there would be no business fluctuations, no periods of general prosperity or general depression and hence no need for a flexible distribution of public works.[7]

This objection may be countered, first, by the statement that the distinction between general and partial prosperity (or depression) should be taken "cum grano salis." The difference between them is a difference in degree rather than in kind. There have always been industries which have flourished during "general" depressions or been depressed during periods of "general" prosperity. All that can be said, therefore, is that under a régime of stable price levels the number of industries simultaneously affected by either prosperity or depression will be smaller than it used to be before, provided this régime fulfils all the expectations of its adherents. This, however, would only mean that business fluctuations, in the sense of fluctuations in the aggregate volume of business profits, will be reduced, not that they will be eliminated. As long as business is conducted for profit, profits will be made; and as long as profits are made, their aggregate volume will show short-time deviations from its trend. Furthermore, as long as these short-time fluctuations persist, the effort will be made to reduce their amplitude, and it is a priori possible that the flexible allocation of public works will be an effective means towards this end.

We may conclude, then, that the flexible distribution of public works may be regarded on grounds of general theo-

[7] Cf. Norman Lombard, "The Proposed Prosperity Reserve," *Bulletin of the Stable Money Association,* (December, 1928), p. 6.

retical reasoning as a sound device for smoothing out business fluctuations, and proceed to consider its limitations in attaining this objective. These limitations are twofold: qualitative and quantitative.

QUALITATIVE LIMITATIONS TO LONG-RANGE PLANNING

THE main qualitative limitation has already been implied in the foregoing discussion, but may now be explicitly stated; it concerns the kind of unemployment[8] which may be relieved by this scheme. Since the flexible allocation of public works provides not only for their expansion in times of depression but also for a corresponding contraction in times of prosperity, it follows that it cannot reduce unemployment "in the long run." To put it in more scientific terms, it cannot reduce the level of unemployment, but only the fluctuations around that level, which are the so-called seasonal and the so-called cyclical fluctuations, It is, of course, possible and even probable that the reduction or elimination of these short-term changes may tend to raise the average level of employment over a decade or more. This indirect effect, however, would take place only after a long period of time.

It may readily be seen that the possibility of alleviating seasonal unemployment is very limited indeed. This unemployment is due to the fact that, in the present state of technique, the operations of the construction industries—which are those directly affected by any changes in the allocation of public construction—are mainly determined by climatic conditions. Recent investigations have, indeed, shown that they are not entirely determined by this factor, that the element of custom enters into the business practices of the industries to a surprisingly large extent. We may expect, however, that this traditionalism will not long persist in the face of the modern trend towards rational business methods. It is possible that the initiative of public authorities may become instrumental in its elimination, but this is the utmost which may be expected as the result of their activities; and it may be doubted whether they are well adapted for the rôle of leaders towards greater business efficiency.

"Cyclical" unemployment is thus the only kind of unemployment which may be effectively relieved by public works. Not all unemployment of this kind, however, can partake of the relief. As we have mentioned already, an extension or

---

[8] We shall deal, in the following discussion, mainly with this aspect of business fluctuations, since it is this aspect in which public authorities are mainly interested.

contraction of public works exercises a direct influence only on the construction industries and the amount of employment offered by them. The cyclic fluctuations of employment in construction industries are, therefore, the only ones for which the hope may be entertained that they can be effectively regulated; the other industries will have to content themselves with whatever stabilizing influence is exercised by the larger orders received from the building trades and by the increased buying power of their workers.[9]

Cyclical unemployment in the construction industries, finally, can be alleviated only in so far as the places in which public construction is expanded happen to coincide with the places in which the volume of private construction falls off. Labor is not exactly immobile, but its mobility is not great. It is obviously impossible to relieve unemployment in the building trades of New York City by increasing the volume of public works in Colorado, or vice versa. The effective relief of unemployment by public works thus necessitates a coördination of public with private construction not only in time, but also in space — a fact which entails a considerable complication of this problem for the government authorities.

Summing up, we may state that the qualitative limitations of a flexible distribution of public construction as a device for alleviating unemployment are (1) that they are able to alleviate cyclic unemployment only, and (2) that they are hampered in this endeavor by the lack of fungibility and the lack of mobility of labor.

QUANTITATIVE LIMITATIONS TO LONG-RANGE PLANNING

WE come now to the problem of the quantitative limitations of public works as stabilizers of business conditions and employment, i.e., to the problem of how much cyclical unemployment can be prevented by the ideal allocation of public construction. On this score two statistical studies have been made — for England and the United States respectively. The results of these appear, at first glance, to be highly encouraging.

Taking a typical pre-war cycle of ten years' duration and assuming that 80 per cent of the total cost of public works consist of wages, Mr. Bowley and Mr. Stuart reach the conclusion that all fluctuations of unemployment could have been eliminated, if £45,000,000 of expenditures had been postponed during the first three years, and if a total of £20,000,000 had

9 Some writers regard these indirect effects as equally important. Cf. **Sidney** and Beatrice Webb, *The Prevention of Destitution,* (London, 1911), chap. 6.

been advanced during the seventh and eighth years.[10]   Since,
according to the same authorities, the average annual expenditures for public works in England amounted to about £30,-
000,000 during the period in question,[11] the first act would
have involved a shift of one half, the second act that of one
third of their average volume.

In a study on public works and cyclical unemployment in
the United States during the period 1919–25 Mr. Dickinson
arrives at results which are somewhat similar to those obtained
by the British authors.[12]   According to him all cyclic fluctuations in employment might have been eliminated if there
had been no limits at all to the shifting of public construction.
If only one half of the public construction undertaken during
each year had been shifted, the amplitude of these fluctuations
would have been substantially reduced.[13]

Two objections against these conclusions suggest themselves
at once.   The first is, whether such a large shift as that en-
visaged by these authors would be technically possible, provided
the authorities were able to foresee the coming development
of the labor market and willing to act accordingly.   The
second is, whether this shift, if possible, would have been desirable in view of what we have learned about the qualitative
limitation of public construction in regulating the demand for
labor.   Public works, as we have seen, exercise a direct influence only on the building trades in the places where they
are undertaken.   If the building trades are fully employed,
it would be obviously inopportune to attempt any further
extension in the scale of public construction.   This would
only serve to subject building activity to an overstrain, which
is precisely what flexible distribution aims to avoid.   For this
reason there may be considerable depression and unemployment prevailing in other industries, or even in the building
trades of other places, while the possibilities of expanding public works are by no means exhausted.

Even if we were willing to wave aside these preliminary
objections as not touching the heart of the matter, there still
remain two criticisms of a more fundamental sort to be directed
against the soundness of the method by which these results
have been obtained.

The first criticism would be to the effect that it is not per-

[10] Bowley and Stuart, *op. cit.*, pp. 367–368.
[11] *Ibid.*, p. 371.
[12] Dickinson, *op. cit.*, pp. 190 et seq.
[13] *Ibid.*, Tables X and XI on pp. 190, 191,

missible to regard the additional employment offered by the
enlargement of public building activities as so much net increase in the total volume of employment available. This assumption disregards the fact that an extension of public works
has to be financed with funds, part of which at least would
otherwise have been used by private enterprise. An increase
in public employment is, therefore, at least partly offset by a
decline in private employment. It is only the difference between these two magnitudes which represents the net increase
in the total demand for labor.[14] The same process of reasoning
would also lead us to infer that the decline in employment
due to the withholding of public contracts in time of prosperity
will likewise be counteracted, this time by an enlargement in
the scale of private operations. Funds set free by the reduction
in public building are likely to be transferred to private borrowers. Moreover, since the competition of would-be borrowers for loans is very keen in times of expanding business
activity, we may expect that all of the funds thus released will
find their way into private use and that, consequently, the
amount of private employment thereby created will be as
large as, or larger than, the amount by which public employment has been diminished.

This last consideration suggests a line of analysis which challenges to a certain extent the commonly accepted views on the
effects of flexible distribution. Students of this subject take
it as a matter of course — one might almost say, as a matter of
faith — that a shift of public construction from good to bad
times is a measure whose sole effect is to ensure greater business
stability, and that the traditional practice of making fluctuations in public construction coincide with the fluctuations in
general business activity has no other result than that of increasing business instability. It is our contention that there
are elements in the first method which make for an increase
in the amplitude of industrial fluctuations and, conversely, that
there are elements in the second method which make for their
alleviation. Fortunately, in justifying this heterodox view, we
are able to base our reasoning on a thesis which also enjoys
universal recognition. If it is true, namely, that an over-
generous extension of credit to private industry occupies a
prominent place among the factors leading from prosperity to
overexpansion and recession — and all students of business
cycles agree with that proposition — then it must likewise be

14 "Of a million pounds borrowed by governmental authorities in bad times
. . . and expended in the employment of labour, not all represents a net addition to the demand for labour." Pigou, *Unemployment,* (London, 1913), p. 174.

true that any factor likely to reduce credit extension to private industry during the later phases of business prosperity will also tend to lessen overexpansion of business activity and mitigate the severity of the following depression. It can readily be seen that the traditional method of allocating public works, in so far as it entailed an increase in public borrowing during the later part of prosperity, has been a factor working in that direction. This increase in public loans would have been impossible without at least a relative decline in the volume of credit available for private industry, the credit system being, as a rule, heavily taxed during that period. Unless we are to assume that the credits set free by a reduction of public works during prosperity in accordance with the principles of flexible distribution would not be extended to private borrowers, we must conclude that the process of industrial overexpansion would be carried still further in this case and that the ultimate break would be more severe. We have no grounds for making that assumption and good reason to expect the opposite to happen, the reason being found in the organization of our banking system into highly competitive units which are dependent for their profits upon a full utilization of their resources. We are thus obliged to conclude that an expansion of public construction in times of high business activity likewise tends to exercise some stabilizing influence on economic conditions. The more credit used for the construction of roads, bridges, public buildings, etc., the less is available for the construction of new or the extension of old plants, for the accumulation of raw materials, and for similar purposes, and the less, consequently, the discrepancy between productive and consumptive capacity at the given price level which marks the end of each boom period. The direct stabilizing influence on business and employment which may be expected from a flexible distribution of public works must, therefore, be compared with the indirect stabilizing effects which the old system of allocating public construction tends to exercise through the medium of the credit mechanism. Only the balance which remains in favor of the first system can be counted as a net gain.

The weight of this consideration as a general argument against the flexible allocation of public works would depend upon the rôle which credit conditions play in determining the state of business, or upon the rôle which the individual theorist is willing to assign to them in this connection. Authors like Mr. Hawtrey, who are inclined to regard the business cycle as a "purely monetary phenomenon," will also be inclined to accept it as a conclusive proof of the uselessness or actual harmfulness of the proposed policy. Others whose views are more orthodox are likely to attach less importance to the point. The foregoing analysis, at any rate, makes it sufficiently clear that in trying to stabilize employment through a flexible distribution of public works we are compelled to sacrifice *some* stabilizing influences which the old method of allocating public works contained. This conclusion, together with that reached with regard to the net increase of employment resulting from an expansion in public construction, justifies the statement that the stabilizing influence on business conditions and employment exercised by a flexible distribution of public works cannot be quantitatively determined, but that it is smaller, and probably much smaller, than the results obtained by Bowley and Stuart, Dickinson, or other authors employing the same methods would lead us to assume.

It is, indeed, possible that the actual influence of flexible distribution may be enhanced by psychological factors. Foster and Catchings, in particular, emphasize this point rather strongly.[15] We doubt whether the government can expect much help from this quarter. There have always been outstanding business men with sufficient vision, courage, and freedom from financial commitments, to use a period of depression for the enlargement of their production facilities, and with sufficient caution to clear their stocks and reduce their scale of operations before the advent of the slump. It is the aim of flexible distribution to increase the number of business executives committed to such a policy. This purpose would be achieved only if the business public could be reasonably sure that the government alone would be able to effect a substantial alleviation of industrial fluctuations by a proper adjustment of its public works program to business conditions. Without such assurance it would be tantamount to economic suicide for the business man to align himself in his decisions with the government, disregarding the momentary economic situation. As it is doubtful whether he can have this assurance, we must also be skeptical as to his willingness and ability to give active support to the government policy.

THE discussion of "the long-range planning of public works" as a device for reducing the fluctuations of business conditions and employment has so far been based upon the premise that public works have been allocated in such a way as to make them most effective in reaching that objective. The obstacles to such an ideal allocation of public contracts, however, are large

15 Foster and Catchings, *The Road to Plenty*, p. 190 et passim.

in number and various in kind. The second part of the present investigation will be devoted to their analysis, for which purpose they will be classified under three headings : those of administrative, technical, and economic character.

I. ADMINISTRATIVE OBSTACLES TO AN IDEAL ALLOCATION OF PUBLIC CONTRACTS

THE first administrative difficulty which suggests itself is that of speeding up the operation of the bureaucratic machinery, of making officials act quickly,[16] a difficulty which will be considered very grave even by those who otherwise are not professional pessimists.

The second difficulty consists in finding a way to make quick action by officials possible, provided the first obstacle has been overcome. At present such quick action by public authorities is well-nigh impossible, on account of the long period which elapses between a proposal for an increase in public construction, the appropriation of the necessary funds by the legislature, the raising of the funds in the prescribed way and, finally, the expenditure of the funds raised. The necessity of a less rigid fiscal system has been recognized by all students of this subject. Apparently the first to emphasize it were the experts whom the French government consulted on this score after the crisis of 1907 and who advanced the following recommendations : [17]

(1). To have appropriations for public works not utilized during the current fiscal year automatically transferred to the next year.

(2). To form special reserve funds in the departments and administrative agencies concerned with public works.

(3). To accumulate a general reserve fund to be used for the expansion of public works in times of severe unemployment.

Almost identical proposals were made in 1921 by the President's Conference on Unemployment in Washington, and given wide publicity, thanks to the efforts of Mallery,[18] Foster and Catchings,[19] and other writers.

Administrative and fiscal reforms of the kind indicated are doubtless necessary for the success of the scheme under discussion. In sponsoring them, however, it is advisable to bear in

---

[16] Dickinson, *op. cit.*, p. 190. Mr. Dickinson speaks of city officials in particular, but the same is true of officials generally.

[17] Rapports présentés au nom de la commission par Mm. Georges Cahen et Edmond Laurent sur les indices des crises économiques et sur les mesures financières propres à atténuer les chômages résultant de ces crises (Paris, 1909).

[18] Otto T. Mallery, "The Long-Range Planning of Public Works" in *Business Cycles and Unemployment,* (New York, 1923), p. 258 et passim.

[19] Foster and Catchings, *op. cit.*, p. 193 et passim.

mind that the reason for the present rigid limitation of public expenditures by legislatures has been the endeavor of the tax-payers to curb public extravagance, and that the advocacy of greater freedom for the government in determining its ex-penditures may be tantamount to proposing a remedy which is worse than the evil.

The greatest administrative obstacle to a proper allocation of public contracts, however, seems to consist in the difficulty of bringing into line the policies of the various authorities by which public contracts are awarded. It would be necessary to perform two tasks in order to bring about this result. In the first place, the federal government as well as the state and city administrations would have to coördinate the activities of all of their departments engaged in the construction and mainte-nance of public works; in the second place, the activities of federal, state and city governments would have to be har-monized with each other.

The difficulty of the first task can be readily appreciated if we recall that there are in the United States, for example, thirty-nine federal agencies authorized to execute some kind of public construction, thirty-five of which belong to nine out of the ten national departments, while four are unattached.[20] Some practical experience in this respect has been gained by progressive German city administrations, like that of Frankfort-on-the-Main, which even before the war had the courage to initiate an attempt at alleviation of unemployment by advance planning of their public works.[21] But these experiences give only an inkling of the obstacles that have to be overcome.

If the first task must thus be considered very difficult, the second one — the coördination of central and local government policies — is truly enormous. Since the bulk of public con-struction is not executed by central but by local governments, it is also apparent that its successful solution is of paramount importance. At bottom this problem is nothing but a par-ticular aspect of the issue which has dominated all constitu-tional struggles: that of local self-government versus centralized control of public affairs. As far as Anglo-Saxon countries are concerned, this issue has been definitely settled in favor of local autonomy and there is no chance that the decision will be re-versed just for this particular purpose. Nor would experience with public works in countries like France, which have gone the other way, encourage such a step. There is, then, no

---

[20] Mallery, *op. cit.*, pp. 246, 247.
[21] Cf. Ernst Bernhard, *Die Vergebung der öffentlichen Arbeiten in Deutschland im Kampf gegen die Arbeitslosigkeit,* (Berlin, 1913).

chance that the federal government will be able to obtain the coöperation of state and city authorities by direct administrative pressure. Some writers like Bowley[22] and Mallery[23] expect to have the same result achieved indirectly, by a skilful use of the greater economic power of the central government, especially if combined with effective propaganda. Mr. Mallery, in particular, believes that federal subsidies or loans to public authorities advanced for the construction of public improvements are "a convenient key to unlock many doors," and that in order to ensure a shifting of public works from good to bad times it is only necessary "that a clause be attached to each federal appropriation . . . . reserving a certain part, say 20 per cent, for expenditure only when the president shall find a period of national unemployment and industrial depression to exist."[24] It is doubtful whether such a clause would be altogether fair to the recipients of the appropriation, since the allocation of their public works — if conducted properly — would have to be determined primarily by the volume and movement of employment in their particular region, which may differ considerably from the fluctuations of "national employment." It is still more doubtful whether such a clause would be effective. Upon closer scrutiny, the following dilemma is found to exist as regards its effectiveness. If the federal appropriations are small compared to the total costs of construction, we may expect that they will not influence the decisions of local authorities to any considerable extent; if, on the other hand, they are large, it is possible, even probable, that they will induce local governments to expand their program of public works beyond the limits set either by economic necessity or by their own resources. English experiences during the post-war years attest the reality of the danger inherent in the second alternative.[25] The power of propaganda, on the other hand, is a factor which may become very large, but the magnitude of which is unknown beforehand. On the basis of past experience it seems likely to be more effective in Anglo-Saxon countries.

II. TECHNICAL OBSTACLES

Of somewhat less importance than the obstacles due to the nature of the agencies undertaking public works are the obstacles arising from the nature of the works themselves. They

[22] Arthur L. Bowley, *The Regularisation of Industry*, (Christian Order of Industry Series, no. 5, Cambridge, 1924), pp. 34 et seq.

[23] Mallery, *op. cit.*, pp. 244 et seq.

[24] *Ibid.*, p. 245.

[25] Cf. Davison, *op. cit.*, pp. 47, 48.

are, however, by no means negligible. The technical problems which arise are not so much those of effecting shifts in public construction large enough to make a considerable impress on business conditions and employment; they are rather those of effecting prompt adjustments of the volume of public works to business fluctuations within the technical limits of their postponement or anticipation. Such an adjustment would be easy if the number of public works undertaken were large, the single undertaking small, and the time of construction short. This is, however, not quite the case; some large-scale public undertakings are in course of construction all the time. Since these are the works which can be most conveniently postponed or most readily anticipated, we may expect that under the long-range planning of public works a period of industrial depression will see the starting of those public constructions which are small in number, and in which the individual undertaking is large in size and the time required for its completion comparatively long. This is the first circumstance to be considered. The second is that the construction of such undertakings, as it progresses, requires an increasing number of workers and an increasing amount of materials, the maximum requirements for both being reached, as a rule, only a considerable time after work has been started. In view of these two circumstances, public works begun during depression may not bring their heaviest demands for men and materials until the following period of prosperity. This increased demand on the part of works started in the past could not be offset by diminishing the volume of current public construction, because, according to our premise, all public construction for which no pressing need exists has already been shifted. It is, then, possible that a flexible distribution of public works will not diminish competition for men and materials during times of active business, but will actually enhance it. The shorter the duration of the "business cycle," the greater will the probability of this become; and a tendency towards shorter periods of depression and prosperity has been apparent during the last decades.

We have so far in our investigation made a sharp distinction between the flexible distribution of public works and the establishment of public relief works in times of general unemployment. In dealing with the economic obstacles to flexible distribution we shall do well, however, to submit this distinction to a more critical analysis.

As we have already seen there are, in the main, three objections commonly advanced against public relief works. They demoralize workers by paying them wages in excess of what they have earned, they entail excessively high costs of construction, and they are frequently of indifferent value to the community when completed. The first two alleged shortcomings of public works are due to a common cause — the inefficiency of workers employed — and therefore can be remedied if their cause can be removed. Past experience, particularly that of Germany, shows that the maintenance of high standards of efficiency among laborers employed on public relief works is quite feasible. All that is needed is a close coöperation between the authorities conducting relief works and the public labor exchanges. Such coöperation enables the authorities to select the men best suited for the kind of work at hand, and it enables the staff of the labor exchanges to keep a record of each worker's performance, a record which the worker will be anxious to keep good for fear of lessening his chances of future employment. As regards the first two points, then, properly conducted relief works cannot be considered much inferior to ordinary public works. With regard to the third alleged drawback of relief works — their questionable value to the community — it may be pointed out that the public authorities will try to make the work undertaken meet some actual or expected need of the community, and that this charge will be correct only if they should fail in this effort. But ordinary public works undertaken according to a long-range program may also fail in this respect, unless the program is infallible in gauging the kind and extent of present or future public needs. They are superior to relief works only in so far as long-range planning offers better chances of adjusting public construction to public needs than the impromptu decisions which have to be made in setting up relief works. To put it succinctly and somewhat paradoxically: public undertakings originally started as relief works will be promoted to the rank of anticipated public works, if they come to serve some need of the community; on the other hand, ordinary public works executed during a period of unemployment, if they prove to be useless in the light of future developments, will be demoted to the rank of relief works.

III. ECONOMIC OBSTACLES

THE economic obstacles to a flexible distribution of public works may be traced to two causes: (1) our uncertainty concerning the future trend of economic events; (2) our uncertainty as to the ultimate effect of measures designed to influence such events as can be foreseen.

The obstacle due to the first cause — the unpredictability of business — has been minimized by certain authors, foremost among them being Mr. Dickinson. In his opinion, "the success or failure of business forecasting has little to do with the whole plan. It would be necessary for some agency to advise public officials when they ought to sell bonds and let contracts. It seems possible to fasten this apparently onerous burden upon a first-class clerk in the Bureau of Labor Statistics at Washington. His duty would be to watch the index of employment and immediately inform the numerous public officials throughout the country whenever the index approached 5 per cent above or below the average of the preceding years.[26]

We are inclined to doubt the effectiveness of this proposal. Our skepticism is based on several grounds. First of all Mr. Dickinson's analysis disregards the existence of regional differences in the fluctuations of employment; secondly, it disregards the powerful psychological forces which are likely to influence the decisions of public officials as well as of business men ; and finally, it disregards the fact that all unemployment appearing during depression is not due to "cyclical" causes.

It is evident that, since the indices of regional employment differ — and sometimes differ considerably — from the index of national employment, such a procedure as that outlined would be far too rigid for its purpose. More important still is the second point, which applies with particular force to European conditions. True it is that after a few years of good business, people are likely to forget the waves of pessimism which sweep a country during a serious depression. But during each period of business stagnation the impression among business men is that the end of all days has come, while in scientific circles the conviction gains ground that the capitalistic system has reached the limits of its growth. The effect of such a mental atmosphere on the decisions of public authorities should not be underrated, and is certainly not of the kind to encourage them to an expansion of their building program.

Assuming, however, that the public authorities have not been infected by the universal spirit of pessimism and continue to believe in a future upward trend of economic affairs, they face the problem of determining how such a future upswing will affect their particular region. To appreciate the difficulty of this problem we must consider that much of the unemployment during times of bad business is due to non-cyclical factors. Among these factors the main is the gradual or abrupt decline of certain industries conditioned by economic changes in the broadest sense of the term. Present instances of this

---

[26] Dickinson, *op. cit.*, p. 200.

kind are coal-mining, the cotton industry, shipbuilding. In regions where such industries are concentrated unemployment will be heaviest; but they are also those in which the need for public improvements will grow less in consequence of the permanent reduction in industrial activity. Unfortunately the distinction between cyclical and non-cyclical unemployment is easier to establish in theory than to observe in practice. Public authorities in such regions are, therefore, likely to err on the side of optimism. Civic pride and consideration for their unemployed will combine to induce them to expand their public works when economic conditions would point to a contraction.[27]

Assuming, however, that the public authorities have been right in deciding upon an expansion of their building activity, they may still commit mistakes in choosing the kind of public improvements to be undertaken. Again Mr. Dickinson seems to us unduly optimistic as regards the difficulty of the latter task. According to him, "The problems in chronological order are — first, to withhold contracts until the state of employment becomes less favorable, and second, to build in advance. Advancing or accelerating the letting of contracts is the more difficult project because it requires knowledge not only of future construction costs, but also of the future need for certain specific public improvements. It seems fortunate that the long-range planning of future construction is much more concerned with postponement, the easier shift."[28]

This statement that the long-range planning of public works will consist in postponement rather than anticipation of them might be challenged at the very outset. Recent experiences of countries like the United States would lend weight to such a challenge. It might be pointed out, for example, that the remarkable prosperity of the country during recent years has been due largely to the rapid growth of the automobile industry, which in turn has been made possible by the rapid increase in road building.* A policy which aimed at postponing an appreciable part of the road-building program would have been obviously unwise under these circumstances; it would have amounted to killing prosperity in the effort to mitigate depression. Speaking in more general terms it may be said that, as industrial activity becomes more dependent for its growth upon a corresponding increase in the facilities offered by public improvements, a policy of postponing public works becomes more questionable for this reason.

* Eds. note: Bielschowsky is referring to "the period of prosperity" which ended in the fall of 1929.

[27] Cf. Davison, *op. cit.*, pp. 54–55.   [28] Dickinson, *loc. cit.*

Even if we were to admit the first part of Mr. Dickinson's contention, we should still have to reject its second part to the effect that there is a considerable or even essential difference between a postponement and an anticipation of public construction. The idea back of this proposition seems to be that, if road building, for example, has been postponed in a period of prosperity to the extent of say $50,000,000, it can be expanded in the following depression by the same amount. Such would indeed be the case under one condition : that the character of economic development remains the same as it has been in the past. An argument that more roads are desirable now because they have been desirable in the past obviously makes this tacit assumption. If this is the case, the anticipation of future public needs does not offer any serious difficulty. If, on the other hand, there is a sudden change in the structure of the economic system, the difficulty of adjusting public improvements to this change is shared by postponed and anticipated works alike. Although there has been a contraction of road building in the past — to use again the example previously chosen — it may now be advisable, in view of the economic changes which have taken place in the meantime, to use the funds released for the building of, let us say, municipal airports. Postponement and anticipation are, in the last analysis, the same thing; the deferring of some present construction to a future date and the advancing of some future construction to the present date both imply the expectation that there will be no changes, or at least no unforeseen changes, in the pattern of public needs.

The difficulty of deciding whether there should be any expansion of public works at all and the difficulty of choosing the right kind of public improvements for this expansion program are the two major economic difficulties which result from our comparative ignorance of future developments. There are also two minor factors working in the same direction.

One of these factors is obsolescence. Even if the authorities have been correct in anticipating some future public need, the particular public improvement which they have constructed to serve this need may become inadequate or useless for this purpose because of technical changes which have taken place in the meantime. This applies with particular force to the so-called remunerative public undertakings like gas and water works, power stations, and the like, which play a large rôle in Europe, where government ownership and operation of public utilities is more common than it is in the United States, and where, for this reason, the temptation of the government to disregard technical efficiency in favor of social considerations is stronger.

The other factor is the change in the costs of construction in so far as it is due to technical innovations. Public authorities which have avoided all the pitfalls mentioned in planning and executing their construction program may still expose themselves to the charge of having executed this program in a wasteful fashion, because public improvements which they have anticipated might have been more cheaply constructed at the later date when methods of construction were more efficient.

This last consideration leads us to the second set of economic obstacles to the long-range planning of public works, obstacles which may be summed up in the statement that this advance planning has to take account not only of the time, place, and kind of construction, but also of the manner in which the work is to be carried out, in order to bring about the desired economic effects. Mistakes which the public authorities may commit in this respect and the consequences of these mistakes are suggested by the theoretical arguments against the flexible distribution of public works which have been discussed above, and which have been rejected on the ground that they do not prove the principle of flexible distribution to be incorrect.

In this connection Mr. Bowley's argument has been countered by pointing out that the shifting of necessary public works from periods of good to periods of bad business will actually result in expanding the total volume of credit available for industry and commerce, because the same amount of public loans will displace less trade issues in time of depression than it would in times of high business activity. Government authorities, however, may allow themselves considerable latitude in determining just what amount of public improvements is necessary; if their construction program is linked with the struggle against unemployment, it is possible, even probable, that marginal proposals will get the benefit of the doubt, and consequently that the volume of public construction will be larger than it would be otherwise, the same being true of the total volume of public borrowing. Since countries where the "cyclic" fluctuations of employment are heavy frequently suffer in addition from a scarcity of capital, the net result of long-range planning would be to accentuate this scarcity of capital and thereby perhaps to alleviate business fluctuations, but only at the expense of prolonging periods of depression and shortening periods of prosperity.

Other mistakes which the public authorities may commit in

carrying out their long-range program of public works are suggested by Professor Cassel's arguments. We have agreed with Professor Cassel that a downward revision of wage rates is frequently imperative in times of depression; we may now add that a downward adjustment of prices is always necessary during such a period. It is again possible and probable that this necessary decline of prices and wages will be delayed by an expansion of public building activity during depression. For a number of reasons — political pressure by the interested groups, social considerations, and lack of business acumen being the most likely among them — public authorities are likely to pay higher prices and wages than entrepreneurs and workers could obtain on the open market. This will encourage merchants and manufacturers to hold on to their commodity stocks for higher prices rather than dispose of them at a loss, and it will similarly encourage the struggle of workers against wage reductions, again with the ultimate result of lengthening the period of depression.

FINALLY the proposition advanced by the adherents of the stable-money school, to the effect that fluctuations in the volume of business and employment are conditioned by price fluctuations, suggests the question whether the conclusions reached so far will have to be modified if the premise upon which they were built should no longer hold.

This premise has been that the fluctuations of prices, business profits, volume of trade, and volume of employment will move on parallel lines. It has been justified inasmuch as most of the business fluctuation in the past conformed to it; on the other hand, we have admitted that the connection between the phenomena in question is purely empirical and by no means necessary on a priori grounds. The reason for its existence has been the fact that past periods of prosperity have witnessed an expansion in the demand for commodities which has been so large as to bring about, first, an increase in the volume of trade, second, an increase in the volume of employment, third, further increases in the volume of trade and employment together with a rise in prices and, finally, a further rise in prices without a further increase in the volume of production or employment; this rise in prices, then, brought about upward adjustments of wages and interest rates — usually belated and inadequate.

It is quite possible that in future a demand will not expand sufficiently to occasion a rise in prices; either because of a stricter credit control, or because of the changed attitude of a business public which has come to estimate the benefits of economic stability more highly than the "easy money" to be made during periods of precipitate business expansion, or because of the greater elasticity of modern productive equipment, which makes it possible to meet even a vastly enlarged demand at stable or lower prices, or, finally, because of a combination between all these factors. The post-war business fluctuations in the United States offer instances of this kind. Thus the period 1925–26 had witnessed an increase in the volume of business profits and the volume of trade together with an actual decline in the volume of employment. The same combination of rising business profits, rising output, and falling prices might have been observed during the second half of 1929 together with a rising volume of employment. In the first period mentioned interest rates were fairly stable, while during 1929 they had advanced to a level which in former times would have heralded the advent of a crisis. In both cases, however, the movement of interest rates has been determined not so much by the demand for credit on the part of industry and trade as by the behavior of that "enfant terrible" among modern economic institutions — the stock exchange. Future business fluctuations may differ from the old "business cycle" in still other respects. It seems, indeed, that in the absence of extreme fluctuations in the demand for commodities we may expect almost all the mathematically possible combinations between the movements of business profits, prices, volume of trade, volume of employment, etc., to occur at the same time.

If such deviations of future business fluctuations from their historic pattern should become more frequent, additional problems in the process of allocating public works with a view to stabilizing business conditions would arise. It is clear, for example, that, once periods of low employment cease to be also periods of low interest rates and low prices, government authorities in trying to counteract a decline of employment by an expansion of public works cannot count upon raising the funds necessary for this purpose on favorable terms. The question at once arises whether they would be justified in following this course of action, even though it involved the payment of high rates of interest and high prices for supplies, and thus amounted to sacrificing the interests of taxpayers to those of the unemployed. Assuming that this question is answered in the affirmative, another question presents itself, namely, whether this policy would bring about the desired result. Is it not possible, for example, that an increase in public orders during a period of rising unemployment which has been brought about by a large-scale application of labor-saving machinery may encourage still further displacements of men by machinery and thus create still more unemployment? [29]

Such questions and many others of the same kind suggest themselves in this connection. None of them can be answered beforehand, and we are not sure whether many of them could be answered after a study of the concrete situation out of which they arise. There is only one thing we may be positive about, namely, that the difficulties of long-range planning, already very considerable indeed, will be multiplied should industrial fluctuations in future fail to shape themselves in the manner of the old-style business cycle.

This brings to an end our discussion of the economic problems involved in the attempt to regulate business conditions by public works. We shall content ourselves with merely mentioning that there are also political problems involved in this scheme, without proceeding to an examination of the latter, except for pointing out that the issues raised by the proposed changes cannot be kept out of politics. It need not be elaborated that even if government authorities overcome all the obstacles and avoid all the dangers which we have enumerated, there will be one danger left which they may not be able to avoid, and one obstacle which they may not be able to overcome — the demagogy of politicians.

CONCLUSIONS

To sum up. The foregoing argument does not, in our opinion, invalidate the principle of flexible distribution as set forth by Foster and Catchings and by the other authors mentioned. It rather points out the very numerous qualifications to which this principle is subject in its practical application. It also implies that these qualifications will vary in importance according to the political and economic conditions prevailing in a given country. On the whole it may be said that the greater the stability, efficiency, and integrity of the governments directing the planning and execution of public works, the smaller the political and economic difficulties involved in this scheme will be. The economic difficulties will be easier to overcome, the larger the capital supply of the country is; that is, the less business expansions are hampered by shortage of funds, and the easier it is to foresee coming economic developments. In short,

---

[29] This is by no means a remote possibility. It should be considered, first, that even the most advanced enterprises do not avail themselves of all known devices for increasing the productivity of labor, and that there are surprisingly large differences between the productivity of labor in different plants of the same industry; second, that the extent to which labor-saving devices are utilized depends mainly upon the actual or expected volume of output.

the less is expected of a flexible distribution of public construction the more it will achieve. It is not "The Road to Plenty;" it is not even a first-rate device for reducing business fluctuations; it must rather be conceived of as the last finishing touch which a highly competent government may put upon a smoothly working business economy. However, if a country still suffers from the political upheaval and the annihilation of wealth which have been the consequences of the late war, and if innovations in technique and business management follow each other with bewildering rapidity, the effectiveness of this device decreases and the dangers connected with its execution increase. The relief of unemployment by means other than charity or doles is an end which will always justify vigorous efforts towards its realization, but the leadership in this fight against unemployment belongs, paradoxically enough, to the countries that are least affected by this social evil, on account of having reached the highest degree of economic and political stability. A clear perception of the limits within which the scheme discussed is workable and of the obstacles to be surmounted on the way to its successful execution will in any event improve the chances of bringing the problem of unemployment nearer to a solution.

(b) *An Analysis of Certain Practical and Theoretical Objections to the Long-Range Planning of Public Works for the Stabilization of Employment.**

PROFESSOR LOUCKS has analyzed in greater detail than has Bielschowsky some of the objections to the increasing of public expenditures for public works in periods of industrial depression. It will be seen that Loucks' conclusions are not in every case identical with those of Bielschowsky.

LONG-RANGE planning of public works for the mitigation of unemployment has been so little used and so superficially analyzed that many of the practical and theoretical problems connected with it remain unsolved. The following discussion attempts to point out and evaluate some of the major objections to long-range planning, especially as it might be used by the City of Philadelphia.[1]

---

* From W. N. Loucks, *The Stabilization of Employment in Philadelphia*, (University of Pennsylvania Press, Philadelphia, 1931), pp. 232–256.

[1] The most complete statements of these objections will be found in "Business Fluctuations and Public Works" by Georg Bielschowsky, *Quarterly Journal of Economics*, February, 1930, pp. 286–319; "A Criticism of Stimulated Construction as a Cure for Business Depression," by E. C. Harwood, *The Annalist*, May 30, 1930, p. 1155.

WOULD AN EXPANDED PUBLIC WORKS PROGRAM ATTRACT WORKERS FROM OTHER PLACES?

IT has been claimed that, if one community were to attempt a stabilization of employment through long-range planning, the result would be the attraction of unemployed men from other communities in sufficient numbers to reduce seriously or completely destroy the effectiveness of the plan in the original community. It is thought that in so far as anything actually is accomplished in the way of creating jobs, the news will spread rapidly to unemployed groups elsewhere. Exaggerated newspaper accounts of these accomplishments and wild rumors which are known to float about during such times will further increase the inflow of job-seekers. The usual immobility of labor is considerably decreased during unemployment periods. Recent experiences of the Ford plants in Detroit demonstrate that unemployed laborers may move in enormous numbers into districts actually or supposedly affording employment opportunities.

An illustrative experience of this sort was that of Vancouver, Canada, during the 1921–22 depression. The unemployed were registered and considerable park improvement, road and sewer, wood-cutting, and rock-breaking work was provided by the municipality. Although the work was clearly of a relief nature, "Vancouver quickly became the assembling place for unemployed men from all parts of Western Canada."[2]

If Philadelphia were to put into operation a program of expanded public works construction during a period of unemployment, there is scarcely any doubt that, in the absence of similar plans in neighboring cities, a marked inflow of unemployed laborers would occur. Philadelphia's location in the center of a highly industrialized region would undoubtedly increase the tendency toward such a movement. This, therefore, is a serious practical problem to which there are three possible solutions:

(1) The development of similar plans by other municipalities, by states, and by the federal government. If such activities were to be undertaken by other neighboring agencies, there would be little or no inflow, either because of the effectiveness of these efforts to create jobs elsewhere, or because the laborers, knowing the ineffectiveness of local plans, would decide that

[2] Quoted from the Annual Report of the Department of Labor of British Columbia, by V. A. Mund, "Prosperity Reserves of Public Works," *The Annals of the American Academy of Political and Social Science*, Supplement, May, 1930, p. 3.

efforts being put forth in other communities were no more productive of jobs.

(2) The development of an attitude on the part of the community that no differentiation should be made between resident and non-resident laborers and that any extra jobs created are a net gain, whether they go to local citizens or to recently arrived unemployed men. It is hardly to be expected, however, that one city, having exerted itself to create additional jobs, would be quite so generous in its attitude toward citizens of neighboring communities.

(3) Probably the most adequate solution, at least until long-range planning becomes much more widespread than it is likely to be in the near future, is for each community to develop a policy of giving preference to local citizens so far as possible. Of course, each contractor will have to be left free to choose his nucleus of technical assistants and highly skilled workmen, but there are several plans whereby it may be made reasonably certain that the major portion of the working force will be composed of local laborers. German cities have experimented with plans for registering the unemployed and requiring contractors working on municipal projects to pick a certain portion of their employees from these rolls, provided properly qualified men are listed thereon.[3] It has also been suggested that bidding contractors be required to agree to take, if men are available, a certain portion of their labor forces from the local labor supply. In such cases the city's only obligation is to check up on the contractor's fulfillment of his promise.

DOES LONG-RANGE PLANNING INVOLVE IMPOSSIBLE OCCUPATIONAL SHIFTS?

OPPONENTS of long-range planning for employment stabilization often resort to the argument that, were jobs to be created by expanding public works, occupational barriers would keep many unemployed workers from benefiting thereby. These critics of the plan are accustomed to say that barbers cannot be turned into bricklayers, clerks into hodcarriers, etc., in a short time if, indeed, they ever can be. These barriers, it is claimed, would so restrict the satisfactory shifting of unemployed workers to the jobs created that any such attempt at stabilization would be effective only within that very small group of occupations connected with the construction industry.

Obviously no such occupational shifts as those suggested are

[3] Otto T. Mallery, "The Long-Range Planning of Public Works," in *Business Cycles and Unemployment*, p. 239; Mollie Ray Carroll, *American Economic Review*, Supplement, March 1930, pp. 20-23.

in the minds of the long-range planning advocates. It should first be noted that workers other than those directly employed upon public works are benefited by expanded improvement programs during unemployment periods, for extra jobs, give extra purchasing power, which becomes demand for many kinds of labor. However, it is true that, so far as only one city is concerned, by far the most significant results of long-range planning are the jobs created directly by the projects undertaken. It is, therefore, quite legitimate to question whether it is possible that large numbers of unemployed persons will be able to shift to such jobs.

Three classes of laborers may be expected to come to the newly-created public works jobs:

(1) Skilled and unskilled laborers who have been employed in various types of construction work but are out of work because of the depressed condition of the private construction industry. Clearly there is no problem of occupational shift in such cases, for the change is from a former or usual job on a private construction project to the same type of job on a public project.

(2) Skilled or semi-skilled workers, usually employed in industries other than construction, whose skill fits them to take jobs on construction projects. For instance, truck drivers in various industries may become drivers of trucks hauling materials and excavated earth; men who have operated power machines may turn to the operation of hoisting, mixing, and other machinery; carpenters and woodworkers from many industries may turn to the erecting of concrete forms, scaffolding, and framework; and even bookkeepers and clerks may become timekeepers and paymasters on public construction projects. The possibilities of shifting between jobs on a given level of skill, and requiring similar muscular capacities, have been greatly underestimated by the critics of long-range planning.

(3) Unskilled manual workers, formerly employed in a wide range of industries. It is for the unskilled group that the greatest number of jobs will be created and occupational shifts will occasion the least difficulties. In fact there would seem to be only two factors restricting this suggested mobility of unskilled manual workers. On the one hand, if employed on inside work, they have probably become accustomed to protection from the climatic conditions of heat, cold, and dampness. Such workers may encounter some difficulties when they attempt to engage in outside construction work. Again, particular types of factory work often cause certain restricted muscular developments which do not meet the usual construction

job requirement for an all-around development. But in general, unskilled manual laborers in large numbers would find no significant hindrances to shifts from their present occupations to construction jobs on the same level of skill. . .

THE fact that some portions of the building trades are strongly unionized might complicate the problem of occupational shifts were it necessary to bring non-union men into unionized occupations. It is conceivable that under such conditions union men would withdraw and seriously disrupt the public works program. This difficulty might become acute if there were a scarcity of union men available for some strategic portion of the work upon which the remainder depended. Although this problem is not to be overlooked, it usually would not constitute a major difficulty in the way of expanding public works during unemployment years. There are several possible solutions, any one of which would be adequate, the choice depending upon the immediate conditions.

(1) The City might refuse to recognize the union's right to demand that all men hired carry union cards, while, at the same time, it might pay union rates of wages to all employees and enforce all union working rules under union conditions. It is very doubtful whether in such circumstances unions would withdraw their members from employment. In fact, present conditions indicate that such a solution, or indeed one still less favorable to the union, would be entirely acceptable. It is said that union men are employed by contractors on municipal construction projects in Philadelphia at wage rates lower than the union scale, despite ordinances requiring that every such contractor must pay union rates, and must make affidavit that he has done so before the City Controller signs a warrant on the City Treasurer in favor of the contractor. The unions involved are attempting neither to enforce these ordinances nor to get union men to withdraw from the employment of these contractors. Such a situation indicates that union rules and policies would interpose no barriers to the carrying out of projects as dictated by a long-range plan. Of course, the situation could change quite suddenly at any time, thereby necessitating a modification of policy on the part of the City, possibly along the lines suggested.

(2) The unions might be induced to issue temporary membership cards to men needed in order to carry on portions of the construction work more rapidly than would be possible with the limited supply of union men. A union might be induced to follow such a policy either by its desire to co-

operate in the mitigation of general unemployment or by its desire to open directly or indirectly as many jobs as possible for members of its own and other unions.

THE contention that long-range planning merely will divert some spendable funds from one use to another is stated as follows by Mr. Georg Bielschowsky: "The first criticism would be to the effect that it is not permissible to regard the additional employment offered by the enlargement of public building activities as so much net increase in the total volume of employment available. This assumption disregards the fact that an extension of public works has to be financed with funds part of which at least would otherwise have been used by private enterprise. An increase in public employment is, therefore, at least partly offset by a decline in private employment. It is only the difference between these two magnitudes which represents the net increase in the total demand for labor."

The validity of this criticism depends, in the first place, upon the way in which, and the time at which, the funds spent by the City are raised. If, for instance, Philadelphia as soon as it had let the contract for the construction of a new building were to levy an immediately payable tax to meet the entire cost, it would be quite clear that the process actually involved a shifting of purchasing power from taxpayer to city. The funds which the taxpayer now must turn over to the City Treasurer otherwise would have been either spent by him for consumers' commodities, deposited in a bank, or used to purchase some investment security. If, in the latter two cases, this purchasing power should not have been held as an unused cash balance by the bank or the concern issuing the securities, it would have been spent for producers' equipment of various sorts. In cases such as this there is much reason for contending that an expansion of public works results merely in shifting purchasing power out of private into public channels of expenditure, and an allowance for this fact materially reduces the net value claimed for public construction projects as creators of new jobs.[4]

But the fact that all construction work done by the City of

---

[4] It should be noted in passing that even though such a procedure would merely shift purchasing power from one use to another, there is still some chance that it would become effective in creating jobs more quickly through the taxation channel than through the private expenditure or investment channels.

forgetting

Philadelphia is financed by the issuing of long-term bonds changes the problem materially, although it does not necessarily mean that all shifting from one possible use to another is thereby eliminated. The City definitely competes with manufacturing, mining, shipping, and other business enterprises for the savings of the investing public. It is, therefore, just as possible that borrowing to finance a construction project will cause a mere shifting of funds from one kind of expenditure to another as it is that taxation will result in such shifting.

The point of primary importance is that, when these projects are financed by loans, investors are furnishing funds which, although it is true, ultimately would have become purchasing power along other lines of expenditure, since they are now being taken up by the City, become immediately effective purchasing power paid out in the prosecution of public improvement projects. Thus, in a sense, these funds may be said to have been merely shifted from one use to another, or from one expenditure to another, but in such shifting, they have been turned into immediately used purchasing power. Had they been left in the original channel of investment, they would have lain for some time, either as bank balances of individuals, unabsorbed by borrowers from the bank, or as corporate balances awaiting expenditure. It should be clear that this lag in effectiveness, if the funds are left to be used by banks and corporations, is occasioned by the fact that during times of depressed business conditions, especially during the early portions of such periods, business men are hesitating to make capital expenditures because of the declining costs of capital equipment, the absence of immediate need for additional productive capacity, and the uncertainty of the future.

Professor J. M. Clark has summarized this point in answering the question : "Can any methods of financing increase the supply of funds in the country out of which the demand for construction and for industrial products must come?" "Funds may," he contends, "be raised by drawing on general balances, by short-term borrowings, or by the sale of long-term securities somewhat earlier than they would otherwise have been sold. (That is, earlier than they would have become effective purchasing power used by issuing corporations had they been left in the hands of corporations rather than shifted to governmental uses.) And the probabilities are all in favor of this being done without giving rise to reactions which would neutralize the effect and defeat the end in view." [5] The same point has been expressed differently by Mr. F. G. Dickinson : "It is

[5] *American Economic Review,* Supplement to issue of March, 1930, p. 18.

true that the sale of construction bonds would absorb some of
the funds that might have been available for industrial production in a period of falling commodity prices." [6]

Professor Clark's references to "general balances" and "short-
time borrowings" are particularly applicable to the City of
Philadelphia. Any funds in the consolidated loan fund of the
City Treasury may be used temporarily to meet capital outlays. If such funds actually are used to carry construction
projects for a time, they can scarcely be said to be diverted from
other users who would have spent them if the City had not.
Philadelphia has been given very extensive privileges with
respect to the flotation of short-time loans. Since such loans
would, when used for temporary financing of public improvements, draw upon temporarily unused bank, personal, and
corporate balances, such uses would occasion no diversion of
purchasing power from any definitely planned line of expenditure, either private or corporate.

The position taken here is that there are temporary stop-
pages of the flow of credit funds into actual purchases of producer's equipment during the early portions of a depression
period. By tapping these reservoirs of credit, consisting of
unused balances of various kinds, an expanded program of
credit-financed public works can do much to increase the
amount of effective purchasing power in the market at any
one time. This increase is obviously temporary. Ultimately
capital equipment must all come from savings, and if such
savings are used for the construction of public improvements,
they cannot be used for the construction of privately-owned
capital equipment. At any one time, however, the speed with
which funds of credit actually are turned into effective market
purchasing power, and therefore into a demand for labor,
may depend primarily upon whether they are used to finance
public construction work already planned and ready to be
started, or are held for the financing of capital improvements
which are contemplated but, for some one or more of a variety
of reasons which are perfectly sound from the standpoint of
the private business concern, are being postponed.

Obviously the effect in terms of jobs would be the same
whether these funds were used for capital improvements by
private concerns or for public improvements by the municipality, provided they were used at the same time in either case.
But so long as private business hesitates during business depres-

---

[6] "Public Construction and Cyclical Unemployment," *The Annals of the
American Academy of Political and Social Science,* Supplement to issue of September, 1928, p. 25.

sions to accept the risks of developing productive capacity in anticipation of demand, and so long as it remains as inefficient as it now is in planning such development, it is perfectly justifiable to look to the construction of public works, the demand for which is not subject to the whims of a competitive market, to convert available credit into jobs at crucial times.

It must be admitted that the complexity of the phenomena being handled in the discussion of this point is not conducive to dogmatic conclusions. If the above analysis is substantially correct, however, there is no reason to believe that sums spent on expanded public works programs during unemployment periods are merely taken from some other use to which they would have been put just as quickly. The fact that Philadelphia finances all such expenditures out of borrowings strengthens this conclusion. Moreover, when it is recalled that only the expenditures of the City of Philadelphia are being analyzed, and that funds expended by this one city are drawn from the general credit market, it seems legitimate to conclude that practically none of the funds which may be thus spent in Philadelphia to mitigate unemployment will be drawn from other immediate local uses, and that the jobs resulting from such expenditures will constitute a net gain in the volume of employment in the City of Philadelphia.

WILL WORKERS EMPLOYED UPON PUBLIC WORKS PROJECTS BE EFFICIENT?

DURING periods of severe unemployment there are factors making for labor efficiency which probably are powerful enough to counterbalance any inefficiency resulting from the shifting of men from their usual lines of activity into enlarged public works enterprises.*

There remains undetermined one phase of this general problem: Would the nature of the work being done develop mental attitudes conducive to inefficiency on the part of the workers? In all probability, the answer would have to be in the affirmative if projects were to be undertaken purely as relief measures or if they were to be merely "busy-work" for the unemployed. If men are set to work at a task created merely to give them work, or if they are ordered to do work in a way obviously designed to be inefficient in order that jobs may be created, it is impossible to keep them from feeling that they are not being paid for work accomplished, but rather because they and their

---

* Eds. note: For a more complete discussion of this point see Loucks' treatment of the costs of construction work during a period of unemployment, *op. cit.*, pp. 209-210 ; 225-226.

families need food. As soon as the connection between personal efficiency and the tenure of the job thus becomes clouded, personal efficiency and effort are likely to wane.

Such difficulties can be overcome by adherence to three fundamental principles in advance planning for public works expansion :

(1) No projects are to be undertaken which would not otherwise have been initiated sooner or later. In other words, pure relief projects can form no part of a long-range planning program. The factors determining whether a project is or is not to be undertaken by the City must be precisely the same whether long-range planning for stabilization is or is not adopted. No condemnation of purely relief projects is implied in these statements. The point to be emphasized is that relief projects, if they are to be employed at all, must be treated as such and kept clearly separate from a long-range program of public works.

(2) The individual contractor must be permitted to retain the right of discharge. This does not mean that he should not be requested, or possibly directed, to give preference to local citizens and family heads. It does mean that workers absorbed by these projects must be given to understand that they are being hired on a purely business basis, that their wages are not charitable relief payments, and that their employment will terminate if they do not meet the standard of efficiency maintained by the contractor.

(3) The contractor must be permitted to determine the size of his laboring force and the methods of work to be used. Any attempt to force him to hire more men than necessary or to use less efficient mechanical devices than are available immediately shifts a project from a business to a relief basis with the possibility of an accompanying decrease in the workers' efficiency.

Should these three principles be followed in all expansion programs there is no reason to believe that the efficiency of workers will show any tendency to fall below that usually found in public construction work.

WOULD AN EXPANDED PUBLIC WORKS PROGRAM BE EFFECTIVE IN A DEPRESSION PERIOD DURING WHICH THE LOCAL CONSTRUCTION INDUSTRY WAS OPERATING AT CAPACITY ?

THE answer obviously is that in such a situation there would be little or no local benefit derived from an expanded program. If the local construction industry were operating at practically full capacity and the local supply of construction labor and equipment were fully employed, attempts to expand public works would bring about one or both of the following results:

(1) Laborers in these lines would be drawn into the City to fill the newly created jobs. Although advantageous for other communities whose workers are thus given employment, and of slight assistance to local industry because the newly employed persons will spend at least some portion of their wages in local shops for locally-made goods, the effects of such expansion would probably be very insignificant and from a local standpoint wholly insufficient to justify an expansion of public works projects.

(2) The projects initiated would suffer from a lack of skilled laborers and machinery for some phases of the work. Although there might be available a large number of unskilled workers for construction jobs, and although there would be considerable likelihood of shifting semi-skilled and skilled workers into construction jobs, a scarcity of skilled and experienced construction workers might hamper key phases of the work and thereby seriously delay progress and decrease efficiency in the carrying out of individual projects. A shortage of necessary special equipment would be no less serious a handicap.

Despite the negative answer to the proposed question, this objection to long-range planning is not a serious one, for the assumed conditions would very seldom exist. The construction industry is in the "equipment industries" group and ordinarily experiences cyclical fluctuations of greater intensity than the average for all industries. It is possible, but not likely, that a situation would develop in which during a general depression and unemployment period, an accumulated demand for construction work would keep that particular industry operating at, or near, capacity. Since such a condition is so unlikely to occur, it may be concluded that during an unemployment period there will be sufficient unused capacity in the construction industry to assure the availability of the nucleus of skilled workers and special machinery necessary for the undertaking of an extraordinary amount of public construction work.

WOULD LONG-RANGE PLANNING STIMULATE OR DISCOURAGE OTHER ATTEMPTS TO SOLVE THE UNEMPLOYMENT PROBLEM?

ALTHOUGH entirely pertinent to this discussion, this question is not of primary importance. Moreover, its very nature forestalls a definite answer. By softening the sting of unemployment, and thereby weakening the incentive to develop a more comprehensive remedial program, it is possible that a successful long-range public works program might retard rather than accelerate progress toward a solution of the unemployment problem.

On the one hand specific illustrative adverse possibilities may be listed as follows:

(1) Wholly or partially successfully long-range planning may create the feeling that the City is taking care of the situation and that private relief, which undoubtedly would still be necessary, is no longer needed.

(2) Successful attempts by local agencies, such as cities, to ameliorate local unemployment conditions may seriously distract attention from the broader and therefore more important aspects of the problem as a national issue.

(3) The feeling of the individual employer that he is responsible for the employment of his working force for a longer period of time than the specific wage-contract period, a feeling now so tragically lacking in many cases, may be weakened still further by the creation of temporary public works jobs at just the time when employers feel the profit urge to dismiss employees.

(4) Temporary relief may distract attention from the fundamental causes of unemployment and plans for their removal. Thus the change which is desirable in the long run may be postponed by temporary but successful stabilization programs.

There are no-less-definite factors tending in the opposite direction:

(1) Individual business men, becoming acquainted with the methods and possible financial advantages of public long-range planning, may thereby be induced to direct their own efforts along similar lines.

(2) An expansion of the City's public works program at a strategic time may serve to "instill confidence" into private businesses. Should the psychological aspects of cyclical business fluctuations prove to be even fractionally as important as they are often pictured, recovery from depression could be considerably stimulated by the launching of a bold program of public works, accompanied by judicious optimistic pronouncements by public officials.

(3) Long-range planning, if used successfully, conceivably may point the way to a realization of the solvability of the unemployment problem. Once a successful, although necessarily limited, attack on the problem can be carried through and some more or less clearly-defined results can be shown,

comprehensive research and programs will undoubtedly gain momentum.

Just which of these sets of forces here indicated one considers to be the more powerful depends in large part upon his philosophy of economic reform.   Is it better to allow conditions to become so bad that a complete reorganization becomes necessary in order to avoid economic ruin, or slowly and systematically to remedy specific ills and little by little shape our economic system into the form of our ideal?   The pragmatic position has so much to recommend it, provided the distant goal is not obscured by temporary or local successes, that one is justified in concluding that all accomplishments of local long-range planning will constitute net advances toward the still remote achievement of a highly stable volume of employment throughout the industrialized portions of the world.

WOULD UNEMPLOYMENT RETURN TO ITS FORMER VOLUME
UPON THE COMPLETION OF AN EXPANDED PUBLIC
WORKS PROGRAM?

A PERFECTLY arranged public works program would be expanded by degrees exactly commensurate with coincidental decreases in employment, so that public construction work would absorb as many as possible of the workers being thrown off by private industries as soon as possible after their dismissal, and would be curtailed during a period of recovery to a degree exactly commensurate at any given time with the degree of business recovery.   Thus workers would be able to shift from private employment to public construction employment during declining business activity and to shift back again during increasing activity.   Obviously, so symmetrical a combination is impossible.   In practically all cases the public works program will get under way less quickly than the volume of unemployment will mount and during recovery, the completion of the special public works projects will, in all probability, either precede or lag behind increasing general business activity. The extent to which unemployment will return to its previous volume upon the completion of a public works program depends in part upon the skill with which officials fit public works into the unemployment period.

If the expanded public construction work itself were the only factor involved, it might be argued that, upon the completion of the projects, the men thus thrown out of work would constitute an unemployed group roughly corresponding in size to that originally absorbed.   However, there are two additional factors to be considered. In the first place, the expanded public works program may be the means whereby lines of business other than the construction industry are stimulated. It is sometimes claimed that properly timed public works can be made the stimulant whereby recovery may begin. Just to the extent that this contention is correct, the revival in business activity resuscitated by the public works expenditures will cause the re-absorption into private industry of those thrown out of work by the retarded public works program.

Such results, however, are almost too much to expect from public works expenditures. It is more likely that expenditures of this kind will not play a major part in the revival of business activity. If only one city's construction program were involved this would be quite obviously beyond question. Nevertheless while the expanded construction work is being done, and while the expenditures on it are creating additional jobs for laborers, those forces, whatever they are, which turn depression into recovery will be getting under way, and presumably by the time the various individual projects are completed, business again will be sufficiently active to absorb into private employment those workers who temporarily shifted into public construction jobs. Therefore it may be concluded that, since business activity usually will be experiencing an expansion when the special public works program is completed, in contrast to the contraction which was under way when the program was initiated, private industries will be in a position to absorb those losing their public construction jobs and the workers then thrown onto the labor market will not constitute an unemployed group.

The same reasoning may be employed with reference to workers thrown out of public construction jobs when, during a period of prosperity, the long-range plan calls for a retardation of improvement expenditures in order to build up a reserve of projects for unemployment years. It is sometimes contended that the resultant shrinkage in public construction jobs would mean the creation of a group of unemployed workers who could return to jobs only when public projects were again speeded up. Since such retardations of public construction work would come only during periods of active business, however, these construction workers would be thrown out of specific jobs on public projects at the very time when private business concerns would be most desirous of securing employees, and they would therefore be absorbed into other occupations requiring their respective varieties of skill.

HOW WOULD LONG-RANGE PLANNING AFFECT THE FUNDA-
MENTAL CAUSES OF BUSINESS DEPRESSIONS?

A TWO-FOLD challenge is sometimes issued to long-range planning advocates. It is contended, first, that since long-range planning affects none of the fundamental causes of the cyclical movement of business activity, it would accomplish nothing by way of stabilizing cyclical fluctuations; and second, that long-range planning, if it were successfully used to absorb some unemployed laborers, would thereby postpone a return to sound prosperity.[7]

These contentions are based upon the well-founded assumption that business depressions are caused by serious or basic maladjustments in the industrial system and that depression does not pass away until these maladjustments have been corrected. The numerous possible maladjustments exhibit great variety and may lie in the field of credit, production, monetary circulation, distribution, etc. An illustrative explanation of a business depression might run along these lines: Some important industry producing consumers' goods rapidly expands its productive capacity because of past favorable marketing conditions and a favorable outlook. After this productive equipment has been put to work, difficulties are experienced in finding adequate outlets for the entire product. In other words, the enterprises in that industry have overestimated the market demand for the product or, the estimate having been correctly made on the basis of the available facts, market conditions have taken an unexpected turn, making the industry unable to dispose of its entire product at a price covering cost of production. For a time the industry continues at nearly capacity production, piling up inventories of finished products in the hope that the condition is temporary. When it becomes apparent that no expansion of sales can be expected in the near future, output is curtailed by entirely or partially closing plants. Purchases of raw materials and supplies are thereby restricted and plants producing them are forced to curtail production. Laborers are thrown out of work in the originally over-expanded industry and in those supplying it with materials. Suspended wages mean decreased sales over a wide range of consumers' goods; producers are forced to restrict their activities, thus setting in motion other chains of similar events. In this case it may be said that a maladjustment has occurred in the business system; one industry has got out of line, and a return of sound business activity cannot take place until over-produced

[7] E. C. Harwood, *op. cit.*, p. 1155.

stocks of goods have been liquidated, over-expanded industries have written off unnecessary capacity, creditors have absorbed losses, laborers have accepted deflated wage rates, etc. In other words, a fundamental maladjustment has occurred and the return of business prosperity must await a fundamental readjustment and realignment of the various portions of the business system.

Long-range planning, placed in such a setting, is pictured as quite impotent to bring about the necessary readjustment. If, for instance, excess stock and capacities in the automobile and allied industries must be liquidated before business activity can revive, it is difficult to see just how an expanded public works program is going to facilitiate the liquidation. And if cyclical maladjustments are as fundamental as has been suggested, it is probably quite correct to contend that public works programs can offer only insignificant assistance in the readjusting process.

It should be noted, however, that a public works program may be the means of keeping the cumulative effects of a maladjustment from spreading still further. As one industry after another is shut down or placed on part-time, purchasing power in consumers' hands is decreased further and further. But deficiencies of purchasing power in the hands of consumers do not affect public works projects and the employment opportunities which they entail. The decision to pave a street, put up a new municipal building, or construct a new subway does not depend upon the prospective condition of consumer demand for the services of the new facilities in the next six months or year. It may therefore be said that public works expenditures during periods of business depression may constitute a quickly thrown up barrier to the further advance of the depression forces set in operation by the original maladjustment.[8] This could scarcely be said to be a remedy for the basic difficulty but rather an expedient tending to offset and weaken the secondary or indirect effects of a maladjustment.

A point of primary importance is that, although an expanded public works program may have only secondary or minor importance as a means of stabilizing business activity, it surely does not prolong any basic maladjustment. It is sometimes contended that if after some fundamental maladjustment has occurred, purchasing power is arbitrarily put into the hands of any group of purchasers, the exercise of this power will

[8] Mr. Otto T. Mallery contends that "at least twenty-seven other industries are dependent for a good part of their prosperity upon public works construction." *American Labor Legislation Review*, March, 1928, p. 78.

merely prolong the period of readjustment by postponing the necessity for liquidating inventories and productive capacity. Thus, if the automobile industry had experienced an over-development, a definitely manipulated expansion of public works would put purchasing power into the hands of people some of whom would purchase automobiles and thereby obscure and postpone what otherwise would have been the clear and immediate necessity of liquidating and writing off losses in the automobile industry. In this way the re-establishment of basically sound and co-ordinated prosperity would be delayed.

Although it is quite clear that the factors involved are so complex as to make this analysis incomplete, the tentative conclusion that an expanded public works program during depression will not materially delay business recovery will be hazarded for the following reasons:

(1) Purchasing power put into circulation through the expansion of public works will be relatively small in comparison with total purchasing power during a depression period. An allowance for the various turnovers of purchasing power after the original construction expenditure would not invalidate this statement. Analysis has shown that if the City of Philadelphia had been following a long-range planning procedure, the wages paid to laborers during the years 1928 to 1930 probably would have been increased by $40,000,000, or about five per cent of the value of the total retail sales in the City during that period.*

(2) The small quantities of purchasing power thus injected into the business system during a depression period will not obscure the fundamental readjustments necessary for the return of active business conditions. And since long-range planning will call for the expansion of public works only after it has become clearly evident that serious unemployment is imminent, it will not soften the force of the *original* jolt received by the maladjusted factors in the economic system. Neither will the extra public works expenditures raise the level of the depression enough to conceal any basic difficulty which may be present.

(3) Of the total effective purchasing power hurried into the market by expanded public works programs, only a small portion will be spent for the purchase of any one commodity, and moreover, most of it will be spent for goods produced by industries not greatly subject to maladjustments. Since by far the largest portion of the workers employed upon the newly-started public works projects will depend entirely upon these wages for a living, they will scatter their resultant expenditures

* Eds. note: For this analysis see Loucks, *op. cit.*, pp. 169-196.

over many ordinary family budget items, chiefly necessities. This will tend to stimulate or rather stabilize demand in the staple industries, the very ones which, because of their comparatively steady demand, are least likely to be over-expanded.

(4) The facilities resulting from the increased public works expenditures will not produce marketable commodities to be sold in competition with private industries. There is, therefore, no danger that an expanded public works program will result in still further production in industries which are already over-expanded.

It may therefore be concluded that, although increased public works expenditures during depression periods probably will not play any material part in the correction of those fundamental maladjustments causing depressions, it is also probable that such stimulation of expenditures will be quite unlikely to retard the necessary readjustments and thereby delay the return of soundly prosperous business conditions. The validity of this conclusion is obvious if the public works program of only one city is considered.

* * *

DEFINITE suggestions for overcoming the administrative difficulties of a program of long-range planning of public expenditures will be given in Part IV, (Financial Administration), Chap. XXIX, Sec. 5 of this volume. These suggestions will be treated as a phase of the general administrative problems involved in the control of public expenditures.

The non-administrative or philosophical aspects of expenditure control, that is to say, those aspects which relate to the proper scope of State functions, and which are fundamental to the determination of the desirable ratio of public to private expenditures, are discussed in the next chapter.

QUESTIONS AND PROBLEMS FOR DISCUSSION

1. Cite examples of ordinary and extraordinary public expenditures. How would you classify the expenditure for the development of the Tennessee Valley? the administration of N.R.A.?
2. Why is much of the expenditure of nations for so-called "preparedness" unproductive in nature? Is the expenditure to maintain a local police force productive or unproductive?

3. "Public expenditures for conducting a war are no less productive than those for the construction of a state railroad." Evaluate.
4. Classify the following expenditures as transfer or exhaustive: Boulder Dam construction; the President's salary; interest on a foreign debt; a shipping subsidy.
5. Summarize the important objections to long-range planning of public works.
6. "Heavy expenditures for public construction in periods of depression have little or no justification since the amount expended by political bodies is subtracted from the amount which otherwise would have been spent by private individuals." Evaluate.
7. Is the main objective of a long term public works program the temporary or permanent alleviation of unemployment?
8. Does it appear that the administrative obstacles to long term planning of public works are insurmountable? the technical obstacles? the economic obstacles?
9. Has the problem of occupational shifts been of serious consequence in preventing the full benefit of the construction program of the United States during the last few years?
10. Is there any reason to believe that workers employed on public projects are less efficient than they would be if employed in private enterprise?
11. Is a city, state, or nation justified in promoting a public works project which is not immediately needed?
12. What data would you desire in order to compare the burden of public expenditures of a political unit at different periods of time?
13. Assuming that you have the absolute power to put a system of long-term planning of public expenditures into operation in a given political unit, state in detail the nature of the data which you would attempt to secure and also the steps which you would take in carrying through such a program.
14. "Public expenditures for useless public projects are by no means burdensome to a nation because such expenditures put money into circulation and no money leaves the country." Evaluate.

SUGGESTIONS FOR RESEARCH

1. A study of some local public works project of recent years. Determine costs, the number of men employed, the need for the project, and the general economic and social effects of the public enterprise.
2. An analysis of the recent $3,300,000,000 public works program of the United States in light of the fundamental principles involved in such governmental activities.
3. A quantitative study of the possibilities and limitations of the long-range planning of public expenditures.

4. Relative merits of bonds, paper money, and specie reserves for financing public works in periods of depression.
5. Political difficulties and long-range planning of public expenditures.
6. An historical study of the relationship between the expansion of armament and national security.
7. The effect of public expenditures on the production, distribution, and consumption of wealth.

BIBLIOGRAPHICAL NOTE

For a presentation of some early opinions regarding the economic effects of public expenditures, see C. J. Bullock, *Selected Readings in Public Finance,* (Boston, 1924), Chap. II, Secs. 6, 7, 8.

Discussions of the economic aspects of (1) ordinary and extraordinary expenditures, and (2) productive and unproductive expenditures appear in C. F. Bastable, *Public Finance,* (London, 1917), Bk. I, Chap. VIII; and H. L. Lutz, *Public Finance,* (New York, 1929), Chap. VI.

The effects of public expenditures on production, distribution, and consumption are treated in H. W. Peck, *Taxation and Welfare,* (New York, 1925), Chaps. VII, VIII, IX. The effects on production and distribution are also discussed in Hugh Dalton, *Principles of Public Finance,* (London, 1932), Chaps. XVIII, XIX.

Much has been written in recent years on the subject of public expenditures and the business cycle. In addition to the studies which have been reproduced in whole or in part in this chapter, the following works are of high quality: J. M. Clark, "Public Works and Unemployment," *Proceedings, American Economic Association,* (March, 1930), pp. 15-29; W. L. Jones, "Federal Expenditures and the Construction Industry," *Proceedings of the Academy of Political Science,* Vol. XII, pp. 735-747; W. I. King, *Employment, Hours, and Earnings in Prosperity and Depression,* (New York, 1930); O. T. Mallery, "The Long-Range Planning of Public Works," in *Business Cycles and Unemployment,* (New York, 1923); V. A. Mund, "Prosperity Reserves of Public Works," *Annals of the American Academy of Political and Social Science,* Vol. CXLIX, (May, 1930), pp. 1-45; "National and World Planning," *Annals of the American Academy of Political and Social Science,* Vol. CLXII, (July, 1932), pp. 114-148; A. C. Pigou, *Industrial Fluctuations,* (London, 1929), Pt. II, Chaps. XIV-XVI; *Planning and Control of Public Works,* (National Bureau of Economic Research, New York, 1931); *Unemployment and Public Works,* (International Labor Office, London, 1931); B. M. Anderson, Jr., "State and Municipal Borrowing in Relation to the Business Cycle," *Proceedings of the Academy of Political Science,* Vol. XII, No. 3, (1927); Sumner H. Slichter, "The Economics of Public Works," *American Economic Review,* Vol. XXIV, No. 1, Supplement, (Mar. 1934), pp. 174-185; and Carl Shoup, "The Creation of Reserves to Offset Fluctuations in Revenues," *Current Problems in Public Finance,* (Chicago, 1933), Chap. V, pp. 125-132.

A novel and challenging argument for increasing public expenditure in periods of industrial depression is presented in J. M. Keynes, *The Means to Prosperity,* (New York, 1933), Chaps. II and III.

For the results of three quantitative studies of public construction and the business cycle, see W. T. Layton and others, *Is Unemployment Inevitable?,* (London, 1925), pp. 52-54; F. G. Dickinson, "Public Construction and Cyclical Unemployment," *Annals of the American Academy of Political and Social Science,* Vol. CXXXIX, Supplement, (Sept. 1928), p. 208; and W. N. Loucks, "Municipal Public Works as a Stabilizer of Employment," *Stabilization of Employment,* Chap. VI, edited by C. F. Roos, Bloomington, Indiana, 1933.

A discussion of expenditure for public works under the National Recovery Program may be found in Magee, Atkins, and Stein, *The National Recovery Program,* (New York, 1933), pp. 26-31.

CHAPTER IV

THE RATIO OF PUBLIC TO PRIVATE EXPENDITURES

A DISCUSSION of facts and economic effects of governmental disbursements having been given in preceding chapters, it is logical now to present a general theory of the proper relationship between public and private expenditure. H. W. Peck's analysis of this question is here reproduced.*

THE problem of the most desirable ratio of public to private goods may be clarified by reference to economic theory. It is not worth our while to go into the controversy between the exponents of the consumption theory maintained by Adam Smith and his followers and the productivity theory maintained by their opponents, the German theorists. The common sense view today is that of relative productivity. If the service can be performed more economically through public coöperation than through individual initiative or voluntary private coöperation, the state agency is said to be relatively productive. Otherwise, it is relatively unproductive. The public goods furnished by the state may be material commodities, personal services, or the immaterial conditions of welfare. The state should furnish those services which it can furnish more efficiently or economically. In the words of Woodrow Wilson, "The sphere of the State is limited only by its own wisdom." The most useful *a priori* contributions to this problem have been furnished by economists who have applied to it economic theories of value. Saxe, Wicksell, and Lindahl have applied to public finance the theories of marginal utility. The most recent work, and one that sums up the trend of this school is *Die Gerechtigkeit der Besteuerung* by Erik Lindahl. Lindahl's important contribution to the tax problem is somewhat weakened by being identified with an attempt to revive the generally discarded theory of individual benefit. . . According to Lindahl, the function of the state is to satisfy public wants, which are a part of the complexus of private wants. Since the public life is thus

* Adapted from H. W. Peck, *Taxation and Welfare*, (The Macmillan Co., New York, 1925), Chaps. IV–VI.

involved with the private life, public economy activity follows the same laws that govern the private economy. The laws of the private economy which are applicable to the problem of taxation are the law of diminishing utility, the law of diminishing productivity, and the law of decreasing intensity of wants in the process of their satisfaction.

The problem of the scope of taxation Lindahl attempts to solve according to the principles of marginal utility, marginal productivity, and supply and demand. The production of public goods should be carried on to the point where utility is just offset by costs, as is the tendency in private economy, or where the marginal satisfaction is the same from both public and private goods. Public goods, like private goods, may be divided into producers' goods and consumers' goods. The productive, or reproductive, forces of the state, such as agricultural experiment, and the statistical investigations of industry and commerce, confer benefits that are measurable in terms of money, of market price, and these activities should be governed by the principle of marginal productivity; that is, they should be carried to the point where money expended for state regulation of private activity ceases to be more productive than if spent directly in private activity. Public consumers' goods, such as public art, public cultural education, and public parks, should be governed by the principle analogous to the marginal utility of the private economy. They should approximate the point where benefits are offset by burdens, or where money spent for public consumers' goods ceases to bring in greater satisfaction than money spent for private consumers' goods. The amount of money that will be spent for these public goods will be determined by the individual's estimate of the satisfaction that he will derive from them. Only the connection between cost and utility is more remote and difficult to ascertain than in the case of private economic life. The wants of great masses of individuals are expressed only through representative government; and if representation is imperfect and political or party forces are brought to bear, the power of economic forces in the determination of taxation is proportionately modified. The problem of the amount of taxation can be determined according to purely economic principles provided that individuals estimate intelligently the benefits that they will derive from state activity, and express their conception of self-interest through the agency of a democratic, representative government.

Lindahl's conclusions are stated in the form of individual benefit, but . . . his arguments are valid only to the end of

group benefit. If public operation of an enterprise will produce a greater net social utility, the services rendered by this
enterprise should belong in the category of public goods. Only
the application of the principle of marginal utility to remote
or widely extended operations is difficult. . .

On the side of production, then, the scope of the state should
be limited by what the Germans call its reproductivity. To
state this doctrine in less technical terms, beyond the necessary
expenditures of the state, the expenditures for defense and for
protection of person and property, public activity should be
extended only in so far as this activity will increase the national
income more than it increases taxes, or will add a greater direct
psychic utility than could be secured by an equal expenditure
for goods privately produced.

To illustrate this ideal reproductivity of taxes, let us consider
seven different hypothetical cases of the effects of taxation on
consumption, savings, and income.

	Income	Tax	Consumption	Savings
(1)	$2500	$100	$1900	$500
(2)	2500	200	1900	400
(3)	2500	200	1800	500
(4)	2700	200	2000	500
(5)	2700	200	1900	600
(6)	2900	200	2100	600
(7)	2900	200	2100	600

Under the first hypothetical case taxes of $100 support the
necessary activities of the state, leaving $2400 which can be
divided between consumption and savings. On the second
hypothesis taxes have been doubled, but the tax revenue has
been wastefully spent, as on wars, or the luxurious expenditure
of a monarch. The net result, in this case, is a reduction of
savings by the amount of the additional tax. Under the third
hypothesis the expenditures are equally unproductive and the
net result is a diminution of consumption by the amount of the
original tax. On the fourth hypothesis the additional state
revenue is productively spent, so that the private income taxed
increases by twice the amount of the additional tax. The net
social profit of $100 in this case goes to increase of consumption.
In the fifth hypothesis the conditions are the same except that
the surplus productivity of the tax goes to increase of savings
and thus expands the fund from which the taxes of the future
are to be drawn. On the sixth hypothesis the surplus government revenue is most efficiently employed in such outlay, for

example, as scientific research or agricultural experiment so
that the individual income increases much in excess of the tax.
This surplus economic energy made possible by efficient public
coöperation would result both in a higher standard of living
and an increase in the total capital goods.   The seventh hypothesis is identical with the sixth except in the assumption that
the second one hundred dollars of revenue in the sixth were
derived from a general property or income tax, and the equivalent revenue of the seventh was derived from an excise tax
on specific articles of consumption which injure the health,
strength, or happiness of the consumer.   Such a sumptuary tax
would not alter the welfare that is susceptible to pecuniary
valuation.   The public revenue, the capital accumulation, and
the individual consumption in terms of money would be the
same.   But the restriction of unwise consumption would leave
a larger fund for the purchase of beneficial goods and services.
There would be an increased consumption of wealth and a
decreased consumption of "illth" to the end of an enhancement
of the general well-being.   The assumption in all of these
hypothetical cases is that the effort required in earning the
income is the same.

To approach the theoretical problem more nearly, let us
distinguish between the public and the private economy.
Fiscal theorists make two main distinctions.   First, the time
range of the public and the private economy is different.   The
individual plans for one or for two lives.   The state exists
indefinitely.   The motives of the public and the private
economy are different.   The private producer aims at profits,
the amassing of wealth; the end of the public economy is the
maximum social utility.   On the basis of these two distinctions
we can go some way in the practical application of the doctrine
of marginal productivity.   The state should do those things
which are socially desirable but which do not bring profit to
individuals, or those things in which there is an incompatibility
between private profit and social weal.   Secondly, the state
should do those things which may bring an economic return
but at such a remote future date that the profit motive will
not be sufficient incentive to economic activity.

A useful classification of public services is that of J. S. Mill
who distinguishes between the necessary and the optional functions of the state.   Woodrow Wilson carries out the same distinction under the terms constituent functions and ministrant
functions.   These he enumerates as follows:

THE CONSTITUENT FUNCTIONS

(1) The keeping of order and providing for the protection of persons and property from violence and robbery.

(2) The fixing of the legal relations between man and wife and between parents and children.

(3) The regulation of the holding, transmission, and interchange of property, and the determination of its liabilities for debt or for crime.

(4) The determination of contract rights between individuals.

(5) The definition and punishment of crime.

(6) The administration of justice in civil causes.

(7) The determination of the political duties, privileges, and relations of citizens.

(8) Dealings of the state with foreign powers; the preservation of the state from external danger or encroachment and the advancement of its international interests.

THE MINISTRANT FUNCTIONS

(1) The regulation of trade and industry. Under this head I would include the coinage of money and the establishment of the standard weights and measures, laws against forestalling, engrossing, the licensing of trades, etc., as well as the great matters of tariffs, navigation laws, and the like.

(2) The regulation of labor.

(3) The maintenance of thoroughfares,— including state management of railways and that group of undertakings which we embrace within the comprehensive terms "Internal Improvements" or "The Development of the Country."

(4) The maintenance of postal and telegraph systems, which is very similar in principle to the third ministrant function.

(5) The manufacture and distribution of gas, the maintenance of water-works, etc.

(6) Sanitation, including the regulation of trades for sanitary purposes.

(7) Education.

(8) Care of the poor and incapable.

(9) Care and cultivation of forests and like matters, such as the stocking of rivers with fish.

(10) Sumptuary laws, such as "prohibition" laws, for example.

The theory of the relative productivity of the public and private economy suggests a competition between these two

agencies in public service. But the distinction between necessary and optional goods indicates that there is a realm within
which these two agencies are non-competing. The necessary
public goods will be provided by the state efficiently or ineffi-
ciently with but little effect from private competition. Protection of persons and property is primarily a function of the
state, although even here the distinction between public and
private goods is not absolute. Private individuals employ de-
tectives and watchmen. But in general what Wilson enumerates as the constituent functions are carried out exclusively by
the government and are not subject to private competition.
The ministrant functions, on the other hand, deal with those
things which the government might leave undone or which
might be performed by either public or private agencies.
Trade and industry might be automatically regulated by free
competition. The regulation of labor might be a matter of
free contract between employer and employee. Public service
corporations can be operated by private individuals, private
corporations, or the public. Sanitary regulations can be carried
on by the state, if it seems desirable, or people may be left to
their own devices. Education can be carried on either by
private or public agencies. The poor and incapable may
be provided for through public institutions or left to private
charity. Forests may be under government management or
left to private exploitation. And as to sumptuary laws many
people still believe that they constitute an invasion of the individual's private rights. . . . The general rule is that the government should provide those services that do not appeal to
private enterprises and those that it can perform more efficiently
than the private producers.

But there are certain functions here classified as optional that
seem to belong more naturally to the public economy. Among
these are sanitation, the maintenance of waterways, forests and
fisheries, and probably education. Sanitation would seem to
be a public function. The combating of contagious diseases
and the enforcement of hygienic regulations are collective
duties. Curative medicine as distinct from preventive measures
belongs to the private sphere. For individuals when they are
sick are willing to pay for the services of trained physicians.
But as to preventive and hygienic measures which are a matter
of invisible germs and the future community health, these may
be beyond the understanding or the personal interest of the
individual man. The welfare of all, however, is involved ; the
well-being of the intelligent and the well-to-do is dependent
in large degree on the maintenance of health conditions among

the ignorant and the poor. Waterways also belong obviously to the public economy. Unlike railroads they are not natural monopolies, and their development offers no inducement to the motive of private profit. The scientific use of forests, especially involving re-forestation, is also a public function, for it takes so long to grow a new tree — fifty to one hundred years — that the motive of self-interest will not induce many to replant. Hence, the serious depletion of forest resources in the United States. The improvement of fishing, especially fish hatcheries, is also a public function, for the fishing grounds, like waterways, are not natural monopolies, and the hatching of fish leads to general rather than to specific benefit. Education, also although less confidently, may be classified as a function of the state. If we look at it from the individual point of view, as in the statistics of the increased earnings of college graduates, it seems to be a matter of special and measurable benefit. As such, it might equitably be supported by individual fees. But when we consider that our whole complex material culture is dependent upon scientific and technological training, the general benefits of education seem to be paramount. The individual benefit view of education is represented by the private school, and the university which is supported by tuition fees and by gifts from its graduates. The growth of the general benefit view of education is illustrated in the development of our free public schools and our state universities. The difference between cultural and practical education corresponds in some measure to this distinction between the public and the private benefit view. Cultural education, which gives a man manners and polish, appreciation of Dante, Shakespeare, or Wordsworth, enriches the private life of the individual man, but does not contribute directly to the maintenance of that material culture upon which the general welfare is directly dependent. This perhaps explains the tendency of our universities which are maintained by tuition and gifts to emphasize the classical and humanistic side of education, and also the practical bent of our state universities and colleges. Cultural education, however, perhaps through its tendency toward diffusion, is coming to be considered more and more a general benefit. Professor Einaudi suggests that the diffusion of culture is a public function because the ignorant man has no conception of its necessity any more than he does the necessity of hygiene.[1] The other ministrant functions of the state may be carried on by the state or left as optional to individual enterprise according to economic and social conditions.

[1] Einaudi, L. *Scienza delle Finanze*, p. 144.

WE [have] reached the conclusion that many of the optional functions of the state should be performed under certain conditions and not under others. Among these conditions one of the most important is the ratio of population to land. His-torically the course of development is from sparse population and free or cheap land to dense population and high-priced land. With the growth of population, society and industry go through a series of readjustments. The first stage is that of hunting, trapping, and fishing — the stage of sparse population. Then as population grows and men have domesticated animals they take up grazing. A higher ratio of population leads to extensive agriculture such as the raising of grain. Subsequent stages are more intensive agriculture, such as dairying and gardening. Among the modern western nations manufacture rises coincidently with the development of intensive agriculture. Then, when this has assumed a large reach and commands a wide market, trade and transportation assume increasing importance, science and the learned professions develop more rapidly, personal services of all kinds become a means to livelihood, luxury trades flourish, and advertising and salesmanship become a wide-spread occupation. An industrial evolution is the outcome of man's effort to adjust himself to a changing environment. By a changing environment is meant a declining supply of land or crude natural resources per man. Industrial evolution, then, means a progressive efficiency in the exploitation of a given amount of land. If man does not evolve industrially, but tries to support an increasing population by the old method on the same land, he will encounter the economic law of diminishing return. This will result in emigration or war. If relief is sought through emigration, the same economic evolution follows as the new lands are settled. If war ensues, surplus population is killed off, until the time when intelligence intervenes to lead the way to the next industrial stage.

There is, also, we may infer, a tendency for government and political ideals to become adjusted to conditions determined by the ratio of population to land. The frontiersman tends to be an individualist because under frontier conditions, or conditions of sparse population, the peculiar individual qualities, energy, courage, initiative, and self-reliance, are sufficient for practical success in life. On the frontier natural resources abound, small-scale methods require the use of but little capital, and the scarce or limiting factor is labor applied to land; so that the uneducated but strong and industrious man can satisfy his wants by the labor of his own hands.

Turner has explained how these frontier conditions developed the peculiar characteristics of the American intellect : "That coarseness and strength combined with acuteness and inquisitiveness ; that practical, inventive turn of mind, quick to find expedients ; that masterful grasp of material things, lacking in the artistic but powerful to effect great ends ; that restless nervous energy ; that dominant individualism, working for good and for evil, and withal that buoyancy and exuberance which comes with freedom — these are the traits of the frontier, or traits called out elsewhere because of the existence of the frontier." [2]

Under these conditions of free land and sparse population many of the ministrant services of the state cannot or need not be rendered. Sanitation is not a pressing problem. Public education is hardly feasible. Even the necessary service of protection to person and property has to be left partly to the resource of the individual man or the temporarily organized group. The frontiersman adheres to his individualism, his confidence in his own unaided strength and wisdom, as long as he attains a fair measure of success in his problem of satisfying his wants. But with the increase in population there come into existence various forces that compel the frontiersman to modify his ideal of individualism. Even from the first, as Roosevelt has pointed out, men felt the need of coöperation in defense — in log rollings and in house raisings.[3] And as population becomes more dense and towns and cities arise, the individual becomes confronted with serious problems which he is unable to solve. Among these are the declining fertility of the soil, the dependence upon transportation, the rise of industrial monopoly, and the prevalence of contagious disease.

The problem of the declining fertility of the soil can be solved temporarily by migrating to new lands farther west. But this solution ends when the wave of pioneers has reached the Pacific. Then there is necessary a change in the methods of farming, and there results a demand for scientists and agricultural experts. With the increased dependence on transportation and the rise of large-scale manufacture, the exploitation of vast resources on a large scale, capital becomes a factor of increasing importance in industry, and management assumes a more and more dominant rôle. The new captain of industry applies the old individualistic ideals to the evolution of American industrial society. The development of corporate combinations into pools, trusts, and agreements proceeds apace until in the early years of the twentieth century it seemed probable

[2] Turner, F. J. *The Frontier in American History*, p. 37.
[3] Roosevelt, Theodore. *The Winning of the West*.

that the outcome of free competition under individualism would be monopoly of the most important natural resources by a small group of wealthy men. Under these conditions individualism declines. The government comes to look less like a necessary evil and more like an institution to perpetuate democratic ideals.

"In brief, the defenses of the pioneer democrat began to shift from free land to legislation, from the ideal of individualism to the ideal of social control through regulation by law." [4] "The western radical became convinced that he must sacrifice his ideal of individualism and free competition in order to maintain his ideal of democracy." [5]

With this admission of the need of government regulation comes a growing sense of the importance of education. Advanced scientific attainment is indispensable; and men are sifted out because of intellectual ability and given the training that will fit them to be leaders and experts. Meanwhile man has adjusted himself to a declining per capita supply of crude natural resources by means of mechanical inventions. Manufacture, or the creation of value by fabricating materials to a high degree gains relatively on agriculture. This makes possible a further increase in population and calls for a more detailed differentiation among the people through the need of scientific, technical, and mechanical skill. Trade, transportation, and personal and professional services increase. Society becomes characterized by specialization and interdependence in place of the simplicity, uniformity, homogeneity, and independence of the frontier family or the isolated village community. As a result, there is need for an increase in the regulative services of the government. Also manufacture, unlike agriculture, operates under the law of increasing returns; the growing nation soon finds that it can create a surplus of manufactured goods. At this point the nation ceases to be primarily agricultural, and becomes also an industrial state.

If there is such a law as the law of the normal expansion of public activities, *pari passu*, with the increase of the ratio of population to land, this may have a pertinent bearing on political philosophy. The individualist is a conservative; he represents the mental attitude engendered by conditions that no longer obtain. The socialist is a radical; he assumes an attitude appropriate only to the dense population, closely integrated and highly evolved civilization of the future. The liberal favors a gradual change or readjustment as experience

4 Turner, p. 277.
5 *Ibid.*, p. 305.

proves feasible. The liberal seems to be right, because the ratio of population to land changes gradually.

Yet if there is law of the gradual widening of state activities, it does not follow that all nations will conform to it inevitably and automatically. This conformity is conditioned upon national foresight and intelligence, upon what Lippmann calls a policy of mastery rather than a policy of drift. Russia at present is an example of a nation that has overreached the evolutionary process. The leaders have tried to set up an order suitable perhaps for a densely populated, highly integrated industrial state, only to find that it is not suited to a society still in the earlier stages of agricultural development. China might be taken as an example of the opposite kind, of a vestigial or belated individualism. Lacking in coöperative enterprises that might mobilize capital, and failing to establish a strong central government, the Chinese have not evolved beyond a highly efficient but excessively individualized type of agrarian economy.

WE have indicated how the increase in the ratio of population to land causes a gradual readjustment of industry so as to use most economically the factors that exist in changing proportions. As the proportion of labor and capital increases in relation to land, there is a gradual transition from the pastoral stage to extensive agriculture, then to more and more intensive agriculture. The development of intensive agriculture is paralleled by the growth of manufacture. When this comes to predominate over agriculture, that is, when the country comes to export more manufactured than agricultural products, we have reached the status of an industrial state. In the United States our industry is fairly well balanced, with a gradual incline toward the side of manufacturing.

The characteristics of the industrial as distinct from the agricultural state are a higher degree of specialization and an increase in large-scale production. These cause a greater dependence on transportation and mining, and require the attainment of a high grade of industrial intelligence. This condition may result in a greater need for the governmental services of protection to person and property, and it more certainly requires an increased outlay for public regulation, sanitation, charity, education, and recreation. Economic and social conditions, however, are not the only factors that should govern the expansion of government activities. Political conditions, especially the relative efficiency of the government, are also important. If the ruling body is corrupt, inefficient, or extravagant, the services of the government, however much economic or social need there may be for them, may cost more than they are worth. If much of the public revenue above that required for the necessary public expenditures, were spent by the monarch on his minions and his dames and his games, the political philosophers would be justified in asserting that the best government was the least government. In the light of the history of the Stuarts in England no wonder Adam Smith was a proponent of *laissez faire.*

PROFESSOR PECK next correlates his theories with facts by a study of some statistics of federal and state expenditures. As a result of his correlation he concludes : *

The vital principle that emerges from this analysis is that per capita taxes in the tax system as a whole may be expected to increase. And this increase in taxation would theoretically proceed at a faster rate than the increase in average wealth and income ; since, if public goods become increasingly developmental or cultural, the expenditures for them would increase faster than total expenditures. This is by analogy with the facts of private expenditure that with the increase of income a smaller percentage is spent on necessities and a larger percentage is available for luxuries or cultural goods. . .

Taxation and public expenditures tend to increase with the growth of population, wealth, and civilization. They bear a direct relation to prosperity, to the growth of specialization and interdependence, to the development of coöperation. They bear an inverse relation to independence in the sense of the ability of families and isolated groups to maintain themselves without frequent contact with others. The ideal of individualism — of atomic individualism, thus appears to be in conflict with other modern ideals. It seems to be vestigial. The true individualism, that which is consistent with industrial evolution and modern ideals, is at one with socialism. Human life attains unity in the personality, which has both individual and social aspects. The progress toward true freedom has not been away from the state, but toward the true form of the state. With the growth of democracy and representative government, taxation becomes voluntary, and public expenditure represents a rough social estimate of the proper distribution of expenditures between public and private goods. The state is increasingly regarded as a necessary instrument for attaining the maximum yield from our national resources.

One word more as to the nature of independence. The in-

* Peck, *op. cit.,* Chap. VI.

dependence of the nomad and the frontiersman means freedom from restraint by man but virtual subjection to the natural environment. This dependence of man on nature means frugal living, hard work, and tragic subjection to the fortunes of flood or drought. With the development of coöperation man gradually frees himself from the immediate dominance of the natural environment. Without public regulation, however, coöperation on a large scale would be impossible. In this sense, taxes may be viewed as the price of effective coöperation, and hence, of social progress.

QUESTIONS AND PROBLEMS FOR DISCUSSION

1. "The principle of diminishing utility proves that in order to secure maximum social·advantage public expenditures and taxes necessary to meet them should be carried to the point where there is an equal personal distribution of wealth." Explain and evaluate.
2. Is there any "one and only" proper ratio of public to private expenditures?
3. Evaluate the doctrine that "the scope of the state should be limited by . . . its reproductivity."
4. Discuss the relative significance of the constituent and the ministrant functions of public services during the past few years.
5. Of what significance is the ratio of population to land in the determination of the proper ratio of public to private expenditures? Consider this question in light of conditions today and compare with conditions of fifty years ago.
6. What bearing does the ratio of population to land have upon the economic philosophy of "rugged individualism"?
7. Outline step by step the reasons stated in this chapter for the conclusion that taxes "may be viewed as the price of effective coöperation and hence of social progress."
8. Does an increase in governmental activities and in public expenditures mean a decrease in the freedom of the individual?

SUGGESTIONS FOR RESEARCH

1. Economic and political conditions and the proper ratio of public to private expenditures.
2. The character and significance of expanding governmental activities.

BIBLIOGRAPHICAL NOTE

The general question· of the proper scope of state functions is dealt with in H. C. Adams, *The Science of Finance,* (New York, 1898), Pt. I, Bk. I, Chap. I ; C. F. Bastable, *Public Finance,* (London, 1917), Bk. I, Chap. I ; H. W. Guest, *Public Expenditure,* (New York, 1927), Chap. III ; and *Current Problems· in Public Finance,*

Chap. II, published by Commerce Clearing House, Inc., (Chicago, 1933).   More specific topics, namely,' (1) the comparison of public and private expenditure ; and (2) the proper ratio of the former to the latter are well developed in Adams, *op. cit.* Chaps. II, III ; Bastable, *op. cit.* Chap. VIII, Secs. 3, 4 ; Hugh Dalton, *Principles of Public Finance,* (London, 1932), Chaps. II, III ; and G. F. Shirras, *The Science of Public Finance,* (London, 1925), Chap. III.   Adams' chapters, cited above, present a stimulating discussion of (1) the relation of public expenditures to industrial, political, and social conditions ; and (2) the relation of public expenditures to the classification of governmental functions.

A concise review of some prominent theories of public expenditure is given in Mabel L. Walker, *Municipal Expenditures,* (Baltimore, 1930), Chap. III.

PART II—PUBLIC REVENUES

CHAPTER V

CLASSIFICATIONS AND FACTS OF PUBLIC REVENUES

1. CLASSIFICATION OF PUBLIC REVENUES *

In the realm of public revenues the attempts at classification have been no less marked than those in public expenditures. Classification has been made according to the base upon which the levy is made, or according to some supposedly inherent difference in the form of revenue itself. The first type of classification, as a levy upon person, income, or property, has caused little difficulty; for it is not hard to decide whether the actual levy is upon one or the other. There seems to be rather general agreement that revenues, other than gifts or penalties, may be divided into fees, special assessments, public prices, and taxes. Many have tried, also, to distinguish between direct taxes and indirect taxes; and it has been in these latter attempts at classification that difficulty has arisen.

The difficulty with the use of the expressions special assessment, fee, tax, and public price has been that many have used no basis of fact in choosing the form of revenue which they have placed in each. If it can be determined that each of these terms possesses definite characteristics which will always distinguish it from the others, however, then such classification may be accepted as satisfactory; and it will fall in the same category as that which divides rocks into igneous and metamorphic.

There seems to be a rather general agreement to the nature of a tax. Those revenues are taxes which are compulsorily levied according to some general rule and which are spent with no special reference to the individuals who have made the payment. The difficulty arises in attempting to find earmarks which will set off the other named forms of revenue from taxes and from each other. To define the boundaries of the

* Adapted from M. H. Hunter, "The Problem of Classification: Public Expenditures and Revenues," *American Economic Review*, Vol. XX (March, 1930), pp. 46-53.

special assessment is perhaps the least difficult. It is similar to a tax in that it is a compulsory levy according to some general rule, and in that the expenditure of the receipts involves some object of common good. A marked difference appears, however, in that the payment is measured on the basis of individual benefit, and that furthermore this benefit presumably takes the form of an increase in the value of real estate. The field in which it is possible to use the special assessment, therefore, is somewhat limited; and it is generally used to secure revenue for the construction of streets, sewers, sidewalks and lighting systems.

What are the special characteristics of a fee that distinguish it from other forms of revenue? Can we ascribe such characteristics to it that it will not be confused with other forms of revenue, and such that it may be recognized by anyone at any time and place? In some respects a fee is undoubtedly similar to a tax and to a special assessment. In the levy of each the prerogative of sovereignty must be invoked while some public benefit is involved in the expenditure of the receipts. A tax and special assessment are compulsory levies, as is also the fee if one wishes to avail himself of the privilege or service for which the charge is made. To the fee, however, may be assigned a very distinguishing characteristic possessed by none of the other forms of revenue; and this characteristic gives it claim to a separate class. The payment of the fee legalizes some action or procures the protection of the government in some definite manner. The payment of a fee is only compulsory in the sense that if an individual wants legally to enjoy the service offered by the government upon the payment of a fee, he must make payment.

A tax is seldom concerned with the legality of the base upon which the levy is made. Failure to pay a tax upon an income does not make the receipt of an income illegal, even though the failure to pay may call forth a penalty. Failure to pay a corporation tax does not destroy the corporation; but there is only one way by which a corporation may come into existence, and that is through the grant of the sovereign power of the state. If a charge is made for the grant of the charter, then there is no legal method by which a corporation can come into existence except by making the payment asked by the government. Every state requires a license to be secured before an automobile can be legally operated, while most states still make automobiles subject to the personal property tax. The first requirement legalizes action; and the operation of an automobile without securing the license places the offender in a very different position under the law than the failure to pay the property tax.

Another important distinction between a tax and a fee is that, while the payment of a fee does aid in carrying on a governmental function for the common good, the government at the same time gives some special benefit to the individual who makes the payment. Neither is anyone compelled to make the payment unless he feels that the benefit received will at least compensate for the payment. No corporation would ever be formed unless the advantage of limited liability, continuity of existence, etc., were as great as the charge for the grant of the charter; no automobile would ever be driven unless the satisfaction obtained therefrom were as great as the charge made for a license; and no mortgage would ever be recorded unless it were considered that the protection thus secured were as great as the charge made for recording it.

In order to attach some distinguishing characteristic upon a fee payment, we may say, that, in addition to being inherent in sovereignty, and while it involves the general welfare and confers some measurable benefit upon the one who makes payment, the payment is not compulsory; but when the payment is made the circumstance which called it forth becomes legal. Under this conception there is no place for a distinction between a fee and a license. It has been said by some that a fee is based upon service, while a license is based upon privilege, and that a license is used for regulation while a fee is not.

Individual cases may seem to indicate some such distinction as the above, but no such generalization can be made. To the individual, a privilege is a service and he will pay for the one benefit just as quickly as the other. In fact, any privilege granted to an individual renders him a service. The idea of regulation, moreover, usually has some place in the motive back of all such levies which fall under fees or licenses. The recording of deeds and mortgages, and other court activities for which fees are exacted have as their background social utility rather than service to the individual. In the case of either the fee or license there is but one legal way to perform an act; that is, by the payment of the required amount. There is no other way legally to become a corporation, to drive an automobile, to record a deed or mortgage, or to engage in many kinds of business, especially in the southern states.

When shall we attach the word "price" to the charge made by a government; and if a charge is a price at one time, can it always be so considered, or does it under some conditions become a tax and under other conditions become a fee?

Governmental units enter into many forms of commercial enterprises which might be operated by individuals, or which
may, in part, continue to be operated by individuals. Some
of such enterprises are education, highways, bridges, the postal
system, railroads, etc. The amount of charge has usually been
governed by the degree of public interest in the conduct of the
industry. If the public interest is negligible, the basis for the
charge may be the same as if the industry were in the hands
of individuals. If the conduct of the industry becomes more
important to the general public, the amount of the charge may
be reduced until the service is given at cost, as the service of the
postal system in the United States. As the public interest
appears still more vital, the charge tends to be reduced until
the returns do not begin to meet the cost. The question arises
as to whether the charge under each of these conditions shall be
designated as price, or whether under some conditions it should
not be called a fee or tax.

Some have designated any charge which does not meet the
cost of giving the service as a fee; while public price can apply
only when the charge just equals cost. Should the charge be
more than cost, it automatically becomes a tax. There is no
logic in such an attempt at classification, either from the standpoint of scientific accuracy or usability. In fact, the mere size
of a charge gives no fundamental basis of difference. Many
individuals sell goods at cost, at more than cost, or at less than
cost; but the charge, nevertheless, is designated as a price.
There is no reason why this same plan should not be followed
in designating the revenue to come under the class of public
price. It is a voluntary payment made for a commercial
service, by individuals who receive a special benefit from the
service. The price is for services which are not prerogatives of
the government, and its payment does not legalize action as
does the payment of a fee. Of course, it may be that the service
will be rendered by a government monopoly, but this does not
alter the fact that it could have been produced by an individual.
Then, too, the acceptance of the service offered by the government, and the payment of the price, is often a matter of choice.
One does not have to pay the government two cents to carry
his letter; he may send it by messenger or by express. If he
wills to use the governmental service, then only does he pay the
price. He may ride on the municipality owned street railway
to the city and pay the price, or to accomplish the same end he
may walk, fly, drive his own car or hire a taxi, and not pay
the public price.

Any charge made by the government for a commercial

service should be designated as a price, just as is a similar charge made by an individual. Any attempt to distinguish between a price and a fee, or a price and a tax, on the basis of relation of costs to charge is incapable of use. One of the many duties of a clerk in the office of the Secretary of State is to grant charters to corporations. The charge for a charter is $10.00. Is this a fee, tax, or price? How are we to arrive at the cost of issuing a charter to a particular corporation? Suppose that we can determine that the cost is just $10.00, and the payment thereby is a price. Yet next year, if the cost should go to $15.00, the payment of the $10.00 a payment identical in every respect with the previous one, becomes a fee; while if it should be more than cost it becomes a tax. Such a distinction, based on relation to costs, makes it impossible to place revenues in their respective classes until costs have been determined, and if costs cannot be allocated, then an attempt to classify is futile.

One explanation of this unsatisfactory plan for classification is that reasoning has been on the basis that things which produce the same effects are the same. Thus when a city charges more than costs for water, and turns the surplus into the general fund it becomes, it is said, a tax upon the users of water. The effect is just the same as if a tax to the amount of the surplus above costs had been levied upon those who consume water. But there is no scientific basis for such a process of reasoning and for calling such a charge a tax. When one sees the leaves of a tree shaking, he may conclude that it is caused by the wind; but when he investigates and finds the cause to be a boy or a squirrel, the fact that the effect caused by the actions of the boy or squirrel was the same as what the wind might have caused, does not make the boy or squirrel the wind.

Little need be said as to the amount of difficulty which has arisen from the division of taxes into direct and indirect. The constitutional fathers might have had some distinction in mind when they decreed that no direct tax should be levied by the federal government unless apportioned on the basis of population. What this distinction was, however, was not known to the Supreme Court; and in the sixties a personal income tax was held not to be a direct tax, and in the nineties it was held to be one. After the adoption of the Sixteenth Amendment, Chief Justice White reached the conclusion that a direct tax, under the meaning of the Constitution, was one levied upon persons or land. The attempt has been to find satisfactory boundaries for these two words, and as yet the attempt has been unsuccessful. When the possibility of shift-

TABLE [A]

RELATIVE IMPORTANCE OF DIFFERENT SOURCES OF INCOME OF THE VARIOUS NATIONAL GOVERNMENTS IN 1928 [a]

(Per cent of total governmental income)

Kinds of income	U.S. (1927)	Great Britain	France	Germany	Italy	Japan	Soviet Russia
Income and property taxes	51.7	38.0	28.4	35.3	26.3	20.2	8.0
Death taxes	2.9	10.3	...	0.6	0.4	1.2	...
Excises	17.4	15.6	10.0	15.0	11.8	26.2	20.0
Sales taxes	...	...	20.3	8.5	4.6	...	...
Other taxes (on production, consumption, and transactions)	...	8.7	23.2	7.6	12.6	...	13.0
Customs duties	14.4	15.3	8.7	9.3	9.9	8.1	4.0
Fees and other administrative revenue	1.7	1.4	2.5	1.4	5.6	3.0	...
Net revenue from public domain and quasi-commercial enterprises	1.4	1.2	2.0	1.8	15.7	25.8	45.0 [b]
Miscellaneous	10.5	9.5	4.9	10.0	3.1	1.7	10.0
Loans	...	...	...	10.5	10.0	3.5	...
Surpluses from previous years	...	...	...	...	...	10.3	...
Total	100.0	100.0	100.0	100.0	100.0	100.0	100.0

[a] Compiled for all the governments except Soviet Russia and the United States from the *Memorandum on Public Finance, 1926–1928,* the Economic and Financial Section of the League of Nations (Geneva, 1930); and for the United States from the same *Memorandum for 1922–1926.* For Soviet Russia, the figures have been obtained (after some adjustments) from G. Y. Sokolnikov and Associates, *Soviet Policy in Public Finance, 1917–1928* (Stanford University Press, California, 1931), Chap. IV.

[b] Some of this is gross revenue, such as the revenue from transportation, mails, telegraph and forests. The revenue from public industry, trade, and banks is a net amount. Sokolnikov, *op. cit.,* p. 224.

TABLE [B]

RELATIVE IMPORTANCE OF DIFFERENT TAXES IN THE UNITED STATES IN 1928

(Per cent of total tax revenue)[a]

In the Federal tax system		In state tax systems		In local tax systems	
Personal income tax	26.2	General property taxes	25.3	General property taxes and special property taxes	92.9
Corporation income tax	38.6[b]	Special property taxes	7.0	Other taxes	2.8
Estate tax	1.8	Poll taxes	0.3	Licenses and permits	4.3
Indirect internal revenue — tobacco, spirits, and oleomargarine	12.4	Income taxes	3.7		
		Inheritance taxes	8.5		
		Other special taxes	3.3		
Automobiles (passenger)	1.5	Gasoline taxes	16.0		
Miscellaneous	2.4	Motor vehicle licenses	17.6		
Customs duties	17.1	Business licenses	17.5		
		Non-business permits	0.9		
	100.0		100.0		100.0

[a] Compiled from Cost of Government in the United States, 1928-1929, National Industrial Conference Board (New York, 1931), pp. 88, 98 and 102.

[b] Includes 0.3 for corporation capital stock tax.

ing the tax as the distinguishing mark proved unsatisfactory, it was suggested that classifications be on the basis of whether the legislator intended that the tax be shifted. But any classification based on the intent of a lawmaker can make little claim to being scientific.

It may be impossible, in making classifications of public revenues and expenditures, to be as accurate in methods as are the classifications found in the natural sciences. But if accuracy be the prime motive in making a classification, then we have been much less accurate than we might have been, both in the choice of terms to denote classes and in defining the boundaries of the terms already chosen. From the methodology used in our classification processes there may be some basis for the query as to whether those writing on public expenditures and revenues have been scientific.

2. Some Forms and Facts of Public Revenues

Supplementing Professor Hunter's classification of public *revenues,* there is given below Professor Studenski's classification of public *income.* Some significant facts of public income are also presented.*

The funds raised by the government for the defrayment of its expenses may be divided into (1) taxes, (2) administrative revenues and semi-taxes, composed of fees, licenses, special assessments, fines and other like imposts, (3) revenue from public enterprises which may be called "commercial" or "quasi-commercial" revenue, (4) loans, and (5) miscellaneous receipts, such as interest on sinking funds, proceeds from the sale of public properties, interest on loans made to the government and the reimbursements of such loans, contributions to pension funds, and other like items which may not lend themselves readily to classification under any of the other headings mentioned. In the case of the component state, provincial, and local governments of a larger governmental unit, an additional class of income sometimes makes its appearance in the form of a subsidy from the larger unit. But this item of income represents really a mere transfer of funds from the larger unit of government to the smaller one, and not an independent source of income. All these five or six classes mentioned constitute the *income* of a government. But not all of them constitute *revenue.* The latter term should be used in the more

* Adapted from W. E. Spahr and others, *Economic Principles and Problems,* (Ray Long and Richard R. Smith, Inc., New York, 1932), Vol. II, Chap. XXXIII. This chapter was written by Professor Paul Studenski.

restricted sense of receipts which increase the assets of the government without increasing its liabilities. Proceeds from loans, strictly speaking, are not "revenue," because they increase the liabilities of the government just as they do its assets. They must be repaid eventually from revenue. The proceeds from the sale of public property and repayments by borrowers to the government of the amount of their loans are also not revenue in the strict sense of this term for, while increasing the cash assets of the government, they decrease its investment assets. They represent merely a change of governmental assets from one form to another.

Revenues may be classified on other bases. Professor Seligman justifies the classification of public revenue into taxes, fees, and prices on the ground of the different nature of the benefits which these revenues confer on those from whom they are derived. Taxes confer primarily common benefits; fees confer partly common and partly special benefits; and prices primarily special benefits.[1]

Another distinction may be made between ordinary and extraordinary income. Some receipts constituting income are ordinary in the sense that they occur from year to year; others are extraordinary in the sense that they appear only from time to time. The first are represented by annual taxes, annual loans, and other regular sources. The second are illustrated by war taxes, war loans, receipts on account of after-war reparations or loans and receipts from the sale of large public properties. Again, some receipts are in the nature of current revenues, others in the nature of capital funds.

THERE is, of course, no "one-best" classification of public income. The proper classification is one which is best suited to the particular *purpose* for which it is to be used. In order to show the difference in the *character* of the principal forms of public income, the following classification is suggested.

    I. Taxes
   II. Revenue from Domains or Commercial Revenues
       (public prices)
  III. Administrative and Miscellaneous Revenues
       1. Fees
       2. Special Assessments

[1] E. R. A. Seligman, *Essays in Taxation* (The Macmillan Co., New York, 1925), 10th ed., p. 431.

        3. Fines
        4. Gifts
        5. Escheats
   IV. Proceeds from Public Borrowing
    V. Proceeds from the Sale of Public Property
   VI. Transfers (funds received by one unit of govern-
        ment from another)

Definitions of public prices (revenue from domains), fees, special assessments, and taxes were given in section one of this chapter. These forms of revenue, together with income from public borrowing, will be discussed, in the order mentioned, in succeeding chapters.

QUESTIONS AND PROBLEMS FOR DISCUSSION

1. Point out the distinguishing characteristics of fees, special assessments, and taxes.
2. "Any attempt to distinguish between a price and a fee, or a price and a tax, on the basis of relation of costs to charge is incapable of use." Explain.
3. Should the proceeds from public borrowing be considered as public revenue? as public income?
4. Should a tuition payment for educational services at a state university be classified as a fee? as a price for public service?
5. "The more important the public service to the people as a whole, the more justifiable is the price policy of charging in accordance with the cost of the service." Evaluate.
6. What are the purposes of a proper classification of public revenues?

SUGGESTIONS FOR RESEARCH

1. A critical comparison of the classification of public revenues of at least six different writers.
2. A critical and constructive study of an existing classification of revenue in some particular state, county or municipality.
3. The history and explanation of changes which may have taken place in the magnitude of different forms of revenue in a particular political unit during a considerable period of time.

BIBLIOGRAPHICAL NOTE

Points of difference in various classifications of public revenues are shown in the following references: H. C. Adams, *The Science of Finance,* (New York, 1898), Pt. II, Preliminary Chapter; C. C. Plehn, *Introduction to Public Finance,* (New York, 1920), Pt. II, Chap. I; and E. R. A. Seligman, *Essays in Taxation,* (New York, 1928), Chap. XIV.

CLASSIFICATIONS OF PUBLIC REVENUES   113

For factual material relating to public revenues, see the following annual publications: National Industrial Conference Board, *Cost of Government in the United States* (New York); *Report of the Secretary of the Treasury of the United States;* United States Census Bureau, *Financial Statistics of States;* also its *Financial Statistics of Cities;* and the series of descriptive studies of tax systems in the principal countries of the world published by the Commerce Clearing House, Inc. (Chicago). In addition to the above references, see the *Memorandum on Public Finance,* (Economic and Financial Section, League of Nations, Geneva), a serial publication.

Recent data concerning Federal revenues are given in National Industrial Conference Board, *Federal Finances, 1923–1932,* (New York, 1933), Chap. II; W. F. Willoughby, *Financial Condition and Operations of the National Government, 1921–1930,* (Washington, D. C., 1931), Pt. III; and National Industrial Conference Board, *Economic Reconstruction Legislation of 1933,* (New York, 1933), pp. 17-20.

CHAPTER VI

REVENUES FROM DOMAINS: LANDED AND INDUSTRIAL

1. PUBLIC RECEIPTS FROM GOVERNMENT OWNERSHIP *

MISAPPREHENSION is rife concerning the financial aspects of government ownership. Conservative persons often write or speak as if government ownership were sure to involve a financial loss to the government. At the other extreme are many persons who believe that large revenues may be derived from this source. Experience shows that both views are wrong. In the typical or average country, the receipts from government property and business just about balance the expenditures. The government's expenditures and receipts bulk large in public accounts, and in some countries, such as India, they are of substantial importance. But on the whole government industry just about pays its own way.

For a period after the war, the federal government offered an apparent exception to this rule. As the result of the war, it was left with a vast quantity of supplies and securities, and in some years very large receipts were received from this source. In 1922, for instance, government property and investments yielded over $500,000. Sales of government property yielded $116,000,000; the Panama Canal produced nearly $12,000,000; the government's share of the earnings of the Federal Reserve bank amounted to nearly $60,000,000; interest and discount, amounting to $57,500,000, were collected; and investments in the amount of $121,000,000 were repaid. Some of these receipts will continue and probably increase. Thus in 1928 tolls from the Panama Canal yielded over $28,000,000; and $208,925,942 were received on account of the indebtedness of foreign governments to the United States. But receipts from Federal Reserve and intermediate credit banks amounted to only $618,367 and sales of war supplies to less than three millions. But the situation of the federal government is abnormal, and the ordinary rule is that gov-

* From R. T. Ely and others, *Outlines of Economics,* (The Macmillan Co., New York, 1930), Chap. XXXV, pp. 768–776.

ernment property and business cannot be expected to make a substantial net contribution to the Treasury.

THE PUBLIC DOMAIN

BY domains we usually mean agricultural and mineral land and forests owned by the State and managed in the interest of the public revenue, although we might logically subsume under the term the streets and other public property of cities, with all the valuable franchises and privileges which go with them. The direct revenue from this source in the United States is not large, and if account be taken of the cost of the public domain and the expense which it has entailed, the net earnings would probably be a minus quantity.

Until a comparatively recent date this was not the case. In early feudal times the king had large estates of his own from the produce of which the government was largely supported, and although he had certain military rights over his subjects, he had very limited rights over their property. Later, the king became a public rather than a private person, and a large part of the crown estate became the property of the public; but even then taxation was relatively unimportant, and the State relied principally in times of peace upon fines, escheats, fees, crown prerogatives (certain dues which the king was entitled to collect as of his own right), and upon the proceeds of the public domain. Blackstone, the great English jurist, writing in 1765, classified taxation among the "extraordinary" revenues of the sovereign; and in some of the German principalities the government was enabled to get along without taxation in times of peace, down to the close of the eighteenth century. Real democracy not yet having been achieved, the people distrusted taxation and resented its imposition, while the sovereign wisely clung to that species of revenue which was independent of the people's caprice. "The public domains," said Bodin, the great political philosopher of France in the latter part of the sixteenth century, "should be holy, sacred, and inalienable either by grant or by prescription."

But as democracy developed and the representatives of the people gained control of the finances, a new policy was everywhere adopted. If State management was uneconomical and wasteful, and if the government could obtain all the revenue needed by taxation, why preserve the wasteful methods of management? Why not turn public property into private property, to be developed and multiplied through the vitalizing force of individual self-interest? *The great truth was realized that the property of individuals, when subject to taxation and regulation, is no less part of the great patrimony of the State than those lands and forests whose title is retained by the government itself.* This doctrine was generally accepted by the greater countries of the world during the eighteenth century, so that Adam Smith, in defending it in 1776, was able to write that "there is not at present, in Europe, any civilized state of any kind which derives the greater part of its public revenue from the rent of lands which are the property of the state." This philosophy was dominant when our national government was created in 1789 and has guided our national policy ever since.

By exploration and occupancy, war, and various cessions, the federal government acquired after the Revolutionary War a magnificent domain of 2,252,244 square miles. During the greater part of the nineteenth century, these lands were steadily alienated, in accordance with the accepted national policy of expediting the economic development of the country. In the early years of the republic, large revenues were expected from the sale of public land; land was sold in large blocks even though it went to speculators. This was followed by an attempt to sell small holdings to actual settlers, the credit system being used with disastrous results; later (1830) the preëmption policy was introduced by which bona fide home-makers were given certain advantages in purchase; and finally came the Homestead Act of 1862 and other laws by which actual settlers were enabled to obtain homesteads practically free of cost. In addition, our land was freely used as bounties to hasten the development of the country; and enormous grants were made to the states and to corporations for the endowment of education and the subsidization of canal, railway, and other internal improvements.

Our general policy was to give the land away or sell it at low prices in small holdings to actual settlers. In the case of agricultural lands, this policy worked reasonably well so long as the commercial value of the land was not disproportionate to the expense and sacrifice involved in the work of clearing and settling; but when good agricultural land became scarce, its distribution at less than market value became demoralizing, for much the same reason that a lottery is demoralizing.

In the case of forest land, it became apparent in the last quarter of the nineteenth century that the policy of alienation, whether sound or unsound previously, was then a mistake. Alienation and private ownership were not producing that careful management which conduces to the greatest use and the greatest social good in the long run. Beginning in 1891, forest reserves were established, and in such reserves, from time to time, practically all of the valuable timberland remaining to the government has been placed. Instead of selling forest land, the government is now permitting timber to be cut on its land in such a way as to preserve the forests.

In the case of mineral land, our experience seems to show that the policy of disposing of public land in small holdings free of cost, or at prices far below their value, is demoralizing and wasteful. Broadly speaking, the policy of alienation in small holdings conflicts with the requirements and necessities of modern industry. In disposing of our lands, we have tried to balk the corporation and the speculator in order to subsidize the settler and home builder. For instance, we have made the recipients of homesteads and mineral claims swear that they are not acting as agents "for any person, corporation, or syndicate," or "in collusion with any person, corporation, or syndicate, to give them the benefit of the land entered," and that the land is not being secured "for the purpose of speculation." Yet for purposes of grazing and in less degree for mining and lumbering, modern industrial methods require that large tracts of land shall be worked together, and that individual claims shall be consolidated. The core of the difficulty was well described by Mr. Theodore Roosevelt, when President, in these words: "It is a scandal to maintain laws which sound well but which make fraud the key without which great natural resources must remain closed. The law should give individuals and corporations, under proper government regulation and control, the right to work bodies of coal lands large enough for profitable development." And he thereafter recommended laws to authorize the leasing, instead of the complete alienation, of coal, oil, and gas rights, as well as grazing rights on the public domain. In recent years, increasing use of leasing arrangements has been made both by the federal and the state governments; and in a few decades, these leases will probably yield handsome revenues to some of the states which have adopted them.

In a rough way, our land policy has been a success, as is shown by the almost feverish development of the country in the last century. But in some respects it has signally failed. In the first place, it has not paid: more money has been spent for the purchase, survey, and care of the public lands than has been received from their sale and lease. In the second place, certain kinds of lands, as we have shown, should not have been alienated. And in the third place, our efforts to give land to the landless have bred corruption, fostered speculation, and endowed private monopoly with public wealth. One has only to recall the convictions of public officers for land frauds, and to read the report of the Public Lands Commission . . . to appreciate the truth of these charges.

Our conclusion may be formulated in the following general rule: only those lands should be wholly alienated whose use and development under private ownership lead neither to monopoly nor to unnecessary exhaustion and waste. Or, in more concrete terms (remembering that the maxim applies only to those lands left to the government, and to the majority of cases, not to every specific case), the rule for agricultural lands should be private ownership and management, for forest lands State ownership and management, for mining and grazing lands State ownership and private management under a lease or royalty system, by which the State shall secure a share of the profits and retain a considerable measure of regulation and control. In disposing of its lands the government should endeavor to charge value received, as gifts of valuable land, or sales at inelastic schedules of prices which place an extreme valuation upon some tracts and an utterly inadequate valuation upon others, lead to speculation and monopoly, having most of the demoralizing features of a public lottery in which the prizes are distributed partly by chance and partly in accordance with the cunning and unscrupulousness of the participators. When Uncle Sam was rich enough — or was supposed to be rich enough — to provide us all with a farm, the policy of giving away the public domain appeared to be in harmony with the principle of equality of opportunity. But when the supply is far below the demand, those who receive gifts by lot or similar methods are in receipt of special privileges. What once seemed fair has, in the course of economic evolution, become unfair and demoralizing.

PUBLIC INDUSTRIES

In the beginning, let us briefly pass in review the principal classes of industrial enterprise in which the modern State engages for the satisfaction of other than State wants; because, obviously, we are not concerned with enterprises like the government printing office, the government navy yards, and in general, those incidental industries whose products the government consumes but does not regularly sell.

First, we find states like Switzerland monopolizing the manufacture of alcohol and certain alcoholic beverages, Japan monopolizing the opium traffic in Formosa, or commonwealths like South Carolina engaging at one time in the retail distribution of intoxicating beverages.   The purpose of the State in engaging in such industries is primarily sumptuary; it is desired to regulate the traffic almost to the point of suppression, perhaps.   Ordinarily a good revenue could be secured, but revenue is a very secondary consideration.   Prices will be placed above the level of highest net profit, and not improbably the ideal of regulating consumption will be so vigorously pursued that profits will disappear altogether.

Secondly, we have the group of so-called "fiscal monopolies." France, for instance, monopolizes the manufacture of matches, cigarettes, and tobacco in general; Japan has recently gone farther than any other country in the creation of fiscal monopolies; while Prussia, Austria, Italy, Spain, and other European countries maintain public lotteries — as did many of the American colonies during the eighteenth century.   The primary object of the State in undertaking these enterprises is public revenue, gain; and naturally a monopoly price is charged, the price which will yield the greatest net revenue.

Next, we have a group of enterprises consisting principally of the so-called "natural monopolies," which the State undertakes not for suppression, not for profit, but primarily for regulation — to regulate the quality of the product, as in the case of water; to maintain effectively what have been called "equitable conditions for the prosecution of private business," as in the case of railways; to prevent monopolistic extortion and corporate abuse, as in the case of lighting companies, the post office, the telegraph, and the telephone; or to prevent crime and preserve intact the foundations of commercial prosperity, as in the monopoly of coinage.   The charges here are ordinarily adjusted to either the "revenue" or the "cost" principle, that is to say, the State will either aim to make a fair business profit such as is secured in competitive private enterprises, or it will endeavor approximately to meet expenses by adjusting its charges to the cost of production.   England, France, and Germany, in ordinary years, obtain handsome revenues from their respective postal departments, but in the United States the accounts of the Post-Office Department usually show a small deficit.

Finally, we have a large and heterogeneous group of industries which are maintained principally for service, for their educational and developmental influence, not primarily for regulation, and not at all for profit, but "for the public good." We include here not only schools and educational institutions of all kinds, but roads and canals; the savings banks and public pawn shops maintained in several countries of continental

Europe; workingmen's insurance; and model manufacturing establishments such as France maintains for the production of tapestries and fine porcelains. In this group charges will sink to a minimum, and in some lines of enterprise, such as education, practically disappear. Revenue here is not only a minor, but is almost a negligible, consideration.

Although we cannot decide in a general way what theory of charges should be followed in particular public industries, it is possible to lay down general rules which will assist us in reaching a correct conclusion in specific cases. Assuming that the industry in question supplies a service rather than a commodity, merely to save words in the discussion, we must first of all inquire: (1) Is the service helpful or harmful in its net social effect? According as it is one or the other, we will incline in our charges toward the gratuity principle or the prohibitive principle. If harmful, however, it is plain that we must not make the charges high enough to encourage smuggling or illicit manufacture. If helpful, on the other hand, we cannot at once decide upon the gratuity principle, but must inquire further: (2) How generally is the service enjoyed? If only a small portion of the community enjoys the service, it would usually be unjust to charge less than cost, because the deficit would be borne by general taxation falling upon the entire community; unless, indeed, the benefit to one restricted class is seen to be of advantage to the whole community in such a degree that the rest of the community is willing to bear the deficit as in the case of public charity.

(3) Assuming that the service benefits the whole community, this is still not sufficient to justify a charge less than the cost of production. The problem is one of comparative costs. We must inquire whether greater benefit would not be secured by charging enough to raise a profit and then distributing that profit through the maintenance of some other gratuitous enterprise, or, if the tax system weighs heavily on the poor, by remitting taxation to the extent of the profit. (4) If all these questions are answered in favor of the gratuity principle, we still must consider what effect gratuitous service will have upon the cost of the service. Will it encourage wastefulness? Free city water, for example, would probably prove impracticable because of waste, but free parks or free education do not lead to inordinate or unnecessary consumption. The question is a vital one, but it is not always to be answered one way, as some critics seem to believe. (5) Closely related to the above is the question of pauperization. Some things the State may safely give away, and some not. The modern city, for example,

may give free band concerts, in our view, to the undoubted edification of the community; but in Rome the public games demoralized the populace. (6) Finally, we have to ask what effect gratuitous service will have on incomes. Henry George proposed that our cities should operate the street-car lines gratuitously, and the argument in its favor is far stronger than might be expected on first thought. But what effect would this gratuitous service have upon the incomes of the laboring classes? Take the case of the worker in New York City earning $5.00 a day. Will his wages remain at $5.00, if street-car service is offered free of charge? Will not the migration to New York be increased, so that wages will fall? And may not the gain ultimately fall to owners of house property in the form of enhanced rents?

All these questions must be answered before the tariff of charges can be adopted, and it is plain that the answers will be determined by the particular conditions of time, industry, and place, particularly by the character of the industry. The nearest approach to a general rule, which can be formulated, may be stated as follows: In proportion as a service or commodity tends to the upbuilding of character and personality, we should, so far as fiscal conditions permit, gradually move in the direction of the principle of gratuitous service. If the service or commodity itself is widely consumed, and is as desirable as any vendible commodities which would probably be purchased from possible revenues yielded by charges for the service, particularly if large consumption is desirable and waste in consumption does not become excessive, the principle of gratuitous service may be recommended.

2. THE STATE AND PRODUCTION

A DISCUSSION of the basic theoretical and practical considerations in the determination of the proper limits of state industrial activity is presented in the following extract.*

THE assumption of industrial functions by the state may have only an indirect bearing upon the subject of taxation; for if the income accruing is sufficient to offset the increased aggregate public expenditures, the result will be of no fiscal significance. Whether or not public management of industry would have a fiscal import would depend upon the purpose of the management and its efficiency. If the purpose were fiscal, the indus-

* From H. W. Peck, *Taxation and Welfare*, (New York, 1925), Chap. VII, pp. 85–104.

tries might be operated as state monopolies, conducted along purely business lines, and yielding surpluses which might reduce the national tax bill. On the other hand, if the purpose were primarily social, the industry would be operated at cost, on a deficit, or the services might be gratuitous. In either of the latter two cases the cost would have to be made good through general taxation of non-public industries.

As regards the attitude toward the public management of industry people may be grouped into three classes. By some the assumption of industrial functions on the part of the state is considered a tendency toward socialism, and socialism is regarded as the ultimate outcome of democracy. Others oppose this movement, as they consider that economic progress will best be subserved by the extension of private enterprise under voluntary association. Others believe that there is a considerable area of industry in which it is debatable as to whether public or private management will be more efficient, the balance being determined by various factors and conditions. The following study represents an analysis of the subject from the point of view of the third group.

INDUSTRIES ESPECIALLY SUITED FOR PUBLIC MANAGEMENT

APPROACHING the subject deductively, it would seem that some industries are more especially suited for public management, those that are of fundamental social importance, that are at the basis of economic life, that provide the general conditions of earning a living — what have been called "the power houses of our economic system." These could be divided into six classes :

(1). Transfer of values, such as coinage and currency.

(2). Transmission of intelligences, such as the post office, the telegraph, and the telephone.

(3). Transportation of persons and freight by roads, canals, ferries, bridges, railroads, etc.

(4). Transfer of products by means of markets, docks, wharves, exchanges, and elevators.

(5). Transmission of power and utilities, such as waterworks, electric power, steam heat, water, and irrigation.

(6). In the sixth class might be included all articles necessary for life which are monopolized under privately managed industry.

Following is an enumeration of what have been considered the earmarks of industries that might be placed under public management :

(1). Those that result in the waste of material resources if left to individual exploitation, such as forests.

(2). Those that return only general rewards for industry, such as fisheries (with the exception of oyster beds), light-houses, harbors, dredging of rivers, building of canals and waterways, etc.

(3). Those that bring an economic return only after a very long time so that there is not sufficient individual incentive, such as reforestation.

(4). Those in which the public is universally interested so that it will keep watch upon public officials and hold them up to a high grade of efficiency, such as the post office, telephone, and telegraph.

(5). Those which have reached a final state of development, so that their operation has become standardized, such as the street electric railway, lighting and power plants, etc.

(6). Those which are simple or routine in their operation.

(7). Those that are natural monopolies.

A serious and impartial study of the relative merits of municipal and private operation of public utilities was under-taken nearly twenty years ago by the National Civic Federation of the United States.[1] Reference is here made to an article in the *Quarterly Journal of Economics,* "The Civic Federation Report on Public Ownership."[2]

The following is the conclusion of the committee as to the expediency of either public or private ownership:

"The Committee takes no position on the question of the expediency of either public or private ownership. The ques-tion must be solved by each municipality in the light of local conditions. . . In some cities the companies may so serve the public as to create no dissatisfaction and nothing may be gained by experimenting with municipal ownership. Again, the gov-ernment of one city may be good and capable of taking care of these public utilities, while in another it may be the reverse. In either case the people must remember that it requires a large class of able men as city officials to look after these matters. They must also remember that municipal ownership will create a large class of employees who may have more or less political influence."[3]

A less impartial attitude toward the subject is taken by Emil

---

[1] *Municipal and Private Operation of Public Utilities,* Report to the National Civic Federation, Commission of Public Ownership and Operation (3 vols., New York, 1907).

[2] *Quart. Jr. Econ.,* Vol. XXIII, (1908–09), p. 161.

[3] *Quart. Jr. Econ.,* Vol. XXIII, (1908–09), p. 164.

Davies.[4] Davies enumerates five principal factors making for the collective operation of further services :

" (1) . The necessity for further revenue on the part of the State or city.

(2) . The protection of the people from excessive charges on the part of a monopoly in private hands or combinations among private traders or concerns.

(3) . The natural extension of existing State or municipality owned undertakings, by the addition of fresh branches of production or services.

(4) . The growing discontent of the workers in industries so vital to the health of the community that the State has to interfere, e.g., coal miners, railway workers.

(5) . The growth of socialist ideas."

The following passage may be taken as a summary of the book : "I trust the numerous examples given in this book will have shown that the whole trend of things is toward a further extension of State and municipal trading, and that although many circumstances and influences may *impede* its onward march, nothing is likely to *prevent* it. Indeed the only remedy visible for many of the evils from which modern society suffers, the only possible solution of the ever more threatening labour difficulty, the only method of enabling the great mass of consumers to meet the ever increasing cost of living is that of nationalizing or municipalizing various services and trades, and thus reducing the tribute paid by the masses to the monopolist, the speculator, the middle-man, or the non-producer." [5]

THE GROWTH OF PUBLIC OWNERSHIP

SINCE the problem is to be solved by municipal experience rather than *a priori* principles, an extended treatment of this subject would necessitate assembling statistics on the recent growth of public ownership. The following quotation giving a vivid and humorous suggestion of the growth of municipal industries will take up all the limited space that can be devoted to the topic in this study :

"I have touched upon merely some of the instances of state and municipal undertakings known to me, and there must be thousands of others of which I am unaware.

"Eliminating the element of time in getting from place to place, it is already possible for a man in any civilized country

---

4 *The Collectivist State in the Making*, p. 203.
5 *The Collectivist State in the Making*, p. 207.

to be brought into the world by a State doctor or mid-wife, reared in a State nursery, educated, clothed, and doctored at a State school, fed at the cost of the community during his school days (except, in London, on holidays and days of public rejoicing). He can earn his living in government work in any country. In most big towns he can live in a municipally owned house. In New Zealand the government will lend him money with which to buy a house, and it will also lend him, free of charge, the plans on which to construct it. If sick, he may be treated by a State doctor or in a State hospital. He may read at a State or municipal library until he goes blind, when the State will take him into a State blind asylum, or until he goes off his head, when he will be cared for in a State lunatic asylum. If unemployed the State endeavors to find him work. In most towns in Italy or in Buda-Pesth, he can buy his bread from a municipal bakery, and in other countries he can get municipally killed meat from a municipal butchery, and flavor it with government salt, after having cooked it over a fire made with State-mined coal. Or he can partake of this meal in a municipal restaurant, drinking municipally brewed beer, wine from the State vineyards, or State spirits. He then lights his State-made cigar with State-made matches, and can read a municipally produced daily newspaper. By this time, feeling more cheerful, he can draw some more money from his account at the State or municipal savings bank, and can visit the municipally owned race course, where he gambles with the State or city, and can end up the evening at a State or municipally owned theatre. If he likes he can even take a municipal ballet girl out to supper, after which he may, if he feel so inclined, confess to a State-supported priest. Then, if he can afford it, he may go to recuperate at a State or municipal water spa or bath in France, Germany, or New Zealand, after having insured his life with a State insurance office and his house and furniture with the State fire insurance department.

"By this time, if a strong individualist, in despair at the encroaches of the State and municipality in every domain of life's activity, he can buy State gunpowder at a State shop and blow his brains out; or if he likes to blow out some one else's, the State, having brought him into the world and made him what he is, will finish the job and kill him, this being a monopoly jealously guarded by the State except in war time. In Switzerland, Paris, or many another city, the municipality will bury him. There is no time on this occasion to follow him beyond this stage, except to mention that the Public Trustee in most countries will probably look after the deceased's affairs much better than he himself did during his lifetime." [6]

It would be possible to assemble an immense amount of opinion or evidence as to the routine unprogressiveness, favoritism, and general inefficiency of governments and on the other hand of the waste and anti-social practices of private industry. But this subject of government management has only an indirect bearing on the problem of taxation.

ARGUMENTS FOR AND AGAINST PUBLIC MANAGEMENT

BELOW is a summary of arguments for and against public management. The following is a summary by J. A. Hobson of the broad objections commonly adduced as fatal to the socialization of industry: [7]

"(1). The want of any safe and adequate provision for financing the socialized industries.

(2). The failure of any industrial government or management in which labor is predominant or strong, or into which State interference enters, to apply adequate incentives to secure the best services of inventors, scientific experts, technical, administrative, commercial, and financial ability.

(3). Defective discipline in mine, factory, field, or workshop, and a related slackness and inefficiency of labor.

(4). Bureaucratic incompetence, formalism, and corruption in any public ownership and control of industry, whether operated by central officials or by trade parliaments.

(5). Inadequate protection of the Consumer against the domination of Producers."

Below is a summary of Hobson's answers to these objections: [8]

Argument 1 is based on the view of many economists that the unequal distribution of the national income favors savings; that economic progress is conditional on inequality. In answer to this it is asserted that large income or income in excess of what is necessary as an incentive to economic activity tends to reduce productivity. First, by enabling and inducing its recipients to live in idleness, or in useless or wasteful activities, it withdraws from production the personal labor represented by this leisure class. Secondly, this surplus income, diverted into higher wages might raise the physical standard of efficiency of the working class. Thus, it might be converted from waste into productivity.

---

[6] Davies, Emil. *The Collectivist State in the Making*, p. 127.
[7] Hobson, J. A. *Incentives in the New Industrial Order*, (1922), p. 39.
[8] Hobson, J. A. *Incentives in the New Industrial Order*, (1922), p. 49.

Against the statement that a tendency toward equalizing incomes will reduce the investment fund is the assertion that a wasteful distribution of income involves a wasteful utilization of capital. The easy accumulation of the rich leads to over-investment — to saving and applying to capital a larger proportion of the general income than is needed as capital to produce the consumers' goods for which under these conditions there is an effective demand. The result is recurring periods of business depression. In other words, the great inequalities in income cause a maladjustment between saving and spending.

The rate of interest and falling prices tend to correct the tendency to over-saving and production in excess of effective demand; but this method of adjustment involves much waste; it is slow, imperfect, and inadequate.

Under the condition of a more equitable distribution of income, the proportion of saving to spending would not be so high. But this does not imply an inadequate supply of new capital; for no reduction in the absolute quantity of savings would take place. Under the condition of fuller employment of the factors of production, and so of increased social income, a smaller proportion of saving might yield as large or a larger amount of new capital.

Under the conditions of a more equitable distribution of income, it will be less difficult and costly to get the necessary new capital, the rate of interest will be less. Under pre-war conditions much saving was of the intra-marginal kind, but about one third had to be extracted at some real sacrifice on the part of the suppliers; and the easy saving was remunerated at a price determined by the difficult saving. Under more equalized conditions of income, though the average sacrifice involved in saving a given proportion of the total income would be higher than under the old system, the sacrifice in doing the most difficult saving might be less. And since a smaller proportion of the larger total income would need to be saved, the price for saving, i.e., the rate of interest might be lower than before.

Again, the remuneration for savings that go to public industries will be paid in the form of interest on bonds rather than in dividends on shares of stock. This will remove a portion of the field of industry from the operations of the risk-taking, speculative spirit; it will provide an ampler field for conservative investment of savings; and so will tend to rationalize and moralize the industrial system. And this increase in safe investment will stimulate thrift. Hobson makes the further distinction between savings for the sake of expanding material capital and savings for the increase of personal capital. This form of saving, investment in education and training, he contends has been underestimated in Great Britain. There is greater need for trained ability in science, finance, and business administration than for material capital.

Another objection to the extension of socialized industry is that under public or bureaucratic management the social savings will not be most economically applied. Hobson answers that only the old, established, standardized industries are to be brought under public management; and that industries in the experimental and developmental stage will remain outside the area of public control. He believes that under state control industry and commerce will be less risky, there will be less secrecy about business firms, less ignorance about stocks and prices in the world market, and less violent and unpredictable changes in the monetary situation.

Hobson's answer to the second objection may be summarized in his own words:

"The charge against the new Industrial Order that it will be lacking in initiative and enterprise is, therefore, met by the following considerations:

(1). The industries proposed for nationalisation, being relatively stable and routine in character, have less use for these qualities than those industries which remain within the sphere of private competitive enterprise.

(2). A great deal of this initiative and enterprise has no rightful place in socialised industry, being directed either to the achievement of profitable victories over trade competitors, or to the establishment of a monopolistic power to tax consumers, or to the performance of successful coups in the financial sphere.

(3). Nationalised industries should, however, be able to attract as much of these creative and progressive qualities as they require from men who combine them with a keen public spirit and a high regard for such distinction as the public services can be made to afford." [9]

The charge that public ownership precludes any form of effective management of industry, and therefore tends to reduce the efficiency of labor, is without warrant. It would be possible for the state, after acquiring ownership over the mines and railways, to lease them out to private companies upon terms that would leave unimpaired the previous incentives to efficiency among the employees; but that is not the problem that confronts us. Within the sphere of public industry must be

[9] Hobson, J. A. *Incentives in the New Industrial Order*, p. 99.

found or devised motives adequate to evoke from the will of the workers productive energy equal to that hitherto evoked by the economic pressure brought to bear in private employment.

What would be the effect of nationalization on the attitude of labor that the British call ca' canny? If it is a consciously anti-capitalist policy, nationalization might call it off. In so far as the desire to spread employment by working slowly is a factor in ca' canny, the greater scarcity of employment under a public service would sap this motive to inefficiency. On the other hand, this advantage might be offset by the removal of the fear of being "fired" for inefficiency.

Another economic claim for public service is the argument that public industry, by removing the profit motive, the insecurity of wages and employment, and the speeding up, and bad workmanship, will give freer scope for the instincts of workmanship. Hobson, however, does not ascribe much weight to this argument; for routine, standardization, and large-scale production will continue to be characteristic of the public services; and industrial efficiency requires that minute specialization and sub-division of labor which do not permit the liberty of personal expression which is the essence of true craftsmanship. The elimination of profiteering will hardly make the work more interesting. The compensations are to be found outside the routine services in the enlargement of leisure and other opportunities that are afforded by the new order.

The most potent incentives for the maintenance of industrial efficiency and progress are derived from representative government. Autocracy is failing in industry as it has failed in politics. The democratic institutions that have displaced political autocracy have plenty of faults; but few deem it practicable to return to the autocratic state. So in industry: as a free citizen who has a stake in the government stands to gain by helping to make it good, so the worker who has some control over the industry in which he works, stands to gain by making it efficient. The details of the participation of labor in industry — whether through social ownership, guild ownership and management in certain trades, capitalism combined with profit-sharing and co-partnership, or capitalism limited by wage-boards or other arrangements — are outside the scope of this study. Some of the probable advantages of the introduction of representative democracy into industry are as follows: There may be some gain from a new social atmosphere, the sense of dignity and responsibility of men who are conscious of working for themselves, their comrades, and the public in an industry which in some sense belongs to them and in a government in which they have a voice.

But the great immediate gains to productivity will come from the development of group self-discipline within the workshop or other industrial unit. The possible limits of the efficiency of industry under the conditions of willing coöperation are seen in the extraordinary productivity during the war, when patriotic and other special stimuli took up all the pre-war slack. This problem of efficient self-government in industry is the central problem of public management. Of course, workshop self-government will not yield perfect discipline, but it will yield better discipline than is probable under private management, in view of the progressive revolt of the working class against autocracy in industry. If industrial democracy does not attain this measure of relative success, state industry will be relatively inefficient, and the project for an extension of public management will have to be abandoned as unfeasible.

In answer to the fifth objection to government management that it will afford inadequate protection to the consumer against the combinations of producers, Hobson avers that this danger may be obviated by giving consumers some representation in the government of the trades which exist to supply their wants, and by linking up more closely the trade unions with the coöperative movement.[10]

LARGE-SCALE INDUSTRY AND GOVERNMENT ACTIVITY

BUT leaving the subject of public management, there is no question that the expansion of large-scale industry requires a certain corresponding expansion of government activity. In the case of public service utilities the government has the choice between regulation and management. This is true of industries that operate according to what economists call the law of decreasing costs or increasing returns. The larger the industrial plant the lower the per unit cost of product. The result of this is struggle for enlargement of an industrial plant, cut-throat competition, and finally combination or integration in some form, and monopoly limited only by potential competition or the danger of public interference. Hence, from the social point of view government management or regulation is a prerequisite of industrial democracy and hence, in the long run, to the existence of industry. Regulation is a necessary and hence a productive factor in industry. When the public

---

[10] For a less sanguine analysis of the scope, limitations, and difficulties of collectivism, see Robertson, D. H. *The Control of Industry,* (1923), Chapters VIII and IX.

saves in reduction of strikes and lock-outs, in modifying the industrial cycle, and in prevention of profiteering in prices and wages, more than it costs them in additional taxes, it is conforming to the economic principle of marginal productivity.

This may be justification for the greater taxes which the federal government exacts from manufacture than from agriculture. In 1918 manufacturing corporations paid the federal government $2,112,044,810 as income, profits, and excess profits taxes while the entire agricultural industry probably did not pay the United States government over $100,000,000 in these classes of taxes.[11] The writer goes on to comment that "it seems highly improbable that in 1918 the Federal Government rendered to the manufacturing industry service valued at more than twenty times that furnished to agriculture." From the social point of view this apparent injustice in the distribution of tax burdens tends to disappear. The growth of expenditures is a concomitant of the development of the industrial state. And the great increase in wealth that results furnishes the source of support for those regulative and developmental activities of the state without which the existence or the prosperity of the new order could not endure. Besides, the acceptable principle of taxation today is not benefit but taxable faculty.

CONCLUSIONS

On the subject of the public management of industries we may formulate our conclusions as follows:

A. CONDITIONS FAVORABLE TO PUBLIC MANAGEMENT

(1). The need of supplying an essential service in a field unattractive to private capital.

(2). The need of conserving certain natural resources which would be wasted under private management.

(3). The need of safeguarding the quality of certain commodities, like milk and water, in which minimum standards of quality can be determined scientifically.

(4). When the competition of a public industry is necessary to restrain a private monopoly.

(5). When considerations of social advantage require that the use of the services should be discouraged, and public opinion will not favor complete prohibition. The policy here to be followed is that of a government monopoly, and a price much in excess of cost.

(6). When social considerations require that the service should be rendered at less than cost, e.g., water.

11 *Income in the United States.* National Bureau of Economic Research. Vol. II, pp. 5–6.

(7). When considerations of social advantage require that essential services be provided free of charge to those who otherwise would go without them on account of poverty, *e.g.*, hospital service, education, etc.

(8). When labor is hostile to private management and in favor of nationalized industry.

(9). When public employment is held in high esteem, so that honor and security of tenure rather than high salaries will attract the highest grade of scientific ability.

B. CONDITIONS FAVORABLE FOR PRIVATE MANAGEMENT

(1). Where dynamic industrial conditions prevail, and private profit is needed to evoke initiative and enterprise.

(2). Where the maintenance of soil fertility is a vital factor, as in the case of agricultural land.

(3). Where the mass of people are so limited in intelligence and social vision that they can respond adequately to no motive but the direct appeal to personal gain : where social coöperation can only be unconscious and indirect.

(4). Where government is inefficient or corrupt, and public opinion divided or indifferent.

QUESTIONS AND PROBLEMS FOR DISCUSSION

1. Explain the fact that there is a greater amount of government enterprise in leading European countries than in the United States.

2. Should our industrial domain be enlarged and relied upon as an important source of public revenue ?

3. According to W. S. Jevons, "nothing but experience and argument from experience can in most cases determine whether the community will be best served by its collective state action, or by trusting to private self-interest."   Evaluate.

4. When a government owns and operates an electric power plant, what price policy should be adopted for the sale of the service ? Should the government attempt to make a financial profit by such ownership ?

5. Is a government ever justified in charging what the traffic will bear when offering service, *e.g.*, transportation, to the public ?

6. Discuss the advisability of having the government own and operate those industries in which there is a marked tendency toward monopoly.

SUGGESTIONS FOR RESEARCH

1. An evaluation of the policy followed by the Federal government in disposing of the public domain.

2. A study of the history, the objectives, the accomplishments, and the possibilities of social benefits of the Muscle Shoals project.

3. The possibilities of tax relief through revenue from landed and industrial domains.

4. Public versus private ownership of oil resources in the United States.
5. Price policies of publicly owned and operated enterprises, in theory and in practice.

BIBLIOGRAPHICAL NOTE

A standard treatment of revenues from landed and industrial domains is H. C. Adams, *The Science of Finance*, (New York, 1898), Pt. II, Bk. I, Chaps. I, II. In this work is given, among other things, (1) a consideration of the factors determining the choice of industries suitable for government ownership and operation; and (2) a discussion of price policies of publicly owned and operated enterprises.

German views on the subject of domains as a source of public revenue are presented in K. T. von Eheberg, *Finanzwissenschaft*, (Leipzig, 1921), pp. 85-118; and Adolph Wagner, *Finanzwissenschaft*, (Leipzig, 1883), Vol. I, pp. 527-792. The early development of domains is traced in Gustav Cohn, *The Science of Finance*, (Chicago, 1895), pp. 82-103, translated from the German by T. B. Veblen.

A wide range of opinion concerning various aspects of the problem of public domains may be found in C. J. Bullock, *Selected Readings in Public Finance*, (Boston, 1924), Chaps. V, VI. A discussion of the extent and potentialities of revenues other than taxes in the United States is given in J. P. Jensen, "Public Revenue Sources Supplemental to Taxes," *Proceedings of the National Tax Association*, (1927), pp. 84-98. H. W. Peck's "An Inductive Study of Publicly Owned and Operated versus Privately Owned but Regulated Electric Utilities," *American Economic Review Supplement*, Vol. XIX, (March, 1929), pp. 197-218, is a valuable reference.

Special studies which throw light on the question of the proper ownership and management of domains are: J. W. Toumey, "Who Should Own the Forests?", *Yale Review*, N.S., Vol. III, pp. 145-156; G. O. Virtue, "Public Ownership of Mineral Lands in the United States," *Journal of Political Economy*, Vol. III, pp. 185-202; W. H. Voskuil, *The Economics of Water Power Development*, (New York, 1928); Edwin Cannan, "Ought Municipal Enterprises to be Allowed to Yield a Profit?" *Economic Journal*, Vol. IX, pp. 1-9; and G. W. Stocking, *The Oil Industry and the Competitive System*, (Boston, 1925). More general works on the question of public ownership and management are: D. Knoop, *Principles and Methods of Public Trading*, (London, 1912); and C. D. Thompson, *Public Ownership*, (New York, 1925).

For the historical development of the public land policy of the United States, see B. H. Hibbard, *A History of the Public Land Policies*, (New York, 1924). A comprehensive treatment of the management of public enterprises in Soviet Russia is given in G. Y. Sokolnikov and Associates, *Soviet Policy in Public Finance, 1917-1928*, (Stanford University, California, 1931).

A stimulating treatise which considers "how far private personal profit in present-day industry works economically, and how far it can be displaced by incentives with a wider, better, and more reliable appeal," is J. A. Hobson, *Incentives in the New Industrial Order,* (London, 1922).

Much valuable material concerning the revenue from public lands in the United States is available in the report of a Committee of the National Tax Association on "Revenue from Public Lands," in the *Proceedings of the National Tax Association,* (1927), pp. 215-242.

CHAPTER VII

FEES AND SPECIAL ASSESSMENTS

1. FEES OR ADMINISTRATIVE CHARGES *

. . . FEES or administrative charges are varied in character, since they are collected in varying amounts by practically every general service organization of practically every part of our government. The wide variations in the receipts among the same type or degree of governmental unit suggest possibilities of augmented revenues.

For the Federal Government, fees are probably relatively less significant than for the states and their local divisions. The consular and passport fees amount to about $10,000,000 annually, and render the State Department nearly self-supporting. Certain fees of the customs service, of the public land registers and receivers and others bring the total of federal fees to probably less than $25,000,000. Considered as a percentage of total federal revenue in excess[1] of $4,000,000,000, this is considerably less than 1%. It does not seem probable that federal fees will increase so as to form a very important part of the total revenue.

The 48 states in 1925 received nearly $119,000,000 from general department earnings, or about $1.05 per capita, and 8% of their total receipts. The extent to which the 48 states, taken together, and to which certain selected states that received more than 10% of their total revenues from fees, made their different departments self-supporting, may be seen from the accompanying table.

Some of these figures are decidedly misleading. For example, the State of Kansas collected through its "highway department" 143% of its cost payments for highways. That appears to be a case of making highways sources of considerable income. But the total amount collected was less than $34,000; and the amount spent was less than $24,000 — both amounts inconsequential. The explanation is that the state constitution forbids the state to engage directly in any internal improvement.

---

* Adapted from J. P. Jensen, "Public Revenue Sources Supplemental to Taxes," *Proceedings of the National Tax Association*, (1927), pp. 85–91.

[1] See, e.g., *First Report of the Director of the Budget*, 1923.

It can therefore spend very little directly, and whatever is collected from miscellaneous sources looms large, relative to the negligible expenditures. No doubt there are other "freak" variations; and some of the variations can be explained away on other bases. But enough of variation remains to suggest that some states might derive additional revenue from fees.

EXTENT OF SELF-SUPPORT IN SELECTED STATES OF GENERAL DEPARTMENTS (PERCENTAGE WHICH EARNINGS WERE OF COST PAYMENTS), 1925

States	All departments	General government	Protection to persons and property	Conservation of health	Highways	Charities, hospitals and corrections	Education	Recreation	Miscellaneous
Maine	15	2	20	9	40	13	8	..	9
Vermont	12	10	21	6	15	16	2	..	2
Minnesota	16	3	32	53	1	28	8	7	1
Iowa	19	13	38	26	1	55	23	12	4
Missouri	24	6	40	38	1	40	11	37	..
North Dakota	14	3	30	34	1	44	7	6	2
South Dakota	16	6	41	32	2	41	10	27	3
Kansas	22	4	72	24	143	18	23	..	5
Maryland	25	54	40	12	6	37	22	..	1
Alabama	31	16	90	7	12	95	15	..	1
Colorado	15	7	48	17	1	11	24	48	18
New Mexico	23	14	25	21	17	3	18	..	250
California	10	11	17	10	..	22	9	36	1
All States	11.5	10	33	16	29	11	9	11	1

Note: Based upon data from *Financial Statistics of States*, 1925.

The 247 cities of 30,000 population or more received in 1925 nearly $67,000,000, or about $1.64 per capita and 2.7% of their total revenue from general department earnings. But 17 cities received more than $3.50 per capita; and Highland Park, Michigan, and Pasadena, California, received, respectively, $5.09 and $5.65 per capita. The extent to which the several departments were self-supporting in all the 247 cities and in those cities that received more than 8% of their total revenue from this source, may be seen in the table following.

It may be argued that the general departments are not organized for fiscal purposes. They are not revenue-producing, but service-giving organizations. That is true in the same sense that it is true that a meat-packing plant exists not to produce fertilizer or toothbrushes. But every well-managed industry exploits its by-products, so long as their sale will yield more than the extra cost of their production. So also should the finance minister use every minor source of revenue whose tapping will cause less sacrifice than the same amount of taxes would cause.

EXTENT OF SELF-SUPPORT IN SELECTED CITIES OF GENERAL DEPARTMENTS (PERCENTAGE WHICH EARNINGS WERE OF COST PAYMENTS), 1925

Cities	All departments	General government	Protection to persons and property	Conservation of health	Sanitation and promotion of health	Highways	Education	Charities, hospitals and corrections	Recreation	Miscellaneous
Detroit	8	7	6	4	2	11	4	24	36	6
Cincinnati	8	10	5	3	1	4	12	1	3	..
Denver	8	26	11	2	..	13	2	10	14	3
Worcester	9	10	1	15	18	10	3	29	10	15
Sacramento	8	..	4	14	52	16	1	5	10	5
Highland Park	11	..	2	18	3	6	3	63	..	48
Berkeley	9	2	3	2	89	41	1	..	10	..
Brockton	10	5	..	13	78	28	2	20	67	..
Jackson, Mich.	14	25	2	62	26	4	2	51	31	..
Pasadena	10	16	3	5	7	57	2	3	10	10
Augusta, Ga.	13	..	2	..	2	9	1	64	..	2
Galveston	15	4	4	..	4	..	..	81	3	..
Columbus, Ga.	19	..	..	42	51	2	17	63	1	..
Fitchburg	8	5	1	12	2	2	20	45	4	13
Lynchburg	10	9	1	4	6	12	8	54	17	..
All cities having population over 30,000	4	9	3	6	5	5	2	11	13	4

Note: Based upon data from *Financial Statistics of Cities*, 1925.

It is obvious that not for every type of service rendered by the government can a fee be charged. Some of them, such as that of the legislature, furnish no occasion for such a fee, and contain no basis for determining the size of the fees. Generally speaking, there can be no charge unless the fee-payer can be identified with tolerable readiness, as being either the recipient of benefit from some definite service or a member of a class whose behavior necessitates the service. Any state or municipal government will furnish examples of organizations whose work is of an overhead, or general character. I have culled from the first Report of the Director of the Budget for the State of Kansas (1927), a number of officers and a number of boards.

The selection of officers includes the governor and the justices of the courts and others. The boards include, among others, the Board of Regents, the Livestock Sanitary Commission, the Board of Health, and the State Historical Society. The appropriations for this group totaled a little over $1,000,000. Not one cent in fees or charges was collected for the services of this group. And there were certain other organizations, such as the Attorney General's Office and the Public Service Commission, whose "earnings" were small. With variations for individual officers or boards, the situation is the same in all states and cities. It is not practical to charge, on a *quid pro quo* basis, for general governmental services. From this source taxpayers can hope for no appreciable relief.

But after all, the general government cost is only a minor part of the total governmental cost. Taking all our governmental divisions as a whole, it may be said that the general government requires considerably less than 10% of the total revenue. And it is probable that the cost of general government will be relatively less in the future than it is now. Nearly all of the new functions of the government are special rather than general. For many of the services, though not for all of them, some charge may reasonably be made. In individual instances this charge will probably not be large, but in many cases it may reasonably cover the entire cost. In some cases it may develop into a tax, when the cost of the service is more than covered. The best example in recent decades of such a development from a fee to a tax is found in our motor-vehicle registration charges, which are now everywhere properly regarded as taxes. In such cases fees represent merely the transitionary state in development of taxes.

I have taken, again from the state budget of Kansas although any other state might serve as well, seventeen boards of the type for whose services heavy charges may be made. The list includes the Athletic Board, the Grain Inspection Department, and the Hotel Commission. These boards collected during the fiscal year 1926 $581,000 in fees, and spent $417,000, or about 70%, leaving $164,000 for the general fund. In the case of an increasing number of these boards, the legislature has in recent sessions required that 10% of the collections be deposited to the credit of the general fund, appropriating the balance for the use of the organization. This is one way of accomplishing two different objects : First, to determine statistically the amount of the collections, with a view to fixing the proper rates ; second, to require these special services to bear not only the direct cost of the agency performing the services but also all or a part of

the overhead cost in which they involve the general government. On theoretical as well as on practical grounds such a
procedure is justifiable.

In between the extremes, on the one hand, the services that
are so general that no charge can be made for them, and on the
other, those services that can bear their full cost, fall the bulk
of governmental services. The cost of the services is partly
met, in varying degrees, from the charges exacted. There is
evidence to show that legislatures and budget-makers are considering the possibility of making the special governmental
services as nearly self-supporting as possible.

Many of our governmental organizations are found upon
analysis to render services of a composite character, some of
which may safely be required to bear their total cost, while
others can bear only a part of it or none at all. Consider, for
example, the institutions of higher learning of the State of
Kansas. The appropriations for these institutions for 1925
amounted to $6,488,000, of which they spent $5,834,000 or
89%. The fees collected, together with minor amounts of
other kinds, amounted to $2,126,000, or about 36% of the cost.

If we analyze the services of, say, a state university, which
we may take as typical of a higher educational institution, into
its elements we see that for purposes of determining fees to be
charged, the services are heterogeneous. And that generalization will hold for nearly all governmental organizations. For
example, the University of Kansas, besides its general instructional service, for which a general fee is charged, maintains a
cafeteria, dormitories, student health service, student extra-
curricular activities, and the like. While probably no one
would argue that this type of services provide a proper occasion
for the levying of a tax, there is no serious objection to charges
for them that will cover their cost. While such services help
to swell the total cost of an educational institution, it is not
regarded as proper that they should swell also that part of the
cost that must be met from taxation.

But not only are such supplementary services more and more
met from fees imposed; the fees for the general instructional
services have almost everywhere doubled during the past decade. At its 1927 session the legislature of Kansas refused to
increase the appropriations for the state educational institutions
for the biennium, over the appropriations for the previous
biennium. If more revenue were required, it was suggested
that the fees might be increased. Accordingly the Board of
Regents authorized an increase. Because of this increase and
because of another increase, made two years earlier for similar

reasons, the general tuition fees have been more than doubled. An inspection of the fee schedules of similar institutions discloses the fact that Kansas is following, rather tardily, a movement that is quite general.

In the tendency to increase the general tuition fees we may discern a principle of much wider application in determining the proper size of fees. Our earliest universities and colleges were endowed institutions, and the first state institutions joined in the practice of giving practically free tuition, or at least of charging nominal fees. This liberal policy served admirably to encourage attendance. We can understand that at that time such encouragement was in the public interest. But today such indiscriminate encouragement is not needed and has, besides, certain drawbacks. Among the hundreds of thousands that matriculate each year at our institutions of higher learning are many who do not have the requisite mentality to benefit from the facilities offered, and also many who for other reasons could more advantageously occupy themselves in some other way. In proportion as it is no longer in the public interest to increase the attendance indiscriminately, may the fees be safely increased, and made to cover a larger part of the cost.

The principle involved is of course that the charging of fees must be subsidiary to the public policy. But public policy, with reference to a given service, may change; and it is not likely to change with reference to all public services to the same extent and in the same direction at the same time. Nothing but constant vigilance and repeated study will develop an acceptable and justifiable schedule of fees.

It is obvious that the so-called "earnings of the general departments" can never equal their cost, at least not all of them considered as a whole. Fees cannot be charged except upon some fairly definite occasion, such as the issue of a marriage license or the inspection of a sample of grain. They cannot be charged unless the fee-payer can be readily identified as having some relation to the specific occasion, either by way of benefiting from the service or giving rise to the necessity for performing it. And finally, they should not be charged when or in such amounts that they will interfere with accepted public policies. The foregoing restrictions require that many public services be rendered free or at less than cost. On the other hand, without doubt, there are many possibilities for additional fees, or for increased fees. Though their payment may cause some sacrifice, it will often be less than the sacrifice involved in taxes to which their non-payment gives rise. It should no longer be possible to ignore the fact that non-payment of justifiable fees involves more than equivalent sacrifice through the exaction of resulting taxes.

2. MOTOR VEHICLE REGISTRATION FEES

A FORM of fee which has acquired prominence in the United States during the past decade is the motor vehicle license fee. Drs. C. H. Sandage and R. W. Nelson treat the historical, legal, and economic aspects of this source of revenue in the section which follows.*

THREE major license fees are at present used by most states in connection with the motor vehicle. These are: (1) registration fees, (2) dealers' licenses, and (3) chauffeur and operator permits. By far the most important of these is the registration fee, or license to use a motor vehicle upon the public streets and highways. Attention will be directed primarily to this one fee because it far outranks the others as a source of revenue, and because the principles involved are equally applicable to other license charges. By way of introduction, it may be helpful at this point to review briefly the legal and historical background of the automobile registration fee in this country.

The automobile and the highway stand in a complementary relationship, in that either would suffer a severe decline in utility if it were divorced from the other. It follows that any exercise of control over one will necessarily affect the other. Hence, in the vehicle's use of the highway the government found a ready means of exercising control over the automobile and its owner. No person need pay a· license fee to operate his automobile on his own premises. It is only because of his use of the public highway that a fee can be imposed.[1] It was quite natural, therefore, that the first type of tax to be levied upon the motor vehicle (other than the personal property tax) was one to regulate the use of highways by that vehicle. The registration fee, or license tax, was the special tax utilized for this purpose.

This type of tax proceeds from the police power of the state. The right of the state to require any person or organization to procure a license to perform certain acts or to conduct a business enterprise which might be detrimental to public health or safety is well-grounded in American law. Any reasonable control over the motor vehicle, through taxation or otherwise, can be exercised in the interests of safety. In the case of

* From C. H. Sandage and R. W. Nelson, *Motor Vehicle Taxation for Highway Purposes*, (Iowa City, Iowa, 1932), Chap. III.
[1] *Kane* vs. *Titus*, 80 Atl. 453.

Schlesinger vs. City of Atlanta, Georgia, the court held that the state can limit and control the use of the highway whenever necessary to "provide for and promote the safety, peace, health, morals, and general welfare of the people,"[2] subject only to limitations of reasonableness and equality.[3]

New York, in 1901, was the first state to impose a motor vehicle registration fee. During that year a total of $954.00 was collected from this source.[4] Following the example of New York, other states quickly joined in the use of this levy. It was the only special tax to be used by all the states prior to 1929, in which year a levy on gasoline was finally given legislative and judicial sanction in Illinois, the last state to adopt such a tax.[5]

The constitutionality of the license fee was called into question shortly after its introduction. It was claimed that there was unfair discrimination between the manufacturer of automobiles and the customer owner. The manufacturer was not required to have a license for each vehicle which he completed, therefore it was argued that a particular class of automobile owners was being singled out for taxation, this constituting class legislation. However, in 1903 the court held, in the New York case of People vs. McWilliams, that there was a clear difference in the two classes of automobile owners and the state was within its rightful powers to tax one and not the other.[6]

The early registration fee was purely a privilege tax and not a tax on property. As a privilege tax it rested upon the police power of the states and not upon the power to tax for revenue purposes. Presumably a privilege tax should be just high enough to cover the necessary costs of regulation, and the early license fees were intended to cover only such costs. However, as the demand for improved roads developed, it appeared that an increase in the license fee would provide an easy and equitable method of raising revenue to aid in the construction and maintenance of highways. Therefore the majority of the states did not long delay in advancing their license fees to figures in excess of the ordinary costs of motor vehicle regulation. This step at once called forth strong opposition from certain quarters, and efforts were made to establish its unconstitutionality.

[2] Schlesinger vs. City of Atlanta, 129 S. E. 861.
[3] In re: Opinion of the Justices, 81 N. H., 566.
[4] Trumbower, Henry R., "Motor Vehicle Fees and Gasoline Taxes," Public Roads, Vol. 5, No. 7, p. 1.
[5] U. S. Bureau of Public Roads, Gasoline Tax Rates, 1929. Illinois had passed a gasoline tax in 1927, but it was declared unconstitutional February 25, 1928.
[6] People vs. McWilliams, 86 N. Y. Supp. 357.

It was agreed that when the state increased a privilege tax appreciably above the cost of administration, it became a levy for revenue purposes and fell under the constitutional requirement of equality and uniformity in taxation. It was claimed that to single out the automobile owner as a source of additional revenue was unreasonably discriminatory, so unconstitutional. The courts, however, upheld the right of the state to levy such increased license fees under its general police powers. In the case of Cleary *vs.* Johnston, a New Jersey case decided in 1909, the court held that, although fees collected were greater than the amounts expended in maintaining the State Automobile Department, the fee was not therefore extortionate for regulatory purposes, nor would it have been unconstitutional had it been imposed as a tax for revenue purposes.[7]

Again, in Kane *vs.* Titus the court went farther and held that, when a license fee was construed to be a tax for revenue purposes, it was not to be regarded as a tax upon the vehicle, but rather upon its operation upon the highway; hence, the constitutional requirements of equality and uniformity in taxation did not apply to such a privilege tax.[8]

It made no difference, then, whether the fee was viewed as a charge representing the exercise of the police power or as a tax for the purpose of raising revenue: the entire license fee was to be construed as a privilege tax and could be imposed without regard to the value of the property involved. Thus the stamp of judicial approval was placed upon the license fee that served in this dual capacity.

The license fee and personal property tax remained the only taxes of importance on the motor vehicle until 1919, the year in which the gasoline tax was introduced. Prior to 1928, moreover, the registration fee occupied first place as a source of revenue, but in that year total receipts from the gasoline tax exceeded the registration fee receipts by $10,798,835. In 1929 this excess was $83,467,976;[9] in 1930 it was $138,978,550;[9] and in 1931 it increased to $192,059,804.[10] This shift in the relative positions of the two levies is attributable to the increased popularity of the tax on gasoline rather than to any decrease either in the amount of the registration fee or the total revenue collections derived therefrom. On the contrary, the receipts from the registration and license fees have had an uninterrupted annual growth. The total collections from this source during

[7] *Cleary vs. Johnston,* 79 N. J., Law 49.
[8] *Kane* vs. *Titus,* 80 Atl. 453.
[9] Obtained from data compiled by the U. S. Bureau of Public Roads.
[10] N.A.C.C., *Facts and Figures of the Automobile Industry, 1931.*

1930 were $355,704,860, a figure that exceeded the collections of 1928 by $33,074,835, and those of 1929 by $7,861,317.[11]

The registration fee schedules of the several states are characterized by an extreme lack of uniformity. In some states the fee covers merely the cost of administration, while in others it furnishes a substantial revenue. The lowest average fee charged in 1930 was that of $4.06 by the District of Columbia, the highest that of $38.15 by Oregon. No personal property tax is assessed against the motor vehicle in Oregon, hence the license fee is properly regarded as consisting in part of such a levy. A like condition prevails in the majority of the states which impose license fees substantially higher than the all-state average.

Table [A] gives the average registration fee by states for the year 1930. The average fee for the entire United States was $13.41, which represents an increase of 2.3 per cent over 1929.

TABLE [A]

AVERAGE AND GROSS LICENSE FEES BY STATES — 1930 *

State	Average License Fee	Gross Receipts from Motor Vehicle License Fees, etc.
Alabama	$13.71	$3,799,761
Arizona †	6.65	734,626
Arkansas	19.45	4,283,959
California.†	4.83	9,858,810
Colorado	6.16	1,901,230
Connecticut	25.04	8,290,404
Delaware	19.79	1,110,047
District of Columbia †	4.06	636,001
Florida	14.69	4,813,495
Georgia	13.12	4,482,257
Idaho	16.78	1,998,290
Illinois	11.26	18,444,247
Indiana	7.25	6,346,879
Iowa	16.31	12,693,621
Kansas	10.23	6,084,348
Kentucky	16.76	5,547,069
Louisiana	16.74	4,609,042
Maine	17.01	3,166,642
Maryland	10.69	3,437,796
Massachusetts	8.41	7,120,583
Michigan	16.93	22,482,412
Minnesota	15.09	11,062,150
Mississippi	12.85	3,046,393
Missouri	13.33	10,150,000

11 *Ibid.*

State	Average License Fee	Gross Receipts from Motor Vehicle License Fees, etc.
Montana	11.71	1,583,276
Nebraska	8.93	3,804,950
Nevada	12.61	373,966
New Hampshire	20.42	2,290,435
New Jersey	18.04	15,382,456
New Mexico	15.20	1,279,623
New York	17.70	40,857,715
North Carolina	15.08	6,835,743
North Dakota	10.70	1,958,662
Ohio	7.55	13,287,352
Oklahoma	11.88	6,536,361
Oregon	38.15	9,617,930
Pennsylvania	18.88	33,112,371
Rhode Island	16.72	2,280,849
South Carolina	13.18	2,878,352
South Dakota	14.43	2,959,913
Tennessee	12.95	4,767,239
Texas	10.22	13,961,362
Utah	7.51	855,584
Vermont	27.62	2,392,152
Virginia	17.28	6,493,989
Washington	17.08	7,616,676
West Virginia	17.66	4,702,812
Wisconsin	16.72	13,083,521
Wyoming	11.24	691,509

* The figures presented in this table and elsewhere in this [section] have been obtained from reports of the U. S. Bureau of Public Roads. The basic data, as found in these reports, are labeled "Motor Vehicle Registration Fees, Licenses, Permits, Fines, etc." Actually, therefore, the figures shown herein involve some small error, in that they include the receipts from permits, fines, and other minor sources, in addition to the amounts derived from registration fees. In the absence of more precise basic data, it has not been possible to eliminate this error, unfortunately. It is believed, however, that the receipts from these minor sources are so altogether negligible in comparison with license fee receipts that their inclusion causes only superficial inexactness in the final figures, rather than serious or consequential error.

† Arizona and California impose flat rate license fees upon passenger cars, but use sliding scales in fixing fees upon commercial vehicles; hence the average license fees for these states do not appear as round figures. The District of Columbia imposes a flat fee upon all types of vehicles; the odd cents attached to her average fee are attributable to the minor levies included in the total receipts from which this figure was derived, as explained in the above footnote.

Each state figure was obtained by dividing the total 1930 motor vehicle license fee collections by the total number of motor vehicles registered in the state during that year. The averages obtained by this method, it is frankly admitted, may not be entirely accurate. It is conceivable that, although states A and B have identical fee schedules, state A would show an

TABLE [B]‡

Method by Which Registration Fees Are Computed in Different States
(January 1, 1931)

State	Passenger Cars	Commercial Cars (Not Common Carriers)
Alabama	Horsepower	Tons capacity
Arizona	Flat rate	Flat rate and pounds unladen weight and kind of tires
Arkansas	Horsepower and pounds gross weight	Tons capacity and kind of tires
California	Flat rate	Flat rate and pounds unladen weight and kind of tires
Colorado	Cost price	Tons capacity
Connecticut	Cubic inch displacement	Tons capacity and kind of tires
Delaware	Pounds gross weight	Pounds gross weight
Florida	Pounds gross weight	Pounds net weight and kind of tires
Georgia	Pounds gross weight	Tons capacity
Idaho	Pounds net weight and number of times registered	Chassis weight capacity and kind of tires
Illinois	Horsepower	Pounds gross weight
Indiana	Horsepower and pounds net weight	Tons capacity
Iowa	Value and pounds net weight	Tons capacity and kind of tires
Kansas	Flat rate and pounds gross weight	Tons capacity and kind of tires
Kentucky	Horsepower and pounds net weight	Pounds capacity
Louisiana	Horsepower	Horsepower and pounds capacity and kind of tires
Maine	Horsepower and pounds net weight	Pounds capacity and kind of tires
Maryland	Horsepower	Pounds capacity and kind of tires (horsepower if on pneumatic tires)
Massachusetts	Horsepower	Pounds gross weight
Michigan	Pounds net weight	Pounds unladen weight
Minnesota	Value	Value and tons capacity
Mississippi	Horsepower and pounds gross weight	Tons capacity and kind of tires
Missouri	Horsepower	Tons capacity

Montana	Net weight	Tons capacity and kind of tires
Nebraska	Pounds net weight	Pounds capacity
Nevada	Pounds gross weight	Pounds gross weight
New Hampshire	Pounds gross weight	Pounds gross weight and kind of tires
New Jersey	Horsepower	Pounds gross weight
New Mexico	Pounds net weight	Chassis weight and kind of tires
New York	Pounds net weight	Pounds net weight
North Carolina	Horsepower	Tons capacity and kind of tires
North Dakota	Factory price, net weight, horsepower and times registered	Factory price, net weight, horsepower, and tons capacity
Ohio	Horsepower	Pounds unladen weight
Oklahoma	Manufacturers' list price	Pounds capacity and times registered
Oregon	Pounds net weight	Net weight and kind of tires
Pennsylvania	Horsepower	Pounds chassis weight and kind of tires
Rhode Island	Pounds gross weight	Pounds gross weight and kind of tires
South Carolina	Pounds net weight	Tons capacity and kind of tires
South Dakota	Pounds net weight	Tons capacity
Tennessee	Horsepower	Horsepower and tons capacity
Texas	Pounds net weight	Pounds gross weight, kind of tires and number of wheels
Utah	Horsepower	Tons capacity and kind of tires
Vermont	Pounds net weight	Pounds gross weight
Virginia	Pounds net weight	Tons capacity
Washington	Pounds net weight	Pounds net weight and pounds capacity
West Virginia	Flat rate, pounds net weight	Tons capacity and kind of tires
Wisconsin	Pounds net weight	Tons gross weight and number of wheels
Wyoming	Horsepower	Tons capacity and kind of tires
District of Columbia	Flat rate	Flat rate

‡ *Facts and Figures of the Automobile Industry*, 1931, p. 41.

appreciably larger average fee than state B, owing to the fact that state A had registered a large number of more costly, heavier, or more powerful cars. Adequate data are not available, however, to make possible a wholly precise calculation in this connection, and it is believed that the method employed herein gives rise to no more than minor inaccuracies.

Not only is there a wide variation in the average license fee, but there exists an equally wide variation among the states in the methods used for computing this fee. These differences are brought out in Table [B]. Some interesting questions and conjectures are likely to result from an examination of this table. Why use horsepower as a basis for levying a registration fee; why a flat rate; why pounds net weight; why cost price; why any particular combination of these factors? Whenever any such variable is chosen as a basis for computation, the resulting fee, obviously, is a variable as among different vehicles. Furthermore, the relative burdensomeness of fees as among different types, models, and makes of vehicle will vary within rather wide limits in accordance with the particular basis of calculation which chances to be used.

The reason for these differences in the bases of computation can best be explained by considering again the purpose of the registration fee. In those states imposing a flat rate the fee is intended to be primarily, if not wholly, a privilege tax of an amount sufficient to cover only the costs of regulation and administration. At present only Arizona, California, Washington, and the District of Columbia adhere to the flat rate basis.

All bases other than the flat rate reflect efforts to utilize the registration fee as a source of revenue — that is, to make it in part a genuine tax. In this event, the burden of the tax may be apportioned among the owners of vehicles in accordance either with the ability theory or the benefit theory of taxation. It is possible to identify certain bases of computation as leaning rather definitely toward one or the other of these principles. The greater the horsepower, the greater the cost price, the greater the cubic inch piston displacement of the motor vehicle, the more valuable it is and hence, in accordance with the ability principle, the more able is the owner to bear a higher tax. As these measures increase, therefore, the size of the fee increases, and thus the principle of ability to pay is injected into the registration fee.

Other frequently used bases are obviously intended to spread the burden among car owners in proportion to the benefits derived from the attendant governmental expenditures. Adherence to this principle results in levying registration fees that are based upon the vehicles' probable use of, or damage to, the highway. Pounds net weight and pounds gross weight are the indices that most clearly reveal this intent. It is highly significant that every state infuses the benefit principle into its method of computing the registration fee on trucks. The District of Columbia alone does not use weight or tons capacity in such computation. On the other hand, twenty states leave out the element of weight entirely in computing the fee on passenger cars.

Frequently, however, no serious effort is made to adhere rigidly to either of these two principles, and the license fee schedule comes to represent an uncertain compromise between the two. This condition is found in some of the states that, not being content to use any one basis of fee assessment, have combined two or more bases. Examples are the joint use of horsepower and pounds net weight; pounds net weight and number of times registered; and value and pounds net weight. The most complex fee base is that of North Dakota, in which are combined factory price, net weight, horsepower and times registered.

DISPOSITION OF RECEIPTS FROM REGISTRATION AND LICENSE FEES

IT is of interest to note the manner in which the funds obtained from registration and license fees are expended. Only a small part is needed and used to cover the immediate costs of collecting and administering such levies. $19,196,926,[12] or approximately 5.4 per cent of the total 1930 collections of $355,704,860 were used for this purpose. The first figure does not quite cover the entire cost of collection and administration, since six states (Arizona, Delaware, Illinois, Minnesota, Vermont, and Wyoming) meet this cost by an appropriation from the general revenue fund; nevertheless, the total cost of collection and administration is nominal as compared with the total receipts. If the levy were made in strict conformity with the theory of a license tax, however, the receipts would not materially exceed the total costs of collection and administration.

The largest part of these receipts goes toward constructing and maintaining the *state* highways, which make up approximately ten per cent of the total road mileage of the nation.

[12] Figure compiled from data sheets issued by the United States Bureau of Public Roads.

These state roads carry from sixty per cent to eighty per cent of the total vehicle traffic [13] and hence are of primary importance to the motor vehicle owner. This system claimed $222,-146,682, or 62.5 per cent of the 1930 receipts.[14]

The local road or secondary road system, which contains about ninety per cent of the total mileage but which is relatively unimportant from the point of view of motor vehicle traffic, received $68,577,899, or 19.3 per cent of the total registration fees.[15] The sum of $36,309,682, constituting 10.2 per cent of all receipts, was used to pay the principal and interest on state and county road bonds.[16] These bonds were, in most cases, issued to hasten the construction of permanent highways, but with the thought that anticipated revenue from taxes on the motor vehicle would meet the necessary payments as they came due.

The remainder of the receipts (2.6 per cent) was used for miscellaneous minor purposes, of which the following are typical : used for city streets ; placed in the general revenue fund ; set aside for traffic control and highway policing ; placed in an auto theft fund.

Thus it is seen that a variety of uses are made of the receipts from registration fees, but that the greater part, or nearly two-thirds of the total, is quite appropriately devoted to state highway purposes.

CRITIQUE OF THE REGISTRATION AND LICENSE FEE

THE registration fee is the oldest of the special motor vehicle taxes and for many years it was the sole one. It is even now surpassed in importance only by the tax on gasoline. It still remains a fundamental part of the taxation program for motor vehicles in most of the states. Nevertheless, its rôle in a balanced taxation program is by no means a settled point — apparently, rather, it is being called more generally into question ; hence there is a point in an analysis of its value in such a tax program.

The legal basis of the registration fee and its variations among the states as to rates and basis of computation have been indicated. It has been noted, further, that the fee may be imposed in accordance with three separate fiscal principles, namely : (1) a privilege tax to cover administrative costs, (2) a

---

[13] This estimate for the entire highway system of the U. S. is made on the basis of information obtained from traffic surveys in the states of Connecticut, Pennsylvania, Ohio, New Hampshire, and Maine.
[14] United States Bureau of Public Roads, period reports of 1930.
[15] *Ibid.*
[16] *Ibid.*

tax for revenue based upon the owner's ability to pay, and (3) a tax for revenue based upon the use made of or damage done to the highway.

The legal status of the license fee is firmly established if its primary purpose is to regulate the person or article assessed. The state's right to levy such a fee is derived from its police power. Presumably, it would be just large enough to cover adequately the costs incident to its administration. Nevertheless, only three states now limit the motor vehicle fee to such an amount. It is true that the courts have upheld the right of the state to increase the size of the fee beyond the point at which it begins to include an element of revenue, but such judicial permission does not settle the question of its proper place in a model motor vehicle taxation program.

A fixed, static fee, such as a license fee must be, cannot measure with any degree of accuracy the use made of the highway, yet this is what some states have attempted to make it do. The fee schedule may be so constructed as to take account of *potential* damage to the highway (by a sliding scale based upon vehicle weight, type of tires, etc.) but *actual* damage attributable to any vehicle will always vary directly with miles traversed. Thus, by virtue of its inherent nature, the license fee cannot be equated, even approximately, with the cost of the highway benefits conferred upon the car owner. Either a gasoline tax or a wheel tax measures the use of the highway with greater accuracy and justice than a flat fee can do. Further, the fee is equally weak if used to measure ability to pay, although less markedly so if it is used in lieu of a personal property tax. In the latter case, however, the tax should be levied on the basis of property value, and not on horsepower cylinder displacement. It would appear, then, that the proper function of a license fee would be to cover the costs of regulation without attempting to raise additional revenue. If this point of view is sound, Arizona, California, Washington, and the District of Columbia seem to be leading the way at present. Those states which combine the registration fee with a personal property tax have adopted much the same position, although in a somewhat less clear-cut manner. It is probable that the future will witness further readjustments in this direction.

3. SPECIAL ASSESSMENTS

A THOROUGH study of special assessment problems in twenty-one cities in New York has been made by A. R. Burnstan.

In spite of the geographical limitations of this study, its treatment of basic economic considerations of special assessments is such as to give it the value of a general work on the subject. Selections from this study are reproduced in the following section.*

Definition of Special Assessments

A special assessment is a levy to defray the cost of a particular public improvement and is theoretically in proportion to, but never in excess of the resulting benefit accruing to the property against which it is levied.[1] The use of the term assessment in this sense is sometimes confusing, because in taxation an assessment is usually valuation used as a basis for the apportionment of a general tax, whereas a *special* assessment is a special levy against definitely-benefited property. It involves a special valuation only in its measure of the increment attaching to property as a result of some improvement.

Variations From True Form

Many variations which have become established in benefit levies are usually included under special assessments, whether they involve a public improvement or not. For this reason it will be necessary in an analysis of these levies to distinguish between the classes of governmental operation financed on a benefit basis. Some of these variations have been short-lived while others have become an accepted part of the governmental plan, as their use has increased.

Importance in Public Finance

The use of special assessments has, in recent years, constantly developed and increased in the field of American public finance. Such levies have been used at intermittent periods in England and continental Europe, but they have never assumed an importance comparable to their position in the United States. This is because special assessment financing is particularly adaptable to new and rapidly-developing communities. Even within this country the extent of their use in newly-settled districts is far greater than it is in the older well-established localities. This is because many communities use special assessments for original improvements only, and do not resort to them in cases involving reconstruction or repairs. It may be

---

* Adapted from A. R. Burnstan, "Special Assessment Procedure," *Special Report of the New York State Tax Commission*, (Albany, 1929), Chaps. I, II, X.

[1] Special assessment is the usual term used to describe this type of levy, but certain New York cities use the expression, "Local Assessment for Public Improvements."

that special assessments are only a transitory phase in the revenue system and as the original construction of a city's improvements reaches completion they will disappear.[2] In struggling new communities the expenses incidental to governmental development are legion and there is a constant demand for the provision of sufficient funds to finance the many improvements of a public nature which are simultaneously forcing themselves upon the governing body. It is obviously impossible to install immediately uniform improvements throughout the city, and it is difficult to decide which projects shall have the preference, because the property adjacent to the improvement will receive a greater advantage than that situated at a distance.

Development of Special Assessment Financing

In the early American colonial cities these problems were more acute than they are in the cities of the present day, because no system had been developed whereby governmental levies according to benefit could be made. Where specific groups of citizens desired a particular public improvement for which the general funds were inadequate, these citizens often did the work at their own expense. When the apportionment of such expense was made, it was only just for the property receiving benefit, to assume a proportional share of the costs. All this was strictly private, and was handled entirely by the property owners concerned.

As the cities grew, public improvements assumed a greater degree of importance, and their control came under the local government. The question of inadequate funds was still present and the idea of assessing according to benefit was absorbed along with the responsibility for construction. As the cities kept pace with the nation's advance the use of special assessments to finance public improvements constantly increased until today under the local revenue collected in the cities of New York state the amount received from special assessments stands second only to that contributed by the general property tax.[3]

Scope of This Study

The problems and questions presented are multiplied when the use of a medium such as the one under consideration be-

[2] The construction of new pavement in New York cities is in some instances approaching completion. Lackawanna, N. Y., has made provision for the paving of all its streets before 1930. This situation would be altered of course by the annexation of any incompletely developed territory.

[3] Comptroller of the State of New York. Bureau of Municipal Accounts. *Annual Reports.*

comes so extensive. To secure an adaptability to local conditions and the peculiar characteristics of each separate case, a flexibility of action is necessary that is bound to produce a variety of practice. While a repetition of exact procedure in different cases is frequently impossible, failure to adhere to certain definite standards of practice has produced most of the modern conflict. Where the same rules are not applied to successive cases the individual property owner is inclined to assume that discrimination is involved. The attempt of many cities to solve the problem locally by constantly altering their methods as each new difficulty arose has only resulted in confusion. The failure to adhere to fixed standards invites political interference and pressure, with a resultant inequitable procedure. The efforts of organizations interested in municipal problems to assist cities in coming to an acceptable solution, have not proved entirely satisfactory because their research has usually been unofficial and designed to solve the problems of a particular city.[4] A few of the states have studied the situation and attempted to specify certain rules and requirements under which their cities should operate. While no definite state law has proven entirely adequate, such legislation has marked the greatest step forward toward an acceptable workable plan.[5] It is the purpose of this study to analyze the situation as it now exists, especially in the twenty-one largest cities of the state of New York, and to make such observations and recommendations as the investigation has suggested. Twenty-one cities were selected for purposes of convenience and upon the assumption that all the important problems of a general nature would present themselves somewhere within this group. Unusual cases were not included, because in such instances set rules could not apply, and the conclusions finally reached should deal with phases of pro-

---

[4] Some of the outstanding studies of this type are :
   1. The Detroit Bureau of Governmental Research. An analysis of the Detroit Special Assessment Sinking Fund. 1925.
   2. Second Analysis. 1927.
   3. The Kansas City Public Service Institute. Special Assessment Problems. 1927.
   4. Cincinnati Bureau of Government Research. Proposed Permanent Improvement Procedure for Highway and Sewer Improvement. 1929.
   5. Rochester Bureau of Municipal Research. The Assessment of Local Improvements. 1929.

[5] The cities of New Jersey report only slight difficulties in their special assessment procedure under the "Act Concerning Municipalities" Chapter 152, Laws of New Jersey, 1917. This act was devised as a model for all New Jersey municipalities to use in the administration of special assessments.

cedure where uniformity would produce a desirable simplicity in operation.*

MODERN PROBLEMS

Local Tendencies Toward Revision of Procedure

THERE are certain problems constantly recurring in the special assessment procedure of the various cities. Most of these could be eliminated if the cities concerned would make some slight changes in their charter provisions and local laws, and then adhere strictly to a selected method of procedure. The tendency of cities, however, is to postpone adoption of these changes until some court action vacates a large special assessment and the city is left to meet the bill from general funds. In cases of this type the charter alteration may take care of only the particular case that necessitated the change. This possibility and many other conditions suggest the need for study of the following questions, the analysis of which might assist in the formulation of some equitable plan of relief.

Present Difficulties Requiring Solution

Has the state power to pass a law that will force its cities to comply with certain standards of operation? Would such a law bring great hardship on some cities, if they were obliged to adopt it immediately and is there an alternative in the passage of a permissive act? Could the legislature pass a model act giving all cities the privilege of adoption, when local conditions warranted?

Is it the right of the property owners to initiate public improvements or does this properly fall within the scope of the activities of the city engineering staff? If the governmental unit initiates, should any provisions for veto be given to the taxpayer?

What are the dangers incidental to the failure to give absolute authority to a majority of the affected property owners?

Would the provision for adequate notice and proper hearing eliminate constitutional rights under the "due process clause," as the chief reasons advanced by the courts for supporting appeals against special assessments?

Are there any specific rules that can be applied in the selection of a basic measure of benefit? Are there not certain factors which should always be considered in the establishment

* Eds. note: Only the summary and recommendations of Dr. Burnstan's study are reproduced here.

of a measure in order to arrive at a proper apportionment? Or do different improvements necessitate the employment of divers bases?

In a city with an active planning commission that is following a definite master plan, how much authority should be given to this commission in the initiation of local improvements?

If a special assessment, because of its size, becomes confiscatory are there plans of limitation that would make such an unfair levy impossible?

Will an advance coördinated economic and engineering study increase the opportunities for an acceptable improvement program?

What are the contributing problems that immediately arise concerning the propriety of financing repairs and reconstruction by special assessments, when property owners are permitted to designate the type and quality of improvement materials?

What is the most advantageous way to pay contractors for construction work and how shall a city carry on its special assessment financing?

Will the delinquencies and the foreclosure of special assessment liens be greatly reduced if a proper collection procedure is enforced?

The Development of Modern Practices

As each city has struggled individually to correct its special assessment deficiencies the practices have varied in proportion to the number of cities concerned. The tendency to correct only the immediate cause of a particular obstruction has resulted in the introduction of a large number of minor changes in charter provisions. This failure to go to the source of the difficulty and correct the general condition of inadequacy, has naturally produced many freak clauses, which, while undoubtedly applicable to the particular case at hand at the time of adoption, are in some instances most inequitable in general application. As a result of this situation succeeding city officials have often assumed discretionary powers in order to permit an unobstructed continuance in the city's improvement program. This has in turn produced another startling result. It has brought about the development, and sometimes the general acceptance, of practices that make no effort to comply with the special assessment requirements of the local law or charter. This fact, when called to their attention, caused general surprise among New York state's city officials who had been moving along smoothly for many years and had assumed that their methods of notice, hearing, and procedure in general were those set down in their respective charters. Since a large percentage of the cost of local improvements in most of these cities was met from general funds property owners were not inclined to question the propriety of the procedure, but in cities where a larger share of the expense has been assessed locally against property deemed to have been benefited, protests have been more numerous. Many property owners who feel that they have been charged an unfair amount, instead of trying to evade payment because the benefit is not commensurate with the cost, resort to a more definite course and demonstrate that the charter provisions governing procedure have not been followed. While the measure of benefit is often debatable there can be no doubt concerning definite charter requirements for notification or for a hearing. It is conditions such as this that have given rise to periodic changes and amendments.

Legislative Attitude toward the Control of City Government

It has, in the past, been the policy of the New York state legislative bodies not to interfere in those municipal activities which are exclusively of local concern. Although under the constitutional provisions prior to 1923, all local laws came before the legislature, their passage was rarely obstructed if they had local endorsement. Under a state constitutional amendment of 1923, many of the legislature's powers were transferred to the local governing bodies, and the state was specifically prohibited from passing any laws pertaining to cities which, in terms or in effect, might be construed as either special or local in character.[6] Because of this policy of non-interference and because of the belief that each city would necessarily work out its own plan of operation in a way that would best fit its particular needs, the legislature has never made any attempt to correct the errors found in special assessment procedure. Since benefit levies have assumed a place of constantly increasing importance in municipal finance it has become evident that a study of the errors and unfortunate experiences of the various cities might prove the need of some state action. It would be possible for the legislature to handle this matter without violating either the spirit or the letter of the state constitution, since the amendment of 1923 provides for the enactment of general city laws that confer upon cities

---

[6] Constitution of the State of New York, Art. 12, Sec. 2, as adopted November 6, 1923. "The legislature shall not pass any law relating to the property, affairs or government of cities, which shall be special or local either in its terms or its effect, but shall act in relation to the property, affairs or government of any city only by general laws which shall in terms and in effect apply alike to all cities . . ."

additional powers of local legislation and administration.[7]
Under this provision it would be possible for the legislature to
pass a model act with a recommendation for its adoption by the
various cities. The legislature, in taking such action would
give evidence not of a spirit of interference, but of a genuine
desire to provide the cities with assistance in solving their individual special assessment problems. A decision as to which
methods of procedure and practice operate with a minimum of
friction between the property owner and the governmental unit
might be reached through an analytical study of the varying
conditions in the cities of the state, especially of those conditions which are more or less common to all cities. A model act,
based on such a comparative study would give much aid toward
insuring the smooth operation of the local fiscal systems. Cities
that adopted this act would eliminate certain difficulties of
procedure encountered in other cities, and would also forestall
those contingencies which usually arise.

Tax Commission's Interest in Assisting the Municipalities

The desirability of some action of this character was felt by
the New York State Tax Commission, which is constantly in
contact with those city officers who are entrusted with the management of municipal fiscal affairs. Through the reports of
these officers and an analysis of the local tax situation it was
evident that special assessment constituted one of the most
difficult phases of municipal finance to administer. It was
clear also that the reasons for this were threefold in character.
First : the local assessment for a public improvement touched
the sensitive pocket nerve of the individual where he felt it
most ; second : the improvement itself was constantly before
his eyes as a reminder that he was a party to its financing.
While general taxes were accepted as a part of the regular
costs of property ownership and maintenance, a special assessment was regarded as an extra charge that might in some way
be evaded. Since these difficulties were of a psychological
nature it was decided that any attempt to alleviate them must
come indirectly, which meant that some method of altering
the property holder's point of view toward this type of compulsory payments must be discovered.

The third irregularity, lack of proper method, promised a
greater possibility of relief. An opportunity was presented
here to effect changes that would standardize procedure to

[7] Constitution of the State of New York, Art. 12, Sec. 5, as adopted November 6, 1923. "The legislature may by general laws confer on cities such further
powers of local legislation and administration as it may, from time to time, deem
expedient."

such an extent as to assure equal treatment to all assessed property. These changes would, at the same time, reduce the operating costs of the cities. This reduction of costs, with its resultant lowering of assessments, would help to solve the first objection by making the property owner's load lighter, and also by giving him a definite expectancy of improvement costs. Following the commission's decision that, in the interest of proper governmental coöperation, such an analysis should be made, the data included in this study was collected and is presented here together with the conclusions reached and recommendations considered desirable.

Universal Character of Special Assessment Problems and Difficulties

The first discovery in the course of the investigation was that special assessment problems were to be found in the cities throughout the United States and were not confined to any particular locality. In addition to the local studies by research organizations referred to in the introduction, there have been some comparative studies by city officials entrusted with special assessment operations in an effort to ease a particular local situation. A few states, which had felt the necessity of general coöperation had passed state laws to provide uniform procedure. All these studies have assisted in the evolution of a just and workable plan. Where state laws have been passed, their operation has presented an opportunity to observe what problems may be dealt with in a general way and what phases are hampered rather than aided by a denial of individual treatment. Still other studies, which have been merely of a statistical nature with no direct resultant action, have served to reveal the seriousness of the situation and have prompted further investigation from which official activity has ultimately ensued.

Observation of the trials and errors of the past gives the present investigator an opportunity to begin at an advanced stage of the problem. Much of the uncertainty has been eliminated through acquisition of the knowledge of the practices which in other states, have proved successful or otherwise under given conditions.

Lack of General Public Interest in Special Assessment Reform

It is surprising that so little public interest has been shown in a reform that would so directly affect the interests of property owners. Special assessments are constantly before the public in any city that is carrying on an improvement program.

Because of the practice of cities closely to ally special assessments and general taxation it is probable that citizens generally regard the former as an undesirable part of the whole system. Because of their failure to question the propriety of taxes they have deprived themselves of possible relief through their failure to establish the impropriety of certain special assessments. This in some cases may apply to the entire assessment while in others it may be merely a question of apportionment. The methods and practices in general property taxation are generally accepted by the lay mind, with the result that a possible saving in special assessments through new methods and practices has been overlooked. With the appearance of many recent articles on the subject, however, the citizen is gradually beginning to differentiate among the basic factors involved, and not only to see the special assessment in its distinctive light but also to recognize some of the possibilities for relief.

In June, 1929, the Committee on Taxation and Assessment of the New York State Association of City and Village Engineers published a pamphlet on the division of expense for public improvements between the city and the benefited property. This report, because of the diversification revealed, was of a rather startling nature, and the circulation of this type of information is serving to make the public conscious of the fact that many phases of special assessment procedure are experimental. This knowledge is responsible for an increasing clamor for a general equitable system.

Expansion of the Use of Special Assessment Financing

With the growing use of special assessments for original construction came their application to allied fields — repairing and reconstruction for example. Although opinion among experts in this field seems to vary, concerning this question, it is the general rule in New York State cities that after property has once been assessed for the construction of an improvement, it is the duty of the city to keep such improvement in order and repair, *i.e.,* subsequent to its initial completion and acceptance. It is assumed that acceptance carries with it an implied obligation on the part of the city. Those who disagree with this point of view contend that repairing such as pavement requires from time to time, involves just as distinct and traceable benefit as did the original construction.[8] In support of the latter

8 Cornick, P. H., Essential Features of a Model Plan for Special Assessments in Proceedings of the Nineteenth Annual Meeting of the Conference of Mayors and other Municipal Officials of the State of New York, 1928, p. 166.

contention it is only necessary to consider the loss in selling value to a piece of property situated in a district where the roads are constantly out of repair.

The courts of the various states have likewise held conflicting views on this question. The Vrooman act of California was amended in 1915 to permit special assessments for reimprovements and the courts sustained such action. The test case involved certain parcels of land against which an assessment had been levied for the laying of sheet asphalt on an abutting street. Within two years, the same street had been torn up, widened and repaved and a second assessment levied. The assessment for the second construction was extended over a larger benefit district and abutting property was assessed for another share. This action was upheld by the court.[9]

At the other extreme on this question is Pennsylvania where the opinions in two court cases held that no paving assessment could be levied on streets previously improved, even though such improvements in one case (1805) involved "turnpiking" and in the other (1832) an application of crushed stone.[10]

Another purpose for which special assessments have been levied is in order to meet current operating expenses, such as street sprinkling or ornamental lighting. As the main thoroughfares of the cities have been paved, street sprinkling has gradually become less important; and the lighting question is now met in most New York cities by establishing a minimum standard for all streets. A district, whose property owners desire additional lighting, is assessed for the surplus.[11]

Special Assessments in the Enforcement of Public Health Measures

One of the chief uses for special assessments in the past has been to meet the costs of sewer construction. Assessment for

[9] Cornick, P. H., Proceedings in Annual Meeting of the Governmental Research Association, 1927, p. 105.

[10] Report to the Reading, Pennsylvania, Chamber of Commerce, by the New York Bureau of Municipal Research, April, 1914, p. 255.

"There are various court decisions which substantiate this contention — *City of Harrisburg versus Segelbaum*, 151 Pa. 172 and *Boyer versus the City of Reading*, 151 Pa. 185 are typical cases in which the city has been restricted from assessing the cost of permanent pavement on account of the original construction of a macadam road.

"It is interesting to find that the overturning of the assessment rights of the city in the Harrisburg case was based largely on a so-called macadamizing of Market Street in 1832 and 1848; and that the decision against the city of Reading in the other case was based largely on the turnpiking of Fifth Street in 1805."

[11] This plan has the endorsement of the New York State Conference of Mayors and is now in general operation throughout the state.

this purpose has been resorted to with increasing frequency notwithstanding the growing tendency to regard sewers as necessary public health provisions, rather than as optional improvements of merely local benefit. Many situations arise where a poor city district cannot afford the cost of a sewer, even though the entire city may suffer if such a sewer is not constructed. If the remainder of the city has been assessed locally for its sewers, the transfer of the cost of the sewer for the poor district to the city at large will of course bring a double burden to some property. Some communities have decided that a flat rate is justified, since as a health measure the benefit to all is equal. The assessment then becomes merely a convenient way to raise funds which might more logically be raised by taxes because any levy involving a general benefit should more properly be on a faculty basis. On such a basis the problem of levying against poor districts would not arise, because the city would be justified in building all its sewers as a general health protective measure from general tax funds.

Sources of Objections to Levies

Most of the higher class communities do not object to special assessments for local improvements, even though the amount of traceable benefit is less than the expenditure involved. Such assessments may merely amount to a transfer in value with an attendant increase of convenience. In a poor community, on the contrary, the same activities may present a delicate economic problem, for even though the same benefits may result, if the payment for them is so great a financial strain that it cannot be met, a resulting loss of property may entirely wipe out the benefit. Even in cases where the payments might possibly be met with the sacrifices involved might so far outweigh the direct benefits resulting from the improvement, that the net result would be a loss instead of a gain. Under circumstances of this character it becomes difficult indeed to justify such special assessments, even though presumably levied on a basis of benefit.

To those cities which have reached their limit in the conversion of open fields into building lots,[12] the question of local improvements in newly developed territory is of no concern unless additional land is to be added to that already within the

[12] Mount Vernon, New York, covers only four and one-half square miles and is fully developed for building. There is no available land remaining for subdivision.

city or a combination made with some adjacent town.[13]   In
some cities there is still much undeveloped land available for
building lots whenever the demand arises.   Such land, when
subdivided, may present many problems to the city if it is
accepted before the usual improvements are installed.

Additional Difficulties Found Only in Newly Developing Cities

To attempt to apply to new territory the same method of
financing that has been used in old established districts, may
lead to many difficulties.   It is necessary first to determine
whether the economic status of the probable new owners will
permit them to meet the costs of contemplated public improvements.   After a subdivision of lots has been made in an industrial district the levy of a special assessment might drive
the new owners from their homes, and the city, not having
made adequate provision in advance, might find itself with
an expensive improvement program to be financed from general funds.   In cities where this contingency arises there must
be devised some plan of regulation that will force the subdivider
to include such charges in his costs, because failure to provide
for such action might disarrange an otherwise smoothly-working
improvement program.

Possible Solutions

Three possible solutions are suggested by a study of the
problems outlined above.

(a).   If it is decided that the individual injury involved is
great enough to warrant some protective measure, recommendations should be made that the legislature pass a restrictive act
under article 12, section 4 of the constitution.

(b).   If it is found that the problems presented could be
solved by a revision of the present procedure, the recommendations should cover a permissive act involving a model local law
with a suggestion that all cities avail themselves of this law as
soon as conditions permit.   This action is possible under article
12, section 5 of the constitution.

(c).   If it is found that the problems in the various cities are
gradually being eliminated by local legislation, recommendations should be made that no state action be taken and each

13 Syracuse, New York, met difficulty with its flat rate sewer payment system
when the town of Solvay was annexed.   The rate had been established on the
basis of past experience in the city of Syracuse, but because of different conditions in Solvay, it was found difficult to apply.

city be left to work out its own local situation, as prevailing conditions seem to dictate.

General Conclusion

THE first and general conclusion is that the special assessment systems in the twenty-one largest New York cities do not operate equitably and should be subjected to change. They are inconsistent in practice, often produce glaring cases of discrimination, and are sometimes used to finance projects that involve current activities of a general character when theoretically they can be properly applied only to public improvements involving a traceable increment to specific property. When special assessments are levied on a fixed rate basis to provide some general protective improvement they are being improperly used. Such activities should be financed with funds raised on a faculty basis. In some cases where such assessments are levied the benefit does accrue to the property but the economic condition of the occupants is such that it prevents the realization of these benefits. There has been no organized effort on the part of the cities themselves to remedy this situation probably because of the lack of information on the subject rather than because of an absence of volition. If, therefore, any relief is to be obtained it is to be looked for through some action, either coöperative or direct, on the part of the state government.

Privilege of Initiation

The initiation of all projects should properly fall to the officials in charge of the city's construction and improvement work. If a group of citizens desire some particular improvement they should be given an opportunity to express their opinion through a petition, and where such a petition embodies the signature of fifty per cent of the affected property holders, the governing body should be *required* to present the proposal for regular consideration. In no case, however, should a property owner's petition be absolutely binding, regardless of the percentage of signers. There are two reasons for this: first, it might cause a deflection from a definitely-ordered program, and second, it would permit a group of property owners to obtain an undue share of neighborhood improvements. These reasons apply only where a portion of the improvement cost is paid from general city funds. In the first instance the forced application of general funds to an unlooked for improvement would cause their withdrawal from some other project; in the latter case a small group would benefit at the expense of the entire city.

Content and Means of Notification

A proper statute covering the special assessment levies must include a provision for adequate notice, and it is desirable that adequate notice in this connection be specifically defined. There are three types of notice in common use today: (1) publication, in a local newspaper; (2) posting, at some spot adjacent to the proposed improvement; and (3) personal notification, usually through the mails. Although no one of these is adequate, the best method is that of mailing to the last known address of the affected property owner. In a small percentage of cases these notices will not establish contact but publication in a local newspaper may remedy this deficiency. Posting is the least effective as it notifies only those owners who happen to have direct contact with the neighborhood wherein their property lies. A notice, while it should contain a complete description of the improvement and define all boundaries should be concise in form and readily understandable. A notice stated in highly technical terms may be thoroughly descriptive to an engineer, and still meaningless to the average property owner. A simple statement of the contemplated improvement with a complete showing of the properties to be affected, may be termed an adequate form of notice. This announcement should be mailed to the last known address of each interested property owner, and supplemented with newspaper publication and posting. If such a notification is made compulsory before any improvement can be constructed, it will fill all reasonable requirements and, from an examination of past cases, it is even safe to assume that the courts would consider this as sufficient, even where contact had failed.

Necessity for Adequate Hearing

The notice is merely the instrument whereby a property owner is informed of a governmental activity that will affect him or his property. It gives him an opportunity to prepare a protest if he feels that this activity is not justified, but the character of the hearing wherein he is permitted to voice his protest is even more important. The first hearing concerns the advisability of the entire project. At this hearing there should be present all maps, estimates of cost and other similar data, that might help to clarify to the property owner every phase of the contemplated improvement. It is also essential

that the city officers, entrusted with the preparation of such
data, should be present to explain and describe how their conclusions were reached, because in many cases objections have
been withdrawn when obstructing property holders have become fully acquainted with the existing facts. If any alterations in the plans are proposed or a question of propriety should
arise there should be a subsequent hearing for the consideration of such changes. When the tentative spread of assessment
has been made another hearing should be held to permit the
affected taxpayers to view and compare the various assessments,
at which time the assessor should explain his method of arriving at the different amounts, where a benefit variable is involved. In cases where the original assessment remained
unchanged this hearing would suffice. If any alterations were
made, the entire roll should be presented in its revised form
at a later hearing. In addition to these regular hearings an
interested property holder should be given the right to have
a review of the assessment, any time before the roll is certified
for collection.

The city would benefit if a system of hearings such as that
outlined above were adhered to because the well-informed
property owner is less likely to raise objections to a proposed
improvement, and the city would therefore save the costs incidental to delay.

The Selection of a Proper Measure of Benefit

The selection of a proper base to use as a measure of benefit
is one of the most difficult and one of the most important steps
in special assessment procedure. There are several measures
now employed, such as "foot-frontage," area, proximity, assessed
value, etc., but there is almost no instance where the definite
amount of benefit can be determined by one of these. Usually
a combination of circumstances controls the situation and it is
necessary to state in a special assessment act or statute some
compulsory considerations in the determination of benefit;
otherwise the taxpayer has no guarantee that a just and unbiased policy will be pursued. The best method would be to
specify several benefit measures that *must* be considered when
the division of the total assessment takes place, then, if one of
these does not apply in a particular case, it can be eliminated.
Such a procedure would force the administrating officer or
board to apply counterbalancing measures. For example, the
popular "front-foot" rule would undoubtedly cause many inequalities if applied alone but if area, value, etc., are applied

as modifying factors, the result will be more accurate and more just.

The determination of benefit is difficult because the same indices of benefit never apply equally to two projects; even improvements of the same character do not produce the same results. The benefit to a business district from a given type of construction can rarely be compared to that resulting in a residential district. Each change of location brings changes in value, and the effect of an improvement will therefore vary in degree. In fact, although the determination of benefit is so complex that a careful consideration of the contributing factors is the only means of producing proper results, the system of measuring benefit must nevertheless be kept flexible, and must permit certain discretionary powers to come into play.

A Planning Commission and a Master City Plan

One of the best guarantees that a city can have of a just and orderly improvement program, is a master city plan. This provision has no place in a special assessment law but is rather an outside contributing factor. A city planning commission with a definite plan is especially helpful in the development of improvements that are to be built in successive stages. For example, in cases of flood control, sewers or any unusual types of work, the influence of a city plan is not felt so greatly as it is in street improvements, where a plan that is to be closely followed can be formulated far in advance. This definite knowledge of the city's attitude toward certain streets or districts permits the owner of property to prepare in advance for such improvements as will occur. Moreover, their cost may be discounted, thus preventing sudden and violent fluctuations in the real estate market. An added advantage of the city plan is the fact that it is sometimes possible to justify, as a part of a whole, an improvement that would not stand individually.

The Effect of Zoning

Zoning comes more properly under the city plan and its relation to the city's special assessments should not come within the improvement laws. While it links up with the local improvements just as definitely as the general plan does, the establishment of an interrelation between the three produces a more workable situation. A zoning ordinance affects the choice of types of material to be used in various betterments. For example: the wear incidental to heavy trucking, in a business or wholesale district, would require a type of pavement construction that would be wasteful in a residential section; the sewage disposal system necessary to a large, tall apartment district would require construction and material in excess of that demanded by a zone of single family dwellings. This determination of type of composition, and the relationship of the improvement to the zones and the general city plan, may all be brought to light in a preliminary survey. Where the selection of the magnitude and class of improvement does not conform to the height area and use zones two conditions result: either the benefit accruing to the adjacent property is not commensurate with the costs of building or the amplitude of the improvement is not adequate to serve the community.

A Preliminary Survey

A provision for an advance study, involving an economic and a physical survey and a coördination of the two, should be required before any improvement project is definitely ordered. Such a study if carefully made would bring to light all the small defects that ordinarily arise to delay the progress of an improvement. It would also answer the question as to the need of the community for the improvement, and would show whether the owners of the benefited property could bear their proportionate share. A topographical study would reveal any unusual cost that might be involved because of peculiar conditions of the terrain and would often halt an improvement where the cost would be out of proportion to the accruing benefit. Many cities have, in the past, become involved in construction of a costly nature that could have been avoided if proper consideration had been given before the improvement was ordered. While there is no way of insuring the proper use of this information after it has been gathered, if its accumulation is made compulsory it will at least assure the taxpayers of a complete advance knowledge of the situation. If they feel that the municipal officers in their procedure are disregarding the facts, they will have certain checks at their disposal. A compulsory survey of this nature should therefore be required in an acceptable improvement statute.

The Individual Project Method of Financing

Three plans of special assessment financing are now in general use. . . The first of these, which permitted the use of special assessment bonds that were not general obligations of the cities of issue, was shown to be too costly to be satisfactory, because the charges for marketing the securities sometimes becomes a major portion of the total improvement costs. This type of security was sometimes forced upon cities where guaranteed bonds would have accelerated an already fast approaching debt limit. The second type of financing referred to was the "revolving fund" whereby all improvements are paid for from a single fund. This system has many possible abuses attached to it. It permits irregularities to exist and accumulate without detection because the actual levy of the assessment is often postponed until long after the completion of the improvement. Moreover it is not self-supporting because the original funds raised at its inception must come either from an issue of bonds or from the general tax funds, and large amounts of cash may be purposely retained in order to place low return deposits with favored banks. The fourth objection is that it becomes a political tool permitting the suspension of all assessments in an election year and causing a corresponding excess the following year.

The third type of financing, and the one here recommended, is that type which forces every project to be handled separately. Under this system bonds are guaranteed by the city of issue but the source of their retirement is special assessments levied because of the particular project against which these bonds were issued. It does not seem proper that such bonds should be included in the regular debt limit of the city, since the funds for their retirement come from a specific source. In case of the default of these specific sources, and the percentage of such default is extremely small, the city merely acts as a guarantor. Another advantage is that under this latter type of financing the assessment is levied immediately upon the completion of the improvement, so that if there are any irregularities present they are instantly detectable.

General and Specific Limitations

If the guaranteed type of special assessment bond which does not come under the general debt limitation is used, it becomes necessary to fix some other check on the issue of these securities. A study of the amount required for the advancement of ordinary improvements will be necessary before a percentage limit can be ascertained. A definite limit will cause the administering officials to use greater care in the selection of improvements for immediate attention. An indiscriminate program might find them with no funds to carry on essential work, because of the fact that less urgent projects had been permitted to proceed.

Another type of limitation designed to protect the property owner from excessive levies is the limit placed on individual assessments. In the past many instances have arisen where the amount of the special assessments has actually exceeded the assessed valuation of the property. New York City has a provision that does not permit an assessment to exceed fifty per cent of the assessed valuation, at the time of the improvement, with other similar limits placed at varying percentages for a given period of years. Such limits are proper if they be applied in some form to prevent too rapid improvement development with resulting assessments of a confiscatory nature.

Designation of Type of Material

The designation of the type of material to be used in improvement construction should be the duty of the city's engineering staff. When a piece of work is officially introduced the plans and specifications should definitely name the class and type of construction material, especially when the improvement will be subjected to excessive wear. . . To allow the affected taxpayers to make this selection might terminate in an evasion of proper expense through the selection of inferior and cheaper material. Specifications of this kind are especially necessary in paving construction where the use of an improper surfacing material may require premature repairing and repaving. If such repairs are charged against general city funds, the group originally benefited is evading part of the cost at the expense of the entire city.

The other reasons for permitting the engineering staff to select the material are their particular qualification in this field of work and also the fact that the city employs these experts for just such service. Their intimate knowledge of conditions enables them to judge accurately, where the untrained property owner would be at a loss.

Difficulties Arising From a State Law

If the recommendations summarized above were included in a compulsory legislative act, the result might be detrimental to some cities, and individuals owning property liable to benefit levies in these cities, might also be exposed to inequitable treatment. Where the cities are concerned there might be instances of major improvements in a state of partial completion, and the introduction of a change of operation would produce a situation involving great additional cost. Likewise in the case of individuals who have paid for the first part of a major improvement, altering the method of procedure would produce a situation where one owner is likely to benefit at another's expense. A provision allowing the city reasonable time in which to comply with the law might overcome these objections. Another obstacle lies in the fact that there may be cities where conditions are so peculiarly local that a state law can never apply. New York City, with conditions that are not comparable with any other city of the state is the best example of this situation.

An Optional Act

A permissive act which the cities of the state may use as a model for their local laws, or adopt in full where local conditions permit, is a more desirable solution than some form of compulsion by the state. It is recommended that this law include all of the provisions suggested in this study which have been found to apply to the general special assessment situation of the state, and the people can bring pressure to bear upon their city officials to adopt those portions of the law that are applicable in their particular case. In this manner the state can give the cities the opportunity to benefit by a comparison of various methods, and still not violate its policy of non-intervention in local affairs.

The Collection of Delinquent Assessments

It is assumed that an equitable system of special assessment procedure would decrease materially the number of delinquent payments. There will undoubtedly always remain a certain portion of the levies that will not be paid within the specified time, but if these levies are well within the selling value of the property, the city need not lose. The special assessment lien is usually combined with the general property tax lien and collection of delinquencies is made as a unit. The improvement in delinquent collection methods, therefore, depends largely upon the devising of an efficient system for the sale of property to cover delinquent taxes. Such a measure, while very desirable, does not fall primarily under a special assessment law.

Criteria for Future Legislation

In conclusion there may be suggested certain criteria for the framing of legislation on special assessments, to be followed in the event of any state action. The necessity for state action occurs only in cases of unsatisfactory local situations which are not likely to improve, but if an individual city can formulate a law fitting its peculiar needs and complying with the general standards, state action may be obviated. Only those characteristics which are common to all special assessments should be dealt with by legislative action. If care is not used in framing the law so that it shall apply to general situations only, the result will be confusion and absence of uniformity. There can be a proper application of special assessment financing only where the benefit is equal to or in excess of the cost. The careful adherence to this principle in dealing with special assessments will cause the elimination of injustice and will conduce to an uninterrupted continuance of benefit levies.

QUESTIONS AND PROBLEMS FOR DISCUSSION

1. It is claimed that "there are many possibilities for additional fees." Cite examples of such possibilities.
2. For what purposes, if any, are fees more desirable than taxes?
3. Explain the prominence of fees in connection with the use of motor vehicles.
4. When an automobile fee is charged on the basis of the cost of the vehicle, is the charge thus made in accordance with the principle of ability to pay?
5. What arguments, if any, may be offered in favor of financing local improvements by special assessments?
6. Explain the fact that special assessments are of greater importance in the United States than in England or continental Europe.
7. What are the sources of objection to special assessment levies?
8. What are some of the administrative difficulties involved in the use of special assessments?

SUGGESTIONS FOR RESEARCH

1. A study of the use of special assessments in the financing of certain improvements in some local community.
2. Motor vehicle registration fees and the benefit theory of taxation.
3. Theoretical aspects of special assessments.
4. The place of gasoline taxes in the financing of street paving.

BIBLIOGRAPHICAL NOTE

General discussions of fees are contained in the following standard works: H. C. Adams, *The Science of Finance*, (New York, 1898), pp. 225-228; M. L. Hunter, *Outlines of Public Finance*, (New York, 1926), pp. 173-180; J. P. Jensen, *Problems of Public Finance*, (New York, 1924), pp. 153-158; and H. L. Lutz, *Public Finance*, (New York, 1929), pp. 235-238. Professor Bullock in his *Selected Readings in Public Finance*, (Boston, 1924), Chap. VII, has assembled a number of outstanding studies of fees in theory and in practice.

For appraisals which give special assessments high rank among the sources of public revenue, see C. C. Plehn, *Introduction to Public Finance*, (New York, 1926), p. 333; and the old and well-known study, V. Rosewater, *Special Assessments*, (New York, 1898). A more critical discussion which shows the defects and limitations of special assessments may be found in H. L. Lutz, *op. cit.*, pp. 241-253. Another able treatment of special assessments is P. H. Cornick's chapter on this subject in A. E. Buck, *Municipal Finance,* (New York, 1930). A useful work dealing with special assessments in a particular state is J. I. Tucker, *Special Assessments in California,* (Los Angeles, 1931). An article which throws light on the economics of special assessments is H. D. Simpson, "The Influence of Public Improvements on Land Values," *Annals of the American Academy of Political and Social Science,* (March, 1930), pp. 120 ff.

The most comprehensive study of special assessments with which the editors are familiar is Ernest H. Hahne, *Special Assessment theory and practice with special reference to Chicago.* This study is an unpublished doctoral dissertation, University of Chicago, 1930. This thesis contains an exceptionally valuable bibliography.

Professor E. R. A. Seligman gives a comprehensive discussion of the betterment tax in his *Essays in Taxation,* (New York, 1928), Chap. XV. R. E. Cushman's *Excess Condemnation,* (New York, 1917), affords a basis for comparing special assessments and excess condemnation as sources of non-tax revenue.

CHAPTER VIII

IDEALS IN TAXATION

1. THE PURPOSE OF TAXATION *

POLITICAL institutions are not ends in themselves. They are organs of social life and are justified in so far as they promote the general social utility. Taxation is a means to the existence of the state; and the justification of taxation is to be found in the end of the state. This end may be phrased as the general welfare or the maximum social utility. There has been some dispute among fiscal writers as to whether the function of taxation were primarily fiscal or social, that is, whether it was primarily to raise the necessary revenue or to change the distribution of wealth, redress inequalities in fortune, regulate industry and control consumption.† A writer in the *Finanz Archiv* has shown that there is really no conflict between these functions of taxation.¹ A tax has three ends, financial, economic, and social. All three are coördinate ends. The financial end of the tax is to maintain the state. The end of state activity is social welfare. The social end of the tax is to promote social welfare. The difference between the fiscal and the social view of taxation is based on the distinction between the immediate end and the ultimate end.

One important function of the state is to mitigate inequalities of wealth. Sociologists have pointed out that inequality seems to be a concomitant of civilization. Inequalities tend to increase with the enlargement of opportunity. Hobhouse has pointed out how slavery is a late development in social

---

* From H. W. Peck, *Taxation and Welfare,* (The Macmillan Co., New York, 1925), Chap. XI.

† Eds. note : Those who hold the view that taxation should not be used for ulterior or non-fiscal purposes argue that : (1) "To mix up with one very important object another different and perhaps incompatible one is to run the risk of failing in both" ; (2) "there is usually another way of accomplishing the desired result' ; and (3) "the use of the taxing power often leads to gross favoritism and special privileges for favored individuals or classes." See C. F. Bastable, *Public Finance,* (London, 1917), pp. 335, 336 ; and H. L. Lutz, *Public Finance,* (New York, 1929), pp. 311–313.

¹ Leon, J. N. "Der Begriff der Steuer," *Finanz Archiv,* Vol. XXXI, (1914), pp. 6–8.

history.[2]   Both military and economic success make for inequality.   Economic advance offers opportunity to men of
ability, and inheritance perpetuates the resulting inequalities
with cumulative effect.   Hence, in modern times, in spite of
civic and political equality, we have contrasts of wealth and
poverty which must be recognized as a social menace.   Hobhouse points out how the Gracchan legislation was an attempt
to save the economic independence of the mass of citizens of
Rome, and how its ill success wrote the doom of the Republic.
To a certain extent this growing inequality of modern times
ought to be checked.   It is a result, not a cause, of economic
progress.   The cause of progress is a greater efficiency of co-
operative efforts, of that organized production which makes
possible specialization and invention — the law of increasing
returns.   Some inequality is doubtless justifiable, as some men
are more efficient than others; but the division of wealth is
not between individuals as such but between one individual
plus society and another individual plus society.   In the words
of Hobhouse, "What can justly be said is not that A of his
own efforts creates so much wealth, and B so much, but that
operating on and with the existing social system the increment
of wealth due to A is greater or less by so much than that
due to B.   Now, if the account were between A and B alone,
that might conceivably determine the basis of remuneration;
but in the account between A or B and Society it fails because
the coöperating society is a major factor in both cases."
    To what extent society is the major factor is evident in the
case of the manager of large enterprises, the most prominent
of the individual forces in the industry.   "The organizer of
industry who thinks that he has 'made' himself and his business has found a whole social system ready to his hand in skilled
workers, machinery, a market, peace and order — a vast apparatus and a pervasive atmosphere, the joint creation of millions of men and scores of generations.   Take away the whole
social factor and we have not Robinson Crusoe, with his salvage from the wreck and his acquired knowledge, but the naked
savage living on roots, berries, and vermin."[3]
    These facts furnish a justification for state interference in
order to modify the distribution of wealth and redress inequalities of fortune.   Since inequalities in wealth are due, to a
considerable extent, to increased economic opportunities made
possible by an evolving material culture, by increased social
productivity, the modification of these inequalities that is nec-

[2] Hobhouse, L. T.   *The Elements of Social Justice,* Chapter V.
[3] *Ibid.,* pp. 162–163.

essary for social harmony should be brought about by the same force that has conditioned them, *i.e.,* the collectivity. . . . This end may be realized, to a large extent, through the medium of increased public expenditures. It may also be brought about, in part, through the machinery of taxation.

This use of taxation to mitigate social inequalities does not necessarily involve the acceptance of extreme theories, such as the compensatory theory or the socialistic theory. It merely justifies public action in modifying the distribution of wealth to the extent that this is required by the principle of the general welfare. The state in redistributing wealth to the end of social harmony applies the principle of distributive justice. The purpose of the state in fixing upon a rate of taxation, either proportional or progressive, is to attain justice. An approximate determination of the proper distribution of the tax burden is, therefore, dependent upon a definition of justice.

Justice, according to Aristotle, is a kind of equality. In order to understand justice we must know what equality means. Equality may be absolute or relative. It may be conceived in several different senses. One is equality of endowment or ability; another, equality of wants; another, equality of rights. Equality in the sense that all men are endowed by nature with equal gifts can be at once dismissed from discussion. On the other hand, the statement that men are equal in the sense that they have equal rights is an allegation that deserves examination. A right is the correlative of a duty. It is a claim on others or on society of such a sort that it would meet the approval of some impartial third person. It is a personal claim which society allows. Is equality of rights absolute or relative? Is equality an equality of absolute magnitude or of proportion? Hobhouse avers that in virtue of certain traits or qualities peculiar to human beings all men have certain equal fundamental rights, such as equality before the law, the right to protection of person and property. Also in the case of special relations to particular people equality means equal reciprocal obligations and equal opportunity to exercise choice in entering into such relations.

If we look away from certain fundamentals common to all human beings, we find that men differ. Equality then becomes a matter of proportion. Individual rights here are relative to merit or desert. Desert may be measured by effort or attainment; or, to use economic terms, by the principle of cost or the principle of utility. If we consider the whole system of rights and obligations, equality seems to be a relative term, but the proportion is less differential than it would be if it were based solely on some standard of individual merit.

The principle of equality, "to each one according to his needs," is also a proportionate rather than a strictly absolute principle. A hard worker would require more food than a light worker. A man of intellectual endowment would need an expensive education. An artist would require beautiful and possibly not inexpensive surroundings. However, there would be less differentiation between the wealth of individuals if equality were based on needs rather than on merit; for to a considerable extent, the needs of human beings are the same — the conditions of physical health and efficiency, and the opportunity for mental and spiritual development to the limits of their capacity. The principle of needs implies a provision for adequate maintenance of useful functions.

As a practical principle of equality Hobhouse suggests that we accept a compromise between need and desert, and in estimating desert consider both effort and attainment. In allotting rewards for services consideration should be taken (1) of the effort made, (2) of the value of the work done, and (3) of the needs of the performers. The relative emphasis on these different aspects of equality is to be determined by reference to the common good.

As to the remuneration of those of special merit or ability, Hobhouse approves of payment in excess of functional costs, in order to evoke the maximum productivity, but he holds that "the movements of remuneration should be diminishing increments tending to stability at some maximum point which can only be determined by experience of the limit of wealth commonly desirable in the interests of the possessor and the community." [4] This limitation of individual earnings is justified by considerations of the greater productivity of the social factor.

In brief, justice, according to one of the most learned and sane of modern scholars, is the impartial application of a rule founded on the common good. It defines individual rights from the point of view of the common good partly on the basis of needs and partly on the basis of merit or ability. Equality requires that the fundamental needs of all citizens should have the first lien on the national income. "When necessaries are short, superfluities must vanish." The general economy should strive to meet the needs of all members of the community in proportion to the urgency, but under such conditions as to

[4] Hobhouse, L. T. *The Elements of Social Justice*, p. 169.

maintain the necessary economic functions. There should be
no method of acquiring wealth except by social service. The
lowest remuneration for work done is that which will maintain
the least capable worker required by the industrial system in
a condition of full civic efficiency. And the highest reward
given for the services of the most able producer should be
remuneration above vital or functional cost; a small margin
in an efficient and highly organized state, a larger margin in a
stupidly and wastefully administered state. In the sense that
it is here used, justice or proportional equality is the principle
of social harmony, purely dependent on, or derivative from
the common good. The sense in which equality is absolute is
that all people are entitled to a standing in the social order
that is based on rules or standards universally and impartially
applied. That is, equality of consideration must be assumed
in determining relative, proportional equality.

2. THE SOCIO-POLITICAL THEORY OF TAXATION

NOWHERE has the socio-political theory of taxation been
more ably presented than in the writings of the great German economist, Adolph Wagner. Professor Bullock, in a
discriminating selection, presents excerpts from Wagner's
works which state concisely the socio-political theory.*

THE modern science of economics not only recognizes the
mutual dependence of public and private economic activity,
and their mutually complementary character; it also renounces
the optimistic view of the present organization of private industry, and recognizes the great evils in the system of free competition.[1] It has come to know that the organization of productive
industry by private initiative, the existing institution of property — especially in land and productive capital, and the distribution of wealth which takes place upon this basis, have a
decisive social influence. It knows that through this process
the power and relations both of individuals and of classes are
determined in modern economic society. At the same time
our science recognizes the influence which the state exercises
directly or indirectly upon the distribution of wealth and position of social classes, by the form which its activity takes, by
the manner in which it spends its revenues, by the kinds of
taxation it adopts, and by the creation of public debts.

* From C. J. Bullock, *Selected Readings in Public Finance*, (Boston, 1924),
pp. 254–258.
[1] *Finanzwissenschaft*, Vol. I, § 27.

From this knowledge our science has developed two demands. In the first place, the state should so order its expenditures, tax system, and loans as to remove certain economic and social evils which have attended them in the past. And in the second place, the state, by adopting appropriate policies, should remedy evils which are not due to its previous action in financial or other matters. From this second demand it follows that, in the domain of public finance, expenditures should increase in order to enable the state to assume new functions; and that taxation, in addition to serving the purely financial purpose of providing sufficient revenue, should be employed for the purpose of bringing about a different distribution of wealth from that which would result from the working of free competition upon the basis of the present social order. It is the modern "social problem," influencing both scientific and public affairs, which is here beginning to work this transformation in the science of finance.

ONE who considers the present economic order unconditionally just, and the only justifiable order, as the liberal school of the Physiocrats and Smith did, must logically consider the existing distribution of wealth, which results from this order, as the only righteous and just distribution.[2] This conclusion the keener thinkers of the school have drawn and definitely formulated. For a person of this opinion the existing distribution of wealth is, therefore, a fact admitting of no further discussion and to be accepted with all of its consequences. One of these consequences is that the expenditure of the same amount of money presses with unequal severity upon persons with different incomes and in different economic circumstances; or, conversely, that the ability of these persons to bear the same expenditure varies according to the conditions just mentioned. It follows, then, that taxation should not alter the existing distribution, which is considered to be just. In this view of the case, therefore, taxation will be confined strictly to the purpose of raising sufficient revenue; and the socio-political theory of taxation, which has already been stated, will be rejected.

The consequences of this view, so far as the concept of justice and the demand for universality and equality in taxation are concerned, is briefly as follows:

(1). The duty of all to pay taxes (universality) is interpreted literally. Every citizen is required, as a matter of principle, to pay taxes, whether his income is small or large, whether it is derived from invested property or from personal exertions. There should be no exemption of the "minimum of subsistence."

(2). Equality in taxation is believed to be proportionality of taxes to income; that is, every one should pay in taxes the same proportion of his income. The result is proportional taxation, or levying the same per cent upon all incomes, and the rejection of progressive taxation of the larger incomes, as well as the equal taxation of funded and unfunded incomes. . .

The theory thus briefly, but sufficiently sketched may be called the purely financial or fiscal theory of taxation, in order to distinguish it from the theory now to be presented. The correctness of the conclusion concerning universality and justice of taxation is not to be questioned if the premise is conceded to be true. This premise is the justice of the distribution of wealth brought about by free competition. The conclusion stands or falls with the premise.

Again referring to my earlier discussion of competition in my Grundlegung,[3] discussion which cannot be repeated here, it is to be said that the premise cannot be admitted to be true,—at least in the universal application given it by the liberal school of economics. . . Therefore the conclusion that the distribution established by competition is not to be disturbed by taxation, is not universally true. We need, rather, besides the purely financial theory of taxation, to establish a second,— the socio-political, by which a tax becomes something more than a means of raising revenue, and is considered a means of correcting that distribution of wealth which results from competition. This is to be brought about particularly by discriminating as sharply as possible between "earned" incomes and incomes resulting from chance or speculative gains. . . And then, with the incomes drawn from ordinary industry, we must distinguish more sharply between income derived from labor and income derived from property; and we must consider that the larger gains, and the accumulation of property which they render possible, usually result more or less from good fortune as well as from the personal contributions of the recipients. Furthermore, only from the socio-political standpoint can due consideration be given to the undeniable fact that the larger incomes represent greater ability to pay taxes than the smaller incomes represent, and that income from property indicates greater ability than income

[3] *Grundlegung der politischen Oekonomie*, especially Bk. V, ch. II. — Ed. [Bullock]

from labor. And, finally, from this standpoint, can be justified the policy of favoring classes of persons with small and precarious incomes or incomes derived wholly from labor, by means of certain exemptions from taxation. Such exemptions necessarily lead to higher taxation of the wealthier classes, but they are, from this standpoint, quite as justifiable as the institutions already maintained, at public expense, for the benefit of the poorer classes, such as schools.

So far as concerns the postulates of universality and equality in taxation, the results of the socio-political theory are as follows:

(1). Universality is not interpreted literally, even for those who are members of the state. It permits the exemption of persons with small incomes, especially incomes derived from labor, from taxation in general or from the operation of certain taxes. This is the social demand for the exemption of a minimum of subsistence. . .

(2). Equality is, in this theory, considered to mean taxation as far as possible in proportion to ability to contribute, which increases more rapidly than the absolute amount of a person's income or property increases. Therefore the socio-political theory demands progressive taxation of larger incomes and the rejection of mere proportional taxation. Furthermore it demands heavier taxation of funded incomes than of incomes derived from labor. . . And, in strictness, only upon this socio-political theory can the taxation of inheritances find adequate justification. For, according to it, the rights of property and inheritance are not mere matters of course and wholly independent of the action of the state, as the liberal school believes them to be. These things are, on the contrary, a product of the legal activity of the state.

3. Appropriate Distribution of the Burden of Taxation *

Until recently "equity" was thought an adequate guide in the philosophy of taxation : and it was generally considered equitable that every one should contribute "on the joint-stock plan" to the expenses of the State in proportion to the income (or, as was sometimes said, the property) which he enjoyed under it. But further consideration showed that while a joint-stock company has no responsibility for the number of shares which each individual holds in it, the duty of the State is of larger

* Adapted from "National Taxation after the War" by Alfred Marshall, in *After-War Problems,* (George Allen and Unwin, Ltd., London, 1917), Chap. XVIII, Secs. 2, 3, 4.

scope. For equity proceeds on the basis of existing rights, as generally recognized: and, though a joint-stock company must accept them as final, the State is under obligation to go behind them; to inquire which of them are based on convention or accident rather than fundamental moral principle; and to use its powers for promoting such economic and social adjustments as will make for the wellbeing of the people at large. A chief place among those powers is held by its control of the distribution of the burden of taxation. The notion that this distribution should be governed by mere equity remained dominant till late in the nineteenth century; but, when the war began, the tide was in full swing towards the notion that the problem is one of constructive ethics; though, of course, on its technical side it calls for careful economic and political thought.

This new notion is indeed largely based on observations which were certainly made two thousand years ago, and probably much earlier, that the happiness of the rich does not exceed that of the poor nearly in proportion to the difference in their commands of material wealth. Sages have indeed frequently asserted that happiness is a product of healthy activity, family affection, and content; and that it is as often to be found in the cottage as in the mansion. But yet a lack of the necessaries of life causes positive suffering, which transcends in a way the lack of happiness; and therefore taxes, which trench on the necessaries of life at the command of any stratum of sober, hardworking people, stand in a class by themselves.

Again, though the upper strata of society do not enjoy an excess of happiness over the lower strata at all proportionate to their superiority in incomes, yet almost every one derives considerable pleasure from an increase of his income, and suffers annoyance from its diminution. For the increase gratifies, and the diminution disappoints, the hope of some enjoyment or of some ambition which is near in sight. In the one case the man feels himself rising in that social stratum to which he is accustomed: the stratum which knows him, and which he knows; the stratum whose wants and thoughts and aspirations are kindred to his own. A clerk is made proud and happy when he can move from a working-class quarter to one in which untidy clothes are not seen; but he does not fret at being unable to move into a fashionable quarter: he is grieved if unable to take his family to the seaside for their wonted two or three weeks; but he does not greatly repine at being unable to travel round the world.

These considerations point to the conclusion that, while anti-social excess in the consumption of alcohol by any class is rightly subject to heavier taxation, those who apply practically the whole of a very small family income to good uses should make little or no *net* contribution to the Revenue. It will not be possible to exempt from taxation all the things consumed by them: but the greater part of what they contribute directly to the Exchequer should be returned to them indirectly by generous expenditure from public funds, imperial and local, for their special or even exclusive benefit. The ever-growing outlay on popular education, old age pensions, insurance, etc., is an expression of the public conscience needed to palliate extreme inequalities of wealth, while yet enabling even the poorest class of genuine workers to remain full, free citizens, with a direct interest in public finance. Their life is an integral part of the national life. If all were equal in wealth and other matters, national life would be something more than the aggregate of the lives of its individual members, and all would need to make sacrifices for it. As things are, while all must suffer (and if needs be die) in time of war for the national life, the purses of the well-to-do alone can be expected to contribute largely to its expenses in time of peace. To do so is merely good business: it is not charity.

We may not shut our eyes to the fact that though as much personal hurt is caused by taking £1000 from an income of £10,000 as by taking £20 from an income of £200 — a matter on which opinions differ — yet the hurt caused by obtaining £1000 of additional Revenue by means of levies of £20 from each of fifty incomes of £200 is unquestionably greater than that caused by taking it from a single income of £10,000. For the fact is becoming ever more prominent to the minds of those who are not specially well-to-do; and it may be a source of some peril to the country, especially in view of the large Revenue that will be needed after the war, unless careful account be taken of the extent to which excessive taxes on capital react indirectly on the people at large. While special provision is made for those whose incomes fall short of the necessaries of life and vigour, every one else must bear a considerable share of the national burdens; but the shares must be graduated *very steeply*. . .

This can be effected only by a very large use of taxes on income and property. No approach towards it has been attained by taxes on particular commodities; for indeed many such taxes press with the heaviest weight on the poorest classes, and with no appreciable weight on the rich; while those which fall chiefly on the consumption of the rich have never been made to yield any large Revenue.

EXTENSIONS OF THE GRADUATION OF THE INCOME-TAX

IN earlier times nearly the whole of most people's incomes was derived from operations known to their neighbours, and a large understatement of income was not likely to escape detection. But modern methods of investment and other causes had made it almost impossible to detect fraudulent understatements, until the plan, now familiar, was adopted of taxing at the source all British corporate incomes; while incomes from stock exchange securities issued abroad are now in effect brought under the same discipline by aid of the agencies of the money market. This has enabled the Inland Revenue officials to give most of their attention to the intricacies of small private businesses, a task in which their methods have greatly improved. Thus the percentage of income demanded by the tax rose long ago much above that which it had originally been thought possible to charge with tolerable safety, unless during the emergency of a war; and yet the evasions are believed to have become relatively small. This plan, however, increases the difficulties of direct graduation of the burden of the tax: so recourse is now had to the indirect method of allowing certain abatements to be made from small incomes before they are assessed to the tax.

In order to carry the graduation above the limit at which no abatement was made a Super-tax was introduced in 1909, surcharging all very large incomes. The collection of that tax derives little aid from the practice of charging at the source; but, as the number of incomes which come under it is small, the officials can give a good deal of time to each of them. The great increases in the income-tax and Super-tax levied during the war, together with the Excess-profits-tax, while throwing no direct light on the probable course of taxation after the war, suggest a hope that the various advances toward graduation made before it, will be sustained and developed after it. In so far as the graduation is effected by abatements, people have a direct interest in submitting statements of their incomes in detail to the income-tax officials: and in this way graduation tends to promote the accuracy of income-tax returns and to diminish evasions.

The exceptional power of adjustment to special conditions possessed by the income-tax extends some way in the direction of taking account of the fact that two persons with equal incomes may have to bear very unequal burdens. Thus insurance premiums are deducted, subject to certain conditions, from income before taxation : and some further deductions, which might advantageously be enlarged, are made on account of young children. There is much to be said for the present plan of regarding the incomes of husband and wife as a single unit for taxation : but the charge levied on that unit should be less than if it had to support only one person.

This inequality between the burdens of taxation on two persons with equal incomes, but unequal responsibilities, extends below the income-tax paying class ; but it is only in that class that a direct remedy is in sight. Among the working classes especially an unmarried man is likely to consume highly taxed alcohol and tobacco in greater quantities than a married man with an equal income ; but in regard to most taxed commodities the married man's expenditure is likely to be the larger. It is true that the married operative is likely to derive more aid than the unmarried from public expenditures on health insurance and on schools. But unfortunately, though the education given by the subsidized schools is often at least as good as that afforded by relatively expensive private schools, even the lower middle classes are induced by convention to hold aloof from them in this country.

If it were possible to exempt from the income-tax that part of income which is saved, to become the source of future capital, while leaving property to be taxed on inheritance and in some other ways ; then an income-tax graduated with reference to its amount, and the number of people who depended for their support on each income, would achieve the apparently impossible result of being a graduated tax on all personal expenditure. Rich and poor alike would be left to select those uses of their incomes which suited them best, without interference from the State, except in so far as any particular form of expenditure might be thought specially beneficial, or specially detrimental, to public interests. The income-tax would then levy the same percentage on the rich man's expenditure on coarse tea and on fine tea, on bread and on expensive food ; and a higher percentage on each than on the poor man's expenditure on anything, unless it be alcohol and tobacco. The way to this ideal perfection is difficult ; but it is more clearly marked than in regard to most Utopian goals.

In pursuing it a watchful eye must of course be kept on the danger that excessive taxes on large incomes may check energy and enterprise. It is true that a man of high genius and originating faculty often values his gains less for their own sake, than for the evidence which they afford to himself and others of eminent power. His energy would not be much affected by a tax which lowered his share, provided it did not put him at a disadvantage relatively to others. The zeal of a yachtsman in a race is not lessened when an unusually unfavourable tide retards the progress of all; and so the business man of high faculty would not be much less eager for success, if taxation took from him and his compeers a considerable portion of their gains.

But the average man desires wealth almost exclusively for its own sake; though some little introspection might suggest to him that what he really cares for is an increase in wealth relatively to his neighbours: and thus the problems of a steeply graduated income-tax run into those of graduated taxes on capital.

LIMITATIONS OF THE SCOPE OF TAXES ON CAPITAL

HEAVY taxes on capital, of course, tend to check its growth and to accelerate its emigration. It is to Britain's credit that she was able to export a great deal of it before the war: but, if her factories had been equipped with as generous a supply of machinery as those of America, her industries would probably have been more productive than they were; and if she is to hold her place in the van of industry after the war, she will need much new capital for her own use. Her natural resources, except in coal and a favourable coastline, are small; and a chief cause of the superiority of the wages of her workpeople over those in other countries of Europe has been the fact that her businesses could obtain the necessary supply of capital at lower charges than anywhere else. Therefore taxes on capital must be handled with caution.

So far as the rights of property have a "natural" and "indefeasible" basis, the first place is to be attached to that property which any one has made or honestly acquired by his own labour. But the right thus earned does not automatically pass to his heirs: the tardy development of steeply graduated duties on inheritance (or "Death Duties") has approved itself increasingly to the ethical conscience and to the practical counsels of administration: and this in spite of the fact that such taxes are generally paid out of capital, for the heir seldom sets apart a sinking fund out of his income. There are considerable evasions, some technically valid, and others not; but they are said to be less than had been anticipated. The annoyance which a man feels on reflecting that his heirs will inherit somewhat less than he has owned does not seem to affect conduct much ; and perhaps some part of the Revenue needed after the war, in excess of that before it, may be safely got by a moderate increase of these duties.

A man's "unearned" income may be derived from inherited property, or from the fruits of his own labour.   Partly because earned income is likely to be subject to heavy demands in making provision for dependents, it is reasonably assessed to income-tax at lower rates than unearned income.   So far all seems well.   But a graduated income-tax falls short of attaining the great ideal of being a graduated tax on lavish "expenditure," because it is levied on what a man saves as well as on what he spends.

The "expenditure" which is contrasted with saving is, of course, expenditure for immediate personal consumption on commodities and services of all kinds ; for that part of an income which is "saved" is spent, if not by the person who saves, yet by those to whom he hands over its use in return for promised income.   Thus all is spent ; but that part which is spent for personal consumption disappears soon after it is taxed, and that part which is turned into income-yielding capital is taxed again fully in the long run.[1]

The duty of each generation to those which are to follow is as urgent as that of the rich to consent to surrender a more than proportionate contribution from their incomes to the national purse ; ethical considerations and those of high policy make alike for the preservation of the capital that is needed to sustain the strength of a country in peace and when assailed by hostile aggression.

Finally, a remark may be made, somewhat dogmatically, on a rather abstruse point, which cannot be fully discussed here. It is, that if a great part of the Revenue is derived from taxes on commodities consumed by the people, then either the standard of living of the people must be lowered, or the taxes must ultimately be paid by their employers ; therefore it must in the main fall on the income obtained from the use of capital in business.   In so far as it does this, it will tend to drive away capital nearly as much as a tax on income derived from capital would, and even more than a tax on all considerable incomes, including those that are earned by professional men and salaried business officials.   All taxes, unless they are

---

[1] Suppose a tax of, say, a shilling in the pound is levied permanently on all income, and £1000 saved yields, say, 4 per cent. permanently : then that £40 of annual income will yield permanently £2 as tax : and the present value of that permanent yield will be £50 — the exact amount of the original tax.

so spent as directly to increase efficiency, tend in the same
direction.

4. EQUITY IN THE DISTRIBUTION OF THE BURDEN OF TAXATION *

MUCH has been written on "the distribution of the burden of
taxation," but the range of questions usually covered by this
title is narrow. Assuming that the incidence of all taxes is
known, and that the necessary statistics of income, consumption, etc., are available, it is possible to determine how the
direct money burden of any tax system is, in fact, distributed
among different individuals and classes. It is also possible to
discuss, in general terms, how this direct money burden ought
to be distributed. In such discussions it is usual to take account of the direct real burdens, which correspond to tax
payments. But the indirect money burdens, and still more
the indirect real burdens, of taxation are not brought under
review. These latter factors require for their consideration
a comprehensive study of the economic effects of taxation,
and any conclusions reached in the narrower field of discussion must, therefore, be regarded as only partial and provisional.

Assuming that a given revenue is to be raised by taxation,
the total direct real burden will be greater under some tax
systems than others.[1] It is an obvious idea that the tax system
should be so arranged, as to make the total direct real burden
as small as possible. This has been called "the principle of
minimum sacrifice," and it has been suggested that it would
be realised by taxing only the largest incomes, cutting down
all those greater than a certain amount to that amount, while
exempting all those less than that amount. Thus all incomes
above, say, £1500 a year would be reduced by taxation to that
figure, and no one, whose income was less than this, would
be taxed at all. We are led to this rough and ready plan
by the conception of the diminishing marginal utility of income.[2] The chief objection to it is that, especially if it were
introduced suddenly, it would probably check nearly all work
and saving, beyond what was required to secure the maximum

* From Hugh Dalton, *Principles of Public Finance*, (George Routledge and
Sons, Ltd., London, 1932), Chap. IX.

1 Also, of course, in so far as foreigners can be made to bear any of the direct
money burden of any of the taxes, the total direct real burden on members of
the taxing community is reduced.

2 Another name for "the principle of minimum sacrifice" is "the principle of
equi-marginal sacrifice." But this is clumsier.

income not subject to taxation.[3] This is an objection based on grounds of economy, that is to say on the consideration of economic effects. But some people would also object to it on grounds of equity or "fairness," and it will be found that, in most discussions of "the proper distribution of the burden of taxation," arguments based on equity are more prominent than those based on economy.

Different people, however, have very different ideas as to what is equitable, and many of these ideas prove to be vague and unhelpful, when it is attempted to apply them to practical problems. "It is equitable that people in the same economic position should be treated in the same way for purposes of taxation." Perhaps; but what differences in treatment are equitable for people in different economic positions? And, moreover, what is meant by the "same economic position?" Clearly a bachelor with an income of £1000 a year is not in the same economic position as a married man with three children and the same income. But by how much must the income of the latter be increased, in order to put him in the same position as the former? Mere considerations of equity provide no answer to such questions as this.

It is, in any case, an error to object, as is sometimes done, to particular taxes, as distinct from the tax system as a whole, as inequitable. For the inequity of one tax, as between different taxpayers, may be cancelled by that of another. There may be inequity in the parts, but equity on the whole. But it is not necessarily an error to approve particular taxes, as distinct from the rest of the tax system, as being in themselves equitable. Thus a plausible case may be made out, on ground of equity, for taxes on "windfall wealth." This form of wealth, of which war profits and "unearned increment" in the value of land are examples, has two characteristics. The first is "undeservedness," in the sense that such wealth accrues to its possessor without his rendering any, or at any rate any equivalent, services in return, and the second is unexpectedness. The first characteristic is thought by many to justify the taxation of windfall wealth from the point of view of equity, while the second . . . justifies its taxation on economic grounds.[4] But it is

---

[3] An example of such a result was the effect on Russian agricultural production of the Russian Government's policy in 1918–20 of requisitioning from the peasants all their foodstuffs in excess of the immediate requirements of themselves and their families. See Dobb, *Russian Economic Development*, p. 119, and also Chapter V.

[4] But, except in a few glaring cases, the attempt to apply the test of deservedness or undeservedness to economic payments leads to great perplexities and illustrates afresh the difficulties and vagueness of the conception of equity. "If we all got our deserts, who should escape whipping?" as Shakespeare asks.

not obviously equitable to tax some forms of windfall wealth, unless all forms are taxed, nor is it obvious at what rates it is equitable to tax such wealth.

Returning to the tax system as a whole, three alternative principles for the equitable distribution of its direct money burden have been suggested : first, the cost to the public authority of the services rendered to individual taxpayers; second, the benefit to individual taxpayers of such services; and third, individual "ability to pay" taxation.

"The cost of service principle" can be applied to the supply of postal services, electric light, etc., by public authorities, and the prices of such services can be fixed in accordance with this principle. But it cannot be applied to services rendered out of the proceeds of taxes, as distinguished from prices. For a tax, by definition, is a payment, in return for which no direct and specific *quid pro quo* is rendered to the payer. The services, if any, rendered to individual members of the community by expenditure on the King's Civil List, on armaments, police or public parks cannot, in fact, be determined and, therefore, the cost of rendering these services to different individuals cannot be determined. Thus the "cost of service principle," however equitable it may seem in the abstract, is not capable of wide practical application.

The "benefit of service principle" fails in the same way. Since the services rendered to individuals by many forms of public expenditure cannot be determined, the benefits to individuals from such services cannot be determined. The principle can, indeed, be applied in a few special cases. For example, the benefit derived by an old age pensioner from his pension is definite enough, and the benefit of service principle is definite enough, and the benefit of service principle would require him to return it to the public treasury in the form of a special tax.[5] If this is equitable, it would be a simpler way of giving effect to equity to repeal the Old Age Pension Acts. Those, who think that this would not be equitable, cannot think that the benefit of service principle without qualifications is equitable. And, if qualifications are to be introduced, it is not clear, so far as equity is concerned, on what principle they are to be based, nor how far reaching they are to be.

The principle that taxation should be distributed between individuals in accordance with their "ability to pay" is, on the face of it, somewhat more practicable. But how is "ability to

[5] Under the cost of service principle, he would be required to repay, not only the amount of his pension, but also a small charge to cover the cost of administration of the scheme.

pay" to be measured? It is usual, in discussions of this question, to consider the "sacrifice" to the taxpayer of paying his taxes, and then to deduce some scheme of distribution of the burden of taxation from some principle concerning sacrifice. The three most common of such principles are those of "equal sacrifice," "proportional sacrifice," and "minimum sacrifice." To these we may add a fourth, which is sometimes expressed by the injunction, "leave them as you find them," or, more precisely, "do not alter the distribution of income by taxation." *Prima facie*, it is not clear, on grounds of equity, which of these four is to be preferred.

According to the principle of equal sacrifice, the direct money burden of taxation should be so distributed that the direct real burden on all taxpayers is equal; according to the principle of proportional sacrifice, so that the direct real burden on every taxpayer is proportionate to the economic welfare,[6] which he derives from his income; according to the principle of minimum sacrifice, already referred to, so that the total direct real burden on the taxpayers as a whole is as small as possible; according to the principle of "leave them as you find them," so that the inequality of incomes should be neither increased nor diminished by taxation.

In order to apply any of these four principles, it is necessary to assume some relation between money income and the economic welfare derived from it. According to the relation assumed, there will result a tax system which may be either proportional, progressive or regressive. Under proportional taxation all taxpayers contribute the same proportion of their incomes; under progressive taxation, the larger a taxpayer's income, the larger the proportion which he contributes; under regressive taxation, the larger a taxpayer's income, the smaller the proportion which he contributes.[7] These terms may be applied, not only to tax systems as a whole, but also to particular taxes. Thus a tax system which is proportional as a whole may contain some taxes which are progressive and others which are regressive, and a tax system which is progressive as a whole may contain some taxes which are regressive, and conversely. Again, a particular tax system may be proportional over a certain range of incomes, progressive over another range and regressive over yet another range, while there are, of course,

---

6 Or "satisfaction," to use an older term not obviously identical in meaning.

7 Another and rather superfluous term sometimes used in these discussions is degressive taxation, which means that all incomes less than a certain amount are exempt from taxation, and that all incomes greater than this amount are taxed proportionately on the surplus. For the latter class of incomes, therefore, degression is a particular case of progression, but in a very mild form.

an infinite number of possible degrees of progression and regression.

Assuming that the relation between income and economic welfare is the same for all taxpayers and that the marginal utility of income diminishes fairly rapidly as income increases, the principle of equal sacrifice leads to progressive taxation, the principle of proportional sacrifice to still steeper progressive taxation, and the principle of minimum sacrifice, as already pointed out, to a relatively high level of exemption and very steeply progressive taxation of those not exempt. The principle of minimum sacrifice, indeed, gives this result, so long as it is assumed that marginal utility diminishes at all with increasing income. Both equal sacrifice and proportional sacrifice, rigidly applied, involve making all members of the community however poor (provided that they have *some* economic welfare to sacrifice) contribute something. But minimum sacrifice does not involve this. Further, the more rapidly the marginal utility of income is assumed to diminish with increasing income, the more steeply progressive must the tax system become, in order to give effect to either equal or proportional sacrifice.

Proportional taxation can only be justified, according to the principle of equal sacrifice, on the assumption that the marginal utility of income diminishes very slowly, and can only be justified, according to the principle of proportional sacrifice, on the assumption that the marginal utility of income does not diminish at all, but remains constant, as income increases. On this last assumption, the principle of minimum sacrifice would lead to no one distribution of taxation more than any other, since the total sacrifice would in all cases be proportionate to the total revenue raised by taxation.

Regressive taxation can only be justified, according to the principle of equal sacrifice, on the assumption that the marginal utility of income diminishes even more slowly than was required in order to justify proportional taxation according to the same principle, or on the assumption that marginal utility does not diminish at all, but remains constant or actually increases. Again, regressive taxation can only be justified, according to the principle of proportional sacrifice, on the assumption that marginal utility actually increases and, on this absurd assumption, the principle of minimum sacrifice would lead to exempting from taxation all incomes greater than a certain amount, and taxing all incomes less than this amount a hundred per cent.

The fourth principle referred to above, that the inequality

of incomes should be neither increased nor diminished by taxation, can only be applied when it has been decided how the inequality of incomes should be measured. It is commonly supposed by its adherents to lead to proportional taxation. But there are strong grounds for holding that, on reasonable assumptions as to the relation of income to economic welfare, this principle also leads to progressive taxation.[8]

It, therefore, appears that, on reasonable assumptions, each of our four alternative interpretations of "ability to pay" leads to some degree of progression in the tax system. This practical conclusion is now generally accepted by modern opinion, which responds readily to the suggestion that considerably the heaviest burdens should be placed upon the broadest backs. A few high authorities of the older generation still cling with a curious fondness to the idea of proportional taxation, and it is time that they have the support, for what it is worth in this connection, of Adam Smith, who held that "the subjects of every State ought to contribute towards the support of the government, as nearly as possible, according to their respective abilities, that is to say, in proportion to the revenue, which they respectively enjoy under the protection of the State." But Adam Smith, though a great economist in his day, wrote nearly a hundred and fifty years ago, and before the discovery of the law of diminishing marginal utility.

It is important to notice that the four principles considered above, in common with all principles of equity in taxation, including the austere principle that "everyone ought to pay something," are only matters of opinion. Failing a clearer and more generally accepted definition of equity than has hitherto been forthcoming, it cannot be proved that they are, in fact, equitable, but only that certain people at certain times think them so. And it is a fact of common observation that opinion on such questions is very liable to change. It has been truly said that current ideas of equity generally amount to little more than "economy tempered by conservatism." Equity often seems to say "No," but hardly ever "Yes," an elusive mistress, whom perhaps it is only worth the while of philosophers to pursue ardently and of politicians to watch warily.

Yet, even on grounds of equity, it may be argued very cogently that "there is at least as good a case for taxation which makes net satisfactions equal as for taxation which makes sacrifices equal. Indeed, there is a better case. For people's

---

[8] See my article on "The Measurement of the Inequality of Incomes," *Economic Journal*, (September, 1920), reprinted as an Appendix to my *Inequality of Incomes* (second edition).

economic well-being depends on the whole system of law, including the laws of property, contract and bequest, and not merely on the law about taxes. To hold that the law about taxes ought to affect different people's satisfactions equally, while allowing that the rest of the legal system may properly affect them very unequally, seems not a little arbitrary." [9] This line of argument discredits proportional sacrifice, along with equal sacrifice. It is neutral towards constant inequality of incomes, and somewhat more benevolently neutral towards minimum sacrifice.

If, however, we look at the problem of the distribution of the burden of taxation from the point of view, not of equity, but of economy, we stand on surer ground, though we may ultimately be led to conclusions less simple in form than those furnished by equity. It has been argued . . . that any system of public finance should be conceived simply with a view to the maximum social advantage in the long run, and it follows that any tax system, as part of this larger system, should be conceived with the same object. But it is a necessary preliminary to the consideration of any tax system from this point of view to consider broadly the economic effects of taxation.

5. Bases of Progressive Taxation *

Progressive taxation of income is now wellnigh universal, and it is difficult to realise that only two decades ago it was still looked upon askance by all but advanced thinkers in this country, and in France it is still viewed with much suspicion. The nineteenth-century economists in the main accepted proportion with an element of degression and an exemption limit, and they regarded any departure from a plain proportional rate as a dangerous and socialistic step leading to confiscation. In 1861 Mill said: "The rule of equality and of fair proportion seems to me to be that people should be taxed in an equal ratio on their superfluities, necessaries being untaxed, and surplus paying in all cases an equal percentage. This satisfies entirely the small amount of justice that there is in the theory of a graduated income tax, which appears to me to be otherwise an entirely unjust mode of taxation, and, in fact, a graduated robbery." [1] In his *Principles of Political Economy* his language is less forcible.

At the same date, Newmarch said graduation was "confisca-

* From Sir Josiah Stamp, *The Fundamental Principles of Taxation*, (Macmillan and Co., Ltd., London, 1929), pp. 38–46.
[9] Pigou, *Public Finance*, p. 60.
[1] 1861 Comm. Q. 3540.

tion, punishing prudence and virtue, taxing a man for being good to himself and doing good to others." [2]

The best known early nineteenth-century view is M'Culloch's oft-quoted remark, "When you abandon the plain principle (of proportion) you are at sea without rudder and compass, and there is no amount of injustice you may not commit." Curiously it was M'Culloch's view that the taxpayers should be left in the same *relative* position in which they had been found. Those who thought of this tax as a definite *payment,* like Sargant, said there was nothing to justify asking a rich man for a shilling for what another gets for ninepence.— One wonders whether Sargant had ever paid a doctor's bill!

Although a progressive produce tax existed in Athens six centuries before Christ, and possibly an income tax in Egypt a thousand years earlier, while in this country there was progression in the fourteenth and fifteenth centuries,[3] the idea only took root sporadically so far as incomes were concerned. In the French tax on a tenant's rental, progression was designed to secure a proportional tax on the income because the ratio of rent to income fell as the income got higher, and also, as Seligman says, "to compensate the lower classes for the other duties." [4]

The principle of progression has, however, never lacked exposition from the time of Montesquieu. Paley, in 1830, gave the first complete English exposition — "We should tax what can be spared." The Dutch writers proceeding from the exemption of the subsistence income gradually reached progression with mathematical forms.[5] By 1894 Seligman, surveying the whole subject with the growing continental practice, was able to urge that the apparent stability or certainty of proportional taxation might really involve the greater arbitrariness, and that the "confiscation" objection had been answered.

The application of progression in the British income tax was delayed far beyond that in the German scheme, probably because the latter system of direct taxation on the individual lent itself more easily to the principle on its practical application than the British system of taxation at the source, where the difficulties are very real, and led to a compromise even at that date.

It was not until the marginal theory was thoroughly worked

---

[2] 1861 Comm. Qs. 747–50.

[3] *Vide* Kennan, *Income Taxation,* chap. i. Also article on "Graduated Taxation," by Prof. Seligman, in *Dictionary of Political Economy.*

[4] Seligman, *Income Tax.*

[5] Seligman, *Progressive Taxation.*

out on its psychological side that progressive taxation obtained a really secure basis in principle. It seems to us now a bare truism to say that taxation is a sacrifice or a "hurt," and that to take away a shilling from the 10,000th £ is not so hurtful as to take a shilling from the 100th £. The principle is based upon the diminishing utility of money or wealth as a whole to its possessor. While the utility of increments of any *particular* commodity may rapidly diminish, and reach zero or even *disutility* (as when a schoolboy has exceeded a fourth helping of plum pudding, or as when we have heard "The end of a perfect day" indifferently sung for the hundredth time), the utility of commodities *in general* does not reach zero so readily. The utility of money, therefore, while continually diminishing to the individual possessor as he has more and more, does not actually become *nil* until the aggregate is enormous, and possibly not even then, for even if a man is surrounded with everything that money can buy, an additional sum may still have some value to him as ministering to his *pride*.

PROGRESSIVE TAXATION HAS ALSO BEEN BASED ON INCREASED PRODUCTIVITY

IT must not be forgotten, moreover, that progression has been justified on the "production" side by reference to the fact that the larger the income the greater its power on being focussed or grouped for the production of further income, and therefore, the more it can be tapped without hurt. This cannot, however, be said to apply to a large income made up of various mixed investments, but only to a business income in the hands of a powerful and highly intelligent direction. This justification has been put forward quite recently for the progressive taxation of businesses according to their size, reckoned by their capital.[6] This, indeed, would be the only way in which the ability arising through power of aggregation could be reached. But if the larger business is not in fact more profitable — what then? If its proceeds formed part of a large number of smaller incomes, the ability, tested on the spending side, is in direct conflict with ability on the production side. But at any rate it may be conceded that direct progressive taxation of businesses is the only true way of reaching greater ability on the "production" side of wealth.

[6] *E. J.*, 1919, p. 419 (S.) ; *Political Science Quarterly*, Mar. 1918.

PROGRESSION HAS BEEN ALLEGED TO BE JUSTIFIED UPON THE "RENTAL" CONCEPTION IN ECONOMIC THEORY

THE latest justification of progression is Mr. J. A. Hobson's doctrine of the taxation of surplus :

If the price or reward of a given factor in production, whether interest or wages, is fixed by the reward payable to the marginal supplier, the superior reward paid to a person with a position of advantage is in the nature of economic rent, and as its withdrawal would not lead to the withdrawal of the supply, it is capable of bearing taxation without further shifting. Mr. J. A. Hobson is, perhaps, our most thoroughgoing exponent of this analysis, and he divides the reward paid into "costs" and "surplus." The taxation of costs cannot in direct theory be achieved — it is thrown off, either because the reward *essential* to maintain the offer is diminished and the offer is withdrawn, or because the efficiency of the agent offered is diminished. For example, if a man is having a bare subsistence wage he may be made to *pay* a tax, but the final burden of it is shifted to the community, for his diminished efficiency reacts on price. Similarly, if the minimum interest which induces a given bit of saving is encroached upon, the saving is withdrawn, the supply of capital diminished, and its general price to others increased. But where tax falls on "surplus" it stays there.[7]

If no economic friction existed, taxation would rebound continually from all elements of costs, shifting and shifting until it all rested finally in "surplus." But friction exists to a most important extent, and there is a rival tendency for taxation to stick where it is first laid on, so that the theoretical result is not achieved, even imperfectly. Mr. Hobson admits that "at present it suffices to register a clear judgement to the effect that it is not feasible or equitable to attempt to earmark and attack for revenue the separate items of surplus as they emerge in the present distribution of rent or dividends or profits."

As the test is not quantitative, it is not possible to discern easily which elements of income possess this peculiar quality of final inability to shift taxes, and which are pure costs. The principle of surplus is therefore not available directly as a practical canon in taxation. But Mr. Hobson presumes that these rental or surplus elements are more likely *prima facie* to exist in the incomes of larger amount — the larger the income the greater the *proportion* of it which is rental and not costs — so that a progressive income tax in a rough way is taxation on the principle of surplus. But in my judgement this assump-

[7] J. A. Hobson, *Taxation in the New State.*

tion is so little likely to accord with the facts that a progressive tax can hardly be based upon it. For an income of £1000 from a happy investment in oil or rubber contains a great deal of surplus, whereas an income of £10,000 from house property or consols contains none at all.[8]

Another writer, R. Jones, boils down all the principles of taxation virtually to one, which is "for the State to take the least useful parts of incomes," which taken in a national rather than a personal sense almost comes to the Hobsonian position.[9]

OBJECTIONS TO THE "DIMINISHING UTILITY" BASIS FOR PROGRESSION

THE principle of regular diminution of utility has not been un-challenged. Sir Sydney Chapman has urged that different schemes of consumption are as a rule variations of certain distinguishable types, which are kept comparatively intact over lengthy periods by habit and social assimilation, though they are never so well defined that their existence cannot be over-looked. Objectively viewed these types may merge into one another, but subjectively — to the individual — they exist as discontinuous. People usually advance in the social scale by distinct steps. He then considers the case of men spending different incomes but aiming at a specific standard of £300 a year. . .

"I do not of course carry this principle of action so far as to distinguish between two incomes of £500, one of which is going to a man who is always 'hard up' because he happens to be at the lower edge of a social group whose habits, etc., are conditioned by incomes falling between £500 and £1000 — say £750 average; while the other income goes to a man who would 'feel' the payment less because he lives on the upper side of a group whose incomes range from £250 to £500, with an average of £350. Such differences in relative sacrifice can never be objectively measured." [10]

You will now understand what Sir Sydney Chapman means when he says that this view involves the hard saying that the marginal utility of money may be greater to a man after his circumstances have improved! "It is a common experience to meet with people who have attained a slight accession of income and whose enjoyment of life has obviously been in-creased quite out of proportion to the accession of income." [11]

8 These paragraphs are reproduced from an Address to the British Associa-tion. *Vide, E. J.*, Dec. 1919.
9 R. Jones, *The Nature and First Principle of Taxation.*
10 1920. Comm. Q. 9603.
11 *E. J.*, 1913, p. 30.

On the practical side Chapman agrees that the difficulty cannot be recognised, and the State must be no respecter of persons but adopt the same fiction as is essential in so much political doctrine and deal with a mode or average type for the whole class. But he challenges the ordinary presentation of diminishing utility on the lines of diminishing sacrifice to the individual, and prefers to put it that wants satisfied by earlier increments to income are of more importance than the wants satisfied by late increments, whether the satisfaction of the former causes more utility or not. We must judge of the value of satisfaction of wants in a moral scheme of consumption. Although this idea works well for a comparison between an income of £200 and one of £2000, it is really only a new way of expressing the degressive idea ; and it does not seem to serve us very well in establishing a charge upon £200,000 at a higher rate than that upon £50,000 per annum when one can hardly distinguish the difference in the social importance of the wants satisfied.†

6. The Taxation of Surplus Elements of Income *

ALL incomes, apart from pensions or certain other fixed allowances, are payments to the owners of some requisite of production in respect of the services rendered by that requisite to the actual production of wealth. Or, put in another way, the monetary value of all goods or services that are produced and sold, after provision has been made for the maintenance and repair of plant, materials and other elements of the capital fabric, is distributed in various proportions as income to the capitalists, workers, landowners, business men, professional men, whose personal activities or property help to produce this wealth. The wealth itself is real income ; the price of it, broken up into various payments to owners of the factors of production, is money income. Much of this income is physically and morally necessary to secure the continued use of the factor of production whose owner receives it. The workers in industry cannot go on working unless a certain wage, enabling them to repair the physical energy they have given out, is continuously paid to them. Nor is it enough that the actual workers at any given time are thus maintained. The subsistence wage must not only keep existing labour in physical efficiency, it must

† Eds. note : Stamp also points out in his *Principles of Taxation*, pp. 48-51, the fact that progressive taxation has sometimes been justified as an engine of social improvement. This view has already been ably presented by Adolph Wagner in section 2 of this chapter.

* From J. A. Hobson, *Taxation in the New State*, (Methuen and Co., Ltd., London, 1919), Chap. II.

provide for a constant flow of young labour into the industry
to take the place of those fallen out from declining powers or
death. This does not, of course, necessarily mean that a subsistence wage for an individual worker, or even the standard
wage in a particular trade, must be enough to enable him to
keep a wife and bring up a family. For there is no physical
or moral compulsion to force a worker to provide a substitute
for himself when he falls out. Nor is it the case that the cost
of bringing up a family to maturity must necessarily be borne
by the wages of a single worker. Moreover, few industries
are recruited entirely from the families of their own members.
Rapidly growing industries will naturally draw their increased
supply largely from industries that are declining, or of slow
growth. It is only true of industry in general that the family
income, to which both parents and during certain periods of
family life one or more children may contribute, must in the
aggregate suffice for this purpose. Here we are considering
wages not from the standpoint of a "labour policy" but from
that of a tax policy.

But the issue of the labour "costs" cannot be settled by
confining our thought to the provision of physical continuity
of labour. In a growing progressive community the crucial
question is, "What is the minimum income any group of workers must receive in order to enable and induce them to continue their output of productive energy, and to provide such
increase of labour-power as will increase that output, so as to
meet the growing demands of a community increasing its numbers and enlarging its wants?" From the standpoint of practical economics this means, "What is the established and
effective standard wage, below which a sufficiently large, skilled
and reliable body of workers cannot be obtained?" The basis
of such standard pay is in part the physiological considerations
already touched upon, in part other conventional or "moral"
considerations, relating to standards of comfort which workers
insist upon as conditions for the regular application of their
labour-power. These standards and the relation of individual
wages to them differ in various trades, in various parts of the
country, and with the different opportunities for remunerative
employment open to other members of the family besides the
chief male wage-earner. But for our present purpose it is
sufficient to recognize that the standard wage in any trade or
locality is a necessary "cost" of production, in that, if it is
not paid, the requisite supply of labour is not forthcoming.
It may perhaps occur to some that there remains a difference
between the wage of physical subsistence, necessary to main-

tain the worker (and perhaps a family), and the supplementary portions which go to make up any standard wage containing elements of conventional expenditure and even including some elements of comfort or luxury, not always conducive but perhaps even detrimental to working efficiency.   It may seem possible that such supplementary wage elements could be broken down under the pressure of wage competition, or could be encroached on by taxation, without affecting the supply of labour. And it must, I think, be admitted that there is some difference in the power of resisting taxation, or capitalist encroachment, between that portion of standard wage which rests on the firm rock of physiological necessity and that which does not.   There have been periods in the industrial history of this and other countries when class standards of comfort have actually been broken down by the application of these outside economic forces.   But for all that, we should be wise not to assign much value to such precedents in considering the actual economic situation of today.   The conventional working-class standards of comfort in this country have been secured by a slow and on the whole continuous process of accretions during several generations, and they have recently been fortified by strong working-class sentiments of "rights."   This moral support for class standards has further been reinforced by economic and political organization.   Taking due account of such considerations, we should be justified in insisting that these standard wages (not merely the money they represent, but the purchasing power, the real wages) form an element in costs of production which is virtually irreducible.   Nay, it is likely that in the post-war economic system the organized power of the workers will be applied effectively to achieve considerable advances upon the pre-war standards, enforcing them by the strike-weapon.   It is sufficient here to recognize that standard wages, however composed and established, form a necessary "cost" which has virtually no ability to bear taxation.   A tax on low standards of wages would entail a loss of physical efficiency in the worker and his family, thus reducing the actual physical supply of labour power.   A tax on the higher standards, reducing those elements of comfort or pleasure which figure most clearly in his consciousness, would be met by a "moral" revolt of organized labour that would have the same injurious reaction upon industry.   Standard wages are therefore necessary elements of income with no true power to bear a tax.

It should be equally evident that in the existing economic system there is a minimum rate of interest, in payment for the production and use of capital, that must be secured to the owners of this capital to induce them to go on supplying it in the required quantities in this country to our industries. It may be that, under a purely socialistic system, if such could be established, no payment of income under the head of interest would be necessary: society would secrete the necessary capital in the ordered arrangements for its annual production. We are not, however, living in this society, but in one that depends almost wholly upon individual voluntary saving and application of savings under the prompting of personal gain. Such an economic system must secure to the individual saver and investor the payment that is absolutely necessary to induce him to save and invest. It would be foolish here to open up the familiar controversies about the nature and springs of saving and the moral justification of interest. It is unnecessary to do so, especially in a discussion confined to our national economy. It may be admitted that a good deal of saving would be effected in this country for the creation of capital, even if no positive interest were attainable. Even in poor and powerless societies many peasants and other people will "save" for nothing, putting their savings in a "stocking." A large proportion of the saving of the rich classes in a developed industrial country is a virtually automatic process of laying aside for investment what is not wanted to support their conventional and personal standard of luxurious consumption. Most of it would go on, even if no interest were obtainable. The same is probably true of a part of the saving of the less well-to-do, who would continue to put aside money during their full earning period of life for their support in old age or infirmity, or even to assist their family after their death. Some of these people, it is rightly urged, would actually save more if interest were lower than it is, because it would be necessary to do so in order to secure a decent livelihood in their later years. But those who would draw from such admissions the conclusion that our national economic system would go on functioning, if no interest were attainable, are in double error. In the first place, there is a general agreement among economists that a considerable proportion of the national saving is evoked by the desire for interest, and varies directly with the rate obtainable. Just as some persons who love their work and would work for the love of it must be paid the common rate of wage or salary needed to evoke the energy of other workers in the same occupations who do not love their work and would withhold their energies if they were not paid, so with the saving classes, the willing savers must be paid at a rate determined by the insistence of the unwilling savers. Moreover, unless

investment of savings in other countries is prohibited (a retro-
grade and injurious restriction upon freedom), the current
world-rate of interest must be paid in this country for new
capital. While, therefore, it is theoretically conceivable that,
even in an economic system where the supply of new capital
was left to individual saving, interest might fall to zero,[1] for
the immediate future it is necessary to secure to the saving
classes as a whole some positive payment, in order to induce
them to withhold enough of their spending power from articles
of immediate personal consumption in order to apply it to
bringing new capital forms into being, and risking their loss
in the processes of investment. In other words, just as there
must be an immunity from taxation for a minimum standard
wage, so there must be also for a minimum rate of interest
upon invested capital.

Profit is notoriously a slippery term, often overlapping and
including elements of interest and rent. On any particular
transaction it is generally taken as the difference between
"costs" and selling price. But, regarded as a form of income,
it is the remuneration of the business man or entrepreneur for
the work of organizing and conducting a business. This would
include the planning of the business, the buying of the requisite materials, plant and labour, the direction of the productive
power along certain channels, the marketing of the product,
and the financing of the various operations. In some businesses, especially in the distributive trades, the success of the
business turns so much upon the arts of buying and selling that
the rate of profit depends mostly upon the difference between
buying and selling prices. In joint stock enterprise, where
nearly all the skilful critical acts of the entrepreneur are done
by a salaried manager, only a portion of the profits goes in
payment for these services ; most of it passes into dividends,
and is thus pooled with interest upon capital. But though
difficult to pin for close definition, profit has a very real existence as a motive force in industry. If it be true that an intelligent and well-informed business man "expects," in putting
his brains, energy and capital, into a particular line of business,
that he will make 10 per cent upon his yearly turnover, any
taxation which defeated that expectation would starve the
trade of business ability and enterprise. This applies not only
to the business man who institutes and "runs" a business, but
also to what we may call the expert or professional investors, as
distinguished from those who merely put their savings in gilt-

---

[1] *I.e.*, the motives which induce peasants to put money by "in a stocking" "for
a rainy day" *might* suffice to provide the socially desirable amount of saving.

edged securities. It may be said that, though this consideration may reasonably set a limit to taxation falling on special
sorts of business profits, any damage done to these trades would
be compensated by others into which their ability and enterprise would be diverted, and that if all "profits" were taxed
indiscriminately, the business men would not allow their brains
and enterprise to lie idle but would take what profits they
could get. There is probably some truth in this view in the
sense that existing business profits possess a large amount of
elasticity. For profits, not wages, as some economists pretend,
have been the "residuary legatee" in the economic system, taking what remains of the product of industry, after the other
factors have been paid their necessary hire. For it is the "entrepreneur" in business who buys or hires at the market rate
all the other instruments and materials, and who, after paying
them their agreed price, keeps the remainder for himself.
Even in a company with a salaried manager this is the case,
though the profiteer is not always the shareholder. Often he
is the group of financiers and directors who floated the company and took out the anticipated profits in advance in the
terms of capitalization.

But the notion of some reformers that somehow or other the
"profits" of business can be eliminated as representing sheer
waste or plunder in the present system is without foundation.
Taking our system as it exists (and we are here not dealing with
another system), it contains many types of business where what
is termed a reasonable rate of profit must be secured to the
men who organize and run them. Large settled businesses
of a routine type can be run either as public services or under
joint stock enterprise by salaried officials. But in new, changing and growing businesses the requisite initiative and energy
will continue to need the personal incentive of speculative
prizes. Fixed salaries will not secure these qualities. Moreover, business ability of a commanding type is more mobile
and cosmopolitan than formerly, and were "profits" too closely
clipped in this country, would seek zones of freer exploitation.

These considerations, applied to profit, whether as speculative gains or as wages of management, need not imply that
profits are in fact kept by effective competition at a minimum,
and that any taxation placed upon them will starve or banish
business ability. On the contrary, there is good reason to
believe that the proportion of the total wealth distributed as
"profits" far exceeds the amount economically necessary to
secure the application of the socially serviceable business ability. For not only is much of this profit predatory or luck

money, but the conditions of such effective competition as applies to ordinary workers in the trades or the professions often have no application in the higher business walks. When, therefore, the Income-Tax Reform of 1913–14 discloses the fact that out of a total income of 1167 millions coming under the survey of Somerset House not less than 483 millions represented professional and business earnings, we may take it for granted that large excessive and fortuitous gains are included in this sum. If to these earnings under Schedule D be added the financial profits and official salaries coming under Schedule B and E (both of which will be much larger in postwar returns), we shall recognize that profits, salaries, professional and official earnings undoubtedly contain a large amount of economically unnecessary income, or, in other words, income with ability to bear taxation. To what extent this taxability applies is a question to which we shall revert presently. Here I am insisting on a recognition of the other side, viz., the fact that all these incomes contain substantial elements of necessary "costs." Profits, salaries, professional earnings, in all the higher grades, may possess large portions of income which if taxed would not disappear, but a large part of this income has the same immunity as other "costs" of production.

The net result of this analysis so far is to establish an all-important distinction between the sorts and sizes of income which rightly rank as "costs" and those which are to be accounted "surplus." It is often said that we possess no means of discovering exactly where "costs" end and "surplus" begins, and that our distinction is a "theoretical" one not suitable for fiscal application. This objection, of course, applies to all distinctions whatsoever, for in all classification there is debatable ground, one species shading off into another. For practical purposes this means the desirability of caution and for allowing a considerable margin of error. It does not mean that the distinction is for practical purposes invalid.

All taxing theory and practice have, in fact, been based upon some amount of discrimination between "surplus" and "costs," though the discrimination has been loose and empirical. Every political financier has been largely occupied with finding sources of income which will not dry up under taxation, and in trying how far he can safely go in taxing them. Moreover, he is more or less cognizant of the sort of taxes which can be safely levied or increased without, as he would say, disturbing industry. Now elements of income which do not "dry up" under taxation and the taxing of which does not disturb industry are precisely what we here call surplus-income.

The classical political economy regarded what is termed economic rent of land as the type of surplus-income, and often confined the term to that income. According to Ricardo, rent was a natural surplus, consisting of the value of the produce of land in excess of the value of the produce of that land which just paid the necessary costs of cultivation. This theory assumed (1) that the worst land in use, *i.e.*, at the "margin of cultivation," paid no rent, and consequently (2) that all economic rents were purely "differential," *i.e.*, measuring the yield per acre over and above the marginal yield. These assumptions, however, as Adam Smith long before had recognized, are incorrect. The total supply of available land for any particular use, or even for all uses, may be so deficient that the worst land may yield a positive rent measuring the pressure of this scarcity of supply. In fact, there are many sorts and uses of land, and in such a country as ours, though the worst (marginal) land for rough grazing in some parts may pay a merely nominal rent, it is not true that the worst wheat-growing land does not pay a substantial rent, still less that the worst market-garden land in actual cultivation pays no rent. Each city has an actual or potential land supply of its own. The worst building sites have a high annual value, directly determined by their value for some alternative purpose such as market gardening or brick making. In a word, rents are not wholly differential: some of them are monopoly prices, measuring the power of the owners of a naturally scarce article to get a high price out of the needs of the public. Such rents taken by the worst building land, or wheat land, or other kinds of land, may be called specific or marginal rents.

These rents, whether marginal or differential, are pure surplus, and have what I here term an absolute ability to bear a tax. This unique nature of land, as he conceives it, is the basis of the contention of the Single-taxer. From the time of the "physiocrats" it has been recognized that rent has no power to shift a tax imposed upon it. The popular mind has, however, no firm grasp of this truth, and persons who ought to know better often speak as if landlords had an unrestricted power to raise rents, so as to throw upon the tenants any increase of taxes and rates to which they are exposed. So far as the landowner is nothing but a landowner, this power does not exist. If rents are sometimes raised "on account of" rises in the rates, it is usually because the properties have previously been under-rented, in the sense that the landlord has not been extracting the utmost that his position would have enabled him to get. The rise of rates, threatening his net income, has led him to look more closely to the economic power he holds and to ask for and obtain a rise of rent which he could, if he chose, have got before.

But there is another consideration. Most land-values, whether agricultural or urban, do not consist wholly of these economic rents. English agricultural land has generally had more capital put into it than would represent its selling value. A good deal, often the whole, of the rent now taken for it may be regarded as interest upon past "improvements." This mixture of rent and interest is, of course, most obvious in the ownership of town properties, and has an important bearing upon taxability. Where the landlord is the house-owner, he is not only a receiver of economic rent but of interest upon capital. In this capacity he has some real power to raise his rent, and so to shift a part at least of the new tax, or higher rate, on to his tenant in the first instance. For, if you tax not only the land value but the buildings and other improvements, you lower the net return on such investments and check the flow of new capital into building enterprises. Though the tax does not immediately reduce the supply of houses in relation to the demand, so that the landlord cannot at once shift any of the new tax or rate on to the rent, he will have the power to do so when the lease falls in, provided that the check upon new building makes a scarcity of houses. How much he can thus shift, and how quickly, depends upon the proportion which ground value bears to building value and the amount of competition there has been in the building business. Where there has been some sort of a monopoly in the development of a town or of a large estate in it, perhaps by the landlord's own enterprise or by a business arrangement with a contracting firm, the capital employed in the housing scheme will have been able to earn a rate of profit or interest considerably greater than would have been the case if building operations were open to the free competition of a number of rival contractors. In other words, some of the economic power of the site owner may be shared by the capitalists and entrepreneurs who helped to develop the estate.

This gives the key to the wider meaning of economic monopoly, or superior business opportunity, from which surplus elements of income are derived. Almost the whole of economic rents, both marginal and differential, could be taken in taxation without causing any reduction in the supply of land for any useful purpose. No owner would withdraw any of his land from its most remunerative use because of the high taxation to which the rent he drew was subjected, provided some fraction remained for him sufficient to induce him to put his land to its best use instead of allowing it to lie idle. A tax upon land value, assessed upon the most remunerative use to which the particular land could be applied, would itself be a strong incentive to compel the owner to put it to this use, for otherwise his residue of rent after he had paid the tax might be nil. Such a tax, therefore, instead of impairing the taxpayer's incentive to apply effectively his factor of production, would actually stimulate such application. Economic rent is a form of income upon which taxation could be put so as to absorb nearly the whole of it. The landowner would have no power to escape any taxation thus directly imposed, or shifted on to it from any source endowed with less ability to bear taxation.

But this taxability is not, as single taxers have contended, a unique property of land values. It is only because these values contain no element of "cost," consisting wholly of "unearned," or surplus income, that this highest degree of ability to bear attaches to them. Other incomes, in proportion as they carry the same element of surplus, also the result of "monopoly" or superior economic opportunity, are similarly susceptible to taxation. I alluded just now to house property which, owing to restricted competition in building operations, was able to make a high return for the capital invested in it. The excess of this return over and above the ordinary market return for such an investment would be just as taxable, and just as unable to shift any of the tax, as would the land values of the sites on which the houses were built. If the capital thus advantageously invested were yielding a net 10 per cent interest, as compared with the (say) net 6 per cent which would suffice ordinary investors in such kinds of enterprise, the extra 4 per cent would stand, as regards ability to bear a tax and inability to shift it, precisely on the same footing with the ground rent. This, of course, would not hold if the tax, instead of being confined to the surplus interest, were levied upon all income drawn from house investments, upon 6 per cent investments as well as 10 per cent investments. For in that case, as I have already pointed out, the flow of fresh capital into building enterprise would be checked, a shortage of housing accommodation would ensue, and all house-owners would be able to raise their rents, including those who had been earning 10 per cent. In other words, this attempt to tax not surplus income only, but also some income which rightly ranked as costs, would enable the owners of surplus to shift the tax on to the tenants as well as the owners whose necessary "costs of production" were assailed by the tax.

This extra 4 per cent is not, as some economic writers describe it, quasi-rent, if by that be meant a feebler or merely temporary imitation of the economic rent of land. The use of the term quasi-rent is applied, by Professor Marshall and others, to the case of capital invested in buildings or any other fixed forms requiring considerable time for their production, which will have a temporary power to raise the price for their use, if a rapid increase in the effective demand for it takes place outstripping for the time all possibility of any corresponding increase of supply. Striking instances of such quasi-rents have been afforded by the experience of these years of war, in which sudden emergency-demands for building, machinery and other plant, have arisen under circumstances where the rate of fresh supplies of such fixed capital not merely could not be accelerated but often had to be reduced. Any existing plant available or adaptable for producing munitions or other war supplies has obviously been put for the time being in an advantageous position as regards its earning capacity, so far as bargaining has not been subject to "control." The income due to this advantageous position is called a "quasi-rent," according to the accepted usage. I would, however, deprecate altogether the shifty epithet "quasi." This temporary surplus income is a short-time rent, as real as any of the more enduring rents or extra-profits, and, what is relevant to our purpose, just as able to bear a tax. In ordinary times, however, such surplus gains are generally of brief endurance. For though any increased pressure of demand for buildings, plant, etc., will give an immediate advantage to the owners of such forms of wealth, translatable into surplus income, this situation will immediately act as a stimulus to direct more capital and labour into these branches of production, so far as they are free of access. This increase in the rate of supply of plant, etc., will normally be rapid enough to prevent the surplus income from rising far or lasting long.

The case from which we started differs, however, vitally from these instances of short business "pulls," or "quasi-rents." The advantage possessed by our owners of house-property, in an area of restricted competition, is based upon a monopoly or lasting scarcity as real as that of land itself. The high return upon such investment has no power to bring into the market an effective competition of new and equally well-placed houses. Upon the foundation of a natural scarcity has been created a scarcity value for this capital, as taxable as rent itself, though it ranks as profit on a business enterprise.

But this is only one instance of a surplus-income due to the possession of some economic coign of vantage, or some superior bargaining power, and associated with other elements of income which are genuine costs and untaxable. Close students of our actual economic structure are aware that the term competitive system is no longer applicable in any high degree to large departments of modern industry, commerce and finance. Everywhere in the more highly organized trades competition is giving place to combination. Were we to follow closely the various processes of production, transport and distribution, by which raw materials are grown, collected, carried, manufactured, and marketed as finished commodities, together with the supplementary processes which feed the main streams of production with machinery, tools, fuel and other subsidiary requisites, we should perceive innumerable places where the free currents were checked, impeded, and held up by powerful organized business groups able to take fixed toll upon the trade as it flowed through the straits where they had planted themselves, or which they had artificially created by the arts of combination. I need not labour the point. But it is to be insisted on that this interference with the free levelling force of competition, keeping prices down to "costs" and incomes down to minimum requirements, cannot be disposed of under the slighting name of "friction," or treated as rare and abnormal. The business system of today is as much combinatory as competitive. It is riddled with financial manipulation, trusts, cartels, pools, conferences, associations, and other arrangements by which businesses of distinct origin combine so as to control prices, and take profits higher than those attainable under free, or as they would call it, cut-throat competition. There is scarcely any large staple branch of manufacture in this country where strong "combines" do not enjoy some such pull. The metal and textile trades, the important new industries of chemicals and electrical apparatus, furnishers to the building trades, the meat, milk and coal distributing trades, tobacco, cinemas and other luxuries, together with many necessaries such as cotton thread and wall papers, are "controlled" in output, prices and profit, by some tight or loose form of combination, ranging from a complete amalgamation to a "gentlemen's" agreement.

Such is the business world in which we are living, and after the war it will be "more so." For everybody is agreed that "wasteful competition" must be got rid of wherever possible:

the enforced combination during war conditions of hitherto competing firms will leave permanent effects. An active policy of Industrial Councils, primarily designed to secure more harmonious coöperation between capital and labour, must issue in closer relations between firms for the regulation of markets and prices. The maintenance of various government "controls" for purposes of "rationing" will make in the same direction of promoting organizations, which are quite unlikely to disintegrate when, if at all, the State removes its hands.

This combinatory character of the new business world must challenge the new State to apply a fiscal policy directed to the conditions under which vast new surplus-incomes will emerge, derived from and proportionate to the new powers of combination. In certain instances the monopoly powers may be so pressing and pervasive, or in other words, the trades may be so fundamental, that the State policy will be one of complete nationalization. But it is unlikely that this process of direct State Socialism can go very far, or very fast, to cope with the new position we describe. The remedy which the State will apply to most cases of surplus-profits due to combination will be a taxation directed to divert large portions of these profits from private hands to the public treasury.

We have here the central problem of the new State finance, how to devise a taxing-system which shall secure as much as possible of these gains of combination without disturbing the energy and initiative of the business men who operate them, or diminishing unduly the flow of the new capital required for their enlargement and improvement.

Many of the surpluses will not be the product of some lucky chance or passing pull. They will flow from the ordinary structure and working of a trade, no longer subject to effective free competition. They will, no doubt, be limited in amount by some consideration of "potential competition" if the surpluses are too exorbitant, as well as by considerations of the shrinkage of demand or recourse to substitutes where available. In other words, monopoly power is never absolute. On the other hand, within their limits the combinations exercise a lasting power to draw excess profits which have the same disability to resist or shift taxation as land itself. Very obstinate is the popular belief that, if you tax a manufacturer or tradesman, he can always take it out of you by raising his prices. But the belief is without foundation in fact. A monopolist or a combination, in control of selling prices, fixes them at the level which he calculates will yield him the maximum net profits on his business. Were he to fix this at a higher level, as he has the power to do, he calculates that he would be a present loser by cutting down demand, or a future loser by stimulating potential into actual outside competition. The fact that a portion of his extra-profits is taken in taxation will not enable him advantageously to raise his prices and throw the tax on the consumer.[2]   High taxation may, of course, lead a combination to look more closely to its control and to be more rigorous in its exactions from the buyer.   Or he may actually raise prices, to his immediate loss, so as to rally public opinion to demand a withdrawal of an unpopular tax.   But, apart from such tactics, there is no tendency for a tax or surplus-profits to be shifted on to the consumer.   It will lie where it is put.

The same capacity to bear a tax, and disability to shift it, apply to that part of earned incomes sometimes termed "rents of ability."   The income of the ordinary working doctor or lawyer is, in ordinary times, considerably higher than that of the ordinary artisan or clerk.   It is sometimes supposed that this follows from, and is the measure of, the higher qualities of skill involved in his occupation.   But there is no validity in the assumption that pay varies directly and proportionately either with the skill or the social utility of work.   An agricultural labourer has much more skill than a bricklayer, but his income is much lower.   A competent journalist is at least as highly skilled as a leading K.C., but does not earn a tithe as much.   Neither what one may call the standard rate, nor the individual rent of ability, is determined in the higher paid callings by intrinsic skill or difficulty.   To some extent the higher standards of professional incomes may rightly be accounted minimum interest upon capital expended in general and professional education and on the subsidies needed for these non-productive years.   If it is the case that a mechanic can attain his full earning capacity at twenty, while an engineer or a doctor has to wait till thirty, spending considerable sums on his keep and training, the interest and sinking fund upon this expenditure contained in the higher standard of professional incomes does not figure as rent of ability.   It is a cost of production of the professional man, and as such is not capable of bearing taxation.   But, in so far as this capital expenditure is only within the reach of a small proportion of our youth, this restriction operates to keep down the number of those entering the professions, and to enable them to organize and bargain more effectively in marketing their services.   To

2 There are rare cases where the imposition of a tax might cause a monopolist to raise his selling prices, but there are as many where it might cause him to lower them.   He has no normal power to raise them.

some extent, no doubt, this tendency is affected by the social prestige and intrinsic interests of the professional life appealing to a very large proportion of the middle and upper classes, and causing some of the professions to be "overstocked." One or two professions, again, notoriously the bar, are so much loaded with subsidised semi-amateurs that anything like a standard rate of income can hardly be said to exist. Moreover, almost all the professions have a considerable fringe of sweated labour. That is particularly true of the clerical, legal, medical and teaching professions. When, therefore, I speak of a standard professional income containing some element of rent or security-value that has a capacity to bear a tax, I must admit that such a standard-rate is far more difficult to discover than in any ordinary trade. And yet, I contend, it is right to assume that some such standard exists in each profession, though it may not be measurable. There is within reasonable limits a size of income which an ordinary professional man in fairly good position looks upon as sufficient and attainable in his particular calling. How much taxable capacity such a standard income possesses, having regard to the conflicting tendencies I have cited, will be matter of much disagreement. Perhaps these "standard incomes" may rightly be deemed too "theoretic" to be available for any taxing-system. But it is necessary to assume them, in order to deal with the individual "rents of ability" which undoubtedly must rank as "surpluses," possessing some considerable capacity to bear taxation.

What is true of the "wages of ability," as they are sometimes termed, in the business and professional classes, is also true of certain favourably placed classes of wage-earners. Though the great majority of wage-earners have no "surplus" income in the sense here given to that term, there are in a good many trades certain skilled or important processes which are so strongly controlled by some organization of labour as to afford an income higher than accords with the grade of skill or strength involved, and higher than would be necessary to evoke a sufficient supply of competent labour for the kind of work. In the engineering and building trades, for example, there have generally been grades of men whose higher rate of pay has been recognized as due to closer organization and stronger power of bargain rather than to any intrinsic skill or knowledge. War experience has notoriously afforded many examples of this scarcity-power to exact a rate of pay containing an element of "surplus."

I may summarize this analysis of "ability to bear" in the following general terms. Those elements of income which

are necessary payments to owners of productive agents, in order
to sustain the productive efficiency of an agent and to evoke its
application, rank as "costs" of production, and have no ability
to bear taxation. The standard wages required to keep a
working-class family on such a level of efficiency and comfort
as will maintain and evoke the regular application of its
labour-power constitute labour "costs." Such salaries, fees and
profits, as are necessary under existing and social economic
conditions to secure the supply of the requisite amounts of
business and professional ability needed for the initiation, organization and management of productive enterprise, must
similarly rank as "costs" of ability or brain-labour. To these
must be added, under any system of private enterprise, the
minimum interest required to evoke the amount of saving and
the application of new capital needed to furnish the plant,
tools and materials for the productive processes.

These "costs" have properly no power to bear a tax. This
does not mean, however, that taxation could not be imposed
on them and might not lie there for a time. It means first,
that if a tax were imposed on any of these "costs" and did lie,
the effort would be to reduce the volume of some productive
power, either by lowering its physical efficiency, or by impairing the incentive for its owner to apply it as efficiently as it
was applied before. Secondly, the reduction in the supply of
any sort of necessary productive power, thus brought about,
must cause such a rise in its price (its wage, salary, profit or
interest) as would defeat the attempt to tax it, by enabling it to
shift the taxation on to those who bought these productive
services, or the products they turned out. The elements of
income which are not "costs" are "surplus." All economic
rents of land, whether "scarcity" or differential rents, all interest, profits, and other payments for the use of capital, brains
or labour, which are due to superior economic opportunities
and are not necessary incentives to secure such use, will rank
as surplus. All forms of surplus have a full ability to bear
taxation. They have no ability to reject or shift it, and all
taxes imposed by a bad taxing policy on "costs" tend to be
shifted on to some form or other of "surplus."

7. THE MINIMUM SACRIFICE THEORY OF TAXATION *

IF taxes were voluntary contributions for the support of the
state, it would be important that we should recognize some

* Reprinted from T. N. Carver, "The Minimum Sacrifice Theory of Taxation," *Political Science Quarterly*, Vol. XIX, (March, 1904), pp. 66–79. Published by the Academy of Political Science, New York.

principle by which to determine how much each individual ought to give. Since the payment of such a tax and its amount would be matters for the individual conscience, it would be pertinent to ask what principle of obligation the individual ought to adopt as his rule of action. But since taxes are not voluntary contributions but forced payments, we need not so much to know what the duty of the individual is as what the duty of the state is: not how much the individual ought in conscience to give, but how much the state ought in justice to take from him, and under what conditions the state ought to take it. In the matter of taxation the state alone is the voluntary agent, and consequently the duty of the state alone is to be determined. It is one thing to say that the individual ought to contribute to the support of the state in proportion to the benefit which he receives, or to his ability to pay, or to his faculty, but it is quite another thing to say that the state ought to make him do any of these things.

These two questions, though distinct, may be resolved into one by assuming that it is the duty of the state to make its citizens do whatever they ought in conscience to do. It would still be the duty of the state which would have to be determined, but under such an assumption that duty would be clear whenever we had found out how the individual ought to act. Such was the assumption upon which states acted in an earlier and darker age, but it has generally been abandoned except in discussions of the basis of taxation, and it is time that it was abandoned even here.

It is doubtless true *in some cases* that the state ought to make the individual do whatever his duty requires, as in the payment of a debt or the keeping of a contract, but there are many other cases where the duty of the state has to be determined on other grounds. It may be that each citizen ought to contribute to the support of the church "according as the Lord hath prospered him," but none of the more advanced nations would think of trying to compel him to do so. It may be the duty of each laborer to join a union, but no state ought to force him into one, much less ought the union to be allowed to appropriate that prerogative of sovereignty to itself. It may be, and very likely is, the duty of each individual "to produce according to his ability and consume according to his needs," but no one but a Marxian socialist would claim that the state ought to make him do so. The illustrations might be multiplied, but enough has been said to show that there are no *a priori* reasons for assuming that because the individual ought to pay for the support of the state according to his ability, for example, that it is therefore the state's duty to make him do so.

It is not to be inferred that the question of taxation is entirely divorced from ethics. Neither is it to be inferred that there are two kinds of moral obligations, one for the individual and the other for the state, nor that the ultimate test of right action is not the same for the one as for the other. A very distinct ethical problem is involved in the question of the apportionment of taxes: *viz.*, what is the duty of the state in the matter? Moreover, there is only one kind of moral obligation, and the same test of right action, whatever that test may be, must be applied in determining the duties of both the individual and the state. But even when a general principle of obligation has been agreed upon, no one is in a position to decide upon the specific duty of either the individual or the state until he knows what would be the general consequences of their various possible acts. Recognizing that each act is, for his purposes, the first link in a chain of causation, he must be able to trace that chain from its initial act to its general results before he can tell whether or not the act in question conforms to his general principle. As applied to taxation, for example, he must know how the effort to collect a certain tax will affect industries and morals and other social interests before he can say whether the state, in levying the tax, would be acting in harmony with the general principle of obligation agreed upon. If, to be more specific, he should find that the attempt to collect a certain tax would discourage certain desirable industries and commendable enterprises, that would be at least a partial reason for condemning it. That is to say, if the industry which is suppressed meets the test of the ethical principle, the tax which suppresses that industry cannot possibly meet the same test.

The question of the general principle of obligation lies so far outside the field of economics that one may be justified in borrowing such a principle ready made from the moral philosophers. Let us therefore accept, for purposes of this discussion, the principle of utility, and assume that the state, as well as the individual, ought to promote the general welfare — or the greatest good to the greatest number. How can the state promote the general welfare in the matter of taxation? In discussing the duty of the state the present writer cherishes no illusions as to the nature of the state. Realizing that the state is merely an abstraction, a convenient name for certain forms of joint action on the part of a multitude of individuals, and that the state can have no duties separate and apart from those of the individuals who compose it, yet the duty of the individual in imposing his will upon other individuals through legislation is so distinct from his duty in other matters that it is much more convenient, and fully as accurate, to speak of the former class of duties as if they belonged to the state itself.

The question of the duty of the state in matters of taxation is, of course, to be kept distinct from the question of its duty in the expenditure of revenue after it is raised. By the expenditure of a given revenue the state may, in various ways, add positively to the general welfare. But it may not be so obvious how the state can, in merely collecting revenue, promote the general welfare. There are certain ways of collecting revenue which are generally believed, and no doubt correctly, positively to promote well-being. When, for example, a tax or a license suppresses or holds in check an industry which is regarded as more or less deleterious, such a tax or license meets the utilitarian test, and is justified only because it meets that test. Writers on taxation generally, even those who uphold the benefit theory or the faculty theory, accept this as a justification, even though it does not conform to their special canon of justice. But if the general utilitarian principle, or the general welfare argument, can, in this special case, override their special canon, why may it not in other cases as well? It is at least an admission that the general utilitarian test is a more fundamental test than that of their special canon. If so, the more fundamental test ought to be applied in all cases.

While, as already suggested, there are certain taxes whose collection adds to the public welfare by suppressing undesirable industries, yet, generally speaking, the collection of a tax is in itself an evil. It is the cost which we have to undergo for the advantages which may be secured by means of the revenue after it is collected. Since a tax is, speaking thus generally, an evil, a burden, a sacrifice imposed, it is obvious that the utilitarian principle requires that that evil, that burden, that sacrifice, shall be as small as possible in proportion to the revenue secured. When the taxes are so levied and collected as to impose the minimum of sacrifice, and the revenue so expended as to confer the maximum of advantage, or when the surplus of advantage over sacrifice, of good over evil, is at its maximum, the state has fulfilled its obligation completely: it has met the utilitarian test.

If it is once admitted that the state's obligation in the matter of taxation is to be determined on the basis of a broad principle of public utility, then it is apparent that the argument in favor of either the benefit theory or the faculty theory must be reconstructed. Instead of basing the argument upon the duty of the individual, as is usually done,[1] the upholder of either of these theories must show that if the state should apportion taxes according to benefits received, in the one case, or according to ability to contribute, in the other, such apportionment would impose the least burden, all things considered. This is possibly the subconscious basis of the arguments of those writers who have championed either of these theories, but it does not seem to have been explicitly recognized by any of them. The champion of the faculty theory, for example, may conceivably have reasoned somewhat as follows :

Major Premise. The burdens of taxation ought to be so distributed as to involve the least possible sacrifice on the part of the community as a whole.

Minor Premise. When each individual contributes in proportion to his ability, the whole burden of taxation is most easily borne — *i.e.,* with the minimum of sacrifice.

Conclusion. It is the individual's duty so to contribute.

Granting the premises, the conclusion follows as a matter of course, so far as the individual's duty is concerned ; but, as we shall see later, the minor premise is not sound, and, as we have already seen, the conclusion is not conclusive so far as the duty of the state is concerned. For, whatever might be true if all men were willing to contribute according to their ability, the fact is that they are not willing so to do. Being unwilling, they will resort to various methods of avoiding such contribution. The attempt of the state to compel them to contribute according to their ability will not be without injurious results : it will cause various changes in the direction of business enterprise. One of the ways of avoiding the necessity of paying a tax is to avoid the occasion which the assessor, acting under the law, seizes upon as a pretext for collecting a sum of money. If, for example, the possession of a certain kind of property is such an occasion, men will tend, within certain limits, to avoid the possession of that kind of property. In so far as men generally try to avoid the possession of such property, or to avoid the other occasions for which the assessor is on the look-out, in so far is industry and enterprise disturbed and readjusted. These disturbances and readjustments may be more or less injurious, or more or less beneficial. If some taxes are to be approved because they repress certain

[1] If such is not the argument, then the leading expounders of these theories are at least guilty of inaccurately expressing their views.

undesirable industries, others must on the same reasoning, be condemned because they repress desirable industries. Since almost every tax has some effect in determining the direction of business enterprise, it is obvious that such considerations must enter into the determination of the duty of the state. The matter is therefore not settled when we have found out what the individual ought to do.

By an argument precisely similar to, though somewhat sounder than, that in favor of the faculty theory of taxation, the socialist could support his claim that the state ought to assume the direction of all industry and apportion to each individual his work and his income.

Major Premise. The individual ought to work for the economic welfare of the whole people.

Minor Premise. If each individual would voluntarily work according to his ability and consume according to his needs, the economic welfare would be promoted in the highest degree.

Conclusion. It is the duty of every individual to produce according to his ability and consume according to his needs.

Both the premises are probably sound, and, if so, the conclusion follows as a matter of course; but like the former argument it is inconclusive when applied to the question in hand, which is: What ought the *state* to do? This question is complicated in both cases by the fact that individuals are not willing to do what the conclusion points out as their logical duty, and will therefore adopt methods of avoiding such necessity if the state should attempt to impose it upon them. Such an attempt would therefore produce unlooked for, and, it is generally conceded, highly undesirable consequences. All this amounts to saying that it is not the duty of the state to try to do anything which it cannot accomplish, or in trying to accomplish which it would work mischief. What is here affirmed regarding the state is equally true of individuals. It is, for example, in the opinion of the present writer, highly desirable that all who read this discussion should agree with its conclusions, but even he does not consider it any one's duty to try to force them to do so — for the simple and only reason that such an attempt could never succeed, or if it did, it would produce other results more undesirable even than disagreement.

McCulloch alone among the leading writers on taxation seems to have grasped this fundamental truth, when he wrote:

It would, no doubt, be in various respects desirable that the inhabitants of a country should contribute to the support of its government in proportion to their means. This is obviously, however, a matter of secondary importance. It is the business of the

legislator to look at the practical influence of different taxes, and
to resort in preference to those by which the revenue may be raised
with the least inconvenience. Should the taxes least adverse to the
public interests fall on the contributors according to their respective abilities, it will be an additional recommendation in their
favor. But the *salus populi* is in this, as it should be in every
similar matter, the prime consideration ; and the tax which is best
fitted to promote, or least opposed to, this great end, though it may
not press quite equally on different orders of society, is to be preferred to a more equal but otherwise less advantageous tax. . .
The distinguishing characteristic of the best tax is, not that it is
most nearly proportioned to the means of individuals, but that it
is easily assessed and collected, and is, at the same time, most conducive, all things considered, to the public interests.[2]

Far from ignoring all ethical considerations, as Bastable suggests,[3] this is a distinct recognition of an ethical principle more
definite and more fundamental than any which Bastable himself recognizes in his discussion, or shows any signs of being
aware of.

Leaving out of consideration for the present all benefits
which the levying and collecting of a tax may confer, such
as the suppression of an undesirable industry or the deepen-
ing of the taxpayer's interest in the affairs of the state, let us
turn our attention to the sacrifices involved. There is, of
course, to be considered the direct sacrifice on the part of him
who pays a tax. Having his income curtailed by the amount
of the tax, his power to consume, or to enjoy the use of wealth,
is correspondingly reduced. This form of sacrifice is the most
prominent, and has, naturally enough, generally appealed most
strongly to writers on taxation. But there is also another form
of sacrifice quite as important and fully as worthy of attention.
Any tax which represses a desirable industry or form of activity not only imposes a sacrifice on him who pays it, but also
upon those who are deprived of the services or the products
of the repressed industry. Taxes should therefore be apportioned in such a way as to impose the smallest sum total of
sacrifice of these two kinds.

While it is essential that both forms of sacrifice should be
considered before reaching any final conclusion as to the best
system of taxation, nevertheless the preliminary discussion may
be facilitated by first considering them separately. If one were
to consider only the first and more direct form of sacrifice,
with a view to determining how the total sacrifice of this kind
could be reduced to a minimum, he would be driven to con-

2 *Taxation and the Funding System,* London, 1845, p. 19.
3 *Public Finance,* London and N. Y., 1895, p. 314.

clude in favor of a highly progressive rate of taxation on incomes, with a somewhat higher rate on incomes derived from more permanent sources, such as secure investments, than upon incomes from insecure sources, such as salaries. From the gross income which comes to him in the form of a salary, the receiver must make certain deductions in the way of insurance premiums, *e.g.,* to provide for the future, before he is on a level, in point of well being, with one whose net income comes to him from a permanent investment. The man with a salary of five thousand dollars would be no better off than another with an income of four thousand from a permanent investment, if the former would have to spend one thousand dollars of his salary in life insurance premiums in order to provide as well for his family as the latter's family would be provided for by the investment itself. Under these conditions, the sacrifice involved in the payment of an equal amount to the state would be equal, though the nominal incomes are unequal.

Leaving such matters out of consideration, a highly progressive rate of taxation would be necessary in order to secure the minimum of sacrifice, and for the following reasons. In the first place, a dollar is worth less, generally speaking, to a man with a large income than to a man with a small income, and a dollar taken from the former imposes a smaller sacrifice than a dollar taken from the latter. Moreover, if after the first dollar is taken from the first man, his income is still greater than that of the second man, the taking of a second dollar will occasion him less sacrifice than would the taking of a first dollar from the second man ; so that if only two dollars were to be raised, they should both be taken from the first man. Applying this principle rigorously, we should continue taxing the largest income until it was reduced to such a level that the last dollar of the remaining income was worth as much to its owner as the last dollar of the next largest income is worth to its owner, and then only should we begin to tax the latter at all. Then the two should be taxed until they were reduced to a similar level with respect to the third largest, before the third largest is taxed at all, and so on until a sufficient revenue is raised.[4]

Such an application of the principle involves the assumption that wants are equal, which, though obviously not true, approximates more nearly to the truth than any other working

[4] For a fuller discussion of this point, see an article by the present writer on "The Ethical Basis of Distribution and its Application to Taxation," in *The Annals of the American Academy of Political and Social Science,* July, 1895.

assumption that could possibly be invented. Since the state must collect a revenue, it must have some definite assumption upon which it can proceed. The question is not, therefore, whether men's wants are equal, but whether there is any rule of inequality of wants upon which the apportionment of taxes could be made with a nearer approximation to the truth. If there be such a rule, it has not yet been discovered. To assume, for example, that the man whose income is greater than five thousand has correspondingly greater wants than the man whose income is less than five thousand, would be obviously unsafe, because there are even chances that the opposite would be true. Where the chances are even on both sides, it is safer to assume equality. Of a given number of men of the same age and the same general standard of health (by way of illustration) it is obviously untrue to assume that they will all live the same number of years, yet it is nearer the truth to assume that than any other definite workable principle. Consequently the life-insurance company acts justly when it assumes that they will live the same number of years, and apportions their premiums accordingly.

This in no way ignores the fact that wants expand with the opportunity of gratifying them. This objection, however, could only apply at the time when the tax was first imposed. At such a time it would doubtless be true that the five thousandth dollar taken from a man with an income of ten thousand would occasion him a greater sacrifice than the taking of the first dollar from an income of five thousand dollars would occasion its owner. But the reasons for this are twofold. In the first place, by taxing the first man so heavily the state would be depriving him of so many things which he was accustomed to enjoying that by the time the five thousandth dollar was reached, the taking of each particular dollar would be keenly felt. The last dollar of his remaining income would represent a greater utility to him than would the last dollar of the five thousand dollar income to its owner. In the second place, by taxing the second man so lightly as compared with his present taxes, the state would be allowing him to consume some things to which he had not become accustomed. The taking of the particular dollar in question would not involve a very high sacrifice, for the reason that it would deprive him only of some enjoyment which had not yet entered into his standard of living. But both these reasons would disappear after the new tax had been in operation for a generation, or long enough to bring the standards of living of the two men to the same level.

Drastic as this method of taxation would be, yet, the writer contends, this is the method which would be logically forced upon us if we should adopt the utilitarian test, and should, in applying it, have regard only to the direct sacrifice on the part of those who pay the taxes, ignoring the indirect forms of sacrifice which a system of taxation inevitably imposes. J. S. Mill, who advocated equality of sacrifice as the rule of justice in taxation, was guilty of faulty reasoning on this point, doubtless because he had not made the analysis which subsequent writers have made into the nature of wants and their satisfaction. He was too good a utilitarian to advocate equality of sacrifice if he did not believe that it would involve the least sacrifice on the whole. This is shown by the following quotation, the italics of which are mine.

For what reason ought equality to be the rule in matters of taxation? For the reason that it ought to be so in all affairs of government. As a government ought to make no distinction of persons or classes in the strength of their claims on it, whatever sacrifice it requires from them should be made to bear as nearly as possible with the same pressure upon all, *which, it must be observed, is the mode by which the least sacrifice is occasioned on the whole.* If any one bears less than his fair share of the burden, some other person must suffer more than his share, and the alleviation to the one is not, *caeteris paribus,* so great a good to him, as the increased pressure upon another is an evil.[5]

The last proposition in the above quotation would be true only of persons whose incomes were approximately equal. If A's income is twice as great as B's, or, to state it more accurately, if A's income were enough greater than B's so that a dollar is worth half as much to A as it is to B, then equality of sacrifice would be secured by making A pay twice as many dollars as B : by collecting $100, for example, from A and $50 from B. But the last dollar of A's remaining income would still be worth less to A than the last dollar of B's remaining income is worth to B : and the last dollar taken from A would occasion him less sacrifice than the last dollar taken from B has occasioned him. Then by taking more than $100, say $110, from A, and less than $50, say $40, from B the same revenue would be raised with a smaller sum total of sacrifice, for the gain to B by this change would be greater than the loss to A. This will appear at once to any one who at all understands the principle of marginal utility. The only conclusion one can draw is that the least sum total of direct sacrifice is secured, not by equality of sacrifice, but by equality of

5 *Principles of Political Economy*, bk. v, ch. ii, sec. 2.

marginal sacrifice. Equality of marginal sacrifice would be secured by so apportioning taxes that, as a general rule, the last dollar collected from one man should impose the same sacrifice as the last dollar collected from any other man, though the total amount collected from each man might impose very unequal total sacrifices.

We are now in a position to test the validity of the minor premise . . . *viz.,* if each individual would voluntarily contribute in proportion to his ability, the whole burden of taxation could be most easily borne — *i.e.,* with the minimum of sacrifice. If one's ability is assumed to be measured by one's income, real and potential, and to vary with that income, then the minimum of sacrifice would not be secured by each one's paying according to his ability. If the rich would volunteer to pay more than in proportion to their ability, allow‚ ing the poor to pay less than in proportion to their ability, the burden would be more easily borne — *i.e.,* with less sacrifice — than if all should pay proportionally. As a statement of individual obligation, even, the faculty theory is untenable, unless modified and defined more rigidly than has yet been done. From the strictly utilitarian standpoint, the individual who measures his obligation to society by his total income is less to be commended than the individual who determines whether he has fulfilled his social obligations by considering, not how much he has given, but how much he has left. The latter type of individual is well illustrated by the example of that religious and philanthropic leader who found, early in life, that he could live in comfort and maintain his maximum efficiency by the expenditure of a certain small income. Later in life, as his income increased, he continued living on his earlier income, devoting all his surplus to the service of society. This is mentioned merely by way of further elucidation of the proposition that if there were no indirect consequences of the attempt to collect taxes, the utilitarian test would require an enormously high rate of progression in the apportionment of taxes, and that, if the state were able to apportion and collect taxes on this basis, it would only be making individuals do what they ought to do voluntarily.

But there are indirect results, the most important of which is, as already pointed out, the repression of certain desirable industries and enterprises. The importance of this consideration becomes apparent when we reflect on the probable consequence of a system of taxation so drastically progressive as that suggested above. If a large share of one's income above a certain sum should be seized by the tax collector, it would tend to discourage the effort to increase one's income beyond that sum. In so far as this reduced the energy of the individual in business or professional life, the community would be deprived of his services. This deprivation would be a burden on the people, all the more regrettable because it would not enrich the public treasury in the least.[6]

Such considerations become still more important when we come to the discussion of various forms of taxation, especially the taxation of various kinds of property. Since different kinds of property come into existence in different ways, taxes must affect them differently. A kind of property which is produced by labor, or comes into being as the result of enterprise, may be very seriously affected by a tax. Tax the makers of it and they will be less willing to make it. Tax the owners or users of it and they will be less willing to own or to use it. They will therefore pay less for it, and thus discourage the makers of it as effectively as if the latter had to pay the tax themselves. In either case, there will be less of that kind of property made and used, and some members of the community who would otherwise have enjoyed the use of it will now be deprived of that use. This is a burden to them, and, moreover, a burden which in no way adds revenue to the state. Such a tax is repressive. On the other hand, a kind of property whose existence does not depend upon individual labor or enterprise, will be less affected by a tax. Tax the owner of a piece of land, and, while you make him less anxious to own it, you will not cause him to abandon it. While you lower its price, you do not reduce the amount of land nor deprive the community of the use and enjoyment of anything which it would otherwise have had. Such a tax is not repressive.

As a general proposition, it is safe to say that, other things equal, a tax which represses desirable enterprises or activities, and thus deprives the community of the use and enjoyment of certain desirable goods, is more burdensome in proportion to the revenue raised than a tax which does not entail such results. In other words, a repressive tax is more burdensome than a non-repressive tax. A proposition much more to the point is that a tax on any form of property or income which comes into being as the result of the productive industry or enterprise of its owner is more repressive than a tax on any form of property or income which does not so come into being. By productive industry and enterprise is meant such

6 See also Ross, "A New Canon of Taxation," *Political Science Quarterly*, vii, p. 585.

industry and enterprise as adds something in the way of utility to the community, and not such as merely costs something to its possessor. Skill in buying land may cost as much study and care as skill in making shoes; but, whereas those who exercise the latter kind of skill increase the number of shoes, it has never been shown that those who exercise the former kind add anything whatever to the community's stock of useful goods. Tax shoe factories and, in so far as it represses the industry, the community will have fewer shoes. Tax the land and the community will not have less of anything than it would have without the tax. What is said of a tax on land could also be said, within limits, of a tax on inheritances. From the standpoint of non-repressive taxation, therefore, both the land tax and the inheritance tax have much to be said in their favor.

Any one who is familiar with the subject of the shifting and incidence of taxation will see at once that there is a close connection between the repressive effects of a tax and the shifting of it. A tax can be shifted, generally speaking, only when it affects the demand for, or the supply of, and consequently the value of, the thing taxed. The more easily a tax affects the supply or demand, the more easily it is shifted. A tax which does either of these things is repressive: it affects supply by repressing production; it affects demand by repressing consumption. A careful analysis of the conditions under which taxes may be shifted is, therefore, very much to be desired.[7] Such an analysis would enable us to form conclusions as to the repressive or non-repressive effects of various taxes.†

As applied to incomes in general, without regard to their source, a progressive, even a highly progressive, tax will occasion, on the whole, less direct sacrifice to the taxpayers than a proportional tax. A progressive tax is therefore to be commended, unless the rate of progression is made so high as to discourage the receivers of large incomes from trying to increase them. If the rate of progression is so high as this, the indirect form of sacrifice, growing out of the repressive effects of the tax, will counteract, wholly or in part, the reduction in the direct form of sacrifice. A moderately progressive income tax would, therefore, seem to be more desirable than a proportional one. But as between different kinds of income and different kinds of property, the preference should be given

---

7 For an attempt in this direction, see the present writer's article on "The Shifting of Taxes," *Yale Review*, 1896. See also Seligman's *Shifting and Incidence of Taxation* for a brilliant survey of the earlier attempts.

† Eds. Note: Such an analysis is given in Chap. IX of this volume.

to those taxes which fall upon natural products, such as land, rather than upon produced goods, and upon increments of wealth which come to an individual through natural causes over which he has no control — inheritances, for instance — rather than upon incomes earned by the individuals themselves. Such taxes are less repressive than most other special forms of taxation, and therefore occasion less sacrifice of the indirect kind.

8. CANONS OF TAXATION *

IN order to evalute specific sources of public revenue or a revenue system as a whole, it is necessary first of all to set up certain standards. It is highly important to evaluate the various fiscal devices as separate units, and it is also imperative that these units be welded together into a system which will function smoothly. It is unreasonable to expect each separate form of revenue to meet every requisite of a good revenue system. Opposition may arise between two or more requisites or canons, e.g., productivity and equity, in the appraisal of a particular source of revenue. The possibility of such a conflict emphasizes the necessity for viewing the revenue system as a whole. A shortcoming in one form of revenue may be offset by a point of strength in another, thereby allowing each to play an important and useful rôle in the system as a unit.

If useful application of the canons of revenue is to be made, the canons themselves must be founded on ideals possible of attainment.[1] Alfred Marshall wrote of the desirability of nourishing ideals in one's heart, but added that one's thought and action must be occupied mainly with the actual, and warned against the temptation to make short cuts to the ideal.[2] A visionary approach cannot result in an objective evaluation of the sources of public revenue.

A reference to canons of revenue brings to the mind of the student of fiscal science the celebrated maxims sets forth in Adam Smith's *Wealth of Nations*, namely, *equity, certainty, convenience,* and *economy.* These maxims bear repetition in full, because modern students of taxation may find in them

---

* By the editors.

[1] In the appraisal of an actual revenue system, e.g., that of a particular American Commonwealth, it is necessary to attach a specific meaning to each canon which is used in the evaluation. This and other problems involved in the appraisal of present and certain potential sources of revenue in terms of selected canons are treated in detail in a study by C. W. Macy entitled, *An Evaluation of Sources of Public Revenue in Iowa,* a doctoral dissertation, Stanford University, 1932.

[2] See *Memorials of Alfred Marshall,* edited by A. C. Pigou, p. 84.

some cardinal principles appropriate for use in solving modern revenue riddles.

(1). The subjects of every state ought to contribute towards the support of the government, as nearly as possible, in proportion to their respective abilities; that is, in proportion to the revenue which they respectively enjoy under the protection of the state. The expense of government to the individuals of a great nation, is like the expense of management to the joint tenants of a great estate, who are all obliged to contribute in proportion to their respective interests in the estate. In the observation or neglect of this maxim consists, what is called the equality or inequality of taxation. Every tax, it must be observed once for all, which falls finally upon one only of the three sorts of revenue [rent, wages, and profits], is necessarily unequal, in so far as it does not affect the other two. In the following examination of different taxes I shall seldom take much further notice of this sort of inequality, but shall, in most cases, confine my observations to that inequality which is occasioned by a particular tax falling unequally even upon that particular sort of private revenue which is affected by it.

(2). The tax which each individual is bound to pay ought to be certain, and not arbitrary. The time of payment, the manner of payment, the quantity to be paid, ought all to be clear and plain to the contributor, and to every other person. Where it is otherwise, every person subject to the tax is put more or less in the power of the tax-gatherer, who can either aggravate the tax upon any obnoxious contributor, or extort, by the terror of such aggravation, some present or perquisite to himself. The uncertainty of taxation encourages the insolence and favours the corruption of an order of men who are naturally unpopular, even where they are neither insolent nor corrupt. The certainty of what each individual ought to pay is, in taxation, a matter of so great importance, that a very considerable degree of inequality, it appears, I believe, from the experience of all nations, is not near so great an evil as a very small degree of uncertainty.

(3). Every tax ought to be levied at the time, or in the manner, in which it is most likely to be convenient for the contributor to pay it. A tax upon the rent of land or of houses, payable at the same term at which such rents are usually paid, is levied at the time when it is most likely to be convenient for the contributor to pay; or, when he is most likely to have wherewithal to pay. Taxes upon such consumable goods as are articles of luxury, are all finally paid by the consumer, and generally in a manner that is very convenient for him. He pays them by little and little, as he has occasion to buy the goods. As he is at liberty too, either to buy, or not to buy, as he pleases, it must be his own fault if he ever suffers any considerable inconveniency from such taxes.

(4). Every tax ought to be so contrived as both to take out and to keep out of the pockets of the people as little as possible, over and above what it brings into the public treasury of the state. A tax may either take out or keep out of the pockets of the people a great deal more than it brings into the public treasury, in the four following ways. First, the levying of it may require a great number of officers, whose salaries may eat up the greater part of the produce of the tax, and whose perquisites may impose another additional tax upon the people. Secondly, it may obstruct the industry of the people, and discourage them from applying to certain branches of business which might give maintenance and employment to great multitudes. While it obliges the people to pay, it may thus diminish, or perhaps destroy, some of the funds which might enable them more easily to do so.† Thirdly, by the forfeitures and other penalties which those unfortunate individuals incur who attempt unsuccessfully to evade the tax, it may frequently ruin them, and thereby put an end to the benefit which the community might have received from the employment of their capitals. An injudicious tax offers a great temptation to smuggling. But the penalties of smuggling must rise in proportion to the temptation. The law, contrary to all the ordinary principles of justice, first creates the temptation, and then punishes those who yield to it ; and it commonly enhances the punishment too in proportion to the very circumstance which ought certainly to alleviate it, the temptation to commit the crime. Fourthly, by subjecting the people to the frequent visits and the odious examination of the tax-gatherers, it may expose them to much unnecessary

† Eds. Note : In 1892, E. A. Ross presented what he termed a "new canon of taxation," namely, the canon of social economy, coördinate and complementary to that of administrative economy. "A tax for purposes of revenue," wrote Prof. Ross, "should have the least possible prohibitive effects." This conception of economy harmonized perfectly with that of Smith, and therefore was improperly called a *new* canon by Prof. Ross. (See E. A. Ross, "A New Canon of Taxation," *Political Science Quarterly*, Vol. VII, (Dec. 1892), pp. 585–597).

In this same connection. H. L. Lutz has written : "It is necessary, however, to take a somewhat broader view of the meaning of economy than that which is expressed in Smith's famous maxim. The economy of a tax must be judged not merely by the relative cost of administration, but as well by the economic effect of this tax on the taxpayer and on the community." (See his *Public Finance*, 2nd ed. p. 278.) However, a careful reading of Smith's discussion of economy reveals the same broad meaning of the term as suggested by Prof. Lutz.

trouble, vexation, and oppression; and though vexation is not, strictly speaking, expense, it is certainly equivalent to the expense at which every man would be willing to redeem himself from it. It is in some one or other of these four different ways that taxes are frequently so much more burdensome to the people than they are beneficial to the sovereign.[3]

Opinions of prominent writers in the field of public finance have differed widely with regard to the importance which should be attached to Smith's canons of taxation. For example, G. Findlay Shirras has written as follows: "These Smithian canons have rightly been regarded as classic. . . No genius . . . has succeeded in condensing the principles into such clear and simple canons as has Adam Smith." Furthermore, "his successors have not, to any material degree, improved on these principles or succeeded in displacing them from the position which they hold in the science of finance."[4] Jensen agrees that Smith's canons "have so far not been excelled;[5] and Bastable has stated that these maxims "have not been found inapplicable to modern conditions, and . . . bid fair to hold their ground in the future."[6]

Other writers, however, disagree with the above views, offering in their place scathing criticism of Smith's canons. As an example of this criticism, the following is quoted from Francis A. Walker: "A vast deal of importance has been assigned by English economists to these [Smith's] maxims. They have been quoted over and over again, as if they contained truths of great moment; yet if one examines them, he finds them, at the best, trivial; while the first and most famous of these cannot be subjected to the slightest test without going all to pieces."[7] In much the same manner, Cohn contended that Smith had merely advanced a collection of simple considerations of common sense such as would find their place in any tax discussion;[8] while Sir Josiah Stamp has said of Smith's canons: "Indisputable as these rules may be, they are now inadequate to the practical task of bringing under judgment the many difficult issues that confront us."[9]

Other critics of Smith attempt to belittle his discussion of taxation maxims by questioning the originality of his views. Though this type of criticism may have little bearing on mod-

[3] Adam Smith, *Wealth of Nations*, Vol. II, Bk. V, Chap. II, Pt. II, pp. 310–312. (Cannan's edition.)

[4] G. F. Shirras, *The Science of Public Finance*, p. 121.

[5] J. P. Jensen, *Problems of Public Finance*, p. 182.

[6] C. F. Bastable, *Public Finance*, p. 413.

[7] F. A. Walker, *Political Economy*, 3rd ed., p. 489.

[8] Gustav Cohn, *The Science of Finance*, p. 535. (Veblen's translation.)

[9] Sir Josiah Stamp, *The Fundamental Principles of Taxation*, p. 4.

ern fiscal problems, it is nevertheless of some interest to the academician and should not pass entirely unnoticed. Robert Jones claims to have found far more than a preshadowing of the maxims of Smith in the writings of Beaumont, Turgot, Verri, Steuart and others.[10] Edwin Cannan concurs in this general notion in words not complimentary to Smith when he states that the celebrated canons "are only four selected out of a larger aggregate number put forward by various writers whose works Smith had read, and it may well be doubted whether the selection was not as much a result of imperfect memory as of deliberate choice."[11] This latter criticism may be too harsh, although it is a well established fact that theories of taxation were seriously considered by many of Smith's predecessors. Though it must be admitted that the canons of taxation as presented in the *Wealth of Nations* were not entirely original with Smith, it is only fair to credit him with ingenuity in simplifying, condensing, and organizing existing knowledge on the subject into useful form. These canons, supplemented by those of productivity and elasticity, both implicit in Smith's discussion, constitute, in our opinion, the requisites of a good revenue system.

QUESTIONS AND PROBLEMS FOR DISCUSSION

1. What arguments, if any, can be advanced in favor of using taxation for non-fiscal purposes? Are such arguments "socialistic"?
2. The state of Iowa recently provided for the establishment of an emergency relief fund of $3,000,000. A portion of the proceeds from the state income and sales taxes is to be turned into this fund. Can this method of using taxation for wealth distribution be justified?
3. What is the social justification of taxes on "windfall wealth"?
4. Cite examples which show the application of the cost of service, the benefit, and the ability-to-pay principles of taxation.
5. Do you agree with the notion that "everyone ought to pay something" toward the support of the state?
6. Explain how the principle of diminishing utility is related to the argument for progressive taxation.
7. "All forms of surplus have a full ability to bear taxation." What is the meaning of "surplus"? Why is it able to bear taxation?
8. What is the relationship between progressive taxation and the principle of minimum sacrifice?
9. Of what practical importance, if any, are canons of taxation?

[10] Robert Jones, *The Nature and First Principle of Taxation*, p. 75.
[11] Edwin Cannan, "Review of the Fundamental Principles of Taxation" (Stamp), *Economic Journal*, Vol. XXXI, p. 349.

Do legislators commonly establish canons for purposes of evaluating actual and potential sources of revenue?

10. "There is a close relation between the shiftability of a tax and its repressive effects." Explain.

SUGGESTIONS FOR RESEARCH

1. Illustrations of progressive, proportional, and regressive taxation in the revenue system of some particular state.
2. An evaluation of one or more sources of revenue in some particular state in light of the canons suggested in this chapter.
3. An evaluation of the arguments which have been offered for and against progressive taxation.
4. The growth of sentiment in favor of progressive taxation.
5. The benefit versus the ability theory of taxation.
6. Popular (as distinct from academic or professional) fiscal theory.

BIBLIOGRAPHICAL NOTE

An excellent historical and critical study of the concepts of justice in taxation is S. F. Weston, *Principles of Justice in Taxation* (New York, 1903). Another study in which ideals in taxation are traced and briefly discussed is Robert Jones, *The Nature and First Principle of Taxation*, (London, 1914). The major portion of Jones' work is devoted to an explanation and defense of what he terms the first principle of taxation, namely, economy.

Discussions of the fiscal versus the non-fiscal purpose of taxation are presented in J. N. Leon, "Der Begriff der Steuer," *Finanz-Archiv*, Vol. XXXI, pp. 489-496; E. H. Vogel, "Grundsätzliches zur theoretischen Frage 'nichtfiskalischer Zwecksetzung' im der Besteuerung," *Finanz-Archiv*, Vol. XLVI, pp. 5-47; and H. A. Silverman, *Taxation, Its Incidence and Effects*, (London, 1931), Chap. I.

The important arguments for progressive taxation may be found in E. R. A. Seligman, *Progressive Taxation in Theory and Practice*, (Baltimore, 1908); H. A. Silverman, *op. cit.*, Chap. IV, Sec. 2; F. W. Taussig, *Principles of Economics*, (New York, 1921), Vol. II, Chap. LXVIII; Gustav Cassel, "The Theory of Progressive Taxation," *Economic Journal*, Vol. XI, pp. 469-480; Sir Sydney Chapman, "The Utility of Income and Progressive Taxation," *Economic Journal*, Vol. XXII, pp. 25-35; and R. F. Harrod, "Progressive Taxation and Equal Sacrifice," *Economic Journal*, Vol. XL, pp. 704-707.

For mathematical and statistical studies of the relation of diminishing utility to progressive taxation see Irving Fisher, "A Statistical Method for Measuring 'Marginal Utility' and Testing the Justice of a Progressive Income Tax," *Economic Essays in Honor of J. B. Clark*, (New York, 1927), pp. 157-193; F. Vinci, "L'utilita della moneta e l'imposta progressiva," *Riv. Itla. di Stat. Econ. e Finan.*, June, 1933; and Ragnar Frisch, *New Methods of Measuring Mar-*

ginal Utility, (Tübingen, 1932). A book which the editors have not yet seen but one in which, according to Professor Carl Shoup (review in Bull. of N. T. A., April, 1933), the theory of progressive taxation is subjected to a searching analysis is A. DeViti de Marco, *Grundlehren der Finanzwirtschaft*, (Tübingen, 1932). The case for proportional taxation is ably presented in C. F. Bastable, Public Finance, (London, 1917), Bk. III, Chap. III. An exposition and defense of the minimum sacrifice theory of taxation is given in F. Y. Edgeworth, "The Pure Theory of Taxation," *Economic Journal*, Vol. VII, pp. 46-70; 226-238; 550-571; also his "The Subjective Element in the First Principle of Taxation," *Quarterly Journal of Economics*, Vol. XXIV, pp. 459-470. Least aggregate sacrifice and equal sacrifice theories are presented in A. C. Pigou, *A Study in Public Finance*, (London, 1928), Pt. II, Chaps. I, IV, V, VII. In J. S. Nicholson, *Principles of Political Economy*, (London, 1897), Vol. III, p. 270 et. seq., the equal sacrifice theory is defended.

General discussions of canons of taxation are accessible in standard text books in the field of public finance, for example, C. F. Bastable, *op. cit.*, Bk. III, Chap. VII; and G. F. Shirras, *The Science of Public Finance*, (London, 1925), Chap. XIV. Specific canons are treated in greater detail in Edwin Cannan, "Equity and Economy in Taxation," *Economic Journal*, Vol. XI, pp. 469-480; C. F. Bastable, "The Rule of Taxation for Revenue as a Canon of Public Finance," *Economic Journal*, Vol. XIII, pp. 505-510; F. A. Walker, "The Bases of Taxation," *Political Science Quarterly*, Vol. III, pp. 1-16; and H. A. Silverman, *op. cit.*, Chap. IV, Secs. 1, 3. The latter volume considers the relative merits of the ability and benefit theories of taxation. A succinct and excellent statement of the case for the ability theory is in Gustav Cohn, *The Science of Finance*, (Chicago, 1895), p. 297 et. seq. (Veblen's translation).

A stimulating and cynical discussion of ideals in taxation is T. S. Adams, "Ideals and Idealism in Taxation," *American Economic Review*, Vol. XVIII, pp. 1-8.

For a discussion of an ideal tax system, see Gerhard Colm, "The Ideal Tax System," *Social Research*, Vol. I, pp. 319-342.

CHAPTER IX

THE SHIFTING AND INCIDENCE OF TAXES

1. CLARIFICATION OF CONCEPTS *

THE problem of the incidence of taxation is one of the most neglected, as it is one of the most complicated, subjects in economic science. It has indeed been treated by many writers; but its discussion in scientific literature, as well as in everyday life, has frequently been marked by what Parieu calls the "simplicity of ignorance." Yet no topic in public finance is more important; for, in every system of taxation, the cardinal point is its influence on the community. Without a correct analysis of the incidence of a tax, no proper opinion can be formed as to its actual effect or its justice. It is, therefore, time for an attempt to be made not only to pass in review the theories hitherto advanced, but to contribute to the solution of some of the theoretic problems while paying special attention to the practical aspects of the discussion.

A word first as to the terminology. In the process of taxing, we must distinguish three conceptions. First, a tax may be imposed on some person; secondly, it may be transferred by him to a second person; thirdly, it may be ultimately borne by this second person or transferred to others by whom it is finally assumed. Thus the person who originally pays the tax may not be the one who bears its burden in last instance. The process of the transfer of a tax is known as the *shifting* of the tax, while the settlement of the burden on the ultimate taxpayer is called the *incidence* of the tax. The incidence of the tax is therefore the result of the shifting, and the real economic problem lies in the nature of the shiftings.

The English fiscal language is somewhat deficient in its nomenclature. While *incidence* conveys to the mind the notion of the ultimate result of the shifting, we have no word in common use to express the immediate result of the original imposition of the tax. "Assessment" of the tax looks upon

* From E. R. A. Seligman, *The Shifting and Incidence of Taxation*, (Columbia University Press, New York, 1927), Introduction.

the process from above downward; but what we need is a term to characterize the processes as seen from below upward. The French and the Italians have the words, *percussion, percussione,* to express this idea of the primary result of the assessment. They, therefore, logically term the shifting of the tax *repercussion*[1] of taxation, the ultimate result of which is the incidence (*incidence, incidenza*).

The English term which best expresses this idea is "impact." We occasionally speak of a tax "impinging" on somebody or something, so that the "impact" of a tax would denote the act of impinging. Moreover, we ordinarily refer to the impact of a projectile in this very sense. The impact of a tax is therefore the immediate result of the imposition of a tax on the person who pays it in first instance. It corresponds to what is often, but erroneously, called the "original incidence" or the "primary incidence" of a tax. There is but one kind of incidence, namely the ultimate incidence, which emerges only when the tax finally settles, or comes to rest, on the person who bears it. We thus have the three distinct conceptions — the impact, the shifting, and the incidence of a tax, which correspond respectively to the imposition, the transfer, and the settling, or coming to rest, of the tax. The impact is the initial phenomenon, the shifting is the intermediate process, the incidence is the result. To confuse the impact with the incidence is as reprehensible as to confound the incidence with the shifting.

Strictly speaking, the impact of a tax includes not only the immediate result of the original imposition, but also the subsequent impinging of a tax on a person who is not the tax-bearer. Thus if a tax is imposed on A, shifted to B, and then again shifted to C, who finally bears the tax, we can properly speak of the impact of the tax first on A and then on B. The impact is transferred or repeated. It is only when the taxpayer is at the same time the tax-bearer that the impact is immediately followed by, or converted into, the incidence. For a similar reason, when the initial taxpayer is also the tax-bearer, the impact of the tax is at once followed by the incidence, without any intermediate process of shifting. But in all cases incidence signifies the result, while shifting, if there is any, denotes the process.

The point to be emphasized is that through the process of shifting, the taxpayer escapes the burden of the tax. There are, however, other methods of escape, which must not be con-

---

[1] They also use the words *translation, traslazione,* which are the same as our "transference" or "shifting." The French also speak of taxes being "rejetés," our "thrown off" or "shifted."

fused with shifting. It is here that both the analysis and the nomenclature of the subject have been exceedingly defective.[2] Let us endeavor to clear up the matter and to suggest what may possibly be deemed worthy of acceptance as the definitive nomenclature.

Whenever there is a shifting of taxation, the tax may be shifted forward or backward. Thus a producer, upon whom a tax has been assessed, may shift it to the consumer, or a seller may shift it to the purchaser. The tax is shifted forward to the consumer or the purchaser respectively. On the other hand, the tax may be imposed in first instance on the consumer or the purchaser, and may be shifted by him to the producer or the vendor respectively. In this case the tax is shifted backward. Finally, when the tax is shifted from the seller to an intermediate purchaser, who then sells to another person, and so on until the tax finally settles on the ultimate purchaser or consumer, we speak of the tax being shifted onward. Taxes, therefore, may be shifted forward, backward, or onward.[3]

To be contrasted, in part at all events, with the shifting of taxation is the capitalization or the amortization of taxation. The chief feature of this phenomenon[4] . . . is the fact that under certain circumstances the purchaser of a taxable object, by cutting down the purchase price, discounts all the taxes which he may be called upon to pay in the future. If, for instance, the ordinary return on investments in securities is five per cent and a tax of one per cent is imposed on a particular kind of corporate bonds selling at par, the price of these bonds will fall from par to eighty. The tax will be amortized or discounted through a depreciation of the capital value of the bonds by a sum equal to the capitalized value of the tax. The new purchaser thus escapes the tax which he is compelled to pay to the government by giving so much less for the bonds.

The few writers who have discussed this phenomenon generally consider capitalization to be a kind of shifting. In a

---

[2] The English and the French writers have done virtually nothing to clear up the confusion. The Germans have done a little, but only a little. More has been accomplished by the Italians, especially by Maffeo Pantaleoni, *Teoria della Traslazione dei Tributi,* 1882, and more recently by Fabrizio Natoli, *Studi su gli Effetti Economici dell' Imposta,* 1909. But their analysis also is not entirely free from objection.

[3] The Germans, since the time of von Hock, in 1863, have been accustomed to these conceptions, which they designate by the terms *Fortwälzung, Ruckwälzung,* and *Weiterwälzung,*—all of them subdivisions of shifting or *Ueberwälzung.*

[4] See Part II, chap. i, § 1 [of Seligman's *Shifting and Incidence of Taxation*].

certain sense, indeed, there is a seeming justification for this view. For the purchaser escapes the tax by throwing it off, or shifting it backward, on the seller. In reality, however, a distinction ought to be observed between shifting and capitalization. Shifting implies a process applicable to a single tax or to a tax each time that it is imposed; capitalization implies a process applicable to a whole series of taxes and takes place *before* any of them, with the exception of the first, is paid. In the case of a dealer who shifts a tax on a commodity back to the producer, the process takes place each time that the tax is levied, and the producer reduces the selling price each time by the amount of the tax. In the case of capitalization the purchaser indeed pays the tax, but the initial possessor or vendor reduces the price by a sum equal to all the future taxes which the purchaser expects to be called upon to pay. In the one case we have the shifting back of a single tax; in the other case we have the throwing back of a whole series of taxes at once. For capitalization implies a change in price equal to the capital value of all anticipated payments. There is, therefore, a marked distinction between shifting and capitalization. If a tax is shifted, it cannot be capitalized; if a tax is capitalized, it cannot be shifted. A tax on houses, for instance . . . if imposed on the tenant, may possibly be shifted back to the owner, but cannot be capitalized; a tax on land, imposed on the tenant, may be capitalized without being shifted to the present owner. Shifting and capitalization are in reality opposite, not complementary, conceptions.

In the case of both shifting and capitalization, however, the taxpayer escapes the burden of the tax through the mediation of the process of exchange. Without the purchase and the sale of the commodity there can be neither shifting nor capitalization. There is, however, a third method of escape possible, which is based not upon exchange, but upon production. Let us take, for instance, the case of a tax imposed either upon a finished commodity or upon the process of producing the commodity. It is possible, under certain circumstances, that the producer, fearing the loss of his market if he should add the tax to the price, will pay the tax and endeavor to recoup himself by so improving the process of production as to succeed in turning out his units of product at a lower cost. In such a case the loss occasioned by the tax may be offset, or perhaps even more than offset, by the gains resulting from the economies of production.

What shall we call such a phenomenon? The Germans term it the "throwing-off" (Abwälzung), while the Italians call it the "rejection" or the "removal" of the tax.[5] All these terms, however, are ill-chosen, because there is nothing distinctive in them. If a tax is shifted, it is also thrown off or removed from the taxpayer. We venture, therefore, to suggest for this phenomenon the term "transformation of taxation." For by virtue of its operation the loss due to the tax is, or may be, transformed into a gain : the tax is transformed into its opposite. The attribute of removal or throwing-off ("rejection") of the tax is common to all three methods of escape — shifting, capitalization, and transformation ; but the attribute of the conversion of loss into gain is found only in the case of transformation.

Whether there is any such phenomenon as the transformation of taxation has sometimes been questioned. The discussion is at least as old as the time of Hume, and has usually been associated with the query as to whether taxes can act as a spur to industry. As a broad generalization, the assertion is indeed open to grave doubt, for taxes on industry must indubitably be regarded on the whole as a drag or burden on industry, rather than as a spur to industry. But while it is doubtless true that under a régime of free competition the quest for profits will impel the individual to make the best use of his opportunities, it is none the less a fact that there have frequently been cases where the attention of the producer was first directed to the possibility of improving the productive process by some new burden which started a whole branch of industry out of its comparative lethargy and caused it to forsake the old rut. Take, for instance, the familiar example of the eighteenth-century Scotch tax on the whiskey distillery which led to such improvements in the process that for a time at least the distillers succeeded in transforming the loss into a gain ; or the case of the European continental tax on beet sugar in the nineteenth century, the burden of which admittedly first directed the attention of the producers to the possibility of reducing the cost of extracting the sugar from the beets. It may be true that the improvements would probably have come about of themselves after a time ; but this does not invalidate the accuracy of the contention that a tax may be the occasion, even if it be not the cause, of a betterment in production. Whenever we find such a phenomenon, we are in the presence

---

[5] The term *Abwälzung* is found first in von Hock, *Die öffentlichen Abgaben und Schulden*, 1863, although the phenomenon itself had previously been described by Rau. Pantaleoni, *op. cit.*, p. 28, calls it *rigetto dell' imposta ;* Natoli, *op. cit.*, p. 22, calls it *remozione dell' imposta ;* Tenerelli, *L'Azione delle Imposte Indirette sui consumi*, 1898, p. 67, calls it *rimozione dell' imposta.*

of the transformation of a tax—the transformation from loss into possible gain.

The literature of finance, however, has thus far failed to put the transformation of taxation into its proper place. Some writers confuse transformation with shifting,[6] whereas, as we are now aware, the two conceptions are entirely distinct. In the case of shifting, the tax is thrown off the taxpayer and settles upon the final tax-bearer. The incidence is on some one else than the original taxpayer. In the case of transformation, on the contrary, the incidence is on the original taxpayer. He escapes, not by a shifting of the tax, but by a transformation of the tax. Transformation depends upon incidence and is a reaction from the incidence. If there is no incidence, there can be no transformation. But if there is a shifting, there can obviously be no incidence on the original taxpayer. Transformation and shifting are hence opposites.

Others, again, confuse transformation with evasion of taxation.[7] This phenomenon, however, as will be seen immediately below, is something entirely different. Others finally seek unduly to extend the sphere of transformation, and include under this phenomenon not only economies through improvements in production, but also savings through changes in consumption[8] which, as we shall see, properly come under a quite distinct head.

The transformation of taxation is therefore a method of escape from taxation which must be classed with shifting and capitalization. Shifting is the most common, capitalization somewhat less usual, transformation rather infrequent. While

---

[6] This is true especially of the Germans. Although von Hock was, as stated above, the first to speak of *Abwälzung*, subsequent writers used this as a general term, synonymous with *Ueberwälzung*. So, *e.g.*, Rau, and Prince-Smith in his essay "Ueber die Abwälzung" in the *Vierteljahrschrift für Volkswirtschaft und Kulturgeschichte*, vol. xiii (1866). Held, in his article "Zur Lehre von der Ueberwälzung der Steuern" in the *Zeitschrift für die gesamte Staatswissenschaft*, 1868, pp. 489 and 492, first called attention to the fact that transformation is really not shifting, but he did not designate transformation by the term *Abwälzung*, which, on the contrary, he continually employed as synonymous with *Ueberwälzung*. See, *e.g.*, *op. cit.*, p. 481, and Part I, Book ii, chap. 6, of this monograph. Wagner clearly describes the phenomenon of transformation, which he calls *Abwälzung*, but he considers it one of the two forms of *Ueberwälzung* or shifting, the other being what he terms *Weiterwälzung*. See his *Finanzwissenschaft*, IIer Theil (1880), § 331, p. 154. The same is true of the later editions. The more recent German writers employ the terms in all degrees of confusion, none of them making the correct distinction. An improvement, however, is to be noted in the recent treatment of the subject by Dr. Mildschuh in the *Handbuch der Finanzwissenschaft*, 1926, who has profited by Pantaleoni and the present writer.

[7] This is true, *e.g.*, of Wicksell, *Finanztheoretische Untersuchungen*, 1896, p. 12.

[8] This error, *e.g.*, is committed by Pantaleoni, *op. cit.*, p. 25.

shifting and capitalization are, as we have learned, separate and even opposite phenomena, both shifting and capitalization possess two attributes which differentiate them from transformation. These are the means of escape and the result. In shifting and capitalization the escape from taxation takes place through the medium of exchange of commodities; in transformation through the medium of production. In shifting and capitalization the taxpayer may escape the burden, but can never receive a benefit; in transformation the taxpayer may not only escape, but may have his loss transformed into a gain.

While shifting, capitalization, and transformation of taxation are three forms of escape from taxation, they are not the only forms. There remains, in fact, one more method of escape from taxation which is even more common than any of those hitherto mentioned — namely, the evasion of taxation. In each of the three methods of escape thus far discussed the government has always received a revenue, whatever may have been the facts as to the taxpayer. Whether the tax be shifted, capitalized, or transformed, it has always been paid by some one. Even in the case of transformation the tax is paid by the producer, and it is of no fiscal concern to the government whether the loss of the producer due to the payment of the tax is transformed into a gain.

In the case of evasion, however, not only does the taxpayer escape the tax, but the government loses its revenue. Evasion of the tax takes place only when there are no proceeds. If the tax is evaded in part, there are no proceeds as to the part which is evaded. Evasion of taxation is tantamount, fiscally speaking, to the absence of taxation. So far as the revenue of the government is concerned, there might as well be no tax. In all other forms of escape from taxation the government still receives its due.

Evasion of taxation assumes several forms — the most important categories being legitimate and illegitimate evasion. The conception of illegitimate evasion is simple. It consists of failure of the legal taxpayer to conform to the provisions of the law. Illegitimate evasion is of two kinds: on the one hand, the taxpayer may fail to conform to the provisions of the law by becoming a smuggler or a "tax-dodger," or by resorting to a variety of other shifts or illegal practices. Secondly, the producer may evade the tax by reducing the quality or the size of the commodity. This involves a change in the process of production similar to that described in the so-called transformation of taxation, but with the important difference that, instead of an improvement in the process, we now have a deterioration. In both smuggling and deterioration, what the taxpayer gains, the government loses.

On the other hand, the evasion may be legitimate, that is, in accordance with law. Legitimate evasion can take place only when the individual escapes the tax by refraining from the consumption of the commodity. Without a diminution of consumption there can be no legitimate evasion. Legitimate evasion, moreover, differs according as it is intended or not intended. Intentional evasion takes places when the legislator expressly desires that the tax be not paid. The object of the tax in such a case is not fiscal, but social. Thus in the case of the American tax on opium or on state bank-notes the purpose of the law is to cause the individual to refrain from using opium or emitting bank-notes. The same would be true of a high tariff. To the extent that the tariff checks, or even prohibits, imports, the tax is not paid and the purpose of the law is thus achieved. On the other hand, the legislator may desire to have the tax paid, but the imposition or the increase of the tax may engender an unexpected and entirely unwelcome falling off of consumption, thus leading to a decrease, or even to the entire disappearance, of any revenue to the treasury. Such cases have been frequent in the excise legislation of all countries. Sometimes, however, we have a combination of legitimate and illegitimate evasion, although the legitimate evasion which is here in question must be of the unintentional type. For manifestly if the government desires that the tax be not paid, non-payment is not in conflict with the law. A good illustration of such a combination of illegitimate and legitimate unintentional evasion is afforded by the experience of the American government with the whiskey tax during the Civil War period, the sudden jump of the tax from fifty cents to two dollars a gallon causing not only a great falling off in consumption, but also a marked increase in frauds on the revenue.

If we sum up the preceding discussion, we can portray the various categories of escape from taxation in the following table : —

Of all these forms of escape from taxation, shifting is the really important one. Evasion of taxation is so simple that it needs little elucidation ; transformation of taxation is too infrequent as to call for only slight consideration ; capitalization of taxation is so closely allied to shifting that it can best be treated in connection with it. In the process that inter-

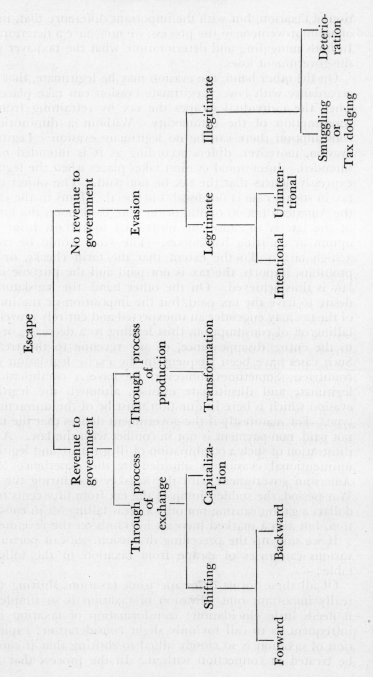

Escape

No revenue to government — Evasion — Illegitimate — Deterioration

Smuggling or Tax dodging

Legitimate — Unintentional

Intentional

Revenue to government — Through process of production — Transformation

Through process of exchange — Capitalization

Shifting — Backward

Forward

venes between the impact and the incidence of taxation, shifting is thus really the phenomenon that calls for an extended study.

In addition to the confusion that has been brought about by the failure to distinguish between shifting and the other forms of escape from taxation, we find another fertile source of error in the failure to distinguish between the shifting of a tax and the incidental burden which may rest on the shifter.

When we consider, for instance, the shifting of a tax as between buyer and seller, or between producer and consumer, the question that concerns us is : Will the price of the article be raised by the imposition of the tax? If the price is raised, we say that the tax is to that extent shifted. But even a complete shifting of the tax does not necessarily mean an entire absence of loss to the seller. Thus, it usually happens that an increase of the price of a commodity leads to a decrease in sales ; and it may happen that these decreased sales, even at higher prices, will yield less total profits than before. In such a case, not only does the buyer pay the tax, but the seller also suffers a loss, even though the tax has been shifted completely.

These incidental burdens may be summed up under the head of pressure of taxation. We should thus have a fourth category to add to the original three mentioned above. . . In tracing the life history of a tax, in other words, it might seem that we should have to distinguish between (1) the impact, (2) the shifting (and other forms of escape), (3) the incidence, and (4) the pressure of taxation. In reality, however, the pressure of taxation is not simply a consequence of the incidence, but may be connected with any of the preceding stages.[9] There may be a pressure or incidental burden resulting from the impact and from the shifting or other forms of escape, as well as from the incidence. And the pressure may be felt not only by those who pay, but by those who do not pay.

That there is a distinction between the incidence of a tax and the pressure of the incidence is obvious. The incidence of a tax marks the final payment by the tax-bearer. Ordinarily, the burden upon the tax-bearer is equal to, or measured by, the amount of the tax which he is called upon to pay. But . . . there are cases where the producer may be able, as the consequence of a tax, to raise the price of the commodity not only by the amount of the tax, but by something more than this amount. In such a case, not only is the incidence of the tax upon the consumer, but the burden resting on the consumer is greater than the amount of the tax. The loss to

9 As has been pointed out by Natoli, *op. cit.*, in his criticism of Pantaleoni.

the tax-bearer outweighs the gain to the treasury. The pressure of incidence includes this extra loss.[10]

The pressure of the impact of a tax may be typified by the illustration mentioned in the last paragraph but two. The producer may shift the tax entirely, and yet his restricted sales may lead to lower profits. This decrease of profit represents the pressure of the impact, which is not neutralized by the shifting of the tax. Conversely, if the tax is originally imposed upon and borne by the consumer, the loss possibly resulting to the producer through the decrease of sales represents the reaction on the producer of the pressure of the impact on the consumer. Again, if the producer who has paid the tax were able for some reason to shift to the consumer only the exact amount of the tax, not including the interest on the amount paid out, this interest lost by the producer would represent the pressure of the impact.[11]

The pressure connected with the process of escape from taxation can be well illustrated in the case of evasion. If a tax imposed on a commodity enhances its price by the amount of the tax, it is possible, and in ordinary cases even likely, that, whether the tax impinges on the consumer directly or through shifting, the consumer will restrict his consumption. He may even be led to abandon the consumption entirely. If this occurs, he, of course, pays no tax, but evades it. Yet in so far as he is compelled to resort to an inferior substitute, or to suffer the complete deprivation of the satisfaction of his want, he undoubtedly undergoes a loss. This is not a pressure of incidence, because, since he pays no tax, there is no incidence; it is a pressure of evasion. The burden of a tax may thus be felt by those who do not pay, as well as by those who do. In fact, as has been well said, "persons who pay a tax are often less injured by its imposition than those who pay no portion of it. The man who goes two miles out of his way daily to avoid a bridge toll would be more benefited by the freeing of the bridge than most of us who pay the toll." [12]

This consideration has led the writer just quoted to suggest

---

[10] Professor Adams, *Science of Finance*, p. 388, seems to overlook this when he says: "Manifestly there can be no payment by a citizen unless there is a corresponding receipt by the government." Professor Bastable, while avoiding this mistake, errs in including this extra loss under the head of incidence, rather than of pressure of incidence. *Public Finance*, 3d ed., 1903, p. 361.

[11] Pantaleoni, *op. cit.*, p. 21, is in error in characterizing this payment of interest as a partial incidence upon the producer. As Natoli well points out, *op. cit.*, p. 37, there can be no incidence without a corresponding revenue to the treasury.

[12] Edwin Cannan in *Memoranda chiefly relating to the Classification and Incidence of Imperial and Local Taxation,* of the Royal Commission on Taxation, 1899, p. 166.

the entire dropping of the term "incidence of taxation" and the substitution in its stead of "effects of taxation."[13] The suggestion, however, has very properly met with no favor whatsoever.[14] By effects of taxation we may mean two things. In the narrower sense, it denotes the immediate consequence of each of the above-mentioned steps. Thus shifting is an effect of impact, incidence is an effect of shifting, and the pressure of a tax is an effect, in turn, of the impact and of the shifting as well as of the incidence. In the wider sense, effect denotes any of the subsequent results of taxation. A tax may have a great many effects. It may diminish industry and impoverish individuals; it may stimulate production and enrich individuals; it may be an unmitigated curse to society; it may be a necessary evil; it may be an unqualified boon to the community regarded as a whole.

These problems are indeed important. They can, however, not be successfully attacked unless we previously solve the question of shifting and incidence. Scientific progress can be made only by a continually closer analysis and finer classification. To discuss nothing but the "effects" of taxation in general would be to render abortive the entire analysis which has been attempted in the preceding pages. This analysis has led us to the conclusion that the problem *par excellence* is that of shifting and incidence. With the wider questions of the general effects of taxation the student of incidence does not

13 "I have no doubt that it is desirable to eschew the use of the term 'incidence of taxation.' It unduly restricts inquiries into the justice and expediency of taxes, since it is always held that the 'real incidence' of a tax is upon the persons who ultimately pay or provide the money for a tax. . . It is therefore far better to consider the *effects* of taxation." Cannan, *op. cit., ibid.*

14 The only writer who seems to lean toward the suggestion is Edgeworth, who begins his series of articles on "The Incidence of Urban Rates" in the *Economic Journal,* vol. x (1900), p. 172, with the words: "Incidence here denotes all those effects of taxation with which the economist is concerned." Yet on p. 132 of the *Memoranda* mentioned in the preceding note Professor Edgeworth quotes with seeming approbation the doubt that has been raised as to whether "an effect of this sort — detrimental to a certain class, without any corresponding benefit to the exchequer — can properly be described as the *incidence* of a tax." Yet surely it is an effect "with which the economist is concerned." On the other hand Bastable thinks that "the expression is far too well established, and also far too convenient to be thus summarily abandoned." *Public Finance,* 3d ed., 1903, p. 361. Natoli says that the "remedy, as everyone can see, is worse than the evil. Once that we have reached the point of separating the phenomena into the effects of incidence and into other effects, not perhaps well designated, but clearly not the effects of incidence, it is taking a step backward to chaos to catalogue every possible effect under a rubric with no precise content whatever." *Op. cit.,* p. 311. Finally, as Row-Fogo says, "the term 'effects' is itself open to objection. Rates may have the effect of injuring the health and morals of occupiers. . . If 'effects' is to supersede 'incidence,' the term will have to be defined more closely. . . 'Effect' includes anything."—J. Row-Fogo, *An Essay on the Reform of Local Taxation in England,* 1902, p. 127, note and p. 131.

primarily busy himself. What he has particularly to investigate is the question: On whom does the tax ultimately fall? When we once know this, we can then proceed to the further discussion of the effects produced by the pressure of taxation on the various classes or individuals. The shifting is the process; the incidence is the result; the changes in the distribution of wealth are the effect.[15]

The discussion of incidence thus depends largely on the investigation of the shifting of taxation. The real problem before us is to ascertain the conditions according to which a tax is shifted forward, backward, or not at all. Only when we understand whither, why, and how a tax is shifted, can we discover its actual incidence; and it is only when we have ascertained the incidence that we can proceed to discuss the wider effects of a tax.

2. The Shifting of Taxes *

When a tax is paid ultimately by some one other than the original payer, the process of transferring it to the person of final payment is known as shifting. The incidence, or actual pecuniary burden, of a tax, *so far as the matter of its payment is concerned,* rests on this last payer. The collection of a tax entails many effects other than a possible shifting of it to others. And the decision whether to levy a tax or not should include a consideration of these effects as well as of its incidence. It is proposed here, however, to examine only the matter of its shifting—a sufficient task.

Shifting is a price process. Unless a tax affects a price, it cannot be shifted, for there is no way of transferring its payment to some one else. Price is the medium for the transfer of tax burdens, just as it is the medium for the transfer of other costs. The shifting of a tax, then, is one more chapter in the theory of price. Thus its examination runs in terms of those familiar fundamentals, supply and demand; for only by affecting supply or demand can price be changed.

The usual analysis of shifting finds the effect of a tax on a price through its effect on the supply of the object taxed. If the supply is changed because of the tax, the price likewise is

---

* From M. S. Kendrick, *Taxation Issues,* (Harper and Bros., New York, 1933), Chap. V.

[15] For a discussion of some of the effects of taxation, see my article entitled "The Effects of Taxation," in the *Political Science Quarterly,* vol. 38 (1923), pp. 1-23, and my volume *Studies in Public Finance,* 1925, chapters on "Income Taxes and the Price Level," "Taxation and Prices," "The Problem of Tax-exempt Securities," and "The Reform of Municipal Taxation."

changed, thus shifting the tax in some degree. If the supply is unaffected by the tax, the price likewise is unaffected by it and no part of the tax is shifted. Thus, in examining the incidence of a tax on land, the inquiry is whether as a result of the tax the supply of land is changed. Commonly the supply of land situation is found to be unaffected by the tax, but the supply of land fertility and of buildings is found to be affected by it. Thereby the conclusion is reached that a tax on the site value of land cannot be shifted, but that one on the fertility of the soil or on buildings may be shifted. Again, in examining the incidence of a tax on a commodity, the question is whether the tax through raising the cost of producing the commodity will operate to limit the supply of it produced and thus to increase the price at which it is sold. Throughout both of these analyses and others, the demand schedule is assumed to be unaffected by the tax.

Possible changes in demand are not considered because the effects of the expenditure of funds exacted by the tax are not examined. And indeed there is, in general, good reason for this omission. The allocation in dollars of any special effect arising from the expenditure of the contribution to the general revenue fund by a given tax object, upon the supply curve or the demand curve of this tax object, may well be a highly artificial task, and in the present state of economic knowledge is probably an impossible one. Therefore, on the whole, the current practice in works on the shifting and incidence of taxation, of treating public expenditures in a rather vague and general way, and incidence of taxation in a most particular and specific way, and of never permitting the twain to meet, is probably justified.

But this is not to say that in all instances such consideration of the incidence of a tax apart from the expenditure of the funds collected in its administration is justified. In opening the question of the effects of public expenditures it is, however, no part of the present task to determine whether the dollars' worth of benefits to the tax-bearer, arising from the expenditure of all or of particular taxes, cancels or limits the burdens imposed by the tax payments which he bears. The view here advanced is expressed with the recognized concept of incidence in mind. This thesis is that whenever the expenditure of the funds gathered by a tax can be ascertained, an account of the effects of this expenditure, if any, upon the supply curve or the demand curve of the relevant tax object, is a necessary step in the determination of the incidence of this tax. By "effects" changes in the supply curve or in the demand curve are meant.[1]

The arguments for such a recognition of expenditure in an analysis of the shifting of a tax is simple. It follows directly from the assumption fundamental to current theories of the shifting and incidence of taxation. Thus, if it be granted, as the current theory assumes, that the incidence of a tax is a function of the particular supply-demand relationship of the object upon which the tax is levied, it follows that any factor introduced by the tax which changes this relationship is pertinent to the question of the incidence of this tax. This conclusion is inevitable — to hold otherwise is to say that the incidence of a tax must be determined by the supply-demand relationship of the tax object which existed *before* and not *after* the imposition of the tax, even though, on account of this tax, this supply-demand relationship has changed. Therefore, if it can be shown that the expenditure of the funds yielded by a tax changes the supply-demand relationship of the object taxed, a consideration of such effects of this expenditure is relevant to the analysis of the incidence of this tax. For it can scarcely be denied that the expenditure of the yield of a tax is a factor introduced by the tax whenever the dependence of a particular expenditure on the particular tax can be traced.[2]

MOST important of all taxes levied in this country is the property tax which still is typically on general property, although exemptions and other exceptions to this rule are becoming relatively more important. Is this tax shifted and if so, on whom is its final incidence?

An examination of this question involves a breaking of the property on which this tax is levied into its various divisions, for the problem of incidence varies somewhat with each. The general property tax is levied on land and its improvements, as buildings, fences, and drains, and on tangible and intangible property of any and every description. Thus it is levied on furniture, books, pictures, jewelry, and other goods, whether in use by consumers or on the shelves of merchants. Likewise, it is levied on stocks, bonds, notes, mortgages, and various other valuable rights to income or to property.

[1] Although these changes are usually shifts in the curve, it is conceivable that the expenditure of a tax could change the nature of the supply curve or the demand curve of the tax object upon which it is levied. Thus a tax on milk spent in acquainting the public with the merits of milk as a food might result in a change in the elasticity of the demand curve for this product as well as in a shift in the curve itself.

[2] This point of view was presented by the writer in an article in the *American Economic Review*, June, 1930.

At least three cases may be distinguished in regard to the levy of the general property tax on land and its improvements: (1) Where the tax is not more than the economic rent of the land. (2) Where the tax is greater than the economic rent of the land but not more than the total rent of the land. (3) Where the tax is greater than the total rent of the land. These cases will be examined for their bearing on the shifting of the tax, first in relation to the collection of the tax, then, so far as is relevant, in relation to the effect of the expenditure of the funds gathered by it.

For the sake of clarity, it is well to indicate what is meant by the economic rent of the land. Ricardo defined it as "that portion of the produce of the earth which is paid to the landlord for the use of the original and indestructible powers of the soil."[3] This definition was framed by a banker before the rise of the science of soils. Nevertheless, it has played a leading part in tax incidence theory. For purposes of economic analysis, it is, however, open to attack. The Ricardian definition finds economic rent to be paid only for the final residuum of "powers" so fixed in the soil as to be indestructible. Whether such an absolute remainder exists or not except in its location, it is probably true that on most soils the cultivator through following the ordinary processes of rotation and of disposition of manure and crop waste maintains the fertility of his soil on a level much above the limit of its exhaustion suggested by Ricardo. Clearly it is to his economic interest to do so. Not only is the productivity of his soil maintained thereby, but his income is made more stable and his labor is used more efficiently because of the spacing of the peak load requirements of the various crops. Such practices are to be clearly distinguished from the renewal of the productivity of the soil by expensive applications of commercial fertilizer or lime and from the construction of fences, buildings, and other improvements. But once the common techniques of agriculture are so distinguished, payment for the opportunity to make use of them in the cultivation of land is as surely economic rent as is payment for location or any other stratum of the indestructible that may inhere in the soil.

(1) What may be said of the possibility of shifting a tax on the economic rent of land so defined when the tax is no greater than the economic rent?

3 Ricardo, David, *Principles of Political Economy and Taxation,* in the *Works of David Ricardo,* by J. R. McCulloch, p. 34. London, John Murray, 1881.

If the land were used by the owner, the annual net worth of its "original and indestructible powers" would still be economic rent. Ricardo and others after him found the landlord illustration useful.

The usual analysis is that such a tax cannot be shifted. The argument runs in terms of the effect of the tax on the supply of land so taxed. It is pointed out that the collection of the tax cannot limit the supply of taxed land, for this supply is not dependent on the actions of landlords. It exists — level, rolling, near or far from market, generous or niggardly in its offering of opportunities — and nothing can be done about it. If it were most profitably cropped to a rotation of corn, oats, wheat, and clover before the tax, it will still be so after the tax. For the fact of collection of the tax has nothing to do with the profits to be derived from this rotation of crops. Owners managing their farms as best they can find nothing in the payment of the tax to make them order their production differently. They produce and sell neither less nor more because of it. Landlords charging their tenants a market rental can obtain no more because of a tax levied on economic rent. The supply of land to be rented and the number of tenants seeking land remain as before. Thus, so far as the collection of the tax is concerned, and rightly, the conclusion of the usual analysis of the incidence of a tax on the economic rent of land is that it cannot be shifted, but remains on the owner of the land.

But let it be supposed that the proceeds of a tax levied on the economic rent of farm land were used to buy up large areas of marginal and submarginal farm land and to retire these areas from agricultural production. Such a use of the funds of this tax would clearly lower the supply of land and the tax might well be shifted in the first instance to consumers through higher prices of farm products, and ultimately most of it to capital-in-general. For funds which now are invested in these lands of low production would find employment elsewhere. This would result in an increased supply of capital relative to other factors and therefore in a lower return on it.[4]

Although no state levies a tax of this description on the rent of land for the purpose of buying land that should be retired from agricultural production, such a procedure and such a tax are by no means impossible. New York State has embarked upon a large program of this kind in which marginal and submarginal hill areas are purchased for reforestation. The cost

[4] It may be objected that the purchase of these lands by the state would be merely a substitute for its purchase by private individuals, and that thereby no more funds would be made available for investment elsewhere. This position is valid on the basis of the assumption mentioned. Such land, however, would be purchased only once by the state ; but now, held in private ownership, it is purchased many times, thus being a sinkhole for the savings of many persons before it is abandoned. Moreover, the state, because of its greater resources and ability to wait, might well put this land to a more productive use.

of this enterprise is not paid for by a levy on property but is derived from other sources. But there is nothing to prevent a state in which property revenues are an important part of state finance from levying a tax on property for this very purpose. For such a tax on the rent of farm land to be shifted, all that is necessary is for the dependence of the expenditure on the revenues from the tax to be established.

But not all the effects of the expenditure of a tax on the economic rent of land need contradict the effects of its payment. Sometimes they accentuate these effects, so far as shifting or the absence of it is concerned. Professor Herbert D. Simpson has pointed out that the development of a boulevard system and other street improvements in Chicago has actually lowered the value of part of the real property affected instead of raising it.[5] He estimated that property at one end of Michigan Avenue suffered a depreciation of $609,198,420 as a result of these improvements. A tax for these improvements levied on the economic rent of this land could not be shifted; the further loss of economic rent caused by the expenditure likewise could not be shifted. Thus the tax through its expenditure would become a still heavier burden. In this particular instance, the property which was depreciated in value had to bear a special assessment for the improvements responsible for its depreciation. The effect was even worse than that of a tax.

(2) The second case for consideration is where the property tax is greater than the economic rent of the land, but less than its total rent. The total rent of the land includes both economic rent and fertilizer, building, or other improvement rents. Since the effect of a tax on economic rent has been analysed, there remains for discussion the effect of a tax on fertilizer and improvement rents. That productivity of the soil which is due to the application of commercial fertilizer is dependent on the willingness of the farmer to make the necessary expenditures. It may be increased or diminished, depending on whether funds for fertilizer are used or withheld. Likewise, a building may be maintained or allowed to deteriorate.

There is opportunity for the collection of a tax on the fertilizer element of the soil or on an improvement to result in the shifting of this tax. This follows from the choice that an owner of real estate has in respect to its upkeep. If because of the tax payment he finds that he can obtain more remunera-

[5] Simpson, Herbert D., "The Effect of Improvements on Land Values," *Annals of the American Academy of Political and Social Science*, March, 1930.

tion elsewhere for his expenditures than by applying commercial fertilizer to his soil or by maintaining or adding to his buildings, he is likely to neglect his soil or his buildings. Eventually this neglect of the soil means a depletion of nutrients dependent on fertilizer. This is equivalent to a reduction in the supply of land other than its situation element. This lessened supply of land leads to a smaller amount of produce which may be sold at higher prices. Similarly, a tax on buildings may be shifted because of the payment of a tax. Funds for maintenance may be spent elsewhere and funds for new buildings may go into other enterprises. Eventually the supply of buildings is decreased and rents rise.

However, a tax on purchased fertility or on an improvement need not be shifted, depending on the expenditure of the funds yielded by it. For example, let it be supposed that the money from a tax on the fertilizer element of the soil is spent to improve the rural roads. It is by no means certain that such a tax would be shifted. For it is conceivable that because of the less costly access to markets resulting from the improved roads, the investment in fertilizer would continue as before, and that the supply of farm products on the market would be maintained as before the levy of the tax.[6]

But suppose the expenditure of the yield of a tax on the fertilizer element or on improvements does not offset or cancel the effects of its payment and that therefore the tax is shifted. On whom does the burden of the higher prices of farm products and the higher rent of buildings fall? The obvious answer is that this burden rests on the consumers of farm products and the tenants of buildings. And clearly these consumers and tenants pay higher prices and rents. But to conclude therefore that the entire burden of the tax rests on consumers and tenants is erroneous. For, to the extent that the prices and rents are high, maintenance and investment funds have been shifted from fertilizer and buildings to other forms of capital. Thus the amount of such capital is increased and its return is lowered until once more it is in equilibrium with that from the taxed capital. It may be said then that the incidence of a tax on some capital rests eventually on all capital.[7] And in

[6] In Coombs, Whitney, "Taxation of Farm Property," *U.S.D.A. Tech. Bul.* 172, p. 62, 1930, it is said that, "If the proceeds of the tax are used, for example, to build a road by which easy and rapid access to markets is secured, then the economic yield of the land will be increased just as much as if it had been possible to add increased fertility."

[7] For the argument that a tax on some capital falls on all capital, I am especially indebted to Brown, H. G., *The Economics of Taxation*, pp. 178-184. New York, Henry Holt & Company, Inc. The view here expressed differs from

most general terms this is true. But it is equally true that those consumers and tenants whose expenditures for farm products and for building space are large relative to their expenditures for other things are final bearers of part of the burden of a tax on fertilizer and buildings. For to the extent that the higher prices which they pay for farm products and the higher rents that they pay for building space are not compensated by lower prices of goods produced in untaxed lines they suffer a net loss because of the imposition of the tax.

One further question before closing the consideration of the second case: Can a tax on fertilizer and improvements which is shifted to capital-in-general be shifted further? If this tax is shifted to all capital, it lowers the return from it. Once borne by all capital, no opportunity exists for a transfer of this burden to any particular kind or class of capital except by removal to another taxing jurisdiction.[8] The only way in which a further shifting of this tax is possible is through less saving. With the supply of capital less, the return per dollar of investment would be greater and some measure at least of shifting would have taken place. But, does a lowered return on capital mean less saving? Would saving be as great with a 3- or a 4-per-cent return on capital as with a 5- or 6-per-cent return? It may safely be said that at present no categorical answer to this question is possible. We do not know the effect of higher or lower interest rates on the total volume of saving.

A more important issue, though, than sheer volume of saving is its direction of investment. Much saving is wasted by being invested in fields already suffering from excess of plant capacity.

This suggests that the issue of whether a tax on all capital can be shifted through a decrease in the volume of saving is also affected by the use of the funds collected by the tax. A possible example to illustrate potentialities in the use of tax funds to sustain the capital supply may be found in the following situation: Let it be supposed that in a certain country a significant share of savings are being employed in industries already overdeveloped, such as soft coal mining, radio manu-

that of Brown in that it recognizes more explicitly the share of the burden borne by consumers of the products of the taxed capital.

The argument that a tax on some capital rests eventually on all capital also finds support in Davenport, H. J., "Theoretical Issues in the Single Tax," *Am. Econ. Review*, March, 1917, footnote pp. 26-28, and in Adams, T. S., the June, 1916, issue of the same periodical, p. 278.

[8] Not examined here because the writer believes it not to be of sufficient importance.

facturing, and tire-making but that some other necessary forms of capital, such as concrete roads, are underdeveloped. In such a situation, a tax on capital the yield of which is spent for concrete roads may make for a better distributed supply of capital and thus operate to cancel or to lessen the effect of the decline in saving due to the imposition of the tax.

(3) The third possibility of shifting to be examined under the tax on land and improvements is where this tax is greater than the total rent. At first thought, such a rate of property taxation may seem impossible. But with the amount of general property tax levy determined by the expenditure of the governmental unit in question and with this tax apportioned on the basis of the selling value of the property, rather than on the income yielded by it, such a rate of taxation relative to rent is by no means an impossible one. In fact, in the poorest of the hill regions of New York State, known as the sub-marginal land areas, such a rate of taxation relative to rent is not only possible but is common.[9]

The effect of a tax so related to income is to make for the final abandonment of the land. The process of abandonment as proceeding in New York State is a slow and cruel process in which family after family fails to make a living and pay taxes. Gradually, with the land's slight fertility depleted in the struggle, agricultural undertakings based on it are abandoned. This abandonment lessens the supply of farm land and therefore of farm products to some small degree. Thus it may be said that a tax of this severity is shifted eventually though very slowly.

The general property tax when levied on tangible personal property, as furniture, jewelry, clothing, books, and pictures in possession of the ultimate consumer, cannot be shifted. There being no further transaction through which these goods pass, no opportunity for shifting the tax is presented. Nor can the expenditure of the funds so obtained have any effect on the matter of the shifting of the tax responsible for them. But when levied on this same tangible personal property of the merchant, as stocks on his shelves or goods in his warehouse, the effect is different. Shifting here is subject to the laws of a tax on capital that can be reproduced. This has been discussed in connection with the incidence of a tax on buildings and soil fertilizer. If the tax is general, the ultimate resting-place of such a tax is on all capital.[10] Whether any of this

---

[9] A detailed description of these areas in economic terms is found in Vaughan, L. M., "Abandoned Farm Areas in New York," *Cornell Exp. Sta. Bul.* 490, 1929.

[10] If the tax is not general, consumers of the taxed goods bear part of it so far as they are not compensated by lower prices for other goods.

tax on capital can be shifted is, as has been indicated, a question of saving and public expenditure.

The general property tax when levied on intangibles, as notes, bonds, stocks, and mortgages, is a tax on capital, and therefore the possibility of shifting it and the questions of incidence involved are matters of the laws of a tax on capital. Whether part or all intangibles are taxed, the ultimate incidence of their taxation is on all capital. The question of further shifting of this tax depends on whether saving is decreased or not, because of the lowered rate of return on capital. The importance of the use of savings in affecting the capital supply has been indicated, and the possibility of the wise expenditure of a tax on capital nullifying the effect of its payment on saving has been examined.

ANOTHER important source of taxation the incidence of which should be examined is the income tax. As has been indicated, the federal government levies both personal- and corporation-income taxes, and a number of states do likewise.

Corporation-income taxes and part of the personal-income taxes are levied on incomes from the economic rent of land and from that part of capital which, being created by individuals, is reproducible and therefore is subject to variations in supply. The incidence of these taxes on income follows the laws of shifting already discussed in relation to a tax on the economic rent of land and on improvements or other reproducible capital.

That part of the personal-income tax which rests on returns from personal exertions raises different problems of incidence. Some description of this tax is a necessary preliminary to the examination of the possibility of shifting it. Not all personal exertions are taxed by the levy on personal earnings made by the income tax. The most general income tax, the federal, provides extremely liberal personal exemptions. Although not all exemptions from state income taxation are so generous, such exemptions always are well above the average earnings of labor. Thus the tax is universally on the incomes of those persons whose earnings place them in a relatively favorable position in the economic order. The federal tax rates are progressive, thereby absorbing a larger percentage of the greater than of the lesser incomes. What may be said of the incidence of such a tax? Does it rest on the preferred group on which it is levied? Or, is it shifted to wage-earners in general, as a tax on some capital rests ultimately on all capital?[11]

[11] Except as has been noted.

Clearly, when first levied there can be no shifting of a personal-income tax which is general in its application as is the federal tax on personal incomes. The only effective escape is to choose an occupation with a lower income, a procedure that involves far greater loss in income than saving in taxes.

In theory, if a state imposed a personal-income tax on earnings, it would seem possible for some persons affected by this tax to move to a state where their incomes would be untaxed, thus to lower the supply of services in the taxing state and to increase the remuneration therefor. But with the liberal exemptions of state income taxation and the moderate rates now in effect, it is doubtful whether any person earning his income by his personal exertions in a given state is so marginal as between residence in this state or in that as to change his residence to another state and to earn his income there because of a tax levied on it by the state of his present residence.

A change of residence to be effective in avoiding the personal-income tax must result in a change of residence for the income as well as for the person, since it is common for a state levying a personal-income tax to tax all personal income derived from within its borders whether by a resident or a nonresident. Thus it is clear that when first imposed there is no shifting of a federal income tax or of a state income tax of the type now levied. The tax rests on its payers. Their personal earnings are lower accordingly.

But what of the future? Is a tax on higher personal earnings, even if general, ultimately shifted through a decreased supply of persons in these better-paid occupations, with the consequences that the rate of their remuneration is raised and the rate of remuneration in lower-paid positions is lowered because of the increased supply of persons in these occupations who, except for the tax, would be in higher-paid occupations? In other words, is the ultimate incidence of the federal and state income taxes, so far as they are levied on personal incomes, on wages in general?

The case against the shifting of a personal-income tax on earnings in the writer's opinion is supported by the strongest *a priori* reasons. These reasons will be examined with respect, first to those persons in the lowest income-tax paying group and second to those in the highest income-tax-paying group.

Perhaps the first significant observation which can be made regarding a payer of a small income tax on earnings is that after the payment of the tax his financial situation always remains better than it would have been had he chosen a low-paid occupation and thus received an income below the exemption. Moreover, this difference between income below the exemption and income above it is probably much more significant than any similar percentage difference between large incomes. Dollars are of more importance when there are few of them. Not only are they of significance for purposes of living but a few more dollars mean an opportunity for saving and thus getting ahead by means of income from investments as well as from earnings. Thus the financial consideration is in itself a powerful argument against any shifting of a tax on personal earnings.

A person choosing between a low-paid occupation and a better-paid one, if influenced in his decision by the earnings of those persons in this occupation who are in the lowest income-tax-paying group and thus in the income-tax group nearest the starting income in this occupation, must, *because of the very fact that he is making income a consideration,* come to the conclusion that if he receives a larger income and pays an income tax he will be better off than if he receives so small an income that no tax is levied on it.

But the financial argument does not stand alone in supporting the position that there is no shifting of the income tax on personal earnings. It is reinforced by other considerations. The better-paid positions, even those which yield incomes barely above the personal exemption, are more pleasant and interesting, if variety of duties, absence of exhausting physical labor, emphasis on thinking, and more of personal initiative are to be preferred to specialization, heavy physical labor, emphasis on brawn and the direction of a boss. Moreover, it is certainly true that these jobs carry with them more prestige than do low-paid jobs. No doubt part of this prestige is attached to the larger income which the better-paid positions command. But it is more than mere dollars. Attainment of the better-paid positions represents a certain achievement, a success that is respected. Moreover, the position itself is commonly esteemed to be of more significance than the low-paid one.

But let it be supposed that a person in considering an occupation looks not to the low incomes realized by most persons in it, but to the high incomes received by a few at the top. Will, for example, the prospective law student refuse to study law, but instead choose to dig ditches because he finds that incomes of $100,000 earned in the legal profession (and in others, for the personal-income tax is general in its application) are taxed to the extent of $25,000 under the progressive rates of federal- and state-income taxes? This is not probable, for two reasons.

In the first place, a person whose ambition vaults so high as to base his choice of an occupation, so far as its financial rewards are concerned, on its top possibilities, *is by the very fact of this emphasis on things financial* precluded from the possibility of going to the other extreme and choosing a low-paid occupation. One who has unbounded ambition for financial success cannot, *for financial reasons,* refuse to try for the highest reward possible for him to obtain, because, on account of an income tax, it is not high enough, and then give up all opportunity for financial success by choosing a low-paid occupation. The two things simply do not go together.

In the second place, the attraction of high earnings is relative. For example, suppose the top personal earnings in any lines to be $50,000. Let this top increase to $100,000. Then $50,000 seems too small to attract. Let it increase to $200,000, and $100,000 becomes small. Once the top rises, then all previous tops shrink in comparison. Yet is there any reason to suppose that a top of $200,000 for personal exertions is more effective in attracting persons into the better-paid occupations than is a top of $50,000? A progressive personal-income tax such as the federal-income tax operates in all lines of endeavor to reduce these tops. But if the matter of a top is relative, then it may well be that the top rewards of all occupations, when reduced in proportion, attract as many persons into these occupations and enlist as enthusiastic an endeavor from them as would be the case if these rewards were proportionately higher.

Much the same line of reasoning follows for persons already in the profession. It is probably true that, so far as they are influenced by the money incentive, they will try as hard to attain a top reward of $50,000 as one, say, of $200,000. But although money reward may well accompany the higher achievements in an occupation, success in it is usually not a matter of money incentive alone. Rather it is one of peculiar genius for the task in hand, a rare mating of man and opportunity, love and enthusiasm for the thing itself rather than for the monetary insignia of success. To the extent that these factors enter the situation, the money element becomes of less importance in accounting for endeavors to reach the top. Thus, for two reasons, the relative significance of top financial rewards and the presence of non-pecuniary elements, it is doubtful whether persons in the better-paid occupations strive less hard to reach the top when some of the cream of that top is skimmed by a tax on personal incomes, provided all personal incomes of the same size in all occupations are taxed likewise.

For these reasons, the writer believes that an income tax on personal earnings can be shifted neither at once nor ultimately, and that its incidence is finally on those who pay it. They suggest to him that the rates of this tax could be made much higher than at present with precisely the same incidence.

A TAX levied on inheritance and estates is a levy on capital. Is it subject to the laws of shifting as on other capital? Clearly in respect to its first incidence, a tax on an estate or on the individual shares received by heirs is similar to a tax on capital. With the estate or the inheritance subject to the tax and its descent to the heirs conditional on the payment of the tax, there is no opportunity for shifting it.

The real question regarding the incidence of the inheritance tax is the effect of this method of taxation on the supply of capital. Sometimes the naïve argument is advanced that such a tax must diminish the supply of capital, for it is levied on capital and in many instances it is paid with the proceeds of a sale of capital. In reply to this, Professor Pigou has called attention to the fact that the object on which a tax is levied is not necessarily the source of its payment by the happy illustration that a tax on beer is not necessarily paid in beer or from resources which otherwise would have become beer.[12]

The fundamental issue is not the immediate one of whether the capital taxed must be sold or not to pay the tax or the source from which the payment comes. Rather as Professor Brown points out, it is the question of saving.[13] Is accumulation less because of a tax on inheritance? Will a man accumulate as much for his heirs and the state as he will for his heirs alone? If the future capital supply decreases due to the tax or is less than it would have been without the tax, then the tax will be shifted in the form of higher interest rates. Ultimately laborers and receivers of economic rent will bear the final burden.

The answer to the question whether an inheritance tax lessens accumulation and therefore capital is not yet out of the realm of "beautiful thoughts." Not enough is known of the mo-

12 Pigou, A. C., *A Study in Public Finance*, p. 159. London, Macmillan & Co., Ltd., 1928.
13 Brown, H. G., *The Economics of Taxation*, p. 209. New York, Henry Holt & Company, Inc., 1924.

tives for individual saving to make the answer to it certain. Is saving explained by the desire to make provision for heirs, love for that power which comes with vast interests, or passion for the game of getting a pecuniary coat of arms, or is saving easier than spending once a certain amount has been accumulated? How much of it is habit, worn comfortably as an old coat and not soon to be laid aside? Is it possible that with inheritance-taxation standards of accumulation change? Thus when a million was enough before, a million, two hundred thousand must be accumulated now in order to leave the million.

Two observations may be made with reference to the incidence of inheritance taxation — one with respect to the way of levying the tax, the other with respect to its expenditure. These are on more certain ground. For the argument that the taxation of inheritance weakens the passion to accumulate (and for other purposes), Professor Rignano has developed a most ingenius plan of taxation whereby the different portions of the estate are taxed at different rates.[14] He proposes to tax that part of an estate due to the testator's thrift and labor at the present inheritance-tax rates; that part inherited from his father 50 per cent; and that part from his grandfather 100 per cent. If thought desirable the rate schedule advocated by Professor Rignano could be changed so that little, if any, tax would be paid on that part of the estate due to the labor and thrift of the testator. Thus by this application of the Rignano proposal, it would be possible to levy an inheritance tax which could not affect the motive to accumulate, since one's personal accumulation, if taxed at all, would be taxed lightly. Only his father's or his grandfather's accumulations would be taxed heavily.

The expenditure of an inheritance tax may also affect the supply of capital. Professor Shultz has pointed out that revenues from this tax may be used for dams, roadways, airplane lanes, and the like, which are additions to the capital equipment of the country.[15] Also he indicates that if the proceeds of this tax are used to pay off loans, they put in the hands of an investing class, namely bondholders, a sum of funds equivalent to that extracted from the inheritors of estates. In regard to the possibility of the inheritance tax operating to check savings and thus to reduce the supply of capital, it may

14 Rignano, Eugenio, *The Social Significance of the Inheritance Tax*, p. 34. Translated by Shultz, W. J. New York, Alfred A. Knopf, 1924.
15 Shultz, W. J., *The Taxation of Inheritance*, pp. 201-206. New York, Houghton Mifflin Co., 1926.

be remarked here that the opportunity of nullifying or at least of lessening the effects of any such decline by a wise expenditure of funds is available through such use of the funds gathered by the inheritance tax precisely as it has been shown to be available through the use of funds obtained by tax on all capital.

THE federal government and the states levy various taxes on commodities. Among these are the federal excises on tobacco, oleomargarine, pistols and revolvers, and other commodities which formerly included automobiles and automobile accessories. The states all levy taxes on gasoline, and a number of them tax tobacco and soft drinks.

The incidence of a tax on commodities is usually examined with respect to three types of cost — constant cost, increasing cost, and decreasing cost under conditions of competition and monopoly.

Constant cost is the simplest of these variations in cost and therefore is the one most useful for purposes of introducing the principles of incidence as they apply to the taxation of commodities. As its name implies, constant cost refers to a status in which the cost per unit remains constant whether many or few units are produced. Thus it is a situation of elastic supply. Using Professor Brown's illustration, and assuming a constant cost per unit of one dollar, at a price of slightly above one dollar a unit an indefinitely large supply of the given commodity will be produced; but at a price slightly below one dollar none will be turned out.[16]

Assuming competition, the general conclusion of authorities on the incidence of taxation is that a tax on any commodity produced under conditions of constant cost is shifted entirely in the form of higher prices charged consumers. This is because all business firms engaged in its production are marginal at the price charged. Under the assumption of constant cost, no opportunity exists for variations in cost between them, and competition forces the price down to a level slightly above cost. Therefore the argument follows that any addition to cost in the form of a tax must be shifted entirely or none of the commodities will be produced.

In a sense this conclusion is valid and in another sense it is most fallacious. If the test of incidence be merely the effect of the tax on the price of the commodity taxed, it is inescapable, for the price is higher by the amount of the tax. But if a wider price test be employed, one that considers not only

16 Brown, H. G., *Economics of Taxation*, pp. 56-62.

the effect of the tax on the price of the commodity taxed, but its effect on other prices, another conclusion is reached. A tax which raises the price of a commodity results in a decline in its consumption, the extent of the decrease varying with the degree of elasticity of the demand curve for the commodity.[17] This decline means a lowering in the return on the capital employed in producing the taxed commodity and ultimately a shift of capital from this industry to others. This employment of more capital in other industries lowers the rates of return on it. Eventually rates of return on the capital employed in other and untaxed industries are in equilibrium with the rate of return on capital employed in the industry whose product is taxed. Thus eventually a tax on a commodity is a tax on all capital, except to the extent that consumers of the taxed commodity are uncompensated by lower prices of other commodities and therefore bear part of the tax.

Doubtless, the reader will note the similarity of this analysis to the one already given that a tax on some capital is a tax on all capital. This similarity of analyses is intended, for in the writer's view the two cases are identical — in the legal phrase "on all fours." The cigarette may be taxed or the cigarette-making machine, but the effect of the tax is the same — *so far as the matter of incidence is concerned.*[18] Other effects there would necessarily be, but these are not effects of incidence. The reason for this parallelism of incidence is that, whether the cigarette or its machine be taxed, the ultimate effects are: a limitation of the supply of cigarettes; a rise in their price; and a shifting of capital from the cigarette-making industry to other lines. And the resultant of these like effects is a like incidence.

The question of possible effects of the expenditure of funds from the taxation of a commodity produced at constant cost on the supply curve or the demand curve of this commodity, and therefore on the incidence of the tax, is not discussed here. No single chapter can include all aspects of the problem of tax shifting. Moreover, the *principle* involved can be demonstrated best by an examination of the incidence of a tax on

---

[17] Possible exceptions to this decreased consumption, if any, are too rare and insignificant to be mentioned.

[18] The cigarette illustration is used for its contribution to the point that it makes no difference "incidence-wise" whether a tax is levied on capital or on its commodity product. No assumption with regard to the nature of cost in the cigarette-manufacturing industry is intended. Some illustration appeared necessary and the writer knows of no industry which operates under conditions of constant cost.

gasoline under conditions of increasing and decreasing cost.[19] This tax is levied in cents per gallon on the sale of gasoline, and the proceeds are commonly used on the roads, with the result that the roads are being steadily improved as funds from it flow into the public treasury.

However, in examining the incidence of this tax, it must be confessed at the outset that any examination of the incidence of the gasoline tax that is made here must be based on hypothetical data. The writer has been unable to find information which established the precise shape of either the supply curve or the demand curve for gasoline. Does the supply curve slope upward or downward with increases in the quantity of gasoline produced? Is gasoline production subject to the law of diminishing returns or to the law of increasing returns? Is the demand curve for gasoline elastic or inelastic, and in what degree? At each price in a given schedule, what quantity of gasoline will be purchased? Facts such as these are usually missing when analyses of the incidence of taxation are made. Consequently, it is usually necessary to substitute hypotheses for realities and to encounter the hazards incidental to such substitution. But the purpose of this analysis is not so much to establish an absolute truth — if such there be — as to suggest a principle. For this purpose hypothetical data will serve to illustrate and, it is hoped, to illuminate, the thought that in some instances the effects of the expenditure of a tax on a commodity must be considered in an analysis of the incidence of this tax.

Returning now to the incidence of a gasoline tax whose proceeds spent on the roads, let it be supposed that the production of gasoline is subject to the law of increasing cost and that Fig. 1 is representative of the relationship of the supply and demand curves both before and after the imposition of the tax. Competition in the industry is assumed.

In this figure the supply and demand curves are indicated by the conventional letters, SS' and DD'. Before the imposition of the tax, OA quantity of gasoline is sold at the price OP.

After the tax, the supply line becomes ST S'T, the T's being introduced to indicate the levy of the tax. According to the usual analysis, the price now becomes OP', and OA' quantity of gasoline is sold. This rise in price is something less than

[19] The writer believes that much can be said in favor of using the terminology, "Law of the Proportion of the Factors," and "Law of Advantage and Size," as used by Davenport, H. J., in *Economics of Enterprise*, ch. 23, but prefers to follow current usage and thus not to complicate further an already complicated matter by the use of an unusual terminology.

the amount of the tax.   Therefore not all of the tax is shifted.

But suppose that, because of the expenditure of receipts from this tax on gasoline, the roads are improved, and that as a consequence of this improvement more gasoline is burned in motor vehicles operating on them, what then may be said of the incidence of the tax?

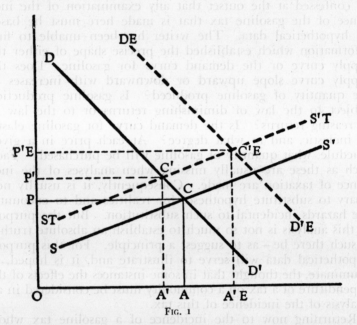

FIG. 1

The curve DE D'E indicates the possible migration of the demand curve on account of the improved roads.[20]   Now the quantity of gasoline sold becomes OA'E, and the price becomes OP'E.   The tax on gasoline has been followed by a rise in price greater than the amount of the tax.[21]   Something more than the amount of the tax has been shifted.

Possibly it should be remarked, parenthetically, that even if consumers of gasoline pay more than the amount of the tax, it does not follow that taxes on gasoline are to be condemned.   Consumers pay more than the tax only because of

[20] It is conceivable that the elasticity of this curve could change also because of the changed conditions.

[21] In interpreting the results of this or of the next analysis given, it should be remembered that they follow from the particular conditions in the figure. A change in the conditions would affect these results.   For example, assuming that the elasticity of the supply curve remains unchanged, the more elastic the demand curve, the less the rise in price because of the tax and the more inelastic the demand curve the greater the rise in price.

a greater use of roads that have been improved with the tax funds. It may well be that they obtain their money's worth or more. But an examination of whether they do or not lies outside the subject of incidence and so would not be relevant here.

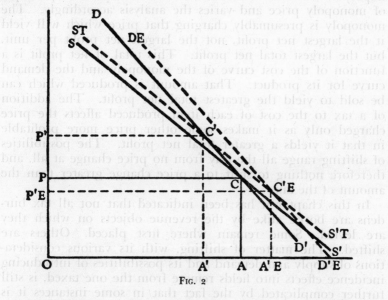

Fig. 2

Perhaps the next question is what happens to the price of gasoline under the above analysis if gasoline is produced under conditions of decreasing cost. Assuming that competition exists, Fig. 2 is a possible representation under the hypothesis of decreasing cost.

In this figure the curves are lettered as in Fig. 1. Before the imposition of the tax, OA quantity of gasoline is sold at price OP.

The usual analysis finds that with the introduction of the tax, the supply curve SS' becomes ST S'T and intersects the demand at C'. This results in a rise of the price to OP' and in a decrease in the quantity sold to OA'. This rise in the price of gasoline is greater than the amount of the tax. All of the tax plus something in addition has been shifted.

The analysis suggested in this paper finds that, because of the improvement in the roads due to the expenditure of the gasoline tax money on them, the demand for gasoline may well be represented by the curve DE D'E instead of by the curve DD'. Because of the conditions of decreasing cost indicated in the figure, the increase in the demand for gasoline results in a price of OP'E, one actually lower than the price existing before the imposition of the tax on gasoline. Nothing of the tax has been shifted.

But suppose gasoline is produced under conditions of monopoly? This consideration introduces the peculiar principle of monopoly price and varies the analysis accordingly. The monopoly is presumably charging that price which will yield it the largest net profit, not the largest net profit per unit, but the largest total net profit. This total of net profit is a function of the cost curve of the monopoly and the demand curve for its product. That amount is produced which can be sold to yield the greatest total net profit. The addition of a tax to the cost of each item produced affects the price charged only as it makes some other price more profitable in that it yields a greater total net profit. The possibilities of shifting range all the way from no price change at all, and therefore nothing to shift to a price change greater than the amount of the tax.

In this chapter it has been indicated that not all tax burdens are borne alike by the revenue objects on which they are levied. Some remain where first placed. Others are shifted. The matter of shifting, with its various considerations of supply and demand and its possibilities of introducing incidence effects into fields remote from the one taxed, is still further complicated by the fact that in some instances it is affected by the expenditure of tax funds.

One last question . . . is, Does it matter on whom the burden finally rests? The answer is clearly in the affirmative. It matters because through discriminations in taxation one industry or economic activity can be discouraged and another can be encouraged. Whether this is good or bad depends on the ideal of what society should be. This is too large a question for examination here. Only the fact that the burden of taxation matters must be indicated. It matters even when a tax on one object is shifted to the other objects in the same group. Thus a heavy tax on buildings, though shifted ultimately to all capital, may be worse than a tax levied directly on all capital. For it makes rents ultimately higher than other prices. The net return to the landlord — rent less taxes — is no higher than the net return on other capital, but the rent paid by the tenant is higher even though compensated to some extent by lower prices elsewhere. To the degree that building should be encouraged such a tax on buildings is undesirable.

QUESTIONS AND PROBLEMS FOR DISCUSSION

1. Point out the differences between tax shifting and tax evasion.
2. Distinguish clearly between the impact, the shifting, the incidence, and the pressure of taxation.
3. State the conditions under which tax capitalization is possible.
4. If the price of a commodity is increased by the amount of the tax levied on its sale, does the seller escape entirely from the burden of the tax?
5. Why is it difficult to speak intelligently about the *effects* of taxation?
6. Upon whom does a tax on the economic rent of land tend to fall? Can such a tax be considered burdenless?
7. If federal income tax rates are increased in the future in order to help finance heavy governmental expenditures, upon whom will the burden of such taxes fall?
8. Discuss the incidence of inheritance taxes. Is the incidence of this form of taxation a factor in favor or its use as an important source of revenue?
9. Of the taxes considered in this chapter, which can be regarded as levies on "surplus"? In general what can be said about the incidence of taxes on "surplus"? Does your answer serve to justify the use of such taxes?
10. "The incidence of a tax on some capital rests eventually on all capital." Explain and evaluate.
11. In order to provide additional revenue for local improvements, the town of Medium, a growing community, has increased significantly its tax rates on general property. Mr. White, a retailer of agricultural implements in Medium, is conducting his business in rented quarters.
    (a) Will Mr. White bear any portion of the increased tax burden? Support your answer.
    (b) If any portion of the tax burden should fall upon Mr. White, will he be able to shift it? Explain fully.
    (c) What form of revenue, if any, could have been collected without any portion of its burden falling upon Mr. White? Support your answer.
12. During the 1931 session of the General Assembly of Iowa, a new state tax law was enacted which levied an excise tax of five cents per pound on oleomargarine sold within the state. The revenue from this tax went into the General State Fund. A large percentage of this fund was expended for public education.
    Assume that, before the enactment of this legislation, you were a member of a committee charged with securing information on the following points: (1) the probable effect of the tax on the price of oleomargarine, (2) the probable effect of the tax on volume of sales of oleomargarine, (3) the amount of revenue which the state might expect to receive from the tax.

State clearly the nature of the data which you would have attempted to collect in order to make the estimates requested by the General Assembly. Give your reasons for selecting these data.

SUGGESTIONS FOR RESEARCH

1. The relation of the incidence of taxation to the theory of value.
2. An inductive study of the shifting and incidence of a sales tax on some commodity or commodities in some particular state.
3. The shifting and incidence of taxes on stock-and-produce-exchange transactions.
4. The shifting and incidence of taxes levied upon monopolies.
5. The measurement of taxable capacity.

BIBLIOGRAPHICAL NOTE

For a history of the theories of shifting and incidence of taxation, see E. R. A. Seligman, *The Shifting and Incidence of Taxation,* (New York, 1927), Pt. I. In Pt. II of this work, Professor Seligman sets forth his own theories. Another general treatise of high quality is Otto Frhr. von Mering, *Die Steuer Überwälzung,* (Jena, 1928). The general principles of incidence and effects of taxation are discussed in H. A. Silverman, *Taxation, Its Incidence and Effects,* (London, 1931), Chaps. V, VI. H. G. Brown in his *The Economics of Taxation,* (New York, 1924), Chaps. IV-X, presents a well-reasoned exposition of the incidence of various forms of taxation. Other good discussions of the same subject are in Hugh Dalton, *Principles of Public Finance,* (London, 1932), Chaps. VII, VIII; F. Y. Edgeworth, *Papers Relating to Political Economy,* (London, 1925), Vol. II, pp. 63-125; Adolph Wagner, *Finanzwissenschaft,* (Leipzig, 1890), Vol. II, pp. 340-372; and T. N. Carver, "The Shifting of Taxes," *Yale Review,* Vol. V, pp. 258-271.

J. A. Hobson, in his *Taxation in the New State,* (London, 1919), Chap. III, makes an analysis of tax shifting based upon his distinction between the "surplus" and "cost" elements in income.

A review of recent German studies which stress the importance of the empirical method in investigations of the shifting and incidence of taxation is Rolf Grabower, "Die Steuerüberwälzungslehre, ein Beitrag zum neuesten Schrifttum," *Vierteljahresschrift für Steuer- und Finanzrecht,* 1928, Heft 3, pp. 453-503.

A discussion of the effects as distinct from the incidence of taxation may be found in E. R. A. Seligman, "The Effects of Taxation," *Political Science Quarterly,* Vol. XXXVIII, pp. 1-23. The measurement of tax burden is dealt with by R. M. Haig in *Report of the New York State Commission for the Revision of the Tax Laws,* 1932.

A consideration of the incidence and effects of taxation in a given country is important and necessary in the determination of its taxable capacity. For discussions of taxable capacity and the problem of its measurement, see Sir Josiah Stamp, *Wealth and Taxable Capacity*, (London, 1923); G. F. Shirras, *The Science of Public Finance*, (London, 1925), Chap. XV; H. A. Silverman, *Taxation, Its Incidence and Effects*, (London, 1931), Chap. III; G. L. Leffler, "Wisconsin Industry and the Wisconsin Tax System," *University of Wisconsin Bulletin*, No. 1, Bureau of Business and Economic Research, Madison, 1930; M. J. Gillen, *A New Economic Yardstick of Taxation and Public Credit for States and their Political Subdivisions*, (A monograph, New York, 1932); and H. M. Groves, "'A New Economic Yardstick of Taxation' in Wisconsin," *Bulletin of the National Tax Association*, Vol. XVIII, pp. 201-202.

References relating to the shifting and incidence of specific forms of taxation are given at the end of the succeeding chapters in which the various forms of taxation are discussed.

CHAPTER X

THE GENERAL PROPERTY TAX

THE most important source of state and local revenue in the United States is the general property tax. An appraisal of this form of revenue by Professor S. E. Leland is reproduced in this chapter.*

THE general property tax is a tax on all property regardless of its nature, at a uniform rate throughout the jurisdiction imposing the tax. The uniformity of the rate has caused this form of taxation to be referred to as taxation under the 'uniform rule,' but even this concept must be carefully qualified because in some instances all property is not uniformly taxed. Certain special property taxes have arisen, which, though levied directly upon property, are assessed and collected by methods not applied to real estate.[1] Included in this class are property taxes levied against corporations based upon the amount of their capital; special taxes imposed upon banks in proportion to capital, or deposits; taxes on investments; and taxes on animals per head. It is necessary, then, to distinguish the general from these special property taxes. This can be done by remembering that the general tax has as its base total individual property holdings upon which a proportional rate is imposed, while the special property taxes are either levied upon a different base or at a rate varying from the general property tax rate. At first, property taxation was of the special type, the land tax being the usual form, but gradually other types of property were included until the tax became one on general wealth.[2] In this form it is found in most of the American commonwealths.

Under the general property tax wealth is ordinarily assessed at full value,[3] but in a few states fractional assessments are

* From S. E. Leland, *The Classified Property Tax in the United States*, (Houghton, Mifflin Co., Boston, 1928), Chapter I.

[1] This definition of special property taxes accords with that used by the Bureau of Census.

[2] Seligman, *Essays in Taxation*, pp. 11-13.

[3] The term 'full value' has been interpreted to mean actual cash value, fair market value, etc. See *Report of Special Tax Commission*, Virginia, 1911, p. 79. *Cf.* especially Rifkind, 'What is Fair Value in Taxation?' *Proceedings*, National Tax Association (hereafter designated *Proc.*, N.T.A.), 1926, pp. 305-13.

allowed. Among the states which have at some time legalized the underassessment of some or all property are Alabama, Arkansas, California, Idaho, Illinois, Iowa, Louisiana, Minnesota, Montana, Nebraska, New Mexico, North Dakota and Washington.[4] In a number of other states undervaluation has in fact been legalized by court decisions although full assessment has been required by constitutional provision or by statute. In such cases complaints are usually made before the courts that the property of the plaintiff is assessed at a higher percentage of value than other property and that the proper authorities have not equalized the value of the complainant's holdings relative to other property under their jurisdiction.[5] When this allegation has been supported by adequate evidence, many of the courts have ordered a reduction of the assessment of the plaintiff's property to the level at which other property in the community is assessed.[6] Here the courts have performed the task of equalization. In the absence of such powers of equalization a remedy at law would appear to be lacking. A few courts, however, have denied relief where the plaintiff's property has not been fully assessed, and have said that the remedy consists in elevating the ratio of other assessments to true value.[7] When the state itself through its assessment machinery has found this impossible such decisions have conferred a right without a remedy. The injustice of such a decision should be obvious.

EXEMPTIONS

UNDER the general property tax certain exemptions from taxation are allowed. The usual exemptions include the property of religious, educational, scientific, and charitable institutions which are not conducted for private gain; property belonging to governmental units, to soldiers, to members of the militia, is exempt in full or in part; individual taxpayers, or families, receive a specific exemption of a small amount of personal property, tools, agricultural implements and machinery. Some states extend the exemption list to include the property of

[4] Fractional assessments adopted as a device for securing classification in California, Louisiana, Minnesota, Montana and North Dakota.

[5] As in *Hoboken Ferry Co.* v. *State Board of Taxes and Assessment,* 128 Atl. (N. J.) 418.

[6] *C. R. I. & P. Ry. Co.* v. *State,* 197 N. W. 114 (Neb); *Tacoma Mill Co.* v. *Pierce Co.,* 227 Pac. 500 (Wash.); *C. B. & Q. R. R. Co.,* v. *Cole,* 75 Ill. 591; *Sunday Lake Iron Co.* v. *Wakefield,* 247 U. S. 350, and many others.

[7] *Mason* v. *Des Moines,* 192 N. W. 129 (Ia.); *Thompson* v. *Devine Independent School Dist.,* 249 S. W. 887 (Tex.); *In re C. R. I. & P. Ry. Co.,* 200 N. W. 996 (Neb.); and a few others.

fraternal orders, agricultural societies, crops in hands of growers, flocks of chickens, and a few animals. Manufacturers are likewise liberally treated in not a few places. Other exemptions could also be cited.[8] The final result is, however, that the general property tax reaches all property, both real and personal, unless it is expressly exempt. This selection of property for complete exemption is not treated as classification, although partial exemptions are considered as a means of securing classification.[9]

EXTENT AND GROWTH OF EXEMPTIONS

THE exemption of property has always been one of the important problems in fiscal democracy. In early times tax exemption was the prerogative of a nobleman. Social stigma was attached to those who paid taxes. After many struggles, the base was widened to include the nobility, but even then the competition for exemption did not cease. Economic groups and interested individuals still strive for tax exemption. Hardly a legislative season passes in any state without a request for preferential tax treatment to be accorded through exemptions. Some of these requests have been inspired by high motives, such as the exemption of educational or charitable institutions, while others have been actuated by a desire to secure a differential advantage, using the exemption as an indirect government subsidy, but regardless of the motive the result has been the same. The exemption of real property from 1880 to 1922 is shown in Table 1.

When it is recalled that these figures do not include exempted personalty, the magnitude of tax exemptions seems staggering. Property exemptions means the heavier taxation of those holdings which are unable to claim this privilege. Little wonder it is that the demand is to keep exemptions at a

8 Interesting variations in exemptions are pointed out by Estcourt, in *The Conflict of Tax Laws*, p. 161. The list of exemptions in various states includes the property of temperance societies, temperance associations, water companies, state fair associations, building and loan associations, coöperative banks, manufacturing enterprises, manufactured products in the hands of the producer, mines of metal, forests, fruit trees, irrigation plants, vessels and steamships, hotels, dwelling houses, family portraits, sewing machines, personal property, money and credits, cash bonds of private corporations, property of Indians, firemen or persons under guardianship, legal reserve of life insurance companies, debts, stock in corporations paying no dividends and insurance companies. Even this does not exhaust the list. For summary of property exemptions see *Tax Burdens and Exemptions*, Research Report No. 64, National Industrial Conference Board, 1923, Appendix A, pp. 131-44. *Cf. Digest of State Laws Relating to Taxation and Revenue*, 1922.

9 See Chapter II, [Leland, *The Classified Property Tax in the United States*].

minimum, but in spite of this the value of exempted property yearly mounts higher.[10]

TABLE 1. COMPARISON OF REAL ESTATE EXEMPTED WITH TRUE VALUE OF TAXABLE PROPERTY [11]

Year	Taxable Property (in millions)	Realty Exempt (in millions)	Per Capita Exempt
1880	$ 41,642	$ 2,000	$ 44 [a]
1890	61,203	3,833	61
1900	82,304	6,212	82
1904	100,272	6,831	84
1912	173,986	12,313	129
1922	300,298	20,505	186

[a] Estimated.

It is difficult to estimate the extent of exemptions in each state because few states require the listing of property which is not taxed.[12] Statistics are, however, available for real estate exemptions in the State of New York, and the experience of this state may be taken as fairly typical of the situation in other localities. Every increase in the assessment of property has been accompanied by a more than corresponding increase in exemptions, as is shown in Table 2. These data show an increase of almost 470 per cent in the assessed value of exempted real property, which exceeds the growth in the assessment of taxable property by 187 per cent.

Recent investigations of tax exemptions in Connecticut show that from 1909 to 1925 the value of exempted property increased 179.49 per cent, while the value of taxable property increased 188.89 per cent.[13] But from 1921 to 1925, the value of exempted property increased 43.5 per cent, while taxable property increased about one-half as much, 23.2 per cent.

For the states as a whole, however, there appears to be little cause for alarm if real estate exemptions are compared with

---

[10] It is practically impossible to make comparisons prior to 1880, as no details of estimates for 1850, 1860 or 1870 were reported. Cf. Estimated Valuation of National Wealth, 1850–1912, p. 43. In 1880 the exempted property was but five per cent of the total so that it can be fairly assumed that the exemptions in those early years did not exceed that figure. Cf. Wealth, Debt and Taxation, 1907, p. 27.

[11] Estimated National Wealth, Wealth, Debt and Taxation, 1922, pp. 17-18, 25-29.

[12] The Bureau of Census has frequently voiced this complaint. Cf. Wealth, Debt and Taxation, 1907, p. 7.

[13] Quadrennial Statement by Tax Commissioner of Property Exempted from Taxation, Connecticut, 1926, p. 11. Value of exempted property: 1909, $144,-200,941; 1921, $280,887,014; 1925, $403,033,410. Value of taxable property: 1909, $837,022,807; 1921, $1,962,763,631; 1925, $2,418,096,161.

the estimated true value of all property.[14]   In 1900 real estate
exemptions amounted to 7 per cent of the total value of all
wealth; in 1904 the ratio was 6.4 per cent; in 1912, 6.6 per
cent; and in 1922 it was again 6.4 per cent.[15] Thus since
1900 the value of taxable property has increased more rapidly
than the real estate exemptions.

TABLE 2. COMPARISON OF REAL ESTATE ASSESSMENT WITH REAL
ESTATE EXEMPTIONS IN NEW YORK, 1900–24 [16]

Year	Assessed Value of all Taxable Real Estate (in millions)	Assessed Value of Exempt Real Property (in millions)	Ratio of Exempt to Total Real Property (per cent)	Ratio of Exempt to Taxable Real Property (per cent)
1900	$ 5,093	$ 723	12.4	14.2
1905	7,312	1,389	16.0	19.0
1910	9,639	1,788	15.6	18.6
1915	11,335	2,521	18.2	22.2
1920	14,595	2,996	17.0	20.5
1924	19,411	4,110	17.5	21.2

ASSESSMENT

Though the problem of exemptions has been very important, the assessment of property has received more attention
from tax officials, and at the same time has been the subject
of much research by students interested in taxation. Valuation
seems very simple until the assessment is to be made; then
the various factors which go to produce value must be considered carefully. The problem would be easily solved if
only one kind of property had to be appraised. Instead, so
numerous are the types of property that a single county
assessor may be called upon to value steel mills, steamship
lines, manufacturing and mercantile concerns, farm property,
city lots and buildings, leaseholds, annuities, securities, as well
as personal and household effects. The valuation of any one
of these is a task which calls for an expert knowledge, which,
at present, the average local assessor cannot be expected to
possess. The mere size of a manufacturing establishment may
make it psychologically impossible for the assessor to reach
its true value, yet the law requires him to attempt a valuation.
In a few states instead of placing the burden of assessment on
the local officials, the taxpayer is required, under a perfunctory
oath, to list his own property. If he turns in an assessment,

14 Jensen, 'The General Prpoerty Tax' (unpublished thesis), p. 105.
15 Estimated National Wealth, op. cit., p. 19.
16 Tax Burdens and Exemptions, op. cit., p. 79; Report of State Tax Commission, New York, 1924.

it may be increased by the local equalization board, but as long as he has listed something, the assessor usually does not trouble him. Under such methods there is little doubt that much property escapes taxation.

Taxable property is generally listed as of a certain day designated by law, and only property owned on that date need be listed. This day has usually been in the early spring, when the farmers have disposed of their crops, or if it comes at a time when the harvests have not been sold, the law generally exempts for that year the crops still in the hands of the grower.[17] One consequence of limiting liability for taxes to property held on a given day is that many taxpayers have been enabled effectually to escape taxation. For example, prior to assessment day some forms of property, such as bank deposits, have been converted into non-taxable bonds, only to be reconverted into cash when assessment day has passed; cashier's checks, which are easily hidden, have been exchanged for deposit accounts in banks; taxable securities have been sold to be rebought after liability for tax payments has passed.[18] Many other devices have likewise been employed.

The frequency of assessment varies. For personal property there is invariably an annual assessment. Real estate is valued annually in a majority of the states, but biennially and quadrennially in others, with not a few states providing for even more infrequent appraisals. Maryland, for example, at one time had assessments only when ordered by the legislature, and it pleased the legislature to have but seven assessments in a hundred years.[19] A peculiar condition, due to the fact that dates for assessments were to be 'at the time ordered by the town,' resulted in thirty-eight different assessment dates in Rhode Island in 1912.[20]

HISTORY OF GENERAL PROPERTY TAX

SELIGMAN has traced the general taxation of property as far back as 596 B.C., when it was employed in Athens during the time of Solon.[21] A more general form was found there about two centuries later (378 B.C.). Early Rome used this method later to abandon the attempt to tax personalty. During the

[17] For date of assessments in various states see *Sixth Annual Report of Board of Tax Commissioners*, Rhode Island, 1918, pp. 27 ff.; *Digest of State Laws Relating to Taxation and Revenue*, 1922.
[18] *Report of State Tax Commission of Maryland to General Assembly*, 1892, p. x.
[19] Girwood, 'Progress Since 1912 Conference,' *Proc.*, N.T.A., 1913, p. 302.
[20] *Report of Joint Special Committee on Taxation Laws*, 1910, pp. 143-44. Uniform date of assessment adopted, *Public Laws*, Rhode Island, 1919, ch. 1735.
[21] For early history, see Seligman, *Essays in Taxation*, 10th ed., pp. 34 ff.

Middle Ages the feudal land taxes were extended to embrace all forms of wealth, the movement being readily discernible in England, Scotland, and on the continent. In some of the American colonies this tax was the rule from earliest times,[22] but in others, as in Virginia, it grew up as the excessive poll taxes oppressed the poor, and called for the measurement of faculty by 'the visible estates in the colony.'[23] In some localities the extension of the land tax precipitated many conflicts between different groups in the colonies,[24] while in others it was thought for a time that the general property tax was in substantial accord with their ideals of justice, and as long as the rate was low it occasioned little hardship even as the sole source of revenue for many states.

Roughly speaking, about the time of the Civil War the property tax rates began to be increasingly severe. In the meantime property holdings were becoming differentiated. largely through the development of corporate ownership which opened new channels for the investment of funds. The appearance of these intangibles, the growth of population, increasing urbanization, and other complications in our economic and social life increased the problems of property assessment. The states, instead of perfecting assessment machinery, began to rely more and more on local valuations, securing their revenue by increasing levies upon these, their main source of support.[25] With the increase in state rates, assessors began to undervalue the property in their districts more than before, in order to minimize the portion of the state burden which their localities would have to shoulder. Recognition of these conditions increased the dissatisfaction with the general property tax.

FISCAL IMPORTANCE OF GENERAL PROPERTY TAX

The seriousness of the defects of this tax can be realized by noting that it has always been the main support of state and local governments in the United States.[26] In 1902 general

[22] Ripley, *Financial History of Virginia*, Columbia Univ. Studies in Hist., Econ. and Pub. Law, vol. IV, no. 1, p. 21.

[23] *Ibid.*, p. 25.

[24] 'This fact marks the beginning of that struggle between great and small landowners, the cause of which lay deep rooted in the origin of private property under the old Virginia Company. This in time crystallized into a sectional as well as a class antagonism ; and lasted until Virginia was finally subdivided into two states.' *Ibid.*, pp. 25-26.

[25] Seligman, 'Sound Tax Reform,' *Chicago Daily News Reprint*, no. 3, 1922, p. 5.

[26] *Cf.* Gottlieb, 'Growth of Local Tax Burdens,' *Bulletin*, National Tax Association, vol. VIII, no. 6, pp. 160 ff. (Hereafter designated as *Bul.*, N.T.A.) Reprinted from *Quart. Jour. Ec.*, Feb., 1923 ; Jensen, *op. cit.*, pp. 6-17.

property taxes in this country amounted to $706,660,000. Twenty years later the collections were $3,321,484,000, or over four times greater than in 1902. The per capita increase and the ratio of general property taxes to the aggregate taxes and special assessments are shown in the accompanying table:

TABLE 3. GENERAL PROPERTY TAX BURDEN : 1902, 1912, 1922 [27]

Year	Aggregate[a] Per capita	Per cent of total[b]	States Per capita	Per cent of total[b]	Cities Per capita	Per cent of total[b]	Counties Per capita	Per cent of total[b]
1922	$30.55	78.7	$3.22	40.1	$20.30	82.8	$7.07	92.1
1912	11.20	79.4	1.44	45.9	14.47	77.5	3.29	91.1
1902	8.35	82.1	1.02	51.0	12.21	86.7	1.85	91.1

a Includes also minor civil divisions not shown on this table.
b Per cent of total taxes and special assessments.

This table shows an increase in the per capita burden of the general property tax for every division of government making use of it. The percentage calculations also indicate that this is the main source of revenue for most governments at the present time. In 1922 the general property taxes furnished over 90 per cent of the total tax revenues in 13 states for state and local purposes combined, between 80 and 90 per cent of such revenues in 21 states, between 70 and 80 per cent in 12 states, and less than 70 per cent in only 2 states.[28] A close examination of the foregoing table, however, indicates that the tax is not contributing as large a proportion of the state revenues as formerly, a tendency which is probably due to the development of special taxes and to the desire to leave this source of revenue more exclusively to the local governments; yet, in the large, this tax is still of primary importance to the states. Its chief importance today, however, comes from the fact that it is the main reliance of local governments. They are relying more both absolutely and relatively on this tax than are other branches of government; their taxes are greater in amount than other levies; and due to their increasing needs and expenditures their tax burden has become correspondingly more severe — all of which emphasizes the fiscal importance of this tax.

DEFECTS OF THE GENERAL PROPERTY TAX

THE defects of the general property tax were recognized almost as soon as it was employed.[29] Complaints of inequalities in the

27 Wealth, Debt and Taxation, 1907, 1913, 1922.
28 Yearbook, U. S. Dept. of Agriculture, 1924, p. 262.
29 The general property tax has been abandoned in most of Europe. It is found in some of the Swiss cantons. Bullock, Selected Readings in Public Finance, 3d ed., pp. 350 ff. Also found in Australia. Seligman, op. cit., p. 141.

assessment of the land tax and the failure to consider improvements emanated from fiscal officers in Virginia prior to 1630. Recognition of these defects led to the establishment of fixed valuation upon land.[30] Undervaluation caused Rhode Island in 1673 to enact the following law : [31]

If the Assembly judge any to have undervalued their estate, each shall be required to give in to the Treasurer a true form of an inventory of all their estate and strength in particular, and give in writing what proportion of estate and strength in particular he guesseth ten of his neighbors, naming them in particular, hath in estate and strength to his estate and strength.

In Massachusetts the poll and property tax system was attacked as early as 1786, while the injustices of local assessments were complained of in 1792.[32] Secretary Wolcott in his report on direct taxes, delivered to Congress in 1796, alluded to the difficulty of obtaining accurate and impartial assessments, and stated that the tax systems were being confined more and more 'to visible and permanent objects.'[33] In 1809, Vermont, attempting to correct the valuation of intangibles, passed a law giving listers authority to assess intangibles at what they thought to be the true amount, if they were dissatisfied with the valuation of the owners.[34] In Connecticut, in 1817, Governor Wolcott delivered a message to the general assembly characterizing the property tax system as ancient and ill-adapted to the needs of the people.[35] In 1820 the legislature attempted to meet the situation by the creation of a board of equalization.[36] Subsequent complaints can be found in practically every state, increasing in intensity and vigor as the mounting tax rates emphasized the intolerable nature of the tax.

The defects of the general property tax fall naturally into two classes : those inherent in the theoretical basis of the tax, and those arising from its administration. The latter class was quickly noted[37] and received first attention, but the causes of failure were more deeply rooted than mere administrative

[30] Sydenstricker, A Brief History of Taxation in Virginia, pp. 61-63.
[31] Ely, Taxation in American States and Cities, p. 141 ; Pottle, 'The State Board and the Local Asessor,' Bul. no. 6, Rhode Island Tax Officials Asso., p. 10 (Feb. 1, 1919).
[32] Bullock, Financial Policy of Massachusetts, pp. 13, 18.
[33] Wolcott, in American State Papers, 1 Finance, 438 (1796).
[34] Wood, Finances of Vermont, p. 32 ; cites Laws of 1809, ch. XLIV, p. 41.
[35] Walradt, The Financial History of Connecticut, p. 61.
[36] Session Laws of 1820, p. 448 ; Revision of 1821, p. 449 ; Report of Special Tax Commission, Connecticut, 1887, pp. 10 ff.
[37] Cf. Seligman, op. cit., p. 19.

difficulties. The fundamental reasons for failure are found in the defects in theory.

A. THEORETICAL DEFECTS

(a) Adopts a False Test of Faculty

THE foremost failing of the general property tax is that it adopts a false test of faculty. It either assumes that property *per se* possesses ability to pay or uses property as the *indicia* of ability. When at first land was used as the basis of taxation complaints were heard at once of the inequality of the tax.[38] The demand for its extension led to the inclusion of all property, which as long as property was but slightly differentiated resulted in a tax fairly proportional to individual faculty. When, however, property holdings lost their primitive character this base became a faulty test.

As property becomes productive, men begin to support themselves more and more from the income which it produces and come to measure taxes in terms of the income of which they are paid. The property tax thus becomes an assessment for a payment made from the returns of property, or out of income.[39] Yet if the property produces no product, the tax becomes one on labor to be paid out of the income from services, or else it takes the form of a capital levy destroying a part of the capital upon which rests the patrimony of the state.[40] The impermanence of the value of wealth renders property a precarious standard of measurement. Changes in demand may destroy the value of goods and the industries producing them. Changes in prices, which are continually going on, may create fictitious wealth which becomes taxable,[41] or may destroy preëxistent values. A share of stock, for example, seldom has a stable market value, so that its price on assessment day may afford little insight into the ability of the owner to meet a tax payment. Again, property is an insufficient index because there may be income without property. Thus, labor and service incomes are without the sphere of property taxation. As between various enterprises, some requiring a large amount of property, others very little, a property index operates most unsatisfactorily.

[38] *Cf.* Seligman, *op. cit.*, pp. 34 ff.

[39] Bastable, *Public Finance*, p. 470.

[40] Resemblance of general capital levies to the general property tax pointed out by Viner, 'Taxation and Changes in Price Levels,' *Jour. Pol. Econ.*, vol. XXXI, no. 4, pp. 508-09 (Aug., 1923).

[41] See Viner, *supra* ; also Bastable, *op. cit.*, p. 470.

If an individual secures property by the result of his labor, he possesses ability to pay prior to conversion into property, so the investment may be no measure of the income from which it is acquired. When the alternative of borrowing is used, property does not represent tax ability. Here there is only an equity which may be entirely offset by liabilities. To use gross property as an index of faculty in such a case is to make tax burdens proportional to liabilities and most oppressive upon poor debtors. Subject to the limitations noted in the previous paragraphs, property cannot be a measure of taxable capacity until the liabilities incurred in its acquisition are extinguished and an unencumbered title is received. To tax both the property and the debt for its acquisition, without offset for the latter, is to tax not only dually but also beyond ability. Allowance of offsets for debts has proved inexpedient because of liability of abuse through the creation of fictitious debts which were deducted from the value of taxable holdings, in many cases leaving dishonest individuals with no taxes to pay.[42] Corporations likewise sought to deduct bonded indebtedness from property values and escaped a large share of their taxes until the practice was checked.[43] The policy now followed by the majority of the states is to restrict the privilege of debt deductions. While this is necessary properly to safeguard the treasury, it renders impossible a complete remedy against double taxation.

Turning from the measure of ability to the obligation to pay for benefits received, property becomes a more satisfactory measure. Though the benefit theory has been discarded as worthless by many writers on public finance,[44] nevertheless it cannot be thrown aside altogether.[45] Under local governments many benefits are conferred directly on property by public expenditures. These benefits often not only enhance the value of the property but frequently add to its net return. In such cases it is only just that the government recoup itself for these benefits from the property or the owners thereof. The property not only receives the benefits but often possesses the ability

[42] Seligman, 'Two Experiments in the Taxation of Franchises,' *Review of Reviews*, Jan., 1904, p. 717.

[43] Hunter, 'Taxation of Public Service Corporations in New York,' *Bul.*, N.T.A., vol. IV, no. 2, p. 36.

[44] Seligman, *Essays, op. cit.*, p. 73; *Progressive Taxation in Theory and Practice*, 2d ed., 1908, pp. 150-57; Plehn, *Intro. to Pub. Finance*, 5th ed., pp. 89-91; Adams, *Science of Finance*, pp. 299-301. *Cf.* Seligman, 'Taxation and Prices,' *Proc.*, Acad. of Pol. Sci., vol. XI, no. 2, pp. 106-106 (Jan., 1925).

[45] Lyon, *Principles of Taxation*, pp. 14-16, 22-23, 26-30; Lutz, *Public Finance*, pp. 273-74; 280.

to pay. When such ability is present it would seem that the value of the property would measure a part of the benefits of governmental services. If the ability were absent, then the index would be faulty or the benefit immeasurable or infinitesimal. Though property may measure benefits conferred, it seems unwise to adopt it as the sole test for governmental obligations.

(b) *Ignores Income from Property*

A corollary of the first defect is that the general property tax ignores the income from property. If all values represented a sum equal to the capitalization of net earnings this statement would be untrue, but much of the property which is taxed possesses value without producing income. Some goods possess value because they satisfy wants though they produce only psychic income. Psychic values are usually discarded in the realm of taxation as being too difficult of measurement. 'Income' in the tax field means income in the form of money or what can be exchanged for money. Since property is composed of income- and non-income-producing types, the taxation of property alone, without differentiation as to class does not correspond closely to the taxation of income. In the assessment of personal effects, income is not involved. Furniture in the home yields no monetary income, yet it is taxed on the same basis as a going concern or as bonds and stocks. As long as property is to be taxed *as property,* non-income-producing types should be taxable if they have value. To do otherwise would be to destroy property taxation *per se.*

An unfairness can be seen, however, by reference to certain enterprises. Some concerns utilize small amounts of property, yet their earnings are large, often out of all proportion to invested capital. Such undertakings may be capitalized for security purposes on the basis of their earning power, rather than on the basis of physical valuations, yet to tax them on the basis of property is to ignore large taxable capacity. To tax such a business according to its property and to tax a competing enterprise on the basis of the large property holdings which its operation necessitates is to subject one to an excessive burden, relatively underestimating, at the same time, the ability of the other. Certain industries, for example, such as express companies, motor transit concerns, and private (refrigerator) car lines, have very little physical property, yet from their investment large returns are received. Other commercial establishments, such as railroads, require vast amounts of property and earn relatively smaller returns. To tax on the basis of property two competing concerns, whose returns are in widely different proportions to the property employed by them, is in effect to subsidize one competitor at the expense of the other. What may seem to be equality of taxation may after all be only equality with reference to a criterion having little relationship to ability to pay taxes.

Some would say that here an intangible value is escaping taxation, but very often such values do not exist, or if present, call for special treatment. Similarly in the case of well-managed and fortunate concerns having the same capital value as like ventures unfortunate and poorly managed no differences in property taxes would appear in spite of a diversity in tax paying ability. These complications demonstrate the futility of the attempted application of the uniform rule.[46] Some have favored classification so that these factors may be considered.

(c) Assumes Property is Homogeneous

A third defect is that the general property tax assumes that all property is socially and economically homogeneous. Time was when this assumption was substantially correct, but the growing complexity of our economic society with its many types of property and objects of ownership has increased the injustice of taxing all property by uniform methods. These difficulties have been accentuated by the rapid industrial development of the country and the rise of intangibles. Inequalities in income became more apparent and property as a test of ability to pay more unsatisfactory. Under these circumstances the uniform taxation of property ignored fundamental differences between very dissimilar types of property. The assumption of the homogeneity of property likewise ignores the differences in the degree of ease of concealing certain classes of property. Nor do the varying costs of protecting different types of property, or the differences in demands upon government services receive the slightest consideration under the general property tax. Obviously, property cannot be assumed to be one economic good to be taxed by a single method. Recognition of this has caused many to advocate the adoption of classification.

---

46 The diversity of the real estate tax burden in New York was pointed out in 1922. It was shown that different businesses paid the following percentages of net income in property taxes : mercantile and manufacturing corporations, 4.5 per cent ; national banks, 1.5 ; state banks, 3.5 ; trust companies, 4.1 ; savings banks, 3.6 ; steam railroads, 24.6 ; electric railways, 38.5 ; telephone and telegraph companies, 12.1 ; gas and electric companies, 20.5. *Report of Special Joint Committee on Taxation and Retrenchment*, 1922 ; *Bul.*, N.T.A., vol. VII, no. 8, p. 254.

(d) Does not Heed Incidence

From the standpoint of justice one of the most glaring defects of the general property tax is its disregard of the incidence of the tax. It assumes that the tax is imposed on a single piece of property whereas numerous economic elements are taxed on which the incidence is not the same. The incidence of the tax on land is very different from the incidence of the tax on buildings or that of the improvements on land. Taxes on commodities intended for resale may be shifted while taxes on articles destined for consumption which are subject to no further transfers cannot be passed on directly. The incidence of taxes on stocks may be a very different thing from the incidence of taxes on certificates of indebtedness. In one case the holder of the stock may pay the tax while in the case of a bond it will probably be passed on to the borrower. Through the process of capitalization the tax on securities may be made to fall on the holder at the time of the tax.[47] These problems in the shifting of taxation are ignored by the general property tax. Only by providing separate methods of taxation for the different types of property can the problems of tax shifting be fairly dealt with and substantial justice accorded.

B. OPERATIVE DEFECTS

THE theoretical defects of the general property tax caused many to be interested in classification, but the four types of operative defects, next to be considered, gave a further impetus to the acceptance of this doctrine. The first to be discussed are the inequalities between taxing districts.

(a) Inequalities between Taxing Districts

The inequalities in the assessment of property as between various counties have been the direct product of the general property tax system. State revenues were derived, in most instances, by rates based upon the total assessment of each county, thereby causing those counties which desired to minimize their contribution to the state to underassess the property in their district so that the state rate would apply to a smaller base than if full-value assessments were employed. The counties which endeavored to enforce the laws calling for assessments at fair cash values were heavily penalized for their honesty. In Virginia, in 1910, the range for county assessments upon real estate was from 18 to 77 per cent of true value, with

47 For a fuller discussion of incidence see Seligman, *The Shifting and Incidence of Taxation*; Bastable, *op. cit.*, bk. III, ch. V.

an average assessment of 48 per cent, while in eighteen prominent cities the range began at 40 and extended to 77, with a
mean assessment of 63 per cent, indicating more uniformity and
a closer approximation to law in the cities than in the counties,
which of course would have been reversed as to personal property.[48] In Nebraska, in 1913, average assessments per county
ranged from 30 per cent to 87.74 per cent of true value, the
percentages showing a tendency to increase as counties in the
eastern part of the state were examined.[49] In Indiana counties
in 1915, the assessments ranged from 20 to 75 per cent of true
value, the average being 45 per cent, with rural counties showing a relatively higher valuation than the distinctly urban
counties.[50] In California, in 1915, the undervaluations ranged
from 20 to 50 per cent. Assessments in six counties ranged
from 20 to 30 per cent; those in thirty counties from 30 to 40
per cent; while sixteen counties assessed their property at
from 40 to 50 per cent.[51] The same situation could be shown
for practically every state in which the general property tax
was used prior to the adoption of reformed administrative
systems.[52]

[48] *Report of Special Tax Commission*, Virginia, 1911, pp. 141-44.
[49] *Report of the Special Commission on Revenue and Taxation*, Nebraska,
1914, pp. 64-65.
[50] *Report of Commission on Taxation*, Indiana, 1916, pp. 233-35.
[51] *Report of State Tax Commission*, California, 1917, p. 253.
[52] A recent comparison of 6105 real estate transfers in Cook County, Illinois,
for 1926 revealed the following ratios of assessed to sales value in different
townships in that county :

Township	Percentage of Assessed to Sales Value
1. South Town (Loop District)	48.3
2. Rogers Park	33.6
3. North Town	33.1
4. Hyde Park	30.3
5. West Town	30.0
6. Jefferson	29.9
7. Lake View	28.5
8. Lake	28.5
9. Calumet	9.9
Average	31.3

(Data taken from *A Study of Assessment Methods and Results in Cook County*,
prepared by the Joint Commission on Real Estate Valuation for the Board
of County Commissioners of Cook County, July, 1927, p. 22.)
In 1924, the following ratios of assessed to true value were found in 22
Illinois counties crossed by the C. & N. W. Ry. (true value computed by means
of sales data); Boone, 41.30 per cent; Bureau, 33.03; DeKalb, 41.4; DuPage,
35.00; Jo Daviess, 39.63; Kane, 42.75; Lake, 23.93; LaSalle, 36.06; Lee, 40.45;
McHenry, 50.03; Macoupin, 38.64; Marshall, 39.58; Mason, 41.87; Menard,

(b) Inequalities between Types of Property

A more serious injustice results from the unequal assessment of different types of property. Though the general property tax endeavors to tax all property uniformly, seldom, if ever, are all classes of property equally assessed.[53] Although the burden upon real estate has become notorious, it has often not been equitably distributed among the various types of property.[54] Tangible personalty has been forced to contribute more than its proportionate share of state taxes, while such objects as bicycles, automobiles, and musical instruments are often singled out for careful valuation.[55] The result usually is their overassessment relative to the property which is not receiving similar attention. In Kentucky, in 1912, for instance, the state was able to secure more revenue from its dogs than from its stocks, bonds and monies.[56] In the same year only about ten

41.63 ; Ogle, 48.25 ; Peoria, 40.18 ; Sangamon, 47.29 ; Stark, 39.52 ; Stephenson, 42.59 ; Tazewell, 35.82 ; Whiteside, 44.98 ; Winnebago, 47.82. Compiled by R. A. Miller, Gen'l Tax Agent, C. & N. W. Ry Co., Chicago.

[53] For example, in 1918 in Illinois the average valuation of horses in Hardin County was $109.77, while in Pulaski County it was $48.51 ; the value of sheep ranged from $13.44 (average) in Menard County, to $3.24 in Pulaski ; traction engines had an average value of $2233.41 in Rock Island County, as compared with an average of $90.12 in Douglas County ; pianos ranged from $124.23 (average) in Hardin County, to $42.69 in Coles County ; clocks averaged $60.75 in Rock Island County to $4.47 in Brown County ; automobiles assessed at $365.79 (average) in Hardin County, $362.91 in Cook County, and at $70.68 in Pulaski County ; household and office furniture per family averaged $110 in McHenry County, $40 in Cook County, and $25 in Edgar and Jefferson Counties. *Taxation in Illinois*, 1918.

[54] This is illustrated by an analysis of 6105 real estate transfers in Cook County, Illinois, for 1926 in which the following ratios of assessed to sales values of various types of property were discovered :

Types of Property	Percentage of Assessed to Sales Value
1. Office and bank buildings	53.4
2. Industrial	38.1
3. Retail and wholesale	36.3
4. Apartment buildings	32.3
5. Hotels, theaters, amusements	31.2
6. Miscellaneous	30.9
7. Combined business and residence	29.5
8. Duplex-family residences	29.4
9. Single-family residences	27.7
10. Vacant land	19.7
Average	31.3

(Data taken from *A Study of Assessment Methods and Results in Cook County*, op. cit., p. 23.)

[55] Lutz, *The State Tax Commission*, p. 123 (bicycles) ; Rhode Island Tax Officials' Asso., 1916, *Bul.*, no. 2, p. 7 (automobiles, especially Ford cars) ; *Cincinnati Enquirer*, June 9, 1915 (automatic pianos in saloons).

[56] *Report of the Special Tax Commission*, Kentucky, 1912, p. 84.

per cent of the bank deposits were returned for taxation in that state. In addition, the complaint is frequently heard that banks are discriminated against and have higher true rates imposed on them than are levied against other property.[57] Indeed, in a number of states banks pay over half of the personal property taxes. In Missouri, in 1911, the owners of bank stock were taxed two or three times as much as the owners of equivalent amounts of other types of property. Like protest against discrimination has been made at various times by other economic groups, such as the railroads,[58] mines and utilities. While this property was being listed, much personal property was not being assessed at all. In New York, for example, the failure adequately to reach personalty was a fact which contributed greatly to the enactment of the income tax in that state.[59] Many other inequalities in the assessment of various types of property could be cited, but enough have been shown to substantiate the conclusion that the general property tax does not equally or uniformly reach the many types of property it endeavors to assess. Likewise it produces an uncontrolled differentiation in tax burdens, resulting in what might be called unintentional classification.

(c) Inequalities between Individual Assessments

Closely akin to the inequalities treated in the preceding paragraph are those which prevail between individual assessments. These may be the result of mistakes in appraisals, political connivance or social influence, but more often they are due either to the different degrees of full reporting on the part of taxpayers or to the psychological inability of the assessor properly to evaluate those things with which he is not familiar. The notoriously small valuations placed on private art collections and on exquisite house furnishings are more properly to be accounted for in this manner than by a desire to curry favor with the rich. Moreover, the same piece of property will seldom be valued for the same amount by two different though equally honest and competent individuals. This was clearly illustrated by the assessment of steel mills in Pittsburgh. These establishments were valued by one assessor

57 Paton, 'State Taxation of Banks,' Proc., N.T.A., 1913, pp. 323-24, 338.
58 Baldwin, 'Taxation of Railroad Property,' Papers and Proc., Minn. Acad. of Soc. Sci., vol. I, no. 1, pp. 123-25, 129-30 (Dec., 1907); 'Taxation of Street Railways in Rhode Island,' Bul., N.T.A., vol. IV, no. 2, pp. 56-57. For undertaxation of railroads, cf. Miller, 'Taxation of Railroad Property,' Papers and Proc., Minn. Acad. of Soc. Sci., vol. I, no. 1, p. 134; Taxation in Illinois, 1918, pp. 16-17; Lutz, op. cit., pp. 73, 168-69.
59 See Comstock, The State Taxation of Personal Incomes, New York, 1921.

for city purposes and by another for county purposes. In most cases there was considerable discrepancy in the valuations, as is shown in Table 4.

TABLE 4. COMPARISON OF ASSESSMENT OF MILL PROPERTIES MADE BY DIFFERENT ASSESSING OFFICIALS: PITTSBURGH, PENNSYLVANIA [60]

Property Assessed	City Assessment	County Assessment
Carnegie Steel Co. (Lucy Furnace)..	$ 927,950	$1,071,380
Clinton Iron & Steel Co.	597,710	468,229
Pressed Steel Car Co. (Allegheny Plant)	500,160	719,730
Carbon Steel Co.	490,450	472,950
Brown & Co.	480,810	484,300
American Steel & Wire Co. (Schoenberger Mill)	1,564,453	1,352,190
Jones & Laughlin Steel Co.	2,761,638	3,165,040

The above table indicates the variable judgments of *different* assessors, without special training, acting without expert supervision and standardized practices, when attempting to value *identical* properties. The same condition prevails when the *same* assessors, under conditions just mentioned, endeavor to appraise *similar,* but not *identical,* holdings. In the assessment of modern office buildings in Pittsburgh it was shown in 1916 that assessed values of structures of like construction, age and desirability when reduced to a cubic foot basis varied from 75.20 cents to 22.07 cents for the sixteen structures for which the comparison was made.[61]

Inequality between individual assessments is also manifest in the valuation of practically identical lands separated only by township or county lines but with the assessments made by different officials. Such examples, which may be of territorial inequalities also, have frequently been cited in Kansas where different assessors have placed unlike valuations on tracts of land adjacent to township lines, as follows: [62]

Township Line	$137	149	129	116	96	70	91	82	70	76	73	Township Line
	$ 78	75	76	62	52	44	45	47	44	44	40	

[60] Data taken from *Report of Committee on Taxation Study,* Pittsburgh, 1916, p. 19.

[61] Cf. *Report of Committee on Taxation Study,* Pittsburgh, 1916.

[62] *Third Report to Legislature, Kansas Tax Commission,* 1913, p. 36; cf. also pp. 35-38.

(d) Inequalities between Amounts of Property

Another defect is found in the inequality between amounts of property to be assessed. Smaller parcels are more easy of assessment than large ones; modest homes simply furnished can be appraised with more facility than the princely mansion; while the small store or manufacturing establishment can be more certainly valued than the larger enterprise. Because of this natural weakness the smaller pieces of property have been taxed regressively. Indeed, the Special Tax Commission of 1916, in Indiana, found that assessments showed a steady decrease in the ratio of the assessed to true value as the worth of the property increased.[63] Investigation of a number of pieces of real estate in the city of Vincennes shortly after the submission of this report revealed the fact that the finest houses in that locality were assessed at one-tenth of their value, while the homes of those economically less fortunate were assessed at approximately three-fourths of their value. In the District of Columbia a few years earlier it was found that small houses were assessed at an average of 90 per cent of their true value while fine residences were listed at 50 per cent.[64] Even considering the ground values alone, the sites of small homes were assessed at a higher percentage of true value than other property.[65] In Wisconsin it was found that 'taking the assessment of persons whose personal property amounted to less than $1000 at 100 per cent, those whose possessions ranged between $1000 and $10,000 were assessed only 82 per cent as high; those who owned more than $10,000 and less than $50,000 were assessed at 60 per cent; and those who owned more than $50,000 and less than $500,000 were assessed at 43 per cent; and all who owned over $500,000 were assessed at only 28 per cent.'[66]

In Virginia the fact that assessment percentages vary inversely with the value of the property has been frequently demonstrated. This was brought out very clearly by the Joint Committee on Tax Revision in 1914 which found that small country tracts were assessed at nearly half of their true value while estates of over $10,000 were assessed at about one-fourth

[63] *Report of Special Tax Commission,* Indiana, 1916, p. vi.
[64] *Report on Assessment and Taxation of Real Estate in the District of Columbia,* House Report, no. 1215, 62d Congress, 2d Session, pp. 5, 20-25.
[65] 'Considering ground values by themselves, those acres occupied by small houses are assessed at 60 per cent of true value (p. 416); those by middle-class houses, at 50 per cent; those by fine residences at 30 per cent; and the large suburban areas at 20 per cent.' House Report, *supra,* pp. 5-6.
[66] Francis E. McGovern, *A State Income Tax,* Address before Conference of Governors, Richmond, Virginia, Dec. 5, 1912, pam., p. 4.

of their value.[67] The same tendency was found in cities but as assessments were larger the difference was less accentuated than in the counties. Table 5 will reveal the facts.[68]

TABLE 5. RATIO OF ASSESSMENT TO SELLING VALUE OF PROPERTY IN COUNTIES AND CITIES BY VALUE OF PROPERTY OWNED: VIRGINIA, 1914

Value of Property	Ratio of Assessment to Selling Price	
	In Counties (per cent)	In Cities (per cent)
Total	33.5	53.1
Under $500	46.7	59.8
500- 1,000	39.0	58.2
1,000- 2,500	36.4	56.5
2,500- 5,000	32.7	56.0
5,000-10,000	31.1	53.0
Over 10,000	28.1	48.2

More recently an extensive investigation in Kansas covering the period from 1913 to 1922 brought out the same tendency toward regressive assessments,[69] as shown in Table 6.

TABLE 6. RATIO OF ASSESSMENT TO SALE PRICE OF REAL ESTATE BY VALUE OF PROPERTY OWNED: KANSAS, 1913–1922

Value of Property	Ratio of Assessment to Sale Price *	
	Real Estate Farm	Real Estate City
Under $1,500	85.7%	97.0%
1,500- 2,999	76.7	89.0
3,000- 4,499	72.9	82.9
4,500- 5,999	70.0	80.5
6,000- 7,499	66.4	76.5
7,500- 8,999	65.3	74.5
9,000-10,499	62.3	70.9
10,500 and over	58.7	69.1
All groups	65.6	73.3

* Weighted average.

It must not be concluded, however, that the regressive character of the general property tax is confined to the taxation of

[67] Report of Joint Committee on Tax Revision, Virginia, 1914, p. 10 ; Snavely, The Taxation of Negroes in Virginia, pp. 71, 72, 75.
[68] Report of Joint Committee, op. cit., p. 10.
[69] Englund, 'Assessment and Equalization of Farm and City Real Estate in Kansas,' Bul., no. 232, Kan. Agri. Exper. Station.

real estate alone. In 1884 the following observation was recorded by a West Virginia tax commission: [70]

By comparing a number of these appraisements (made for probate purposes) with the tax assessment made next prior to the death of such person, we find that a man with a personal estate valued immediately *after* his death at $200 was rated immediately *before* his death at $178; while a man whose estate appraised at $5000 was rated at only $1500; this is to say, if the man of small means was rated in the same proportion as the man of large means, he would pay taxes on only $60 whereas he now pays on $178.

These conclusions which may have evidenced only erratic assessment have been more recently substantiated by investigations in Wisconsin. Special assessors sent out by the tax commission to check the accuracy of assessments in two counties discovered considerable evidence of regression as a result of over two thousand appraisals of personal estates.[71] The evidence, presented in Table 7, shows that holdings valued at under $1000 were assessed at a much higher percentage of true value, and therefore, were taxed at a greater effective rate, than more valuable holdings, and that as the estates increased in value the ratio of assessed to true value declined. Regression, then, seems to be found in the taxation of both real and personal property under the general property tax system.

TABLE 7. INSPECTIONS OF PERSONAL PROPERTY IN TWO WISCONSIN COUNTIES CLASSIFIED ACCORDING TO THE VALUE OF THE INDIVIDUAL HOLDINGS [72]

Value of Holdings	Number of Inspections	Values Assessed	True	Ratio of Assessed to True Value (per cent)
Under $1,000	918	$ 355,870	$ 595,968	59.72
1,000- 9,999	1210	1,430,295	2,913,912	49.08
10,000- 49,999	84	650,865	1,800,622	36.15
50,000-499,999	25	826,261	3,207,027	25.76
500,000 and over	2	343,950	2,832,942	16.92
Total	2239	$3,607,241	$10,550,471	34.19

ASSESSMENT OF INTANGIBLES

THE attempted assessment of intangibles under the general property tax has been a tale of continual failure, dating back

70 *Preliminary Report of the West Virginia Tax Commission*, 1884, quoted by Ely, *Taxation in American States and Cities*, p. 174.
71 Cf. Adams, 'Income Tax as Substitute for Property Tax,' *Proc.*, N.T.A., 1910, pp. 108 ff.
72 *Proc.*, N.T.A., 1910, p. 110.

almost to colonial times,[73] and has been the chief reason for the agitation for a classified property tax. The value of taxable intangibles ranges from at least a fourth to over a hundred per cent of the remaining total assessable wealth, but never in the experience of any state has this class of property been listed with even an approach to completeness. Because of its mobility and the ease with which it can be concealed its assessment depends largely on the honesty of the taxpayers and the efficiency of the administrative system in that locality, but even under model supervisory conditions assessments have been inadequate. In Massachusetts, in 1908, only 10 to 20 per cent of the intangibles were reached.[74] In Nebraska, where this type of property should have constituted at the very least one-fourth of the total assessment, it never reached one-twentieth of the assessment in three decades.[75] When related to the assessment of personalty, intangibles, in that state, in 1911 comprised but 20.95 per cent of that assessment,[76] indicating that tangible property bore the brunt of the tax for personal property, just as real estate was the main support for total revenues. In Virginia, in 1910, it was estimated that only about 75 per cent of the intangibles were reported, but inasmuch as the total assessment of intangible property in 1910 was $93,607,498, while bank deposits were $117,788,748 this estimate was liberal indeed.[77] Moreover, the money which was taxed was listed at only 6.21 per cent of its real value. It is not surprising, therefore, that in Baltimore in 1914 there was assessed $35,000-000 more of intangible property than in the whole Commonwealth of Virginia with its assessment of $157,138,100, the largest assessment during the preceding five years.[78] In Wyoming [79] in 1910, after deducting mortgages, only $421,919 in money and unsecured credits was turned in, though bank deposits aggregated over eighteen million dollars. After 1910 mortgages were exempt from taxation and the assessment of money and credits showed a continuous decline falling to $198,431 in 1914, though it rose slightly after that date.[80] In Austin, Texas, in 1911, credits assessed amounted to $688,391, or 3.5 per cent of the total assessment, while money assessed was but

---

[73] For more detailed treatment of taxation of intangibles see [Leland, *The Classified Property Tax in the United States*], Chapters V and VIII.
[74] *Report of Special Tax Commission*, Massachusetts, 1908, p. 34.
[75] *Report of Special Committee on Revenue and Taxation*, Nebraska, 1914, pp. 53-58.
[76] *Ibid.*, p. 57.
[77] *Report of Special Tax Commission*, Virginia, 1911, pp. 61-63.
[78] *Report of the Joint Committee on Tax Revision*, Virginia, 1914, p. 52.
[79] *Report of Tax Commissioner*, Wyoming, 1910, pp. 13-14.
[80] Cf. *Biennial Reports of Commissioner of Taxation*, Wyoming.

0.65 per cent of the aggregate valuation with but 2.5 per cent of the bank deposits in the city appearing on the tax duplicate.[81] The same condition was typical of the entire state. Using the year 1880 as a base (100) the index number of bank deposits rose by leaps until in 1914 it was 11,125, while the index number of the assessment of money increased to but 305.[82] In North Dakota the assessment of money decreased as the number of banking institutions multiplied. In 1893, when there were but 106 banks in the state (with deposits of $6,708,-181), money was assessed at $745,338, while in 1912, with 733 banks (having deposits of $70,302,584), the assessment was but $224,167.[83] The reports from other states indicate the same chronic disability of the general property tax to reach intangibles.

Though difficult to discover, intangibles, when found, are ordinarily very easy to assess. The value of money can be exactly decided once it is located. A bond, a mortgage or certificate of stock likewise can be accurately valued, at least in most cases, by means of stock market quotations. The result is that when it is assessed, intangible property is more heavily taxed than other pieces of property.[84] The difficulty has been not to assess it but to locate it. In Indiana, in 1916, the average assessed value of property was 40 per cent of true value, but when intangibles were located, they were assessed at 75 per cent of their value,[85] and probably would have been listed at full value but for the confiscation of the income-return due to high rates. In Virginia, in 1914, the Tax Commission pointed out that this class of property when assessed paid 'an average tax that is more than twice as high as that on tangible personalty and nearly three times as high as that on real estate.'[86] This condition coupled with the high tax rates causes the taxpayers to conceal this property in order to prevent confiscation. A clear idea of the effect of these rates upon the income from securities may be seen from the situation in Chicago. If the general property tax was strictly enforced upon true valuations of securities the following percentages of net income from in-

81 Wooldrige in *Bul.* no. 236, Univ. of Texas, pp. 134-35.

82 Miller, 'A Financial History of Texas,' *Bul.* no. 37, Univ. of Texas.

83 *First Report of the N. Dak. Tax Commissioner to the Governor and the Legislature of the State of North Dakota,* 1912, p. 44.

84 Supplementary Report by Richard T. Ely in *Report of Maryland Tax Commission,* 1888, pp. 143-44 n.; Taussig, 'Taxation of Securities,' *Pol. Sci. Quart.,* vol. XIV, p. 110.

85 *Report of Committee on Taxation,* Indiana, 1916, pp. vi-vii. See pp. 396-99 for confiscatory nature of the tax rates in Indiana.

86 *Report of Joint Committee on Tax Revision,* Virginia, 1914, p. 53.

vestments bearing given rates would be taken by the 1925 levies :

TABLE 8. PERCENTAGE OF NET INCOME FROM INVESTMENTS BEAR-
ING GIVEN RATES OF RETURN TAKEN BY TAXES
IN CERTAIN CHICAGO SUBURBS : 1925

Chicago Suburb	Tax Rate per $100 of True Value [a]	Per Cent of Income from Investments Taken in Taxes		
		6% Invest-ment	5% Invest-ment	4% Invest-ment
Cicero	$6.485	106	130	162
Glencoe	6.27	104	125	157
Des Plaines	6.265	104	125	157
Oak Place	5.91	99	118	148
Bellwood	5.89	98	118	147
Brookfield	5.765	96	115	144
Forest Park	5.705	95	114	142
Maywood	5.665	94	113	141
Arlington Heights	5.18	86	104	129

[a] Since assessments were made at 50 per cent of value, this conversion was necessary.

The confiscation of values under the general property tax is tantamount to a recurrent capital levy and is repugnant to current notions of justice in taxation. When intangible prop-erty has been omitted, other property has been required to pay too great a proportion of the state taxes ; when it has appeared on the tax duplicates, it has been taxed too heavily. Under either possibility the general property tax has failed to mete out justice. This furnished an additional reason for classi-fication.

DEFECTS IN ASSESSMENT OF REAL ESTATE

BECAUSE of the failure of the general property tax to reach those pieces of property which are intangible and easily hidden, many have concluded that the assessment of real estate is compara-tively easy, as well as substantially just. Even in the taxation of this class of property there has however been little justice. Not only has some land not been assessed but likewise much of it has been undervalued. Being tangible and immovable it has been said that 'no one can dispute the fact that all land is taxed,' [87] yet numerous instances can be cited where vast tracts

[87] Wolcott, 'Tax Rates in Indiana and Their Tendency,' 2d Annual Confer-ence on Taxation in Indiana, Ind. Univ. Bul., vol. XII, no. 15, p. 61 (Jan. 15, 1915) ; also p. 66.

of land have never appeared on the tax duplicate. In Kentucky, much taxable land has not appeared on the assessment roll. In 1912, for example, in 33 counties there were more acres in farms than were assessed in tracts,[88] but since the creation of the tax commission this situation has improved. In Charleston, South Carolina, an investigation showed that at one time from one-half to two-thirds of the land and about one-half of the buildings had not been assessed at all.[89] No excuse can be given for this state of affairs, yet it has been the by-product of a laxly administered general property tax.

For real estate, the problem is generally rather one of relative over- than under-assessment, with the result that in many localities the general property tax has degenerated into virtually a tax on real estate and tangible personalty alone, with realty shouldering the greatest burden. In Illinois, for example, realty represents about 40 per cent of the taxable wealth but has been called upon to pay approximately 80 per cent of the taxes.[90] The burden of taxes on real estate in Oregon is indicated by the fact that from 1906 to 1916 this class of property paid not less than 74 per cent of the general property taxes and in two years bore over 79 per cent of the load.[91]

Due to the fact that much property has escaped taxation and that improper valuations have prevailed, most states have, at one time or another, endeavored to increase the assessed valuation of their property. Tax commissions have usually pointed with pride to the increases which they have made. All too often, however, these increases have resulted in saddling a greater burden on real estate with a resulting relative decrease in the load carried by other property. In the state of Texas, in 1913, the assessed value of all property was $148,-197,941 greater than its value in 1912; 62.51 per cent of the increase fell on real estate, while the increases on other classes of property were as follows: cattle 4.78 per cent, vehicles 1.93 per cent, banks 2.39 per cent, railroads 7.88 per cent, money and credits 5.23 per cent.[92] In Alabama, from 1909 to 1914 the aggregate valuation of property increased about $100,000,-000, nearly three-fifths of which was due to city lots.[93] In

[88] Cf. *Report of Special Tax Commission*, Kentucky, 1912, p. 34.
[89] *Report of South Carolina Tax Commission*, 1915, pp. 22-26; cf. Lutz, *op. cit.*, p. 585.
[90] *Bul.*, N.T.A., vol. X, no. 3, p. 78.
[91] Cf. *Report of Tax Commission*, Oregon, 1911, p. 117; 1913, p. 79; 1917, p. 48.
[92] *Fifth Report of Tax Commission*, Texas, 1913, p. 36.
[93] Lutz, *op. cit.*, p. 557.

other states, as in New Hampshire and New Jersey, the increases have been more or less constant, changing but little the relative position of real estate and intangibles.[94] In view of this tendency alone it is little wonder that the owners of real estate so strenuously oppose increases in the general property tax assessments.

EFFECTS OF GENERAL PROPERTY TAX

Not a little of the opposition to the general property tax has arisen from the various effects produced by this form of taxation, to many of which reference has been made. These effects have been for the most part unintentional and unexpected. In the taxation of mortgages and mortgaged property the aim was to tax both the mortgagor and the mortgagee, but the result was that this tax was shifted to the mortgagor by means of an added interest premium, increased usually slightly more than the amount of the tax. When valuations were raised or when the tax rate on land was increased these additions were capitalized so that the increases would fall on the present holders of the land. On bonds and securities the same thing would probably have happened but the decrease, if any, was very slight owing to the universality of tax-dodging. The fear of discovery with its penalties, or the decline in values due to the tax, caused some to invest in non-taxables who otherwise would have purchased industrial securities. This influence on investments has been severely criticized as a material handicap to private enterprise. Tax officials in some places recognized, for example, how adversely trust companies were affected and consequently entered into gentlemen's agreements with them under which intangibles were valued at less than the legal requirement, the result being a form of extra-legal classification.[95] Moreover, the high general property tax rates in various localities have prevented new enterprises from locating there, and have furnished the incentive to others to move to states where assessments and tax rates are lower. Similarly, the high rates of the general property tax, or the activity of honest officials has brought about some movement of the rich from one locality to another. The popular fear of the removal of wealth to other states has been a factor leading to extra-legal arrangements to modify the severity of the tax. It has also led to the condoning of under-valuations for all types of prop-

[94] *Ibid.*, pp. 115, 554.
[95] Cf. Chapter II [Leland, *The Classified Property Tax in the United States*].

erty. These practices have been approved because they accorded greater justice to certain taxpayers than full rates literally enforced, but likewise they may have produced disrespect for other laws and led to perjury in other governmental dealings. When, therefore, classification measures were proposed in such states reference to these conditions afforded an argument in favor of the adoption of legal classification.[96]

SOLUTION BY EQUALIZATION

CORRECTIVES for the general property tax were applied first from the administrative side. It was thought that severe penalties and resort to tax inquisitions would help the local officials eliminate many of the defects.[97] These penalties included heavy fines, the doubling of assessments, even terms of imprisonment, reënforced in several states by the use of tax ferrets,[98] yet the desired results failed to appear. Local boards of equalization were created to aid the assessors. The movement spread until there appeared district and state boards of equalization which attempted to establish equality between interterritorial assessments and to equalize the assessments between classes of property and between individuals.[99] No matter how good the equalization, these boards could not undo the injustice of a poor assessment. Undervaluations continued in spite of them and the inequalities between individuals and between different classes of property continued largely as before. The failure of equalizations can be seen from the experience of practically every state. In Illinois the failures have been a scandal.[100] On many occasions not a single change has been made in local assessments and frequently the valuations of real estate and personal property have not been altered.[101] In Ohio from 1846 to 1900, instead of increasing the local valuations, the Ohio State Board of Equalization lowered them, the decreases ranging from three to one hundred and twenty-

96 See Chapter V [Leland, *The Classified Property Tax in the United States*].
97 Cf. Lutz, *op. cit.*, pp. 7 ff. For summary of penalties see *Digest of State Laws Relating to Taxation and Revenue*, 1922.
98 Carver, T. N., 'The Tax Inquisition System in Ohio,' Am. Ec. Asso., *Economic Studies*, vol. III, pp. 162-212 ; Angell, 'The Tax Inquisition System in Ohio,' *Yale Review*, vol. V, pp. 350-73 ; Brindley, *Financial History of Iowa*, vol. I, p. 341 ; also chs. 14, 15 ; Viner, in *Government of Kentucky*, vol. I, p. 260.
99 The equalization movement is carefully traced and analyzed in Lutz, *op. cit.*
100 Cf. *Report of Efficiency and Economy Committee*, 1915, Ill., pp. 102-04 ; Richberg, 'Tax Dodging in Illinois,' *New Republic*, vol. I, no. 10, pp. 21-22 (Jan. 9, 1915).
101 *Report of Efficiency and Economy Committee*, 1915 ; Fairlie, *Revenue and Finance Administration in Illinois*, p. 105 ; cf. *Reports of State Tax Commission*, Illinois.

six million dollars.[102] Limitations on tax rates also proved ineffective in producing equitable as well as adequate assessments.

THE TAX COMMISSION

THE final approach to the problem from the administrative side came with the creation of the centralized tax commission. This movement began in Indiana, in 1891, with the creation of the State Board of Tax Commissioners, spreading rapidly until today such bodies are found in about forty states.[103] The earlier state equalization boards failed because of inadequate powers [104] or because their personnel was without vision as to the seriousness of the problem confronting them or because the boards were manned by exofficio members. Many times the desire for low assessments for their own districts [105] was stronger than the wish for the improvement of the tax situation generally. The movement for centralized administration sought to correct these defects by giving the tax commissions broad powers of assessment, supervision and control over local officials. The office of tax commissioner was made appointive, the commissions were frequently bi-partisan and the salary was made sufficiently large to attract the service of competent men. As a result of the activity of these tax commissions, the general property tax improved, though all of the inequalities were by no means eliminated.

OTHER REFORMS

THE partial failure of these administrative correctives led to the advocacy of four other well-defined lines of reform : solution by exemption ; separation of the sources of state and local revenues ; state income taxes ; and the classification of property for taxation. At various times each of these reforms has held sway, commanding a considerable following of advocates.

SOLUTION BY EXEMPTION

THOSE who favored solution by exemption thought that it was useless to endeavor to reach intangible property under the

[102] Lutz, *op. cit.*, p. 51.

[103] Lutz, *Public Finance*, p. 250.

[104] Lutz, *The State Tax Commission*, pp. 6, 130-31. In commenting on the failure of equalization, the Special Tax Commission of 1916, Indiana, said 'our one expert has collected more and better information as to the working of the tax laws in six months than the State Board has collected in a quarter of a century.' *Report, op. cit.*, p. vi.

[105] This seemed to be the case in Ill. Fairlie, *Taxation and Revenue Systems in Illinois*, p. 65.

general property tax. Since its attempted taxation had been a fiasco they favored the exemption of that property which could not be adequately assessed by present methods. Some extended the demand for exemption to all personal property not only because of its ease of sequestration but also because much of it was representative property and because a part produced no income save satisfactions in use. Not a few thought that the exemption of personal property would make an entering wedge for the single tax.[106] Some have advocated the exemption of personality because they believed that other methods of reaching this property were superior to the general property tax. Those who favored state income taxes did not think that both incomes and intangible personal property should be taxed, so the exemption of the latter was advocated in the interest of justice.[107] The solution by exemption alone was objected to by many who felt that it was unfair to exempt those whose wealth was in the form of intangibles.[108] Others opposed the project thinking it would necessitate the assumption of an additional burden by the farmers and the owners of tangible wealth.

SEPARATION OF SOURCES

THE advocates of separation approached the problem from another angle.[109] The competitive undervaluations of property between counties were thought to be due to the fact that state funds were derived from levies upon local valuations. Therefore, it was proposed to remove the incentive to undervaluation by segregating the sources of state and local revenues, and, if possible, by assigning the general property tax to the local governments alone. In case the revenues from other sources were insufficient for state purposes, then state property levies might be employed as an emergency device. Far from curing the defects of the general property tax this method tended only to remove the territorial inequalities in assessments, which are unimportant in many states because of the smallness of the

106 Cf. Chapters VI and VII, [Leland, *The Classified Property Tax in the United States*].

107 Adams, 'The Wisconsin Income Tax,' *Pol. Sci. Quart.*, vol. XXVIII, p. 584; *Preliminary Report of the Committee Appointed by the National Tax Association to Prepare a Plan of a Model System of State and Local Taxation*, 2d Imprint, Jan., 1923, pp. 31-32.

108 Fairchild, *Proc.*, N.T.A., 1913, p. 85; Girwood, A. C., 'Better Methods of Legislation and Administration vs. Radical Changes in the Tax System,' *Bul.*, N.T.A., vol. II, no. 4, p. 107.

109 For extended discussion of separation cf. Mabel Newcomer, *Separation of State and Local Revenues in the United States*, Columbia Univ. Studies, vol. 72, no. 2 (1917).

state rates. The remaining defects are left to the local governments for solution.[110]

HOWEVER much the preceding reforms have found favor, the state income tax as a solution for the general property tax problems has been coming into its own. Very early in American history the colonial income or 'faculty' taxes appeared.[111] Massachusetts was among the first of the colonies to employ them, the early acts dating back to 1634 and 1646. The method spread until before many years 'faculty' taxes were found in one form or another in Connecticut (1650), Rhode Island (1673), South Carolina (1701), New Hampshire (1719), Vermont (1778), and Virginia (1777). Following these early presumptive taxes came attempts to levy upon income proper, beginning in Pennsylvania (1841) and spreading to Maryland (1842), Virginia (1843), Alabama (1843), Florida (1845) and North Carolina (1849). The need for revenue not only caused their adoption, but also led other states to incorporate income taxes in their revenue systems during the Civil War and Reconstruction periods, during which time Missouri (1861), Texas (1863), Georgia (1863), West Virginia (1863), Louisiana (1865), Kentucky (1867), Delaware (1869) and Tennessee (1883) adopted this mode of taxation.

Some of these laws were general acts, others were special; some used progressive rates, some proportional rates, others a mixture of the two. These taxes were for the most part short-lived. Those which did survive lapsed into inactivity with only occasional attempts at revival, but even at such times the revenue derived from them was so insignificant in some instances as barely to meet the collection costs.[112] The failure of these income taxes was due to the administrative features of the laws. Local administration of a tax for state purposes led to laxities and inequalities; under such circumstances self-assessment failed and the taxpayers were successful in their efforts to escape payment. The result was that most students

---

[110] For relation of classification to separation cf. Chapter XVII, [Leland, *The Classified Property Tax in the United States*].

[111] On income taxation see Seligman, *The Income Tax*, 1911; 'The Income Tax in American Colonies and States,' *Pol. Sci. Quart.*, vol. X, no. 2 (June, 1895); Kinsman, 'The Income Tax in the Commonwealths of the United States,' *Am. Ec. Asso.*, 3d Series, vol. IV, pp. 1 ff., 110-11 (Nov., 1903); Kennan, *Income Taxation*; Comstock, *op. cit.*

[112] Oklahoma income tax of 1908 had a yield of less than $5000 annually. Comstock, *op. cit.*, p. 15.

of public finance lost faith in the income tax as a source of state revenues.[113]

Present state income taxes received their impetus from the success of the Wisconsin act of 1911. Other states were quick to follow her lead until at the present time [1923] income taxes are found in Connecticut, Delaware, Massachusetts, Mississippi, Missouri, Montana, New Hampshire, New York, North Carolina, North Dakota, Oklahoma, South Carolina, Tennessee, Virginia, and Wisconsin — fifteen states in all.[114] . . .*

CLASSIFICATION AND THE GENERAL PROPERTY TAX

In this chapter the rise and fall of the general property tax has been hastily sketched. Its extent and importance to American commonwealths has been indicated. Its defects, theoretical and operative, have been pointed out. It has been shown that it has succeeded but slightly better under ideally perfected administrative conditions than under crude defective methods elsewhere in vogue. The obsolesence of this form of taxation due to industrial and social changes has further aided its degeneration. The high rates which have come with increased governmental activity have aroused the public to the need of reform as well as to the resulting injustice caused by this archaic transformation from past generations. As it stands, therefore, relative to the classification movement, the general property tax has been a major cause awakening interest in tax reform, and it has itself been the thing to be reformed. But for its defects, classification and separation probably would not yet have been devised, our vast administrative improvements would not have been undertaken, and the movement for the state income tax would not have been hastened. Classification, therefore, relates directly to the correction of the general property tax defects. It seeks to solve the problem of adjusting the tax burden to varying capacity to pay taxes and varying capacity to evade taxes as between different classes of property by dividing property into groups so that each group can be taxed at a different rate if need be. Its success is to be judged on the one hand by the manner in which these are solved, and on the other, by its achievement of approximate relative proportionality.

---

[113] Seligman, *The Income Tax*, 1911 ed., pp. 418-29 ; Essays, *op. cit.*, p. 651 ; Comstock, *op. cit.*, pp. 18, 21-22 ; Kinsman, *loc. cit.*, pp. 115-21 ; Kennan, *op. cit.*, pp. 235-36.

[114] Cf. Witte, 'Federal and State Income Tax Laws,' *Bul.*, N.T.A., vol. IX, no. 2, pp. 43-46 (Nov., 1923).

* Eds. note : See Chap. XV of this volume for further information on state income taxation.

QUESTIONS AND PROBLEMS FOR DISCUSSION

1. Is the general property tax in the United States based upon the ability or upon the benefit theory of taxation?
2. "The industrialization of the United States has left the general property tax with little, if any, justification." Evaluate.
3. If a property tax is designed to be a *general* property tax, is there any justification in allowing certain exemptions?
4. What are the most important administrative defects of the general property tax?
5. If the administrative defects of the propery tax could be eliminated, do you think the use of this tax could then be justified? How might some of these administrative defects be eliminated?
6. What objections can be made against the taxation of furniture in a private home? Would the same objections apply to the taxation of furniture in a hotel?
7. If a tax is to be levied on intangibles, how should the value of such property be determined?
8. What must be the conditions in the money market to enable a mortgagee to shift a tax on the mortgage to the mortgagor by means of an added interest premium?
9. In a certain city, the property of a manufacturing concern is valued at $20,000,000 for fire insurance purposes. The home of Mr. A in the same city is valued at $7,500 for insurance. For taxation purposes, the corporation's property is valued at $2,500,000; and the home at $3,500. The assessment officials justify this discrimination by claiming that low taxes attract industry, and thus build the city. Is there any economic justification for such discrimination?
10. "In operation the general property tax discriminates against the rural and in favor of the urban population." Evaluate.

SUGGESTIONS FOR RESEARCH

1. Centralized assessment of property in theory and practice.
2. Reasons for the importance and persistence of general property taxation in the United States.
3. The relation between the general property tax and tax delinquency in some particular state which makes extensive use of the general property tax.
4. The general property tax and the farmer.
5. The general property tax and industrial fluctuations.
6. A comparison of rural and urban tax burdens in some particular state.

BIBLIOGRAPHICAL NOTE

Excellent references on the general property tax can be cited almost without end. Here, however, only a few valuable works are mentioned.

E. R. A. Seligman, in his *Essays in Taxation*, (New York, 1928),

Chap. II, contends that "the general property tax as a main source of public revenue is a failure from the triple standpoint of history, theory and practice." J. P. Jensen's *Property Taxation in the United States,* (Chicago, 1931), is an exhaustive treatment of the subject suggested by the title. This work contains an extensive bibliography on property taxation. The theoretical and practical defects of the general property tax are ably presented in M. S. Kendrick, *Taxation Issues,* (New York, 1933), Chap. III.

A selected and annotated bibliography, useful for the student of property taxation, is "Taxation and the Farmer," *Agricultural Economics Bibliography No. 25,* United States Department of Agriculture, Washington, D. C., June, 1928.

For some results of a study of taxation of farms in the United States, see the *Year Book* of the United States Department of Agriculture, 1932.

An important question concerning property taxation is discussed by E. H. Spengler in his study, "Is the Real Estate Tax a Benefit Tax?", *Report of the New York State Commission for the Revision of the Tax Laws,* 1932.

A valuable article for the student of property taxation is K. M. Williamson, "Taxation of Real Estate : Survey of Recent Discussion," *Quarterly Journal of Economics,* Vol. XLVIII, pp. 96-128.

CHAPTER XI

THE CLASSIFIED PROPERTY TAX

THE classified property tax is, according to Professor S. E. Leland, "the ad valorem taxation of property by its segregation into groups or types and the application to these various classes of different effective rates."* The status of this form of taxation is discussed in this chapter.

1. STATUS OF THE CLASSIFIED PROPERTY TAX IN THE UNITED STATES †

PARTIAL CLASSIFICATION OF REAL PROPERTY

WHILE Minnesota and Montana are the only states today using general classified property tax systems applicable to all tangible property, most of the states have provided for special taxation of some classes of real property and tangible personal property. The classes of real property most frequently segregated for special taxation are forests and mines.

Forest Taxation. The application of the general property tax to forest areas is held to be particularly burdensome. The return from an investment in forest lands, whether mature forests or immature growing forests or areas to be reforested, is usually a deferred return. Taxes paid currently along with interest and other charges accrue and accumulate during the period of waiting.

The taxation of mature forests and of immature second growth at ordinary property tax rates may tend to stimulate cutting, thus contributing to overproduction, depressed prices, wasteful utilization, and depletion of natural resources. In the case of reforestation projects such taxation may prove a deterrent to a form of enterprise which, however laudable, has to contend with the inertia of a public generally indifferent to projects that do not promise an early return on the investment.

Experiments with tracts under forest management in New

---

* S. E. Leland, *The Classified Property Tax in the United States,* (Boston, 1928), p. 41.

† Adapted from *State and Local Taxation of Property,* (National Industrial Conference Board, New York, 1930), Chap. I, pp. 21-49.

York State indicate that, in general, planted forests will yield pulpwood in thirty years and low-grade lumber in fifty years. When the interest on investment over such a period of years is added to the cost of insurance against fires and to the market risks, it is not difficult to understand the reluctance of private persons and corporations to invest in this form of enterprise. The burden is further increased by general property taxes, which must be paid annually out of funds supplied by the investor and not returned to him until the investment begins to yield income at a time many years in the future.

For these reasons most states with extensive forest areas have adopted special methods of taxing investments in growing timber. In 1926 the federal government created the Forest Taxation Inquiry, a section of the Research Branch of the Forest Service, Department of Agriculture. This organization, under the directorship of Professor Fred R. Fairchild, has been studying the problems of forest taxation and expects to publish its final report some time during 1931 or as soon thereafter as possible. In view of the wide extent of this survey, final conclusions on the subject of forest taxation should be postponed until the findings of the inquiry are made public.

The consensus of opinion at the present time, however, seems to indicate that the most satisfactory solution of the forest tax problem will be found along the lines of separating the land from the timber; imposing an annual tax upon the land, based upon its bare land value; and imposing a severance or yield tax upon the timber equivalent in amount to the taxes that would be imposed under the general property tax during the period of growth, but based upon the value of the stumpage at maturity and collected at the time of cutting. As the fiscal policies of most governmental units containing large forested areas are based on the collection of an annual property tax on the standing timber, the change to a yield tax basis will in many cases require substantial readjustment of local fiscal systems.

Mines. There has been a strong tendency in many of the states to provide for the special taxation of mines and mining property. This policy has been adopted in Colorado, Idaho, Minnesota, New Mexico, South Carolina, and Wisconsin. Several other states also have provided for separate assessment of mineral properties. . . They indicate a tendency to substitute the more efficient central assessment for the less efficient local assessment of mining property.

In some states in which the tax laws do not provide for the special taxation of mining properties, this is actually accomplished by the administration. Arizona provides an interesting example. Formerly a specific bullion tax was imposed in this state, but with the law creating the tax commission in 1912 this tax was removed, and since then mines have been subject to the general property tax. Later attempts to bring back the bullion tax have been strongly opposed by the tax commission. In valuing mines the commission has made extensive use of the capitalization of earnings. The basis of the assessment has been a changing average of annual earnings. Until 1922 this average covered a period of five years, but in that year the period was increased to ten years. The periods used since that time have varied. This system has been opposed by the mining companies, but has been supported by the tax commission. In 1924, however, the latter requested that the office of state geologist be created to assist the commission in valuing mining property, estimating the extent of ore bodies, and the like. This recommendation was not followed by the legislature. The commission was forced to defend several court actions brought by the larger mining companies, and finally in 1925, when faced with a case that could not be defended because of inadequate funds, the commission retreated from its previous stand and decided to recognize other factors in its valuations. Since then assessments have been based on all information available to the tax commission, but net income is still an important factor in the tax base.

The demand for special taxation of mineral properties rests on two claims: first, that minerals are natural resources which have come into the hands of persons who have contributed nothing to their values beyond making them more accessible; second, that minerals are diminishing or disappearing assets, and consequently the state under the general property tax will receive less revenue from a tax on mines than from a tax on indestructible properties such as agricultural lands. Whatever validity these claims may possess, it is still doubtful that they justify special treatment. The first claim applies with equal force to all cases of private appropriation of land and other natural resources. In respect to the second claim, it should be pointed out that in the long run the value of every piece of property depends on its potential income-earning capacity. In general, capital value means capitalized income; the income that is capitalized is the entire future income. Consequently, a tax on capital value, provided the normal relationship between value and income exists, is a tax on the entire future expected income, and a tax on property with a limited future income yield will necessarily produce less revenue than a tax on property with a perpetual income yield. It is difficult, however, to find in this consideration a reason for the imposition of a supertax on property with a limited future income yield.

In 1920 the Special Committee on Mines Taxation reported to the National Tax Association on a model system for taxing mines. They found no justification for the classification of real property, and held that mines should be subjected to the normal ad valorem rates. Their particular objection to the substitution of income or other types of taxes for property taxes was that this would deprive local governments of an important elastic source of revenue. As to the imposition of special burdens on mines, the committee stated:

"We believe that mines should be taxed for revenue only and condemn the supertaxation of mines on the one hand, and on the other exemption or undertaxation. A classification of real estate for taxation opens the door to exploitation of the numerically weaker elements in the population by the dominant elements. . . The prevailing constitutional rule of uniformity so far as it applies to real estate is a wholesome restraint of the misuse of legislative power by a dominant element or class, and in our opinion it should be carefully guarded in all proposed amendments which purpose only the exclusion of intangible and personal property from the application of this rule." [1]

Minnesota provides an example of both the supertaxation of mines and the possibilities of ad valorem taxation. Besides the high property taxes, Minnesota also imposes an occupation tax amounting to six per cent of the gross ore output less certain deductions. This tax amounts to a roughly determined net income tax. If the mine is operated by any person or organization other than its owner, the owner pays a six per cent royalty tax on all royalties received from the operator. Mining corporations also pay the normal corporate excess tax. The result is a peculiarly burdensome system of supertaxation.

On the other hand, Minnesota also provides an outstanding example of the possibilities of satisfactory assessment under an efficient central administrative organization. The conclusion of the National Tax Association committee was ". . . that ad valorem taxation of mines by state and local jurisdictions, under direct administration of a state tax commission or tax commissioner, is a thoroughly practical method of taxing mineral wealth. . . What has already been done under centralized

[1] *Proceedings* of the 12th Annual Conference on Taxation under the auspices of the National Tax Association, 1920, pp. 407 and 408.

administration in Michigan, Wisconsin, Minnesota, and Arizona can be done in other states. . . Every problem of assessment and administration that could conceivably arise anywhere occurs in principle in the application of the system in these states. They have all been satisfactorily met." [2]

Other Real Property. Some states provide for special taxation and for separate assessment of other types of property. Several states provide for special methods of taxing oil lands or oil royalties. Another common provision is that privately owned equities in government lands shall be taxed, as in Idaho, Michigan, and Minnesota.

PARTIAL CLASSIFICATION OF TANGIBLE PERSONAL PROPERTY

As in the case with real estate, most of the states make use of special methods for the taxation of some specific types of personal property.

Motor Vehicles. Special treatment is most common in the case of automobiles. During recent years all the states have enacted laws imposing license taxes upon motor vehicles and consumption taxes upon motor vehicle fuels. In Idaho, Iowa, New York, Oklahoma, Oregon, and Vermont these special taxes have displaced the property taxes, and all motor vehicles are exempt from the latter. In New Hampshire a local license fee equivalent to a property tax is imposed. Few of the remaining states rely upon ordinary valuation methods for the assessment of motor vehicles. Connecticut, Louisiana, Maryland, Massachusetts, Minnesota, Missouri, and Wyoming assess automobiles on the basis of their list prices, but allow specific depreciations according to the age of the vehicle. This is also the practice of some assessors in Indiana and Ohio. Maine uses practically the same system, except that the tax is imposed upon the full list price at rates varying according to the age of the vehicle. Nevada, South Carolina, and District of Columbia tax automobiles on the basis of the values recorded in the National Used Car Market Report. The remaining states tax motor vehicles as general property.

Much difficulty has been encountered in some states in attempting to list motor vehicles. In Arkansas approximately one fourth of the motor vehicles escape listing. Georgia has a special provision intended to force local officials to assess automobiles. Automobiles must be registered, and there seems to be no good reason why they cannot be listed for property tax purposes. The suggestion is frequently made that in-

[2] *Proceedings* of the National Tax Association, 1920, p. 410.

creased license fees be substituted for property taxes. The
simplicity of this solution cannot be denied, but the justice
of the proposal is questioned. A license tax is essentially
a regressive tax, that is, the tax amounts to a much larger
proportion of the value of a low-priced car than that of a
high-priced car. Hence, such a tax is held to be inequitable.
If the ad valorem method is applied to other taxed property,
there seems to be no reason why it cannot be applied to automobiles, providing the proper administrative machinery is set
up. There are difficulties, but they should not be insurmountable. A requirement that a tax receipt for the past
taxable year must be shown at the time a license is granted
would seem to be a satisfactory solution. Because of the movement and sale of vehicles some qualifications in the law would
be necessary. For instance, if an owner has brought a car
into the state since the last preceding tax day and if he can
prove that fact, he should probably be exempted from the
property tax receipt requirement. With certain qualifications
of this nature, it would appear to be possible to retain the
ad valorem tax on motor vehicles, and to enforce it with
almost if not the same efficiency as is achieved in the listing of
real estate. Of course, once the automobiles are listed they
can be valued in most cases much more easily than real estate
can be valued. The National Used Car Market Report and
other similar publications will provide valuations sufficiently
accurate for tax purposes.

Other Types of Tangible Personal Property. The special
taxes on automobiles have been adopted for the purpose of
facilitating valuation. They partake to some extent of the
character of specific taxes. The same type of property tax
is frequently used in the case of livestock, vessels, and agricultural products. Arizona, Kentucky, Montana, New Hampshire, and Wyoming have provided for the special treatment
of livestock. Livestock is also treated separately in Colorado
by an extra-legal agreement of assessors under which they assess
animals at flat valuations per head which may differ considerably
from their actual values. In Kentucky this special treatment
has resulted from the separation of state and local revenue
sources and takes the form of a special mill tax imposed by
local units. In Wyoming the tax has the character of a specific
tax, as it is imposed upon fixed valuations.

Vessels are treated separately by Connecticut, Maine, Michigan, Missouri, New Hampshire, Rhode Island, and Wisconsin.
Several other states exempt them entirely. The usual form is
a specific tax on tonnage. This special treatment applies in

most cases only to vessels operating in interstate commerce. Such vessels can be registered in either of several states at the option of the owner and will ordinarily be registered and therefore listed for taxation in the state imposing the lowest tax.

Finally, there are four states in which very little tangible personal property of any kind is assessed, namely, Delaware, Massachusetts, New York, and Pennsylvania. In Delaware this has resulted from the administrative break-down of assessments, as the law provides for taxation of general property. Massachusetts exempts all tangible personal property except machinery used in business. In New York all personal property of corporations, other than public utilities, is exempt, and in actual practice little personal property of any kind is taxed. Pennsylvania has exempted all tangible personalty except ordinary passenger vehicles.

Inventories. The special taxes discussed so far have applied to specific classes of property regardless of ownership. There remains an important provision found in many of the tax laws providing for special treatment of the inventories of manufacturers and merchants. The usual provision is that these inventories shall be taxed at their actual values at general property tax rates, but that the tax base shall be the average annual inventory. This method of assessment has been adopted in Alabama, Arkansas, Colorado, Iowa, Kansas, Louisiana, Maryland, New Hampshire, New Jersey, New Mexico, Ohio, Oklahoma, South Carolina, Tennessee, Wyoming, and District of Columbia. In some states it applies to manufacturers, in some, to merchants, and in some, to both. These provisions of course are not always strictly enforced.

EXEMPTION OF TANGIBLE PROPERTY

THE uniform rule provisions were written into most of the state constitutions during the latter part of the nineteenth century. These provisions usually compelled the uniform taxation of all taxed property, but allowed the legislatures considerable freedom in the exemption of property. The exemption of a small amount of household goods and the exemption of property used for educational, religious, and charitable purposes were common. Property owned by the Federal Government was universally exempted because of the implied prohibition of the Federal Constitution.

Various additional classes of property have been added to the exempt list during the more recent period. Exemption from property taxes does not necessarily imply exemption from tax-

ation. Expediency has led to the substitution of other taxes
for the general property tax on certain classes of property, as
has been previously explained. In these cases there is no exemption from the burden of government. In other cases, however, the legislatures have given up the attempt to tax property
that cannot be readily discovered and appraised and have
turned to entirely distinct tax bases to make up the loss in
revenue incurred through exemption.

The exemption of property owned by state and local governments is also common. Almost half the states exempt their
own property and the property of their local governments by
constitutional provisions, while about eighteen have provided
for such exemptions by statute. In these cases state property
is, of course, exempt wherever located. Where local property
is exempted by state law, it is usually also exempt wherever located. Some local units exempt their own property from local
taxes when located within their own borders.

Finally, there are cases of exemption of specified kinds of
property used by certain industries. These may be called developmental exemptions. Examples are farm or manufacturing machinery, exempted for the purpose of encouraging
production. Developmental exemptions are granted in many
states. Alabama, Connecticut, Georgia, Iowa, Kentucky,
Maine, Maryland, Mississippi, Oklahoma, Tennessee, and Virginia exempt products of domestic agriculture, while Arkansas,
California, Idaho, Maryland, Oklahoma, and Tennessee exempt
growing crops. At least two states, Alabama and Mississippi,
have provided for the exemption of manufacturing establishments. In the latter case the exemption is limited to the first
five years of the existence of each establishment. In Georgia,
Kentucky, New York, Rhode Island, South Carolina, and Vermont the local units are authorized to grant exemptions to
manufacturing establishments. In each case the exemption
must be limited to a definite period, usually five years.

Every year new demands for the exemption of property from
taxation are presented to state legislatures. The value of exempt property is increasing at a more rapid rate than the
value of taxed property. A study of tax commission reports
and other documents indicates, however, an almost universal
opposition on the part of tax officials to the further extension
of exemptions.

Reasons for Exemption. The reasons for the exemption of
these different types of property are many and varied. The
subject of tax exemption in all its ramifications is too broad for
thorough treatment here. No study of property taxation

would be complete, however, without at least a brief summary of the reasons for the exemption of the particular classes of property mentioned above and of the arguments for and against such practice.

The reasons for the exemption of public property are partly legal and partly economic. Although the Constitution contains no express prohibition of the taxation of the property or the agencies of the Federal Government by a state or its municipalities, or of the taxation of the property or the agencies of a state or its municipalities by the Federal Government, both these forms of taxation have been rendered unconstitutional by the so-called "doctrine of implied prohibitions." The reason is expressed in Chief Justice Marshall's dictum that "the power to tax is the power to destroy." Congress, however, may permit the taxation of federal properties or of federal agencies. It has at times permitted both, the most important example of the latter at the present time being the statute permitting the taxation of the real estate of national banks. A state may also permit the taxation of its property by its municipalities, as does the State of New York. It may also tax its own properties, but unless the statute clearly states that state properties are taxable, they are construed by the courts to be exempt.

The economic justification of the exemption of public property is that such property is used for public purposes and is not used for profit. In the case of the taxation of such property by the governmental unit that owns it such taxation is held to be a needless waste of administrative effort.

For several reasons many writers oppose the exemption of public property. The opposition is based chiefly on two grounds. First is the claim that many government-owned properties, such as public utilities, while perhaps not used for profit in the ordinary sense, are, nevertheless, commercial properties operated in competition with private business and should be compelled to show on their books costs of operation comparable with those necessarily incurred by their private competitors. Second, is the opposition to exemption that comes from governmental units within whose boundaries are located properties of other governments. Thus Arizona objects to the exemption of federal lands, and points to the fact that, while general property taxes provide more than three fourths of the state revenues, over seventy per cent of the land of the state belongs to the Federal Government and is non-taxable. This case is unusual, and the state government incurs little expense within the federal-owned area. Much more common situations are those of the capital city, in which much property is withdrawn from the municipal tax roll by the state government, and of the municipality that owns a water or power plant or some other quasi-commercial property within the boundaries of another. Here tax exemption is opposed on the ground that it permits the residents of one community to benefit without cost from the governmental services provided by those of another.

Almost all states exempt a certain amount of the personal property of each individual. There are two reasons for these exemptions. It is generally believed that the poorer classes should be exempt from taxation, and it has been proved by experience that taxes on very small amounts of property do not yield sufficient revenue to defray the cost of administration. There seems to be little objection to such exemptions. In some cases tax officials even exceed their authority by allowing in practice greater exemptions than are permitted by the law.

Properties used for charitable, religious, educational, and similar purposes are exempted for both social and economic reasons. It is held that such uses of property are meritorious and should be encouraged. These exemptions are also supported by the argument that, if private organizations did not perform these services, it would be necessary for the state to provide for their performance at the public expense.

Few deny that charitable, religious, and educational institutions perform useful public services. Yet strong opposition to the exemption of these properties comes from various sources, particularly tax officials and business groups. Judging by the opinions expressed in published reports, tax officials generally oppose this class of exemptions. They point to the rapid rate at which property, particularly land, is being withdrawn from the tax roll. Each year a larger proportion of all property becomes exempt, and, as exemption of social organizations extends, the relative tax burden borne by industry and by individual taxpayers increases.

A further claim, made by both tax officials and competing business men in some states, is that when property is once placed on the exempt list it tends to remain there even though it be in part used thereafter for commercial, profit-making purposes. This claim is now being urged by hotel associations in several states. This is an objection to the practice of allowing unlawful exemption, rather than to the principle of the law itself.

The second reason for social exemptions, that exempt organizations relieve the public of the cost of services that would otherwise be performed by governments, has also been subjected to vigorous criticism. In the first place, this claim cannot logically be applied to churches in the United States. Then, as regards schools, hospitals, charities, and similar groups, it is frequently contended that, if the citizens pay for these benefits through taxation for the support of governmental services, they do so voluntarily, rather than at the option of small private groups, as is the case when they pay through the increased burdens resulting from exemptions. It is pointed out that taxpayers' organizations throughout the United States are actively engaged in attempting to curtail the rapid increase of the cost of government, particularly that resulting from the adoption of programs of governmental luxuries, such as educational experiments and other desirable but unnecessary services of the type in which private organizations so frequently specialize. Furthermore, it is claimed that such services as are within the proper sphere of government should be performed either by the government under public control or by private groups paying their share of the tax burden. This claim is made particularly in opposition to the exemption of schools and colleges operated by churches and other private bodies.

The position of practically all writers on the principles of taxation may be summarized in the following statement. The exemption of particular properties or classes of property from taxation restricts the tax base and consequently increases the tax burden borne by other property or by payers of taxes other than the property tax. Unless it can be shown that the taxation of any particular class of property is not feasible, the interests of equality will best be served by denying it exemption. A well-conducted charity may actually relieve a community of caring for its poor through a governmental department, and a private school may draw students away from the public schools and thus relieve the community from part of the costs of the latter. Yet when a church or a private school is exempted from taxation, the members or patrons of that church or school enjoy the protection of government without cost to themselves, but at the expense of other, and uninterested, taxpayers. These benefiting groups may be expected, providing they can afford to build properties of high tax values, to have tax-paying ability, and they should contribute to the costs of the benefits they receive as do other taxpayers. In short, exemption always means a shifting of tax burdens from one group to another group, and consideration should be given to the latter as well as to the former.

The reason for the exemption of business property is always the encouragement of business, usually farming or manufacturing. Opposition to this type of exemption comes from both tax theorists and tax officials, and rests on approximately the same grounds as opposition to the social exemptions. It is held that taxes form a part of the normal overhead costs of most businesses, and that these costs should be divided among business concerns without favoritism. Most economists question the claim that public benefits are derived from the growth of industries that are unable to bear their fair share of the cost of the government.

There remains the exemption of particular types of property, such as automobiles or musical instruments. The reason for exemption in such cases is merely expediency. Equitable administration of property taxes on such property has been found to be difficult.

Usually the revenue lost by exemption is made up by increasing the taxes on other property or other bases. Here there seems to be little opposition providing it is clearly shown that equitable taxation of a particular class of property is not feasible.

It will be seen that the arguments for exemption range from those based purely on moral principles to those based wholly on expediency without consideration of equity. The arguments against exemptions likewise vary, but most of them rest on the desire to broaden the tax base as much as possible and on the claim that every exemption narrows the tax base and therefore results in an inequitable shifting of tax burdens from one group of taxpayers to another group.

TAXABLE SITUS

THE problem of taxable situs is not so serious in the case of tangible property as in that of intangible. In some instances double taxation has resulted from conflict of jurisdictions. Usually, however, it cannot occur except in the case of a few particular types of property, such as cattle, that are commonly moved from one jurisdiction to another during the tax year, and the statutes of most states contain provisions covering such situations.

Real estate is uniformly taxed at its location. There is, however, no uniformity in the definition of the taxable situs of personal property. The old common law rule was that personal property was taxable at the domicile of its owner, but the states generally have enacted laws making location the taxable situs of most classes of tangible personal property. It is difficult to classify the states in this regard, as the statutory provisions usually apply only to particular classes of property, and many of them are conditional in character. About fourteen states, however, tax most tangible personal property at the domicile of the owner, while about thirty states now tax the bulk of such property at its location. Frequently the statutes provide that property is to be taxed at its location, if the owner has a place of business there ; otherwise, that it is to be taxed at the owner's domicile. In Georgia tangible personalty is taxed at its location, if its owner owns real estate there ; otherwise, at the owner's domicile. Similar qualifications of the statutory provisions are common. The practice, however, as is so frequently the case with taxation systems, often varies from the letter of the law. With or without extra-legal agreements, assessors frequently list property according to their own judgment as to the merits of the case.

CLASSIFICATION AND SPECIAL TREATMENT OF INTANGIBLE PERSONAL PROPERTY

THE most serious deficiency of the general property tax has resulted from the impossibility under this form of taxation of reaching intangible property. The increasing importance of this type of property during recent decades has led to the adoption of many plans designed to help or to force the assessors to place such property on the tax rolls. Penalties for non-listing have been increased ; assessors have been given added powers of investigation ; and other special types of property taxes have been devised. Out of the many reforms that have been adopted and the mass of literature that has been published on this subject there have come several significant methods of treating this type of property. Before describing these, however, it is necessary to discuss briefly the commonly accepted theories regarding the proper method of treating intangibles.

Principles Involved. An examination of the numerous official reports discussing the failure of the general property tax and urging the adoption of new methods that will prevent the escape of intangibles naturally suggests the question why, if taxation is so difficult, intangibles are not exempted. Several legislatures have already accepted this solution. It has long been urged by economists.

The demand for exemption rests on stronger grounds than that of mere expediency. Writers on taxation have almost without exception opposed the taxation of intangible property as an unjust form of double taxation. Documentary evidences of property rights are not wealth. Many forms of intangibles amount to nothing more than equities in tangible property that is already subjected to the property tax. Such representative property includes mortgages and most other credits, such as bills and notes; money, other than gold; bank deposits; and corporation securities. Justice clearly demands the exemption of mortgages and other debts secured by tangible property and of corporation stock and other evidences of ownership of tangible property, if the intent of the legislature is to tax all persons equally on the basis of their ability to pay as measured by ownership of property.

In the case of corporation bonds, the double taxation is less evident, and some persons who consider it desirable to exempt corporation stock hold that the bondholder's interest is sufficiently different from that of the stockholder to justify taxation of bonds. The bondholder receives a fixed return not ordinarily dependent on the profits of the enterprise. Therefore, to exempt bonds appears to some persons as an unjustifiable discrimination in favor of a large group of property owners with considerable ability to pay taxes. Yet careful consideration of the position of the bondholder seems to lend support to the contention that bonds should be exempted.

The line of distinction between corporation stock and corporation bonds at the present time is not clearly defined. Both contain elements of ownership and elements of credit; both represent equities in corporation property; and it is probable that the burden of a tax is distributed in much the same manner in one case as in the other. The removal of a property tax imposed on bonds, assuming that such a tax had previously been enforced against a substantial majority of bondholders, would undoubtedly be reflected immediately in the bond market. It would be impossible to forecast the exact extent of the effect, yet it is certain that the prices of bonds would rise. The result would be that the yields, measured as percentages of market values, would fall. Corporations would thereafter be able to borrow money at lower interest rates, and the gross incomes of bondholders would be curtailed by approximately the amount of the tax formerly paid and deducted from gross incomes. The stockholders would gain, as the cost of operating capital would fall and profits would consequently rise. This gain would, of course, be partly offset by the increase of the burden on tangible property and other tax bases. This burden, however, would be more equitably distributed than formerly.

It seems evident that the taxation of either stocks or bonds, in addition to the taxation of the property of the issuing corporations, is a clear case of double taxation — in fact, a particularly onerous type of double taxation, in so far as a substantial part of the bond tax as well as the other two taxes must be borne by the stockholders. It may be held that corporation stock, at least in some cases, represents a right to share in the dividends of a corporation, if earned, rather than an equity in the corporation's assets. Such is, of course, always true in the case of income bonds. In these cases such securities obviously represent income rather than wealth and consequently are not proper subjects of property taxation. The conclusion is that, if the avoidance of every element of double taxation be desired, all equities in tangible property and all debts secured by tangible property, that is, all representative property, should be exempted.

Some mention should be made also of the case of government securities. The exemption of government bonds from the income tax has been opposed generally by writers on taxation. The reason for such opposition, however, lies in the fact that income taxes are imposed at progressive rates. Such is not the case under the property tax, and therefore the exemption of government bonds from property taxes is of relatively slight importance. It would be idle to discuss the exemption of federal securities, as this is required by the Federal Constitution and there is little probability that this requirement will be repealed. It would seem that state and local bonds should be exempted on grounds of expediency, if for no other reason.

There remain several classes of intangible property that are not representative of tangible property and may properly be viewed as additional evidence of tax-paying ability. The most important types of non-representative intangibles are such sources of income as business good will, patents, and copyrights. Under an ideal system of taxation it is probable that property taxes would be imposed on these classes of non-representative intangibles and on all tangible property.

It would make little difference whether taxes were imposed only on the persons in possession of the property or were distributed among all persons owning equities in it, but they should not be imposed on both groups. For instance, if a mortgage is taxed, the amount of the mortgage should be deducted from the valuation on which the property is taxed. It is evident that, while the taxation of credits and the deduction of their amounts from the valuation of the property by which they are secured satisfies the principles of justice, a simpler method would be the exemption of the credits and the taxation of the tangible property on its full value. The incidence of the tax would ordinarily be the same in both cases.

In the states that tax mortgages in the hands of the holder and allow deduction of the amount of the mortgage from the assessed value of the property, the tax is nevertheless usually borne by the mortgagor, to whom the mortgagee shifts the burden either directly or in the form of higher interest rates.

While such an ideal system could not be criticized on the grounds of justice, it would be in part unworkable. Personal equities in patents and copyrights and the good will of unincorporated businesses can never be assessed even by the most efficient administrative methods. It is possible, however, to tax corporation good-will by means of corporate excess taxes. In this case the security market sometimes provides an adequate measure of the taxable value. While the enforcement of corporate excess taxes has not been, in fact, particularly successful in many of the states that have used it, this form of taxation presents no inherent and insurmountable difficulties to an efficient and adequately supported assessor.

The ideal system of property taxation, as modified by expediency, would, therefore, include the taxation of all real property, such forms of tangible personal property as can be assessed in practice, and perhaps corporate excess. Such a tax might be held to be unequal in that stockholders of corporations would be discriminated against and other owners of nonrepresentative intangible property would be favored. Such discrimination, however, would be of slight significance as compared with the discriminations now resulting from most of our state and local tax systems. Moreover, in most cases in which intangible property has been exempted the states impose personal income taxes, and where this is the case income that is not reached by the property tax does not escape taxation entirely. Finally, so far as patents and copyrights are concerned, it would be impossible for a state to tax these sources of income because of the implied prohibition of the Federal Constitution.[3]

Special Taxes on Intangibles. While twelve states have exempted the bulk of intangible property from taxation, fourteen states have adopted a different and more widely discussed method of reform, namely, the classified property tax. This provides for the taxation of intangibles at a low rate in lieu of taxation at the general property tax rate. This type of plan has been very popular among tax reformers during recent years. . .

Intangible property is uniformly assessed at its full value. The rates imposed upon this valuation vary from 1 mill to 7.5

[3] *Long* v. *Rockwood,* 277 U. S. 277.

mills. The most common rates are 3 and 4 mills, levied annually.

A similar type of tax is the mortgage-recording tax imposed in eight states. The purpose and the effect of such a tax are similar to those of the annually imposed low-rate tax, except that the administration is simplified by the fact that the tax is imposed only once, at the time that the mortgage is recorded. Moreover, such a tax is frequently easier to enforce because the laws in many states provide that unrecorded mortgages may not be presented as evidence in court. The burden in these cases is not adjusted so closely as in the case of the annual taxes. In some cases the rate of tax is adjusted roughly according to the life of the mortgage. . .

Mention should be made here of the experiments of New Hampshire and Tennessee. These states have exempted intangibles from property taxation, but have enacted income taxes imposed only upon income received from the intangibles formerly taxed. It may be expected that the tax revenues will be slightly greater under this method of taxation than under the general property tax, chiefly because of the substitution of central for local administration. When only the income from intangibles need be reported, it is doubtful that enforcement is facilitated to a greater degree by this method than by the low-rate property tax. If income, however, is considered a better tax base than property value, the income tax form is obviously more equitable.

The theory behind these mill taxes and mortgage-recording taxes is that taxation of intangible property at low rates will induce the owners to list such property for taxation. Under the general property tax system the rate is fixed at a figure that will yield sufficient revenue to meet the budget requirements. The rate, therefore, depends on two factors, namely, the budget requirements and the total assessed value of property. The bulk of the property taxed is undervalued. Therefore, the nominal property tax rate is always much higher than the effective rate at which tangible property is taxed. In the case of intangibles, however, undervaluation is, if not impossible, at least less common than in the case of tangibles. Therefore, the effective rate approximates the nominal rate on intangible property. It is usually claimed by the proponents of the classified property tax that this is the reason why intangible property is not listed, and it is further claimed that, if taxes did not take so large a percentage of the income from such property, it would be listed and assessed.

This claim is usually supported by statistics showing that

the amount of property assessed and, in some cases, the actual taxes raised have increased under classification. No recognition is, however, usually given to the fact that the normal rate of increase of assessment under the general property tax before the adoption of classification would in some of these states have resulted in equally large assessments under the old method. Furthermore, it is usually admitted by the low rate advocates that much of the increase of assessments under classification laws must be attributed to the centralization of administration that has accompanied every enactment. Classification supporters have never made a satisfactory attempt to show that any state has, through classification, succeeded in placing substantially all intangibles on the tax roll. Nor, finally, has any one of this group ever shown any good reason other than fiscal expediency why representative intangibles should be taxed at all.

Listing of intangibles not taxed at the source is uniformly left to the property-owners. It would not be possible in the United States to give assessors the inquisitorial powers that would be necessary to enable them to discover such property. The system, except in a few cases in which property is held in trust by an organization whose accounts are open to the assessors, is one of self-assessment, and consequently it places a premium upon dishonesty and a penalty upon honesty. The penalties imposed by law are usually high, but they are seldom enforced. The failure to list intangibles is nowhere viewed as a crime by either the taxpayers or the assessors. This being the case, it is hopeless to expect that substantially all the intangible property will be listed, whatever the rate of taxation may be. If it is impossible to clothe the assessor with power to enforce listing, and so long as this duty is left to the taxpayer, the attempt to tax intangibles takes on the character of an appeal for voluntary contributions rather than that of a demand for payment of a tax. Modern governments are not financed by voluntary contributions. Therefore, in the final analysis, all classified property tax systems, as applied to most types of intangibles, must be viewed as makeshift measures. A more workable and equitable system of taxation would seem to be the complete exemption of all intangibles, except possibly corporate excess. As has been pointed out, furthermore, experience with corporate excess taxation has been anything but satisfactory.

Money and Deposits. Most of the states tax money and deposits, although money is exempt in 11 states; commercial bank deposits, in 14 states; and savings deposits, in 17 states.

Low-rate taxes are imposed upon money in 10 states and District of Columbia; upon commercial deposits in 11 states and District of Columbia; and upon savings deposits in 9 states and District of Columbia. The remaining states — 27 in the case of money, 23 in the case of commercial deposits, and 22 in the case of savings deposits — tax these items in the same manner as other personal property.

Solvent Credits. It is difficult to classify the methods of taxing solvent credits[4] because of the classifications under state laws, but, in general, bills and notes receivable are exempt in about 12 states, while they are subject to low-rate taxes in about 11 states and District of Columbia. In the remaining states an attempt is made to tax them as ordinary personal property. About 11 states and District of Columbia impose low-rate taxes of either the annual type or the single registration type upon bonds other than those of governments or business corporations, while in about an equal number of states bonds are exempt. There appears in the state laws governing credits a tendency to exempt those forms which are most clearly seen to be representative property. It is frequently the practice to exempt all solvent credits secured by tangible, or in some cases real, property. . .

Mortgages. The tendency to exempt representative property is evident also in the taxation of mortgages. These are exempted more frequently than is the case with any other type of intangibles except corporation stock. They are exempt at the present time in 23 states. In 10 states and District of Columbia they are subject to low-rate taxes of either the annual or the registration variety. They are still taxed as ordinary personal property in 12 states. In Colorado, Connecticut, Indiana, Massachusetts, Nebraska, New Jersey, and Vermont mortgages are taxable, but provision is made for the deduction of the mortgage assessment from the valuation of the property by which it is secured. In all these cases the mortgage contracts usually provide that the tax be paid by the mortgagor, so that such provisions amount, in fact, to exemption of mortgages. In Indiana this deduction is limited to $1000, or half the value of the real estate, whichever is the smaller. In Mississippi, Vermont, and one county of Maryland the right to deduct the mortgage assessment from the valuation of the tangible property depends on the rate of interest paid on the mortgage. A peculiar provision of the Connecticut law indicates the tendency to recognize in the

4 Including bills, notes, accounts receivable, non-mortgage corporation bonds, etc.

statutes the fact of unlawful undervaluation. While the law provides that Connecticut tangible property is assessable at its full value, it provides also that mortgages are taxable to the extent that the face values of the mortgages exceed the assessed values of the Connecticut properties by which they are secured.

Securities of Business Corporations. The tendency to exempt representative property is illustrated further by the practice in regard to the taxation of securities of most business corporations. Shares of stocks of most domestic corporations are now exempt in 32 states. These exemptions are frequently limited, however, to domestic corporations whose property is taxed within the taxing state—a further illustration of the tendency of states to attempt to tax property outside of their boundaries. In about 13 states the individual owners of the capital stock are exempt, but a tax equivalent to a property tax on the stock is imposed upon the corporation in the form of either a capital stock tax or a corporate excess or capital tax. Bonds are more frequently taxed than stocks, and they are also more frequently subject to low-rate annual or registry taxes.

Bank stock is now exempt in 17 states. In 6 states the tax is collected from the banks. Bank stock is subject to low-rate taxes in only 5 states. The failure to include bank stock in the low-rate taxes results from the provision of the federal statutes, Section 5219, R. S. U. S., which prescribes four methods of taxing national banks. One of these methods is a tax on the capital stock, and, as the four methods are mutually exclusive, if the capital stock is taxed, no other tax may be imposed upon a national bank. Hence, the imposition of a low-rate capital stock tax upon the securities of national banks would result in serious undertaxation. The limitations on the taxation of national banks are generally reflected also in the systems of taxing state banks and trust companies. In general, where a low-rate tax is imposed upon intangibles, the stock of national banks, and frequently also of all other banks, is exempted, and some other method of taxing such institutions is adopted.

CONCLUSIONS

SEVERAL tendencies in the taxation of general property are evident. Little change has taken place during the last half century in the taxation of real estate, except for the classification of particular types of real estate, such as mines and forests. In the case of mines classification has not gone far, and special taxation usually represents an attempt to provide a new method of administration rather than an attempt to adjust the tax burden. In the case of forest property, classification represents an attempt to adjust the time of payment of the tax rather than its amount. The same is true of tangible personal property. Such classification plans as have been adopted usually represent attempts to provide easier methods of enforcement rather than to relieve this property from taxation. In the case of intangibles two tendencies are discernible. The first is the tendency toward a low rate of taxation resulting from the belief — (1) that intangibles bear a higher burden of taxation under the general property tax than does other property, which is normally underassessed, and (2) that more intangibles will be listed under a low-rate tax than under a tax imposed at normal rates. The second is the tendency to exempt intangibles, particularly those types that are clearly seen to be merely representative of equities in tangible property. The latter tendency, however, is limited by the attempt to tax income sources in other states.

Under the ideal system of taxation . . . a state would tax all real estate, all tangible personal property that can be assessed, and all non-representative intangibles. The two reasons in favor of the low-rate taxation of intangibles, cited in the preceding paragraph, appear to be fallacious. If intangibles are overtaxed under the general property tax, this is because tangible property is undervalued and not because there is any difference between tangible and intangible property as regards relation of earnings to capital value. The remedy for this situation would, therefore, seem to be the improvement of tax administration rather than the imposition of special low-rate taxes. As regards the second reason cited, it has been stated that the attempt to induce listing by special concessions means an attempt to finance government by voluntary contributions rather than by taxation.

The policy of exemption seems to be more equitable than low-rate taxation of intangibles, if equal distribution of tax burdens is the goal. Taxation of representative intangible property which, as stated, includes practically all the intangibles ordinarily taxed, means double taxation, and, under modern forms of corporate organization, if a tax is imposed upon each additional evidence of property rights, may mean further extended multiple taxation. Double taxation does not necessarily result in unequal taxation, providing the double taxation be universal and uniform. If, however, the double taxation resulting from the taxation of intangibles is to be made universal and uniform, all tangible property must be taxed, and all rights to tangible property must be taxed as well. Under such a plan taxes would be imposed upon deeds and upon rights to wealth not represented by documentary evidence, as well as upon mortgages, securities, and other evidences of wealth. Such a system of taxation would be absurd. The taxation of all intangible rights to wealth is both impossible and unnecessary. The same result can be achieved by the taxation of all assessable tangibles and the exemption of all intangibles. Such a plan will result in inequalities to the extent that non-representative intangible rights exist. Such inequality can perhaps be remedied in part by the taxation of corporate excess, but the most logical conclusion seems to be that the injustices resulting from the exemption of all intangibles will be of slight significance as compared with the injustices and the administrative chaos that obtain under the prevailing system.

One qualification of the general position of authorities on public finance which has been reflected in this report should be mentioned in passing. The perfect tax system will be realized, if ever, at a time in the far distant future. As has already been stated, it would not be difficult to devise a satisfactory plan of distributing the burdens of government if a legislature could start with a clean slate. But it is necessary in every state to revise tax laws upon the basis of those that now exist; and for this reason the adoption of perfect forms is in most cases impossible. This factor applies particularly to the attempts toward the modification of the present methods of taxing intangible property. Much as the exemption of such property may be desired, it is in many cases fiscally and politically impossible. It is difficult to convince the owner of real property that a bondholder, for instance, cannot, under any method of taxation, be forced to bear any substantial property tax burden. It is also impossible, in many states, to discard the present taxes on intangible property without replacing the revenue now derived therefrom. If no other source of revenue is provided, the exemption of this class of property will result in the increase of taxes on tangible property.

As previously pointed out, the actual burden of the taxes now imposed on intangibles must necessarily fall on owners of tangible property. Therefore, the exemption of intangible property without substitution of other revenues, while it would probably result in an increase of property tax rates, would really mean a more equitable distribution of burdens on property, because it would cause the substitution of higher and more equitably distributed direct burdens for the present less equitably distributed indirect burdens on tangible wealth. Yet the political impossibility of enacting any measures that would result in this increase in direct tax rates, together with the constitutional impossibility of this increase where the rates are limited, may necessitate substitution of other revenues. It is commonly felt throughout the United States that property tax burdens should be reduced in any case by the substitution of other revenues for property taxes. If this is true, the revenue lost by the exemption of intangible property from general property taxes should be made up in some way other than the increase of tangible property tax rates.

There are several possible alternatives. In the case of revenue from individual holdings of intangible property, personal income taxes or sales taxes may be substituted. In the case of revenue derived from corporate holdings of intangible property, corporation income taxes or other business taxes may be substituted. Where it is not possible to find any other substitute, a low-rate tax on intangible property may be the best alternative. This much can definitely be stated for the low-rate tax on intangibles: the distribution of the burden is wider under most low-rate or classification tax systems than under most general property tax systems. Furthermore, it is possible that in the future systems may be devised under which substantially all of some classes of intangible property may be assessed for taxation. In some states intangible property taxes imposed "at the source" have been satisfactorily administered. This has frequently been the case with bank deposits and bank stocks. Such is also the case with some mortgage-recording taxes. Kentucky may be taken as an example. Here the banks pay the taxes on bank deposits and bank stocks, and they may in turn collect these taxes from their stockholders and depositors. Where such a system is used, the administrators may reasonably hope to secure a substantially complete assessment of the property so taxed. It is possible that imposition of taxes at the source may be extended, and wherever this is feasible satisfactory assessment may be expected. Thus, it must be concluded that, while the taxation of intangible property must in most cases be considered double taxation, and, if double taxation is to be avoided, most intangibles must be exempted, the classification of intangible property and the taxation of such property at special low rates is at least a step in the right direction.

Finally, the argument for the substitution of an income tax for a property tax on intangibles remains to be considered. The question is frequently asked whether a state should adopt a low-rate tax on intangibles or an income tax. The question implies that the one is a substitute for the other. There is no reason why this should necessarily be the case.

Two states, namely, New Hampshire and Tennessee, have substituted income taxes, imposed only on the income from intangibles, for property taxes on intangible property. In the opinion of some of the foremost American tax administrators there seems to be less reluctance on the part of taxpayers to report income from intangible property than to report the property itself. Aside from this possibility there would seem to be only a slight advantage in this limited form of income taxation, as compared with the more usual low-rate property tax.

There appears to be no good reason for viewing income taxes and low-rate property taxes as alternatives. Where general personal income taxes are imposed, the income from real property is not exempted. If it be assumed that intangible property should be included in the property tax base, the imposition of an income tax affords no additional reason for exempting intangibles from property taxes that would not hold equally for other property. If it be held that the taxation of intangible property amounts to unequal double taxation, such property should be exempted whether an income tax be imposed or not.

Modern property taxes are in fact objective. The income tax, on the other hand, according to the usually accepted view, is a personal tax. The total net income of the individual, from whatever source derived, is held to be a measure of his ability to contribute to the support of government. The fact that the sources of that income have been reached by property taxes is wholly irrelevant, as such taxes are objective and are usually justified on other grounds, namely, the benefits of government to property and the privilege of property ownership. It is true that there may be double taxation, in the sense that two taxes must be paid out of the same income fund, but there is no double taxation in the sense that the same jurisdiction imposes two taxes on the same tax base.

The merits of income taxation are not under discussion in this study. It may be that the addition of a personal income tax will result in a wider and more equal distribution of the aggregate tax burden in accordance with ability to pay, and it is true that exemption of intangibles is now common, though not universal, in the income tax states. Nevertheless, the income tax cannot be regarded as a proper substitute for property taxes on either intangible or other property. If the avoidance of partial double taxation is to be desired, intangibles should be exempted whether or not an income tax be adopted.

2. A CASE AGAINST THE TAXATION OF INTANGIBLE PROPERTY *

FIRST let us note that it [the taxing of stocks, bonds and mortgages] often taxes both the property itself and the evidence of ownership of that property. For example, a corporation may own property in one State, and as a corporation pay taxes on this property to the State in which it is located. But some of the stockholders may live in another State, and be compelled to pay taxes on the value of their stock. Obviously these stockholders suffer from double taxation — being taxed by one State on their property, and by the other State on their stock certificates, or evidence of ownership of that property.

A somewhat similar, and in some respects a worse, evil than that just illustrated is represented by the taxation of bonds and mortgages. Let us assume, to illustrate this point, that Smith and Jones each own a $10,000 house in a city in which the tax rate is 2 per cent on the full value of the property. If each has his house fully paid for, and has no other taxable property, each will be compelled to pay $200 in taxes. But suppose that Smith had only $5000 when he built his house and Jones had $15,000, and that Smith borrowed $5000 from Jones, giving the latter a $5000 mortgage on his house. As the general property tax is applied in many States, Smith would be allowed no abatement in taxes for his $5000 debt, or mortgage. He would pay his tax of $200 just the same, which would amount to 4 per cent of his actual equity in the house. But this is not the worst. Jones, as owner of the mortgage, would be compelled to pay a 2 per cent tax on that, or $100, and this tax he might be able to shift to Smith. He might have the opportunity of investing his $5000 at a reasonable rate of interest in some tax-free investment, this usually being possible under our present systems of taxation. The rate he might obtain on his tax-free investment, would be, let us say, 6 per cent. If, now, Smith wants Jones' $5000 as a loan he must pay the 6 per cent that Jones would get by investing his money elsewhere, and in addition the 2 per cent required to pay the tax. Therefore Smith would pay in taxes altogether $300, although he owned only $5000 worth of property, while Jones would pay only $200 net, although he owned $15,000 worth of

* From L. A. Rufener, *Principles of Economics,* (Houghton Mifflin Co., Boston, 1927), pp. 758-760.

property, including the $5000 which he lent Smith on the mortgage. Smith would actually pay taxes at the rate of 6 per cent on the value of his equity in his house, while Jones would pay at the rate of 1 1-3 per cent on his property. Real examples like this are easy to find and represent that gross form of injustice which compels the poor man to pay taxes at a higher rate than the rich man.

Some States, as West Virginia, tax bonds and mortgages, but not stocks of corporations. This has the unfortunate effect of inducing investors to buy more or less speculative stocks instead of sound bonds and mortgages, in an attempt to avoid the tax.*

* Eds. note: Another argument which has been advanced against the taxation of intangible property is to the effect that such property does not constitute economic wealth. An illustration of this point is given in Hastings Lyon, *Principles of Taxation*, (Boston, 1914), p. 32. Here Lyon writes: "If Smith owes Jones $1000, Jones has a right against Smith and Smith owes an obligation to Jones that constitutes *property*. Jones owns this property. The fact that Smith owes Jones does not constitute *wealth* at all. Otherwise a group of people, sitting in a room together, say, could become wealthy far 'beyond the dreams of avarice' by solemnly making mutual promises to each other. In this way a nation could increase its wealth to any extent."

QUESTIONS AND PROBLEMS FOR DISCUSSION

1. Show how property is classified for taxation in some particular state.
2. Is there any justification for exempting from taxation the property owned by churches? by endowed educational institutions?
3. Can the exemption of industrial property from taxation be socially justified on grounds that it encourages production?
4. What do you think of the argument that the taxation of intangibles is an unjust form of double taxation?
5. Does it seem reasonable and fair to tax intangibles at a low rate merely to encourage the owners to list them for taxation?
6. In view of the many problems involved in the taxation of intangibles, would you favor the complete exemption of intangible property from taxation? all forms of intangible property or only "representative property"?
7. Do you believe that income taxation should be substituted for the taxation of intangibles?
8. Have the low-rate taxes on intangible property been successful in increasing the amount of such property assessed?

SUGGESTIONS FOR RESEARCH

1. The taxation of intangibles and the concept of property.
2. The place of the classified property tax in state and local taxation.
3. Suggestions for improvement in the assessment of intangible property.

4. The results of property classification for taxation in the United States or in some particular state.

5. Exemption versus low-rate taxation of intangible property.

BIBLIOGRAPHICAL NOTE

The outstanding treatise on the classified property tax in the United States is S. E. Leland, *The Classified Property Tax in the United States,* (Boston, 1928). One of the many excellent features of this book is the comprehensive bibliography which it contains.

Two scholarly articles on the classified property tax have been written by Professor C. J. Bullock. They are: "A Classified Property Tax," *Proceedings of the National Tax Association,* (1909), pp. 95-105; and "The State Income Tax versus A Classified Property Tax," *Proceedings of the National Tax Association,* (1916), pp. 362-384.

The nature and extent of the classification of property for taxation purposes in the United States are given in J. P. Jensen, *Property Taxation in the United States,* (Chicago, 1931), Chap. VII. Valuable material on the subject of classification in various American states may be found in the *Proceedings of the National Tax Association.* The *Proceedings* for 1928 are deserving of special mention.

A stimulating argument for the taxation of tangible and intangible property at different rates is presented in Hastings Lyon, *Principles of Taxation,* (Boston, 1914), Chap. III.

CHAPTER XII

*TAXATION OF LAND VALUE: THE SINGLE TAX
AND THE INCREMENT TAX*

1. THE EARLY DEVELOPMENT OF THE SINGLE TAX CONCEPT *

Meaning of the single tax. By the single tax is meant a
policy under which all the public revenue is to be raised by the
single tax on land value. One of the most persistent misin-
terpretations of the single tax is that of assuming that it means
a tax to be raised on real estate rather than on land values.
Land value is defined as the value of land itself irrespective of
all improvements, such as ditching, draining, fencing, the planting of trees, and the erection of buildings. In short, everything done on the land itself to improve the value of an estate
is classed as an improvement and, under the single tax, would
be exempt from taxation. This leaves nothing except the
location value and the fertility value to be taxed.

*The physiocrats, believers in the "rule of nature," believed
in the impôt unique.* The original advocates of the single tax
were a group of French economists called physiocrats. It was
their belief that land was the original and fundamental source
of all wealth, and that the rent of land was the only real surplus
wealth which the community ever produced. From their point
of view, rent was due to the bounty of nature. They believed
that every other tax must eventually be paid out of rent anyway, wherever it may have been laid by the government. If
we tax the products of industries, there is no surplus out of
which the tax can be paid; as a result we either raise their price
or depress the price of raw materials. If we tax labor we must
raise wages accordingly; if we tax enterprise we must raise
profits. Every tax, therefore, is shifted from one to another
till it reaches the landowner, who alone has a surplus out of
which it can be paid. The landowner cannot shift it any farther, and, since he must ultimately pay the tax, the physiocrats
argued that it was better for him to pay it directly in the first
place than indirectly after several shiftings from one person
to another. They regarded the single tax as a good system of

* From T. N. Carver, *Principles of National Economy,* (Ginn and Co., Boston, 1921), pp. 731-733, 737, 738.

330

taxation for raising revenue, not as an engine of social reform.

The classical economist regarded rent as a peculiar income.
The idea that landowners who live entirely upon the rent of
land are in a peculiar sense nonproducers is by no means new.
Adam Smith wrote,[1] in 1776, "As soon as the land of any country has all become private property, the landlords, like all other
men, love to reap where they never sowed, and demand a rent
even for its natural produce." And again, "They [the land-
lords] are the only one of the three orders whose revenue costs
them neither labor nor care, but comes to them, as it were, of
its own accord, and independent of any plan or project of their
own."[2] Economists from Adam Smith down have generally
agreed on this point, though they have not generally agreed
that this is the great cause of poverty, nor that the abolition of
ground rent would be a social panacea.

Ricardo, in developing his theory of rent, laid emphasis upon
the fact that rent arises from the niggardliness rather than from
the bounty of nature, thus taking a position opposed to that of
the French physiocrats. This niggardliness shows itself in two
ways: first, the land is always limited in area; second, its
productivity is limited. On any given area the amount of any
crop which can be produced is limited; and even before that
limit is reached, diminishing returns are received from successive applications of labor and capital. Because of these
limitations upon the productivity of the best land, poorer and
poorer land must be taken into cultivation as the demand for
products increases. The fortunate possessors of the better
grades of land are then in a position to demand a rent for their
land.

*The single tax made an engine of social reform by Henry
George.* It was the late Henry George, in his book entitled
Progress and Poverty, who seized upon these ideas to make
the single tax an engine of social reform. He began his inquiry
by pointing out that even in the midst of plenty, poverty still
persisted. He stated that though the productive power of the
world had increased many fold through mechanical improvements, nevertheless large numbers of people remained in
poverty. In fact, he went so far as to insist that increasing
numbers were compelled to live in conditions of increasing
squalor. . .

The argument for the single tax as an engine of social reform
rests on three general propositions. In the first place, since
those who receive rent because of the location of their land cre-

[1] *Wealth of Nations,* Bk. I, chap. vi.
[2] *Wealth of Nations,* Bk. I, chap. xi.

ate nothing in return for the rent they receive, their incomes are merely subtracted from those of the rest of society. If their incomes should be taken away, this would not in any degree diminish the total productiveness of the community. . .

In the second place, it is alleged that a great deal of land is kept out of use for speculative purposes and that a high tax on land values would force this land into use. . .

A third argument for the single tax is to the effect that when a large amount of revenue is raised from a tax on land, there is no necessity for so high a tax — probably no necessity for any tax whatever — on other things. This reduction of taxation on other forms of property would serve as a stimulus to greater production.

A BASIS upon which to judge the validity of the foregoing and of other propositions of the single taxers will be afforded by the next section of this chapter.

2. THEORETICAL ISSUES IN THE SINGLE TAX *

THE temper and point of view of the following discussion will perhaps be made clearer if I set out with a confession of faith :

I believe that the principle at the heart of the single tax agitation — that the fiscal revenues should be derived from the social estates (the regalia principle in ultimate essence), from sources to which the justifications for private property do not attach — is right and vastly important. The rents of mines, forests, waterfalls, franchises, town lots, and also, if practicable, of agricultural lands, should be retained as fiscal properties. Not a society single-taxed, but a society free from all taxes of any sort, is the logic of the principle — a goal well within the reach of a wise and provident public policy. One needs in this connection to recall only the school land properties of the West, the mining wealth set aside for the University of Minnesota, the immense areas of prospective agricultural land forming the endowment of the University of Texas, the salt mines publicly owned in Germany, the royalties which Canada is collecting from very considerable portions of its mineral wealth. As ethical basis, whatever other bases there may conceivably be for private property, the single taxer logically finds nothing but the right of the individual to himself and to the results of his activity — the simple recognition of the meaning of personality and of the ethical relations which it prescribes. That

* From H. J. Davenport, "Theoretical Issues in the Single Tax," *American Economic Review*, Vol. VII, (March, 1917), pp. 1-30.

one has produced an item of wealth, or has it by the voluntary transfer of some one that has produced it, affords the sole ethical claim to it. This is doubtless a labor theory of the ethical right of property. Nothing, therefore, which is natural bounty can rightly have been allowed to serve as a source of individual income, to fall into the category of individual ownership.

I believe also that all times have been propitious times, the present a right time no less than any earlier time, for establishing the provision that future increments of earning power from natural resources shall not be permitted to fall into the hands of private owners.

But I don't know what course is now wise in repair of the blunders that are past. Confiscation, at any rate, a program which shall impose on any casual present owner of original natural bounty the penalty for a general and institutional blunder, appears to me to be an incredibly unethical position for a school of thinkers whose essential doctrine is one of practical ethics. Remedies, however, I do not despair of; the most promising of these being an extreme extension of inheritance taxation. In view of the fact also that the ad valorem and property tax methods of state and local taxation subject to fiscal claims only something like one fifth of the total taxable income of society, I am sure that much is possible through the development of state income taxation. If the transfer of the public estates into private ownership was a blunder, the returns from new taxation may well be applied to the purchase of permanent ground rents in the public interest.

These payments could well be fixed at the present worth of ground rent charge for approximately the expectation of life, or even for the possible duration of life, of the actual owner. The principle of escheat or of the inheritance tax carried to its ultimate logical extreme would take care of the residue of value.

THE TAXATION OF RENTAL VERSUS THE TAXATION OF CAPITAL VALUE

NONE, therefore, of the objections which I shall offer to the typical and usual single tax analysis should be taken to constitute a fundamental or essential criticism. I am, for example, sure that, when the purpose is to appropriate for society a certain rental, the only wise method is to proceed directly against the rental as such, rather than by an ad valorem tax upon the value derivative from the rental. In those cases where the property burden is in present command of the revenues upholding its market price, the results of the ad valorem tax do not seriously depart from those attending a direct appropriation of the rent.[3]

But in the degree that prospective changes in earning power find expression in a present worth of market price, it is practically disastrous and theoretically inept to make the present value the basis or the determinant of the present contribution to the public treasury. For the purposes of the single tax program the ad valorem policy is singularly inappropriate; not so much that to take the rent leaves, so far, no value to tax — saws off on the hither side the limb on which one is sitting — as that it strikes at the very heart of the equities involved. After society has taxed for years a town lot not yet within the area of practicable improvement, but yet valuable by its prospect of availability — has collected from the owner annually as the years have passed, say, 1 per cent of the present worth of the expectation that the owner will finally enter into the enjoyment of the income — is it not clear that society has foreclosed itself from later asserting its right to appropriate these revenues entirely? In cases of this sort, ad valorem taxation barters away for present

[3] Nevertheless extreme absurdities and impracticabilities, falling still something short of mathematical impossibilities, forbid reaching by ad valorem methods any considerable fraction of the earning power of the property.

Suppose, for example, that a piece of property, by virtue of its net annual revenue of $50, bears a market price of $1000. Each new tax, changing the net return to the owner, must change the market price. Thus, if $10 is to be obtained for the fisc out of the revenue attaching to the land, the land, as retaining a net earning power of $40, will be worth $800. The rate of taxation necessary to get the $10 is not 1 per cent, but 1¼ per cent, else the land will stand upon the tax books as over-appraised to the extent of $200. This may not be a serious matter; is not, indeed, serious in the ordinary ad valorem collection of approximately one fifth of an income. But see how the case appears with the single taxer's attempt to pursue the method to the extent of his ultimate purpose:

											Per cent
With $20 taken and	$30	left, price is	$600;	rate	to	yield	$20	is	3⅓
"	30	"	"	20	"	"	"	400	"	"	"	30	"	7½
"	40	"	"	10	"	"	"	200	"	"	"	40	"	20
"	45	"	"	5	"	"	"	100	"	"	"	45	"	45
"	46	"	"	4	"	"	"	80	"	"	"	46	"	59½
"	47	"	"	3	"	"	"	60	"	"	"	47	"	78⅓
"	48	"	"	2	"	"	"	40	"	"	"	48	"	120
"	49	"	"	1	"	"	"	20	"	"	"	49	"	245
"	49.50 "	"	.50 "	"	"	"	10	"	"	"	49.50 "	495
"	49.75 "	"	.25 "	"	"	"	5	"	"	"	49.75 "	995
"	49.99 "	"	.01 "	"	"	"	.20 "	"	"	49.99 "	24.995

This, by the way, is an opportune time to confess the error in an earlier assertion of mine that this ad valorem method can avail to appropriate at the outside limit only one half of the annual rental. This blunder was cogently exposed by Professor Edgar H. Johnson in the *Quarterly Journal of Economics* of August, 1910. That I never replied was due to the fact that I could not. Conceivably, indeed, I suppose, there might be a case with even a better reason. Mr. Johnson's article, however, was in tone and temper entirely cordial and courteous. He merely had me cornered—and still has.

revenue the public right to the future revenue; in substance, hypothecates future resources to obtain present funds. Thus the single tax position amounts not merely to the inequity of intending to repudiate the contract but at the same time to the absurdity of the present announcement of this intention.

But not only does the single taxer's plan of burdening the present shadow of the future income, at the same time with intending to appropriate this same income when it accrues, amount to an attempt to enjoy two taxes where only one can possibly be equitable (either of which, in fact, both by the test of justice and by the working of economic forces, must replace the other), but also from a theoretical point of view gets into even a worse case: the taxation of a present worth in the absence of a present income, or any taxation disproportionate to present income, is an affront to the fundamental principle of taxation in general.

When shall the individual contribute to the public income for the maintenance of public activities? When he has some income to contribute. From what sources shall society's current expenses be financed? From society's current productive power, the social income. Taxation is merely a method of redistributing the applications of the productive powers of society to the creation of a wider variety of goods — more of some, the goods of public providing, less of the goods of private production; it is a transfer of private income to the state in order to provide more goods of security or education, in place, say, of butcher's meat or of the entertainment provided by the movie show. To tax at present an income which does not exist at present, and thus to support the current state expenditures at the cost of future productive activity, is a fiscal improvidence similar to that of two centuries ago when the English government permitted the owners of lands to purchase for cash a perpetual exemption from imperial taxes. Carried far enough this kind of fiscal policy would mean that a government had sold itself unto death through encumbering its expected revenues in aid of immediate receipts.

Current revenue is the only proper object of current taxation, as is frankly recognized in both the theory and the practice of income taxation. It is, however, fairly to be said that this single tax fallacy is merely a derivative from the larger theoretical error which vitiates the general property tax as a whole. The blunder merely becomes the more serious as the share of the income aimed at through taxation is larger. In some respects, moreover, the effects are even more serious in their general economic aspects than in the purely fiscal. Ad valorem taxation consistently applied amounts to almost an absolute veto on all investments promising remote returns. Present progress in forestry taxation is based upon the recognition that ad valorem taxation tends to discourage the growing of new trees precisely as it has prompted the exhaustion of the accumulated supplies. For the purpose of the present analysis, the planting of trees amounts to the purchase of a deferred annuity through the payment of a series of annual premiums, with only this difference, that the old age provision is a contingent annuity rather than an annuity approximately certain. Computing, then, that the general property tax upon an ordinary property appropriates one fifth of its income, it must follow that a rational tax upon a forest should at the maturity of its particular harvest appropriate one fifth of that harvest. To subject the undertaking to an annual tax is to compel the investor to submit in advance to an interest-bearing encumbrance on his putative future harvest. And precisely so with mines; the tax is a direct incentive to what is socially an untimely and wasteful exploitation.

The extreme of folly in this method of taxation is perhaps best illustrated in the case of a single-payment purchase of an old-age annuity. An outlay of $1000 at the age of 30 will provide approximately $250 at 60 years of age, if the buyer survives to that time, and thereafter the same sum for each successive year for the term of his life.[4] By assumption, here is a property worth $1000 immediately upon the purchase of the right. The state claims, say, $10 in taxes the first year. The purchased right increases in present worth not only by its interest accumulations but by the greater prospect of survival to the end of the tontine period. Each year, therefore, it pays a higher tax; not that it has yet afforded its owner any income or ever certainly will, but that a contract for a contingent future income has an increasing present worth. This annual increase of value is not, in fact, an income but merely the larger present worth of the hope of one day enjoying an income — precisely as the increase in the value of a field of grain as it approaches the time of harvest is not a daily receipt of income but a daily increase in the present worth of the future income. To be sure, if the owner sells in advance of the harvest, he ceases to be an investor in prospective income and the buyer takes his place. A rediscount of the note has occurred, the seller getting the advantage of the interest earned, but not yet due, as the sum of the past increases in the present worth of an income the receipt of which still lies in the future. The income

---

[4] Mutual Life rates, 3 per cent actuarial basis.

from the field of grain accrues solely at harvest. So again, to tax a provident and wealthy father of a family and at the same time to tax the prospective inheritor of the father's wealth on the basis of the increasing present worth of the hope of the sometime demise of the progenitor, is to make the general property tax a means of rampant extortion and injustice. When present value is merely a present-worth shadow of a future income, this value is a property, it is true, but a property the taxation of which should be postponed by virtue of the very fact that the income is postponed. It is time enough to make an individual income contribute to the general income when there begins to be an individual income.

But it is obvious that from all of this nothing follows more serious than that, as the single taxer aims solely to appropriate the rent, he would best do nothing but directly to take it. His indirection of method is unnecessary. His adoption of the principle and the machinery of the ad valorem property tax is a deal worse.

BUT the single taxer may find still other folk for company in his perplexities. If the appropriation of the rent must wait till there be rent to appropriate, what shall be done with the fact that, so long as there is no established policy of appropriation, purchasers must be proceeding in the confidence — or speculating in the hope — that appropriation will never take place? Thus, if appropriation finally does take place, there is inevitable disappointment and the charge of confiscation. The rule with taxation is similar to the legal rule : it is even more important to have a clear rule than to have a right one. Precisely this same difficulty presents itself in the regulation of public utility rates, and precisely the same line of treatment is indicated. Nothing will serve but the utmost certainty, promptitude, and consistency of action. With stocks, as with lands, anticipated earnings are capitalized into current market prices and undergo indefinite transfer — a traffic in the substance of things hoped for. To permit undue present earnings is to lead investors to part with their funds in the hope of the continuance of these earnings. To intervene later in order to bring an end to what ought never to have had a beginning amounts to the sudden confiscation of values long generally traded in but now lodged deflated in the hands of those investors least shrewd of political forecast. Thus, where the policy of rate regulation is unsettled, stock prices register the outcome of a great gamble on the very question of what this policy is going to be. When faith in public drowsiness flourishes, or when confidence grows that adverse legislation can be controlled, stocks rise; when public opinion stirs, or some truculent executive gets especially strenuous, there befalls a stock panic. Financial and industrial stability come to be dependent not merely on the confidence, but on the justified confidence, that never will society actually arrive at the refusal to be further plundered.

But no advocate of the restriction of corporate gains has so far ever argued that his purpose could be accomplished through any early or late application of the ad valorem tax. If an exclusive privilege or a permit of overcharge increases earnings by $50,000, the property goes up by $1,000,000 in price. To subject this increment of price to a 1 per cent ad valorem tax is to reclaim only $10,000 out of $50,000 overcharge.

With either land rents or with franchise gains, therefore, all increment must be claimed by the state promptly upon its emergence. To anticipate the increment by taxation is nonsense. To delay is to delude investors and thereupon finally to penalize them for being deluded.[5]

ETHICAL ASPECTS OF THE SINGLE TAX PROGRAM

THE general condemnation — my condemnation also — of the single-tax demand for the confiscation of past increments rests substantially on the conviction that an institutional situation — long established and generally recognized rules of the competitive game — should constitute a social obligation to protect that player who proceeds in conformity with the rule and in reliance on it. If some change needs be made, if a reform is to come, the society that established the institution, rather than the individual who uncritically has acquiesced in it, must bear the cost of getting over to the better way. The principle of vicarious atonement, however acceptable among systems of faith, deserves definite repudiation here. Surely if another will assume my bond, pay my taxes, serve my sentence, discharge my fine, I may make shift somehow to acquiesce. The best place to have a boil has been wisely declared to be on some one else. But justice does not necessarily impose what self-seeking might

---

[5] The doctrine of vested interest should be recognized in public affairs as the expression of the principle known in legal reasoning as the doctrine of estoppel. It was substantially under this doctrine, applied against the public, that overcharge rates were sustained in the famous Consolidated Gas Company case. By acts of commission certainly, if not by acts of omission, the public may cut itself off from the right to protect itself against an entirely obvious plundering. Privileges of overcharge may become irrevocable under conditions falling far short of the obligation of contract. Perhaps, indeed, the rationale of the obligation of contract itself is ultimately this same principle of estoppel, the creation of a justified belief or expectation which it would be unethical to disappoint.

approve. Confiscation remains none the less robbery, if there
is such a thing anywhere, even though the title of the first holder
were achieved through an obvious crime and the first authorized transfer were an authorized wrong. To justify confiscation by pointing to the emancipation of the slaves in America
merely serves to put in question the ethics of emancipation.
The English had already recognized the plain moral dictate
of indemnity — a dictate none the less plain for us in America
that it was later disregarded in the exigencies or the barbari-
ties of war.

Viewed in the large, doubtless, land is human opportunity
rather than human achievement, primary equipment rather
than product. The single taxer insists, and rightly and wisely
I again agree, that most or all of this original bounty should
have been held as a joint possession and heritage among men,
in equal and common right, to the end that, so far forth, there
be always for all men an equality of opportunity. The fiscal
requirements of society, the expenses of the joint community
life, should be to the utmost possibility covered by the payments into the common treasury of the funds derived as rent
from the social estates. Under competitive institutions this
appears, indeed, to be the only practicable way of validating
the principle of common property. Since we do not as a community farm the land, or live on it, or mine it, or hunt over
it, the only socialization practicable is the socialization of the
competitive return. In theory, indeed, the single taxer of the
strict observance would permit no other sort of socialization.
He is an individualist of the most radical type, even to the
degree of questioning the strict ethical propriety of the social
appropriation of any income due to individual activity. Accurately, therefore, he should profess himself not as a believer in
taxation but rather as a contemner of all taxation. He intends
an untaxed society. The right of society to the rent of the land
he holds to be fundamentally conditioned on the fact that no
individual can make good any claim in his own behalf. In
ultimate doctrine this no-tax advocate is the direct antithesis
of the socialist — finding social property justified only where
individual property cannot be supported. So far, indeed, is
he an individualist that even the working of the social estates
he will leave to competition, socializing only the receipt of the
rent. Nor even in the collection of the rent is he willing to
make the state a landlord; he aims, indeed, at the appropriation
of the rent by methods which shall preserve the essential features of private property and the incentives and guarantees of
private husbandry — cultivating ownership. Tenant cultiva-

tion he regards, in truth, as one of the especially evil aspects of the present system. The privilege of cultivating land should not be confined to those wealthy enough to buy it, or depend later on their consent. Thus, while the socialist finds no individual production nor the ethical necessity of individual ownership anywhere, the single taxer finds nowhere any righteous type of property which is not upheld by the title of individual productive effort. With opportunity equalized, whatever any one produces in his competitions with others is ethically to be accounted his own production. If opportunity is an actual auxiliary in the process, all his fellows have equal access to it and share in it. Thus, the single taxer socializes land — after his peculiar methods — not because he is a socialist but because he is not. It is only the principle of individualism that finds a peculiar ethical right and duty to socialize treasure trove, jetsam and flotsam, and estates without heirs.

Not altogether irrelevant, therefore, is the objection to the single tax policy that the revenues which it would make the exclusive support of the fisc may turn out inadequate. But the single taxer's confidence that the revenue would be adequate does not require justification as hope or demonstration as accomplishment in order to prescribe that, before other sources of revenue are exploited, this be made to render its utmost return. Harsh necessity may enforce resort to other devices; but for none of these can he discover so clear an ethical warrant or any unquestionable warrant. His tax need logically be unique only on the condition that it is adequate.

But that so many of the contentions of the single taxers are acceptable can avail to approve their program only so far as it is a forward-looking policy. It does not follow as just that society shall now proceed to do what society admittedly ought once to have done, but did not then do; that the penalties of delay shall be visited not upon society as a whole, to which as a whole has attached the responsibility of delay, but, instead, on whatever individuals, after centuries of free and active trading, happen now to be the actual proprietors. It was society that imposed buying as the condition of independent exploitation, offering nowhere to any individual the permission of control under high exactions in favor of the state. If it be indeed true that this fiscal reform is of transcendent importance — I myself believe it to be wise — let it speedily come. But never a great reform need come after this wise, unless by the fact that those who so greatly want it want it only on terms that others pay for it. Doubtless it is true that under the stress of war the state may force some men to death upon the firing line for the general good, though the jurisdiction of the majority for this purpose and to this extremity may be hard to establish. But fiscal reform can come, if it be worth the price, without this hit-or-miss selection of scapegoats. The minimum social sacrifice does not prescribe or permit the expropriation of the few, but only the spreading of the burden widely, as the theory of insurance should easily suffice to prove. Largely viewed, land may be and doubtless is a bounty of nature, whatever that may mean. But to its actual present owner it represents something quite other, a property into which have flowed income and savings of indefinitely various sources — most of them forms of wealth about which the single taxer draws his sacred circle. He holds that the unearned gains were the good fortune of the earlier holders who escaped their doom by selling to me or to you — gains which have undergone investment and reinvestment into houses, herds, factories, libraries, merchandise, steamships, and are now safe in their inviolability, buttressed about by utmost sanctities, certified to as properties assured against public claim no matter into whose hands they have fallen — thief, beggar, or prostitute. And all this by the sole fact that somewhere back in the chain of title there was a holder whose claim was ethically worthy of public approval, he having brought this wealth into being. And thus, by force of his original merit, somehow inexplicably attached to the property, all later owners are rendered safe. Thereby is justice construed as relative not to persons but to properties. Originally it was personal, to be sure, but later it became somehow appurtenant to things. It is the kind of property that a buyer purchases, not the source of the funds with which he purchases, that determines whether he shall be protected, even were these funds representative of earlier gains through unearned increments. But selling any possible sort of property, no matter what or when the fish he has caught, or the grain he has grown, or the cloth he has woven, or the house he has builded, let him beware what things he shall now buy with these funds of unquestioned title. If his righteous earnings go into land, society may any day dispossess him. And likewise let later investors beware; if they buy from him this land over which the sword has hung suspended but has not yet fallen, he shall go away safe with the proceeds and they shall become subject to the menacing confiscation — shall fall into this pit of calamity contrived and set by society for the trapping of the unwary. Not only shall no man henceforth obtain further gains of unearned increment, but, buying now, any man may forfeit all of his

earlier accumulations, no matter whence he had them. That
fortunate man, however, who has already cashed in his objectionable gains shall be forever safe, resting in the vestments
and odor of sanctity, if only he be wise enough to extend no
further his operations in unearned increments. And under
similar limitations he may pass along to any later vendee this
same age-long immunity, he and they forever sheltered under
the merit of an original impeccable possessor. But those men
to whom the gainer through unearned increment shall sell,
shall indemnify society for the titles it alienated, making good
to it the gains of all preceding title-holders, settling in full the
score of the centuries. Thus it appears to be a sheer error that
holds guilt to be personal. Instead, it is solely an attribute of
things, and is of the general character of magic and taboo,
houses that are haunted and ass-skins that are accursed. And
thus the naïve childlike fancies of a primitive age survive to
make ridiculous the policies of a great reform.

Not less faulty in logic, if not quite so closely akin to the
animism of primitive superstition, is the commonplace objection to the public retention of all kinds of ground rent: that
unearned increments in society are many, land increments only
one out of a larger class, and that therefore it is unjust and
indefensible to prohibit this one, while leaving the others to
flourish. And thus it appears again that justice, equally with
merit or crime, inheres in the relations of things. And yet it
must be clear that whatever is accomplished towards the elimination of privilege and the equalization of opportunity is so
far good. Remedy must begin with something; it is well to do
the next thing next, especially if this next thing be the most
important and the least difficult thing. Burglary need not be
continued or highway robbery tolerated, awaiting the time that
murder or counterfeiting shall be no more. No crime, or
better no criminal, may claim to go free till all other malefac-
tors are jailed — a vested right in one's particular graft or
iniquity.

Not much more respectable is the theory that, if unearned
increments are to be claimed by the state, unearned decrements
must be made good — say, for example, that if you be denied
gain on your little speculation, I must be repaid the loss on
mine. At any rate, it must be obvious that, if there is to be no
gain for speculative operators, there will be no speculators. To
retain the land rent for society, whatever and whenever it may
be, is so far to leave nothing to invest in or to gamble about
or to lose by — an illustration of the ancient truth that, if you
will sit always on the ground, you can never fall off.

LITTLE more to the purpose are the objections: (1) that the single tax violates the principle that burden should conform to capacity, and (2) that it provides no fiscal elasticity. But if the revenues are merely prices for the use of special advantages attaching to exceptional opportunity — a device to establish equality where else there would exist differential advantage — and are in ultimate theory not taxes at all but methods of making taxation unnecessary, the rule of capacity as an ethical guide becomes inapplicable, because irrelevant. It is even more important that revenue be stable than flexible. If in the long average these regalia revenues are adequate, deficit financiering will take care of any temporary stress; if they are inadequate, such supplements as must be sought will easily provide the elasticity.

The foregoing discussions, however, are intended merely to clear the ground for other issues, some of them appreciably more difficult and all of them more distinctly technical in character.

WILL SINGLE TAX BURDENS SHIFT?

ADVOCATES and opponents concur in the belief that they will not. As shifting, the single taxer would not desire the tax or the opponents object to it. It would be merely another indirect tax.

The theory for the case is clear. Taxes shift only through changes in market price. If the tax affect neither demand nor supply, it must be neutral as to prices. Only because, when hat factories are taxed, there will result a diminished supply of factories and forthwith of hats, is the tax a shifting tax — the hats higher priced to buyers. If a tax on land leaves the land supply unchanged, it will leave the volume of products unchanged and their prices unchanged. There is no way directly or indirectly whereby the rent should be affected or the price of products modified.

So runs the authoritative Ricardian doctrine. And in the large, doubtless, it is correct; and, for urban lands, accurate almost beyond criticism. It is not, however, quite so satisfactory in its applications to agricultural land. With urban land, certainly, there can be no response of supply to changes in burden. The lands will neither be more if taxes are low or less if taxes are high. It is a matter of mere superficies, a geographical or surveying fact. Not so, however, with the fertility aspects of agricultural land. As hat factories will not be built excepting to the degree that the higher taxes can be collected from consumers, or must, under the same limitations, be allowed to go to decay for lack of renewals and upkeep, precisely so will the fertility of the land — quite as easily worn out or renewed — be affected by any exceptionally severe treatment at the hands of the fisc. It is only position rents that really conform to the Ricardian description of the "original and indestructible powers of the soil." The skinning of land, the mining of its fertility, is as commonplace a fact as the digging of peat or the mining of coal.

The theoretical merits or demerits of the single tax will, therefore, be best examined in connection with urban conditions or with situations requiring substantially the same analysis. Whatever be the truth as to agricultural rents, they are a very minor matter in the problem. The ground values of New York City outrun in appraisal all the real estate of the country, inclusive of improvements, west of the Mississippi.

AGRICULTURAL TECHNIQUE, TRANSPORTATION, AND RENT

IT is, in fact, precisely the enormous increase in urban rents that leaves safe Henry George's argument that improvements in transportation and improvements in the arts of production, together with all influences of progress in general, make for the growth of ground rent. The Ricardian analysis, with its tacit assumption of a practically inflexible per capita consumption of food and of raw material in general, leads inevitably to the conclusion that improvements in transportation and improvements in agricultural methods work to diminish rather than to increase agricultural rent. I have elsewhere shown how hazardous for any purpose, with the facts at present available, is the entire economic analysis of these rural land rent tendencies. Agricultural improvements tend to reduce the rural population and probably, though inappreciably, to lower agricultural rents [6] as a world total.

Quite other, however, and astonishingly divergent in point of degree, is the trend of modern forces towards the increase of urban rents and urban prices — site values, terminal values, franchise values. The errors of analysis on either side of the present controversy with regard to rural land need not further seriously concern us.

WILL URBAN GROUND RENTS BE LOWERED?

CLEARLY not, for precisely the same reasons that they can neither be increased nor shifted — unless in a relatively inappreciable degree as the effect of certain minor influences yet to be taken into account. The single tax program intends merely

[6] See my *Economics of Enterprise*, p. 455.

a change in the recipients of the rent, substantially a new land-lord, the state, rather than a change in the earning power of the land. There is so far, then, no justification for the propagandist assertion that wage receipts will be advanced, the incomes of cultivators augmented, or house rents lowered. The main significance of the change sums up in making the landed proprietors pay the taxes in place of the wage-earners, the cultivators, the tenants and the consumers, who before have done most of the paying. So much as this, however, should reasonably well fulfill the aspirations of any single taxer. Taxes in the United States run at something like $85 per bread-winner.

SOME small effect on interest rates and thereby some effect on the prices of durable goods might be experienced. The range of investment for fluid funds must contract to the extent that lands either disappear or diminish as possible lines of investment, employing no new funds or a smaller volume of funds. On the other hand, the wider range of untaxed investment, e.g., in plant and improvements, should employ a larger volume of funds and employ these funds on terms of a much larger contribution to the economic output of goods. Interest rates should in the balance somewhat advance.

PRICES TO CONSUMERS

. THAT the effects upon consumers must be approximately nil will become increasingly evident with a more careful attention to the fundamental principles of the shifting process. No tax ever shifts, be it repeated, excepting through changes in market prices; no price can change excepting through modifications in demand or in supply. There is obviously nothing in the situation to affect seriously the volume of consumer's demand; nothing again to affect the supply of land — urban land, note again — position utilities; therefore no possibility of higher rents to tenants; no room for the recouping of these rents from consumers, even could they be imposed; no new opening for the landlords to organize for the joint protection; no owner who is now disposed or could ever have been disposed to forego his rent for the benefit of other owners; no single item of land before worth occupancy that can now wisely be abandoned; no item that before was not worth occupancy that could now be gainfully improved. An acre or area tax might retire items of supply at or near the margin of occupation. But the appropriation of a fraction of the rent or a percentage tax upon the selling price will prompt the abandonment of no single piece of land; any percentage of nothing, no matter how high, can be no appreciable burden. Only those production goods the supply of which will be modified by the imposition of a tax can present the phenomenon of shifting; a shifting which, should it occur, must be in part at the cost of the consumer and in part at the cost of the complementary productive factors. Taxes on position rents or values cannot shift, precisely because space remains a constant.

SPECULATION AS RETARDING IMPROVEMENT

IN the main, however, the foregoing analysis should rouse no protest from any instructed single taxer. He defers to no one in his loyalty to the Ricardian analysis; going so far, indeed, as to accept the Ricardian error that declares fertility taxes to be non-shifting. It is solely by discouraging land speculation and the attendant speculative withholding of land from use that he looks for higher wages or lower prices. True, the earth is still no larger nor the lands encircling the city more in area, but the supply of land available for use must be larger when once the speculators have been compelled to let go. The single tax, as he insists, will bring it about that they will let go.

I believe this contention to be entirely valid for whatever there is in it. Speculators are an appreciable influence in creating land scarcity — only that this influence is not much more than appreciable, so far at least as rural lands are concerned. In cities, speculation avails for something more, though even · in the city it is, in the main, not the activities of speculation but the presence of a speculative situation that must be held responsible for most of the vacant land. Of agricultural lands in speculative ownership there is an enormous area; but of this land there is little that is held idle, and this little itself near to the extensive margin of cultivation, on the outer fringe of things, where the social waste from the forfeited use is inconsiderable. High priced farming land gets cultivated no matter who owns it; and if not well or providently cultivated, the single taxer should not greatly labor the point; his plan would go far to make this bad condition general.

More serious are the speculative aspects of land holding and land improving in urban centers. So far, clearly, as the outlook for increasing earning power and higher prices tempts a particular class of operators to invest, a class of men with neither the disposition nor the resources for improvement, some land must be retarded in its improvement — those operators who intend a mere gain in price as a return upon investment outbidding the competing offers of the long-run investor. To remove the inducements to speculative purchase by cancelling all prospect of the private enjoyment of whatever rent or increases of rent shall attach to the land, is obviously to exclude this speculative demand.

But even the more clear is it that to fix the tax, whether present or prospective, at anything short of the entire earning power — to leave a shell of individual property and income — is merely to make the gains still greater in proportion to the investment necessary to control them and is to foster the greater speculative activity that goes with operations on margins. Some share of the furious speculation in single tax cities like Vancouver is to be accounted to this influence.

THE clue, however, to most of the incredible confusions of the analysis attending the theoretical discussion of the relations between the lure of the unearned increment and the progress of city improvement is to be found in the failure to distinguish between what the speculators are accountable for and what speculative conditions inevitably impose and determine. A host of things have been charged or credited to the speculator, or to the speculation attending land uncertainties, or to the hurry of land seekers, that are due merely to the uncertainties themselves, and would manifest themselves if there were no speculators and no "sooners" — if, even, the state had constituted itself the sole landlord and were everywhere and at all times precise in its appropriation of rental incomes.

The wonder is, then, not that so much of the theoretical discussion so far has on the whole been wrong, though much of it has been so, but that so much more of it has been right — the contestants really not succeeding in joining issues, each chiefly in error in his conviction that the truth which he holds opposes the truth of another.

In the large, however, certain disagreements can be made to look like seriously held differences in fundamental theory. The single taxers are fairly unanimous in the assertion that the effect of the lure of the unearned increment is to retard improvements, especially in cities. Professor A. S. Johnson, on the other hand, holds that, but for the quest of gain through the rise of lands, the American frontier would today be somewhere in Ohio or Indiana, that the state appropriation of land rents works to retard improvement.[7] Professor R. M. Haig reasons as to urban lands that to cut into the unearned increment by higher taxes would stimulate investment.[8] Professor T. S. Adams takes by implication the view of Professor Haig,

[7] *Atlantic Monthly,* January, 1914.
[8] *Quarterly Journal of Economics,* vol. XXIX (Aug., 1915), p. 829.

urging that by accelerating his improvements, in the faith that
the rise in the price of land will indemnify the deficit in interest
which his untimely improvements occasion, the landowner not
only subjects himself to a sacrifice in order to procure the gain
from the land, but also renders in return for his gain a *quid
pro quo* of service to society through the lower house rents at
which the larger supply of house room must find occupants.[9]

The single taxers' views excepted, the general opinion would
so far appear to be that whether society takes the increment or
leaves it, in either case the processes of improvement are accelerated.

Professor B. M. Anderson, however, offers as a possible basis
of compromise the view that, whether or not society shall take
the increment or shall leave it, there can be in no slightest
degree either stimulus or retardation of improvement.[10]

But no matter how far a perverse ingenuity may succeed in
making these authorities appear to disagree, the issues are not
clearly joined — the disagreements rather apparent than real.
In the main these writers are discussing different things : *e.g.*,
the effects (a) of doubt as to what is to happen ; (b) of doubt as
to the extent to which it may happen if it happen at all ; (c) of
certainty as to that which must happen but has not yet happened ; (d) of uncertainty as to the date of fulfillment of this
certainty ; (e) of speculative activity as to (a), (b), (c), or (d) ;
(f) of the effects of the larger taxes on some one or other of (a),
(b), (c), (d), or (e).

So much as this, at any rate, should be fairly clear : if improvements are to be fostered by the single tax, this must take
place, in the main, not through subjecting the land to more
burden but through imposing less upon the improvements. It
is easy to see how building must be more, if this more of building
comes to carry with it less penalty of taxes, and how also, with
more building, house rents should be lowered. But it is not
so easy to see how, merely because the tax is greater on the
land but no less upon the house, there should come about
more houses. There is nothing in this to make building
cheaper, or land more plenty, or the burden less that goes
with the utilization of the land. Nor is there any way through
improving the land to diminish the burden attaching to the
ownership of it. Funds will be invested in improving land
whenever the return is large enough to justify their use. Precisely what the land tax has to do with the case it is difficult
to see. With the tax cutting into the net return of the land

9 *American Economic Review*, vol. VI (June, 1916), p. 271.
10 *Quarterly Journal of Economics*, vol. XXVIII (Aug., 1914), p. 811.

whenever it comes to yield its return, or making greater the burden of holding it till the time when it will yield its return, the price at which an investor would buy the land, or a holder be willing to sell it, must fall by an amount to express the present worth of the increased tax. But all this has nothing to do with the question of when an improvement will pay such a return as to justify the making of it. The tax is a loss against which nothing will avail as escape — selling, building, or holding. It is just so much less that the land will earn, no matter who uses it, or when, and therefore a definite reduction in its present worth whether for sale or improvement or holding. This I take to be the substance of Professor Anderson's argument — a cogent and irrefutable argument for the purposes of his problem — the significance of the greater tax burden upon lands or rents, but not at all the significance of prospective changes in these rents.[11]

Nevertheless the truth may be that the first and the immediate and temporary effect of the inauguration of the heavier tax would be to start improvements. Were the tax so thoroughgoing as to eliminate the speculative class entirely, or even a tax so burdensome as, by crippling their marginal unpreparedness, to compel any considerable part of them to let go, the lands must pass into the hands of a different set of owners, men with different policies and purposes of handling, previously outbid by the speculators but now permitted to buy at prices fitting their purposes and expressive of the present worth to them of the future earning powers as they estimate them for purposes of improvement. The fall in price would therefore be somewhat greater than the ordinary theories of capitalization would indicate. The owners are now a building variety of owners — the property now offering itself at prices adapted to their estimates of a wise building policy. There is clearly room here, in this redistribution of proprietorships, for a temporary acceleration of building.[12]

[11] He does, however, actually deny any significance to these rental changes. "That the increment, which is a constant factor whether the land is built upon or not, should have any influence on a decision to build or not to build, is, on the face of it, impossible. . . If the tax is a constant factor, whether the land is built upon or not, in what way could it affect the decision to build? A special tax on unoccupied land alone would cause more building, but factors which are constant regardless of the decision do not count among the pros and cons. It should be added, however, that since buildings are, under our general property tax, in fact more heavily taxed than most other forms of capital, an application of the single tax would relieve buildings of a disproportionate burden, and so somewhat stimulate building at the expense of other forms of enterprise" (op. cit., p. 813).

[12] Possibly also a tax newly imposed and catching unprepared holders who

But with the period of readjustment completed, the capitalization process will have digested any increase of taxes into lower prices — a capitalization process, however, now conducted, on the demand side, by builders less optimistic than were the speculators as to the prospective gains in the price or in the earnings of the land. The only substantial change therefore must accrue through the elimination of the speculative operators — assuming all the while, of course, the sort of tax that would entirely eliminate them.

But it still remains true, as the single taxer asserts, that the effect of speculation in city lots is to hold vacant a considerable body of property that the building investor might otherwise have utilized earlier. The scattering and sprawling growth of a growing city is in the main due to the fact that the city *is* growing and that many properties are being wisely held vacant waiting for the time to arrive when the appropriate improvement will justify itself as a long-time investment. Different men judge differently as to the appropriate time as well as to the appropriate degree of investment. The fact, however, that many buyers purchase with the sole purpose not of improving but of selling at higher prices to those who will improve, holding in the belief that the rate of increase in the selling price will afford an attractive return, not merely attaches to much of the property prices unattractive to building investors, but, by what amounts to a temporary restriction of supply of property, compels some investors to move farther out, if they are to make improvements at all. These speculative activities have therefore some bearing to accentuate the straggling growth of the city, to make ground rents higher, and to impose serious municipal wastes in the supply of street, sidewalk, water, light, and sewer services.

have purchased not for resale but for later improvement, in the expectation of moderate *ad interim* burdens, men to whom still the land is worth more for use than they could have for it by selling it, men who come now in presence of the problem of whether it be wiser to build forthwith than to wait — it is possible that these men, trapped in mid-process, may some of them build earlier because of the tax. If so, these are men to whom their enhanced *ad interim* costs are exceptionally severe burdens and who would therefore have been outbid by the demand prices of other men, had this larger tax been in clear and definite prospect.

But as to the truth of the case in this particular regard, I confess myself much in doubt. When one of these owners builds, he must have the extra ground tax still to pay — his annual cost, say, $50 higher as occupant than he had expected. But he has no way to evade ; must sell at a reduction which capitalizes the loss, or must hold under the same sum of increased burden, or must build still subject to this same larger tax. Thus there seems to be no change in the differential attractions of building and not building, each alternative merely shrinking $50 in its net volume of service.

BUT it must be obvious that this general argument — impregnable as I believe it to be — with regard to the effect of the larger tax, has nothing to say as to how far the restriction of improvements may be due to an existing uncertainty as to the amount of improvement which will turn out later to be best adapted to the land, or as to the kind of use for which the land will later come to be sought. Either retardation or acceleration may result from the various possible estimates of these future uses or earning powers. If, for example, it seems probable — but not certain — that next year a viaduct or a bridge will make accessible my pasture tract yonder, I shall wisely decide to postpone the erection of a barn till I know definitely what is to happen and when — perhaps, therefore, till the thing has really happened. Cancel my hopes, and up will go my barn. Confirm them, and I may forthwith begin my laying of sidewalks, planting of trees, grading of streets. Or, on the other hand, I may still decline to move in any direction till I make out whether these lands may not be marketable for terminal purposes or manufacturing sites. Or again, having settled in my mind that the uses are to be residential and that I myself shall finally do the building, I may still hesitate greatly and delay long as to whether I shall the more wisely build cheaply or dearly — balancing the chance of having to rebuild on such a higher scale of expensiveness as shall better fit the ultimate market, as against the danger of loss by making my improvements even more expensive than the prospective demand will turn out to justify.

These effects of speculative conditions — not of speculative operations and not of the pressure of taxes — are especially evident in certain quarters of growing cities, as, for example, upon South State Street, in Chicago, where midway between the established center of trade and the nearby decent and decaying resident sections, persist in shaky survival several blocks of cheap buildings, starved of upkeep, tenanted by saloons, cheap restaurants, peep-shows, catch-penny enterprises, museums of anatomy, and whatever other cover of varied iniquity the city authorities will overlook. These are typical slums in typical locations. Why are not the shacks removed? They pay satisfactorily enough, in view of the fact that the time has not yet arrived for building anything better. But even now something far better would pay, if only it were yet certain how good it must be to pay best in the long run. But fairly certain is it that the sort of building which ten years hence ought to be there must for several years afford inadequate returns — an extreme misfit for the intervening time. It is wise to wait. But equally certain is it that whenever the time does come to act, the building must be projected somewhat beyond the justification of the immediate demand. Delay is certain, for a time; and not less certain, at the proper time, is the acceleration. No tax would appreciably affect the problem. The same influences, now of retardation and now of acceleration, would be present and in full force no matter even were the state a rack-rent landlord, or were the sites available only as leased land or on terms of perpetual ground rents.

It seems, indeed, quite clear that no one improves in order to reap the advantages of rising prices or rising rents, in the sense that, as Adams and others argue, the landowner looks to the appreciation of the land to make good his losses on his building. To build is the only way to utilize the earning power of the land. Whenever one builds he does it in the way which will afford the best return upon his building investment. In accomplishing this he must recognize that the investment in improvements must be duly proportioned to the investment in land—that to get a high earning power out of land, high-cost improvements must go with it, and that, when the earning power of the land is changing, any improvement that fits it at any one time must turn out a misfit for the later time. His only resource is to make the best compromise possible between the long-time and the short-time adaptation. So far as he goes in emphasis of the long-time aspect, he does this in the faith not that he will get a rise in price to offset his loss in building, but that this is the only way to achieve the maximum return on his entire investment. The increasing earning power of land advises a more expensive improvement in the present. Whenever he builds he must plan in view not only of immediate return but of the later higher return, making such allowance as he may for the uncertainties of the future. But the earlier he builds, the more cheaply he must build; the later, the more expensively. Were the prospect one rather of retrogression than of progress, as, for example, in a currently prosperous placer-mining camp, the buildings must be cheaper than the immediate demand justifies, in partial adjustment to a later period when they must correspondingly overrun.

When the prospects are speculative equally in the directions of rising and of falling income power, so much the more do the improvements vary in retardation or acceleration according to individual estimates of ultimate adjustments. Weighing as best he may in his estimate of present worths the difference between belief and certainty, each holder enters into a hazard of putative future incomes—his investment in excess of the purchase price of the lot being a more or less irrevocable adventure in building costs. The degree of hazard in this adventure is affected by the nature and the degree of the various chances involved.

I DO therefore agree with the single taxers that speculation in some measure restricts the supply of land, that in some fraction of its many effects it works to retard improvement. I agree also with Anderson that the taxes have nothing appreciable to do with the case; but I nevertheless insist that prospective changes in earning power have much to do with it. I agree with both Haig and Adams that prospective increases in earning power do, in some share of their many effects, appreciably stimulate building operations — insisting, however, that an obverse sort of stimulation would attend a prospective fall in earning power; that the amount of the tax imposed upon the land would have little to do with it; the effort to reduce to personal gain the unearned increment nothing to do with it.

And, finally, I agree with Johnson that the lure of unearned increment has been a continuous incentive to pioneering, even though speculative operations in the premises have been, as the single taxer rightly asserts, an incubus on the activities both of pioneering and of exploitation. But I hold that Johnson's deduction is in point of degree a gross exaggeration. The lure of increment merely induces a fringe of pioneering "sooners," some tens of miles in advance of the extensive margin of purely agricultural enterprise. It is a sort of twilight zone, a No Man's Land, an area of adumbration along the frontier margin, attending this margin as the shadow the subject, not directing or placing or determining it. That my shadow is some feet west of me at each moment of the forenoon does not indicate that by noon it will have preceded me into the next county. It is merely true that without the inducement of the prospective rise of land incomes and land prices, the American frontier would for all of our history have been some fifty or a hundred miles in the rear of where it actually has been.[13]

But all this is entirely aside from the question of whether it might not have been as well or better that the frontier should

---

[13] The policy of land grants to railroads has had, doubtless, larger effect. But, even here, the same principle applies, only that the area of pioneering railroad adventure is often greatly wider, even to the extent of marking out ribbons of narrow occupation entirely across the continent. Extending vertically outward beyond the extensive margin of gainful agriculture on either side of it will always be found the intermediate area of individual adventure in the quest of the lure. It is, however, not so obvious that the land grants to railroads should be declared unearned, or the gains achieved regarded as lacking any social *quid pro quo*.

now be in Ohio. It is not obvious that the rapid preëmpting of government land, to the point that now the age of free land in the world is mostly past, has been so distinct a blessing. To whom precisely? To you or to me? Or to which one of our landless sons? It must have been rather to that vague retreat of unprecise thinking, the country or society — that gets some good from growing more, or more widely or more thickly : the thinking that discovers, for example, that because this country "owns" the Philippines, includes more people, and totals more wealth, and therefore can collect and spend more taxes, you or I must be somehow better off; or that it is matter of congratulation to any one but the land grabber that the city or state should grow; or, again, that the death of a few millions of men more or less is an economic loss of, say, $2000 each to the survivors, or to the earth, or to society, or to the cosmos, instead of to themselves.

But should not this evident fact that the unearned increment has attracted enterprising men horizontally further forth mean also that it has pushed building adventures higher into the air? Having located cabins deep in the woods or far out on the prairies, why may it not have added further and earlier stories to the skyscrapers? Well, if in order to get title to the city lots, men had to build on them or live on them, such must have been the influence. Or if to hold the business sites, men had also to sit wind-buffeted on the cornices of their sky-scrapers, thereto they must have climbed and have clingingly, continuously, numbly and coldly sat. It was the fact that men were physically tied to these promises of title, had to occupy their homesteads and preëmptions and work their timber claims, that took these men further out into the wilderness, and held them there; and, being there, they had to work there, since their labor, as different from their investment, had to be done each man in his own presence.

ARE THERE UNEARNED INCREMENTS?

And did not these pioneers pay well in privations, lonesome-ness, and danger for all that they got? Verily — but paid to whom? and on terms of what *quid pro quo* of service? Whether the rewards be defended either as moderate indemnity for the privations undergone or as return upon foresight and energy in pushing forward to grasp an offered prize, the question still remains whether the prize was wisely offered. It is the central problem of institutional policy in the economic field to limit and apportion private gain to social service.

Neither shrewdness nor wisdom connotes an ethical value or affords secure warrant of rightness or service.

But both Johnson and Adams make much of these privations as being of the nature of services rendered to the state, or to society, or to humanity at large and in general. There need be no question that, inasmuch as the lands were offered on terms of these privations, and inasmuch as the terms and conditions were fulfilled, there can be nothing now for the case but to abide by the contract — that confiscation here is as immoral as any other variety of robbery. But still again, as institutional policy, what have these privations to do with the case? Was the land placed there by these adventuring geographers? Or retained there by their safe anchoring? Or improved for some one else by their labors — or even for themselves? Or saved from any menacing disintegration or decay? Recall that the purpose of the argument must be to show that it was wise social policy, as a human gain in the large, that these land seekers should be induced to hurry forth and get there first; that in some phase of social accounting these individual privations constituted an inevitable debit incurred in the securing of some greater social gain.

Adams, indeed, takes this position quite uncompromisingly and on distinctly economic grounds rather than as deduced from some vague, conjectural values in the field of sociology or politics or patriotism. Through this pioneering, "Farmers and farms are more numerous, farm products more plentiful and farm [product?] prices lower, because of the unearned increment. The latter is diffused . . . in part to the purchasers of farm products." [14]

But I submit that the net social result of sending men out where "the farmers work for less than day's wages, if we measure his reward in annual income alone," is, so far, to waste the labor of each man. Allowing for the productive energies employed in moving his product from its remote place of growing to the market, the result in terms either of price or of nutriment would have been greater had he remained on the hither side of the extensive margin. If in either case he would have farmed, food is scarcer and dearer for his change of place. If he were an artisan, but now as pioneer turns perforce to amateur agriculture, the loss in some other kind of product, in which the prices are now higher for consumers, must far outweigh the increase in agricultural product. In the form of a mortgage on the future we have been paying the pioneers for wasting their time.

[14] *Op. cit.*, p. 279.

But I do most cordially agree with Professor Adams that the owners of the "much unused and presently unusable land . . . upon which they are willing to pay taxes, only because they expect to reap and benefit by the unearned increment," have really in this way and to this extent rendered a *quid pro quo* to their fellow men — to this extent, therefore, have ethically made good their titles and are receiving increments not un-earned but fairly purchased; though still I question the institutional wisdom in the case.

But from this fact of these various payments Professor Adams deduces an argument in support of the general property tax as fair and just both in principle and in working, as deriving revenues from commendable sources, and as affording generous returns. I should have deduced precisely the opposite con-clusion. But in the background of the thought there is evi-dently a principle on which he and I are in substantial agreement. He is genuinely pleased, as also am I, that some of the unearned increment has thus been intercepted for public purposes; only that he is glad of the particular method, the while that I regret it. Each of us is thus a single taxer in essential spirit.

In the main purpose and emphasis of Adams' article, however, I more than cordially concur. I believe that he has done the science of taxation an immeasurable service in exploding for all time, not the general doctrine of the capitalization of taxes, but a bastard offspring from it — the notion that every purchaser of a property already overtaxed buys unaffected by the general property tax, holds his property quit and free of tax burdens, and may now be called upon, through the imposition of further taxes, to be initiated into the great brotherhood of the duly burdened. Most economists, I believe, have been uncom-fortably conscious in their noses of a fallacy somewhere in the near vicinity, but have not been entirely successful in locating it, or in applying the appropriate remedial or preventive formula. Such at all events has been my own case. The doc-trinal essentials, however, are easily at hand in a correct notion of what capital is and of how it functions in the capitalization process.[15]

---

[15] Since this article was submitted and accepted Professor Seligman in the December number of *The American Economic Review* has put in question cer-tain of Adams' positions. Still, however, the ultimate issue appears to turn upon the relation between property taxes and interest rates. The disputants substantially agree that those who buy taxed property get as good bargains at the prices paid as those who buy untaxed property. The prices merely reflect the net incomes in prospect. But Adams — agreeing with Seligman that to reduce a net income is proportionately to reduce the value of its property basis

It must be added that even were it true that the capitalization process would justify the imposition of further taxes as a matter of justice between persons, it would still be disastrous in its effect upon the general welfare. There is no such thing as justice between properties; but it is nevertheless important that investments be by taxation so equally affected in their incomes that the distribution of investment shall not by fiscal policies be fostered in some directions and impeded in others — unless, of course, it be for specific reasons desirable to discourage certain lines of investment.

WILL THE SINGLE TAX CONGEST URBAN POPULATIONS?

YES and no, depending on what one means by the term; and depending partly, also, on whether the tax be applied locally or generally.

To shift taxation from all other property to land amounts in general to the putting of the tax on what can not move and exempting those things that can stay, go, or come. As between cities, it is a competitive method of bonus or premium.

and that there can be, because of the tax, no difference in the *rates* of return to different investors — yet holds that the very fact of taxation upon property must be ranked among the influences restricting the net returns from property and thereby restricting interest rates. These tax burdens upon the investors manifest themselves precisely in the fact that they make net incomes dearer, in terms of present purchasing prices. The investor gets less income from his money. There is a burden, therefore, not precisely on him as the purchaser of property, but rather on him as the holder of funds the earning power of which is restricted through the existence of property taxes.

Seligman, as I interpret him, holds that taxes on property — or, perhaps, taxes on some sorts of property — have no effect to harm investors in other properties. Any purchaser after the tax buys subject to the tax, buys at a price appropriate to the reduced net earning power of the property, and buys on a capitalization rate which is independent of the tax on this property or on other classes of property.

At the logical extreme, therefore, Adams should argue that a property rendering a $50 income must be worth, on a five per cent basis, $1000 as present price; that this property, under a general property tax, would change to, say, a $40 income discounted on a four per cent basis; that no change in price would occur but only a change in the net earning power of the invested funds. Seligman, on the other hand, should argue that the property would be bought at $800, its income of $40 remaining at a five per cent basis upon the new and actual investment price.

So much of this, at any rate, is clear; the rates of return upon different investments cannot be different because of the varying tax burdens on the different properties. All investments must be equally affected, in the sense that all are equally taxed or that none is taxed. Adams says that all are taxed under the guise of the lower interest rates which the imposition of the tax must bring about. Seligman appears to say that all are free from tax by virtue of the purchase of diminished incomes at proportionately diminished prices; smaller investments but unchanged rates.

To assert that in my opinion both disputants are wrong would be an awkward way of formulating my conviction that the entire analysis requires a change of venue, or better, a new method of approach. I should say:

It is equivalent to a general and perpetual tax exemption for
all dwellings, factories, equipment and stocks, and for investment in general, other than the land that cannot get away.
No more effective competitive device for promoting city growth
could be devised, as long as competitors refrain from adopting
it — irrespective, of course, of any question of what is the use
of it to any one but the landowner.

Vancouver inevitably made a great growth of population and
business through it — inevitably attracted thereby an inflow
of laborers and industries in structural lines, stimulated therewith a great advance in the rentals of land, and thus inevitably,
since the appropriation of rents was only partial, fostered a
frantic speculation, which finally, when the slackening building activity threw laborers out of employment and speculation
receded, ended in a colossal collapse and liquidation. But the
town was there, a much larger town — if it be to any one's purpose to personify and congratulate a town. A partial single
tax is a dangerous thing.

But does it congest population? It builds the city higher

(1) That no property tax, even one so general as to affect all existing
properties, would in the slightest affect the interest rates of the market, if
only new investment funds and other openings for new investments were left
untaxed. Such a tax would amount merely to a *pro tanto* confiscation of the
incomes on the burdened properties without in the slightest changing the
capitalization rates.

(2) That were the tax only upon new funds for investment or only upon the
new properties derivative from the investment of these funds, the capitalization
rate would fall approximately *pro tanto* and the previously existing properties
would rise in market price without any slightest change in the incomes
derivative from them, but with changes solely in the *rates* of return.

(3) That were the tax imposed upon all properties, old as well as new, the
net incomes would fall, and probably, though not certainly, would fall in
something like the same proportion with the fall in rates of interest. No
great change in present worths would result, with the exception that the less
durable of income-bearing properties would suffer relatively less.

(4) That for any purposes of the capitalization analysis, the concepts of
property, of capital, or of investment must be so widened as to include not
merely all operating funds in rent or other gain-seeking activities, but all the
time-using methods or properties in which funds may be expended : all the
durable goods like houses, autos, and furniture, which, as affording future
incomes, absorb present investment funds ; all banking activities and insurance ;
all lending to state or other consuming borrowers ; all outlays in promotion,
publicity, salesmanship, organization, speculation ; in short, all gain promising
or income rendering or income earning employments of money or of banking
credit.

If, therefore, Adams is to be interpreted to include new investment funds
and new investment properties in his tax, he is right in asserting that the
capitalization rates must be affected ; and wrong, merely in including previously
existing properties as within the causal field. Seligman, also, must be declared
to be correct in denying that property taxes necessarily affect interest rates ;
and wrong, merely if he be interpreted to deny that taxes on new investment
funds and new investment properties are also to be regarded as outside the
casual field.

as well as wider, more people to the acre and more acres. But, essentially, it is not the tax that congests the population, but the growth of the town. With increasing demands and higher prices for shelter, building increases at both the intensive and the extensive margin.

Consider, however, what would be the effect if all towns followed in equal degree and by similar methods the single tax principle. There could be no marked disturbance in the ratio of the total urban to the total rural population or, by assumption, any redistribution of urban population between cities. On the face of it, the sole advantage would appear to be that the landowners would be compelled to transfer their rent rolls to the state, all other property owners going free. But this process of setting all other property free of tax would also mean the freedom of future improvements. It would for a time amount to a gift to the owners of existing houses with a corresponding stimulus to the supplying of more houses, at lower rates per unit of service. This larger supply of houses could only be achieved through increases both at the intensive and the extensive margins. Building would go higher and extend more widely — more house room for the money and a larger consumption of house room relatively to other goods.

HOW ABOUT THE DRYING UP OF BUILDING LOANS?

It has been speciously argued that inasmuch as most building operations are financed through borrowed funds secured primarily and mainly by the ground values, the land tax would mean that the supply of loan capital would be driven out of building enterprises. I confess that for a time this seemed to me cogent and valid reasoning. But see how easy it is open to flank attack, and how disastrously it works for its opponents. I have, say $1,000,000 and am projecting a building. I must first buy my lot, costing $1,000,000, and then through the pledge of it procure money, another million, with which to build. But, if I could have the lot on terms of paying the annual rent tax on it, I need borrow nothing. The rents would as well pay the $40,000 of tax on the land as they would pay the same amount of interest on my building loan. I am now independent of the loan market. A great argument was this.

The wisdom of the entire exemption of improvements from taxation is obviously tied up with the question of the property tax in general. In the past, under the actual working of the general property tax, improvements have been subjected to especially heavy burdens, investment in buildings therefore

relatively retarded, and house room thereby made especially
dear. Any remedy to be applied should be carefully guarded
against undue emphasis in the opposite direction. No ordinary tax is bad or good unless as part of a system. Investments in improvements should presumably bear the rate of
burden common to other lines of wealth that are flexible in
supply. In fact, however, most other lines of investment do
actually evade the general property tax as well as other state
and local burdens. So long as this remains a fact, investments
in buildings should wisely be left entirely exempt. Ideally
all ordinary incomes, property or other, should participate in
contributing to the public revenues — but as incomes, not as
property bases of incomes. Nothing can be more unwise than
the relative freedom of personal property incomes from public
burdens. The personal property tax should disappear only
with the disappearance of the property tax in general.

    I trust that the necessary limitations of space — occasionally
betraying me, I fear, into seeming dogmatisms of statement —
may serve at the same time as my excuse, if need there be, for
unintentional inadequacies in reporting the positions that I
have subjected to criticism or attack. In spirit, at any rate,
if not in actual accomplishment, I hold argument to be never
rightly a game for victory, or anything more or less or other
than always a coöperative investigation. It is a pleasure, therefore, to adopt for my present purposes the following admirable
words from the genial and brilliant paper of Professor Adams,
against which I have directed certain objections. I also may
"have written more dogmatically than I feel, and more emphatically than the rules of polite controversy warrant." But
"if the position taken be unsound, it will bring down surer
and swifter retribution, a speedier recognition of the true doctrine." Not less perhaps for us single taxers of the looser
observance than for our fellows of the stricter faith, is it to be
desired that we continually exercise ourselves in the amenities
of discussion.

3. The Unearned Increment Tax

(a) An Argument for the Increment Tax

Professors Bye and Hewett, after an analysis of the single
tax, write as follows concerning the taxation of unearned
increment : *

* From R. T. Bye and W. W. Hewett, *Applied Economics*, (F. S. Crofts &
Company, New York, 1928), pp. 546-547.

OUR previous analysis supports the Single Tax contention that land rent is an unearned income, and we have seen that this is one source of large fortunes. It is therefore good policy to restrict the further derivation of incomes from this source. Many, and probably most, economists support this view, but are keenly aware of the injustice of taxing away the vested interests of present land owners. They are, therefore, inclined not to disturb the rents already attached to land, but they do favor the so-called *unearned increment tax,* which would appropriate future increases in land values. As the rent-yielding capacity of a piece of land rises, due to the growth of the community or other causes, an annual tax could be laid upon it sufficient to confiscate this purely unearned increase, without in any way disturbing the present value of the land and the income derived from it. The desirability of this is strengthened by the fact that authorities on public finance are now generally tending toward the view that land is a more suitable object for taxation than the improvements erected upon it. Hence it is believed wise gradually to reduce the tax on real estate improvements while increasing those upon the bare land itself. In time this might be carried to the point where the improvements were no longer taxed at all and the land taxes were so large as to absorb the major portion, if not the whole, of the land rent. If this increase in land taxation was made so slowly that the burden in any one year would not be oppressive, and in such a way that the major part of it would fall upon succeeding generations, the injustice to those who have invested savings in land would not be serious. Another possibility would be for the law of inheritance to be so changed as to provide that all lands transferred at death should henceforth be subject to a tax sufficient to appropriate the rents thereof.

But land taxes should never be made the sole source of public revenue, partly for the reason . . . that they would not prove sufficient, and also because there are other taxes equally desirable from a social point of view. Besides, land rents are not the only unearned incomes. . . It is therefore reasonable to tax these other revenues, or appropriate them in some way to the social use.

Practical difficulties involved in the taxation of unearned increment are discussed by Professor Taussig in his *Principles of Economics,* 3rd edition, Vol. II, pp. 108-112. One important difficulty which he considers is that of making allowance for the general movement of prices. On this point he writes : "If all prices double, money rents of land may be expected to double also ; more slowly, it is probable, than the prices of most commodities, but in the end with substantially the same rate of advance. The special causes affecting each particular plot meanwhile will still be in operation, causing its site rent to rise or perhaps to fall,— to diverge more or less from the general trend of prices and of rents. How disentangle the increment which economic theory and social policy would wish to set aside?"

(b) Do We Avoid Trenching on Vested Rights by Taxing only Future Increases in Land Values? *

DESPITE the apparent condemnation by a large proportion of text-writing economists, of the single tax, there yet seems to lurk a feeling, at least among those who really *want* to be "liberal," that something should be done about land rent. But how can something be done without interfering with the sacred rights of ownership intuitively determined? The answer of many economists is, to tax *future increases* in the value of land. To do this, it is supposed, would not interfere with vested rights because it supposedly would not lower the salable value of land. In the simple phraseology of Professor Fairchild's book, written for high-school pupils, "there is nothing unjust about this." [16]

And yet, this also resembles "changing the rules of a game, while the game is in progress, to the disadvantage of one contestant." For the adoption of such a policy on any extended scale would be likely . . . to lower the current salable value of land in comparison with other goods. Indeed, considered as a mathematical proposition the argument is just as convincing for reduced present value of land consequent upon a definitely promised tax on *future increment* of value as for reduced present value consequent upon a definitely promised increased taxation rate upon the entire value of the land. The purchaser of a piece of land, in buying it and in determining the maximum price he can afford to pay — as, also, the seller in determining the minimum price he can afford to take — considers as well the possibilities of future increases in value as the

---

* From H. G. Brown, *The Economic Basis of Tax Reform*, (Lucas Bros., Columbia, Missouri, 1932), pp. 320-331.

[16] P. 527. It may be noted in this connection that Fairchild, Furniss and Buck, in their joint textbook, *Elementary Economics*, second edition, New York (Macmillan), 1930, also seem to oppose increase of taxation on the value of land in general, while favoring some tax on future increases of value. See pp. 154-155.

present rental yield. A piece of land may sell for about $1000, not because of any present yield, but because of the estimate that, after fourteen years, it will yield a net annual income of $100 and be worth (capitalized on a 5 per cent basis) approximately $2000. Suppose that, on the day after a purchaser has possessed himself of such a piece of land at a price of $1000, it suddenly and unexpectedly becomes evident that half of the increment in value, at the end of fourteen years, is to be taken in taxation! Would not the present salable value at once fall to $750? And if the increment tax were to be 100 per cent, would not the present value at once become $500? Yet economists like Professor Fairchild — who is here referred to not as an isolated errant writer but as *following the beaten track* — can say on the same page [17] that discriminatory taxes on land "would be an injustice" and, of a tax on future increases in value, that "there is nothing unjust about this"!

In truth, in a rapidly growing country, the present value of a very large part of the land is probably affected by the estimate of or the reasonable hope of future increases. Even land which actually does not rise in value may have high present value because of the expectation of such a rise, and the partial destruction of this expectation by a prospective increment tax might lower its present value. Suggest, for such a country, *any rate whatever* of taxation of *future increments* and it becomes at once possible for the mathematician, if he has the requisite data, to work out a lower (at first) but gradually increasing rate on the entire value of land, becoming eventually high enough to absorb the entire rental yield, which would lower the present salable value of land, on the average, *no more than the increment tax.* This conclusion will be obvious to any mathematician. Indeed, it requires only a very little knowledge of mathematics to grasp it. There is no occasion for any one to be vainglorious over his comprehension of it. But many, if not most, of the American economists who have become prominent as the authors of text books, not only do not mention it but write as if it were untrue.

Professor Taussig seems clearly to understand that the value of a piece of land is affected by its expected future rent. Thus, he states [18] that in a growing city "an advantageous site will command a price more than in proportion to its present rent, because it is expected that the rent will increase still further as the years go on." A little further on,[19] refer-

[17] P. 527.
[18] *Principles of Economics*, 3d rev. ed., Vol. II, p. 104.
[19] *Ibid.*, pp. 107-108.

ring specifically to "the problem of vested rights," he says:

"To the present owners the capitalized value represents an investment or an inheritance. . . . The whole institution of property may indeed be overhauled; . . . but unless the system of private property be remade, the existing rights to land, as they have been allowed to develop through the centuries, must be respected."

And yet, after having thus pointed out that present values are affected by prospective future increases of rent, and after having indicated his respect for the doctrine of vested rights, Professor Taussig proceeds to defend the taxation of future increments![20] "The question is different," he says, "as regards the rise in rent that is still to come. There is no vested right in the indefinite future."

Professor Bullock argues with more definitely conservative qualification but in a somewhat similar vein. He points out that Henry George advocated seizing "gradually the present economic rent of land" or enough of it to defray all public expenditures.[21] He then proceeds to insist upon the confiscatory and unjust nature of the reform.[22] Following after this he contends that "to adjust municipal taxation in such a manner as to intercept a considerable part of the future unearned increment from land would be a safe and probably a desirable policy."[23] But Professor Bullock has not left unconsidered the possibility that purchasers of land have paid, in the purchase price, for anticipated future increases in value. For he goes on to say:

"The purchase price paid for land in a progressive city is somewhat greater than its capitalized present rental value, since the purchaser can and must pay more in view of the prospective increase of the rent. Some part of the future increase, therefore, is reflected in present capital values, and should be left to the present owners."[24]

But what part of the future increase is *not* reflected in present capital values? Are present capital values of land arrived at in any other way than by discounting all anticipated future rents? Does Professor Bullock think that these rents are in part discounted and in part not, or does he think that the anticipated increases are, on the average, less than the realized increases? And if he thinks the latter, for what reason? Or

---

[20] *Ibid.*, p. 108.
[21] *The Elements of Economics*, 2d ed., pp. 324, 325.
[22] *Ibid.*, pp. 326-28.
[23] *Ibid.*, p. 329.
[24] *Ibid.*, p. 329, footnote.

does Professor Bullock suppose that a part of future land-value increments is unanticipated in such a sense that to establish definitely the policy of taxing heavily this part, would leave every purchaser of land perfectly confident that not any of the tax would fall upon him and perfectly willing, therefore to pay as much for the land as if such a tax were not promised? [25]

[25] Perhaps, however, Professor Bullock supposes that there are cases where the rise of land value is so utterly unexpected that no anticipation of it, no remotest hope of the possibility of it, has had any previous effect on the value of the land. To plan for the taxation of such an entirely unanticipated increase in land value would presumably have no effect upon the salable value of any land when the policy was announced. But in view of unanticipated declines in land values, also, such a policy would presumably reduce the *average* rate of return on investments in land below a "reasonable" rate. And if, when they buy land, people are ordinarily influenced by the thought that there are possibilities of gain as well as chances of loss, then a tax on such gain, if the tax is to have no least influence on present salable values, must be on only such parts of the gain as have been in no sense contemplated or considered by sellers or purchasers of land. Whether or not a means could be devised to distinguish any such part of any gain from the rest, it will be obvious that a tax on so limited a value is, considered as a source of public revenue, unimportant and, considered as an engine of economic reform, utterly futile. And, indeed, if the investor thinks of the possibility of unexpected gains as offsetting the possibility of unexpected declines, a foreseen tax on the gains, with no "compensation" for the declines, would certainly lower the salable value of land.

But no matter if all future land-value increases are considered as subject to taxation, no matter how high the rates of tax on such increments and no matter how *quickly* the salable value of land might be affected and "vested rights" infringed, in the *long run* the salable value of land could not be made to fall as much and the opportunities for widespread land ownership rendered as favorable as by gradually increasing the tax rate on land values in general.

In passing, it may be worth while to allude to the contention sometimes made that an "unearned increment" is necessary to keep farmers in their business. Then what keeps the increasing proportion of tenant farmers in the business? And is it likewise necessary in other lines to keep everyone in a specific business? If no one received any "unearned increment" would each person leave his business for some other business in which he likewise would not receive it? But, as we have seen, if land values were taxed the yield to owners of land would be as high a per cent of what their land would then sell for as now — a higher rate, perhaps, because of the reduction of other taxes.

After meeting this objection, viz., that farmers must have an unearned increment, it seems curious to find some economists, who apparently do not venture to support generally increased land-value taxation, demanding that *railroads* shall be *prevented* from securing "unearned increment" but that the means of prevention shall be rate regulation instead of taxation. It is proposed that railroad rates shall be regulated on the basis of original cost of plant without regard to what the land necessary would now cost. But there are a number of serious objections to such a proposal. In the first place, if we say, in effect, to landowners, that they have a chance at an unearned increment provided they use their land in any other way but no chance for it if they use it for railroads — or that railroads which purchase land cannot have the same chance as other purchasers — then the tendency is to discourage railroad construction as compared with other uses of land. In the second place, if two railroad lines are built through a given territory, one at a later date than the other and paying a higher price for its land, such a system of rate regulation would tend to justify higher rates on the second-built railroad than on the first, with consequent discrimination in favor of the shippers on the

Except as we suppose that landowners, owners of monopolies, etc., *underestimate* the future possibilities of income from their property — and they are, perhaps, as likely to overestimate — there is certainly no possibility of ever giving the non-land-owning and non-monopoly-owning public *anything whatever,* even through purchase, without trenching on the "vested rights" of the owners.[26] The landless must continue to pay owners for the privilege of living on or working on their land or they must pay the owners, in advance, not only the capitalized value of the present rent but the capitalized value of any future increases in the rent which the owners may have a reasonable prospect of being able to charge.[27] Similarly, consumers must continue to pay monopoly prices to the owners of monopolies or else they must pay such owners, in advance, the capitalized value not of the present monopoly profits only but, if increased prices may be looked for in the future, of the estimated additional future profits also. Why must professional economists continually try to evade the issue, insisting at one moment that vested rights — which are merely rights to expected future income — must be respected and in the next moment discussing sympathetically the proposition to take a part of such expected future income for the public?[28] Is economic science now

first-constructed road. And no system of taking from successful railroads a part of their increased returns from superior efficiency can possibly be as satisfactory as a system of taxing them and all other persons and corporations on their economic rent (potential rent in the case of unused land) or land value. (For a fuller discussion of this problem see the author's review, "Sharfman's *American Railroad Problem*" in the *Quarterly Journal of Economics,* February, 1922, pp. 323-334, and relevant passages from *Economic Science and the Common Welfare,* fifth edition, Part I, Chapter VII, § 8.

26 We are here supposing that the property owners in question have bought their property in the confidence that public policy would not change. If they have paid less because of the expectation of change, does such change trench on their "vested rights"?

Possibly the statement above in the text should be qualified. Besides the direct loss to consumers of monopoly goods from extortionate prices, there is also the disadvantage to persons who are prevented by these prices from buying the monopolized goods and who so contribute nothing to the monopoly gains, i.e., who are injured but not exactly exploited. If there is any advantage at all to the public in so buying out a monopoly it can only lie in the termination of this incidental disadvantage or injury. Does speculative holding of land thus similarly injure even where there is no direct exploitation? But economists who say that speculative holding is no especial evil and those who say that it does good are not the ones to argue that the public would derive even any incidental advantage from buying out the owners of land.

27 It may be of passing interest to a very few readers to note that this point, although apparently overlooked by most current writers of economics texts, was clearly understood by Henry George. See his book, *The Science of Political Economy,* New York, (Doubleday and McClure Co.), 1898, p. 195.

28 Professor T. S. Adams is both more consistent and more conservative. He seems very clearly to go the whole way and to be definitely opposed to the taxing even of future increases of land value as unfair to "the man who has purchased land at a price or value determined by capitalizing unearned incre-

where the physical sciences were before the days of Newton, Kepler and Galileo?

A heavy tax on future increase of value might conceivably infringe upon "vested rights" as much as or more than a gradual increase of taxation on land values in general. But *if we are primarily interested in building the best possible future society, we shall prefer the latter.* For however greatly "vested rights" may be infringed upon by an increment tax, in the *long run* the salable value of land cannot be made to fall as much and the opportunities of the ambitious poor to get started in life cannot be made as favorable by such a tax as by a gradually increasing tax on the entire rental value of land.

In practice this so-called increment tax or tax on future increases of value has amounted to little. The British act of 1909 applied only to land which was sold at a gain to the seller (thus discouraging sales), except that increases in value as determined by a revaluation or re-assessment after twenty years, were to be taxed. Long before the twenty years were up, an overwhelmingly Conservative parliament repealed the law. Such laws involve administrative complications and difficulties. As revenue producers they are likely to be so disappointing as to lead to their abandonment. As means to economic reform they are too hopelessly inadequate to arouse the enthusiasm of any one who really comprehends the nature of the evils in our economic order.

But scarcely any least glimmering of light on the real and important advantages of increased land-value taxation shines through the dark smoke-screen of confused reasoning with which, however unconsciously and unintentionally, the majority of writers on public finance have surrounded this subject. And so what the historian, Buckle,[29] remarked as being frequently true of the so-called educated, can perhaps be fairly asserted of many present-day students of economics who, ambitious to understand the economic laws of taxation and the effects of taxation on human welfare, have sought aid from the standard text books on public finance, viz., that the progress of their knowledge "has been actually retarded by the activity of their education," that they are "burdened by prejudices, which their reading, instead of dissipating, has rendered more inveterate," that their "erudition ministers to their ignorance" and that "the more they read, the less they know."

ment." See his article, "Tax Exemption through Tax Capitalization," *American Economic Review*, June, 1916, p. 281.
    29 Henry Thomas Buckle, *The History of Civilization in England*, reprinted from the second London edition, New York, (Appleton) 1894, Vol. I, p. 195.

QUESTIONS AND PROBLEMS FOR DISCUSSION

1. Distinguish between the single tax and the increment tax.
2. State and evaluate the arguments for the single tax as an engine of social reform.
3. If unearned increments should be claimed by the state, would it be just to force land owners to bear the burden on unearned decrements?
4. "The single-tax program would tend to abolish taxation." Explain and evaluate.
5. If only future increases in land values were to be taxed, what would be the effect on vested interests?
6. Discuss the question of the taxation of rental versus the taxation of the capital value of land.
7. Discuss some of the ethical problems involved in the single-tax program.
8. How does Professor Davenport answer the argument that the single tax provides no fiscal elasticity?
9. Will the single tax decrease land speculation? Will it force idle land into use?
10. Can single-tax burdens be shifted? on urban land? on agricultural land?

SUGGESTIONS FOR RESEARCH

1. A critique of the tax theories of Henry George.
2. The single tax and the distribution of wealth.
3. The incidence of increment taxes.
4. The increment tax versus special assessments for financing local improvements.
5. Administrative problems connected with the single-tax program.
6. A comparison between the socialist program and the single-tax program.
7. A history of the single-tax movement in the United States.
8. The single tax in practice.
9. Increment taxes in practice.

BIBLIOGRAPHICAL NOTE

A comprehensive treatment of the nature, theory, and practice of land value taxation is Yetta Scheftel, *The Taxation of Land Value*, (Boston, 1916). This book contains an excellent bibliography. Another scholarly treatment of land taxation is M. M. Stockwell, *Some Problems of Land Taxation*, (Urbana, Illinois, 1927). R. T. Ely and E. W. Morehouse, *Elements of Land Economics*, (New York, 1924), contains a valuable chapter on land taxation. The economics of urban land taxation is discussed in H. B. Dorau and A. G. Hinman, *Urban Land Economics*, (New York, 1928), Chaps. XXII, XXIII. The problem of the taxation of bare-land values is analyzed in J. R. Commons, "Progressive Tax on Bare-Land Values," *Political Science Quarterly,* Vol. XXXVII, pp. 41-68.

There are many excellent discussions of the economic and social aspects of increments in land values. Among these are W. H. Dawson, *The Unearned Increment,* (London, 1910); and F. W. Taussig, *Principles of Economics,* (New York, 1921), Vol. II, Chap. XLII, Sec. 7, and Chap. XLIV, Secs. 5, 6.

The outstanding work on the single tax is, of course, Henry George, *Progress and Poverty,* (New York, 1881). A recent and valuable study of Henry George and his theories is George Geiger, *The Philosophy of Henry George,* (New York, 1933).

A stimulating article on the single tax is H. G. Brown, "The Single-Tax Complex of Some Contemporary Economists," *Journal of Political Economy,* Vol. XXXII, pp. 164-190. The ethical, economic, and practical defects of the single tax are emphasized in E. R. A. Seligman, *Essays in Taxation,* (New York, 1928), Chap. III.

The single tax movement in the United States is described and appraised in A. N. Young, *The Single Tax Movement in the United States,* (Princeton, N. J., 1916).

The selected and annotated bibliography, "Taxation and the Farmer," referred to in the bibliographical note for Chap. X, contains many references on the taxation of land values.

A discussion of the incidence of increment taxes may be found in C. C. Plehn, "A Study of the Incidence of an Increment Value Land Tax," *Quarterly Journal of Economics,* Vol. XXXII, pp. 487-506; and Sir Josiah Stamp, "The Incidence of Increment Duties," *Economic Journal,* Vol. XXIII, pp. 194-205.

CHAPTER XIII

THE INCIDENCE OF REAL ESTATE TAXES

In addition to the brief discussion of the shifting of taxes on land and improvements, presented in Chapter IX, the importance of taxes on real estate justifies the reproduction of the more comprehensive study of the incidence of real estate taxes by H. D. Simpson.*

In the widespread discussion of real estate taxes in recent years, little consideration has been given to the shifting and incidence of these taxes. When this aspect of the problem has been referred to, it has commonly been assumed that taxes on buildings are shifted in greater or less degree to the tenants; high rentals have frequently been explained on the ground that they contain a large element of taxes. Where any scientific reconsideration of theories of incidence in this field has been attempted, it has commonly taken the form of questioning the traditional theory with regard to taxes on land and of efforts to demonstrate that taxes on land value may in reality be shifted in much the same way as taxes on other commodities.

The writer's observation of the real estate and building field over the past decade has suggested that herein scientific treatment should be exactly reversed; that while there is little ground for modifying the long established theory of land taxes, there are grounds for seriously questioning the usual application of the theory to taxes on buildings. A full discussion of this broad field of incidence can of course not be attempted in a single article; but the grounds for adhering to the established theory in the one case and questioning it in the other will be outlined briefly.

TAXES ON LAND VALUE

In general, taxes are shifted only by reducing the supply of a commodity and consequently raising its price. The question, therefore, is whether a tax on land value can have the effect of reducing the supply of land, in the sense not merely of

---

* From H. D. Simpson, "The Incidence of Real Estate Taxes," *American Economic Review*, Vol. XXII, pp. 219-230.

physical quantity of land but the amount available for sale, rent, or use; that is, the market supply.

Special Land Taxes.   It is a commonplace to observe that even a land tax, if not a general tax applicable to all land in a given jurisdiction or competing area, will be subject to the same processes of shifting as any ordinary tax.   A tax laid only on certain classes or uses of land will reduce the supply available for these particular uses, wherever alternative uses exist. A heavy tax on golf courses would reduce the supply of land devoted to that use, as would a tax on subdivisions, on tobacco land or wheat acreage, or on any other specific classification of land.

We rarely have such arbitrary classifications in modern times; but we not infrequently have situations in which differences in the administration of a tax or in the economic situation of the taxpayer result in real differences in the pressure of a tax upon different areas, with consequent movement of land and resources from one use to another.   The effect of assessment policies on the transfer of agricultural land to subdivisions is an illustration of such a situation.   In this case, if the amount of agricultural land affected is sufficient to have an appreciable effect upon the production of fruit and vegetables for the local market the result must be that some part of the tax on these lands is shifted to the consumer in the form of higher prices for these products.[1]

All this has been recognized in a general way in the accepted theory of incidence.   But the writer is convinced that actual inequalities of *pressure,* in consequence of differences in assessment and administration and in the competitive relationships of different land uses, have developed over much larger areas than have yet been recognized; and that these differences have had more substantial effects upon transfers among alternative uses and consequently upon the *shifting of land taxes* than the prevalent theory of incidence has commonly conceded.

Definite conclusions in this field, however, will have to await more extensive and more rigid research than has yet been carried on.   Consequently further discussion in this portion of our enquiry will be limited to the operation of general taxes on land.

General Land Taxes.   So far as land is subject to processes of production, heavier taxes will discourage these processes, whatever they may be — draining, filling, excavation, grading, and so forth.   To the extent of this discouragement, the pro-

[1] See *The Valuation of Vacant Land in Suburban Areas,* Simpson and Burton, Institute for Economic Research, 1931.

duction of these particular classes of land will be diminished; and prices, rentals, and prices of products will be raised by the effect of *that amount* of diminution.

The problem hinges upon "that amount of diminution" in the production of land. There have been somewhat extreme points of view on this subject, and it has sometimes been maintained that land is subject to "production" in the same way as other commodities. In support of this view, it has been urged that not only clearing, filling, grading, and the ordinary physical processes of preparing land for occupation and use should be classed as production of land; but that railroad construction, transport facilities, and steamship lines which provide access to land resources, inventions and technological processes for utilizing the products of land, provision of markets for the products of land, and the speculative holding of land for future utilization — all constitute processes of "producing" land. From this premise it follows that if the "supply" of land is dependent upon these various processes of production, any factor, such as a tax on land, which lessens the incentives to its production, will have the effect of reducing the supply and thereby shifting the tax, much as a tax on any other object of production might be shifted.

Two observations upon this point of view may be offered.

(1) The first is that whether one wishes to call such general activities processes of *producing* land or not is immaterial, since these are the underlying processes of production of all commodities. The difference lies in the fact that whereas the value of land and manufactured commodities alike depends upon the maintenance of these underlying processes, manufactured articles require, in addition, a variety of specific operations and costs, without which they will not be produced. It is these specific costs that we have in mind when we speak of the influence of costs of production on prices and on the shifting of taxes. Railway and highway construction across the Middle West and steamship transportation across the Atlantic to carry American grain to European markets were all parts of the cost of "producing" the Mississippi Valley, if one wishes to put it that way. They represented likewise a part of the costs of making St. Louis the center of an important shoe manufacturing industry. But over and above all such common and general costs, the production of shoes requires not only a variety of specific operations and costs, but requires the constant repetition of these operations and costs. It is the absence of these costs that differentiates land from freely

reproducible commodities and that creates fundamental differences in the incidence of taxes.

(2) Our second observation is that those who apply the above
argument to the incidence of taxes on land appear to have overlooked the obvious fact that *past processes* of production of
land, whatever they may have been, have now been embodied
in the land and can have no effect on present and future incidence. One might concede that the whole earth was produced by Atlas or some other embodiment of human resources;
and that had it not been taxed, he might have made a bigger
and better earth than he did. But all that creative effort has
now been permanently embodied in land — it makes no difference whether we prefer to lump it under some more general
term, "capital," or what we call it — and taxes now can have
no effect on the quantity of land resulting from this past production.

The only way in which taxes can now affect the "production"
of land and thereby be subject to the ordinary processes of
shifting is in so far as they may affect potential future production of land. In Florida at the present time there are some
37,000,000 acres of land. The only way in which taxes on the
value of this land will reduce the quantity of land in Florida
is in so far as such taxes may retard the future production of
additional acres in that commonwealth. Needless to say, the
amount of such future additions to the land supply of Florida
is going to be very small; and *that fraction of this amount
which will come or not come according as it is taxed or not
taxed* is a still smaller fraction. This, of course, does not
preclude a vast amount of shifting of land resources back and
forth among alternative uses, according to the varying pressure
of taxes and other costs upon particular uses. But most of
us will probably feel that the total amount of land available in
Florida over the next hundred years is going to be pretty
much the same, regardless of the varied tax policies which may
be adopted in that time.

In that case, the tax cannot be embodied in the costs of
production and passed along to the purchaser, tenant, or consumer. The tax becomes a fixed charge upon the land in
exactly the same way as a mortgage and reduces by some corresponding amount the net value of the land.

Conclusion — Taxes on Land. The writer finds it difficult,
therefore, to come to any other conclusion than that the prevalent theory of the incidence of land taxes, as it has been worked
out for the past hundred years or so, still holds substantially
true; that modifications in its application will not be found in

any existing differences of philosophy with regard to the character of land or the nature of its supply; but that research may well be made into those fields where differences in the pressure of a supposedly general tax will bring about movements among alternative land uses that may make some shifting even of land taxes possible.

TAXES ON BUILDINGS AND IMPROVEMENTS: GENERAL THEORY

THE general theory here has always been that so far as taxes, like other costs, limit the amount of building, they reduce the supply and make the shifting of some portion of the tax possible. With this theory, as a statement of general tendency, the writer has no ground for disagreeing. But two comments will be offered, one upon the conditions of its application, and one on its significance from the standpoint of tax policy.

Conditions of Its Application. It is the economist's task to keep theory and experience in neighborly juxtaposition and to note constantly the coincidences and divergencies of the two. In the great building expansion of the past decade it is an unhappy commonplace to observe that much of this construction has been highly speculative. Much of it has been carried on without reference to costs — of labor, materials, financing, or otherwise. The speculative element may possibly have been larger in Chicago, where the writer has had somewhat unusual opportunity for close observation of the movement, than in many other cities; but it has been a large element in Detroit, Cleveland, New York, and quite generally throughout the southern and western states — so much so that cities where it has not been present would be distinctly the exceptions.

Throughout this building expansion, in the urban areas, at least, it would be extremely difficult to discover any way in which taxes have had any effect upon the amount of commercial and industrial construction or even upon the residential construction carried on by real estate and commercial companies. The writer has quoted elsewhere the statement of a representative of one of the largest development companies in Chicago, in 1927, that "we don't figure on taxes at all." And that was the truth throughout most of this period. Speculative profits, actual and anticipated, were so liberal, that taxes seldom entered into the decision when or where to build or whether to build or not.

It was the familiar case of surplus throughout a supermarginal field of activity, where costs were no longer determining factors. And if one sought diligently for a "marginal producer," whose option might determine the limit of production on the basis of costs, one found these marginal producers (marginal in every economic and business sense) frequently the most reckless of all.

Unreasonal and unorthodox as this may appear, the explanation is surprisingly simple. Shifting assumes a margin of production, which sets a limit to production under given conditions of cost, demand, and so forth. A tax raises this margin and cuts off production at an earlier point, thereby raising the price. But this analysis is after all only a description of the supposed behavior of producers under a given set of conditions. It assumes that producers will have sufficient intelligence to know where this margin is and "gumption" enough

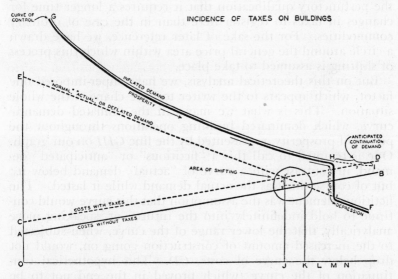

to stop when they get there. But what is going to happen if they have neither? And if, furthermore, there really is no way in which to detect this margin, since the demand for buildings cannot register itself in homogeneous or comparable quotations, like commodity prices, from day to day or month to month? And if, still further, this is not a sporadic or exceptional situation, but very nearly the "normal" condition in the United States, so far as commercial building operations are concerned?

Probably the best clue to what is likely to happen is what has been happening for the past decade; and we have undertaken to represent this in the accompanying graph. Here lines *AB* and *EF* represent the familiar supply and demand curves, respectively. *AB* represents the cost of constructing and operating buildings, without taxes; *CD* the cost with taxes; *x* the margin of production without taxes, and *x'* the margin with taxes. *Kx* represents the level of prices or rentals for building accommodations, without the tax; *Jx'* represents the supposed higher prices or rentals, which in the usual theory would eventually be established as a result of the tax. *P*, therefore, represents the portion of the tax that is shifted, and *q* the portion that remains with the property owner.

This is accepting the normal process of shifting and incidence in the case of any commodity whose supply is limited by the costs of production. It has been customary to apply this analysis to taxes on buildings and improvements, with only the perfunctory qualification that it requires a longer time for changes in taxes to register here than in the case of ordinary commodities. For the sake of later reference, we have drawn a circle around the general price area within which this process of shifting is assumed to take place.

But on this theoretical analysis, we have super-imposed one factor, which appears to the writer to have changed the whole situation. This is what we may call the "inflated demand" curve, which dominated building operations throughout the period of prosperity, represented by the line *GHI* on our graph. One is tempted to call this a "fictitious" or "anticipated" demand, in contrast with a curve of "actual" demand below it; but of course this was the actual demand while it lasted. The fictitious element was the assumption that this curve would continue to hold indefinitely into the future; or, speaking more analytically, that the lower range of the curve, when subjected to the increased amount of construction going on, would not drop below the curve of costs, *CD*. This hypothetical continuation of the curve (which proved in the end not to be there) we have represented by the dotted extension *HI*. *y* represents the point at which this anticipated demand *might have intersected the cost curve, if it had continued far enough, and established another area of shifting.*

As a matter of fact, before it reached any such point of equilibrium, the boom collapsed, and prices and rentals dropped to some lower curve of "normal" demand, but intersecting this curve at a still lower point now on account of the additional construction thrown on the market in the interim by ultra-marginal producers, *K, L, M;* and *N.*

Alongside of line *GH,* dropping abruptly from *H* to *z,* and thence following the line *zF,* is another line designated "curve of control," meaning thereby to indicate the factors that have actually governed building operations throughout past periods.

In the boom period, extending in most cities from 1923 to 1929, the actual demand for building accommodations, in the sense of demand for actual use, had little, if anything, to do with the magnitude of building operations. Nobody knew what the actual demand was, and nobody seemed to care greatly. The only curve that development and construction companies and finance concerns saw was the rainbow curve of an unlimited future demand that would continue to fill their buildings or take properties off their hands at advancing prices. In other words, the ordinary demand curve *ceased to function as a market factor* and was replaced by a much higher curve of anticipated demand. It would be more accurate to say that in most fields of building any actual demand curve, in the sense of demand for actual use, ceased to exist; and a demand based, even in the minds of consumers, on anticipated uses took its place.

This psychological curve governed building activities until the collapse of the boom. Thereafter psychology dropped to the level of actual demand, intersecting that curve at a lower level, as we have pointed out, on account of the additions to the supply of buildings in the meantime. Needless to say, this deflated "normal" demand now governs the building situation. In the diagram a static graph, representing theoretically a momentary demand and supply situation, is unavoidably combined with the histogrammatic element in the control curve; but if it succeeds in making our meaning clear, the cartographic anomaly may perhaps be tolerated.

It means, in so far as this describes the situation accurately, that the factors which actually have governed the volume of construction have not been such as to set up any level of marginal costs which could make shifting possible. The ingredients out of which to construct a parallelogram of shifting and incidence have not been present. The expansion, collapse, and depression in sequence have carried the building industry completely around the area of any possible shifting, and have landed it in a trough of acute over-supply and deflation, where any shifting is obviously out of the question.

An interesting problem in market analysis is afforded by the segment zF. Is this in reality a continuation of the curve GH, whose elasticity broke under the increased supply represented by L, M, and N? Or is it a projection of an entirely different curve Ez? Among real estate men the consensus of opinion (translated into academic terminology) is that zF is not merely the bottom of an inelastic curve or a curve whose elasticity gave way rapidly throughout its lower ranges; that if this increased supply of building had been thrown upon the market in 1926 or 1927, while the demand curve might have dropped rapidly, it would not have fallen to anything approaching the level of z; that the segment zF is therefore a projection from a very different curve, Ez, brought about by radical changes in the purchasing power and economic position of "consumers," as well as changes in the supply of buildings. In any case, it does not affect our inference that the factors which have governed construction throughout the past decade, and probably for a much longer period, have created surplus profits throughout one period and deficits throughout the other, both of which would make shifting impossible; and the swiftness of the collapse would seem to have precluded the maintenance of any intervening purgatory long enough for one to shift any taxes in the course of his descent.

The preceding discussion applies to commercial building operations and buildings of all kinds for business purposes. In the case of single-family residences, however, built by owners for the purpose of residence, taxes have been a serious factor, one upon which the prospective home builder has generally "figured" long and earnestly. But a home-owner occupying his own home cannot shift the taxes, for the simple reason that there is no one farther down the line to whom to shift them. It happens, therefore, that the one conspicuous field of building in which taxes have been a serious deterrent is a field in which shifting has already been precluded by the nature of the ownership and use.

Consequently, while the writer would subscribe to the general theory of incidence, as it has commonly been worked out by economists, and entertains no illusions about seriously modifying the elements of this theory, he has been forced by observation over the past decade to the conclusion *that the building industry does not afford the conditions which make an application of the theory possible.* The people who do the building have not behaved as, under the theory of incidence, they are expected to, and as they should have behaved if they wanted to shift their taxes.

Of course, there are relatively static districts, sufficiently stabilized to avoid speculative movements and sufficiently isolated by their location or character to avoid the consequences of inflation and deflation elsewhere; but they are very rare. Special situations also may be figured out, involving peculiar processes of shifting, some of which the writer has endeavored elsewhere to trace. One such situation is interesting, because it illustrates the fact that a tax which cannot be shifted itself may become a factor in the shifting of some other tax.

The impact of a tax depends on many other considerations than its amount. A lump-sum tax will ordinarily develop more prophylactics than the same amount of tax spread over an indefinite number of small payments; a direct and visible tax more than an indirect and invisible tax; and a permanent tax more than one which offers a gambling chance of discontinuance or modification. Now, it happens that the tax on private homes occupies the less favorable position in all these alternatives. In the first place, it is a painfully direct tax; whereas such portion of the taxes as the tenant pays on an apartment building are so indirect and unrecognized that it is necessary to write labored papers like the present one in order to determine whether he really does pay them or not. In the second place, it is a lump-sum tax, with "delinquent" and "penalty dates," which the ordinary home-owner has to begin to mark on his desk calendar months ahead; whereas any taxes the apartment dweller pays are at least spread evenly over the twelve months of the year. In the third place, when one builds a home, he realizes that he is assuming not only a mortgage, interest payments, repairs, and other responsibilities of a permanent investment, but also an annual tax bill, whose recurrence is as certain as anything in life; whereas, if he rents an apartment, while he may be fully convinced that the owner is shifting some of the taxes, he is at least free to move at any time to some other location where rents are lower, salaries higher, or facilities more convenient.

The consequence is that even if assessments and taxes were exactly the same in the case of homes and apartments, the pressure of the tax would be *a greater deterrent* to home building than to apartment building and renting. This means a greater demand for apartments than would be the case without the tax; and to this extent the tax on homes has the effect of making it possible to shift a portion of the tax on apartment buildings.

But notwithstanding all of these special situations, it is apparent that in most sections of the country throughout the past decade the *supply of buildings has been governed by factors and conditions which make the application of the usual theory of incidence impossible;* and that, in consequence, the taxes on buildings and improvements have not been shifted to any appreciable extent, as one would expect, and as the writer himself has taught his classes for years.

It is true that what we have said about taxes on buildings

applies in greater or less degree to many other fields of production in which there has been excessive speculation. But the background of the problem is in reality something broader even than speculation — it is the "business cycle" itself. And the effect of the business cycle, throughout both its upward and downward movements, in suspending more or less indefinitely the conventional analysis of shifting and incidence in those fields of production whose movements are correlated closely with the general phases of the business cycle, is a problem to which the writer hopes to contribute somewhat further. This, however, is beyond the scope of the present paper; and in the meantime the building field may serve to exemplify this larger problem.

Significance of Shifting from Standpoint of Tax Policy. One other thing which developments of the past decade have clearly suggested is that even where these taxes may be shifted more or less in accordance with the customary theory, the significance of this fact is much less than has commonly been assumed. Shifting means shifting the "burden," as we have always been careful to explain, though the "payment" is still made by the party upon whom the tax was originally levied. But there are business relations, of importance to the community as well as to the individual directly concerned, in which the *payment* may be more significant than the *burden.* Let us take a hypothetical illustration, of a kind that can be reproduced in actual business thousands of times, except that in our illustration we shall concede the shifting of the taxes.

Suppose that a small apartment building, built four or five years ago at an actual cost of $125,000, is now worth only $90,000, because similar buildings can now be constructed at the lower cost. Suppose that the supply has now been adjusted to the actual demand; and that both have been adjusted so nicely to costs that rentals are now on a cost basis. Assume that this means a rental of 10 per cent on the value of the property, of which 2 per cent represents taxes and 2 per cent insurance, repairs, and current costs, leaving 6 per cent (on $90,000) for interest on the investment (at current value); so that taxes are entirely shifted to the tenants, and it is possible to show that none of the "burden" of real estate taxes rests upon the building owner.

But suppose the building was financed at the time of construction to the amount of $100,000, with an interest charge of $6000, including both first and junior liens — not excessive financing for well located, established types of building. But the second mortgage is due; it may even have been renewed once in that time; and the holder is refusing to renew without some reduction of the principal. The rental is yielding, on our supposition above, something less than sufficient to cover taxes and interest and of course nothing for payment of principal. *The fact that the burden of the tax is shifted to the tenant* does not prevent the disastrous results *of a heavy concentration of fixed charges on the equity;* and the tax, under most of our property taxes, falls entirely on the equity.

The result is what has happened thousands of times all over the United States in the past few years. Equities have been wiped out and properties sacrificed through forced sale or foreclosure, with disastrous effects upon real estate values and real estate credit, which in turn have precipitated failures of banks and financial houses and entailed the loss of millions of dollars by people who have supposed that they had no connection with any real estate investments whatever.

The harm here is not the onerousness or injustice of the tax, but the financial and industrial dislocation to which it contributes. And it does not help the situation to say that it is due to speculation and overbuilding. Some speculation, overproduction, and deflation are inevitable as long as we have our unstable price level. And no matter who is responsible, conservative as well as speculative builders are involved in the losses, and the whole community suffers the consequences.

Taxes are a factor in this process, not on account either of their amount or their incidence, but on account of the rigidity of their payment, *which even a complete shifting of the tax will not alleviate.* These conditions happen to be particularly fresh in mind on account of our recent experiences; but the rigidity of real estate taxes has worked hardship for many years and in many fields, entirely aside from any of our recent experiences. It has wrought havoc in farm taxes. And altogether it is probable that the rigidity of real estate taxes has been more painful and costly than their amount, large as this is. This fact makes the shifting of taxes, to whatever extent it may take place, of considerably less significance in this field than it might have in other fields of taxation.

Implications. If these conclusions are sound, they convey two implications, one applicable to the real estate owner, the other to the rest of us.

The first is that the real estate owner may substantially reduce his taxes by taking steps to remove the flagrant speculative elements and speculative practices from his field. It is these elements that have prevented him from shifting his taxes in the past. If he will remove these elements and get the building business established upon some stable basis in relation to costs, he will thereby give the orthodox laws of incidence at least a gambling chance to operate, which in the past they have not had. We sometimes speak of the impossibility of repealing economic laws; the building business, through the habitual behavior of its members, has seemingly repealed the laws of incidence in this field; and this paper may be construed as a plea for a return to "law abiding" habits in the field of economic law.

The second implication is that since realtors and builders will probably not heed this plea; and since, even if they do, shifting the real estate taxes will not eliminate the harmful consequences of the unyielding rigidity of these taxes, it behooves the rest of us to move, with such haste as we may, toward the adoption of less rigid forms of taxation. Our modern financial and industrial mechanism requires forms of taxation that will have a smaller "load-factor"; taxes in which the *payment*, regardless of the "ultimate burden," will have less of the character of an unvarying fixed charge and will be adjusted with some reference to the business situation and financial capacity of the taxpayer.

QUESTIONS AND PROBLEMS FOR DISCUSSION

1. What is meant by the "production" of land? What is the bearing of this point upon the incidence of a tax on land?
2. Do inequalities in assessment of land for taxation purposes have any effect on the problem of incidence of a land tax?
3. In the long run will building construction be governed to any degree by taxes on buildings?
4. Will a home-owner occupying his own home be able to shift a tax levied on this property? If he leases the home to another and rents an apartment for himself, who then bears the burden of the tax on the home?
5. Why is the pressure of a tax a greater deterrent to home building than to apartment building?
6. State the generally accepted theory of the incidence of taxes on buildings and improvements. Follow this with an explanation of the modifications which "speculation" has made necessary in the conventional analysis.
7. "The rigidity of real estate taxes has been more painful and costly than their amount, large as this is." Explain.

SUGGESTIONS FOR RESEARCH

1. A study of the shifting and incidence of real estate taxes in some particular municipality.
2. The shifting and incidence of a tax levied exclusively on land used for a particular purpose — wheat growing for example.

3. The shifting and incidence of taxes on buildings (in some particular locality) and the business cycle.

BIBLIOGRAPHICAL NOTE

Some of the outstanding studies which deal specifically with the incidence of taxes on land are : H. G. Brown, *Economics of Taxation*, (New York, 1924), Chap. VIII ; Whitney Coombs, "Taxation of Farm Property," *United States Department of Agriculture, Technical Bulletin*, No. 172, (February, 1930), pp. 61-65 ; and M. H. Hunter, "The Burden of Land Taxes," *Proceedings of the National Tax Association*, (1924), pp. 298-305.

The question of the incidence of increment taxes is ably discussed in C. C. Plehn, "A Study of the Incidence of an Increment Value Land Tax," *Quarterly Journal of Economics*, Vol. XXXII, pp. 487-506 ; and Sir Josiah Stamp, "The Incidence of Increment Duties," *Economic Journal*, Vol. XXIII, pp. 194-205.

For a more general discussion of real estate taxation, see K. M. Williamson, "Taxation of Real Estate : Survey of Recent Discussion," *Quarterly Journal of Economics*, Vol. XLVIII, pp. 96-128.

CHAPTER XIV

TAXATION OF NATURAL RESOURCES

1. THE SEVERANCE TAX *

To any student of political science who, for the first time, examines the revenue system of the average American state, the most striking phenomenon he finds is the multiple character of the taxes provided for.

The discussion of any taxation problem is opportune in view of the gathering momentum of the eternal quest for more prolific sources of revenue. The present federal, state and local fiscal resources are strained to the breaking point.

It is opportune also for the further reason that the dire experience of financing the Great War has brought home to this nation, and to the other less fortunate participants, the importance of the conservation of material resources.

In the foundation stones of the typical fiscal edifice are recognized the well-known outlines of the general property tax; but upon and around this substructure there has been erected an incongruous variety of gingerbread work in the form of numerous supplemental taxes.

It happens that in three of the six states composing the Southwestern Political Science Association there has recently come into public notice the unique form of taxation which is the subject of this sketch.

In Louisiana, Texas and Oklahoma the prominence of the special tax which it is my purpose briefly to discuss marks these commonwealths as veritable laboratories for experimentation in this particular field of public finance. Before generalizing upon the principles involved in the structure and administration of the tax in question, let us analyze and describe six of these interesting specimens in the following order :

> The Oklahoma Gross Production tax.
> The Louisiana Severance tax.
> The Texas Gross Receipts tax
> The Alabama Tonnage tax.
> The Pennsylvania Output tax.
> The Minnesota Occupation tax.

* From George Vaughan, "The Severance Tax," *Bulletin of the National Tax Association*, Vol. VII, pp. 243-250.

THE OKLAHOMA "GROSS PRODUCTION" TAX

THE present Act, approved February 14, 1916, was an amendment to Chapter 107, Laws of 1915. It requires every person, firm, association or corporation mining asphalt, lead, zinc, gold, silver or copper ores, or producing petroleum or natural gas, to file sworn quarterly statements with the state auditor showing the location of each mine or well operated by the affiant during the next preceding quarter, the kind and amount and value of production. At the same time he must pay the auditor a tax equal to one-half of one per cent on the gross value of ores and three per cent of the gross value of oil or gas, exceeding royalty interests.

The auditor is given express power to ascertain by his own investigation whether the taxpayers' return is true and correct.

Payment of the tax is by the statute declared to be "in full and in lieu of all taxes by the state, counties, cities, towns, townships, school districts and other municipalities upon any property rights attached to or inherent in the right to said minerals, upon leases for mining of the natural products named, and upon the mining rights and privileges for the minerals aforesaid belonging or appertaining to land, upon the machinery, appliances and equipment in and around and actually used in the operation of any well or mine, also upon "the oil, gas or ores . . . during the tax year in which same is produced, and upon any investment in any of the leases or other property" connected therewith.

The State Board of Equalization upon its own initiative or the complaint of the taxpayer, may take testimony to determine whether the taxes imposed by the Act are greater or less than the general advalorem tax for all purposes, would be on the property of such produced subject to taxation, including the value of the lease, machinery, equipment, etc., used in the actual operation of the producing mine or well; and the board must then raise or lower the rates herein imposed conformably. An appeal is afforded to the Supreme Court if taken before the tax has been collected and distributed.

Collection of the tax, if delinquent, is by the sheriff under a warrant of the auditor, on the property of the taxpayer connected with the production being subject to levy therefor as upon execution.

The tax is a lien upon the property of the taxpayer until paid and recovery may be had by suit. The gross production tax becomes delinquent thirty days after the expiration of each quarter, whereupon a penalty of eighteen per cent per annum attaches.

THE LOUISIANA SEVERANCE TAX

THE present act (No. 31, approved June 30, 1920), levies a license tax for 1920, and for each subsequent year, "upon each person, firm, corporation or association of persons engaged in the business of severing natural resources from the soil or water." All forms of timber, turpentine, and other forest products, and minerals, such as oil, gas, sulphur, salt, coal and ores, marble, stone, gravel, sand and shells are specifically included.

The tax is collected quarterly by the parish tax collectors and paid into a special account known as the "Severance Tax License Fund." The license to operate in each quarter is based on the market value of the quantity severed in the last preceding quarter annual period.

There must be filed within 30 days after the expiration of each quarter, with the supervisor of public accounts, sworn statements of the business conducted by the taxpayer, showing the kind, location, quantity and cash value of the natural resources so severed or produced. A duplicate statement must be filed with the tax collector of the parish where the resource is taken and a license tax paid equal to two per cent of the gross value of the total production during the preceding quarter.

Payment is made by those actually engaged in the operation of severing, whether as owners or lessees. Provision is made for verifying by the supervisor of the statements, and for ascertaining the facts where no statement has been filed. The license tax becomes delinquent after the lapse of the 30 days for making report. It is expressly enacted that "the payment of the license tax shall be in addition to and shall not affect the liability of the parties so taxed for the payment of all state, parochial, municipal, district and special taxes upon their real estate and corporeal property.

The supervsior has power to compel the production of books and records of the taxpayer, if necessary to ascertain the amount of the tax. Collection by distraint against delinquents, as in the case of general license laws, is provided for, and false swearing is made punishable as for perjury. Quarterly sworn statements are required from all purchasers of natural products severed from the soil, under penalty of from $50 to $500 for each omission to report.

THE TEXAS "GROSS RECEIPTS" TAX

THE Texas law is the conventional type of license tax upon gross receipts, and the present law (in force since 1907) includes within its purview a multitude of businesses and occupations. It does not include forest products, but Article 7383, covering petroleum, reads as follows:

"Each and every individual, company, corporation or association which owns, controls, manages or leases any oil well within this state shall make quarterly, on the first days of January, April, July and October of each year, a report to the comptroller of public accounts, under oath, showing the total amount of oil produced during the quarter next preceding and the average market value thereof. Said individuals, companies, corporations and associations, at the time of making said report, shall pay to the treasurer of the state of Texas an occupation tax for the quarter beginning on said date equal to one and one-half per cent of the total amount of all oil produced at the average market value thereof, as shown by said report."

Failure to report is penalized in a sum not exceeding $1000; and delinquencies incur a penalty of 10 per cent, to be recovered by suit by the attorney general. All taxes levied by this chapter are expressly declared to be in addition to all other taxes now levied by law.

THE ALABAMA "TONNAGE TAX"

THE Alabama license tax law is very similar to that of Texas, and the tonnage tax on coal and iron ore mined is typical of some hundred or more occupation taxes, and appears in the published laws of 1919 as Schedules 66 and 67, making the following provisions:

"Every person, firm, corporation, partnership, joint-stock company or association engaged in the business of operating a coal mine shall pay to the state treasurer for the use of the state a license or privilege tax, by the 20th day of each month, for the privilege of operating such coal mine during the current month in which such payment is due, an amount equal to two cents per ton on all coal mined during the last preceding month in which such mine was operated, according to the run of the mine, but no such tax shall be paid to any county in the state, providing this shall not apply to wagon mines which do not load said coal in or on railroad cars, boats or barges."

A similar tax of three cents per ton is levied for the privilege of operating an iron mine during the current month in which such payment is due. . . But no such tax shall be paid to any county in the state.

Additional provisions require sworn monthly reports of tonnage output; make the operation of unreported mines or on which the license tax is not paid or is past due, a misdemeanor punishable by a fine of from $10 to $500 and "sentence to hard labor for the county for not more than six months and require sworn statements from purchasers or consignees of coal and iron ore for transportation or use under like penalty."

The validity of this law has been sustained.

THE PENNSYLVANIA OUTPUT TAX

THE recent Pennsylvania law, approved May 11, 1921, is a short act and makes it the duty of the individual, superintendent or officer in charge of any mine to assess a tax of one and one-half per cent of its value on every ton of anthracite coal when mined, washed or screened and ready for market.

Before February 1 the mine official must make written report to the auditor general of the number of gross tons taxable and the assessed value thereof during the preceding calendar year, and the amount of tax thereon. Upon failure of such report to the auditor general, the state treasurer levies the tax upon information and may require the taxpayer to produce books and papers. Payment of the tax into the treasury of the commonwealth must be made within 60 days from the date of the settlement of the account under a penalty of ten per cent. After it is due the tax bears interest at one per cent per month until paid. False statement is punishable by a fine of $500 and imprisonment of one year or both.

The legality of the law has been assailed in the Supreme Court of Pennsylvania in the pending suit of *Heisler* v. *Thomas Colliery Co.*

THE MINNESOTA "OCCUPATION TAX"

THE latest of a series of acts providing a tax on the output of mines in Minnesota was approved April 11, 1921. It imposes "An occupation tax equal to six per cent of the valuation of all ores mined . . . in addition to all other taxes. The occupation tax is payable on May 1, based on the report for the preceding calendar year due to be filed on February 1. The Tax Commission primarily administers the law, but enforcement is lodged with the attorney general. Books and records must be exhibited on demand of the tax commissioner. All the taxes go to the general revenue fund.

Tonnage tax legislation, so called, had been before every session of the Minnesota legislature since 1907. That the vast iron ore deposits in northern Minnesota are a state heritage and that the people are entitled for that reason to a considerable additional revenue from this source, and also in view of the rapid depletion of the merchantable ore bodies, was the chief contention of the proponents of the supertax measure.

The opposition claimed that the mines are now paying a super-tax, in that ore is assessed at 50 per cent of full value under the classified assessment law, while other property is assessed at from 25 to 50 per cent of full value, the average being about 33 1-3 per cent. Discrimination against the northern part of the state and in favor of the agricultural regions to the south and west was also urged.

The present tax in Minnesota, it is seen, is an unblushing super-tax, not on mere tonnage, but on the valuation of the output. Its estimated annual yield is over $2,000,000. When we consider that the mining properties of that state already pay in advalorem taxes more than $18,000,000 annually, it is likely that the law will be tested in the highest court of the land.

EXAMPLES OF THE TAX ELSEWHERE

THOUGH bearing the name of "severance" tax in Louisiana alone, the exaction finds a counterpart in a number of states and in foreign countries. A few examples suffice to show the analogy.

In Great Britain a two per cent royalty is paid directly to the crown on the output of gold-mining. In Canada, the different provinces have regulations of their own, Nova Scotia imposing a two per cent tax paid to the crown on all minerals produced; in Ontario, Act of 1907, net profits are the basis of the tax and a flat rate of three per cent is levied on profits above $10,000. The total revenue of the province in 1917 from mining sources was $1,731,720.

In Mexico there are three kinds of taxes: first, on the mining property; second, on the metals produced; and third, on smelting, assay and coining. The first tax is largely upon the unit of ore, called the pertenencia, the annual rate being graduated, beginning with $6 per pertenencia from one to five, and increasing until the rate is $18 per pertenencia over 100. In addition to the federal tax, the individual states in Mexico may assess a tax on production of metals not to exceed two per cent advalorem.

ANNUAL YIELD

SOME idea of the productiveness of the severance tax in Louisiana and of the similar exactions in some of the other states is conveyed by the following official data :

Oklahoma —

1915	$ 681,413.00
1916	2,640,945.00
1917	3,417,982.00
1918	3,448,473.00
1919	4,212,220.00
1920	6,989,925.00
1921	7,858,945.00

Louisiana —

1916	52.00
1917	100.00
1918	888.89
1919	3,238.18
1920	2,862,354.51
1921	1,590,520.28

Texas —

1919	1,868,280.00
1920	3,877,965.00
1921	4,847,793.00

Alabama —

1920	469,578.00
1921	366,076.00

Minnesota —

1921 (estimated)	2,000,000.00

Pennsylvania —

1921 (estimated)	7,000,000.00

West Virginia —

1921 (estimated)	2,500,000.00

A typical quarter-annual statement of the yield in Louisiana is added to show the species, quantity, total values of the products involved and the tax yield of each :

Product	Quantity quarter ended December 31, 1921	Total Value	2 per cent Tax
Timber (feet)	606,320,583.00	$4,043,016.04	$80,858.74
Turpentine (barrels)	65,417.50	196,252.50	3,925.05
Oil (barrels)	5,226,564.32	8,564,646.59	171,292.67
Gas (cubic feet) ..	15,838,095,717.00	465,313.77	9,306.22
Sulphur (tons) ...	275,485.00	2,479,365.00	49,587.30
Salt (tons)	61,735.66	29,603.49	1,852.06

Product	Quantity quarter ended December 31, 1921	Total Value	2 per cent Tax
Gravel (tons)	293,054.63	131,874.66	2,637.48
Sand (tons)	66,379.66	29,848.24	596.97
Shells (tons)	53,429.16	27,820.32	556.40
		$16,030,740.61	$320,612.89

THE RATIONALE OF THE SEVERANCE TAX

AGITATION for the enactment of a severance tax has been prompted in several states, mainly by consideration of the necessity of conserving our natural resources. The theory has been that owing to the limited supply of the basic resources, which have been accumulated by the gradual operations of nature, definite restriction should be placed by the state upon their utilization. Even though held under private ownership, all waste or extravagant depletion should be prohibited, and a specific tax upon such products, when and as "severed from the soil," would tend to retard undue consumption.

This theory, while sound, perhaps, when addressed to the general public policy of the state or nation, may or may not hold good when borrowed and applied by the Revenue Department. Let us see.

LEGAL STATUS

THREE general classes of taxes have found exemplification and judicial approval in this country, viz.: (1) a property tax, i.e., one based on capital value; (2) a business or privilege tax, and (3) an income tax. For many years the field of the privilege tax has been invaded by both federal and state governments, while that of the general property tax has been preempted by the states. The income tax has of late been jointly appropriated by the commonwealths.

Constitutional restrictions must often be reckoned with in the selection of any proposed tax. As far as the federal constitution controls, these restrictions are few but far-reaching. These federal inhibitions are that no person shall be deprived of property without due process of law (amendment No. 5) construed to apply to acts of congress only, and repeated in the Fourteenth Amendment as respects the powers of the states, with the added bulwark of "equal protection of the laws." Most state constitutions expressly require "equality and uniformity in taxation"; but in certain others, notably in New York, Rhode Island, Connecticut and Vermont, no restrictions exist, and the legislature is left to prescribe with a free hand any system of taxation which will not offend the principles of natural justice.

But the privilege or occupation tax does not fall within the purview of "equality and uniformity" requirements. Indeed there are very slight limitations upon the character of any privilege tax a state may choose to adopt in devising its internal revenue scheme.

A distinguishing feature is, however, that the privilege tax is paid in advance. Its payment is a condition precedent to the lawful performance of the act or to engaging in the business for which the tax or license fee is exacted.

Notable instances of business taxes are, the franchise tax on corporations, the federal capital stock tax, and occupation taxes familiar to all, and applicable to the businesses or professions of individuals or corporations.

A PRIVILEGE, NOT A PROPERTY TAX

It is within the class of the privilege or occupation tax that the severance tax belongs. In every state where it exists the tax is levied expressly upon or for the privilege of carrying on certain business transactions. For this reason, and in the absence of the iron-clad shackles of property taxation, there is a great disparity in the ultimate burden imposed by the tax under consideration.

In Oklahoma, for example, the tax is levied on the gross production of oil and gas and of certain minerals, but it is in lieu of property taxes on the equipment or machinery at the mines or well. In Texas, where the corresponding exaction is expressly declared to be a privilege on "gross receipts," there is no relief against the concurrent operation of the general property tax upon the same property.

The Louisiana severance tax is also an impost laid over and above the general property tax. Indeed, the present compromise rate was reached in 1920 by Governor Parker after prolonged negotiations with the oil interests. The state had been clamoring for a four per cent rate, but the concession of two per cent was finally made in recognition of the fact that payment of the severance tax in no way affected liability for general taxes. The recent anthracite coal levy of six per cent in Pennsylvania is superimposed upon the general property tax.

The point must be emphasized that there is no relationship between the privilege and the property tax. Indeed the body of the law adjudicating these two classes of taxes has been separately developed, so that the principles upon which the taxes rest are recognized to be distinct.

Neither does it avail as a matter of law to say that the privilege tax results in imposing a final burden heavier than that borne by other business interests whose operating property is of the same value. The tax is a *quid pro quo* exacted in return for a privilege; it is not a levy upon property itself. Hence it is that although the Pennsylvania tax means an additional burden of $7,000,000 upon the anthracite coal industry in that state and thus augments substantially the total tax account of the operators, it is not likely on that ground to be held unconstitutional. The fact, if true, that no privilege tax is imposed upon other Pennsylvania business interests representing corresponding capital investments will not vitiate the tax upon the industry selected. "A state may have a policy in taxation," says the Supreme Court of the United States, in the Fort Smith Lumber Company case (251 U. S. 532).

IS CONSERVATION A SOUND BASIS FOR A FISCAL TAX?

THE question then recurs as to whether the idea of conservation is a proper and legitimate basis for any form of a tax, and if so, to what extent may the machinery of taxation be put in motion by a public policy of conservation.

If natural resources, accumulated by the slow development of the ages, are a heritage of the race and not merely of one generation, then certainly a privilege tax by the sovereign is justified on the sheer ground of self-preservation. Wanton destruction of timber, with no provision for reforestation, will in time transform the virgin forest into a howling desert.

No less authority than Gifford Pinchot has recently declared that an area in the state of Pennsylvania equivalent to the entire domain of New Jersey is now without trees, either present or prospective, and is hence a desert and of no useful value. No one who has traversed the states of Colorado and Nevada and other Western states and gazed upon the abandoned mining camps, has failed to perceive of what little value such waste spaces are after the severance of the mineral contents from the majestic mountain sides.

The conclusion, therefore, follows that, if upon no other ground, a severance tax is eminently justified for regulating and controlling the rate of exhaustion and the method of utilizing the resources of forest, field and mine.

Such a tax, moreover, incidentally provides authoritative statistical data so that periodic inventories may be had of our remaining wealth. The recent financing of the Great War showed the supreme necessity of an intimate knowledge of the material and economic resources of state and nation. The government could not commandeer its resources without the co-operation of the states and of their local subdivisions. And so any extensive program of conservation must depend upon the articulation of the massive federal machinery with the minuter instrumentalities of the states.

Granted, then, that a privilege tax for severing natural products from the soil is justified from considerations of conservation, the question arises as to how far the state may go. May she impose an additional burden under the guise of conservation for the real purpose of furnishing funds for public purposes? Or, must the rate be only nominal?

WHAT IS A PUBLIC PURPOSE?

THESE questions strike deeply into the heart of political science. What is a lawful purpose, and what are the objects to which public funds may be dedicated? This field has broadened immensely within the last decade, not only from the state viewpoint, but from federal as well. Today it is not uncommon to see the government engage in affairs which a generation ago were regarded as strictly of a private nature. There is a pronounced trend toward socialism that we cannot gainsay.

Important phases of these activities are a broader program of education, transportation and labor regulations, public welfare, including health and the conservation of human life. Surely all of these functions are economically sound and worthy. If, then, the government is to undertake new and ambitious tasks, there must be tapped an adequate source from which enabling funds are to be drawn.

Recent years mark a tendency to let down the bars of constitutional control entirely in support of education. In my own state an amendment will shortly be voted upon which lifts all restrictions upon the amount of school taxes leviable.

Such tendencies merely indicate that so far as the public weal is concerned the sovereign's control is paramount. She has unquestionably the power to legislate with respect to the rights of private ownership. Indeed, property is not an absolute but merely a relative right. No man has a right to use his property or to waste or destroy it to the injury of his neighbor. *Sic utere tuo ut non alienum laedas.*

The owner of a large timber tract has no moral or legal right to waste or extravagantly utilize that forest for his own enrichment by destroying the seeds of a commodity which could serve the future generations of the race. Neither has a corporation or an individual the right to tap underground reservoirs of oil and gas and permit valuable commodities to waste and lose their service to humanity.

Then if the doctrine is sound that a fiscal tax on output is justified, and can be levied as a privilege exaction, there would seem to be no serious obstacle in the way of employing the severance tax further as a supplemental source of revenue. In amount it should be sufficient, when combined with the inadequately administered property tax, at least to equate the burden of the affected industry with that of other business interests whose operations augment and do not exhaust our economic wealth.

EXPEDIENCY AN INFLUENTIAL FACTOR

An administrative motive frequency prompting the adoption of an output tax on commodities is the technical difficulty of securing a reliable appraisal of hidden values. And so we reach the *argumentum ad convenientem*.

A scientific valuation of natural deposits often involves quite a large expenditure of money. Unfortunately but few states have had an enlightened conception of the far-reaching value of an appraisal. As a result of a penny-wise-and-pound-foolish policy, many thousands of dollars in revenues are annually lost because of the crude and inadequate methods pursued in valuing mineral property for taxation.

SEVERANCE TAX A COMPROMISE

As a matter of convenience in administration, therefore, and to offset or compensate in a degree for the enormous public loss though lack of an accurate appraisal, the severance tax may intervene as a satisfactory compromise to all concerned. While in most states it is impossible under present constitutions to provide that the severance tax shall be in lieu of the general property tax, yet the practical effect of the addition of the severance tax will bring about the desired result otherwise lost because of the incomplete valuation under general schedules.

To illustrate: In the state of Louisiana, where rich pools of oil have been recently discovered, it would be impossible accurately to appraise the oil leases, whether developed or not. Even if such an appraisal were attainable, it is doubtful whether taxing officials would have the courage to put in the assessment rolls the true values so ascertained. Yet the expedient of the severance tax enables the state immediately to secure a proper division of the realized income flowing from this peculiar property.

Such division of income will, from year to year, correspond roughly with the amount of the tax the property itself upon an adequate valuation should have yielded. Indeed, a difference favorable to the taxpayer is perceived in that the annual tax payments are adjusted in accordance with actual income realized, and hence are less burdensome than under the pure property tax plan. A delay in developing or in the marketing of the product would not carry with the lean years the unrequited burden of taxation.

CONCLUSIONS

OUR examination has been limited to only a few of the numerous existing statutes analogous to the so-called severance tax of Louisiana, which imposes special taxes upon the business of severing natural resources from the soil.

We conclude, from this tentative investigation:

(a) That the enactment of such a tax is within the power and is a legitimate and proper function of any state whose constitution does not prohibit privilege taxes.

(b) That the tax as exemplified in this study is a privilege or license tax and not one on property.

(c) That it is justified primarily as a regulatory provision of public policy in the broad interest of conservation of economic resources.

(d) That it is further warranted as a purely fiscal or revenue agency, supplemental to or as the complement of the antiquated and inadequate general property tax.

In the language of Alexander Bruce, writing in the *Pennsylvania Law Review*, "Patriotic citizens are beginning to resolve in the affirmative the question, 'Am I my brother's keeper,' and to recognize the existence of a common humanity and of a state and national solidarity. They are beginning to evince a concern for the generations that are to come and for the states and the nation of the future, which those generations will compose. They are coming to realize, as never before, that the welfare of the state is the highest law; that the whole is made up of the sum of all its parts, and that if the individual citizen suffers and is retarded in growth and development, the state itself is to that extent weakened and undermined."

2. THE TAXATION OF FORESTS *

THE taxation of forests involves two distinct problems, relating respectively to growing forests and to mature or virgin

* Adapted from "Report of the Committee of National Tax Association on Forest Taxation," F. R. Fairchild, Chairman, *Proceedings of the National Tax Association,* (1922), pp. 130-139.

forests. We shall divide our following discussion into two parts accordingly.

THE TAXATION OF GROWING FORESTS

THE idea of [a] former committee [of the National Tax Association] was to find a method of taxation that should take the place of all existing taxation upon forests. This meant practically to find an equitable substitute for the general property tax. It was recognized that theoretically such a substitute might be either (1) an annual tax on the original capital value of the forest — what the foresters call the "expectation value" — which practically amounts to the value of the bare land, or (2) a tax on the yield of forest products, whenever obtained. In the first alternative the rate of the tax should be the prevailing rate of the property tax on wealth in general. The yield tax, in order to impose a burden equivalent to the tax on other wealth, should be at a rate determined by dividing the prevailing rate of the property tax by the rate of interest. Thus, if the rate of interest were five per cent, an annual tax on original capital value at one per cent is equivalent to a yield tax of twenty per cent. Recognizing the practical obstacles to both of these alternatives, the former committee proposed a compromise, involving an annual tax on the land, at half the rate of the prevailing property tax and a ten per cent yield tax on forest products. This recognized the principle that a combination of the capital tax and the yield tax should impose the same total burden as would result from either of these taxes alone ; hence the rates recommended.

In the opinion of your committee analysis of this plan brings to light two features to which may be ascribed its failure to gain more general acceptance. In the first place, the yield tax under American forest conditions would necessarily be irregular as a revenue producer. In spite of practicable devices for correcting this irregularity which were suggested,[1] the public and the legislatures have been extremely cautious about accepting any plan which even remotely threatens to introduce an element of uncertainty or irregularity into the local revenue system. This is undoubtedly the chief obstacle to the practical acceptance of the yield tax.

The other feature which appears as an obstacle to the adoption of the former plan is this : The plan, as proposed, was a compromise between the annual land tax and the yield tax. As such, it gave a reduced land tax, at half the rate paid by

[1] Cf. Fairchild, "Suggestions for a Practical Plan of Forest Taxation," *Proceedings of the National Tax Association*, Volume VI, 1912.

other property, to be made up later by the yield tax. This was, at the start, a concession to the forest land owner. It could be granted only where there was reason to expect the future yield tax. It was essential to make careful provision to prevent resort to the law as a means of escaping taxation on agricultural or other non-forest land. The plan therefore involved complicated provisions, seeking to restrict its application to true forest lands, limiting it to lands not exceeding a certain value, requiring that the lands be properly planted or otherwise stocked with suitable species of trees and that the young forests be properly maintained. The special forest tax was optional, to come into force only after application by the owner and inspection and approval by the state forester, and to terminate whenever the owner should desire to withdraw or the state forester should decide that the forest was not being properly maintained. All of this meant complicated procedure and red tape and has doubtless gone far to cool the interest of the forest owners in the plan.

Of course any arrangement which involves a concession in the way of reduced taxation must be safeguarded in some such way as this. Some of the earlier plans of forest tax reform involved special favors to the forest owner, in return for certain specified management of his forest, under a contract with the state. Forest owners have been very reluctant to bind themselves by such contracts and the laws containing this feature have everywhere failed to produce results. But even where there is no intention to give any ultimate favor to the forest owner, the presence of an initial concession requires some safeguard against abuse. Hence nearly every plan of forest taxation that has appeared in the last ten years has involved restrictions upon its application similar to those contained in the plan of the former committee. This is believed to have been the chief reason for the failure of all these plans to obtain more general acceptance. Your committee believes that it is of the utmost importance to develop a plan which shall be of universal application; which shall be compulsory and not optional, and which shall not be hedged about with the red tape of applications, inspections, and official sanctions.

This goal, which seemed quite unattainable to those of us who were working on the problem ten years ago, has we believe been brought within our reach by certain developments of the past decade in the general field of taxation. Two things have happened. One has been the unexpectedly rapid disintegration of the general property tax, with the corresponding rise of taxes upon incomes and earnings. The other is the development of new ideas regarding the whole system of state and local taxation, under the inspiration and guidance of the model tax committee of the National Tax Association.

These developments have greatly simplified the problem of forest taxation. The old general property tax was intolerable in its application to growing forests. The task was to find some substitute, assuming that the general property tax would long continue for other property in general. The one great achievement of our earlier efforts was to develop the idea of the yield tax. Yet, rather curiously, the practical outcome has been not the adoption of a special yield tax for forests, but the remarkable spread of the income, earnings, or yield basis for taxation in general. While we have been struggling to secure the yield principle as a special concession to the forests, the general tax reform movement has caught up with us.

The problem of today is no longer to find a special method for taxing forests in lieu of all other taxation, but to fit the taxation of forests into a general tax system which is itself destined to rest more and more on the yield or income basis. For example, the model tax committee proposes a system of state and local taxation resting on three foundation stones : (1) the individual income tax, (2) the property tax, upon tangible property only, and (3) the business tax. The individual income tax would of course treat forest incomes like any other income. The forest owner can have no grievance here. So far as the peculiarities of his business are concerned this is the most favorable kind of tax for him. There is no special problem for us here. Likewise the business tax, where such a tax is in effect, will rest upon the income or yield basis, the one best suited to the peculiarities of forest enterprise. Some special adaptations to the business of forestry may be desirable, but at any rate the yield principle is secure.

The only problem remaining is to find a modification of the property tax which shall be suited to the peculiarities of forest enterprise. The weaknesses of the ordinary property tax as applied to growing forests have been carefully studied and the results presented in previous reports and papers before these conferences, to which reference has been made. Reference has also been made to the generally accepted remedy ; namely the combination of an annual tax on the land and a yield tax. As has been pointed out, the annual tax on the land, at the rate of the ordinary property tax, is all the burden that can fairly be placed upon the growing forest. To impose an additional yield tax is excessive. Those who have proposed this have apparently had the feeling that to grant entire exemption of growing timber, without any compensation, was too great a concession or else have had in mind the mature forests, which as we shall show must be called upon for more than the land tax. As regards growing forests there is no principle either to justify a yield tax or to measure its amount, if the land is already subject to annual taxation like other property. Such an additional yield tax is justified only in consideration of a reduced rate of the land tax, as proposed by the committee of 1913.

When we were seeking a special forest tax, in lieu of all other taxes, it was felt that the annual land tax at the regular rate, paid for many years in advance of an income from the forest, was a serious hardship. Now we are assuming that forests are to be subject to the individual income tax and the business tax, and we are seeking only an adaptation of the property tax. This is not the whole tax on forests but only a part of the system. The simple solution becomes practicable and not unduly burdensome ; i.e., the annual tax on the land only, at the regular rate of the property tax, with entire exemption of growing trees. No additional yield tax is required so far as the property tax is concerned. With such a tax, there remains no necessity for any optional feature, for applications or inspections, for contracts or official interference with the owner's management of his forest. The law would apply to all lands and would simply have to provide that in assessing real estate no account should be taken of the value of growing trees.

The yield tax would appear, not as an additional tax in lieu of the property tax, but in the place of the business tax. The forestry business is fairly simple. It is doubtful if the complicated system that has been worked out for manufacturing and mercantile business is necessary or desirable for forests. The simple tax on the stumpage value of forest products corresponds fairly well to a tax on net income and would probably be the best means of applying the business tax principle to the forest. The rate of the yield tax should correspond to the rate of the business tax on other enterprises. Five per cent is suggested as a reasonable rate where circumstances do not indicate the proper rate.

We summarize our plan for the taxation of growing forests as follows :

(1) The law shall provide criteria for determining what is "mature timber."

(2) All trees other than mature timber shall be exempt from taxation, and in assessing land no account should be taken of the value of any trees, except mature timber. Forest lands

shall be assessed no higher than similar bare lands in the neighborhood.

(3) All forest products (with the exception of certain small quantities taken by the owner or the tenant for his own use) shall be subject to a yield tax, at a rate corresponding to the business tax on other businesses. The rate would perhaps ordinarily be in the neighborhood of five per cent. The yield tax should be administered by state officers, and the proceeds ordinarily distributed to the towns or counties.

(4) It is assumed that if there is an individual income tax, forest incomes will be treated exactly like other incomes.

(5) Certain administrative problems will arise, particularly in connection with the yield tax. Since this matter has been fully treated in previous reports and addresses, already referred to, the committee regards further discussion unnecessary. No serious obstacle is to be anticipated.

At two points this plan may require further defense. (1) The old general property tax was defective because (a) by taxing the total value of land and trees it imposed an excessive burden upon the growing forest and (b) it placed on the owner the inconvenient obligation to pay annual taxes for years before any income was realized. The first of these defects is avoided by exempting the trees. The second remains, though greatly reduced. Under all the circumstances it is felt that this inconvenience must be accepted by the forest owner. In return he is guaranteed a reasonable tax burden, made up of a small and fairly certain annual tax on his land and a yield tax at a definite rate.

(2) The chief objection to the yield tax, as already stated, is the irregularity of the resulting revenue. This difficulty is present in the committee's plan. It should be noted, however, that the irregularity resulting from a moderate yield tax (in the neighborhood of five per cent) combined with a steady annual tax on the land is quite different from the result of an exclusive yield tax (at the rate of twenty per cent or thereabouts). If nevertheless this difficulty appears serious, there are ways by which it may be avoided. Six possible methods were suggested by the chairman in his address before the sixth conference, in 1912. It is not necessary to rehearse them here. One of these suggested methods, involving advance annual payments by the owner, to be later deducted with interest from the yield tax, has recently been taken up and skillfully developed by Mr. Murphy of the Forest Service. The committee believes that in most states the irregularity resulting from the yield tax as recommended will not be serious, whereas for any

state which finds this a serious matter there are adequate remedies.

THE TAXATION OF MATURE TIMBER

OUR discussion thus far has related to the growing forest only, with the purpose of devising a method of taxation which shall be equitable to all parties concerned and shall not be an obstacle to the reforestation of cut-over lands or the development of new forests. The mature forest presents quite another problem. We are here dealing with a full grown product. Two cases appear, depending primarily on whether the timber is actually marketable or not. By marketable timber we mean mature timber which is accessible and so located, with respect to market and transportation facilities, that its immediate marketing is possible. Whether it actually is being marketed depends upon the owner's judgment as to the most favorable time. There is nothing in the theory of the property tax to affect adversely marketable mature timber. A property tax fairly drawn and administered with even-handed justice upon all owners of taxable property would give the owner of such mature timber no ground for complaint. Of course the obvious rejoinder is : "there ain't no such animal." This ideally perfect property tax exists only in the imagination. The real property tax, as we know it, is badly drawn and more badly administered. Its application is unequal and unjust. If forests of marketable mature timber are taxed more heavily in proportion to their true value than other classes of wealth, the forest owners have a grievance, but it is in no way different from the grievance of any other property owner, under similar treatment.

On the other hand, when timber is so located that its present marketing is not possible, the situation is in theory similar to that of the growing forest. We have here a form of capital whose income is deferred to the more or less distant future. It is true that the timber is mature, but if other causes beyond the owner's control defer its marketing, the result is the same. It is the fact of the necessarily deferred income, rather than the particular cause of that fact, which makes the annual tax on capital value work injustice. The reasoning in support of this conclusion has been presented heretofore in other reports by the chairman.[2] There are in certain parts of the United States large forest areas containing mature timber whose location is so inaccessible or so remote from markets or transportation

[2] Cf. *Report of the National Conservation Commission*, 1909, Vol. III, pages 611-615 ; Fairchild, "Forest Taxation," *Proceedings National Tax Conference*, 1908.

facilities that its marketing is now and may long continue to be a physical impossibility. To collect from such forest capital an annual property tax, assessed upon the true value from year to year, places an excessive burden upon the owners. This result is inherent in the nature of the property tax and not (as in the case of marketable timber) due to faulty wording or administration of the law.

Careful investigation made ten to fifteen years ago showed that on the whole, forests had not up to that time been taxed excessively. Probably they had, on the whole, been assessed more leniently than other classes of wealth. But it was pointed out at that time that the epoch of lenient taxation was drawing to a close and that heavier and even excessive taxation might be expected in the near future. The past decade has fully justified this prophecy. Tax burdens in general have become enormously heavier, and there is plenty of evidence to show that in the great virgin timber states at least the burden has been increasing more rapidly on timber than on other wealth. The owners of large tracts of mature or virgin timber have reason to be alarmed.

What makes the matter one of public interest is this: The mature forests represent a national resource of vital importance to the well-being of the people. This store of wealth has been gradually built up by nature during many past years. Its utilization has for some time been proceeding more rapidly than its restoration by natural growth and plantation. The store is diminishing and virtual exhaustion may be foreseen in the not distant future. It must be repeated that taxation is not the cause of this condition and that no change in tax methods will materially alter the situation. This is not primarily a tax problem. Taxation becomes a consideration in one way only. If, through the faulty administration of the property tax, mature timber is subjected to an excessive burden of taxes, the owner, already burdened with heavy carrying charges, may find himself forced to market timber before the economical time, suffering loss himself and hastening unduly the depletion of the nation's forest resources.

Of course, by this same token, the forest owner would benefit and the exhaustion of the forests be perhaps retarded by special favors in the way of reduced taxes or entire tax exemption. But this is a program which your committee has refused to consider, standing firmly on its purpose to find a tax system which shall place on forest owners their fair burden of taxation — no more but also no less — as compared with other taxpayers. It is not believed that the public interest as a whole has anything to gain through the granting of special tax favors to this class of taxpayers.

On the other hand, the forest owner is entitled to fair treatment. He has the right to ask two things : (1) that his total tax burden shall not be excessive, as compared with other taxpayers, and (2) that the amounts exacted from him shall not be arbitrary and uncertain. The latter consideration is possibly even more important than the former. It is especially vital to the forest owner whose income may be long deferred, while interest and other expenses run steadily on. There is danger that the just taxation to which the forest owner is entitled may be denied him, either through the inherent defects of the property tax as applied to forests whose cutting is necessarily deferred, or through the assessment of marketable timber at values relatively higher than are placed upon other taxable wealth.

The problem of taxing mature timber has not received the study which has been devoted to the taxation of growing forests, and the solution is not so obvious. The former committee (in 1913) made certain tentative recommendations, while admitting frankly that it was not prepared to say that its plan would fit the conditions in those states of the Pacific coast, the south, and the extreme northeast where the most extensive areas of virgin forest are found and where the problem is most serious. The sub-committee of the National Conservation Congress also made suggestions, likewise somewhat tentative.

In seeking a solution, your committee starts with these principles : (1) Mature timber should be taxed so far as is equitable and possible on a par with other wealth and business. (2) If there is an individual income tax, it should relate to forest income the same as any other income. (3) Where there is a special business tax, it should take the form of a yield tax for forest enterprise. These principles are the same as have been recommended for growing forests and their discussion in that section applies generally here. (4) The property tax as applied to marketable mature forests should be the equivalent of an annual tax upon the land and trees, assessed in the same ratio to true value as prevails for other taxable property in general, and at the same rates as are applied to other wealth. (5) The property tax, when applied to forests of mature timber which will not be marketable till some time in the future, should take account of the fact of deferred income.

It is the practical application of the last two principles which presents the difficult problem. As has been pointed out, the owner of marketable mature timber has no reason to complain if the property tax is applied to his forest on even terms with other kinds of property, but this is not enough for the owner of unmarketable mature timber. Yet the legal separation for taxation of these two classes of mature timber is probably impracticable. There would be too much of personal judgment involved, and disputes and unequal treatment would almost certainly follow. What we must seek is an equitable method of applying the property tax or its equivalent to all mature forests.

From the point of view of the forest owner, the most favorable solution would probably be the pure yield tax, but the pure yield tax will not do, for two reasons at least. (1) The owner of marketable mature timber, who chooses to hold it uncut, for sale in the distant future or as a pleasure park or hunting ground, must not be permitted thus to postpone his tax contribution indefinitely or avoid it altogether. (2) The resulting irregularity of public revenue would be a serious matter, especially in those localities where virgin timber composes a large part of the taxable wealth, these being the very communities where the problem of the taxation of mature timber is most acute. As has been observed heretofore in this report, there are ways of adjusting this irregularity of revenue, but nevertheless the public appears unwilling to take the chance. There are other serious difficulties, both theoretical and practical. We are quite safe in concluding that the pure yield tax is not the solution.

The combination of an annual land tax and a yield tax meets about the same objection. The principal value of a mature forest is in the timber rather than the land. Introduction of the annual land tax, therefore, fails to meet the objections to the pure yield tax. At best it mitigates them slightly.

Taking everything into consideration, your committee is of the opinion that the only practicable solution of the problem of taxing mature forests is to seek to make the property tax as equitable and convenient as may be. In particular every effort should be made to insure a fair assessment of forest property. This means not only an accurate valuation; it requires also that the assessed value of forest property shall not bear a higher ratio to its true value than the prevailing ratio of assessed valuations to true value of all taxable property. Assessment at the hands of a state officer or board would doubtless assure uniformity and certainty in the assessments. There is always the danger, however, that such efficient assessment, by arriving at the true value of forest property, will unjustly burden such property, as compared with other property not so efficiently assessed. Equality in taxation must be real equality, not merely formal.

It is admitted that this solution is more favorable to the forest of marketable timber than to that which is for the present not marketable. But the committee has thus far been unable to discover a practicable means of reconciling this discrepancy. As a matter of fact, the inequality would probably exist more in theory than in practice. It is hardly to be supposed that the assessors would take pains to raise the assessment of unmarketable timber each year, to take account of the approach to the date of cutting, the possibility of this being what makes the property tax unjust to such forests. If the assessors seek honestly to value all mature forests on the same basis as other taxable wealth it is probable that little injustice will be done. If such treatment could be guaranteed, the owners of mature timber would probably have little reason to complain.

QUESTIONS AND PROBLEMS FOR DISCUSSION

1. Why is the severance tax called a privilege, not a property tax?
2. Is it legitimate for the State to use taxation as a method of conserving natural resources?
3. Would you advocate a tax on the production of petroleum for the purpose of raising state (as distinct from federal) revenue?
4. Why is the general property tax not suitable as a method of taxing growing forests? Is it more adaptable to mature timber lands?
5. What may be said for and against the yield tax on forest lands?
6. Does a heavy tax on mature timber land tend to cause its undue depletion?
7. What method of taxation would you advocate for mature forest lands which are not accessible to markets for timber?

SUGGESTIONS FOR RESEARCH

1. The taxation of mineral lands in theory and in practice.
2. The taxation of natural resources in some particular state.
3. The difficulties of harmonizing public and private interests in the taxation of forests.

BIBLIOGRAPHICAL NOTE

A general treatise dealing primarily with the taxation of forests and mines is George Vaughan, "Taxation of Natural Resources," *Proceedings of the National Tax Association,* (1922), pp. 425-447. For a comprehensive study which traces the development of mine taxation in the United States and which compares the various methods of taxing mineral lands, see L. E. Young, *Mine Taxation in the United States,* (University of Illinois, Urbana, 1917). The problem of mine taxation is also discussed by C. R. Howe in, "The

Taxation of Mines and Mineral Properties," *Proceedings of the National Tax Association*, (1927), pp. 353-359. A study of mine taxation, with particular reference to Minnesota, is R. G. Blakey, *Taxation in Minnesota*, (Minneapolis, 1932), Chap. IX. In Chapter VI of this work is given a discussion of forest taxation.

Some of the best material to be had on the subject of forest taxation may be found in the United States Department of Agriculture, *Progress Reports of the Forest Taxation Inquiry*, especially Nos. 2 (1928), 4 (1929), 16 (1932), and 18 (1933), F. R. Fairchild, Director. Other useful studies of forest taxation are : H. H. Chapman, "The Taxation of Forest Property," *Proceedings of the National Tax Association*, (1921), pp. 36-47 ; O. F. Barnes, "Proposed System of Forestry Taxation," *Proceedings of the National Tax Association*, (1922), pp. 143-149 ; E. T. Allen, "Forest Preservation and Its Relation to Public Revenue and Taxation," *Proceedings of the National Tax Association*, (1927), pp. 404-411 ; and F. R. Fairchild, "Forest Taxation in a Cutover Region," *Proceedings of the National Tax Association*, (1927), pp. 367-394.

The *Proceedings of the National Tax Association* (1928), pp. 347-370, contain a number of articles dealing with the problem of taxation and reforestation.

An argument for the gross-production tax on oil properties is presented in Frank Orr, "Taxation of Oil Properties in Oklahoma," *Proceedings of the National Tax Association*, (1920), pp. 36-40.

CHAPTER XV

INCOME TAXATION IN THE UNITED STATES

INCOME taxation, while having its greatest development in the twentieth century, dates back to antiquity. It is now an important form of public revenue in several countries. An outline of the development and principal characteristics of income taxation in the United States, both Federal and state, will be presented in this chapter.

1. DEVELOPMENT AND DESCRIPTION OF THE FEDERAL INCOME TAX *

HISTORY OF THE FEDERAL INCOME TAX

THE first bill providing a Federal income tax in the United States was passed by Congress July 1, 1861. It levied a 3 per cent tax on all monetary incomes above $800. The amount of exemption was subsequently reduced to $600 and a slightly graduated scale adopted. The revenue derived from this tax rose from $2,741,858 in 1863 to $72,982,159 in 1866, after which it gradually decreased until 1877. The original tax law of 1861 expired in 1870, was reenacted for an additional period of two years, and then discontinued. While effective, this income tax yielded nearly 25 per cent of the total internal revenue of the Federal government.

The income tax of 1861 was attacked almost immediately on constitutional grounds; it was held that it was a direct tax not duly "apportioned" as provided in the Constitution of the United States. But in 1880, the Supreme Court of the United States decided that this tax was not a direct tax within the meaning of the Constitution, and so declared it constitutional.[1]

The next attempt to levy a Federal income tax was made in 1894. The tariff law of that year provided for a Federal income tax in addition to various other sources of revenue. The constitutionality of the law was again questioned, and this time the Supreme Court reversed the decision on the Civil War income tax, holding that the tax, in general, was a direct tax and must, therefore, be apportioned according to population.

* From S. H. Patterson and K. W. H. Scholz, *Economic Problems of Modern Life,* (McGraw-Hill Book Co., Inc., New York, 1931), pp. 301-308.

[1] *Springer* vs. *United States,* 102 U. S. 586.

In view of this decision of the Supreme Court of the United States, it became increasingly apparent that a direct Federal income tax could be made possible only by a constitutional amendment. The agitation for such an amendment began in 1909 and continued until the requisite three-fourths of the states finally ratified it in 1913. In spite of this amendment, the constitutionality of that portion of the Federal Revenue Act of 1913 providing for an income tax was contested in the courts. It was contended that the progressive feature of the income tax, classifying taxpayers according to their wealth, was unwarranted, unjust, and unreasonable. The decision [2] of the Supreme Court, however, upheld the law in every respect.

Thus, the Federal income tax, after half a century of attack, criticism, and protest, became an established institution and was incorporated in the Federal revenue system of the United States. For the fiscal year ending June 30, 1929, 58 per cent of the total Federal revenue receipts was derived from individual income and corporation-profit taxes. The accompany-

FEDERAL INCOME AND PROFITS TAXES [3]

1918	$2,852,324,865.89
1919	2,600,783,902.70
1920	3,956,936,003.60
1921	3,228,137,673.75
1922	2,086,918,464.85
1923	1,691,089,534.56
1924	1,841,759,316.80
1925	1,761,659,049.51
1926	1,974,104,141.33
1927	2,219,952,443.72
1928	2,174,573,102.89
1929	2,331,274,428.64
1930	2,410,259,230.28 [4]

ing table indicates the productivity of Federal income and profits taxes since 1918. Chart [A] shows graphically the relative importance of this tax.

PROVISIONS OF THE FEDERAL REVENUE ACTS OF 1926 AND 1928 PERTAINING TO PERSONAL INCOMES [*]

The Tax Rate. As compared with the personal income tax provisions of the Federal revenue acts passed by Congress since 1918, the Revenue Act of 1926 reduced the normal and surtax

[2] *Bushaber* vs. *Union Pacific Railroad*, 240 U. S. 1.
[3] *Annual Report,* Treasurer of the United States, 1929, pp. 8 and 420.
[4] *New York Times,* Aug. 25, 1930.
[*] Eds. note: For changes made by the Revenue Act of 1932, see editors' note at the end of this section.

CHART [A]
Federal Tax Revenue Receipts by Sources

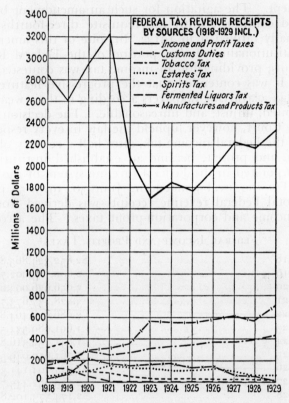

FEDERAL TAX REVENUE RECEIPTS
BY SOURCES (1918-1929 INCL.)
——— Income and Profit Taxes
—·—·— Customs Duties
—··—··— Tobacco Tax
·········· Estates' Tax
––––– Spirits Tax
— — — Fermented Liquors Tax
—×—× Manufactures and Products Tax

rates on individual incomes to their lowest levels since the
World War. The following table, taken from compilations by
actuaries of the Treasury Department, shows how personal income taxes (including both normal and surtaxes) have been
reduced since 1918.

Taxes on Specified Net Incomes up to $100,000 (For Married Men Without Dependents)

Net incomes	Tax under Act of 1918	Tax under Act of 1921	Tax under Act of 1924	Tax under Act of 1926	1926 tax as per cent of 1918 tax
$ 3,000..	$ 60	$ 20	$ 7.50	$ 00.00	0.00
4,000..	120	60	22.50	5.63	4.69
5,000..	180	100	37.80	16.88	9.37
6,000..	250	160	52.50	28.13	11.25

Net incomes	Tax under Act of 1918	Tax under Act of 1921	Tax under Act of 1924	Tax under Act of 1926	1926 tax as per cent of 1918 tax
8,000..	530	340	105.00	56.25	10.61
10,000..	830	520	165.00	101.25	11.91
15,000..	1,670	1,060	515.00	311.25	18.64
20,000..	2,630	1,720	975.00	618.75	23.53
30,000..	4,930	3,520	2,275.00	1,778.75	36.08
40,000..	7,730	5,840	3,995.00	3,198.75	41.38
50,000..	11,030	8,640	6,095.00	4,878.75	44.23
60,000..	14,830	11,940	8,635.00	6,798.75	45.84
70,000..	19,130	15,740	11,535.00	8,958.75	46.83
80,000..	23,930	20,040	14,835.00	11,258.75	47.04
90,000..	29,230	24,840	18,495.00	13,658.75	46.73
100,000..	35,030	30,140	22,575.00	16,058.75	45.84

The Federal Revenue Act of 1926 provided for a reduction of the normal tax rates from 2 to 1½ per cent on the first $4,000 of net taxable income ; from 4 to 3 per cent on the next $4,000 ; and from 6 to 5 per cent on the remainder of the net taxable income.[5] Surtaxes which, under the Revenue Act of 1924 progressed up to 40 per cent of the net income in excess of $500,-000, were scaled down to a maximum of 20 per cent on net incomes in excess of $100,000.

Under the Revenue Act of 1924, net incomes in excess of $100,000 and not exceeding $200,000 were subject to a surtax rate of 37 per cent.   Thus, a maximum surtax rate, which under the 1924 Revenue Act pertained only to net taxable incomes exceeding $500,000, now applies to all net taxable incomes above $100,000, although the rate has been halved. Consequently, persons with net taxable incomes of $1,000,000, who under the Revenue Act of 1924 were required to pay approximately 43 per cent of their net income to the Federal government in the form of normal and surtaxes, under the present revenue act must pay only 24 per cent of this income.   This represents a reduction of no less than 43 per cent of Federal income taxes for a specified tax period on personal incomes of $1,000,000.

On the other hand, the corresponding reductions on net incomes between $30,000 and $60,000 are only about 20 per cent.   It may, of course, be contended that heretofore persons with relatively smaller incomes were not bearing their proportionate share of the Federal tax burden.   But a compari-

[5] By special act of Congress, the normal tax rate on the first $4000 of net taxable income was reduced to one-half of 1 per cent for the year 1929, in view of the large accumulated surplus in the United States Treasury.

son between the surtax rates in the Revenue Act of 1924 and those in the Act of 1926 shows that the present rates of Federal taxes on personal incomes very definitely favor persons of large means. The reductions in rates of surtaxes appear somewhat at variance with the "faculty" principle of taxation.

Not only have normal and surtax rates been reduced under the Revenue Act of 1926 and continued under the 1928 Revenue Act, as compared with those provided in Federal tax laws since 1918, but the amount of personal exemption has also been increased. Single persons may claim an exemption of $1500 (formerly $1000) and married persons, living with husband or wife, are allowed $3500 personal exemption, (formerly $2500). In addition, a personal credit of $400 may be claimed by the taxpayer for each dependent (children under 18 years of age and others depending for their chief support upon the taxpayer).

It has been estimated that, as a result of the increase in personal exemptions, about 2,300,000 individuals who formerly paid Federal income taxes are now relieved of such taxes. Relief from taxes and tax reductions are always popular with the average taxpayer. The fact that the Federal Revenue Act of 1926 reduced personal income taxes "all along the line" has, in most circles, forestalled adverse criticism of the lower surtax rates, which favor primarily persons with large incomes.

Distinction between Earned and Unearned Income. The Federal Revenue Act of 1924 was the first Federal tax law which attempted to differentiate between "earned" and "unearned" incomes for purposes of taxation. The theoretical basis for drawing this distinction is the principle of "equality of sacrifice." Theoretically, it requires effort to acquire an earned income, while unearned incomes are assumed to have been obtained by their recipients without effort on their part.

The theoretical justification for distinguishing between earned and unearned incomes for purposes of taxation can scarcely be questioned, but the practical application of the principle involves difficulties. How is earned income as distinct from unearned income to be ascertained? The Revenue Act of 1924 [6] defines earned income to mean "wages, salaries, professional fees, and other amounts received as compensation for personal services actually rendered. . . If the taxpayer's net income is not more than $5,000, his entire net income shall be considered to be earned net income, and if his net income is more than $5,000 his earned net income shall be considered to be less than $5,000." The same clause is contained in the

---

[6] Sec. 209, 1.

Revenue Act of 1928, with the further provision that in no case shall earned net income be considered to be more than $30,000 (in the 1924 Revenue Act this maximum was $10,000). The Revenue Act of 1928 [7] allows a further credit of 25 per cent on the tax on earned incomes, in addition to all credits against the tax under previous revenue acts.

The theoretical distinction between earned and unearned income cannot be claimed to be the practical basis for the differentiation in the Federal revenue law between these two classes of incomes. For tax purposes, all net incomes of $5000 or less, regardless of source, are considered as having been earned, and no net incomes exceeding $30,000 are regarded as earned incomes. Thus, the distinction between earned incomes and unearned incomes, made in the present income tax law, is applied in a somewhat arbitrary manner. Not until incomes for tax purposes are definitely classified with reference to their origin or source, (such as incomes derived from labor services, from capital investments, from land, from gifts, and the like), as is done in the income-tax laws of various European countries, notably Great Britain and Germany, can an adequate distinction be drawn between earned and unearned incomes for purposes of taxation.

Concept of Net Taxable Income. The present Federal income-tax law provides that all citizens of the United States and all persons residing in the United States whose gross incomes are $5000 or over, regardless of the amount of their net income, or whose net incomes are $1500 (or over) if single, or $3500 (or over) if married and living with husband or wife, shall make returns of their incomes with the Collector of Internal Revenue, not later than the fifteenth of March of each year.

To arrive at net taxable income for tax purposes, certain items, such as interest paid on personal loans, taxes paid other than Federal income taxes, losses of property by fire, storm, shipwreck, theft not compensated for by insurance, uncollectible debts and contributions or gifts made within the taxable year to organized religious, charitable, scientific, literary, or educational institutions are deductible from gross income. The reason for allowing these deductions is to arrive at the net money income of the taxpayer, representing his increased net claim to the social product realized during a definite tax period.

It is this net money income which constitutes the taxpayer's taxable income. In order to relieve the recipients of small taxable incomes of the burden of direct Federal taxation, specific personal exemptions are allowed, before arriving at the net

7 Sec. 31b.

income subject to the Federal income tax. The distinction between net taxable income and net income subject to tax should be carefully noted in this connection.

CORPORATION INCOME-TAX LEGISLATION

NOT only have individual net incomes been subject to Federal income taxes since 1913, but corporate incomes also have been taxed. As early as 1909, an "excise tax" on corporations, measured by net corporate profits, was imposed by the Federal government. This tax yielded on an average of $32,000,000 annually while in force.

When the individual income tax law was passed in 1913, the corporation income tax, in the form of a tax on net corporate profits, was incorporated in the law. In March, 1917, the corporation income-tax law was expanded to include a tax on so-called "excess profits" of corporations, and on Oct. 3, 1917, was superseded by the War Revenue Act, which levied war excess-profits taxes on incomes not only of corporations, but also of individuals and of partnerships. As war fiscal measures, the war-profits and excess-profits taxes were very successful. The combined yield of corporate income and excess-profits taxes in the calendar year 1917 was nearly $3,000,000,000, and in 1918 over $4,000,000,000. The various war-profits and excess-profits taxes were repealed in January, 1921, but net corporate incomes of business corporations were subjected to a uniform annual rate of 12½ per cent, which was increased to 13 per cent under the Revenue Act of 1926, but lowered to 12 per cent under the Revenue Act of 1928.[*]

In the Federal income-tax legislation enacted since 1913, there appears to be an attempt made to treat corporations, partnerships, and individuals alike. The legal interpretation that a corporation functions as a "natural person," is retained in the Federal income-tax law. Thus, the term "person" is defined in the Revenue Act[8] of 1926 to mean "an individual, a trust or estate, a partnership, or a corporation."

However, in the sense in which the concept income is applicable to individuals, it is impossible to apply it to corporations without considerable confusion of thought. Individuals have net monetary incomes which they can employ either to purchase present enjoyments or gratifications, or save for the future. Corporations, on the other hand, are legal entities, creations of the state, ultimately benefiting individuals, who

---

[*] Eds. note: For changes made by the Revenue Act of 1932, see editors' note at the end of this section.

[8] Sec. 2.

derive incomes from them; and as such artificial legal creations, the psychological significance of income to individuals,
a flow of commodities or services to gratify human desires,
is inapplicable to them. Corporations have receipts, expenditures, profits, and losses, the title to which is ultimately vested
in individuals, as is evidenced by the securities they hold.

Specific exemptions and progressive rates of taxation, levied
on net incomes of corporations, have no relationship in principle to similar provisions as to individual net incomes. One
corporation, having net profits in any one year of $100,000,
may distribute these among a few individuals of large means.
Another, with precisely the same net profits for the same taxing
period, may apportion these among several hundred stockholders of moderate means. To allow the same exemptions
and impose the same rates of taxes on both net corporate incomes is unjust. This inequity is only in part offset by the
graduated scale of surtaxes on personal incomes, and with
every further reduction in surtax rates becomes more pronounced.

Certain practical difficulties in the administration of a corporation profits or income tax must also be borne in mind.
How is the net profit or net income of a corporation to be
determined? If figured on invested capital, how is the amount
of invested capital to be ascertained? No uniformity in accounting systems exists at present, which would make possible
an accurate comparison of "net incomes" of different enterprises for tax purposes. The tax on net earnings of corporations has been characterized as follows: [9]

To avoid serious inequality and evasion the tax on net earnings
would require for administration a thorough examination into the
accounts of every corporation taxed, together with strict rules how
these accounts should be kept. . . It would be a continual source of
irritations between the corporation and the taxing officials. . . The
practical difficulties in the way of imposing a tax on net earnings
seem overwhelming.

The economic consequences of heavy taxes on corporate
earnings should also be noted. It has been estimated that
possibly 10 to 15 per cent of the annual capital formation in
the United States results from the direct reinvestment of corporate earnings. To the extent that these earnings, rather
than personal incomes, are absorbed by taxes, they are not
directly available for reinvestment in private corporate enter-

[9] The *Report* of the Special Commission on Taxation of Corporations, State
of Connecticut, 1913.

prises. The net loss in production resulting from such curtailment of capital formation may cause considerable hardship
to certain classes of consumers.

In view of both theoretical and practical objections to taxes
on net earnings of corporations, it is debatable whether they
will form a permanent part of the Federal revenue system.
From the point of view of the government, they have been
very productive, but they are inequitable, for they impose an
unequal burden on industrial enterprise. Moreover, they can
be evaded by an undue increase of many items of expenditures,
salaries, reserves for depreciation, concealed investments and
the like. As stated above, the income tax has been introduced
as a permanent feature of our Federal tax system. It should
now be established on sound economic principles and should
further clarify the concept of income in its application to tax
legislation.

Eds. note: Professor R. G. Blakey and Gladys C. Blakey, in *American Economic Review*, Vol. XXII, p. 622, give the changes which the Act of 1932
made in the Federal income tax. These changes are presented below.

The personal exemptions for individuals in the 1932 law are: $1000 for
single persons; $2500 for husband and wife, and $400 for each dependent. In
the 1928 law these are $1500, $3500, and $400, respectively.

The normal rates on net incomes of individuals under the 1932 law are 4
per cent on the first $4000 above exemptions and 8 per cent on the remainder.
In the 1928 law the rates are: 1½ per cent on the first $4000; 3 per cent on
the second $4000; and 5 per cent on the remainder.

A credit of 25 per cent is allowed in the case of "earned" incomes by the
laws of 1924, 1926, and 1928, but this credit is eliminated from the 1932 law.

Surtax rates in the new law begin at 1 per cent on parts of income in
excess of $6000 and increase by steps of 1 per cent on each $2000 bracket of
income until they reach 47 per cent on the $98,000 to $100,000 bracket. Thence
the brackets increase in size and the maximum rate of 55 per cent is reached
on amounts of net income in excess of $1,000,000. In the 1928 law, surtax
rates begin at 1 per cent on parts of net income in excess of $10,000 and
reach a maximum of 20 per cent on amounts in excess of $100,000. In other
words, the 1932 act provides for a maximum of 63 per cent (8 per cent
normal and 55 per cent surtax) upon parts of individual net income in
excess of $1,000,000 as compared with 25 per cent (5 per cent normal and
20 per cent surtax) in the 1928 act.

Lower personal exemptions; the elimination of the "earned" income credit;
decreases in allowable deductions, especially for security losses; and the tightening of administrative provisions, all tend to increase the income taxes even
more than is indicated by the changes in rates.

The corporation income tax rate is changed from 12 per cent to 13¾
per cent. If a consolidated return is filed for affiliated corporations, the
tax is to be 14½ per cent for 1932 and 1933. The exemption of $3000 allowed
by the 1928 law to corporations with net incomes of $25,000 or less is left out
of the 1932 law.

2. DEVELOPMENT AND DESCRIPTION OF STATE
INCOME TAXES *

HISTORICAL

FORERUNNERS of income taxation in the commonwealths of the United States may be found in the "ability" or "faculty" taxes used in several of the American colonies. Some of the older laws included certain classes of income with property in an attempt to tax the sources of income which could not be reached under property tax laws. Others attempted to reach income of certain professions and trades in order to reach a class of taxpayers who were escaping under the prevailing tax systems. Little success was achieved with the income tax by the states until 1911 when Wisconsin entered the field with a law which was a success from the first. Taxation on the basis of income had been tried in Massachusetts, the Carolinas, New Hampshire, Oklahoma and Delaware prior to 1911. The tax in Virginia and the Carolinas has a long history but failed to develop strength on account of ineffective administration. Mississippi enacted an income tax law in 1912, modelled in part after the Oklahoma Act of 1907 and the South Carolina law of 1902. In 1915, Connecticut passed a law taxing corporations which was modelled after the federal income tax law. In 1917, four states entered the field imposing laws on the basis of net income ; Montana passed a license tax on mercantile and manufacturing corporations measured by net income, Missouri a tax on persons and manufacturing and business corporations, New York a franchise tax on mercantile and manufacturing corporations, and Massachusetts a partial income tax reaching certain classes of income. In 1921 Delaware enacted a law taxing persons on their entire net income, and North Carolina, after adopting a necessary constitutional amendment, passed a general income tax law better adapted to modern conditions. In 1923, New Hampshire passed a law placing a tax on the income of intangibles, and Tennessee imposed an excise tax measured by net income on manufacturing and mercantile corporations. Mississippi modified its law in 1924, making it a general income tax law and bringing it into line with the more modern developments of income taxation. In 1929, four states passed income tax laws : Arkansas enacted a general income tax law ; California an excise on financial, mercantile and manufacturing corporations ; Oregon

---

* From *State Income Taxes*, (National Industrial Conference Board, New York, 1930), Vol. II, Chap. XIV.

a personal income tax and an excise tax on mercantile, financial, and manufacturing corporations and income from intangibles ; and Washington an excise tax on financial corporations. It is thus seen that the period from 1911 to the present has shown a decided tendency for the states to incorporate into their tax systems some form of taxation on the basis of net income. . .

In general, one or more of the following motives have influenced state legislatures in the adoption of income taxes : (1) to tap a new source of revenue, (2) to equalize the burden as between a property-owning class and a non-property-owning class possessing taxpaying ability, (3) to introduce into the tax system a more accurate method of ascertaining ability to pay taxes, (4) to reach intangible property which could not be successfully taxed under existing property tax laws, (5) to introduce conveniently a progressive element of taxation into rates of the tax system, (6) to tax national banks in compliance with Section 5219 of the Revised Statutes of the United States, and (7) to reach the income of property which could not be taxed otherwise because impliedly prohibited by the Federal Constitution or expressly forbidden by the federal law.

BASIS OF ASSESSMENT AND LEVY OF INCOME TAXES

A VARIETY of conditions exists among the states in the scope of the levy and assessment of personal income taxes. The tax is imposed in three states on residents on the entire net income from within and without the state ; in nine states, on residents. on income from sources within and without the state and on non-residents on income derived from within the state ; in one state, on certain forms of income received by residents ; in two states, on the income from intangibles received by residents ; and in one state only on income derived from within the state by residents.

All taxes in which net income determines the amount to be paid are in this study included under the heading of income tax, although the tax may have been imposed on the right or privilege of doing business. The legislative characterization of a tax as a franchise, excise, or income tax is not always conclusive as to its nature when a question of constitutionality is raised in the courts. The legislatures of some of the states have probably been influenced to enact the tax on business in the form of an excise to avoid state constitutional restrictions growing out of the rule of uniformity, and complications arising out of the commerce clause of the Federal Constitution. Although the income tax laws have been attacked on the ground of violating the uniformity clauses of the state constitutions, in nearly all cases the laws were upheld. The commerce clause of the Federal Constitution protects interstate commerce from tax burdens imposed by the states. It has been established by a decision of the United States Supreme Court that a tax on net income of a domestic corporation which includes net income derived from transactions in interstate commerce does not contravene the commerce clause, but it has been held in a later case that an attempt by a state to impose an excise tax on the net income of a foreign corporation which transacts only an interstate business does violate the commerce clause of the Federal Constitution.

Until a more recent decision of the United States Supreme Court, many believed that income from tax-exempt securities could be reached by imposing a tax upon the right to do business, the amount of the tax to be determined by the net income including the interest from tax-exempt securities, but the Court has declared such a law unconstitutional as an attempt to circumvent the prohibition against a direct tax on exempt income.

EXEMPTIONS AND DEDUCTIONS

COMPENSATION received by federal employees and officials and interest on the obligations of the Federal Government are exempt from state income tax laws. Early decisions of the United States Supreme Court laid down the rule that the Federal Constitution impliedly prohibits the state or the Federal Government from taxing the governmental instrumentalities of the other. The reasoning of the Court in these decisions was that a dual system of government, such as ours, cannot exist if one of the co-sovereignties possesses the power to embarrass or destroy the other by means of taxation.

The existence of exempt income interferes with the use of income as a measure of the taxpayer's ability to pay or as a relative measure of his obligation to the state. It is unlikely that this situation can be remedied at present, since the remedy depends upon an amendment to the constitution for which there is little support. Further extension of tax-exempt income may be prevented in certain cases, if the courts construe the income derived from the increasing governmental proprietary activities as taxable the same as in the case of a private agency.

The states generally exempt income from state and local securities from the income tax, and it is difficult to avoid this procedure since each state is in competition with other states as well as with the Federal Government for a market for its securities.

The state income tax laws are similar to the federal income tax law in expressly exempting certain receipts resulting from capital transfers from the category of taxable income, such as the proceeds of life insurance policies, workmen's compensation awards and damages for injuries. While the laws purport to tax only income, and not capital transfers, such capital transfers are generally expressly exempted in order to clear away any possible misconstruction by the taxpayers and courts.

The states are divided in their requirements for taxing interest on savings deposits. The prevailing practice is to make such income taxable. The motives for exempting income from savings are: (1) to encourage savings by taxpayers of small income, (2) to encourage capital to remain in the state or to prevent it from migrating to a competing state. When income is used as a relative measure of the individual's obligation to support the state, the omission of any portion of the taxpayer's income interferes with the proper spread of the burden. This becomes an economic problem for the individual state to solve for itself, guided by existing conditions.

Nearly all the personal tax laws provide for the exemption of a certain amount of net income, the exact amount in each case depending upon the marital status and number of dependents supported by the taxpayer. The factors which influence the amount of personal exemption in the various states are: (1) the level of income within the state, (2) convenience of administration, (3) yield, (4) minimum of health and comfort, and (5) uniformity. The evidence points towards no substantial increase in personal exemptions in the near future. There was a tendency for the states adopting income tax laws after the Federal Government entered the field to use the same exemption in order to simplify the administration of the tax, but most of the states have been unable to follow the Federal Government in increasing the exemptions.

Opinion is divided on the question of whether personal exemptions should be lowered or raised. Some favor reduction of the exemptions because they believe (1) that the tax could be made more productive, since there is considerable ability to pay a tax which is not reached under present exemptions, and (2) that a direct income tax is instrumental in bringing home to citizens the obligation to the state in which they are domiciled and therefore should reach as many as possible. On the other hand, there are those who argue (1) that any further lowering of the exemption in certain states would impinge upon the amount of income necessary to support a family in health and decency, and (2) that the cost of administering the tax on the lower incomes would be prohibitive. It is difficult to reach any general conclusion as to the merits of these arguments, since so much depends upon a careful analysis of the conditions prevailing in the particular state in question. However, legislation and current opinion seem to run generally against further increasing the personal exemptions in the states.

A study and comparison of the principal deductions from gross income under the state income tax laws indicate that the states have been influenced by the federal law, which has likewise been followed in the definition of net taxable income. A few of the states have followed the federal law in disallowing interest on the obligations incurred in purchasing tax-exempt securities, but this precaution seems to be more a matter of imitation, since little avoidance of the tax could be accomplished under the low rates prevailing under state laws. Little uniformity exists in the allowance for the deduction of taxes. No state allows the deduction of taxes which tend to increase the value of the property, such as special assessments. Four states allow all other taxes, but among the remaining states various combinations are to be found. The uneven effects produced in the yields have led some states to disallow the deduction of income taxes.

The states follow the federal law generally in the allowance of deductions for losses incurred in connection with the taxpayer's business, losses incurred outside the business venture for profit, and losses resulting from casualties.

The reduction of taxable income by allowing the taxpayers to deduct contributions for educational, charitable and religious purposes follows an old precedent. The disposition to exempt these activities is based upon their widely-recognized social value to the people in general. However, these allowances are looked upon with disfavor by some of the advocates of the ability theory, since they interfere with the use of income as a measure of the relative burden of the tax. The states are far from uniform in providing for allowances for contributions. Six of the states follow the federal law in allowing deductions for both general welfare organizations and governmental bodies, but two of these limit the deductions to 10% of the net income without the benefit of the deduction. Among the other states a variety of provisions exist, some allowing no deductions of any kind.

The most prevalent method of treating dividends under the state income tax laws is to require the taxpayers to report all dividends as gross income and then to allow the deductions of dividends received from corporations subject to an income tax of the state imposing the tax. This practice is based upon the theory that unjust double taxation results if the income which is the measure of the tax of the corporation also serves as an indication of the ability of the stockholder to pay an income tax. In all the states except New York, dividends taxed under the same act are deductible. In New York the tax on corporations on the basis of net income is considered an impersonal tax, the same as a tax on real estate, and is therefore distinguished from a personal income tax. The Committees of the National Tax Association on a Model Plan have recommended that dividends be taxed in the hands of individuals, on the ground that the individual should be taxed on the basis of his entire ability to pay without reference to the source of the income, and that the tax paid by business be regarded as its contribution to the government for its protection or benefits received, but this recommendation is contingent upon the adoption of the Model Plan by all the states as a complete tax system. It is frequently overlooked that, under the prevailing plan of deducting dividends, inequities of burden result from the use of different types of rates for corporations and individuals, and the question may very well be raised whether the present plan does not result in greater inequity of burden than taxing all dividends in the hands of individuals at a rate that is uniform in its application.

COLLECTION AND ENFORCEMENT OF THE TAX

An objection is sometimes raised to the use of the income tax by the states on the ground of the legal difficulties of collection and enforcement. Under the existing state income tax laws, this objection cannot be said to be serious. It is only occasionally and with regard to certain types of income that any question arises. The question of whether a state may tax the interest paid to a non-resident creditor by a resident debtor has been seriously questioned on principle, but the rule is fairly well settled that only the state in which the creditor is domiciled can tax such income.

The states have very generally followed the federal law in requiring information at the source, which has, generally speaking, proved effective in the collection of the state income taxes. New York is the only state which requires withholding at the source, and this is used only in the case of non-residents.

DOUBLE TAXATION RESULTING FROM OVERLAPPING
JURISDICTIONS

ONE of the most serious handicaps in the use of the income tax by the states is the economic conflicts which arise because of overlapping jurisdictions. Although only twenty of the states, not all of which are contiguous, tax persons or corporations on the basis of net income, these difficulties are already becoming apparent. Many of the inequities arise out of the lack of uniformity in the income tax laws of the different states. As the number of states adopting income taxes increases these conflicts will multiply, and a situation comparable to that when the inheritance tax spread throughout the states will ensue, unless remedial measures are introduced. One of the most perplexing problems arises out of the fact that part of the states tax residents on their entire net income and also non-residents on income earned within the state, while other states tax residents on their entire net income from within and without the state but do not tax non-residents on income earned within the state. Still others tax residents on income earned within the state only. Numerous inequities of burden arise out of the conditions produced by these different methods of imposing the tax. Uniformity in method of taxation among the states would solve most of the problems of inequity of burden, but the economic conflict between the debtor and creditor states stands in the way of uniformity. The debtor states refuse to surrender the revenues derived from income earned within the state by non-residents, while the creditor states refuse to give up the revenues from income earned without the state by their own residents. The only method of escape from this difficulty for which there is any precedent lies in the direction of state reciprocity. Each state has its own peculiar economic problem to solve, but nevertheless it will find it necessary to cooperate with other states in arriving at some arrangement to avoid the most serious conflicts. The experience of the states in reciprocity agreements with respect to state inheritance taxes points to this method of procedure in dealing with state income taxes.

In the taxation of corporations, inequity of burden arises principally out of the variety of methods of allocation of income in effect in the different states. Some of the states favor a special accounting by the individual business to show what income is earned within the state; others apportion income in whole or in part by a mathematical formula. At the present time, some combination of eight or more factors is used

in constructing these formulas, although sales, tangible property and expenses are the three most frequently used. It is
vital to the success of the corporation income tax that a uniform method of allocation or accounting be worked out and
agreed upon by the income tax states.

RATE STRUCTURE

ALL the states imposing a personal income tax use progressive
rate schedules, except Missouri and New Hampshire. The
effective rates in Missouri are slightly progressive owing to the
personal exemption or abatement. Otherwise, little uniformity exists among the states in rate structure. All the states
imposing a personal income tax, except Missouri, Massachusetts, New Hampshire, and Tennessee, use graduated rates.
The number of steps or brackets in the graduation of income
for rate purposes ranges from three in New York to twelve
in Wisconsin; Georgia has adopted the graduation of the federal law. The highest effective rate on persons is in effect in
Georgia, where the rate on a net income of one million dollars
or more is one-third that of the federal income tax, or 8.34%,
and the next highest is found in Wisconsin, where the effective rate is 6.96% on a similar income. The lowest rate (1%)
on net incomes of one million dollars or more is found in
Missouri. Progressive rates on the income of individuals are
ordinarily explained on two different grounds. First, a progressive rate is more productive than a flat rate, since a flat
rate sufficiently high to produce substantial revenue would
be an excessive burden on small incomes and would tend to
destroy the source of the tax, while it would bear less heavily
on the higher incomes. A second ground is that income is
regarded as the best measure of personal capacity to share the
burden of a tax and that this capacity increases as the amount
of income increases.

Massachusetts is the only state which now makes any distinction between funded or "unearned" income and unfunded
or "earned" income, although the distinction was more recently introduced into the federal income tax law.

The states have looked unfavorably upon this distinction in
rate structure, presumably because (1) the heavy real property
levies of the state and localities do in effect place a heavier
burden upon funded income in addition to the income
tax, and (2) experience has shown that this differentiation
complicates the rate structure and renders the administration
more difficult.

Only two states, Mississippi and Wisconsin, have applied progressive rates to the net income of corporations. In other states, flat rates, ranging from 1% in Missouri to 5% in Oregon, are in effect. Where the same progressive rates are used for corporations and individuals, it is not possible to shift from one form of business organization to another to avoid the tax, but the use of progressive rates for corporations cannot be justified on any theoretical basis. The use of moderate flat rates by the different states prevents certain inequities of burden which result from overlapping jurisdictions. Low flat rates may also in certain cases prevent the migration of an industry from one state to another. In a few of the states a minimum tax has been engrafted upon the income taxes. This provision not only furnishes a compromise between the two leading theories underlying the business tax, but also prevents extreme fluctuations in revenues between poor and prosperous years.

The allowance of an offset of property taxes paid against the income tax, usually spoken of as the "property offset," has been tried and abandoned in Missouri, North Dakota, Mississippi and Wisconsin. In 1929, California, Oregon and Washington introduced the "property offset" into their tax laws. A number of objections have been raised to the use of such an offset: (1) it reduces the yield or wipes it out without materially reducing the cost of administration; (2) it interferes with the application of the progressive income tax rates; (3) it leads the taxpayer to attempt to change the classification of property when the taxpayer is allowed to offset the taxes on one class of property only; (4) its use permits evasion of the tax by the property owner who pays no income tax. However, the inclusion of the offset in the initial law has probably aided in its adoption by preventing the placing of a heavier tax burden on property. In California, Oregon, and Washington, it serves to equalize the burden between national banks and other corporations subject to the income tax, since national banks cannot be compelled by the states to pay a personal property tax. It also serves to lighten the burden for corporations paying both a property tax and an income tax.

The income tax rates can be conveniently adjusted to meet the fluctuations in the demand for revenues. The experience of the states has demonstrated that rates can be easily changed by merely providing that a flat percentage of the tax, as calculated under the existing schedules, be added or subtracted. However, this method results in flattening out the progression. Wisconsin has reduced the flattening-out effect by increasing the rates in the schedule on incomes above a fixed minimum.

THE ADMINISTRATION OF INCOME TAXES

THE great majority of the income tax states have centralized the tax administration in a state tax commission or a tax commissioner. However, there is found a variation among the states from almost complete decentralization to practically complete centralization. The experience of the states points emphatically to centralized administration as the most successful method. In some of the more populous states, such as New York, the administration has been localized with a view to bringing the administration closer to the taxpayers, but the authority of the local administration flows from the Tax Commission.

Income is a broad base and involves technical and complicated questions of accounting, economics and law, calling for an intelligent, trained, and experienced personnel. A combination of all these qualities can seldom be found in locally-elected tax officials. Moreover, a uniformity of action is required which cannot be secured in a decentralized system. Several of the states select their employees under civil service rules, and, according to the testimony of tax officials in these states, the results have been gratifying.

The cost of administering the income taxes in the various states for which cost figures are available compares favorably with that of other taxes requiring technicians of a high order. The modal cost for the income tax in general, as estimated in the various states, falls between 2.5% and 3% of the collections. There is a tendency for the cost of collection to decrease in the individual states, especially as the amount of collections increases. The cost of administering the corporation income taxes is much lower than that for the personal income tax, which may be attributed to the larger incomes returned by corporations.

The experiences of South Carolina, Connecticut and Georgia throw light on the much discussed question of harmonizing the state and federal income tax laws. In these states almost complete uniformity with the federal law was required by law. South Carolina experienced difficulty in ascertaining the amount of additional assessments levied by the Federal Government, and the law was repealed. In Connecticut and Georgia, the amount of revenue which can be collected is to a large extent dependent upon the action of Congress, over which the state alone has practically no control. However, the difficulties experienced by these states do not disprove the value of uniformity between the state and federal laws, for there are many features which can be made uniform with beneficial effects on the administration of both the federal and state laws without tying up too closely with the federal law. The numerous cases arising under the federal law for interpretation aid in the clarification of the state laws when they are the same, and such uniformity would greatly aid the taxpayer by eliminating many of the divergent and conflicting provisions arising under the two sets of laws. Moreover, a state report based upon the federal report should be of considerable aid to those states which do not have an adequate office staff to give the reports a thorough examination.

DISTRIBUTION AND FINANCIAL RESULTS

DIFFERENT methods of distribution of the proceeds of the income taxes are used to meet certain fiscal and political exigencies within the states. The most common method is for the state government to retain the proceeds to be used in meeting its expenses. From an administrative standpoint, this method is simplest. Another method in use is to distribute a portion of the proceeds to the localities from which the returns are received, the remainder going to the state. If this method is used without further safeguarding, it may lead to undue accumulation of revenues in certain wealthy communities. Still another plan is to distribute the proceeds to the localities on the basis of assessed value of property. Real property alone has been used in some instances, while in others total real and personal property was made the basis of distribution. The outstanding advantage claimed for this method is its effect in raising the valuation of property for property tax purposes. In some states, the proceeds have been distributed on the basis of school population. None of the above methods can be said to fit into the tax systems and fiscal policies of all the states. The method of distribution is a problem peculiar to the conditions existing within a particular state when the income tax is introduced.

The state income tax has not been used by any state as a major source of revenue for either state or local purposes. However, income tax receipts form an increasing proportion of the total state and local tax receipts, as well as the revenue used for carrying on the state government. It is significant that a number of the states are collecting substantial revenues from income taxes, notwithstanding the fact that the Federal Government levies high rates and derives the major amount of its revenues from this source. If the federal rates are substantially lowered, the states may be encouraged to avail themselves of this method of raising revenues to a greater extent that in the past. As the demands for revenue continue to increase and the states face the inadequacy of their present sources of revenue, it seems reasonable to expect that they will turn to the income tax. Certainly the income tax can now be said to be beyond the purely experimental stage as an effective method of raising revenues. As already noted, the revival of the income tax was made possible by efficient centralized administration. In this connection, it is significant to note that in general the best financial results have been obtained in the states with well-organized administration.

THE BURDEN OF THE STATE INCOME TAX

THE theory is now widely accepted that the burden of a general income tax ordinarily rests upon the taxpayer upon whom the tax is first imposed. The question of the escape from a state income tax by an individual or business unit narrows itself down largely to a question of residence or location. For instance, an individual wage earner may find himself in a state having an income tax to which he is subject. Assuming that he could find work in another state, otherwise equally satisfactory, where no income tax was levied, he would be influenced to change his domicile. A similar situation arises in connection with a business. The choice of a location of a business may turn upon the existence of an income tax within the state. If the choice of location was between two states, one imposing a substantial income tax in addition to a property tax and the other imposing a property tax as its principal tax on business, other conditions being equal, the business would locate in the state levying only the property tax. It should not be overlooked that the total tax differential is the important consideration and that the income tax is only one factor in this. Moreover, it should be kept constantly in mind that tax differentiation is only one of the factors entering into the determination of the location of industry.

When an income tax is introduced into a state under certain conditions, it may result in lightening the relative burden of the agricultural classes. This would be true if all or a part of the receipts went to defray the expenses of state government, supplanting a corresponding levy on property for state purposes. This is explained by the fact that the per capita farm cash income is lower than that of the urban populations, and therefore is relieved to a greater extent by the exemptions as well as by the fact that the smaller incomes fall within the lower brackets of a progressive rate structure.

Both state and federal income taxes are sometimes referred to as class taxes because they reach a relatively small percentage of the population, but it does not follow that a state income tax is discriminatory. The states use the income tax generally as a supplementary or special tax, and in order to determine whether it rests with inequitable burden upon certain classes, the effect of the tax system as a whole must be studied. A number of arguments have been advanced for introducing an income tax into a state tax system : (1) the income tax reaches a class of taxpayers who would otherwise pay little or nothing to the support of government, (2) it lends itself to the graduation of rates, (3) with the use of higher rates on the higher incomes, the tendency of the burden of other taxes to bear with undue weight upon the smaller incomes is overcome to a certain extent, and (4) the income tax draws upon a surplus fund arising from community earnings which can be diverted to government use with the least sacrifice.

QUESTIONS AND PROBLEMS FOR DISCUSSION

1. Should a distinction be made between unearned and earned income for taxation purposes?
2. Is there any justification for taxing the income of corporations as business institutions if the income of other forms of business organization is not taxed?
3. Why are most income tax rates progressive?
4. Is it unfair double taxation to have one's income taxed by both the national and state governments?
5. What are the objections to an offset of property taxes against an income tax?
6. Should the proceeds from a state income tax be used for any special purpose, *e.g.*, educational support?
7. Do you believe that the cost of national emergency measures, such as the relief of distress, should be paid ultimately out of receipts from income taxes?
8. Discuss the income tax in light of the canons of equity and economy in taxation.
9. Should the revenue from state income taxes be used for some particular purpose (education for example) or should it be used to cover the general expenditures of the state?

SUGGESTIONS FOR RESEARCH

1. The nature and extent of present state income taxes in the United States.
2. A comparison of the nature and extent of income taxes in leading countries.

3. An evaluation of methods of distribution of the proceeds of income taxes.
4. An evaluation of the bases of assessment and levy of state income taxes.
5. The need of and means to greater uniformity in state income taxation.
6. The economic effects of state income taxes.
7. Administrative problems of state income taxation.
8. The relation of Federal and state income taxes.

BIBLIOGRAPHICAL NOTE

An outstanding study of the "history, theory, and practice of income taxation at home and abroad" is E. R. A. Seligman, *The Income Tax,* (New York, 1914). An excellent article on this subject by the same author recently appeared in the *Encyclopaedia of the Social Sciences,* Vol. VIII, pp. 626-638. Professor Seligman gives an extensive bibliography in his book and at the end of his article. A work which makes clear the points of difference in the British and American income tax concepts and methods is H. B. Spaulding, *The Income Tax in Great Britain and the United States,* (London, 1927). General studies of the income tax in the United States which are of value to the student of taxation are : J. J. Klein, *Federal Income Taxation,* (New York, 1931) ; and R. M. Haig, *The Federal Income Tax,* (New York, 1921).

A comprehensive treatise on state income taxation in the United States is Alzada Comstock, *State Taxation of Personal Incomes,* (New York, 1921). The development of income taxes in American states from 1911 to 1918 is treated in Alzada Comstock, "Fiscal Aspects of State Income Taxes," *American Economic Review,* Vol. X, pp. 259-271 ; and H. L. Lutz, "Progress of State Income Taxation since 1911," *American Economic Review,* Vol. X, pp. 66-91. The development of this form of taxation from 1918 to 1929 is reviewed in T. C. Bigham, "Fiscal Aspects of the State Income Tax since 1918," *American Economic Review,* Vol. XIX, pp. 227-245. Changes in state income tax rates from 1930 to 1932 are given in J. W. Martin, "Changes in State Income Tax Rates, 1930-1932," *Bulletin of the National Tax Association,* Vol. XVII, pp. 145, 146. The history and characteristics of the income taxes in the various states are ably set forth in the National Industrial Conference Board, *State Income Taxes,* (New York, 1930), 2 Vols.

The Wisconsin income tax of 1911, the forerunner of successful state income taxes in the United States, has been analyzed in T. S. Adams, "The Significance of the Wisconsin Income Tax," *Political Science Quarterly,* Vol. XXVIII, pp. 569-585. The effects of the state income tax upon industry in Wisconsin are shown in G. L. Leffler, "Wisconsin Industry and the Wisconsin Tax System," *University of Wisconsin Bulletin,* (Madison, 1930). A recent study of the historical and economic aspects of state income taxation in the United States is R. G. Blakey, *Taxation in Minnesota,* (Minneapolis, 1932), Chap. XV.

The *Proceedings of the National Tax Association* contain much useful information on state income taxation and its growth. See particularly H. L. Lutz, "Some Aspects of the Problem of Uniform Income Tax Legislation," (1920), pp. 284-301 ; and the Roundtable Discussion of State Personal Income Taxes, (1928), pp. 436-477.

A useful though rather old bibliography on income taxes is the "List of Recent References on the Income Tax," *Library of Congress,* (Washington, 1921).

CHAPTER XVI

SOME PROBLEMS IN INCOME TAXATION

1. SIMPLIFICATION OF THE FEDERAL INCOME TAX *

First we shall take up the proposal to disregard capital gains and losses in computing taxable income.† In many respects this is one of the most far-reaching of all simplification proposals. It involves consideration of the definition of income and of the possibility of doing away with the complicated and troublesome valuations which clog the administrative machinery. Certain aspects of this problem can be illustrated by a second major problem of simplification and equity; namely, the taxation of corporations in such a way as (1) to prevent discrimination as between corporations, partnerships, and individuals and (2) at the same time to prevent evasion of surtaxes upon undistributed earnings.

At the beginning of this discussion it may be well to remember that the income tax derives its great support from the general belief in its essential fairness. Any proposal for simplification is foredoomed to failure if it flouts unduly the reasonable considerations of equity. Perhaps the great majority of people believe that the income tax is more equitable than almost any other tax. Particularly they believe that it is more nearly in accord with ability to pay than tariffs and excises which, prior to 1914, were almost the sole sources of federal revenues. In supporting his income tax amendment to the Wilson Tariff Bill of 1894, Congressman McMillin of Tennessee said: "My friends, are we going to put all this burden on

---

* Adapted from R. G. Blakey, "Simplification of the Federal Income Tax," *American Economic Review, Supplement,* Vol. XVIII, pp. 102-119.

Eds. note: The fact that some of the data in this article are not up-to-date does not diminish its theoretical importance. For provisions of recent Federal Revenue Acts, see: R. G. Blakey and G. C. Blakey, "Revenue Act of 1932," *American Economic Review,* Vol. XXII, pp. 620-640; and *Federal Income Tax Regulations, Revenue Acts, 1928 and 1932,* (Washington: Government Printing Office, 1929 and 1933).

† Eds. note: Capital gains and losses are generally defined as gains or losses, respectively, resulting from the sale or exchange of capital assets, e.g., stocks, bonds, and real estate. Recent Federal Revenue Acts have defined "capital assets" as property held by the taxpayer for a period of two years or more.

the things men eat and wear and leave out those vast accumulations of wealth?"

The ill-fated tax of 1894 was only the beginning of a twenty-year struggle which finally resulted in the adoption of the Sixteenth Amendment to the Constitution (1913) and the subsequent series of income tax statutes. The insistent and general demand for the income tax has not been confined to the United States, nor did it originate here. With growing popular control of government, the masses in most civilized countries have been adopting this method of shifting some of the tax burdens from their shoulders on to those of the richer classes. Ability-to-pay has been the watchword. The idea embodied therein has sunk deep into the popular mind. All proposals for tax modification must, therefore, consider the strength of this popular demand.

THE PRESENT CONCEPT OF INCOME AND ITS LOGICAL IMPLICATIONS

In its main outlines the argument for simplification by omitting capital gains and losses runs somewhat as follows. The Sixteenth Amendment to the Constitution provides for the taxation of income, not of capital. The Supreme Court does not permit Congress to define income as it may chance to please; it has power to tax as income only what is actually income.[1] Economically or theoretically, capital gain is capital, not income; therefore it should not be included as income for taxation. From an administrative standpoint it is very difficult, if not impossible, to measure capital gain because such measurement requires valuations as of March 1, 1913, or/and of some other date more or less remote. The assignment of capital gain to the year or years "realized" results in discriminatory rates of taxation and its taxation at any rate is harmful to business inasmuch as it is a penalty upon sales or exchanges of real estate and other capital assets. The adoption of the proposal to disregard capital gain and loss would remove all of these difficulties, particularly it would do away with the valuation difficulty which is chief of all troubles connected with income tax administration and adjudication.

It will be admitted that the administration of the income tax would be greatly simplified if it could be rid of valuation problems, but we may inquire into the validity of the contention that capital gain is not income and, further, whether its omission from income taxation would eliminate or lessen the problems of valuation.

[1] *Eisner* v. *Macomber*, 252 U. S. 189, decided March 8, 1920.

Some of the arguments of different economists which are in point here may be briefly summarized. It is argued that income is not what one receives but what he spends, consumes, or the satisfaction he derives from consumption. Capital is not income, rather it is the capitalization (reflection) of expected future income. Appreciation of capital is not income but capital. Separation of increment from capital is a necessary condition of the emergence of income. "Its (income's) three essential characteristics are: *receipt, recurrence,* and *expendability.*"[2] An opposing definition is: "Income is the money-value of the net accretion to economic power between two points of time."[3] Obviously this last definition would include capital gains as income whereas the other definitions would not.

We do not wish to enter into a long discussion of the nature of income and of all the controverted points connected therewith; rather we prefer to consider the matter briefly from a somewhat different approach from that usually taken. The concept of income is dynamic, rather than static, as is often

[2] Among other references the following may be consulted in this connection.
Fisher, Irving, "The Rôle of Capital in Economic Theory." *The Economic Journal,* pp. 511-537, December, 1896. *The Nature of Capital and Income,* p. 427, 1906. "Are Savings Income?" *Publications of the American Economic Association,* pp. 21-47, April, 1908. "A Reply to Critics." *Quarterly Journal of Economics,* pp. 536-541, May, 1909. "Comment on President Plehn's Address." *American Economic Review,* pp. 64-67. March, 1924.
Fetter, Frank A., "The Nature of Capital and Income." *The Journal of Political Economy,* pp. 129-148, March, 1907.
Seligman, Edwin R. A., "Are Stock Dividends Income?" *American Economic Review,* pp. 517-536, September, 1919.
Plehn, Carl C., "Income, as Recurrent, Consumable Receipts." *American Economic Review,* pp. 1-12, March, 1924.
Flügel, Felix, *The Income Tax,* 1927.
Hewett, William Wallace, "The Concept of Income." *Journal of Political Economy,* pp. 155-178, April, 1925. *The Definition of Income and Its Application in Federal Taxation,* 1925.
Fairchild, F. R., "Federal Taxation of Income and Profits," *American Economic Review, Supplement,* pp. 148-170, 1921.
Adams, T. S., "Evolution v. Revolution in Federal Tax Reform," *Proceedings of National Tax Association,* XIV, 327-331, 1921.
Mills, Ogden L., "The Spendings Tax," *Proceedings of National Tax Association,* XIV, 327-331, 1921.
Houston, D. F., *Annual Report of the Secretary of the Treasury,* 1920, p. 34. The three last-named authorities argue for discrimination in favor of savings rather than that they are not income.

[3] Haig, R. M., "The Concept of Income," *The Federal Income Tax,* pp. 1-28, 1920.
Schanz, Georg, "Der Einkommensbegriff und die Einkommensteuergesetze," *Finanzarchiv* XIII Jahrg. 1 Band. Quoted by Clarence Heer in an unpublished manuscript on the history of income tax theory.
See also "Report of Committee of the National Tax Association on the Simplification of the Income Tax," pp. 62-74, 1927. (Published in 1927 *Proceedings of the National Tax Association,* pp. 108-172.)

assumed. Like the concept of value, it changes with time and purpose. It has taken us long to learn that there is one value for taxation and another for rate regulation. In fact, the use of the term "value" in the latter case causes great mischief. Similarly the income concepts of economists, accountants, and lawyers differ according to their purposes. As in the case of value, there has been a shifting of the use of the term and the application of it to different things in such a way as to cause much confusion. Under primitive homogeneous agricultural conditions of a practically self-sufficient economy, a gross-income concept without money valuations or much thought of capital or depreciation might have been entirely workable. Taxes could be levied in terms of day's work, sheep, wheat, or other commodities merely by number or quantity without much reference to values.

But in modern society, capital bulks large and economic relations are complex. Division of labor and exchange are characteristic of economic life and money values are almost universal. Both income and capital are measured in terms of money. All accounts are kept in such terms. There may remain a few individuals who still think in primitive terms and count their income in bushels of corn or head of sheep; and there may be others who calculate and spend their gross receipts as profits, regardless of depreciation or inventory values. Perhaps all of us have known some individuals and cities that have gone on the rocks following such concepts of income.

But our present civilization could not well maintain itself, much less progress, if it did not set up a net-income concept; if it did not allow for both "ordinary" current business expenses and also for depreciation of capital. In fact, depreciation is a cost of producing income, just as much as expenditures for raw materials and labor. Depreciation, like out-of-pocket expenses, can be made good only by deductions from gross income that might otherwise have been used for current or future consumption. That is, depreciation is a deduction from potential capital. At the time it comes into one's possession there is no difference in kind in the wealth later designated "capital" or that designated "income." Whatever portion of receipts or "income" an owner sets aside for satisfying future wants is thereby made "capital"; it does not cease to be income for the year of its receipt because it has been earmarked "capital."

To arrive at net income, therefore, it is necessary to determine the amount of depreciation, as well as of other costs

of producing income. Some times depreciation is calculated
upon physical bases. If a building is supposed to last twenty
years, a depreciation rate of 5 per cent is assumed. But obsolescence may alter this rate materially. This is another way
of saying that depreciation is not fundamentally a physical, but
rather a value, phenomenon. To use an old illustration : there
may be shrinkages in quantity of apples, or wine, or other commodities stored for later use and yet no economic depreciation.
In an economic world with a money economy, depreciation is
measured in terms of money. Values at two different dates
must be compared. Furthermore, the valuations that are required for determining depreciation serve also for determining
appreciation. Without valuations one cannot know whether
there has been depreciation or appreciation with the passing
of time, much less can one know the extent of the depreciation
or appreciation. If the calculation shows depreciation, practically all agree that it should be deducted from gross income to
arrive at net income. If, on the other hand, appreciation appears, is it to be disregarded because it is difficult to determine ?

If it lessens his taxes, no business man objects to the deduction of depreciation from gross income on the ground that it
is difficult to estimate. He insists upon its deduction and
usually endeavors to calculate it to his own advantage. But
when it comes to appreciation, his own ox is gored ; so a different theory of income must be evolved. He argues that
capital gain is something different from income and hence
should not be taxed. Furthermore, it is so difficult to measure
that it is not practical to tax it anyway. He stresses and magni-
fies the difficulties into reasons for abolishing the tax, even if
he has to hire economists, accountants, and lawyers to assist
him in the job. This does not imply the conscious use of
bribery. It is easy for all who have been brought up under
the influence of theories and practices of English business,
economics, accounting, and law to be swayed by such theories
and practices, although they contain inconsistencies. Those
who take the trouble to understand and adjust themselves to a
system long perpetuated become its defenders, particularly if
they are its beneficiaries. So we have strenuous American
defense of an expedient that was adopted by England when she
expected her income tax to be temporary.

Much of the capital gain had in mind by those advocating
its omission consists of gain from casual sales or from sales
of property held a long time. Not only is there English
precedent for special treatment of capital gains, but even our
own law gives them exceptional treatment. For example,

capital gains are defined in the statute as those which arise from conversion of property held two years or more. If the gain is from property held one year and 364 days, it is not a capital gain. The real justification for exceptional treatment of such gains is administrative rather than theoretical. It is much easier to keep track of a regular dealer than of one who makes an occasional transaction; especially is it difficult to make the proper valuations if the property has been held a long time. But it is obvious that any period such as two years, ten years, six months, or six days is arbitrary. The essential nature of the gain is the same regardless of the length of time property has been held or how often transactions are made. Though the valuations which must be made in order to measure such gain may be difficult to determine, they are nevertheless the same valuations as those required to determine depreciation or appreciation in the calculation of "ordinary" income from capital.

Probably it is the proper future *use* of income, rather than its *nature*, when it first comes in that is the real reason that many think that capital gains are not income. The *use* concept of income will be discussed at greater length later, but it is in point here to call attention to the fact that in a highly de- veloped money-exchange economy such as ours, capital gain can be used by an individual owner like any other income. Any form of wealth is convertible into any other form of wealth through the exchange medium. Capital gain or any other economic gain that comes in is income unless one perverts the original meaning of income. What one does with income after it comes in does not destroy the fact that it was, is, and always will be income for the income period in which it was received.

It may be questioned whether or not capital appreciation due to a lowering of interest rates increases ability to pay taxes. For example, the selling value of a bond or farm or other capital may increase and yet the annual yield therefrom remain stationary or even decline. If the bond should be sold and reinvested, this would not normally change the rate of return. What benefit or increase in ability to pay taxes accrues to the owner by virtue of a higher rating of the capital value if the owner really gets no more annual return? He may even finally have the bond redeemed at the same face value that it would have been redeemed at whether the selling value had gone up meantime or not.

It will be of some aid perhaps to divide the discussion of this question into three parts: (1) Is the owner of such appreciated

capital better able to pay taxes in the year of accrual than he
was previously? (2) Is he better able to pay taxes than others
whose capital does not appreciate? (3) As a long-time proposition, is he better able to pay taxes because of this appreciation?

With respect to the first question, it is clear that if he has
a capital appreciation, he can sell what he has for more than
he could before, so that in the year of its accrual, he has at his
command more purchasing power to use as he chooses.
Clearly, for the one particular period in which capital appreciation occurs, the owner has greater economic ability than
he would have had without the appreciation.

It is obvious also without further discussion, that for the year
in question, he has greater economic ability than other taxpayers whose capital failed to appreciate, other things being
equal.

Let us now consider the third question; that is, whether or
not the appreciation of capital increases long-time ability to
pay taxes. The answer to this question should be divided into
two parts depending upon whether it is assumed that the lower
interest rate and the consequent appreciation are permanent, or
whether they are temporary. If the appreciation is permanent
and the annual income from the capital is not changed, the
owner obviously has the same annual income as before and
just before the end of his life or at any other time can cash in
for a larger sum; that is, has greater ability to buy or pay for
anything than if there had been no appreciation. It may be
thought that he cannot realize upon capital appreciation soon
after it accrues without destroying his capital and thereby
destroying all subsequent incomes. If, however, before the
appreciation occurred he had sold and consumed all of his
capital he would have prevented the accrual of all future incomes from such capital. If he had sold and consumed only a
part of such non-appreciated capital, he would have eliminated
a proportionate part of otherwise possible future income. But
if his capital appreciates, he is in a position to secure more
consumption goods now if he sells all. Or if he wishes to sell
only a part, it will take a smaller proportion of the larger total
to secure a definite amount of present consumption goods than
before the appreciation. He will consequently have left a
larger proportion of the total which will give rise to a larger
future annual income than would have been the case if his
capital had not appreciated. In this case, therefore, appreciation of capital has resulted in greater ability to pay.

But suppose the appreciation has been temporary only. In
such a case, there may be no long-time net increase in ability

to pay, but this does not mean that including capital gains in taxable income necessarily works injustice or is necessarily contrary to the fundamental tenet of income taxation. Always in theory and usually in practice, the deduction of capital losses is coupled with the inclusion of capital gains in calculating net income. If the appreciation is followed by depreciation within the same taxable year, they counteract each other and only the net or difference is reported as affecting income. But if appreciation is reported one year so as to increase the income of that year, then when depreciation appears later it is a deduction from "ordinary" annual income. The sum total of such deductions allowable aggregate all original capital, plus appreciation. Thus it is seen that the inclusion of capital gain does not result in double taxation. The inclusion of capital gains and losses in income calculations in this most unfavorable situation does not run contrary to ability to pay.[4] In nearly all other cases it is obviously thoroughly supported by this criterion.

In general it may be said, that if depreciation in the case of machinery or other capital goods is to be allowed as a deduction from gross income to arrive at taxable net income, logic requires similar handling of all other forms of capital depreciation and, furthermore, it also requires the inclusion of all capital appreciations as a part of income.

The Supreme Court included "realized" capital gains in the definition of income when it said : "Income may be defined as the gain derived from capital, from labor, or from both combined, provided it be understood to include profit gained through a sale or conversion of capital assets."[5]

The administrative difficulty of measuring "realizable" as opposed to actually "realized" capital gains doubtless was the fundamental reason for not including the former in the definition. Logically any valuable or exchangeable gain which comes within one's ownership is income whether actually exchanged or not. If it is not actually "realized" though "realizable," it is as if the owner had sold capital and then had reinvested in the same thing. There is just as much reason for assuming income in such a case as where a person actually sells property and invests the proceeds in something else. As a matter of fact, it is not the sale or conversion of property which brings in the income ; the appreciation or gain already exists ; the sale merely discloses and measures it. Income is

---

[4] General price changes involve related but somewhat different problems, which limited space forbid taking up here. The same is true with respect to the effect of yearly exemptions and graduated rates.

[5] *Eisner* v. *Macomber*, 252 U. S. 189, decided March 8, 1920.

coincident with value appreciation. But, the practical application of a tax requires measurement; so the Court was constrained to say that there is no income until it is measured. This is not logical though it may be practical.

As already stated, however, the difficulties of determining capital gains and losses add little or nothing to the existing difficulties of determining "ordinary" net income from capital. Practically the same valuations are required in both cases. If there are greater administrative difficulties in determining appreciations than depreciations it is probably because the parties concerned fight harder and longer about valuations which result in increased taxes than they do about those which lessen taxes.

If there were a regular and universal practice of keeping accurate inventory records and basing income tax returns thereon — in other words, if the accounting of all were as good as that of the best business houses and as good as the best business management requires — the whole valuation problem connected with both depreciation and appreciation, including capital gains and losses, would be greatly simplified for tax purposes. There would still remain the difficulty of making valuations where market values are not well established. This is a difficulty now in connection with "ordinary" depreciation and obsolescence, even though in such cases it does not always assume such proportions as in the case of some capital-gain valuations.

As a matter of fact, the evils of inaccurate valuations can be over-emphasized. Fluctuations in income due to unstable prices of inventories can be lessened by the use of averages, though England's experience with averages has not been altogether satisfactory. If too much depreciation is allowed one year, this reduces possible allowances for succeeding years. If certain valuations make capital gains somewhat too large, the bases for calculating future gains are increased, hence future capital gains and taxes thereon will be smaller. After basic valuations are once made, there should be much less difficulty in keeping them up to date than there was with respect to their original establishment. Much of the basic information necessary for future valuations has already been accumulated in connection with past tax laws. To throw this away is unnecessary waste and very bad policy.

We may digress a moment to consider a complicating factor. In truth, one of the chief inequities and hence one of the main causes of manipulation and difficulty in connection with the taxation of capital gains is due to something other than valuation but closely connected with it; namely, to varying tax rates. This same variation of rates complicates also the corporation tax problem which we wish to mention later. Because of difficulty in valuing capital appreciations and the consequent failure to include them in computations of income each year, such gains tend to be lumped in one or a few years and thus occasion the application of heavier tax rates than if the gains were distributed over a series of years as they accrued. Both graduation and changes in rates occasioned by amending revenue acts not only cause discriminations but result also in constant pressure for tax reduction and in manipulation in order not to "realize" income except at the most favorable times. Stability in the tax law and its rates would lessen this evil. Fortunately, the further we are removed from war conditions, the greater becomes the possibility of normal stability.[6] The special rate of 12½ per cent upon capital gains is an attempt to meet part of the difficulty. This removes some of the restraints upon sales and exchanges of capital assets and compromises the problem of discriminations, but it does not meet it much more equitably than does the flat tax on corporations to be discussed hereafter.

As already stated, the impelling reason for the inclusion of capital gains in taxable income is the democratic belief in the "ability-to-pay" criterion and the set purpose of the people to put a substantial part of tax burdens upon those making such gains. The larger share of capital gains is probably made by the corporations and the well-to-do. In any case it is difficult to deny that capital gain usually increases the recipient's tax-paying ability. A capital loss has the opposite effect. The ability-to-pay idea gets its popular support on the grounds of individual equities. The measure of tax liability is not *social* income but *individual* income. The tax is personal. In our money régime, capital and income are interchangeable. Otherwise, money would not be a measure of both — capitalization would not be possible. Altogether it seems difficult to maintain that *any net accretion* to wealth is not income within the logical meaning of that term as popularly used, despite some popular inconsistencies.

EVOLUTION OF THE CONCEPT AND DEFINITION OF INCOME

LET us consider the evolution of the idea of income. We have already suggested that income is a dynamic rather than a static

---

6 The suggestion that income tax rates should never be changed but that all variations in needs for revenue be met by changes in rates of other taxes, however, seems to be the result of a rather narrow view. This might simplify income tax administration at too great a cost. See *Report by Committee of the National Tax Association on Simplification of the Income Tax,* pp. 42-44, 1927.

concept. The controversies over definition are due largely to different interests, private and public. The purpose to be achieved is the dominating factor. The *use* of income — what comes in — rather than the *nature* of income is the real question at issue. In order to secure the desired use of income, the continual attempt is made to shift the definition from the original literal and natural meaning. Today, one speaks of his income without a qualifying term, no one in a modern community understands him to mean gross receipts or even gross income, but rather net income measured in money terms. Not all are entirely agreed as yet as to just how "net" should be defined, because they are not agreed upon the proper use of what comes in. But nearly all agree that it is net income rather than gross income that constitutes the essence of income. This may be said to represent approximately the present status in the evolution of the term. As already shown, this definition has great survival value because it helps to maintain the capital required for our present state of capitalistic civilization.

But this concept is attacked and modified by others with different *use* concepts of income. The "clear-income" or "surplus-income" idea is gaining force and is being put into practice in some form in most countries by means of "exemptions," "credits," and other deductions from net income. Another concept of income which is a very thinly-veiled effort to control the use of what comes in is the definition which makes income coincide with expenditure, consumption, or the psychic reactions from consumption. By defining income not as what comes in, but as only that portion which is devoted to a certain use, we can levy taxes so as to encourage what we favor and discourage what we do not favor. It is not necessary, however, to put the exemptions into the definition, nor is it necessary to tax all income; we can keep our natural definition and tax only income used in a certain way. But modifying the definition is a very successful psychological trick which has accomplished wonderful results. As a matter of fact, much of the merit of the term "capital" is psychological. The race has made a tabu of the term. To label anything that comes in as "capital" is to say, "This thou shalt not touch; however much thou desireth it to satisfy present cravings, it is reserved for ministry to future wants." Those who would exempt savings and those who deny that savings are income stand side by side with respect to income tax legislation. Both are saying in effect, that private or/and public interests require more encouragement for the accumulation of capital than the usual concept of net income without exemption of savings.

Let us digress again and further. A double purpose may be served at this point by citing certain aspects of another major problem of simplification as an illustration of the important part played by economic and social policy in modifying the definition of income or in making exemptions for tax purposes. It makes little difference in effect whether undistributed corporate earnings are favored by exemption or by exclusion in the framing of the definition of income. In either case, corporate and social capital creation is promoted. The main problems concerning the taxation of corporations turn upon this question of social policy.

Let us outline the situation. Corporate income is taxed now at the flat rate of 12½ per cent. Distributed earnings are exempt from the normal tax but subject to the surtax in the hands of recipients. Partnership income as such is not taxed at all but the aggregate individual income of the partner, including non-partnership income as well as partnership profits, whether distributed or not, is subject to the regular normal and surtax rates applicable to other individual incomes. It is obvious that many small stockholders are in effect subject to higher taxes than non-stockholders having equivalent incomes. Exemptions combine with graduated rates to magnify the inequity. On the other hand, wealthy stockholders, usually among the directors of corporations, can nullify surtaxes by leaving earnings undistributed ; in fact, it is generally believed that corporations are thus availed of to evade taxes on a large scale. So far no one has succeeded in putting a provision in the law which will meet all of the difficulties. We might treat corporations as we treat partnerships, as England does practically with respect to the normal tax. But this would complicate administration rather than simplify it. Every stockholder subject to taxes at less than the corporate tax rate could make claim for refund. For example, in a typical year under the British practice,[7] 2,515,000 persons were chargeable with income tax ; 1,991,000 claimed repayment ; and in 1,500,000 cases repayments were made. Not all but a large part of these refunds were due to the tax withholding by corporations. The 50 per cent penalty of our own law has seldom been enforced, largely because of the difficulty of determining the reasonableness of accumulated reserves in the form of undistributed earnings. The bill now before Congress attempts to meet the situation by several devices which may or may not improve the situation. Provision is made for special treatment of the "per-

[7] Spaulding, H. B., *The Income Tax in Great Britain and the United States*, p. 235, 1927.

sonal holding company," which would be taxed 25 per cent upon undistributed profits, in excess of 30 per cent of the net income of any year. With respect to other corporations, the "reasonable-needs" clause is still retained but the penalty is reduced to 25 per cent instead of the unreasonably high and almost unenforceable rate of 50 per cent. Corporations accumulating more than 60 per cent of income must file detailed reasons for net accumulations and from time to time thereafter must file reports of actual disposition of the amounts so accumulated. Shareholders have the option of being taxed as partners and may thus avoid the 25 per cent penalty. The commissioner of Internal Revenue or any collector may require any corporation to report "accumulated gains and profits and the names and addresses of individuals or shareholders who would be entitled to the same if distributed, and the amounts that would be payable to each." [8]

There is much more detail and qualification which it is unnecessary to add here. The point is that the bill has been cluttered up with a lot of new phraseology. It may or may not simplify administration. That is yet to be seen. In any case, it does not meet all the difficulties; it is a compromise.[9] The controlling corporation directors whose incomes, if distributed, would get into the upper brackets can still keep undistributed at least the 30 per cent, in some cases 60 per cent, which would otherwise be subject to the highest surtaxes. This should be enough to satisfy most tax evaders. It is true that the extent of evasion may be reduced by these provisions. If so this is all to the good but it still remains to be seen how many loopholes can be discovered in the many qualifications with which the provisions are hedged about.

But Congress could go much further than this and achieve real simplification. If it saw fit, it could refuse to compromise and do away with all of the important difficulties in this connection except one. Suppose it should eliminate the taxation of corporate incomes except for a flat tax upon undistributed earnings equivalent to (or greater than) the combined normal and surtax rates applicable to the highest brackets of the individual income tax. Suppose that it taxed all distributions in the hands of individuals. The rate applicable under the present law would be 25 per cent (or more). As a result there would be no discrimination as between partners and stockholders with respect to distributed earnings. Whether stock-

[8] 70th Congress, 1st Session, House of Representatives 1, Secs. 104 and 148.
[9] The same is true of a recent amendment to levy a graduated instead of a flat tax upon corporations having incomes of less than $15,000.

holders were large or small, there would be no inducement for wealthy directors to accumulate earnings to avoid surtaxes. There would be no yearly problem of accounting for undistributed earnings allocated but not actually distributed to stockholders. It is true that there would be inequality if all income were not distributed and there would be a great temptation to distribute funds which should be retained in the business. This is the one great and perhaps fatal drawback to the scheme. It is possible, of course, that sufficient capital for expansion could be secured by sale of stocks and bonds, but psychologically we are probably not yet prepared for such a step. Not enough of us have sufficient self-restraint and wisdom to save the capital that we as individuals and as a society need. We must have corporations or governments or other agencies or devices to make us save in order that we may have the capital to maintain and improve our economic status. Certain income must be exempted from taxation by definition or otherwise in order to achieve the private and public ends thought desirable.

From the standpoint of equity alone, there is no good reason at all for taxing corporations as such. Ultimately, all tax burdens are personal, but for reasons of administration and also for other reasons of economic or social policy, in our present stage of development it seems desirable to collect some taxes from corporations. We may rationalize and explain a corporation tax as a franchise tax, citing special benefits accruing to corporations as justification. But taxes cannot be apportioned according to benefit any more accurately than according to ability to pay. As a matter of fact, the benefits, if any, accrue in the form of increased income to individuals. Getting nearer to real reasons, corporations are easy marks and taxes on them may be quite fruitful in yield, even if provocative of great administrative difficulties; so we tax them, despite the inequity. A chief source of government revenue and of society's capital supply must not be destroyed by a rigid attempt to attain equity, if this means the sacrifice of something else more important.

In the last analysis these are questions of economic or social policy and are determined much like other related questions. Social regulation, whether of public utility rates, hours of labor, issuance of currency, imports of foreign goods, or taxation, is concerned with the public control of private property. Taxation is an outstanding example of such social control. It is concerned with questions of what shall be done by government and what left to private enterprise, how costs and benefits of public activities shall be distributed, how such distributions shall be modified by questions of administration and also by questions of business and social policy. If society decides that proper public policy demands greater encouragement of capital accumulation it may exempt from taxation savings or/and capital gains, either by specific exemption or by changes in the definition of income comparable to changes already evolved. In fact, it might define income as expenditure or superfluous expenditure when we have reached that stage. Under such a definition of taxable income, it is possible that we might do away with the necessity of making many troublesome valuations. To determine income it would be necessary only to have every one keep account of his "consumption" expenditures, eliminating therefrom his investment expenditures. It will not take a great deal of thought to recognize the administrative difficulties involved in this method. But if we should adopt the method suggested by the foremost advocate of this income concept,[10] we would calculate income very much as now, except that we would deduct savings. This latter method would mean very little simplification. In fact, with even more stress upon saving and capital building than the present net-income concept involves, we would be fully as unable as now to rid ourselves of that great hindrance to simplification; namely, valuation. In truth, the only way to escape from economic valuation is to escape from the economic world.

But valuations are exceedingly difficult to make. The more capital we have, the greater the risks of making mistakes as to future wants and their satisfaction, hence the greater the difficulties of determining values. But increasing accumulations of capital are required by our increasing demands for services. We are caught in a chain of complexities and cannot escape by crying "back to the simple life." The actual trend of practically all tax legislation, especially of income tax legislation, is away from simplicity for the sake of equity, or for the sake of some social policy. This is almost inevitable because the problems of taxation are so close to life itself.

CONCLUSIONS AND RECOMMENDATIONS

BEFORE making concrete suggestions we should summarize a few facts which we have not time to discuss in detail. The work of the Bureau of Internal Revenue has been badly clogged. Much of this has been due to war and excess-profits taxes abolished in 1921. Most of the old cases have been "closed," though forty thousand of the "closings" have been merely un-

[10] Fisher, Irving, "The Income Concept in the Light of Experience," p. 17 (English reprint from Vol. III of the *Weiser Festschrift*, 1927, Vienna).

loadings upon the General Counsel, the Board of Tax Appeals, and the Courts. The Board of Tax Appeals is said to have a sufficient grist ahead of it to prevent consideration of new cases for four years if no additional petitions are filed. Up until October [1928], new petitions filed were exceeding disposals but a new special advisory committee established in the Bureau has succeeded temporarily at least in disposing of old cases as fast as new appeals are being added. How long this situation will last is unknown.

The great accumulation of unsettled cases may be laid either to the complexities of the law or to incompetent personnel, or to both. Income has been difficult to determine, legal and illegal evasion and attempts at evasion have been common, "closed" cases have been reopened by appeals, reversals of rulings, court decisions, etc. Of prime importance has been the matter of personnel. The turnover has been tremendous. The Bureau has been a training school for those receiving better offers on the outside. Many of the best men have thus been drawn away. Those remaining have had more than they could do. New men require time to learn the ropes, often they have not known precedents, or have not chosen to follow them. Reversed decisions have reopened many old cases. Young and inexperienced men overloaded with cases have had to fight able and experienced representatives on the outside. Often they have made mistakes and have not commanded confidence and respect of the taxpayers and their representatives. They have feared to take responsibility and settle cases. The whole Bureau seems to have shrunk from taking responsibility. It has encouraged Congress to complicate the law by loading it down with details. Much of the present congestion before the Board of Tax Appeals is due to failure to settle cases in the Bureau. Perhaps nothing would improve income tax administration so much as a proper personnel which could and would make good decisions upon matters which are now sidestepped by filing appeals. The way to meet the situation is not to evade it but to face it. We should have a personnel competent to make, and willing to make, good valuations as well as to face the other difficult problems that good administration requires.

In emphasizing the prime importance of personnel there is no intention of minimizing the desirability of statutory simplification in so far as considerations of equity permit. . . Some simplifications have already been made, notably through the abolition of the excess profits tax, the reduction of tax rates and the raising of personal exemptions (not all of which we approve, by the way). Other simplification amendments are under consideration and, if continued, the Congressional Joint Committee on Internal Revenue Taxation and its advisory committee will doubtless propose still other simplifications.* Even the situation with respect to personnel appears to be improving. There are no longer so many outside openings with such large inducements for Bureau resignations. The outside demand for income tax experts is less and the supply is greater. Furthermore, the pending bill proposes unusual salary increases for about a hundred of the top men of the Bureau staff.

There is no denying the faults of our income tax statutes and of their administration. But many of the difficulties could not be avoided under the stress of war demands and in view of our political organization. All in all, we are inclined to regard as somewhat exaggerated the claims of those who insist that the income tax is being rapidly undermined and is doomed to early impotence. Possibly the wish is father to the thought in some cases. We are reminded of the early criticisms of the British income tax and of the many times in recent years when it has been cited to emphasize the faults of our own tax. We admit that it has some superiorities. Especially is the administrative personnel superior and subject to much less unwise political pressure. We have already profited much by British experience and we can profit still more.[11] But the superiorities do not all lie on the English side. In fact, there has been a very definite tendency of late for the British to take some lessons from American experience. To mention only one example, there is a slow but perceptible shift toward the American position on the matters of depreciation and appreciation.

Those most impressed with the merits of the British system and most pessimistic about our own income tax might read with profit a recent comparison of British and American taxes by Mr. Spaulding, a Canadian unusually familiar with the laws and practices of both countries. From this book we quote the following brief excerpts:

"The enactment of an entirely new income tax statute every few years has great advantages. It keeps the law of income tax in one convenient statute; it permits of minor improvements in drafting without the necessity for a separate Act; and it frees the legislators from the inertia inevitable where an entirely

* Eds. note: See "Report of the Joint Committee on Internal Revenue Taxation," *House Miscellaneous Documents*, 1, 70th Congress, First Session, 11, (Washington: Government Printing Office, 1930).

[11] One suggested simplification with respect to earned income credit taken from British law has just been rejected by the Ways and Means Committee, though the reason therefor is not clear. It appears to be political.

new income tax Act occurs perhaps only once in a century. The result is that the United States income tax law is a modern, carefully drafted and logically arranged statute, whereas the British law is antiquated, ill-arranged and obscure and ambiguous in its provisions. . . The actual procedure frequently does not follow the statutory procedure. . . The situation is different in the United States. The revenue laws are modern and comprehensive, and practice is in accord with statute. . . The British policy is to have knowledge of the law and practice concentrated in official circles. It is felt that the less taxpayers know, the less possibility will there be of evasions and contentions. . . The Inland Revenue officers are supplied with manuals and detailed explanations of the law, but these are not available to the public. . . It speaks highly for the officers . . . that they are almost universally respected and that there are practically no complaints [of discrimination]." [12]

Let us summarize briefly. We have taken one or two of many possible examples to illustrate the general problem of simplification. It is not so simple as the term sounds. Furthermore it is contrary to public policy to carry simplification to extremes. After we have gone as far as practicable in simplifying the statute, it is still necessary to improve political organization, particularly administrative and legislative competence, in order that we may meet the complex problems upon which advancing civilization depends. Ultimately substantial improvement depends upon advancement in general intelligence and morals. Our legislators and administrators are persons of our own choice, swayed by the pressure which we all put upon them. More immediately, there is strong argument for continuation of the Joint Congressional Committee with its advisory committee of laymen who are tax experts. Their interrelations with both Congress and the Treasury have been fruitful to date; their services are possible of much extension and intensification.

Taxation is political in all the senses of that term. It is political all through its legislative and administrative phases, and even before legislation begins. It is a large part of the complex art of living together in vast multitudes in modern capitalistic society. Reforms are not reforms unless they will work. When the Golden Rule is not in general usage, practical men will make suggestions that will work in a society as it actually exists. It is important to have the best possible means of getting such practical suggestions.

[12] Spaulding, H. B., *Income Tax in Great Britain and the United States*, pp. 14, 23, 247, 290, 1927.

There should be a small group of able men, possibly headed by one man, who would take up the study of income tax improvement in a comprehensive and thorough fashion. This matter is of sufficient importance to justify undivided and continuous study, rather than spasmodic and hasty attention just before or pending the passage of some particular law. Furthermore, it needs the attention of some who are not weighed down with details or with handling a multitude of other matters, either public or private. This particular problem should be the main business, the long-time, continuous business, not merely the occasional consideration, of some competent man or men having both ability and public spirit. They should confer with and seek the advice of practical men, theorists, taxpayers, legislators and anyone else who can make fruitful suggestions. They might well have an expert board of referees. They should be able to command the confidence and secure the co-operation of legislative and administrative leaders. They should be both theoretical and practical in the most significant senses of those terms.

Improvement is not likely to be meteoric. Those who ask for the demolition of our present system and the erection of an entirely new structure hardly expect to be taken literally.[13] We do not expect either immediate demolition or a heavenly inspiration that will lead to the perfection of the income tax. Rather we look for gradual improvements as dictated by experience, both in text of statute and in administration. Well-planned and continuous consideration by a small but capable group might well develop a leadership for both official and public opinion that would quicken the pace of progress in these matters.

2. A Suggested Income Tax Policy

Suggestions for the improvement of Federal income tax policy, more extreme than those made by Professor Blakey in the preceding section, have been set forth by Professor J. B. Canning and Dr. E. G. Nelson. Their suggestions are reproduced below.*

* Adapted from J. B. Canning and E. G. Nelson, "The Relation of Budget Balancing to Economic Stabilization : A Suggested Federal Treasury Policy," *American Economic Review*, Vol. XXIV, pp. 26-37.

13 "The most important consideration, occurring to the minds of the members of this committee is the genuine need of demolishing the entire present structure of our income tax system in order to build anew along simpler and sounder lines a structure more adaptable to present and future conditions." *Report of Committee of National Tax Association on Simplification of the Income Tax,* p. 1, 1927.

CRITICISM OF SOME PRESENT PRACTICES IN INCOME TAXATION

A SURVEY of the comments on our experience in taxing incomes under the 16th Amendment will disclose a consensus among writers on public finance and among legislators on the following points: (1) that some kind of income tax is necessary; (2) that the taxpayer's annual tax should be either a function of his income for the taxable year or a function of his "average" annual income; and (3) that tax rates on income should be progressive. Further agreement among experts is limited to a profound discontent with the results of the successive tax acts.

Mostly the criticisms that have appeared deal with particular sections of the acts or with particular tax effects. An excellent case has been made out for abandoning the tax on the incomes of corporations and for taxing shareholders, at both normal and surtax rates, on corporation dividends.[1] If this were done, it cannot be doubted that natural persons of equal income — in the sense in which the acts determine income — would be more evenly burdened and that the burden would increase uniformly with increased income. But if the system of determining taxable income is fundamentally erratic and unsound, uniformity of burden distribution with respect to that income measure is a dubious merit.

Both the Treasury and the Congress have been ridiculed for their failure to estimate reliably the successive annual yields. During the late boom astonishing surpluses persisted despite tax rate decreases and despite extravagant expenditures. The astronomical magnitudes of deficits and prospective deficits, despite increased tax rates and cuts in expenditures, inspired panic in the last administration. This panic, more than anything else, handicapped federal effort to arrest the plunge of economic depression. But the successive surpluses and deficits do not prove a grievous fault in the estimators; neither do they prove the unreliability of income taxation; rather they illustrate, as we shall show, the freakish character of the measure of income which has been adopted in all the acts.[2]

The feature of the income tax measures most frequently attacked is, perhaps, the tax on gains from the sale, or other conversion, of so-called capital assets. Some of the critics go no further than to advocate the deleting of the provisions which

[1] H. L. Lutz, "The Treatment of Dividends in Income Taxation," *Journal of Political Economy*, XXXIII, pp. 129-154.

[2] For a statement of one statistical fallacy that lies at the root of much of this freakishness, see J. B. Canning, "A Certain Erratic Tendency in Accountants' Income Procedure," *Econometrica*, I, 52.

authorize alternative determinations of tax liability. This, in our opinion, would make a bad condition much worse.

Many have advocated more drastic changes. They propose exempting all gains resulting from conversions of capital assets and disallowing, as deductions, all losses incurred in such operations. Few who make these proposals appear to have considered it necessary to define "capital assets." Seemingly they either suppose everyone knows what a capital asset is, or else they vaguely suggest that a capital asset is one "not held primarily for resale" or is one "not utilized in a trade or business," or is one that "has been held a long time."

All these suggested criteria for distinguishing capital assets are superficial and useless. The first is so open to abuse and fraud and so obviously provocative of tax litigation as to condemn it without extended consideration. The adoption of the second, though less conducive to fraud and litigation, would be a mere abuse of legislative power.[3]

The third criterion, "assets held a long time," is interesting because of the conclusions to which one is inevitably led by a study of it. How long is "a long time"? Consider first some examples of the operation of our revenue acts under which anything less than forever is not a long time.[4] In 1920 a certain farmer sold his farm to a neighbor for $50,000. He had bought the farm six years earlier for $25,000. Six weeks later but before the end of the year, not finding any other investment to his liking, he bought back his farm for $55,000. The seller invested his "profit" in more land. In March, 1921, these farmers learned to their sorrow that they had suffered taxable incomes, arising out of these two transfers, of $30,000. Shortly afterward both farmers ceased paying income taxes, though they have lived comfortably. Both farmers, if they sold now, could show "deductible losses" which they do not need. If six years (but not six weeks) were, by the revenue acts, "a long time" one farmer would merely have been out of pocket the $5000 price advance, but his neighbor, taxed on a

---

[3] Suppose A, B, and C to hold all the shares in X corporation and to constitute a majority of the board of directors and suppose that they simultaneously buy shares of Y both for X's account and for their private accounts. Suppose that all these shares in Y are later sold. Any reason assignable for exempting A, B, and C from tax burdens on their gains on direct private account is equally assignable for exempting them, as shareholders in X, from a tax burden with respect to X's gains. If they are losers upon conversion of Y's shares, it is equally absurd to make either loss deductible and the other non-deductible.

[4] The later acts provide optional schedules of rates with respect to gains arising from the conversion of certain sorts of assets held more than two years. Only those whose taxable net incomes are large can benefit by a choice between the options.

$5000 gain, could ask the nasty question, why is my capital gain not exempt also? In both cases real taxes were paid; in neither case did their net income rise above the level of mere expectancies. Their "real incomes" were affected only to the extent of taxes paid.

Consider an illustration of the operation of deductible losses on assets held "a long time." That J. P. Morgan and his partners should have paid no federal income taxes for the last two taxable years appeared, for some occult reason, to be regarded by newspaper men as a fact of great news value. But payment of income taxes by these bankers for the years 1931 and 1932 would have been an act of incredible stupidity. Merely by selling securities held a "long time" and buying others in the distressed markets of those years they could establish deductible "losses" numerically greater than their concurrent "gains." Such transfers, though sufficient to *establish* a legal loss, might have been made even though the reward of tax exemption had been absent.

It has not been made to appear that the gentlemen in question were constrained to reduce their real incomes during these years. We do not know that the extent of their command over future real income was impaired. In years of declining markets it is not impossible for shrewd men of great fortune steadily to increase their purchasing power over future real income even though the *number* of dollars employed to express their net estate in their assets declines during the interval.

The only way in which a "long time" could be defined, in order to make it impossible for the two farmers to suffer taxable incomes and our bankers to enjoy deductible losses would be to declare any time at all a long time. That is to say, Congress could abandon the present kind of income measuring altogether. We have concluded not only that length of holding time will not serve as a criterion but also that there is no other criterion, satisfactory in public finance, for distinguishing "capital assets" from assets that are not capital assets.

Superficially considered the dissatisfaction with our revenue acts under the 16th Amendment seems to spring from a great diversity of causes. The inequitable distribution of burden wrought by the tax on corporation incomes, the unreliability of the Treasury's yield estimates, and the freakish distribution of tax liability and of tax burden wrought by the tax on capital gains seem, at first sight, to be quite unrelated. In our opinion, they all spring from one defect, viz., the needless adoption of a measure of income that is wholly unsuited for determining tax liability.

THE PROPOSED MODE OF MEASURING TAXABLE INCOME

THE only concept of income, as yet proposed, that is adequate for quantitative economics was given to us in 1906 by Irving Fisher. In his much neglected book, *Capital and Income,* he has given us also the ablest discussion of the quantitative aspects of income ever written. Unfortunately he has not discussed the application of his theory to taxation beyond a few meager notes; and even in these he seems greatly to have under-estimated the ease of taxing final objective income.[5]

Professor Fisher's concept is that the income of any person, in any definitive objective sense, is to be measured by a balance of (a difference between) the services and disservices of things and persons directly experienced by the person whose income is in question. The positive increments, the final objective services, consist solely of such services as the nutrition of food, the sheltering of houses, the entertainment afforded by players, etc., and include all such services. The negative elements consist of such adverse experiences as labor, (not work, but the undesired fatigue of working), pain, etc. All other economic events derive both their existence and their quantitative significance from the final objective income balances expected ultimately to result from them. Neither a dollar received nor the receiving of a dollar is income in this fundamental sense; the receiving of a dollar merely confers upon the recipient the power to command, at some future time, an increment of service or the power to ward off an increment of disservice.

We do not know how to make any direct objective measurement of income, even in this fundamental sense, that permits provable annual summations. One can measure nutrition, shelter, etc., after a fashion but the units of measure are not interconvertible in the sense in which inches are convertible into yards, meters, etc. Because of this incommensurability it is necessary to resort to indirect measures or indexes.[6]

For a single person or for a living group, such as the family, in a pecuniary society one may reasonably assume that money

---

[5] *Capital and Income,* pp. 250-254 and 398-403. In a number of his papers he refers to the subject but the discussion is not carried beyond the range of the references given here.

[6] Certain measures of "money income" — *e.g.,* of a bondholder's money income — appear to be highly objective and precise. Superficially they are, but only in the sense that if one evaluates the constants in the formulas one obtains unique, numerical results. The economic significance of these numbers depends very little upon the degree of precision of the money income *figures.* The sole economic significance of such a number depends on the degree to which its value assists the beneficially interested person reliably to forecast the associated increment to his final objective income.

spent to obtain these direct services — or, what comes to the same thing, spent to obtain objects which are to render these services — is laid out in a manner roughly conducive to maximizing the present worth of final incomes.

By regarding each particular money outlay as an index of the value of the services expected from the thing purchased and by distributing each outlay in a series the terms of which are proportionate to the rates of use of the thing purchased, one obtains a living expense series. By summing the concurrent terms of these living expense series one obtains a time series representing cost of living (and, hence, value of final income) in successive time intervals. The techniques of modern accounting now restricted almost altogether to enterprise affairs are entirely adequate for finding such an index of final objective income of domestic groups. These techniques are, in fact, immeasurably more satisfactory for this use than they are for the uses to which they are commonly devoted.[7]

It is vain, of course, to hope that such an index can ever, except by accident, become precisely proportional to final objective income. But we have the best of *a priori* grounds for supposing that it will seldom be grossly in error either for individuals or for a population. It cannot have a systematic error. The only errors the index can have arise from (1) incompleteness in the accounting analysis in individual cases, and (2) the assumption that, in a given household, funds will be laid out with equal skill in successive years.

The first kind of error need never be great; and even the crudest accounting procedures provide for an automatic cancelling of all errors of this kind within relatively short time intervals. In all accounting procedures the summation of all dollar outlays during the existence of an enterprise (or a domestic establishment) will be equal to the summation of the income debits for the like periods.[8]

Though the second sort of error is inevitable, the change in skill of domestic management in a given household from year to year cannot be supposed to account for any great change in the number of dollars' worth of uses enjoyed. For a large population, neglecting changes in the cost of living, the summation of errors of this kind must be extremely small relatively to the total real income.

The data employed in calculating the index consists entirely

---

[7] For a brief treatment of the application of accountancy to the measurement of final objective income see J. B. Canning, *The Economics of Accountancy*, pp. 163-168.

[8] For a treatment of this matter see J. B. Canning, "A Certain Erratic Tendency in Accountants' Income Procedure," *Econometrica*, I, 52.

of objective facts. Uses have occurred and payments (or commitments to pay) have been made. The accounting task of
determining this index of income and of tax liability can be
made much less burdensome to taxpayers than the corresponding task as taxable income is now determined. At present the
income accounts most suited to determining net income figures
of enterprise often require an adjustment to obtain the single
item, statutory "income from trade or business," more laborious
to make than the entire task of measuring income by the mode
recommended here.[9]

The index proposed deals with an income that has been
finally and objectively realized ; and the index is objectively
provable at the time of its evaluation. The measurement of it
involves no forecasting beyond that implicit in the outlays
made or promised. In domestic establishments this forecasting, when serviceable articles are bought, is, in point of time,
very close to the service events forecast. Moreover, the forecasts are made either by the person who is to enjoy the service
events or by one to whom those beneficially interested are inti-
mately known, e.g., by a housewife buying food for her household. The accountant who evaluates the index is a mere clerk.

By contrast with the index proposed, the index of income
now relied upon is freakishly erratic. It is *wholly* a forecast —
never an objective determination of provable facts. The forecasting is mostly done by accountants and by corporation
managers, that is, by persons to whom the ultimate beneficiaries
are often wholly unknown. Moreover, it is usually done without the least knowledge of the time by which any final income
will have occurred to any person.

To illustrate this, let us suppose the case of a corporation
whose income accounts are kept in such a manner as to make
the annual balance equal to its statutory taxable net income
minus the tax liability. Suppose, further, that for a given
year the accountant finds a net income figure of $100,000.
This figure means that a $100,000 increment of power to pay
dividends, at some future time, is supposed to have been acquired within the year as a result of enterprise activities brought
to some particular stage (usually sales) during the year. It is
of such increments that surplus accounts are built up.

Dividend paying power in excess of shareholder contributions, is, in fact, limited to the excess of the corporation's money
receipts over money payments, other than transfer between

---

[9] All too often taxpayers, rather than incur the expense of adjusting their
business income, keep accounts suited to determining tax liability but unsuited
to their enterprises — an obvious ill effect of the revenue acts.

shareholders and corporation, during the corporate life. That this power is positive cannot be proved, as a fact, until the corporation has ceased to exist. The magnitude of the increments of dividend paying power credited to surpluses are mere forecasts based upon assumptions about the future volume of the corporation's operations and about the favorable or unfavorable future conditions of the market for goods and services in which the corporation will operate in the future. These assumptions are never explicitly stated; but they are implicit in the accountant's procedures.

Even if the increment of dividend paying power credited to surplus should turn out, ultimately to be correct, the accountant does not know when the associated dividends will be paid, nor to whom they will be paid, nor whether the recipients will reinvest them or utilize them in their households. He does know that a tax burden, proportionate to the increment will fall at once upon the holders of junior shares and that it will be distributed among them in proportion to their several interests but independent of their economic circumstances and programs.

One need not, in these times, labor the point of the unreliability of these forecast earning increments and of their summations up to any particular time. The vanishing not only of huge corporate surpluses but of the entire net proprietary interest together with the scaling down of creditors' rightful expectancies is a common spectacle in the receivership and bankruptcy cases now in process of adjudication. All those surpluses represent taxed net incomes that never had, and never will have, a real existence in any shareholder's economic experiences. They consisted of "the substance of things hoped for, the evidence of things not seen."

Even in an economic society subject to such violent perturbations as those we have experienced in the last two decades, the real economic income of the population has been relatively stable; it has been, perhaps, the least disturbed of all economic series. The red ink which has recently been spread over the accounts of the motor and motor fuel industries has no equivalent counterpart in the rate of automobile use. The physical volume of fuel and tire sales show that car-miles run has declined but little. The building trades are in a deplorable state but we enjoy about as much house *use* as we did in 1928. It is said that the value of shares listed on the New York Stock Exchange (priced at market) fell by nearly $80,000,000,000 between the high point in 1929 and the low point of 1932. A mere barter exchanging of all such shares in 1929 followed by a mere trading back in 1932 would have given rise, in the interim, to tax-deductible losses of $80,000,000,000; for all those shares have a "fair market value" at all times. A correspondingly great decline in real economic income would imply the extermination by starvation of a major portion of the population. Only the most profound unawareness of the unreliable character of accountants' enterprise income data could have led us to tolerate our present measure of tax liability when a highly reliable and simpler measure was available.

No serious question of the adequacy of the proposed tax basis can be raised. Year by year, of course, there could be vast differences between the aggregate measure proposed and the aggregate measure now relied upon. But if the summations of the two measures were to be made for a given population over a long period of years the difference between the two summations would be small in comparison with either summation. The difference would be the sum of two variables: (1) the increase (or the decrease) in value of material wealth held by the population; and (2) the sum of errors in the estimates of the two income measures. But large rates of increase (or decrease) of national wealth in relation to national real income cannot long be sustained. And, as the length of the interval of observation increases the absolute sum of errors of estimate in the two income summations will become smaller in relation to the income summations.[10] Aside from the possible temporary addition of capital levies, it is impossible for any tax basis or any set of tax bases to exceed that of final objective income or "real income."

Only a brief sketch of the tax rate system contemplated is given here.[11] The system would include the following features:

(1). The taxpayer unit would be (as now) the family.

(2). Income increments below the minimum necessary to maintain the family in efficient condition should be (as now) exempt.

(3). The rate system should be progressive, the progressions having regard for number of members in the family.

10 In both measures of income the chief kind of error is, in the long run, self-compensatory. If a merchant overvalues his closing inventory of $1000, his enterprise income figure for that year will be $1000 too large and the next year's figure will be too small by the same amount. The sum of the two years' income figures is therefore free of this particular error.

11 The present writers have recently concluded a two-year statistical study, financed in part by a grant of funds from the Laura Spellman Rockefeller Foundation, of taxation under the 16th Amendment. They hope, in the near future, to offer papers, based on that study, dealing with a tax rate system and with the administrative problems that would arise if their proposals were adopted. They expect to show that a great simplification of our tax system is easily possible.

(4). The income tax should be supplemented by a tax (payable by the donor) on gifts and by a tax upon transfer by will, by trust, or by operation of law at death. These tax rates also should be progressive and become large for large transfers.[12]

The advantages of the system proposed as compared with that now in use may be summarized as follows:

(1). An income tax becomes payable only with respect to income that has actually been enjoyed in a real economic sense rather than with respect to current increased hopes of future income enjoyment. This should minimize injustices to individual taxpayers arising from mistaken forecasts.

(2). Final objective income, for a whole population and for families within it is, in general, much more stable than the current index. This should make Treasury estimates more reliable.

(3). Tax burden is distributed with respect to sacrifice rather than with respect to source of income (as in the case of the corporation tax) and with respect to expected sacrifice (as in the case of the tax upon individuals).

(4). No incentive to sell in markets already depressed by distress selling or by panic, in order to minimize taxes, is afforded.

(5). No premium is put upon borrowing on collateral during market booms, since the tax liability is independent of prices realized in concurrent enterprise or investment operations.

(6). If year-by-year budget balancing is abandoned, the Treasury can throw in the weight of its borrowing and lending operations and of its revenue collections and disbursements as dampers against the successive booms and depressions which we may otherwise expect.*

(7). The form of tax proposed here should be well suited to concurrent use in federal and state finance. Very great convenience to taxpayers and very great savings in the costs of tax administration could result from the adoption by states of income tax acts differing from the federal act only in the rate schedules and in the geographical limits of tax jurisdiction.

---

12 This is not double or multiple taxation in an objectionable sense. If tax burden is to be distributed in accordance with the sacrifice principle the tax liability must be determined by purchasing power over future income, that is, by a summation or integral of income rather than by a *rate of utilizing* that power. To minimize the errors of forecasting we propose merely to defer tax *liability* until increments of the power to command income have become definitively provable. The money cost of real income and of gifts together with the money value of the estate left at death constitute a measure of a taxpayer's total pecuniary power to command income. We propose a system that brings the whole of the power to command income within the tax bases but defers the *tax* increments until the *power* increments are provable.

* Eds. note: The discussion of this point by Canning and Nelson is not reproduced here. See their complete article for analysis of this problem.

3. The Treatment of Capital Gains and Losses in Income Taxation

In addition to the suggestions of Professor Blakey in sec. 1, and of Professor Canning and Dr. Nelson in sec. 2, of this chapter, Professor H. M. Groves has offered a concrete proposal for the treatment of capital gains and losses in income taxation. His analysis of this problem follows.*

THERE are at least two quite distinct kinds of income recognized by the federal income-tax law. This can be made clear, perhaps, by the use of a simple illustration. Suppose we assume the case of two successful physicians who have had, we will say, a regular income from their professions of $100,000 a year during the last ten years. One of the two physicians, Dr. Jones, has spent all of his income each year. The other, Dr. Smith, has made it a rule to invest 20 per cent of his earnings. Ignoring the interest from the investments, this would mean that by 1933, Dr. Smith would have invested $200,000. Toward the close of 1932, let us say, he decides to sell his securities either to realize ready cash or to buy other securities. He sells his holdings for $100,000. He has realized a $100,000 capital loss.

This $100,000 capital loss may be offset against the $100,000 income which Dr. Smith earned in his profession. Thus as our law now stands, Smith will have no taxable income for 1932 and no taxes to pay in 1933. Dr. Jones will show his usual income of $100,000. This does not mean, of course, that Dr. Smith has nothing with which to pay his current bills, including tax bills. On the contrary, he has quite as much money to spend as ever and except for what he lays aside for new investments quite as much money to spend as Dr. Jones. He may even decide to build a yacht in 1933. But he has nothing on which the government can require him to pay taxes.

Now there are plenty of good social reasons why Dr. Smith should pay some taxes in 1933 on his 1932 income. It may happen that in 1933 the government faces an emergency and is trying desperately to balance its budget. The government may be very much embarrassed by the fact that it can collect

* Adapted from H. M. Groves, "Yachts without Income," *The New Republic*, Vol. XXLV, (July 19, 1933), pp. 254-255.
  Eds. note: According to Professor Groves, "A capital gain occurs when an individual sells a stock or a bond or real estate which he has purchased either as an investment or a speculation and sells it for more than he paid for it. And a capital loss occurs when he sells for less than the purchase price."

nothing from the many Dr. Smiths in spite of their obvious ability to pay. At a time when many who normally have an income have nothing with which or upon which to pay taxes, a large number with abundant income will go entirely un-taxed. The Dr. Joneses, too, may complain bitterly when they find that they are called upon to support the government not only as usual but with additional emergency rates of taxation while the Smiths, who are no less prosperous, have nothing to pay.

It will be said, of course, that we have presented only half of the picture; that had Dr. Smith disposed of his securities in 1929 he might have realized a large capital gain. The gov-ernment would then have had its innings and Smith would have had much more taxes to pay than Jones. This is true. But it does not alter the fact that in 1933, when taxes are most needed, the government has less even than the true current income of its citizens to tax.

Looking at the federal income-tax figures, it is easy to see what havoc the capital gains and losses feature of our income tax has played with the national revenues. The national in-come has dropped from 40 to 60 per cent below the peak, according to various estimates. On the other hand our income-tax base has so shrunk that with the 1928 rate and exemptions our individual income-tax receipts for 1933 were estimated at only about one-eighth of the 1929 receipts. A larger share of this disproportionate drop must be due to our method of treat-ing capital gains and losses under the tax law.

What is to be done about this situation? Several alternatives suggest themselves. One is to ignore capital gains and losses entirely in taxing income. This is what the British do. How-ever, this alternative is open to the objection that speculative gains are allowed to go untaxed. They represent ability to pay of the first order. A nation which has no unearned-increment taxes cannot lightly consent to ignore this kind of ability when it taxes income.

A second alternative is to tax only capital gains and ignore capital losses. It may not be unjust to tax A's good fortune and pay no attention to B's misfortune. We do this in other taxes. But it does seem unjust to tax A upon his fortunate ventures without taking some account of his unfortunate ones.

This brings us to a third alternative which is to separate income into two classes, capital gains and other income. For purposes of simplifying administration and of graduating the rates, the two bases may be combined to calculate an indi-vidual's tax bill. However, it should be recognized that these two species of income must not be crossed so that capital losses may be offset against anything but capital gains.

A precedent for this procedure was established in the Revenue Act of 1932, when income was so classified that losses on securities held less than two years were allowed as an offset only against similar gains. It would be simple and feasible to extend this same rule to all capital gains and losses.

The principal problem arising under this alternative is that of the period during which offsets are to apply. Capital losses of a given year may be allowed as an offset against *capital* gains of the same year; or net capital losses of a given year may be allowed as an offset against *capital* gains of the next three or five years. There is much to be said for the latter of these procedures, since losses and gains are periodic and a single year is too short to cover the periodic fluctuations. It is important to point out, however, that future losses should not be allowed as an offset against past gains, but only present losses against future gains. To do otherwise would involve the government in wholesale refunding of taxes and would produce a high degree of fluctuation in federal revenues. The offsets would occur during depression periods whereas prosperity is the strategic time to apply them. . .

There has been talk [recently] about shortening the period during which losses are allowed as an offset against gains. The unsoundness of our present law lies not in the period during which losses are good for offset; rather it lies in the fact that one kind of loss is offset against another kind of gain. Unless this fact is clearly recognized and acted upon, we may still expect to see our millionaires building expensive yachts out of current income while an impoverished government collects no taxes from them whatever.

4. Income as a Measure of Tax-Paying Ability *
"ABILITY" TESTED BY INCOME

When Adam Smith said that "the expense of Government to the individuals of a great nation is like the expense of management to the joint-tenants of a great estate who are all obliged to contribute in proportion to their respective interests in the estate," he might be held to have blessed the benefit principle; but his better known pronouncement, "The subjects of every State ought to contribute towards the support

* From Sir Josiah Stamp, *The Fundamental Principles of Taxation*, (Macmillan and Co., Ltd., London, 1929), pp. 12-17.

of the Government as nearly as possible in proportion to their respective abilities; that is, in proportion to the revenue which they respectively enjoy under the protection of the State,"[1] is a clear enunciation of the ability principle. Moreover, we learn that he would test "ability" by reference to "revenues," *i.e.*, incomes.

"ABILITY" TESTED BY OTHER MONETARY MEASURES

PEOPLE are so used to the idea of ability being measured by income that they are in danger of forgetting that there are other tests having rival claims to notice, which have indeed served as sole tests or partial tests of ability, and which have even been regarded in their place as superior tests. There is, for example, the test of "consumption," *i.e.*, expenditure, whether out of capital or income and capital wealth. We are now so wedded to the income conception that even those capital taxes we possess, such as death duties, and the expenditure taxes, such as the taxes on tea, sugar, etc., we endeavour to express in terms of a tax upon income, in order to make comparisons of the total taxation borne by one class of individual with that paid by another, in relation to the amount of their respective incomes This was recently done by Sir Herbert Samuel in his address upon the "Taxation of the various Classes of the People."[2] When we have summed up the taxation of all kinds borne by an "average" person with £300 a year and found it to be so much in the £, and have performed a similar operation upon the average income of £3000, we feel we are in a position to make a valid comparison, but not before. We do not find it so easy to think of the taxation borne by a *fortune* of £6000 compared with one of £60,000, probably because the great majority of people have little capital wealth beyond their home and their insurances, and our comparison would therefore be too limited. Neither does it come easy to us to consider taxation according to the relative amounts *spent*. Nevertheless there is an important school of thought which would alter the tax on incomes to a tax on sums spent, on purely economic grounds, if that were practicable. So if Brown is comparing his taxation burdens with Jones's he will make little allegation of hardship except by reference to relative incomes. "I pay £30 a year out of £400 income, whereas Jones pays only £80 out of £800." But such a mode of thought has not until recent times been common

[1] Adam Smith, *Wealth of Nations*, v. chap. ii. (2).
[2] *Journal of the Royal Statistical Society*, Mar. 1919.

in America, nor has it been very prevalent in France.[3] The
task of reducing a miscellaneous set of taxes into terms of a
tax on incomes is an intricate one, rarely attempted by the
ordinary individual, and unless his thought is naturally and
readily led along that line by the existence of a tax on incomes,
he does not easily think of comparative hardships in that way.
Mr. Hull, in introducing the United States Income Tax in
1913 to Congress, remarked, *"By this method alone* could
every citizen see and know that taxes are being imposed equitably and according to ability to pay." . . . "The masses of
people are now paying most of our tariff taxes, and most of
our State and local taxes . . . those who have been the vic-
tims *without being able to know the extent thereof,* will welcome the proposed tax."[4]

It will probably be easiest to consider first the problems
raised in the mind of the individual by the attempt to tax
according to ability to pay, when it is to be achieved by a tax
on incomes. This will lead the way to a consideration of the
bearing of other kinds of taxation upon the problem of ability
to pay.

"ABILITY" MAY BE SUBJECT TO FIVE TESTS

THE problem of ability to pay might appear at first sight to be
adequately dealt with by putting the question, "How much
have you got coming in?" This I refer to as the *Quantitative*
aspect. But under the stress of modern high rates of taxation
this can only be regarded as a beginning to a series of questions, and we must ask, "Over what period?" A commercial
traveller, for example, having had a fine week on the road,
might be thinking only of his recent experience and answer,
"I'm doing at the rate of 1000 a year." This point must be
dealt with under the heading the "Time Element." Then
follows the question, "Are you sure it was pure income, without any wastage or return of capital?" which is a matter to
be referred to hereafter as the *"Economic"* or *"Pure Income"*
aspect. Even at this stage the true verdict as to comparative
ability cannot be pronounced. We must ask, "How do you
get it?" because we want to know whether it has any reserve
behind it, or whether its continuance depends entirely upon
the continuance of the worker himself. This may be termed
the *"Precarious"* or *"Earned"* income *discrimination.* Then
follows the highly personal question, "Are you free to *spend*

---

[3] *Vide* article on "Graduated Taxation," by Prof. Seligman, in *Dictionary
of Political Economy ;* also "The Income Tax," by the same writer.
[4] *Congressional Record,* May 1, 1913, p. 837.

it all how you like, or have you unescapable family claims upon you?" and to this aspect may be given the title "Domestic Circumstances." [5]

Finally, there would be some who would ask, "Did you get anything in excess of the sum required to induce you to give your service or lend your capital?" This may be called the *Economic Surplus Distinction*.

THESE ELEMENTS HAVE ONLY RECENTLY BEEN RECOGNISED

. . . It is quite clear that in these days we do not feel that we have dealt adequately with the question of "ability" until these several distinct aspects have been reviewed. It is not merely in the pure taxation of *income* that we now expect to find them properly recognised, but also when the whole system of taxation is reduced to its net aggregate effect upon the individual we consider the claims of justice have not been met if the differences of ability here indicated are ignored or inadequately recognised.

Now it is difficult for the rising generation of students to realise how extraordinarily complex the connotation of the term "ability" has become in the last few years. Twenty years ago any ordinary text-book, on coming to the question of taxation, informed us that our income tax was based on the principle of "ability to pay," merely because Jones with an income of £10,000 paid ten times as much taxation as Brown with an income of £1000. Apart from a little degression, and the exemption limit at the bottom of the scale, we had a flat rate of 8d. in the £, without any allowances for differences of income or personal circumstances of any kind. Beyond the scarcely heeded teaching of a few advanced writers, the great mass of the people had no instinctive feeling for anything else. All these questions slumbered peacefully under the gentle weight of such a burden, but as the pressure set up by the Boer War and the growing consciousness of the necessity for wider State functions steadily increased, one by one they woke up and became vocal, until they reached the shrieking chorus that we hear to-day.

QUESTIONS AND PROBLEMS FOR DISCUSSION

1. What are some of the difficulties involved in arriving at a proper definition of income for taxation purposes?
2. What problems may arise in allowing unrestricted deductibility of capital losses in computing income for purposes of taxation?

[5] *Edinburgh Review*, Oct. 1919 (S.).

3. Do you believe that the income tax should be supplemented by a tax on gifts, the tax to be paid by the donor?
4. Is income a satisfactory measure of ability to pay taxes? Show how the answer to this question depends upon one's concept of income.
5. It has been suggested that capital loss deductions be limited to the amount of capital gains in computing income for taxation purposes, and that in no case should capital losses be charged against current income. What do you think of this proposal?
6. Suppose that Mr. A received an income, after expenses, of $25,000 during a certain year. This income was the result of professional services rendered. The owner of the building in which Mr. A's offices were located also received an income after all expenses, including depreciation, of $25,000. Do you believe that the incomes of these men should be taxed equally?
7. How is it possible to tax only income which has been finally and objectively realized? What are the advantages and the difficulties of taxing income in this manner?
8. Does capital appreciation due to a lowering of interest rates increase tax paying ability?

SUGGESTIONS FOR RESEARCH

1. The income concept for purposes of taxation.
2. Capital gains and losses in income taxation.
3. The income tax and the distribution of wealth.
4. The treatment of stock dividends in income taxation.
5. Defects in the present method of income taxation by the Federal government.
6. The treatment of funded (unearned) and unfunded (earned) income in income taxation.

BIBLIOGRAPHICAL NOTE

In addition to the generous list of references cited in the footnotes of Professor Blakey's article reproduced in this chapter, the following will be found useful: E. R. A. Seligman, *Studies in Public Finance,* (New York, 1925), Chap. V; H. C. Freeman, "Stock Dividends and the New York Stock Exchange," *American Economic Review,* Vol. XXI, pp. 658-671; A. C. Whitaker, "The Stock Dividend Question," *American Economic Review,* Vol. XIX, pp. 20-42; also his "Stock Dividends, Investment Trusts, and the Exchange," *American Economic Review,* Vol. XXI, pp. 275-280.

Able discussions of the concept of earned and unearned income are: W. I. King, "Earned and Unearned Income," *Annals of the American Academy of Political and Social Science,* Vol. XCV, pp. 251-258; and Sir Josiah Stamp, "The Meaning of Unearned Income," *Economic Journal,* Vol. XXV, pp. 165-174.

Some aspects of the taxation of capital net gains are treated in M. S. Kendrick, "The Tax on Capital Net Gains," *American Economic Review,* Vol. XIX, pp. 648-651.

For a discussion of the income concept in accounting theory, see J. B. Canning, *The Economics of Accountancy,* (New York, 1929) ; and R. H. Montgomery, "Accounting and the Concept of Income," in *Lectures on Taxation,* (Chicago, 1932), Sec. 3.

An attempt "properly to limit a technical income tax concept as much as possible," and to carry through this concept to its full consequences, is made by Knut Wicksell in "Inkomstbegreppet i skattehänseende och därmed sammanhängande skattefrågor," *Ekonomisk Tidskrift,* Arg. XXIV, (1922), sid. 127-154.

Constructive criticisms of the federal income tax may be found in W. H. Blodgett, "Frailties of the Net Income Tax," *Bulletin of the National Tax Association,* Vol. XVII, pp. 109-111 ; I. L. Shaw, "How Income Tax Methods may be Improved," *Bulletin of the National Tax Association,* Vol. XVI, pp. 269-275 ; and "Report of Committee of the National Tax Association on Simplification of the Income Tax," *Proceedings of the National Tax Association,* (1927), pp. 108-167.

In the *New Republic* for Jan. 24 to Feb. 14, 1934, inclusive, Professor Harold M. Groves offers some very significant suggestions for "A Tax Policy for the United States." In the issue for Feb. 14th, he treats, among other things, the objections made to the taxation of capital gains and offers a suggestion relative to the *rate* at which such income should be taxed.

An excellent critical analysis of the Federal taxation of capital net gains is Edward G. Nelson, *The Federal Tax Determined by Capital Net Gains ; A Critical Analysis with Suggestions for Practical Reform,* (published doctoral dissertation, Stanford University, 1932).

CHAPTER XVII

THE INCIDENCE AND SOME EFFECTS OF INCOME AND EXCESS PROFITS TAXES

THE incidence of a personal income tax has been treated in Chapter IX. The importance of income taxation, as shown in Chapter XV, justifies a more comprehensive discussion of its incidence and effects.

1. THE INCIDENCE OF THE INCOME TAX *

INTRODUCTORY: THE COMMITTEE'S WORK AS A WHOLE †

"THE keynote of my plea," wrote Marshall, "is that the work of the economist is 'to disentangle the interwoven effects of complex causes'; and that for this, general reasoning is essential, but a wide and thorough study of facts is equally essential, and that a combination of the two sides of the work is alone economics proper." [1] This dictum of Marshall has nowhere been more rigorously adhered to than in the Report of the Committee of Lord Colwyn on National Debt and Taxation in Great Britain. [2] In addition to the Report itself the Committee has published a volume of Appendices, comprised mainly of statistical memoranda, and two volumes of Minutes of Evidence, consisting of the testimony submitted by representative economists, business men, and governmental officials. The Report will long be regarded as a documentary source of great importance; for the task of the Committee was performed in a singularly detached and impartial manner, and the inquiry comes at a strategic interval since the close of the World War, making it possible to analyze its economic consequences in the cold light of experience.

Viewed as a whole the Report is, says Professor Keynes, "a vindication of the British System of Taxation as it now is." [3] Matters relating to the public debt and questions of taxation

* From T. R. Snavely, "The Colwyn Committee and the Incidence of Income Tax," *Quarterly Journal of Economics*, Vol. XLII, (August, 1928), pp. 641-668.

† Paragraph headings have been inserted by the editors.

[1] *Memorials of Alfred Marshall*, p. 437.

[2] *Report of the Committee on National Debt and Taxation*, H. M. Stationery Office, 1927.

[3] *The Economic Journal*, xxxvii (June, 1927), 198.

have been treated "separately as well as in conjunction." While technical problems of administration were regarded as outside the reference of the Committee, consideration in detail was given to numerous schemes for debt reduction, as, for example, the capital levy. No attempt is made to minimize the heavy burden of taxation, but it is instructive to note the Committee's conclusion that the general standard of living of the working classes has not fallen below the pre-war level. Except for the inordinately high duty on sugar, indirect taxes are found to be justifiable and the burden of direct taxation to be "less crushing than is frequently represented." In the main also the tax system is exonerated of blame for the post-war position of industry.

One of the most interesting and valuable contributions made by the Committee will be found in that part of the Report which treats of the incidence of income tax. As might have been expected, the testimony submitted on the question of whether income tax enters into prices was markedly divergent in character. The mental adzes were whetted to the sharpest edge in the contest between the economists and business men on this issue, with the result that both sides frequently resorted to economic theory in an effort to establish the validity of their claims. In the main, however, the business men contented themselves with general statements, while the economists rested their case both on *a priori* economic doctrines and on important statistical evidence.

The purpose of the present paper is, first, to review the conclusions of the Committee on the incidence of income tax; second, to consider the validity of the reasoning by which these conclusions were reached; and third, to examine the criticism recently offered by Professor D. H. Robertson, in an article, "The Colwyn Committee, the Income Tax and the Price Level."[4] It is obvious that the incidence of an income tax is not only a "very intricate" problem and one requiring "great powers of abstract economic analysis,"[5] but that it goes to the heart of theories of price determination. It is part and parcel of the problem of cost of production and price.

TESTIMONY OF BUSINESS MEN THAT A GENERAL INCOME TAX IS ADDED TO PRICES

THE definition of incidence followed by the Committee excludes the popular usage of the term, which, in addition to the initial burden of the tax, covers its "whole range of con-

[4] *The Economic Journal*, Dec., 1927.
[5] *The Fundamental Principles of Taxation*, by Sir Josiah Stamp, p. 130.

sequential effects."[6] For the purpose of analysis, it is regarded as desirable to restrict its meaning to the immediate burden of the tax, thus conforming to the customary demarcation between direct and indirect taxation. It is important to note, however, the precaution taken by the Committee in maintaining that the establishment of incidence is only a preliminary step in appraising the effects of a tax. Whether the bearer of the tax may ultimately gain a compensating advantage, whether the broader reactions may have a deterrent effect on saving and enterprise — these are questions which lie beyond the realm of incidence *per se.*

Having thus defined incidence, the Committee weighed the evidence in support of the view, on the one hand, that "a general income tax cannot be shifted by the person on whom it is laid," and on the other hand, that "it can be shifted and is in fact shifted, in the form of an addition to price."[7] Of the business men who testified, several expressed the opinion that the tax is passed on directly to prices, while most of them stated that prices would be materially affected either directly or indirectly. The latter case would operate in the consequential effects of a tax through a contraction of supply. They were prone to regard all distinctions between the incidence and effects of a tax as of little significance, if not, indeed, fallacious. Under cross-examination the business men, although at times "baffled to fight better," were unable to substantiate their assertions and were forced to be content with stating them as articles of faith.

Typical of this point of view is the statement by Mr. P. D. Leake that, ". . . apart from current price fluctuations due to changes in supply and demand, the general level of selling prices must inevitably be based upon the cost borne by employers incidental to production, and this cost includes the employer's disproportionate burden of progressive taxation."[8] Again he says, "Income tax, falling as it does almost wholly upon employers, is an unscheduled and unacknowledged factor in the cost of production which causes high prices to be maintained."[9] Mr. R. S. Wright, representing the National Union of Manufacturers, held the opinion, "that the difference between direct and indirect taxation hardly exists in actual fact";[10] and Mr. E. B. Tredwen, of the London Chamber of Commerce, in answer to a question by Lord Colwyn, said: "It works in this way. In many cases I have declined to do

6 *Report,* p. 106.　　　　　9 *Ibid.,* i, 331.
7 *Report,* p. 108.　　　　　10 *Minutes of Evidence,* i, 93.
8 *Minutes of Evidence,* i, 333.

business because the reward for doing it would be inadequate."[11] Sir Hugh Bell believed that income tax has an indirect influence and ultimately would have a deterrent effect, "so that I should not carry on my business."[12] Finally, Mr. Leake, quoted above, declared the "body of economics today which centers around the marginal principle" (posited by Sir Josiah Stamp) to be "erroneous," and "not applicable to matters of taxation."[13]

REFUTATION BY ECONOMISTS

IN contrast with the foregoing, the economists were unanimous in the view (with one notable exception to be mentioned later) that an income tax cannot be directly passed on to prices. The monopolist cannot normally shift the tax with impunity, for the reason that the price has already been fixed at the point which will yield a maximum monopoly revenue. The competitive trader, on the other hand, labors under still more difficult conditions. Hedged on all sides by forces beyond his control, he cannot directly raise his prices or limit his supply. Thus Professor Pigou testified that, "as income tax is assessed on the profits resulting from trade and industry, and if, as may be presumed, people are already charging the prices that yield them the best profit, the removal by the state of a proportion of the profit will not tempt them to fix prices differently."[14] Relative to its indirect effects, through a contraction of the supply of capital and business initiative, Professor Pigou agreed with Sir Josiah Stamp, that income tax would be "only a particular case of a general class of discouragement attaching to anything if you do not have the reward of your labor."[15]

Space forbids consideration of similar testimony offered by many eminent economists. We must note in some detail the line of reasoning pursued by them. The arguments in the main are grounded squarely on the determination of price in relation to the marginal cost of production. If there is some variance among the witnesses in their conception of what marginal cost really is, nevertheless the reasoning is premised on the assumption that an income tax falls on profits which arise as a differential surplus above the no-profit concerns, whose costs essentially govern prices. For example, Mr. W. T. Layton held that income tax does not "directly become an item in the cost of production," and that, under competition, pro-

11 *Ibid.*, ii, 518.
12 *Ibid.*, ii, 604.
13 *Ibid.*, i, 337.

14 *Ibid.*, i, 41.
15 *Minutes of Evidence*, p. 48, Qu. 629.

duction "continues up to that point where the last‚unit of output makes no contribution towards profit and therefore nothing towards the revenue of the State. This is the unit of production which determines prices, which should therefore be unaffected by a tax on those units which yield some profit." [16] The determination of prices thus tends to focus on marginal costs. Mr. Layton, it should be said, minimizes the indirect effects of the tax, placing very little importance on the view that there is some relation between a given rate of profit and the exertion of effort or the assumption of risks.[17]

Similarly, Professor Seligman postulates marginal cost as the controlling factor in normal price, and establishes profits on a differential cost basis.[18] Some producers have relatively high costs of production, and *vice versa*. The monopolist, by raising the price, would suffer a loss both in the decline of profits and in payment of the tax. Hence the tax cannot be shifted. Such differences as ordinarily exist between conditions of monopoly and competition, however, are resolved in the case of a general income tax. If the tax be progressive, the supertax-payer cannot boost the price beyond that maintained by his competitors who are subject to the normal tax rate only. The excess above the normal rate can surely not be shifted. The same effect will follow for a normal and even a proportional tax, since "the price at which the whole supply will be sold tends to be fixed at the point of greatest cost." [19] In fact, Professor Seligman gives the marginal cost theory an extreme interpretation when he says: "At any given time the normal price will tend to equal the highest cost of production." [20]

The most refined analysis of the marginal theory, and that which had great weight of authority with the Committee, is undoubtedly to be found both in the evidence-in-chief and in a special memorandum submitted by Mr. W. H. Coates, who was for some time Director of Statistics and Intelligence in the Inland Revenue Department. Mr. Coates, although quite

[16] *Ibid.*, p. 177.

[17] Mr. Layton also stated the matter as follows: "I think I put something like the orthodox view here — the orthodox economic view, not the universal view among business people — that on the whole the tax on income ought not to affect economic action for the reason stated, viz., that prices and the amount of production are determined by the cost of output at the margin where no profit is made, that the Income Tax is a tax on the surplus, and that production will continue under competition to the point where profit stops." (See *Minutes of Evidence*, i, 186, Qu. 2543 and 2544.)

[18] "Income Taxes and the Price Level," *Proceedings of the Academy of Political Science*, vol. xi, No. 1. Reproduced as Appendix xii, Report of the Colwyn Committee.

[19] Appendix xii, p. 120.

[20] *Ibid.*

familiar with Marshall's theory of normal price, evaluates it as belonging to a "stage that is rarely reached in the actual conditions of life." [21] Indeed, according to his interpretation, it is the contention of the business school that price is determined by production in the hands of representative concerns. Although not in accord with this principle, he himself starts with Marshall's laws of marginal utility, demand, and the law of substitution,[22] and builds gradually to the point that "price (*i.e.*, actual price) is always hovering in the neighborhood of that line on which neither profit nor loss is made. . . . Hence the price realized for the marginal increments of supply bears no tax. Yet those marginal increments of supply settle the general price. So the general price also contains no element of tax, and the producer does not recover from the customer any part of the tax that he, the producer, will bear on the result of his productive activities." [23]

Thus it is a part of the general assumption that every producer carries his production to that margin where additional increments will yield neither a profit nor a loss.[24] But what if profits become unsatisfactory because of the tax? The eventual result is not an addition of tax to price, but a tendency toward contraction in supply. Yet if the tax be applied *generally,* the latter effect is of doubtful consequence. It may be that meanwhile there would follow some psychological change in the estimate of reward necessary for a continuance of production. Obviously the issue must be decided, if at all, empirically, that is, by discovering which of the two points of view is more in accord with the facts.

This Mr. Coates attempts to do through a statistical examination for stated years of corporate income tax returns, which were accessible in the Inland Revenue Department. Within the limitations of the data, his analysis is a finished piece of work. At the very least, one can only say of it that it demonstrates beyond doubt the potential contributions to economic theory which may be found in the Inland Revenue Department and in the Bureau of Internal Revenue. Its importance was

21 Appendix xi, p. 68.

22 Marshall, *Principles of Economics,* eighth edition, pp. 93, 99, and 341, respectively.

23 Appendix xi, p. 68.

24 Cf. also the following : "No doubt each producer has a marginal amount of production, that is, a variable quantity the production of which he may hesitate to undertake. And if all producers were equal in ability, the marginal production of any commodity might well be spread over the whole area of production, with a constant tendency on the part of each producer to determine his marginal production by the test of net profits after payment of income tax." (Appendix xi, p. 70.)

noted by Professor J. M. Keynes as follows: "The data at the disposal of Mr. Coates have enabled for the first time the *a priori* conclusion of the economists to be subjected to a statistical test — and the test whatever it is worth is very interesting indeed — from which it emerges undamaged." [25]

Because of the general instability of the market valuation of capital assets, the ratio of net profits was calculated, not on the basis of a unit of capital employed, but on that of a unit of turnover. Consistency required also that the returns of individual and partnership traders be excluded, since "earnings of management" are here reported as profits. Such earnings in the case of joint stock companies are deducted in determining net profits. Joint stock companies were listed under seven trade groups, as follows: cotton, wool, iron and steel, metals, food, wholesale distribution, and retail distribution. The percentage of profit to turnover was calculated for the income tax years, 1920–21, 1922–23, the year 1921–22 having not been chosen because of the radical fall in the price level of that year. Comparisons were also made between the pre-war year, 1913–14, and the post-war years, 1922–23. The years were subdivided into quarters. Cases were classified according to the percentage of profit, ranging at intervals of 5 per cent from those concerns suffering losses of not less than 10 per cent for the first class, to those reporting a profit of 20 per cent or more in the eighth class. Tables were thus prepared showing the dispersion of individual concerns within each class.

The Committee interpreted the results shown by the investigation as affording "strong confirmation of the view that price is determined by considerations into which the income tax does not directly enter." [26] Mr. Coates found no manifest tendency toward a corresponding fall in prices when the standard rate of income tax was reduced from 6s. to 5s., or one sixth, between 1920–21 and 1922–23. Decidedly the most "relevant characteristic," however, is the wide dispersion of firms over the entire percentage range. A considerable proportion of the total production is found at or near the margin. For the year 1922–23, approximately 14 per cent of the total turnover sold at a price below the cost of production.

One is forcibly struck also with the general similarity, over the entire range, of the profits dispersion which was found for the pre-war year, 1913–14, in comparison with the post-war

[25] *The Economic Journal*, xxxvii (June, 1927), 199.
[26] *Report of Committee*, p. 114.

year, 1922–23. For the aggregate of seven industrial groups the following coefficients were obtained: [27]

	1912–13	1922–23
Median	4.61	4.11
Lower Quartile	2.53	1.24
Upper Quartile	7.67	8.46
Skewness	plus 0.19	plus 0.20
Average or mean	5.80	5.43
Mean deviation from median	3.59	6.01

The wholly abnormal conditions which prevailed during this decade might naturally lead one to expect the appearance of many cross-section movements within the seven industrial groups. Such we are told was the case. We note, for example, the aberrations in the cotton industry. In the main, however, internal fluctuations of trade groups tended to cancel. While there is a marked similarity in the profits dispersion for the two years, a glance at the upper and lower quartiles indicates that the dispersion in the latter year was considerably widened.

THE ECONOMIC THEORY ON WHICH THE COMMITTEE'S DEDUCTIONS WERE PREMISED

FROM the foregoing summary of the Committee's conclusion, and the expert testimony brought within its purview, we may turn to an examination of the economic theory on which its deductions are premised. Disregarding sundry variations of statement, it is clear that the reasoning is posited finally on the assumption of some special relation — some casual nexus or governing force — between marginal cost of production and price. Hence it is pertinent to inquire whether the arguments, as enumerated, are in harmony with current doctrines of normal price. (Singularly enough, both the economists and business men frequently appealed to the writings of Marshall to substantiate their claims.) Is the marginal statement incompatible with sound economic theory, and are the conclusions of the Committee, therefore, untenable?

Professor Robertson, in the article referred to above, has advanced some important criticisms against the mode of reasoning accepted by the Committee. Certain of the arguments are labelled by him as fallacious, and others as involving "at the very least a radical departure" from the Marshallian principles. Thus he finds, "a certain looseness in Professor Seligman's conception both of what constitutes the 'costs' of the marginal producer and of the sense in which the profits of the

[27] Appendix xi, p. 92.

intramarginal producer constitute a 'producer's surplus.'"[28]
A similar misconception is attributed to Sir Josiah Stamp and
to the "elaborate and ingenious" analysis of Mr. Coates.

There is abundant justification, of course, for the position
that a bald statement of the marginal cost theory is inconsistent with Marshall's teaching. He states clearly enough
that marginal cost is not significant for normal supply price
under conditions of increasing returns. He counsels us for
these conditions to avoid the use of the term "margin" altogether. It may be used when considering short-run fluctuations of price, since demand is here the dominant factor; and
since a material increase in production for short periods always "conforms to the law of diminishing and not increasing
return."[29] The forces of both demand and supply may doubtless be profitably studied at the margin, but their marginal uses
are inter-related factors with price and are in position of both
cause and effect.[30] The cost of production which Marshall
conceives as being in closest proximity to price in the long run,
and which is therefore normal, consists, for a given volume of
production, in the aggregate expenses incurred by a representative producer.[31] When a business is managed by entrepreneurs of normal or average ability, when it has no special
advantages or disadvantages as regards internal and external
economies of operation, and when the capital has had sufficient
time to reach a full stage of fruition — then the business has
become a typical or standard concern in the industry, and the
"marginal supply price is that, the expectation of which in the
long run just suffices to induce capitalists to invest their material capital, and workers of all grades to invest their personal
capital in the trade."[32]

Aggregate expenses of production are in turn divided into
prime and supplementary costs, the former including in everyday terminology, such direct expenses as "wages, coal, material,
wear and tear of plant, etc." The latter is made up of general
charges, such as "interest on capital employed; depreciation

---

[28] The Economic Journal, Dec., 1927, p. 566.

[29] Principles of Economics, pp. 410, 411. See also Appendix H, p. 805.

[30] The general theory of value developed by Marshall in his Principles is
reaffirmed in his last work, published thirty years later. "Values in domestic
trade," he says, "are governed by the general relations of demand and supply. . .
The margin itself governs nothing; its position is governed simultaneously with
value by the broad forces of demand and supply. But the manner in which
those forces control value can best be studied at the margin." We are told
unequivocally in the subsequent paragraph that the margin is the best place
for studying the "influence of cost," and likewise the "influence of demand."
(Money, Credit and Commerce, Appendix H, p. 321.)

[31] Principles, pp. 317 et seq.

[32] Principles, p. 497.

of buildings, machinery, etc., otherwise than by actual wear and tear; salaries of officials and others who cannot conveniently be discharged at short notice; and the whole cost of building up the organization of the business both internally and in relation to its customers. And over all, allowance must be made for the earnings (i. e., excess of profits over interest on capital, and insurance) of the heads of the business." [33] The supply of a commodity will tend to be increased as long as the price offered is sufficient to cover the expenses of production, including fairly good profits for the managerial functions. [34]

Economists have been quick to perceive that in the world of facts the normal trend of price is not set by the very highest cost at which any part of the product is brought to market. Because of unforeseen or unavoidable conditions, some producers can always be found who are conducting operations at a considerable loss. This is true in good as well as bad years, and appears to be characteristic in the length and breadth of competitive industry. Aside from the circular reasoning involved, such an interpretation of marginal cost would bring it to a *reductio ad absurdum*. Obviously price is not set by the cost, let us say, of that fractional percentage of a commodity which may have been produced at a loss of 20 or 50 per cent. Few economists would gainsay the fact, also, that there is no final causal relationship emanating from marginal cost (in whatever sense) to price. One may call to mind Professor J. M. Clark's statement: "The idea that price is governed by marginal cost of production may be reduced to a tautology; the marginal producer is the producer whose cost of production is equal to the normal price." [35] Marshall breaks "the circular concatenation of phenomena" only by "appealing to the *real* forces underlying what may be called the solar equilibrium of the whole economic system." [36]

The true Marshallian theory, as we are reminded by Professor Robertson, predicates normal price as an average or mean around which momentary price fluctuates. Some producers, having been blessed as preferred children in natural resources and exceptional facilities, and having been endowed with surpassing business ability, fall at the lower end of an ascending costs scale. At the higher end of the scale is the marginal concern; one that is "working under the least advantageous

[33] *Industry and Trade*, p. 191. For a discussion of direct and indirect expenses, see J. M. Clark, *The Economics of Overhead Costs*, pp. 56 et seq.
[34] *Ibid.*, p. 195.
[35] *The Economics of Overhead Costs*, p. 13.
[36] Paul T. Homan, *Contemporary Economic Thought*, p. 235.

conditions in respect of the assistance it derives from the strictly limited resources of nature, *but under average conditions as regards managerial capacity and human qualities in general.*" [37]

Each producer pushes his output to that limit at which the price in conjunction with the quantity demanded will not "spoil the market." Marginal producers who are hanging on the edge of a precipice because of incompetent management are doomed to disappear, to be followed later by others whose management has likewise become less effective. (To Marshall a cyclical rise and fall in industry appears to be a sort of natural order.) But these are not *marginal* in the sense that they govern normal price, so that their full costs are returned, including profits of management.

The conception of normal price as a mean or average is supported by both Professor Taussig and Professor Pigou. [38] In his illuminating study of prices, conducted during the turbulent period of the World War, Professor Taussig found confirmation of the theory that "normal or long period price" conforms to marginal cost whenever variations in cost arise from natural forces rather than from business capacity. [39] That is, normal price is here determined by cost to that marginal firm which is managed by an enterpreneur of "representative ability." On the other hand, when variations in cost occur because of differences in business capacity, normal price "may be expected rather to conform to average cost." In the latter case, which is characterized by decreasing cost of production, the marginal producer is hastening toward his own elimination. Let the sporadic instances of extreme high costs be disregarded. Even so, the "dominant price-determining position" is held, not by the marginal producer, but by the representative firm.

Sir Josiah Stamp and Mr. Coates have been chided by Professor Robertson for having forsaken, or having misunderstood,

[37] H. D. Henderson, *Supply and Demand*, p. 59. See also, Professor Taussig's article in the *Quarterly Journal of Economics*, vol. xxxiii (Feb., 1919).

[38] For Professor Pigou's theory, see *The Economics of Welfare*, 2nd ed. (1924), pp. 193 and 755 ; *Industrial Fluctuations*, pp. 167-171. Cf. also, *The Economic Journal*, xxxvii (June, 1927), 187.

[39] "Price-Fixing as Seen by a Price-Fixer," *Quarterly Journal of Economics*, xxxiii (February, 1919), pp. 225 et seq. It is important to note that Professor Taussig arrives at an opposite conclusion from that of Mr. Coates on the relation of marginal cost to market price. (Cf. Memorandum of Mr. Coates, Appendix xi, part ii, section 8, p. 68.) For Professor Taussig tells us that, "The doctrine of price determination by the marginal producer is not to be considered as applying to anything but a *long-run price* [italics mine]. It has no bearing on the short-period, or seasonal price. Only over a period of years does marginal cost have a determining influence on price. . . The price actually obtaining in any season for a given commodity may be higher or lower than the marginal cost figure reached on the 'bulk line' basis" (p. 226).

the marginal doctrine as taught in Marshall's value theory. Nowhere, he tells us, has Marshall implied that normal value is specially related to the cost of production of the "most inefficient and unfortunate producers," or that "costs do not comprise a substantial element of profit."[40] Mr. Coates is held to have argued that "the magnitude of net profits" is of no concern in the determination of price. Professor Robertson continues: "That, as Mr. Coates points out, the output of the least efficient producers forms part of the total output whose magnitude helps to determine price is, of course, evident; but to argue from this that there is some special relation between price and the costs of the least efficient producers is a complete *non sequitur.*" Thus Mr. Coates is presumed to have departed from Marshall's teaching in underestimating the resistance against cutting prices in a manner to "spoil the market"; and secondly, in assuming all short-periods to be attended by subnormal demand.[41]

Now I venture the belief that Professor Robertson has presented an *ex parte* interpretation of the term "marginal" as expounded by Sir Josiah Stamp and Mr. Coates. It is doubtless true that the latter has subjected himself to certain inconsistencies of reasoning through a failure to relate his long-period and short-period theory of price. He includes the entire assortment of extra-marginal producers within the marginal cost group, thereby omitting to discard the few extreme instances of high-cost producers, whom Professor Taussig designates as part of the "flotsam and jetsam of economic life."[42] Mr. Coates, indeed, appears to regard his marginal cost theory as incompatible with any doctrine of normal price.

Be that as it may, the essential fact is that Mr. Coates, for sufficient reason, has examined only joint-stock companies. Professor Robertson has ignored the significance of this. The no-profit line of corporations for which wages of management have been figured as a part of overhead costs is an altogether different thing from that of single entrepreneur and partner-

---

[40] *The Economic Journal* (Dec., 1927), p. 569.

[41] *Ibid.*, pp. 570, 571. The fallacy of arguing that the ultimate highest cost is marginal is admirably stated by Professor Robertson as follows: "But the fact that some firms are working at an actual loss, while it raises no additional difficulties on the theory that there is a special relation between price and the costs (including profit) of the representative producer, makes nonsense of the theory that there is a special relation between price and the costs (excluding profit) of the 'marginal' producer. For the latter doctrine loses entirely its apparent simplicity of outline when we discover that in fact the 'marginal' producer is not a man who is making neither profit nor loss, but a man who is making a loss of an undefined and unpredictable amount" (p. 572).

[42] *Quarterly Journal of Economics*, xxxiii, 219.

ship firms in which such calculations are not entered. Yet aside from a few types of industry, for example, agriculture, the preponderance of business is conducted under corporate organization. The doctrine of profits is at least simplified and brought into juxtaposition with the business world, if we regard profits as a residuum over and above wages of management. Thus, throughout his paper, Professor Robertson finds himself imperatively using the phrase "excluding profit," or "including profit," to give his words precision.

One may ponder, after all, on the width of the zone between representative firm cost and marginal cost under a proper accounting system for corporations. Professor Bullock maintains that, under conditions of competition, "it is not the average cost or the cost to a representative firm, but the marginal cost of production that is decisive in fixing the normal value of all commodities. In this respect, manufactured goods differ in no way from the products of the farm or the mine ; and it is at this point that our law of varied costs finds its all-important application." [43] Professor P. G. Wright finds that, under Walker's rent of ability theory, the "marginal entrepreneur operating in a conceptual society becomes Marshall's representative firm operating in an actual society." [44] The only dissimilarity between the two theories, he thinks, is that one is moulded to hypothetical, the other to actual, conditions. From a study of Marshall's particular expenses curve, Professor R. C. Meriam concludes that, even for commodities produced under decreasing cost, "the supply price at the equilibrium point is the cost of the most expensive unit of the equilibrium output. The normal price is thus the marginal cost, in the best sense in which the term is used." [45]

When thus conceived, marginal cost is a quite valid reason for the "a priori distinction" between the "effects of a tax on raw materials and a tax on profits." If it can be verified that a substantial proportion of a commodity is produced close to or below the margin,— as much as, let us say, one fifth or one fourth of the output,— then the more favored producers cannot with impunity foist the income tax onto price. For, *ex hypo-*

[43] "The Variation of Productive Forces," by C. J. Bullock, in *Quarterly Journal of Economics,* xvi (August, 1902), 503.

[44] "Cost of Production and Price," *Quarterly Journal of Economics,* xxxiii (May, 1919), 562. Professor Wright concludes that the term "marginal" is faulty in that it is "too uncompromising" and suggests "the absolute highest cost"; while the term "representative" is "too compromising," since it suggests an average or modal cost, p. 563.

[45] "Supply Curves and Maximum Satisfaction," *Quarterly Journal of Economics,* xlii (Feb., 1928), 173.

thesi, every entrepreneur carries his production to the point where additional units actually or potentially yield a diminished total net profit. Whereas, therefore, marginal and submarginal producers are unaffected by the tax, super-marginal producers are actuated by a compelling force against imposing it. That force is the fear of "spoiling the market"—used in an opposite sense from that of Marshall. If it be valid to assume that an expansion of supply will not be effected by super-marginal producers from the fear of demoralization of the market, it must be valid to assume that a contraction of supply, when a substantial proportion of the production is at or near the margin, will not be attempted for the identical reason.

It is the differential aspect of profits that will not down. The implication of marginal cost (as here defined) is clearly indicated, and the existence of firms at or below the margin becomes a crucial factor in the relative elasticity or inelasticity of supply. Professor Robertson reckons with unwarranted levity when he holds it erroneous to range producers in hierarchical order of magnitude of their costs. Short of empirical proof to the contrary, the differential element of profits, taken in conjunction with the *post hoc* relationship of profits to price, bulwarks the faith of the economist with prima facie evidence that is unassailable.

But a tax on raw materials is a general charge applied in advance of price. The entire schedule of supply is *directly* affected through the imposition of the tax. Submarginal firms which do not add the tax labor under an accentuated disadvantage, while those above the margin will elevate price to the point which will again leave them the highest net return. If diagrammatic representation of normal price is here found to be difficult under the assumption of a single competitive price, the fault lies "not in our stars but in ourselves." It will be well to examine the premises on which normal price is thus postulated. In my opinion, Professor Pigou does not "presuppose monopoly conditions" in maintaining that, when an equilibrium in competitive prices has been established at a point which will yield the best profit, . . . people will not charge higher prices because a proportion of the profit has been taken by the State.[46] For income tax acts as an impediment to supply, not directly, but vicariously through its modification of the sources of capital investment and through a change in the psychological estimate of that rate of

[46] *Minutes of Evidence,* i, 41, sec. 30.

reward which is regarded as just worth the effort and sacrifice put forth.[47]

Certain economists to whom the theory of the representative firm is not unacceptable have customarily taught that there is an element of surplus in profits, arising from differential costs, which, in contradistinction to a tax on raw materials, will be reached by a general income tax. Acting as an expositor of Marshall's doctrines for business men, Mr. S. Evelyn Thomas views profit as a "rent of ability," which is "measured upwards" from the level of the entrepreneur who earns a normal profit."[48] In a recent text for students, a similar idea is expressed as follows: "Fortuitous profits above the average cost of production, good and bad years taken together, may be taxed away without affecting the supply of the commodity."[49] Even Mr. J. A. Hobson, lauded by Professor Robertson as the lone economist to sustain the "unwonted rôle of champion of Marshallian orthodoxy," seemingly holds that profits as a surplus above a normal line may be caught within the net of a general income tax.[50]

Factual data bearing upon the truth of the representative firm are not plentiful, but the little that has been brought out of darkness is less reassuring than the economist might wish. The statistical inquiry conducted by Mr. Coates for British joint-stock companies indicates that typical industries showed a steady gradation of concerns from those experiencing wide losses to those realizing large profits per unit of business.[51] Yet

[47] Marshall appears nowhere to have expressed in writing his views on the incidence of a general income tax. Professor Robertson states that he has searched his works in vain for an expression of opinion. He quotes the following passage from Marshall's *Official Papers* (p. 357) in substantiation of his arguments: "Generally speaking, the incidence of taxes on profits is widely and evenly diffused; they run over rapidly from one part of a trade to another, and from one trade to other trades."

I, also, have searched Marshall's works for an expression of opinion, and with no better results. He states at one point that it is prudent to keep "a watchful eye," lest energy and enterprise be checked by excessive taxes on large incomes; but adds in the same paragraph that the "business man of high faculty might not be made much less eager for success by taxation, which took from him and his compeers a considerable portion of their gain" (*Memorials*, p. 351). It is not unlikely that Marshall reasoned on income tax in an analogous manner to that of rent, to wit: "It is *wisest not* to say that 'Rent does not enter into the cost of production'; for that will confuse many people. But it is *wicked* to say that 'Rent *does* enter into cost of production,' because that is *sure* to be applied in such a way as to lead to the denial of subtle truths, which, in spite of their being subtle, are of the very highest importance scientifically and also in relation to the practical well-being of the world." (Letter to Edgeworth, *Memorials*, p. 436. The italics are Marshall's.)

[48] *Elements of Economics*, 2nd edition, p. 289.
[49] *Principles of Economics*, by F. W. Garver and A. H. Hansen, p. 637.
[50] *Minutes of Evidence*, vol. i, Qu. 1565 et seq.
[51] Appendix xi. Cf. *Minutes of Evidence*, ii, 637, sec. 10.

in the industries represented, probably no less than 80 per cent of the aggregate business is of corporate organization. Professor Robertson thinks that Marshall would not have been surprised at this; but Mr. J. M. Keynes holds that the "magnitude of the dispersion . . . is so considerable as to do some damage to the conception of the Representative Firm." [52]

The valuable study of prices which Professor Taussig made in the United States during the World War has already been noted. Cost data were obtained by the Price-Fixing Committee from schedules sent to the several producers by the Federal Trade Commission. Considering the emergency conditions which prevailed, the figures are regarded by him as reasonably authentic. The typical industries were found to be competitive, and "in all these the same phenomena commanded attention, namely, that of marked differences in cost for different producers — a gradual shading from low cost producers at one extreme to high cost producers at the other." [53] The usual cost curves were easily discernible.

SUBSIDIARY ARGUMENTS

Turning from the main lines of Professor Robertson's criticism, we may mention briefly his objections to certain "subsidiary arguments" developed in the hearings before the Committee. There is one common deficiency which he finds characteristic of them all. They are alleged to apply quite as much to local rates or to an impost on raw materials. The first was stated by Sir Josiah Stamp as a corollary of the quantity theory of money. Assuming that there is no change in the quantity of commodities countered against it, how can a general income tax be attended by higher prices? Mr. Hobson had no impromptu answer to this question, but after deliberation replied that it might occur through a "shrinkage of supply." [54]

Such a contraction of supply, while theoretically possible, under the quantity theory, is based on the hypothesis that those upon whom the tax falls will experience generally an indisposition to effort and also an unreadiness to assume investment risks. But it is hazardous to presuppose the unwillingness of producers to accept a diminished net return on the ground that the reward of their labor is unsatisfactory. Such a conclusion is unjustified until proved by the facts themselves.

[52] "The Colwyn Report on National Debt and Taxation," *The Economic Journal*, xxxvii (June, 1927), 205.
[53] "Price-Fixing as Seen by a Price-Fixer," *Quarterly Journal of Economics*, xxxiii (Feb., 1919), 218.
[54] *Minutes of Evidence*, i, 127 n. See also *Ibid.*, ii, 652, Qu. 9060.

There is a strong presumption against it; for, if a considerable proportion of entrepreneurs are not affected, the tendency toward a contraction of supply by one group of producers would be followed by an expansion of supply by another group, thus endangering the market.[55]

In the present objection, therefore, the very point which it has been assiduously sought to prove is nimbly recorded as a fact. As has already been maintained, if there is *any* differential element of profits which may be measured above *some* margin or level of cost of production, then the contention is not "equally applicable" to local rates and to a tax on goods in various stages of production. Under the tenet previously advanced by Sir Josiah Stamp, there could not, in reality, be a contraction of supply until some impediment — through a tax or otherwise — acted adversely upon the motivation to production. We cannot avoid paying hostages to the force of a single competitive price. There is no escape from the dilemma that, if the tax be added to price without alteration in the supply schedule, equilibrium will be established, through the magic of currency, at a higher price level, but the relative position will be unchanged. A shrinkage of supply would ensue only as a dubious by-product. The argument remains as before.

Professor Robertson's rebuttal to the second minor proposition involves a like material fallacy. Under varying rates of super-tax, or a progressive scale of normal rates, the question what income tax becomes a part of costs is entirely apropos.[56] The problem is not one of finding an algebraic formula which will measure the effect on prices of a differential income tax on "various sources of supply." Such a statement really beclouds the issue. The argument of the business men tended to hinge upon the *rate* of income tax in relation to the effect upon price.[57] Hence the Committee was moved to ask, "What

[55] The Committee was apparently unanimous in the view that it would be difficult to experience a general increase of all prices, consequent upon increased income tax, unless the volume of the currency is expanded. In the Minority Report it is declared that "The only remaining way in which increased Income Tax would raise the general level of prices would be by causing a reduction in the volume of production proportionate to the increase in the price level. In this event, however, manufacturers and merchants would lose in reduced sales all that they had hoped to gain in increased prices." (*Report of the Committee*, p. 379, sec. 98.)

[56] The question was stated by Sir Josiah Stamp as follows: "If there is anything in that, I would ask what Income Tax it is that goes into the cost, is it the low Income Tax that small people pay, or is it the high Income Tax which rich people pay, or is it the normal rate of income tax which a company deducts from a dividend? (*Minutes of Evidence*, i, 48, Qu. 621.)

[57] See, for example, *Minutes of Evidence*, i, 337, Qu. 4700.

rate?" Whether under the conception of marginal cost or that of the representative firm, the question is relevant. The analogy drawn between the effect of a tax on raw materials and a tax on income becomes hardly more than a jejune assertion.

The hypothesis that the income tax is added to price leads to a third impasse from which there is no easy extrication. This relates to a nation's foreign trade. Let it be assumed that because of the tax there is a general rise in the prices of domestic commodities. Then, as foreign producers are not subjected to the tax, the equilibrium will be broken and imports will increase. On the other hand, exports, at higher domestic prices, will diminish. Under these circumstances, it would follow that, if the gold standard were maintained, gold would be exported, interest rates would rise, and the price level would be lowered.[58] The prima facie conclusion is that the tax would not be entered as a part of costs, and no evidence was adduced before the Committee to contradict it. In a modified form the opposite view is supported by Professor Robertson — which again hangs upon the validity of postulates regarding normal price that earlier in his paper he labored to prove.

The weight of authority attaching to the statistical investigation of Mr. Coates can unfortunately be made to depend somewhat upon one's theoretical predilections. Despite the high degree of correlation, extraneous factors which could not be eliminated might have influenced the results. I am disposed to agree with Professor Robertson that the statistical evidence obtained does not prove finally that income tax was not added to prices for the years considered. Nevertheless, the evidence itself, within its limitations, weighs heavily against this supposition. With an increase in the rate of income tax by 328 per cent, between 1912–13 and 1922–23, the median rate of profit on sales declined from 4.61 per cent in 1912–13 to 4.11 per cent in 1922–23. If income tax may be added to price, ipso facto, at the will of the entrepreneur, I doubt whether the conditions prevailing in the "very bad year" 1922–23 would have thwarted the impulse to glean such harvest as there was.

But has the tax as applied to the income of securities effected a rise in the rate of interest? The data inspected do not

[58] *Minutes of Evidence*, ii, 652, Qu. 9040. For a discussion of the quantity theory of money under international prices, as bearing upon this point, see *International Trade* by F. W. Taussig, pp. 198 et seq. Cf. also J. W. Angell, *The Theory of International Prices*, chap. 13.

warrant a confident answer to this question either in the affirmative or in the negative. A high degree of correlation (plus 0.893) is found between the gross yield of consols and an index-number of prices during the 100 years from 1825 to 1924.[59] For the short period from 1908 to 1924, the coefficient of correlation is plus 0.90. For the latter period, the correlation between wholesale prices and the net yield of consols after the deduction of income tax is found to be somewhat less, namely, plus 0.74. On the other hand, no close correlation is found for the period from 1885 to 1913, between the same index prices and the rate of income tax.[60] While there is some "implication" from these figures that income tax has not been added to the gross yield of consols, Mr. Coates rightly makes no claim that there is any relationship of cause and effect between the variables.

CONCLUSIONS

WE arrive at the conclusion that the Colwyn Committee was not in error in its deduction that a general income tax cannot normally be passed directly into prices. This deduction is not at variance with sound doctrines of cost of production and price determination. The view of the Committee that the influence of income tax on price will be manifested only through its indirect, consequential effects, is strongly supported by *a priori* reasoning and by such fragmentary evidence as statistical investigations have revealed. The distinction made by economists between the incidence of a general income tax and a tax on raw materials is not, as some writers have maintained, in conflict with economic theory. It needs only to be said, as the Committee pointed out, that minor exceptions, local and temporary in nature, will be found to the "broad economic argument," but these are neither extensive nor important. Such exceptions will occur primarily as the result of some "stickiness" in the adjustment of the forces of competition, or because of a previously existing slack in the competitive price structure.

As to its indirect consequences, suffice it to say that an income tax will, if the rates are made inordinately high, tend to affect the supply of capital and business ability, and to contract the volume of production. Ultimately it must have an influence

[59] Appendix xi, pp. 101, 102.
[60] *Minutes of Evidence,* ii, 675, Qu. 9330. Professor Robertson, however, asserts that there is a very high degree of correlation (plus 0.94) between the rate of income tax and the price level for the period, 1908–24. *The Economic Journal,* xxxvii (Dec., 1927), 579.

upon price. The tax will tend to affect the supply of these factors in a two-fold manner. It will, first, diminish the economic capacity for saving and thus restrict the scope of individual enterprise. In the second place, it may chill the motivating forces of the individual for saving and for the exercise of business initiative. Both the "physical" and "psychological" effects of the British income tax, however, under the high rates imposed during and since the World War, were found by the Committee, notwithstanding the fact that many business men voiced an opinion to the contrary, not to be of great importance. The danger that sources of new capital would be dried up, that pioneering and hazardous enterprises would not be ventured upon, has proved under the high postwar rates, to be more mythical than real. Assuming the tax to have had some adverse effect upon the capacity to save, in the long run there must be balanced against this effect the use to which the revenue is applied. Much of the expenditure used in cancellation of the internal debt is at once reinvested; while a considerable proportion of the revenue devoted to social purposes is subsequently poured back into channels of production.

The fear of a detrimental psychological influence has proved to be no less unfounded. More than is generally realized, a tax bearing high rates acts, within a limited range of incomes, as a spur to greater effort. The likehood that the incentive to exertion will be dampened may easily be exaggerated. In considering effects of this nature, one must not fail to comprehend the significance of the universality of a general income tax within a given sphere. Formerly, too, the burden of risks in industry was confined to a few adventurous persons, but today the corporate type of business organization is predominant and risks are more widely scattered. The corporation, or joint-stock company, is not as sensitive to the imposition of high rates as is the individual entrepreneur. Finally, the reward which is required as a motivating force to business activity is itself a variable factor. The rate of profit demanded in business is determined in a measure by custom. It turns "entirely upon the reaction of people to the conjuncture," in which they live and work. Business men of the younger generation, not accustomed by contrast to a régime of "low taxes" or "low prices," may find themselves, when ushered into an era of high income taxation, relatively unaffected.

2. Relation of an Excess Profits Tax to Instability of Industry *

[A] most interesting and fascinating project is one which has to do, not with the taxes which have been levied during the last decade, but rather with what might have been accomplished with taxes which were abolished at the beginning of the decade. One of these especially deserves attention. It is the excess profits tax. Had it been allowed to remain as a part of the fiscal structure of our federal government, it might well have served to check, if not to eliminate, one of the principal causes of the depression, so far as those causes are economic in character. Beginning with 1922 the excess profits tax was abolished. But the tax on gains from the sale of stocks, bonds, and real estate was retained. This was probably one of the most grievous errors that has been made in the field of taxation in our whole history. Especially serious was this blunder from the point of view of economic stability. The greater the emphasis we lay on stabilization, the more is this action in abolishing one tax and retaining the other to be deplored.

If taxes are ever employed as a means of stabilizing industry, it will probably be discovered that they must be directed at the curbing of credit expansion. If they are to do this, they will have to be so levied as to do everything possible to check speculation in all fields that involve the construction of durable goods. They will have to be aimed particularly at speculation in real estate and in the security markets. Taxes levied upon economic surpluses should be the best way of accomplishing this. All returns to entrepreneurs which are larger in amount than is necessary to induce the managers to apply themselves with all diligence to production and the improvement in productive process should be shared with the public treasury. The term surplus here is used in the sense in which J. A. Hobson uses it in his book *The Industrial System*.

During our participation in the Great War we did exactly this. Under the stress of need for funds for the prosecution of the war and the public conviction that industrial profits were unconscionably large, we devised and enacted a tax on excess profits which produced $2,505,000,000 in the single year 1918. There were loud complaints as to its repressive industrial effects. But the years 1919 and 1920, with their boom in industrial activity, proved these complaints to be ground-

* Adapted from David Friday, "Taxation and Economic Stability," *Research Memorandum : Industry and Trade,* (Social Science Research Council, December, 1932).

less. The rates were lowered for those years, but even in 1920, when depression overtook us during the latter part of the year, it yielded just under a billion dollars. In 1921 the profits of all corporations declined to practically nothing; but the excess profits tax yielded $335,000,000. This tax was collected entirely from corporations which were earning a rate upon their invested capital which was higher than was economically necessary.

Such a tax relieves the industry which is struggling for the time being with unfavorable circumstances of a temporary nature and with the problems of change. It places the tax upon industries which have income which is beyond any level that is necessary for the motivation of ownership and risk-taking.

As a result of the statistical material which became available during the period of excess profits tax administration, we know that a wide diversity prevails in the rate of profits from one industry to another; and between establishments within the same industry.* In an industrial structure which is characterized by the importance and rapidity of change which marks American industry, there will always be a number of entrepreneurs who are in that stage of the growth curve in which profits are abnormally large. During the period from 1922 to 1929 this was true to an unusual degree. The growing profits of these industries translated themselves into increasing security prices upon the stock exchanges of the country. Toward the end of the period, many of these industries found it much cheaper to secure funds by the issue to the stockholders of rights to subscribe to new stock than to secure new capital through the issue of bonds. Some of the more important industrial organizations even issued stock in order to get money with which to redeem their outstanding bonds. This movement of speculative values certainly would never have gone to the lengths to which it did if an excess profits tax had been retained. Perhaps we should have an excess profits tax which is stepped up as the profits of industry mount. Of course it automatically does this if it is graduated, as ours was during the war period.

The ease with which funds could be secured in a period of inflated stock values undoubtedly contributed greatly to the expansion of plant, and so to the demand for durable goods. This operation had two further effects which contributed to instability. The investor who bought stocks and who exer-

* Eds. note: For interesting data on this point, see David Friday, "The Shifting of Taxes on Personal Incomes and on Profits," *Proceedings of the National Tax Association,* (1924), pp. 310, 311.

cised his rights to subscribe to stocks became indebted to brokers or to the bank on security loans in very large amounts. The complaint that stock speculation and brokers loans were withdrawing money from industry was the exact obverse of what was really true. Bank credit was flowing into industry by way of the stock market; but industry did not become indebted to the banks. Instead the stockholders and speculators were obligated to the banks. The banks themselves depended, not directly upon the industry for repayment, but upon the value of the stocks and in some slight measure upon the personal credit of the stockholder. In this manner the whole financial structure became overburdened with short-term loans, mostly payable upon demand. That is one of the difficulties with the whole world today. It had built up, during a period of prosperity, a short-time credit structure which could not possibly be liquidated except by diverting the income of the debtor to the liquidation of these credits in very large amounts. This naturally curtailed the debtor's purchases of commodities, and so brought stagnation in demand and in industrial production.

The situation was aggravated by the retention of the tax upon the gains made from securities and real estate. It is generally charged, by bankers and others, that the desire to escape these taxes contributed to the rise in stocks. In order to escape the taxes people did not sell as the market rose to inflated heights. There is probably truth in this assertion. But the desire to escape taxes did not prevent speculators from taking profits. During the five years, 1925–1929, no less than $17,685,-000,000 of such gains were reported to the federal treasury on income tax returns. This was an average of three and a half billion dollars a year. The determination of what taxes were paid on these gains awaits the results of research. But it can hardly have been less than two billion dollars, or an average of four hundred million dollars a year. Had this sum been collected from the corporations through an excess profits tax, instead of a tax on gains from the stockholders, the resulting industrial process would certainly have been vastly different than it was. And the situation today, from the standpoint of economic stability, would in my opinion have been an entirely different one. . . .

The results of an investigation into the industrial effects which would have been exerted by a continuation of the tax on excess profits will probably furnish the key to the manner in which taxes may be employed for the stabilization of production and employment. It is likely to have much greater significance than the use of taxes for the purpose of re-distributing income directly.

Incidentally, the tax on excess profits would show much greater stability than does the tax on gains. One of the difficulties with the latter tax is that it not only sinks to zero in times such as these; but that its losses neutralize income from other sources. A research project which would trace out the probable effects of excess profits taxes; and contrast them with the industrial consequences of a tax levied on speculative gains would probably get closer to the heart of our industrial process and to the secret of its disturbances than any other field of investigation which might be undertaken. Economic change and fortuitous profits are in all likelihood the foundation of our difficulties. The ten billion dollars of taxes which governments divert to the public use could well be used to offset many, if not most, of the deleterious effects which they exercise upon economic stability.

[Another question is] whether taxes can be employed directly to restrain the over-exuberant production of durable goods in times of prosperity. For example, ought we to levy an especially high rate of insurance premium for unemployment relief in the industries which are engaged in the production of durable things? If we were to go in for a general scheme of unemployment insurance, this question would become a very practical one. Would it be possible to go a step further and prevent by taxation the peaks of production which lead to subsequent depressions? It is probable that what merit there is in this suggestion would be found to be embodied in the taxes on excess profits and income; but at any rate the general problem should be kept in mind, as it is the very core of economic stabilization. . .

The usual dictum with respect to taxes has been that they should be so levied as to do the least possible injury to industry. Our generation is bound to find that generalization quite inadequate for its ambitions. What we are asking ourselves is how taxes can be levied in such manner as to confer an actual benefit upon industrial society. The benefit which we want most just now is stability.

QUESTIONS AND PROBLEMS FOR DISCUSSION

1. Is there any basis for the argument that income taxes are added to prices?
2. Develop the argument that an income tax is not shifted.
3. What factors must be considered in determining the economic effects of progressive income taxes?

4. What benefit would arise if an excess profits tax would "restrain the over-exuberant production of durable goods in times of prosperity"?
5. "Taxes should be so levied as to do the least possible injury to industry." Evaluate.

SUGGESTIONS FOR RESEARCH

1. The economic and social effects of excess profits taxes.
2. The incidence and effect of a state income tax in some particular state in the United States.
3. Income taxation and industrial stability.
4. Income taxes and the canons of equity, productivity, and economy.
5. The economic and social effects of progressive taxation.

BIBLIOGRAPHICAL NOTE

For a discussion of the incidence of an income tax under competition and under monopoly, see H. A. Silverman, *Taxation, Its Incidence and Effects,* (London, 1931), Chap. VII. The effects of the income tax on saving and incentive are discussed in Silverman, *op. cit.,* Chap. VIII. The incidence of taxes on profits and wages is treated in E. R. A. Seligman, *The Shifting and Incidence of Taxation,* (New York, 1927), Pt. II, Chaps. V, VI, and pp. 385-388. Professor Seligman in his *Studies in Public Finance,* (New York, 1925), Chap. III, develops his theory of the shifting and indirect effects of an income tax.

The incidence of taxes on labor incomes and on income from capital is ably treated in H. G. Brown, *The Economics of Taxation,* (New York, 1924), Chaps. V, VII. A stimulating analysis of the incidence of income taxes is David Friday, "The Shifting of Taxes on Personal Incomes and on Profits," *Proceedings of the National Tax Association,* (1924), pp. 306-314. A valuable reference on the subject of the incidence and effects of corporation income taxes is the National Industrial Conference Board, *The Shifting and Effects of the Federal Corporation Income Tax,* Vols. I, II, (New York, 1929, 1930).

An excellent reference for the student of income taxation is the *Report of the Colwyn Committee on National Debt and Taxation,* (London, 1927). The incidence of the income tax is discussed, pp. 108-121. The effects of this form of taxation are studied, pp. 121-169. An exceptionally fine article based upon this report is D. H. Robertson, "The Colwyn Committee, the Income Tax and the Price Level," *Economic Journal,* Vol. XXXVII, pp. 566-581.

Additional material on the incidence and effects of income taxes may be found in references listed at the end of Chapter IX.

CHAPTER XVIII

ESTATE AND INHERITANCE TAXATION

1. ESTATE AND INHERITANCE TAXATION IN THE THE UNITED STATES *

FEDERAL ESTATES TAX

A FEDERAL estates tax was first adopted in 1916. Under the Revenue Law of 1921, it is levied by the Federal government upon the transfer of property at the death of the owner. It differs essentially from an inheritance tax, as popularly understood, since it is levied against the decedent's undivided estate, regardless of the amount of individual inheritances or the relationship of the beneficiaries. In 1929, 45 of the states of the Union had enacted inheritance-tax legislation. Only Alabama, Florida and Nevada have levied no inheritance taxes.

State inheritance taxes are commonly based on the separate legacies, and the rates usually differentiate between several classes of heirs. The Federal estates tax, on the other hand, applies to the decedent's entire estate, after allowing for certain deductions, such as funeral expenses, administration claims, public bequests, and an exemption of $100,000. Under the Revenue Act of 1926, a progressive tax is levied on the remaining net estate, ranging from 1 per cent on a net valuation of $50,000 to 20 per cent on a net estate valuation in excess of $10,000,000.

Since its adoption in 1916, the Federal estates tax has shown considerable productiveness, as is indicated in the following statistics :

YIELD OF FEDERAL ESTATES TAX [1]

Year	Yield
1917	$ 6,076,575
1918	47,452,879
1919	82,029,983
1920	103,635,563

* From S. H. Patterson and K. W. H. Scholz, *Economic Problems of Modern Life,* (McGraw-Hill Book Co., Inc., New York, 1931), pp. 308-309 ; 321-323.
[1] United States Treasury, *Annual Report,* 1929, p. 420.

YIELD OF FEDERAL ESTATES TAX — *Continued*

Year	Yield
1921	154,043,260
1922	139,418,846
1923	126,705,206
1924	102,966,761
1925 [2]	108,939,895
1926 [2]	119,216,374
1927	100,339,851
1928	60,087,233
1929	61,897,141

A Federal tax on inheritance was adopted as a war measure at the time of the Civil War, but it yielded relatively little revenue. The maximum return was reached in 1870, when $3,091,825.50 was collected. In 1872, the Federal inheritance tax was discontinued, but it was revived in 1899 and continued until 1908. During this interval the maximum yield, that of 1901, was but slightly in excess of $5,000,000.

In view of the often voiced dissatisfaction with the highly progressive rates of the Federal estates tax, Congress reduced them very materially under the Revenue Act of 1926. The common arguments advanced in favor of a reduction or an abandonment of the Federal estates tax are to the effect that highly progressive rates on large estates tend to destroy individual initiative and thrift, and so result in a net loss to the community. It is also contended that such rates are intended to equalize the distribution of weath, and so savor of socialism. Finally, it is held that the estates tax is objectionable because it is a tax levied on capital and not on income. These popular arguments against a Federal estates tax, however, cannot be supported by actual facts.[3]

Most modern governments have included estates taxes, death duties or inheritance taxes of one type or another in their fiscal programs. The general tendency appears to be in the direction of increasing, rather than decreasing, these taxes, even though there may be a temporary reaction to highly progressive rates.

As tax measures, estates taxes embody practically all the features of a "good" tax. . . From the standpoint of the taxpayer they are burdenless and cannot easily be evaded. They are levied according to the faculty principle of taxation. From the point of view of the government imposing them they are open

[2] Includes gift taxes in 1925 and 1926.

[3] A convincing refutation of these arguments is contained in a study of Federal taxes made by Ernest M. Patterson, in the special taxation supplement to *The New Republic*, Nov. 4, 1925, p. 26 f.

to the one objection that they are not certain as to time and amount. They are economical to collect, and from the point of view of the general public, possess the merits of tending to decrease inequalities in the distribution of wealth and of not being a burden on industry, unless the rates are such that the lump sum payment of the taxes will constitute an actual drain on industrial capital. To avoid the possibility of imposing undue hardships on an estate, the Revenue Act of 1926 provides that the Commissioner of Internal Revenue may extend the time of payment "not to exceed 5 years from the due date." [4]

* * *

STATE INHERITANCE TAXES

THE first state inheritance tax in the United States was adopted by Pennsylvania in 1826. Since then, other states have from time to time passed inheritance tax laws, until today 45 states in the Union derive a portion of their revenue from inheritance taxes. All of these laws have certain basic features in common.

In the first place, state inheritance taxes are not "estates" taxes, such as the Federal estates tax . . . since they are taxes based on separate legacies and not on the estate as a whole. Secondly, legacies to direct heirs, such as parents, wife, husband, or children of the legator are usually taxed at a lower rate than those to collateral heirs. For example, the New York inheritance-tax law imposes a rate of 1 to 4 per cent on net bequests to direct heirs (the rate varying with the size of the bequest). The corresponding rates on bequests to non-relatives are 5 to 8 per cent. In some states, legacies to direct heirs are exempt entirely from the inheritance tax. Such is the case in Maryland and Texas. Furthermore, a minimum exemption is usually allowed. As a rule, gifts to religious, educational, and charitable institutions are not taxed. Finally, rates are generally progressive, increasing with the size of the bequest and the remoteness of the relationship.

On what grounds can highly progressive tax rates on collateral inheritances be justified? It is contended that, from the point of view of the beneficiary, an inheritance tax is burdenless, since whatever he receives is so much unearned income to him. Again, from the point of view of the testator, the desire to leave a large estate to distant relatives or friends plays an unimportant rôle in gratifying his acquisitive tendencies. Tax or no tax on collateral inheritances, he would in all

[4] Sec. 305b.

probability be inclined to save and to accumulate wealth just the same. The incentive to produce and to save is not destroyed by such a tax.

There are many people who question the right of the state to levy heavy taxes on inheritances, contending that such taxation represents a confiscation of private property. They seem to confuse the right to possess property and to enjoy the benefits of property during life with the right to transfer property at the time of death. The latter right is essentially modern. It is not necessary to go far back into history to discover that property left at the time of death reverted to the state or to the ruler as a matter of course.

When the owner of property dies, his ownership ceases. The disposition of the property subsequently becomes a problem of social, rather than individual, significance. No one has an absolute right to the property, although most modern states safeguard the rights of certain direct heirs in the estates of the deceased, "but always under definite limitations designated to promote the general well-being." [1] The deceased cannot be permitted to determine what shall be done with the property, regardless of the interest of the living. It does not appear unjust for the state to assume the right to a share in the property which it has safeguarded during the lifetime of the deceased, to be employed for the benefit of the whole community. The share thus appropriated by the state is neither a burden on the deceased, nor does it impose a burden on the heirs, since it is not the product of their labors.

The argument is frequently advanced that too high rates of inheritance taxes will discourage the accumulation of property. The validity of this argument can be accepted only with qualifications. If the rates of inheritance taxes are moderate and a reasonable amount is exempt to assure a continuation of the accustomed standard of living to the direct heirs of the testator, it is doubtful whether progressive rates will appreciably retard the accumulations of further wealth and impair the industrial efficiency of an individual. Only excessive rates or multiple taxation of the same property will tend to discourage the accumulation of property.

One of the outstanding weaknesses of inheritance and estates-tax legislation in the United States today is the fact that the inheritance tax laws are not uniform. They lack uniformity not only in respect to rates, but also in respect to the bases on which the taxes are levied. Some states levy the inheritance tax at the domicile of the decedent, others impose the tax upon

[1] Seager, *Practical Problems in Economics*, p. 541.

the situs of the physical property, while still others impose the tax on evidences of ownership.

"Suppose an individual dies in state A, who was a citizen of state B, owned $100,000 worth of bonds of a corporation chartered in state C, the actual property of which was in state D, while the bonds were in the safety vault in state E. The inheritance-tax law of A taxes the property of every decedent of the state, B that of every citizen, C the bonds of corporations chartered within the state, D the property where located, and E the situs of the bonds." [2] In addition, the Federal government takes its share of the property. A hypothetical case can be worked out according to which the combined state inheritance taxes and the Federal estates tax, as provided in existing laws, would theoretically absorb over 100 per cent of the value of the estate.

It is obvious that such chaotic conditions should be remedied. Uniform inheritance taxes, levied on a common base, can be secured only by coöperation among the various states. If the individual states mutually agreed to abolish their present inheritance taxes and allowed the Federal government to tax estates uniformly, the latter returning a certain percentage of the taxes thus collected to the individual states, the outstanding objections to present inheritance taxes would probably be removed.

Furthermore, to remove the possible discouragement to the accumulation of wealth, the rates could be made to vary not only with the degree of relationship and the size of the estate, but also with the number of times the property exchanged hands through inheritance. In other words, the rate might be made "progressive in time," increasing each time the property passed from testator to beneficiary, until after several generations the original estate would finally pass entirely into the hands of the state.

It has been suggested that such a scheme would not discourage the accumulation of wealth so much as do many of the present inheritance taxes. The real problem is to obtain the consent of the states to any such proposal, and to devise a practical basis for administering such a tax and for redistributing the revenue thus collected.

As fiscal measures, inheritance taxes possess practically all the qualities of a good form of taxation. Nevertheless, as was pointed out in discussing the Federal estates tax, they are open to the objection that they are uncertain as to time and indefinite as to the amount of revenue yielded.

[2] Hunter, *Outlines of Public Finance,* p. 327 f.

2. INEQUALITY AND INHERITANCE TAXATION *

INEQUALITY AND INHERITED WEALTH

THE phenomenon of inherited wealth is at once very curious, very important and very much neglected. "For half a century and more, the rights and responsibilities of living men may be determined by an instrument which was of no effect, until the author of it was in his grave and had no longer any concern with the world or its affairs. The power of the dead hand is so familiar a feature in our law, that we accept it as a matter of course, and have some difficulty in realising what a very singular phenomenon it really is." [1] Under almost all systems of law, where the ownership of private property is concerned, the living are allowed to step into the shoes of the dead, either under wills or under various legal rules of succession. This is a very curious fact.

It is also a very important fact. We have seen that, within the framework of the capitalist system, the chief cause of the inequality of incomes from property is the fact that some persons receive much larger amounts of property through inheritance and gift than others, and that the effects of inherited property in maintaining the inequality of incomes from work are also very great, since the children of those who inherit property inherit better economic opportunities, in the form of better chances than they might otherwise have had, and than others have, of health, education, and comfort. Thus "the institution of inheritance promotes social stratification through its indirect effects not less than through its direct." [2] Each year about one-thirtieth part of the total accumulated private wealth in existence changes hands owing to death, and in a period somewhat over thirty years practically the whole will have changed hands. The mere deaths of individuals hardly affect the wealth of the world, and in no way directly affect the mass of material wealth. [3] So, too, the great and growing fund of knowledge and skill is hardly affected by individual

---

* From Hugh Dalton, *Some Aspects of the Inequality of Incomes in Modern Communities,* (George Routledge and Sons, Ltd., London, 1929), pp. 281-286; 311-327.

[1] Salmond, *Jurisprudence,* p. 422.

[2] Taussig, *Principles of Economics,* II, p. 248. Moreover, "mere continuance of prosperity is likely to increase the inequality of incomes resulting from inequality of inheritance." (Cannan, *Wealth,* p. 184.)

[3] "It is a law of our nature," said a speaker at a political meeting some years ago, "that just as we cannot bring anything into this world, so none of us, not even the richest, can carry anything out." "And if you could, it would melt!" commented a member of the audience. For an alternative view, compare Mr. Hilaire Belloc's Poem, *Dives and Lazarus,* (*Versus,* pp. 1-2).

deaths and, subject to trivial limitations, this fund is at the free disposal of all. But with the bulk of the material wealth of the world it is otherwise. Its disposal is limited and its proprietorship is determined by the laws of inheritance, in such a way that great wealth is handed down from one generation to another, and poverty likewise is handed down.

We have seen that under modern conditions there is no tendency, apart from the effects of taxation, for great fortunes to break up in the course of a few generations. The statement of Leroy Beaulieu that it is as hard to maintain as to create a fortune [4] is ridiculous, and is akin to the argument that it is undesirable to pay off the National Debt, because by so doing we should deprive widows and elderly spinsters of a safe investment. In spite of taxation, it is generally quite easy for any reasonably prudent person, not only to maintain a large fortune intact, but by saving and judicious investment steadily to increase it. As Dr. Watkins truly says, "keeping riches once gained is easier than ever before. . . The rich by inheritance have a position which they can lose only by a destructive tendency amounting almost to madness." [5]

Though very curious and very important, the phenomenon of inherited wealth has been very much neglected, especially by professional economists.[6] "Few economists," says Professor Graham Wallas, "think with satisfaction of the degree to which the less urgent desires of the minority who have inherited wealth are now satisfied before the more urgent desires of the majority who have not inherited it." [7] It would be more true to say that few professional economists appear to think of this aspect of the distribution of wealth at all. Their thoughts on this subject at any rate are usually confined to stray comments or *obiter dicta,* which are often neither particularly illuminating nor particularly profound. The importance of the question has been most vividly present to the minds of many, who can make small claim to the title of economist. "I am astonished," said de Tocqueville, "that ancient and modern writers have not attributed to the laws relating to succession a greater influence in the march of human affairs. . . They should be placed at the head of all political institutions, for they exercise an incredible influence upon the social conditions of peoples." [8] The grounds of de Tocqueville's astonishment are no less valid

[4] *Répartition des Richessés,* pp. 261-262.
[5] *Growth of Large Fortunes,* p. 159. Compare Taussig, *Principles,* II, p. 168.
[6] Compare Part II, passim, and especially Chapter VII, §§ 8-11 above, [in Dalton, *Inequality of Incomes*].
[7] *The Great Society,* p. 312.
[8] *La Démocratie en Amerique,* Vol. I, Ch. III, pp. 74-5.

today, in spite of the fact that he imagined that America would continue to be a land of moderate fortunes evenly distributed.[9]

It is important to avoid false analogies between the inheritance of private property and other forms of inheritance in economics, politics and biology. For such false analogies are very commonly met with.[10] Certain analogies, which are not logical connections, are apt, indeed, to impress the modern mind. It is not, for instance, to be expected that, when "the hereditary principle" has been practically abolished as regards political power, it will be much longer ignored as regards economic power. Yet, as an example of how even an intelligent man could look at inheritance a century and a half ago, we may still read with interest Burke's letter to the Duke of Richmond in 1772 : "You people of great families and hereditary trusts and fortunes are not like such as I am, who . . . are but annual plants that perish with our season, and leave no sort of traces behind us. You, if you are what you ought to be, are the great oaks that shade a country, and perpetuate your benefits from generation to generation."[11] More recently one of Meredith's characters found himself able, in the spirit of Burke, to "venerate old families, when they are not dead wood," but the capacity for even this conditional "veneration" is probably growing rarer. For reason begins to suggest that all families are really equally old, though unequally notorious, and even that, the worthier any family may be of "veneration," the less its members should need the economic prop of inherited wealth.

But the full realisation and constructive criticism of this institution are surprisingly slow to arrive. "The question of inheritance," said Stein in 1850, "is the question upon the discussion of which the entire future of the social form of Europe will rest during the next two generations."[12] He has proved quite wrong. Many thinkers of high reputation still talk, or

9 *Ibid.*, Vol. II, Part III, Ch. I, and Vol. IV, Part IV, Ch. VIII.

10 See, for example, the remarks of Schmoller, quoted in Part II, Ch. VI, § 4, above, [in Dalton, *op cit.*]. Even Mr. Hartley Withers (*Poverty and Waste*, pp. 49-50) after observing that "the owner of inherited wealth above all men is bound to be extremely careful of the use that he makes of it. . . For he owes everything to the care that his fellow-creatures take of him. He may think that he owes it all to his great-grandfather, but herein he errs," seems to encourage confusion of thought when he continues, a few sentences later, as follows: "When the case has thus been decided against the owner of inherited wealth, and he has been cautioned as a suspicious character, let us then go on to recognise that we are nearly all of us owners, if not of inherited wealth, at least of inherited earning power." For there is no genuine analogy between inherited wealth in this sense, and inherited earning power.

11 Quoted by Hammond, *The Village Labourer*, p. 24.

12 *Geschichte der Sozialen Bewegung in Frankreich*, II, pp. 226-7.

remain silent, about the law of inheritance, as though it had fallen immutable from heaven into the Garden of Eden.

In fact, law and custom regarding inheritance show great variations both in the same country at different times and in different countries at the same time. Law imposes an outer limit and custom an inner limit, within which the effects of the institution operate. The outer limit of law is sometimes crossed by illegal evasion, and the inner limit of custom includes such so-called "legal evasion" of the intentions of the legislator, as gifts of property among the living, designed to evade the operation of rules of law. Both law and custom are expressions of public opinion, but expressions in which the same weight is not necessarily attached to different sections of public opinion. A divergence is specially likely to appear in a politically democratic country with a markedly unequal distribution of property.

The law regarding the inheritance of property may be divided into two parts, the fiscal and the non-fiscal law. The fiscal law regulates the taxation of inherited property, whether at the moment of inheritance or at other times. The non-fiscal law regulates the extent to which, if at all, freedom of bequest is permitted, and the rules which determine inheritance, in so far as freedom of bequest does not operate, including rules of intestate succession.

* * *

THE COMPARATIVE FISCAL LAW OF INHERITANCE AND ITS COMPARATIVE EFFECTS

A SPECIAL form of the fiscal law of inheritance is the Law of Escheat, by which, under certain conditions, a dead person's property reverts to the State. This law has a certain historic interest, but at the present time in this country only applies to intestate estates, in cases where there are no relatives, however remote. It has been proposed by Bentham, Mill and others that the present rights of "collaterals" to inherit on intestacy should be abolished, and the field of operation of the Law of Escheat correspondingly extended.[1] But such a provision would stimulate will-making, and its effect is not likely to be great.

It is conceivable that a society might have developed from primitive conditions into modern civilisation with a law of inheritance, under which wills were more or less completely pro-

---

[1] Compare Part II, Chapter III, § 5, and Chapter V, § 3 above [in Dalton, *op. cit.*].

hibited, and the rights of inheritance of relatives limited to
small amounts, the bulk of the property of deceased persons
escheating to the sovereign, that is to say, in later stages of
development, to public authorities. But the political power
and "class consciousness" of the rich have everywhere contributed to prevent any such historical development.

We may now turn to the more practically important question of the taxation of inherited property.[2] Such taxes may
be divided into two classes, according as they are imposed on
property actually changing hands at death, or on inherited
property at other times. It will be convenient to begin by
considering the first class, to which the term "inheritance tax"
is usually confined.

Nearly all modern communities have inheritance taxes in
this sense, but this part of the fiscal law of inheritance differs
from other parts and from the non-fiscal law, in that it changes
much more rapidly and much more markedly from year to
year. The law of legitim in its various forms, and the various
legal restrictions imposed on freedom of bequest in the English-
speaking countries, have remained substantially unchanged
during the past half-century, but inheritance taxes during this
period have everywhere been changing and developing.[3]

Three principles of graduation are found, singly or in combination, in most of the inheritance taxes actually in force.
The first is graduation according to the total amount of property left by the dead person, larger amounts paying a higher
proportionate tax than smaller amounts. This principle is
applied, for example, in the British Estate Duty. The second
is graduation according to the total amount received by individual inheritors, larger amounts again paying a higher proportionate tax than smaller amounts. The third is graduation
according to the relationship of the inheritor to the dead person, a near relative paying a lower proportionate tax than a
distant relative, and the latter a lower proportionate tax than
a stranger, on an inheritance of given amount. Both the second
and third principles are applied in the British Legacy Duty,

---

[2] Professor Graziani rightly points out (*Teorie e Fatti Economici*, p. 103) that
a tax on inherited property is to be regarded simply as part of the tax system,
and defended as such, and not, as Bluntschli and other "theorists of the State"
have argued, on the "metaphysical" ground that "the State" has rights as coheir
with individuals to the property of the dead. Compare also Graziana, *Natura
Economica Delle Imposte Sulle Successioni* and Nitti, *Scienza Delle Finanze*,
pp. 677-680.

[3] The best general account of inheritance taxes is that given by Dr. Max West
in his book, *The Inheritance Tax*, first published in *Columbia University
Studies*, Vol. IV. A second edition appeared in 1908. The premature death
of Dr. West in 1909 is a serious loss to students of this subject who were looking
forward to a new edition of his book.

and all three principles are applied in State inheritance taxes in the United States.[4]

The first principle differentiates against large estates, but not between different methods of distribution among inheritors. The second principle differentiates in favour of a fairly equal distribution among a large number of inheritors, as against a more unequal distribution among the same number, or as against concentration among a smaller number. The third principle differentiates in favour of a distribution among near relatives, and against inheritance by strangers. Such differentiation, in all three cases, operates both through the actual operation of the taxes, in which these principles are applied, and also, though probably to a smaller extent, in the effect produced upon the minds of testators by the knowledge that the taxes will so operate. Mill's proposal to limit the amount which any individual may inherit might be enforced as a particular case of the second principle, the tax being so graduated as to take 100% of all inheritance in excess of the limit laid down. The first principle is the easiest to apply administratively, and it is chiefly for this reason that it figures more prominently than the second or third in the British system of death duties. Randolph Churchill, when Chancellor of the Exchequer in 1886, was anxious to reform the death duties by getting rid of both the first and third principles and relying entirely on the second, but the Treasury officials raised administrative difficulties, which resulted, in combination with Churchill's ill-calculated resignation, in the dropping of the scheme.[5] Harcourt, in his reform of the death duties in 1894, relied mainly on the first principle, and incidentally abolished a previously existing differentiation in favour of inheritors of realty as against inheritors of personalty.

The comparative effect of the three principles on inequality can best be considered by assuming that a given revenue is to be raised by an inheritance tax, in which only one of the principles is applied. It is clear that, except in very exceptional circumstances,[6] the naked adoption of the third principle will do less to diminish inequality than the adoption of either the first or the second. But such naked adoption implies the taxation of bequests for benevolent purposes at the same

[4] Compare Bancroft, *Inheritance Taxes for Investors*, Read, *Abolition of Inheritance*, pp. xiii, 293-4, Ely, *Property and Contract*, I, pp. 417 ff. The first principle is applied in the United States Federal Inheritance Tax.

[5] See Mr. Winston Churchill's *Lord Randolph Churchill*, II, Chapter XV.

[6] *E.g.*, if the generality of strangers benefiting substantially under wills are very much poorer than the generality of relatives, and if, among the latter, near relatives are considerably richer than remote.

maximum rate as bequests to individual strangers. If clothed
with the qualification that publicly advantageous bequests of
the former sort are to be untaxed, or taxed at a relatively low
rate, the application of the third principle will do more to
diminish inequality than if it is adopted in its naked form.[7]
But it will not do *much* more, unless such public bequests
are of considerable quantitative importance, and, unless their
importance becomes very much greater than it is at present,
even in the United States, the third principle is likely to be
decidedly inferior to either the first or the second, as a means
of reducing inequality.

As between the first and the second principles, the adoption
of the second is likely to diminish inequality more than the
adoption of the first, if the scale of graduation is roughly the
same in both cases. But, if a given revenue is to be raised,
it will be necessary either to have a higher maximum rate, or a
lower minimum exemption, or a somewhat steeper graduation,
under the second principle than under the first. Even so, the
advantage seems to lie with the second.

Turning to the comparative effects of the three principles on
production, it does not seem that there is much to choose
between them. As compared with other practicable methods
of taxing the relatively rich, Professor Pigou argues persua-
sively that an inheritance tax has "strong claims upon the
attention of statesmen." [8] His argument is irrespective of
whether our first, second, or third principle is adopted in framing such a tax. From the point of view of production, the
case for the inheritance tax is especially strong, if its payment
has been completely insured against in advance, so that there
is no temptation to those who have to pay it to sell part of
the inherited property in order to raise the money, and stronger
still, if the insurance premiums are likely to be paid with money
which would otherwise have been spent and not saved.

It is also important to remember that the effect of this, or
any other, tax in checking production may be more than offset
by the way in which the public authority, which imposes it,
deals with the proceeds. If the latter are treated as capital or,
as is sometimes said, "devoted to capital purposes," such as the
reduction of the National Debt, or the planting of trees, the
net effect of the raising and spending of such revenue will gen-

---

[7] In many states of the United States, bequests to benevolent and charitable
institutions are exempt from taxation. See Underwood, *Distribution of Ownership*, pp. 151-2, where it is also pointed out that many of the states put an
additional tax on bequests to non-resident aliens.

[8] See *Wealth and Welfare*, pp. 352-354 and 375-377.

erally benefit production.[9] The belief, not always well founded, that an inheritance tax tends to "fall on capital" to a greater extent than other direct taxes, is so common that it is often proposed that its proceeds should be thus treated. "The State," says Professor A. S. Johnson, "can adopt the same policy which every prudent person recommends to the private heir. It can treat capital acquired through inheritance as a fund to be maintained intact. Let the State set apart, as a permanent investment fund, the proceeds of all inheritance taxes, and depletion of the national capital will at once cease." [10] This may be a good policy, but not precisely for the reason given.[11]

There is, however, a fourth alternative principle, which might be, though it has not hitherto been, adopted in framing an inheritance tax. This has been propounded by Professor Rignano in his remarkable and curiously little known book, *Di un Socialismo in Accordo colla Dottrina Economica Liberale*.[12] This principle is that of an inheritance tax, which shall be "progressive in time," or, in other words, such that the rate of tax shall increase with the number of times that the property subject to it has already changed hands through inheritance. Thus, to take the illustration given by Professor Rignano himself,[13] suppose that the inheritance tax on a first transmission by inheritance is one-third, on a second transmission two-thirds, on a third transmission the whole. Suppose that A, who receives nothing by inheritance, acquires by work and saving property of value a, which he leaves by will to B. Then the tax will be $\frac{1}{3}a$ and B will receive $\frac{2}{3}a$.

Suppose that B, by his own work and saving, adds a further amount b to his inheritance of $\frac{2}{3}a$, and leaves the whole by will to C. Then the tax will be, as to the $\frac{2}{3}a$, two-thirds and, as to

---

[9] In the cases both of raising and of spending, we need, for completeness, to take account not only of the effects of the fact, but of the effects of the expectation of the fact. But the latter are probably not very important, as far as the "spending" of public revenue on capital purposes is concerned.

[10] *Journal of Political Economy*, 1914, p. 169.

[11] An example of how not to carry out this policy is furnished by the decision of Mr. Austen Chamberlain that his 4% Victory Bonds, 1919, issued at 85, shall be accepted at their par value in payment of death duties. Under this plan an attempt is made to improve the national credit at the expense of the real, if not the apparent, yield of the death duties. For, unless the market value of Victory Bonds rises to par, which for some time to come is unlikely, those who pay in these Bonds will escape part of the death duties. For example, if the market value is 75, Mr. Chamberlain will receive, as the equivalent of £100 of revenue, what he could have bought in the open market for £75, while the burden of death duties on the taxpayer will be reduced by 25%.

[12] The page references which follow are to the French edition. Compare Part II, Chapter VII, § 14 above, [in Dalton, *op. cit.*].

[13] *Op. cit.*, p. 42.

the b, one-third. Therefore the total tax will be $\frac{4}{9}a + \frac{1}{3}b$, and C will receive $\frac{2}{9}a + \frac{2}{3}b$. Suppose that C, by his own work and saving, adds a further amount c to his inheritance and leaves the whole by will to D. Then the tax will be, as to the $\frac{2}{9}a$, the whole, as to the $\frac{2}{3}b$, two-thirds, and as to the c, one-third. Therefore the total tax will be $\frac{2}{9}a + \frac{4}{9}b + \frac{1}{3}c$, and D will receive $\frac{2}{9}b + \frac{2}{3}c$. And so on indefinitely, each person's addition, if any, to his inheritance being wiped out by taxation in the course of three transmissions. "In effect, on the death of the grandson of each accumulator, or more generally of the heir of his immediate heir, the State would have nationalised a third of the personal fortune of the deceased, seven-ninths of that accumulated by his father, and the whole of that accumulated by his grandfather. One could modify these rates and adopt any scheme of progression which seemed most suitable." [14]

Professor Rignano thus puts forward this principle of taxation in general form, noticing certain other proposals which have been made as special applications of it.[15] He claims that it affords the only practicable method of nationalising private capital, while at the same time stimulating, rather than discouraging, work and saving by private individuals.[16] Such a tax, however, apart from the desirability of using it as an instrument of nationalisation, which we may regard for the moment as an open question, has certain obvious merits. We may therefore begin by enquiring into its practical applicability.

The chief practical problem, which is involved, is that of distinguishing, on the death of any person, between that part of his property which is due to his own work and saving and that part which is due to the work and saving of various individuals from whom, directly and indirectly, he has inherited. Professor Rignano points out that this division of the dead person's property into different parts, for the purpose of ap-

14 *Ibid.*, p. 47.

15 For example, the proposal of Huet, *Règne Social du Christianisme* (1853), p. 271, that no one should be allowed to leave by will anything beyond what he had acquired by work and saving during his own lifetime, or in other words, that property should be transmissible once by inheritance free of tax, but that at the second transmission the State should take the whole. Also Russell Wallace's proposal, in his *Land Nationalisation*, that the State should assume ownership of all land, and guarantee the proprietors' current incomes therefrom for two lives, but not longer. A tax on Professor Rignano's principle may be contrasted with a special tax on "War Wealth." The former discriminates against wealth created a long time ago ; the latter against wealth created a short time ago. The main argument for the former is economic, for the latter sentimental. The contrast illustrates the distinction between economy and equity.

16 *Ibid.*, pp. 40-41 and 48-49.

plying different rates of taxation, need only be "a quantitative and not a qualitative division." [17]   That is to say, no attempt need be made to trace particular pieces of land, or particular blocks of shares, in their passage by inheritance from one proprietor to another. It will be sufficient to divide the dead person's property into various parts according to their total value. This procedure will, indeed, be necessary, since particular property rights change hands, not only by inheritance and gift, but also by sale. If, however, the division is made on the basis of values, it will be necessary, ideally, to make an allowance for changes in value, which are due, not to the action of the proprietor, but either to changes in the general rate of interest, or to changes in the relative value of different sorts, or particular pieces, of property. If such an allowance is not made, the alleged advantages of a tax on this principle will not be fully realised. In practice, it would be possible, though difficult, to allow for the effects of changes in the general rate of interest, but almost impossible to allow for the effects of other changes. This, however, should not be fatal to the application of the principle, though it would lead to a certain number of "hard cases," and also, in the opposite sense, to a number of "soft cases," of which less is likely to be heard.

Apart from this question of allowances, the practical application of the principle involves little more than a sufficiently elaborate system of book-keeping by Government tax-collectors. It will be necessary for the latter to keep records showing the amount of property received by individuals by inheritance, and probably also by gifts *inter vivos*, and the sources of such receipts, *i.e.*, whether the latter consist of property already inherited, and if so, how many times already inherited. There seems no doubt that a modern state could create an adequate system of book-keeping of this kind, if the results were held to justify the cost and trouble involved. Nor would the cost and trouble be so great as might be imagined at first sight. For, in the first place, there would presumably, though Professor Rignano does not suggest it, be a minimum value fixed, below which inherited property would not be taxable, no matter how many times it might already have changed hands by inheritance, and, in view of the very unequal distribution of property in modern communities, the number of individuals, for whose property elaborate records would be necessary, would be only a small fraction of the population. In this country at the present time it would probably be less than half a million. In the second place, as regards inheritance, though not as

[17] *Ibid.*, p. 43.

regards gifts *inter vivos,* Professor Rignano rightly points out that a complete record of an individual's property and its distribution at his death, involving entries in the accounts of all substantial beneficiaries, would afford sufficient data for the application of his principle.[18] There seems no reason to suppose that the fiscal book-keeping necessary to carry out the scheme would, at the worst, be one-tenth part as elaborate and expensive as that involved in the administration of the National Health Insurance Act.

The adoption of the scheme might also be facilitated by other changes in the law. Thus Professor Rignano suggests that Bearer Bonds might be prohibited,[19] and Professor Pigou throws out, but does not develop, the suggestion that "it might even be necessary for a law to be passed requiring all legacies to be settled, in such wise that the heirs could not touch the principal."[20]

Even if it were to be decided that the principle, in its more elaborate or drastic forms, is not administratively practicable, it might still be possible to introduce it in a simplified form by making a distinction between a person's own savings and his inheritances and gifts, whether direct or indirect, and by imposing at his death two rates of taxation, a lower one for his own savings and a higher one for his inheritance and gifts.[21] In the discussion, which follows, of comparative effects, the latter principle will be referred to as the simplified Rignano principle, and will be contrasted with the full Rignano principle, which will be taken to involve at least three, and possibly more, different rates of tax according to the number of hereditary transmissions. Following the analogy of the terms "earned" and "unearned" income, we may conveniently speak of a person's own savings as his earned property, and of his inheritances and gifts as his unearned property.

We may now compare the effects on inequality and on production of raising a given sum by means of an inheritance tax based on the full Rignano principle, or on the simplified Rignano principle, with the effects of raising the same sum by means of an inheritance tax based on the first, second, or third principles discussed in . . . this chapter. It will be noticed that neither form of the Rignano principle involves any gradua-

---

[18] *Ibid.,* p. 59.
[19] *Ibid.,* p. 58.
[20] *Wealth and Welfare,* p. 377.
[21] If it is found impossible to allow for fortuitous changes in the value of property, such savings, for purposes of taxation, will be increased by any fortuitous appreciations of any property held by him, and diminished by any fortuitous depreciations.

tion according to amount, except presumably the exemption of inheritances below a certain amount from the operation of the tax.

The effects on inequality of a tax on the Rignano principle depends upon the proportion at different points of time between the totals of earned property and of unearned property, and further, if the full principle is being applied, upon the proportions between the totals in different categories of inherited, or unearned, property, which it is proposed to tax at different rates. Other things being equal, the effect of such a tax in diminishing inequality will be greater, the smaller is the proportion of earned to unearned property, and, if the full principle is being applied, the larger is the proportion of inherited property to be taxed at the highest rate to total property in private hands. It is clear that, in general, a tax based on the full principle will diminish inequality more than a tax based on the simplified principle. Since a tax based on the Rignano principle could not easily be made retrospective, owing to the need to set up fresh administrative machinery, which could only operate easily on events taking place after it was set up, the effects of such a tax could only make themselves felt gradually, and comparisons with the effects of a tax based upon the other principles, which we have been considering, could only, therefore, be made after a certain period had elapsed. In the absence of knowledge as to the proportions between the amounts of different categories of property just referred to, it does not seem possible to make any very confident predictions as to comparative effects on inequality. But it seems likely that a tax based on the simplified Rignano principle would generally do more to diminish inequality than a tax based on the third principle, but less than a steeply graduated tax based on either the first or the second principle. On the other hand, if the proportion of earned to unearned property was small, and the proportion of property taxable at the highest rate was large, a tax based on the full Rignano principle might very likely diminish inequality as much as a pretty steeply graduated tax based on either the first or second principles. These comparisons, however, are speculative and uncertain.

But, as regards comparative effects on production, we can stand on firmer ground, and it is here that the strongest argument for the adoption of the Rignano principle is forthcoming. Professor Pigou, in his carefully balanced comparison of the effects of different sorts of taxes upon production, concludes, as regards the plan proposed by Professor Rignano, that "there can be no doubt that a given revenue could be obtained by this plan, in such wise that the expectation of the levy of it would invoke a smaller restrictive effect upon the supply of waiting than is associated with the existing system of death duties." [22] More roughly, a tax on the Rignano principle diminishes the *will to save* less than other types of inheritance tax of equal amount. This seems clear enough, but it is not all that can be said on the matter. For it is arguable that the will to save may, as a result of the adoption of a tax on the Rignano principle, be actually increased, and also that the will to work may be stimulated.[23]

Professor Rignano himself contends that a tax according to his plan would lead to more work and saving by those whose property would on their death be subject to it, than would take place, if there were no inheritance tax of any kind in force.[24] "Experience teaches us," he says, "that the possessors of great fortunes, being able to leave to their children the property which they themselves received by inheritance, are in no way stimulated to increase these still further. Generally they spend their considerable incomes in luxury and pleasure. . . It is the existing right of bequest which leads them to dissipation instead of stimulating them to save, even when they are very far seeing and very much attached to their families. But these men would conduct themselves quite differently, if one said to them, 'take care; of the wealth which you have yourselves inherited, you will only be able to leave to your children a small fraction, or even nothing at all, whereas of that which you have yourselves accumulated, you will be able to leave a very considerable part.' This argument would dispose them more than any other to economise their foolish expenditure and to transform part of their income into beneficent productive capital. Furthermore, whatever his social position, an affectionate father would be far more stimulated to work and saving, when each hundred francs that he made would represent for his children a value double or treble that of each hundred francs of his own inherited property." [25]

22 *Wealth and Welfare*, p. 377.

23 Professor Pigou (*ibid.*, p. 365 n.) deliberately leaves out of account "as of secondary importance, the indirect effect of the expectation of diminished resources in inducing the rich to do more work." As regards inheritors it may generally be of secondary importance. The argument in the text is concerned with those who work or save in order to leave property to their children.

24 *Ibid.*, pp. 40-41 and 65 ff. He quotes (p. 65), while disagreeing with, Professor Wagner's opinion that a heavy inheritance tax, even of the ordinary kind, would actually stimulate saving by parents desirous of leaving an adequate fortune to their children.

25 *Ibid.*, pp. 67-68.

This line of argument is very plausible. It resembles Professor Gonner's argument that a fall in the rate of interest tends to increase saving, since more saving than before is now necessary in order to secure an amount of property yielding a given income.[26] The latter argument indeed fails, partly because, owing to the very unequal distribution of property in modern communities, a comparatively small number of rich people do the bulk of the saving and invest, for the most part, merely income surplus to habitual expenditure. These are tempted to save more by a higher, and less by a lower, rate of interest. Those who invest in order to secure from their investments a certain minimum income and tend, therefore, to save more when the rate of interest falls, though perhaps more numerous, are less rich than the former class, and their savings much less important in the aggregate. If the latter class predominate in the will to save, the former predominate in the power to save.

But Professor Rignano's argument is stronger than Professor Gonner's. For he suggests, in effect, that the adoption of his plan would place many members of the former class in the position of the latter class, and would reinforce their power to save with a strengthened will to save.[27] Looked at from another angle, the effect of the adoption of his plan would be to raise the marginal utility of savings made by themselves, while reducing the marginal utility to them of the savings inherited from previous generations. For the marginal utility of either sort of savings depends largely upon the power of leaving them to their children. Moreover, Professor Rignano relies upon an increased stimulus to work among those desirous of leaving property to their children.

It is not easy to be sure whether Professor Pigou is right in thinking that an inheritance tax on Professor Rignano's plan would discourage saving, but discourage it less than other sorts of inheritance tax, or whether Professor Rignano is right in thinking that such a tax would actually stimulate work and saving. But it is clear that, from the point of view of its effects upon production, a tax based upon the Rignano principle is superior to a tax based upon any of the other three principles considered at the beginning of this chapter, and it is also clear that, if administratively feasible, a tax based upon

[26] Compare Gonner, *Interest and Saving*, p. 67, and Marshall, *Principles*, pp. 234-5.

[27] Some light might be thrown on the matter by a study, if the facts were available, of the conduct of life tenants of property, which at their death is to pass away from their family, as compared with tenants in fee simple. Probably such life tenants work harder and save more, as a general rule, than similar tenants in fee simple.

the full Rignano principle is better than one based upon the simplified Rignano principle.

We may now turn to a difficulty which presents itself in connection with all inheritance taxes, namely, the possibility of evasion of the tax by the transfer of property by gifts *inter vivos*, that is to say, by gifts from one living person to another. In principle, such gifts should be treated, for purposes of taxation, on the same footing as inheritances, for to acquire property by gift is substantially the same thing as to acquire it by inheritance. In practice, it seems hardly possible either to tax all such gifts as inheritances, or effectually to prohibit them altogether, as has sometimes been suggested.[28] But various considerations suggest that the seriousness of the problem is less than might be imagined. Small gifts *inter vivos* need not trouble us. They are only glorified tips and of no concern to either tax-gatherer or statesman. Substantial gifts, on the other hand, will generally be traceable, and consequently taxable. In countries where the law of legitim prevails, gifts *inter vivos* are not allowed to defeat the law, nor are fictitious sales for a nominal purchase price, by means of which gifts are often sought to be concealed.[29] Somewhat similar problems of "disappearing assets" have been successfully dealt with by British lawyers in connection with the law of bankruptcy and the law of trusts. And already under the British law, gifts made within three years of death[30] are subject to death duties.

Moreover, if we adopt a tax on the Rignano principle, the inducement to evade the tax by gifts *inter vivos* will be to some extent diminished, since such gifts will tend to diminish that part of a person's property, which at death will pay the lowest rate of tax, while, if in addition we adopt the plan that all inherited property must be settled on trustees, we reduce the possibility of gifts still further.

In any event, the desire of rich men to die *visibly* rich, and their disinclination to part with control over their property, the human weaknesses of vanity and love of power, will always strongly check the tendency to make gifts *inter vivos*. And such gifts as do take place, as has already been noted, are likely somewhat to diminish both production and inequality and to increase the welfare derivable from a given expenditure. Harcourt in 1894, when it was foretold that one of the effects of

---

[28] Compare Rignano *op. cit.*, p. 27.

[29] Compare the American case *In re Gould*, where a father assessed the value of his son's services in his business at five million dollars, but the Court held that the alleged contract was illusory, and that the five million dollars were a gift, and liable to inheritance tax. See Read, *Abolition of Inheritance*, p. 298.

[30] And charitable gifts within one year of death.

his increased death duties would be to cause fathers to give their property away to their sons during their lifetime, replied, "I am on the side of the sons." [31]

So far we have been considering inheritance taxes in the ordinary sense, that is to say taxes imposed on inherited property at the moment of its inheritance through the death of its previous owner. It remains to notice that it is possible to impose a special tax upon inherited property, or the income therefrom, at other times than when property changes hands by reason of death. Given an administrative system, under which every individual's holding of inherited property was known, there would be no difficulty in imposing such a tax, and its general effect would be similar to that of a tax on the Rignano principle upon property passing at death. One of the simplest methods of imposing such a tax would be by an amendment of the income tax, distinguishing three categories of income, instead of two, as at present, namely, income from work, income from earned property, and income from unearned or inherited property, and taxing the second category at a rate intermediate between the first and third. This would go some way to meet the objection to the present income tax, which has been dwelt upon by Professor Pigou [32] and others, that it differentiates against saving. It may be objected that this distinction between earned and unearned property is not strictly equitable, since the possession of a large amount of unearned property facilitates the accumulation of earned property. But it is equally true that the possession of a large amount of property facilitates the acquisition, through expensive training, and otherwise, of a large income from work, and this fact does not invalidate the broad distinction between earned and unearned income.

3. THE ECONOMIC EFFECT OF DEATH DUTIES *

ONE of the things most frequently urged against a tax is its effect in preventing the accumulation of capital, or in wasting capital. The Estate Duties have to meet such a criticism, and a little detailed examination may serve to indicate the line of approach to such a subject.

All taxation appears to affect capital accumulation, because

* From Sir Josiah Stamp, *The Fundamental Principles of Taxation*, (Macmillan and Co., Ltd., London, 1929), pp. 144-155.

[31] A student in one of my W.E.A. tutorial classes, who is also on the side of the sons, has suggested to me that a tax on individual inheritances might be graduated, not only according to the amount inherited, but also according to the age of the inheritor, an addition of, say, 1% being made to the duty for each year by which the inheritor's age exceeds 45.

[32] *Wealth and Welfare*, p. 370.

if, *ceteris paribus,* it ceased to exist we should all have more either (1) to spend in consumption or (2) to save as capital. It is unlikely that (1) would monopolise the new fund, for even if it tended to do so the increased demand for consumable goods would in itself set up an increased demand for fixed capital to provide them. This net loss of saving capacity through taxation may be called "y." But, of course, all other things would *not* be equal, and the cessation of Government expenditure might so adversely affect the possibilities of effective saving, that accumulation of capital wealth would be actually retarded. A potent factor in successful accumulation and maintenance of capital is the setting aside of part of individual funds for collective use. This gain of saving capacity through Government expenditure may be called "x."

Hence we have the compulsory postulate at the outset that capital will be better situated by a certain definite sum being raised in taxation than if it were not raised, the net gain being x-y, a positive quantity. That definite sum having to be raised, the question is:

If part of the sum is raised by Death Duties, will it be less advantageous to capital wealth than if the whole sum were raised by other taxes? Do Death Duties (1) annihilate accumulated capital, or (2) prevent accumulation, and if so, do they do so more than other taxes?

I propose no inquiry into the value of "x," but will deal entirely with "y" to see if non-recourse to Death Duties will put "y" at a minimum, and therefore (x-y), the capital gain, at a maximum. (Here it is necessary to point out that "Capital Gain," x-y, is not synonymous with *total national gain.* Even if one concludes that Death Duties adversely affect capital, and more so than other taxes, they may have other effects on national well-being which are fully worth it. Accumulation of savings is not the only important factor in well-being and the nation might easily save too much. I am not concerned with the wider inquiry.)

The first superficial observation when a payment out of an estate is made is that the capital value of that estate is reduced — the difference of capital has "gone." The reply that capital can only be embodied in material goods, and that these all remain the same, nothing having been burnt or destroyed, and that only a change in the title to use has taken place, so that the *National Capital* is unchanged, is only a little less superficial, and does not meet the point. For, of course — leaving the Government out of the question for the moment — there is at any given time a fund of immediate fluid savings offering itself for embodiment in fixed forms, and it is out of this that the estate duty payment comes. A pays the Government by selling land to B, who buys it by selling shares to C, who has not consumed all his income in the year current but was looking for an investment for the balance. If C had not bought the shares he would have supported a *new* investment, and, let us say, built a house. So even if no existing capital form is annihilated, we can at any rate say that a new capital form has been prevented from coming into being.

But, of course, we cannot ignore the question as to what the Government does with the money. If it builds the house that C could not build, then the net effect on national capital is nil—there is merely a transfer from individual wealth or rights to collective wealth or rights, just as there would be if, wanting a building for offices, the Government took over, as its tax, the ownership of an existing building. But if the Government drops the money into the sea there is a net loss in national capital, and C's potential house is never erected; just as there would be if the Government burnt the building that it had taken over.

In either case, therefore—destroying existing capital, or preventing accumulation of capital—we are concerned with Government action. Hence arises Plehn's warning that to regard death duty as current revenue and not to treat the yield as a permanent endowment for a specific purpose is an improvident proceeding, "inasmuch as the tax is drawn from accumulated capital and not from current income." It "would seem wise to use the income solely for buildings or improvements of an enduring character." But, of course, the *specific* application is not necessary—if the Government is spending in "permanent improvements" or objects of a capital nature the equivalent of the death duties it is as broad as it is long, and the other sources of revenue, which appear to be coming out of income and not capital, are assignable to non-permanent expenditure. No doubt opinions differ as to what constitutes capital expenditure, down from permanent military or naval works through battleships, to a completed land valuation, or a real but intangible organisation for National Insurance, but the two last mentioned would not appear in any ordinary computation of national capital, and, therefore, may reasonably be held to be no substitute in this connection for the cotton mills that might otherwise have come into being. Gladstone held the view, prompted, I believe, by J. S. Mill, that death duties applied to the reduction of National Debt remained "capital" still. The community are in debt to A, and discharge the debt by buying

War Loan with the death duty from B, who sells a house to pay the duty, A buying the house with the proceeds of the War Loan. A is in the same "capital" position as before, B is the loser by a house, and the community are the gainers by the liability discharged. This accords with the usual treatment of the National Debt in computations of national wealth.[1]

So much for the immediate effect of the transfer of wealth. There is annihilation of existing capital only in rare cases. There may be prevention of immediately potential capital if the Government has no equivalent capital expenditure.

But the last position is not peculiar to Death Duties. By our postulate the money has to be raised. If it is not paid by death duties on the wealthy, assume that it may be obtained as income tax on the middle class. The tax may then prevent them from saving what they were in the habit of doing, they may be pushed out of the new investment field and we may thus get an equivalent prevention of immediately potential capital. Or assume the revenue is obtained from the poor. If it does not come out of potential savings it must lessen consumption expenditure. This may or may not be efficiency-expenditure, but if it is, it reacts on productive capacity not only for the labourer himself, but reduces also the total industry-dividend, the share of the employer, and therefore the saving fund of the wealthy. *There is no proof that the immediate effect of taking revenue as death duty reduces immediately potential fixed capital more than an income tax which may equally trench upon potential savings.*

But the dynamic aspect over a series of years must now be considered in addition to the static position for a single year which is all we have so far treated.

Even if transferring wealth from individuals to the community does *not* affect the grand total at the moment, or even if there is little difference between transferring the house that a man has already saved (death duties) and the sterling that a number of people might just be going to invest (income tax), the knowledge that saved wealth will some day be transferred may powerfully affect the desire to save.

A completely confiscatory duty would almost stop most types of saving.

At one time it was thought that death duties would "tend to diminish the funds destined for the maintenance of productive labour," but that view is to my mind tainted with the "wages fund" fallacy. Mill considered the amount which would be derived by a high duty would be but a small pro-

[1] *Vide* "The Wealth and Income of the Chief Powers," *S.J.* 1919 (S.).

portion of the annual increase of capital in a wealthy country like ours, and its abstraction (and annihilation) would but make room for saving to an equivalent amount.[2] I agree with the first part of his view, but the second I think can only be assumed given certain conditions as to the rate of interest. It might be true in times of rising prices and trade activity, but not in times of stagnation. Sidgwick thought that the bad effects are "not likely to be at all equal in proportion to the similar effect that would be produced by extra taxes on income, in fact, the limits of taxation on inheritances will be practically determined rather by the danger of evasion than by the danger of checking industry and thrift."

Bastable urges the same point, and considers, too, that the "equal amount of taxation would have to be imposed in other directions, and would in some degree trench on capital."

In the case of a mortgage on an estate raised to pay the duty, when the efforts of the owner to redeem it in fifteen years cause him to reduce expenditure, reduce wages and discharge servants, the result does not seem to differ essentially from what might follow an equivalent annual tax for fifteen years.

At the root of the whole matter lies the question : Will a man save less or more per annum if he has to pay a lump sum at death instead of an annual tax?

Now to the extent to which he himself turns the lump sum into an annual tax, by specific insurance provision, there is no difference. If he would have paid the income tax out of potential savings, out of consumption expenditure, or partly out of each, so equally may he be expected to bear the annual equivalent of the death duty. If this is widely done, death duties are not specially disadvantageous in their effect upon accumulating capital in comparison with an income tax.

Bastable regards the estate duty as a capitalised income tax, and many others have held this view. Seligman contests the point, but his objection, in my judgement, only amounts to showing that this cannot be used as a theoretical justification for the duty, because of the divergent rates of income tax that would result from the uncertainty of length of life. It does not alter the argument that if all persons pool their risks in insurance the tax may in fact be a general community income tax. But we have to recognise that to a considerable extent it is *not* turned into an income tax by the individual, and it is over this field of inquiry that most difficulty arises.

Apart from what the Government may do with the money,

[2] Mill, *Principles,* V. ii.

and from the individual point of view only, most writers seem to feel that the duty falls on accumulated wealth rather than on income, though admittedly the economic position of society and the habits of the people are important factors.

Professor Cannan has said : "Perhaps, on account of a certain obvious peculiarity of the time at which they occur, death duties discourage accumulation somewhat less than annual taxes, and consequently are rather more favourable to the non-propertied class. If they are graduated they necessarily tend to cause greater equality of wealth."

Now, it may be demonstrable that two burdens are actuarially alike, and yet the psychological appeal to the taxpayer may be very different. The bearing of this possibility upon this subject has not been really finally worked out and agreed, but Professor Pigou has recently treated it with some fulness.[3] He says :*"It has now to be observed that the check on the supply of waiting, brought about by the expectation of death duties, is likely, ceteris paribus, to be considerably smaller than that due to the expectation of the former kind.* Let us suppose that a million pounds has to be raised by taxation upon the fruits of industrial investment. It is indifferent to the State whether this annual sum is collected by a tax on the annual returns of all enterprises, or by a tax confined to the annual returns of enterprises that have been established for some time. The choice between the two methods is not, however, indifferent to the persons concerned in the enterprises. Since these persons discount future taxes precisely as they discount all future events, the expectation of taxes levied after the second method will have the smaller restrictive influence upon the quantity of waiting supplied by them. The fact that distance in time introduced a considerable chance that the investor may no longer be living when the postponed tax falls due, greatly emphasises this difference. Hence, there is a special and not generally recognised advantage in taxation by the method of a time limit. Delay in the levy enables the State to collect a given annual sum, in such wise that the expectation of the levy exercises a smaller restrictive influence upon the supply of waiting, and, hence, upon the magnitude of the national dividend, than would occur if the levy were immediate.

THE argument, however, is not yet exhausted. It has to be observed, further, *that the superiority of postponed, over immediate, taxes is enhanced, when the levy is made, not after a*

[3] Pigou, *Wealth and Welfare*, p. 374, etc.

distinctive time, during which there is a chance of the occur-rence of the investor's death, but definitely at his death; for, obviously, a certainty influences conduct more strongly than a probability. Furthermore, there are additional reasons why this form of postponed tax should impose a relatively small check upon the supply of waiting. In some measure the stim-ulus to accumulation consists in the hope of the distinction afforded by dying very rich. That stimulus is not interfered with by death duties."

Further points may be added to those put forward by Pro-fessor Pigou if we once admit that our income tax differen-tiates against savings-use in favour of consumption-use. People may be divided into two classes: (1) Those who are ambitious to die as rich as possible; (2) those who are indifferent to the actual sum left at death.

In the case of (1), as Mr. Carnegie has urged,[4] the death duties have no effect on saving. In the case of (2), prospective death duties may militate less against saving than equivalent income taxes, because there is always the chance of living to a good age, and being able to avoid death duties by division *inter vivos* at a late, but not too late, period, and a good many people may take this chance of "no tax at all," when no dif-ferentiation exists (for them) against savings-use. (But if many actually succeed, and realise their hope, then in order to main-tain the total yield, the death duties rates must be *pro tanto* higher than the income tax rates.)

The whole fund of saved capital is a resultant of many dif-ferent psychological forces, which do not answer in the same way to changes in conditions. The behaviour of those who are saving against risks or against being worse off, those who are saving to be better off, and those who save without effort or self-sacrifice out of superfluity, will be very different. The net effect of all motives together cannot be finally determined. If taxes are paid out of pure economic (unearned) surpluses they have less tendency to shift effects to other factors of pro-duction and other social classes than if they are paid out of "earnings" (salary, interest, or profits), which have functional value in inducing full maintenance of the producing agent.

Despite these psychological considerations, however, on the whole, I think there may often be a tendency to curtail expend-iture to meet an *annual* income tax, and to keep on saving and thus in the long run add more to capital than would be the case under the death duty régime. The very fact that the total annual yield is made up of a large number of compara-

4 Carnegie, *Problems of To-day.*

tively *small* "doses," and that to each individual the payments are regular, must, I think, assist this tendency. In so far as this is true, death duties trench more upon the annual new investment fund and less upon the consumption expenditure than income taxes would do, but not to any marked extent. Of the £26,000,000 raised, a large part would be covered by insurance and have the same annual incidence as an income tax. Of the balance only a small part, probably not more than two millions, would be paid out of savings, where it might under an income tax have come out of consumption expenditure. This in relation to the total annual savings of about £350,000,000 is almost negligible. People greatly exaggerate this matter, because they forget that the money must be raised somehow; and *from the gross effect of the death duties on capital, they fail to take off the effect that other equivalent taxes would also have upon saving.*

(1) As a broad conclusion, therefore, apart from other economic effects of death duties, even current expenditure of the proceeds is likely to add to the nation's power of accumulation more than the actual *capital* it takes from individuals.

(2) *Immediate effect on realised savings.* (*a*) In so far as Government expenditure is in permanent works or reduction of debt there is only a transfer of capital. (*b*) If it is not so spent, savings may be "wasted," but if the money had been raised by other taxes, potential saving might have been "wasted" to just the same extent, and no special disadvantage attaches to death duties.

(3) *Ultimate effect on stimulus to saving.* Owing to powerful countervailing considerations the net effect is only slightly against the death duties as compared with other taxes. Reverting to the idea with which I opened, the death duties may leave "*y*" almost at a minimum. This is only an expression of personal views and no reliable body of received opinion exists.

QUESTIONS AND PROBLEMS FOR DISCUSSION

1. What essential differences are there between estate taxes and inheritance taxes?
2. Discuss the validity of the contention that highly progressive tax rates on large estates tend to destroy individual thrift and initiative.
3. In what sense may an inheritance tax be considered burdenless?
4. Evaluate the argument that taxation of inheritances represents a confiscation of private property.

5. What practical tax problems arise because of lack of uniformity of inheritance tax laws in the various states?
6. Is it possible for an inheritance tax to be shifted? (Review Chapter IX.)
7. Compare the three principles of graduation commonly used in inheritance taxation.
8. In your opinion is the Rignano principle just? Is it practicable?
9. Show by means of a hypothetical example how the Rignano principle might operate in the taxation of inheritances.
10. Do estate and inheritance taxes violate the canon of convenience? If so, is there any way in which they may be made to conform to it?

SUGGESTIONS FOR RESEARCH

1. The inheritance tax and inequality in the distribution of wealth.
2. The economic effects of estate and inheritance taxes.
3. Reciprocity and uniformity in estate and inheritance taxation.
4. Federal versus state inheritance and estate taxes.
5. The proper use of revenue from estate and inheritance taxes.

BIBLIOGRAPHICAL NOTE

An old but comprehensive and valuable work on inheritance taxation is Max West, *The Inheritance Tax*, (New York, 1908). A recent and outstanding study which treats the subject of inheritance taxation as a phase of the broader problem of the economics of inheritance is Josiah Wedgwood, *The Economics of Inheritance*, (London, 1929). A brief but able analysis of the economic aspects of inheritance taxation is Sir Josiah Stamp, "Inheritance as an Economic Factor," *Economic Journal*, Vol. XXXVI, pp. 339-374. A useful treatment of death taxes is presented in W. J. Shultz, *American Public Finance and Taxation*, (New York, 1932), Chaps. XXXI, XXXII. Chapter XXXI deals with the history and present status of American death taxes; Chapter XXXII is a critique of death taxes. Another useful reference of general nature is M. H. Hunter, "The Inheritance Tax," *Annals of the American Academy of Political and Social Science*, Vol. XCV, pp. 165-180.

Outstanding analyses of the incidence of estate and inheritance taxes are: *Report of the Colwyn Committee on National Debt and Taxation*, (London, 1927), pp. 169-172; and H. A. Silverman, *Taxation, Its Incidence and Effects*, (London, 1931), Chap. IX. For Professor Kendrick's analysis of the incidence of inheritance taxes, see *supra*, Chap. IX. See also the general references at the close of same chapter.

The economic effects of estate and inheritance taxation are ably treated in the following works: *Colwyn Committee Report*, 172-

199; H. A. Silverman, *op. cit.* Chap. X; J. A. Hobson, *Taxation in the New State,* (London, 1919), Pt. I, Chap. VI; Sir Josiah Stamp, *Some Economic Factors in Modern Life,* (London, 1929), Chap. II; A. C. Pigou, *A Study in Public Finance,* (London, 1928), Pt. II, Chap. XIII; T. S. Adams, "Effects of Income and Inheritance Taxes on the Distribution of Wealth," *Proceedings of the American Economic Association,* 1914, pp. 240-244; and Glenn S. Hoover, "Economic Effects of Inheritance Taxes," *American Economic Review,* Vol. XVII, pp. 38-49.

For the development of inheritance taxation in foreign countries, see Alzada Comstock, *Taxation in the Modern State,* (New York, 1929), Chaps. XI, XII; and R. M. Haig, "Inheritance Taxes: Methods Applied and Proposed in other Countries," *Proceedings of the National Tax Association,* (1925), pp. 48-57.

Some legal aspects of the inheritance tax in the United States are presented in the first section of *Lectures on Taxation,* Roswell Magill, editor, (Chicago, 1932).

State inheritance taxation is treated in H. A. Millis, "The Inheritance Tax in American Commonwealths," *Quarterly Journal of Economics,* Vol. XIX, pp. 288-301.

Problems of reciprocity and uniformity in estate and inheritance taxation are discussed in the following: C. W. Gerstenberg, "Inheritance Tax Uniformity through Federal Administration," *Proceedings of the National Tax Association,* (1920), pp. 78-89; G. B. Winston, "State and Federal Relations in Inheritance Taxation," *Proceedings of the National Tax Association,* (1924), pp. 246-252; E. R. A. Seligman, *Studies in Public Finance,* (New York, 1925), Chap. VIII; and in *Reports of Committees of the National Tax Association on Reciprocity in Inheritance Taxation,* (1927), pp. 415-433; (1929), pp. 200-224. A model plan for inheritance taxation is set forth in the *Proceedings of the National Tax Association,* (1922), pp. 398-411.

In the *Proceedings of the National Tax Association,* (1925), pp. 128-146, Professor C. J. Bullock presents an article entitled, "The Future of Estate and Inheritance Taxes in the United States."

CHAPTER XIX

THE TAXATION OF BUSINESS

1. THE TAXATION OF BUSINESS ENTERPRISES *

CRITICISM OF THE PRESENT SYSTEM OF BUSINESS TAXATION

IN making a critical analysis of the taxation of business, it is not necessary to argue that business should be taxed as an entity. As Professor T. S. Adams says : "The justification for this class of taxes is plain. Business is responsible for much of the work which occupies the courts, the police, etc. New business creates new tasks and entails further public expense." In other words, organized society is a sort of silent partner in every business enterprise and may rightfully demand a share of the product for public purposes.

We must all agree that business enterprises should be taxed, but is the present system of taxation of business enterprises in the majority of our states equitable and just to all parties concerned ? That the present system is unjust and inequitable can easily be shown by a few illustrations.

(1). Consider the present method of taxing mercantile enterprises under the general property tax system. Ignorance or neglect on the part of local assessors results in glaring inaccuracy and inequity in the valuation of mercantile stocks of goods. In the same community one merchant may be assessed for the full value of his stock of goods, while another may escape with a mere fraction of full valuation. Furthermore, in competing communities, merchants may be subject to such differences in tax levies as to hamper free competition to a very marked degree.

(2). Inequities arise as between incorporated and unincorporated enterprises. We have greatly magnified the supposed advantages conferred by the corporate form of business organization, particularly in the case of certain types of mercantile and manufacturing enterprises. One illustration will suffice. Here are two retail clothing stores in the same city ; one of them incorporated and the other a partnership. Both are doing the same volume of business. Now, from the standpoint

* From E. S. Todd, "The Taxation of Business Enterprises," *Bulletin of the National Tax Association,* Vol. XVII, (October, 1931), pp. 15-20.

of taxation, what peculiar power has the incorporated enterprise, either in the way of enhancing its profits or of managing the enterprise that warrants the imposition of a so-called "franchise" tax upon the incorporated enterprise while the unincorporated enterprise goes scot-free from such a burden? There is no such peculiar power. Of course, a corporate enterprise acts as a legal entity and thus has certain advantages in connection with the securing of new capital, etc.; but these legal powers confer no superior managerial ability, nor do they imply any greater obligation to support government than in the case of unincorporated enterprises.

(3). Inequities have arisen on account of the misunderstanding of and the misuse and abuse of the term franchise, as applied to corporations, particularly to public service corporations. The dictionary defines franchise as a right or privilege conferred by a superior jurisdiction or government and not belonging of common right to the members of the public. As applied to corporations, it may mean merely the right *to do* or *to be;* or it may be specifically defined, as in some states, as an intangible something representing the value of the "corporate excess,"—that is, the difference between the value of a corporation as derived from the capitalization of its earning power and the value of the corporation as expressed by the par value of its stock.

The general idea seems to be that the state grants to the corporation a bundle of intangible rights, loosely called the franchise. For taxation purposes, it has been assumed that the corporate franchise is a peculiar species of intangible and therefore rightfully subject to special taxes. All of our states, therefore, impose a so-called franchise tax for the privilege of incorporating. In reality, however, this is not, or rather *should not be,* a tax at all, but a license fee covering the bare costs of state supervision of corporations.

The granting of franchise rights, however, has unfortunately been the convenient and constitutional means for imposing so-called franchise taxes which are pure property or income taxes. In other words, the police power has been invoked, by a process of legal fiction, to impose taxes disguised under other names.

The franchise tax has been particularly misapplied in connection with public utility corporations. In the case of the public utilities, the fiction still prevails that the term "franchise" connotes something very peculiar in nature, conferring some magic power on these corporations and placing them upon a plane of special advantage and privilege which other types of corporations are unable to occupy. There was probably a great measure of truth in this notion in former times, but it would be hard to prove that these corporations possess many peculiar privileges in our day. For example, the possession of a franchise affords no opportunity for any public service corporation to enhance its profits through the manipulation of production or prices or through the curtailment of service, for the reason that all these matters are controlled and regulated by some grade of government.

In other words, the corporation franchise has become an exceedingly intangible kind of property. Nevertheless, most of our states have used and increasingly misused and abused the very convenient franchise tax "to beat the devil around the bush" ; — that is to say, the states, by a process of legal fiction, have succeeded more or less in imposing tax burdens on corporation property and on gross or net income, merely by calling the tax not a tax but a regulation of the corporation through the franchise.

In so far as the taxation of corporations engaged in interstate commerce is concerned, there are indications that the states must call a halt on the excessive abuse of the franchise tax. For two or three years, now, the federal Supreme Court, in various decisions involving such taxation, has, by implication, warned the states that the Supreme Court would hereafter "go behind the returns," when such cases come up for consideration. In other words, the court will not be hoodwinked by the mere label attached to the tax but will look at the reality behind the tax.

On January 6, 1930, the court rendered a momentous decision in the case of the *New Jersey Bell Telephone Company v. State Board of Assessors of New Jersey*. New Jersey, in 1900, imposed a so-called franchise tax on gross receipts, and the rate was gradually increased from 2% in 1900 to 5% in 1920. The Telephone company contested the tax, in so far as it involved interstate commerce, on the ground that it was a license tax and as such could not be measured by receipts from interstate commerce. The lower state court upheld the tax, declaring that earnings were "merely the measure of the value of the franchise." The state supreme court upheld this decision and the case was appealed to the federal Supreme Court.

The federal Supreme Court, in its decision (January 6, 1930) reiterated the rule that a state may not tax, as such, gross earnings derived from interstate commerce or impose a license fee or other burden upon the privilege of engaging in interstate commerce. Therefore the court could not sustain the tax "if it was not one on property but was in fact upon the gross receipts from interstate commerce or a license computed thereon." The court further criticized the use of the terms franchise and franchise tax as not being indicative of an intent to impose a property tax or a tax in lieu of such a tax.

The court also found this tax base inconsistent with the taxation, at its true value, of the right to use the streets and highways, inasmuch as the property used to produce earnings included lands, buildings, etc. Therefore, the tax on gross earnings was *out of all proportion to the naked use of the streets.* There follows, then, this very significant statement: "The elements of value resulting from appellant's power of eminent domain and possession of a going concern and of a regulated monopoly cannot reasonably be deemed to be the sole or even a distinct source of the gross earnings by which the tax is measured."

The court therefore decided that, in so far as gross receipts were concerned, the tax was "at least void." Is the whole tax void? While the court did not so declare, it certainly opens the door to many interesting questions such as I have sought to raise in the discussion of this topic. The chief point I would raise is this: If now, by decision of the federal Supreme Court, it is implied that the corporate franchise is no longer an important source of gross earnings as applied to interstate commerce, then why should we not apply the same reasoning to state taxation of corporate enterprises? Has not the time come when we must consider the franchise as a kind of intangible that must go the way of all other intangibles, as respects taxation?

A CONSTRUCTIVE PROGRAM

By exposition and illustration we have thus far tried to point out that the chief defects in the taxation of business enterprises are owing to three causes, namely: The inequities in the taxation of mercantile enterprises; the illogical distinction between incorporated and unincorporated enterprises for the purpose of taxation; and the loose and illogical use of franchise taxes on public utilities. Let us now turn to the question of adjusting business taxes, so as to secure equity between the various types of enterprises and between business on the one hand and other subjects of taxation on the other.

(1). Our first question is whether we can lay down any rules of procedure that would and should apply to all types of business enterprise. I believe that we can do so. In the first place, every type of business enterprise, incorporated or unincorporated, should pay a tax on its real estate at the local rate where the real property is situated. Whether the total revenue thus derived should be devoted solely to the support of local government will depend on the extent to which we shift the burden of local public expenditures to the state. In this manner, so far as realty is concerned, every individual and every business enterprise will be on an exact basis of parity as respects the carrying of the tax load.

(2). Secondly, every type of enterprise, as well as every individual, should be exempt from all taxation on tangible personalty. Such a procedure would automatically exempt from taxation all farm implements, live stock, household goods, mercantile stocks of goods, factory machinery, etc. (The state registration license taxes on motor vehicles have nothing to do with this proposition. Of course all motor vehicles would be exempt as personal property; but the proposal to set up a state license tax on motor transportation rests on a different economic basis which is not germane to the present discussion.)

The arguments for the elimination of all tangible personal property taxes may be summed up as follows:

(a) It is difficult to estimate what the law terms a "fair value" of such property.

(b) Few assessors have the technical ability to appraise such property.

(c) Gross and inequitable discrepancies appear in the valuations of personal property in competing jurisdictions and even in the same jurisdiction. This is true particularly in the case of mercantile stocks of goods.

(d) There is easy and constant evasion of such taxation which leads to ridiculous evaluations and discrepancies.

(e) The reason in large part for such evasion is the thought, perhaps unconsciously held, that personal tangible property is to a very small degree a criterion of ability to pay. For example, one merchant with a small stock of goods on a given assessment day may be far better able to pay than another merchant with a far larger stock.

(f) Elimination of tangible personalty would to a great degree lessen the difficulties of tax officials in administering the tax system.

(g) Other and far more equitable means can be devised to compel every individual and every enterprise to shoulder his fair share of the public burden.

(h) On the practical side, we have the testimony of those states which have turned away from such taxation and of the recent expert commissions that have studied the subject. For example, a special committee reporting to the National Tax Association in 1919 says: "The tax officials of a state like Wisconsin have become so impressed with the difficulty of

taxing tangible personalty at the same rate as realty that they
have recommended the total exemption of this class of property. A classified tax on tangible property is not a vital feature of a tax program." Again, New York's experience, with
the receipt of only nine-tenths of one per cent of its entire
revenues from this source, leads that state to propose the entire
abolition of such taxation. The California Tax Commission
in its report (February 1, 1929), says: "The future property
tax must be impersonal. Ultimately it should be on realty
alone, gradually eliminating all personal property." The
special Utah Commission (Nov. 30, 1929) says: "Classification
of tangible property is to be condemned because of the inconsistencies and difficulties involved."

(3). Third, every type of business enterprise and every individual should be exempt from taxation on every species of
intangible property. This exemption would include not only
stocks and bonds and bank deposits, but also franchises, patents,
accounts and notes receivable, etc. The arguments for such a
proposal are conclusive.

(a) The taxation of intangibles is contrary to fundamental prin-
    ciples of taxation.
(b) Ownership of intangibles is not in itself a criterion of ability
    to pay.
(c) Exemptions are so common that a large body of potential tax-
    payers go scot-free from any direct tax burden.
(d) Evasion is so common as to lead to gross inequities.
(e) Administrative difficulties are great, even when we resort to
    low flat rates on intangibles.
(f) There are better and more equitable means of reaching the
    individual or corporate owners of intangibles than through
    the direct tax on intangibles.
(g) The testimony of such states as New York and the conclusions
    of many recent special state tax commissions is to the effect
    that we should give up any sort of direct tax on intangibles
    and substitute either income or production taxes.

(4). Having shown that all business enterprises should be
treated alike in connection with tangible and intangible property, we now face the further question whether we can treat
all enterprises alike when we consider a constructive plan for
their taxation. Our first question is whether we should make
any distinctions among incorporated enterprises for taxation
purposes. Let us first take the case of the public utilities.
What reason is there for treating public utilities in any other
manner than manufacturing corporations? If our analysis of
the nature of the corporation franchise is valid, there is no such
reason. Indeed, this fact is now recognized by our leading

tax authorities and by the procedure in our most advanced states.

As far back as 1907, Mr. W. H. Gardner, speaking at a conference of the National Tax Association, said: "We may set aside franchise taxes as relics of past methods from which the community may or may not have the wit to free itself."

In 1913, at a similar conference, Professor Bullock of Harvard said: "There is no good reason for the separate classification of public service corporations. Taxation of such corporations should be the same as that imposed on property subject to the full rate of state and local taxation."

A special committee of the National Tax Association reporting in 1922 stated that with the general principle of regulation, there is no longer a valid reason for considering taxation from the standpoint of special privilege or monopoly, or for taxing public utilities more heavily than other classes of corporations. Stating the matter positively, the committee recommended that the taxation of public utilities should be as nearly as possible on an equality with other kinds of business. "Equality, however, does not necessarily connote uniformity in rates."

Again, a special Utah Tax Commission, reporting in November, 1929, recommends that all business enterprises conducted for profit, except insurance companies, shall be taxed alike, and that such a tax must be "a substitute for the present unfair corporation license taxes."

Must we segregate insurance companies? Probably so, from the standpoint of expediency. The whole question of the treatment of life insurance, however, demands our most careful and unbiased study, before we can come to any definite conclusions on the matter.

How about the national banks? It is scarcely necessary to say that nothing can be done looking to a final solution of the problem of bank taxation until Congress legislates to relieve the states from the difficulties imposed by the Macallen decision.

(5). The second question is whether we shall make any distinction between incorporated and unincorporated enterprises, for taxation purposes. There is no longer any logical reason for such distinction. Note the following testimony:

(a) A committee of the National Tax Association, reporting in 1926, declares that the distinction between corporate and other business enterprises should be abolished.

(b) The Special California Tax Commission, in its February 1929 report, says: "Theoretically, a system of business taxes should not be simply a series of corporation taxes, but as broad as business itself."

(6). The third and final question is this: "If we relieve business enterprises from taxes on tangible and intangible personalty, if we give up the present so-called franchise and excise taxes on corporations, can we find a just and equitable common base for all business concerns?" Without any theorizing on the matter, may I present a few witnesses.

(a) In 1917, at the National Tax Conference, Professor T. S. Adams said: "Perhaps the most severely logical form of business taxation would be one upon gross business at different rates for the various classes of trade and industry, which rates would be determined by the normal or average relationship between net income and gross business in each class of trade or industry. Net income taxes would be simpler."

(b) In 1930, a committee of the National Tax Association, reporting on business taxes, declared in favor of a tax on net income at a moderate flat rate; and again in 1926, a similar committee advocated the same plan. Again in 1928, a similar committee advocated the taxation of partnerships and corporations at a flat rate on net income.

(c) In 1929, a committee of the National Tax Association suggested that an income tax be imposed on corporations and that it should be based on the following principles:

(i) Must yield sufficient revenue.
(ii) Ease of administration.
(iii) Adaptation to our system of dual government.
(iv) Must respect constitutional limitations.
(v) Must conform to past experience and present trends.

(d) The Special California Tax Commission, in its final report, February 1929, declared: "When we adopt a business tax, the base should be net income."

(e) Mr. C. J. Tobin, speaking before the 1929 National Tax Conference, said: "The franchise taxes [in New York] are too complicated. A gross-net earnings or net income tax on all corporations is preferable." At the same conference Mr. J. Frank Zoller said: "The business tax ought to be entirely in lieu of personal property taxes and should be imposed upon all business, whether operated at a profit or loss." [Mr. Zoller favored a production tax, at least for enterprises showing no net income.]

CONCLUSIONS

LET us now briefly review the road we have traveled. We have tried to show:

(1) That the old general property tax or its remnants is as unfair and inequitable to business as it is to the owners of realty or to individuals.

(2) That all subjects of taxation suffer equally from the futile attempts to tax personal tangibles and intangibles.

(3) That our present franchise taxes are archaic and out of tune with modern fiscal ideas and ideals.

(4) That, as a beginning of tax reconstruction, we should abolish all taxes on tangible and intangible property, including franchises and all so-called "privilege" taxes on all forms of business enterprise.

Finally, we come to the conclusion that, for business, some form of income or combination income-production tax is inevitable, as the only solution of the problem of business taxation. Our conclusions are based on the following propositions:

(1) That an income tax, in this day of scientific accounting, can be estimated with a fair degree of accuracy.

(2) That the tax cannot be shifted.

(3) That the tax will not be evaded or cannot be evaded by the vast majority of enterprisers.

(4) That the tax has been increasingly successful wherever tried.

(5) That practically all tax experts and administrators are agreed that it must be the next step in the evolution of taxation.

(6) That it is the only way to bring order and system and unity in the construction of a tax system which seeks to do justice to the three mainstays of government: realty, personal incomes, and business enterprisership.

2. The Taxation of Business Corporations *

I interpret my subject as covering not only the taxation of the corporate entity, but also the taxation of stockholders, since obviously corporate stock represents merely corporate assets, and any consideration of the tax burden to be imposed upon the corporation can be significant only in conjunction with a consideration of the tax burden to be imposed upon the stockholders.

ACTUAL TAX SYSTEMS IN VOGUE THROUGHOUT THE UNITED STATES

In practically all jurisdictions real estate owned by corporations is taxed in the same manner and at the same rates as real estate owned by individuals. (And it may be noted that throughout this discussion the term "individuals" is to be understood as including all non-corporate entities owning property and transacting business.) With some restrictions and exceptions the same statement may be made with respect to tangible personal

---

* From J. W. Mudge, "How Business Corporations Should be Taxed," *Bulletin of the National Tax Association*, Vol. XVI, pp. 105-114.

property. So far, however, as concerns other elements of corporate value, the tax methods used are almost as numerous as the taxing jurisdictions. Even if minor differences be ignored, there are at least the following basically distinct classifications:

(1). On the corporation side: (a) No taxation whatever; (b) A specific, arbitrary annual fee, small in amount and collected from all corporations alike; (c) A fee based upon authorized capital stock and usually comparatively small in amount; (d) A tax upon the so-called corporate excess, arrived at by deducting from the entire value of the corporate assets of all kinds (very generally determined by reference to the market value of the stock) the value of tangible property independently taxed; (e) A tax based upon and measured by corporate net income.

(2). On the stock side: (a) Exemption of all corporate stock; (b) Taxation of all corporate stock; (c) Exemption of stock in domestic corporations and taxation of stock in foreign corporations; (d) Taxation of what may be called the stock excess, arrived at by deducting from the full value of corporate stock that portion thereof corresponding to corporate assets independently taxed; (e) Exemption of stock as property but taxation of dividends received; and perhaps also there should be added, (f) Theoretical taxation of stock but practical exemption through non-enforcement of the law.

All the described methods of taxing the corporate entity are combined in different ways with the several methods of taxing corporate stock.

In this field of corporate taxation our New England states have well exemplified their traditional independence, and illustrate, among themselves, a large proportion of the more important types above described.

SHOULD CORPORATIONS BE SUBJECT TO ANY FORM OF SPECIAL TAXATION?

THE first question to be disposed of would seem to be: Should corporations be made the subject of any kind of special taxation? Why is it not sufficient, in jurisdictions where property taxation is in vogue, if the several types of property possessed by the corporation be taxed in exactly the same way and to exactly the same extent as similar property held by individuals, or, in jurisdictions having an income tax system, if corporate income be taxed in exactly the same way and at exactly the same rate as income received by individuals? The question may be subdivided: First, should corporate business be more heavily burdened than unincorporated business? Second, should the *form* of the burden imposed upon corporations be different from the *form* of the burden imposed upon individuals?

The first subdivision of the question appears to be fairly simple. Corporations should be more heavily burdened provided, and only provided, they possess, as corporations, some asset not possessed by individuals. The only such asset, so far as I am aware, is the so-called corporate franchise, or right to transact business as an artificial entity with limited liability. There can be no doubt that this is an element of some value. However, the amount of its value is not capable of mathematical demonstration and accordingly the extent to which its possession justifies the imposition of additional tax burdens will always be a subject of controversy. For purposes of my discussion I am not interested in it because it involves merely the amount or rate of the tax burden, whereas my subject, as I interpret it, is not concerned with the amount of the burden but rather with the method of its imposition, its incidence and allocation.

The second subdivision of the question, namely, should the *form* of the corporation tax be different from the *form* of the tax on individuals — must, I think, be answered in the affirmative. The reason why corporate taxation is bound to take different *forms* from those taken by individual taxation has little to do with any peculiar values possessed by the corporation but results instead from the circumstance that all corporate values have a double representation, first, in the corporate entity and second, in the naural entities, the stockholders. The reason why this double embodiment of values leads to a system of taxation for corporations fundamentally different from that employed in the case of individuals may be indicated as follows:

When the tax assessor considers the individual as a subject of taxation, he finds him possessed of real estate, tangible personalty, and corporate securities. Each of these types of property he can tax to the individual. When he considers the corporation he finds the corporation possessed of the same types of property. In the case of the corporation, however, he finds something else,—namely, outstanding capital stock. Furthermore, he finds that the total market value of this capital stock substantially exceeds the total value of all the assets which he has been able to identify as independently owned by the corporation. The capital stock is, of course, owned by the stockholders but it must represent, says the state, something owned by the corporation because the stock, of necessity, represents merely that which is possessed by the corporation. What is this excess value? Well, in part it may be ascribed to the corporate franchise, the right to do business in a particularly convenient and attractive form, with limited liability. More probably, however, it represents what may be termed good-will, or a business earning power in excess of the earning power of the specific assets independently identifiable as owned by the corporation. At any rate, that it exists is proved to the state's satisfaction by the actual market value of the corporation's outstanding stock, and the state thereupon undertakes to tax it. Is there anything of a parallel nature in the case of the individual merchant or manufacturer? There is no corporate franchise, of course, but there may well be good-will, or exceptional earning power. However, any such good-will is not, as in the case of the corporation, definitely identified and valued by the existence of outstanding capital stock, and accordingly the state finds it impracticable to tax it and does not tax it. This is one reason for the divergence of corporate tax methods from those applicable to individuals.

Now turning to the stockholder: Suppose that I, a resident of Massachusetts, own a manufacturing plant in Vermont. Vermont taxes me in respect of that plant because of its location in Vermont. Massachusetts cannot tax me in respect of it, in spite of my residence in Massachusetts, because the law does not recognize an individual's ownership of tangible property as something distinct and apart from the property itself and fairly subject to taxation in the state of the owner's residence when that state is different from the state of the location of the property.

Suppose, however, that I incorporate my manufacturing plant. Vermont continues to tax it, this time against the newly formed corporate entity, but now, under the decisions of the United States Supreme Court, Massachusetts can also tax me, in respect of the stock, in spite of the fact that in substance the stock represents merely the same ownership of the tangible property which ownership the Supreme Court refuses to permit Massachusetts to tax me for directly. This recognition of corporate stock as an independent subject of taxation at the situs of the owner, without respect to the situs of the property, and the refusal to recognize an analogous situation in the case of the individual, is the second reason for the divergence of corporate tax methods from those applicable to individuals.

ALTERNATIVE AVAILABLE METHODS OF CORPORATE TAXATION

ASSUMING, then, that the taxation of corporate values as such, on a basis measured by their total worth, and by methods peculiarly adapted to the peculiar nature of the corporation, is an essential part of our national tax system, it remains to consider what form of such taxation is to be preferred.

By way of preliminary, let me say that I believe the special system should not be applied to tangible assets, either real or personal. Such assets can be identified with equal ease (or equal difficulty) whether owned by corporations or individuals, and it seems to me that they should be directly taxed by the same methods in either case. Our problem thus becomes: What form of taxation should be adopted for that part of the corporation's total wealth which exceeds its tangible property?

In a general way I believe the options between which we must choose may be summarized as follows: First, the tax may be levied upon the corporation alone, or upon the stockholders alone, or it may be levied upon both the corporation and the stockholders. Second, the tax may be levied upon the corporate excess as property or it may be levied upon the income.

Let us consider, first, whether the tax should be levied on the corporate entity exclusively or on the stockholders exclusively, or partly on each. In passing upon this question I think it will be profitable to consider with special care two particular problems: first, that of double taxation, and second, that of uniform taxation as between the several States.

DOUBLE TAXATION

FIRST, consider the matter of double taxation: The first objection to one of my suggested alternatives — that of taxing both the corporation and the stockholders — may be that it is double taxation. Now, there are various kinds of double taxation, some of which it seems to me are inherently vicious and some of which are not vicious at all. Double taxation which results from the fact that two jurisdictions each claim the exclusive right to tax the same subject matter is inherently vicious because it necessarily leads, or tends to lead, to excessive taxation, for the reason that each jurisdiction will tend to levy the maximum tax which it believes the property involved can stand assuming that no other jurisdiction taxes it at all. On the other hand, so-called double taxation which represents merely the frank recognition by all parties that a certain property value exists in duplicate form or phase, whether in the same State or in different States, each phase being fairly answerable on some basis to the jurisdiction where it exists, and the right of each jurisdiction to tax being recognized by the other jurisdiction, is not vicious because duplication of the tax levy under these circumstances is not likely to lead to the imposition of an excessive or unfair aggregate burden. Now applying that to the case of the corporation and its stockholders, assume that X dollars is concededly a fair tax burden to be imposed upon the total assets of a certain corporation. That wealth is not more greatly burdened by the imposition of a tax of one-half X dollars on the corporation and a tax of another half X dollars on the stockholders. On the other hand, a tax of two X dollars would be legitimately objectionable even if imposed on the corporation alone, the stockholders being exempt, or on the stockholders alone, the corporation being exempt. In other words, the real objection, and the only legitimate objection, is to excessive taxation upon any given subject matter, not to a sub-division of the tax upon different forms of the same underlying subject matter, this latter not being really double taxation at all.

Another form of so-called double taxation which this double embodiment of corporate wealth (first in the corporation and second in the stockholder) makes possible, is taxation by different jurisdictions. That is, instead of the situation where the corporation and the stockholders are both in a single State (the situation which I have assumed in my first illustration) we may have the property and business of the corporation located in one State — for example, Vermont — and the stockholders residing in another State — for example, Massachusetts. As before, we may have a tax levied on both the corporation and the stockholders but this time one tax levied by Vermont and the other by Massachusetts. Is such double taxation objectionable? It seems to me again, just as in the case where the same State taxes both the corporation and the stockholder, that it is objectionable only provided the aggregate of taxes levied, by Vermont on the corporation and by Massachusetts on the stockholders, is excessive. That is, if a total burden of X dollars levied by Vermont, assuming both corporation and stockholders are confined to that State, would not be excessive, it does not become excessive because levied partly by Vermont and partly by Massachusetts. The problem here, however, is obviously different because where the two taxes are levied by different jurisdictions there is more danger that the aggregate will be unscientifically ascertained, and therefore either excessive or insufficient — more probably excessive, whereas if a single State is levying all the taxes the aggregate can be made such as that State, at any rate, considers to be proper on the basis of some carefully worked out and presumably scientific principle. This point, however, should be borne in mind : it does not at all necessarily follow, because two States are taxing what is in substance the same thing, that the aggregate of taxes levied by the two States will be excessive, because just as at the present time certain States refrain entirely from taxing, for example, resident stockholders in foreign corporations whose property and business are located elsewhere, because of their assumption that such corporations are adequately taxed at the situs of their property and business, so it is equally possible for the States although levying taxes on both the corporation and the stockholders, to levy each tax with the assumption that the other tax will also be levied somewhere and by some jurisdiction, and to moderate the size of the levy in each case accordingly. And note that the exercise of such moderation would be fiscally practicable for the reason that each State would tax both corporations and stockholders — that is, would tax both corporations having property and business within the State and also resident stockholders of corporations having neither property nor business within the State — and consequently could easily afford, without endangering its aggregate revenues, to curtail very substantially, the burden laid on each.

Before leaving the matter of double taxation attention should be called to the following point : I have suggested that taxation of both the corporation and the stockholder, although in a sense double taxation, is unobjectionable because it presupposes that the taxation of both is deliberate and is so controlled as to rates that the aggregate tax burden is not excessive, each tax being levied with clear recognition that the other will also be levied. But suppose the stockholder is itself a corporation which in turn has its own stockholders. Clearly, if in such a case a tax is levied on the original operating corporation — the corporation which holds the underlying property and transacts the underlying business — and two more taxes are levied on corporate stocks representing the same basic assets, in one case stock held by an intermediate corporation (either a holding corporation or a corporation which has bought the stock for investment) and in the other case the stock held by the individual owning the stock of the intermediate holding or investing corporation, then three taxes are levied, and since we are assuming that the rates of tax on the first corporation and on the stockholders are gauged so as to be fair as between themselves, the third tax, levied on the intervening corporation, will necessarily constitute an excessive burden. It therefore follows that any system involving the division of the corporate burden between the corporation and the ultimate stockholder should provide for this situation and by some machinery should relieve the intervening corporation of the tax. The bill introduced this year into the Massachusetts legislature for a thoroughgoing change in the Massachusetts system of taxation (which bill provided for a system of taxation partly upon the corporation and partly upon the stockholder) was, it seemed to me, subject to objection for this reason. That is, it provided no relief or exemption for intervening holding or investment corporations.

UNIFORMITY IN TAXATION AS BETWEEN THE STATES

I WOULD like now to pass to a consideration of the matter of uniformity in State taxation. A desideratum of primary importance in corporate taxation is, very clearly, at least a fair degree of uniformity as between the several States. One of our greatest national assets is our economic solidarity, the absence of tariff barriers as between the several States, and the resulting freedom of commercial intercourse without interruption at State lines. Any factor which raises obstacles to untrammelled business intercourse throughout the nation or places artificial and widely varying burdens upon the exercise of business activity in one State as against another, thus tending to direct business into artificial and unnatural channels, goes some distance towards minimizing that basic advantage. Our national constitution protects us against interstate tariff barriers, whether affecting individuals or corporations, it protects both individuals and corporations against State burdens upon interstate commerce, and it protects the individual citizen against burdensome restrictions upon his right to pass from State to State in the pursuit of his business activity; but it furnishes little protection to incorporated business against harassing and varying restrictions and burdens, particularly tax burdens, based upon the exercise of the corporate franchise in conducting business within the territories of the various States.

As Justices Holmes and Hughes of the United States Supreme Court have said:

"No doubt it would be a great advantage to the country and to the individual States if principles of taxation could be agreed upon which did not conflict with each other, and a common scheme could be adopted by which taxation of substantially the same property in two jurisdictions could be avoided. But the Constitution of the

United States does not go so far."   (*Kid* v. *Alabama,* 188 U.S. 730; *Hawley* v. *Malden,* 232 U.S. 1.)

Since the law furnishes no protection in this field it is particularly important that the States should voluntarily work out some solution of the problem. They have as yet made almost no progress towards doing so. An important step in advance toward the goal of uniformity will, however, be made if there is developed some formula for a system of taxation such as should theoretically be acceptable to every State because covering adequately everything which any State has an equitable right to tax and covering nothing which any State, in deference to the rights of its neighbors, has not an equitable right to tax. If agreement can be reached upon the main characteristics of such a system then even though the States may be, as they almost surely will be, very slow in enacting it into law, the tendency, so far as State taxes are changed from time to time, will almost inevitably be in the right direction and toward the adoption of the principles and details of such a system.

Now very many of the differences in our State systems of corporate taxation (differences which destroy any semblance of uniformity) result from the fact that certain States have tried, and certain other States have not tried, to avoid what they consider double taxation of corporations; and still other States, while attempting to avoid double taxation of corporations within their own jurisdictions, have not attempted to avoid it when other jurisdictions were taken into consideration. If these differences, absolutely fatal to any hope of uniformity, are to be eliminated, it must be by agreement on some system capable of universal adoption by all the States with fair results. Three such systems are conceivable, as follows:

First, a system whereby every State taxes corporations and every State exempts stockholders; second, a system whereby every State taxes stockholders and exempts corporations; third, a system whereby every State taxes both corporations and stockholders but taxes each on a basis which assumes and allows for taxation of the other. Which of these systems is preferable? It seems to me that the third system is preferable for this reason: any one of the three systems is satisfactory if universally applied, but it is hardly conceivable that either of the two first systems would be universally applied, whereas it is quite conceivable that the third system might be universally applied. The reason it is unlikely that all the States would agree on a system involving the taxation of corporations and the exemption of stockholders, or the taxation of stockholders and the exemption of corporations, is because the selfish interests of different States would lead them in different directions. Thus, the selfish interest of a State in which there was a considerable concentration of inactive wealth (in the form of stock) would lead to insistence upon the taxation of stockholders, whereas the selfish interest of a State in which corporate plants and business were concentrated and resident stockholders comparatively few, would lead to an insistence upon the taxation of corporate property and business. It is much more likely that all the States could be brought to uniformity on a system for taxing both corporations and stockholders, each on a more moderate scale than if only one were taxed. Furthermore, it seems to me that the various States having these divergent interests in different phases or forms of corporate value are justified each in insisting upon the taxation of that which it finds within its own borders.

With respect to this matter of uniformity of taxation I would like to make reference particularly to the following point: some States, conspicuously my own State, Massachusetts, ascribe what seems to me undue importance to the State of the business corporation's organization. That is, although considerable progress has been made in eliminating the discrepancies which formerly existed there are still conspicuous differences in the methods employed in taxing domestic and foreign corporations. It seems to me that the perpetuation of such differences constitutes a mistake, and a mistake which is fatal to uniformity. The selection of the State of incorporation, in the case of business corporations, is a purely formal matter, a mere matter of drafting papers, in no way affecting the substance of the corporation's existence, business activity or value. It should not, therefore, be made the basis of a substantial differentiation in taxation unless such differentiation is necessitated by constitutional requirements. That the differentiation is not necessitated by any constitutional requirement appears to be indicated by the fact that certain States have in effect, and not successfully subjected to constitutional attack, systems which make no such differentiation. To illustrate what is meant: Massachusetts computes corporate excess in a radically different manner in the case of domestic and foreign corporations. If the corporation is a Massachusetts corporation its corporate excess is the value of its *entire* capital stock minus certain intangibles and substantially all tangibles except Massachusetts merchandise, whereas if it is a foreign corporation its corporate excess is the value of a *part* of its capital stock, allocated to Massachusetts on the basis of the employment of property, minus certain intangibles and taxed tangibles located in Massa-

chusetts. The result of this difference in the method of computation is that the corporate excess taxable to a corporation
operating under a Massachusetts charter may be substantially
greater than the corporate excess taxable to a corporation otherwise the same but operating under a foreign charter. For this
and also for other reasons Massachusetts presents a good example of a tax system which is not capable of uniform adoption. That can be illustrated by the following example:
assume that a certain corporation has capital stock with a market value of $1,500,000, with tangible property worth $500,000,
and with an annual income of $100,000, all of which annual
income is annually distributed in dividends to the stockholders.
If we assume that the present tax laws of Massachusetts were in
existence uniformly in all the States then the total tax burden
for the corporation and stockholders would be either $7,500,
$12,500, $13,500 or $16,000, depending upon the State of in-
corporation and the location of property and business.

One or two further points should be referred to in connection with the matter of uniformity:

First, before any system of taxation can hope to be uniformly
acceptable to the several States the problem of allocation as
between the several States must be solved. That is, whether
the tax base be corporate excess or corporate income, some
formula must be found, which shall be generally acceptable to
the several States, for the allocation between them of the total
corporate excess or the total corporate net income. Various
formulae for such allocation are at present employed, and the
subject is one of great difficulty. There is no reason to suppose, however, that it is not a problem perfectly capable of a
solution which ought to appeal to the great majority of the
States, at least, as fair. That problem is outside the scope of
this address. Likewise outside the scope of this address is the
group of problems centering around the treatment of subsidiary corporations. . .

Then another point involves the matter of the allocation of
the burden as between the corporation and the stockholders.
Up to the present time I have suggested merely that it should
be allocated between them. Should it be allocated equally or
on some other basis? Obviously a State having a preponderance of corporate property and business will be tempted to
allocate a larger proportion of the burden against the corporation, whereas a State with a preponderance of investors will
be tempted to allocate a larger proportion to the stock. Furthermore, States which have in effect a system of graduated
rates, or surtaxes, for the taxation of individuals, will find the

problem somewhat further complicated by that factor. All of these matters constitute, of course, difficulties (doubtless insuperable difficulties) in the way of absolute uniformity in the way of State taxation, but they surely do not render unreasonable the hope for attainment of a very considerable degree of uniformity.

Finally, in order to guard against misunderstanding, let me point out that by uniformity of taxation as among the several States it is not meant that each State should levy corporate taxes at the same rate. The revenue needs of different States vary greatly, some States needing a much greater income per unit of values within the State than others need, and naturally the rates of taxation levied by such States will vary widely. Such variance is in no way inconsistent with uniformity, which requires merely that the total tax burden, whether large or small, necessitating high rates or low rates, should be allocated as among the several subject matters of taxation on a uniform basis, so that, for example, if one State taxes both corporations and stockholders all States should tax both corporations and stockholders, even though the aggregate burden in one State is materially more or less than in other States, and so that if one State allocates the burden roughly equally between the corporation and the stockholder, all States should make at least an approximately similar allocation, and so that if one State allocates corporate excess or income on the basis of property and gross receipts, all States should allocate on substantially the same basis.

TAXATION OF PROPERTY AS AGAINST TAXATION OF INCOME

It having been decided, at least tentatively, that the business corporation should be subjected to taxation in duplicate form, a portion of the total burden which may be considered fair being placed upon the corporation and another portion upon the stockholders, the question remains: should the burden be placed upon or measured by the property (in the case of the corporation the so-called corporate excess and in the case of the individual the market value of the capital stock) or should the burden be placed upon or measured by the income?

It appears to be fairly obvious that the taxation of property and the taxation of the income from property are in reality substantially the same so far as concerns the ultimate burden. Since property is primarily valuable on account of the income derivable from it, the property is taxed when the income is taxed. In the taxation of individuals there are some fields where no real option is presented as between property taxation and income taxation, one type and only one being appropriate to the situation. Thus, in the case of real estate, property taxation is clearly indicated because of the circumstance that much real estate does not produce income, being either unimproved or used for residence purposes. A similar situation exists in the case of tangible personal property, where property taxation is indicated rather than income taxation. On the other hand, in the case of salaries and wages, income taxation is the only possibility since it is obviously impracticable to tax the personal human faculties, bodily and intellectual, which correspond to the property which produces the income. In the individual taxation field, intangibles constitute about the only form of property where there is a real option as between property taxation and income taxation. However, in the field of corporate taxation the situation is quite different, since substantially all the property of corporations is used in the production of income, and corporations do not earn wages and salaries, and furthermore, the exceptional earning power of corporations represented by their so-called goodwill can be taxed either directly as income or in the property values reflected by the market values of their capital stocks. Therefore in the case of corporations there is a real option as between the taxation of property and the taxation of income.

How should that option be exercised? From the viewpoint of corporations in general, it would seem that a tax on income is to be preferred because such a tax is levied on the basis of ability to pay, thus being light in years of adversity and heavy in years of prosperity, and presumably most corporations would prefer to be taxed heavily on their prosperity rather than encounter the risk of being taxed out of existence in case of adversity.

From the point of view of the taxing power it might be urged that a tax on property was to be preferred because a tax based on property is stable whereas a tax on income will fluctuate widely, producing heavily in boom years and meagerly in years of depression. This objection does not seem to me to be of primary importance for the reason that real estate bears by far the largest share in the aggregate burden of State taxation and any deficiency or excess in the proceeds of an income tax, resulting from fluctuations in income, can rather easily be adjusted by slight increases or decreases in the rate of property tax assessments; or if deemed fairer, the adjustment could be made by a temporary change in the rates of the income tax itself. Furthermore, variations in the income base might be reduced, and at the same time a highly desirable advantage gained from the point of view of equity and fairness, by levying the tax upon average income over a period of years.

A third important point of distinction between a corporate income tax and a corporate property tax is this : if property be used as the corporation tax base it is very difficult to apply to individuals any similar or analogous tax burden. That is, so far as there is any property base for the tax on corporate excess it must necessarily consist of two things, the corporate franchise or right to carry on business, and the goodwill or exceptional earning power. Usually the primary source of value in the corporate excess is exceptional earning power. Now, while individuals have goodwill — in other words exceptional earning power — it appears to be impracticable to tax them upon it as property. Therefore, if the property base is used for the taxation of corporations, no parallel tax can be applied to individuals. On the other hand, if the base of the corporation tax is income it is a very simple matter to collect an analogous or parallel tax from the individual. This strikes me as important for the reason that through the imposition of an income tax on both corporations and individuals it becomes possible, first, to eliminate discrimination against corporations if that be the State policy, and even if that be not the State policy it becomes possible to define the desired differentiation very clearly and simply, so that it may be easily and definitely understood by the business man when considering the relative advantages and disadvantages of the individual or corporate method of conducting his business activities. In the bill introduced this year into the Massachusetts Legislature, for a general revision of our tax system, corporate income was taxed. to the corporation at 4% and dividends on corporate stock representing the same income when passed on to the stockholder, at 3%, or a total of 7%, whereas business income received by individuals and partnerships was taxed at 1% only. It is true, however, that as against this discrepancy unfavorable to the corporation, allowance must be made for the fact that corporations were not taxed, although individuals were, upon their merchandise. Whether that is a full offset, a partial offset, or an excessive offset, may be a matter on which opinions will differ. If provisions were made for the taxation of merchandise and similar property owned by corporations in the same manner as provided in the case of individuals, the rate of tax on corporate incomes being reduced by way of offset, it would then become possible to determine the exact amount of the discrepancy and its incidence.

A fourth point of distinction between taxation of corporations through the medium of a property tax and through the medium of an income tax relates to difficulties of administration. An income tax is much more easily administrable, both from the standpoint of the State and of the corporation, because it requires no special computation other than that required by the necessity of allocation within and without the State, the computation of income itself being required in any event for Federal purposes. By adopting the obvious expedient of accepting for State purposes the income determined for Federal purposes, with certain minor modifications, the great bulk of the auditing burden is eliminated.

Against a system for taxing corporations exclusively upon income, it is sometimes urged that pursuant to that method the corporation which is temporarily losing money will pay no tax, in spite of the fact that it continues to receive protection for its property and business. However, it should be remembered that even such a corporation would continue to be taxed upon its tangible property. Furthermore, it would be in no way inconsistent with the general system here proposed if a minimum tax were provided to cover such cases.

Finally, one further distinction should be noted between the use of income, on the one hand, or property, on the other hand, as the taxation base. Under present systems where property (that is, the corporate excess in the case of the corporation and the stock in the case of the stockholder) is employed as the taxation base, an attempt to do complete equity is frequently made by the granting of a deduction against the property base equal in amount to the value of the tangible property independently taxed. If the base used be income, the allowance of this offset or deduction cannot be effected quite so directly. However, it would seem that satisfactory provision might still be made by reducing the income to be taxed by an amount bearing the same relation to the entire income as that borne by the assessed value of the taxed tangible property to the value of all the corporation's property. And if this method of fixing the deduction should be found to be difficult of administration, as it well might be, then the deduction might be determined by taking some fair percentage (for example, 5% or 6%) of the assessed value of the tangible property, on the assumption that such amount fairly represented the contribution of income ascribable to the tangible property. It may be noted, in passing, that the propriety of the adjustment here suggested may require careful consideration from various viewpoints.

In conclusion, then, the suggestions contained herein may be summarized as follows:

(1). The burden of corporate taxation (other than that imposed on tangible property) should be divided between the corporate entity, on the one hand, and the stockholders on the other hand, each State levying a tax on all corporations, whether domestic or foreign, owning property or transacting business within its borders, based upon the amount of such property and the extent of such business, this tax being levied wholly without regard to the residence of the stockholders; each State also levying a tax upon all resident stockholders based upon their stock holdings in both domestic and foreign corporations, this tax being levied wholly without regard to the location of the corporation's property and business. Obviously each tax thus levied can be and should be substantially less than any single tax now levied upon either the corporation alone or the stockholders alone. The reason for preferring this system has been already clearly indicated. It is in brief that the divided system is much better adapted to uniform adoption by all the States because it permits each State to collect the tax to which the character of the State population and the location of corporate property and business entitles it.

(2). The taxes to be levied, one on the corporation and the other on the stockholders, should each be levied with respect to and measured by income — in the case of the corporation by the corporation's net income fairly allocable to the taxing State, and in the case of the stockholder by corporate dividends. In the case of both taxes a deduction may be allowed based upon the amount of tangible property independently taxed. The reasons why such taxes (namely, taxes on income) seem preferable to taxes with respect to and measured by property have also been already indicated. They are in brief as follows: first, the tax on net income throws the burden of the tax where it can be most easily borne, in accordance with the principle of ability to pay; second, the tax on net income can be administered with much greater economy, certainty and efficiency than a tax on property and is much less vexatious to the taxpayer; third, the tax on income is the only tax which, for practical purposes, can be applied alike to the corporation and to the stockholder and to the unincorporated recipient of general business income, and therefore is much more likely to result in an equitable allocation of the total tax burden; lastly, while at first sight it might appear that a tax based on income would be less stable and continuously productive than a tax based on property, little weight attaches to this consideration because of the ease with which discrepancies in the revenue produced by the income tax on corporate wealth can be adjusted by slight increases or decreases in the tax on real estate, or even by slight adjustments in the rate of the income tax itself.

(3). Whether the aggregate of the described taxes should be the same as the taxes collected from unincorporated business, and to what extent, if to any extent, the possession of the corporate franchise justifies the collection of taxes on corporate income at rates in excess of those on income from unincorporated business, is not within the scope of this address. Another very difficult question which is not within the scope of this address is the question by what means, if any, we may mitigate the undoubted hardship involved in the process of effecting those changes in the status of certain types of property necessary to the substitution of the proposed system in place of existing systems, thus subjecting to taxation types of property at present exempt and acquired by present investors at prices reflecting the tax exemption which must be forfeited if the proposed system is to be substituted for a different system now in force.

Finally it should be borne in mind that the suggestions for a tax system or method herein contained have not been made with special reference to the situation or requirements of any particular state, and it is fully realized that in most instances (either for historical reasons or because of state constitutional provisions or special situations of various kinds) anything like the adoption of the entire system, even if deemed correct in theory, would be impracticable except as a result of a very gradual process of adaptation.

3. Economic Aspects of Bank Taxation *

The past decade has witnessed a unique conflict in the taxation of commercial banks. The conflict is not yet ended, and no solution, not even a workable arrangement, is in sight. The agreement that has been arrived at between the two bargaining committees of the American Bankers Association and of the Association of States on Bank Taxation is not yet enacted into law. And if it does become law, it will have to run the gauntlet of all the vicissitudes incidental to a new tax. It is a very complicated measure.

* Adapted from J. P. Jensen, "Economic Aspects of Bank Taxation," *Proceedings of the National Tax Association,* (1930), pp. 297-303.

Perhaps we should say that all the economic aspects of bank taxation should have been presented earlier as far back as ten years ago, or at any rate so far back as to be of use in shaping the various amendments of Section 5219,† and in arriving at the present compromise of the two bargaining committees. One might go further and say that there is little or nothing new that can be said. Yet it is certain that the last word has not been and will not be said for some time. Perhaps there is no last word. Surely if there is one, it cannot be said until a more stable equilibrium is developed than that which exists today.

THE POLITICAL ASPECTS

It may be trite to say that the factors that have produced the present confusion have not been economic. The present situation has grown out of the dual form of government under which we live. This political situation we shall of course continue to have. From it we cannot escape. Any system of bank taxation we may adopt must fit into the system of banking with banks chartered by two different governments.

The political factor may not have been barren of good effects; but surely the net result, at least at the present time, is far from good. Section 5219 practically prescribed the general property tax for the shares of bank stock. It did practically prescribe uniform taxation, at least in contemplation of law, in most of the states. And this uniformity, in the past may not have been an unmixed evil. But it is certain, in my opinion, that Section 5219 has compelled the states to retain the general property tax longer than they otherwise would have done. The prolongation of that outgrown system of taxation is a serious charge to bring against the political factor in bank taxation.

Except for the restraining force of Section 5219 it seems reasonable to suppose that we should have been further along in arriving at a workable method of taxing banks. Consider the insurance business, by way of comparison. There is no Section 5219 for taxes on insurance companies. They are financial enterprises no less specialized than the commercial banks. Being free to adapt taxes on insurance companies to the economic characteristics of the insurance business we have evolved at least a stable and workable premium tax. The taxes

† Eds. note: Section 5219, United States Revised Statutes, provides that a state "may (1) tax said shares [of national banking associations located within its borders], or (2) include dividends derived therefrom in the taxable income of an owner or holder thereof, or (3) tax such associations on their net income, or (4) according to or measured by their net income." In addition to any one of the above methods, local taxation of real property is permitted.

on gross premiums on insurance companies are as uniform and as simple, and as suitable for their purpose as the taxes on the shares of bank stock ever were among the several states. In the absence of Section 5219 we should expect to have made equal progress in taxing banks.

It is also reasonable to suppose that, in the absence of Section 5219, we should have been able to dispose of the discrepancies that now exist, and are strikingly apparent from a comparison of the taxes on banks with the taxes on other financial corporations such as building and loan associations and the various forms of finance companies. The problem of establishing equality in the taxation of commercial banks as compared with the taxation of other financial corporations is far from being an academic question.

ECONOMIC ASPECTS

WHAT are the economic aspects of bank taxation? Possibly the inquiry should be limited to this: What are the economic aspects of bank taxation that can be given due recognition under Section 5219 as it now is; as it will be if amended as proposed; or how ought it to be amended so as to give recognition to all the relevant economic aspects of taxes on banks?

It is easier to approach the question if we first rephrase it so as to read: What taxes on banks are economically sound? It may be said that a tax on banks, to be economically sound, must produce substantial equality, on some reasonable basis, between the banks and other business enterprises which, like the banks, are neither particularly vicious nor unusually meritorious from a social point of view. It is not essential to economic soundness of a tax on banks that it shall be the same in form as those on other business enterprises. But it is essential that the tax shall bear some reasonable relation to some relevant aspect or aspects of banks and other business enterprises. And the most relevant aspect of all business enterprises would appear to be the business income.

A tax that is unsound economically is socially detrimental. A tax that bears a grossly unequal relation to the net business income of economically similar business enterprises reduces the aggregate net services which these enterprises bestow upon society. The value of the services bestowed upon society by the relatively overtaxed enterprises is curtailed to a greater extent than the value of the services of the relatively under-taxed enterprises is augmented by the discrepancies in the tax burden. There is a net social loss.

Now the social loss sustained in this way cannot be demonstrated fully here. I must content myself with using an actually existing condition as a demonstration. Such a demonstration will be more intelligible than elaborate theoretical proof. It happens that such a demonstration is ready at hand and may be had by a comparison of the taxes on commercial banks with those on building and loan associations. It is not my wish to foster ill-will between cousins in the family of business enterprises we call financial corporations. But the demonstration is too convenient, and should be too convincing, for me to neglect it.

It is a matter of common knowledge that building and loan associations have shown a remarkable growth during the past decade. The total assets have increased from about $1,769,-000,000 in 1917 to $7,000,000,000 in 1928. The number of persons who are investors has increased from 4 of each 100 in 1917 to 10 of each 100 in 1928. It is perhaps not equally well known that the commercial banks have shown a relatively much slower growth, where they have shown any growth at all. The building and loan associations owe a part of their growth, perhaps a large part, to their preferential position with respect to taxation on their business. On their business as such, in most states they pay practically no taxes. Moreover, they pay practically no federal taxes. The commercial banks enjoy no such preference. On the contrary, they are relatively overtaxed in most of the states. It is not necessary at this point to show that the banks are overtaxed in comparison with non-financial corporations, although I think that can readily be proved in the states where the bank shares are taxed as general property. It is enough for the present argument if the commercial banks are overtaxed in comparison with building and loan associations. And that is surely true, at least in the general property tax states.

Now the business of the commercial banks and that of the building and loan associations are both, and to my mind equally meritorious. But the gain that has accrued to patrons of the building and loan associations, whether investors or borrowers, by reason of the virtual tax exemption which their business enjoys has been more than offset to the patrons of the commercial banks by reason of the heavy taxes which banks pay.

THE GENERAL PROPERTY TAX ON THE SHARES

TURNING now to a brief economic analysis of the specific taxes permissible under Section 5219, let us first consider the property tax on the shares as general property. The original Section 5219 was enacted at a time when the general property tax, both as required by state constitutions, as provided for by statute law, and as cherished (if any tax can be cherished) by public opinion was at its zenith. With the then prevailing philosophy of property taxation, though never with the prevailing practice, Section 5219 was in harmony. Had Section 5219 been drafted fifty years earlier, it *might* have been different. Had it been drafted in 1930, it surely *would* have been different. It is thus an historical accident that we happen to be saddled with an incubus that blocks tax reform, to some degree, in every direction.

By their works shall taxes, like men, be justified. But the property tax on shares as general property has not been so justified, if we accept as a test substantial equality of taxation as between banks and other business enterprises. For it has singled out the commercial banks, in the general property tax states, as the only business corporations, with the possible exception of certain public utilities, to be taxed on the basis of the full value of all their property. The result is partly due to the requirements of the law, and partly due to the facts that these requirements are not and cannot be met in practice. Let me take first a very clear case as a demonstration.

It has been my privilege recently to examine at close range the Colorado state tax system. Though the Colorado constitution contains the uniformity clause of the general property tax in some form, the shares of stock of all corporations, except banks, are declared to be not property for purposes of taxation. The shares of banks are therefore by law the only corporate shares taxable as property. And, with the possible exception of certain centrally assessed public utilities, there is no provision elsewhere in the law of the state for taxing the so-called corporate excess which the corporate shares may be said to represent.

Now the situation is not far different in the states in which the tax law requires, in part, all or some of the corporate shares to be taxed as property. For it is, of course, familiar that these shares are not so taxed in practice. Whether the law requires it or not, the intangibles, other than bank stock, almost universally escape the general property tax. This means that in most of the general property tax states the banks are, again with the possible exception of the centrally assessed public utilities, the only corporations that are taxed on the basis of their total value, including the intangible value of the enterprise. For very few of the general property tax states provide for taxation of this intangible value of general corporations

But the discrimination extends farther. It is well established, I believe, that intangibles, where they are reached for taxation at all, tend to be assessed at percentage of their value nearer 100 per cent than is the assessment ratio for tangible property. But bank stock is always assessed because of the method of assessment. If then the bank-owned real estate is assessed at, say 60 per cent and the bank stock is assessed at, say 90 per cent of full value; and if the assessed value of the real estate is deducted from the assessed value of the shares, in arriving at the value taxable to the banks, the result is the same as if aggregate taxable value were assessed at 90 per cent to the banks. Hence the banks can neither participate in the prevailing evasion of taxes by non-listing of intangibles, nor participate in the prevailing undervaluation on tangible property. The surveys of bank taxation made by the American Bankers Association's Committee on State and Local Taxation of Banks demonstrate that in fact that type of double discrimination exists partly because of the administrative procedure and partly because of the requirements of the law.

There is still another way in which the property tax on the shares as general property discriminates against the commercial banks. It is a strange paradox in Section 5219 that it does not require tax-exempt assets of the bank to be excluded in arriving at the value of the shares of bank stock for property taxation while in arriving at the taxable income for income taxation, a much lighter tax than the property tax, income from such exempt assets clearly must be deducted under alternative 3, and probably, at least possibly, must be deducted under alternative 4 of Section 5219 as it stands now. In general such exempts are not taxable to other taxpayers, at least not on a property basis.

So it has come about that Section 5219, originally intended as a safeguard to the banks against excessive taxation by the states, has become a device by which they are, at least in the three forms mentioned above, denied or deprived of the relief from property taxes which are available to other taxpayers.

It has been said that the banks could not possibly be overtaxed by a system of property taxes on bank shares as general property. The assets of the banks, particularly those represented by deposits, correspond to the merchandise of a merchant, or the stores of a manufacturer, or the livestock of a farmer. They are the working capital of the bank, even if they are balanced by claims of depositors, with which the banks do business, and on which they make money. But this argument overlooks all of the three factors I have mentioned above, which result in discriminations against the commercial banks.

This argument is rooted in the general property-tax philosophy, and assumes that all property is alike or assumes that it may be taxed as if it were alike, which of course is far from true. The intangible property, taxed fully to the banks, but generally not to other taxpayers on a general-property basis, differs from tangible property in two significant respects. In the first place, nearly all of the intangibles represent tangible property, directly or indirectly, which has presumably been fully taxed without deduction for debt. This fact should argue for their exemption no matter by whom the intangibles are held. In the second place, and for the present purpose most important, the fact that intangibles generally escape, and that the owners do not expect to pay the tax, while the owners of tangible property, especially real property, know that they must pay the tax, has important consequences. Other taxpayers can own and hold the intangibles tax-free, while banks cannot. But the yield must be the same to the banks as to others.

In short, the value of intangibles as general property is not a proper basis for their taxation. And the hardships to the banks result from the fact that this inequitable basis of taxation can be enforced against them, has been so enforced against them in the general property tax states, but cannot in general be so enforced against other taxpayers.

TAXATION OF BANKS ON AN INCOME BASIS

But if the present property tax on the shares as general property is inequitable as applied at present, the basis of income for taxation runs to the other extreme. If it should develop that alternative four, the excise tax measured by net income without deduction, or at least without more than a proportional deduction, of the income from tax-exempts, in arriving at the taxable income, is permissible, then there is, as is generally understood, a possibility for adequate taxation of the banks, compared to other business enterprises, especially if an offset of personal-property taxes should be permitted, and if a personal-income tax should supplement the corporate excise-income tax. But all of that will stand or fall with the treatment of the income from the tax-exempt sources.

SPECIAL TAXES ON BANKS

If the Macallen decision should be applied in all its rigor to the taxation of banks on an income-tax basis, then income taxation as applied to banks would be impracticable. Since the tax on shares as general property is inequitable we cannot expect, nor ought we to hope that it will be retained. There is then left only some special form of tax on the banks. The proposed amendment to Section 5219 would make such a tax possible, as is in use in Virginia, Kentucky, and Nebraska. There is an important difference between a special property tax on the shares at a uniform intermediate rate and a general property tax on them. The former can be placed at such a rate that it will satisfy the banks. Yet that method has all the undesirable features of a compromise measure. Other compromise measures are possible conceivably, but as they are not proposed, they are not proper measures for discussion now.

4. The Taxation of Public Utilities [*]

THE PROBLEM OF TAXATION OF PUBLIC UTILITIES

Present methods of taxing public utility corporations. The most striking features of the existing taxation of public utility corporations are (1) the extraordinary variety in the methods followed by the several states, (2) the duplication and confusion arising from the decentralized taxation of property by the local jurisdictions, and (3) the lack of any guiding principle in the taxation of the public utilities and in the place of such taxes in the tax system as a whole.

As to the first, it is quite safe to say that there are as many varieties of public utility taxes as there are states, indeed, more, since the same state frequently uses different methods for different classes of utilities. From this bewildering collection of tax methods it is possible to select three types which stand out as of enough importance to merit special consideration. These are (1) the *ad valorem* basis, (2) the capitalization basis, and (3) the earnings basis.

Under the *ad valorem* basis the tax is imposed upon the value of the property of the corporation. This was the original method of taxing corporations under the general property tax. In the beginning, the valuation was made and the tax imposed by the local bodies, in exactly the same way as for natural persons. This crude method has now been generally abandoned. As employed in progressive states today, the *ad valorem* method involves a more or less expert valuation of the property of the corporation as a whole, made by a state board or officer, generally followed by apportionment of the taxable value thus determined among the local taxing districts. In determining

---

[*] Adapted from a "Report of the Committee of the National Tax Association on The Taxation of Public Utilities and upon the Interstate Apportionment of the Tax," *Proceedings of the National Tax Association,* (1922), pp. 162-179.

the value of the corporation's property a variety of evidence is used. It is safe to say that at present the most weight is given to the earning capacity of the corporation; in other words, the value of the property is determined primarily by capitalizing the corporation's net earnings.

The *ad valorem* basis is the one most widely used. About half the states rely on it exclusively for the taxation of railroads. Nearly as many use it as the exclusive tax for telephone and telegraph companies. About a dozen states use it as the only method of taxing street railways and water, gas and electric companies. *Ad valorem* taxes are used in connection with other methods in many other states.

The capitalization basis involves the imposition of a tax upon the value of the securities of the corporation. This sometimes includes only the value of the stock; in other cases, and more correctly, the value of both stock and bonds is used. It is safe to say that this basis has generally proved unsatisfactory, and is today of declining importance. Only three or four states rely upon this method alone for the taxation of one or more of the classes of public utility corporations. About half a dozen states use this in connection with other methods.

Next to the *ad valorem* basis, the earnings basis is the one in widest use. The amount of the tax is stated as a certain percentage of the earnings. The rate of the tax is generally fixed with the idea of making the tax correspond, at least roughly, with the burden of the property tax on taxpayers generally. The rate is apt to be different for different classes of corporations. The earnings tax is almost always based on gross earnings. The gross earnings basis is used for the taxation of railroads, of street railways, of telephone and telegraph companies, of water, gas and electric companies in a considerable number of states.

The confusion and duplication arising from the taxation of the property of public utility corporations by the several towns and counties is notorious. What could be more absurd than the taxation of a great railroad system or a telegraph company upon odd bits of its tracks or odd sections of poles and wires in hundreds of small local taxing districts? The local assessors are usually quite powerless to value such property, even if there were any such thing as a real value of odd bits of tracks or lines, apart from the value of the whole plant. The corporation must take account of thousands of different assessments and thousands of different levies at as many different rates. It receives thousands of separate tax bills for amounts varying from hundreds of dollars down to a few cents. It must employ an army of tax agents to protect its interests. An enormous burden, quite in addition to the actual amount of its taxes, is thus placed upon the public utility corporations.

The lack of any guiding principle is obvious from even a cursory study of the present methods of taxing public utilities. The extraordinary diversity of methods is not merely the result of difference of opinion regarding the means for producing a desired end. It represents lack of agreement upon fundamental matters of principle. What are the economic characteristics of the public utility? On what principle are the charges for its services determined? How does legal regulation of its charges distinguish the public utility from other businesses? What is the relation between rate regulation and taxation? How is the taxation of public utilities to be fittted harmoniously into the general tax system? These are questions which must be considered in formulating any rational system of public utility taxation and in apportioning the taxes upon public utilities engaged in interstate business.

The model tax system. As a condition of its problem, the committee has assumed the tax system outlined by the committee on a Model Tax System. This system includes three taxes: (1) an individual income tax, (2) a property tax upon real estate and perhaps tangible personal property, but not on intangible property, and (3) a business tax. The committee's problem is to develop a plan for the taxation of public utility corporations which will fit harmoniously into this general system. As a practical consideration, the committee has had to take cognizance of the fact that the system of the model committee is not now actually in effect in any great number of states and that its general adoption will necessarily be a slow process. Moreover, there is the feeling among members of the committee that the taxation of tangible personal property is very probably destined to hold even a less important place in the future American tax systems than has been assigned to it by the model committee, although the committee itself seems not to regard it as essential. Large classes of tangible personalty are already virtually exempt from taxation by default and there is evident a growing movement to grant legal exemption to many, if not all, kinds of tangible personalty. The possibility that some states may see fit to classify tangible personalty and to tax certain classes at low rates is also to be reckoned with. These possibilities are indeed recognized by the model committee. The committee has accordingly undertaken to develop a plan for taxing public utilities which would be in harmony with the ideal system of the model committee generally, rather than an isolated plan for public utilities in particular; and at the same time a plan which would have sufficient elasticity to make possible its adaptation to present day conditions in at least a majority of the states, without necessarily waiting for the complete adoption of the model tax system.

TAXATION IN RELATION TO THE ECONOMIC NATURE OF PUBLIC UTILITIES

The economic nature of public utilities. In general, public utilities are distinguished from other business enterprises by two important characteristics. (1) They are in possession of certain special privileges received from government; the power to obtain land through condemnation; the right to use the public streets for their tracks or pipes, or wires, etc. These privileges very frequently give the public utility a monopoly. (2) The public utilities are under obligation to render adequate service to the public and to make reasonable charges for such service. This double obligation is now generally enforced by government, through commissions or other public agencies, having power to regulate the character of service rendered and the rates charged. Public regulation of rates and service may now be assumed as the normal condition.

In the days before legal regulation became the accepted principle, the privileged position of the public utilities was often made the ground for advocating especially heavy taxation of public utilities, on the theory that there should thus be recovered for the public as great a share as possible of that which rightfully belonged to the public. With the general acceptance of the principle of regulation, this reason for taxing public utilities more heavily than other kinds of property has ceased to exist.

Three theories of taxation of public utilities. Upon the assumption of legal regulation we may have three theories of taxation of public utilities. In the first place, it is possible to subject the public utilities to heavy taxation — heavier than is borne by other kinds of property. Because of its privileged position the utility is assumed to be able to pass these taxes on to the consumers of its services, and the regulating authority will allow rates high enough to permit such shifting and to leave to the utility a fair profit on its investment. Or, put in other words, rates will be high, with taxes high enough to take substantially all profits above a fair return. This is in effect a tax on the consumer of the service, with the public utility acting as tax-gatherer for the government.

In the opinion of the committee, this theory is not sound. It is fair neither to the consuming public nor to the utility. The use of transportation, gas or electricity, telephone or telegraph service or the service of any public utility is not a fair measure of taxpaying ability. Some men are required to travel constantly in the conduct of their businesses ; others travel little. Some persons must travel daily to and from their work ; others have no such necessity. It is recognized that in the course of time economic adjustments, for example in rents, tend to soften such irregularities, but it is not believed that such adjustments are either certain enough or prompt enough to overcome the initial injustice. Public utility services, moreover, are generally necessities, and their use as a measure of tax obligation imposes a degressive tax burden, increasing in relative severity as one goes down the economic scale. From the side of the taxed utility this theory is unfair, for the reason that the mere permission to charge high rates does not always carry the power to shift heavy taxes. If rates are already as high as the traffic will bear, it is futile to attempt to shift taxes by raising rates, even though the increase be perfectly legal. Finally, this theory may lead to serious interstate inequalities. It is not easy to justify a tax imposed by one state and shifted to consumers who are residents of another state.

The second theory of taxation of public utilities goes to the opposite extreme. It would exempt the utility entirely, to the end that the service may be given the consumers at the lowest possible rate. This theory, in the opinion of the committee, is also untenable. The public utility enjoys certain services from the government, in the protection of its property and otherwise, like any other property owner. The government is compelled to incur certain expenditures, in order to render its services to the public utility. This governmental service must be regarded as one of the costs of furnishing the service by the public utility. It forms the basis for a tax upon the public utility, a tax which may be passed on as a fair charge upon the consumers. Whereas the first theory would impose upon the utility consumers an unfair share of the cost of government, which ought to be borne by the general body of taxpayers, this theory would put upon the general taxpayers a government cost which should be regarded as part of the costs of furnishing the public service, and should therefore be borne by the consumers.

The third theory, in the committee's opinion the sound theory, would place the taxation of the public utilities as nearly as possible on an equality with other kinds of property and business. The general principle of equality in taxation will be questioned by few. It has had repeated support at these conferences. A heavy burden of proof rests upon him who advocates departure from the principle of equality in any particular case. The committee fails to find any valid argument for departure from this principle in the case of the taxation of public utilities.

Two points need to be emphasized in this connection. (1) It should by now be well recognized that equality does not require uniformity either of method or of rate. Equality relates to the actual burden of taxation. It may be the result of a judicious variety of tax methods. As will be shown later, there is good reason for taxing public utilities by methods distinct from those applied to other property or businesses. This implies no departure from the principle of equality. (2) It cannot be too strongly insisted that equality must be real equality and not merely formal. Because the statutes declare that all property, real and personal, tangible and intangible, shall be taxed at the same rate, it must not be assumed that all property is actually so taxed. For example, the development of an efficient process for the centralized assessment of all the property of public utility corporations may produce, not equality, but gross inequality, because of the simple fact that equally efficient methods of assessment are not applied to all the taxable property of other taxpayers.[1]

Measure of the burden of taxes on public utilities. If the principle of equality is to prevail, the burden of the taxes upon the public utilities should correspond to the taxes levied upon other kinds of property and business. The model tax system embraces (1) an individual income tax, (2) the property tax, and (3) a business tax. How may the taxation of the public utilities be fitted into this system?

It should always be remembered that we are seeking to find a fair measure of the contribution to be demanded of the public utilities, but do not have in mind application to such corporations of the same methods of taxation which are applied to other taxpayers in the model system. What we seek at this point is a measure of the burden, not the method.

(1). As regards the individual income tax, there is no special problem. This is a tax on individuals, not on corporations. It will not be imposed on the incorporated public

[1] The importance of the prinicple of equality was ably discussed by a former committee on the taxation of public service corporations, which reported to the national tax conference of 1913. (*Proceedings*, seventh conference, pp. 372-383). With the arguments and conclusions of that report, the present committee is in substantial agreement.

utilities. On the other hand, being a tax on virtually all incomes, regardless of their source, it will fall upon the stockholders and bondholders of the public utility corporations, with respect to their dividends and interest, as in the case of other corporations.

(2). Under the property tax, the burden borne by the public utilities should correspond to that of other property owners. Possession of property by the public utility should measure taxpaying obligation to the extent that similar property is actually taxed to other owners. It may be assumed that real estate is everywhere taxed. (We do not here mean technical legal real estate, but ordinary economic real estate; that is, land and buildings.) But the fact of assessment at less than true value must not be overlooked. As a measure of tax obligation, the public utility's real estate must not be valued at its true value, while real estate in general is differently assessed. Or, if this is done, allowance must be made elsewhere. The same rule applies to the tangible personal property of the public utility. Such property should be a measure of tax obligation to the extent, and only to the extent, that tangible personalty is actually taxed to other owners. References must be, not to the formal statute, but to the facts of prevailing practice, with due allowance for under-assessment and complete escape of much tangible property, as well as for legal exemption. It is assumed that there will be, in the model system, no taxation of intangible personal property. The possession of such property by the public utility should therefore not be used as an index of tax obligation, and in valuing the property of the utility as a whole, no account should be taken of franchise or other intangible values.

The preceding paragraph, while stated with reference to the model tax system, nevertheless furnishes the general rule for all cases. Its acceptance need not await the complete adoption of the model system. For example, if intangibles, or certain classes thereof, are taxed, such property in the possession of the public utility should be given corresponding consideration. On the other hand, any state which sees fit to exempt tangible personalty, in whole or in part, has only to be consistent by disregarding such property in determining the tax obligation of its public utilities. In general, property of all sorts may be used to measure the tax obligation of the public utilities, to the extent that similar property is actually taxed in the hands of other owners, due account being taken of exemptions, actual as well as legal, evasion, and under-assessment. The necessity of having regard to such excrescences will continue so long as the general tax system remains in its present imperfect state. We cannot safely put a new patch of efficient public utility assessment upon the old tax garment.

(3). In addition to the contribution as measured by property, the public utilities should be called upon for a contribution corresponding to the business tax. Here also the rule of equality must govern, and those states which do not impose a business tax upon other business cannot fairly exact a corresponding contribution from the public utilities.

(4). Finally, the peculiar position of the public utility, as a privileged and regulated enterprise, appears to the committee to require a special tax treatment in order to carry out completely the principle of rate regulation. This topic will be further developed in the following section.

Why do the public utilities require special treatment? In the preceding section the principle of equality has been applied to the taxation of public utilities as compared with other kinds of property and business. The question may arise: Why not accomplish equality by simply subjecting the public utilities to the same property and business taxes as are applied to property and business in general? Why is special treatment required? The answer depends upon two considerations — (1) the character of the property of the public utility, and (2) rate regulation.

The property of the ordinary public utility is peculiar on account of (a) its highly technical character, (b) the fact that its value can generally be appraised only as a whole plant, not in separate parts, and (c) its widespread location in many local tax jurisdictions.

These peculiarities make the assessment of public utility property a special problem. The local assessors are generally not qualified for the task. The property cannot be valued in little bits. Central assessment is a necessity. With central assessment comes the danger, already referred to, that public utility property will be fully and accurately valued, while property in general is largely undervalued or overlooked. Indeed the whole problem of assessing the property of the great public utilities is so complicated and difficult that the property basis seems likely to be displaced by other more effective methods of taxation. At any rate, the ordinary methods of the general property tax are wholly inapplicable to the public utilities.

It was these peculiarities of public utility property that early led to the break-down of the old general property tax as applied to the public utilities, compelling the substitution of centralized for local assessment and the invention of special methods of taxation.   That is to say, the weaknesses of the general property tax were earlier discovered and remedies earlier attempted in the case of the public utilities than with respect to other kinds of property.   Much progress has been made.   Tax technique has been perfected and valuable experience gained.   In spite of the inherent difficulties, it is safe to say that in many states the taxation of public utility corporations has reached a technical efficiency far beyond what has anywhere been attained in the administration of the general property tax.   To name only random examples, witness the *ad valorem* taxation of Wisconsin and the gross earnings taxes of Minnesota and Connecticut.   These advantages should not be thrown away.

The second consideration which points to special treatment of the public utilities is the matter of rate regulation.   Rate regulation and taxation must go together and supplement each other.   Rate regulation should be such as to enable the public utility to earn, in the long run, a fair return on all its property and to secure fresh capital as required for the proper maintenance and development of the enterprise.   The actual ruling of the supreme court is a reasonable return on the fair value of the property at the time the rate regulation is applied.   The legal rates must permit profits greater than the normal in the good years to offset smaller profits or losses in other years.   Changes in the legal rate limits occur at more or less long intervals.   In the interim changed conditions may permit of higher profits than were contemplated.   Again rates may be limited by general rules applying to several corporations.   Rates sufficient for the least favorably situated may give high profits to those in more favorable circumstances.   Taxation should be relied upon to take for the public a part of the extra profits made under unexpectedly favorable conditions or by the more fortunate corporations.   Such a tax should be levied upon pure economic profits, after allowing a reasonable rate of interest upon all the capital invested, whether owned or borrowed.   A tax on this basis may be at fairly high rates, but not so high as to take away from the utilities the incentive to economy and efficiency required in the interest of the public as well as of the utilities themselves.

PROPOSED METHOD OF TAXING PUBLIC UTILITIES

Ad valorem basis vs. *earnings basis.   Gross* vs. *net earnings.* In the foregoing sections of its report the committee has undertaken to formulate certain principles to govern the taxation of public utilities. In particular we have sought a guide to measure the amount of the tax contribution of the utilities. The remaining task is to develop the most effective means for putting these principles into effect. Experience in the taxation of public utilities has now gone far enough so that the choice of a tax basis is practically narrowed down to two: i.e., the *ad valorem* basis and the earnings basis.

The *ad valorem* basis, in spite of its use by the majority of the states, is open to serious objections. Whatever the process employed for obtaining the value of the corporation's property, the operation is difficult and expensive. To be properly performed, it requires a large staff of experts familiar with the technical details of the business and the corporations involved. At the best, the element of personal judgment must always enter to a large degree.

There are also serious theoretical questions involved, first, as to the valuation of the physical properties, and secondly, as to the use to be made of the facts regarding financial condition, earnings, etc. The vice of the real operation of the *ad valorem* system is in the extremely arbitrary and unequal results. When occasion demands, wholly arbitrary and inexplicable changes are made without any rational basis. And the trouble is that there is no practical method of securing judicial review; (1) because of the subject matter, (2) because of the utter impossibility of equalizing where there is no similar property with which to make comparison. The almost entire absence of the possibility of equity is the disturbing factor.

Finally, the fact remains that the value of property alone is not a true measure of a corporation's worth or of the taxes it should pay. The thing that really gives worth to a corporation is its earning power. It is significant that so many of the states which rely upon the *ad valorem* basis have found it necessary to take account of earnings in arriving at the value of the corporation's property.

The *ad valorem* basis lacks simplicity. It is apt to become arbitrary. Its administration is difficult and expensive. It is not an accurate measure of the obligation or ability to pay taxes. It does not succeed in placing the burden of taxation equitably.

The tax on earnings is strong at the points where the *ad valorem* basis is weak. The earnings of a corporation are the real basis of its worth and its taxpaying ability. The earnings tax involves the fewest theoretical difficulties and is simple and inexpensive to administer. Earnings are a matter of fact, about which there will generally not be disagreement. The determination of net earnings does involve certain difficulties, but in general the element of personal judgment is relatively small as compared with the property tax. The earnings tax is simple and clear, it usually fluctuates with the prosperity of the taxpaying corporations, and it is generally equitable between corporations.

The outstanding facts in recent tax history are the concentration of public opinion in favor of taxes upon incomes or earnings and the rapid development of such taxes. In legislation the federal government has taken the lead in taxing corporate and individual incomes. Several states, notably California, Minnesota and Connecticut, have led the way in the taxation of public utility corporations on the basis of gross earnings. A number of states, among which Wisconsin and New York are leaders, have made progress in the successful taxation of individual incomes and the net incomes of business corporations. The present tendency is without doubt in the direction of income and earnings taxes, which confirms the conclusion in favor of the earnings basis for the taxation of the public utility corporations.

The next question has to do with the relative merits of net earnings and gross earnings as the basis of the tax. The situation may be summarized briefly, as follows: Net earnings are the fairest and most accurate measure of the ability to pay taxes, an important advantage of this basis. On the other hand, the gross earnings basis has the advantage of greater certainty and simplicity. Gross earnings are a matter of fact, clearly shown on the books, about which there will seldom be difference of opinion. Determination of net earnings requires the deduction of a great variety of expenses, involving some exercise of judgment and the possibility of disagreement and evasion. Ten years ago this argument was generally decisive in favor of the gross earnings basis. Today it is not so strong. Under the compulsion of the federal income tax, those public utility corporations whose accounts were not already prescribed by the interstate commerce commission have been led to put their accounting systems into order. Since the federal returns of these corporations are subject to inspection by the officers of any state imposing an income tax upon them, there would appear now to be much less practical difficulty in the way of the tax on net earnings than formerly, though the advantage of extreme simplicity still remains with the gross earnings basis.

The decision between the two bases really rests upon a more fundamental question as to the theory of the corporation tax. Is the obligation to contribute to the support of the state to be limited to those corporations that make profits? If so, the net earnings tax is indicated. On the other hand, if it is intended that the corporations shall contribute, whether they make profits or not, if taxes are to be regarded as one of the necessary costs of business, the gross earnings tax is the proper method. Obviously the government must function in years when business is poor as well as in years of prosperity. If certain sources of revenue decline or fail, other sources must make good the loss.

Taxes may be classified into two groups: (1) Those which are paid only out of profits or net income, such as the individual income tax and the income taxes imposed by certain states (e.g., New York and Connecticut) on business corporations, and (2) those which continue with fair regularity, regardless of profits or which may even be increased in years of business depression, to make good the losses from other sources; the only important example (aside from the gross earnings tax on corporations) is the property tax. The question is: Into which class shall the tax on public utility corporations be put? It is simply the practical question of how far the states can safely go in narrowing the basis of taxes upon which they may rely for a regular income, regardless of fluctuations in business prosperity. There is a strong tendency in this direction. The general property tax seems tending to become practically a tax on real estate only. The center of gravity of the revenue system is rapidly moving to the side of net income and net earnings taxes. There is danger that the states may find themselves dependent upon an irregular income — too great in some years, and insufficient in others, and that the property tax may not be elastic enough to stand the strain of the lean years. It is this consideration that dictates caution in going over completely to the net earnings basis.

The practical consideration of government necessity would seem therefore to preclude the complete adoption of the net earnings basis. On the other hand, the gross earnings basis may fairly be charged, on behalf of the tax-paying utility, with neglect of the principle of ability to pay. In particular it puts a heavy burden upon the utility whose net earnings are small or entirely lacking. It is to be noted that in this respect the gross earnings tax is no worse, indeed is probably better, than the property tax. Nevertheless, this is a real defect.

The earnings tax, gross or net. In the opinion of the committee the dilemma which thus arises may be met by a combination of gross and net earnings taxes. A tax on net earnings could be imposed at a certain rate, with the proviso that the amount of the tax should never be less than a certain moderate percentage of the gross earnings. This is the same thing as providing two taxes, one on gross earnings, at a moderate rate, the other at a higher rate on net earnings, with the proviso that in each particular case the tax collected shall be the higher of the two. For example, the law might provide a tax of ten per cent of net earnings, the amount of which should never be less than two per cent of gross earnings. The same result would be accomplished by providing that each utility should pay either ten per cent, or any other per cent, of its net earnings, or two per cent, or any other per cent, of its gross earnings, whichever were the greater. The committee, of course, uses these particular rates merely for the sake of illustration.

The effect of such a tax may be illustrated by the following example:

Gross Earnings	Net Earnings	Tax	Resulting Ratio of Tax	
			To Gross	To Net
$100,000	Not over $5,000	$2,000	2%	40% or over
100,000	5,000 to 10,000	2,000	2%	40% to 20%
100,000	10,000 to 15,000	2,000	2%	20% to 13⅓%
100,000	15,000 to 20,000	2,000	2%	13⅓% to 10%
100,000	20,000 to 25,000	2,000 to 2,500	2 % to 2½%	10%
100,000	25,000 to 30,000	2,500 to 3,000	2½% to 3%	10%
100,000	30,000 to 35,000	3,000 to 3,500	3 % to 3½%	10%
100,000	35,000 to 40,000	3,500 to 4,000	3½% to 4%	10%

Virtually the same result could also be obtained by means of a gross earnings tax at a progressive rate, starting with a moderate rate where net earnings bear a small ratio to gross or are non-existent, and increasing with the increase in the ratio of net to gross. For example, such a progressive tax on gross earnings might be at the following rates:

Every company shall pay an annual tax which shall be based on gross earnings and which shall be the percentage of gross earnings fixed herein:

(a) When it has no net earnings or its net earnings do not exceed 5 per cent of its gross earnings — 1 per cent;

(b) When its net earnings exceed 5 per cent of its gross earnings but do not exceed 10 per cent — 1¼ per cent;

(c) When its net earnings exceed 10 per cent of its gross earnings but do not exceed 15 per cent — 1½ per cent;

(d) When its net earnings exceed 15 per cent of its gross earnings but do not exceed 20 per cent — 1¾ per cent;

(e) When its net earnings exceed 20 per cent of its gross earnings but do not exceed 25 per cent — 2 per cent;

(f) When its net earnings exceed 25 per cent of its gross earnings but do not exceed 30 per cent — 2¼ per cent;

(g) When its net earnings exceed 30 per cent of its gross earnings but do not exceed 35 per cent — 2½ per cent;

(h) When its net earnings exceed 35 per cent of its gross earnings but do not exceed 40 per cent — 2¾ per cent;

(i) When its net earnings exceed 40 per cent of its gross earnings — 3 per cent.

The operation of these rates may be illustrated by the following example:

Gross Earnings	Net Earnings	Ratio Net to Gross	Rate	Tax	Resulting Ratio of Tax to Net
$100,000	Not over $5,000	Not over 5%	1%	$1,000	.20 or more
100,000	5,000 to 10,000	5% to 10%	1¼%	1,250	.25 to .125
100,000	10,000 to 15,000	10% to 15%	1½%	1,500	.15 to .10
100,000	15,000 to 20,000	15% to 20%	1¾%	1,750	.116 to .087
100,000	20,000 to 25,000	20% to 25%	2%	2,000	.10 to .08
100,000	25,000 to 30,000	25% to 30%	2¼%	2,250	.09 to .075
100,000	30,000 to 35,000	30% to 35%	2½%	2,500	.083 to .071
100,000	35,000 to 40,000	35% to 40%	2¾%	2,750	.78 to .068
100,000	Over 40,000	Over 40%	3%	3,000	.075 or less

Such a combination tax is a reasonable compromise between the gross earnings basis and the net earnings basis. Being based primarily upon net earnings, the tax takes account of the varying abilities of the several utilities. On the other hand, the requirement of a certain minimum contribution from each corporation upon the basis of gross earnings, meets the public requirement of regular and dependable revenue.

Such an alternative gross or net tax is in harmony with the principles laid down as a guide for measuring the amount of the tax contribution of the public utilities. By proper adjustment of the rates applied to gross and net earnings respectively, the burden of the tax may be made to correspond fairly with the burden of the property tax upon other taxpayers.[2] In

[2] For a full discussion of this principle and its application, cf. the report of the California tax commission of 1906 and the report of the Connecticut special commission on taxation of certain corporations of 1913 (especially pp. 6-14).

determining this rate, the fact must, of course, not be over-looked that much intangible property and also a good deal of tangible property escapes taxation under the general property tax. As we have already emphasized, the tax on public utilities must correspond not to a property tax which reaches all kinds of property, but to the property tax as we know it, under which there is widespread escape of many forms of tangible and intangible personalty. While not quite so rigid as the property tax, its amount will be fairly regular from year to year. This regularity may be further enhanced, to the advantage of both the government and the utilities, by taking as the base the average of the earnings of several years (e.g., the past five years) instead of a single year. The alternative gross or net tax may be used, therefore, to exact from the public utilities that contribution which is due from them on account of the possession of property, while securing the great advantage of certainty and simplicity, which are lost if the tax is imposed directly upon the property. On the other hand, the rate of net earnings may be so adjusted as to take account of both property and business taxes.

The tax on net earnings may also be made to serve to take some part of the profits of the more favorably situated utilities, as required by the principle of rate regulation. The more exact way to accomplish this end would be by means of an additional tax upon pure economic profits, meaning the profits remaining after allowing a fair rate of interest upon all the capital employed, whether owned or borrowed. While making no positive recommendation, the committee is inclined to favor such a tax and believes that this idea is likely to gain favor as the scientific regulation of public utilities progresses.

The tax on real estate (i.e., actual real estate, land and buildings, not technical legal real estate). One further matter must be considered in this connection. That is the question of the taxation of real estate. The simplest way to tax the public utilities would be to impose the alternative gross or net tax as an exclusive tax. No further taxation of the utility's property, either real or personal, need be required. This is the method followed, for example, by Connecticut in the taxation of railroad corporations; a gross earnings tax is imposed in lieu of all other taxation of property used in the railroad business. The alternative gross or net earnings tax may thus be used as the exclusive tax exacted from the public utilities, with rates so adjusted as to meet all the requirements of equality and in large measure also the requirements of rate regulation.

The committee is firmly convinced that with the earnings tax there should be no taxation of the franchise or intangible property of the public utilities, and preferably also no taxation of tangible personalty. It is probable, however, that most states will see fit to continue the taxation of the real estate at least, of the public utilities. In that case the amount of the tax on real estate should be allowed as a deduction from the alternative gross or net earnings tax, or else adequate allowance for the real estate tax should be made in fixing the rates of the earnings tax. The basic gross or net earnings tax should be the measure of the tax contribution of the utilities, except, of course, in individual cases, where the real estate tax alone (allowed as a deduction) might exceed the entire earnings tax. This rule is clearly required by the principle of equality which has been laid down. It is also necessary to insure the constitutionality of the gross earnings tax when applied to earnings from interstate commerce, a topic which is discussed in the next section. If real estate is taxed at all, it should include only land and buildings, not the right of way.

Constitutionality of the gross earnings tax. Doubt is sometimes expressed of the constitutional power of a state to impose a tax measured by gross earnings derived, in whole or in part, from interstate commerce. Such doubt can arise only from misapprehension of the decisions of the United States Supreme Court. This subject has been thoroughly studied by numerous authorities. The conclusions from the decisions of the Supreme Court are quite clear. They may be stated briefly as follows:

First of all, there is no question of the general principle that all laws which impose taxes directly burdening gross receipts from interstate commerce are in violation of the Federal Constitution and void. The right of a state, however, to impose taxes upon the property of corporations within its borders is unquestioned, even though the corporations be engaged in interstate commerce. Again, a state may value the property of corporations by the "unit rule"; that is, may ascertain the total value of the entire system and then apportion to the state in question a share of the entire property, according to the ratio of the mileage within the state to the total mileage of the system, or according to the ratio of business done within the state to the business of the whole system. Finally, in lieu of the tax on property, a state may impose a tax on earnings, and in reaching such a tax, gross earnings from interstate commerce may be used. It is also possible to use net earnings, and in this case no difficulty arises from the use of earnings from interstate commerce, as was clearly held in the decision in *U. S. Glue Co.* v. *Town of Oak Creek,* 247 U. S. 321.

There can be, therefore, no doubt of the legality of a properly drawn tax based upon gross and net earnings. All that is required is that the amount of the tax, if based upon gross earnings and if exclusive, should not be greater than a tax upon the property of the company as compared with taxes imposed upon property generally in the state.[3] Such a tax will be regarded, not as a tax upon earnings, but as a tax upon property, using earnings as a means to reach the property. The committee has been careful to insist that the above requirements be met in the recommendations which it makes.

INTERSTATE APPORTIONMENT, TAX RATES, ETC.

THIS brings us to the question of interstate apportionment The committee has only recently reached an agreement on the general plan for the taxation of public utilities, which proposes an arrangement that is novel in certain important respects, particularly in that it provides an alternative gross or net tax, in substitution for a property tax. This plan involves difficult questions of apportionment, and the committee has not yet had the opportunity to test out and check up the precise manner in which the various simple arbitrary rules of apportionment will operate. Since the particular object of the apportionment is to avoid duplicate taxation, are niceties important or is any good rough-and-ready rule enough? Consequently it is not prepared to give a specific recommendation as to which of these rules is best suited to accomplish the task in the most acceptable manner. It, therefore, requests an opportunity to study this subject further.*

It would also like time to develop further the method to be employed by the state in determining the proper rates for the alternative gross or net tax, in order that the burden imposed shall fairly approximate the burden imposed upon other classes of property taxed in other ways. Who shall determine the rate? Who shall equate it? Shall it be left to the legislature or not?

* Eds. note: The question of interstate apportionment of taxes on public utilities is dealt with by the same committee in its report published in the *Proceedings of the National Tax Association,* (1923), pp. 403-419.

[3] In case of a gross earnings tax which is not exclusive, that is, which is imposed in addition to taxes on the property of the corporation, the legal situation is by no means so clear. There appears to be a difference of opinion as to how the Supreme Court might regard a non-exclusive gross earnings tax. This furnishes another strong argument in favor of the exclusive earnings tax.

QUESTIONS AND PROBLEMS FOR DISCUSSION

1. Should business institutions be subjected to special taxes?
2. List the various methods of taxing business institutions in the United States.
3. What are some of the objections to the property tax as a method of taxing corporations?
4. Should a corporation be subjected to a heavier tax than other forms of business enterprise — e.g., a partnership?
5. What may be said for and against the taxation of gross receipts of corporations?
6. Discuss the difficulties involved in the taxation of banks.
7. Should public utilities be taxed at a heavier rate or in a different manner than other forms of business?
8. Is it feasible to tax the net income of public utilities?
9. What problems arise in the valuation of public utility property for taxation purposes?
10. Suppose that an electric light and power plant located in Omaha, Nebraska, furnishes service for residents of Council Bluffs, Iowa, located just across the Missouri River. What tax problems would arise in such a case?

SUGGESTIONS FOR RESEARCH

1. The fiscal and ethical bases for the taxation of corporations.
2. The corporate excess tax.
3. General versus classified business taxes.
4. The taxation of public utilities.
5. The taxation of municipally owned utilities.
6. The shifting and incidence of various forms of business taxes.
7. The allocation of corporate income for the purpose of state taxation.

BIBLIOGRAPHICAL NOTE

The general principles underlying business taxation are presented in T. S. Adams, "The Taxation of Business," *Proceedings of the National Tax Association,* (1917), pp. 185-194; and in Sec. V of a Report of the National Tax Association on "A Plan of a Model System of State and Local Taxation," *Proceedings of the National Tax Association,* (1919), pp. 451-457. The history, principles, and some problems of corporation taxation are discussed by E. R. A. Seligman in his *Essays in Taxation,* (New York, 1928), Chaps. VI, VII, VIII. A recent study of the National Industrial Conference Board, *State and Local Taxation of Business Corporations,* (New York, 1931), analyzes the various methods of taxing corporations and discusses certain economic aspects of this form of taxation.

The perplexing problems involved in the taxation of banks as business institutions are treated by many writers. The following references on this subject will be found useful: R. M. Haig, "Should Banks be Taxed, and How?", *Proceedings of the National Tax*

Association, (1929), pp. 385-401; J. H. Gilbert, "The General Property Tax as Affected by the Bank Tax Situation," *Proceedings of the National Tax Association,* (1928), pp. 218-227; W. H. Blodgett, "Weighing the National Tax Burden by Comparatives," *Bulletin of the National Tax Association,* Vol. XVI, pp. 70-78; and W. H. Hitchcock, "How Should Banks be Taxed?", *The Tax Magazine,* Nov. 1930.

For material relating to the taxation of public utilities see : H. D. Simpson, "Taxation of Public Service Industries," *Journal of Land and Public Utility Economics,* Jan. 1925, p. 44 et seq.; M. G. Glaeser, *Outlines of Public Utility Economics,* (New York, 1927), Chap. XXVI; and the following references in the *Proceedings of the National Tax Association :* C. C. Plehn, "The Taxation of Public Service Corporations," (1907), pp. 635-648; and the Report of the Committee of the National Tax Association on "The Taxation of Public Service Corporations," (1913), pp. 372-383. Another useful reference, though old, is D. F. Wilcox, "Taxation of Public Utilities," *Annals of the American Academy of Political and Social Science,* Vol. LVIII, pp. 140-148.

A discussion of the incidence of business taxes may be found in J. F. Zoller, "The Incidence of Business Taxation," *Proceedings of the National Tax Association,* (1924), pp. 315-326. The incidence and effects of one form of corporation taxation are treated in the National Industrial Conference Board, *The Shifting and Effects of the Federal Corporation Income Tax,* 2 Vols., (New York, 1929, 1930).

The problem of standardizing business taxes is dealt with in Reports of Committees of the National Tax Association on "Standardization and Simplification of the Business Taxes," *Proceedings of the National Tax Association,* (1927), pp. 323-342; and (1929), pp. 152-191.

A recent report which treats a special phase of corporation taxation is R. S. Ford, "The Allocation of Corporate Income for the Purpose of State Taxation," *New York State Tax Commission Report,* (Albany, 1933).

The special taxation of business profits is discussed in an article under the same title by Sir Josiah Stamp, in *Economic Journal,* Vol. XXIX, pp. 407-427.

CHAPTER XX

THE TAXATION OF COMMODITIES

1. General *versus* Selective Sales Taxes *

IT is my thesis that an acceptable tax apportionment cannot be had by means of any one tax, or two or three taxes, each purporting to tax everything and everybody and to treat everybody alike. I believe that this undiscriminating faith in superficial uniformity and universality has done harm to the cause of tax reform.

Of course really uniform and universal taxation is desirable, as far as practicable. It should be presumed, and non-uniformity and non-universality should be capable of justification. It is axiomatic that if equals are treated alike, the results are equal; but it is equally axiomatic that if unequals are treated alike, the results are unequal. The difficulty with the popularly favored uniform and universal taxation is that it is applied to objects that are significantly unequal. Our experience with the so-called general property tax should have taught us that fact. There can seldom be any good reason why two parcels of real estate in the same tax district should not bear the same tax; but there is valid objection to treating them alike if one of them is mortgaged and the mortgage is also equally fully taxed. That the objects are reducible to a common denominator, such as market value or volume of gross sales, cannot always justify uniform and universal taxation. Such common denominator does not always eliminate the inequalities resulting from improperly uniform and universal taxation.

THE GENERAL SALES TAX

THE latest tax for which a universal and uniform application is sought in the American commonwealths is the sales tax. Particular sales taxes on tobacco, beverages, and sometimes other articles the federal treasury has long used. For state revenue the sales tax on gasoline has attained in a decade a phenomenal success; and in a scattered and somewhat desultory fashion selective sales taxes on tobacco, amusements, soft

---

* Adapted from J. P. Jensen, "General versus Selective Sales Taxes," *Proceedings of the National Tax Association*, (1929), pp. 403-412.

drinks, and other articles appear in several states.[1] On the whole they have not been very satisfactory.

General sales taxes have, until recently, been unfamiliar subjects to the American legislator. They are, of course, very old. Adam Smith denounced them roundly. Sales taxes of a somewhat general scope there were, before the recent war, in Mexico and the Philippines, and possibly elsewhere. In the United States, however, as far as I can learn, a federal general gross sales tax was not proposed until the period of the Civil War. Serious as was then the fiscal emergency, it was not deemed serious enough to warrant the introduction of a gross sales tax.

Then came the recent war with its fiscal emergencies in every belligerent and many neutral countries. Sales taxes more or less general in scope took their places alongside of capital levies and other fiscal devices. The experience of these countries with general sales taxes has been treated[2] by Professor Buehler of Vermont. I think his conclusions may be fairly summarized as follows: They were regarded as emergency taxes, opposed by many classes, and retained only because revenue from any other source is not available, but they will probably disappear or be so modified as to lose their character as general sales taxes. They have been productive of considerable revenue, and the cost of administration has not been excessive. But they are regressive in their incidence and repressive upon business.

In the United States a federal general sales tax has been advocated during the past decade as a substitute for the personal and corporate income taxes. Repeated efforts in Congress have failed to secure its adoption. Its advocates have now turned to the states, and during the past four or five years taxpayers of means have been asked to contribute money to a fund, perhaps to several funds, for the promotion of the sales tax. Business men have been circularized with propaganda. Besides, property taxes have been rapidly rising. The gasoline tax, which is, of course, a sales tax, has demonstrated its capacity. The seed fell upon fertile ground; and if I mistake not there is a widespread, though undiscriminating, sentiment in favor of general sales taxes for state purposes.

Measuring the results in terms of sales taxes actually adopted, there is little to report. The selective sales taxes, discussed by Professor Miller as excise taxes in 1926, and with which certain states, particularly in the South, are still experimenting,

[1] See E. T. Miller, "State Excise Taxes," *Proceedings*, 1926, pp. 224-37.
[2] *Jour. Pol. Econ.*, April, 1928.

were probably adopted largely independently of the general sales tax propaganda. The same is doubtless true of the West Virginia gross sales tax of 1921, amended in 1925. And it is certainly true of the Pennsylvania mercantile license tax of long standing, whose abolition was urged by the special tax commission in 1926. The only tax which might possibly have been so influenced is probably the Georgia tax on gross incomes. . .

In fact there does not appear to be a single state whose taxes have been influenced appreciably by the propaganda for the general sales tax, except possibly Georgia. But the propaganda was back of the unsuccessful attempts to adopt general sales taxes in at least two states, Kansas and Tennessee, possibly others as well. The Kansas bill would tax all sales and all gross receipts of money, at the rate of ½ of 1 mill on the dollar. The Tennessee proposal was similar in its general outline. Both failed. As far as I could learn, even more meagre success was attained elsewhere, except in Georgia, where the rates range from ½ to 3 mills.

The explanation, in view of the prevailing sentiment, is probably something like this. So long as it can be discussed in the abstract, a general sales tax appeals because of its simplicity. It has the apparent advantage of universality and uniformity, which are popularly supposed to produce equality. But as soon as the legislature begins to apply it to an actual local situation its fundamental defects appear even before it is adopted.

THE GENERAL SALES TAX AS A STATE TAX

A GENERAL sales tax for state purposes is a local tax. State boundaries do not exist, practically speaking, for trade and industry. National boundaries do, as is familiar to every exporter or importer who must get his goods over a tariff wall. A large share of the shortcomings of the general sales tax, as indeed of almost any sales tax, may be charged to the circumstance that it is a local tax. The shifting cannot take place with the same ease, if at all, as if the tax were national. If we are to have general sales taxes, they should be imposed by the national rather than the state governments.

It is assumed by the advocates of the general sales tax, as a substitute for the income tax, that it would be shifted forward uniformly and become a part of the price of consumers' goods so that everybody would bear taxes in proportion to his consumption. The resulting increase in the cost of living is of course unfortunate, they say, but then the sales tax is better than the income tax, which is also shifted forward so that consumers bear it, and do so without knowing it. These people have become staunch, though not very logical or discriminating, disciples of the diffusion doctrine of taxes, at least of the income tax. They argue that the sales tax is superior to the income because of the certainty of its shifting. All of it and no more will be shifted. The taxbearer will know exactly how heavy his tax burden is, which is said not to be true of the income tax.

Now this assertion of incidence is false. If the sales tax were national, doubtless a great part of it would be shifted forward. But the shifting even of a national sales tax would be very uncertain. If, however, the tax is levied by a state surrounded by other states that do not have such a tax, the incidence becomes exceedingly uncertain, variable and complicated. Since the incidence of the general sales tax as a local tax is significant, I propose briefly to indicate what I think would happen in a state whose neighbors impose no such tax. For I believe that whatever of experimentation there is to be with the general sales tax will be done by states under such conditions.

At one extreme are the sales taxes paid by the extractive industries, that is to say, farming, forestry and mining. Such taxes will not be shifted appreciably but will be capitalized and will reduce, by the amount of the present value of all such expected taxes, the value of the natural resources which these industries are exploiting. These products are sold in a market not affected by the tax. There would be probably some shifting if the entire supply were taxed equally. But, as an example, it is agreed, I believe, that the Minnesota 6% tax on the privilege of mining iron ore and on royalties is so capitalized. Likewise the West Virginia tax on coal, oil, and gas, as well as the severance taxes found in a few other states, must be capitalized rather than shifted. Such taxes, if heavy under the local conditions, or if improperly imposed, may cause the exploitation to cease by forcing the plants to shut down, but there can be very little if any shifting. The argument sometimes advanced in West Virginia that taxes paid by the mine operators of the state are reimbursed by consumers in other states is misleading.

At the other extreme are the mobile industries and activities, ever shifting from one state to another, seeking locations having the most favorable conditions of raw material, transportation, labor supply, etc. For industries that are completely mobile, which, of course, is true of relatively few, there must be shifting of the tax or the industry will move out. This does not always necessarily mean dismantling a plant. All that is necessary may be to divert orders to plants in other states owned by the same corporation.

Between the two extremes, on the one hand the industries that are necessarily located in the taxing state, and, on the other, those that are free to move away from any threatened tax, fall most business activities. And for them it may be very difficult to say how far they can shift the tax if at all, or whether they must capitalize it, or move away, or shut down.

But, for one very significant purpose, it makes little difference whether the sales tax is capitalized or shifted forward. So long as it is a local, that is, state tax, it will be a burden upon the fixed property of the state directly or indirectly, very much as the property tax was before it. For the tax, if paid, is either capitalized or shifted. In so far as the tax is capitalized, as will be the case, largely, with the sales tax on industries exploiting natural resources, the tax directly reduces the value of such property. In so far as the tax is shifted forward it must increase the cost of living in the state; and, if labor is at all mobile, the labor cost will be increased, as will other items of cost. This fact will make the state a less desirable place in which to carry on business. And while the tax would in this way hardly precipitate an immediate wholesale industrial exodus from the state, it would in time check the industrial development sufficiently to lower property values.

It is clear, therefore, that in a sense, and in a degree, the sales tax will fail to accomplish the purpose for which, as a state tax, it is chiefly sought. Property owners assert that property values have been depressed through the rapidly increasing non-shiftable taxes on property; and this assertion is correct. They seek relief from the property tax through the general sales tax. But, for the fixed property of the state as a whole, it appears that there will be no such or very little relief. The taxing authorities give relief with one hand, in reducing the property tax rate, and take it away with the other hand, in imposing the sales tax.

Of course, no labor and no capital employed in a state is completely and instantly mobile. Also, residents living on their income cannot instantly remove to other states in order to escape a sales tax. Yet, some degree of mobility these factors have, and in time the tax will strongly tend to come to rest on local fixed property. During the interval labor and resident capitalists may be required to bear a higher cost of living; mobile capital, until it may be removed, to accept a lower return; and these contributions may temporarily redound to the benefit of the fixed property that must remain. During the interval there is capitalization of the tax.

If it is true that the burden of the local general sales tax will rest on the local fixed property, as did the tax on property which it partly displaces, then it might be said that there can be no good and no harm in a general sales tax; but that statement is not necessarily or even probably true.

In the first place, the burden of the sales tax on local fixed property might be heavier than would an addition to the existing property tax designed to raise the same revenue. For there is the extra cost of collecting the sales tax, which an addition to the property tax levy would not entail. Again, as I propose to show presently, the sales tax might cause an uneconomical dislocation within, as well as an exodus from the state of its business enterprises.

In the second place, even though the burden, on local fixed property as a whole, imposed by the general sales tax were exactly equal to that burden of which the property is relieved by the reduction in the property tax levy, there would still be some classes of property and certainly many individual taxpayers whose property would be more heavily burdened by the sales tax than by the property tax, while others would be correspondingly relieved. That certainly would be true if the sales tax were imposed at a uniform rate on all sales as in case of the proposed Kansas and Tennessee sales-tax proposals. For the amount of the property employed in different classes and units of business varies widely, from next to nothing to a very large percentage of the volume of the sales. And if the rates of the sales tax were to vary widely as they do in West Virginia, from, for example, a very low rate on sales at wholesale to a very high rate on sales of gas and oil, there would of course be an opportunity for equalizing partly the sales-tax burden with the burden of the property tax on the various classes of property and business. But there would also be the opportunity for making the sales-tax burden especially heavy on some classes and very light on others. It is agreed, I believe, that the sales taxes on mineral products in West Virginia has reduced the net income, and hence the capital value of these resources, far more than they would have been reduced through a property-tax levy designed to produce an equal revenue. For the seven years in which the sales tax has been in force in West Virginia the extractive industries have paid about 44% of its total yield, and since the rates, beginning in 1925, are higher than in 1921 on the extractive industries, these industries are now paying probably about 50% of the yield of the sales tax. This is, of course, a higher percentage than they would pay on the basis of the property tax. And this discrimination is intentional in West Virginia, being the local equivalent of the preference for the severance tax in other states. A sales tax, whether general or selective, produces effects similar to those produced by a general classification of property for taxation at different rates on each class. But it cannot be expected to bring noticeable relief to the property owners as a group.

HETEROGENEITY OF GROSS SALES

IF we are to have sales taxes for state purposes, and perhaps there are no good reasons why they should not contribute a moderate part of the state revenue, I venture the prediction that they will take the form of selective sales taxes rather than general sales taxes on all sales at a uniform rate. The gross sales, including, as proposed in Kansas and Tennessee, the gross income from professional services, are too heterogeneous in respects that are highly significant for taxation purposes. These differences may be pointed out briefly as follows:

In the first place goods sold vary in respect to the number of sales intervening between the first and the final processes of production. Consider wheat, for instance, a product that would have been seriously affected had the proposed Kansas gross sales tax become law. It would have been taxed to the farmer, the local elevator, the railroad, the speculator, the miller, the baker, the retailer, and possibly others in the normal process of production. All the things entering into the production of wheat, and into the various processes of converting the wheat into bread on the consumer's table would also be taxed. For this phenomenon the term "pyramiding the tax" has been coined. That is a bad name because it appears to imply that the taxes paid are all shifted forward, becoming a part of the final price. In this particular case there would be so many taxes that it would certainly be economical to avoid most of them by shipping the wheat out of the state, except possibly small amounts for consumption in the interior parts of the state. Interior grain markets, primary elevators, flour mills and bakeries are all more or less mobile industries. They could hardly continue long in the state. For the wheat growers could always ship out of the state, thereby avoiding the tax, by making the only sale an interstate transaction. The curtailing of industry within the state would mean reduced sales, and decreased tax revenue.

There are of course articles whose normal sales in the state are fewer in number. Imported articles would seldom be sold in the state except at retail, for the wholesale transaction could usually be made an interstate transaction, thereby avoiding the tax. This probably is the worst feature of the gross sales tax, at a uniform rate. It is pyramided unequally on different industries, and on different products of the same industry in the state. And it would fall most heavily on the native products of the state and their basic industries as compared with the imported ones. Few states would knowingly pursue that kind of tax policy.

In the second place, industries differ in their mobility, a circumstance pointed out above in another connection. Extractive industries must be carried on where the exploited minerals or farm lands are located. Likewise retail sales must (though not always nor equally) be made where people live. The intermediate processes are more mobile. But that is precisely the kind of industrial activity that is eagerly sought by every promoter of any state. It is also the kind of industry whose presence increases the amount of pyramiding by increasing the volume of intrastate sales. It is, in short, particularly vulnerable to the effects of a gross sales tax. It is seldom economical for a state to pursue a tax policy that would discourage its manufacturing industries.

The gross sales tax would, in case of manufacturing, operate in the same way as an increase in the freight rates into and out of the state. When one considers the vigorous opposition to higher freight rates, affecting one locality only, he can visualize the energetic opposition to sales taxes that will hinder a state's mobile industry in competition with that of other states.

In the third place, gross sales differentiate themselves with respect to their location. Sales made near the borders of a state not having a gross sales tax are handicapped in comparison with those made in the interior, in that the possibility of being made an interstate transaction, and therefore tax-free, is increased. It is not accidental that the most vigorous opposition to the West Virginia gross sales tax, particularly as presented by the Wheeling Chamber of Commerce, came from the northern panhandle. There was even a threat on the part of these four counties to start a movement for secession from West Virginia and for attaching themselves to Pennsylvania. The fact that Pennsylvania already has a mercantile license tax based upon retail sales indicates the opposition to a gross sales tax as compared with a retail sales tax. Nor was it accidental that the protests against the proposed Kansas

gross sales tax, in so far as any one took it seriously enough
to protest, came from border towns such as Leavenworth and
Atchison. It so happens in many states that the border towns
and cities are the most important. They may be trusted to
block a tax that would handicap them in comparison with the
interior.

In the fourth place, the uniform gross sales tax, and this
would be true of a uniform retail sales tax also, will operate
unequally upon enterprises because of the nature of the marketing process. Convenience goods must be sold where consumed, while other goods may be marketed via the mail-order
route; or the highways and motor vehicles may readily take
the customer to the market over the state line. Here one type
of enterprise is set against another. In the conflict between
them the tax is likely to fail of adoption.

In the fifth place, and this is important, and it is too familiar
to require extended elucidation, the gross sales bear no necessary relation to the net earnings out of which the taxes are
paid. For any class of industry, and for individual business
units there are good times and hard times. The net return
will now be large and now small; the gross sales will vary
relatively little; and the tax will be to pay in any case. Forward shifting may be relatively easy during the good times but
difficult when stocks accumulate on the shelves. The tax
therefore accentuates an already unfortunate condition. The
same of course is true of a property tax, but it is not true of
an income tax.

Another aspect of the same inequality, equally important,
is that the gross sales bear varying ratios to capital employed
and to the rapidity of the turnover; and this inequality would
also obtain in case of a retail sales tax at a uniform rate.
Personal service enterprises employ little or no capital; while
others, such as steam railroads and hydroelectric plants, employ relatively much. A uniform rate on all sales, and even
on all retail sales, would scarcely be accepted as fair.

In the sixth place, and finally, goods vary in social desirability. They are, more or less, necessities or luxuries. It
may be true, though for want of definite information it is not
pressed here very strongly, that necessities such as bread are
the object of more successive sales and of greater rapidity of
turnover, and therefore of more taxes in the taxing state than
is true of luxuries. If this is true the gross sales tax will be
more regressive than a uniform retail sales tax which in itself
is regressive. This cause of regressiveness can be partly eliminated by means of the substitution of selective taxes at dif-

ferent rates. If there are, as is probably true, certain articles the consumption of which is to be discouraged or encouraged, then such a purpose would be checked by a uniform sales tax, whether on all or only on retail sales.

CONCLUSIONS

ONE would run but little risk in predicting that a uniform gross sales tax or even a uniform retail sales tax will not long be found satisfactory in any state. Not all sales, not even all retail sales, are equally good tax-bearers, though their suitability as tax-bearers will vary from time to time and from place to place. To tax all sales alike is to tax some less and some more than the traffic will bear. Taxation in excess of what the traffic will bear occurs when business, because of the tax, is uneconomically checked in, or diverted from the state. Assuming that a given amount of revenue is to be raised through state consumption or sales taxes, a minimum of checking or diversion of business can be approximated by imposing the taxes on selected tax-bearers, and by adjusting the rates experimentally.

Let me employ, for the sake of exposition, an analogy from the field of freight-rate making — an analogy which is not to be carried too far. We do not pay, nor permit to be charged, a uniform freight rate per ton-mile, or per dollar-mile of traffic carried. If such a uniform freight rate were to be charged no one familiar with the transportation could doubt the results. There would be an enormous decrease in the low-class traffic, accompanied possibly by a far from compensating increase in the high-class traffic, though there might even be a decrease in all classes of traffic. There would be a tremendous decrease in the aggregate of transportation services; and the transportation agencies would be hamstrung in their capacity to render service. The per-ton-mile cost would increase. Society would sustain a decided economic loss. In some such way the uniform gross sales or the uniform retail sales tax would check the effectiveness of productive enterprise in the isolated taxing state.

Let me employ one more analogy, this time within the field of taxation. No one today would advocate a uniform import duty on all imports, as a suitable tariff policy for an industrially developed country. Yet the British customs duties were for centuries, but during recent centuries they have not been, largely in the form of a uniform *ad valorem* duty. China presents another, more recent example of ill-fitting uniform *ad valorem* customs duties, imposed against her will, and over her protest, by foreign powers in control of her customs. These experiences, whose lessons are at least partly applicable to the question of state sales taxes, it would be well to consider. All the more so since the checking and diverting effects of a sales tax are greatly accentuated by the fact that the tax in question is a state rather than a national tax.

I have not raised the question of whether, theoretically, consumptive taxes, as such, are a suitable element in an ideal system of state and local taxation. When properly adopted much can be said for such taxes yielding a moderate share of the total state and local tax revenue. I have rather sought to throw light on the question of how the well-informed practical politician might fit the consumption tax into his state's tax system, in the best interests of the state. I am led to the conclusion that uniform general sales taxes are the worst; uniform general retail sales taxes, the intermediate; and selective sales taxes, with suitably adjusted rates, the least objectionable for the purpose. If legislators should nevertheless adopt the worst of these three alternative forms of sales taxes, it will be because they must, or think they must, make concessions to those who believe or affect to believe that sales taxes should be spread uniformly, and universally over all sales or all retail sales. It is perhaps inevitable that some experimentation with general sales taxes be carried on, but every citizen should devoutly hope that the experimentation may be done by some other state than his own.

2. Some Problems in State and Local Sales Taxation *

In the presentation of some of the problems involved in state and local sales taxation the following assumptions are made as to the topic under discussion :

First, that the tax to be discussed is either a general sales tax or a comprehensive mercantile retail sales tax. Special taxes on selected commodities such as tobacco, soft drinks, etc., require separate treatment.

Second, that the tax, if levied, would be intended to produce a substantial amount of revenue, so that the rate would be, say, from one-half of one per cent to one per cent for a general sales tax, or from one to three per cent for a retail sales tax. If the rate were extremely low, a small fraction of one per cent, many of the problems discussed herewith might not arise.

---

* Adapted from Carl Shoup, "Some Problems in State and Local Sales Taxation," *Proceedings of the National Tax Association*, (1931), pp. 401-407.

Third, that enough money would be spent in administration so that the amount of evasion would not be great.

Grounded on these basic assumptions, the following discussion will be concerned in general with what may be called problems of unequal treatment raised by the sales tax. Unequal treatment does not necessarily imply unjust discrimination. The point raised here is that the sales tax, sometimes thought of as a simple uniform levy, would, it appears, result in unequal treatment, especially if levied by states or local bodies. Therefore, this possible unequal treatment should be carefully considered by legislators to determine whether it serves to counterbalance other inequalities in the tax system and so rounds out a well-balanced system as a whole, or whether it adds to similar unequal treatment in other parts of the existing system. Each state and locality must, of course, find its own answer to this question.

There are many ways in which unequal treatment might manifest itself, but for purposes of this paper attention will be centered on three main points, as follows: exemption limits, turnover and profit margins, and consumers' purchases.

If either a general sales tax or an ordinary retail sales tax be levied, an exemption of some sort seems advisable from the administrative point of view. To support this statement one may examine some data showing the distribution of business concerns under the sales tax, by income groups. One way to put the question is: what percent of total turnover or total tax receipts is furnished by the top one per cent of taxpayers, or the top two per cent, and so on? If a country with a general sales tax has about five million taxpayers, for instance, under that tax, how much of the total taxable gross receipts is accounted for by the 50,000 concerns having the largest turnover? Germany has had a comprehensive general sales tax for some years which includes within its scope the gross earnings of professional men (doctors, lawyers, etc.) and gross receipts of farmers. The exemption limit has been very low.[1]

Statistics for the year 1926 show that 0.65 per cent of all the tax returns accounted for 55.16 per cent of the total gross receipts.[2]

[1] Exempt are those whose annual tax would not be over 5 marks — mostly small farmers. The rate of the tax in 1926 was one per cent up to March 31st; 0.75 per cent after that date.

[2] "Total gross receipts" includes a certain amount of tax-free turnover (for instance, export trade), but does not include such tax-free turnover as bank or insurance transactions or receipts of government railways. The figures in the text were taken from *Umsatz und Umsatzsteuer in Deutschland nach den Umsatzsteuerveranlagungen 1926 bis 1928*, compiled by *Statistischen Reichsamt*. Verlag von Reimar Hobbing, Berlin, 1931, page 27. See also appendix D [not reproduced here. See Shoup's study, p. 412].

This indicates, of course, the extent to which business is concentrated in the hands of large firms, but it also poses an interesting administrative problem. The same statistics show that 36.79 per cent of the returns accounted for 95.81 per cent of the total turnover. To put it another way, 63 per cent of the total number of taxpayers could have been exempted with a loss of, roughly, only 4 per cent of the tax revenue.[3]

Data on the French sales tax indicate much the same state of affairs. For the year 1922, 1.71 per cent of the taxpayers supplied 54.58 per cent of the total revenue from the tax, and 78.44 per cent of the taxpayers could have been exempted with a loss of only 10.12 per cent of the revenue.[4]

Since these data are for foreign countries, one might wish comparative statistics for the United States. These will be available shortly from the Census of Distribution. At present one can only cite the Trial Distribution Census of 1927, the data being for 1926, which showed in the eleven cities which it covered that of the 79,778 independent retail stores covered, the top 0.72 per cent accounted for 36.75 per cent of total sales; and the bottom 46.56 per cent accounted for only 5.24 per cent of the total sales.[5]

As to industry, the Census of Manufacturers for 1927 indicates that manufacturing firms with an annual output of less than $5000 constitute at least 22 per cent of the total number of manufacturing establishments in the United States, yet these 22 per cent account for less than one per cent of the total factory output measured in dollars.[6]

The concentration of trade revealed by these figures is much greater than the concentration of taxable income under the federal individual income tax. The booklet, *Statistics of Income for 1928*, shows that the top 1.056 per cent of taxpayers (those with incomes over $50,000) accounted for 25.02 per cent of total net income,[7] in contrast, for instance, with the German experience cited above, where the top 0.65 per cent of all returns accounted for 55.16 per cent of the total turnover. This result might be expected in view of the larger number of

[3] The above data include returns from farms. If industry alone is considered there is shown a still greater concentration of turnover in the hands of a few concerns. The data for commerce alone (*Handel und Verkehr*), on the other hand, show less concentration than the average for all three groups. (See appendix D) [not reproduced here. See Shoup's study, p. 412].

[4] Shoup, C. S., *The Sales Tax in France*, (Columbia University Press, New York, 1930), page 74.

[5] Retail and Wholesale Trade of 11 Cities, Domestic Distribution Department, Chamber of Commerce of the United States, Washington, D. C., 1928, page 73.

[6] Biennial Census of Manufacturers, 1927, U. S. Department of Commerce, Washington, D. C., 1930, page 6.

[7] But 78.04 per cent of tax paid, owing, of course, to progressive rates.

small income receivers who are not subject to the federal tax, and it throws some light on the administrative problem involved in a comprehensive general sales tax which has no exemption limits.

From a purely fiscal point of view, it seems hardly worth while to bother with the 63 per cent of the taxpayers in Germany who furnished only 4 per cent of the tax revenue, or with the 78 per cent of the taxpayers in France who furnished only 10 per cent of the revenue. The tax department's time and efforts might better be disposed of elsewhere, unless there is some compelling reason in equity for allowing no such exemption.

The sales tax is supposed to be passed on to the consumer; is this aim defeated if a dividing line is drawn so that a merchant with, for instance, $10,000 a year turnover [8] (that is, about $33.00 a day) is exempt, and therefore prevents his tax-paying competitors from passing on the tax through higher prices? Or is there less direct competition among the large and small concerns than is sometimes thought, so that in effect the exemption line would divide the consuming public into two classes — those who would (ultimately) pay the sales tax and those who would not? It would be out of place to attempt to answer these questions at this moment, but the problem must be faced squarely in the framing of any sales-tax law.

The second phase of this discussion, turnover and profit margins, is concerned with the possible different effects of a uniform sales tax upon different types of firms. The well-known basic fact upon which this point rests is as follows: Two firms, each making the same per cent of profit on net worth, may have very different ratios of profit to gross sales. This is because one firm turns over its stock rapidly, say, 8 or 9 times a year, while the other firm in a different line of business must perforce turn its stock slowly, say once or twice a year. Here again certain data may lend point to the statement. These figures represent the five-year average experience of large, well-established concerns in different lines of business, concerns which have been able to borrow money on the open market.[9]

As a sample, there may be considered the experience of

---

[8] The 46.56 per cent of all dealers, noted above in the remarks on the Census of Distribution, had annual turnover of less than $10,000.

[9] The data used in the following paragraphs were taken from tables compiled by the Bank Service Department of the National Credit Office, New York City. These tables show five-year comparative ratios of firms in 27 different lines of business and cover the period 1925-1929. Owing to the nature of the averages developed, there are certain statistical limitations to their use, but these limitations are apparently not enough to invalidate the statements made in the text above.

firms in seven types of business. In each of these seven groups the percent of profit to net worth averaged between six and eight per cent, so that each of these types of business was (for the firms covered) about on a par with all the other types — no one business was much more or less profitable than any of the others. Despite this fact, one line of business (retail lumber dealers) showed 5.60 per cent profit on sales, while another type (meat packers, not including the "Big Four") showed only 1.68 per cent profit on sales. Both of these lines of business showed almost precisely the same percent of annual profit on net worth. The answer is, of course, that the type of business with the large profit margin on sales (retail lumber) had a very slow turnover of its circulating capital, owing to the nature of the business, while the type of business with a small profit margin on sales (meat packers) made up for this fact by turning over its capital more quickly — again, because the nature of the business permitted, even demanded, it.

Another group of types of business may be cited : those types showing a percent of profit on net worth of between 8 and 10 per cent. The profit margin on sales ranged for this group from 1.21 per cent (factories) to 6.57 per cent (retail furniture dealers).

The argument which these data are offered to support is, of course, as follows : A uniform sales tax is a much greater burden, calculated as a percent of profits on net worth, for firms in one type of business than it is for firms in another type of business, even though both types of business are equally profitable, as that term is ordinarily used. The quick turnover firm feels the tax much more keenly than does the slow turnover firm. A sales tax of one per cent, if not shifted, would take 80 per cent of the profits in one line of business and only 20 per cent in another, and so on.

It may be said that the above data are of little significance because the sales tax, after all, is passed on to the consumer and is not a burden on the business firm. It should be remembered, however, that one can never be certain that this will always be the case, especially with a state or local sales tax and especially in the first few years of its existence. Furthermore, if both the quick turnover and the slow turnover concerns raise their prices by, say, one per cent, may not the quick turnover concern lose a greater percent of its trade, owing to a slackening in demand, than will the slow turnover concern? May not a slow turnover, wide profit margin (on sales) type of business, imply a sluggish, inelastic type of consumer demand which will not react much to a variation of one per cent in the price in one direction or the other? Contrariwise, may not a quick turnover, narrow profit margin type of business, imply a fluid, elastic type of consumer demand which responds readily to a one per cent change in price? Again, without attempting to answer all these questions, one may point out the possible differences in the effect of a uniform-rate sales tax on firms in different lines of business.

The third phase of the discussion, consumers' purchases, concerns the type of goods and services which are purchased by different classes of consumers and which might be subject to a sales tax. The purpose of this examination is to ascertain what percentage of the goods and services used by consumers would be subject to a mercantile and manufacturing sales tax, and what differences in this respect there might be as among certain classes of consumers. Again, it seems best to cite a few figures, for although these data have certain definite limitations they may give a tone of reality to the discussion.

Suppose, for instance, that one is considering a retail sales tax which is comprehensive as to all ordinary mercantile transactions, but which is not collected upon payments for house rents, for services rendered by rate-regulated public utilities, for insurance, or for professional services of doctors, lawyers, etc. If the tax were shifted to the consumer, what percentage of his total expenditures would be thus taxed, and are there any differences as among consuming classes?

Several studies of consumers' expenditures have been made in the past: for the purpose of the present discussion, only three will be referred to, namely, those concerning (a) the cost of living of federal employees in five cities, (b) the standard of living of farmers in several states, (c) the standard of living of Ford Motor Company employees in Detroit. All of these studies have been made within the last few years by departments of the Federal Government.[10]

Consider, for instance, the record of expenditures made by 105 families of Federal employees in New Orleans, the male head of the family in no case receiving more than $2500 a year from the government, but usually receiving in addition some outside income. If one goes through the items (average expenditure per family) one by one, separating those which would be subject to a retail sales tax, as outlined above, from those which would not be, one arrives at the conclusion that 37 per cent of the total expenditure of the average family

---

[10] For details and description of sources, see appendices A, B, C. [These appendices are not reproduced here. They may be found in *Proceedings of the National Tax Association*, (1931), pp. 407-412.]

would be free of sales tax. A similar study of 101 families in New York City shows 39 per cent of the expenditure to be non-taxable. Rental payment (actual or imputed) accounts for nearly half of these tax-exempt expenditures. Nearly the same percentage was shown by 100 families of Ford employees in Detroit having an average total expenditure of $1,719.83 per year.

A difference may sometimes be observed when one turns to farm families, owing to the fact that in many cases the farm itself furnishes much of the family's food. A study of farm families' expenditures published in 1926 shows that for 1130 farm families studied in Alabama, South Carolina and Virginia, the value of family goods consumed averaged per family $1550 a year; and of this amount 59.5 per cent would not be subject to the type of retail sales tax under discussion, in contrast with the 37 and 39 per cent figures for certain city dwellers in other states noted above. The figures for farm expenditure do not include any amount spent for business purposes, such as expenditures for farm equipment, seed, field labor, etc.

As to higher income groups, no similar data are available, but it seems a fair presumption that the percentage of non-taxable income would be higher, owing to greater savings.

Although the above data indicate, perhaps, no more than what has always been generally surmised, they call to mind two important questions of policy which states and localities must decide in framing either a general sales tax or a retail sales tax.

First, suppose that one assumes that most of the tax, no matter how broad its scope, could be passed on to the consumers. Is there, then, any reason for extending it beyond ordinary mercantile and manufacturing transactions to include receipts from the sale of transportation, water, gas, electricity and professional services? The above data, at least, indicate no reason for doing so, as concerns the relative burden among urban families of the lower income group, since data gathered from three different locations — New Orleans, New York and Detroit — show in each case about the same percentage of total expenditures subject to the ordinary mercantile retail sales tax. However, not all the data contained in the sources from which these figures have been drawn have been analyzed in this paper. Other students of the question might pursue this matter further and arrive at more illuminating results.

Secondly, is it desired to use the sales tax as a means of imposing a somewhat greater burden on the urban dweller than

on the farm resident? Here again, caution is needed in dealing with the very restricted samples noted above, especially in
view of our uncertainty of where the final burden of any tax
rests. But the differences indicated by the figures above are
great enough at least to raise a presumption that under a sales
tax the urban family would bear a somewhat heavier burden
than a farm family with approximately the same real income.
This factor might, therefore, be taken into consideration by
any state or locality which wishes to make a sales tax an integral part of its tax system, unless further study shows it to be
counterbalanced by other factors inherent in the situation.

In summary: The data presented above serve to illustrate
three chief problems to which attention must be given by any
state or locality planning to levy a sales tax at a fairly high rate,
and they all center around the possibility of unequal treatment of different groups of business men or consumers. Unequal treatment may arise, first, because it is administrative
wisdom to exempt the smaller business firms; secondly (insofar as the tax is not passed on), because of inherent differences
in profit margin on sales; thirdly (insofar as the tax is passed
on), because of differences in taxable expenditures per family,
differences which occur both among families on the same income level (rural *vs.* urban) and among families on different
income levels. There are, of course, other possibilities of unequal treatment, especially as resulting from out-of-state competition, but no time is available to discuss that problem here.

In conclusion, it is to be emphasized that unequal treatment
resulting from a sales tax does not necessarily mean injustice.
The entire tax system of the state or locality must be considered
as a whole, and when it is so considered, it might in certain
cases be found that the unequal treatment accorded by a sales
tax was a necessary ingredient to counterbalance discrepancies
in other parts of the system. That problem is not entered into
here. The point of this paper is rather that, for good or ill,
the sales tax, although levied at a uniform rate, is not a truly
uniform tax when viewed as a burden upon the persons concerned.

3. Customs Duties *

Prior to the imposition of the corporation profits tax in 1911
and the individual income tax in 1913, custom duties were
more productive of Federal revenue than the so-called internal-
revenue duties. Before 1860, custom receipts were frequently

* Adapted from S. H. Patterson and K. W. H. Scholz, *Economic Problems of
Modern Life,* (McGraw-Hill Book Co., Inc., New York, 1931), pp. 296-299.

in excess of the total ordinary Federal expenditures. During the ten years from 1902 to 1911, customs yielded an annual average of 53 per cent of the tax receipts of the Federal government, as compared with 47 per cent yielded by the internal-revenue taxes. The revenue receipts from duties on imports for the fiscal year ending June 30, 1929, on the other hand, were but 17 per cent of the total tax revenues of the Federal government.

In general, the relative importance of custom receipts to total Federal receipts from direct and indirect taxes has decreased during the past century and a half. In spite of the fact that they have increased greatly in absolute amount, import duties have shown considerable fluctuation from time to time, varying not merely with general industrial conditions within the country, but also with prospects of either war or peace and of possible changes in tariff legislation.†

CHART [A]

FEDERAL REVENUE RECEIPTS FROM CUSTOM DUTIES

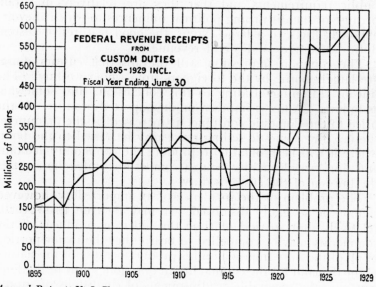

FEDERAL REVENUE RECEIPTS
FROM
CUSTOM DUTIES
1895-1929 INCL.
Fiscal Year Ending June 30

Annual Report, U. S. Treasury, 1929, *pp.* 402, 403.

Chart [A] depicts these fluctuations during the 35-year period from 1895 to 1929 inclusive. At best, custom duties offer but a comparatively uncertain source of Federal revenue,

† Eds. note : See R. F. Hoxie, "The Adequacy of the Customs Revenue," *Journal of Political Economy,* Vol. III, pp. 43-64, for an excellent discussion of this point.

since they are affected by so many disturbing influences. For example, in times of a great national crisis, such as a war, when governmental expenditures ordinarily increase, revenue from customs will tend to decrease rather than to increase, because of the disruption of normal peace-time trade. This fact is clearly shown in the accompanying chart. In 1898, at the time of the Spanish-American War, custom receipts decreased from $176,544,127 the preceding year to $149,575,062, while, in 1918, custom receipts dropped to $182,758,989 from $225,962,393 in 1917.

The wars of foreign nations, as well as those in which our nation participates, affect Federal receipts derived from import duties. The effect on our trade of the outbreak of the World War is reflected in the decreased import duties collected in 1914 as compared with 1913, the figures for the respective years being $292,320,014 and $318,891,396. As pointed out above, tariff revisions may also cause fluctuations in receipts from customs. The fact that custom revenues tend to decrease at the very time when additional funds are needed to meet urgent public requirements and that they are relatively uncertain because of the disturbing political influences to which they are exposed offsets, to a large extent, the good features of custom duties as sources of Federal revenue.

The common impression still prevails that custom duties are largely borne by the foreigners from whom we buy. The line of reasoning, leading to this conclusion, runs somewhat as follows. A tax is imposed on an imported product. If the price to the domestic consumer is increased by the amount of the tax, the domestic selling price may be raised to the point where it will be profitable to produce the commodity at home and thus crowd out the foreign competitor, unless he assumes the burden of the customs duty.

The problem of the incidence of an import duty, however, cannot be so easily dismissed. It may be true that over a relatively short period of time the seller or producer of the commodity may be compelled to bear either the major portion or all of the duty imposed on his product because of the nature of the demand for the commodity in question. But in the long run . . . the inevitable readjustments of conditions of supply will tend to shift the burden of customs duties, even as internal excise duties are ultimately shifted, to the consumers.

. . . . When duties are imposed on foreign products imported into the United States for the purpose of restricting such importation, it is obvious that they cannot be productive of revenue if they fulfill their full protective purpose. A tariff which is high enough to be prohibitive can yield no revenue. Consequently, a so-called "protective tariff" may not logically be regarded as a part of the revenue system of a country. In general, it may be concluded that within certain limits the larger the amount of actual protection to domestic industries, the smaller the resultant revenue to the home government, and the greater the loss to, or the burden on, the domestic consumer. From the point of view of public revenue, therefore, our present tariff system is open to the criticism that the income it affords to the government is out of proportion to the burden it imposes on the taxpayer in the form of higher prices of commodities.

Custom duties for fiscal purposes are open to objections not merely because they are uncertain and because it is difficult to ascertain the incidence of such duties, but also because they can be evaded, in whole or in part, either by smuggling or by misrepresentation.

Moreover, as compared with internal revenues, they are uneconomical taxes to collect. For the fiscal year 1929 the total cost of collecting $100 of various kinds of custom duties was $3.42, while the total cost of collecting internal revenue taxes was but $1.17 for every $100 collected.[1]

Finally, customs duties are not levied in accordance with the principle of ability to pay. To the extent that they are placed on essential commodities or necessities they impose a disproportionately heavy burden on individuals with small incomes and so fail to satisfy our sense of justice in taxation.

In spite of these many objections, customs duties will in all probability continue to be an important part of the Federal revenue system in the future, although perhaps relatively less important than in the past. As sources of public revenue they possess the virtue of high productivity under normal conditions, as well as of convenience of payment. These factors apparently impress legislators sufficiently to advocate their retention as a part of the Federal revenue system.‡

QUESTIONS AND PROBLEMS FOR DISCUSSION

1. Define the different forms of sales taxes.
2. What is meant by the statement that sales taxes are repressive? Is this feature objectionable?
3. Evaluate a general sales tax in light of the canons of productivity, economy, and equity.

[1] U. S. Treasury, *Annual Report*, 1929, pp. 419 and 825.

‡ Eds. note: For recent changes in the nature and extent of Federal excise taxes and customs duties, see National Industrial Conference Board, *Federal Finances, 1923-1932*, (New York, 1933), Chap. II.

4. It is said that "to tax all sales alike is to tax some less and some more than the traffic will bear." What is meant by this statement?

5. Do you believe that the use of the general sales tax is justified in meeting emergency expenditures, e.g., costs of proof relief?

6. It is claimed that a sales tax is "painless." What is meant? If we may assume that the tax is borne largely by the consumer do you believe that a 2 per cent tax on the sales of all commodities, including necessities, is painless?

7. The general sales tax is often defended on grounds that it makes all people tax conscious. Evaluate this argument.

8. Discuss the forms of industrial discrimination which arise under a state general sales tax. Which, if any, of these forms of discrimination would exist under a federal general sales tax?

9. During the 1931 session of the General Assembly of Iowa, a new state tax law was enacted which levied an excise tax of five cents per pound on oleomargarine sold within the state. The revenue from this tax went into the General State Fund.

Assume that before the enactment of this legislation you were a member of a committee charged with securing information on the following points: (1) the probable effect of the tax on the price of oleomargarine, (2) the probable effect of the tax on volume of sales of oleomargarine, (3) the amount of revenue which the state might expect to receive from the tax. State clearly the nature of the data which you would attempt to collect in order to make the estimates requested by the General Assembly. Give your reasons for selecting these data.

10. Assume the free importation of Canadian No. 1 Hard Spring wheat, and also the following data relative to (1) the U. S. demand for No. 1 Hard Spring wheat, (2) the long-run supply schedule of Canadian No. 1 Hard Spring in the U. S. market and (3) the long-run supply schedule of U. S. No. 1 Hard Spring in the U. S. market.

Normal Demand Schedule for No. 1 Hard Spring Wheat in U. S. Market		Long-run Canadian Supply Schedule		Long-run U. S. Supply Schedule	
price per bushel	amount taken	price	amount offered	price	amount offered
.30	65,000	.30	3,000	.30	2,000
.40	60,000	.40	7,000	.40	3,000
.50	55,000	.50	15,000	.50	5,000
.60	50,000	.60	30,000	.60	20,000
.70	45,000	.70	40,000	.70	30,000
.80	40,000	.80	60,000	.80	40,000

Problem : If a tariff of 20 cents per bushel is levied upon Canadian No. 1 Hard Spring wheat, what will be the effect upon the price of No. 1 Hard Spring wheat in the U. S.? How much revenue should the U. S. expect to receive from her 20 cent tariff? Explain fully any significant modifications which should be made in your results. If in return for tariff protection the farmers in the U. S. had agreed to restrict their production to the pre-tariff amount, what would have been the effect of the 20 cent tariff on the price of No. 1 Hard Spring wheat in the U. S.? (Review Chapter IX.)

SUGGESTIONS FOR RESEARCH

1. The growth of the sales tax in the United States.
2. The incidence of a sales tax.
3. General versus selective sales taxes as sources of state revenue.
4. Administrative aspects of sales taxes.
5. The economic effects of sales taxes.
6. The effects of sales taxes in some particular state.
7. Sales taxes versus income taxes for state revenue.
8. The shifting and incidence of customs duties.

BIBLIOGRAPHICAL NOTE

An outstanding work which treats the history and theory of sales taxation is A. G. Buehler, *General Sales Taxation,* (New York, 1932). Another general treatise which deals with the economic, constitutional, and administrative aspects of general sales taxation is National Industrial Conference Board, *General Sales or Turnover Taxation,* (New York, 1929). The sales tax as a form of revenue in foreign countries is discussed in C. S. Shoup, *The Sales Tax in France,* (New York, 1930); and Alzada Comstock, *Taxation in the Modern State,* (New York, 1929), Chaps. VIII, IX, X.

The sales tax as a form of state revenue in the United States is treated in Robert M. Haig and Carl S. Shoup, *The Sales Tax in the American States,* (New York, 1934); National Industrial Conference Board, *Current Tax Problems in New York State,* (New York, 1931), Chaps. VIII, IX, X; and A. G. Buehler, "The General Sales Tax as a State Revenue," *Bulletin of the National Tax Association,* Vol. XV, pp. 258-262. Beulah Bailey in the *Tax Digest,* Vol. II, (August, 1933), pp. 268-275, summarizes in chart form the characteristics of present sales taxes in American commonwealths. Two special studies of value on state sales taxation are: "Mississippi's General Sales Tax," *Bulletin of the University of Mississippi,* Series XXX, No. 3, January, 1933; and W. S. Hallanan, "West Virginia Sales Tax," *Proceedings of the National Tax Association,* (1921), pp. 103-109. In the *Proceedings,* (1922), Mr. Hallanan contributes another article on the West Virginia sales tax, based upon a year's administrative experience. For the history and theory of luxury taxation, see R. B. Tower, "Luxury Taxation and its

Place in a System of Public Revenues," *Special Report of the New York State Tax Commission*, No. 4, (Albany, 1931). The possibilities and limitations of sales taxes on selected commodities and of retail and general sales taxes are discussed by C. S. Shoup in Memoranda 6 and 7 of *Report of the New York State Commission for the Revision of the Tax Laws*, 1932.

Arguments for and against the sales tax have been presented by many writers. Two important references in which such arguments are presented are E. R. A. Seligman, *Studies in Public Finance*, (New York, 1925), Chap. VI; and W. A. Paton, "The Pro and Con of a Sales Tax," *Administration*, Vol. II, pp. 367-372.

The operating aspects of the retail sales tax are presented in A. C. Willemsen, "Operating Aspects of the Retail Sales Tax," *Harvard Business Review*, (October, 1932). The legal aspects of excise taxes are discussed in L. H. Porter, "State Excise Taxes as Limited by the Federal Constitution," *Proceedings of the National Tax Association*, (1923), pp. 116-124.

A general analysis of the incidence of sales taxation is Gordon Hayes, "The Incidence of a Sales Tax," *Annals of the American Academy of Political and Social Science*, Vol. XCV, pp. 207-212. The incidence of duties on imports and exports is treated in Alfred Marshall, *Money, Credit and Commerce*, (London, 1923), Bk. III, Chaps. VIII, IX, X. The incidence and effects of customs and excise duties are examined in the *Report of the Colwyn Committee on National Debt and Taxation*, (London, 1927), pp. 209-232.

The relationship between the shifting and incidence of taxes on commodities and the laws of cost is analyzed in Alfred Marshall, *Principles of Economics*, (London, 1916), Bk. V, Chap. XIII; H. G. Brown, *The Economics of Taxation*, (New York, 1924), Chaps. III, IV; and T. N. Carver, "The Incidence of Costs," *Economic Journal*, Vol. XXXIV, pp. 576-588. The validity and usefulness of the laws of cost as an approach to the problem of shifting and incidence are questioned in E. D. Fagan, "Tax Shifting and the Laws of Cost," *Quarterly Journal of Economics*, Vol. XLVII, pp. 680-710. The relationship between statistical laws of supply and demand and tax shifting is treated in Henry Schultz, "Cost of Production, Supply and Demand, and the Tariff," *Journal of Farm Economics*, Vol. IX, pp. 192-209. Mathematical analyses of the problem of the incidence of taxes on commodities are F. Y. Edgeworth, *Papers Relating to Political Economy*, (London, 1925), Vol. I, pp. 132, 143 ff., and Vol. II, pp. 93, 401, 427; Harold Hotelling, "Edgeworth's Taxation Paradox and the Nature of Demand and Supply Functions," *Journal of Political Economy*, Vol. XL, pp. 577-616; and Raymond Garver, "The Effect of Taxation on a Monopolist," *American Economic Review*, Vol. XXII, pp. 463-465.

For additional references on shifting and incidence of taxes on commodities, see references at the close of Chap. IX, — especially Otto Frhr. von Mering, *Die Steuer Überwälzung;* and E. R. A. Seligman, *The Shifting and Incidence of Taxation*.

CHAPTER XXI.

SELECTED PROBLEMS IN TAXATION

1. TAXATION AND CHANGES IN PRICE LEVELS *

CHANGING price levels give rise to important theoretical and practical problems of taxation which have received no systematic treatment and only occasional mention in the economic literature on taxation and on price levels. The adequate theoretical presentation of the case for or against a particular tax often demands consideration of the special conditions resulting from the upward or downward swing of the general price level. Tax laws are almost invariably written in pecuniary terms. They may not operate in the manner intended by the legislators or they may even operate in a manner directly contrary to that anticipated by the legislators and productive of gross inequalities if provision is not made therein for changes in the value of the monetary unit. The relation of taxation to price levels is a problem of sufficient importance to merit a greater measure of attention from students of government finance than has been vouchsafed to it in the past. This article is an attempt to open up the subject in the hope that it will lead to further discussion of the general problem and its detailed manifestations.

INCOME TAXES

To take up first the bearing of fluctuating prices on income taxation, a careful reading of a number of current income-tax laws has not disclosed to the writer a single important instance of deliberate provision for adjustment to changing price levels. In a few instances, isolated provisions in these acts permit of some degree of adjustment, but this effect appears to be a happy coincidence not anticipated by the drafters of the acts.

Exemptions.— First, and most obviously, the specific amounts granted as exemptions to small incomes and for dependents have no rational basis unless they take into account the purchasing power of monetary incomes. The degree of adequacy for its intended purposes of a given exemption will vary inversely with fluctuations in the general price level.

* From Jacob Viner, "Taxation and Changes in Price Levels," *Journal of Political Economy*, Vol. XXXI, pp. 494-520.

Progression.— If the rates of an income tax are progressive the severity of the tax will increase as prices rise and will decrease as prices fall, even though the statutory rates remain unaltered, provided that monetary incomes in general vary in some degree of conformity with variations in the purchasing power of the monetary unit. The table presented below gives in Column I the schedule of rates of a hypothetical progressive tax and in Columns II and III a series of incomes in the years 1915 and 1920, respectively, and the taxes payable thereon, constructed on the assumptions that between 1915 and 1920 there was a 100 per cent rise in the general price level and that monetary incomes were exactly adjusted to this rise in prices, so that real income for all individuals remained unchanged.

I	II			III		
Tax Rates on Amount of Income	Total Income, 1915	Tax	Percentage of Total Income	Total Income, 1920	Tax	Percentage of Total Income
Not exceeding $1,000—exempt	A. $ 5,000	$ 200	4.0	A. $10,000	$ 450	4.5
$ 1,001–$ 10,000— 5 per cent	B. 10,000	450	4.5	B. 20,000	1,450	7.25
$10,001–$ 20,000—10 per cent	C. 20,000	1,450	7.25	C. 40,000	5,450	14.9
$20,001–$ 50,000—20 per cent	D. 50,000	7,450	14.9	D. 100,000	27,450	27.45
$50,001–$100,000—40 per cent						

The table demonstrates clearly enough that a rise in the price level increases the severity of a progressive scale of rates, even though the statutory rates are not increased. It can readily be demonstrated by arithmetical illustrations that, with a given progressive series of rates, the degree of increase in the severity of the rates will vary directly (although not necessarily in exact proportion) with the degree of rise in the price level, and that, with a given percentage of rise in the price level, the degree of increase in the severity of the rates will vary directly (although not necessarily in exact proportion) with the rate of progression in the tax law. In other words, the extent to which an increase in prices will increase the severity of progressive taxation depends upon both the percentage of increase in the price level and the rate of progression in the tax law. The greater the rise in prices and the greater the steepness in progression, the greater will be the increase in the severity of the tax. The reverse propositions also hold true: a fall in the general price level accompanied by a corresponding fall in money incomes will result in a decrease in the severity of a given progressive schedule of rates; the steeper the rate of progression in the tax and the greater the fall in prices, the greater will be the decrease in the severity of the tax. It follows that, assuming the national real income and its distribution to remain the same, the maintenance of a given progressive scale of rates in a general income tax during a period of rising prices will bring into the state treasury an increase in money revenue more than proportionate to the increase in the price level, and during a period of falling prices will result in a decrease in the money revenue more than proportionate to the fall in the price level. As a period of rising prices is probably also generally a period of increasing real income, and a period of falling prices a period of decreasing real income, the variations in the monetary revenue yield of a progressive income tax resulting from changing price levels will be still further accentuated.

A proportional income tax, on the other hand, aside from any exemption provisions it may contain, will not vary in its severity with changes in the price level to which money incomes adjust themselves, and the money revenue which it yields to the government will vary in exact proportion to the variations in the purchasing power of the monetary unit. This irregular and arbitrary variation in the severity and the productiveness of progressive income taxation during a period of changing price levels — from which proportional taxation is exempt — must be regarded either as a hitherto unnoticed objection to the progressive principle or as an argument for the frequent adjustment of the schedule of rates to allow for changes in the value of the monetary unit. Even if the latter alternative be chosen, it still remains true that such adjustment would be difficult to establish in practice, whether by statute or by administrative rule, and that it is not needed in connection with proportional taxation.

Capital gains.— One of the difficult problems in connection with income taxation is the propriety of including capital gains in taxable income. In general, writers on this topic definitely take either one position or the other, although logically the problem bristles with difficulties which should restrain the attempt to find in theory a categorical answer. Where the capital gain arises from the appreciation in value, as compared with the original cost, of an income-yielding asset, it can reasonably be argued in opposition to its taxation that such gain is the result of the capitalization of future income which will in due time pay its full measure of taxation. This argument does not hold, however, for those gains which are not reinvested by the recipients, but are used as current income. In such cases, failure to tax such gains either when they accrue or when they are realized results in the total escape from taxation of genuine income with full tax-paying ability. Since the income tax is assumed to be a general tax, it cannot be objected that the taxes on the future income yield of the sold capital asset were discounted in the sale price. There will normally be no shifting of a uniform tax upon all kinds of income. If there is a probability of lower tax rates in the future and if consideration is given to the difficulty of tracing the use to which the recipient of a capital gain puts the proceeds, there is ample justification for a compromise, such as is attempted in the American Revenue Act of 1921, between the full taxation of realized capital gains (as in the American Revenue Act of 1919) and the total exemption from taxation (as in the British income tax) by taxing capital gains more moderately than income in general.[1] An additional reason for the more moderate taxation of capital gains is that apparent capital gains may merely represent the reappraisal of a capital asset in terms of a dollar of less purchasing power. No acceptable concept of income will include as income the rise in monetary value of a capital asset which represents merely the fall in the value of the monetary unit and is not indicative of increased purchasing power in general.[2] During a period of rising prices, a lower rate on capital gains than on ordinary income can be justified, therefore, as a rough attempt to offset the taxation of fictitious gains resulting from the fall in the value of the monetary unit. This conclusion remains valid even though it be admitted that, given a constant current interest rate, there will probably be a tendency of variations in the value of income-yielding capital assets to lag

[1] The United States Revenue Act of 1921 provides that at the election of the taxpayer realized capital gains may be taxed separately from ordinary income at a rate of 12½ per cent. There is no justification in principle for restricting the relief from full taxation of capital gains to those whose taxable incomes are otherwise large enough to make them subject to rates higher than 12½ per cent. A more equitable method of granting relief would have been to permit a deduction for capital gains of a stated percentage, say 50 per cent, of the amount of tax to which they would have been subject in the absence of the relief provision. This principle holds, even though the object of the relief provision was not to afford a closer approximation of equity, but was to facilitate property deals.

[2] "A man who sold an asset in 1920 which he had purchased in 1914, making an apparent profit of 100 per cent and receiving his pay in fifty-cent dollars is, under our statute, subject to tax on his gain, although that gain is only apparent and not real. Moreover, the situation is particularly unjust under our present system. If complete periodical revaluations were used in determining income there would still be relative equality as between different taxpayers. But as the situation now stands, the transactions are closed in a haphazard and uneven fashion. A man who happens to sell out at the peak of the price curves is taxed very unequally as compared with the man who continues his transaction until a period of lower price levels."— R. M. Haig, "The Concept of Income," in *The Federal Income Tax* ("Columbia University Lectures," 1921), p. 17.

behind variations in their monetary yield. The owners or buyers of capital assets probably do not at once fully capitalize an increase or a decrease in monetary income, partly because of inertia, and partly on the logical ground that a rise or a fall in yield may prove to be of short duration. Another justification for the taxation of capital gains at specially low rates is suggested by the point made by Professor Powell, that, as capital gains are taxed only when realized, under progressive taxation a ten years' accumulated gain realized in one year will be subject to a greater tax than the same gain realized evenly year by year.[3]

During a period of falling prices, on the other hand, there may be a genuine capital gain, though the market value of the capital asset remains constant or even falls. In a period of rapid deflation of a depreciated currency, a considerable measure of such capital gains may well be concealed by the general downward trend of prices.

Inventories.— In the taxation of business incomes, taxable income is generally measured by the increase in net worth between the beginning and the end of the fiscal period plus any intermediate distribution of earnings. Accounting practice generally demands that net worth be estimated on the basis of the cost price minus depreciation of fixed assets; the cost or market value, whichever is lower, of inventories; and the book value of other assets, adjusted, generally, by reserves for possible losses. During a period of rapidly rising prices, market values of inventory will generally exceed cost values, but if the "cost or market, whichever is lower" basis is used for valuing inventories, the rise in the market values of inventory will not affect the income as shown by the accounting records until the profit is actually realized through sale at the higher prices. The accountant's case for this method of valuing inventory rests mainly on the argument that the acknowledgment of losses as soon as they become prospective, and the admission of gains only when they are actually realized, promotes conservative business practice.

There are four possible basic methods of valuing inventories: at cost; at market; at cost or market, whichever is lower; or at cost or market, whichever is higher. Of these, the last-named is rarely, if ever, employed. It is sometimes held that for purposes of taxation it does not matter which method is used, since any loss or gain in market value not reflected in the inventory

[3] Thomas Reed Powell, "Constitutional Aspects of Federal Income Taxation," in *The Federal Income Tax* ("Columbia University Lectures," 1921), p. 83.

or any loss or gain in inventory valuation not reflected in market value will ultimately be offset by gains or losses shown by sales.[4]

Under ordinary circumstances, however, and especially during a period of changing price levels, it does make a difference for taxation, even in the long run, whether one method or another of inventory valuation is used. To illustrate the significance of choice of method of taking inventories during a period of changing price levels, the following hypothetical cases are presented. Case A applies to conditions of rising prices followed by falling prices; Case B applies to conditions of falling prices followed by rising prices.

CASE A

Inventory of Stock Purchased in 1920, as of December 31, 1920	Sale Price in 1921, after Deduction of Selling Expenses, etc.
Cost, $100,000 Market, $150,000	$100,000

In Case A, if inventory were taken in 1920 at market value, or at cost or market, whichever was higher, there would have been admitted as income in 1920 a gain of $50,000, and there would have been deductible in 1921 a loss of $50,000. If the tax was proportional, if the rate was the same for both years, and if there was for the entire business in both years a net taxable income, then, and only then, would these two items offset each other for purposes of taxation. If there was a net loss for the entire business in 1921, there would be no opportunity in that year for the deduction of the tax paid in 1920 on what later proved to have been a fictitious gain.[5] If the tax was progressive, and if total net income in 1921 before deduction of the loss was not in the same taxable grade as total net income in 1920 after inclusion of the inventory gain, the deduction of the $50,000 loss in 1921 would either more than offset or would less than offset for taxation purposes the addition of $50,000 gain in 1920. In any case, the Treasury would have had the use for one year of the tax on the $50,000 temporary inventory gain. Valuation of inventory for taxation on the

[4] Cf. U. S. Revenue Act of 1916, Form 1031. "In case the annual gain or loss is determined by inventory, merchandise must be inventoried at the cost price, as any loss in saleable value will ultimately be reflected in the sales during the year when the goods are disposed of." Cf. also, A. A. Ballantine, "Inventories" in *The Federal Income Tax* ("Columbia University Lectures," 1921), p. 172: "The effect of admitting inventory losses, even wrongly, is *merely* to postpone profits from one year to another, while the effect of failure to admit them is to treat as income that which is really capital."

[5] The provision in the Revenue Act of 1921 (Sec. 204) which permits deduction of net loss in one year from net income of the next succeeding two years meets this problem in part, but only in part.

basis of market, or of cost or market, whichever is higher, tends to hasten the liability to taxation on gains during rising prices. If, as in the case given, a rise in prices in one year is offset by a corresponding fall in the next year, valuation on the basis of market or of cost or market, whichever is higher, tends also to increase the total amount of tax paid in the two years, since taxable income is probably greater in the year of high prices. If the rise in prices continues, inventory valuation according to either of these two methods tends to advance the liability to pay taxes, but under progressive taxation it probably operates to lessen the total amount of tax paid over a period of years, for rising prices generally bring increasing monetary incomes. When incomes are rising and taxation is progressive, the sooner the tax is paid on any particular item of gain, the lower will be the tax rate thereon. During a period of rising prices or rising tax rates, or both combined, these methods of inventory valuation would tend over a number of years to reduce the tax yield to the government.

In Case A, if cost, or cost or market, whichever was lower, was used as the basis of valuing inventory, there would be no taxable gain in 1920, and no loss in 1921. If prices continued to rise in 1921, however, either of these methods of valuing inventory would postpone taxation until the gain was actually realized. During a period of rising prices, if the tax was progressive, and still more if the tax rates were increasing, these methods of inventory valuation, by postponing liability to taxation to the years in which the rates were higher, and the net incomes greater, would tend to increase the tax yield to the government.

CASE B

Inventory of Stock Purchased in 1920, as of December 31, 1920	Sale Price in 1921, after Deduction of Selling Expenses, etc.
Cost, $100,000 Market, $50,000	$100,000

In Case B, if inventory were taken in 1920 at cost, or at cost or market, whichever was higher, no loss would be deductible in 1920, and there would be no taxable gain in 1921. If inventory were taken at market, or at cost or market, whichever was lower, a loss of $50,000 would be deductible in 1920, and there would be a taxable gain of $50,000 in 1921. As has been sufficiently demonstrated in connection with Case A, it would be highly improbable that for taxation purposes the loss in one year would be exactly offset by the equivalent gain in another year. If prices, instead of recovering in 1921, continued to fall, business incomes probably would fall also. Inventory valuation on the basis of market, or cost or market, whichever was lower, would tend to hasten the admission of losses. It would thus permit the appropriate tax deductions to be made in the years of higher incomes, and, therefore, of higher taxation.

The British income tax, in general, permits inventory valuations to be made only on the basis of cost or market, whichever is lower.[6] American federal income taxation started out with an attempt to determine income without reference to inventories, proceeded to the cost basis, and finally, when lower price levels were threatened, permitted, in the interest of the taxpayers, the use of the cost or market, whichever is lower, basis. As has already been pointed out, this basis of inventory valuation under progressive taxation tends to reduce the revenue yield during a period of falling prices, and this tendency is further accentuated if the period of falling prices is also marked by reductions in the statutory tax rates. This tendency, it should be noted, is independent of and additional to the similar tendency resulting from the decline in money incomes. On logical grounds this method of inventory valuation is open to criticism from the treasury point of view, inasmuch as under it inventory gains are reportable only when realized, whereas inventory losses are deductible as soon as they are reasonably certain to accrue. It is not practicable, however, to treat losses in any other manner. Many types of losses cannot be definitely proved to be such until long after they are written off the books, and this applies to inventory losses where the sale of the depreciated goods is indefinitely postponed in the absence of a market, or in the hope of a return of better times.

Depreciation.— A depreciation reserve which conforms to the standard accounting practice of distributing the original cost of the property minus the ultimate salvage value over the useful life of the property will not be sufficient during a period of rising prices to provide for physical replacement unless replacement costs lag behind the upward trend of prices. Where accounting practice fails also to sanction the periodic reappraisal of fixed assets during a period of rising prices so as to take account of appreciation, the maintenance of a depreciation reserve inadequate to take care of physical replacement, together with the failure to write up capital investment, will tend to give an exaggerated appearance of prosperity to the concern and will act as a stimulus either to increased distribution of earnings or to overexpansion of plant facilities.

[6] R. M. Haig, "The Taxation of Excess Profits in Great Britain," *American Economic Review Supplement,* Vol. X, No. 4 (December, 1920), p. 45.

	1915	1920
Capital	$100,000	$100,000
Net income before depreciation	15,000	30,000
Depreciation allowance	5,000	5,000
Net income after depreciation	10,000	25,000

In the foregoing illustration it is assumed that prices rose by 100 per cent between 1915 and 1920, that the fixed assets of the corporation remained unchanged physically except for full replacement of worn-out plant, and that whereas $5000 was sufficient to provide for such physical replacement in 1915, $10,000 would be necessary in 1920. On the usual accounting basis the data in this illustration would indicate that the firm could distribute $25,000 as dividends in 1920 without encroachment on capital, as compared with $10,000 in 1915. In any case, under the usual income-tax law, the taxable income of the corporation would have to be reported as $25,000. After physical replacement, however, the money income in 1920 would be only $20,000, and in terms of real income there would have been no change from 1915. A fictitious profit to the amount of $5000 would be taxed as income to the corporation and, if $25,000 was distributed as dividends, a distribution of capital assets to the amount of $5000 would be taxed as income to the shareholder. There would be no offset when there was actual need of physical replacement at a money cost greater than the original cost and greater, therefore, than could be met from the depreciation reserve, since income-tax laws under such circumstances forbid a readjustment for taxation of earlier depreciation allowances proved in course of time to have been inadequate to provide for physical replacement. Such is specifically the case in the American federal income tax, where the Treasury regulations permit only of such deductions for depreciation as will suffice, with the salvage value, to provide at the end of the "useful life" of the property its original money cost and not its replacement cost.[7]

During a period of falling prices, if the cost of replacement of worn-out capital goods declines with the general price level, a depreciation allowance on the standard original-cost basis will enable the taxpayer to deduct each year from taxable income an amount greater than is necessary to replace his original physical investment. If the monetary income of the concern prior to depreciation falls *pari passu* with the fall in the general price level, the net monetary income after allowance for depreciation will fall more than proportionately with the fall in

[7] U. S. Treasury Department, *Income Tax Regulations 62*, 1922 ed., Art. 161.

the price level, and the burden of taxation upon the concern will be lower, even under proportional taxation, in terms of purchasing power, although its real income remains the same. Allowance for depreciation on the original-cost basis tends, therefore, to increase the real burden of taxation during a period of rising prices and to decrease it during a period of falling prices.

WAR-PROFITS AND EXCESS-PROFITS TAXES

SOMEWHAT similar problems arise in connection with war-profits or excess-profits taxes, which use either pre-war income or invested capital as the basis for calculating taxable profits. In the case of the use of pre-war income as a basis for measurement of war-time excess income for purposes of war-profits taxation, if prices from the pre-war year to the given tax year in general rise by 100 per cent, the monetary income of a business representing the same physical investment as before the war should also increase by 100 per cent if the business is merely holding its own. Nevertheless, the British excess-profits tax and the American war-profits tax of March, 1917, both of which used pre-war profits as a basis of measurement, treated increases in monetary income resulting merely from the general rise in prices, and in many cases not fully compensating for the fall in the purchasing power of the monetary unit, as excess profits properly subject to special taxation over and above the general scheme of income taxation. An appearance of justice was given to such taxation by the accepted accounting practice of making no allowance for appreciation of capital assets and by the common impression that any war-time departure from this practice had for its only purpose the illegitimate evasion of legitimate taxation.

In the present American excess-profits tax, which bases the rates of the tax primarily on the percentage of earnings to invested capital, the various items included in invested capital must be valued at their cash value at the time at which they were acquired. Their valuation "is not to be based upon the present net worth of the assets, as shown by an appraisal or in any other manner." [8] If, between the time of acquisition by a firm of its capital assets and the year of taxation, prices in general have risen, and if the monetary earnings of the firm have kept pace with the rise in prices, these earnings will be a correspondingly increased percentage of invested capital at its original cash value, but they will not necessarily show any change in their percentage to actual net worth on a market

[8] *Ibid.*, Art. 831.

basis. In other words, the law, in its assumption that the monetary unit has an unchanging significance for taxation and in its refusal to admit appreciation of capital assets for purposes of income or profits taxation, decrees a basis for measurement of percentage of profits to invested capital which, during a period of rising prices, exaggerates the true proportion which the former bears to the latter. On the other hand, during a period of falling prices the failure to require writing down of capital assets for purposes of taxation to adjust them to the increased value of the monetary unit operates to minimize the proportion which profits bear to the net worth of the invested capital, and thus to lessen the burden of the tax. Where the tax system includes both taxes on capital gains and excess-profits taxes, the taxation of capital gains upon an accrual instead of upon a realization basis would have the double merit that it would prevent the lumping of accumulated capital gains in a single year, and that by sanctioning the periodic reappraisal of capital assets it would offset, in part at least, the exaggeration of the ratio of earnings to invested capital during a period of rising prices.

INHERITANCE TAXES

In connection with inheritance taxes, which normally fall upon any particular estate or succession only at long intervals, if prices are changing and if the tax rates are progressive, the proportion of the estate going to the state will be different in one year from what it would have been in the next or the preceding year, even though the statutory rates remain the same. During a period of rising prices the state will be taking an increasing proportion of the estates, and the proportion going to the state will fall with a fall in the general price level. As in the case of progressive income taxation, the revenue productiveness of a progressive inheritance tax will vary with, but more sharply than, the variations in the general price level, and the steeper the progression the greater will be the accentuation of changes in revenue as prices change. A proportional inheritance tax will adjust itself closely, except in so far as exemptions are concerned, in its revenue yield and in its real burden on the beneficiaries of the inheritance, to the changes in the price level. If there is a residuary legatee, and if the tax law or the will provides that the tax shall be paid either out of the estate before distribution or by the residuary legatee, a rise in prices which is reflected in the money value of the estate will proportionately increase the absolute amount of tax on the residuary legatee, if the tax is proportional and will more than proportionately increase the absolute amount of tax if it is progressive. On the other hand, if the will was made at a much earlier period and if the shares were defined in absolute and not in percentage terms, the rise in prices, as reflected in the value of the estate, will also increase the relative share of the residuary legatee in the estate.

PROPERTY TAXES

THE operation of proportional property taxes should not be disturbed by changes in price levels if the taxes are levied on the basis of annual and not of capital values. Other things being equal, the annual value of property should correspond in its fluctuations with the changes in prices in general. Where, as in the United States, the capital value of property is the base for taxation, the effects of changing price levels on the severity of the tax and on its productiveness of revenue may be somewhat different. Aside from the fact that the change in values will probably be reflected in changing assessments only after some delay, the capital value of property will vary in exact proportion with the variation in its income yield and therefore, by assumption, with the changes in general price levels, only if capitalization of income yield is solely on the basis of current annual yield. As this is not the case, and as capital values probably lag considerably behind both upward and downward changes in income yields and in general price levels, the taxation of property on its capital value at a constant porportional rate during a period of changing prices should generally result in the proportion of the tax to the income from the property diminishing during a period of rising prices and rising during a period of falling prices. It should generally result, likewise, in a less than proportionate increase in the revenue to the government from the taxation of property at a constant percentage during a period of rising prices and in a less than proportionate decrease during a period of falling prices, as compared in each case with the variation in the general price level.

CAPITAL LEVIES

SO-CALLED "capital levies" have been the subject of considerable discussion in Europe as means of reducing the burden of war indebtedness, and in a number of instances have been enacted into law. The proposals take two main forms: first, that a special non-recurrent tax be put upon new capital values created during the war period; and second, that such a tax be put upon the entire body of capital in the country.

The first form, that of a special tax on the war-time increase of wealth, is very much like the ordinary tax on capital gains, such as, for instance, under the American income-tax laws. It differs, however, from the latter in two respects. It is levied upon an appraisal basis as of a specified date, regardless of whether the capital gain had been, or could be, realized through sale, and it is a non-recurrent tax, assessed once for all in a specified year, although it may be payable in instalments over a series of years. The bearing of price levels on such a tax is covered by the discussion of a general tax on capital gains. The only additional consideration which its special features suggest is that the presumptive severity of its rates and its restriction to a single year make all-important the status of the price level in that year. A capital levy of this sort with a given progressive schedule of rates would impose a burden of very different magnitude if it were levied on the basis of the increase in capital values from 1913 to 1919 as compared, say, with the increase from 1913 to 1922. On the other hand, since the tax is non-recurrent, any allowance made by the legislators for the influence of changing prices on capital values need also be made only once. Such allowance, logically, could take either of the following forms: (a) a deduction from the money values of the post-war capital corresponding to the decline from the pre-war period in the value of the monetary unit; (b) recognition, in the form of a lower schedule of rates than would otherwise be imposed, of the fact that some of the war-time increase in capital values was more apparent than real.[9]

The second form which proposals for a capital levy take, namely, that of a tax on the whole body of capital in the country, closely resembles a general property tax, except that the former is non-recurrent, and, in the usual proposals, is to be levied at severe and progressive rates. This form avoids the difficulty of a double appraisal, pre-war and post-war, of capital values. It does not give rise, therefore, to the problem of adjustment to changes in price levels. If it be objected that in the assessment year the capital values are inflated, and that these values will later fall, there is the obvious rejoinder, if the

---

[9] A progressive tax on the war-time increase of wealth was imposed in Italy in 1919-20. The British Board of Inland Revenue in 1920 vouched for the practicability of such a tax, and declared that the change in the value of the pound afforded "no justification for a general allowance in determining the amount of wealth subject to the proposed duty." ("Increase of Wealth [War]" [Cmd. 594] as reported in *Economic Journal*, June, 1920, p. 260.) The report is not available, and the grounds for this position are not known to the writer, but if in drawing up the schedule of rates the legislators bore in mind the influence on capital values of a fall in the value of the monetary unit, as is pointed out in the text, no formal allowance would be necessary.

tax is payable in the year of assessment or shortly thereafter, that it will be paid in correspondingly depreciated money. If the tax is a severe one, however, payment in a single year would be a serious hardship to many taxpayers. The same difficulty is present in connection with levies on war-time increases of wealth. To meet this problem, the advocates of such taxes often concede that the taxpayer should be granted the privilege of paying on the instalment plan over a series of years, but with interest added.[10]

When the capital levy is payable in instalments, a rise in the value of the monetary unit, such as is to be expected in the post-war period, will force the taxpayer to pay the tax in more valuable money than that in terms of which his capital was assessed. The law may permit compounding of the payments in the first year — the Italian laws do. This does not, however, fully meet the problem. Some types of wealth have a ready market and are easily divisible, so that their owners can dispose of enough of their holdings to pay the full tax at once. Other types of property, however, can be sold only with difficulty and at a great sacrifice, so that to their owners such recourse is scarcely open. This is particularly true of peasant proprietors, who cannot easily divide up their small estates, and who are extremely reluctant to dispose of them altogether, because they thus separate themselves from their only certain means of livelihood.[11]

In the Italian law, which permits the payment of both types of capital levy in instalments spread over a long period, the problem is partially met for the general tax on wealth by a provision for the periodic revaluation of the wealth. This, however, raises another problem in its turn. Since the tax is

10 The German Capital Levy Tax of December 31, 1919 (Reichsnotopfer) provides for the taxation, with minor exceptions, of all wealth on the basis of the assessed valuation as of December 31, 1919, at steeply progressive rates. There is no general privilege of postponement of payment, but in cases where serious hardship would result from the demand for full immediate payment, the tax administrators are permitted at their discretion to grant postponement. (Cf. Quarterly Journal of Economics, XXXIV (1920), 545 ff.) The Italian tax on the war-time increase in wealth permits of payment in instalments spread over twenty years. The Italian law, in addition, imposes a tax of the second type, namely, a general tax on wealth, also levied at progressive rates, and payable in instalments spread over thirty years. This tax provides, however, for revaluation of wealth at stated intervals during this thirty-year period, so that except for the fact that the reassessments are not annual, that the rates are progressive, and that there is a presumption, if not a pledge, that the rates will not be changed, it very closely resembles in its general features the American general property tax. (Cf. Economic Journal, XXIX (1920), 296 ff.)

11 This is, in essence, the basis of a criticism of the Italian laws made by C. Gini, "A Levy on Capital : the Italian Law," Economic Journal, XXIX (1920), 296 ff.

progressive, and there is at least an implied pledge that the rates will not be changed, the severity of the tax and its productiveness to the government will diminish with each successive valuation, if the value of the lira rises. As the estates shrink in value in terms of lire, they will fall more and more below the grades subject to the high rates.

LAND-VALUE TAXES

CHANGING price levels have an important bearing also on the single-tax program for the special taxation of land values. The single-taxer rarely makes proper allowance for the influence of rising prices on the value of improvements as well as on monetary land values. He consequently almost always underestimates the proportion of the total land value at the end of a period of rising prices — and therefore also of the annual land value — which is properly attributable to the improvements. If unimproved value of the land is measured by the total value minus the original cost of the improvements, all of the increase in the monetary value of the land which is due to rising prices is attributed to the unimproved part of the land. This can be justified only on the theory that improvements on — or in — the land are exempt, or for purposes of taxation should be assumed to be exempt, from the price tendencies affecting all other commodities. Granting the logic of the single-tax argument for the appropriation by the state of all the economic rent, for improved land the determination of economic rent should be based on a formula which takes cognizance of the effect of changing price levels on the monetary values of both site and the improvements thereon.

Similar problems arise in connection with the taxation of the future increment of land values. All such taxes, actual and proposed, define the taxable increment for a given piece of land as the increase in its price between some base-date and some future "occasion" for taxation. Many of the laws make no allowance for the influence on land prices of changing price levels. A rise in the price of land will not indicate "unearned increment" of the sort which such taxes are intended to reach if such rise is not in excess of the rise in the general price-level. Moreover during a period of falling prices there may be genuine unearned increment even though the price of the land falls, provided its fall is less than proportionate to the general decline in prices. A law taxing unearned increment of land values on the basis of comparisons with the prices of a basic date, even though the tax is only a fractional one, may take from the landlord much more than the total real increment

during a period of rapidly rising prices and, even though the
rate of the tax is a full 100 per cent, may permit unearned
increment wholly to escape taxation during a period of falling
prices. The imperial German increment value tax of 1911
permitted an addition of from ¾ to 2½ per cent per annum
to be made to the purchase price of land from which increment
is calculated to compensate the landowners for, among other
things, a rise of value which may be in part due to a decrease
in the purchasing power of money.[12] This arbitrary allowance
is not a very scientific adjustment of taxation to the problem
here under discussion, but it is at least an attempt in that direction. There is no provision of the law, however, which meets
the problem of increments of value being concealed by a rise in
the purchasing power of the mark.[13] It would be interesting
to know whether this law has survived, without amendment
to permit of fuller adjustment to changing price levels, the
post-war period of depreciation in the value of the mark. The
lack in this German tax of more elaborate provision for adjustment to changing price levels is made more serious by the fact
that its rates are progressive, increasing with the increase of the
percentage of increment to purchase price, and that the effects
of changing price levels on the severity and the productiveness
of the tax are thus accentuated.

The need which has been pointed out, in connection with
taxes on land values, for caution lest there be attributed solely
to the "economic" land an increase in value really due in part
to the rise in the monetary value of the improvements applies
also to the increment taxes which differentiate between economic land value and the value of improvements and aim to
tax only the increase in the former. The New Zealand authorities appear to have worked out most carefully, in connection with the New Zealand tax of this character, rules for the
separate assessment of land value and improvement value, respectively, but their rules require that the improvements be
valued at cost or market, whichever is lower.[14] In thus at-

12 "This whole provision is designed to meet objections urged against the
strong retroactive feature of the law. During a period ranging from twenty-
six up to a maximum of forty years the monetary standard of value can decline
very materially in purchasing power. Relative to a higher general range of
prices a large apparent increase in land values may be real only in part or even
totally deceptive. . . Hence the allowance of a small steady annual rate of
interest upon purchase price and improvement costs."— R. C. Brooks, "The German Imperial Tax on the Unearned Increment," *Quarterly Journal of Economics*, XXV (August, 1911), 694-95.

13 This is pointed out by Brooks, *ibid.*

14 "The amount at which improvements are to be valued is defined by the
Act as the sum by which they increase the selling value of the land, *provided
that the value must not exceed the cost*, although it may be below the cost if

tributing all of the rise in the value of improved land to the bare land, the law intensifies the effect of the basic error of accepting as taxable value increment an increase in the price of land which is due to the fall in the value of the monetary unit.

IMPORT DUTIES

It is only in connection with import duties that taxing authorities and writers on taxation have given much attention to the problems arising out of changes in price levels. Even here, however, the display of interest has been due more to the obvious influence exerted by changing prices on the manner in which import duties achieve their non-fiscal purposes than to their effects on the taxpayer or on the Treasury. Interest has centered particularly about the different manner of operation under changing prices of specific and ad valorem duties. As Gregory points out, "Specific duties do not respond, as ad valorem duties do, to changes in the price level. Whether prices rise or fall 20 per cent, the ratio of the duty to the price remains the same with ad valorem duties, but changes in the specific duties inversely to the price movement."[15] Gregory states that it is arguable that the specific duty yields a better result, because the ad valorem duty, which fluctuates in its absolute amount with fluctuations in the price of the imported commodity, increases the burden of the duty on the importer when the price burden has increased and decreases the duty burden when the price burden has decreased. But Gregory's entire discussion rests on the implied assumption that only the price of a particular commodity is changing, all other prices and all money incomes remaining the same, and he gives no consideration to the broader problem of the method of operation of specific and of ad valorem duties when *all* prices are changing. During changes in the general price level, an unaltered schedule of ad valorem duties adjusts itself automatically to the change in the price levels so as to maintain the same relative degree of severity on the taxpayer and to bring into the Treasury the same amount of purchasing power. Specific duties, on the other hand, become more severe on the taxpayer during a period of falling price levels and less severe during a period of rising price levels; their relative productiveness during periods of rising and of falling prices, respectively, in terms of purchasing power, will be uncertain and will depend

their condition warrants it."— A. C. Pigou, *Economics of Welfare* (London, 1920), p. 611. (Italics his.)

[15] T. E. Gregory, *Tariffs, A Study in Method* (London, 1921), p. 120.

on the elasticity of demand for the imported commodities and on the effects on domestic production of the changing severity of the rates on imports. During a period of rising prices, import duties intended to be protective will be more likely to accomplish their purpose of hindering foreign competition if they are ad valorem than if they are specific; specific duties will require constant revision if they are to exert the same measure of protective influence. The French government has endeavored to maintain its system of specific import duties through a period of rapidly rising prices and, at the same time, to maintain its productiveness in terms of purchasing power and its protective effect, not by repeated legislative revision of the rates, which would have been a source of great inconvenience, but by establishing an administrative commission with the power to multiply the specific rates in the statutory tariff by "value coefficients" corresponding to the changes in price of the particular groups of commodities. This is not, at least from the administrative side, a virtual substitution of the ad valorem for the specific method. The valuation is done only at intermittent intervals, and for classes or groups of commodities. Actual imports need only to be classified and need not be valued.

Where tariff rates are a combination of specific and ad valorem duties or are otherwise more complex than the simple specific or ad valorem duty, the effect of changing price levels on their method of operation is also more complex. Only one such type of rate will be given here as illustrative of the general character of the problems which arise. The classification of commodities for purposes of customs taxation at specific rates is sometimes made on the basis of their prices. For example, in the American tariff, sugar candy and confectionery not specially provided for are dutiable, if valued at fifteen cents per pound or less, at two cents per pound; if valued at more than fifteen cents per pound, at 25 per cent ad valorem.[16] If it be assumed that the fixing of the dividing line between the two classes at fifteen cents per pound was at the time of the enactment of the tariff law not wholly arbitrary, but conformed to some logical plan, this point becomes too high if prices fall, and too low if prices rise.[17]

[16] Tariff Act of October 3, 1913, No. 180.
[17] Unless, of course, it is intended to conform with some other part of the tax law. The specific duty of two cents on sugar candy under fifteen cents per pound may be intended to prevent sugar from entering the United States in the form of candy at a lower rate than it would be subject to as sugar.

EXCISE TAXES

EXCISE taxation is affected by changes in price levels in fundamentally the same manner as import duties.   Because the main
purpose of excise taxes is a fiscal one, the effect thereon of
changing prices has not, however, been given the same amount
of attention.   Ad valorem taxes will respond in their revenue
yield to changes in price levels, and the real burden on the
taxpayer will not be affected by changes in the prices of the
taxed commodities which correspond to changes in the general
price level.   Specific taxes, on the other hand, will become
more severe in their burden as prices fall, and lighter as prices
rise.   The effect of changing prices on the revenue productivity
of specific taxes will depend on the elasticity of demand for the
taxed commodities.   It being assumed that the price changes
in the taxed commodities conform exactly, except for the tax
element in price, to changes in the general level of prices, a
rise in prices will cause a relative fall in the burden of taxation
and will tend, therefore, to stimulate consumption of the taxed
articles.   Conversely a fall in prices will tend to check their
consumption.   The monetary yield of specific excise taxes will
tend to vary in partial correspondence with changes in the
price level, rising when prices rise and falling when prices fall,
but, in each case, unless the demand for the taxed commodities
is highly elastic and the tax very severe, the variation in monetary yield will tend to be less than proportionate to the change
in prices.   If, as is generally the case, the commodities taxed
have very inelastic demands, the modifications in the severity
of specific taxes resulting from changes in price levels will have
but slight effect on the consumption of the taxed commodities
and therefore on the monetary yield of the taxes.

Where an attempt is made to introduce progression into ad
valorem excise taxation by grading the taxed commodities according to price and imposing higher ad valorem rates on the
higher-priced grades, falling prices will tend to counteract the
effect of the grading, and rising prices will tend to accentuate
it.   Where an attempt is made, as in the American excise on
tobacco, to modify the regressive character of specific excise
taxes by grading the taxed commodities according to price and
imposing higher specific duties on the more expensive grades,
falling prices will likewise tend to counteract the effect of the
grading, and rising prices to accentuate it.   A so-called luxury
tax which is imposed only on commodities which exceed
specified prices will be somewhat similarly affected by changes
in the price level.   Rising prices will tend to broaden the in-

cidence of the tax, and falling prices to restrict it, for if prices are rising, an increasing proportion, and if prices are falling, a decreasing proportion, of the range of commodities will be found above the basic prices selected as marking the border line between luxury and non-luxury, or taxable and non-taxable, commodities.

THE EFFECTS ON TAXATION OF CHANGES IN INTEREST LEVELS

IN connection with taxes which rest on the assessment of capital values, such as property taxes, taxes of capital gains, inheritance taxes, and land-value taxes, changing interest levels give rise to problems closely resembling those resulting from changes in general price levels. Invested capital will tend to vary in price in inverse proportion to variations in the current rate of interest. A fall in the current rate of interest will result in an increase in the value of such property without increasing the taxpaying ability, on an income basis, of the owners thereof. An increase in the value of property, due to a fall in interest rates, will make the owners subject to increased capital gain and general property taxation, without increasing the flow of income out of which the tax must generally be met. In the same way, the value of an estate will be returnable at a higher figure when the interest rate is low than when it is high, and the amount of inheritance tax payable thereon will vary accordingly, although there will not be a corresponding variation in the income which the legatee will derive from the estate. Conversely, a rise in the current rate of interest will tend to bring about a fall in the value of invested capital, and to reduce the amount of tax payable under taxation resting on capital values, although the income yield of such capital will not be affected thereby.

This tendency of capital goods to vary in value in inverse proportion to variations in the interest rate is of special significance in connection with the taxation of the increment in land values. A fall in the current rate of interest will operate to increase the value of land without increasing the ability of the landowner to pay taxes from the income derived from the land. A subsequent recovery in interest rates will tend to wipe out the increase in value of his land, perhaps after a substantial part of that increase had already been appropriated by the state. On the other hand, a rise in the interest rate will tend to reduce the capital value of land, without reducing the annual income which its owner derives therefrom. These considerations suggest the desirability that attempts to reach unearned increment of land be directed rather to taxation of the increase in rent yields than of the increase in capital values, but with special provision for the taxation of idle land.[18]

CONCLUSION

THIS discussion has, with a few minor exceptions, assumed throughout that when the price level changes all prices change in the same proportion. If provisions of general application were introduced into tax laws in order to permit of adjustment to changes in the value of the monetary unit, such provisions would undoubtedly meet only partially, if at all, the problems presented by individual cases of variation from the general price trend. If it could be demonstrated with reasonable certainty that there are always normal well-defined tendencies for certain sectional price levels to move counter to, or only in partial sympathy with, the general trend of prices, it might be necessary to take account of such tendencies in any attempt to adjust taxation to changing prices.

It may be objected that injustices to taxpayers in the application of tax laws resulting from failure to make proper allowances for changes in value of the monetary unit tend, in the long run, to be offset by unintended generosity to them when the price trend reverses itself. It has been sufficiently demonstrated in the foregoing argument, however, that there is in many cases no probability that a reversal in the trend of prices will fully repay either the Treasury or the taxpayers, as the case may be, for the unreasonable losses incurred when prices had been moving in the other direction. Moreover, men may die, or may go out of business, or the basis for taxation may change, before the scales of justice which had been unduly tipped in one direction acquire a compensatory bias in the other. Reversals in the trend of the price level are not necessarily, or, if only substantial price changes are considered, are not even usually, matters of a few years. The "long run" may be a very long run, too long to permit of substantial compensation being made to the same individuals who have suffered an original injustice, or of additional demands for taxation being made upon those who had in an earlier period unreasonably escaped therefrom. In any case, even though this were a decisive objection to any plan for adjusting the taxation system to the conditions resulting from changing price levels, it would not be an adequate explanation of the absence of such plans in the past. For to the legislator, as to the average taxpayer

[18] Cf. F. W. Taussig, *Principles of Economics*, II (1912), 103, 4.

and to the main body of accounting practice, a dollar is always
a dollar, regardless of its purchasing power. There has not
been in the past any general recognition of the existence of
such problems in taxation as have been discussed above.

The writer has concerned himself mainly with an attempt to
define the problems and has not felt any obligation to devise
solutions therefor. In the course of the discussion, however,
some suggestions were made which might, perhaps, be capable
of practical application. Any comprehensive attempt to prevent changes in price levels from affecting the tax system in
such a manner as to impose illogical and undesirable burdens
on either the taxpayer or the Treasury must, in its general lines,
follow one or another of three possible administrative methods.
First, the rates in the tax law could be periodically revised, so as
to keep them in proximate adjustment with the trend of price
levels. Second, there could be embodied in the texts of the
laws provisions intended to make automatic allowance for the
effects both of rising and of falling prices. Such provisions
might, perhaps, provide for the use of price index numbers in
the assessment of taxes. Third, a considerable measure of
discretion could be given to the officials intrusted with the
administration of the taxes, with power to make proper adjustments, whether in defense of the legitimate interests of the
Treasury or of the taxpayer, for the effects of changing price
levels. Decision between these alternative methods can well
await further analysis of the nature of the problem and of the
possible devices for meeting it.

Perfect and complete adjustment of taxation to changing
price levels is, it must be confessed, an unattainable ideal. It
may even be true that any attempt to bring about even a partial
though substantial degree of adjustment would meet with insuperable administrative difficulties. The task would unquestionably be far from simple.[19] But new tax proposals have

---

[19] Cf. R. M. Haig, "The Concept of Income," in *The Federal Income Tax*
("Columbia University Lectures," 1921), p. 17 : "If it were possible to modify
the concept of taxable income so as to eliminate this variation in the value of
money it would certainly be desirable to do so. The prospect for a complete
solution of the difficulty pointed out, however, is identical with the prospect
for a perfect monetary standard. But an approximate solution might be realized
if we were able to evolve a satisfactory index of the level of prices. If it were
accurately known what the change in price levels in a given year had been, it
might be possible to qualify the results shown by a comparison of the balance
sheets for the beginning and the end of the period in such a way as to eliminate
the influence of the changing standard. But even this refinement is not likely
to be introduced soon. Indeed, the desirability and urgency of its introduction
is dependent largely upon the complete solution of the accounting problem,
which solution is certainly not imminent."

almost always to meet the anticipatory objection that they are beyond the administrative powers of the government.[20] Our leading authorities on taxation appear at the moment to be in almost unanimous agreement that a comprehensive sales tax would involve the government in insuperable difficulties of administration. But in Canada such a tax, under conditions much more unfavorable than those existing in the United States, has been working smoothly from its very inception. There applies to special provisions in tax legislation such as are suggested above, what Sir Josiah Stamp, from his ripe experience as a tax administrator, says of taxes in general:

It will be found generally that if a tax is believed to be practicable over a considerable part of the field to which it is to be applied, and the impracticability is confined to a minor part, most states will embark upon the scheme, and by a sacrifice of logical principle at the point of difficulty and the adoption of a few conventions will satisfy the equities roughly.[21]

Even though there be accepted the conclusions of this paper to the effect that the absence in tax legislation of provisions for adjusting taxes to the changing conditions resulting from changing price levels is a source of serious inequities, it must be admitted that there is a strong presumption against adding further to the intricacies and complexities of taxation. In any case, it may be asked, why treat symptoms instead of causes? If changing price levels prevent ordinary tax laws from working well, why is this not rather an added argument for the search for means of stabilizing prices, instead of an argument supporting further elaboration of tax laws? The answer to this question turns, of course, upon the relative difficulty of stabilizing price levels as compared with adjusting tax laws. Until the development and installation of some scheme for the stabilization of prices is more of a practical possibility than it appears to be at the present, the possibility of adjusting taxation to changing price levels, even at the cost of further complication in tax laws, is at least deserving of more consideration than it has yet received.

[20] "The first argument that is brought against every new proposal departing from conventional lines is nearly always that it is 'impracticable.'"— Sir Josiah Stamp, The Fundamental Principles of Taxation (London, 1921), p. 95.
[21] Sir Josiah Stamp, The Fundamental Principles of Taxation, (London, 1921), pp. 95, 96.

2. THE PROBLEMS OF HIGHWAY FINANCE *

HIGHWAY economy does not mean highway parsimony. Where highway improvements will be worth more than their cost, it is true economy to make the necessary expenditures; it is extravagance to withhold them, or to spend less than the minimum necessary adequately to finance such highway improvements as are economically justified. Retarded highway development means costly maintenance of outworn highways, excessive operating costs to automobile users, and arrested growth of such industrial and pleasurable activities as are dependent on advanced means of transportation. But there are many other avenues of waste in highway finance, some of which have been much traveled. Our experience with the special problems of automobile highway construction and maintenance has been, perhaps, of too short duration to permit of the detection of all of these avenues of waste, or to justify the dogmatic formulation of the principles which should be followed at every time and in every place in the expenditure of funds. Some problems, however, have been more or less clearly discerned, and for a few of these the available fund of experience has already disclosed effective remedies.

No primary highway should be constructed or substantially improved until after an economic survey of existing and potential traffic, conducted by competent technicians, along the lines developed by the federal bureau of public roads and the more efficient of the state highway commissions, has shown that the improvement is economically warranted and has indicated for what volume and character of traffic it should be designed. The existing volume of traffic, prior to the making of the improvement, should not, of course, be alone relied upon in making the necessary decisions, for the prospective growth in population and in production should be taken into account, as well as the stimulus to traffic resulting directly from the more economical or more convenient mode of transportation brought about by the improvement itself. The mode of construction and especially the type of surfacing to be used should be decided upon only after reference to the results of local research with respect to the comparative costs of construction and of maintenance of the different types. Consideration

---

* Adapted from "Report of Committee of the National Tax Association on the Problems of Highway Finance," *Proceedings of the National Tax Association,* (1924), pp. 413-431.

Eds. note : While there are later reports on this subject (see bibliographical note at end of this chapter), the able treatment of the fundamental economic aspects of the problem dictates the reproduction of this earlier study.

should always be given to the possibility of the economic utilization of nearby building material resources, or of other means of transportation than the automobile highway.

The rule that no highway should be constructed or substantially improved until after a scientific survey has shown that the expenditure is economically justified, should be strictly enforced and should be made the means of guarding against any unnecessary or unwise extension of existing transportation facilities beyond the reasonable needs of the state or its facilities for payment. It should constantly be borne in mind that one of the urgent needs of American government at the present time is for a reduction of tax load and a check to the expansion of government indebtedness, with its attendant evils of reckless expenditure, impaired credit, a flood of tax-exempt securities and the legacy to later generations of a debt-liquidation problem of serious proportions. The state and local governments should be on their guard lest in their well-deserved enthusiasm for highways they carry their highway programs beyond their real needs or beyond their means for financing them.

Highway construction and improvement should follow a central and systematic plan, in order that individual projects shall eventually develop into a coördinated highway system instead of a haphazard collection of blind alleys and scraps. Once it has been decided, upon the basis of a careful survey, that a proposed highway project is immediately warranted by the traffic needs and potentialities, construction of its main framework, as rapidly as is consistent with the maintenance of competitive market conditions for bond flotations, labor, and materials, is economically urgent, since every mile of improved road adds to the value of the remaining mileage of improved road to which it is supplementary. Piecemeal construction often means wasteful gaps, which lessen the serviceability of what has already been built, trunk lines without feeders to bring traffic to them, feeders without access to trunk lines.

It is often desirable that sufficient right-of-way should be acquired, when an improvement is first planned, to permit of widening of the road surface at some later date, to meet the demands of increased traffic without excessive cost for land purchase or condemnation. This practice is especially desirable in urban terminal areas, where successive widenings of the highways are most likely to become urgent and where, in the absence of such precaution, subsequent widenings are liable to require expensive purchase or condemnation of buildings.

On highways in the neighborhood of urban centers of population there is likely to be a pronounced peak-load of traffic on summer week-ends and roads which may provide generous accommodation to traffic at other times may at such periods be seriously congested. It is not economically justifiable to try to meet all the demands for ample highway accommodation for peak-load traffic of this character. Where the congestion is, however, confined to a limited mileage, usually the outlet roads for large cities, the provision of a few miles of wider or additional terminal roads, linking up the city streets with the rural highway system, will often be sufficient to reduce the peak-load congestion to tolerable proportions, without involving unduly excessive financial burdens on the state. Many urban automobile owners have no opportunity to utilize the rural highways except at week-ends and whatever can reasonably be done to meet their needs should be done.

No highway should be constructed or improved without immediate provision being made for the necessary maintenance to keep it in first-class condition. Adequate maintenance is necessary not only to make possible the complete and satisfactory utilization of the highways but also to preserve the original highway investment. The construction of expensive highways, which are then permitted to break up and disintegrate, because of a desire to "economize" on maintenance costs, is highly wasteful procedure. Another form of waste of highway facilities which is unduly prevalent is the failure to maintain the roads in condition fit for traffic during the winter months. Clearance of snow from the roads is not always economically justifiable, but where winter traffic would be present in volume sufficient to justify snow clearance if the roads were cleared, and is absent only because they are not cleared, there is a wasteful loss to the community during a part of each year, because of the enforced idleness of its highway investment.

The problem of the heavy motor truck is a difficult one that has led to many popular misconceptions as to the causes of undue damage to the highways. The heavy truck will here be considered to be the truck whose weight, unloaded, is five tons or over and whose weight, with a standard load, is eleven tons or over. Studies made by the bureau of public roads, in coöperation with state highway departments and others, show conclusively that the chief causes of highway deterioration are adverse weather conditions, which result in a breaking up of the sub-base, bad soil conditions, lack of maintenance and overloading of the road or the vehicle. Mere gross weight is not in itself the determining factor. Where the potential volume of freight traffic justifies the construction of roads designed to carry such vehicles, heavy trucks provide an efficient and economical means of freight transportation. But heavy traffic can do great damage to improved roads not designed for such traffic, if weather and soil conditions are adverse, or if traffic regulation is not adequate. The construction of roads, capable of handling, without excessive maintenance costs, a substantial amount of such traffic requires heavy additional expenditures for extra depth of surfacing and width of road. Sufficient economic justification for the construction of roads designed to handle heavy truck traffic ordinarily exists only in limited areas, such as densely populated industrial centers and trunk routes connecting large urban districts not too distant from each other. On ordinary improved highways not designed for such traffic, heavy trucks should be admitted only where there exist emergency or special needs for their operation, and only under special permit and subject to close regulation by the highway officials as to character and distribution of the load, condition of the tires, speed, condition of the roads, etc. Under such regulation even a light-surfaced road can carry a substantial amount of heavy truck traffic without excessive wear on the road.

There cannot be entirely effective maintenance of our public highways, and above all, there cannot be reasonably economical maintenance expense, unless there is adequate legislative provision for the regulation of traffic and adequate machinery, energetically administered, for the enforcement of such legislation. To prevent the uneconomic and unjustifiable wear and tear of highways, size, weight, load, speed, and tire-condition, regulation of motor traffic have been found absolutely essential. Effective traffic regulation on the other hand, is not possible, without considerable centralization of highway control. The tendency is strongly in the direction of absolute state control over primary improved roads, and it is a desirable tendency. Uniformity of regulation is desirable not only for the various parts of the highway system within a state but also between states, and the latter type of uniformity can be secured only by voluntary coöperation between the highway authorities of the different states. The regulatory code should not be too rigid and should preferably be left to administrative authorities, subject to broad legislative limitations. The variables to be considered as to type of traffic, type of road, season of year, volume of traffic, special circumstances, etc., are too numerous to be dealt with in adequate detail and with sufficient flexibility by legislation. Careful investigations by federal and state highway officials have shown that the great bulk of damage to roads is done by abuse rather than by reasonable use thereof. Traffic regulation should be directed, in the main, to fostering the maximum use of the available highway facilities and should have a punitive trend only against unreasonable use of roads.

To secure proper direction and economic control of highway expenditures a substantial degree of centralization is necessary. Prior to the coming of motor transportation, roads were, with a few outstanding exceptions, built and maintained by the local communities. The first influence of the advent of motor transportation was to secure the extension and improvement of these local roads, so as to facilitate communication between neighboring communities. Later the counties, and still later the states, assumed some measure of responsibility for and authority over the road system, mainly in order to develop chains of local roads connecting the larger cities. Every state in the Union has now some form of highway department with powers of control ranging from complete authority over minute details of state and local expenditures for construction and maintenance, to merely advisory functions for the state highway and no jurisdiction whatsoever over local roads. The trend, however, is decidedly in the direction of greater centralization, in inevitable response to the needs of the situation. In very recent years all the states, with the coöperation of the federal bureau of public roads, have planned and have made substantial progress in the construction of thoroughly coördinated systems of improved highways, providing both through routes of state and national importance and systems of secondary roads subsidiary to these through routes. Some states have initiated purely state projects, going beyond the federal plan.

The inevitable consequences of local control of primary roads are piecemeal construction, inadequate and varying construction and maintenance standards, lack of coördination and the continuance of costly gaps in the system, excessive costs, because of lack of knowledge of recent developments and of the results of scientific tests and investigations. There should be state control of all roads which are not almost wholly of a strictly local character, serving merely the community in which they are situated. As population and motor traffic grow, more and more of what are now local roads will be absorbed into the state highway systems and should come under state control or supervision. Even before local roads are placed under any degree of mandatory state supervision, the state highway departments should develop facilities for giving to local authorities in systematic fashion guidance with respect to most suitable road materials, mode and location of road construction, material and labor prices, bond flotations for roads, maintenance standards, etc.

THE BORROWING *vs*. THE PAY-AS-YOU-GO METHODS OF HIGHWAY FINANCING

THE modern automobile highway is in large part a "permanent" improvement. The location, right-of-way, subgrade, drainage, and many of the structures are permanent, and competent engineers estimate the permanent portion of improved highways to account for from forty to sixty per cent of the total construction expenses. Maintenance expenditures should be sufficient to preserve the improvement in as good shape as when first constructed. The generally accepted rule that the maturity of bonds for financing improvements should not extend beyond the life of the improvement fails, therefore, to set an adequate limit to the resort to borrowing to finance highway construction, and guidance must be sought in more fundamental principles, in determining the extent to which borrowing is justified.

During the initial period of construction of an extensive system of improved highways, densely populated and rapidly growing states, and states where the immediate need for the construction of improved highways is urgent, it would be unwise to attempt to finance highway construction wholly or even in large part from current tax revenues. If current revenues are relied upon under these circumstances, there will result either an intolerable tax burden on the community or else there will be an unreasonable retardation of highway construction, entailing to the community the loss for many years of the advantages of improved means of highway communication. Such a financial policy would be likely to lead, moreover, to piecemeal construction, with the result that the utility of each mile of improved road will for many years be reduced, as compared to the possibilities if, once the system were carefully planned, a program of rapid completion of its general framework were embarked upon. States and localities, however, which have already made considerable progress in highway construction and have already passed the peak of new annual mileage, should move gradually toward the pay-as-you-go basis. This could be accomplished, partly by shortening the maturity of new bond issues and partly by increasing the proportion of new construction costs met out of current revenues. Maintenance and reconstruction costs should, under all normal circumstances, except perhaps where the reconstruction involves a substantial improvement in the more permanent features of the old road, be financed from current revenues.

In more sparsely settled states, where road mileage per capita is great, where there are no large urban centers of population, and where industry is mainly agricultural and specializes in the production for distant markets of a few staple products, the local roads to the railroad stations are by far the most important part of the highway system. In such states the demand for road construction and improvements will continue for decade after decade at a comparatively uniform rate, and improved roads should not be constructed much ahead of the growth of population to utilize them. In such states road construction should be financed with little or no recourse to borrowing.

Loans incurred for highway construction should not have a longer maturity than thirty years, and preferably not more than twenty years, and should be of the serial bond type. While a substantial proportion of the original cost of highway construction is properly to be regarded as a more or less permanent investment, this is not sufficient to justify the resort to bond issues of indefinitely long maturities. Resort to bond issues, with excessively long maturities, is liable to stimulate reckless and wasteful expenditures, since the resistance of the taxpayer to bond issues is much less than to increases in tax levies. In any case, there is comparatively little advantage in the annual cost during the first twenty years, of paying for an improvement on a twenty- as compared to a forty-year basis, but there is a tremendous difference at the end of the twenty years, depending upon whether the one maturity or the other had been chosen. The accumulation of debt, without provision for its early liquidation, impairs the credit of the borrowing agency and if funds are later needed for emergencies or for the new activities which democracy is constantly demanding of government, they will not be obtainable or will be obtainable only at usurious rates. We cannot see clearly enough into the future to be certain that new transportation needs or facilities may not develop which will render obsolete much of our present huge investment in automobile roads. There is always the danger that a highway has not been properly planned and that it may have to be rebuilt in another way or in another location. "As the highway systems are completed, the traffic will become more and more organized, and concentrated on the improved highways. If these systems are not properly selected, they will have to be revised and so much of the investment jeopardized." [1]

PRINCIPLES OF TAXATION FOR HIGHWAY PURPOSES

UNTIL the latter half of the nineteenth century main highways or trunk lines were largely privately constructed and operated and were financed by tolls levied upon the users of the road. Local roads were constructed and maintained, as now, by the local governments and were financed out of the general local revenues or by special local road taxes, payable in labor or in cash. Unsatisfactory maintenance of the trunk roads by their owners and the exaction of extortionate tolls led gradually to the taking over of the roads by the local or county governments, but in the earlier stages even state roads were often financed out of tolls levied on the users. The inconvenience and irritation of the toll system to road-users, the growing recognition of the general utility of highways, and the general acceptance of the principle that government services should be financed by taxation levied on the ability principle, were all contributing factors in bringing about an almost complete abolition of the toll system and the financing of roads out of the general revenues of the local, and, later, the state governments. To-day there survive only slight traces, here and there, confined largely to bridges, of the once-dominant toll system.

The advent of the automobile brought the need of a greatly improved and extended highway system and threw upon the state and local governments a great additional financial burden which, because of their inadequate and obsolete revenue systems, they were ill-prepared to assume. A partial solution was sought in a return to the benefit principle of taxation, a part of the cost of highway financing being thrown on the direct users of the highways, but in the form of special automobile license or registry taxes, and in the last few years, of gasoline taxes, without resort again to the abandoned toll system. The tendency toward imposing on highway users an increasing portion of the cost of highways is becoming more marked each year. In 1914 the federal and state special taxes on motor vehicles amounted to only five per cent of the total highway expenditures; in 1921 this percentage had increased to about twenty-five; in 1923 it reached approximately thirty-eight per cent; and in 1924 it promises to equal or surpass forty-five per cent. Since about forty per cent of the highway expenditures are met

---

[1] Thomas H. Macdonald, Director of Federal Bureau of Public Roads, in address before United States Chamber of Commerce, May 16, 1922.

by borrowings, the time is rapidly approaching when special motor vehicle taxes will equal the expenditure on highways, both primary and local, from current tax receipts.

The varying circumstances in which different states find themselves, with respect to highway burdens, and the fact also that American public finance is not governed to any important extent by formulas, meritorious or otherwise, but is largely the product of historical traditions, inertia, and the play of political factors, make it academic to present any rigid formula as the proper solution of the problem of apportionment of highway costs. Your committee is not prepared to recommend any fixed percentage of total highway expenditures as the proper percentage to be financed by special taxation of motor vehicles. The different stages of highway development reached by different states, the difference in the relative burden of highway finance in different regions, because of differences in the density of population, in per capita mileage of roads, in climatic conditions, in availability of highway building materials, in per capita ownership of automobiles, make different distributions of the burden politically inevitable and probably also theoretically equitable, and no one formula will best suit the needs of all the states. But for all states, except those at the very inception of their program of improved highway construction, special taxes on highway users should be sufficient to defray a substantial part of the costs of construction and of interest on highway indebtedness, as well as all of the maintenance costs of primary highways. The tendency in highway finance is strongly in the direction of placing on highway users an increasing proportion of the burden of highway finance. We approve of this tendency, not only as an inevitable resultant of the pressure of facts, but as thoroughly consistent with equity and with expediency.

Roads of a purely local interest, serving only local needs, should be financed out of local revenues, obtained either from local general tax revenues or from special assessments on adjoining land. When such local roads, however, are improved and absorbed into the state highway system and lose their purely local character, they should be financed out of state funds, derived mainly from motor vehicle taxes. Special assessments ordinarily have no place in the financing of primary roads. They should be used in connection with the financing of local roads, only to meet part of the construction cost and the amount of the assessment should never be greater than the increase in the market value of the adjoining land which would unmistakably and immediately result from the improvement.

We do not regard as within the scope of our task a consideration of the problem of the financing of city streets.

Special motor vehicle taxes for highway purposes represent a return to the principle that those who derive direct benefit from government services should contribute to the cost of such services, in proportion to their benefit therefrom. Some modern writers on public finance have largely thrown this principle overboard, and find little or no proper scope for its application beyond its limited use in the levy of fees and special assessments. The trend of taxation practice for other than highway activities has during the last few generations also been decidedly away from the benefit principle and toward the principle that government services should be made freely available to all and should be financed by taxation according to ability. The field of highway finance presents almost the only instance — if not actually the only one — in modern American financial history, of the sharp reversal of the trend from benefit taxes to ability taxes. Is this reversal of the trend justified? If so, has it gone too far or should it go still further?

The abandonment of the benefit principle was due in the main to the influence of the modern concept of the social solidarity of the people, which appeared to justify the policy of requiring the more prosperous classes to pay the cost of services which the poorer classes would in large part enjoy. Under the influence of popular pressure, governments extended their functions so as to include new types of activities, expensive to finance and many of them distinctly serving the masses of the people rather than the wealthier classes. The poor could not afford to meet the cost of these new activities, without making serious sacrifices. The main objects and results of the shift from the benefit to the ability principle were, therefore, (1) to enable the government to provide for the masses, services whose costs the latter could not or would not directly defray, and (2) to shift the burden of financially supporting the more general activities of government from the population as a whole to the relatively wealthy classes.

To the extent that the great rise in highway expenditures has been incurred on behalf of the non-industrial automobile use of roads, the ordinary argument for the application of the ability principle fails altogether to apply. There is not any problem here of making a government service freely available to the poorer classes, who otherwise could not afford to avail themselves thereof. The really powerful arguments against the benefit principle of taxation, namely, that it shifts burdens to those who are not able to bear them and that it therefore makes impossible the financing of such government activities as are predominantly for the direct benefit of the masses, have, therefore, a narrowly limited applicability to this phase of the modern problem of the financing of automobile highways.

In the case of commercial and industrial automobile use of highways, the situation is not essentially different. The benefits of the improved primary highways accrue immediately to the automobile owners, in the form of lower transportation costs, and will in general be passed on to consumers in the form of lower prices or else will be absorbed as extra profits by the producers or the owners of productive property. To the extent that the general public shares in the benefits of cheaper transportation, special taxation of highway users will be passed on to them. In the last analysis, owners of industrial automobiles will shift any special automobile taxes imposed on them who derive the economic benefit from the highway improvements.

There can be no reasonable ground for doubt that the direct benefits from highway improvements go in the first instance to the automobile owners or to those who are directly served by automobile transportation. These are not, of course, the sole beneficiaries of the highways, but they are by far the chief ones. That there are secondary benefits from the use of highways, which accrue to others than those immediately served by highway transportation, is not a valid objection to the financing of highways on the benefit principle. No one would contend, because there are secondary benefits from the existence of a suitable water supply, which accrue to others than those who actually make use of the water service, that it is unfair to finance a municipal waterworks by special charges on those who are directly served by it. If any municipality ever departs from the benefit principle in financing its waterworks, it is not because of the existence of indirect and secondary benefits to the general community from the water system, important as these are, but to relieve the poorer classes of the necessity of meeting the cost of the direct benefits accruing to them. Where electric or steam railroads are operated by the state, it has not been generally regarded as inequitable to the direct users of these public works, that the special charges to users should be sufficient to finance the enterprises. But there are indirect and secondary benefits accruing to others than the direct users, in the case of railroad transportation, as much as in the case of highway transportation.

Were the issue in the case of highway finance really between the ability principle and the benefit principle, it would not much matter, in so far as the equitable distribution of the burden of highway costs was concerned, which method was chosen, since either method would, in the ultimate analysis, probably result in about the same distribution of taxes. But the real alternative in state and local highway finance in the United States is between the benefit principle and the general property tax. It has been repeatedly disclosed by careful investigators that the general property tax works out in practice at a higher rate on small parcels of property than on large. A large fraction of the property tax on improved real estate and on personal property, moreover, is unquestionably shifted by the first taxpayer to the masses of the population, in the form of higher house rents and higher prices for commodities and services. It is altogether probable that with the existing distribution of ownership of automobiles, the financing of primary highways by special taxes on highway-users will conform more closely to the ability principle than will the resort to the general tax revenues of state and local governments for highway funds.

The argument from expediency also justifies the resort to automobile taxation as a means of financing highways. In most of the American commonwealths the existing revenue systems are already strained to the utmost to meet the calls for revenue from the expanding programs of government activity. The tax burdens on real estate and on the farmers in general are already as great as they can reasonably be expected to be able to bear. The great need in state and local finance is the discovery and adoption of means to lighten the tax load on the overburdened classes. To finance highway expenditures out of general revenues means in practice to finance them by additional taxes on tangible property, real and personal. Under existing conditions it is much more equitable to place the burden of highway finance on those who use the highways in proportion to their use, rather than on property owners, irrespective of their use of the highways.

The payment by highway users of all maintenance costs of primary highways and of a substantial portion of construction costs and interest on indebtedness incurred in the construction of primary highways is well within the limits of their reasonable capacity. The motor vehicle registrations in 1923 in the United States totalled 15,092,000 and will undoubtedly pass the 17,000,000 mark in 1924. Although primary highways now comprise not more than ten per cent of the total road mileage of the country and probably will not exceed for a long time twenty per cent of the total mileage, they account for eighty-five to ninety per cent of the total highway costs. The average levy per automobile, which would pay all maintenance and interest costs and would provide a generous fund for amortization of construction costs of primary roads would not greatly exceed the average special tax burden per automobile now imposed. The annual registration of automobiles is increasing more rapidly than the annual highway expenditures, so that the average levy per automobile which would be necessary to finance all the highway costs, for *secondary* as well as primary roads, is progressively diminishing. If the expenditures of automobilists on the upkeep of their cars, on gasoline, and on garage hire be considered, it is not unreasonable to hold that an annual levy, adequate fully to meet the program laid down in this report, would not be beyond their ability to pay and would not exert an appreciable adverse influence on the rate of development of automobile transportation. While your committee does not recommend that the cost of purely local roads should be met by special motor-vehicle taxation and while it does not regard it as immediately practicable that even all primary road costs should be financed by motor-vehicle taxes, it regards with approval what appears to be a tendency in this direction and welcomes progress toward that goal, especially for states and counties which have completed or are approaching the completion of the construction of their primary system of improved highways.

The resolution of the National Tax Association authorizing the appointment of this committee, instructed it to consider the question of "the coördination of the taxation of transportation agencies using highways with other transportation agencies." Motor transportation, whether of passengers or of freight, and whether as a common carrier, for hire, or for personal use, is not wholly competitive with other modes of transportation, but is, to an important and growing extent, complementary to them; but even where it is essentially complementary, the sound method of determining where one shall begin and the other shall end is through the free play of supply and demand, after each type has met all the costs properly attributable to it. If any type is permitted to escape meeting any of the costs with which it can properly be charged, the result is an artificial stimulation of the favored type, which leads to its expansion beyond its natural economic limits and is unfair to competing methods of transportation and to the general taxpayer. If the program of highway finance laid down in this report were executed, your committe is of the opinion that all justification would be removed for charges against motor transportation that it is being subsidized in its competition with other transportation agencies.

APPORTIONMENT OF HIGHWAY COSTS BETWEEN FEDERAL, STATE AND LOCAL GOVERNMENTS

OUR report has already urged the importance of centralized control over the planning, construction and maintenance of primary roads. But under the American type of political organization, no great measure of centralization of financial control is feasible, unless it is accompanied by the assumption on the part of the central authority of a substantial measure of responsibility for financing the activity in question. Except through centralized financing, moreover, it is impossible to apportion the costs of a coördinated highway system, in even rough accordance with the territorial distribution of benefits from highways or with the territorial distribution of ability to pay.

Federal aid to highways has been valuable under these circumstances. By its highway grants the Federal Government has secured the opportunity of giving advice, of laying down minimum engineering standards of construction and maintenance, of assuring the development of a nationally coördinated highway system, and also of lightening the burden for those states of sparse population and long distances, which are crossed by important national automobile routes, but which could not reasonably be expected to meet the full cost thereof from state and local revenues. It is important that federal aid should never be given, without conditions being attached which will assure their proper utilization, but the administration of federal highway aid by the federal bureau of public roads, under the able direction of Mr. Thomas H. Macdonald has been of a highly satisfactory character and is entitled to the commendation of all who are interested in the full and scientific development of the American highway system.

The Federal Government has collected in special taxes on motor vehicles and parts, to June 30, 1923, a total of $589,-012,000, but during the same period has spent on highway aid to the states and on forest roads, including administrative expenses, a total of $264,782,000, or only forty-five per cent of the receipts from motor vehicle taxes.* Your committee recommends that the Federal Government should derive the revenues which it devotes to highways from the special taxation of highway users, Mr. Brosseau, [a member of the committee], however, dissenting. These federal taxes should, if possible,

* Eds. note : For later data see National Industrial Conference Board, *Federal Finances, 1923-1932*, pp. 25-43.

take some form other than an ad valorem tax. To the extent that its aid is granted to projects constructed primarily to serve the purpose of national defense or to open backward regions to colonization, the Federal Government would be justified in using funds derived from general tax revenues. But the Federal Government should not levy taxes on motor vehicles as such in excess of what it spends on highways. The reduction in the taxes on motor vehicles and on motor vehicle parts effected by the Revenue Act of 1924 meets, therefore, with our approval. We recommend the total elimination of the remaining federal excise taxes on motor vehicle parts.

Similar considerations to those discussed above, in connection with the relation between federal and state highway finance, apply with even greater force to the relation between the states and the political subdivisions.[2]

The counties, and even more so, the smaller political subdivisions, are no longer proper units of highway finance, so far as the financing of primary roads is concerned. Dependence on local revenues for a substantial portion of the cost of primary highways means either gaps in the highway system, because some localities are laggard in making financial provision for improved highways, or the overburdening of some localities with excessive taxes or debts. Local financing of primary roads inevitably results in serious territorial inequalities in tax burden, because of varying relations of mileage and local traffic population and per capita wealth. Where the state develops main highways, through the linking up at its own cost of local roads, localities which had been backward in improving their roads escape their due share of the cost and localities which had shown more than the average degree of enterprise in constructing improved highways bear an undue share of the cost. In those instances where the finances of local governments have become seriously involved, as a result of highway expenditures, it has usually been because they have assumed a disproportionate share of the burden of financing the primary highway system and have not received adequate aid from the state. The problem of highway finance, however, is becoming less serious for the local political units. The states are rapidly increasing the amount of highway aid which they grant to the localities. The construction and improvement of highways generally operate to raise the economic status of districts hitherto backward, because of their lack of advanced means of transportation. Government studies have shown that

[2] With the exception, perhaps, of cities, whose street finance problems do not come within the range of this report.

the improvement of main roads tends to lessen the volume of traffic on local roads and thus reduces the maintenance burden falling on the local governments.

For purposes of highway finance, roads should be classified as local and primary highways, according to whether they serve purely local needs or the needs of wider areas. Local roads should alone be financed by the locality, whereas primary roads, serving a wider area, should be financed by the state. The principle here is sound in theory but is difficult of application. As the extension and improvement of the highway system progresses, it approaches ever more closely to being a unified whole, requiring control and financing on that basis. It is desirable, therefore, and it becomes more urgent with every expansion of the highway system, that highway costs be met as far as possible from state revenues, derived from state taxes, uniformly levied throughout the state. It is impossible to render exact justice as between the different localities, but the nearest approximation thereto can be made, especially as between, on the one hand, sparsely settled or poor rural districts, through which run expensive primary highways, and on the other hand, the urban centers, which provide much of the traffic for these highways, if the state government assumes the entire burden of financing primary highways, leaving to the counties the financing out of local tax revenues of local roads not constructed or maintained in condition to be satisfactory for through motor traffic or used solely, or almost so, by traffic originating and terminating within the immediate locality.

Where the state provides all or part of the funds for financing the primary highway system but the actual expenditures are made by the local governments, careful consideration should be given to the mode of apportionment of the state aid to the local governments. As in the case of federal aid, conditions should always be attached to the grants, to assure that the expenditure will be made in the manner best designed to carry out the state highway program. Apportionment of state funds to the localities, according to a rigid and arbitrary formula, whether it be in proportion to population, road mileage, area, local highway expenditures, or equally to counties, all of which methods have been used, either singly or in combination with others, by one or more states, is bound to operate unsatisfactorily, for no one formula, no matter how carefully devised, can make adequate provision for the varying needs of different localities. A number of states fix the method by which apportionments shall be made by a special legislative act for each apportionment. This is preferable to the fixed-rule method, but is open to the objection that it leads to political log-rolling and unscientific allocation of the funds. At least twelve states leave the apportionment of the funds to the state highway officials, subject to such broad limitations as the legislatures deem essential. Your committee recommends this last method as the one best designed to secure a scientific and equitable apportionment of state funds.

MOTOR VEHICLE TAXES

ALL of the states levy registration taxes on motor vehicles and some three-quarters of the states levy gasoline taxes in addition. There is no uniformity between the states, either as to the bases for determining the taxes or as to the rates of tax. The states base their registration taxes on value, cubic-inch displacement, weight, gross weight, or horse power, or on a combination of two of these. One state levies a flat license fee, uniform for all motor vehicles. One state levies a registration tax based on value, weight, horsepower, and previous number of registrations. Where horse power or weight is used as the basis, some states levy a flat-rate tax per unit of base; other states make the rate per unit rise progressively as the base rises; a few states make the rate per unit fall as the base rises. Some states levy heavier rates on automobiles with solid tires than on automobiles with pneumatic tires; other states do not. The gasoline tax rates vary from one cent per gallon to four cents per gallon. Some states tax all gasoline, whether used to propel motor vehicles on the highways or not; other states make varying exemptions for gasoline consumed otherwise than as motor vehicle fuel. Whether gasoline taxes are levied or not does not always appear to influence the rates of the registration taxes levied on automobiles. ‡

If only one motor vehicle tax were to be levied, the gasoline tax would appear to be preferable to the registration tax. The factors of most importance in estimating the costs accruing to the state from automobile traffic are the mileage traveled, the gross weight of the vehicle and the speed at which it is driven, and the amount of fuel consumed reflects in some measure all of these factors. The gasoline tax is conveniently paid, easily collected and easily administered. It is the only practicable mode of reaching highway users from other states than that levying the tax. Even where the tax is opposed at first by motorists it wins their approval, or at least their

‡ Eds. note: For later data see C. H. Sandage and R. W. Nelson, *Motor Vehicle Taxation for Highway Purposes*, (University of Iowa Study), 1932, especially pp. 25-27, 58-59.

toleration, after it has been in effect for some time and they have grown accustomed to it. There is a marked tendency toward general adoption of the tax and toward a two-cent or a three-cent, rather than a one-cent rate. The yield of the tax has been moderate so far, but with the increases in rates recently introduced and the adoption of the tax by more of the states, it has been estimated that it will yield over $50,000,-000, in 1924, as compared to approximately $30,000,000 in 1923, and $12,700,000 in 1922. A three-cent tax on all the gasoline consumed in the United States by automobiles would net at least $150,000,000. §

Registration taxes appear to be necessary, even where gasoline taxes are in effect, in connection with the regulation of motor vehicle ownership and operation. They also are useful, because they can be devised to take more fully into account the influence of weight of car, weight of load and type of tire on highway wear and tear, than does fuel consumption. A further factor in favor of the levy of registration taxes, even when gasoline taxes are levied, is that highways in general are constructed on a scale sufficient to accommodate the peak load of traffic and an automobile which is in the garage most of the year, and therefore consumes little gasoline, but is operated on the highways when traffic is at its peak, escapes its due share of taxes if it is taxed only on its gasoline consumption. A greater measure of uniformity between the states in the bases used for levying registration taxes is, however, highly desirable. Gross weight, by which is meant the weight of the vehicle loaded with a standard load, is the best, as it is the simplest base. Where weight or gross weight is used as the basis of taxation, your committee recommends that the rate of tax, per unit of weight, should be graded upwards as weight increases, the gradation of rates to be determined on the basis of engineers' tests of the comparative wear and tear on the roads and use of road space per ton of the different weight vehicles. Since the primary purpose of motor vehicle taxation now is to make the highway user meet in whole or in part the cost of the construction and maintenance of automobile highways, there is no justification for registration taxes which take into account the value of the vehicle, such as ad valorem taxes, taxes which make allowance for the depreciation of the vehicle, or horsepower taxes, intended to reflect the value of the vehicle. Even though there may be some relation between value of the vehicle and wear and tear on the roads, the latter can be better

§ Eds. note : For recent data on this point see Sandage and Nelson, *op. cit.*, pp. 24-33.

taken into account by other means than through taxation on the basis of value or some index of value. It is not reasonable to ask that the rates of tax, whether for gasoline taxes or for registration taxes, should be uniform as between the states, since the different financial requirements for highway purposes of the different states justify different rates of taxation. It is recommended, however, that each state, before fixing its rates of taxation, should survey the financial requirement for highway construction, interest on highway indebtedness and highway maintenance (including its grants in aid to the counties and after allowance for what is to be received as federal highway aid), should determine what proportion of its highway expenditures is to be met by motor vehicle taxation and should adjust the rates accordingly. It is also recommended that the counties levy no charges in connection with chauffeurs' or operators' licenses and that the states levy no such charges, other than very moderate license fees not exceeding $1 each.

The levy of ad valorem rates on automobiles as personal property under the general property tax is not considered to be a special tax on motor vehicles or to have any direct relation with the problem of highway finance, and is therefore not regarded as falling within the scope of our report. Where motor vehicle registration taxes are levied in lieu of personal property taxes, only such parts of the registration tax revenues are to be regarded as special taxes on highway users as are in excess of the amounts which automobiles would pay under the personal property tax, if they were not exempt therefrom.

There is no uniformity in usage as between the states in the disposal of revenues from special taxes on motor vehicles. In most of the states they are used solely or mainly for highway purposes, but in some states important fractions thereof are diverted to other than highway purposes. Some states segregate their motor vehicle tax funds for construction purposes, others for the payment of interest on and the amortization of highway indebtedness, others for road maintenance expenses, and still others reserve them for highway purposes in general, without further statutory specification. Many states distribute the proceeds of the motor vehicle taxes in part to the counties; other states reserve them wholly for their own use.

Your committee recommends that each state determine what proportion of its highway expenditures it proposes to finance from the proceeds of special taxes on motor vehicles and that it do not levy taxes on motor vehicles in excess of the rates necessary to produce such amounts of revenue, and it further recommends that in no instance shall the special taxes on motor vehicles exceed in amount the total highway expenditures of the state, after deduction of the amounts received as federal highway aid, but including the amounts distributed to the counties for highway purposes. Your committee cannot recommend, however, the rigid segregation by statute of the proceeds of motor vehicle taxes for use solely for highway purposes. Segregated treasury funds increase the interest expense of the government, by cutting down the supply of available cash. It is important for the economical administration of state funds, that special funds be eliminated entirely and that all receipts be placed in one general account. The proper balancing of highway expenditures and motor vehicle tax revenues should be provided for in the preparation of the state budgets rather than by rigid statutory requirements.

3. INTERNATIONAL AND INTERSTATE ASPECTS OF DOUBLE TAXATION *

THE movement inaugurated by the League of Nations at the suggestion of the International Chamber of Commerce to foster and encourage international agreements designed to prevent, or, at least, minimize, double taxation, has been going on for eight or nine years. Professor Seligman . . . participated with Sir Josiah Stamp and a group of other international economists in a report made in 1923, as I recall, which attempted to lay down what might be called the theoretical principles of the subject. Thereafter the matter was turned over to a group of so-called government experts, and for five or six years since that time they have been having conferences on the subject. The League of Nations has recently created a permanent Fiscal Committee on this subject designed in general to encourage the adoption of these international agreements, to work out some of the more difficult technical questions which arise in connection with this movement, and, perhaps, if requested by the interested parties, to decide disputes arising in the interpretation of agreements actually made.

The interesting fact about the present situation, as I see it, is that the movement is reaching a stage of practical fruition.

There have been concluded, I should say, at the present time about twenty of these broad bilateral conventions between pairs of nations, looking to the elimination of double taxation, particularly in the field of income taxation, but in some cases extending into the field of direct property and capital taxes. In addition, there have been adopted a considerable number

* From T. S. Adams, "International and Interstate Aspects of Double Taxation," *Proceedings of the National Tax Association,* (1929), pp. 193-198.

of more restricted agreements, covering disputed points in income or property taxation, or providing for administrative coöperation. In other words, the practical movement is gathering headway and momentum, and unless I am mistaken the time is not far distant — I should say in six or eight years — when tax-wise Europe will be covered with a network of these bilateral conventions, under which the business men of the contracting nations will be virtually free from the irritation and burden of double taxation. That, I think, is plainly written on the wall.

The United States has not concluded any broad or general reciprocal agreement. Under our existing federal law we possibly could not conclude such agreements. Whether such agreements could, theoretically, be concluded by our treaty-making powers is a nice question of constitutional law; but whatever may be the answer of the theoretical lawyer to that question, we probably shall not conclude agreements of that kind in practice without some additional legislative sanction or authorization. And this consideration brings us to one of the practical aspects of the subject under discussion. At the next session of Congress amendatory legislation authorizing the executive officers of the government to conclude arrangements of this kind will, I hope, be introduced. I hope further that those of you who are in position to assist this legislation will after examination become convinced of its wisdom and its helpfulness, and do what you can to secure its adoption. It will enable the business men of this country to compete on somewhat fairer terms with the business men of those foreign countries which have the benefit of conventions or treaties of this kind protecting them from the burdens of international double taxation.

One of the other practical achievements of this movement has been the adoption of reciprocal arrangements between the great maritime nations of the world, by which the shipping industry is freed from double taxation.

The taxation of a foreign shipping company under a national income-tax law is a particularly difficult thing, as will appear if you stop to think of the problem presented. A tramp steamer comes from abroad and stopping, perhaps only a few days, takes a lucrative cargo from New York, and moves off, perhaps not touching again at the port for eighteen months or more. The allocation of shipping profits to particular ports is intrinsically difficult. After the war the difficulties presented were unusually great. By a fortunate movement originating on the part of the United States, the proposal was virtually made to the world that this country would release or exempt the ships of other countries if they took the same attitude towards our own vessels. That reciprocal proposal has been virtually accepted by all the great maritime nations of the world; and today the shipping industry is practically freed from the evil of international double taxation. I have no doubt that the industry of air transport will in a short time have the benefit of this same reciprocal exemption, and that this new industry will grow up without ever having been subjected to the burden of double taxation.

I want to speak a word now about the technique of this subject, the machinery adopted to achieve the end of preventing or reducing double taxation. The work of the governmental experts conducted under the auspices of the League of Nations, up to the present time, has been largely confined to the formulation of what might be called model treaties. They have been attempting to formulate a series of draft conventions or model treaties suitable for adoption by pairs of countries which desire to get rid of double taxation. In other words, the device which has been adopted to correct this evil is what is known in the chatter of the diplomatist as the bilateral convention. I think there are elements of danger in this device or mechanism of solution. The agreement will usually be between two nations. They are to adopt for themselves and for their residents or nationals only, methods of solution by which double taxation can be averted.

Now, in the long run, whatever solutions are adopted by different pairs of nations, it is probable that Nation A in concluding a bilateral convention with Nation B will adopt some solution different from that which it might adopt in a similar treaty with Nation X. And if this piece-meal bargaining goes on for twenty years or more, as it is likely to go on, it may possibly result in a tangle of conflicting solutions applicable to the nationals of different countries, which will be highly complicated and highly mysterious, and about as bad as the situation that now exists. In short there is in my mind, looking to the longer future, the strongest reason for the adoption of one uniform solution, if we could get it, or the settlement of this problem by a multilateral convention, in which a large group of nations would adopt the same solutions for the detailed problems which have to be settled.

Here I may note one of the results of the experience of the governmental experts in drawing up these model conventions

or treaties which impresses me as both interesting and significant. The experts who have formulated these conventions
are, except for the American representative, government officials, in most cases the heads of the tax systems of the several
countries. . . These experts have guarded zealously the rights
and interests of the nations which they represented. They
have preferred and fought for solutions which would benefit
their own countries, making minor compromises and concessions from time to time.

In the field of income taxation, for instance, there have been
worked out three separate solutions. In other words, three
model treaties are recommended adapted to countries with different interests and different forms of taxation. Now, here is
the point which interests me profoundly : on practically every
subject except the taxation of bond interest and dividends
from shares, they have come to a virtual unanimity of opinion.
Income arises in hundreds of forms ; compensation for personal
service ; rent of all types ; interest of all kinds ; annuities ; royalties ; pensions ; gains and profits from hundreds of distinct
trades, professions and businesses. The treatment of all these
classes of income has been discussed and debated at length,
from the standpoints of a score of different countries with
divergent interests and different methods of administering the
income tax. And as I have said, the experts have ended by
endorsing three model conventions which in form and appearance are very different. But in substance they differ,
practically, on nothing except the taxation of income from
transferable securities. This agreement has been reached unconsciously almost. As a matter of fact, many of the experts
did not realize, until it was pointed out to them, that these
three treaties, representing the main types of solution for these
problems, were substantially similar except for the treatment of
income from transferable securities.

I gather from this experience that it is entirely practicable
for the great nations of the world to get together and adopt a
uniform multilateral treaty by which double taxation could
be eliminated, except for these items of bond interest and
dividends. But this experience suggests something more. It
indicates, I believe, that if a similar movement were put under
way in the United States, the evil of double and multiple taxation in the field of income taxation could be averted. State
income taxation, in this country, is in the stage of development.
Double taxation in this field is not now a grave evil. But it
will spread as state income taxes multiply unless the states
coöperate in a way which they have never tried in the past.

European experience here is reassuring. It suggests that the technical problems involved are susceptible of a common or uniform solution.   In short, if able and zealous representatives of the various states got together, mindful of the economic interests of their own commonwealths — selfish, if you want to put it that way — and if they stayed with their problem long enough, the chances are that there would happen to that group of Americans exactly what is happening to the representatives of the great European nations of the world after six or eight years of conference; in short, that they would, except upon one or two items relating primarily to stocks and bonds, come to something approaching a unanimity of decision and treatment.

It would be an appropriate and helpful thing for this Association to do for the American states what the League of Nations has done for the European states, *i.e.,* promote a movement to eliminate or prevent double taxation by calling together representatives of the several states for the purpose of drafting a uniform law or a reciprocal agreement or both for the prevention of double income taxation.   This would do more than restrict, or tend to restrict, double imposition in the field of income taxation.   It would bring about in the end a broader and keener understanding of the necessity for equity and fairness and legislative restraint in the imposition of taxes. We talk about equity and fairness in taxation.   Any man who has mixed in taxation widely knows that it is a unique experience to get on the part of legislative bodies a full and open and whole-hearted recognition of the equities involved.   Politics plays its part, partly a proper part and partly an improper part. The taxpayer has something to seek and get, partly proper and partly improper.   The administrative authority has his bias. He seldom is as disinterested as he thinks he is.   Equity goes by the board, largely because it is lost sight of.   It gets lost in the shuffle.

Now, according to my experience, there is no means or instrument by which to get recognition of the equitable, disinterested, scientific point of view in taxation as potent as this argument based on the desirability of eliminating double taxation.   There is something in the legislative mind which recognizes that if one taxpayer is being taxed twice while the majority of men similarly situated are being taxed only once, by the same tax, something wrong or inequitable is being done which, other things being equal, the legislator should correct if he can. In my experience with legislative bodies I have found that you can accomplish more for equity and justice in taxation in the name of eliminating or preventing double taxation, than with any other slogan or appeal.

Another fact is worth noting, which the European experience has brought to light. Much double taxation is caused not by unfair treatment of the foreigner, but by unfair and thoughtless treatment of the citizen by his own state or country. More double taxation of the unjust variety is inflicted upon the taxpayer by his own government than by foreign governments. This is true both theoretically and practically. More relief from double taxation can be given to your own nationals than you can give to aliens.

The explanation is simple. Every state insists upon taxing the non-resident alien who derives income from sources within that country, and rightly so, at least inevitably so. Now, then, in due course of time, citizens of the home state inevitably invest abroad and derive income from foreign sources. The average state refuses to acknowledge in this situation the right of its own citizen to a proper exemption on income derived from foreign sources. It insists upon taxing income at source or at origin when earned by the non-resident or the foreigner. It adopts this attitude as a principle. But it refuses to recognize when one of its own citizens or nationals gets income from a foreign source that he inevitably will be taxed abroad. As a necessary corollary of the principle of taxing at source or origin which it has adopted, the home state owes an exemption of some kind to its own citizen or resident who derives income from a foreign source or sources.

In the midst of the war, when the financial burden upon the United States was greater than it had ever been, I proposed to the Congress that we should recognize the equities which I have just noted, by including in the federal income tax the so-called credit for foreign taxes paid, by which an American deriving income from a foreign source and taxed thereon could credit the foreign tax against the American tax dollar for dollar with due safeguards which prevented the abuse of that privilege. I had no notion . . . when I proposed it, that it would ever receive serious consideration. I expected it to be turned down with the reply which I have received so often from legislative committees: "Oh, yes, Doctor, that is pretty good, but the finances won't permit it." But to my surprise, the credit for foreign taxes was accepted and approved, because it touched the equitable chord or sense, and because double taxation under the heavy war rates might not only cause injustice but the actual bankruptcy of the taxpayer.

Equity in taxation is not always clear and plain. I see my

own equities through a telescope, but the other fellow's equities through a microscope. This is true of me and you as well as the legislator. But the worst forms of double taxation are clearly and plainly inequitable. They constitute the opening wedge and by driving them home continuously into the consciousness of legislative bodies, a very great deal can be accomplished to put our tax systems on a fairer and more appealing basis.

The subject of double taxation is rather prosaic. It is not dramatic or thrilling, and I shall not try to endow it with a fictitious interest. I leave the subject with you then with this one moral:

The European movement to eliminate double taxation has reached the practical stage. It is getting results in and for Europe. It is expedient, apart from other considerations, for the United States to find an acceptable and unobjectionable way of getting into the European game. To do so will require additional federal legislation.

4. Separation of State and Local Revenues *

The history of American state finance in the last thirty years reveals two major movements, one against excessive uniformity, the other against excessive decentralization. It has been found on the one hand that a uniform rate of taxation cannot successfully be applied to all forms of property, and we have the irresistible movement for classification of taxes. It has been found on the other hand that inter-community enterprises or property cannot successfully be taxed by local officials, and we have the inevitable movement towards central assessment and the emergence of the state tax commission.

Surveying these movements, many students of taxation have essayed to project them into the future — always a necessary but a difficult and dangerous thing to do. These prognosticators have evolved as their ideal the separation of the sources of state and local revenues, which Professor Seligman would extend to cover the federal as well as the field of commonwealth finance. The tax whose base is broad is to be given to the superior jurisdiction; the tax whose base is narrow is to be used exclusively by the local jurisdictions. Concretely, in state

* Adapted from T. S. Adams, "Separation of State and Local Revenues," *Annals of the American Academy of Political and Social Science*, Vol. LVIII, (March, 1915), pp. 131-137.

Eds. note: In spite of the fact that Professor Adams' factual data are now out of date, the political and economic wisdom of his article justifies its reproduction here. See bibliographical note at end of this chapter for more recent references.

finance the central government is to take over the tax on insurance companies, on railroads and similar enterprises carried on in all or nearly all parts of the state.   The local governments are to be given for their exclusive use the general
property tax, with an indefinite measure of home rule, so that
they may abolish or modify the tax on personal property.   The
proposition apparently is that no tax shall be used in common
but shall belong exclusively to the jurisdiction to which it has
been assigned.

Much of this program is obviously sound and in strict accord
with fundamental tendencies, the reality of which cannot be
questioned.   The only difficulty is to determine its proper
limits.   Some seven years ago at the first meeting of the National Tax Association [1] the writer suggested that this program,
as it was then generally formulated, was extreme, and likely to
result in as much harm as good, if not carefully guarded.   And
events since that time have apparently warranted the position
then taken.   Professor Seligman, for instance, a few years ago,
expressed his approval of "a separation of state and local taxation, with local option on the part of the localities to tax or
to exempt from taxation whatever classes of property they saw
fit." [2]   At the present time Professor Seligman approves of only
a very narrow measure of home rule.   Other advocates, who a
few years ago endorsed the whole program of separation without modification, now suggest the retention of at least a small
state tax on general property in order to avoid the danger of
extravagance, which unquestionably accompanies the program.
The chief danger, however, lies in the possibility that the reaction against the iron rule of uniformity under which most
states have labored in the past, may prove excessive and extreme.   The principal error of the "separatists," as the writer
views it, lies in the proposal or implication utterly to divorce
state and local tax jurisdictions.

That there is justice in the demand for some measure of local
fiscal freedom, I would be the last to deny.   It is now generally
recognized that no tax is fit to be applied to all kinds of property and business.   By the same token no tax is fit to be applied
to all of the diverse territorial districts of the same state.   In
the average American commonwealth today we have every
variety of social life from the city slum to the frontier.   This is
true even in some of the original thirteen states.   We must
have territorial classification for the same reason that we must

1 *State and Local Taxation, First National Conference under the Auspices of
the National Tax Association*, [1907], vol. i, p. 514.
2 *Political Science Quarterly*, vol. xxii, pp. 312-313.

classify the subjects of taxation. One way to establish such territorial classification is by carefully limited local home rule under such regulation that it cannot be abused. Thus the local governments could not safely be given the right to impose new taxes on business as they see fit. Business is now divided among so many jurisdictions that to give each the right to devise new methods of taxing it is merely to invite double and multiple taxation. But the various local districts might safely be given the right to exempt specified classes of personal property and even to select from a small number of specified local taxes, set aside for their potential use by the state legislature.

But the element of centralization is just as essential as the element of local autonomy, and much more necessary at the present time. This is particularly true with respect to tax administration. In no domain of public administration are distance, removal from local pressure and local political intrigue, so important as in tax administration. The strength of the assessor is as much increased by outside protection and control as it is weakened by lack of local knowledge. In short, we must have a mixture of local and central control in tax administration.

Many advocates of separation find their ideal in the present divorce of federal from state taxation. Federal taxation has its elements of strength because of this very divorce, but it has its elements of weakness as well, arising from the same origin; and federal taxation would be stronger if it were linked up more closely with state taxation. The administration of the federal inheritance tax during the Spanish War was woefully weak in many respects. Many estates subject to the tax escaped because of the lack of local knowledge. Merely to enforce a federal inheritance tax properly would require the federal government to duplicate administrative machinery which the state governments already possess. On the other hand, at the present time state inheritance taxation is suffering greatly from the lack of control by a superior and higher jurisdiction. All this illustrates the principal truth which it is desired to emphasize here, that the ideal is not separation but joint administration and control; that we could not divorce state and local taxation even if we tried, and we ought not even if we could. The central administration needs local knowledge. The local administration needs backing and control from the central body. Any other plan involves duplication of machinery and excessive cost of administration.

Let me illustrate: There is a widespread notion that the federal government controls interstate commerce and many court decisions have been rendered, which apparently prevent the state governments from taxing the earnings of interstate commerce. But the property of going business concerns, and its earnings, are inseparable. The same property to a successful business concern is worth more than to an unsuccessful business concern, and the state governments taking advantage of this truth have so imposed and defined their property taxes as to touch and tax earnings from interstate commerce. Again a state income tax on earnings derived from interstate commerce might be unconstitutional. But I do not see, under the rulings of the federal courts, how the states could be prevented from using an excise tax or something akin thereto, measured by or with respect to earnings derived from interstate commerce. The proposition of exclusive jurisdiction fails. Joint and harmonious control is the only true solution.

Moreover, it may be denied in the most emphatic way that it is necessarily a bad thing for two jurisdictions to use the same tax. If the tax is already high, it may be unwise for another jurisdiction to clap on a sur-tax. And there are other circumstances in which it would be palpably unwise for two jurisdictions to use the same tax. But just as frequently it is a good thing for two branches of government to use the same basis of taxation. Local criticism helps the central authority to be efficient, and central criticism helps the local administrator to be effective. This is particularly true of the income tax. Central control is needed to prevent double taxation and to protect the fearless assessor; local knowledge is absolutely indispensable to prevent evasion. The federal income tax would be stronger if every state in the union had a state income tax, provided of course that the two administrations worked in harmony and that the aggregate rate were not excessive. The development of the income tax in Europe plainly proves this point. And anyone who has administered an income tax must realize its truth regardless of historical or practical confirmation.

The same is true of the taxation of real estate. Many large manufacturing plants are located in small villages which cannot afford to employ an assessor expert enough to value such property. The cheap way is to have a corps of expert assessors for the whole state. Here are two low grade iron mines side by side. The operating company in the one case has valuable connections with iron furnaces and large consumers and because of this fact it can operate the mine at a profit. The other company has no such connections and cannot mine its ore profitably. How are the two mines to be assessed; and what local assessor is fitted to handle such difficult cases? Again

in some thinly settled districts there are mines or large manufacturing plants the taxation of which frequently supplies more
money than the local district can utilize wisely. All these
things call for intimate linking up of the central and local
jurisdictions.

In the writer's opinion it is idle and academic — in the worst
sense — to say that we can have general or central supervision
over local taxes without the central jurisdiction making active
use of the same basis of taxation. Theoretically, yes — practically, no. What local government in the United States would
brook continual control and supervision by a state body which
had no vital or real interest in the taxes and assessments concerned? On the other hand, what American legislature would
make the appropriations necessary to maintain an effective
central commission unless that commission were actively engaged in supervising assessments which the state government
itself was to utilize?

The same line of thought applies to the "state equalization."
Much fun has been poked at this in the past, because in most
places the state equalization was made by an *ex officio* board
which had no serious interest in, and no real knowledge of, the
work it was called upon to perform. But just as soon as the
state equalization is undertaken seriously it becomes the opening wedge of tax reform. In a large number of states in which
the greatest improvement in tax administration has been made
in the last five years, the necessity of making a state equalization has proved the beginning of tax reform. The knowledge
acquired in this work is exceedingly valuable to local officials
and frequently can be obtained in no other way.

Both the state and local governments need to use the same
basis of taxation not only to secure administrative coöperation,
but also to prevent extravagance on the part of the state government. To give the taxation of the large corporations exclusively to the state government for its support is good neither
for the corporations nor for the state government. It concen-
trates corporate influence at the state capitol. If the corporations are unusually strong they may be powerful enough to
keep state expenditures down and thus get off with an un-
fairly small share of the general tax burden. If they are weak,
special corporation taxes may be pushed unjustifiably high and
the state government spend too much money. Above all
things, the state government needs the criticism and check that
come from the farmer, the home owner and other small taxpayers, who constitute the majority of the electorate. To deprive this class of its immediate interest in the expenditures of

the state government is openly and deliberately inviting extravagance.

This last assertion is probably proved by the financial history of the last decade. I cannot speak with certainty because statistics are not available, but I venture to predict that when the next census volume on wealth, debt and taxation appears, contrasting state expenditures in 1913 with those in 1902–1903, it will be found that the increase in expenditures has been greatest in those states which either have achieved separation or have approached it most closely. New York, California, New Jersey and the other states in which separation has been most nearly achieved will be found, I believe, greatly to have outstripped their competitors in rapid expenditure.

This is the deepest vice of separation—it does not separate. When the sources of revenue are segregated, the state government is apt to find itself for a short period on "Easy Street," with ample revenue easily secured. But the spending ability of the average state legislature is great and within a short time the new sources of revenue are likely to be exhausted and the state legislature to find an irresistible temptation to lay on a small state tax once more. Substantially this has happened in New York and California. It is irrelevant to say that in these cases the state tax has been necessitated by extraordinary expenditures. The answer is that the absence of a state tax levy invites such expenditures.

Finally it should be noted that neither experience nor theory warrants the belief that the mere abolition of a state tax will greatly improve assessment work. In the tax bill of the average American taxpayer the state tax accounts for only 11 per cent of the total. The remainder, 89 per cent, represents county and local taxes, and it is primarily to avoid these that the assessor is subjected to the pressure which so frequently makes his work inefficient. Many, if not most, of the states which have made marked improvement in assessment work during the last five years are states with a comparatively high state tax and using the device of state equalization. Arizona, Colorado, Minnesota, Michigan, Ohio, West Virginia and Washington are merely some of the states without "separation" which have greatly improved their assessment work in the past five years. In Wisconsin for a number of years the state tax practically disappeared. During those years little improvement was marked in the local assessments. Later the state tax was increased and the local assessment work rapidly improved. The city of Milwaukee went to a full value basis in the latter period when the state tax was quite an important factor. In states like Maryland and Virginia where there is no central control[3] or state equalization and where the ratio of true to assessed values varies from twenty to ninety per cent among the various counties, the imposition of a high tax is obviously an important factor in demoralizing local assessments. But what these states need is not separation but central control. Pennsylvania has had something akin to separation for many years. The quality of its local assessment work is, from all the writer can learn, below rather than above the average.

If space permitted it would be desirable to point out in detail that for the state government to take over enough sources of revenue to accomplish separation would in the average state deprive the local government of property or other sources of taxation which they cannot afford to spare. A realization of this fact, I understand, prevented a recommendation of separation in the recent admirable report of the Kentucky commission. The truth is that while there is no very rigid or exact connection between the property within a given jurisdiction and the necessary governmental expenses of that jurisdiction, there is a very real connection of this kind which cannot be wholly disregarded. There is more reason perhaps for the retention by the state government of all taxes on steam railroads than in the case of any other form of property or industry. But even in this case serious injury may be done to particular local jurisdictions. Take a small city or village in which important railroad shops are located: They may constitute and frequently do, a large part of the property of this place, and the principal expenses of the local government may arise from the provision of proper schooling and fire protection for the district occupied by the railroad shops. To deprive this jurisdiction of all taxes from this source is inequitable and unwise. In short, while there are some taxes, including that on steam railroads, which are particularly adapted to state use, modifications and exceptions must be made even with reference to this tax and when we further extend the sphere of exclusive state taxes we almost always encounter serious trouble.

5. The Relations of Federal, State and Local Finance *

The relation of intergovernmental finance in the United States is a problem almost as old as the commonwealth itself. It is a

* From S. E. Leland, "The Relations of Federal, State and Local Finance," *Proceedings of the National Tax Association*, (1930), pp. 94-106.

[3] In Maryland, since the recent establishment of a strong state tax commission, this is no longer true.

problem which has frequently been discussed at the conferences of the National Tax Association[1] and in the reports of its various committees.[2] Probably little that is new can be said.

The problem of the fiscal relations between governments is but part of the larger problem of intergovernmental relations which arises whenever a people are governed by more than a single political unit. The problem is rendered complex today by the overlapping of competing local political jurisdictions organized functionally and territorially in every state. In Illinois, for example, there are two and a fraction governments for every 1000 people. If this ratio prevails throughout the country, there are over 250,000 governments whose interrelations must be taken into account. Further complications arise from the unequal distribution of wealth and income among individuals, territories and economic groups.[3] As a result of this fact, capacity to support government is also unequal. The attempt locally to maintain governments where taxable capacity is lacking results in little net gain to those governed. Political units of this type soon degenerate, yet their existence is often prolonged by "doles" from the state. The maintenance of *independent* governments in regions where surplus taxable capacity exists is no less undesirable from a social viewpoint, since such districts resent attempts to tax their wealth for the benefit of non-residents. Thus, the maintenance of complex governmental structures gives rise to numerous social, economic and political problems.

The interrelations among units with independent or quasi-independent political spheres are generally accidental. Recognition of mutual difficulties or the anticipation of common gains has, however, led to amalgamations. Independent political spheres have vanished as more powerful groups have con-

---

[1] See, for example, E. R. A. Seligman, "Relation of State and Federal Finance," *Proceedings, National Tax Association,* 1909, pp. 213-26; H. P. Willis, "Relation of Federal to State and Local Taxation," *Proceedings, National Tax Association,* 1907, pp. 201-10. Discussion on the Relations of Federal and State Taxation, *Proceedings, National Tax Association,* 1909, pp. 239-64. General Discussion, Relation of Federal and State Taxation, *Proceedings, National Tax Association,* 1919, pp. 128-46.

[2] As, for example, Report of Committee on Double Taxation and Situs for Purposes of Taxation, *Proceedings, National Tax Association,* 1914, pp. 233 ff.; Preliminary Report of the Committee Appointed by the National Tax Association to Prepare a Plan of A Model System of State and Local Taxation, *ibid.,* 1919, pp. 426 ff.; Report of Committee on Simplification of State Taxation of Business Concerns, *ibid.,* 1926, pp. 155 ff.; *ibid.,* 1927, pp. 323 ff.; *ibid.,* 1928, pp. 398 ff.; *ibid.,* 1929, pp. 152 ff.; Report of Committee of National Tax Association on Reciprocity in Inheritance Taxation, *ibid.,* 1927, pp. 415 ff.; *ibid.,* 1928, pp. 478 ff.; *ibid.,* 1929, pp. 200 ff.

[3] See especially, Blough, *The Geographical Problem in Wisconsin Taxation, Bulletin* No. 39, Wisconsin Tax Commission, June, 1930.

quered their neighbors. The evolution of modern states has been accompanied by a concentration of power, the unification of functions and the centralization of the means of support.[4] Purely local government has been displaced by units operating in larger territories. Nationalism has endeavored to weld these bodies into a union but the process in the United States has not been completely successful. The division of powers among our governments is anomalous. The central government possesses only delegated — largely defective — powers. The states which have powers reserved to them are so circumscribed on the one hand by constitutional limitations and on the other by the interstate character of our economic and social system that effective government, social control, or even financial administration is impossible. The central government is unable to expand its functions or develop its fiscal system because of constitutional limitations and the practical antagonisms of lesser nigh-sovereign states. The localities, particularly those of metropolitan character whose functions and budgets exceed those of the states of which they are a part, possess practically no sovereign powers, are mere agencies of the states and are so restricted in the choice of fiscal measures that the taxable capacity found within their borders is seldom available to finance local government. The framework of government thus erected has become a matter of custom, as well as of law.[5] Change comes slowly, experimentation is made negligible, and the crossing of territorial as well as functional boundary lines is rendered difficult.

The ideal relationship between federal, state and local revenue systems is one of unity. The financial system of a nation should be highly, if not completely, integrated. The tax system should rest upon a diversified base, the net operative effect of which should be taxation under the principle of progression or ability to pay. Every tax need not be on the basis of individual faculty, as benefit charges should be freely incorporated in the system. The revenue system should be under the control of a single governmental unit — the national government — so as to secure uniformity of laws, administration and burdens, and to make possible effective adjustment of tax loads as chang-

[4] Cf. Bastable, *Public Finance* (3rd ed. revised and enlarged, 1922), pp. 113 ff.

[5] Compare : "in the main the structure of local government and the way in which local problems are handled have not been changed since the state was created. In fact, some aspects of present institutions have not been altered since the English established the provincial government of New York after driving out the Dutch in 1664 . . . the main features of county government have not been changed in the 146 years since New York became a state . . . where changes have been made they are of a patch-work character."— *Report of Special Joint Committee on Taxation and Retrenchment,* 1923, pp. 11, 12, 13.

ing economic conditions and governmental needs may require. The administration of such a system should be centralized, or located where maximum efficiency can be secured. The revenue receipts produced by the system should be shared with all governmental units in such proportions and amounts as to maximize the social utility of government.

The ideal which has been stated will be very difficult of attainment. Nevertheless, the immediate undertaking should be so as to relate governments, their functions and financial structure that this ideal may be gradually approached. A logical first step is the integration of governments.

No form of government or its structure is an end in itself. In the beginning, government was created to satisfy common needs and administer to collective wants. Its value continues only so long as general welfare is enhanced — a thing which is often obscured by the fetishes attached to particular forms and theories of government, such as that of the United States, the nature of which was determined when the country was but a fringe of small agricultural settlements along the Atlantic coast. Collective wants were then few and the demands upon government were simple as well as local in character. Since the colonial period, economic and social changes have taken place, the population has multiplied many times, its wealth and income have increased, the territorial area to be governed has been enlarged, new functions have been engrafted upon the old political structure, new units of government have been created, changes in transportation, communication and the general level of education have transpired. Economic life is national, or even international in character, freely crossing political boundaries except where artificial political trade barriers have been erected. Economic activity thus occupies a field practically divorced from that of the American state. As a result government trails industry in the technique of service and the sating of wants. While industrial integration has been going on, the opposite tendency has dominated governmental policy. The governmental sphere no longer is coextensive with the sphere of economic activity.

The first problem, therefore, is to bring our political structure into harmony with our economic unit. This calls for governmental integration and the enlargement of the territorial base for government. The place to begin is with the abolition of the township.[6] In Iowa, for example, there are

[6] For similar recommendations see *Report of the Joint Legislative Committee on Economy and Taxation*, Ohio, 1926, pp. 249 ff.; *Report of New York Tax Commission*, 1928, pp. 10-11; Compton, *Fiscal Problems of Rural Decline*, pp. 178 ff.

1675 townships, in Kansas 1500, in Ohio almost 1400, in Michigan 1376, in Illinois 1327, in Missouri 1299. In Ohio the number of townships within a single county varies from 8 to 28; the area of each is about 30 square miles and the population outside of municipalities averages under 1000.[7] These governments, many of which cannot support themselves, and whose primary function has been the building of township roads and the maintenance of one-room schools, perform no functions which cannot and should not be performed by larger political units. The time has come when this New England tradition should be discarded.[8]

Along with the abolition of townships should go special school districts, road districts, sewer districts, mosquito and pest abatement districts, and similar subdivisions. In Illinois in 1918 there were 12,000 school districts.[9] In 1925 there were 1,488 road districts[10] and over 16,000 governments of all kinds.[11] Too frequently have these units been organized for the purpose of avoiding the provisions of tax-rate and debt-limit laws. This type of financial gerrymandering has led to extravagant support of functions in some districts while in others there was a lack of financial resources. State aid for education has been designed to correct this mal-distribution of tax resources but aids, on such a basis, do not strike the heart of the problem. The remedy is governmental reorganization and the abolition of special districts rather than their ameliorated perpetuation through state grants.

The abolition of county government should also be seriously considered. Many counties possess too few people and too little wealth to justify the maintenance of government. These "pauper counties" have often relied upon grants from the state for their support, as in Kentucky and Virginia.[12] At the opposite extreme, counties containing metropolitan cities are so dwarfed in their functions that their existence is superfluous, as will be seen more fully in subsequent paragraphs. The movement to abolish or consolidate counties is thus appearing in the largest and most populous, as well as in the least populous and poorest counties. The number of counties alone furnishes a *prima facie* case for their consolidation. In Ken-

---

[7] *Report,* Ohio, *supra,* p. 249.

[8] This is applicable, of course, only to certain northern states, as township government was never a characteristic of local government in the South.

[9] *Administration of Public Funds in Illinois,* p. 20.

[10] Auditor of Public Accounts, *Statement of Indebtedness of the State of Illinois and the Political Subdivisions Thereof,* January 1, 1925, p. 3.

[11] *Ibid.*

[12] Cf. *The Government of Kentucky, Report of Efficiency Commission,* Vol. I.

tucky they number 120. Virginia and North Carolina have 100, Missouri has 114, Kansas 105, Indiana 92, Ohio 88, whereas Massachusetts has 14, Connecticut 8 and Rhode Island 5. The number of officials required to run these petty governments is enormous. In Indiana, in addition to over 1000 township trustees, there are "276 county commissioners, 644 county councilmen to watch the county commissioners, 3048 members of the advisory boards as sort of guardians over the 1000 and more trustees," and in addition over 1000 elected county officials —"an average of 54 officers to the county." [13] The financial burden of supporting this staff of officers is enormous. Their support constitutes a permanent charge against taxpayers before any services for the benefit of citizens are performed. In New York, for example, over 36 per cent of the expenditure of counties and over 20 per cent of the expenditures of towns from 1918 to 1921 went for the support of general government, constituting practically an overhead cost antecedent to the performance of governmental functions.[14]

The inability of many counties to support government has resulted in frequent attempts to correct the situation by the granting of state aid or the extension of state functions. The counties have been principally concerned with the construction of roads, the development of educational facilities, the maintenance of a few charitable institutions and the administration of justice, functions which are rapidly being taken over by the state.[15] Possibly small and impecunious counties should be consolidated as the first step in a program of economy and efficiency, but in the end they should be abolished as units of government, their functions being transferred to the state. Where local administrative areas are required for the effective performance of functions hitherto performed by localities such areas should be created by the state but their boundaries and functions should be flexible, changing as conditions may require. This step will leave city government in its present position; its sphere should be widened so that adjacent areas socially and economically affected by city action may be under control of urban units.

---

13 Miller, "Cost of County Government," *United States Daily*, Oct. 2, 1930.

14 Davenport, *An Analysis of the Cost of Municipal and State Government*, p. 79. In 1923 excessive costs for administering local poor relief in New York were pointed out.— *Report of the Special Joint Committee on Taxation and Retrenchment*, 1923, pp. 71 ff. See also pp. 82 ff.

15 Cf., e.g., *State Expenditures, Tax Burden, and Wealth*, a report by the Special Joint Committee on Taxation and Retrenchment, New York State, 1926, pp. 65-8.

State governments, too, cannot escape the need for change. There are already too many states. Our economic and social life passes over state political boundaries, leaving the states impotent to regulate it. No longer can single states adequately tax by simple formulae the property of interstate corporations. Their attempts too frequently result in obnoxious double taxation, in impediments to commerce and the free movement of capital. Conventions to promote uniformity in state legislation must be held, committees like those of the National Tax Association must work for reciprocity and the elimination of double taxation, and the courts must be prevailed upon to erect standards of acceptable state legislation. Recently the courts have shown a disposition to impose limits upon state tax powers which may sooner or later bring uniformity in state tax policies relating to interstate business.[16] But promising as this course of action appears, it cannot prevent the movement of capital and industry to escape taxation when tax subsidies are offered, nor can it eliminate the evil of competitive tax exemption or competitive mal-administration. Treaties between states under the compact clause of the Federal Constitution offer some promise for the future. Regional government has possibilities which should be investigated. Greater hope, however, would inhere in a reconstitution of states territorially or in the complete elimination of state government as it now is and the substitution therefor of administrative districts under federal control, local autonomy and local experimentation being secured by state or regionally-elected administrative councils. Perhaps the details of such a scheme are both imperfect and impractical but the problems of today call for a very different type of government than we now have. The needs of economic classes, of territories specializing in manufacturing, commerce and agriculture cannot be met by our federal geographical form of government. It is time that the utility of its structure be examined and that it be adapted to current conditions.

The problems of the metropolis call for similar treatment. The human relations in these centers cross township, county, state and frequently international political boundaries. The metropolis cannot regulate the actions of those who come within

16 As, for example, in *Frick v. Pennsylvania*, 268 U. S. 473 (1925) ; *Rhode Island Hospital Trust Co.* v. *Doughton*, 270 U. S. 65 (1926) ; *Safe Deposit and Trust Co. of Baltimore* v. *Virginia*, 280 U. S. 83, *United States Daily*, Nov. 26, 1929 ; *Farmers Loan and Trust Company* v. *Minnesota*, 280 U. S. 204, *United States Daily*, Jan. 8, 1929 ; *Baldwin* v. *Missouri*, 281 U. S. 586, *United States Daily*, May 27, 1930.

its sphere save as its political jurisdiction is coextensive with the boundaries of its economic and social life. In such areas the elimination of political subdivisions is imperative. A city can only govern itself when it controls or is itself the source of local political power. When independent governments exist within and around it, it can neither exercise its political power nor control the financial burdens which competing governments place upon its citizens. The necessity for unity has led to the abolition of county governments in many urban centers, such as Denver, San Francisco and New York. Pittsburgh recently attempted to consolidate all of the governments within Alleghany County, but the plan was defeated.[17] St. Louis is working upon such a consolidation. The situation is perhaps at its worst in Chicago. In the city there are eight principal governments and over a score of minor ones.[18] There are twenty different authorities dealing with parks and recreation having jurisdiction within the limits of the city of Chicago.[19] There are two operating and six non-operating townships within the city limits.[20] There are five separate civil service commissions engaged in the task of hiring public employees. In Cook County, outside of the limits of Chicago there are 9 cities, 76 villages, 30 townships, 192 school districts, over 30 park districts, over 40 road and bridge districts, 2 sanitary districts, and enough additional subdivisions of government to aggregate 415 separate, independent units, each having power to levy taxes and borrow money.[21] If the area of metropolitan Chicago — its trade and social area — is made the basis of the calculation, the territory embraced exceeds 5000 square miles with a population in excess of 4,000,000.[22] In this area there are 1600 independent governments including 4 states, 16 counties, 203 cities, 166 townships and 188 drainage districts.[23] The question has been quite properly asked, "How can 4,000,000 people manage 1600 governments and attend to their own

[17] Cf. Miller, "The Pittsburgh Consolidation Charter," *National Municipal Review*, Vol. XVIII, No. 10, pp. 603-09 (Oct., 1929).

[18] Merriam, *Chicago*, p. 90.

[19] Beyle, *Government Reporting in Chicago*, p. 62.

[20] *Preliminary Report on Problems of Government Simplification, Administrative Processes and Fiscal Affairs of the various local taxing agencies in Chicago and Cook County*, prepared by Advisory Board of Estimate and Apportionment of Local Public Expenditures, appointed by the Board of Cook County Commissioners, 1929, p. 12.

[21] *Ibid.*, pp. 13, 16.

[22] Merriam, *op. cit.*

[23] The independent governments were classified by Merriam as follows: States 4, Counties 16, Cities 203, Townships 166, Park Districts 59, Sanitary Districts 10, Drainage Districts 188, Miscellaneous 1027 — Total 1673. *Ibid.*, p. 91.

affairs ?"[24] The same questions confront the residents of every county and city, only in lesser degree.[25]

From a fiscal standpoint this condition, among others, has prevented the development of an equitable municipal tax system. Local governments have been forced to rely upon the general property tax as their major source of revenue. Real estate has been the backbone of this tax; personalty has largely escaped; thus the intangible wealth and income present in the community has contributed little or nothing to the support of local government. In a majority of the states income taxes are lacking so that personal ability represented by income is not reached even for state purposes and the federal income tax with its liberal exemptions fails to tax many persons who should pay for governmental support. With objective taxes at their command, subordinate political units have multiplied and all governments have so increased their levies that the property-tax burden has become intolerable both on the farm and in many urban communities. The state governments have diversified their own revenue systems but have little improved the local tax base. Equalizations and state administration have made the property tax more equitable. Several have distributed to the localities a portion of the proceeds from income taxes. Others have made grants-in-aid either to equalize given services or to stimulate the spending of larger amounts for desirable social activities.[26] But little has been done by the state to develop a well-balanced municipal tax system or to decrease the cost of local government.

A few states have attempted to minimize the cost of local activities. Central purchasing departments have been created. Audits of accounts have been commenced. Administrative control over local tax levies and expenditures have been undertaken but these relief measures do not strike at the roots of governmental folly — the creation of a multiplicity of political subdivisions. A logical next step, therefore, appears in the integration of governmental units. Meanwhile the transference of government functions should take place. This course should be determined relative to the nature of public wants stated by government, the allocation being determined by ability most economically to satisfy the demand for governmental services.[27] This will necessitate the distribution of functions on other than an historical or accidental basis,

24 *Ibid.*, pp. 91-92.
25 Cf. Frazer, "Northern New Jersey Seeks Solution of Regional Problem," *National Municipal Review*, Vol. XIX, No. 9, pp. 593-98 (Sept., 1930).
26 Cf. *Annual Report of the State Tax Commission*, New York, 1928, pp. 26 ff.
27 Cf. Bastable, *op. cit.*, p. 113.

and should do much to improve the quality of government.

The principal obstacle to be encountered in increasing centralized administrative control over local governments or in attempting to integrate governments or their functions is the belief in the efficacy of local autonomy. This doctrine was an important feature of American democracy in days of the hamlet and the village, in the age before industrialism produced the metropolis. At that time existing transportation and communication facilities required small governmental units. Local autonomy meant a political government chiefly concerned with personal matters of no great moment to be settled by forensics rather than the research which is now requisite to the proper settlement of complicated public problems. When governments did less and cost little, local autonomy was a tolerable principle for governmental action, but when costs are high and the demand for governmental service exceeds the capacity to serve, it is important that governments be efficient and that maximum social utility be considered before local autonomy.

The integration of governments should be accompanied by the integration of fiscal systems. This is a departure from the traditional reform of twenty-five years ago. Early sessions of this Association were spent debating the advantages of separating the sources of state and local revenues.[28] Most of these alleged advantages have failed to materialize and such as have occurred are the result of centralized administration.[29] The gains to the state have been offset by losses to local governments.[30] The results from integration are more hopeful.

The property tax which is now locally administered under state supervision should be made a state-administered tax.[31] The assessors and their supervisors should be made state officials under civil service rules. Their valuations should be made by appraisal methods under approved techniques assuring uniform standards of assessment. Territorial inequalities would be eliminated and the necessity for equalizations could

[28] Cf. Seligman, "The Separation of State and Local Revenues," *Proceedings of National Tax Association*, 1907, pp. 485-514 ; Adams, "Separation of the Sources of State and Local Revenues as a Program of Tax Reform," *ibid.*, pp. 589-92 ; Thompson, "Separation of State and Local Revenues," *ibid.*, 1915, pp. 42-49 ; Plehn, "Results of Separation in California," *ibid.*, pp. 50-58.

[29] Leland, *The Classified Property Tax in the United States*, p. 406. Cf. Lutz, *Public Finance*, p. 252 ; also in *Proceedings of National Tax Association*, 1925, pp. 51-52 ; *ibid.*, 1926, pp. 298-302 ; *Final Report of California Tax Commission*, 1929, pp. 44 ff.

[30] Lutz, *loc. cit.*, 1926, pp. 299-302 ; *Final Report of California Tax Commission*, 1929, pp. 44 ff., 68 ff. ; Tunell, *The California Revenue System* (Reprint, 1929), pp. 3-4, 20-23.

[31] Cf. Seligman, *op. cit.*, pp. 664-668.

be dispensed with. The demand for local knowledge from local assessment officials, which is seen as an obstacle to state administration of property taxes, is tantamount to a request for no administration whatever.[32] The employment of approved assessment techniques is far better than the hiring of local assessors with their store of personal information and their groups of friends and political associates. Card files can soon displace the faulty memories of part-time elected assessors. With an impersonal assessment force the quantity and quality of assessed valuations should improve. The responsibility for equitable valuations is thus placed directly upon the state government with its specialists in taxation — the tax commission — in control. The interest of the state in the maintenance of the system could be guaranteed by the maintenance of a state tax rate. Local needs could be met, in part, by local additions to the state tax rate. This proposal reverses the present arrangement under which the state, using the local tax base, adds its levy to the local levy. The proposed shift would eliminate many of the evils now present in the general real estate tax.

Local revenues from the property tax should be supplemented by funds distributed from the proceeds of income and faculty taxes. These taxes must be administered by units other than the local government, but the proceeds from given taxes do not necessarily belong exclusively to the administering unit. Administrative functions should be placed where they can best be performed — funds should be used where they will most increase the benefits from government.

Such a proposal leads to the suggestion that income and inheritance taxes should be placed under the control of the federal government.[33] These federal taxes should be made in lieu of the state taxes with rates and exemptions accordingly adjusted. Or, as an alternative, the states might be permitted to add their rates up to certain maxima to those of the federal government.[34] In any case the federal government should

32 Professor Seligman, however, has emphasized the need for local administration as follows : "Secondly, the efficiency of the administration. Certain taxes like real estate taxes are specially adapted to initial local administration, because the assessment takes place under the eyes of the individual taxpayer. In many other cases, however, the farther away we get from local administration the better the chances not only of securing expert officials, removed from the dependence upon local prejudice, but also of making allowance for certain inevitable gaps in any local administration." *Ibid.*, p. 670.

33 Cf. Seligman, *Essays in Taxation*, 10th ed., pp. 379, 677 ; Leland, "The Future of the Estate Tax," *National Income Tax Magazine*, January 1926, pp. 9 ff. ; Schultz, *The Taxation of Inheritance*, Chapter XXI.

34 But cf. *Report of the Special Joint Committee on Taxation and Retrenchment*, New York, 1925, p. 20.

share the proceeds from these taxes with the states,[35] which in turn would divide them with the localities. If such a plan were adopted, uniformity in income taxation would be secured at one stroke, double taxation and jurisdictional conflicts would be eliminated, tax competition would be ended and the integrated income tax could be equitably adjusted to reach all classes and all sizes of incomes. The greatest difficulty would be the development of an equitable distribution formula, but this could be developed by experimentation and research. The fiscal adequacy of such a tax system would be such as to guarantee to all governments as much as they are now getting from the same sources. With that as the initial guarantee and with future prospects of increased returns, the objections on the part of state governments might be overcome. At all events the gains appear to outweigh the losses.

The federal government should also undertake the taxation of interstate business.[36] Considerations of uniformity and equity, as well as the impossibility of adequate state taxation, make this course desirable. The federal system should also be supplemented by the development of a gift tax to stop the avoidance of present taxes now under federal control. From time to time the system might be extended but the aim should be to develop a tax base which rests fundamentally upon the ability basis, allowing limited benefit charges to be imposed by state and local governments. These local levies should be supplemented by subventions from the proceeds of progressive taxes imposed under federal authority.

The next step, of course, would be to transfer all tax functions save limited local licenses for regulatory purposes and special assessments for permanent improvements to the federal government, abolishing all other taxes and supporting intermediate and local government on the basis of subventions and grants. The danger in giving complete financial control to the central government could be obviated by allowing the distribution to be determined by an administrative council or governing board selected by state or regional districts. Distributions to localities could be similarly protected. The lack of clear-cut lines between federal, state and local functions and expenditures makes both governmental and fiscal integration an ideal solution for the present chaos in intergovernmental, functional and fiscal relations.

The plan here suggested is beset with difficulties and is probably impossible of attainment short of a complete reorgani-

[35] Seligman, *op. cit.*, pp. 386-87.
[36] Cf. Seligman, *op. cit.*, pp. 380-82.

zation of federal, state and local government. A reorganization of government within the state is within the range of immediate possibilities but the rearrangement of states, even fiscally and territorially, is so remote as to be quite visionary. And although the statement of an ideal — though a revolutionary one it may be — is beneficial, of greater practical significance are the things which can be done here and now, all of which promote the integration of governments and the integration of their fiscal systems.

A logical first step in the program of unifying government is the abolition of the township. This can be readily followed by the consolidation of counties and the adoption of a regional basis for local government. This step is of especial importance to metropolitan centers, the governments of which should be consolidated into a single unit with a territory large enough to enable the metropolis to control those who proximately come within its sphere of influence. Sufficient consolidations of this type have already taken place conclusively to demonstrate the merits of the proposal; their extension to other areas would appear to be beneficial. And, while township elimination and county consolidation are taking place the gradual transfer of many functions, such as education, highways, and the administration of justice, to the state government should be commenced. As the activities of the state are thus increased the benefits of further functional integration can be easily measured.

These changes should also be accompanied by the gradual integration of fiscal systems and administration. The property tax which for decades has been the prevailing source of state and local revenue should be made a state-administered tax. The office of township assessor should be abolished and a full-time local assessor appointed by the state officials under civil service rules and state control should undertake the tasks of local assessment. These valuations should be state valuations to which the state and local levies could be applied. Income, inheritance and other faculty taxes should be developed not only to supplement the existing real property tax, but also to reach that personal ability to support government which now largely escapes taxation. The income and inheritance taxes especially should be transferred to the federal government for administration and control, but a division of revenues with the states, and by them to the localities, should be assured. The taxation of interstate business and income appears logically to belong to the federal government, and in order to secure greater uniformity and equality of taxation such taxes should be surrendered to the federal government, division of revenues again being insured. Here, too, the gains to accrue from further integration can best be measured when the benefits resulting from these transfers have appeared. And while the ideal relationship between the various fiscal systems of American governments may appear visionary, these more immediate steps appear to be within the range of possible attainment. At least they offer possibilities for bringing our governmental structure more into harmony with existing social and economic institutions.

QUESTIONS AND PROBLEMS FOR DISCUSSION

1. Discuss the effects of a change in the price level upon the severity of progressive income taxes.
2. What bearing do changing price levels have upon the general problem of capital gains in income taxation?
3. If the profits of a business concern in terms of dollars double within a year's time and the general price level increases at an equal rate, is it fair to tax the new business income at a rate higher than that which prevailed before the increase in profits?
4. In 1928 Mr. A inherited an estate consisting largely of stocks and bonds. For inheritance tax purposes the estate was valued at $10,000,000. The law allowed him three years in which to pay the inheritance tax. Before the end of the three-year period the market value of the estate was less than the amount of the tax. Can this situation be justified? Can it be prevented? If so, how?
5. Would there be economic justification for an increment tax on land values if the price of land changed in accordance with the general level of prices?
6. Do you believe that the administrative difficulties involved in attempting to adjust taxation to changing price levels are insurmountable? Would you favor complete abandonment of an attempt to make these adjustments?
7. Point out the advantages and the disadvantages of the borrowing and the pay-as-you-go methods of highway financing.
8. What principles of taxation are usually applied in financing highways? Is there a place for the ability-to-pay principle?
9. What efforts have been made to eliminate international double taxation?
10. What are some of the problems of interstate double taxation which confront the people of the United States today?
11. What suggestions can you offer for the elimination of the evils of national and international double taxation?
12. Present the arguments for and against the separation of state and local revenues.
13. Why is there such pressing need for the integration of federal, state and local fiscal systems?

SUGGESTIONS FOR RESEARCH

1. The fiscal aspects of a managed currency.
2. The income tax and the problem of double taxation.
3. Motor vehicle license taxes for highway use.
4. Highway financing in some particular state.
5. The coördination of state and local revenue systems.
6. The results of the separation of state and local revenues.
7. Federal versus state administration of income, inheritance, and sales taxes.
8. Suggested reforms for municipal revenue systems.
9. Why not a single tax on incomes?
10. Federal and state aid for education.

BIBLIOGRAPHICAL NOTE

A recent volume which gives "a detailed exposition of the two complementary forms of motor vehicle taxation, license taxes and fuel taxes, their development, the measure or base of these taxes, their administration, the financial results, and the disposition of the proceeds" is National Industrial Conference Board, *Taxation of Motor Vehicle Transportation,* (New York, 1932). Another general work dealing with highway finance is Sigvald Johannesson, *Highway Economics,* (New York, 1931). A valuable article on highway economics is Shorey Peterson, "Highway Policy on a Commercial Basis," *Quarterly Journal of Economics,* Vol. XLVI, pp. 417-443. Several studies on highway finance have been published recently in the *Proceedings of the National Tax Association.* Among these are: G. C. Dillman, "The Financing of a Complete Highway System," (1930), pp. 112-121; J. W. Martin, "Neglected Aspects of the Taxation of Commercial Motor Transportation," (1929), pp. 487-518; and Reports of Committees of the National Tax Association on "Taxation of Motor Vehicle Transportation," (1929), pp. 468-487; (1930), pp. 135-166; (1931), pp. 357-371. On the financing of city and village streets, see W. M. Anderson, "The Gasoline Tax for City and Village Streets," *Minnesota Municipalities,* (Dec. 1932). Statistical data showing "recent changes and present practices in highway finance" are given in Malcolm M. Davisson, "Trends in Highway Finance," *Bulletin of the National Tax Association,* Vol. XIX, pp. 226-232.

The principal work on double taxation is E. R. A. Seligman, *Double Taxation and International Fiscal Coöperation,* (New York, 1928). The subject of international double taxation is ably treated by Sir Josiah Stamp in *Encyclopaedia of the Social Sciences,* Vol. V, pp. 224-225. Another useful reference on this subject is League of Nations, *Report of Committee of Experts on Double Taxation,* (Geneva, 1923). A preliminary report on double taxation and other problems of duplication in federal and state taxation has been made by a Sub-Committee of the Committee on Ways and Means, 72nd Congress, Second Session, 1933.

Mabel Newcomer's *Separation of State and Local Revenues,* (New York, 1917), is the most complete and valuable study on this subject. Two important, though less comprehensive, analyses of this subject are : C. J. Bullock, "The Separation of State and Local Revenues," *Quarterly Journal of Economics,* Vol. XXIV, pp. 437-458 ; and J. W. Martin and C. M. Stephenson, "Aspects of the Movement toward Separation of Sources of State and Local Revenue," *The Tax Magazine,* Jan.-Feb., 1933.

The interrelation of federal, state and local fiscal systems is discussed in the following references : R. M. Haig, "The Coördination of the Federal and State Tax Systems," *Bulletin of the National Tax Association,* Vol. XVIII, pp. 66-74 ; W. J. Shultz, *American Public Finance and Taxation,* (New York, 1932), Chap. XXXIII ; Mabel Newcomer, "Tendencies in State and Local Finance and Their Relation to State and Local Functions," *Political Science Quarterly,* Vol. XLIII, pp. 1-31 ; Ruth G. Hutchinson, *State Administered and Locally Shared Taxes,* (New York, 1931) ; M. S. Kendrick, *Taxation Issues,* (New York, 1933), Chap. VI ; H. C. Adams, *The Science of Finance,* (New York, 1898), Pt. II, Bk. II, Chap. VI ; and Preliminary Report of a Committee of the National Tax Association upon a "Plan of a Model System of State and Local Taxation," *Proceedings of the National Tax Association,* (1919), pp. 426-469. At present a Committee of the National Tax Association, with Professor Bullock as Chairman, is revising this report. A progress report of this Committee appears in the *Proceedings,* (1932), pp. 286-290. The problem of coördination of federal, state and local revenue systems is dealt with in *Report of the New York State Tax Commission,* (Albany, 1927). Valuable suggestions on this same problem may be found in A. A. Young, "Personal and Impersonal Taxation," *Proceedings of the National Tax Association,* (1915), pp. 426-470.

PART III—PUBLIC CREDIT

CHAPTER XXII

NATURE AND DEVELOPMENT OF PUBLIC CREDIT

THE general nature of the institution of public credit, a brief summary of its historical evolution, and some pertinent facts relating to current indebtedness of leading governments are presented in the following discussion by Paul Studenski.*

THE NATURE AND FUNCTIONS OF PUBLIC LOANS

PUBLIC loans are not, strictly speaking, revenue since they increase the liabilities of the government just as much as they do its assets and must eventually be repaid from revenue. Yet they are an important part of governmental income. They also provide an important occasion for governmental expenditures, since they necessitate the payment of interest and the repayment of principal. They must be considered as a special financial category, represented both on the income and the outgo side of a governmental budget.

Public loans perform a twofold function in modern governments and are of two basic types. First of all, they supply the government with funds for the financing of extraordinary expenditures for which the regular revenue is insufficient. Loans of this nature permit the distribution of the costs of extraordinary expenditures among taxpayers over a period of time. Instead of being assessed immediately for the full amount of these expenditures, taxpayers are assessed immediately only for the interest on the amount borrowed and the annual amortization or redemption charges, aggregating only 6 to 8 per cent of the total sum. Every year thereafter until the debt is liquidated, this charge is paid by the taxpayers who, as a class, are constantly undergoing changes as old ones die or move to other jurisdictions and new ones take their places. Loans of

---

* Adapted from Walter E. Spahr and others, *Economic Principles and Problems*, (Ray Long and Richard R. Smith, Inc., New York, 1932), Vol. II, Chap. XXXIV, pp. 520-535. This chapter was written by Professor Paul Studenski.

this nature, therefore, are really deferred taxes, or more correctly, taxes distributed in time. These loans are known as *long term or permanent loans.*

Secondly, loans supply the public treasury with funds necessary to meet (a) temporary deficits in the treasury arising during certain months each year due to the uneven flow of revenue, and (b) budgetary deficits resulting from unforeseen expenses, or deficiencies in revenue, or from the fact that necessary expenses were left out of the budget. These loans must be repaid a few months later when tax collections grow larger, or, in the case of budgetary deficits, ordinarily from the next budget. Loans of this nature enable the treasury to meet the government payroll and other expenses from month to month in a regular manner despite the irregularity of the flow of revenue, and they make possible a smoother operation of the budget and a closer adjustment of it to actual conditions.[1] These loans are known as *temporary or short term loans.*

Between these two types, there is sometimes found an intermediate type of loans, frequently called short term loans which run for a period of three to five years. In a sense they are really subsidiary to long term loans due to the fact that they are usually issued in anticipation of the time when it may be convenient to float a long term loan, and are converted when the latter loan is floated. They are also used sometimes to refund a portion of a maturing long term debt, thus, in effect, securing an extension of time for its payment, and permitting its gradual retirement. Loans of this nature may be called *intermediate loans.*

Public loans are floated by the sale of bonds or notes to the investing public, directly or through banks. These bonds or notes are issued usually in convenient denominations of say $100, $500, or $1000 and are bought and sold in the market just like any other securities. They call for the payment of interest at a specified rate and, in this country, for the repayment of principal on a certain date.

Besides their functions in the public economy, public loans perform certain incidental functions in the private economy. Government bonds represent, as a rule, the safest form of investment available. They are bought, therefore, by those investors to whom safety of investment is more important than large returns, by many recipients of fixed incomes, by savings banks, and pension and trust funds, and by the wealthy who wish to invest in securities the income from which is partially

---

[1] Loans to meet budgetary deficits are often abused and lead to a habit of over-expenditure, but this need not be entered into here.

or wholly free from taxation. In addition, they are also the most liquid form of investment, particularly when they run for short terms, being more easily and quickly converted into cash than any other kind of securities. Because the bonds combine these two characteristics of safety and liquidity, commercial banks not only invest large proportions of their capital and surplus in such securities but also use them as a means of building up a liquid secondary reserve when they have surplus funds available. This practice enables them to receive some return on their funds when there is no commercial demand for them and at the same time they can convert them at a moment's notice into cash when the opportunity for the commercial use of their funds reappears. In addition to serving various other purposes, government bonds are also used in this country as a basis or security for the issuance of national and Federal reserve bank notes (when the latter kind was issued). These various functions performed by government bonds in the private economy have become so essential that the complete retirement of the public debt not only would hamper but would actually prevent the performance of some of the most essential business activities. As our financial and investment mechanisms are constituted at present, it appears that government bonds must be issued even though government loans be unnecessary.

THE BASIS OF PUBLIC CREDIT

PUBLIC credit, like private, rests upon confidence in the willingness and ability of the borrower to discharge his obligations to the lender. Unless the lenders have confidence in the government's possession of both these qualifications the sale of bonds is rendered difficult if not impossible. Such confidence implies faith in the integrity of the government, that is, in its intention to execute scrupulously all its debt obligations; faith in the stability of the government; and faith in its financial soundness and the continued prosperity and tax-paying ability of the people. There is a limit in every government beyond which taxes cannot be levied. If a people finds itself so impoverished by economic adversity that it is unable to pay the required taxes a government may find itself seriously embarrassed if, indeed, its continued existence is not endangered. Under such conditions it may default on its payments of interest or principal of the debt, with the result that bondholders are subjected to losses. Manifestly, public credit is adversely affected when there is danger that such conditions may obtain.

If a government's credit is poor, it may still be able to sell its bonds, but only at a price considerably below par or with a very high rate of interest as an inducement to purchasers. Occasionally governments are unable to secure a loan under any circumstances. On the other hand, where confidence in the integrity, stability, and financial soundness of the government and the tax-paying ability of its people is present, the government in normal times has no difficulty in securing loans at low rates of interest.

Public loans, unlike private, are generally unsecured. If the State defaults on its payments of interest or repudiates the principal of its debt, the bondholders ordinarily have no legal remedy. The State is sovereign and, as a rule, cannot be sued without its consent. A State that repudiates a debt, of course, will not consent to be sued. But even if the constitution of the State should contain a clause permitting the holders of its obligations to sue it (a rather rare occurrence), there is still the possibility of the State's changing the constitution in order to pave the way for repudiation. And even should the remedy be available and an award rendered by the court in favor of the bondholders, there is the difficult question of securing the enforcement of the award. Municipalities generally can be sued, although they exercise delegated powers of the State. This is due to the fact that the states (in the United States) quite generally make municipalities subject to suit.

Bondholders ordinarily may do but two things in the case of default or repudiation of a debt by a State. One is to refuse to lend more money to it and to persuade other investors to do likewise. Investors, particularly banking institutions, very frequently act in unison in cases of this nature. Faced by a threat of a complete withdrawal of credit, the defaulting government may start negotiations with the bondholders and make some arrangements for a gradual and at least partial fulfillment of its obligations to them. The second remedy is political in nature. Where the defaulting or repudiating State is their own, the bondholders may combine to secure a change of government and the adoption of measures looking to the satisfaction of their claims. It is a well-known fact that the framing and adoption of the Constitution of the United States was due in no small measure to the activities of the holders of the Revolutionary debt who had not received any interest on their almost worthless bonds for years and whose only hope of receiving payment on them lay in the substitution of a strong and financially sound central government for the inept and bankrupt central government then existing. Where the defaulting or repudiating debtor is a foreign State, the bondholders may appeal to their own government for protection and secure political intervention on its part. If the debtor is a small and weak country it will readily yield to pressure, and either take appropriate measures towards the resumption of payments or will submit to the financial control by the creditor State. Should it fail to do either of these things, military intervention may follow. Generally, the pressure exerted is cloaked in diplomatic language and the military intervention, if unavoidable, is justified on some political ground and not merely on the failure of the other State to pay its debts to the private citizens of the intervening State. This is due to the fact that the right of a State to interfere in the affairs of another sovereign State because of its non-payment of debts to private parties is not definitely established in international law. It constitutes a use of governmental powers for the benefit of private interests and is regarded by many authoritative jurists as an illegitimate interference with the sovereignty of another State. The theory underlying this opinion is that the citizens who invested their funds in the bonds of a foreign government have done so voluntarily and should have been aware of the legal limitations of this type of investment.

Municipalities, on the other hand, can be sued though they exercise delegated powers of the state (in the United States). This is due to the fact that the states quite generally make them suable by a specific provision of the law or of the charters granted to them. But even in their case, the legal remedies available to investors are often limited, and the properties of the municipalities cannot be attached, as can private properties, in order to secure the enforcement of a court award. The most potent remedy in municipal defaults frequently is found to be an appeal to the state legislature, which may establish practically a receivership over the affairs of the defaulted cities and secure in the course of time a partial or full payment to the bondholders.

If a monarchy gives way to a republic, if a country or city is subdivided into two or more new countries or cities or annexed to another country or city, it is generally assumed that the government's obligation, legally or theoretically, does not expire on such a change but passes to the new government or governments which assume control over the territory. In actual practice, however, the new government or governments may refuse to assume the debt of the old on the ground that the former government was despotic and existed contrary to the will of the people or was purely provisional in nature. The Soviet government in Russia took this position and the United

States refused to recognize the Soviet government, in part on the ground that this position was contrary to the accepted principles assumed to exist in international relations among civilized States. Whatever the legal merits of the issue, it is evident that investors assume large risks in lending money to a government which does not rest on a firm constitutional basis.

Because public credit, even more than private, rests upon confidence it is necessary for governments which wish to maintain good credit standing to avoid assuming any obligations which they may not be able to fulfill, to discharge faithfully all obligations undertaken, to keep their finances in a sound condition, and use the taxpaying abilities of the people with discretion, and in a way likely to increase them, so that no occasion for default should ever arise. Being generally more permanent in nature than private enterprise and having the powers of taxation at their disposal, governments are in a better position to provide against the possibility of default and are better able to assure lenders of a more meticulous performance of their obligations towards them than are private borrowers. Cases of default or repudiation are much more rare in the case of government loans than in the case of private loans. Hence, public credit is generally much stronger than private, and governments ordinarily can borrow with greater facility and on more favorable terms than can private parties in their jurisdiction.

OTHER INFLUENCES DETERMINING THE STATUS OF PUBLIC CREDIT

THE status of public credit also depends upon (a) the existence of an ample supply of loanable capital in the home country or abroad; (b) the existence of an efficient credit organization in the country and the world; and (c) the condition of the money market at home and abroad at a given moment.

As will be shown further below, the institution of public credit, just as the institution of private credit, could develop only with the development of capital on a substantial scale. The government of a poor and undeveloped country, which lacks capital, must necessarily look for its loans in the wealthier countries which have loanable funds. The government of a wealthy country generally will find all the capital it needs at home.

If governments are to borrow under favorable conditions there must also be a sound and efficient banking system, well-managed stock exchanges, a good system of communications, an efficient press, and other facilities for the dissemination of financial information and the quick investment or withdrawal of funds. In a country in which these facilities are present and efficient, the institution of public credit occupies a more important place in the economic system than in a country in which they are less efficient or totally lacking.

The conditions of the money market change. The relationship between the factors of demand and supply in the market for loanable funds is constantly shifting as a result of changes in general business conditions, such as those found in periods of business expansion or recession, and as a result of gold movements, speculative orgies, and so on. Since governments must depend upon these money markets to a large extent for their funds, the ease with which they can borrow is determined, in no small degree, by money market conditions at the time the loan is floated.

THE DEVELOPMENT OF THE INSTITUTION OF PUBLIC CREDIT

PUBLIC credit is a relatively recent institution, accepted and established generally throughout the world only in modern times. Governments in the Middle Ages and even in ancient times borrowed from time to time, but such transactions embodied few if any of the significant characteristics of modern public credit.

When the sovereigns during the Middle Ages needed money they borrowed from their noble vassals, from the Church and wealthy monasteries, from rich merchants who had accumulated gold and silver coins from various countries, and from professional money lenders. They borrowed, in other words, on their personal credit from small groups of wealthy men and not from the "public," which was impecunious. They often bothered little about the payment of their debts, repudiated them freely, or dealt summarily with those creditors who demanded payment. Under the circumstances, the few wealthy men who were in a position to lend money to the sovereign had little confidence in his promise of repayment and were seldom willing to lend voluntarily. Most loans were forced loans and were regarded by the lenders as being as good as lost. When the few voluntary lenders assumed the risk of lending money they usually lent for short terms (a few months or years), or on the security of valuables or the right to collect a certain revenue, and at high interest rates.

Loans incurred in later periods and in more civilized countries naturally took more advanced forms than those incurred in early times and in less civilized nations. With the advent of the money economy, accompanied by the development of trade and the importation of gold and silver from South America into Europe, the States as well as individuals developed an ever growing need for money and there appeared at the time a supply of loanable funds. The great States which emerged from the Middle Ages — France, England, Spain, Holland — which began to wage war on one another and needed large sums of money to that end, managed to secure large loans by mortgaging their revenues or properties, by forcing those who supplied them with materials to accept promissory notes in payment for them, and by printing bills of credit which were a cross between paper currency and a bond. They also secured large funds from the masses of the people by resorting to state lotteries and tontines (annuity systems) and selling shares in them, on a large scale. These devices, in the main, were large, popular gambling schemes, and yet they contained the germ of the arrangements which made possible, some years later, popular loans. Out of these various early forms developed eventually the modern institution of public borrowing. It could reach its present highly developed state only with the growth of two important factors — general confidence in the government and the supply of loanable funds.

Public borrowing assumed its modern aspects and began to develop very rapidly in England, America, France, and other countries only in the eighteenth, and the beginning of the nineteenth, century, following the great political revolutions and reforms, which, in each case, established representative government on a firmer foundation, introduced respect by the government for private rights, liberated economic forces for a capitalistic development, vested the government with wide powers of taxation, and introduced a substantial amount of order in the finances of the government. Not only were the requisite political and economic conditions for the expansion of public credit now present but the need for loans on the part of governments also had increased greatly.

Wars assumed greater magnitude and required much larger loans. In addition, capital outlays, which have come to assume great importance in modern governments, came to be financed by means of loans. Having borrowed in war time, it was natural for the national governments to resort to the same expedient in peace-time whenever the regular revenues fell below expectations and budgetary deficits appeared, or whenever unusually large expenditures had to be made for the construction of great railways, waterways or telegraphs, the building of a large fleet, or the purchase of a vast territory from another country — expenditures for which the regular revenues seemed insufficient and which had to be financed outside the regular budget. It was natural also for state (or provincial) and local governments which were confronted with emergencies, to resort to borrowing. They were forced by the rapid industrial and urban developments to expand their activities greatly and to spend large sums for such construction work as that associated with canals, roads, public buildings, water works, sewers, and so on. They could not raise the capital required for these purposes from their current revenues, or impose additional levies large enough to provide it without making taxation oppressive. Borrowing was the only avenue open to them.

The issuance of bonds for capital outlays soon became an established practice in national, state, and municipal finance. A notion developed in some governments that every capital outlay should be financed by borrowing and that taxation should be confined to defraying the operating expenditures of the government and the interest and redemption charges on the debt. In the United States this notion became the gospel of municipal finance.

The public debt became a permanent institution. Nearly every government today is heavily in debt and pays large amounts annually in interest and amortization charges. Some of the debts are very old and in some foreign countries are never retired or at least are not retired rapidly enough to offset new loans and to cause any material reduction in the total indebtedness of the government. The bulk of the British national debts of 1914 was incurred during the wars against the French more than a century before.[2] By the time the loans incurred in one war are reduced somewhat, another war occurs and new and much larger loans are incurred, so that the total debt is pyramided and reaches ever greater heights. In addition, while the debts incurred for capital outlays are being amortized, new loans for new and larger capital outlays are incurred annually with the result that the possibility of reducing the debt radically is steadily declining from year to year. Most governments have become greater if not permanent debtors.

GROWTH OF PUBLIC DEBTS ILLUSTRATED STATISTICALLY

THE influence of wars on the growth of national indebtedness throughout the leading countries of the world is brought out clearly in Table [A]. Every sudden jump of the debt was due

---

[2] Hugh Dalton, *Principles of Public Finance* (George Routledge and Sons, Ltd., London, 1930), p. 243.

TABLE [A]

GROWTH OF THE INDEBTEDNESS OF THE PRINCIPAL NATIONAL GOVERNMENTS FROM 1700 TO 1930

(In millions)

Year	Great Britain (pounds)[b] $4.8665	France (francs)[a] $.193 .0392	United States (dollars)[c]	Russia (rubles)[d] $.5146	Germany (marks)[e] $.2382	Italy (lire)[f] $.193 .0526	Japan (yen)[g] $.4985	Canada (dollars)[h]	Belgium (francs, belga)[i] $.193 .139	Total (dollars)[j]
1700	16	1,200								309
1763	133	2,750								1,178
1800	500	725	83	53						2,683
1816-20	861	3,590	90	214						5,083
1840	843	4,682	10	463					304	5,313
1870	798	12,310	2,036	1,854	397	8,300	5	78	682	11,158
1900	639	30,109	1,023	6,193	2,418	13,431	502	265	2,709	17,337
1914	708	33,558	968	8,811	5,158	15,766	2,584	336	4,277	22,145
1920	7,879*	297,369	24,061	32,300*	91,710	74,496*	3,278	2,249	25,237*	123,986
1930	7,596*	459,000*	15,922	2,943	11,321*	87,949*	5,942	2,141	52,034*	92,230

a G. F. Shirras, Science of Public Finance (Macmillan and Co., Ltd., London, 1925) pp. 489 and 650; National Debt, the Treasury Department of Great Britain (1896); Annuaire Statistique de la France (1929), p. 406 (comparative tables); Statesman's Yearbook (1931). * Foreign debt included.

b Annuaire Statistique de la France (1929), p. 166; Shirras, op. cit., p. 520; Statesman's Yearbook (1931). Rentes viagères not included. The last figure is for the year 1929.

c Wealth, Debt and Taxation (1880), the United States Census Bureau, p. 274; and the Annual Report of the Secretary of the Treasury of the United States (1930). These figures include only interest bearing debt.

d J. Petrunkevich (Ed.), Voprosy Gosudarstvennago Khosiaistva (St. Petersburg, 1907), chapter by P. P. Migulin on the Russian National Debt; and Statesman's Yearbook (1916) and (1931).

e Annuaire Statistique de la France (1929), p. 406 (comparative table); Statesman's Yearbook (1931). * Drop due to revaluation of the mark and partial repudiation. Reparations and non-interest bearing treasury notes are not included.

f Annuaire Statistique de la France (1929) and Statesman's Yearbook (1931). * Foreign debt not included.

g Annuaire Statistique de la France (1929); Statesman's Yearbook (1931).

h Ibid.

i Edm. Nicolai, Étude Historique de la Dette Publique de la Belgique (Brussels, 1921); Statesman's Yearbook (1931). * Foreign debt included.

j In the cases of France, Italy and Belgium the figures of total debt for 1920 and 1930 were computed on the basis of the newly established values of their money which are indicated at the top of their respective columns.

to some war. In addition, there has been a fairly steady climb of indebtedness in most countries since 1870 as a result of frequent annual deficits in the budgets occasioned by the rapid increase of expenditures for the military and naval establishments.

Thus of its 850 million pound indebtedness outstanding at the end of the Napoleonic War, Great Britain redeemed only 354 million pounds by 1914, that is, in the course of a century, but at the same time it added 310 million pounds to its debt, of which 35 on account of the Crimean War and 140 on account of the Boer War were the largest items—so that its total debt in 1914 was smaller than in 1817 by only 144 million pounds. The World War increased the indebtedness eleven times.

The other leading countries did much worse. After the Revolution and the Napoleonic régime cut the indebtedness incurred by the old monarchy by repudiation and repayment, France's indebtedness resumed its upward climb and never ceased to move in that direction. War indemnities imposed on her by the Peace Treaty of 1815, various annual deficits, and finally Napoleon III's military adventures, caused France to borrow so much that its debt increased from 1 billion francs in 1814 to 12 billions in 1868 and then, under the influence of the Franco-Prussian War, to 20 billions in 1878. Then followed loans for the construction of railroads and other internal improvements and the expansion of military and naval establishments, which increased the debt to 33 billions by 1914. The World War and its consequences increased France's indebtedness to the stupendous sum of 477 billion francs by the end of the year 1927.

The German Empire started with a small indebtedness of 397 million marks which was a consequence of the Franco-Prussian War. The small amount was due to the fact that the greater part of the expense of the war was borne by the states individually. During the succeeding decades Germany borrowed almost annually to cover budgetary deficits caused by a rapid growth of military and naval expenses. By 1914 her imperial debt amounted to 5 billion marks. The World War and its consequences increased her funded debt to 92 billions, created a floating debt (non-interest bearing treasury notes) of 35 quadrillions and a reparations' obligation of an indeterminate number of billions. Repudiation and adoption of a new monetary unit in 1924–1925 cut the funded debt to 7 billion reichsmarks and eliminated the floating debt, but budgetary difficulties during the years 1925–1929 necessitated some new loans. The total debt, domestic and foreign, exclusive of reparations, amounted to 9 billion reichsmarks in 1929.

TABLE [B]

GROWTH OF FEDERAL, STATE, AND LOCAL INDEBTEDNESS IN THE UNITED STATES FROM 1790 TO 1931 [a]

(In millions of dollars)

Year	National	State	County	Municipal	Total	National wealth	Per cent ratio of debt to national wealth
1790..	$ 75	...	...	...	$ 75	.....	..
1800..	83	...	...	...	83	.....	..
1810..	53	...	...	...	53	.....	..
1820..	91	...	...	...	91	.....	..
1830..	48	$ 26	...	...	74	.....	..
1840..	10	175	...	$ 20	205	.....	..
1850..	63	190	...	(b)	(b)	.....	..
1860..	65	257	...	200	522	16,100[c]	3.2[d]
1870..	2,331	353	$ 188	328	3,202	30,069[c]	10.7[d]
1880..	1,919	297	124	702	3,042	43,462	6.7
1890[e] .	852	211	145	781	1,989	65,037	3.1
1902..	969	235	197	1,433	2,834	98,000[f]	2.9
1912..	1,028	346	372	3,105	4,851	187,739	2.6
1922..	22,156	936	1,273	6,481	30,846	320,804	9.6
1926..	19,573	1,328	9,475		30,376	342,471	8.8
1927..	18,422	1,445	10,185		30,052	336,125	8.9
1928..	17,468	1,502	11,106		30,076	360,062	8.4
1929..	16,743	1,577	11,875		30,195	361,800	8.3
1930..	15,985						
1931..	16,481						

[a] Compiled from the reports on *Wealth, Debt and Taxation,* the United States Census Bureau, for the years 1880, 1890, 1902, 1913, and 1922, and from the *Cost of Government in the United States, 1929–1930* (National Industrial Conference Board, New York, 1931), pp. 40 and 44. The figures include non-interest bearing notes (less gold reserves) and various temporary debts.

[b] Data not available.

[c] Taxable wealth only.

[d] Ratio of debt to taxable wealth only.

[e] The figures are for the year 1891. The figures for 1890 are not available.

[f] Estimated. The figure for 1900 is 88,517 millions and for 1904 — 107,104 millions.

Russia incurred her first loan under Catherine the Great in 1769, and became a heavy borrower in the nineteenth century in consequence of the Napoleonic War and, especially, later military campaigns, railway construction, indemnification of the landowners for the liberation of the slaves, and annual budgetary deficits generally. The Russo-Japanese war and its immediate consequences cost Russia 3 billion rubles of which close to 2.5 billion rubles were obtained through loans. At least one-half of Russia's loans, since she began to borrow, have been foreign loans. The World War caused that government's indebtedness to increase from 8 to 32 billions, but this debt was repudiated as a result of the revolution which ushered in the Soviet government. In 1925 the Soviet government began to borrow internally for its industrialization program and budgetary deficits with the result that by 1929 it had a domestic debt, of an entirely new origin, amounting to 2.6 billion rubles.

In the United States, as shown in Table [B], the Federal government began operation in 1789 with the debt of the Revolutionary War of 75 million dollars on its hands. Scarcely had it managed to cut it in half when the War of 1812 plunged it further into debt and increased the amount to 125 millions. The prosperity of the succeeding twenty years enabled the government to liquidate this debt by 1835, but a turn in economic conditions which precipitated a series of budgetary deficits during the succeeding two decades, and the war with Mexico, led to a new debt so that by 1860 the Federal debt amounted to 65 million dollars. The Civil War produced an indebtedness of two and a half billion dollars. The retirement of this debt proceeded at a moderate rate during the first fourteen years, very rapidly during the following ten, and very slowly after that. When the World War broke out, there was still outstanding a portion of the Civil War debt and of those loans incurred since that war for budgetary deficits, the Spanish-American War, the construction of the Panama Canal, and other purposes. The debt amounted to 1 billion dollars and the loans of the World War raised it to 24 billions. The operation of the sinking fund and direct redemption reduced the debt to 16 billions by 1930, when the business depression and consequent budgetary deficits, combined with advances to veterans on their certificates, necessitated new loans which, momentarily at least, gave a new upward turn to the debt. Foreign governments owed the United States, in consequence of the loans extended to them during the World War, 11.3 billion dollars and agreed to pay their debts together with interest computed in some cases at a very low rate, in annual instalments over a maximum period in most cases, of sixty-two years.[3] The execution of these agreements, however, is

---

[3] These agreements have been negotiated since 1923 but not all of them have been ratified. Under the terms of the Young Plan and the Statutes of the Bank for International Settlements the payments of the principal debtor countries are

very uncertain for there is a strong movement on foot abroad in favor of the cancellation of all inter-governmental obligations growing out of the World War. It is possible, therefore, that the American taxpayers will not receive much relief from this source and will have to bear the entire burden of the debt incurred in part for the benefit of the allies, themselves.

States and municipalities in the United States have been borrowing primarily for the financing of capital outlays. The states began to borrow for these purposes in the 1820's. After plunging deeply into debt for the construction of canals, promotion of railway construction, and other enterprises (increasing their indebtedness from 26 million dollars in 1830 to 175 millions in 1840), they nearly wrecked their credit and were forced for a time to discontinue any further borrowing or to borrow on a very modest scale. Except for some additions caused by the Civil War, the total state debt remained practically the same during the period 1860–1900, despite the rapid growth of the country. In the present century, however, the states resumed borrowing on a large scale, largely due to the heavy expenditures they had to assume for highway construction, made necessary by the automobile. They have been forced recently to curtail their borrowings due to the adverse turn in business conditions, the tightening of the loan market, and the general demand for a reduction in the costs of government.

Municipalities began to borrow extensively in the 1830's when, as a result of the construction of canals and railways, they began to grow rapidly. Loans were incurred for water supplies, sewers, pavements, and other facilities By 1840, the cities had a debt of 20 million dollars, by 1860 — one of 200 million dollars. The era immediately after the Civil War was one of particularly rapid expansion of municipal borrowing. Municipal indebtedness reached the 328 million mark in 1870, and the 702 million mark in 1880. This over-expansion impaired municipal credit and ushered in a period of abstention from borrowing which lasted throughout the eighties and part of the nineties. The following thirty years, with some interruptions, was a period of renewed activity in municipal borrowing. The growth of municipal indebtedness was particularly rapid during the decade following the World War,

to run uniformly until 1988. For the funding agreements between the United States and the foreign governments see the *Annual Report of the Secretary of the Treasury of the United States* for the years, 1925–1931. For the terms of payment under the Young Plan see *Bank for International Settlements : Documents.* Introductory Note and an Address by Melvin A. Traylor (First National Bank of Chicago and First Union Trust and Savings Bank, Chicago, 1930).

reflecting the rapid expansion of municipal activities in general during this period of prosperity. Following the business crisis of 1930, many municipalities found themselves in financial difficulties and some of the smaller ones defaulted on their bonds. Retrenchment in municipal borrowing has followed.

The significant features of the past history of public indebtedness in the United States, which may characterize also its development in the future, may be stated as follows: (1) public indebtedness in the United States has been increasing more or less continually for the past century, although at a very irregular rate. Such reductions as may have been effected from time to time, in the total amount of it have been temporary only. (2) At least 75 per cent of the national indebtedness has been incurred because of war, while almost all of state and local indebtedness has been for public improvements. (3) Although the national indebtedness has invariably declined in times of peace, state and local indebtedness has invariably risen. (4) The relative importance of war debts and public improvement (or productive) debts has been changing alternately, the former predominating in times of war and the years immediately following war, the latter growing in importance and eventually reaching the foremost place in times of peace. (5) The volume of new public loans has been fluctuating in a periodic or cyclical manner, being affected by alternating war and peace periods, times of business prosperity and business depression, and other periodic changes in political and economic conditions. (6) The ratio of the total public indebtedness to the national wealth has fluctuated between 12 per cent in times of war and 2.5 per cent in times of peace. The burden of the public debt on the national income has invariably declined in times of peace, due, in part, to the rapid increase of national wealth and income.

QUESTIONS AND PROBLEMS FOR DISCUSSION

1. Discuss the nature and functions of public loans.
2. What action may a bondholder take if a municipality defaults on the payment of interest on its bonds?
3. In what respects is the success of a government borrowing program dependent upon an efficient banking system?
4. What rôle in federal finance has been played by the Federal Reserve System during the last few years?
5. How does the condition of the money market influence a government's financial program?
6. Trace the relationship between the development of representative government and the institution of public credit.

7. Discuss the trend of federal, state, and local indebtedness from the Civil War to the present.
8. Would there be public borrowing under a socialistic or communistic government?

SUGGESTIONS FOR RESEARCH

1. The effect of the growth of representative government on the development of the institution of public credit.
2. The nature and extent of borrowing by the federal government since 1929.
3. The functions of the Federal Reserve Banks in the borrowing operations of the federal government.
4. Municipal borrowing in some particular state.
5. An historical study of the relation between the magnitude of public borrowing and industrial fluctuations.
6. The nature of national and local debts compared.

BIBLIOGRAPHICAL NOTE

A good discussion of the general characteristics of public debts can be found in Hugh Dalton, *Principles of Public Finance,* (London, 1932), Chap. XXI.

In H. C. Adams, *Public Debts,* (New York, 1890), Pt. I, Chaps. I, II, III; and E. L. Bogart, *War Costs and Their Financing,* (New York, 1921), Chap. I, one will find valuable discussions of the institutional background of public credit.

The general historical development of public credit in the different countries, as presented in the following books, will be found useful: C. F. Bastable, *Public Finance,* (London, 1917), Bk. V, Chaps. I-IV; D. R. Dewey, *Financial History of the United States,* (New York, 1931); R. A. Love, *Federal Financing,* (New York, 1931); A. D. Noyes, *Forty Years of American Finance,* (New York, 1909); also his, *The War Period of American Finance,* (New York, 1926); G. F. Shirras, *The Science of Public Finance,* (London, 1925), Chaps. XXXV, XXXVI; Paul Studenski, *Public Borrowing,* (New York, 1930), Chap. I; and W. F. Willoughby, *Financial Condition and Operations of the National Government, 1921–1930,* (Washington, D. C., 1931), Pt. V. A report of the National Monetary Commission, *The Credit of Nations,* (Washington, D. C., 1910), by F. W. Hirst, traces the development of public credit in Great Britain, Germany, France and the United States to 1909.

An outstanding historical and analytical study of national debts arising out of the Great War is H. G. Moulton and Leo Pasvolsky, *War Debts and World Prosperity,* (New York, 1932).

For factual material on public credit see The National Industrial Conference Board, *Cost of Government in the United States,* (New York, published annually); and also its study, *Federal Finances, 1923–1932,* (New York, 1933), Chap. III; the *Annual Report* of the Secretary of the Treasury of the United States; The United

States Census Reports on *Financial Statistics of States* and *Financial Statistics of Cities,* (both published annually); and *The Internal Debts of the United States,* edited by Evans Clark, (New York, 1933), Chaps. VIII and IX. In addition, the *Memorandum on Public Finance,* (Economic and Financial Section, League of Nations, Geneva), a serial publication, provides a comprehensive review of credit and other fiscal conditions in many of the principal nations of the world.

CHAPTER XXIII

MODERN THEORIES OF PUBLIC CREDIT

A CONCISE exposition of the theories of public credit of several leading writers in the field of public finance has been made by Dr. Shutaro Matsushita. His discussion is given below.*

PROFESSOR C. F. BASTABLE, who is one of the most distinguished English writers on public finance, maintains that public credit is only one form of credit in general, and is governed by the same fundamental principles which control private credit. If the resources obtained through public credit are not applied for economic production, there is proportional loss to the material power of the state. Such borrowing means reduced income in the future until the debt is paid. Just as an individual can only rightly borrow on the expected strength of his clear income in the future, so a state can only rightly borrow on the expected strength of its clear future revenue. And in a modern state, that strength, in the last analysis, depends upon the capacity of the people to pay taxes. As to the mechanism of public credit, the analogy, according to this writer, still holds. A state has to enter the money market and compete with private loan issues for the flotation of its issues. The rate of interest demanded by the creditors will depend upon their estimation of the government's good faith and financial strength.[1]

Although this general conclusion is amply corroborated, says Professor Bastable, and may be utilized in dispelling certain fallacies on the subject, there are some special features of public economy that impart to public borrowing certain peculiarities, especially in the case of the central government. He describes these peculiarities somewhat as follows:

In the first place, the sources of private wealth are in property or personal earning power; it is from them that all private incomes are derived. But the revenue of the state is, for the most part, derivative; that is to say the state can compel the

---

* From Shutaro Matsushita, *The Economic Effects of Public Debts*, (Columbia University Studies in History, Economics, and Public Law, New York, 1929), Chap. II.
[1] See C. F. Bastable, *Public Finance*, 3rd ed., pp. 658-59.

individual tax-payers to provide the necessary funds.   Borrowing is used, therefore, when heavy taxation is for the moment
undesirable, and is the more desirable since public credit rests
on a broader and more enduring foundation than private
credit.   In the second place, in public finance it is difficult
to make a sudden retrenchment of customary expenditures.
Therefore, when a deficit is foreseen, and new taxes are not
for the moment available, borrowing is always necessary.[2]
Thirdly, and most important of all, there is the peculiar legal
position of a debtor state.   Unlike all private persons, a state
may declare whether or not it will fulfill its debt obligations.[3]

With reference to the last-mentioned peculiarity of public
borrowing, however, Professor Bastable adds the following
explanatory statement:

Though released from legal liability, the sovereign state is in practice under very powerful inducements to pay its way.   In the first
place, if its creditors are foreigners, a failure to fulfill its agreement
lays it open to remonstrance on the part of the foreign States affected, and possibly to even more rigorous measures. . . With regard to native creditors there is an obvious interest on the part of
the state to do nothing that will injure them, and whatever political
power they possess will surely be used in their own defense.
Stronger than either foreign or domestic influence is the economic
sanction that protects the security of loans.   The repudiating State
shuts itself out from the future use of credit for the sake of a temporary gain. . .[4]

Coming down to the subject proper, Professor Bastable says
that if a public loan is contracted for an industrial undertaking, such as construction of railroads, its influence on the state
economy may be imperceptible.   Private enterprise might just
as well do the work, and therefore, from the economic standpoint, a public loan is unnecessary.   We cannot quite accept
this opinion of Professor Bastable.   What he says is true if
we assume that all industries are carried on just as economically
by private enterprise as by public enterprise.   But often the
contrary is the case.   We must remember that in private enterprises there are often doubled or tripled expenses due to separate organizations and to competition; discriminatory freight
rates (for instance) affecting other industries; over-production
or under-production as the case may be, due to lack of coördination; the labor strikes arising from the payment of insufficient wages to the working-men; and so on. . . Suffice it to

[2] Bastable, *op. cit.*, pp. 659-60.
[3] *Ibid.*
[4] *Ibid.*, p. 661.

say here that, in our opinion, the public loan for industrial purposes has become one of the most important subjects in public economy, and its economic consequences are far-reaching. The tremendous growth of public utilities in recent years is an outstanding proof of the existence of the differences in economic effects between public and private ownership.

Professor Bastable goes on to discuss the effects of loans applied for unproductive purposes, such as wars. Here a fund of capital is used in producing goods and services applied to acts of destruction. Of course this holds true even when war expenses are met by taxation. We must therefore consider, says this writer, the effects that are directly traceable to public loans; and he brings out the following points:

(1) It is only partly true that the loan is made out of capital, while taxation is obtained from income. There is no clear-cut distinction between income and capital. For this reason, according to different conditions the public loan affects income as well as capital, and taxation affects capital as well as income. "Large public borrowing stimulates saving and thereby checks expenditure on enjoyments, while oppressive taxation reduces the fund from which new savings are made, and so far hinders the accumulation of capital." [5]

(2) A loan is responded to voluntarily while taxation is compulsory. The loan, therefore, puts less immediate pressure on the individual citizens. [6]

(3) "The equitable distribution of heavy taxation is not easily attained. Where very high imposts are laid, some classes and persons are likely to suffer unduly. The division of the charge over a longer period by the use of borrowing makes the proper apportionment of the burden far easier, and more especially allows of sufficient time for its full consideration." On the other hand, some urge that the policy of paying all expenses out of taxation checks the government from indulging in extravagant and wasteful outlay. [7]

Finally, Professor Bastable enumerates his general conclusions:

On the whole, then, the rules applicable to the treatment of abnormal outlay for other than economic purposes may be stated as follows: (1) Expenditure should, as far as possible, be met out of the annual receipts, and therefore increased outlay should be balanced by heavier taxation. (2) In the case of non-recurrent expense of large amount, a loan is preferable to a serious disturbance

[5] Bastable, *op. cit.*, p. 673.
[6] See *ibid.*, p. 674.
[7] See *ibid.*, pp. 674-75.

of the normal tax-system, and may fairly be employed.   (3) Where the abnormal expenditure extends over a series of years, the various forms of taxation should, speaking generally, be adjusted to meet it.   (4) This general principle, however, fails where either (a) it would be impossible to secure an equitable division of the heavy taxation necessary, or (b) where the limit of productiveness with regard to the several taxes would have to be exceeded, or finally (c) where for political reasons it is inexpedient to press heavily on the tax-payers.   Under any of these conditions resort to loans as a supplement to the tax revenue even for a somewhat lengthened period is defensible.[8]

Professor A. C. Pigou discusses public loans in a more specific way than Professor Bastable.   In Part 4, Chapter VIII of his book *Economics of Welfare,* he discusses the comparative effects of taxes and loans on the national dividend.   He argues that it is clear that, under either system, to the extent that the funds required are obtained from consumption (in excess of what is needed for efficiency) or from the formation of new resources (without decreasing the efficiency of the people or machinery employed), the national dividend of the future is not adversely affected.   But to the extent that they are drawn from any other source, the future national dividend is damaged "to the full extent of the interest loss which the depletion of the capital implies."   The first problem that confronts us, therefore, is to determine how great a difference the choice between the loan system and the tax system makes to the source from which the funds obtained are in fact drawn.[9]   For the sake of clearness it must be remarked that in either system "the extent to which the various sources are drawn upon will be affected by the nature of the cause which renders the raising of the money necessary."   If the government thereby enters upon some profitable (that is, productive) enterprise the people will neither economize in their expenditures nor make extra exertions to provide the money, because they expect lower taxes in the future.   On the other hand, if the cause of the need for fund is a war, the people will economize more and work harder, because there is neither lowering of tax nor increased social income in sight.   Thus far, the effect is the same whether money be raised by loans or by taxes.

Now, one of the reasons why differences in the effects are brought about, according as one or the other method is used, is the fact that the people overvalue the benefits of the interest they are to receive on their bonds and undervalue the sacri-

[8] Bastable, *op. cit.*, pp. 678-79.
[9] See *supra*, p. 647 [refers to Pigou's *Economics of Welfare*].

fices (that is, taxes) they have to make in the future to pay off public debt. So the result is that they do not, under the loan policy, economize in their consumption, nor do they make increased exertion. (Here, Professor Pigou seems clearly to overemphasize the human instinct of fear, yet almost to disregard the other instinct of the love of gain, as stimulating to economy and to greater activity.) In the second place, the taxes have never been high enough to absorb all the interest accruing to government bonds held by the wealthy class. Therefore, the rich are less likely to curtail their expenditures or to exert themselves more. The result is a diminution of the future national dividend. In the third place, concerning future taxes for the purpose of debt payment, we know that these taxes, being long-enduring, are foreseen; and the expectation of them must tend to check production and injure the national dividend, as long as they last. It is clear, then, that in several ways, "the levy of any given sum of money by a loan is likely to prove more injurious to the national dividend of the future than the levy of an equal sum by taxation." [10]

"However," says the same writer, "caution is required before they are applied to the controversy between advocates of loans and advocates of taxes as a means of financing war." [11] In his opinion, since wars may last for a number of years, the tax method will reduce the exertions of the people insofar as they think "a large part of the fruit of any exertions they may make will be absorbed by the state." On the other hand, there is a point in favor of tax policy in that "the tax plan will cause the people actually living and working at the time the expenditure is being undertaken to contract their consumption and to increase their productive efforts to a greater extent than they would do under the other plan." [12]

Professor Pigou finally comes to this rather ambiguous conclusion: "Hence, we conclude generally that, from the standpoint of the national dividend, and apart altogether from political difficulties, taxation affords a *somewhat* better method than loans of raising money for emergencies. *How much* better it is, it is not, of course, possible to say."

In Chapter IX of the same book, Professor Pigou unsuccessfully attempts to refute Professors Seligman and Scott and comes to a more definite conclusion that, from the standpoint of a sound distribution, a great war ought not to be financed predominantly by loans, the interest on which will afterwards

---

[10] Pigou, *op. cit.*, p. 647.
[11] *Ibid.*
[12] See *ibid.*, p. 652.

be met by ordinary taxes. Rather a large part of the costs should be met by taxation levied at the time, on principles such as to lay a far greater part of the burden on the wealthy class than is usual under ordinary forms of taxation.[13]

Doctor Hugh Dalton is another prominent authority on public finance in Great Britain. With reference to a foreign debt, Dr. Dalton believes that its real burden depends upon the way in which that burden is distributed among the people. If the required money payments are made mainly by the rich, the burden will be less than if they are made mainly by the poor.

Putting it another way, the money payments are used by the external creditors to obtain goods and services, which would otherwise have been at the disposal of members of the debtor community. The latter are, therefore, deprived of goods and services to this amount, and the amount of direct real burden will depend on the way in which this deprivation is distributed.[14]

According to this writer there will be a direct and real burden of internal debt if the share of the burden of taxation borne by the rich is smaller than the proportion of public securities held by them. There will be a direct real benefit if the burden shared by the rich is larger. But as a matter of fact, in nearly all modern communities, owing to a vast inequality of incomes, public securities are held for the most part by the wealthier classes. On the other hand, taxation, no matter how progressive, is seldom so sharply progressive as to counterbalance among the rich classes the incomes which they obtain from public securities. In almost all cases, therefore, an internal debt also involves a direct and real burden.[15]

As to the indirect burden of a foreign debt, Dr. Dalton maintains that it arises from the check to the productive power of the community, due first to the taxation necessary for the payment of debt charges, and second, to the probable check to public expenditures which would promote production.[16] Internal debt involves similar indirect burden.

One reason for this is that the taxation required for the service of the debt tends to check production, insofar as it reduces taxpayers' ability and desire to work and save. Another reason is that short-sighted 'economies' in desirable social expenditure, which also tend

---

13 See *ibid.*, p. 664.
14 Hugh Dalton, *Public Finance*, p. 189.
15 See *ibid.*, pp. 191-92.
16 See *ibid.*, p. 190.

to check production, are particularly likely to be made when heavy taxation is required to meet debt charges.[17]

Dr. Dalton believes that taxation will probably reduce personal efficiency more than the receipt of debt charges will increase it. "There would thus be a net loss in ability to work, while ability to save would be unaffected by the transfer of income." He also believes that the assured yearly income to the bondholders will tend to reduce their desire to work and save.[18] However, as Prof. Bastable has stated, much depends upon the amount of taxation as well as the particular kinds of funds affected by the taxes, and therefore, we cannot accept Dr. Dalton's statements without some reservations. . .

With regard to war debts, Dr. Dalton gives us a clear exposition of their evil economic consequences to the following effect: It is a peculiarity of a period of war that the general level of prices and the rate of interest are unusually high. The former is due to reduced production coupled with the increase in paper money; while the latter is due to the shortage of capital combined with the large government borrowing. As prices fall, after the war, the amount of real wealth corresponding to a given money payment increases. Hence, when interest is paid on public debts, the transfer of real wealth from taxpayers to public creditors increases, and therefore, both the direct and the indirect burdens of the debt increase. Again, as the rate of interest falls, the prices of all public securities rise, and the money cost of repayment of a given amount of principal increases. Here again, therefore, the direct and the indirect burdens of the debt increase. If the fall in prices and the rate of interest occur simultaneously, the burden is so much the greater.[19] Dr. Dalton therefore favors "straightforward taxation as the chief means of financing war."

On repayment of public debts, the same writer expresses the following opinion: The rate at which a foreign debt should be paid off depends upon the wealth of the debtor community in relation to the amount of the debt. If the wealth of the debtor is great and the amount of the debt small, the debt should be repaid faster, and conversely. The rate at which an internal debt should be repaid depends upon different considerations, because here the repayment involves, not a diminution of wealth, but merely a transfer of wealth within the community. Here there is a good reason for rapid repayment

---

[17] Dalton, *op. cit.*, p. 192.
[18] See *ibid.*, p. 194.
[19] *Ibid.*, pp. 194-95.

regardless of the wealth of the community or the size of the debt. Indeed, in contrast with the case of an external debt, the argument for rapid repayment is stronger, the greater the burden of the debt, which means, in general, the greater its size.[20] If the debt is repaid slowly, the burden of interest payment will decrease slowly, while there will also be a long-enduring burden of sinking-fund payments. The probability is, therefore, that there will be a long-continued check to productivity and to beneficial public expenditure. If, on the other hand, the debt is paid off rapidly by means of a special but short-lived taxation, the burden of interest payment will diminish rapidly, while the additional burden due to taxation for repayment will not last long. The check to productive power of the community and to beneficial public expenditure will, therefore, be removed within a comparatively short time.[21]

Professor H. C. Adams, in his *Science of Finance,* states that public credit is the source of *anticipatory* revenue as contrasted with revenue that is direct or *derivative,* and every question that arises concerning it must be judged in the light of this fact. Moreover, industries and taxation are almost always limited in their view to the ordinary and ever-recurring fiscal needs of the state, while credit, correctly employed, offers a means to obtain a fund for some unusual object or to meet a demand of an unusual amount. In his opinion, therefore, if any state resorts to public credit for other purpose than to anticipate an orderly income in the future, it will sooner or later face a serious financial difficulty.

The industrial effect of public borrowing, therefore [says Professor Adams] must show itself in the fact that capital which might develop or sustain industries under the direction of private control is taken over by the state ; and if, . . . the capital borrowed is put to a non-industrial use, it is evident that the demand made by the state for funds through the placement of its bonds will disturb the orderly development of industry, if indeed it does not check that development or proceed so far as to cause the fall of industries already established.[22]

The same writer discusses loans for emergencies somewhat as follows : [23] When a government faces a sudden emergency, it is justified in resorting to a loan at least to bridge over the period between the levy of new taxes and the time at which

20 Dalton, *op. cit.,* pp. 201-202.
21 See *ibid.,* p. 202.
22 H. C. Adams, *Science of Finance,* pp. 520-21.
23 See Adams, *Public Debts,* pp. 83-85.

those taxes yield sufficient revenues. The reasons are : (1) The government needs a large extra fund immediately. But it takes a considerable time before new taxes become remunerative,— at best it takes many months, and at the worst it takes many years, and they become remunerative when the emergency pressure is gone. (2) The evils arising from a sudden great increase in the rate of taxation more than counterbalance the benefits. Indeed, we should always bear in mind that the expenses of wars or other emergencies are ultimately to be paid through the instrument of taxation. For an emergency, however, this instrument cannot be immediately and wholly relied upon. In any permanent system of taxation among modern nations, it usually happens that the rates of many taxes are so fixed as to yield the greatest possible revenues under the existing conditions. Therefore, a sudden increase in rate does not increase revenue; it may even cause a decrease in revenue. There are other taxes which are more elastic and which may be resorted to for the purpose of immediately increasing the revenue : for instance, excise or tariff. But the merchants, traders and manufacturers are much disturbed in their business calculations, and that may cause a decrease in production, not to mention a sudden rise in prices. Therefore, a violent change in the rates of even these taxes is inadvisable.

As to the method of financing public works,[24] Professor Adams, assuming that a certain public work is justified, believes the only economical method of raising a fund for its completion is public borrowing. Taxes could never secure a large enough fund within the time in which the work should be completed. The work should be done without interruption and within as short a period of time as possible, because every delay means the loss of the benefit derivable from the capital already invested, as well as the loss due to the damage usually sustained by any half-finished work. One might ask, why not raise the necessary fund by an extraordinary tax if that were possible? Professor Adams' answer is as follows : (1) That such a tax seriously disturbs the business relations of the community, (2) that it runs counter to one of the fundamental principles of public finance, viz., that a sound revenue system should be stable. The shock and the burden of a sudden tax are better replaced by a loan which distributes both of them more smoothly over a period of years. Moreover, in the last analysis, heavy taxation cannot eliminate the element of loan from the community. Except for the small contribution by way of diminished personal expenditures, the tax for the most part

24 Adams, op. cit., pp. 95-99.

is derived from employed capital. Now, in order to replace that portion paid out as taxes, business men must borrow from the possessors of free capital. Therefore, from the standpoint of the general welfare of the community, if the government can contract a debt on better terms than private persons, government borrowing is much to be preferred.

Professor W. M. Daniels [25] believes that it is doubtful whether any formula — that is, a rule telling the financier when to resort to public debts — can prove of much real assistance. He doubts the importance of Professor Adams' classification.[26] In his opinion, since interest is paid to the public creditors out of current taxation, the merit of any particular borrowing can be decided only by weighing the benefits accruing from the proceeds of the loan and the sacrifice (that is expressed in higher taxes) and comparing the two. But such benefits are often very imperfectly measurable in money terms. The inference is, therefore, that the economic effect of a particular public debt is to that extent indeterminable. Professor Daniels' criticism does not seem to us quite well-founded. A precise measurement of the economic effects of a public loan, if possible, is certainly very desirable and very useful. For our practical purposes, however, it is not essential in determining the financial policy or in giving judgment upon its general economic effects.

We have thus far reviewed the opinions of the several writers on the general questions of public loans, and these necessarily have been expressed in but little more than summary statements. We now come to a writer who gives us an exhaustive discussion of a specific phase — perhaps the most important one — of public loans.

In Chapter XXIII of his *Essays in Taxation, Professor E. R. A. Seligman* discusses the question of "Loans versus Taxes in War Finance."

The fiscal problems of the war [says this authority] may be divided into those of a general and of a specific character. War expenditures can be met in three ways : by taxes, by loans, or by paper money. The specific problems have to deal with the nature and the details of each of these expedients ; the general problem is concerned with the principles that underlie the preference among the respective methods. Inasmuch as paper money is by common consent to be regarded as the last resort, the general problem at issue

---

[25] See his *The Elements of Public Finance*, p. 295.

[26] On pp. 78-101 in his *Public Debts*, Prof. Adams maintains that loans may be used to cover a temporary deficit, to meet a fiscal emergency and to meet demands arising from public works.

here pertains to the choice between loans and taxes and the relative proportions in which each is to be employed.[27]

Professor Seligman then goes on to tell us of the changes in the method of war financing between the past ages and the present. Speaking of the financing of the World War, he brings out the fact that by far the greater part of war expenditures were met by the belligerents through loans, the proportion raised by taxation ranging from 17% in Great Britain to zero in France. He asks: in spite of suggestions by economists and others that the war cost be met by taxation, why did the belligerent governments follow the loan method primarily? In answering this question, Professor Seligman first raises and answers the question, "What are war costs?"

It is obvious [says Professor Seligman] that a distinction must be made between the money costs and the real costs of a war. The *money costs* of a war are the actual outlays of the government for war purposes, that is, the surplus above the general expenditures in time of peace, making due allowance for changes in the purchasing power of money. . . The *real costs* of a war are to be measured by the diminution of the social patrimony and by the diversion of current social output from productive to unproductive channels, i. e., by changes both in the fund of accumulated wealth and in the flow of social income.[28]

But, says the same writer, in order to go to the root of the nature of real costs, we must analyze further. He analyzes them into two elements, objective and subjective. By objective costs he means the sacrifice or pain of physical and mental exertions, and abstinence, or the foregoing of enjoyments. The real wealth of a community depends upon net sacrifices, or, net subjective costs. And by net subjective costs Professor Seligman means the exertions and abstinences which are over and above those economically worth while to make. The important criterion in the economic welfare of a community is, therefore, the net subjective cost or sacrifice. "This is as true in war as in time of peace."[29]

Now, applying this idea to war, Professor Seligman continues:

The true costs of a war are the net sacrifices or subjective burdens which result from the transition from a peace economy to a war economy, and which are connected with the fundamental processes

27 Seligman, *Essays in Taxation* (9th ed.), pp. 715-16.
28 *Ibid.*, p. 717.
29 See *ibid.*, p. 720.

of production and consumption. They consist, on the one hand, of all those efforts involved in the transfer of enterprises and investments from the ordinary channels of production to the new fields of primary importance in the war. They consist, on the other hand, of all those efforts involved in the reduction and the change of consumption which will serve to counterbalance, in part at least, the inevitable reduction of social output. The net result measured in terms of aggregate sacrifice or subjective cost constitutes the real burden of a war. The problem that confronts us is to analyze the results of various fiscal expedients upon these changes in production and consumption from the point of view of the subjective costs or the real burdens resting on society.[30]

Professor Seligman then raises the question : Can war costs be diminished in the present or be shared with the future? And he answers : — Except for certain limitations and exceptions, the objective costs can neither be diminished nor shared with the future, because the commodities and services are now produced and now consumed. The exceptions and limitations are such things as (a) the using of fixed capital without adequately providing for its upkeep, thereby causing deterioration of the plants, the machines, etc., (b) the capital fixed for war purposes only, leaving so much less capital after the war, (c) overworking of labor, resulting in less energy and efficiency after the war. When it comes to the subjective costs, however, the situation is quite different. Subjective costs may be reduced without shifting any of the burden to the future, or they may be partly diminished and partly shifted to the future. Obviously, neither of these consequences is obtainable by the method of taxation,— the reason simply being that the present taxpayers bear the burden, although the future taxpayers may also bear some burden.

"Is the same true," asks the same writer, "in the case of loans? Are the subjective costs or sacrifices of the community in any way lessened by government borrowing? This brings up for consideration the theory of public credit."

Professor Seligman then proceeds to discuss private and public credit. The use of private credit for productive purposes, that is for business enterprise, diminishes the individual's subjective sacrifice for the obvious reason that he expects a future profit. But even a private credit for the purpose of consumption diminishes the individual's subjective sacrifice because of his underestimating the future and because of the possibility of gradual repayment. "The social utility of credit is therefore quite clear. It increases the wealth of the com-

[30] Seligman, *op. cit.*, p. 720.

munity by lessening the subjective sacrifices of certain individuals and putting at the disposal of the community funds where they will be utilized to the greatest advantage, thus decreasing costs and increasing output." [31]

After discussing the differences between private and public credit the same writer says that all the advantages of private credit hold true of public credit. On public credit, he says:

Its utility consists in the fact that, through borrowing from those in possession of the capital rather than taxing all the members of the community, whether or not they have the capital, it lessens subjective costs or sacrifices and puts at the disposal of the government those services in the community with which it can most easily dispense.[32]

Why cannot taxes take up that same capital? he asks; and then he answers, "In order to invalidate this statement it would be necessary for the government to take by taxation from each individual absolutely everything above the necessary means of subsistence. Only then would this particular argument as to the advantage of loans over taxes lose its force." [33]

Professor Seligman further proves that this diminution of subjective costs of the community may lead to greater social production, or, what is the same thing, to a decrease in objective costs to society. Then he says, "If, then, it is true that the utilization of public credit may involve a lessening of subjective costs or real burdens upon the community, can it in the second place accomplish this by transferring a part of the burden to the future?" [34] After proving the fallacy of the contention that the sacrifice imposed upon the future tax-payers is counterbalanced by the benefit to the bondholders, Professor Seligman says, "We may, therefore, consider it as established that it is possible, not only to diminish the subjective sacrifice on the present, but also to put a share of the burden upon the future. It has also been established that the device of public credit necessarily accomplishes the second result in effecting the first." [35]

Finally, this writer asks: "Ought the burdens of a war to be shared with the future?" After analyzing and comparing the

31 Seligman, *op. cit.*, p. 724.
32 *Ibid.*, p. 726.
33 *Ibid.*, p. 726.
34 *Ibid.*, p. 729.
35 *Ibid.*, pp. 731-32.

various sorts of government expenditures, he maintains that war expenditures should be classed as recurring, extraordinary expenditures, and comes to the following well-balanced conclusion:

The conclusion, therefore, would be that in the case of a great war it would meet all the demands of justice to put part of the burden upon the present tax-payers and to shift the remainder upon the tax-payers of succeeding years, with the understanding that all the charges of the war will finally have been met before the period when the recurrence of a similar outbreak is within the realm of probability. This conclusion in other words shows the essential legitimacy of utilizing both loans and taxes in times of war.[36]

Professor Carl C. Plehn expresses his fundamental conception of public loans in a summary way, as follows:

Much attention has been given by different authorities on public finance to the economic effects of public borrowing. The consensus of opinion is that public borrowing does not, as was once taught, create new wealth except indirectly, through the use made of the capital taken when it is used productively. Nor, on the other hand, does public borrowing in itself directly destroy wealth. The money borrowed may be devoted to some form of rapid consumption, as in war. In this case the destruction of wealth is determined by the line of expenditure decided upon, not by the borrowing merely. . . As in the case of a spendthrift who mortgages his patrimony for wasteful extravagance, so in the case of a nation which borrows for war, the evil that arises is from the waste of war, not from the borrowing. For a state to borrow for a productive purpose has no other economic effect than for a private corporation to do the same.[37]

On the difference between public and private debts, *Professor M. H. Hunter* tells us that in private enterprise the squandering of funds or failure of the undertaking, frequently means the inability to meet liabilities. In the case of a state, however, liabilities can be met from the general taxing power. As long as taxes can be secured, the interest and the principal of debts can be paid. The ability of an individual to meet a liability depends upon the success of his particular industry, while the ability of the state to meet liabilities depends upon the success of industry in general. It is because of this broad patrimony that the state is often able to secure funds on better terms than individuals.[38]

---

[36] Seligman, *op. cit.*, p. 736.
[37] See Carl C. Plehn, *Introduction to Public Finance*, 4th ed., p. 349.
[38] See M. H. Hunter, *Outlines of Public Finance*, p. 391.

The same writer believes it is among the advantages of borrowing as against taxation in financing a war that the people feel less hurt; and also that idle capital can be utilized more quickly and to a fuller extent.[39] On the disadvantages, he says that borrowing increases the cost of war in a two-fold manner: (1) Government has to pay higher prices for goods, (2) people have to pay higher prices for commodities. The reason for this is the increase in the purchasing media. Increased prices work hardship on the people of fixed incomes, i. e., on wage-earners in general. On this last point, a word should be said as to the validity of Professor Hunter's opinion. . . Although public borrowing is almost always followed by inflation, this is not the necessary consequence of public borrowing. If public loans were made from the real savings of the people, inflation need not follow at all. But of this, more later.

Professor Hunter further believes that public borrowing does not shift the burden of war to the future. "There is no question," says he, "but that war entails a burden upon the future — the sinking of battleships and merchant marine, the destruction of factories, cities, mines, railroads, and agricultural lands, which otherwise would have been handed down to posterity, is conclusive evidence that war places a burden upon the future. The contention, however, that the burden may be shifted has, in reality, no foundation. In only one way can this be possible." And he mentions foreign loans.[40] "It is impossible to eat one's cake and have it too — one cannot spend his money for goods and at the same time turn it over to the government to purchase war materials."[41]

True, it is incontrovertible that the material burden of the war — taking the nation as a whole — cannot be shifted. But, as Professor Seligman ably contends, its 'psychological burden' can be shifted to the future. A person going through a surgical operation today cannot 'shift' today's loss of blood; but through the use of anesthetics his pain can be shifted to the following days. The shock at operation might have killed him. And so it seems with loans, as against excessive taxation, in war time. Assuming that future burdens are distributed equally, to a cold mathematical logic there is nothing more absurd than to insist that it is more soothing for a person to give up all the future income of a thousand dollars as an increased share of future taxation than to give up those thousand dollars now and be free

39 Hunter, *op. cit.*, p. 449.
40 See *ibid.*, p. 452.
41 *Ibid.*, p. 453.

from that future increase in taxation. Yet that is precisely the situation when we take the people as a whole. Whatever the government borrows today, we have to provide from today, and we only receive in return a "shadow" of claim called bonds. But our present and our future incomes are diminished to the extent that our government shoots them off from the mouths of cannons. (We have assumed that future taxes are to be distributed equally. To the extent that the wealthy classes bear relatively less burden than the poorer classes, they gain more under the loan policy than under the taxation policy.)

However, taking human nature as it is, in a period of war when every encouragement must be given to increased production, it were perhaps wiser for a practical financier of a nation to preserve the people's optimism even though it may be based largely upon illusory thinking. In this connection it is interesting to notice that a large part of that optimism is, consciously or unconsciously, based upon the expectation of victory, for no nation would enter a war if it were sure of defeat.

Professor Hunter seems to be an ardent theoretical supporter of the taxing policy instead of the loan policy. His statements under the heading "Exaggerated Objections" are admirable.[42] But he recognizes the practical difficulties of exclusive reliance on taxation.[43]

In the opinion of *Professor N. G. Pierson,* whenever, at the time of its flotation, no proper measures are adopted to insure the redemption of a loan, that loan is *permanent.* On the other hand, if, at the same time with the issue of loans, taxes are increased or expenditures are reduced to such a degree as must automatically effect the repayment of the loan at the end of a certain period, that loan is *temporary,* even though it should take the form of a long-term debt.[44] He maintains that permanent loans should only be contracted for the purpose of such expenditures as are certain to yield revenues amounting to at least the interest on the loans. If a more liberal policy be pursued in the use of permanent loans, there results a chronic deficit, and a chronic deficit is a chronic evil, constantly increasing and resulting in a steady growth of taxation.[45]

On war loans, Professor Pierson gives us the following admirable view :

[42] Hunter, *op. cit.,* p. 456.
[43] See *ibid.,* pp. 458-61.
[44] N. G. Pierson, *Principles of Economics,* English translation, vol. ii, pp. 607-8.
[45] See *ibid.,* pp. 608-9.

The mistake usually made by public financiers in time of war has not lain in having recourse to loans. That was no mistake; it was necessary. It would be all the more necessary in these days, for the cost of a war is far greater than it used to be, and could not possibly be defrayed at once by means of taxation. Where the mistake lay, was in not at once devising measures for extinguishing the debt within a certain number of years. . . Each generation should bear its own burdens, in order that the National Debt may not swell to extravagant proportions. If the burdens are distributed over a certain number of years the fulfillment of this requirement becomes possible.[46]

According to this writer, what has been said concerning war cost is also true of other extraordinary expenditures. Schools for large towns mean annually recurring expenditures. In small towns and villages they are truly extraordinary expenditures, and therefore can properly be met by loans. "What must be avoided, is the spreading of the debt over too long a period." Again, if ultimate advantage is considered, it is much more preferable to issue bonds at par, because by so doing both conversion and redemption can be made more easily.[47] In cases of small loans or where the future generation gains increasingly greater benefit, the annuity system (that is, the system in which payment is the same year after year until the debt is extinguished completely) is harmless. However, for large loans, the yearly redemption of the largest possible sums is much to be preferred, for thereby the burdening of future generations is avoided.[48]

Professor Pierson, contrary to Adams and others whom he refutes, advocates the system of obligatory periodical payments as offering greater guarantee to the observance of debt repayment.[49] He opposes total extinguishment of debt by increased taxation because the benefits to be derived are remote, and present sacrifices are great. For countries of poor credit, however, where high rates of interest are paid, the endeavor to repay the whole debt is advantageous in that it improves the credit of such countries and enables conversions. In countries of good credit it will suffice for this purpose to apply surpluses of prosperous years.[50]

Leroy-Beaulieu believes that public borrowing is in itself neither good nor evil; "or rather," says he, "we should frankly say, the ability for a state to contract debts is a good, an incon-

[46] Pierson, *op. cit.*, pp. 623-24.
[47] See *ibid.*, pp. 624-26.
[48] See *ibid.*, pp. 629-30.
[49] See *ibid.*, pp. 630-37.
[50] See *ibid.*, pp. 637-44.

testable good." The public credit is a respectable power and is useful like private credit, but it is a power which can be abused. Beaulieu, however, refutes the idea that internal debts are under any circumstances not harmful. He explodes the sophistry of Voltaire and Melon, somewhat as follows:

This is how one can demonstrate the falsity of that sophism: it is very true that one of the consequences of public borrowing is to levy on the taxpayers by means of a tax a certain sum which is afterwards distributed to the bondholders for the claim of the interest. If the person held himself to such a superficial view of it, he might find that the state is indifferent to such things, as there is there no loss of the public fortune since certain nationals by the name of bondholders receive that which is paid by the other nationals by the name of taxpayers. These people expostulate that the nation itself would not be impoverished. But it is necessary to push the analysis further: Suppose no borrowing were done. The taxpayers would keep for themselves the surplus of the tax which is destined to pay the interest to the annuitants. On the other hand, the annuitants would have in their possession the capital which they lend to the state in the case of a loan, and, whether they should themselves put this capital to account or whether they should intrust it to some enterprisers or manufacturers, they would draw from it interest almost equal to that which the state pays when it borrows. Thus, in the case where a public loan is contracted, the annuitants acquire the interest of the capital lent to the state only at the expense of the taxpayers who pay them. In cases where no borrowing is done the taxpayers keep the money which they might otherwise have had to pay as tax to pay the interest on the borrowed sum: and the annuitants, having left in their hands and putting to account the capital which they might have lent to the state if it had borrowed, are not deprived of their interest. One sees the difference between the two cases: when there is a loan, one of the parties is injured; when there is no loan, each of the two parties — the taxpayers and the annuitants — has at its disposal the sum which in the case of a loan belongs only to one of them. . . When there is a loan the right hand, that is to say the taxpayer, passes its money to the left hand, that is to say the annuitant; where there is no loan, each of the two hands rests completely, which is preferable.[51]

Beaulieu's above argument does not hold in one particular case, and that is when the loan is made for a purpose directly

[51] See Leroy-Beaulieu, *Traité de la sicence des finances*, 8th ed., vol. ii, pp. 227-28.

contributing to the productive capacities of the taxpayers, so that they are more than compensated for their increased burden of taxation.   Loans for public utilities are examples of such a case.

This same writer contends that public borrowing is useful if it is for the purpose of public works such as railroads, canals, ports and establishments of public instruction; if the government brings into these enterprises some standard and judgment; and if the works have been judiciously selected and executed with economy.[52] If, on the contrary, the capital which the state has borrowed and which the annuitants have parted with is wasted in the pleasures of the court, in ostentatious buildings or in foolish enterprises, then it is clear that society will be impoverished, because the capital which the annuitants have been deprived of will absolutely cease to exist or will only be represented by some unproductive works such as palaces, jewels, etc.[53]

A loan, then, will be useful or harmful to society in general, [says Beaulieu] according as the state will have preserved and employed usefully or wasted and destroyed the capital the possession of which the annuitants will have abandoned.   But, since in the past the passions of the sovereigns and the errors of the governments have had the effect of dispersing the product of most part of the loans in useless expenditures, many minds have been swept off to condemn public credit, absolutely, as an instrument of evil.   This conclusion is exaggerated.   It is as good as to say that it were desirable that man had no senses because he often errs by his senses.[54]

Beaulieu admits that public loans stimulate the spirit of saving, and he cites as examples the two great loans after the Franco-Prussian War.   But he cautiously adds that that portion of the loan which represents — considered from the side of the annuitants — an economy which they would not have made if the loan had not been issued, is always only a very small part of the total amount of the loan.   If, then, this loan has been wasted in useless expenditures, it is a folly to argue as an advantage that it has stimulated national economy.[55]

Again, in this writer's opinion, one of the other economic and financial effects of public loans in the country has been to

52 Leroy-Beaulieu, *op. cit.*, pp. 228-29.
53 See *ibid.*, pp. 228-229.
54 Ibid., pp. 229-30.
55 See *ibid.*, pp. 230-31.

spread among the mass of the people the knowledge of and the desire for securities, consequently to generalize credit and also the spirit of enterprise.

It is incontestable [says Beaulieu] that the public loans have been, from this point of view, means of initiation. In all the civilized countries the inhabitants of the rural districts and in general the thrifty men of the lower class have had and still preserve some habit of distrusting the investments in securities. They are afraid to let go of their savings ; they dare not lend to the companies whose conditions of existence they do not know, nor to the individuals whose solvency they suspect. Also they bury their savings in some hiding places and leave them most often unproductive. The public loans — above all, those which are put in circulation through the process of universal subscription — break through these habits little by little. As the state is the only personage of a country whose solvency everyone might *grosso modo* esteem, the most timid people concluded by daring to lend to it. Then, after having thus familiarized themselves with the securities, they feel less dislike for them. From the annuities of the state, they pass to the securities of municipal loans, and to the securities of the railroad companies. It is thus that public loans have served in Europe as initiators to the credit of the joint-stock societies and of the collective enterprises. . .[56]

In spite of all this, the writer says, however, that the repeated issues of great public loans have, with time, given them a bad direction. The more a country borrows, the more the credit is concentrated in the capital city or the seat of principal exchange of the country. There is thus produced a centralization of capital which peculiarly harms local enterprises. The people complain that the savings of the rural communities are absorbed, as soon as they are created, by the public loans which dissipate them often in pure waste, and by such companies as the Land Trust of Paris, which employ them in constructing luxurious buildings in the cities. It is so much lost, they say, to agriculture, to the fecundation of the soil, to the production of the necessaries of life. For this reason, many persons in France have come to believe that the expansion of public credit is an evil. Although there is a great deal of truth in these recriminations, says Beaulieu, the cause of these is not the public credit itself; it is its excessive concentration and the intemperate abuse of the national loans. Public credit, when correctly used, has permitted a great number of collective enterprises which have profited the whole country and especially the

[56] Leroy-Beaulieu, *op. cit.*, pp. 231-32.

rural districts, in particular the network of lines of communication.[57]

Although Beaulieu has great confidence in public loans, he is not oblivious to some of their unfortunate results. He recognizes that the frequent public loans save capitalists from the necessity of seeking a useful employment for their capital, and thus tend to check their spirit of enterprise. He also admits that public loans have always resulted in raising the rate of interest in the country by diminishing its disposable circulating capital, which in turn has increased production costs of industries, reduced the profits of the merchants, and rendered difficult the creation of great works of public utility by the individuals or by joint-stock companies.[58] (This writer proves the point by French statistics.) In a country which issues large loans, it is probable that the fixed capital will be less well maintained than if the loan had not taken place. Whether there is a compensation for this reduction of circulating capital and this impoverishment of fixed capital depends upon the use which is made of the capital borrowed. However, says Beaulieu, the diminution of the circulating capital in a country is ordinarily less than the sum borrowed for several reasons: (1) public loans always stimulate saving to a certain extent; (2) large public loans always bring out of the safes, the writing desks, the straw mattresses, and the old stockings, a part of the metallic reserve which is a country's dormant capital; (3) public loans are often subscribed to, to a great extent, by foreigners.[59] Beaulieu here refutes Condorcet's view that it is to be regretted if a national loan is subscribed by foreigners because the interest will be paid and consumed outside of the country:

Indeed, if the interest goes out of the country upon its being paid, it should not be forgotten that the capital of the loan has entered the country. . . This capital, it is true, could be wasted — what happened in the past with many loans of the state. But it would have been equally so if the capital had been taken from the country, and then the means of production would have been reduced: while, if the means of production were not diminished, the revenue only would have been diminished. In supposing that a state must borrow, there is an advantage and not a disadvantage in what it borrows from outside, provided that it does not borrow at an excessive and ruinous rate. But it is very rare that a state can borrow from outside in a permanent manner and for a long duration.[60]

[57] See Leroy-Beaulieu, *op. cit.*, pp. 234-35.
[58] See *ibid.*, p. 237.
[59] *Ibid.*, pp. 239-40.
[60] *Ibid.*, p. 240.

Beaulieu thus rightly contends that the foreigner comes to the aid of the nation which borrows, even if temporarily, and saves it from reducing its circulating capital as much as would have been necessary if that foreign aid had not come.[61]

He continues to discuss at length the influx of foreign capital as an indirect result of a large public loan. He proves by statistics that the reasons for this are : (1) national securities are popular among foreign capitalists, and (2) the securities of all kinds including foreign, fall in price because of the domestic monetary situation, and that therefore the foreigners come to buy them up as much as they can. He says that the huge operation of the payment of five billion francs by France to Germany at the end of the Franco-Prussian War was effected through the working of this latter factor.

According to *Adolph Wagner,* government expenditures and revenues are divided into ordinary and extraordinary. Ordinary expenditures are those involved in maintaining legal protection and in promoting culture and welfare, etc., and they recur year after year. Ordinary revenues are those obtained generally from taxation. Ordinary expenditures must always be covered by ordinary revenues. Extraordinary expenditures are those occasioned by abnormal difficulties, such as wars. Extraordinary revenues are those obtained through national loans. Extraordinary expenditures are preferably to be covered by extraordinary revenues.[62] Nevertheless, says Professor Wagner, we cannot declare ourselves unconditionally for the utilization of the national credit to cover extraordinary needs, because the effects of taxes and of national debts on the position of individual economies and national economy can be different. It is evident that those means of reimbursement are most advantageous which work most favorably on the national economy in drawing commodities from the individual economies. Whether and how far such differences exist between taxation and debt assumption is still to be proved, the answer depending upon whether the law of applicability of national credit in the national finances has to experience more or less limitation against the position that all extraordinary expenditures — on account of their more lasting effects in themselves — might be covered by national debts.[63]

Professor Wagner then goes on to distinguish three kinds of loans according to the kinds of capital from which they flow :

[61] Leroy-Beaulieu, *op. cit.,* p. 224.
[62] See Adolph Wagner, *Finanzwissenschaft,* 3rd ed., pp. 143-52.
[63] *Op. cit.,* p. 153.

(a) Loans from truly disposable capital of domestic national economy ; (b) loans from capital of foreign national economy [debt to
foreign country] ; (c) loans from domestic capital which are first
drawn by loan from productive employment elsewhere in the home
country. Always supposing that the loan is admissible for the
kind of expenditures which have to be covered with it, in general,
from the standpoint of the particular national economy, the loans
of the first and second kinds may be preferred to taxation. On the
other hand, conversely taxation must be chosen instead of a loan
of the third kind.[64]

Even for the covering of extraordinary expenditures, this
writer prefers taxation everywhere except where loans of the
two above-mentioned kinds are possible, and when without such
loans the capital might be wasted in bad undertakings or
speculations.[65] He also prefers foreign loans to loans at home
where capital is drawn from productive employment. The
reason he gives is obviously that thereby domestic production
is increased or at least its diminution is prevented. To Professor Wagner it is immaterial in this regard whether the proceeds
of the loans were used productively or unproductively, for without such foreign loans, a corresponding diminution of capital,
and hence of production, would take place at home.[66] We
remember that Leroy-Beaulieu also was of this opinion. Although some writers seem to oppose foreign loans except in
cases of extreme necessity, we agree with this broad view of
Beaulieu and Wagner. . .

Professor Wagner reiterates the evil effects of loans obtained
from capital productively employed. The capitalists, according to him, are induced to participate in the loan by the
prospect of greater gain than they draw from the employment
hitherto made of their capital — the supposition of his discussion. A particular motive for real limitation of consumption,
for greater thrift in order to form new capital, and for increased productive activity is not, therefore, engendered in
these classes by the loan, but perhaps it is by taxation. By loan,
consequently, that part of the national income, or national
wealth, which the state withdraws from the individual economies to cover its financial need is threatened to be transferred
to the disposal of the state at the cost of the classes of people
who possess no capital and who did not participate in the loan ;
above all, at the cost of the mass of the workingmen. By the
equal taxation of all classes, the possessors of capital must bear

[64] Wagner, op. cit., p. 154.
[65] See ibid., pp. 155-56.
[66] See ibid., pp. 157-60.

their share of this burden and are spurred on to make good again this loss in income or capital, which the tax imposes on them, through suitable regulation of their consumption and their saving and through increase of their productivity.[67] What Professor Wagner says is generally true in practice, but theoretically it is not necessary for the poorer classes alone to bear the burden. If the increase in tax burden after and on account of the loan is equitably distributed, we could still retain all the advantages of the loan without bringing hardships on the poorer members of society. Those who are fighting against tax-exemption of national bonds have precisely this point in view. . .

The same writer reverts to the question of the advisability of the actual use of national credit according to the particular kinds of extraordinary expenditures, and he says that war costs had better be met by taxation or foreign loans and in certain cases by loans which come from disposable capital of the domestic national economy; that the national economic capital investment, such as that for administrative reforms, etc., is also better covered by taxation because its favorable effects are not easily measurable; and that the private capital investments, that is, the investments for government-owned industries, are better covered by loans.[68]

Professor Wagner finally discusses the specific case of war loans. He considers that loans are very costly in war time because they have to be floated at high rates of interest; that loans sometimes do not suffice or are not contracted quickly enough; that therefore the precautionary measures which are to be taken for this purpose are the establishment of a national treasure (war treasure) and the arrangement of a system of extra (war) taxes.[69] The same writer also discusses at length the subject of war treasure and defends it. In his opinion, if the amount is moderate the service which it performs — namely, preservation of greater security for the state and for the national economy — outweighs the loss incurred by way of interest losses, etc. A further advantage of it lies in the ability of the government thereby to secure better conditions for its war loans. It is surprising to us that so great an authority in public finance as Professor Wagner should entertain such ideas on the use of a war treasure. . . The war treasure has been discarded by practically all other authorities on public finance as an inadequate and uneconomical system of war finance. An imme-

[67] Wagner, *op. cit.*, pp. 163-64.
[68] *Ibid.*, pp. 165-66.
[69] See *ibid.*, pp. 170-73.

diate need for a fund at the outbreak of a war can be easily met by the government by the issue of treasury certificates or some similar device. The modern war loans, also, are so large that the conditions of their flotation are very unlikely to be affected at all by the government's possession of a relatively small fund in the form of a war treasure; rather . . . they are conditioned upon the permanent credit of the government.

QUESTIONS AND PROBLEMS FOR DISCUSSION

1. Do you believe that the principles of private credit are applicable to public credit?
2. Should funds obtained through public borrowing be directed only into so-called reproductive channels?
3. When is it legitimate for a government to borrow?
4. Discuss Pigou's conclusion that "taxation affords a *somewhat* better method than loans of raising money for emergencies."
5. What does Dalton mean by his contention that the real burden of a public debt "depends upon the way in which that burden is distributed among the people"?
6. What is the importance of the indirect burden of a nation's foreign debt?
7. What factors determine the rate at which an internal public debt should be paid off?
8. How would you attempt to weigh the benefit resulting from the expenditure of the proceeds of a public loan against the sacrifice involved in the resultant higher taxes?
9. How may public loans stimulate the spirit of saving?
10. Do you agree with Wagner's views on the proper use of taxes and loans for financing public enterprises?

SUGGESTIONS FOR RESEARCH

1. The nature and proper use of public credit.
2. The development of the theories of public credit.
3. Private and public credit compared.
4. Popular (as distinct from professional or academic) theories of public credit.
5. A comparison of the views of Alexander Hamilton and Albert Gallatin on the nature and purpose of public credit.

BIBLIOGRAPHICAL NOTE

For the student who is interested in further study of the theory of public credit, the following references, which provide direct and complete statements of the views discussed in this chapter, are especially recommended: C. F. Bastable, *Public Finance,* (London, 1917), Bk. V, Chap. V; Paul Leroy-Beaulieu, *Traité de la Science des Finances,* (Paris, 1883), Vol. II, Bk. II, Chaps. I, IV; A. C.

Pigou, *Wealth and Welfare*, (London, 1912), Pt. IV, Chap. VIII; also his, *A Study in Public Finance*, (London, 1928), Pt. III, Chap. I; and Adolph Wagner, *Finanzwissenschaft*, (Leipzig, 1883), Vol. I, pp. 144-173.

Early theories of public credit may be found in C. J. Bullock, *Selected Readings in Public Finance*, (Boston, 1924), Chaps. XXII, XXIII; and Shutaro Matsushita, *The Economic Effects of Public Debts*, (New York, 1929), Chap. I.

CHAPTER XXIV

ECONOMIC EFFECTS OF PUBLIC CREDIT: THE PURPOSE OF BORROWING

In this and the remaining chapters on public credit, attention will be given to the economic effects of governmental borrowing. These effects are dependent upon the purpose, the nature, and the method of repayment of public debts. In the present chapter the relationship between purpose and economic effects will be discussed.

Students of public finance agree that it is legitimate to borrow, to some extent at least, for the following purposes: (1) the covering of temporary deficits; (2) the financing of capital outlay; and (3) the meeting of emergency expenditures. The discussion of purposes (1) and (2), as presented in Professor Paul Studenski's excellent treatment of public credit, follows.

1. TEMPORARY DEFICITS AND CAPITAL OUTLAYS *

THE USE OF SHORT-TERM LOANS TO COVER TEMPORARY DEFICITS JUSTIFIED

SHORT-TERM loans made to cover temporary deficits in the treasury due to the uneven flow of revenue from month to month are clearly justified. It is impossible to synchronize completely the rate of expenditures with the rate of revenue collections from time to time. The expenditures are bound to run at a more even rate than the collections, only a portion of which are continuous in nature. Most of the direct taxes are paid annually, semi-annually, or quarterly and concentrate in certain months. It would be possible, of course, for a government to accumulate a reserve and to borrow from it, thus avoiding payment of interest. But an arrangement of this nature has at least two disadvantages. One is that taxpayers would be deprived of the use of their funds which might have earned a larger rate of interest than the two, three, or four per cent which

---

* From Walter E. Spahr and others, *Economic Principles and Problems*, (Ray Long and Richard R. Smith, Inc., New York, 1932), Vol. II, Chap. XXXIV, pp. 540-545. Sections written by Professor Studenski.

they would earn for the government while on deposit in the banks or invested in the government's own bonds. The other disadvantage is that the management of this fund may require a greater amount of skill than the average financial officer of the government may be able to display, and the government may suffer losses through the mismanagement of the fund.

Short-term loans are also justified when used to cover temporary budget deficits due to unforeseen emergencies necessitating additional expenditures or to miscalculation of revenue or a sudden fall in revenue. Such contingencies are bound to occur, and the issuance of short-term loans to be liquidated in the next budget constitute an effective way of taking care of them. But the privilege of engaging in such temporary financing must not be abused. Every effort must be bent on reducing the occurrence of such contingencies, since otherwise the budget will cease to be effective. Furthermore under such a loan policy interest charges become excessive and the form of financing current expenditures becomes more expensive than that of taxation.

Loans should never be used in lieu of taxes in the financing of expenditures for current services or for the payment of interest on loans, for such a policy increases government costs and debts in an unreasonable manner and is the surest road toward bankruptcy.

JUSTIFICATION OF LOANS IN THE FINANCING OF CAPITAL
OUTLAYS

THERE are, broadly speaking, three ways of financing capital outlays: one is to finance them entirely from loans; the other is to finance them entirely from current revenues; and the third is to use both of these resources regularly or from time to time.

Many national governments follow the all-loan policy of financing capital outlays and take care of them in the extraordinary budget which they maintain for this and other, supposedly exceptional, purposes. Most of the municipal governments in this country also follow the all-loan policy in the financing of these outlays. They issue usually a separate loan for each separate object, (say) $1,000,000 issue for certain street improvements, $2,000,000 issue for the enlargement of the water supply, $1,200,000 issue for the construction of certain schools, and so on. The all-loan policy is usually defended on the ground that the properties constructed or acquired by these outlays will render service for many years; that it is only fair that all the successive generations that will use these properties and will be benefited by them should pay for them; and that only financing them by loans can accomplish this result, since loans alone can shift charges to the future and the loans can be made to run for the entire life of the particular properties so that interest and amortization charges on them will be payable each year during their life.

This justification of an all-loan policy cannot stand close analysis. Its principal faults lie in the fact that it stresses one phase of the situation — that of equitable distribution of costs between present and future users — and ignores other no less important phases and considerations. An all-loan policy is unwise from the point of view of economy. It leads to a far too liberal and careless authorization of capital outlays and expenditure of capital funds, since taxpayers are inclined to offer much less objection to expenditures financed from loans than to those financed from immediate taxation. It increases unduly the costs of the capital outlays to taxpayers in the long run, inasmuch as interest charges are added under it and over a long period of time they make up in the aggregate a very substantial addition to the cost.

The all-loan policy is unwise also from the point of view of financial safety, since public credit may be used to finance minor projects with the result that it may prove insufficient in time to finance emergencies or the more important projects which may arise. It also results in a far too rapid accumulation of debt and annual debt charges during prosperous times or periods of rapid growth of the community, with consequent embarrassment in times of depression.

The all-loan policy is unsound, in the next place, because it is based upon a very one-sided conception of what is an equitable distribution of burdens between the present and future generations of taxpayers. Under this policy charges are distributed between the present and the future in an equal manner, without regard to differences in the tax-paying ability of the community at different times. Finally, such a policy is based upon a very inadequate notion of the benefits which society derives from capital outlays and the properties acquired or constructed by their means. In this notion, each outlay on property constructed or acquired is a separate undertaking, benefiting primarily the future and, hence, a proper charge primarily on future years. The properties are not viewed as they should be — in the aggregate and in their interrelation as parts of, or additions to, an existing and evergrowing governmental plant which renders services currently. Neither are the outlays for them considered as parts of a continuous process of expenditure for the reconstruction' and expansion of that plant. If these outlays were appraised properly it would have been apparent that such improvements go largely to replace worn out property, and that the benefits obtained from them are largely of current nature ; that they constitute only in part a net addition to the plant which will render benefits mainly in future years ; and that the distribution of charges for such outlays according to benefits, between different generations of the users of the plant may be attained as well and much more simply and economically if each generation adds its proper share of improvements for the replacement of, and additions to, the plant and pays for them currently, borrowing merely for any excess amount of them.[1]

In a few cases, however, an all-loan policy may be justified as, for example, in communities which are yet in a relatively undeveloped state and lack the means for raising by taxation even a part of the costs of the capital outlays. It may be justified even in the most prosperous and developed communities in times of a business depression, when it is important to keep taxes low and yet execute a large amount of public works. But it is certainly not justified in the case of all communities and at all times.

The very reverse of the policy just discussed is the no-loan policy of financing capital outlays. It really antedates the all-loan policy, which may be said to have been introduced, at least in the case of local governments, because of the failure of the no-loan plan. Still the no-loan policy has never ceased to have its advocates who have kept on looking with dismay upon the growth of governmental borrowing and have kept on demanding that the government return to what they consider a safer practice. There have been but few instances of a return to this policy, and these, furthermore, have seldom been of lasting nature. According to the advocates of this policy governments must never undertake any improvements unless they are ready to pay for them at once, for to do otherwise is to invite extravagance. "Pay-as-you-go," they say, is the only sound policy for governments to follow. The fault with this policy lies in its extreme conservatism. It may be a good policy to follow for communities with very large tax resources or characterized by a very slow growth, or, temporarily, for those which have overborrowed, but it is not a good policy to follow for

[1] For a more detailed discussion of this question see Paul Studenski's *Public Borrowing* (National Municipal League, New York, 1930), pp. 38-39, and 67-68.

other communities and in normal times.   It results usually in
extreme conservatism in the matter of authorization of expenditures for public improvements.   Extensive projects meet
with formidable opposition on the part of taxpayers who are
unwilling to tolerate the large increases in taxation which the
execution of these projects would make necessary.   Important
community needs, therefore, go unsatisfied and the development of industry and commerce is hampered in the end because
of the lack of proper governmental facilities.   A community
that abstains from borrowing and denies itself the use of the
additional resources for productive work, which borrowing
would place at its disposal, may be condemned to a slow development, just as would be a private enterprise that refuses to
avail itself of the facilities of modern credit.   But this abstention from borrowing usually breaks down in the end, as a result
of pressure from citizens who feel the need of the particular
improvements.   Exceptions are made from time to time as a
result of popular demands, and they become, in time, so numerous that the rule ceases to be operative and the community
drifts into an all-loan or part-loan policy in its financing of
capital outlays.

Some governments combine taxation and borrowing in the
financing of permanent improvements either intermittently or
regularly from year to year.   The government of the United
States finances capital outlays, as it does current services, ordinarily from current revenues, and only resorts to loans when
the revenues prove insufficient to cover the aggregate expenditures.   Sometimes it issues special loans in the case of some
exceptionally large outlays such as the outlays for the purchases
of Louisiana and Florida, the subsidy for the construction of
transcontinental railroads, and the construction of the Panama
Canal.   Some municipalities regularly raise by taxation a certain amount for capital outlays and supply the excess by means
of loans.   A few regulate the proportion of the two sources to
be used according to the tax-paying ability of the community,
using taxes more extensively and loans less widely in times
of plenty, and taxes less extensively and loans more widely
during bad times.

Under the part-loan policy public credit is used more effectively and with closer regard to the primary functions of public
credit than under the all-loan policy.   Public debt is kept
within reasonable limits and a substantial amount of the community's credit is reserved for emergencies and future needs
of greater scope.   Capital outlays are planned more carefully.
The community neither rushes headlong into extravagant

projects nor refuses to proceed with necessary improvements. It steers a middle course between extreme boldness and extreme caution. The burdens of capital outlays are distributed equitably between the successive generations of taxpayers, both in accordance with the benefits obtained by them from the outlays and in accordance with their tax-paying ability. So far only a few local governments in this country follow such a policy, but their number is likely to increase, for the tendency in government financing is likely to be toward long-range planning and such a policy is more consistent with such planning than either of the other two policies described.

To summarize: Public loans for capital outlays are justified in so far as they (1) enable the government to meet outlays of an emergency nature and of extraordinary size, such as those for flood prevention, purchase of vast properties or territories, and construction of especially great works; (2) facilitate the execution of socially productive permanent improvements in general (whether self-supporting in part, or entirely, or not self-supporting at all), by furnishing funds for them over and above the amounts which taxpayers are willing, or can be made, to supply; (3) assure the execution of projects requiring years of financing, by providing funds for them in advance and thus eliminating the uncertainties and possible delays and reconsiderations attached to the system of financing such projects by annual appropriations from taxes; (4) make possible the maintenance of a more or less stable tax rate from year to year; (5) enable the government to expand its capital outlays as rapidly as the development of private industry and commerce may require; and (6) make possible an expansion of public works in times of business depression in order to afford employment to idle capital and labor and help to revive and stabilize industry.*

Public loans in the financing of capital outlays are unjustified to the extent (1) that they may be used to finance extravagantly conceived and socially unproductive public works; (2) that they may be used in place of legitimate taxation and extend the public indebtedness beyond the point of safety; (3) that they leave no reserve credit for emergencies, and (4) that they work to sustain and accentuate an already too great expansion of industry, commerce, and government activity. Public loans are most effective when used in conjunction with and not in substitution of taxes in the financing of capital outlays.

---

* Eds. note: Full consideration is given to (6) in a preceding section of this volume. See Pt. I, Chap. III, Sec. 2.

2. Emergency Financing

With respect to financing emergencies which require revenues in amounts impracticable to raise by taxation, borrowing is generally resorted to as a means of providing a part of the necessary funds. A modern war is typical of such an emergency. Therefore, the effects of public credit in emergency financing are well illustrated by borrowing in time of war.

The determination of the proper extent of borrowing in war finance is dependent upon a comparison of the economic effects of this fiscal device with feasible alternatives, namely, taxation and the issuance of irredeemable paper money. A discussion of the economic effects of bonds versus taxes is now presented. This will be followed by an analysis of the effects of irredeemable paper money.

(a) The Effects of Bonds and Taxes in War Finance *

Vague and erroneous ideas about war finance are perhaps more general than about any other matter of such vital importance in the great struggle which we have entered. Even among those otherwise well informed, including many in business and banking itself, the prevalence and persistence of incorrect and even fallacious ideas regarding the fundamentals of war financiering are little short of amazing. Editors of our leading journals and directors of financial institutions point out almost daily our inability to meet the expenditures of a great war during the war period and the advisability of postponing part of the cost to the future so that posterity, which shall share the benefits, may share also its burdens. They have failed to distinguish between internal and foreign financing; they have failed to grasp the significance of President Wilson's war message in its urgent appeal to Congress to resort to taxation and "to protect our people, so far as we may, against the very serious hardships and evils which would be likely to arise out of the inflation which would be produced by vast loans."

After pointing out the advantages of an initial bond issue, this article will undertake to show, first, how a continued resort to borrowing will inflate our purchasing medium and cause prices to rise exorbitantly, as taxation will not; second, why the cost of our part of the war not only can, but must, be met during the war period and that no part of the burden can really

* Adapted from Roy G. Blakey, "Effects of Bonds and Taxation in War Finance," *The South Atlantic Quarterly*, July, 1917, pp. 236-247.

be postponed; third, how adequate funds may be raised by taxation without resort to further bond issues; fourth, why the taxation policy will be more just and mobilize our resources more effectively than will a continuance of the bond policy; and, fifth, why the taxation policy will make easier necessary readjustments after the war.

Practically all economists admit the desirability of an initial bond issue at the outbreak of war to secure funds quickly while taxation machinery is being put in order. Furthermore, a successful $7,000,000,000 bond issue will impress ourselves, our friends and our enemies; it will give our movement a tremendous momentum from the very start. In some ways it will make the diversion of labor and capital to war industries more natural and gradual than would too heavy taxation at the outset. But the continuance of the bond policy as the chief method of raising funds would be exceedingly unwise.

According to *The Annalist,* the cost of living has risen 64% in the twelve months ending May 5, 1917. This means that a man with a fixed wage or salary of $1000 has had his income cut to $610 as compared with a year ago, or to $529 as compared with pre-war conditions. This is in addition to the cut caused by high prices which had been our chief complaint for several years prior to 1914. Of course, those with large incomes could spare one-third or one-half of the total and still have left much more than a minimum of subsistence, but few of us realize the sacrifice involved for the great majority of families of this country, for their incomes are considerably less than $1000 a year. For many of them it means poor health, disease, destitution, and even death in the case of many children, and perhaps in the case of even women and men in the poorer quarters of our cities. It means also more crime as well as a less efficient labor force and hence the undermining of national power at its very foundation.

Why bond issues cause an increase in prices as taxation does not is far from clear to many who have not studied banking. Hence it is desirable to present a few fundamental principles. Bank deposits are of two kinds. When a man puts a thousand gold dollars in a bank, he is given a deposit account. This is a "real deposit" and it is in this sense that many people think of the term "deposit." But there is another kind of deposit which is even more important in practice. Suppose a man goes to the bank to borrow a thousand dollars. He gives his note for a thousand dollars, and he might take out a thousand gold dollars; but he does not. Instead, the bank gives him a deposit account for $1000 on which he may draw. This is a "book deposit." If the man is unsophisticated, he may imagine that the bank sets aside 1000 actual dollars to pay the checks which he will draw, but that is not the case. It merely sets aside a small reserve, probably $200, which makes his $1000 deposit account good, because when this man gives his grocer a ten dollar check, the grocer presents it at the bank but does not usually ask for cash. Instead he asks that it be deposited to his account. The first man's account is debited $10, and the grocer's account is credited $10. No actual money has been used. If the grocer gives a clothier a $10 check, the latter presents it to the bank and, instead of asking for cash, has it deposited. The sum on deposit is still $1000. No money has been used. A few who receive checks will ask for actual cash, but the bank has found by experience that a small reserve, say $200, is all that is necessary to keep the thousand dollar deposit account going. In other words, when the bank loaned this man a thousand dollars, it merely gave him a book account which involved the use of only $200 of actual money. It may be said to have created $800 of credit purchasing power which is used to buy more goods just the same as real money. The important point for our purpose is that the man's ability to borrow depended upon his giving security.

That is why a bond issue means more purchasing power than does taxation. It is primarily because a bond is security upon which the holder can borrow at the bank.

On the other hand, if the government takes $1000 from a man in taxes, his credit or purchasing power is lessened to the same extent as the government's is increased. He cannot borrow on the security of his tax receipt.

The man with a bond worth $1000 can, and very often will, borrow at the bank. Suppose he borrows $800; to lend him $800 the bank does not have to give up 800 actual dollars. Instead it gives him a deposit account of $800 and, inasmuch as most of those who present checks do not ask for actual cash but have their checks credited to their deposit accounts, the bank can keep this $800 in checks floating by setting aside, say, only $200 of actual cash. In other words, this bond issue transaction has resulted in increasing the government's credit by $1000, in decreasing the man's credit by only $200 and in decreasing the bank's reserve by only $200; that is, there has been a net increase of credit currency (checking deposit accounts) of $800, in contrast with no net increase if taxes had been adopted instead of bonds.

If the man had given up $1000 in taxes, he would have ceased to compete with the government and other buyers of commodities and labor to that extent; but when the government gives him a bond for his $1000, he is still enabled, by borrowing at the bank, to enter the market for goods and labor to the extent of $800. The competition of the bondholder with the government inevitably forces up the prices which must be paid by both. Thus the government's cost of conducting the war and citizens' costs of living are increased. In the illustration, the bank sets aside $200 of actual cash as a reserve to support the $800 of credit extended to the bondholder. This leaves $600 as the net increase in the purchasing power of society as a whole.

Inflation will not take place unless the floating of bond issues causes more borrowing at the banks. Hence objectors have asked whether many wealthy men will borrow at the banks or sell their present securities yielding 4 to 6% in order to provide funds for investment in United States bonds yielding $3\frac{1}{2}\%$. One hard-headed banker is quoted as replying to such a question, "I don't know. I've sold $300,000 worth in the past few days to enter an initial subscription for that amount." [1] Perhaps many who buy United States Bonds will not borrow at the time to do so, but, if they have any other money borrowed at the time, or, if they borrow anything in the future before they realize on their bonds, such borrowing will have much the same effect then as borrowing to buy bonds, because such borrowing would not have been necessary if the funds had not been spent for bonds. Furthermore, even if they have spare funds and do not need to borrow to buy bonds, their buying of bonds prevents their lending to others, who are thus forced, directly or indirectly, to borrow more from the banks and inflate the purchasing medium more than would have been the case with no bond issues. It is not a question of whether bond issues will cause inflation or not, but a question of the extent of the inflation.

The above illustrations show the possible results of bond issues that are taken by the public. As a matter of fact, if bonds are issued, a large part of them will be taken by banks. It is likely that the Federal Reserve Banks will buy these bonds wholesale by giving the government checking accounts to the extent of the bonds. This will cause immediate inflation to the amount of the checking accounts thus created, less reserve requirements, that is, possible inflation to about 80%, or even to 100%, instead of to 60% of the bond issue, as outlined in the previous illustration.

As the government draws checks on these bank accounts to

[1] *The Annalist*, April 16, 1917, p. 536.

meet its requirements, the banks will try to recoup themselves by retailing the bonds to the public. To the extent that they succeed, the bonds get into the hands of the ultimate investor who can use them as security for bank loans. In so far as the banks are unsuccessful in this distribution, the government is almost certain to permit them to issue bank notes on the basis of the bonds left in their hands, if the financial strain becomes severe. Such bank notes will cause inflation even worse than that due to the checking accounts of the public based on bond collateral.

The effect of inflation is cumulative. The more bonds that are issued the greater the inflation and the higher the rise in prices; the higher the prices, the quicker the funds are exhausted and the greater the need for more bond issues with still greater inflation and prices.

Bond issues sold at home do not, in fact, lighten the present burden of a war nor do heavy taxes necessarily increase its weight more than bonds. Perhaps there is no more common fallacy regarding the burden of a severe war than that it is so great that it cannot be met in the short time in which it is being fought. Corollary to this is another very popular fallacy that, even if a war could be paid for at the time, part of the burden should be put off until the future in order that posterity, which shares the benefits, should also share the burdens.

The truth of the matter is that a war, however great its cost, not only can, but must, be paid for during the war period, if the nation does not expect to draw upon foreign countries. If the war should be a long contest, the equipment which we have on hand at the beginning is an insignificant fraction of what we shall have to devote to its prosecution. Munitions, food, clothing, and practically all that is necessary to wage the war will have to be produced as we fight. They must be paid for by somebody during the war period unless the government is to seize them without payment.

What a war really means is a diversion of labor from the industries of peace to the industries of war. We cannot continue producing and consuming all of the commodities to which we have been accustomed and, at the same time, divert a large part of the forces which have been used in their production to military purposes. This obliges us, of course, to give up some things, the things that are least necessary luxuries. The corollary of this is that everyone who demands luxuries and unnecessaries is thereby keeping men from the firing line or from the production of equipment for war or from the production of the necessities of life. This not only means a smaller force to fight against the enemy, but it means a higher cost of necessities and also a higher cost of everything which the government has to buy.

If the government is to pay for the labor which it diverts and for the commodities which it uses, it must secure its funds in one of two ways, either by taxing or by borrowing. In either case, it can secure these funds only from those who have more than a minimum of subsistence unless it is to press down the masses of its people below that minimum. If the government takes money in the form of taxes from a man, it gives him a tax receipt and owes him nothing further, but, if it secures the same amount by borrowing, it gives him a bond which it promises to repay in the future, with interest. If the government takes as taxes a large part, or even all, of income above a minimum of subsistence, it causes no more sacrifice than it does when it conscripts a man for the firing line. This is especially true in the case of special war profits. If, instead of taking this income by taxation, the government promises to pay it back with interest, the sacrifice is insignificant.

It is now clear in what sense the burden of a war financed at home can be put upon posterity. If a father sustains great losses, the burden is put upon his children in the sense that they do not receive as great a heritage as they would have received otherwise. If a nation sustains a great loss, posterity receives an impaired heritage. Both the present generation and all future generations suffer. But in the sense that is usually meant, the future cannot bear the present's burden. Munitions not yet created and men not yet born cannot be hurled against the enemy's lines. It is true that some of our citizens may advance money in return for bonds and be repaid by the citizens of the future, who will include the soldiers who are fortunate enough to return. But this merely means taking the burden off one part of our citizens and putting a double burden upon another part. The nation as a whole cannot put off the burden. This is evident when we consider that if all the bonds should be cancelled there would be no change in the amount of commodities or property within the nation. There would merely be a cancellation of the obligation of one part of the citizens to another part of the citizens.

As has been intimated above, the extraordinary expenditures of the war should be met in large part by taxation upon special war profits and surplus incomes. It would be unwise to increase most of our customs duties greatly, because they fall upon people largely in proportion to their consumption of

necessities and not in proportion to their ability to bear burdens
of taxation.

To meet the enormous needs of war, we may well lower the
income tax exemptions from $3000 and $4000 to, say, $1500
and $2000 or even less, and we may well increase the rates
upon the larger incomes, especially upon those above $50,000
or $100,000.   In extreme need taxation might take all incomes
above a minimum of subsistence without involving any more
sacrifice than in taking men for the firing line.   Doubtless it
would be more expedient not to take all, but to leave as large
a proportion as is feasible in order to encourage efficiency.   Of
special profits caused by the war itself, the government might
first exempt a maximum profit of 6% or 8% and then take all
of the excess above that amount if necessary.   But here, too,
it would be expedient to exempt a certain percentage to stimulate efficiency.   It should be observed that both of these proposed taxes provide for exemptions at the bottom, that both
of them are advocated for the war period only, and that neither
of them confiscates capital now in existence, but that they
merely propose to take a part of surplus income during the
war.

The experience of the warring nations shows that such taxes
are feasible.   For example, during the fiscal year just closed,
Great Britain has raised nearly three-fourths of a billion dollars from her "excess profits tax" and nearly a billion dollars
from her income tax.   It has been estimated that the incomes
of the United States are probably two or three times as great
as those of Great Britain and the profits even greater in proportion.   In other words, from these two taxes as now framed
in Great Britain, we could probably raise 3½ to 4 billion dollars a year.   They should form the backbone of our emergency
revenue system, also.   If to them we add other taxes and other
measures which are suggested below, we could finance our
part of the war entirely, if need be, by taxation.

But taxation is not only a method of raising revenue, it is
also a method of cutting down demand for luxuries and unnecessaries, of diverting labor and capital from places where
least needed to military purposes.   In the present emergency,
such a national waste as the liquor business should not merely
be discouraged by heavy taxation, but should be eliminated
entirely.   The taxation of luxuries which are not to be absolutely prohibited will cut down their consumption, and the
taxation of surplus incomes will have a similar effect by reducing the means for purchasing luxuries.   Estimates have been
made of the value of commodities and services produced in the

United States which could be dispensed with either permanently or temporarily. The items include such things as artificial flowers, pleasure cars, billiard tables, many furnishings, clocks, many articles of clothing, silks, laces, feathers, plumes, jewelry, extravagant millinery, musical instruments, patent medicines, alcoholic liquors, coffee, tea, many private and public buildings, *et cetera*, amounting to from $7,000,000,000 to $10,000,000,000 annually, enough to finance the war.

But there is much objection to heavy taxes. Besides the fallacious ideas which have been discussed above, the most common and serious objection is that taxation will not raise funds quickly enough and that it will injure industry and business much more than will bonds. It is true that time is required to get the machinery for new and heavy taxes in working order so as to bring in their maximum yield; hence the initial issue of short time bonds or treasury notes is justifiable. Such bonds or treasury notes, however, should be in large denominations and interest bearing, in order to keep them out of general circulation as paper money.

The most serious objection to a policy of heavy taxation is its effect upon industry. This objection takes several forms. In the first place, it should be pointed out that many people who make this objection have not drawn the proper distinctions between general taxes upon surplus incomes and net profits, on the one hand, and taxes upon commodities, property, and even special taxes upon income and profits, on the other hand. A tax upon property or upon the products of that property — for example, upon a sugar factory or upon the sugar turned out — would make that property or that commodity less profitable and would tend to drive producers out of that line of industry into others which were taxed less heavily. But if the tax were general and evenly distributed upon all property and all commodities, it would not drive enterprise out of one industry into another, because both would be taxed in the same way, and if they were equally profitable before the tax was levied, they would be also equally profitable after it was levied. But from an administrative standpoint it would be almost impossible to levy taxes on different properties and commodities in such a way as to distribute them equally. Hence such taxes might cause a considerable disturbance in business.

Even in case of a special tax upon incomes or net profits from certain lines of business, there would be a tendency for those in the taxed lines to go over into those industries whose profits were not taxed. But the case is different with a *general* tax upon net profits and incomes. This tax applies to net profits and incomes from whatever source derived. Whatever the rate of the tax, it is to the interest of the taxpayer to make the highest possible net profit. If the tax leaves him any part of his net profit, that is, if it is anything less than 100%, the greater his total profit the greater will be his remaining share after the tax is deducted. Before the tax was levied he presumably went into that industry in which he could make the greatest possible profit. If, because of the tax, he goes into any industry in which the total net profit is less, his share of the net profit after the tax is deducted will also be less. In other words, a general tax upon net incomes offers no inducement for a man to go out of one industry into another.

But even heavy general taxes upon net incomes may hurt business by taking funds for the government which would otherwise be used for repairs or for extension of plants. In the case of war the government must get funds somewhere. The question is whether the government shall take part of the funds which would ordinarily go for the repair and extension of plants or whether it shall take part of the funds which people would use for consumption. It is evidently in the public interest to take these funds from consumption in so far as this consumption is of luxuries. But it is of very questionable wisdom to take such funds from the consumption of necessities, especially if, as is probable, this will mean depriving the masses of a standard of living which is necessary for health and efficiency. It is probable, however, that nearly all the funds needed could be secured through the elimination of the consumption of luxuries. It would be unfortunate to take funds that would really hamper business, and it would be equally, or even more unfortunate, to sap our national labor strength at its foundation.

A typical business man has objected to the injury which heavy taxation would cause business by saying: "While I might pay 25% of my income in taxes, it would be impossible to give up 60% of it without incurring bankruptcy." This man, like many others, has a net income of perhaps $100,000, but he knew in advance that he would have such an income and hence had made contracts involving its use. Not all this $100,000 net income, nor even one-fourth of it, is what may be called free. He had agreed to use a certain part of it to pay for land which he had bought, other parts for interest on certain debts, other parts for life insurance, et cetera. It is true that most of these payments are investments of a sort, but he is under contract to pay them and may be bankrupted by foreclosures if he has to give up too large a part of his income in taxes.

This is a real difficulty, but it involves a problem of administration rather than a matter of principle. In many cases the investments which men like this one are making are bringing in current income out of which they could pay taxes, but if, as in many other cases, the free income would not be available for a few years, the taxes could be advanced by the banks on the security of the investments of present income. These investments will become remunerative, or can be liquidated in time to repay the loans of the banks. The government might even instruct the Federal Reserve Banks and the national banks to arrange for such advances of taxes.

It has been objected also that very sudden and heavy taxes would cut down consumption with great rapidity in some lines and thus lead to bankruptcy, much temporary unemployment, and much confusion. Bond issues, by causing inflation, would avoid this sudden change and consequent depression, it is claimed. The government in bidding for commodities and men would raise prices for those things which it wanted. These higher prices would result in diverting industry in the desired directions gradually instead of suddenly. There is much weight to this claim, although, even those who advance the idea, urge very heavy taxes as well as bonds and admit that bond issues sacrifice justice for the sake of expediency. The present writer is in thorough agreement with this. But the fact is that we are not faced with a prospect of raising all funds through taxation. We have already authorized $7,000,000,000 in bonds. The policy here advocated is the raising of as large a proportion as possible of all future requirements through taxation.

We have already indicated incidentally some ways in which a proper tax policy will promote national efficiency as bond issues will not. The maintenance of an adequate standard of living, which is threatened by the inflation consequent upon bond issues, is of prime importance. Taxation as a means of forcing economies and of diverting labor and capital to the places most needed is scarcely of secondary importance, though the advantages of taxes over bonds are not so great in this case.

But what is of more importance in promoting national efficiency is the justice of the taxation program. All serious objections to taxes are based upon expediency; very few deny their justice. All admit that taking surplus income by taxation involves very much less real sacrifice than conscription of men. Justice makes for national solidarity and power. Men will enlist in greater numbers and will fight with greater zeal if they know that those at home, both rich and poor, are also sacrificing their all for the cause.

Not only would the tax policy mobilize our forces more effectively during the war period, but it would also leave our industries much better prepared to meet the readjustments which must follow the war. Prices have already soared skyward. The more bond issues, the further they will rise. The higher they go, the further they will have to drop after the war. Hence the greater the danger not only of a financial panic but also of a prolonged depression with unemployment and all its attendant evils. The reduction of heavy war taxation at the end of the struggle would encourage consumption and hence call for employment of returning soldiers and labor freed from munition making. If we raise prices during the war by bond issues and levy heavy taxes after the war, incomes will then be cut and consumption curtailed at the very time when we shall have a large free labor force capable of producing for larger consumption.

The problem . . . is not one of raising all funds by the one method or by the other but rather one of the proper proportion between the two. How much shall what is economically feasible give way to what is politically practicable? How much shall social justice be sacrificed to administrative expediency? The answer depends almost solely upon the general understanding of the issues involved.

(b) Irredeemable Paper Money in War Finance *

So long as the issue of inconvertible paper money merely displaces an equivalent or nearly equivalent amount of metallic money, under the operation of Gresham's law, its issue may be no special burden on the people of the issuing country. The government buys goods and services with the paper money. Thus this money gets into circulation. In doing so it tends to bid up prices. Such higher prices encourage buying abroad where prices have not thus risen. The result is increased monetary obligations to foreign countries and a flow of gold to them. Thus, instead of a great rise of prices in the paper-money-issuing country alone, there is a smaller rise of prices affecting many or all countries. The paper-money-issuing country has given up gold to these other countries and has secured, in its stead, goods of various kinds. But the loss of the gold is made good by the paper money which takes over the money function. In spending this money when first

---

* Adapted from H. G. Brown, *The Economics of Taxation,* (Henry Holt and Co., New York, 1924), Chap. I.

printed, the government has got from the citizens various goods and services; but in sending abroad for goods and services a substantially equivalent value of gold, the citizens have largely recouped their losses. Although the people of the country have now only paper money in place of the gold, they are not, on that account, necessarily any the worse off, since with the paper money they will presumably be able to carry on business as effectively as if the money were gold. For in order that anything should circulate as money and have value in the purchase of goods, it is only necessary that each[1] person shall have confidence that, if he accepts such money from others in selling goods or services, he can, in his turn, get others to accept it from him; and that the quantity of such money shall be limited. Experience seems to show that, when an established government issues inconvertible paper money which it makes legal tender, such money actually does pass from hand to hand in the exchange of goods and services and performs the ordinary functions of money; and that the value of such money declines greatly only if it is over-issued in quantity.

But if there may be a question whether a government is really taxing its citizens when it issues not more than enough inconvertible paper money to push out of circulation a metallic money of bullion value equal to its monetary value, there is no possible doubt that it is taxing its citizens if it continues to issue the paper money beyond that point. Thus, to illustrate, suppose that there is, in the United States, $4,000,000,000 in inconvertible paper money and that all metallic money has been driven out of circulation through the operation of Gresham's law. Suppose that then the government issues another $4,000,000,000 of paper money. This new issue clearly cannot make the country as a whole any richer. It cannot facilitate the importation of goods from abroad because foreigners will not accept the money[2] and because there is no longer any gold money in circulation which can be displaced by the use of paper and so sent abroad for goods. The only effect the paper money can have is to raise prices. As there is twice as much money to spend, approximately twice as much of goods and services would be demanded at the previously prevailing prices. But no such increased volume of goods can be produced. Demand for goods must, therefore, exceed sup-

---

[1] Most persons — not necessarily *every* individual.

[2] This statement may be somewhat qualified. People outside of Germany have accepted depreciated German marks — have, in some cases, made it a point to invest in them — as a speculation, hoping that they would rise in value.

ply unless and until prices approximately double. And this is what prices will tend, rapidly, to do.[3]

When prices have doubled, the people of the country will be getting money incomes roughly twice as large as before and paying prices for goods approximately twice as high as before. In this there is obviously no advantage. But, on the other hand, in this fact there is no loss. Yet if such paper money issue by government is a kind of taxation the citizens of the country must lose somehow as much as the government gets. Where and how is this loss suffered?

For the government to issue $4,000,000,000 of paper money when there is already $4,000,000,000 of such money in circulation and no gold or other metallic money capable of being displaced, and for the government so to buy approximately $4,000,000,000 worth of goods, is for the government to compete against citizens for the purchase of goods. Thus, if we suppose the velocity of circulation of money (the average number of times a dollar changes hands during a year in payment for goods) to be 26, then, with $4,000,000,000 in circulation, about $4,000,000,000 would be spent in two weeks. But if, during such two weeks, the government puts into circulation another $1,000,000,000, which it has had printed for the purpose, and so purchases supplies and services, it to that extent outbids the citizens who are trying to buy these things for themselves; and these citizens, as individuals, can purchase, with the $4,000,000,000 spent by them, only some four-fifths as many goods as it would otherwise be possible for them to buy.[4] The government takes the other one-fifth. Thus, the government practically gets, in effect, a fifth of the output of industry during such a period. And this is abstracted from the people. Hence, the citizens may properly be regarded as being, to that extent, taxed for government needs. The extra $1,000,000,000 spent because of the new issue, bids up prices. The government *bids against* the citizens for goods. Demand for goods, at prevailing prices, exceeds supply. Prices therefore rise to such a point that the $4,000,000,000 spent by the

---

[3] Recent experiences in Germany and Austria have shown that, under rapid inflation, prices rise more than in proportion to the increase in monetary circulation. Velocity of circulation of money is increased.

[4] We are here supposing, for simplicity, that none of the new $1,000,000,000 put into circulation by government is spent a second time before the expiration of the two weeks ; also the assumption is made that the velocity of circulation of money has remained unchanged with the increase in inflation. This latter assumption violates the recent experiences in many counties of Central Europe, where under rapidly increasing inflation the velocity of circulation has increased greatly and prices have risen much more than in proportion to the increase in the monetary medium.

people individually buys less than before and the government gets the reduced purchasing value of $1,000,000,000.

When the government has spent its $1,000,000,000 of new money, it can tax the people no more in this way without a further issue. There is now $5,000,000,000 in circulation instead of $4,000,000,000. Prices of goods and services are, on the average, according to our assumption, twenty-five per cent higher than before. Money incomes are larger but it costs more to live. Some will be better off, but, on the average, the people of the country are neither better off nor worse off than before *except for the wealth and services abstracted from them by the government when the new money was first put into circulation*. But if the government, during the next two weeks, puts into circulation *another* $1,000,000,000, and then another, and another, it thus continues to tax citizens through outbidding them for goods in addition to setting in motion a whole series of expropriating influences which derive their force from the rapidity rather than the extent of the inflation.

In order, however, that the government may tax citizens an equal amount with each new issue, these issues must become progressively larger as prices become progressively higher. Thus, after $8,000,000,000 is in circulation, a new issue of $2,000,000,000 is necessary if the government would take even approximately a fifth of the industrial output of the next spending period (assumed to be two weeks), as $1,000,000,000 new issue was necessary when only $4,000,000,000 was in circulation. And so a government which long attempts to finance itself in any such way causes prices to rise in geometric ratio until finally, perhaps, the money becomes worth no more than the paper on which it is printed. If, however, the money issued continues to be used, even the difficulty that the value of the money tends to approach that of the paper it is made of is not insurmountable. For the government can print, as exemplified in Central Europe, ever larger denominations — instead of increasing the number of original denominations — and so, in effect, introduce successively new official standards. The time when the money is completely discredited may be long in coming, as we see from the case of post-war Germany where money has increased and prices have risen rapidly year after year, yet where the inconvertible paper money — they have no other in circulation [5] — continues to be used, the limit, if any, to the process seeming to lie in its rapidity rather than in its extent.

If, with paper money inflation, all prices should rise equally

[5] Stabilized since the above was written.

and with equal swiftness, the burden of the inflation tax would be distributed over the public in proportion to purchases. Paper money issue as a means of financing government would then resemble, in respect of its ultimate incidence, taxation of commodities in general or a general sales tax as being a burden on consumers as such.

However, in practice prices do not ordinarily rise with equal rapidity or in equal degree [6] and, therefore, the burden is not distributed in proportion to consumption or to purchases-in-general. Upon some classes the burden falls with crushing weight while other classes may gain, at the expense of the classes who lose, more than the gaining classes contribute to the government. All the classes with fixed money incomes lose at such a time : the recipients of salaries, which are apt to change but slowly; the recipients of rentals which have been determined in advance by contracts applying over a period of years ; the recipients of interest on bonds, which continue to pay the same number of dollars, francs, marks or kronen a year however much these standards of value may depreciate.

But, on the other hand, other classes may actually gain. Thus the borrowing business enterpriser finds that, with prices rising, he gains at the expense of lenders and, perhaps, of recipients of salaries. He borrows (say) $50,000 to build a factory, pledging an interest payment of $2500 a year. At first, his direct outlays for current production come to $60,000 per year and the salable value of his output is $70,000. He pays his interest of $2500, sets aside $1500 for a sinking fund, and $2000 for depreciation and has $4000 left for himself. But suppose prices in general to double! Then his outlays for production become $120,000 and the salable value of his output $140,000. But his interest is, by contract, still only $2500. Also, his debt is still only $50,000 despite the fact that each dollar is worth only half what it was before. On this account he does not need to increase at all the annual contribution of $1500 to his sinking fund. Doubling his allowance for depreciation — a new plant would now cost twice as much — he still has left for himself $12,000. With prices doubled, he needs $8000 a year to be as well off as he was before with $4000, but he has $4000 *in excess* of this. The lender, however, is still receiving $2500 interest though now he should be receiving $5000 to be as well off as before ; and also, on the same basis, the debt should now be reckoned as $100,000 in-

[6] Cf. Fisher, *The Purchasing Power of Money,* revised edition, New York (Macmillan), 1911, Chapter IX.

stead of $50,000, so that it would take $3000 instead of $1500 a year to provide the sinking fund necessary to pay it. In other words, the $4000 net gain a year of the borrower is balanced by a $4000 net loss a year of the lender.

During a process of inflation financing, the government, as we have seen, is continually outbidding the public for goods, so that prices rise faster than, on the average, individual incomes increase. Part of the net $4000 gain of the borrower of our illustration may thus be abstracted from him by a further rise of prices consequent on the bidding for goods by government through a new paper money issue. It is conceivable, indeed, that further issues might come so fast and prices so rapidly as to leave him worse off with $12,000 than he was previously with $8000. But such further issues and further rise of prices would add more to the injury of lenders. It follows, then, that this method of taxation — for we have seen that inflation is really taxation — is a method by which the lending class not only pays taxes to government but also, in addition, loses to the borrowing class; while at the same time it is a method by which the borrowing class may gain at the expense of lenders far more than it contributes to government.

These inequalities from inflation are, of course, a consequence partly of men's failure to realize that the value of the monetary standard may vary, and they are due partly to men's inability to foresee in what direction and how great the variation will be. Could the lender both realize the significance of a declining value of the monetary unit and foresee such a declining value, he would refuse to lend except at a very high rate of interest measured in such depreciating money. But during long periods of comparatively stable prices, the habit of counting on this stability and making long-term contracts in expectation of it becomes all but universal.

If government finance through paper money inflation is, as we have shown, in effect taxation, and if it is taxation of so unequal a kind as actually to benefit some classes (or tax them only a little) while perhaps taking from other classes more than it yields to government, why is paper money inflation ever adopted for the finance of war or any other emergency? Such a question may well be asked by one who expects to see governments act intelligently and for the general interest. It is unlikely to be asked by those whose knowledge of human nature and whose study, in history, of the past actions of men, have taught them in how slight degree men understand the nature of the economic forces to which they are subjected and how much they are swayed by prejudice, and, what is most pertinent from the standpoint of a government, how much more important it is for political reasons, to avoid unpopular taxes than to impose just ones. Since the goods and services secured by government through competitive spending of new paper money issues are, in effect, obtained by taxation which may actually profit some citizens as well as the government, it is reasonable to suppose that as much or more wealth and services could be obtained by more equitably adjusted taxation. If existing taxes are not high enough to secure the needed revenue, then they can be raised higher as an alternative to money inflation. But a government may fear to lose popular support if it definitely thus increases the tax rate, since such an increase can be clearly seen and will be understood by citizens to be an increase; while the putting into circulation of inconvertible paper money taxes them insidiously without their being, as a rule, for some time aware what is the cause of their new poverty. The rise of prices will be attributed to scarcity of goods, to demands of organized labor, to "profiteers," to "war demands," etc., and few will realize until the inflation has become very great, if they ever do, what is the real cause of the rising prices. Indeed it is more than probable that many of the legislators themselves who are instrumental in initiating the inflation will not realize. For men who are chosen as representatives of the voters to make the statute laws of a country, though they are often plausible in manner and effective in speech making, frequently understand the laws of our economic life no better than they understand differential calculus or physiological chemistry. Being themselves ignorant of the complex forces of economics they the more readily accept current fallacies and even themselves initiate such fallacies by way of attempted explanation of the rising prices. According to the influential sentiment of their constituents and their own bent — whether "radical" or "conservative" — they may attribute the evils for which their own action is responsible to the "profiteering" of captains of industry or to the "exactions" of organized laborers *et al.*

(c) Other Questions of the Effects of Government Borrowing

IN the concluding pages of this chapter there is presented Professor H. G. Brown's stimulating discussion of two important questions of the incidence of government borrowing.*

* Adapted from H. G. Brown, *The Economics of Taxation,* (Henry Holt and Co., New York, 1924), Chap. II, pp. 37-46.

CAN THE BURDEN OF FINANCING A WAR BE IMPOSED ON POSTERITY?

IN examining [the] contention [that the financing of a war or other emergency by borrowing, rather than by taxation, puts the burden — or part of it — upon posterity], we shall assume two cases : one, when the borrowing is done outside the borrowing country; two, when the borrowing is done inside the borrowing country. In the first case, no denial can be made of the accuracy of the contention, so far as the people of the borrowing country are concerned. Thus, certain of the allied countries borrowed, during the recent war, of the United States. This enabled these countries to have, for the time being, additional supplies of munitions, food, etc., for which their own people did not have to pay. But if, eventually, the loans are repaid, then the people of these countries must bear a burden in excess of their current governmental expenses. And if this repayment, though made, is considerably deferred, a burden rests upon another generation, in these allied countries, than those who fought the war. Whether the gains from the war — or the losses prevented by it — are such that they can afford so to pay, or whether they are likely to have new wars of their own and to be overwhelmed with burdens and obligations new and old, we shall not inquire. We need only note that, under the assumed circumstances, it is undoubtedly possible for the people of a country to impose a burden upon their descendants.

Consider, now, the other case, when the borrowing nation (or nations) borrows only from its own people. This case was substantially realized during the World War by the borrowing of the United States. In this case the contention that the burden of an emergency expense can, by borrowing, be thrown upon posterity, must be declared to be altogether false. Thus, to illustrate, we shall suppose the sum borrowed by the United States from its people, exclusive of sums borrowed to loan the Allies, to have been, in round numbers, $10,000,000,000. This loan was made by citizens of the war generation, who, in making it, presumably had to curtail their expenditures in other directions but who received government bonds as a pledge of repayment. The question is whether they are ever repaid. It can be shown that they are not except if, as a group, they *repay themselves*.[1] For if there is no repayment until a

1 See, for example, Sprague, "Loans and Taxes in War Finance," *The American Economic Review*, Supplement, March, 1917, pp. 199-213, especially p. 206, and Davenport, "The War-Tax Paradox," *The American Economic Review*, March, 1919, pp. 34-46, especially pp. 37-39.

new generation has reached maturity, then, obviously, the lending generation never gets repaid since, when repayment is made, many of the lending generation are dead. While if repayment is made soon, then members of the lending generation are themselves the bearers of the taxes.

Let us discuss the problem in the light of an hypothetical concrete case. Smith, living during the World War, buys, we will suppose, $1000 worth of Liberty bonds in 1918. Suppose repayment to be made in 1928, Smith being still alive, and suppose that Smith's purchase of bonds was substantially in the same proportion to the purchases of others as are his tax obligations to the tax obligations of others. Then when it comes time to pay Smith back the $1000 of money which he lent, he must contribute $1000 in taxes to provide the means for such repayment. Or, if the loan is paid back from the proceeds of an amortization fund gradually accumulated, then he has had to contribute to this fund. In fact, therefore, he never gets back the $1000 although in probably ninety-nine cases out of a hundred he does not realize this. So far as Smith is concerned, conditions would have been the same had he been asked to pay the $1000 as a tax in the first place. For though he ostensibly merely loans it, he is equally deprived of the privilege of spending it for himself; the annual (or semi-annual) interest received is matched by annual payments of tax and the final repayment of principal is, as we have seen, likewise, in effect, a mere taking of money out of one pocket and putting it into another.

In practice, of course, the taxes paid by different persons to provide means for redeeming the bonds issued, have no necessary relationship to the value of the bonds bought by these persons. A person who bought few bonds may, if he has, when repayment is made, large taxable income, pay much toward the redemption of the bonds bought by others; and a person who bought many bonds may, if he has, at the time of repayment, only a small taxable income, pay little.

Hence, although it can be truly said that the people as a whole have lost as effectually as if the money had been raised by taxation and, when they are paid back, really have to do the paying themselves, this cannot be said of each individual among them. And so, the person whose patriotism or sense of duty inclines him to lend money to his government during a war, need not fear that he will have to contribute more towards paying it back than if the lending were done by others. If he does the lending, his later taxes will be largely devoted to paying himself back. But if he does *not* do the lending, his later taxes will be devoted to paying others back.   As an individual, then, he may fairly consider that lending does not cost him more than not lending.   But the whole people, considered collectively, might as well contribute frankly by taxation as to camouflage the situation through government bond issues.

We shall next suppose, however, that the period of repayment of the bonds is deferred, so that the repaying is done by a later generation.   In that case it should be equally clear that the original lenders of the funds are never really reimbursed and it should be clear that the later generation, considered as a whole, is not burdened.   Certainly there is no way by which a later generation can reimburse a generation which has passed away.   Smith has loaned his $1000 to the government.   He has received only the annual interest paid for by taxes on his own generation, perhaps on himself.   Before the principal is due, he dies.   The government bond is inherited by his son. Thus, when redemption is undertaken, and taxes are levied on the new generation to consummate it, the funds so raised are paid *to* the new generation.   Smith's son — along with his contemporaries — meets the taxes that are required to redeem his bond.   If any of the older generation are still living, they will contribute to the repayment, probably in proportion as they received such repayment.[2]   If none of them are living, the new generation will do all the paying but, also, it will do the receiving.

ARE GOVERNMENT BONDS A MORTGAGE OF THE MASSES TO THE CLASSES?

DURING the recent World War, persons of liberal and radical persuasion were, in large part, advocates of the scheme of having the funds necessary raised entirely or almost entirely by taxation rather than by bond issue.   They reasoned that sharply progressive income taxes could be levied on the well-to-do, taking for government purposes practically all their surplus above their reasonable requirements for current consumption, that the funds required by government would be more certainly obtained by taxation — a compulsory method — than by borrowing and, particularly, that to secure the funds by borrowing would mean heavier later taxation of the poor to provide repayment of the bonds.   One thing is clear, viz.,

---

2 It is, of course, admitted that, with many of the older generation still living, a tax discriminating specifically against the newer generation would force them to contribute largely towards the repayment of the original lenders.   Also, a non-discriminatory tax, in a country growing rapidly by immigration, would force the immigrants to contribute toward the redemption of bonds owned by the original inhabitants and their offspring.

that if the needed funds are provided at once, by taxation, a large part or most of these funds will necessarily be provided from the incomes of the relatively wealthy. The poor have little to spare. It is not possible to squeeze much from them. A *taxation* system of money raising, therefore, if much is raised, and especially if nearly the maximum amount possible is raised, *must* involve very sharply progressive taxation. The funds so raised cannot, of course, be invested in the capital of private business but neither could like sums raised by borrowing be so invested.

If, however, the money needed is raised by borrowing, then it becomes possible to put more of the burden of the emergency financing on the poor. For although the poor have only a small surplus and cannot contribute much in taxes during the few years that an expensive war continues, nevertheless they can contribute something each year for an indefinite future *after* such a war is over. This annual contribution can then be used to pay interest on the bonds owned by the wealthy and, if it is desired eventually to retire the bonds, can be used to repay the principal. Herein lies the meaning of the contention that war finance by bond issue means "a mortgage on the masses to the classes." [3]

Doubtless war finance by means of bond issues might mean a mortgage of the masses to the classes and perhaps, in large part, this is what the American Civil War bond issues did mean. Tariff duties, levied on articles of general consumption and falling largely on the masses were the means of securing a great part of the money needed for the redemption of these bonds. But financing by bond issues need not inevitably mean this. For the taxes later levied to pay back the bonds might be made, as at the present time for example, progressive and sharply graduated, or they might be levied only on large incomes or large property, or only on specific kinds of property or specific kinds of expenditure, or could be otherwise so adjusted as not to fall upon the masses.

That some of the above kinds of taxes might indirectly fall upon the masses by discouraging accumulation and raising the rate of interest is not here denied. This may or may not be the case. . . But, at least, the taxes above suggested do not in the first instance so fall.

The suggestion of a "capital levy" to pay off the war debts, which has been advocated in Great Britain and elsewhere, is perhaps largely motivated by the desire to make the wealthy

[3] Cf. Davenport, article above cited on "The War-Tax Paradox," especially pp. 39-41.

pay off these debts. By a capital levy is meant a tax on the owners of property too heavy to be paid out of annual income. To pay such a tax property owners would have to sell a part of their holdings. The part sold would presumably be purchased, in the main, by the owners of bonds whose bonds were being redeemed. In general, the property-owning classes have been antagonistic to the scheme. Yet if the bonds were to be redeemed, eventually, by heavy taxes on the income from their property, the question might plausibly be raised whether they might not as well relinquish some of this property at once and thereafter avoid taxation on the rest (except to meet costs of current governmental services). But if repayment of the bonds is to take place gradually over a period of years, there is considerable probability that at least a part of the necessary funds will be raised by taxes falling upon others than the owners of property.

Whether or not a progressive tax on incomes might in some degree be shifted, ordinarily, upon the poor by discouraging capital accumulation and raising the rate of interest, the fear of such a result should perhaps not operate as an obstacle to such taxation during a war. For in war time, at least in such a time as that of the recent World War, little or nothing can be spared for the increase — if, even, for the upkeep — of capital not needed for war purposes. And whether people pay heavy taxes to government or lend "until it hurts," makes no difference either in how the funds secured are used or in how much private-business capital citizens can accumulate during the emergency.

QUESTIONS AND PROBLEMS FOR DISCUSSION

1. Under what conditions is it justifiable for a government to borrow in order to meet deficits?
2. Is it true that public loans are "most effective when used in conjunction with and not in substitution of taxes in the financing of capital outlays"?
3. What are the advantages of an initial bond issue in financing a war?
4. How may the issue of bonds for the purpose of financing emergencies lead to inflation?
5. If a government borrows from its own people in order to finance a war, is the financial burden of the war passed on to future generations?
6. If you wished the present generation to bear as little as possible of the financial burden of a national emergency expenditure, what method or methods of financing would you employ?
7. If you desired the most equitable distribution of the financial

burden of emergency expenditures among members of the present generation, what method or methods of financing would you select?

8. Evaluate the advantages of and the objections to heavy taxes during a war period.

9. What is meant by the statement that social justice may be sacrificed to administrative expediency in financing an emergency?

10. In what manner do issues of inconvertible paper money which push out of circulation a metallic money of bullion value equal to its monetary value place a burden upon the citizens of the country? Are all citizens affected adversely?

11. Under what conditions, if any, might war financing by means of bond issues mean "a mortgage of the masses to the classes"?

12. Assuming the propriety of the following public expenditures, would you meet them by borrowing or by the use of current revenues? Support your choice in each case:
    (1) maintenance of municipal playgrounds in a large city
    (2) police and fire protection
    (3) street paving
    (4) construction and maintenance of a large "consolidated" rural school building
    (5) elimination of railroad grade crossings
    (6) municipal construction made necessary by a severe earthquake
    (7) the purchase by a municipality of a privately owned utility corporation.

SUGGESTIONS FOR RESEARCH

1. The fiscal effects of irredeemable paper money.
2. Loans versus taxes in war finance.
3. The economic effects of public borrowing for poor relief.
4. War finance in theory and practice.
5. A study of war financing in some belligerent nation during the Great War.
6. The purposes of federal, state, and municipal borrowing.

BIBLIOGRAPHICAL NOTE

The question of the purposes for which a government may legitimately borrow is considered in the following works: H. L. Lutz, *Public Finance,* (New York, 1929), Chap. XXVI, pp. 591-598; Shutaro Matsushita, *The Economic Effects of Public Debts,* (New York, 1929), Chap. IV; A. C. Pigou, *A Study in Public Finance,* (London, 1928), Pt. III, Chap. I; and Paul Studenski, *Public Borrowing,* (New York, 1930), Chap. V.

Concerning the place of borrowing in war finance, much valuable material is available. For excellent statements by those who advocate "taxation to the bone" and borrowing to a minimum for war purposes, see T. N. Carver, *Principles of National Economy*, (Boston, 1921), Chap. XLIX, and O. M. W. Sprague, "Loans and Taxes in War Finance," *Proceedings, American Economic Association*, (1916), pp. 199-213. Other views regarding the proper ratio of taxation to borrowing in war finance, for the most part less extreme than those of Carver and Sprague, are expressed in E. L. Bogart, *War Costs and Their Financing*, (New York, 1921), Chap. X ; C. J. Bullock, "Financing the War," *Quarterly Journal of Economics*, Vol. XXXI, (May, 1917), pp. 357-379 ; and E. R. A. Seligman, "Loans versus Taxes in War Finance," *Annals of the American Academy of Political and Social Science*, Vol. LXXV, pp. 52-82.

The results of war financing by bank credits are ably presented by R. G. Hawtrey, *Currency and Credit*, (London, 1919), Chaps. XIII, XIV, and A. C. Pigou, *A Study in Public Finance*, (London, 1928), Pt. III, Chaps. III, V.

A general historical study of federal financing in the United States, which contains valuable material relating to policies of war borrowing, is R. A. Love, *Federal Financing*, (New York, 1931). The financing of the American Civil War is treated exhaustively in W. C. Mitchell's splendid work, *A History of the Greenbacks*, (Chicago, 1903).

For a comprehensive bibliography on borrowing for the financing of public expenditures in periods of industrial depression, see list of references at the end of Chapter III.

CHAPTER XXV

WHO PAID FOR THE WAR?

Professor Jacob Viner has made an inductive study which shows among other things the economic effects of borrowing in war finance. This study is reproduced below.*

In a recent article Professor Davenport presents a striking argument in support of the thesis that labor has already paid the main cost of the war and, moreover, will pay it over again in the future.[1] Briefly summarized, his argument runs as follows : The cost of the war must be met out of contemporaneous income ; as there was no war-time increase in production, the war needs must have been supplied, therefore, from a decrease in consumption ; the upward tendency of prices during the war period was more marked than the similar tendency of money wages ; this lag of wages behind prices resulted in a great increase in profits ; these profits were lent to the government to finance the war ; the war loans will be repaid by taxation which will fall chiefly on the working classes ; labor will in this manner pay the cost of the war twice over, once to the capitalistic class in the form of inflated profits, and once to the government to provide it with revenue wherewith to repay the borrowed war-time profits.

Professor Davenport's conclusions are assuredly not in keeping with the general impression regarding the incidence of the war burden. Complaints of excessive taxation and of class discrimination have come mainly from the business world, and the current attempts of labor to secure wage increases have been widely excoriated as profiteering by government officials, the press, and to a less extent by economists, to say nothing of manufacturers' associations and chambers of commerce. But most of the problems raised for discussion by Professor Davenport are fundamentally quantitative in character ; they are subject to inductive verification if statistical data can be found covering the points of relative wage and price advances ; war-

* Jacob Viner, "Who Paid for the War ?" *Journal of Political Economy,* Vol. XXVIII, January, 1920, pp. 46-76.

[1] H. J. Davenport, "The War-Tax Paradox," *American Economic Review,* March, 1919.

time production, income, and consumption; and the sources of government revenue. Where statistics are not available, facts of common knowledge may be at hand, whereby the reasoning of Professor Davenport, largely a priori in character, may be tested. What follows is mainly an attempt to use the available factual material to test the accuracy of his conclusions, and to throw further light on the incidence of the war cost.

WAR BURDEN CANNOT BE TRANSFERRED TO FUTURE

The reasoning that the cost of the war, for a country which cannot or does not borrow from abroad, must be borne from current income, is generally accepted by economists. What is not yet existent cannot meet a present need. The economic war burdens created by a present generation cannot be transmitted to the future, to be borne by subsequent generations. Financing through loans does not postpone the burden, but merely provides the lenders of present income with a promise that the government will at a later date transfer to them in repayment portions of the future income of other members of the community. The amount of the current drain upon national income is not altered by the method of financing used by the Treasury, unless of course the method used affects the relative degree in which contributions to the Treasury are made out of income and capital resources.

Professor Seligman, it is true, discovers a fallacy in such reasoning, arising out of an alleged failure to discriminate between objective and subjective sacrifices.[2] The bondholder, he claims, incurs little or no net subjective sacrifice in surrendering his funds to the government, since he would have invested his surplus income in any case, and is compensated for such temporary surrender of his funds by the receipt of interest. If he were to contribute through taxation, on the other hand, there would be an immediate subjective sacrifice. To the extent, therefore, that recourse is had to borrowing instead of taxation, to that extent the amount of immediate subjective sacrifice is reduced. When in the future the burden of taxation is placed upon the citizen in order that the government may redeem its bonds, there is no offsetting subjective benefit to the bondholder, but on the contrary he suffers a further burden in being obliged to find a new field for the investment of his funds. The burden placed on the taxpayer of the future in order to redeem war bonds, Professor Seligman concludes, is

2 E. R. Seligman, "Loans versus Taxes in War Finance," *Annals of the American Academy of Political and Social Science*, XXV (Whole No. 164), 63 ff.

therefore not offset by a contemporaneous benefit to another group, but is an initial sacrifice toward financing the war. which sacrifice, by means of loan financing, had been hitherto postponed.

But this reasoning, it appears to the writer, is open to serious criticism, and is not a valid objection to the position generally taken by economists. The sacrifice involved in lending is the postponement of consumption during the currency of the loan ; the sacrifice involved in the payment of taxation is the permanent surrender of means to consumption; the difference between lending and taxpaying is in the future, not in the present. If the loan were repudiated upon maturity, the bondholder would readily perceive the benefits arising to him from repayment, and the fact that he takes such repayment as a matter of course does not appreciably subtract from the amount of subjective satisfaction derived from it. If Professor Seligman's reasoning were accepted and given its logical applications, all consumers' surpluses would be lightly regarded by economists, since, except when the consumer is in danger of, or in process of, losing them, they secure only very fragmentary recognition in consciousness.

In one sense only can the economic burden of the war be handed on to a future generation, and that is by a diminution of the bequest made by the war-time generation to succeeding ones, whether this diminution be absolute or only in comparison with what would have been handed on if there had been no war. The war expenditures must be met out of current goods, but these goods may be part of the capital resources instead of part of the current net income. Through consumption of existing stocks, through failure to maintain and to replace depreciating plant and equipment, through the more intensive exploitation of natural resources, the capital of a belligerent may be partially destroyed by war, even though no invader crosses its borders. An analogous situation arises if the resources existing at the outbreak of the war are maintained undiminished, but the increase in these resources which would have accrued in normal times does not take place owing to war-time conditions. In each case the next generation is poorer than it would have been if there had been no war, or if the war cost had been met without making inroads upon the wealth accumulated in the past and without reducing below the normal rate the amount added to these past accumulations during the war period.

CAPITAL RESOURCES OF NATION NOT IMPAIRED BY WAR

THERE is little evidence, however, to suggest that the capital resources of this country have been significantly impaired as a result of the war. Stocks of goods in warehouses and in retail stores may have been smaller at the signing of the armistice than prior to the entrance of the United States into the war; statistics are not available for a reliable judgment. But such statistics as have come to the writer's notice indicate that for many raw materials and foodstuffs, including such important commodities as copper, cotton, tea, coffee, wheat, the stocks on hand at the cessation of hostilities were unprecedented in volume. Buildings, railroads, highways, were not kept at their pre-war standards of maintenance and repair; extensions were undertaken at very much below the normal rate. But new capital in enormous quantities was turned into the construction and equipment of the greatly enlarged shipbuilding and shipping, chemical, dye, ordnance, and munition industries, was absorbed in the development of hitherto unexploited mineral and timber resources, and was used to purchase American securities held abroad, to make foreign loans, to build up a great reserve of gold obtained from abroad. Some of this new accumulation has proved to be of little value for peacetime purposes; the cases of conspicuous depreciation have received considerable publicity; but the bulk of it remains as a valuable addition to the working equipment of the United States.

Professor Friday has estimated, largely from data collected by the Treasury for fiscal purposes, the capital savings of the nation during the war period as compared with 1912.[3] He finds the new savings in 1917 and 1918 to have been 18 and 22 billion dollars respectively, as compared with new savings of 6.5 billions in 1913 and of 9 and 14.5 billions in 1915 and 1916 respectively. He gives no estimate for 1914. If the amount of new savings for 1913 be taken as a normal pre-war figure — it appears to have been greater than the figure for the immediately preceding years — the total accretion of capital was in excess of the normal rate by 27 billions of dollars in the two war years[4] and by 10.5 billions in the two given years of neutrality.[5]

These figures are subject to correction from two directions before they can be accepted as satisfactory indexes of the total

[3] David Friday, "The War and the Supply of Capital," *American Economic Review Supplement*, March, 1919, p. 91.
[4] $(18 + 22) — (2 \times 6.5) = 27$ ($= 8.5$ on the basis of 1913 prices).
[5] $(9 + 14.5) — (2 \times 6.5) = 10.5$ ($= 7.8$ on the basis of 1913 prices).

amount of the national income withheld from civilian consumption during the war period.   Because of the depreciation
in the standard of value since 1913, the figures for the later
years exaggerate the real volume of new savings.   On the other
hand, the estimates are based largely on income returns made
for taxation purposes, and as the period was marked by a sharp
rise in the rates of taxation, there was an undoubted tendency
toward undervaluation of income.   These two sources of error
thus tend to offset each other.   It will be shown later that the
amount of increase in new savings indicated by Friday's figures
was sufficient to meet the cost of the war.[6]   If the increase in
national income over the normal pre-war rate can be shown to
have been equal to this increase in national savings, then the
war cost was met without any reduction in the national average
standard of living.

INCREASE IN NATIONAL PRODUCTION IN WAR YEARS

PROFESSOR DAVENPORT claims, however, that there was no increase in production during the war period, and that the war
cost was met by a decrease in consumption.   Although no
means are available for an estimate of the normal percentage of
employment of the labor and capital resources of the nation
during normal times, it would be generally admitted that, on
the average, through a peace-time period long enough to cover
both the prosperity and depression phases of the business cycle,
very considerable percentages of both labor and capital are
idle and unproductive.   During the war period there was an
approximation to complete utilization ; labor worked full time
and even overtime ; plant and equipment were utilized to near
their utmost capacity ; intensive training enabled many men to
turn from unskilled to skilled labor ; the period of production
from the extraction of the raw material to the turning out of
the finished article was shortened through more rapid turnover
of stocks at each stage.

The loss in the labor supply through the withdrawal of men
for the army and navy was offset by the entrance of women into
industry, by the postponement of retirement of the older employees and by the earlier entry of youths into industry, by the
entrance into the ranks of labor of men non-productively occupied in normal times.   In England, where a much greater
percentage of the male population was withdrawn for military
purposes, a recent official statistical survey showed that the industrial labor force was practically maintained by the entrance

[6] The possibility that some of these savings may have lost their value after the
cessation of hostilities has already been indicated.

of women into industry, and by the postponing of retirement of older employees and hastening of entry into employment of youths. Between July, 1914, and July, 1918, approximately 5,000,000 men in England entered military service out of a total male working population at the outbreak of the war of 10,500,000, a withdrawal from the male working force of about 47 per cent of its numbers. The replacements by 1918, including, however, demobilized soldiers, lacked only 6 per cent of equaling the withdrawals. Owing to the smaller number withdrawn for military service in this country, the greater annual accretions of workers, the larger reserve supply of labor, there was probably no net reduction in the total number of workers as a result of the war. As compared with 1913 and 1914 there may have been a substantial increase.

There is some danger, however, of exaggeration. Production was already near its peak in 1916, or prior to the entrance of the United States into the war, and a comparison of the war years with the years of neutrality would not give as favorable results as would a comparison with the pre-war years. Moreover, the recruiting of labor for the war industries was effected in large part through withdrawals from other industries or from household work. Professor Wolfe states that "most of the women who went into war industry came from other industries in which they had previously gained a livelihood," and that "the three important non-industrial sources were doubtless (1) domestic service, from which came considerable numbers for the factories; (2) teachers, 100,000 of whom are said to have left the low pay of the schoolroom for clerical and munitions work; (3) wives and mothers of soldiers." [7] The male labor for the war industries also came mainly from the other industries. But with a labor force at work in approximately its maximum numbers, at almost full time, utilizing the increased capital equipment of the country to an extent approaching maximum capacity, and all under especially high pressure, there is strong presumptive reason to believe that the war-time production in this country was substantially greater than the pre-war production and at least as great as the production during the period of neutrality.

More concrete evidence of an increase in production during the war period is available, however. Professor Wesley Mitchell, basing his estimates on the figures of production and importation for ninety staple raw materials, weighted both for differences in relative importance and for differences in the

[7] A. B. Wolfe and Helen Olson, "War-Time Industrial Employment of Women in the United States," *Journal of Political Economy*, XXVII (October, 1919), 640.

"fabrication factors" or costs of conversion to finished goods, has devised an index number for production during the war period from 1913 to 1918, which, taking 100 as representing the production in 1913, shows aggregate production to have been 99 in 1914, 107 in 1915, 111 in 1916, 114 in 1917, and 116 in 1918.[8]

There are several factors which may tend, under certain circumstances, to make an index such as this, based as it is on both production and import statistics for raw materials, exaggerate the amount of increase in production during the period under investigation. The inclusion of raw-material imports is essential if due weight is to be given to fabrication of raw materials. But if imports of raw materials should increase during the period more rapidly than their domestic production, the resulting index would exaggerate the degree of increase in production. Conversely, a decrease or a slower rate of increase in imports as compared with domestic production of raw materials would operate to make the index minimize unduly the increase in production. But imports of raw materials, in terms of quantities, appear to have increased in about the same proportions as domestic production during the war period. As the fabrication cost is generally much greater than the raw-material cost, the possibility of substantial error arising from this source cannot be very great.

A possible source of more serious error is to be found in the probable tendency during the war period for a substitution of the manufacture of coarse and bulky war materials out of the raw materials instead of finely finished consumer's goods. The *Census of Manufacturers of 1914* was used by Professor Mitchell to determine the increment of value added to raw materials in the process of fabrication. The decline in the relative importance of cost of fabrication as compared with cost of production of raw materials in the period subsequent to 1914 would tend therefore to make Mitchell's index exaggerate the amount of increase in production. Against this, however, there is to be balanced the counter consideration that a smaller proportion of this country's exports consisted of crude and partially manufactured products and a greater proportion consisted of fully manufactured articles during the war years than during the period antecedent to the outbreak of hostilities. The resulting increase in the amount of fabrication for export done in this country finds, I think, no expression in Professor Mitchell's index, but is probably adequately corrected by the

[8] Wesley C. Mitchell, "History of Prices During the War, Summary," *War Industries Board Price Bulletin No. 1*, p. 45.

failure of his index to account for reduction in the amount of fabrication undergone by raw materials as a whole in the war period.

A third source of possible error arises from the fact that the index, since it is based wholly on figures of production of tangible goods, would not account for variations in the production of non-material services. There was undoubtedly a decrease in the amount of personal services such as domestic help, waiters' services, education, etc., rendered during these years, and the importance of such material services in the national dividend can easily be underestimated. It has already been suggested that a substantial fraction of the increased labor at work in the war industries was withdrawn from the "personal-service industries." On the whole, however, it is probably safe to assume that these factors of error, some operating in one direction and some in the other, come near enough to counterbalancing each other, and that Mitchell's index may be accepted as a true enough measure of the trend for our purposes.

There was therefore increased production during the period subsequent to the outbreak of hostilities, and this increase was maintained throughout the period of American participation in the war. But unless this increase in production was of itself sufficient to meet the costs of the war, it would still be true that there was either a war-time decrease in civilian consumption or a decrease in capital resources or both. There was no decrease in capital resources. As shown, the probability is that there was an increase. Was there a decrease in national consumption?

NO DECREASE IN AVERAGE NATIONAL STANDARD OF LIVING DURING WAR PERIOD

To the casual observer, there was not apparent any marked reduction in the average standard of living during the war period. On the contrary, there were many surface indications that the nation was living better, more comfortably, in enjoyment of more conveniences and luxuries during the war period than ever before. It appeared from rough statistical calculations made during the war by government bodies in Washington, that coffee, tea, cocoa, chocolate, soft drinks, cheap jewelry, talking machines, silk shirts, among other commodities of like character generally classed as luxuries, were being consumed in unprecedented quantities, and from such evidence the impression became widespread that the nation as a whole and labor in particular were thoroughly enjoying the war. But figures of consumption, when only a short period is covered, are almost

always, because of the only methods usually available for their
compilation, of slight value even as showing a trend. Increased production and increased imports may indicate only an
increase in stocks and not in actual consumption. In the case
of coffee and tea, paradoxical as it may seem, the general policy
of restriction of imports was itself the cause of increased imports, which went into stock, but appeared in most estimates
as increased consumption. The restrictions on imports were
not applied to these commodities, but the importers, not believing that their special good fortune would last, took full
advantage of their opportunity and made greatly increased imports in anticipation of future restrictions. In the case of tea
at least, importers who had throughout the war period used up
valuable shipping space in anticipation of the imposition of
restrictions, shortly before the armistice, found themselves embarrassed by overgreat supplies and besought the imposition of
restrictions on further imports "in order to economize shipping."

In the absence of satisfactory statistics of consumption some
aid may perhaps be derived from Veblen's doctrine of conspicuous consumption. Increases of spending power would be
more likely to be widely advertised, and decreases to be concealed from the vulgar gaze. This would be the easier since
the items in which there was unquestionably great decrease in
average consumption during the war period, as for example
house-room and personal services in the home, were often such
as would not attract general attention. Professor Davenport
thinks there was a reduction in consumption. Professor Friday has stated his belief in an increase in consumption of somewhere in the neighborhood of 12½ per cent, but without
indicating whether this estimate was intended to cover military
as well as civilian consumption.[9] It appears to be a widely
held opinion that there was a considerable increase in consumption during the war period. There is ground, however, for
believing that the truth lies somewhere between, that there was
no marked decrease in national consumption and no marked
increase. This, of course, does not preclude the possibility
that there may have been a considerable war-time redistribution of consumption, some groups increasing their consumption and others decreasing it. With regard to this possibility,
something will be said later.

[9] "Such statistics as are available show that consumption has not increased
more than 12½ per cent during the same (i.e., the war) period." — *American
Economic Review Supplement*, March, 1919, p. 91.

WAR COST COMPARED WITH WAR-TIME INCREASE IN NATIONAL INCOME

A MORE satisfactory method of approach to the problem whether the military expenditure demanded a reduction in the national standard of living is available through a comparison of the war cost with the war-time increase in national income. If the increase in national income was as great as the expenditure on the war, and if the capital resources at the end of the war were about what they would have been if the war had not taken place and the 1913 rate of accumulation had continued throughout, it would follow that there was no reduction in average national consumption. There follows an attempt at a quantitative comparison of the total war cost, the total war-time increase in national income, and the total private savings from income during the war period.

The national income for the United States for the year 1913 has been estimated by Anderson as 34.8 billions of dollars.[10] In the following table an estimate of annual national income is given for the years 1914 to 1918, obtained in terms of 1913 values by multiplying Mitchell's physical-production index for each year by Anderson's figure for the national income in 1913.

Year	Total Physical Production, W. C. Mitchell's Index	Aggregate value Yearly National Income, on Basis of 1913 Prices in Billions of Dollars
1913	100	34.8
1914	99	34.5
1915	107	37.2
1916	111	38.6
1917	114	39.7
1918	116	40.4

The estimate of 34.5 billions as the aggregate national income in 1913 appears reasonable when compared with King's estimate of 30.5 billions for 1910,[11] with Friday's estimate of 6.5 billions as the new savings from income in 1913,[12] and with Mitchell's estimate of 17.4 billions as the value of the fabricated products of ninety raw materials produced in 1913.[13] The acceptability of Mitchell's index of production has already been discussed. The figures of gross production which result are accepted also as indicating gross income. Professor Anderson,

---

10 B. M. Anderson, Jr., in the *New York Times Annalist*, January 6, 1919.
11 W. I. King, *Wealth and Income of the People of the United States.*
12 See *supra*, p. 743.
13 W. C. Mitchell, *op. cit.*, p. 45.

although he admits the correspondence between production and income under normal conditions, claims that this correspondence ceases under war conditions, on the ground that soldiers, although withdrawn from production, still receive income. He concludes, therefore, that the diminution of production which results from the withdrawal of men for the army from industry is not accompanied by a corresponding diminution of national income.[14] But there is obviously a fallacy in this reasoning. Where does the income of the soldiers come from if not out of national production? The income of the soldiers represents an equivalent subtraction from the income of the civilian population, but the national income remains what national production makes it.[15]

The period from the entrance of the United States into the war to May 1, 1919, which is a convenient terminal date for our purposes, is longer than two years by 24 days. Assuming that real national income has been accruing during 1919 at the same rate as in the early part of 1917, the total income for 1917 and 1918 plus 24 days' income at the 1917 rate may be taken as the total national income during the war period. At the 1913 level of prices, this gives a figure of 82.7 billions.[16]

The general staff has reported an estimate of $21,294,000,000 as the total cost of the war to the Treasury of the United States to May 1, 1919.[17] A calculation based on the monthly ordinary expenditures of the Treasury throughout this period indicates that approximately 10 per cent of this expenditure occurred in 1917, 60 per cent in 1918, and 30 per cent in 1919. Conversion

---

[14] New York Times Annalist, January 6, 1919.

[15] Professor Anderson, in the article cited, has himself made estimates of the annual national income for the years of the war period, but in terms of yearly prices calculated on the bases of Dun's price index and his own production index. His figures recalculated in terms of the 1913 price level throughout give the following results:

Year	B. M. Anderson's Production Index	National Income on Basis of 1913 Prices in Billions of Dollars
1913	100.0	34.8
1914	92.9	32.3
1915	97.8	34.0
1916	114.7	39.9
1917	116.7	40.6
1918	110.9	38.6

[16] $39.7 + 40.4 + 2.6 = 82.7$.

[17] New York Times, May 18, 1919. Professor Bogart at about the same time independently reached an estimate of $22,625,000,000 as the total war cost. E. L. Bogart, "Direct and Indirect Costs of the Great World War," Preliminary Economic Studies of the War, No. 24, p. 267, Carnegie Endowment for International Peace. It would be proper to add, however, the amounts spent by semi-public organizations in war relief, welfare work among soldiers, etc. These would probably total considerably over a billion dollars.

to the 1913 basis of prices with the use of the Bureau of Labor Statistics Wholesale Price Index gives a total war cost for the period, in terms of 1913 prices, of 10.4 billions of dollars, or 12.6 per cent of the war-time national income.

In 1917 and 1918 there were annual increases in national income over the 1913 rate of 4.9 and 5.6 billions of dollars respectively, in terms of 1913 prices. To this should be added 0.3 billion of dollars increase for the 24 days by which the period taken as the war period exceeded two years, estimated on the basis of 1919 income being equal to 1917 income, making a total increase of income for the war period above the 1913 rate of 10.8 billions.[18] The increase of income during the war period as compared with the 1913 rate of income was almost exactly equal to the cost of the war.

The total increase in the rate of new savings from income during the years 1917 and 1918 above the 1913 rate, when reduced to the 1913 basis of prices, was 8.5 billions of dollars.[19] If to this figure be added an allowance for the new savings in the additional 24 days by which the war period exceeded two years and a further allowance for a substantial amount of undervaluation of income in the returns upon which Professor Friday's estimates were based, there would result as an estimate of the total amount of new savings during the war years a figure not appreciably less, in terms of 1913 prices, than either the total amount of increase in national income during the same period, namely 10.8 billions, or the total cost of the war to May 1, 1919, namely 10.4 billions.

As compared with 1913, there was therefore no decrease in the average national standard of living and no impairment of capital resources, and the war cost was met from the increase in national income resulting from an increase in national production.[20]

Professor Davenport appears to have reached his conclusion that the war expenditures necessitated a reduction of the national standard of living, partly on the assumption that there

[18] $4.9 + 5.6 + 0.3 = 10.8.$
[19] See *supra*, p. 743.
[20] Purchases of war bonds would, of course, be entered as private savings and be included in the gross figure of national savings. If the remainder of the increase in new savings were not used indirectly or directly to provide funds for the prosecution of the war, there would result a net increase in capital resources. The remainder of the war cost would be met, however, by a decrease in consumption. To this extent the conclusions reached here are subject to modification. But 70 per cent of the war cost, including loans to the Allies, was financed by the flotation of bonds. Of the remaining 30 per cent which was financed from tax revenue, a good part must have been paid out of savings from increased incomes.

was no increase in production, partly as the result of an over-estimate of the proportion of the national income necessary to meet the war cost. On the basis of an estimate of 40 billion dollars as the national income in 1914 and of a war budget of 15 billion dollars presumably for each year of war, he arrived at the figure of 40 per cent as the ratio of war cost to total national income. To take income, even assuming no increase since 1914 in real income, at the 1914 price level, and to set against it war expenditures at the inflated price levels of the later years, is to exaggerate in unjustifiable degree the real extent of the war burden. Moreover, his figure for war expenditures, even in terms of 1917 and 1918 prices, is unduly high, unless the loans to the Allies are included. These will be considered later.

It may be objected that the increase of population during the period from 1913 to 1918 required an increase in national income if the 1913 standard of living were to be maintained. The census estimate for the increase in population from 1913 to 1917 is about 5,000,000, or approximately 6.7 per cent of the population in 1913. But the increase in these war years is estimated at practically the pre-war rate, whereas immigration declined heavily and emigration increased. Moreover, in calculating the income necessary to maintain the pre-war standard of living among the civilian population, deduction must be made of a sum sufficient to meet the normal consumption of the several million soldiers and sailors and such of their dependents as were maintained out of the war budget. To charge their consumption against both the civilian budget and the war budget is to count it twice. If allowance is made for these factors, the increase in population may be disregarded without serious error.

On superficial examination it might appear that similar allowance should be made for the consumption of all whose maintenance was provided either directly or indirectly out of the war budget. But the estimate of national production was based on the index of production, including the production of ordnance, munitions, and other war material. If the consumption of the war workers were to be deducted from the national consumption, on the ground that it was provided for out of the military budget, their production would then have to be deducted from the amount of national production, and the figure for national income would be reduced correspondingly. The civilian workers produced the income for both themselves and the military forces. Both the civilian war workers and the military forces received their income by means of the war budget, but the claims of the war workers on the war budget were offset by their additions to the national income.

LOANS TO THE ALLIES AND THE PROFITS OF NEUTRALITY

So far only the war cost has been considered as a drain upon income. But by May 1, 1919, the United States had lent to the Allies approximately 9 billions of dollars. Although these are properly to be considered as investments and not as expenditures, it is nevertheless true that in so far as income available for consumption is concerned lending to the Allies would have exactly the same effect as expenditure outright on the war program. This would lead to the conclusion that while there was an increase in national income during the war period adequate to meet the war budget without necessitating a lowering of the standard of living, nevertheless it was necessary, to meet the demands on the United States for credits to the Allies, that there should be a restriction of consumption.

There is still to be considered, however, the increase in national income during the period of American neutrality. Taking 1915, 1916, and the latter half of 1914 as covering the period of neutrality, there was an increase in income on the basis of 1913 prices of 2.4 and 3.8 billions respectively in 1915 and 1916, and a loss for the whole of 1914, all of which may be taken as having occurred in the latter half of the year, of 0.30 billions, a total gain in income of approximately 6 billions. The loans to the Allies were made chiefly in 1918 and 1919. On the basis of the 1913 price level they would amount to approximately 4.6 billions. The United States produced enough in the war years to meet the war cost, and produced more than enough in the years of neutrality to extend the credits to the Allies without encroachment upon the average national standard of living.

THE SOURCES OF THE GOVERNMENT WAR-TIME REVENUE

PROFESSOR DAVENPORT claims that the war cost was met chiefly by borrowing from the capitalist class the excess profits which inured to them through the widened gap between prices and wages. Of the total expenditures of the United States government from April 6, 1917, to June 30, 1919, amounting to $32,427,000,000, about 29 per cent was met from taxation and other revenues than loans.[21] In these expenditures were included the loans to the Allies, which would ultimately be re-

21 Letter of Secretary Glass to Congressman Fordney, July 9, 1919, in *Federal Reserve Bulletin*, August 1, 1919, p. 725.

paid, and government investments in ships, War Finance Corporation stock, federal land bank bonds, and other income-yielding assets. This would leave an increase in indebtedness as a result of the war of considerably less than 23 billions of dollars if loans to the Allies be not deducted. If these loans be deducted, the net increase in indebtedness would be considerably less than 14 billions of dollars. It still remains true, however, that the cost of the war was met temporarily chiefly by loans instead of taxes.

The war loans in spite of their superficially wide distribution were absorbed mainly by the wealthier classes and by financial institutions. The small subscriptions bulked large only for the last three loans, and many of the small holdings were soon transferred to the traditionally investing classes at a loss to the original subscribers. It still remains to be proved, however, that the funds which the wealthier classes subscribed to the war loans were war profits, in excess of normal, and obtained through the lag of wages behind prices.

There is a remarkable scarcity of reliable data upon which to base conclusions with regard to changes in the distribution of the national income among the various economic groups. This is particularly true with regard to the income of professional classes, of domestic servants, of real estate owners, of farmers, and of unorganized labor. An attempt follows to utilize such material coming from official or otherwise unquestionable sources as has come to the attention of the writer.

PROFITS DURING THE WAR PERIOD

PROFESSOR FRIDAY presents the following figures for the net income before taxation of corporations in the United States for the years 1913 to 1918, consisting in part of returns of the Commissioner of Revenue and in part of estimates based on published reports of the corporations.[22] For purposes of comparison, the Bureau of Labor Index for Wholesale Prices is also included in the table.

The increase in corporation incomes for every year in the period was thus relatively much greater than the rise in prices. The increase in the returns of two hundred and twenty-four industrial corporations for which Professor Friday could find continuous data was relatively so much greater, however, than the increase in corporation earnings in general as to indicate that not all kinds of corporations fared well during the period, and that while abnormal profits inured to industrial concerns

[22] David Friday, "The War and the Supply of Capital," *American Economic Review Supplement*, March, 1919, p. 89.

as a whole, other corporations, especially those operating public utilities, suffered from an increase in costs not wholly compensated for by increases in the prices they were permitted to charge for their services. It should also be noted that returns are prior to taxation, and that the increasing rates of taxation in the later years made substantial reductions in the percentages of increase in net income. On the other hand, these returns were made primarily for taxation purposes, and there would be operative, therefore, a tendency to make them as small as possible. Moreover, under the involved provisions of the tax laws, "taxable income" was often an uncertain quantity, with somewhat distant relationship to real income. Many income-tax returns were made low, in the hope that there would be no protest from the Treasury, and in the reasonable certainty that any demand for an upward revision would not come until some time had elapsed. In the interval the use of the funds could be enjoyed. Other returns were made unduly low because of honest misunderstanding of the requirements of the tax legislation. It is a widely held opinion that the income-tax returns of 1917 and 1918 have still considerable scrutiny to undergo before their final approval.[23]

Years	Net Income of All Corporations in the United States in Millions	Percentage Increase Over 1913	Net Income of 224 Industrial Corporations in Millions	Percentage Increase Over 1913	Bureau of Labor Wholesale Price Index
1913	$ 4,340	....	$ 507	....	100
1914	3,711	14.5	381	− 24.9	99
1915	5,184	19.4	664	31.0	100
1916	8,766	102.0	1,364	169.0	123
1917	10,500	141.9	1,750	245.1	175
1918	9,500	118.9	....	....	185

While corporation incomes as a whole have risen more rapidly than prices, interest payments on bonded obligations incurred prior to 1914 have remained at the pre-war rate. The bondholders as a class received the same money income in 1918 as in 1914 on their old investments. This must have resulted in a greater increase in corporation income distributed among common shareholders or charged to surplus available for distribution as dividends in the future than in corporation income as a whole. For the economic group deriving their income from corporation earnings, the war brought increased real

[23] Since this was written, Professor T. S. Adams, Tax Adviser to the Treasury, has estimated at $1,000,000,000 or thereabout the amount of additional tax revenue which would accrue from careful auditing of tax returns. This amount is, of course, much less than the amount of undervaluation in the tax returns represented thereby.

earnings if they were shareholders, decreased real earnings if they were bondholders, brought fortunes to shareholders in industrial concerns, misfortune to both shareholders and bondholders in public utilities.[24]

THE CONTRIBUTION OF INDUSTRIAL LABOR TO THE WAR COST

IN the following table two indexes for wages during the years 1913 to 1918 are compared with the rise in wholesale prices and in the cost of living:

UNION RATES OF WAGES PER HOUR [*]		WHOLESALE PRICES §		AVERAGE WEEKLY EARNINGS IN N. Y. STATE FACTORIES. ALL EMPLOYEES, OFFICE AND SHOP †		COST OF LIVING IN COUNTRY AS A WHOLE EXCLUDING AGRICULTURAL COMMUNITIES ‡	
Date	Index	Date	Index	Date	Index	Date	Index
				June, 1914	100	1913	100
May 1, 1913	100	1913	100	June–Dec., 1914	98	July, 1914	101
May 1, 1914	102	1914	99	Jan.–Dec., 1915	101	Dec., 1914	103
May 1, 1915	103	1915	100	Jan.–Dec., 1916	114	June, 1915	103
May 1, 1916	107	1916	123	Jan.–Dec., 1917	129	Dec., 1915	104
May 1, 1917	114	1917	175	Jan.–Dec., 1918	160	June, 1916	110
May 1, 1918	133	1918	197	Jan.–April, 1919	176	Dec., 1916	118
		Jan.–April, 1919	201			June, 1917	129
						Dec., 1917	142
						June, 1918	158
						Dec., 1918	174
						Spring, 1919	175

* United States Bureau of Labor Statistics, *Monthly Labor Review*, March, 1919, p. 119.
§ *Ibid.*, February, 1919, p. 104, and November, 1919, p. 153.
† New York State Industrial Commission, *Labor Market Bulletin*, September, 1919.
‡ *Monthly Labor Review*, October, 1919, p. 1, and November, 1919, p. 193.

No other comprehensive indexes of the trend of wages than those presented above have been found. The Bureau of Labor index of union rates of wages per hour is compiled from the minimum rates agreed upon by labor and employers. In some cases higher rates than these were in effect, but these minimum rates were usually the prevailing rates.[25] This index does not reveal the amount of increase in actual earnings in so far as

[24] The relative trend of index numbers published by various newspapers for bond prices, industrial shares, and railroad shares on the stock market since 1913 confirms this conclusion.

[25] "Union Scale of Wages and Hours of Labor," *United States Bureau of Labor Statistics Bulletin No. 214*, May 15, 1916, pp. 10, 11.

"The union scale, as the term is here used, is a statement, either written or definitely understood, of wages and hours of labor agreed to or accepted by an organization of union men and an employer or group of employers, under which agreement, express or implied, union men actually are working. The union scale usually fixes the limit in only one direction. It sets a minimum wage and a maximum of hours for a regular day's work. . . As a general rule the union scale represents the prevailing wage of a locality for efficient labor."

such increase is due to fuller employment or to payment of higher rates for overtime work. On the other hand, a recent study of the length of the workday reveals a widespread tendency since 1913 toward a reduction in the number of hours worked each day.[26] This index fails also to throw any light on the trend of earnings of unorganized industrial labor.

The New York state index for average weekly earnings is based on returns for one week in each month including the fifteenth of the month, and is obtained by dividing the total weekly pay-roll by the total number of employees on the pay-roll for the given week. It should represent accurately the average earnings actually received by factory workers in New York state, office workers included. But the New York experience may not have been typical of the country as a whole. Moreover the average weekly earnings indicated by the statistics upon which the index is based were so low in the early years of the war period [27] that they suggest the question whether the workers covered by this index do not include an unusual proportion of cheap factory and office labor, and especially of female labor, than is typical of American industry as a whole. If such be the case it is also a possibility that the classes of labor which were relatively most poorly situated with regard to earnings at the outbreak of the war may have profited most as a result of the war conditions.

For the purpose of reaching conclusions with regard to the earnings of labor as a whole, this index has the further defect that it does not include non-factory labor, such as transportation workers, employees in the building trades, government employees, and wage earners in mercantile establishments and in offices not connected with factories. Finally, it is open to question in the absence of further data whether an index of earnings for New York state is fairly comparable with an index of cost of living for the country as a whole. For all these reasons, confident conclusions cannot be based on these data alone. They must be used, therefore, only as suggesting and not as proving conclusions.

Two issues, largely independent of each other, are involved in the comparison of wages with prices. In a search for the source of expanded war-time profits of business enterprise, and of its relationship with the remuneration of labor, the relevant comparison is between rates of wage and wholesale prices. A third factor, of possibly quite considerable importance here, is the relative effectiveness of each unit of labor in the war

[26] *Monthly Labor Review*, November, 1919, pp. 197, 198.
[27] They were $12.48 in 1914 ; $12.85 in 1915.

years as compared with the pre-war period. Data on this point are not available. Pointing in the direction of decreased effectiveness are the emergency redistribution of labor from old occupations to new; the extension of industries of importance to the military program under disadvantageous emergency conditions; the not infrequent reports of ca' canny practice among labor during the war period; and probably increased rates of turnover of labor. Suggesting increased effectiveness are the intensive training of hitherto unskilled labor for skilled work; the patriotic stimulus; the increased use of labor-saving devices; the full utilization of existing plant, appliances, stocks of materials, and administrative and executive organizations. Which of these sets of factors predominated it appears impossible to say. That the net change, whatever its direction, was important, is unlikely.

The second issue is concerned with the welfare of the laboring classes and more especially the integrity of their standard of living during the war period. Here a comparison of earnings, and not *rates* of wages, with cost of living, and not wholesale prices, is pertinent. The indexes given above show an approximately complete correspondence until 1918 between the increase in earnings in the state of New York and the increase in cost of living for the country as a whole. In the one year, 1918, there appears to have been some lag of earnings behind cost of living. This indicates, what has already been suggested, that the contribution of labor to the cost of the war was made through increased production and not to any important extent, if at all, through decreased consumption.

Comparison of the increases in rates of wages indicated by these indexes with the rise in wholesale prices shows that rates of wages per hour failed by a great margin to keep up with the rise in prices in 1917 and 1918. This lag of wages, an important element in costs of production, behind the prices secured by the manufacturers for their products points to an important source of the great increase in the earnings of industrial corporations during the war period. Price inflation, as Professor Davenport claims, does appear to have operated to reduce the rate of return to labor and to transfer this saving in cost to the employer in the form of increased profits.

Not all of the increase in profits necessarily was secured at the expense of labor. As has been pointed out by Professor Moulton,[28] in those lines of manufacture in which there was increased output from the same plant, there was a saving in

[28] H. G. Moulton, "War Finance and the Price Level," *Journal of Political Economy*, XXVII, 701.

overhead cost per unit which would have enabled producers to maintain profits even though prices of their products did not rise in full proportion to the increase in wage rates. But even though it be granted that all the savings in overhead resulting from increased output should be added to the profits of the producer, and that labor had no claim to a share in these, it would still have been true that the additional margin of profits resulting from the lag of wage rates behind prices was obtained at the expense of labor. As there is no question that these extra profits were to some extent invested in war loans, to that extent at least Professor Davenport is justified in his claim that these profits represented a contribution by labor to the cost of the war, paid to the employers, and lent by them to the government. To some extent, however, these profits were taken by the government as income and excess-profit taxes, and except for the stimulus to price expansion resulting from this method of indirect contribution, the ultimate results were to this extent what they would have been if labor had been directly taxed to the same extent.

RATES OF WAGES, WEEKLY EARNINGS, AND FAMILY EARNINGS

PROFESSOR MOULTON, in the same article,[29] states that the problem whether the increase in the monetary income of the laboring classes resulted in an increase of real wages depends upon whether prices increased more rapidly than family monetary income, and proceeds to express the opinion that during the first year of the war (i.e., the first year of American participation therein) the *family* money income increased more rapidly than did the price level among many classes of laborers. Unquestionably the rise in money wages was not equal in all industries and for all occupations. In some industries, real earnings per employee went up, in some they fell. But for industry as a whole the best available data indicate constant weekly real earnings per employee until 1918, and a fall in real earnings in 1918. On what grounds can it be claimed that *family annual earnings* rose, while *individual weekly earnings* remained constant, or even fell?

Professor Moulton claims that at the time of the entrance of the United States into the war there was a considerable volume of unemployment in the country and a great deal of part-time work, that the first effect of the war was to decrease the number of unemployed, that a second effect was to increase the number of days per year worked by those already employed,

29 *Op. cit.*, p. 709.

that a third effect was to provide overtime work at higher rates of pay, and that a fourth was to draw more members of the family into the wage-earning classes. Production, however, as indicated by both Mitchell's and Anderson's indexes, and as a matter of current knowledge, had already very nearly reached its height by 1916, and there was little margin either in equipment or in labor for further expansion. The Bureau of Labor Statistics index for employment for thirteen of the most important industries shows an unquestionable increase in the number on the pay-roll following the entrance of the United States into the war for only one, the iron and steel industry, and substantial decreases in employment in most of the others.[30] This indicates that shipbuilding and other war industries in which expansion came after the entrance of the United States into the war, obtained their supplies of labor from the nonessential industries. There was no important army of unemployed to be utilized. Nor is it any more probable that there was an unusual amount of part-time work just prior to April, 1917, unless it was voluntary on the part of the workers. Moreover, the index for weekly earnings given above shows the full effect on earnings of any increase in the number of hours worked per week, including overtime work at higher rates. The net amount of overtime work done during the war period is probably generally overestimated. There was widespread complaint on the part of the employers during the war that employees were working overtime hours at overtime pay one day in order to absent themselves from work next day. There remains the possibility of increased earnings through working more weeks per year. But as compared with 1916 there could have been but a slight decrease in involuntary unemployment in 1917 and 1918. The increase in the number of wage-earners in the family could not have been a factor of great importance. As has already been indicated, most of the female labor recruited for the war industries was withdrawn from other employments. There was left, as an emergency source for additional wage-earners in a country without a male idle class, only the youths who had not reached the age at which they would ordinarily have entered into industry.

There seems little reason to suppose, therefore, that the trend of family earnings was very much different from the trend of individual earnings. Moreover, if standard of living is in question, where wages are maintained at the same real level or are only slightly increased by dint of loss of home life and home conveniences or by the cessation of schooling by

[30] *Monthly Labor Review,* January, 1919, p. 140.

youths, or even by increased hours of labor, there results a distinct loss in the standard of living, the increase in monetary, or even real wages, notwithstanding. This loss is more apparent, although not more real, where entrance of the women folk of the household into industry increases the monetary expense of the domestic economy.

One possible factor operating to increase family earnings, not already considered, but which should be accounted for in an index of average weekly earnings, is the movement of wage-earners from poorly paid nonessential occupations to well-paid war work. But to whatever extent this factor and the ones already considered may have increased the family earnings, it still remains true that prices rose more rapidly than rates of wages, that profits consequently increased faster than prices, and that labor made its contribution to the cost of the war in large part via war profits lent to the government. In this respect, however, industrial wage labor was in a not very different situation from that of the salaried classes or the bondholder class in general, or of all those, bondholders and stockholders alike, who were financially interested in public utilities. The entrepreneur paid interest on his bonded indebtedness at the pre-war rate. He bought transportation, power, heat, and light from franchise corporations, and he hired his salaried employees at rates only slightly above the pre-war levels. He sold his own products at the war-time level of prices.

THE CONTRIBUTION OF AGRICULTURAL WORKERS TO THE WAR COST

THE following table presents wage and price data for agricultural laborers and farmers. The data collected are not adequate material upon which to base any very confident conclusions. The annual amount of crop yield, for instance, is involved before any opinion on the share in the war cost borne by the farmer can be reached. In so far as price factors are concerned, however, these figures indicate that the rise in the prices of the things which farmers sell was greater during the war period than was the rise in the prices of the articles which farmers buy, and was also greater, on the whole, than the rise in the wages of farm labor. The farm laborers seem to have fared better than their brethren in the city factories. For both groups the rate of wages rose less rapidly than did the general price level. On the other hand, there was probably a smaller rise in the cost of living of the farm laborer than in that of the city dweller, and his rate of wages rose more rapidly than did that of organized industrial labor. For the farm laborer as for the city laborer, but in less degree, the rise in prices appears to have operated to increase the profits of his employers partly at his expense.

FARM WAGES AND PRICE INDEXES *

YEAR	WAGES OF MALE FARM LABOR †				YEAR	PRICES OF ARTICLES FARMERS BUY ‡	YEAR	PRICES OF FARM CROPS TO PRODUCERS †	PRICES OF MEAT ANIMALS †
	By the Month		Day Labor at Harvest						
	With Board	Without Board	With Board	Without Board					
1913	100	100	100	100	1913–14	102	1913	100	100
1914	98	99	99	98	1914–15	104	1914	89	103
1915	99	99	99	99	1915–16	112	1915	93	94
1916	109	108	108	107	1916–17	124	1916	141	111
1917	135	133	132	131	1917–18	162	1917	194	164
1918	163	155	169	166			1918	224	192

* Compiled from *United States Department of Agriculture Year Book*, 1918, pp. 698, 701.
† 1913 = 100.
‡ Five-year average, 1909–10 to 1913–14 = 100. Read from graph.

WAR-TIME INCOME FROM URBAN PROPERTY

RENTS on urban property increased quite generally during the war period, but the percentage of increase appears to have varied greatly according to the class of property and its location.[31] The average percentage of increase in rents for urban property of all kinds for the country as a whole was unquestionably considerably less than the average rise in commodity prices or in cost of living. This would indicate that the urban landlord also suffered a decrease in real income as a result of price inflation. At least two-thirds of the costs involved in property ownership consist — or did before the war-time rise in costs of maintenance and operation — in interest on capital invested, and much of the invested capital is borrowed on mortgage at pre-war rates of interest. Here again the property-owning group divides itself into two subgroups, of which one may have profited from the general rise in prices, and the other unquestionably lost. The legal owner — the property-entrepreneur he may perhaps be designated — was protected in large measure from the effects of a rise in the costs of maintenance, management, and fuel, by the rise in rents such as it

[31] Cf. "Wartime Changes in the Cost of Living," *National Industrial Conference Board, Research Report*, No. 9, pp. 22 ff. This report estimates the average rate of increase in the rent of workingmen's houses, from 1914 to the summer of 1918, at 15 per cent.

was, and by the mortgage contracts whereby much of the capital
he controlled was intrusted to him for management at pre-war
rates of interest. But for the mortgage-holder, as for the corporation bondholder, there was nothing to mitigate the loss
in real income arising from a constant money income and rising
prices.

THE DISTRIBUTION OF THE WAR BURDEN

LABOR contributed a large part of the war cost. How large a
part there has been no attempt here, with the inadequate
statistical resources available, to discover. Its contribution was
made mainly in the manner indicated by Professor Davenport,
namely through a lagging of rates of wages behind prices, and
a consequent increase in profits. Some of these profits were
taxed away by the government; much of what remained was
lent to the government. But the reduction in real rates of
wages did not involve a serious impairment of the standard
of living of labor and appears to have left it on the average at
the 1913 level, since all, or most, of the fall in real rates of
wages was made up, as compared with 1913 and 1914, by increased employment. The increased war-time profits came,
therefore, not at all or only to a slight extent out of a reduction
in consumption by the working classes, but was provided mainly
by a war-time increase in national production. This increase
in production resulted from the increased utilization of both
the capital and the labor resources of the nation, and was sufficient not only to permit of the financing of the war without any
impairment of the average national standard of living, but to
make possible at the end of the war the possession of capital
resources equal to what they would have been if there had been
no war and if production had continued throughout this period
at the pre-war rate. But even among wage labor there were
certain classes of labor who profited from the war conditions,
with the result that a study of average conditions does not
reveal the extent to which the remaining classes of labor lost.
Munitions workers, shipyard workers, garment workers, emergency employees of the government, shared with the employing
class in the increased war-time prosperity. School teachers,
most of the civil-service employees, salaried employees in general contributed most heavily.

That part of the war cost which was not contributed by
clerical and industrial labor was probably contributed in largest
part by those other groups such as bondholders, investors in
public utilities, mortgage holders, and those engaged in professions to whose services there accrued an income at a consid-

erably reduced real rate. The members of these groups were
not able to make up the deficiency, as labor could, by increased
effort, and therefore the war burden fell more heavily upon
them than upon wage labor. There is some evidence, also,
that the wages of agricultural labor lagged behind prices. Any
increase in farmers' profits of which this may have been a cause
was contributed only to a very small extent to the funds made
available, whether by taxation or by loans, for the prosecution
of the war. Owners of urban property did little more than
hold their own against the rise in prices. The mortgage holders, who provide at least half the capital invested in real estate,
received little or no increase in their money income to offset
the rise in prices. There are practically no data of value,
bearing upon the trend of middlemen's earnings or of professional incomes during the war period, and therefore these important shares of the national income have not been considered
here.

AFTER-THE-WAR TAXATION

PROFESSOR DAVENPORT's expectation that the repayment of the
war loans will be effected through taxation which will fall
mainly on the masses is, it is to be hoped, more speculative than
prophetic. If the taxation system by which the loans will be
repaid turns out to be in substance that which prevailed in pre-
war days, he will be confirmed in his prediction. The pre-war
federal tax system, with import duties and excise taxes on
tobacco and liquors as its main sources of revenue, was certainly
not progressive; it was possibly even regressive in its incidence.
With the greater numbers in the lower economic classes than in
the higher, and with the greater expenditure on commodities,
relatively to total income, of poor than of rich, the bulk of the
revenue came from the poorer classes. The taxes may even
have deducted a larger share from small incomes than from
great.

The continuance of income taxation as an important source
of revenue appears, however, to be inevitable. It is a good
practical rule for income taxation as at present practiced that
every considerable increase in the amount of revenue to be collected through an income tax results in an increase of the rate
of progression of the tax. When taxes are not concealed nor
uncertain in their incidence, the political resistance to greater
taxation is much more vocal and effective on the part of the
many poor than on the part of the few rich. In the modern
democracy, the path of least resistance to the collection of increased revenue leads to the greater taxation of the larger in-

comes. The only feasible way of keeping such taxation within narrow limits by imposing a great share of the burden on the shoulders of the poor is to distribute the repayment of the war debt over a long period. There are practical limits, both narrow and inelastic, to the amount of taxes which can be collected in any one year from the working classes. But just as the poor who cannot pay cash for pianos can pay for them on the instalment plan, so the spreading of repayment of the debt over a long period of years can be effectively employed to assure substantial contributions from the working classes to the repayment to the wealthy classes of the war loans. Whether Professor Davenport's expectations will or will not be fulfilled may depend mainly upon whether a long or a short period is decided upon for the redemption of the war debt.

It is to be noted that the continuance of the present graduated taxation results during a period of rising prices in an increase from year to year in the percentages of the large incomes taken away in taxes, even though the nominal rates of taxation and the real incomes remain the same. Thus, if an income of $10,000 is subject to a 10 per cent tax and an income of $20,000 is subject to a 20 per cent tax; if the price level rises 100 per cent in a given year; if the money income just keeps pace with the rise in prices; then the same real income is taxed 10 per cent in the first year and 20 per cent in the second. Even if the present price level is maintained and no further rise occurs, the rates of taxation now levied bear more heavily at present and will bear more heavily in the future upon the large incomes than they did when the war-tax legislation was enacted. This factor may tend of itself and without further legislation to make the tax system more steeply progressive in the future. On the other hand, a fall in the price level, if accompanied by a corresponding fall in money incomes, will make the present tax system less steeply progressive.

If the war debt is repaid from the proceeds of taxation falling mainly on the wealthy, the excess war profits will practically be canceled, and the imposition on labor of a double burden will be avoided. Considerations of social justice seem to point to such a result as a consummation devoutly to be wished. But no tax system can be so well devised as to correct with impartial justice the economic inequalities resulting from inflation.

INFLATION AND WAR FINANCE

THE problem of war taxation was not so much one of the distribution of the war burden as of taxation versus loans, although, of course, the one problem was involved in the other. Admitting that the practical situation made it necessary that certain economic groups should pay for the war, was it also necessary that their contribution should inure in large part as profits to certain other groups, then to be turned over to the government as loans instead of as taxes? The answer to this rests on the degree of incentive necessary to induce capital to enter financially risky ventures essential to the war program. Some added profit was probably unavoidable if the full co-operation of capital and of business enterprise were to be secured. No bribe would have been too great to pay for the results accomplished, if a lesser bribe would not have sufficed. But a lesser bribe probably would have sufficed.

Finally, the point may be raised that the economic groups which contributed most heavily to defraying the cost of the war, through the tendency of their rates of remuneration to lag behind price movements, may reimburse themselves in a subsequent period of falling prices for such sacrifices as they may have made during the war period. In so far as *rates* are concerned, there is strength in this argument. But whereas the entrepreneur gains through increased profits from rising price levels, he is enabled by reducing the scale of employment to free himself, in part at least, from the losses resulting from continued production at falling prices but undiminished rates of wages and interest. Fluctuating price levels injure those economic groups whose rates of remuneration are comparatively inelastic, regardless of the direction of the price movement. When prices fall, they lose through unemployment. When prices rise, they gain somewhat from fuller employment, but lose in real earnings per unit of service. There can be no thought of reimbursement at this late date. But Professor Davenport asks, on behalf of one of the economic groups which contributed in undue proportion to the defraying of the war cost, the least that can be asked, that it shall not be obliged to pay twice over.

QUESTIONS AND PROBLEMS FOR DISCUSSION

1. State Professor Davenport's argument relative to the burden of war costs.
2. What is meant by subjective and objective sacrifices? Can it be shown that the immediate subjective sacrifice in financing a war is greater if funds are raised by taxes than if raised by loans?
3. To what extent can the economic burden of a war be passed on to a future generation?
4. What support is there for the contention that production actually increased during the World War?

5. How do you account for the fact that the national income, in terms of 1913 values, increased during the War?

6. In what manner did industrial labor contribute to the costs of the World War? agricultural labor?

7. Should war profits be taxed heavily during a war, or should a government secure control of them through the sale of government bonds?

8. If a war leaves a government heavily in debt, what kinds of taxes should be levied to retire the obligations?

SUGGESTIONS FOR RESEARCH

1. Direct and indirect costs of war.
2. The effect of war on capital resources.
3. The contribution of labor to war cost in some country other than the United States.
4. Effect of the World War on the distribution of wealth in the United States.

BIBLIOGRAPHICAL NOTE

Special attention is called to H. J. Davenport, "The War-Tax Paradox," *American Economic Review,* Vol. IX, (March, 1919), pp. 34-46 for the complete statement of the deductive analysis upon which Professor Viner's inductive study was based. The quality of the reasoning in the article by the late Professor Davenport is praiseworthy.

A concise and scholarly discussion of direct and indirect costs of war, and also of its material and immaterial costs, is E. L. Bogart, *War Costs and Their Financing,* (New York, 1921), Chap. XIV. In his treatment of war costs in terms of human life and vitality, Professor Bogart calls attention to D. S. Jordan, *The Blood of the Nation : a Study of the Decay of Races through the Survival of the Unfit,* (Boston, 1910) and *War and the Breed : the Relation of War to the Downfall of Nations,* (Boston, 1915) ; V. L. Kellogg, *Eugenics and Militarism,* (London, 1912), and *Military Selection and Race Deterioration,* (Oxford, 1916).

CHAPTER XXVI

ECONOMIC EFFECTS OF PUBLIC CREDIT: THE FORM OF BORROWING

1. ECONOMIC EFFECTS DUE TO THE NATURE OF PUBLIC DEBTS *

FROM the foregoing survey of the opinions of many prominent writers on public finance, it seems well established that public debts are in themselves neither good nor bad.† Consequently their economic effects always depend upon the purpose for which the debt is incurred; upon the nature of the loan, including the amount, the terms, etc.; and finally, upon the industrial, social, and political conditions of the country.[1] For that reason no sweeping general conclusions can be drawn from the study of this question. Implicitly or explicitly we have to employ constantly our familiar economic idiom "other things being equal," and thus try to draw particular conclusions out of particular situations. And from the sum of these conclusions a few generalizations may be ventured which may be called "the economic effects of public debts."

It must be stated, first of all, that there is no direct or immediate economic effect upon a country if the debt transaction is followed merely by an adjustment of credits. Thus, when an old debt is paid with the proceeds of a new debt, or when a floating debt is cancelled by the issue of bonds, or again when one country settles an account with another, there follows in each case simply an adjustment of credits. There might be administrative expenses and some financial loss (due to slight changes in interest rates) to the government, but broadly speaking, there will be no significant economic effects arising in those cases, for industry is not directly affected by such transactions because none of the control of the actual capital of the country is transferred and consequently there is no readjustment in the application of labor. A good historical example, often mentioned by writers on public finance as one of such debt trans-

---

* From Shutaro Matsushita, *The Economic Effects of Public Debts*, (Columbia University Studies in History, Economics, and Public Law, New York, 1929), Chap. III.

† Eds. note: See Chap. XXIII.

[1] See H. C. Adams, *Public Debts*, p. 53.

actions, is the French loan after the war of 1870 to pay one billion dollars of indemnity to Germany.[2] In this case, France sold her rentes as well as her holdings of foreign securities by means of an international refunding operation and was able to leave unaffected her domestic capital invested in current industry. French foreign trade was not appreciably affected, nor was production disturbed, and the country's industry was carried on smoothly.

It is clear, then, that a public loan directly affects industries only when it involves the transfer of domestic capital, and the degree to which industries are affected depends upon the amount of capital transferred. Let us now consider the kinds of debt transactions which involve the transfer of the control of domestic capital, and their economic effects. One of them is the so-called "forced" loan.

FORCED LOANS

HISTORICALLY, there are many forms of forced loans, but of these the issue of legal-tender notes is the most common and at the same time the principal method of forced loans, and therefore, the only one requiring discussion for our practical purposes. When these government notes are suddenly issued, there is an increase in the medium of exchange without any commercial necessity for such an increase — in other words, there is an inflation of the currency. Prices will rise, commercial relations will be disturbed, and creditors will suffer severely. Prices rise because there is an augmented supply of money to carry on exchanges, without any necessary increase in the commodities to be exchanged. Commercial relations are disturbed because merchants and manufacturers must readjust themselves to the sudden rise in the prices of goods. Creditors suffer, because the same nominal amount of money does not have as much purchasing power as before. Moreover, as is always the case in a period of rising prices, wage-earners suffer because the rise in wages always lags behind the rise in prices. If, then, this form of forced loan is carried out far enough, Gresham's law will be brought into operation and the precious metals will either be driven out of circulation or be used at a premium. The evil effects of an excessive forced loan are so obvious that a government should never resort to this method until all other methods of borrowing have been exhausted. A more moderate example of the evil effects arising from forced loans is the condition of the United States during and after the Civil War, when the government issued

2 Adams, *op. cit.,* pp. 54-57. Also Leroy-Beaulieu, chap. iii.

a large amount of greenbacks ; and a more extreme example is the financial condition of all the principal countries of Europe immediately after the World War. We are familiar with the fact that even today the franc, the lira, and the ruble are worth only a fraction of their par values.[3] Nor does the government itself gain much in the end, for what it saves by not needing to pay interest is counter-balanced by the enhanced prices of the goods and the services which it must purchase.

Let us take an example from the recent war. The Currency Act of 1914 empowered the British Treasury to issue Currency Notes to an unlimited amount. The banks came into possession of them through their depositors, who were paid by the government for goods and services. The banks, thus possessed of new cash, either made new advances to their customers or subscribed for Treasury Bills and other government securities. The money so received by the government was again spent by the government and returned to the banks through their depositors. The banks only kept a portion of this money as cash reserves and again invested the remaining sum in government securities, the process being repeated again and again, until deposits in banks increased many times over. This of course meant an increase in purchasing power without any necessary increase in production. Hence, there followed inflation, high prices and other evil consequences.[4]

SHORT-TERM LOANS

SOMETIMES governments contract loans for a few months, in anticipation of revenues in the near future. These short-term loans are floated by issuing what are variously termed in different countries as Treasury Bills, Treasury Certificates, etc. There are two great advantages to this sort of borrowing. One is the ease with which it can be done. There are many business men and banks who are glad to invest their temporary surplus funds in such government certificates. The government can also often hand over these certificates to private contractors in payment of its dues. The other great advantage of certificate borrowing (the term commonly used in the United States for this kind of loan) lies in its economy. The saving effected by the government comes in two ways. In the first place, the government can ordinarily obtain the temporarily idle funds in private hands at a relatively low rate of interest. In the second place, too large an accumulation of idle surplus in the Treasury is avoided by certificate borrowing, because,

---

[3] This part was written before recent stabilizations of those currencies.
[4] See T. J. Kiernan, *British War Finance*, p. 93.

unlike when it issues bonds, the government can borrow almost any small amount according to its need.

On the other hand, there are several dangers to a large floating debt at very short term.[5] First, there is a financial danger in that the time for redemption comes quickly and the government may not be able to repay a large sum. If, at the same time, capital is in great demand by industry and commerce, and if confidence in the government is shaken, the renewal of the loan would require higher rates of interest or some other advantages which would be burdensome to the future financial management of the country. Secondly, from the economic point of view, short-term floating debt presents some grave disadvantages to a country: — (a) The Treasury having great facilities to borrow at short term, these borrowings are liable to become habitual. In other words, the debt at short term has a tendency to become permanent by means of unlimited renewals. The capitalists are thus induced, if the rate of interest or the advantages are considerable, to confide their funds to the Treasury in a permanent manner. This is to the detriment of the banks of deposits and discounts. The banks no longer having as many deposits, the rate of discount of commercial paper is raised, and the means of bank credit become more difficult. This increases the net costs of products, which in turn entails a rise of prices and of the cost of living.

(b) Even if the individuals continue to make deposits in the banks, the existence of a large short-term debt at high interest incites the banks to place their funds of deposit in Treasury certificates instead of making discounts and running the risks which they require. That is an operation very profitable for the banks but very disadvantageous to commerce and industry. The banks pay a small interest to the depositors and purchase the Treasury certificates bearing a sufficiently high interest; they benefit thus by the difference between the interest they pay to their depositors and the interest they receive from the public treasury. This operation, therefore, turns away the banks of deposits and discounts from their proper social mission, which of course is harmful to commerce and industry.

(c) Another economic danger of the existence of a large floating debt at short term is the inflation that it provokes directly or indirectly. Direct inflation may be brought about in three ways: (1) The Treasury certificates may be used by the public as a purchasing medium, in which case those certificates are virtually transformed into paper money. (2) If the holders of

<hr>

[5] See *Revue de Science et de Législation financières*, Jan.-Mar. number, 1925, pp. 100-102.

these certificates deposit them in banks and create deposit-credits thereby, the result is an increase in the instruments of payment without a necessary increase in the amount of business. (3) When the Treasury uses its certificates to pay its creditors, and if the creditors of the Treasury discount at the national bank of issue the certificates they have received, or if they consent to some advances, the bank will be induced to issue some paper-money – in other words, to create a direct inflation. To the extent that these creditors hoard the certificates there is no influence on inflation.

(d) Whatever may be the use which is practically made of Treasury certificates, there is a constant menace of inflation on account of the existence of a large public debt at very short maturity. For, any event that arrests or slackens the renewal of Treasury certificates has the evil consequence of an issue of paper-money. If such an event does once occur, from that time on the increase of Treasury certificates in circulation will shake the confidence of the foreign holders of those certificates and, indirectly, of the foreign holders of national money, which in turn will adversely affect the national rate of exchange.

So much for the theory. Let us now turn to facts. In the first half of the World War, the British government made enormous issues of 3-, 6-, 9- or 12-month Treasury Bills which drew money only from the financiers and professional money dealers. Had the government issued bonds (which it did later) it would have drawn the money of the people out of their real savings, and at a lower interest rate than that of the Treasury Bills. The rate of interest paid by the British government for this kind of credit increased steadily from 2¾% in April, to 5½% in January, 1917. Moreover, the amount of Bills outstanding at the end of 1915 was £380,000,000, while at the end of 1916 the figure had risen to £1,148,000,000.[6] According to Mr. Kiernan, the British government's control of the money market by the over-issue of Currency Notes and Treasury Bills resulted in a discouragement of thrift, in higher prices, in profiteering by the moneyed classes and in a relative decrease in wages.[7]

During the World War the United States also made the following short-term borrowings in the form of "Treasury certificates of indebetedness" : [8]

[6] See T. J. Kiernan, British War Finance, p. 93. Also, Kirkaldy, British Finance, 1914–1921, pp. 153-54.
[7] Op. cit., Chap. iv. Cf. Colwyn Report, Ev. p. 277, E in C. : 2.
[8] See J. H. Hollander, War Borrowing, p. 27.

Amount	In anticipation of
$50,000,000	1917 Income Tax
868,000,000	First Liberty Loan
2,320,493,000	Second Liberty Loan
1,624,403,500	1918 Income and Excess Profits Taxes
3,012,085,500	Third Liberty Loan
4,659,820,000	Fourth Liberty Loan
157,552,500	1919 Income and Excess Profits Taxes

The United States government lost the advantage of obtaining low interest rates through this means of borrowing by using it, not as a temporary measure just before the funded loans were floated, but as an ever-recurring measure in anticipation of each successive loan. (See above table.) Furthermore, the advantage of avoiding a Treasury surplus was largely lost by the early adoption and continued use by the government of the policy of a mounting Treasury balance.[9] The evil effect of the excessive use of short-term borrowing in the United States was seen even after the war when on April 30, 1920, the floating public debt (exclusive of War Savings Securities) still amounted to $2,994,272,555 — all outstanding in the form of Treasury certificates of indebtedness, bearing high interest ranging from $4\frac{3}{4}\%$ to $5\frac{1}{4}\%$.[10]

Again, a persistent resort to certificate borrowing by the United States government exerted a strain on the money market, which was harmful to business. As long as the Treasury pursued during the war the justifiable policy of a mounting balance, and as long as the banks could counteract the withdrawals from "certificate-created deposits" by preferential rediscounting with the Federal Reserve Banks, monetary strain was avoided by certificate borrowing. But this advantage soon disappeared when the dwindling Treasury balance compelled the Treasury to withdraw its deposits as fast as the banks granted them, while the banks' profits were wiped out by such a rapid withdrawal. The banks, working as they did with low reserves, were thus strained in their resources and the money market was hard pressed. Federal Reserve Banks had to be utilized, followed by a further reduction in the reserve ration and finally by a resort to deliberate credit restriction.[11]

During the World War, the French government made considerable use of short-term loans in the form of Treasury Bills,

[9] Hollander, *op. cit.*, p. 201.

[10] See J. H. Hollander, "Certificate Borrowing and the Floating Debt," in *The Weekly Review*, vol. ii, May 22, 1920, p. 552.

[11] See *ibid.*, pp. 553-54.

which were renamed early in the war "National Defense Bills." [12]   At first these were issued to mature in three or six months or a year.   But later, bills of even one month's maturity were also issued.   These Treasury Bills were very popular and were bought to a large extent by the working classes out of their small savings.   They were at first issued in denominations equivalent to $20, $100, and $200, but later in as small denominations as 5 francs and 20 francs.   In 1914, $312,000,000 worth were issued; in 1915, a net addition of some $839,000,000 was made; in 1916, a net addition of $1,089,000,000; in 1917, a net addition of $1,345,000,000; in 1918, by November 30, the total outstanding issue had increased to $6,357,000,000. This amount was reduced by almost 2 billion dollars in December, 1918, by means of a new permanent loan.   However, the issues of the Treasury Bills steadily increased in 1919, so that by the end of that year the total outstanding amounted to about 9½ billion dollars.

According to an authority on French war finance, the Treasury Bills provided for nearly 29% of the French war expenditures.   The chief factors which prevented the use of such an enormous amount of short-term loans in France during the World War from giving rise to disastrous economic results were: The extreme patriotism of the common people; [13] their strong habit of saving, causing them to hoard the Bills instead of using them as a currency; and the timely issue of long-term loans. [14]

In the last war, the German government also made large use of Treasury Bills. [15]   In all, about $18,000,000,000 of these bills was issued during 1914–1918.   The fact that scarcely any resort was made to taxation during the war for meeting the costs of the war, but that the above short-term loans were bolstered up by long-term war loans amounting to $24,640,000,000 is sufficient to explain the enormous inflation in Germany during and immediately after the war.

From what has been observed above in theory and practice concerning short-term loans, it is certain that they are, at best, but temporary expedients.   Unless their amounts are relatively small and unless they are promptly redeemed by the issue of long-term loans (if not by taxation), they are sure to bring about inflation, government discredit, and other related evil effects.   It must be admitted, however, that the conduct of

[12] See H. E. Fisk, *French Public Finance in the Great War and Today,* pp. 15-16.
[13] But *cf.* Bastable, *Public Finance,* p. 686.
[14] See H. E. Fisk, *French Public Finance in the Great War and Today.*
[15] See E. L. Bogart, *War Costs and their Financing,* pp. 187-194.

the European countries in the last war with reference to their short-term loans was determined, at least in the beginning of the war, largely by their miscalculation as to the possible duration of the war.   When they finally came to realize that the war was going to last much longer than they had expected, the evil effects of the Treasury borrowing were rampant, and all that could be done was to prevent their further spread.   Taking too much advantage of its facility had made the Treasury borrowing lose its other great merit — economy.

PUBLIC BONDS

By far the most important form of public debt transactions which involve the transfer of the control of capital is the issuance of bonds.   What are the economic effects of public borrowing by bond issues?   The answer differs according to several considerations, chief among which are (1) the rate of interest; (2) the period of the loan; (3) the convertibility; (4) the size of the bonds; (5) the taxability; (6) domestic or foreign loan.

(1) *The Rate of Interest:* [16] — If public bonds are issued at the normal market rate of interest, there will be no disturbance of industry and trade.   They will be bought with the fund of free capital which otherwise might be used for consumption or for investment in private business.   No special competition is established between public and private securities, and therefore, we may conclude that the issuance of such bonds is followed by no unusual economic effects.   This is especially true in the beginning of a war or a period of business depression when there is always business uncertainty and when industrial entrepreneurs hesitate to expand their business.   This is a very opportune period for the government to obtain the country's fund of free capital without affecting the market rate of interest.   We are of course speaking on the assumption that the public loan in question is of such moderate amount as to be easily absorbed by the money market.   If a huge loan is floated in time of peace for industrial purposes, there is a likelihood that private competition will ensue.

Suppose the government needs more money than it can obtain by offering the market rate of interest.   If its credit is good, it will obtain the needed money, provided the amount is not altogether too large, by paying a high rate of interest. What will be the effects on industry?   The results depend chiefly upon the nature and the importance of the funds that

---

[16] See Adams, *Science of Finance*, p. 521.   *Cf.* Wagner, *Finanzwissenschaft*, p. 154 *et seq.*

are thus obtained. Undoubtedly, some money will come from the funds of individuals which would otherwise have been spent in consumption. That means that the commodities which would have been bought by the individuals will not now be bought, or in other words, the demand for those goods will be diminished.[17] Other things being equal, the industries engaged in producing those goods will be depressed. Less capital and labor will be employed in them. The commodities most likely to be affected will be those of comfort or luxury, because it is hardly conceivable that the people will curtail the use of the necessaries of life in order to invest in government bonds, nor is it likely that the people can accumulate to any appreciable amount that money which normally goes to purchase the necessaries of life. To speak in concrete terms, such things as automobiles, radios, paintings, and the like will be dispensed with, and the money will flow into the government treasury.

Now, such an effect will be very serious for the country, so that the government is unlikely to resort to such a loan except in cases of emergency such as wars or the reconstruction works carried on at the present time in war-devastated regions in Europe or the quake-stricken regions in Japan. In such cases, the men thrown out of private employment will be employed by the government and moreover the circulating capital unemployed will be diverted to this field: for instance, in manufacturing war materials in time of war, or in manufacturing lumber, bricks, iron frames, etc., in reconstruction work.

Let us take another case. Suppose the money obtained by the government through a high rate of interest comes from the people who had invested in industries which are on the verge of making no profit or only a low profit at the time. Of course only circulating capital is thus obtainable, because fixed capital cannot be transferred to the government. It might be asked, would not the government be able under those conditions to obtain such a fund at a normal rate of interest? The answer is in the negative, for this reason: unless the interest accruing to the circulating capital from the high rate of interest of the government bonds amounts to a larger sum than the profit from the fixed capital, the people will not buy government bonds, but will keep on investing the circulating capital in industries in order to keep fixed capital employed.

The proprietors of the businesses which are on the verge of no profit will sell their buildings, machinery, equipment and

---

17 This statement must be modified to the extent that such a loan incites the individuals to greater activity and thus enables them to earn greater income than before.

the goods on hand for what they will bring and invest the proceeds in government bonds. As to those industries which have been made unprofitable through the change in demand (on account of war or similar causes), the owners will for the time being suspend their activities and invest all their available free capital in the government loan.

The raising of this kind of fund, then, is very advantageous to the community, (1) because it gives opportunity for a change of investments to those who need it, and (2) because the manufacturers whose businesses have been made dull will also have a chance to buy the bonds with their free capital.

The third source from which the government can obtain funds through a loan bearing a high rate of interest is the profits of the prosperous industries. The chance given them to invest their surplus capital in lucrative bonds incites them to greater activity and efficiency. The source of those profits is either intensified labor or labor-saving inventions. Either is highly desirable as an effective means of increasing production.

Thus we may come to the conclusion that, provided the exigency requires the floating of such a high-rate loan thereby disturbing business relations, it aids in readjusting business relations again and in encouraging production — production, however, in a new direction.

Suppose a government has to raise a fund by a loan with an abnormally high rate of interest. The effects are very harmful, both to the government and to the community. By so doing the government will tend to absorb all the capital invested by the marginal producers, and thus to dry up the sources of taxation. Moreover, a greater burden is laid yearly on the revenue in order to pay off the interest. Looking at the matter from the standpoint of the community, the general scale of prices will suddenly rise and speculation will follow. The industries producing goods that respond quickly to industrial changes will gain unusual profits, while those that respond slowly will lose heavily. The commodities which the workingmen consume respond most quickly to any change in commercial conditions, but labor responds very slowly. Hence, while prices rise fast, wages will lag behind, and the employers will reap the extra profits at the expense of the workers. For these reasons, only the most urgent necessities can justify the flotation of such a loan.

Generally speaking, therefore, loans at the market rate of interest will be followed by no very important industrial results, provided that the amount of the loan is moderate. Loans at a rate higher than market rate will disturb to a certain extent the placement of capital; but if the occasion of the loan is (as in the case of a war) such as to cause a readjustment of already disturbed conditions of trade and industry, such a loan is positively advantageous. But if the rate of interest is so high that it becomes itself a powerful cause of commercial disturbance, it will have serious consequences.[18] In particular cases, however, there are many factors which operate to modify the above conclusions. For instance, the marginal producers will theoretically abandon their business and invest in lucrative government bonds; but actually there will be many business men who, for psychological and sentimental reasons, will tenaciously adhere to their low-profit undertakings. Again, when the rate of interest paid is very high, foreign investors will come in to compete with domestic capital. Furthermore, when a government contracts a considerable loan at a high rate of interest, the benefit is not always on the side of the capitalists alone. For, such a loan almost always has two consequences: higher taxation (of which the rich bear the greater share) and extensive employment of workingmen in government works. Witness the situation in Japan after the great earthquake.

(2) *The Length of the Period*: — The time for which a public loan should run depends primarily upon the purpose for which it is contracted. Loans are contracted to cover casual deficits, to cover emergency expenditures, or for public investments. When loans are contracted for the casual deficits of the government they are necessarily of very short duration. A few months or a few years at most ought to be sufficient to bring about the fiscal readjustment through increased revenues. The very purpose of the loan regulates its duration, and therefore, it is not necessary to discuss deficit-filling loans in this place.

When it comes to loans for emergencies such as a war or some natural calamity, the duration of the loan has important economic bearing. In the first place, the rate of interest differs according as the bond runs for 10 or 20 years or for 40, 50 or more years. Considered alone from the point of view of the rate of interest, it is usually preferable for the government to issue bonds of shorter duration because they can be issued at a lower rate of interest. Although it is true to a certain extent that the investing public is loath to have the principal paid back so long as the investment is secure, yet a loan of too long a duration arouses a feeling of insecurity in the minds of the investors, because they are unable to surmise

18 See H. C. Adams, *Science of Finance*, p. 526. Also *cf.* Wagner, *Finanzwissenschaft*, pp. 162-64.

the condition of the country so many years in advance. Hence they will demand a higher rate of interest, which means a greater public burden. Again, loans of very long duration are liable to cause an ever-mounting public debt, because a need for contracting another loan may arise before the existing debt will have been repaid. There is only a negative advantage in a loan of very long duration in that the government can avail itself of the falling market-rate of interest to convert its bonds into those bearing lower interest. For these reasons, public bonds should not run for a longer period than 25 or 30 years at most.

Another purpose for which a loan is contracted by the government is, as stated above, investments. Government investments may take two forms: commercial or non-commercial. Under the former comes the purchase or the building of railroads, canals, etc., or the manufacture and sale of tobacco, salt, liquor, etc. Under the latter comes the building of roads, bridges, public schools, hospitals, etc. With a commercial investment there is no objection even if the loan becomes permanent, because the profits from the investment in question will more than pay for the interest, and therefore, there is no burden on the public because of the debt. Public railroads in Prussia and Japan offer good examples of this kind of investment.

The case is different with non-commercial government investments. Here the primary consideration is to adjust the life of the loan to the probable life of the object of investment. In other words, the loan should be repaid within the period in which the object of the loan (a schoolhouse, a bridge, a hospital, or what not) endures. In a country like the United States where the government is quite decentralized, the non-commercial government investments occupy a very important place in the finances of the municipal and the State governments. In recent years, especially, the trend has been toward a greater and greater expansion of governmental works in this direction, and the question has become very important. For this reason we see it discussed quite often in various State and local government reports and in periodicals.

Several years ago, lively discussions on local government loans took place under the subject "The Pay-as-you-go Plan." Writers who are in favor of public loans for public improvements argue that there is nothing financially unsound in borrowing money by the issuance of bonds in order to provide funds for worthwhile improvements, if the term of the bonds is less than the reasonable life of the improvement and if adequate provisions are made for paying such bonds at maturity either by the serial or the sinking-fund method. If the loan is for necessary improvements, it will either save the money or create the value to pay the debt and interest. It does not at all lay the burden on future generations; the improvements will pay for themselves.[19]

In one of the recommendations made by the Municipal Research Bureaus of Cleveland, Minneapolis, St. Paul, Duluth, Kansas City and Portland (Oregon) in their reports for 1922, the point is brought out that the term of the bonds should be limited to the life of the improvements.[20] Mr. L. W. Lancaster also mentions the fact that in Massachusetts one of the features of the laws enacted for local financing is, that, with regard to permanent indebtedness the principle that debts should be paid back within the life-time of the improvement is recognized.[21]

From the above considerations it is clear that the length of the period for which a public debt runs has important economic effects. Debts that are incurred for casual deficits take care of themselves through the conditions of their existence, but other debts, such as those incurred for emergency expenditures or public investments, should be carefully planned. Loans made for industrial purposes may follow the rules of private business finance, that is to say, so long as the undertaking is self-supporting the bonds may be made perpetual or at least may be of very long term. But in cases of loans for emergencies or public improvements the danger of a mounting debt is so great that they should not run longer than the life of the improvements, or for emergency loans, no longer than twenty-five or thirty years. If such limits are exceeded, not only will there be a heavier burden for future generations but public credit will also be undermined.

Thus far we have spoken of the bonds for definite periods of time. There are, in addition, two kinds of bonds which are less common or are almost obsolete and which have indefinite periods of time. They are the so-called *"perpetual"* bonds and the *terminable annuities*.

Before the World War by far the greater part of European debts consisted of the "perpetual" bonds. English consols and French rentes are good examples. These bonds have no definite date set for their repayment, but they are redeemable at any time by the government, subject to certain limitations

19 See *National Municipal Review*, June, 1924, p. 336.
20 See *ibid.*, vol. xi (1922), pp. 385-89.
21 See *ibid.*, March, 1924, p. 163 *et seq.*

for the security of the lenders such as obligation to give a previous notice of the intention to redeem, or to make a promise not to redeem for a certain length of time. There are advantages and disadvantages to "perpetual" bonds. As to their advantages: In the first place, the government is relieved from the risk of demands for repayment of capital, and has only to provide for the payment of interest. An extraordinary burden can be divided into any number of smaller payments to suit the financial capacity of the government in the future period, and consequently its pressure is distributed so as to be less onerous. Yet the creditor is in no way prevented from realizing the capital value of his loan, because he can always go to the stock exchange and sell his bonds at the market price. Again, with the improvement of its credit, the government can reduce the original rate of interest by means of its conversion privileges.[22]

On the other hand, there is a strong argument in favor of the amortizable loan over the "perpetual" loan. Undoubtedly, there are dangers to a large debt without a definite period of repayment. Each expenditure, whatever it may be, has no unlimited utility. Each debt should not, therefore, escape from the rule of repayment. To contract a "perpetual" debt, is completely to lay aside the rational period of repayment. Besides, from the standpoint of the lenders, there are two disadvantages: (1) The fact that no one can tell what will be the economic, political or social situation in the distant future; (2) the opposition of the taxpayers, which may even expose the lenders to the danger of repudiation, when the conditions of the loan become too disadvantageous for the former.[23] As an objection to a loan in perpetuity it may be said that if a government is left free to deal with the repayment of the debt, it may never repay. The reason is that politicians are afraid to incur unpopularity by levying heavy or new taxes in order to repay the debt. They are, therefore, always ready to shift the burden to the future. Another objection arises in connection with the process of repayment: if the prices of securities at the market are above par the repayment becomes burdensome.[24]

After weighing both the advantages and the disadvantages of perpetual bonds, it seems that, provided a strict enforcement of a sinking-fund provision is made, the perpetual bonds can

[22] See C. F. Bastable, *Public Finance* (1903 ed.), pp. 688-89.
[23] See *Revue de Science et de Législation financières*, Jan.-Feb.-Mar. number, 1925, pp. 111-13.
[24] See *ibid.*, p. 118.

be utilized advantageously by the government with loans for non-commercial or semi-commercial investments, such as the extension of the postal system, the building of canals, etc. With war loans, however, the danger of non-repayment or at least of gradual accumulation of debt is so great that it seems best not to resort to this form of loan.

Terminable annuities: — These may be divided into two classes, viz., the annuities which cease at the end of a certain number of years, and life annuities. According to one writer of repute, the trouble with the former type of annuities is that the principal is returned in such small fractions that the individual lenders will have spent their capital at the end of the period of annuity. If the individuals wish to avoid this they must take the trouble to calculate and to save annually that portion of the annuity which corresponds to the fraction of the capital return. But most individuals are loath to take such trouble, and therefore, the terminable annuities are not convenient for general investors. For this reason, they are more often taken up by large business concerns such as insurance companies, railroad companies, landed companies, etc. The government usually pays these companies their expenses incurred for borrowing in their turn from the public in order to subscribe to the government loan. Private companies rarely have credit as good as the state. Hence, this indirect borrowing by the government is more costly to its treasury than direct borrowing from individuals. The fact should be admitted that a regular annual payment of a small sum (as compared with the principal) will extinguish the total debt within a given period of years. This may at first seem a great advantage, but that very fact often tends to government waste, especially when the loans are quietly made through large companies, as already mentioned.[25]

An argument, considered by some persons as decisive, is often advanced in a period of crisis of national credit in favor of an indirect loan to the state under the form of terminable annuities discharged to an establishment. It is somewhat as follows : It may be that at a given moment the financial situation of the state may be such that the issue of a direct loan would strike a blow at public credit. For example, the public debt may be very heavy ; and public opinion may be hostile to loans. If the treasury borrows directly, this addition to the debt will entail a rise in the rate of interest and will lower the prices of the bonds already issued. If, on the other hand, one proceeds

[25] See on this point *Revue de Science et de Législation financières,* April-May-June, 1925 number, pp. 193-201.

by way of an indirect loan through the intermediary of an establishment other than the state, those consequences will not appear, because the public will not perceive that there is really a national loan. The necessary loan can be issued and the financial market will not be disturbed.

Nevertheless the facts do not conform to the argument. When an establishment borrows for the benefit of the state, it always gives as security and guaranty the terminable annuity promised by the Treasury, when it appeals to the public or to the bankers. In both cases the borrowing establishment recognizes that it has less credit than the state, since the loan is granted to it only because the annuity is promised by the state. Thus, it will have to submit to conditions more onerous than those which would have been made for a direct loan of the state. The rate of interest of the indirect loan will be $\frac{1}{2}$ or 1% higher than in the case of a direct loan. Furthermore, it does not conform to facts to assert that an indirect loan, contrary to a direct loan, exercises no influence on the market prices of the public bonds already in circulation and does not modify the conditions of the financial market. By an indirect loan through the public or the bankers, capital is absorbed; there is a new investment offered at a rate of interest more advantageous than that procured by the existing bonds of the state. There is no reason why this rise in the rate of interest should not have the effect of depreciating the public bonds. For public bonds do not enjoy a special favor on the stock exchange; they rise and fall in value as the interest rate rises or falls. The government can indeed oppose this movement for a time by extraordinary measures such as an obligation to make certain investments in its own securities, purchases in the exchange, funds of maintenance, etc. These expedients, however, have only a temporary effect. In the end—at the close of a few days or a few weeks—the public bonds may suffer the counter-blow of the variations of the interest rate on the market. If, therefore, the indirect loan inevitably raises the rate of interest, public bonds will necessarily be depreciated.[26]

Aside from the foregoing objections, since the capital lent is returned to the lenders in driblets, the terminable annuities have the indirect effect of checking the saving of capital and of encouraging thriftlessness. Thus, considered from all angles, terminable annuities are an uneconomical kind of loan and, therefore, should not be used except for urgent necessity or in specially favorable circumstances when the demand for them by large business companies or individual possessors of large

26 See *supra*, pp. 201-203 [in work mentioned in footnote 25]

amounts of liquid capital is sufficient to enable the government to issue them at a reasonable rate of interest. As a matter of fact this form of loan is now almost obsolete.[27]

Life annuities are a special form of terminable annuities. They were a popular form of loan in France and Great Britain under the designation "tontine" (named after its originator Tonti). The idea of the tontine is very simple. A group of persons of very nearly the same age lend to the government a certain sum. The government is then obliged to pay each year to each lender of the group a constant annuity, including the interest and the amortization charge. The share of each deceased annuitant devolves upon the survivors, until finally, when the last survivor of the group dies, the annuity ceases. According to a French writer, this contrivance is never advantageous for the Treasury unless the lives of *all* the participants without exception are shorter than the *average life* which has served as the basis of calculations for the fixing of the annuity. But this has never been the case, because the participants in the tontines are always persons who are of excellent health and of great physical vigor. The last survivors have always exceeded the average taken for the basis of calculations. This method of loan has been a great loss to the national treasury for the reason that a few long-lived survivors can claim the entire amount of the annuities of the whole group to which they belong.[28] This objection can be partly removed by limiting the sum to be attributed to the survivors, but then the system will lose much of its popularity. Be that as it may, when the government is in a stringent financial condition the perpetual bonds serve the purpose of raising funds better, because they do not require for the time being any amortization charges and, therefore, less burden is imposed on the strained treasury. Tontines, however, are now obsolete.

(3) *Convertibility:* — Ordinarily, bonds of short duration such as ten or fifteen years have no conversion privileges attached to them by the government. On the other hand, perpetual bonds and bonds of long term enjoy this privilege. When the state makes a large loan, it does so, more often than not, under the stress of a great necessity. Such is especially the case with war loans. Under such circumstances the rate of interest that it is compelled to pay is high. Therefore, when the strenuous period is past and the country's financial and economic conditions return to normal, the market rate

27 At present the French government is using it to a limited extent to relieve war-sufferers.

28 See *supra*, pp. 237-47, especially p. 238. [in work mentioned in footnote 25]

of interest always falls.   Then is the time when the government can use its so-called conversion privilege over its bonds. The saving to the government, and hence to the taxpayers, through this process of reducing the rate of interest on the public bonds is very great.   Conversion is a process in which the government offers the public creditors the choice of redemption of their bonds or the exchange of them for bonds of lower interest.   Needless to say, this assumes that the government is enjoying good credit.

With reference to the process of conversion, the government should always bear in mind several important considerations. First of all, the capital of the debt should not be increased, unless there is a sufficiently counteracting gain, because the future burden is thereby increased.[29]   Secondly, the conditions of conversion should be stated simply so that they may be easily understood.   Thirdly, the best time for the operation of conversion is the beginning of a period of returning prosperity that usually follows a period of business depression.   There is then plenty of free capital and the rate of interest is low so that the success of conversion is assured.[30]   Fourthly, the condition of the new bonds to be issued in exchange for the old ones should not be such that the new bonds cannot be redeemed or reconverted for too long a period.   H. C. Adams criticized the refunding act of 1870 of the United States on this score.[31]

In England the process of conversion has been made use of ever since 1717, when the rate of interest on the public debt was reduced from 6 to 5 per cent.   In 1727 a further reduction of 1 per cent was made, by which the government realized a saving of £400,000 per annum.   In 1749, Pelham succeeded in reducing the interest on part of the debt to 3½ per cent for seven years, and 3 per cent afterwards.   Next year the interest on the rest of the debt was reduced to 3½ per cent for five years, and 3 per cent afterwards.[32]   "In 1822, £152,000,000 of 5 per cent stock was converted into 4 per cents, and in 1830 further reduced to 3½ per cents.   The old 5 per cent stock (£76,250,000) was reduced to 3½ per cent, to which rate a small balance of 4 per cents (about £10,000,000) was also reduced in 1834."[33]   By the firm administration of Sir Robert Peel, government credit was enhanced, and in 1844, the 3½ per cent stock — which amounted at this time to £248,000,000 — was converted into 3¼ per cent for ten years and 3 per cent

29 Cf. Italian consolidation act of November 1926, described, infra.
30 See Bastable, Public Finance (1903 ed.), pp. 706-707.
31 See H. C. Adams, Public Debts, p. 226 et seq.
32 See Bastable, Public Finance, pp. 631-32.
33 Ibid., p. 636.

afterwards.[34]   In 1888, Lord Goschen succeeded in converting practically the whole of the 3 per cent stock — amounting to £558,000,000 — into new stock bearing 2¾ per cent interest till 1903, and 2½ per cent from that date for twenty years.[35] The conduct of the British government after the World War with reference to conversions is subject to criticism, because the capital sum of the debt has been increased without a corresponding gain in interest reduction, etc.[36]

In France, two important cases of conversion occurred under the Second Empire.   The first was the conversion of the 5 per cent stock to the amount of £140,000,000 into 4½ per cent, bringing £700,000 per annum of gain to the government. The second conversion was that of 1862.   In this case the government took the unjustifiable course of issuing the new bonds below par for a premium, so that, although it gained £6,300,000 as a premium, it increased the debt of the nation by nearly £64,000,000, besides preventing the chance of further conversion for many years to come.   In 1883 the old 5 per cent bonds were converted into 4½ per cents without any increase of capital, and in 1894 this was again converted into 3½ per cents.   Since the capital of the debt at this time was approximately £271,000,000, the gain to the state through these conversions was over £2,700,000 per annum.[37]   In France, however, on account of the fact that the state creditors have been so numerous and have been so scattered among all classes, the government has often faced strong opposition to its employment of the conversion process.[38]

In the United States the system of conversion was applied by the refunding act of 1870.   By this Act the Civil War debts bearing 6 per cent or more of interest were converted into 5, 4½, and 4 per cent bonds, maturing at different dates.[39] Again, by the refunding provisions of the Act of 1900, the treasury was authorized to issue thirty-year two-percent gold bonds to refund the outstanding three-percent bonds of 1908 (Spanish War loan), the four-percent bonds due in 1907, and the five-percent bonds due in 1904, totaling $839,000,000.   But the bonds were converted for a premium so that the benefit to the government was not so great as the low rate of interest might indicate.   Inducements were also given to the banks by exempting them from the tax on their note-circulation if they

---

[34] Bastable, *op. cit.*, p. 636.
[35] See *ibid.*, p. 639.
[36] See Colwyn Report, pp. 44-50.
[37] See Bastable, *Public Finance*, pp. 647-48.
[38] See *ibid.*, p. 646.   Also, p. 649.
[39] See Adams, *Public Debts*, p. 231.

held the new 2-percents as security.   By December 31, 1900, $445,940,750 of bonds was refunded; the premium paid was $43,582,000 and the saving of interest was $54,548,000.   Making no allowance for the loss of circulation tax, due to exemption privilege given to banks, the net saving to the government due to this refunding operation amounted to $10,966,000.[40] Through subsequent conversions, by 1916 nearly three-fourths, $721,000,000, of the total interest-bearing debt of the United States bore the low interest rate of 2 per cent.[41]   Of the World War loans, the following conversions have been made: In March, 1927, some $1,360,000,000 of the second Liberty 4¼ per cents were refunded into 3½ per cent Treasury notes of 1930–1932; in June of the same year, some $245,000,000 of the same were refunded into 3⅜ per cent bonds of 1943–1947; and in September, some $368,000,000 were refunded into 3½ per cent Treasury notes of 1930–1932.[42]

The recent conversion operation (November, 1926) of the Italian government has really been for the purpose of consolidating the floating liabilities rather than to reduce interest charges.   More than 20,500,000,000 lire (approximately $879,-450,000) of the floating debt have been converted into 5 per cent bonds.   The exchange was made on the basis of 116 lire 50 centesimi of the new loan for every 100 lire of ordinary Treasury bonds; 113 lire of the new loan for every 100 lire of the five-year Treasury bonds; 112 lire of the new loan for every 100 lire of the seven-year Treasury bonds.   Holders of the nine-year Treasury bonds had the option of converting their bonds into the new loan at the rate of 107 lire 50 centesimi of the loan for every 100 lire of bonds.   In view of the further fact that the new loan was offered to the public at 87 lire 50 centesimi for each nominal 100 lire of the loan, the Italian government has increased the principal of its debt by this operation, but it has gained an advantage through the fact that it will have no bonds maturing prior to 1931–1934.[43]   It is doubtful whether the government ultimately gains by such a conversion.

From what has been said above concerning conversions, we see in the first place that a sound government credit is the indispensable prerequisite for the effective use of the process of conversion, and in the second place, provided proper caution is taken for the avoidance of the increase in the principal of

40 See D. R. Dewey, *Financial History of the United States* (8th ed.), pp. 471-72.
41 *Ibid.*, p. 497.
42 See *Federal Reserve Bulletin*, Oct., 1927, p. 693.
43 See New York *Times*, Nov. 8, 1926.

the debt, for the preservation of further future conversion opportunities, etc., conversion is a valuable financial instrument
of the state, by which it rectifies and retrieves its disadvantageous dealings of the past, which it was forced to enter into
under strenuous circumstances.

(4) *Size of the bonds:* — At first thought the question of the
'size' of bonds may seem an insignificant one, but a further
consideration shows us its due importance, especially in case
of war loans. Professor Plehn writes in his book [44] of the experience of the United States government with "popular" loans
during the Spanish-American War. The government issued
the bonds in denominations as low as $20. About 320,000
persons offered or made subscriptions, and the sum tendered
the government amounted to about $1,400,000,000. It is true
that the cost of this method of floating the loan was relatively
high, but the government gained by strengthening its credit
thereby. The popular loan of $200,000,000 of 1898 was,
therefore, a signal success. As Professor Plehn tells us, it demonstrated the perfect solvency of the government; it gave the
country a financial prestige which went a long way toward
hastening the end of the war; and it so strengthened the credit
of the government that, had the war unfortunately continued,
it would have been able to obtain funds to almost any amount
on the most favorable terms imaginable. With a 3 per cent
bond selling at 105 during the actual continuance of military
operations, a nation may safely regard its credit as unimpaired.[45] The popular Liberty Loans of the United States
during the World War are too well known to need description.

Other countries also tried popular loans during the World
War. At the beginning of the war the British government
borrowed all the necessary funds from the bankers and the
moneyed classes. But when it realized that the war was going to be prolonged, the government found it necessary to
appeal to the whole people. In order to attract small investors
the Post Office was authorized to sell small denomination bonds
of $25 and $125 and also scrip vouchers of $5, $2½ and $1¼
which could be applied on the purchase of the bonds.

The first loan had been taken principally by the large financial institutions and wealthy subscribers, the total number of
subscribers being only 100,000, but the second loan was taken
by 1,100,000 subscribers, and at the same time the amount was
almost doubled.[46] The war savings stamps, the lowest denomi-

---

44 See Carl C. Plehn, *Introduction* . . . , pp. 432-34.
45 *Supra*, p. 434 [in Plehn].
46 E. L. Bogart, *War Costs and Their Financing*, p. 161.

nation of which was 25 cents, and the war savings certificates, the lowest denomination of which was $5, were also used to raise war funds from the poorer classes.

The governments of the other countries also resorted to bonds of small denominations. Thus the bonds of lowest denominations in various countries were as follows: Hungary — $10, France, Italy and Austria — $20; Russia and Germany — $25; and Canada and the United States — $50.[47] Taking the largest number of subscribers for any one loan in each country, the results in approximate figures were as follows: United States — 21,000,000; Great Britain — 5,000,000; France — 7,-000,000; Italy — 490,000; Canada — 1,000,000; Australia — 220,000; Germany — 7,000,000.[48]

Such a popularization of bonds in each country, except Germany, was extremely beneficial in that it aroused the spirit of thrift and economy, to say nothing of patriotism. Moreover, the beneficent influence of popularized public borrowing is felt not only during the war but also after the war. For, to the extent that the public debt is scattered among all classes, class antagonism is avoided, and the people in general are more willing to aid the government in its post-war economy.

(5) *The Taxability of the Bonds:* — A government's gain from a low interest rate of its bonds is often lost through their tax-exemption. Tax exemption of government securities is not a new phenomenon in public finance, but this subject has assumed fresh importance since the World War on account of the appearance of the so-called 'surtax.' Those who favor 'tax-free bonds' maintain that there are, among others, two great advantages in them. In the first place, the government will be able to issue its bonds at a lower rate of interest than it would otherwise be able to do. In the second place, other things being equal, the government will be able more readily to sell its bonds than if they were subject to taxation. Both these points are undoubtedly true as far as they go. If, for instance, a rich prospective investor had the choice either of investing in sound private securities yielding 5 or 6 per cent but at the same time liable to an income tax lopping off 50 per cent of the yield, or of investing in a government bond at 3 or 3½ per cent but without tax burden, he will certainly choose the latter. Again, tax-free government bonds — especially if they are long-term — will be more readily saleable to the rich investors in view of the fact that the governments of

[47] Bogart, *op. cit.*, p. 156.
[48] *Ibid.*, p. 157.

all the important countries in the world are applying more and
more the principle of progressive taxation.

Over against its advantages there are many serious disadvantages in the exemption of government bonds from taxation.
To begin with, the government in fact loses more in tax than
it gains in obtaining a lower interest rate. To be sure, if the
government bonds are moderate in amount, they can be absorbed by the highest-income group and the government can
reap the full benefit by way of lowered interest. For instance,
under the Revenue Act of 1918, to a person receiving an annual income of $1,000,000, a hundred-dollar 5-percent Liberty
Bond was worth over $143 of 5-percent private bonds, because
on private 5-percent bonds he was taxed 77 per cent on his
income. Did he in fact have to pay so much for the Liberty
Bond? Certainly not. Why? Because the government, in
order to sell not millions but billions of its bonds, was compelled to resort to much lower bidders. Now, to a person receiving an annual income of $10,000 the same 5-percent Liberty
Bond was worth only around $105, because on a similar pri-
vate bond he had to pay 14 per cent tax on his income. Under those circumstances, therefore, the million-dollar income
receivers will have had to pay only around $105 instead of
around $143. As a matter of fact, this was approximately the
situation, as was shown by the fact that, in 1920, federal farm
loan bonds sold at not above 108 although they have sold
steadily above par.[49] Whatever amount the high-income receivers gained in this way, the government lost in revenue. A
writer on government finance made a statistical analysis of the
government's gain due to lower interest rate on account of
the tax-exemption condition, and the loss due to decrease in
tax receipts. His conclusion was that the federal government
would have received $57,600,000 in 1924 if the securities were
taxable. But it paid $23,500,000 less interest than would have
been necessary had the securities not been exempt. There
was, therefore, a net loss to the government of $34,100,000.[50]
According to Professor Seligman (writing in 1925), the loss of
revenue to be incurred by the United States Government on
account of tax-exempt bonds up to 1926 promised to be at least
$300,000,000.[51] When we add to this the loss of revenue borne
by State governments, the situation is indeed grave.

In the second place, and directly due to the situation re-

[49] See *Bulletin of the National Tax Association,* vol. vi, no. 3 (Dec., 1920), pp.
76-78.

[50] See *Political Science Quarterly,* June, 1926 (vol. 41), pp. 271-80, "The Cost
of Tax-Exempt Securities" — A. F. Hinrichs.

[51] See E. R. A. Seligman, *Studies in Public Finance,* chap. vii.

ferred to above, tax-free bonds create a privileged moneyed-class which becomes a parasite to the general taxpayers of the country. Its evil effects are two-fold : on the one hand, there will be an inequitable distribution of income, while production is decreased on the other hand because of the retirement of the possessors of money from active participation in industry. Secretary Mellon's annual report for 1923 tells us that large incomes of $300,000 or over took refuge from surtaxes in the haven of tax-exempt bonds. According to the Secretary, there were, in 1916, 1296 taxpayers with incomes over $300,000 ; that in the next five years the numbers declined rapidly, thus : 1015 in 1917, 627 in 1918, 679 in 1919, 395 in 1920, and 246 in 1921 ; that their aggregate net income in 1916 was $992,-000,000, while it had dwindled to $153,000,000 by 1921.[52] Although Mr. Mellon's surmise is refuted by some,[53] there is no question but that the rapid decline in those large incomes was partly to be accounted for by investment in tax-free bonds.

In the third place, tax-exempt government bonds set up unfair competition against private securities.[54] With no immediate prospect in sight of a radical lowering of the present high income tax, it is natural that tax-exempt government securities have an advantage in the market over the securities of private borrowers. The private companies, therefore, would have to pay higher rates of interest. The result will be either that production will be decreased (or at least prevented from increasing) or that prices will rise. In either case, the public will suffer an economic loss.

Lastly, tax-exemption of government securities is a menace to the system of federal revenues and taxation. The present system of taxation in the United States (as well as in all civilized countries) is based upon the principle of 'ability to pay.' But the ability of an individual to pay depends largely upon his income. Now, it is a well-known fact that the majority of great private fortunes consist of securities in one form or other. Public securities are increasing more and more in number and value. It is estimated that they are increasing at present at the rate of one billion dollars a year. If they continue to be exempt from taxation, the evil consequences are not far to seek even though the effects are partly attenuated by the higher prices of the securities which the bondholders are compelled to pay.

[52] *Annual Report of the Secretary of Treasury*, 1923, p. 12, Table II.

[53] See the *New Republic*, Jan. 23, 1924, pp. 220-21 ; also, see the same for Jan. 27, 1926, under the title "Those Vanished Fortunes, the great Mellon Myth about the Tax-exempt Bonds" — C. O. Hardy.

[54] See *Secretary of Treasury's Report for 1924*, p. 10.

From the above considerations it is obvious that tax-exemption of public bonds is economically unjustifiable as well as financially unsound, and therefore, it should not be utilized as a means of popularizing government bonds. It is far better to pay a higher rate of interest, if necessary, because then the government can apply conversion and other means of diminishing its burden due to a high rate of interest. Moreover, as has been stated in a previous section of the present chapter, a high rate of interest on government securities will be a powerful stimulus for thrift and economy on the part of the people of small means, while 'tax-free bonds' offer no such stimulus to them, because they are very little affected by income taxes. Despite the obvious faults of the tax-exemption of government bonds, a bill prohibiting the future issue of tax-free bonds was defeated on February, 1924, in the United States House of Representatives. Its defeat was chiefly due, however, to political reasons.

(6) *Foreign Loans:* — Thus far we have tacitly assumed that the public loans were made within the country. In concluding this section, a few words should now be said of foreign loans. Some writers oppose foreign loans because they entail heavy payments of goods and services to foreign countries by way of interest payments and repayments of the principal. One cannot eat one's cake and have it too, and so, provided that such loans were made for necessary purposes, they are in the main advantageous.[55] Broadly speaking, however, in our age when the means of transportation and communication have been so highly developed, in the long run there is not much difference in economic effects whether a country borrows at home or abroad. The fluidity of capital is so great that economic adjustment will sooner or later take place. Yet there is some difference between the temporary economic effects of a foreign loan and those of a domestic loan : and this difference is by no means unimportant.

Provided a country's credit is good and there is abundant loanable capital in foreign countries, there is no reason why such capital should not be borrowed. For greater production is thereby attained at home and at the same time the demand for the products is assured by the circumstances of the situation. If on the contrary the government borrows from lenders at home, there will be so much less capital available for private industries. Less production will take place, which in turn — through a rise of prices — will entail less consumption at home and less demand for domestic products in the foreign

[55] *Cf.* Bastable, *Public Finance,* pt. 1, sec. ii, pars. 76, 77 and 78 ; also, p. 679.

markets.   To be sure, foreign capital will in time flow into the country through private borrowings, but only after the domestic production has suffered a temporary diminution and, also, after a higher rate of interest has been paid by private borrowers.   In case of an emergency such as war, the beneficent effect of a foreign loan is even more pronounced.   Domestic industries are thereby given time to adjust themselves to new conditions, while the government need not wait for domestic production to satisfy its sudden abnormal demand for war materials of all kinds.   Moreover, the inflation of currency and the abnormal rise in domestic prices are prevented because the commodities imported will be paid for by the proceeds of the foreign loan.   The Allies obtained just such a benefit when the United States entered the World War and made large loans to them, although in that case of course the internal economic conditions of the allied nations were already badly disturbed, and the only thing the loans could do was to prevent their aggravation.

There are on the other hand some disadvantages in making foreign loans in times of emergency.   In the first place, the temporary relief and plenty due to a foreign loan are liable to check the people from making a greater exertion and economy which they otherwise would have made.   Nothing has a more wholesome effect on a country than for the people fully to realize the gravity of an emergency, be it a war or a natural calamity.   In the second place, the interest rates of foreign loans are usually high in cases of emergency because of the lender's apprehension for the future condition of the borrower and because of the needy situation of the borrower.[56]   This of course means that the future burden on the people will be heavy.   In case of war, when a country's very existence is at stake, the government cannot afford to be swayed by such disadvantages.   But in case of a natural calamity such as a deluge or an earthquake, if the task is to rehabilitate the country's parks, museums, capital buildings and the like, it is not necessary from an economic standpoint to resort to a foreign loan with a high rate of interest.   If domestic capital barely suffices to regain the country's productive efficiency, social improvements can be made out of domestic capital as it gradually accumulates in the future.   For these and other less important reasons,[57] which may be omitted, it seems to us that, as a general rule, foreign loans for exigencies should be resorted to only to the extent of preventing violent industrial disturbances

[56] America's loans to the Allies were exceptions.
[57] Given by Bastable in his *Public Finance*, pt. 1, sec. ii, pp. 79-80.

in the transition from ordinary to extraordinary conditions and of giving an initial encouragement to the people — a "handicap," as it were, given in an economic race with foreign countries.

When it comes to foreign loans for industrial undertakings in time of peace, the case is very different. If, for instance, a country wishes to develop its industries or to open up its natural resources but has not enough capital, there is — considered from an economic standpoint alone — no reason why it should not borrow capital from foreign countries. There are obviously two great advantages in such a loan. First, the rate of interest charged will be relatively low because the undertakings in question are sound business propositions. In the second place, the gains arising from the undertakings will far outbalance the sums of interest to be paid on borrowed capital. Especially will this be true in the case of developing natural resources. The countries in point are China, Russia, Mexico and the South American Republics.[58] Were it not for political considerations of both the would-be lenders and the would-be borrowers, there is no reason why those countries should not borrow all the capital they could from foreign countries, in order to open up their natural resources and to develop their industries. For, once their industries are established and developed, the gains that arise will be immensely greater than the temporary loss due to debt charges.

There is another point which has a very important economic bearing upon a country, although it is more directly of a political than of an economic nature. If a country borrows a large amount of money from another country there is likelihood that the creditor country will grant more readily what is known in international politics as a "most-favored nation" treaty. Wars, also, are more likely to be avoided, because international debts are often repudiated as a result of the severance of diplomatic relations. All these facts tend to the economic advantage of the debtor country.

We may come to the conclusion then, that foreign loans, provided they are made at a reasonable rate of interest, are advantageous to a country because they help to prevent industrial disturbance, inflation, and decrease of production at home in times of emergency; and that, in time of peace, they serve to develop domestic industries and to increase domestic production in general.

[58] Notice the recent endeavors of Soviet Russia to attract foreign capital.

2. TAX-EXEMPT SECURITIES

A DISCUSSION of the economic effects of tax exemption of government securities, more comprehensive than that which appears in the preceding section, was given by the late Professor Thomas S. Adams in an address before the Conference of the National Tax Association in 1922. The major portion of his address is presented below.*

IN its principal aspect I feel that I can do nothing more than emphasize . . . the seriousness of the social problem that is likely to be created if there arises in this country a situation in which the wealthiest men — the men most able to bear taxation — get themselves, by reason of the existence of these tax-free bonds, into an isle of safety, in which they are absolutely sheltered from the burden of supporting government, to which, as Justice Holmes of the supreme court has said, they owe their protection and in some senses their lives. It is necessary that the richer classes of the country pay taxes and be known and seen to pay taxes. There are many direct and indirect ways that are open by which it is possible to reach the very wealthy elements of the country, and I feel . . . that this question of the creation of class conflict, of hatred for the wealthier classes of society, is perhaps the most important phase of this problem. . .

I was interested to find out [in a previous study] how rapid under the federal law the escape of very wealthy members of society was by reason of the tax-free bonds, and while the figures which I am about to quote did not describe this with scientific accuracy, in a rough way they represent what is happening. There was reported for the year 1916 by persons having an annual income of three hundred thousand dollars or more, practically nine hundred and ninety-three million dollars of net income. I am talking about the very rich now. The same thing would be true of any other group. I took that group because in treasury discussion at Washington it has been usual for a number of years to regard the people with incomes of three hundred thousand dollars or more a year as typical of the very rich. Now, by 1919, after years of unexampled prosperity, during which the incomes of neither the rich nor the poor in this country were shrinking, but in which they were manifestly growing, the reported taxable income of

* From Thomas S. Adams, "Tax-Exempt Securities," *Proceedings, National Tax Association*, 1922, pp. 262-267.

that group had shrunk to four hundred and forty millions of dollars. In other words, there was a reduction to less than one-half of what there had been four years earlier. While that is to be explained partly by the variety of methods of avoiding federal taxes by the very rich, it has to be principally ascribed, in my opinion, to the influence of the tax-free bond. The testimony of bankers and of experts, and of people who advise the wealthier members of American society, is universal as to the extent that they are investing their new wealth in increasing amounts in tax-free securities, and as to their growing habit of transferring their old wealth to tax-free securities. That puts in concrete form the seriousness of this problem.

Now, President Harding and others have called attention to other baleful effects and results of the possibility of investing in tax-free securities, of which there are probably fifteen billions outstanding at the present time, in one form or another, enough certainly to take all the investments of the very rich people of this country, or sufficient to practically exempt them from taxation. The evils are first of all the unfair competition in which it places private industry. I want to stop to discuss that a moment, because I think it has sometimes been exaggerated, and that it ought to be placed in its proper light. Quite obviously, if you think about it, the man who buys state, local or exempt federal bonds is not wholly tax-free. I like . . . to concede all that is strong in the opposing case, if I am talking for anything. The man who buys a municipal bond or a state bond is not wholly tax-exempt. It is perfectly obvious that the so-called legal exemption feature of that bond makes him pay a higher rate of interest than he would otherwise pay. The city or the state floats its indebtedness at a lower rate of interest than it would otherwise pay. To that extent the individual is paying, because he takes a lower interest rate. He is paying some tax indirectly. Now, that is true, and it is also true that cities are enabled to borrow at lower rates of interest because of the tax-exemption feature, and it is true that the federal government is enabled to borrow at lower rates of interest. Now, in talking over carefully the real evil of the tax-exempt bond, we ought not to attempt to deny those facts. It is also true that the competition between the public borrower and the private borrower is not quite as unfair as it seems on the face, but it is nevertheless true that this thing is a grave evil, and that public bodies — states, municipalities, and the federal government — lose far more in taxes than they gain in reduced interest; it is a losing proposition, and must be a losing proposition wherever you have a system of progressive taxation, and that is easily demonstrable. It is also true that private industry does suffer from unfair competition by reason of this exemption; and worst of all, this exemption, in my opinion, perverts the normal and natural habits of investment.

Municipal and state and public securities of this country are gilt-edged; they offer the best security, the nearest approach to absolute safety that we have. They ought to be investments of those persons who have small amounts to invest, in which safety is paramount. Now, what happens is that under the existing situation the very rich become the principal owners of these bonds; the men who ought to be taking the grave industrial chances — who ought to be investing in the hazardous things — who ought to be supplying the money for those dangerous investments which are legitimate and necessary, but which ought to be invested in and be supported by the people who can afford to lose. The oil schemes, the dangerous mining ventures, are getting in increasing degree the investments of the poor, and the rich, who ought to carry those grave risks, are turning from them to invest in tax-free securities. Thus the normal habits of investment have been perverted.

It is also true that many of our private enterprises which have through past habit and custom been accustomed to rely for support upon the well-to-do investor, find that he now is seeking the tax-free bond. The testimony of investment bankers and brokers is all unanimous to the effect that the ordinary customers, to whom they have turned to support the railroads, the industrials, and to take over the new bonds that must be issued from time to time, are no longer available. In those ways private industry has been seriously handicapped.

I return just for a moment to the assertion I made a moment ago, that while the states and cities, by reason of this exemption feature, are enabled to borrow more cheaply than they can borrow without the exemption feature, it is nevertheless a losing game for the state and city. I think that is plain if you stop to think a moment. You have federal taxes running from 58 per cent down. The highest rate in the federal income tax is a little less than 58 per cent. Now, let us take a very wealthy man, subject to a 50 per cent tax, and then take another man less wealthy, subject to a 25 per cent tax; let us suppose, just for the purposes of convenience, that the rate on absolutely secure taxable investments is five per cent. Now then, the man paying a 50 per cent tax, if he invests in taxable securities, is going to net two and one-half per cent. That is all he is going to get. He is going to pay fifty per cent in taxes, half of his interest. He could then afford, if necessary, to lend to states and cities and to the federal government, on tax-exempt federal securities, at two and one-half per cent. It would net him just as much as a five per cent taxable bond. But, the important point is that there are very few, relatively speaking, of those men who are paying the fifty per cent tax, and if the states and cities want to float all the bonds that it is necessary for them to float, they have to seek classes of taxpayers that are paying a smaller tax. They have to come down and get into the market of the people who are subject to twenty-five per cent taxes. But to the man who is subject to only a twenty-five per cent tax, this exemption is worth one-quarter of five per cent, which is one and one-quarter per cent. All he will bid for this privilege of exemption is one and one-quarter per cent; and if you go down to the man subject to only twenty per cent income tax, the exemption feature is worth only one per cent, and that is all he will pay for it. Now then, to float the large volume of state and municipal securities — and they must be floated — you have to appeal to the taxpayers subject to from fifty per cent taxpayers down to the forty, thirty, twenty-five and twenty per cent, and you are going to sell your privilege of exemption at that figure which will appeal to the lowest of the classes of taxpayers to which you must sell. In other words, all you are going to get for your exemption privilege is one per cent, but every taxpayer subject to more than twenty per cent tax is going to save more in taxes than he loses in taking the smaller interest rate. That is the reason why under any system of progressive taxation, an exemption feature must cost the government more in taxes than it saves them in reduced interest payment.

There are one or two other features of this discussion less commonly alluded to, to which I want to refer. I have hopes that every state tax official here will become an ardent advocate of this federal constitutional amendment,* for the reasons to which I have alluded and because I think this exemption creates a grave social problem.

I want to say to you state tax officials that I think there is one feature of this campaign against the tax-exempt bond which is unfair and more or less untrue, and I for one want to refute it, and that argument is this: federal officials are very fond of stating, and corporation officials are very fond of stat-

---

* Eds. note: Professor Adams is here referring to a resolution adopted by the National Tax Conference at Bretton Woods in 1921, calling upon Congress to submit to the states for ratification an amendment to the Federal Constitution prohibiting the exemption from income taxation of the interest on future issues of federal, state, and municipal obligations.

ing, that the tax-exempt feature has greatly stimulated public borrowing, and they have intimated that the cities and counties and states of this country have, since the cessation of the war — largely by reason of their ability to borrow at low rates — gone into a period of debauch — of borrowing and spending money like drunken sailors. I don't believe in any such nonsense. I don't believe that the cities and states of this country are borrowing money merely because they can borrow it a little more cheaply. As a matter of fact, the explanation of the enormous output of municipal and state securities after the war is the simple fact that the states and cities of this country had, like patriotic organizations, left off all their development work during the war; roads and schools and institution after institution were in bad shape, and they needed money, and they went out and borrowed it, just as the industries of this country did. That one particular argument I have personally no patience with, and it is not necessary to the making of an absolutely convincing case for the desirability of passing this constitutional amendment.

Now, I have only one other aspect of the subject, which I say is an aspect not so frequently referred to, that I want to mention. The amendment which has been proposed, the resolution which has been introduced and which has been referred to, strikes me as most eminently fair. It seems to me to be a gentleman's proposition. It extends to the states all the powers which the federal government asks, and it keeps entire faith with the taxpayers of this country, by not attempting to remove the exemption under which the vast volume of tax-exempt securities was sold. I think that is right. I don't believe that we could have removed that exemption, and it is absolutely necessary to retain it for reasons of fairness and good policy. The states and the federal government should be put upon an equal footing in this regard, namely; that after the passage of the amendment the states shall have the power to tax federal issues and the federal government shall have the power to tax state and municipal issues.

But, there are fifteen billions or more of tax-free securities outstanding. This is the last aspect of the problem to which I want to refer: Until they are retired, or for fifteen or twenty years or so, we must labor under the disadvantage of having outstanding all the time this enormous volume of securities which anybody can buy at any time, thus securing tax exemption. I personally am not so certain that there is any sound or equitable reason why for fifteen or twenty or twenty-five years we should endure this evil, which is just as large an evil now as it will be twenty-five years from now. I believe that in addition to the prompt adoption of this constitutional amendment, very serious thought should be given to the question of whether now, at the present time, by an exercise of legal ingenuity, we may not devise ways and means of overcoming this disadvantage.

A Voice (interrupting): How about changing the terms of a contract?

Professor Adams: I don't want to change the term of the contract. A violation of good faith, sir, is just as obnoxious to me as it is to you. I would not want to remove one scintilla of the exemption which has been given. The holders of state and federal bonds have been exempted from income taxes, but there are methods which are absolutely free from the slightest taint of violation of good faith. I mention one of them merely. Its possibilities grow with me every day, not only from this standpoint, but from other standpoints. That is the substitution for our graduated income tax of a graduated tax on expenditure, taking the place of our federal surtaxes. Now stop, some of you, and very seriously, from day to day, for the next six months or so, consider the possibilities of that. You would have a tax that would absolutely be exempting, for instance, the saved income; you would be stimulating thrift; you would have a tax indirectly and in essence, but not in any literal sense, that would be applicable to the interest from state and municipal bonds when it was spent. There would not be the slightest violation of good faith. I mention this as simply one expedient. I could mention five or six other expedients by which indirectly we could get some income from the people who hold exempt bonds. For instance, one method is this: you all know that the corporation excise tax, adopted in 1909, and approved by unanimous vote of the supreme court of the United States, applied to and was measured by the entire income of corporations, including all interest from municipal bonds. There is much possibility in the adoption of excise taxes. The point I want to make is this: let us get that amendment; let us protect the next generation from the evil under which we suffer; and then also let us give serious thought to the question of whether by the adoption of taxes on expenditure or by excise taxes, we cannot legitimately — because we don't want even to consider anything we cannot do legitimately — whether we cannot, without violation of good faith — because we don't want to consider anything else — levy other kinds of taxes perhaps that will meet this particular evil.

3. EXTERNAL AND INTERNAL DEBTS

A BRIEF treatment of the distinction between the economic effects of foreign and domestic loans was given in the first section of this chapter. A more thorough analysis of this problem, however, has been made by the late Professor Allyn A. Young in connection with a study of the War Debts. The excellence of Professor Young's analysis, together with the world-wide importance of the subject, warrants its reproduction at this point.*

How far is it true that a large domestic or internal national debt, as contrasted with an external or foreign debt, is a relatively negligible burden? Does the payment of an internal debt, requiring merely the transfer of wealth or income from some persons to others *within* the same country, put no formidable strain upon that country's economic energies? How far is it true, by way of contrast, that Germany's capacity to make reparations payments, or the capacity of any nation to make large foreign payments, is narrowly and rigidly limited by its ability to maintain a favorable balance of commodity exports over commodity imports?

At first the very real differences between the burdens imposed by external and by internal debts were ignored in popular discussions and flouted in the policies of governments. That fact explains and justifies the emphasis competent critics, in increasing number, have put upon those differences. But despite the great value of the educational work they have done, some of these critics have drawn too straight a line between the two kinds of debts.

We may find a helpful approach to the problem if we look first at several different ways of appraising a country's ability to pay a heavy and burdensome foreign debt.

In the first place, there is the now familiar method which relies upon an inventory of a country's present foreign assets coupled with an estimate of its capacity to maintain a favorable balance of trade through a series of years. This latter estimate is generally based upon an analysis of the country's pre-war trade and its possible rate of growth, together with a consideration of the degree in which the war has affected the country's productive resources and its markets. This is the method used by Mr. Keynes in *The Economic Consequences of the Peace*,

* From Allyn A. Young, "War Debts, External and Internal," *Foreign Affairs*, (March, 1924), pp. 397-409.

and by Messrs. Moulton and McGuire in *Germany's Capacity to Pay*. In competent hands it leads to important results. It is worth observing that, despite the highly conjectural character of some of the figures that must be drawn upon, the better estimates that have been made in this way are not far apart.

Such studies of a debtor country's possible balance of trade are indispensable. They are a necessary preliminary to any reasoned judgment upon that country's capacity to make foreign payments. But it is wrong to rest content with them — to regard them as complete and adequate estimates of capacity to pay. They make no room for the play of various elastic factors. In particular they take no account of the readjustments in the economic and financial relations of the different nations of the world that are bound to be brought about as a result of the very operation of paying a heavy foreign debt.

In the second place, we may turn to the arguments of those who hold that the effort to pay a large foreign debt has the curious effect of greatly increasing the debtor country's real capacity to pay — provided that the currency of the debtor country is inconvertible paper. Under such conditions, it is even contended, a country's ability to make foreign payments is really limited only by its ability to produce more than it consumes. The gist of the argument is as follows: To make payments on its external debt the government must buy foreign bills of exchange in large quantities. The price of such bills, and along with it the prices obtained (in domestic currency) for exported goods, will be pushed up rapidly, so that finally a considerable differential will be established between the general domestic price level and the prices that can be had for exports. This differential operates, so the doctrine runs, virtually as a bonus on exports. It will induce business men to turn a larger share of their energies to producing goods for the export rather than for the domestic market. Why should German producers, for example, sell goods at home when more *marks* could be got for them by selling them (or other goods produced at no larger cost) abroad for credits in dollars or pounds or francs which could then be sold to the government at high prices? So long as this bonus on exports can be maintained by the pressure of the government's continuing demand for the means of making foreign payments, so long, in a quasi-automatic way, the country's production of goods for the export market will be increased, while in equal measure its production of goods consumed at home will be decreased. Its capacity to pay, therefore, will be limited in the long run only by its maximum productive capacity on the one hand and its minimum domestic industrial and subsistence needs on the other.

Now this theory is based upon a perfectly sound principle, but it runs that principle into the ground by fantastically exaggerating its possibilities. The first of the two methods we have considered, taken by itself, is too inelastic. This second method errs in the other direction. It ignores a number of very important inelastic factors. It takes no account, for example, of the inelasticity of the demand of the world's markets for the exports of any one country or of the inelasticity of that country's demand for imports. It passes over the fact that a country like Germany must shape its exports very largely from imported raw materials and that the prices that must be paid for imported goods, in domestic currency, generally rise at least as rapidly as the prices that can be realized for exports. It disregards the way in which such price differentials react upon the whole structure of industry and finance within the debtor country. It forgets the inevitable lowering of the standard of living and the disintegrating effects of maladjustments in the delicate interrelations of the country's system of prices. Financial and industrial wreckage, rather than an increasing export surplus, is the certain result of the pressure of an unduly large foreign debt.

Furthermore, even though some of the advantages claimed might be secured by export industries if export and domestic prices and the differential between them could be maintained at a moderate and stable level, such advantages would disappear when, as would be inevitable, the export and domestic price levels continued to advance. An *increasing* differential between export and domestic prices will not always stimulate exports. Some exporters will prefer to wait for a higher differential later. Some importers, on the other hand, will be induced to bring in foreign goods, at whatever cost, in order to sell them later when the margin between the prices of imports and the general level of domestic prices is larger.

A third method of approach to the problem of the maximum manageable size of a foreign debt is suggested by the proposals that Germany's payment should be made in a lump by turning over shares in German industries to Germany's creditors. There have been some such proposals, on the part of Germans, that have had an official or semi-official character. A distinguished German statistician, Dr. R. R. Kuczynski, has gone even further, proposing a heavy capital tax upon German property of whatever sort, the proceeds, in the form of mortgages, bonds, shares, and the like, to be handed over *en bloc* in acquittance of reparations obligations.

It is going too far to hold that such methods of payment "do not constitute actual payments at all."[1] I do not suppose that it is claimed by Dr. Kuczynski or by others who have made similar proposals that a final or *economic* payment could be achieved by such a transfer. A *legal* payment might conceivably be made and a receipt in full secured by assigning or transferring securities which would themselves be nothing more than evidences of debt. A public debt might be converted into a mass of private debts. The contention merely is that the final economic settlement of the debt could be reached more easily and more efficiently if it were removed from the field of international politics, and if the mechanism of the payment were controlled by the free play of economic forces, rather than by the attempts of governments to collect the payments in one form rather than in another.

There is no reason to doubt the sincerity and good intentions back of these proposals, and it is in some respects a matter for regret that any large reliance upon such methods is neither wise nor practicable. The difficulties, both political and economic, are manifold. For one thing, the assets thus secured, if large and miscellaneous, would shrink greatly in value in the markets of the world.

Back of such proposals, nevertheless, there is a thoroughly sound notion which supplements and corrects the rigid export-surplus doctrine. If the reparations debt were fixed at a reasonable amount and if Germany were left free to find her own ways and means of payment, it is fairly certain that a situation would develop in the end which would somewhat resemble — though on a reduced and moderate scale — the situation which these proposals contemplate as the result of a single operation. By the time the reparations payments were completed, other countries — not Germany's present creditors alone — would hold considerable amounts of German securities, both public and private. In various ways, planned or spontaneous, a fairly large proportion of the reparations debt would be refunded into these other forms. Legal payment would be completed and the German Government acquitted of its liability long before the final economic payment had been made. Indeed, the continual shiftings of the world's balances of international debts and payments might make it impossible to say with certainty at any one time that the final payments *had* been made.

It is likewise difficult to think that France will receive any

[1] Moulton and McGuire, *Germany's Capacity to Pay*, p. 18.

large part of her share of reparations in the form of such manufactured goods as Germany might produce. It is distinctly
more probable — her own external debts aside — that France's
increased imports, like Germany's increased exports, would be
diffused over the whole surface of world trade, and that her
foreign holdings of various sorts, her investments in other parts
of the world, would be measurably increased, although not
necessarily in exact proportion to the increase of Germany's
"refunded" foreign liabilities. Such changes in the world's international balance sheets would, beyond doubt, react upon
and modify the currents of international trade in commodities,
— but the discussion of such matters would take us far afield.

All the differences between external and internal debts are
bound up with the fundamental fact that the former call for
foreign payments. Such payments create problems in foreign
trade and foreign exchange. So long as the payments continue,
the debtor country, except so far as it can refund the debt, must
produce more than it can consume or add to its accumulated
domestic capital. The monetary units in which payment must
be made and which therefore measure the amount of the debt
are not within the arbitrary control of the debtor government.
Domestic inflation makes these foreign monetary units dearer,
not cheaper. Deliberate repudiation, complete or partial, of
external debts is not, as a rule, practicable. Such are some of
the more important characteristics which external debts have,
but which internal debts lack.

Let us turn now to points which they have in common. We
note, in the first place, that the payment of an internal, as of an
external debt, requires taxation, calling for sacrifices and exercising a repressive effect upon trade and industry.

In the second place, there is an analogy — not merely fanci-
ful, although it would be easy to push it too far — between a
country's taxpayers and the holders of its internal debt, on the
one hand, and debtor and creditor countries, on the other.
Taxpayers and holders of the public debts are, in part, two
different groups. The interest and principal of the debt enter
into the balance of payments as between the taxpayers and the
owners of government securities. For many years the taxpayers, as such, must produce more than they can consume or
save, while the government's creditors will receive more than,
at the time, they are producing. If the debt absorbs any large
proportion of the national income, as in France, England, and
other European countries, the resulting reactions upon the distribution of incomes, upon the general standard of living, upon
the demand for goods, and upon the general structure of in-

dustry, may be considerable.   Much depends, of course, upon
the way in which the burden of taxation is apportioned,
upon whether taxes fall more or less heavily upon necessities,
upon luxuries, upon incomes, or upon accumulated capital.
But at the best the strain upon the country's economic activities is likely to be heavy, even though the complications and
special difficulties attending transactions in foreign exchange
are absent.

In the third place — and this I believe to be the most important point of similarity — heavy internal debts, like external
debts, strike at the heart of a country's economic life by bringing disorder into its currency.   That inflation, unbalanced
budgets, and disordered exchanges have been among the chief
factors delaying Europe's economic recovery is pretty generally
known, but it is not so well understood as it should be that the
sequence of cause and effect, particularly in the period following the war, has not been inflation, unbalanced budgets,
disordered exchanges, but unbalanced budgets, disordered exchanges, inflation.

Before the war the world had an international money — gold
— which not only stabilized (albeit imperfectly) but tied and
held together the currencies of the great commercial countries.
The mechanism of international payments operated with deceptive ease and smoothness.   The price system was, in very
large measure, international.   The market for loanable funds,
whether of long or short maturity, was also, in a very considerable degree, international.

At present a large part of the western world is cut up, artificially, into separate economic districts within which purely
national currencies rule.   The worst thing about these new
artificial barriers is that they fluctuate continuously and un-
certainly — inviting hazardous speculation, but discouraging
the steady flow of trade.

The war was financed, as we know, partly by taxes and to
some extent by voluntary savings, but mostly by diluting the
purchasing power of money.   Inflation was the mechanism by
which war debts, we might say, were created.   All this is now
very generally understood.   But there appears to be no adequate appreciation of the intimate and necessary connection
between debt reduction, on the one hand, and the deflation
and stabilization of paper currencies, on the other hand.

This relation between debts and the status of paper currencies holds whether the debts be external or internal, although the mechanism by means of which the increase or
decrease of the debt operates upon the currency is different in

the two cases.   Consider, for a moment, some of the monetary effects of a burdensome foreign debt.   The wrecking of Germany's monetary system affords an instructive example.

The Government's demand for foreign funds, added to similar demands on the part of importers and of others having foreign payments to make, was greatly in excess of the available supply.   The only way of securing foreign exchange was to bid its price up to a point where some of the competing demand was eliminated.   The price of dollars, of sterling, and of francs went up out of all proportion to the difference between the domestic purchasing power of marks within Germany and the domestic purchasing power of the other currencies in the countries in which they circulated.   But the prices in marks of imported and exported goods — of goods, that is, for which there is an international market — were driven rapidly up by the advance in the price of foreign exchange.   Tied to the prices of the international market in a thousand indirect and intricate ways, the domestic price level, though until recently lagging considerably behind, advanced haltingly but irresistibly.   Inflation, though accelerated by an unbalanced budget, followed — it did not precede — the advance of prices.   During the past four years the per capita circulation of money in Germany, measured in terms of its domestic purchasing power, has been much smaller than before the war.   Measured in terms of its gold value the shrinkage of the currency has been even more striking.   In large measure inflation has been the result rather than the cause of the depreciation of the value of the currency.

I have reviewed these matters again in order to give point to the emphasis I shall put upon what I believe to be the indispensable key to an understanding of the vagaries of the behavior of the depreciated currencies of Europe.   I refer to the dominating part played by speculation.   It makes all the difference in the world whether men's actions are prompted by the belief that a depreciated currency will increase in value or by the belief that its future trend will be downward.

The turning point in Germany's financial fortunes came in the first half of 1922, following upon the adverse decision with respect to Northern Silesia, late in the autumn of 1921.   Up to that time many people in and out of Germany had maintained a persistent if unreasoned faith in the future of the mark.   That circumstance measurably retarded the inevitable decline of the mark, and did much to lighten Germany's financial burden.   It made exports of German goods larger than they would otherwise have been.   It led people in other countries to make large speculative purchases of marks and of securities payable in marks. It was one of the things that induced persons in other countries to invest heavily in German property. During that period, it is safe to say, Germany's imports of capital, in various invisible forms, were distinctly larger than her invisible exports. Part of the favorable balance was available for reparation payments.

This misplaced confidence in the future of the mark waned rapidly after the failure of the attempt to stabilize its value in December, 1921, and a complete reversal of the general trend of speculation followed. With a bear market for marks the difficulties of the German Government were multiplied. Then came the unrelenting drift of events into the reparations crisis of a year ago, with its costly and ominous sequel.

With the conviction once established that the value of the mark, in terms of other currencies, was bound to continue to depreciate, its depreciation was accelerated. Commodity exports were retarded and imports stimulated. The direction of the current of invisible elements in the balance of international payments was reversed. Capital began to flow out of Germany more rapidly than into it. The rapid decline of the mark under the pressure of these forces only added to their strength. The mechanism of financial disintegration worked in a cumulative way.

Some absurdly exaggerated stories are afloat respecting the amount of German capital that has gone during the last year and a half into bank deposits and into the purchase of securities in the United States, Canada, Switzerland, and other countries with relatively stable currencies. But underneath these exaggerations there is reasonable ground for presuming that Germany's exports of capital have been significant in amount.

We do not have to attribute these developments to a concerted plot on the part of German business men, abetted by the German Government, to evade their reparations obligation. It is reasonably certain, of course, that the fear of drastic taxation helped to create a preference for foreign holdings. But the major compelling force back of the export of German capital has been the loss of confidence in the mark. The particular methods by which such transactions are effected do not matter greatly. The general result is that the foreign credits created by exports and in other ways are allowed to remain abroad instead of being offered for sale to the government. In any case the transaction is essentially a bear operation in marks. As such it is easily explainable. It is wrong only in so far as it involves a violation or evasion of the laws regulating the purchase and sale of foreign bills of exchange.

I cannot believe that the real attitude of the French Government toward this matter, or, at any rate, the attitude of the economic advisers of the French Government, has been correctly reported, or that it is adequately expressed in the official statements of that government. A very definite impression has been given that the French Government objects to the removal of "wealth" from Germany, and that it insists that ways and means of bringing it back again must be found. This, it appears, is a problem upon which one of the committees of experts now attached to the Reparations Commission is at work. On the face of it this attitude is paradoxical, for so long as German wealth remains in Germany it can be used only with difficulty for reparations payments. German-owned dollars, francs, and sterling, on the other hand, are precisely the stuff out of which reparations payments can easily be fashioned.

The real ground of the French complaint must be that these privately-owned foreign funds, which have been accumulated at such heavy cost to Germany, might, at no greater cost, have been acquired by the German Government and then applied to the payment of reparations. The French Government does not really desire that these foreign funds be brought back into Germany in the form, let us say, of imports of merchandise. Its real and legitimate interest is that the German Government should be able in some way to possess itself of these foreign assets and turn them over to Germany's creditors.

It is impossible that this legitimate end should be obtained by ferreting out these foreign holdings or by any amount of pressure and intimidation. But it would be accomplished promptly and easily if a stable monetary system could be established in Germany. With the motive for the concealment and expatriation of funds destroyed, the German Government could get hold of them by paying a fair market price in German currency.

It will be granted, perhaps, that the history of the German mark illustrates and confirms the principle that a stable currency and an excessive external debt are incompatible. A similar relation holds as between a country's currency and an excessive internal debt, although only a part of the mechanism by which external debts affect the price level operates when the debts are internal. An excessive internal debt makes it difficult to balance the budget, and an unbalanced budget calls for further advances by the banks, or for further sales of government securities, attended by an increase in the volume of bank credit. These new creations of purchasing power, as we know, exert a continued upward pressure on prices.

Here again, speculation plays a very important part. The movement of prices in a period of continuing inflation is not a direct effect of the sheer mechanical impact of the offer of new supplies of money in the market for goods and services. Speculation anticipates these consequences, and, by anticipating them, puts into operation a new mechanism of its own. Except in the initial, and perhaps the very last, stages of inflation, the price of foreign exchange and of imports and exports generally keeps in advance of the general movement of domestic prices, even when external debts are not exerting a steady pressure upon the foreign exchange market. The general level of domestic prices, though again lagging behind, follows the course marked out for it by the appraisal of the value of the country's currencies in the international market. Thus, for example, fresh issues of paper money to cover a deficit in the budget may, merely by altering the expectations people have formed respecting the deflation or stabilization of the currency, lead to a sharp advance of prices, which in turn will call for and in a manner justify further creations of bank credit. In a similar way, any really effective steps taken toward deflation will produce a powerfully cumulative downward influence. Under a régime of inconvertible paper money, it is barely a step from a stable to an extremely unstable equilibrium. So far as I know, all of the world's experience with inconvertible paper money illustrates and confirms these principles.

The bearing of these considerations upon what we may call the international problem of national debts is obvious. The stabilization of European currencies (I do not mean their drastic deflation), is the indispensable prerequisite to the economic recovery of Europe. The one indispensable instrument of stabilization is the balancing of budgets. The burden of debts, external and internal, blocks the way. If the debts can be taken care of, the monetary situation would take care of itself. This is what makes of national debts, seen as an aggregate, an international problem — and no shutting of our eyes to it will alter the fact.

I am not one of those who believe that the payment of the interest and principal of an international debt does more harm than good to the nation receiving the payment. Nor do I believe that the payment of an international debt strengthens rather than weakens the nation making the payment. But I am convinced that the present debts of European nations, including reparations, interallied debts, and internal debts, are so large that, as they now stand on the books, they cannot be paid in full. Moreover, no considerable part of them can be paid without perpetuating and perhaps increasing the disorders of the currency. There is, I grant, one possible alternative. These debts might within the next generation be reduced to manageable proportions by the persistent use of taxation of unprecedented severity. I doubt that this is politically practicable. Even if it were, I doubt that the game would be worth the candle. There would be long periods of business depression, lowered standards of living, and new injustices in the distribution of wealth. It would be better to release the world's economic energies; to permit deflation to be accomplished, so far as it is desirable, by increasing the volume of production and trade rather than by drastic reductions in the volume of the currency.

On the whole there is less pessimism respecting the general economic condition of Europe than there was a few years ago. Despite the enforced retrogression of Germany during the past year, Europe as a whole continues to go forward and not backward. But her complete recovery will be delayed indefinitely if there are to be either further increases of debt and further inflation, or a steady general reduction of debts and deflation of currencies.

The whole subject of international debts, including their relations to internal debts, would profit by a candid and open international discussion. The central unifying theme which would bind the different parts of the discussion together would be the stabilizing of the world's currencies so as to get rid, so far as possible, of the distorting and destructive influence of international currency speculation, and to provide a dependable mechanism of international payments.

The United States cannot always hold itself aloof from such discussion, if only because, as the ultimate creditor, it holds what may prove to be the master key to the whole problem. I do not question the present wisdom of the policy regarding the debts owed to us which President Coolidge has reaffirmed. The debts of other countries as well as of England are valid and binding international obligations. We are right in insisting that they be recognized as such, that they should be rated higher than a mere offset to Class C German reparations bonds. But it is one thing to consolidate our power; it is another thing to use that power wisely.

These considerations gain weight from the fact that the uncertainties of Germany's creditors respecting the relative status of one as compared with that of each of the others have done as much to delay a reasonable solution of the reparations problem as have their doubts concerning Germany's attitude, and more than any disagreement respecting the aggregate amount Germany can pay. Reciprocal jealousies, disputes over priorities, maneuverings for positions of advantage, are dominant elements in the sorry history of the last four years. Reparations are hardly more an issue between Germany and her joint creditors than they are a bone of contention among the creditors themselves. Each of the creditor countries appears to have been mainly concerned, first of all with small immediate gains that could be used for political window-dressing at home, and, second, with the ultimate *net* advantage secured.

My argument does not necessarily lead to the conclusion that our own claims should ultimately all be cancelled. It merely means that they should not be viewed as a separate, inviolable, and sacrosanct item, as something apart and distinct from the general structure of external and internal debts. We should be candid enough to admit that in this, as in other ways, the reparations problem is in part our problem, that it is part and parcel of the problem of the whole international debt structure and its future. We should be prepared to make whatever modifications and adjustments are necessary to bring the whole body of debt into manageable form. Along that course lie our own interests, as well as those of Europe.

QUESTIONS AND PROBLEMS FOR DISCUSSION

1. What are some of the problems which arise in connection with short-term government loans?
2. Discuss the relation of the rate of interest to the economic effects of public borrowing.
3. What are the advantages and disadvantages of perpetual bonds?
4. What are the economic and psychological effects of issuing bonds in small denominations?
5. Discuss the advantages and disadvantages of tax-free bonds.
6. External debts create problems in foreign trade and foreign exchange. What are some of these problems?
7. If the United States government owed $5,000,000,000 to England and chose to pay the amount in full, how might it be done and what would be the economic effects of the transactions?
8. Professor Pigou states that "in conceivable circumstances a nation might be able to meet internal debt up to the whole amount of its wealth without suffering any direct injury, while at the same time to meet any foreign claim at all would involve some of its members in starvation." Do you agree? Support your answer.

SUGGESTIONS FOR RESEARCH

1. The taxation of government securities.
2. Short-term loans in practice.
3. The economic aspects of Allied Debts.
4. External debts and foreign trade.
5. Perpetual bonds in theory and practice.

BIBLIOGRAPHICAL NOTE

Descriptive and analytical studies of the forms of public credit have been made by H. C. Adams, *The Science of Finance*, (New York, 1898), Pt. II, Bk. III, Chap. I, pp. 520-526; C. F. Bastable, *Public Finance*, (London, 1917), Bk. V, Chap. VI; H. L. Lutz, *Public Finance*, (New York, 1929), Chap. XXVII; W. J. Shultz, *American Public Finance and Taxation*, (New York, 1932), Chap. VII; and Paul Studenski, *Public Borrowing*, (New York, 1930), Chap. VI. Bastable, Lutz, and Shultz discuss the difference in the economic effects of forced, patriotic, and business loans. The influence of length of term of a loan is well shown by Bastable, Lutz, and Studenski. The rate of interest as a factor in the economic effects of public borrowing is ably presented by Adams. Other factors relating to terms of issue and methods of floating government loans are discussed by Bastable, Lutz, and Shultz.

For the economic aspects of tax exemption of government securities as a special problem of public credit, see C. O. Hardy, *Tax Exempt Securities and the Sur-Tax*, (New York, 1926), Chaps. III-VI; K. N. Robins, "Evils of Tax Exemption as Applied to Securities," *Proceedings, National Tax Association*, (1919), pp. 477-486; W. A. Rowe, "Tax Exemption of Government Bonds," *American Economic Review*, Vol. XVI, pp. 653-659; and E. R. A. Seligman, *Studies in Public Finance*, (New York, 1925), Chap. VII.

Material in Hugh Dalton, *Principles of Public Finance*, (London, 1932), Chaps. XXII and XXV supplements the discussion of external and internal debts which is given in this chapter. One of the many excellent treatments of the economic effects of the external debts arising out of the Great War is H. G. Moulton and Leo Pasvolsky, *War Debts and World Prosperity*, (New York, 1932).

CHAPTER XXVII

ECONOMIC EFFECTS OF PUBLIC CREDIT: THE REPAYMENT OF DEBTS

A SUCCINCT argument by Professor C. F. Bastable for the redemption of public debts runs as follows : *

A study of the conditions and limitations under which public borrowing is alone admissable naturally leads to the conclusion that the maintenance of a permanent debt ought to be avoided. If loans should be contracted only under great pressure, and to prevent the exhaustion of the agency of taxation, and if, while they exist, they act as a drag on the financial power of the State, it cannot be disputed that their speedy redemption must be eminently desirable.

A more recent statement of the case for the repayment of government obligations is that of the Colwyn Committee on Debt and Taxation. The conclusion of this Committee that a steady reduction of public debt is desirable, while given in connection with the post-war situation in England, agrees in principle with that of Professor Bastable. The reasons stated by this Committee for debt reduction are : †

(1) The maintenance and improvement of the national credit, particularly with a view to paving the way for future conversion operations ;

(2) The desirability of reducing the debt in view of the possibility of a future national emergency requiring the State to incur further borrowing :

(3) The risk of the burden of the debt charge increasing beyond the present point, should the level of prices fall in the future.

---

* C. F. Bastable, *Public Finance*, (Macmillan and Co., Ltd., London, 1917), p. 698.
† *Colwyn Report of Committee on National Debt and Taxation*, (London, 1927), p. 329.

Repudiation of public debts, on the other hand, enjoys little or no support from contemporary economists. The case against repudiation is based upon both ethical and economic considerations.* It is argued that repudiation is unethical in that it penalizes the individual who has purchased the obligations of the repudiating government, thus discriminating against him in favor of holders of sound investments. The economic objections to debt repudiation are (1) impairment of the credit of the defaulting government, and (2) in the case of external debts, danger of retaliatory action against it. This retaliation may take the form of trade discrimination, or in extreme instances, military aggression.

1. Repayment and Conversion of Public Debts

Repudiation being unwise, repayment and conversion are the principal courses of action by which a nation may alter the conditions of its indebtedness. A recent treatment of the two latter fiscal devices has been made by Dr. William Withers. His discussion follows.†

(a) The Sinking Fund: Its Form and Functions

THE INTEGRATION OF THE PRICE AND SAVINGS ASPECTS OF RETIREMENT IN RELATION TO SINKING FUND POLICY

Since the war the sinking fund has been vindicated as a means of debt retirement in both theory and practice. ‡ Of the three other most commonly discussed methods the levy on capital has now ceased to be an important issue, repudiation has only occurred in countries that were very badly off financially (even Germany having revalued her debt), and in some countries little advantage is expected to come from any future conversions. It is upon the sinking funds that the nations of the world have come again to rely for the alleviation of their debt burdens. Furthermore . . . there is not much optimism

---

* See Hugh Dalton, *Principles of Public Finance*, (George Routledge and Sons, Ltd., London, 1932), Chap. XXIII, pp. 259-262.

† Adapted from William Withers, *The Retirement of National Debts*, (Columbia University Studies, New York, 1932), Chap. XI, pp. 311-325.

‡ Eds. note : In local finance the use of serial bonds rather than sinking funds is a growing practice. The advantages generally claimed for the former are : (1) no trustees required for administration ; (2) no accumulation and reinvestment of funds necessary ; (3) no miscalculations possible since bonds mature and must be paid ; and (4) permits adjustment of redemption dates to nature of the project financed.

about fortunate changes in price or about the growth of population. What light then does the integration between the price and saving aspects of retirement throw upon sinking fund policy and the methods of retirement suggested since the war?

. . . Sinking funds have four functions: to insure payment of the debt, to make payment regular, to establish the form and character of payment and to guide the speed or rate of payment. Possibly a fifth is to maintain national credit. . . The American fund does indicate the rate of payment and establish conditions of regular payment. The same may be said of the British sinking fund provisions. In France much more is done through the sinking fund laws to insure payment. The degree of persistence in carrying out sinking fund law is greatest in the United States, less great in England, and least in France. The degree of effort exercised through law to maintain sinking fund payment is, however, in the reverse order. In the United States it was not thought necessary to establish a separate constitutional sinking fund body such as exists in France or to lump interest and retirement funds together in a fixed annual charge as in England.

The one most important function of sinking funds is to set the rate of retirement. The accomplishment of this function has been limited by the great use of the surplus in the United States and the frequent alterations of the fixed charge in Great Britain. It might appear from this that the determination of the rate of retirement is not the most important function. Those who regard the rate of retirement as the central problem, however, would be more likely to attribute this failure in the United States and Great Britain to vacillation in administrative policy. But it is more reasonable to suppose that the sinking fund should not determine the rate of retirement through the mere establishment of a given percentage or annual charge once and for all. Rather should sinking fund laws set up some mechanism by which a varying rate of retirement may be followed, and yet this variation may not be totally arbitrary. Of course there is much to be said for Pigou's opinion that no one can set a definite time limit to the payment of the debt, that the debt should not be paid off more rapidly than is convenient and that this convenience would have to be determined in the course of the payment.[1] But to leave this entirely up to "convenience" is too indefinite and has led in the past merely to the payment of surplus and this

[1] *Colwyn Report, Minutes of Evidence*, par. 6083.

in turn to no payment at all.   The common solution has been to establish a sinking fund and let "convenience" be represented by the additional appropriation of surplus.   It would seem, however, that by the estimation of the trend of savings and by a general investigation of business conditions at the time of the adoption of the sinking fund some rate of retirement might be tentatively determined.   Surplus could be applied in addition but this surplus should surely not be as large as the sinking fund.   In case the surplus is very large, the sinking fund should either be increased or the taxes lowered.

The sinking fund should not only be set up in relation to the volume of saving; it should be varied in amount as the volume of saving changes.   "Convenience" should be accounted for, but in some definite way.   Unless certain other public expenses seem obviously more important or the greater retirement of debt seems likely to cause undue financial difficulty, debt retirement should proceed more rapidly in case of an increased volume of national saving.   An index of the volume of saving might be devised.   In case this increased two per cent the fund should increase two per cent unless the Treasury could give adequate reason for not doing so.   Account should also be taken of the rate of saving.   If it was apparent that the trend of saving was not increasing, then the Treasury should seriously consider whether the sinking fund was not too large.

It is, therefore, apparent that the rate of retirement need not be set arbitrarily in the beginning and that some definiteness may be introduced by sinking fund law into the adjustment of debt payment to varying economic conditions.   In this way it may be possible to satisfy partly the demand that business conditions be considered in the rate of debt payment. This demand has been made by a great number of persons. Secretary Sherman, for example, long ago contended that the sinking fund should be allowed to lapse in bad times if replaced when good times returned.[2]   Pigou believes that debt payment should vary with good and bad times or that at least taxes for retirement should not be increased during a depression.[3]   There is, of course, the danger that politics may enter into the debt policy if the connection is not made definite by law.   Professor Seligman,[4] Mr. McKenna and the National Chamber of Trade in Great Britain also favor an adjustment

---

[2] Ross, *Sinking Funds*, p. 83 *et seq.*
[3] *Colwyn Report, Minutes of Evidence*, p. 43.
[4] Seligman, *Studies in Public Finance*, p. 80.

of the rate of payment to variations in business conditions. Witnesses for the last even suggested that retirement should be adjusted to the net savings of the nation.[5] But they treated the whole matter as though the debt funds were not returned to business and held that the capital needs of the community must be taken into account. Schuster in his testimony before the Colwyn Committee said, however, "Debt repayments through the sinking fund should be carried on continuously and quite irrespectively of considerations of good and bad trade." This he advocated in order to insure the regular and continuous retirement of the debt and because the maintenance of the sinking fund was the "best means of maintaining confidence. . ."[6] It was also declared by other witnesses that it would be difficult to anticipate periods of good and bad trade and that a suitable method of adjustment to these periods was the employment of budget surplus.[7] Professor Macgregor also holds the latter view. These objections do not preclude the possibility of some systematic modification of the sinking fund according to the variations in the rate of saving provided some surplus financing is continued. The alteration of the sinking fund could take account of the trend of saving and the surplus of cyclical variations in the conditions of business. Thus the sinking fund should be a guide to the rate of retirement, but it should not be an unintelligent guide. Some adequate and systematic relationship should be set up between the rate and volume of saving and the sinking fund.

Two plans for linking debt retirement with business conditions have been suggested. Bowley advocated the establishment of a joint sinking fund and public works fund of £100,000,000. All of it was to be spent on debt retirement during good years, but only £45,000,000 during bad years. In the latter the remaining £55,000,000 was to be spent for public works, a committee indicating, some time ahead, the nature of public works to be supplied. The second plan, that of Hobson, was merely to vary the amount of debt retirement with some index of the volume of business.

A number of questions arise in connection with sinking funds which the preceding pages may help to answer. The first of these is: how may the function of guiding the speed of payment and insuring payment both be achieved? The Colwyn Report stated that the sinking fund should be both a guide and a minimum below which debt retirement should

5 *Colwyn Report, Minutes of Evidence,* p. 246.
6 *Colwyn Report, Minutes of Evidence,* p. 9.
7 *Colwyn Report,* evidence of Coöperative Congress, p. 304.

not fall. But it is hard to establish such a minimum unless borrowing for sinking fund purposes is prohibited. Borrowing to pay sinking funds has occurred in England, France and the United States since the war, but in the United States only in the most recent years (1930–31). In the United States and England sinking funds may be guides but they certainly do not establish a minimum amount to be paid for debt retirement in any real sense. Mr. Gillett, speaking before the House of Commons in regard to a sinking fund law, said,

As far as the principle of accumulation is concerned there is no doubt that after it has run for a certain number of years, the favorable position created is such that, human nature being what it is, there is always the danger of those lapses from financial virtue which have been so properly stigmatized as raids. I cannot myself visualize accurately a situation where the government in 1978 will be providing £355 millions for the service of the debt while knowing that the government of 1979 will not have to provide a penny. That is hardly how it will work. But still I believe it will be a good guide within the lifetime of many of us here, if we push ahead with a figure of £355,000,000 a year.[8]

Whatever one may think of laws to prevent borrowing for sinking fund purposes, they are no longer popular with the leading nations of the world and if debt payment is to be enforced it will not be enforced by this method.

More popular since the war have been the use of special funds and the attachment of special sources of revenue. Germany and Great Britain have used special sinking funds since the war and some economists have advocated them on theoretical grounds. Dalton, for example, thought that special funds would be more difficult to raid because in order to meet the needs of the nation borrowing would be necessary and this would cause much adverse publicity.[9] He preferred this method of enforcing retirement to the attachment of special revenues. France represents the outstanding post-war example of such an attachment.[10] Without discussing the old argument on these two measures and without repeating again our discussion of a third, namely constitutional independence of the sinking fund, it can be said that their employment arises in the main from two conditions, a low state of political *savoir faire* and heavy taxation relative to the growth of national income. If the debt is retired in proper relation to the growth of saving, at least one reason for these measures will have been

[8] Parliamentary Debates, *Official Report*, vol. 219, p. 563.
[9] *Colwyn Report*, p. 404.
[10] Eds. note. Withers covers this point in Chap. IV of his study.

withdrawn. The other reason for their use is a matter for education to remove. If before this is accomplished the use of these measures is found successful in practice, their use will have to depend upon the conditions present at given times and places.

Another proposal made in England to insure payment is the conversion of the debt into terminable annuities. In Mr. J. St. Loe Strachey's plan these were to run for one hundred years. The Colwyn Committee expressed their conclusions about Mr. Strachey's plan as follows: "It (the plan) resolves itself into a question whether the demand for a security of this type might be such as to enable the government to issue on terms advantageous to itself. We ourselves are not very hopeful." [11] Cannan also favors the conversion of the whole debt into annuities, as Stafford Northecote tried to do in 1875. On the whole, however, both England and France have made relatively little use of annuities and they are apparently no longer an important means of debt retirement.

PUBLIC AND PRIVATE CREDIT CONDITIONS IN RELATION TO SINKING FUND POLICY

A SECOND question with regard to sinking funds is, how should their operations be related to public and private credit conditions? The improvement of public credit has of course been considered one of the most important functions of the sinking fund for a long time. Plehn pointed out that the earliest American sinking funds performed this function even though they did not succeed in retiring the existing debt.[12] Witnesses before the Colwyn Committee asserted that the maintenance and improvement of national credit was one of the main purposes of the sinking fund. Pigou believed that repayment would enable the government to borrow more cheaply. Stamp thought that the price of government bonds would be raised by a plan of consistent debt retirement, that it was desirable to remove debts in order to meet future emergencies, and that taxation for removal should precede the emergencies. It is apparent then that many economists have praised the effect of sinking funds in improving the conditions of public credit. It is, however, possible that too much emphasis may be put upon the improvement of public credit. If taxation for retirement has a tendency to stimulate the accumulation of capital, this will tend to lower the loan price of capital to the

---

[11] *Colwyn Report*, p. 320.
[12] Plehn, *Introduction to Public Finance*, 3rd ed., pp. 410-411.

government and to the general public. As a matter of fact, the public credit is frequently the effect of the more important factor, i.e. the accumulation of capital. The great loan operations of the United States should show the enormous potentialities of public credit to meet emergencies and should raise the question of whether or not the importance of rapid debt payment to preserve the public credit for emergencies has not been over-emphasized. . .

In so far as [debt] retirement stimulates saving the rate of interest will have a tendency to fall. In one sense the burden of debt may be reduced at a progressive rate even without a cumulative sinking fund. It thus appears that if taxation is devised in such a way as to stimulate rather than retard capital accumulation and if every effort is made to keep the rates of interest paid by the government as low as general credit conditions warrant, the general character of the relationship between the sinking fund and public and private credit will be satisfactory.

THE FORM OF THE SINKING FUND

A THIRD question relates to the form of the sinking fund. Should it be cumulative or non-cumulative, based on a percentage or on a given absolute figure? It should be obvious that in one year the interest and the sinking fund may be lumped together to represent the total burden of debt. If during the first years after a war a nation can support this burden it should be able to do this in later years when times are better. The sinking fund should therefore always cumulate the interest of bonds already paid. This policy has been adopted in the sinking funds of both the United States and Great Britain since the World War. As we pointed out above, the sinking fund might well be made greater as the volume of saving increases. It might also be desirable to include the interest saved by conversion or refunding. Where there is a fixed annual debt charge, as in England, this sort of cumulation is provided. In regard to the percentage base, it would seem that where a debt has been created for unproductive purposes or for a capital investment of indefinite maturity, it would be best to suit payments to general economic conditions and not to a certain percentage of the capital of the debt. A definite amount representing a certain proportion of national savings and determined in the beginning by a careful investigation would seem most reasonable.

THE SINKING FUND AND CHANGING PRICES

A FOURTH question refers to changes in prices. What account should the sinking fund take of these changes? There should be two important aspects to the answer of this question. These refer to price changes in which the debt plays a part and to price changes independent of debt payment. Since the burdens of debt arise from deflation rather than merely from falling prices, it is necessary, . . . to investigate the causes of falling prices in order to determine whether deflation is occurring. Debt retirement should be retarded if it is plain that it is causing deflation. Where the deflation is not due to debt retirement, should the rate of retirement be adjusted to the deflation? Several possible modes of adjustment have been suggested. One of these is that the amount of payment should be stabilized on a commodity basis. Glenday has suggested that if the price level falls the amount to be paid back should decrease.[13] Keynes has a plan of issuing debt in such a form that the interest and capital are payable in a fixed commodity value. Professor Hall also believes that the fall in prices must be taken into account in determining the amount of debt payment. Dalton favors the issue of debt with a rate of interest variable with the changing price level. This plan, he believes, would make it unnecessary either to decrease the amount of debt during times of falling prices or to issue a greater quantity of paper money in order to prevent a decline in prices. The objections to a variable rate of interest are, he thinks, rapidly decreasing.[14] It seems reasonable to conclude . . . that since falling prices do not necessarily represent increased debt burden and since there are objections to variable interest and debt capital, debt policy should advocate measures to prevent or retard deflation rather than tie debt issues to a fixed price level.

Although measures to prevent deflation may be advisable, the conscious use of inflation to pay the debt would not be wise. . . The outstanding example of this practice was provided by Germany in 1923. Alfred Hoare and a Mr. Stilwell have advocated inflation to remove debt in England. Hoare advocated that the government build up a treasury surplus by the issue of paper money and then convert the debt at a lower rate of interest by offering to pay it off in this money. His scheme was first expounded in an issue of *Sperling's Journal* as early as October, 1918. Hartley Withers objected to his

13 *Colwyn Report, Minutes of Evidence,* par. 4777.
14 Dalton, *Public Finance,* p. 180 *et seq.*

plan on the ground that it would penalize thrift.[15]   Withers
also discussed Stilwell's "Great Plan, How to Pay for the War,"
which consisted of a large issue of inconvertible paper.   Of
these plans he says: "Not only would they defraud the debt
holder by paying him off in currency enormously depreciated
by the multiplication that would be involved; but they would
also by that depreciation throw the burden of the debt on the
shoulders of the general consumer through a further disastrous
rise in prices. . ."[16]

Another interesting aspect of the relation of retirement to
deflation arises out of the fact that they may represent conflicting aims in public policy.   In Great Britain deflation has
been pursued as an end in itself.   The prestige of returning
the pound to its pre-war rate of exchange has, according to
some economists, cost her a great deal.   M. E. Robinson, for
example, believes that deflation was accomplished at the expense of the needs of tax and debt reduction.[17]   In an earlier
chapter it was seen how ready even a Labour chancellor of the
exchequer was to sacrifice debt reduction to the maintenance
of the gold standard at pre-war exchange.   The choice of these
objectives depends upon national preferences but it seems to
the writer that from the standpoint of the public debt a case
might have been made for devaluation in the early post-war
years. . .

(b) The Reduction of Debt Burden through Conversion and Refunding

IT is seldom possible for public officials to take advantage
of conversion unless the market rate of interest has fallen for
government loans and lower interest rates will be accepted.
This fall may not necessarily be due to debt retirement, but,
as was pointed out above, it may be.   At any rate the advantage due to conversion or refunding is not due essentially to
conversion but to the fall in the rate of interest that makes
it possible.   Conversions are not so much influences as effects.
Furthermore, in post-war debt history relatively small use has
been made of conversions.   This has resulted to a large extent
from the fact that the advantages from conversions do not
appear to be very great.   Conversion was used in both France
and England largely to improve the state of debt maturities.
Since 1926, in England, at least, conversions have appeared to
have very little further potentiality for the reduction of debt

[15] Withers, *War-time Financial Problems*, chap. xv.
[16] *Ibid.*, p. 222.
[17] Robinson, *Public Finance*, p. 160.

interest. Dalton in his testimony before the Colwyn Committee said that in the ten years after 1924 the following amounts and their respective rates of interest would fall due, totalling altogether £4106 millions: £165 millions at 5½ per cent, £2698 millions at 5 per cent, £134 millions at 4½ per cent, £256 millions at 4 per cent, £63 millions at 3½ per cent and £16 millions at 3 per cent. Since the rate of interest could not be expected to fall much below 4½ per cent for such loans he thought that only about £15 millions annually could be saved by conversions. Actually more has been saved, but only by the process of conversion with increased capital. Somewhat more hopeful is Shirras, who has estimated that if the British debt could be reduced to a three per cent basis, £100 millions of interest could be saved a year.[18] Rates of interest in Great Britain have not allowed the country to make such great savings.

Refunding in both France and the United States has, however, very considerably reduced the burden of high interest rates. This has been especially true of the French short term debt. . . The history of the reduction of interest in the United States is given in writings dealing more directly with the post-war history of debt management.[19] On the whole it seems that conversion has lost in popularity and that the American methods have gained.

There are, as Shirras and others have pointed out, three factors involved in the conversion of debt: prices, interest and taxes. Many economists have coöperated in the course of time to build up a number of criteria for conversion. Among these are: the capital of the debt should not be increased by conversions; conversions should be simple; they should be accompanied by the guarantee of no immediate reconversion; they should lead to consolidation and uniformity of debt and help to reduce the floating debt; and they should help to establish convenient maturities.[20] The Colwyn Committee and most of the witnesses appearing before it supported these criteria of conversion. Cannan and Pigou were particularly outspoken in their criticism of conversion above par. In English Parliamentary debates, Pethick-Lawrence and Dalton have interrogated the government to learn how much increase in capital has resulted from conversion above par. It thus appears that although most of the traditional criteria of conversion have

---

18 Shirras, *Public Finance*, p. 537.

19 See Hendricks, *Federal Debt, 1919–1929* and Love, R. A., *Federal Financing*.

20 See Shirras, *Public Finance*; Bastable, *Public Finance*; Matsushita, *Economic Effects of Public Debts*; Leveque, *Les Conversions de dettes publiques*.

been reaffirmed since the war, that most emphasized in theory, and most ignored in practice, is conversion at par. Conversion at par, it seems to the writer, takes on a new significance in the light of the previous discussion. So long as the policies indicated in regard to the sinking fund are followed, the burdens of debt may perhaps be reduced to a minimum, but if the government is forced by the nature of its loans to pay an excessive rate of interest, a new and needless element of burden is injected into the situation. The function of conversion and refunding is to remove as completely as possible this arbitrary element. When the price of government bonds considerably exceeds par the presence of this element may be indicated. Leveque, who has written a comprehensive theoretical work on conversions, concludes that conversions are best at par because they do not increase capital, controvert the borrower's interests or impede future conversions. All of these arguments are sound, but still more important is the fact that if through conversion or refunding bonds are kept near par, the arbitrary element of excessive interest is kept out of the burden of debt. Leroy-Beaulieu thought that every conversion should be made with view to a succeeding one. This means in terms of our interpretation that no conversion should prevent a future adjustment of government to market interest rates. A close contact with the money market is required. This adjustment would be hampered not only by inefficient conversions but by the original issue of the bonds at a discount. Long ago H. C. Adams also pointed out the need of a technique to keep debts at par. Conversions constitute one of these techniques and they should not be used in such a way as to prevent parity.

2. INTERNAL WAR DEBT AND A SPECIAL LEVY

A SPECIAL levy as a method of debt repayment or reduction received considerable attention following the Great War. A comparison of the economic aspects of this form of taxation with those of orthodox finance has been made by Professor A. C. Pigou. His comparison appears below.*

IN the rush and difficulty of a modern war statesmen are certain, for political reasons, to rely predominantly upon some form of borrowing — we need not now distinguish between normal loans and loans through bank credits — rather than upon taxation. This was the course followed in every country —

* Adapted from A. C. Pigou, *A Study in Public Finance*, (Macmillan and Co., Ltd., London, 1928), Part III, Chap. VI, pp. 286-307.

even in the United States of America — during the Great War. It is a course that leaves as its aftermath a very difficult financial problem. When a country has a large internally held national debt there are four lines of action open to it : (1) repudiation ; (2) provision for the service of the debt by currency expansion ; (3) a large special levy ; (4) provision for the service of the debt out of annual taxes. When, for any reason, political or other, method (4) is excluded and the choice is between the other three, the case for a special levy is enormously stronger than it is when method (4) is not excluded. In England method (4) is actually at work, which proves it to be feasible, and, therefore, the case for and against a special levy stands on a different plane from what it would occupy if our national debt were, say, two or three times as large as it is. I shall postulate a situation of this kind, where repudiation and finance by currency expansion are both ruled out, and the choice lies between quick repayment of large masses of debt by a special levy and the service of debt out of taxes over a long series of years. I assume that, whichever plan is adopted, the intention will be to distribute the burden among people of different degrees of wealth in a roughly similar manner.

GRADUAL DEBT REPAYMENT VERSUS QUICK REPAYMENT BY A SINGLE LARGE EFFORT

To give concreteness to my discussion I shall relate it to the actual debt of the United Kingdom. Foreign debt, the service of which *may* perhaps be nearly provided for out of payments to us in respect of our own claims on foreign governments, I shall leave out of account. As a convenient round figure, we may put the effective debt of Great Britain and Northern Ireland at some £6000 million, all held internally. With a debt of this magnitude at 4¾ per cent, so long as none of the principal is repaid, £275 million would have to be raised every year to provide the interest. Nobody proposes, however, that the principal shall be left outstanding as a debt for ever. A large national debt weakens the financial position of a State and makes it difficult for it to raise money to meet any emergency with which it may be confronted. Consequently, it has always been the policy of prudent governments in time of peace steadily to reduce debt. When the British debt, in the years before the war, stood at the comparatively low figure of £700 million, there was no dispute about this. Every year more revenue was raised than was needed for current expenditure and the payment of debt interest, and the balance was devoted, through the agency of a sinking fund, to reducing the principal of the debt. It is agreed that a policy at least as strict as this must be followed now. In addition to revenue for interest payment further revenue must be raised for the repayment of principal. This means that at first we shall require, say, 310 millions annually, and then, as the debt is gradually paid off, a smaller annual amount. That is "orthodox" financial policy. In contrast with its stands the rival policy of a large immediate special levy to redeem debt. That policy agrees with orthodox policy in refusing to allow the principal of the debt to remain outstanding permanently. It differs from it only as regards the period over which repayment should be spread. Whereas orthodox policy would repay a small fraction of the principal debt every year and would complete repayment in a period of fifty or a hundred years, the policy of a special levy would repay a very large fraction of the principal — if it were practicable, it would repay the whole — by a single tremendous effort. This is the fundamental issue, to which all questions of the form and method of a special levy, if it is decided to make one, are subordinate. Is it, on the whole, more to the national advantage to discharge a great slice of debt by a single levy at once, and so to do away with the obligation to pay interest on it in the future, or to repay the debt gradually and face large interest charges for a long term of years? This issue it is the business of the present chapter to examine. I shall arrange my discussion in three parts: I shall study first the effect of a special levy policy without reference either to equity or to administrative technique; secondly, distributive fairness by itself; thirdly, technique by itself.

THE ALLEGED ANALOGY BETWEEN INTERNALLY HELD NATIONAL DEBT AND DEBT DUE FROM INDIVIDUALS

BEFORE this programme is attacked, however, it is desirable to clear out of the way a popular argument which rests on misunderstanding. The problem to be faced, it is said, has an exact analogy in individual life. A man in debt to the extent of £6000 borrowed at 4¾ per cent has to choose between paying interest and reducing the principal of his debt slowly — orthodox finance — and paying off the whole debt at once — the policy of the special levy. It is impossible to decide which of these two courses would be more advantageous in any general or absolute sense. The right choice depends on the circumstances of the debtor. If, however, he has contracted the debt in resisting an attack by a powerful neighbour, and if, in the course of the contest, his resources have been strained to breaking-point, the issue is not doubtful. He *must* repay gradually,

for the simple reason that he *cannot* repay at once. The United
Kingdom, the argument runs, is in exactly this position. Impoverished as we are by the losses of the war and its aftermath, the enormous payments, which a special levy would
involve, are wholly beyond our means. This analogy, plausible
as it sounds, misses a vital distinction. Whereas the individual we have been imagining owes the whole of his debt to
other people, the British nation owes the predominant part
to itself. So far, no doubt, as it is indebted to foreigners, its
position is analogous to that of an individual debtor. But,
so far as it is indebted to British citizens — and it is this aspect
of the debt with which we are here concerned — its position
is quite different. To repay debt of this kind involves no
drain on the resources of the community as a whole, because,
though one part of the community transfers resources to another part, the community as a whole pays nothing. It
follows that, whereas the impoverishment of an individual
may make it impossible for him to pay off the principal of a
debt due from him, and the impoverishment of a community
may have the same effect on it so far as its debt is held by foreigners, this impoverishment cannot make impossible the repayment by the community of a debt held by its own members.
This becomes obvious when we reflect that the community can,
if it chooses, impose on each of its members a levy exactly
equivalent to that member's holding of State debt. Thus, the
analogy between internally held national debt and debt due
from individuals is not a valid one.

THE EFFECT OF DRASTIC REDUCTION OF INTERNAL NATIONAL DEBT ON PRODUCTIVE ACTIVITY

LET us then consider the effects that may be expected from the
imposition of a special levy to take over part of the tasks of
orthodox debt finance. . . Distributional considerations and
difficulties of technique being ignored, the raising of revenue
coupled with its expenditure in debt repayment implies some
net sacrifice. For, apart from lump-sum taxation, which [is
not] feasible on any important scale, all tax announcements reduce the supply of work, and so check production; [1] whence it
follows that the damage done by raising a revenue R, expressed
in money, must be greater than R. If the rates of taxation in
a given country are high, not only absolutely, but also relatively to those ruling in other countries, the damage will be
intensified by a tendency on the part of some rich people to
take themselves and their capital abroad. When to income tax

[1] See Pigou, *A Study in Public Finance*, Part II, Chap. V, 2.

and death duties are added various sorts of commodity taxes, there will follow, besides a diminution in the quantity of productive effort, a disturbance in its direction — a diversion of resources from the sorts of production that people would favour if left to themselves — and, therewith, in general, a further element of real loss. It follows that, whatever the amount of the internal debt, some advantage to national well-being will follow if it can be eliminated by a process which does not itself involve a real cost. There is a further presumption that the advantage of eliminating a large internal debt would be more than proportionately greater than that of eliminating a small one ; because, while a certain amount of money can be raised by taxation of a kind and degree that is only slightly obstructive, as more and more money is required, resort must be had to worse and worse kinds of taxation and to more and more oppressive rates. There can, therefore, be no reasonable doubt that the elimination, by some costless process which did not modify distribution, of, say, £3000 million, the amount proposed under the Labour Party's Capital Levy scheme, of the existing internal debt of Great Britain would increase our national well-being.

This merely qualitative result is, however, of little help as a guide to policy. The process of elimination would not in fact be costless, and we need, therefore, before we can decide whether it is worth attempting, to form at least a rough idea of the *scale* of the gain which might be looked for. Now, if the contention . . . that the supply of work is in general fairly rigid, be accepted, it will follow that large sums can be raised by direct taxation for the service of internal debt with very much less damage to work and enterprise, and so to economic welfare, than is implied in the conventional complaints of business men about the oppressive effects of such taxation upon industry. In the matter of saving it is even arguable that the net effect of debt service transfers — presumed to include some annual repayment of principal — will, when distributional as well as announcement effects are taken into account, be favourable rather than the reverse, since the repaid principal will almost certainly be devoted to new investment, while the funds to make repayment will be provided at least in part by economies in consumption.[2] *   Hence, even though the repayment of £3000 million of internal debt, implying the remission of

---

* Eds. note : By announcement effects, Professor Pigou means effects on human conduct. For a discussion of the announcement and distribution aspects of taxation, see Pigou, *op. cit.*, Part II, Chaps. IV, V and VI.

[2] See Pigou, *op. cit.*, Part II, Chap. IV, 10 footnote.

some £150 million of annual revenue now required for the service of it, *i.e.,* half of the present yield of our income tax and super-tax, enabled us to cut down rates of income tax and super-tax by a half, the net benefit would be on a very much smaller scale than is popularly supposed. High rates of direct taxation — when the proceeds are retained inside the country — are not really very damaging, and even a substantial cut in them is not, therefore, very beneficial.

There is also a further important consideration. To remove by repayment of internal debt the need for revenue equal to half the yield of our present income tax and super-tax would not enable us to reduce the rates of these taxes in anything approaching that proportion : and a like proposition holds good of death duties. The reason is that, under British methods of assessment, interest on war loan is assessable to income tax and war loan holdings to death duties ; so that repayment of internal debt, by wiping out this income and associated capital, would reduce correspondingly the amount of income and of capital in respect of which income tax and death duties are subsequently levied. *Prima facie,* indeed, this consideration only suggests that the cut in tax rates made possible by the repayment of internal debt through a special levy would be *a little less* proportionately than the cut in revenue requirements. This suggestion is, however, a grave understatement. It ignores the fact that, since any special levy for debt repayment is certain in practice to be steeply graduated, the assessable income and capital destroyed by it would, in the main, consist of income and capital subject to high rates of super-tax and death duties. This matter has been studied in detail by Sir Josiah Stamp. Writing in 1923, and basing himself on a levy scaled in the manner proposed by the Labour Party, he concluded, as the result of a careful and detailed study : "For some time to come, the total annual loss of duties would be in the neighbourhood of £90 million to £98 million, and, as the saving in revenue (consequent upon debt repayment) was put at about £140 million, the net gain lies between 42 and 50 millions. In other words, approximately two-thirds of the levy is wanted to 'pay its own keep'" ; [3] and its effect in enabling rates of taxation in the future to be reduced is only one-third of what it seemed likely to be at first sight. The income tax could not, in short, in consequence of a £3000 million levy, be reduced by more than 1s. in the £. A more recent calculation, carried out by the Board of Inland Revenue for the Committee on the

[3] *Current Problems in Finance and Government,* p. 265.

National Debt and Taxation, is in close agreement, allowing for changes in the rates of taxation as between the dates of the two estimates, with that of Sir Josiah Stamp.[4]

THE PROSPECTS OF AN AUTOMATIC FALL IN THE RATES OF TAX NECESSARY FOR THE SERVICE OF THE BRITISH DEBT UNDER THE GRADUAL REPAYMENT METHOD

EVEN this, however, is not all. The aforesaid £50 million of budget savings can only be regarded as net savings on the assumption that, were methods of orthodox finance to be continued instead of a special levy, the burden of the debt, allowance being made for its gradual repayment under a sinking fund, would remain what it is now. If there is reason to believe that, under orthodox methods, relief would soon be forthcoming to the extent of, say, 5d. in the £ on income tax, the net benefit to be assigned to a special levy policy is represented by a reduction in income tax per £, not of a shilling, but of something intermediate between a shilling and 7d. Hence, it is important to inquire whether in fact, under orthodox finance, any substantial relief is to be looked for. Under this head three principal factors call for study.

First, it is often urged that, as the world in general, and this country in particular, recover from the effects of the war, the rate of interest at which it is possible to borrow money will fall : that, therefore, the government may hope to effect a conversion of its long-term debt, replacing, perhaps, 5 per cent obligations by obligations of 4½ per cent or even 4 per cent. In so far as it succeeds in doing this, the amount of revenue, which will be needed to provide interest on any given amount of war debt, will be proportionately reduced, and, consequently, less high rates of taxation will suffice. This consideration is obviously relevant. But it is very difficult to determine how important it is quantitatively. A 1 per cent cut in interest rates would represent a gross saving of some £50 million a year, or a shilling off the income tax. In view of the long-dating of most government borrowing, and of the fact that conversions, no less than a special levy, commit ravages on the future yield of any given rate of income tax, it is certain that no saving on that scale would be possible even after the lapse of a long term of years. In the course of the next decade it would be unreasonable to look to a saving from true conversions — conversions which purchase a reduction of present interest merely by

[4] Cf. *Report of the Committee on National Debt and Taxation*, p. 254.

the offer of higher ultimate capital payments are not true conversions — of more than a few million £s annually.[5]

Secondly, in spite of the prolonged period of post-war difficulty, there is ground for hope that the productive power of
this country will continue to increase in the future as it has
done in the past. Increased productivity will involve increased
incomes, and so, it is argued, will make it possible to raise the
same revenue as now by means of much lower rates of taxation.
There is in this contention an important element of truth; but
some qualification is necessary. Plainly, if our national debt
were contracted in terms of commodities, an increase — to take
an extreme case, a doubling — of the productivity of the United
Kingdom *must* make it easier to budget for the annual debt
charges. Whereas, before the improvement, these charges absorbed, say, one-twelfth part of the real income of the people,
after it they might absorb, say, one twenty-fourth part; and
the rates of taxation associated with them might be roughly
halved. But the national debt is contracted in terms, not of
commodities, but of money. This complicates the issue. If
increased production has no effect in reducing prices, money
incomes will increase in the same proportion as production increases, and the rates of taxation needed to yield a given revenue will be diminished to exactly the same extent as they
would be under a system of payment in kind. In fact, however, an increase of production tends, other things being equal,
to cause a fall in prices, and if, as is to be expected, the increase
is not confined to this country, but is worldwide, a very considerable fall. But, when prices fall, a given volume of production is represented by a smaller money income. If, for
example, production doubles, but at the same time prices fall
by a quarter, the sum of real incomes will be doubled, but the
sum of money incomes will only be increased to one and a
half times the former amount. This does not prevent the increased productivity from having its full effect in lowering the
rates of taxation needed to finance *normal government expenditure,* because a government, which still wishes to buy the same
quantity of things and services as before, will now require only
three-quarters as much money revenue. But the position is different as regards *government expenditure on debt charges.*
The money revenue needed to meet these is the same as it was
before. Real incomes all round have been doubled, but money

5 The Committee on National Debt and Taxation (Majority Report), after a
careful study of the position, conclude : "We are of opinion that the review we
have made of the possibilities of savings from conversions does not justify the
placing of any great reliance upon such operations as a means of effecting a
really appreciable mitigation in the early future" (p. 67).

incomes have only increased in the proportion of 3 to 2. Consequently, the rates of taxation required to finance war debt will not be halved, but only reduced in this latter proportion. It should be added that an increase in productivity up to double its existing amount in any short period would be a very exceptional occurrence, for it appears that in recent times the average increase has been about 3 per cent per annum.

There remains a third consideration pointing in a sense opposite to the above. As a consequence of the war, the value of gold in terms of things has greatly fallen throughout the world; in other words, gold prices have everywhere greatly risen. It may be that in future years gold prices, which are, of course, now equivalent to sterling prices, will, through the operation of causes acting on the side of currency, move, by slow degrees, nearer to the pre-war level than, on the average of slumps and booms, they stand now. If a fall of prices due to currency causes comes about, the money incomes, representing given real incomes, of the people must fall correspondingly. Hence, in order to raise a given money revenue to meet debt charges, the government will have to impose rates of taxation higher — perhaps much higher — than are required now. The heart of the matter can be set out in a crude statement thus: if prices are halved through currency causes, the tax-payers will have to pay to fund-holders the equivalent of twice as many things as they have to pay now: fund-holders will gain and tax-rates will increase to exactly the same extent as they would have done if prices had remained constant and all war obligations had been doubled in amount. The imposition now of a special levy to wipe out debt would obviate this danger. If general prices are due to fall seriously, this is a very important matter. The future of prices cannot, however, be forecast with any confidence. The Committee on National Debt and Taxation conclude: "We think that the evidence is sufficient to indicate that present conditions do not point to any very strong or definite movement in general prices, such as would be required to affect in any important degree the case for or against a capital levy."[6] Even this guarded statement is, perhaps, over-confident.

It is plainly impossible to measure statistically the three factors considered in the preceding paragraphs. They are all exceedingly uncertain. *Probably,* however, no one of them is of large significance. It, therefore, seems a reasonable, as it is, beyond doubt, the only practicable policy to set them off against one another, in effect assuming, in the absence of

[6] *Report,* p. 258.

knowledge, that they roughly balance. If we do this, we shall conclude, on the basis of Sir Josiah Stamp's analysis [as mentioned above] that the real effect of wiping out £3000 million of internal debt would be to allow of a cut of about 1s. in the £ off income tax or some equivalent cut off other taxes, and so to increase economic welfare to the small extent which we were led to contemplate prior to the analysis of the present section.

ARGUMENTS AGAINST THE POLICY OF A SPECIAL LEVY FROM THE POINT OF VIEW OF ITS INDIRECT EFFECTS ON PRODUCTION

AGAINST this benefit from the *consequences* of a special levy there have to be set any ill effects that may be attributable to the levy itself. It is sometimes argued that, since a single levy to wipe out debt must be enormously larger than the contribution of any single year under the orthodox system, the greater size of the levy would cancel the benefit of its less frequent imposition. This contention is, as it stands, invalid. A special levy to wipe out debt must be assessed on the basis of existing facts, on the capital that people have now, or on the income that they have now, or, at all events, by reference to some objective criterion that is known now. Consequently, whatever different individuals have to pay — it does not matter whether they have to pay at once or are allowed to pay in instalments — is fixed independently of their future conduct. Thus, a special levy of, say, 200 per cent of a man's current income is roughly equivalent in yield to a permanent income tax of 10 per cent. But, whereas the permanent 10 per cent tax implies that one-tenth of whatever he may get in the future by work or saving will be taken by the government, under the 200 per cent single levy, he will have to pay a definite amount, fixed once and for all; and, however much he may increase his income in the future, he will not have to pay anything more. Unless, therefore, people are afraid of further levies, the levy plan cannot do damage in the way contemplated. It may, indeed, be answered that the imposition of a large special levy for the purpose of paying off debt will create an expectation that it will be repeated, not merely to wipe off any debt that the first levy may have left standing, but also, it may be, for purposes not connected with debt redemption at all. This expectation will discourage people from saving and so adding to the capital stock of the country, and this check to capital will react injuriously on productivity. The injury wrought in this way will, it is urged, be very great. It cannot, moreover, be prevented by any assurance of the Cabinet, or even of Parliament, that a repetition of the levy is not contemplated, because no government can effectively bind its successors. There is force in this argument. But it is open to an effective rejoinder. So long as a "capital levy" forms a plank in the programme of an important political party, the fear that a levy will be imposed exists already. It is even arguable that, when once a levy had actually been made, people would feel that things were settled, at all events for a considerable time, and would, therefore, be actually less fearful of the future than they are now. This objection to a special levy is not, therefore, very formidable.

A second line of argument sometimes adopted is as follows. Hitherto, we have proceeded on the tacit assumption that government policy as to expenditure in the future would not be altered as an indirect consequence of repaying internal debt through a special levy. It may be urged that in fact policy will be altered — and that in an injurious manner. When the annual revenue needed to provide interest and sinking fund on the debt has been reduced, the result will be, not lessened taxation, but increased extravagance on the part of the government. Having found that it is possible to maintain, for example, an income tax at a standard rate of 4s. in the £, the government will merely use the saving on debt service as an excuse for more spending; so that in the end, instead of the levy being a substitute for high annual taxes, it will turn out to have been an addition to them! This argument is, from a practical standpoint, a very important one. There can be no doubt that, when so large an amount of revenue has to be raised that the tax system is strained, this fact strengthens the hands of the opponents of public wastefulness. The argument that "the country cannot afford unnecessary officials," and so forth, has a greater backing of votes when the budget is 800 millions than when it is 200 millions. It is true that against this must be set the attitude of mind of the spending departments themselves. With a budget of 1000 millions, such a sum as, say, 10 millions seems a bagatelle, whereas, with a 200 million budget, it is a grave matter. This consideration is, however, outweighed by that just set out. To wipe out £3000 million of internal debt would certainly, on the whole, weaken the country's defence against government extravagance. This, however, is not the complete case. Not all sorts of government expenditure are waste. A government may easily be accused of extravagance because it has increased its expenditure on educational services, the payment of old age pensions, or other socially ameliorative enterprises. The cry, "We cannot afford

this," may, in short, be directed against good things as well as
against bad. It may even happen that it is more effective
against the good things : that the Treasury, for example, has
greater success in vetoing a 10 million increase in educational
charges than in clipping, to the extent of 10 millions, the wings
of some unduly grandiose ministerial establishment. This is
a real danger. There are, of course, limits to the extent to
which it is for the national advantage for the government to
spend money on social betterment. But the limits are chiefly,
though not entirely, dependent on the proportion between the
real income of the country and the real, or exhaustive, expenditure which it undertakes through the agency of the government.
So far as the budget is swollen by charges connected with internal debt, budget expenditure does not correspond to this
real expenditure, because . . . money raised to meet these
charges is not spent in any ordinary sense, but is merely transferred from one group of citizens to another. This fact not
being generally realised, there is a presumption that the existence of large transfer expenditure to finance internal debt
will cause expenditure on social betterment to be checked more
than it ought to be. Hence, if it should happen that new government expenditure is undertaken in consequence of the relief to the budget brought about by debt repayment, it is
gratuitous to assume that it will all be mere waste. Some of
it, at least, is likely to be expenditure which ought to be undertaken, but has not been undertaken hitherto because of the
technical difficulty of enlarging an already enormous budget,
coupled with the inability of the public to understand the distinction between taxation for exhaustive expenditure and taxation for interest on internal debt. It is true that good
government expenditure, equally with bad, involves a forcing
up of tax rates. But, since good expenditure is, almost by
definition, expenditure the advantage of which is greater than
the disadvantage involved in raising the money for it, this
increase of rates cannot be taken to cancel the original lowering of the rates for which a levy is responsible. The whole of
that lowering must be counted to the levy for righteousness,
even though the country decides, after the lowering has been
accomplished, to put rates up again in a cause that it considers
worth the damage to production that high rates involve. The
case for keeping debt unrepaid, as a means of dragooning
spendthrift governments, is thus not made out.

A further objection to the device of a special levy is based
on the dislocating effects likely to be produced by the actual
process of collecting the very large sum that the levy contem-

plates. Upon this matter there has been considerable misapprehension. It has been asserted, for example, that any levy
plan necessarily involves withdrawing an enormous amount of
capital from industry, thus robbing it of its means of life. This
is not so. Industrial capital consists of factories, machines,
materials, and the stores of goods out of which real wages come.
None of these are withdrawn from industry by a special levy.
The utmost that can happen is that so much purchasing power
is taken by the government from one set of people (the payers
of the levy) and handed over to another set of people (holders of
war loan) inside the same country. This has no direct effect
on the supply of capital to industry as a whole. So much being
granted, it is next argued that working capital would, nevertheless, have to be withdrawn in large masses from *particular
industrial concerns,* that this capital would probably not be
immediately replaced, and that, therefore, many concerns might
be forced to close down. This argument is more substantial
than the other. It points to a real difficulty. But the difficulty
is much smaller than the argument suggests. The reason is
that the main part of industry, in this country at all events,
is in the hands of public companies, and that these companies,
not being subject to the levy (though, of course, their shareholders are subject to it), cannot suffer any withdrawal of
capital. There remain private concerns. So far as the owners of these possess resources outside their business — war stock,
for example, that is not serving as security for loans — sufficient
to meet the levy upon them, their business need not suffer.
On the strength of an *ad hoc* investigation made for them by
the Board of Trade the Committee on National Debt and
Taxation write : "It seems safe to conclude that, in the case
of private trading concerns (including private limited companies), the assets which proprietors could pledge for bank
advances are, in the aggregate, far in excess of those actually
so employed." [7] None the less, there must, of course, be a
number of firms practically the whole of whose resources are
locked up in their business, either directly or as collateral for
loans. If such firms had to meet a large levy all at once, they
might be broken, and their business largely destroyed. For
such firms it would be necessary to make special provision.
This could be done by permitting the Treasury, when good
cause was shown, to accept payment (with interest) in instalments spread over a definite number of years. There is no
reason, and, indeed, it would be very undesirable, that this
method of payment should become the normal one. But it

[7] *Report*, p. 271.

might appropriately be used for the relief of hard cases. In
like manner, for imposts, if any such were included in the
special levy, upon professional men and others whose wealth
consisted of the immaterial capital of personal qualities, the
government would, no doubt, have to be content with a series
of annual payments rather than with a large lump sum. With
reasonable arrangements on these lines there is little danger
that a special levy would damage any concerns by withdrawing
real capital from them.

There remains the argument that, even though a special
levy would not injure industry directly through real capital,
it would injure it indirectly through finance. In order to raise
the money to pay their quotas, people, it is said, would be compelled to throw securities on the market to such an extent as
to cause a serious fall in values, and the ensuing slump would
dislocate arrangements for loans on collateral, with inevitable
repercussions upon industry. This argument rests, in part at
least, on a misconception. Even though the levy had all to be
paid in actual cash, since the proceeds would be employed in
paying off holders of war loan, these people would presumably
have about as much money seeking securities as the payers
of the levy had securities seeking money. Any momentary gap
between the time of the levy and the time of using it to buy war
loan could easily be adjusted through the banks. There is,
therefore, no reason to fear anything like a general slump in
values, though, of course, some particular securities might
suffer somewhat relatively to others. But this is not the whole
matter. There would be no need to require payment of the
levy in cash. Payment in war loan stock would be even more
acceptable to the Treasury, and payment in other first-class
securities not less acceptable. Arrangements might also be
made, as under the German Capital Levy law, by means of a
specially created institution for holding property on behalf of
the State, to permit people who so desired to pay in other less
readily marketable securities, or even in some forms of real
property. Thus, no serious difficulty and no appreciable injury to industry through repercussions from finance *need* arise.
It must be confessed, however, that a successful propaganda of
misunderstanding, or hostility on the part of bankers, might
easily bring about a financial panic, and so, for a time, general
disorganisation. I conclude, therefore, that in a *favourable
atmosphere* the damage attributable to the actual process of
collecting a special levy would be small; there would be
nothing of significance to set on the debit side against the
benefits associated with the shilling cut in income tax which a

£3000 million levy would render possible. If, however, a special levy were imposed in an unfavourable atmosphere, the damage done by the process of collecting it might be very large, and would very probably outweigh the whole of the advantages looked for from it.

DISTRIBUTIONAL FAIRNESS OF A SPECIAL LEVY AND OF ORTHODOX FINANCE COMPARED

I NOW turn to the second part of my problem . . . namely, the merits or otherwise of a special levy, as compared with orthodox finance, from the point of view of equity. We are supposing, it will be remembered, that the general scheme of distribution as between people of different grades of wealth is to be as nearly as possible the same under both plans. The essential fact is that a special levy takes from a number of people a large sum at one blow instead of a succession of smaller sums over a period of years, the lump sum method striking them over this period of years by depriving them beforehand of property which would otherwise have yielded them income. Thus, whereas with orthodox finance the burden imposed on different people is adjusted to their capacity in each year as it comes, under the special levy method the distribution of it is determined once for all at the beginning of the period, without regard to any changes in fortune that different people may subsequently undergo. If equal intelligence is applied to devising a plan for a special levy and a plan for continuing taxes respectively, it is inevitable, therefore, that the special levy plan should work out less fairly than the other. Thus, while, of course, it is as easy to graduate a special levy as to graduate an income tax, it is impossible to take adequate cognisance under it of family needs. Under an income tax a bachelor, a father of five living children and a father of five children who have died are appropriately treated both in each several year and over the whole period of their lives. Under a special levy two men who are bachelors at the moment the levy is made must be treated alike, although during the period covered by the effects of it one may continue a bachelor and the other may become possessed of an enormous family. This inequality of treatment occurs equally whether we include or do not include allowances for children in the structure of the special levy law. Allowances, if made, can only take account of a man's family as it stands at the moment of the levy, not of what it is going presently to become. In like manner, whereas under income tax a man who comes into a piece of good fortune is taxed in consequence of it, under a special levy, if that good fortune occurs immediately after the levy law has been framed, he is necessarily treated in the same way as the man to whom no corresponding good fortune comes at all. Distributional errors of this type are inevitable under a special levy, whatever basis of assessment is chosen for it.

Again, under the only form of special levy which has hitherto been widely advocated, namely a levy assessed upon material capital, there is a serious inequity as between owners of this capital and owners of the immaterial capital of large personal earning power. Since a special levy for debt repayment is a substitute for future taxation to provide for debt service, it is plainly proper that those who have the power to earn income, since they will benefit from the reduction of future taxation, should bear a share of the levy. Unless they are made to do this, the imposition of the levy will have the effect of substantially altering the burden borne by different citizens, to the advantage of those possessing the immaterial capital of capacity to do profitable work and to the disadvantage of those possessing material capital as ordinarily understood. This shifting of burden is exactly similar to that which would occur if the policy of a levy were rejected in favour of the orthodox system of annual taxation, but the rates on investment income were largely raised, and those on earned income largely reduced. Of course, it is open to any one to maintain that the existing discrimination between the rates of income tax on the two sorts of income is less favourable to earned income, even when account is taken of death duties, than it ought to be. But, if this be so, the right policy is to readjust relative rates in whatever manner is thought proper : nobody can believe that the right adjustment would be attained through a levy, of arbitrarily determined magnitude, confined to material capital. It is, indeed, not difficult to imagine a form of special levy which should be based both on material capital and also on the immaterial capital of trained earning power. It would, however, be unreasonable to require the revenue officials to value for assessment such an entity as immaterial capital. The present worth of a man's capacity to earn so much income depends on the man's expectation of life, and so would be different for men in similar occupations but of different ages. Account would have to be taken too of prospects of promotion ; and, in strictness, not merely of existing capacity, but also of capacity to acquire capacity. Clearly, this is impracticable. A second-best solution would be provided by a levy on capital coupled with a special tax upon earned income ; or, what comes to the same thing, followed by a reduction in the taxation of investment income but not in that of earned income. This arrangement, however, is not one that a democracy, interested to *relieve* earned income at the expense of investment income, is at all likely to adopt. Hence, a special levy, which in the nature of things must be somewhat less fair than continuing taxation, is likely in practice to prove *much* less fair.

ADMINISTRATIVE DIFFICULTIES

THE third and last division of my subject-matter concerns administrative technique. It may be laid down at the outset that any levy law is practically bound to prove unworkable if introduced during a period of violent fluctuations in the value of money; for such fluctuations will upset the whole intention of the law in the interval between its passage and its application. We assume then reasonably stable monetary conditions. On that assumption, the technical problem to be tackled depends on the particular form of special levy that is chosen. The main difficulty presented by a capital levy in the ordinary sense, whether standing alone or coupled with special imposts upon earned incomes, is the need under it for a large-scale valuation of capital wealth. The hardest problem arises in connection with life interests, which, according to Sir Josiah Stamp's estimate, affect somewhere between 15 and 20 per cent of the wealth that would come under the levy.[8] Since the capital value of these can only be calculated by reference to the actuarially probable length of the life-tenant's life, the valuations must necessarily turn out wrong in the great majority of individual cases. "The life-tenant A has a valuation of £70,000 on his expectation of life, say, 17 years, and has other property £30,000. Assume that he pays £35,000, the bulk of which he raises by mortgaging his whole independent property. He dies the following year, and, instead of being worth £30,000, his estate is wholly bankrupt and his dependents penniless. B's reversion is valued at the residual £30,000, on which he pays, say, £5000. The following year he comes into the full interest and has really been undercharged by a very large sum."[9] Even here, however, there is a way round. In a note prepared for the Committee on National Debt and Taxation the Board of Inland Revenue writes: "An alternative course would be for the levy to be imposed, not on the separate interests of individuals and payable out of their estates, but on the whole value of settled property and payable out of the

8 Cf. *Current Problems in Finance and Government*, p. 232.
9 *Ibid.*, p. 231.

settled fund, the rate of duty both for the settled fund and for
the free wealth of the life-tenant being found by aggregating
the value of the settled property with the life-tenant's other
property." [10]   This way of treating the settled property would
agree with that now in force for the Estate Duties, and so would
introduce no new principle. Where no life-interests are involved the problem of valuation is less difficult. For some
sorts of property, indeed, it is easy. Thus in respect of capital
possessions, the titles to which are held in the form of securities, a simple return could be required, and it could be checked
to some extent by the information already in the hands of inspectors of taxes. For securities for which there is a wide
market values could then be satisfactorily determined by reference to the prices that had ruled in the market over some
assigned period. For securities that are not often dealt in it
would be more difficult to make a fair valuation. For property
not represented by securities there would have to be an appraisement by government valuers. Private businesses, houses,
furniture, jewellery, works of art and other such things would
all, so far as it was decided to include them under the levy,
need to be treated in this way. It would be impossible to
carry through such a general appraisement quickly, and it
could hardly fail to prove both irritating and expensive. The
difficulties, however, are not insuperable. At least three alternative ways of dealing with them are available. First, all
persons *prima facie* liable to levy might be required to send
in a valuation of their properties by some assigned date. On
this valuation they might be assessed in the first instance.
Thereafter, government appraisers might set to work and gradually, during the course of several years, might go through
these private valuations and, where necessary, correct them.
After the proper valuation had been finally determined, any
adjustment required on account of the corrections might be
effected by payments from the tax-payer to the Exchequer, or
vice versa. Secondly, the levy might be assessed in the first
instance on the basis of those kinds of property only, the valuation of which presents no difficulty. Such things as furniture,
jewellery and works of art might be left over till each several
property came up for valuation in the natural course at the
owner's death. Then the ordinary death duty assessment
might be supplemented by a further assessment in respect of
postponed special levy upon these things. The disadvantage
of this method is, of course, that it makes difficult the proper
graduation of the levy. The rate of levy should vary with the

[10] *Report,* p. 249.

aggregate size of different properties. If only a part of these properties is brought under review when the main levy is assessed, this cannot be done. Any error that results might, however, be corrected by manipulating the rates at which the supplementary levy is assessed later on. Thirdly, elements of property which are exceptionally intractable to valuation might be left out of assessment altogether, on the ground that, though this would, undoubtedly, be unfair, yet a certain amount of unfairness must, as in all tax matters, be endured in order to avoid administrative complications. Clearly, no one of these devices is wholly satisfactory, and this fact is, so far, an argument against the imposition of a special levy based on capital.

A special levy based, not on capital, but on current and recent income as the object of assessment would be free from these valuation difficulties; for all that the taxing authority would need to know is already filed in connection with ordinary income tax. Considerations of equity, however, practically rule out of account a special levy assessed in a merely mechanical way upon incomes. It would be essential to arrange for the imposition of different rates upon (given amounts of) different kinds of income, and this would involve complicated inquiries into the nature of the sources from which incomes arose. These might well bulk so large that this apparently simple form of special levy would in practice prove extremely complex.

GENERAL SUMMARY

IT is not necessary to say much in general summary of this long discussion. During the period immediately following the war I personally was of opinion that, if it had been possible to pass with general assent, or with such measure of assent as was accorded to the Excess Profits Duty, an Act providing for a levy adequate to wipe out a substantial portion of the war debt, this would, on the whole, have been to the national advantage. At the present time, or as regards the near future, I do not advocate such an Act, for the following reasons.* First, if it was passed, its execution would be impeded by strong and organised opposition, perhaps backed by some of the banks, and, in view of the great technical difficulties to be overcome in any event, it could not successfully surmount this. Secondly, such an Act, passed belatedly a number of years after the return of peace, would make people much more fearful of further levies to follow the first than it would have done if passed in intimate connection with the ending of the war. Thirdly, whereas in

* Eds. note : This was written in 1928.

the boom that followed the war prices stood at a level from which it was highly probable there would be — as in fact there has been — a large recession, so that to refrain from repayment of internal debt then meant allowing its real value, and so the rates of tax required to provide for its service, to increase very greatly, at the present time there is no strong reason to expect a heavy fall in prices in the near future. Lastly, British industry is still in an abnormally depressed condition, and in these circumstances anything which might render business men nervous, even if the nervousness would be, in the main, unreasonable, is to be deprecated.

QUESTIONS AND PROBLEMS FOR DISCUSSION

1. Compare the merits of perpetual bonds, sinking fund bonds, and serial bonds in national (as distinct from state and local) financing.
2. If a sinking fund is to be established, what factors should determine the amount to be placed in this fund in each period?
3. Discuss the relationship between debt retirement plans and business conditions.
4. Does debt retirement stimulate saving?
5. What advantages may arise as a result of reducing a public debt through conversion?
6. How would a drastic reduction of an internal national debt directly and indirectly affect economic activity?
7. State and evaluate arguments for and against a special levy in the United States for the purpose of reducing the federal debt.
8. "Debt, whether private or public, is always a burden, and it should be the first interest of a nation to wipe out the entire national debt." Evaluate.

SUGGESTIONS FOR RESEARCH

1. An evaluation of possible methods of repaying the national debt of the United States.
2. Debt-reducing operations of the federal government from the close of the World War to 1929.
3. Methods of debt repayment and reduction of some particular state or of the municipalities of some particular state.
4. Sinking funds versus serial bonds.
5. The technique and economic effects of the repayment of external debts.

BIBLIOGRAPHICAL NOTE

Valuable material relating to the question of the advisability of the repayment of public debts may be found in H. C. Adams, *Public Debts,* (New York, 1890), Pt. II, Chap. V; C. F. Bastable, *Public Finance,* (London, 1917), Bk. V, Chap. VII; Hugh Dalton, *Prin-*

ciples of Public Finance, (London, 1932), Chap. XXIII; and *Colwyn Report of Committee on National Debt and Taxation,* (London, 1927).

Concerning the method of repaying or reducing public indebtedness, general discussions are available in H. L. Lutz, *Public Finance,* (New York, 1929), Chap. XXVIII; G. F. Shirras, *The Science of Public Finance,* (London, 1925), Chap. XXXVII; Shutaro Matsushita, *The Economic Effects of Public Debts,* (New York, 1929), Chap. V; and the *Colwyn Committee Report.* An original work is William Withers, *The Retirement of National Debts,* (New York, 1932). This work is a constructive exposition of the relationship between debt repayment and theories of debt burdens. It also contains an extensive and useful bibliography.

Paul Leroy-Beaulieu, *Traité de la Science des Finances,* (Paris, 1883), Vol. II, Bk. II, Chaps. IX, X treats amortization and conversion of public debts.

For discussions of the theoretical and practical aspects of the capital levy as a means of debt repayment or reduction see Hugh Dalton, *The Capital Levy Explained,* (London, 1923); J. A. Hobson, *Taxation in the New State,* (London, 1919), Pt. II, Chaps. II and III; Sir Josiah Stamp, *Current Problems in Finance and Government,* (London, 1924), Chap. XI; *Colwyn Committee Report,* (London, 1927), Pt. II, pp. 246-328 and Pt. IV, pp. 397-412; and articles by Sydney Arnold; A. A. Hook; A. A. Mitchell; A. C. Pigou; and W. R. Scott in the *Economic Journal,* Vol. XXVIII.

A comparison of the economic aspects of the capital levy with those of currency depreciation is made by J. M. Keynes in his *Monetary Reform,* (New York, 1924), Chap. II, Sec. 2.

The capital levy in practice is treated in Alzada Comstock, *Taxation in the Modern State,* (New York, 1929), Chap. XV; J. Jastrow, "The German Capital Levy Tax," *Quarterly Journal of Economics,* Vol. XXXIV, pp. 462-472; B. S. Chlepner, *Le prélèvement sur le capital dans la théorie et la pratique,* (Brussels, 1925); and Lew Ping Yeh, *L'impôt sur le capital en pratique,* (Paris, 1924).

The subject of municipal debt administration is dealt with in A. E. Buck, *Municipal Finance,* (New York, 1930), Chap. XIV. This chapter was written by Luther Gulick.

An important historical account of public debt repudiation is W. A. Scott, *The Repudiation of State Debts,* (New York, 1893).

W. F. Willoughby in his *Financial Condition and Operations of the National Government, 1921–1930,* (Washington, D. C., 1931), Chap. XVII treats the subject of federal debt reduction during the period, 1921–1930.

PART IV
FINANCIAL ADMINISTRATION

CHAPTER XXVIII

FINANCIAL ADMINISTRATION: GENERAL CONSIDERATIONS

1. FINANCIAL ADMINISTRATION *

FINANCIAL Administration is that part of the government organization which deals with the collection, preservation and distribution of public funds, with the coördination of public revenues and expenditures, with the management of the credit operations on behalf of the state and with the general control of the financial affairs of the public household. The term also refers to that part of fiscal science which is concerned with the principles and practises involved in the proper administration of state finances.

Several factors have contributed to the increasing importance of the administrative aspects of public finance in modern times: first, the ever widening scope of state activities and consequent growth of public receipts and expenditures; second, the democratization of political institutions and the establishment of parliamentary control over the public purse; and, finally, the recent tendency of applying a more simplified and rationalized procedure to the business of public administration.

The main principles underlying a sound system of financial administration are: unity of organization and centralized responsibility; strict compliance with the will of the legislature as expressed and formulated in the budget; simplicity, promptness and regularity of functioning; and, finally, an effective but not too complicated system of control over all stages of the financial operations. No system of administration is complete without a trained and reliable personnel, the recruiting of which is a task equal in importance to that of proper organization itself.

The various systems of financial administration are products

* From Gaston Jèze, "Financial Administration," *Encyclopaedia of the Social Sciences*, (The Macmillan Co., New York, 1931), Vol. VI, pp. 234-241.

of slow growth; their development is closely associated with that of political institutions. For a long time England and France were the only countries which endeavored to build up a satisfactory financial administration. The constitutional law which regulates the financial administration of England is the Exchequer and Audit Departments Act of June 28, 1866, "an Act to consolidate the duties of the Exchequer and Audit Departments, to regulate the Receipts, Custody and Issue of Public Moneys, and to provide for the Audit of the Accounts thereof," supplemented by regulations contained in the Treasury Minute of March 2, 1867. In France the laws which regulate the financial administration are included in the *Règlement général sur la comptabilité publique,* the first edition of which was published in the *Ordonnance royale du 31 Mai 1838* and the last edition on May 31, 1862. Other countries followed the French or the English example; the French, adopted chiefly on the continent, is more lucid and systematic than the English, but less satisfactory. In adopting it some countries profited from experience and improved on it; for example, Belgium in the law regarding public accounts of May 15, 1846, and the general regulation concerning public accounts of December 10, 1868; Italy in the laws of February 17, 1884, and the regulation of May 4, 1885, concerning the administration and the general public accounts; and Germany in the law of December 31, 1922, concerning the regulation of the budget of the Reich, the codified text of April 14, 1930, and the ordinance of August 6, 1927, concerning the service of the Treasury of the Reich.

Of all countries Great Britain has undoubtedly worked out the most detailed and unified system of handling her fiscal affairs. The central organ of administration is the Treasury. Since 1612 the Treasury has been organized in the form of a board, consisting of the first lord of the Treasury, a title ordinarily given to the prime minister, the chancellor of the Exchequer and a variable number of junior lords of the Treasury (usually three). Actually, however, the chancellor of the Exchequer is the only head of the Treasury. Under his supervision is a trained personnel whose coöperation insures the continuity of tradition and prevents technical errors. The most important members of the staff are the permanent secretary to the Treasury, whose task it is to direct the administration, and the permanent financial secretary, who controls the other governmental departments. These two important officials also have carefully selected staffs.

The Treasury centralizes the estimates of expenditures of all governmental departments. The chancellor of the Exchequer is the official financial counselor of the crown; he requests the appropriations for all national expenditure from the House of Commons and thus exercises a strong control over the other ministers. The House merely votes on the estimates of expenditures; its members do not possess the right of initiating expenditures or of demanding an augmentation of the credits. The credits are always granted according to the demand of the chancellor of the Exchequer.

The Treasury exercises a continuous and direct control over the financial activities of all governmental departments. In fact, the House of Commons grants the credits to the crown and not to the ministers. It is incumbent upon the crown to state whether a credit is to be used or whether certain expenditures are to be made, and the Treasury is the organ through which the crown makes its will known. Accordingly, before making any expenditure a minister must obtain authorization from the Treasury. If it is found by a department that the credits which it had obtained are insufficient, it must forward a written statement to the Treasury in order that the latter may decide whether the expenditures might not possibly be deferred or whether it could present a "supplementary estimate" to the House of Commons. Finally, it is the task of the Treasury to supervise the efficiency of all governmental departments, to which it may issue instructions.

The Treasury supervises the collection of the public revenues and the public debt service, but separate agencies are charged directly with the two respective tasks. It supervises the preservation and distribution of the public funds, which are kept in the Bank of England. The Treasury maintains a current account with the Bank, to which all the receipts collected by the agents of the revenue departments are forwarded. Upon orders from the Treasury the Bank effects transfers to the accounts of the various accounting officers, especially the paymaster general. The practice of depositing the government funds with the Bank of England helps to keep the public funds in circulation and minimizes the restrictive effect of heavy tax payments on the money market.

The comptroller and auditor general, a very high and powerful public official, although nominated by the crown is considered an agent of Parliament and not of the Treasury. He can be recalled only by Parliament, and his salary does not depend upon the annual vote of credit. He takes care that the Treasury withdraws funds from the account of the Exchequer with the Bank of England only in conformity with the will of Parliament; every withdrawal of funds requires his authorization, which is known as a grant of credit by the comptroller and auditor general.

The Treasury has the power of contracting short term loans in order to balance temporary deficits.   These loans are either advanced by the Bank of England, in which case they are called ways and means advances, or raised by bankers through the agency of the Bank of England (through the sale of Treasury bills).   In case of productive capital expenditures the Treasury may be authorized to issue Exchequer bonds, which are of greater duration than Treasury bills and are usually repaid from the earnings of the investment.

The Treasury does not directly audit the public accounts. It publishes weekly financial statements about receipts, payments and the status of the Exchequer.   In addition each year it submits financial tables to Parliament informing it of the financial situation.   The auditing of the accounts is performed by a committee of Parliament, the Committee on Public Accounts, chiefly with the assistance of the comptroller and auditor general and one official of the Treasury.   This committee also supervises the financial activities of the Treasury. . The observations which it makes form the basis of the Treasury minutes, which are instructions forwarded by the Treasury to the various departments.   A collection of all instructions given since 1857 has been published in the *Epitome of the Reports from the Committees on Public Accounts 1857 to 1910, and of the Treasury Minutes Thereon* and forms an excellent digest of English public accounting.

In France the system of financial administration is directed by the minister of finance.   Until 1925 there existed unity of administration, but in that year for reasons of political opportunism there was established side by side with the Ministry of Finance a Ministry of the Budget, the principal duty of which is to prepare the budget and present it to parliament.   This dualism has not produced good results.   The minister of the budget is inferior in position to the minister of finance and is not superior to the other ministers.   Although the latter submit to him a proposal of their expenditures, the minister of the budget has no special power to control them.   The authority and responsibility of the minister of the budget and the minister of finance are impaired by the finance commissions of the Chamber of Deputies and the Senate, which possess the right to modify the financial measures of the government. The proposals discussed by parliament are more often those of the commissions rather than those of the government.   Finally, every deputy has the right to propose new expenditures as well as additional credits. The legal restrictions intended to prevent gross abuse are ineffectual. According to the constitution senators do not possess the right to propose an increase in the credits, but in practice the Senate circumvents the constitution by voting a nominal reduction of the credit. When the modified budget is again submitted to the Chamber any deputy can propose the additional credit desired by the Senate. Under such conditions the authority of the minister of finance and the minister of the budget depends entirely upon their personalities. The French budget has no responsible author; it is the offspring of an unknown father.

The Ministry of Finance does not exercise a direct, permanent and effective control over the financial activities of the other ministerial departments. Each minister uses the credits granted to him without interference from the minister of finance. Where additional appropriations are necessary, the minister of the budget demands them from parliament in agreement with the interested minister. Because of the weak position of the minister of the budget and the preponderant influence of financial commissions, deputies and senators additional credits are of considerable importance in France. In 1890 the legal power of controlling expenditure was granted to the minister of finance. An official of the Ministry of Finance, a *contrôleur des dépenses engagées,* supervises the expenditures of each minister. Every project which involves expenditures must be submitted for the countersignature of that official, who examines its conformity with the law and the credits voted by parliament, but not its expediency. The *contrôleur* has the right to comment on the efficiency of the methods employed. In case the countersignature is refused an appeal is taken to the minister of finance, who renders the final decision. A minister who knowingly incurs expenditures without the indorsement of the *contrôleur* is held civilly and criminally responsible for his action according to the law of August 10, 1922; the law, however, has never been enforced. The *contrôleur* does useful work but lacks the authority necessary to render his service effective.

The minister of finance is in charge of the collection and distribution of the public revenues. The custody of the public funds, however, is entrusted to the Bank of France, and the money thus remains in circulation. The Treasury has a current account with the Bank, to which the revenue collectors forward the public funds. The minister of finance, on the other hand, gives instructions to the Bank for placing the necessary amounts at the disposal of the paymasters. The creditors of the state receive pay orders from the respective ministers, which are honored by the accountants only if they bear the countersignatures of the *contrôleur* and the Direction du Mouvement Général des Fonds du Ministère des Finances. The first confirms the authority of the minister in regard to this expenditure, while the second guarantees that no creditor is given a pay order without previous verification of the fact that the national Treasury contains the amount necessary for honoring it. Every month after calculating the funds at his disposal the minister of finance informs each minister of the amount up to which he may issue pay orders during the following month. The accountants are held personally responsible in case they honor orders which lack the correct form. The extent of their personal responsibility is, however, determined in the last instance by the minister of finance.

The minister of finance is the only authority charged with securing compliance with the law and the will of parliament. There exists no authority comparable to the office of the comptroller and auditor general in England to prevent the minister of finance from violating the will of parliament. He has the power to incur public expenditures regardless of their legality. His orders, even if unlawful, must be obeyed by the comptrollers of expenditures and the accountants. He has the power of releasing the accountants from their responsibility. Moreover, the law of August 10, 1922, authorizes the government to open credits, by a decree of the Council of the Ministers, for expenditures required in the interests of public security, providing the credits are subsequently ratified by the parliament; the fact that the government frequently makes use of this power considerably decreases the effectiveness of the parliamentary control. The legal prerequisites which insure the publicity of the financial transactions are disregarded. For instance, in 1929 the public was astonished to learn that the national Treasury had at its disposal reserves of approximtely 20,000,000,000 francs which were unknown to parliament. In 1930 a law was enacted which vainly tried to establish a control over the Treasury; its provisions, which are very poorly drawn, are not enforced.

The minister of finance is in charge of the administration of the national debt as well as of the issues of public loans. In order to balance the temporary deficits of the Treasury he floats short term loans in the form of Treasury certificates. Until 1928 the Bank of France gave the Treasury a standing non-interest bearing advance of 600,000,000 francs, which was indirectly abolished when the franc was stabilized.

The minister of finance supervises the public accounts of all ministerial departments and even examines the statements of the accountants before they are forwarded to the Cour des Comptes for the final verification. Actually, these statements are forwarded to the Cour des Comptes only after a delay of several years; the verification is therefore ineffective. Parliament is completely uninterested in the matter.

Although the financial administration of Germany is influenced by the French system, nevertheless German tradition favors the institution of powerful executives confronted by an impotent parliament. This tradition is evident in the very considerable power granted to the minister of finance as the head of the financial administration. His share in the preparation of the budget is larger than in France, although not so large as in England; he himself draws up the budget of the receipts and for the preparation of the budget of expenditures he utilizes the proposals which the other ministers submit to him, and which they formulate uniformly according to a model prescribed by him. He possesses the right to criticize the proposed expenditures of the other ministers. In the case of a conflict decision rests with the Council of Ministers; the minister of finance may, however, demand that the council take a new vote at a meeting at which all the ministers are required to be present. The credit requested by a minister against the advice of the minister of finance is granted only if the majority of the ministers are in favor of it and if the chancellor of the Reich votes with the majority. The plan of the budget approved by the Council of Ministers is then submitted to the Reichsrat, a body composed of delegates from the states, where it is examined by a commission headed by the minister of finance. The latter may ask that modifications proposed by the Reichsrat be submitted to the Council of Ministers, who may approve or reject them. The project approved by the government is next submitted to the Reichstag. Although the budget commission of the Reichstag may tend to encroach upon the prerogative of the minister of finance, it lacks the power of the Finance Commission of the French Chamber and cannot propose a new budget. Every member of the Reichstag has the right to propose additional expenditures; actually, however, the right is exercised by the strong political parties in their negotiations with the government. In 1931 the regulations of the Reichstag were changed and its members prohibited from increasing credits or reducing receipts without indicating the ways and means of reëstablishing a balance. If in order to comply with these regulations a reëvaluation of the receipts is proposed, it must be submitted to the approval of the government. Moreover, if the Reichstag augments the credits demanded by the minister of finance, the increase must be submitted to the approval of the Reichsrat. If the latter does not render its decision or vetoes the increase the president of the Reich must either submit the matter to the referendum of the electoral body within three months or order the Reichstag to reconsider the matter; in the latter case the increase is sustained only if it is supported by a majority of two thirds. So far the second course has always been followed. Even if, as usually happens, two thirds of the members of the Reichstag vote for the increase, the president of the Reich may decree a referendum by the people. Finally, article 48 of the Weimar constitution of August 11, 1919, authorizes the president to promulgate the necessary ordinances in case the Reichstag should reject the budget or in case it should be dissolved before it can vote. Thus on July 18, 1930, when the Reichstag was dissolved after having rejected the budgetary proposals of the government, fiscal ordinances were promulgated by the president of the Reich and the budget for 1930 was established by decree subject to a subsequent law.

Actually the German method of financial administration has not been successful in securing a balanced budget. All budgets since that for 1924 have resulted in deficits. The deficit of an ordinary budget must figure as an ordinary expenditure in the second budget thereafter, which means that new taxes are to be raised in order to cover the deficit. In reality the deficits have been covered by loans, especially short term foreign loans; this has given rise to a floating debt which in August, 1930, exceeded the sum of 1,300,000,000 marks.

The minister of finance does not possess the power, as does the chancellor of the Exchequer in England, to control his colleagues when the budget is carried into practice; his position in this respect resembles that of the French minister of finance. He is not even authorized, as in France, to place comptrollers of expenditures beside each minister; the ministers have their own special officials who account for their expenditures. The system of the monthly distribution of funds is modeled after the French pattern. The minister of finance decides upon the total amount to be passed for payment, but no control guarantees that the limit is not exceeded; the only check consists in a refusal of the accountants to honor orders beyond the amount determined.

The minister of finance is in charge of the collection of most revenues. In the Ministry of Finance there exist departments and subdepartments which direct the assessment and collection of taxes and other revenues subject to his jurisdiction. The local treasuries forward the funds at their disposal to the central Treasury, either by depositing them with the Reichsbank to the account of the Reich or by postal checks. The amount due the Reich from its postal checking account is cleared through the Reichsbank. Certain treasuries are authorized to maintain an account with the Reichsbank. On the whole the part played by the Reichsbank in financial administration is inferior to that of the Bank of England or the Bank of France.

The minister of finance issues the public loans authorized by the Parliament and has charge of the conversion of debt. The administration of the national debt is reserved to an independent organ, the Reichsschuldenverwaltung. Up to 1924 the temporary deficits of the Treasury were covered by advances from the Reichsbank against unlimited Treasury certificates; but since that date the Reichsbank has been permitted to open credits for a maximum period of three months up to the amount of 100,000,000 marks, which must be entirely refunded not later than July 15 following the end of the financial year (March 31). Furthermore, the Reichsbank may discount Treasury certificates of three months' maturity up to the amount of 400,000,000 marks, providing the certificates bear the signature of a solvent person. The Treasury may also grant short term loans to the Railroad Administration and the Post Office Department, both of which enjoy a large degree of financial autonomy.

The financial administration possesses no organ whatever to insure compliance with the laws and decisions promulgated by the Reichstag, but in every administrative branch a "special budget officer" or a "budget office" nominated by the minister or by the head of the respective department has charge of that function and works under the supervision of the minister at the head of the respective administrative branch. The Reichstag itself is not interested in the compliance with its decrees. Expenditures exceeding the budgetary credits are made without authorization from the Reichstag and at times are submitted for approval only after the financial statements have been published. Yet even in such cases the Reichstag has given its approval without comment.

Since May, 1929, the minister of finance has published a monthly account of receipts and expenditures as well as a Treasury report and a statement concerning the floating debt. With the assistance of other departments he also draws up the budgetary accounts of the Reich which are published and submitted to the Reichstag. The accounts rendered by the accountants are submitted to the autonomous Rechnungshof, which has power to investigate the proper execution of the budget, the compliance with the law, the proper handling of expenditures by the administration and finally whether unnecessary or excessive expenditures were incurred. This body has also the right to decide on the introduction of reforms and incorporates its observations in an annual report addressed to the government. After the accounts and the reports of the Rechnungshof have been submitted to the Reichsrat and Reichstag these bodies pass resolutions by which they release the government from responsibility. Actually the Reichstag is not interested in exercising control.

The financial administration of the United States was very deficient up to the passing of the Budget and Accounting Act of 1921. The preparation of the appropriation bills was in the hands of the numerous committees of the House of Representatives and the Senate. There was no interest in balancing receipts and expenditures. The Treasury did not possess the legal power to examine the demands for expenditures of the various departments, to prevent the grant of expenditures recognized as unnecessary or to check the misuse of credits granted. Congress maintained that the appropriations were compulsory for the government and by no means optional and that the government was compelled to spend the amount it had been granted. Logrolling, the pork barrel, inconsistency and waste were the outstanding characteristics of the management of the finances of the United States.

The legislation of 1921 reorganized the entire system of financial administration. Although the English system was accepted as a model it was not followed in every detail. It would have been impossible, for example, to give to the secretary of the Treasury the power possessed by the chancellor of the Exchequer in England. The forces which resisted any radical change were the preponderant position of the president, the subordinate position of the ministers as simple assistants to the president, the large measure of financial control granted to Congress by the constitution and finally the strength of a tradition more than a century old.

The task and responsibility of preparing, elaborating and presenting the annual budget are vested in the president. In this task he is assisted by the Bureau of the Budget, created by the law of 1921. The function of the Bureau corresponds to that of the permanent secretaries to the Treasury in England;

its task is to coördinate, revise and increase the estimates of the various departments and services, a function which practically amounts to a control of the entire administration. The Board of Estimates, a division of the Bureau of the Budget, is charged especially with maintaining the connections with all branches of the federal administration. In every branch of service there is a special official, the budget officer, nominated by the head of the service, whose task it is to prepare the estimates and to deal with the Bureau of the Budget. The executive departments are compelled to supply the Bureau of the Budget with all the information which it desires and the director, assistant director and duly authorized employees of the Bureau have the right to examine the books of all departments and services.

Credits are granted to each department or service. The head of a department or service has the right to employ them without consulting the Bureau of the Budget, but no official or administrative branch may use them for a new purpose without consulting the Bureau of the Budget and receiving its approval. On the other hand, immediately upon the publication of the budget and before June 30 each service must inform the Bureau as to the "Apportionment of Appropriations" — the monthly, trimestrial or other apportionment of its credits which it intends to make. Any subsequent change in the apportionment must also be reported to the Bureau and endorsed by it. Besides, every service must inform the Bureau at the end of each trimester of the amount actually spent during the period. The coördinating agencies, commissions of officials headed by the chief coördinator and supervised by the director of the Bureau of the Budget, serve the purpose of finding the most economical way of using the credits granted by Congress, of insuring the most rapid and most simple functioning of the federal service and of eliminating friction and delay.

Because of the preëminence of the president and the Bureau of the Budget the position of the secretary of the Treasury cannot be compared with that of the chancellor of the Exchequer or of the ministers of finance of France or Germany. The secretary of the Treasury proposes to the president the creation or the reduction of taxes, loans and other financial measures. He has complete supervision and control of the collection and preservation of public funds. The absence of a central bank in the United States formerly raised great problems in the matter of the custody of the funds. At first they were deposited in various banks, but favoritism on the part of Treasury officials and frequent bank failures led to their segregation in Treasury vaults. The economic waste and disturbing effects caused by the withdrawal of large sums of money from circulation brought about, however, a gradual return to the bank deposit system in the years following the Civil War. With the passing of the Federal Reserve Act in 1913 the Federal Reserve Banks were designated as fiscal agents and government depositories, although the secretary of the Treasury retained the right to select other banks as well. In 1920 a division on deposits was created and charged with all matters pertaining to the designation of depositories. The present policy is to maintain the national banks as depositories only in places which are remote from Federal Reserve Banks or their branches and in which a depository is necessary for pay roll purposes. In 1928 the secretary of the Treasury was authorized to designate state banks and trust companies to carry public deposits and act as fiscal agents of the government.

The Treasury is also charged with carrying on credit operations on behalf of the government. The short term borrowing is effected through the sale of Treasury certificates and Treasury notes issued usually in anticipation of revenue. These operations help the Treasury in distributing the public expenditure more evenly and to that extent have a stabilizing effect on the economic life of the country.

The control and auditing of financial operations are vested in the General Accounting Office established by the law of 1921. It is under the supervision of the comptroller general of the United States and the assistant comptroller general, both of whom are nominated by the president for fifteen years subject to the approval of the Senate. They may be recalled only with the consent of both houses of Congress. The General Accounting Office is to a certain extent an agent of Congress; its function may be compared with that of the comptroller and auditor general of England. Since 1921 its power has been considerably increased. It prescribes the forms and methods of accounting which must be employed by every department and service, as well as the forms of the accounts and the methods for their examination; actually, it has introduced very important simplifications by making uniform the methods of accounting and recording. It has the right to demand information from any office and to examine on the spot every ledger and document. It investigates whether expenditures and collections are effected in conformity with the law and the will of Congress. Similarly, upon the request of the services and particularly the pay-masters it interprets the provisions of the laws governing the budget and decides whether a certain credit

may be employed for a certain purpose. Congress alone possesses authority to change its interpretations. In spite of its
extensive jurisdiction it does not exercise the same power as a
comptroller of expenditure in France. Its control extends
only to the orders issued by the chiefs of the various services
previous to the actual making of payments, but even this sort
of control is not general. The General Accounting Office for-
wards to the president of the United States and to Congress
reports in which it proposes measures intended to render the
working of the federal services more simple and economical.
Both houses and their committees as well as the Bureau of the
Budget frequently ask the Office to investigate certain problems and to report on its findings. If the Office discovers that
certain expenditures or the terms of a contract infringe upon
the law, it is its duty to notify Congress of this fact through
a special report.

In addition to these functions the General Accounting Office
exercises various competencies in the interest of which it is
divided into several sections. The Claims Division investigates private claims, based on administrative acts, which the
services are unable to satisfy because of the lack of credit. If
the General Accounting Office considers the claims justified,
it makes recommendations in their favor to Congress. The
Audit Division is in charge of the examination and the auditing of the accounts of all departments including the Post Office
Department. The Office of the General Counsel has the task
of giving legal advice, especially on questions of interpretation
of the budget regarding the appeal taken by a service against
the decision of other sections of the General Accounting Office.
The Records Division is in charge of the archives, i.e. the preservation of accounts, contracts, checks and other documents.

2. THE NATURE AND FUNCTIONS OF A BUDGET *

AMONG the specific proposals brought forward during recent
years for the improvement of the methods of administration
of the national and state governments, that calling for the
adoption by these governments of a proper budgetary system
is much the most important. The adoption of this device as
an instrument of administration is more than important; it is
vital if an efficient and economical administration of public
affairs is to be had. Few will question the statement that no
government can have an efficient administration unless it has
evolved an efficient system for the administration of its finances

* From W. F. Willoughby, *The Problem of a National Budget,* (Brookings
Institution, Washington, D. C., 1918), Chap. I.

and, conversely, that that government which has evolved such a system has traveled a long way on the road toward the achievement of a satisfactory system of administration generally. This assertion can be pushed yet further by adding to it the statement that no system of financial administration can prove satisfactory that is not based securely upon what is known as a budget. We are thus brought to the position where the budget is erected into the central or determining feature of the whole problem of securing governmental efficiency. It remains to prove this thesis.

ESSENTIALS OF A BUDGET

IT is a remarkable fact that great as is the amount of study that has for years been given to the question of the budget in foreign countries, and extensively as the question has been discussed in recent years in this country, no general agreement appears to have been reached as to the precise meaning which should be attached to the term "budget." To some of the numerous writers on the subject a budget is a mere statement of estimated revenues and expenditures. Others going to the opposite pole make it synonymous with a revenue and appropriation act. The former conception is most commonly found in American commentators, while the latter, springing naturally from the close relation between the estimates and the legislative acts under European parliamentary systems, is to be found most clearly in European writers, particularly the French.[1]

As used by the writer throughout the following pages the term corresponds to neither of these conceptions. Were the budget a mere estimate of revenues and expenditures it would be palpably absurd to characterize the simple and relatively unimportant matter of the preparation of such an estimate as the master problem of our public administration. On the other hand, not only does the concept of the budget, as hereafter developed, not include the formal statutory authorization for the collection and expenditure of money, but it is believed that serious consequences result from confounding the budget

---

[1] Thus, M. Leroy-Beaulieu writes: "A budget is a statement of the estimated receipts and expenses during a fixed period; it is a comparative table giving the amounts of the receipts to be realized and of the expenses to be incurred; it is, furthermore, an authorization or a command given by the proper authorities to incur the expenses and to collect the revenues." "The budget of the state," says René Stourm, "is a document containing a preliminary approved plan of public revenues and expenditures." "The budget in modern states," according to M. G. Jèze, is a forecast and an estimate of all the public receipts and expenses and, for certain expenses and receipts, an authorization to incur them and to collect them."

with the act of revenue and appropriation and attempting to provide for both estimates and statute in the same document.

What then is a budget, as the term is here used? On analysis, the administration of the financial affairs of a government will be found to involve a continuous chain of operations, the several links of which are (1) estimates of revenue and expenditure needs; (2) revenue and expenditure acts; (3) accounts; (4) audit; and (5) reports.[2] An estimate is first made of the expenditures that will be required for the due conduct of governmental affairs during a fixed period (this period being almost universally fixed at one year), together with a statement as to the manner in which it is proposed that the money to meet these expenditures shall be raised. On the basis of this estimate, revenue and appropriation acts are passed giving legal authority for taking the action determined upon. Following this the accounting department of the government opens up revenue and appropriation accounts corresponding to the items of the revenue and appropriation acts. The data recorded in these accounts are then subjected to examination and scrutiny by the auditing department for the purpose of ensuring that they are accurately made, and that they correspond to the real facts and represent a full compliance with all provisions of law. The information furnished by these accounts is then summarized for the period to which they relate and is given publicity in the form of reports. Finally, on the basis of the data contained in these reports, new estimates for the next year are made and the circuit is begun again. In this chain of operations the budget finds its place as the instrument through which these several operations are correlated, compared one with the other, and brought under examination at one and the same time. It should be at once a report, an estimate and a proposal. It is the document through which the chief executive, as the authority responsible for the actual conduct of governmental affairs, comes before the fund-raising and fund-granting authority and makes full report regarding the manner in which he and his subordinates have administered affairs during the last completed year; in which he exhibits the present condition of the public treasury; and, on the basis of such information, sets forth his program of work for the year to come and the manner in which he proposes that such work shall be financed.

2 For a more detailed analysis of the operations involved in the administration of the financial affairs of a government, see Chapter I, "Analysis of the Problem of Financial Administration of a Government:" *The System of Financial Administration of Great Britain:* W. F. Willoughby, W. W. Willoughby and S. M. Lindsay, *Studies in Administration,* Institute for Government Research, 1917.

That the significance of past operations and the purpose of proposals for the future may be clearly seen, this document must be complete and detailed. It must cover all the financial operations of the government and cover them in such a way that the relationship between past action and proposals for the future revenues and expenditures and assets and liabilities may be clearly seen.

The most important feature of a budget is that it shall be all-comprehensive. It must bring together in one consolidated statement all the facts regarding the financial condition of the treasury and the revenues and expenditures of the government, past and prospective. It is obviously imperative that the appropriating authorities, in considering the problem of financing the government, shall know the total revenues that are available. Furthermore, the work of making provision for the financial needs of a government involves the consideration of relative as well as of absolute values. The problem presented is that of allotting or apportioning funds, the total amount of which is more or less fixed, to purposes in proportion to their relative importance or immediate urgency. To do this effectively it is necessary that the whole problem of financing the government should be considered at one time.

It is thus of the essence of correct budgetary practice that the general budget of a government should bring together in one all-comprehensive showing a complete statement of all government revenues and expenditures, but it does not follow that use may not be made of special or subordinate budgets for particular services whose operations it is desirable to segregate from those of the government generally considered. . . There are certain services of the national government of a purely industrial or commercial character and not related to the general operations of the government, such as the Panama Canal, the Alaskan Engineering Commission, etc., the financial operations of which, from both the revenue and the expenditure side, should be carefully segregated from those of the government generally considered, by presentation in the form of subordinate budgets, tied to the general budget by items showing the net proceeds resulting from their operation, or the appropriations required to meet their deficits, as the case may be. The expenditures of these services do not constitute a part of the cost of government in the same way as those which have to be made for the general conduct of government affairs, and their inclusion in the general budget thus tends to give a false picture of the progress of the cost of government. It seems clear, therefore, that the segregation of these revenues and expenditures in subsidiary budgets results in a more informative showing of the general financial conditions and operations of the government, and in no way does violence to the principle that the general budget should present a comprehensive showing of the financial conditions and operations of the government.

A second point, which is in the nature of a corollary to the first, is that the budget, in respect to both its estimate and its report features, should be in the form of a balanced statement. The balancing of revenues and expenditures is rightly deemed to be of the essence of a budget. In this way only can the relationship between the two sides of the national accounts be established, and the effect of the action had, or proposed, upon the financial situation of the government be made known.

CONTENTS OF A BUDGET

As already indicated, the central and basic element in a budget is the balanced statement of estimated revenues and expenditures for the ensuing fiscal period, comprehensive, complete and detailed. In connection with each item of this estimate should be given a report of the corresponding revenues and expenditures for the last completed year, and the provision for the year in progress. Such a statement may be termed the budget proper, as it is to this statement alone that the term budget, as already stated, is frequently applied. Standing by itself, however, such a statement falls far short of furnishing the information which the fund-granting authority should have before it. At least three major classes of additional information are indispensable.

In the first place, the budget proper should be accompanied by a balance sheet showing the resources and liabilities of the national treasury at the beginning and close of the last completed official year. A considerable difference of opinion exists among students of public finance regarding the scope and character that this statement should have. There are those who believe that the attempt should be made to value and list all the physical properties of the government; its lands, buildings, equipment, battleships, stores, etc., and to include the totals of such lists in the balance sheet. The writer is in thorough accord with the position that it is desirable that a government should maintain records furnishing as complete information as is feasible of the amount and value of all of its property. He believes, however, that it would be a great mistake to include any statement of the value of this property in the budgetary balance sheet. Only in small degree is any of this property available for the payment of national obligations, or, at least, those representing the current cost of financing government operations. The greatest asset of a government, that of the tax-paying ability of the inhabitants of the country governed, cannot possibly figure in any such statement. The purpose of the budgetary balance sheet is that of furnishing the information that must be had if the significance of operations during the past year and of those proposed for the year to come is to be seen. It is desirable for this reason that the balance sheet should confine itself to a presentation of the actual treasury resources and obligations. Every effort, however, should be made to make this presentation complete. Especially should it contain a showing of outstanding obligations in the form of bonded indebtedness and similar fixed charges. In a supporting statement should be given the details regarding these obligations, the date on which each obligation was incurred, the purpose to which the proceeds were applied, the rate of interest carried, the terms of repayment, the special security, if any, offered for the guarantee of the payment of interest and the repayment of principal, etc.

Next, as a necessary aid to an understanding of the facts and proposals presented, the budget should include a series of tables and explanatory texts summarizing and analyzing the revenue and expenditure data presented from a number of points of view. The budget proper can obviously present a classification of these figures on only a single basis; whereas, for their proper consideration, classification and analysis on several different bases are, as will shortly be more fully pointed out, indispensable. The most desirable form of classification to be used in these tables will be described at length in the succeeding section.

Lastly, these financial statements should be accompanied by the administrative reports of the chief executive, the heads of departments and other officers in charge of the several services of the government. The writer is aware that this proposition — that the annual reports of administrative officers should be made an integral part of the budgetary statement — is a novel one. At least, he has not seen the suggestion that this be done. A moment's reflection, however, will show that this is a desirable and logical requirement. We have already taken pains to point out that the budget is as much a reporting as an estimating operation. The financial statements contained in the budget proper give, and can give, but the bare figures showing the financial results of these operations. In order that their significance may be seen it is essential that they should be accompanied by statements showing the results in terms of work accomplished or to be accomplished, the necessity or utility of such work, the problems that have had to be met, the methods that have been or will have to be employed, etc. The administrative reports thus furnish the means through which the figures contained in the budgetary statements may be understood. Without them it is difficult, if not impossible, for intelligent consideration to be given to them.

To recapitulate: As an aid to the understanding of the facts contained in it, the budget proper should be accompanied by supporting documents which, together with the budget proper, constitute what may be designated a budgetary statement, in order to distinguish it from a budget as that term is more usually employed. Of these, the following are the most important: (1) A balance sheet showing the resources and liabilities of the government at the beginning and close of the year reported upon; (2) summary and analytical tables serving to bring out the important features of the showing made from the various viewpoints from which it is desirable to have the revenue and expenditures of a government considered; (3) the report of the chief executive in the form of a general budgetary message, and (4) the administrative reports of the heads of the several administrative departments and services.

A budgetary statement is then a collection of documents through which the information regarding the condition of the treasury and financial operations, past and prospective, are brought together, coördinated and compared in such a way that intelligent action can be had in the way of adopting a financial and work program for the future. The actual adoption of such a program is, however, a distinct operation and finds expression in distinct documents known as revenue and appropriation acts. To confuse the two, as is done by most writers on finance, obscures the question and is responsible for much of the misapprehension that now exists in regard to the true nature and functions of a budget.

CHARACTER OF EXPENDITURE DATA NEEDED

It has already been pointed out that the budget proper, consisting of a statement of estimated and actual revenues and expenditure, cannot, no matter how minute the detail in which it is drawn up, present all the information needed by the fund-granting authority; for it is necessarily framed upon but a single basis of classification; whereas a proper consideration of past and estimated expenditures requires that they be analyzed and classified upon several different bases.

The writer is of opinion that it is desirable that data regarding the cost of governmental operations should be had from at least five distinct standpoints, namely:

(1). Funds
(2). Organization units
(3). Activities
(4). Character of expenditure
(5). Object of expenditure

As the first step in securing cost data classified under these five heads, the funds, organization units, activities, character of expenditure and object of expenditure of the government, must be analyzed and a standard classification established under each head.

The necessity for classifying expenditure by *funds* is obvious. Most, if not all, governments receive and have the administration of moneys which are not available for general governmental purposes. These consist of moneys received by it on deposit, gifts for particular purposes which the government has accepted and obligated itself to administer in conformity with the deeds of gift, special grants which it has itself made of lump sums as endowments or specified items of income, or of current revenues for special purposes. Each of these constitutes a special fund, the operations of which must be carefully segregated. All governments also make provision for their expenditure needs by grants or appropriations for particular purposes or the support of particular services. Each such grant constitutes a "fund." When the grant is in the form of the dedication of certain receipts to certain purposes, such funds have a current income as well as outgo. Manifestly, accounts should be so kept and reports so rendered that the revenues and expenditures on account of each fund can be clearly determined.

Secondly: It is desirable to know the precise cost entailed in maintaining and operating each *unit of organization,* that is, of each branch of government, each department, each bureau or other subdivision of a department, and, finally, of each operating unit, such as a hospital, an army post or a lighthouse. Without such data it is impossible definitely to locate responsibility for expenditures, to exercise control over actual operating units, to secure efficiency and economy through the comparison of relative costs for similar or analogous units or for the same unit for a series of years, or intelligently to prepare estimates and make appropriations for future needs.

The classification of the organization units of a government means the listing of all the divisions and subdivisions of the government in their proper relations of superiority, coördination or subordination. In the typical modern government this means, first, the division of the government, viewed as an organization, into its four grand divisions of the legislative, the judicial, the executive and the administrative branches; second, the subdivision of each of these branches into its coördinate major divisions, as, for example, the subdivision of the administrative branch into the departments composing it; next, the subdivision of each of these departments into its constituent coördinate bureaus, and these, in turn, into their coördinate subdivisions, continuing this operation until the final working units of the office, station, hospital, lighthouse, army post, etc., are reached. In making this classification, care must be taken to include in the same division only coördinate units, since one of the main purposes is to show the line of authority. If this principle is adhered to, a clear showing is made of the subordinate units composing each division of the government.

Thirdly: It is equally important that expenditures should be known in terms of *activities* or work to be done; how much, for example, is it proposed to devote to the protection of the country from foreign aggression, how much for protection against internal disorder or the prevention and detection of crime, how much for the promotion of education, how much for the protection of the public health, how much for the development of means of communication, how much for the development of the national resources of the country, the promotion of industry, agriculture and commerce, and the many other things which the modern government undertakes for the welfare of its citizens. Many services of a government in performing their general functions engage in a number of specific activities. For example, the Bureau of the Census of the national government collects, compiles and presents statistics of population, agriculture, manufacturing, mining, transportation, production of cotton, municipal finance, births and deaths, wealth, debt, and taxation and many other matters. It is desirable to know the cost of procuring and presenting each of these classes of data.

It is not necessary to discuss in detail the problem of listing and classifying the several activities of government. Though the work to be done is analogous in character to that of listing and classifying the units or organization, its accomplishment presents greater difficulties. This is due to the fact that here we do not have fixed conditions to deal with. The activities of government are exceedingly varied and may be classified in many ways. It is necessary, therefore, to decide regarding not only those activities of the government which are deemed to be of sufficient importance to warrant their being distinguished from other activities, but the principle of classification to be employed.

Fourthly: Information should be available regarding the *character* of these expenditures; that is, how much goes for (1) capital outlay; (2) fixed charges; and (3) current expenses.

By capital outlay is meant those expenditures which result in the acquisition of fixed properties, such as land, buildings or equipment, or that result in the reduction of fixed or long-term liabilities, such as bonded debt. In other words, capital outlay comprises those transactions which go to increase the net capital investment of the service either by increasing its fixed properties, or by decreasing its bonded debt.

By fixed charges is meant expenditures which are required to carry on current activities but in respect to which the administrative and appropriating authorities have no choice of action since they constitute obligations created by previous administrations which must be met. Examples of fixed charges in governmental operations are: interest on bonded indebtedness, pensions, and grants and subsidies to subordinate governmental units. Expenditures for such items as rent, taxes, insurance, etc., should not be treated as fixed charges, even though they represent fixed obligations, since they constitute integral items of current expense and should appear under that head.

By current expenses is meant those expenditures that are required to carry on the current activities of the government and which do not result in the production or acquisition of assets or in the liquidation of liabilities. Current expenses are distinguished from fixed charges in that they are essential to the conduct of current activities and are subject to administrative and legislative discretion, whereas fixed charges are a compulsory burden, the result of obligations created in prior years.[3]

---

[3] Though accountants are agreed that, in all undertakings of importance, public and private, the threefold distinction of expenditures according to their character here set forth is one that should be made, they are not always in agreement in respect to where the line should be drawn between the three. Thus, many accountants assign expenditures for rent, insurance, taxes, etc., to fixed charges instead of current expenditures. In the opinion of the writer, this practice, if one keeps firmly in mind the purpose in view in making the threefold distinction, can scarcely be justified, certainly not when the undertaking is of a governmental character. The distinction as drawn above, it will be observed, rests primarily upon a time factor. Capital outlays represent expenditures the benefits of which accrue largely in the future; fixed charges represent expenditures made on account of benefits received in the past; while current expenses represent expenditures for present benefits. It is quite likely also that all accountants will not agree with the definition above given of the three classes

Finally, if an adequate check is to be had upon expenditures, data should be at hand regarding the *object* of the expenditures; that is, how much goes for each category of things, services or materials purchased; how much, for example, in the way of salaries for personal service, how much for transportation, how much for heat, light, power and every other kind of service or material made use of by the government. The making of a classification of this kind is a task of considerable magnitude and involves the settlement of a large number of perplexing questions in respect to the places that should be assigned particular commodities or objects of expenditure. Fortunately, however, it is a work which has been performed by all large corporations and by not a few governments in the United States; and the existence of their classifications saves a large part of the work that would otherwise have to be performed by other organizations desiring to develop such a classification. One of the most complete schemes of this character is that made by the President's Commission on Economy and Efficiency.

If information regarding expenditures is available from these several standpoints the operations of government may be studied and planned from almost any desired angle.[4] It is possible to determine not only the cost and needs of a particular service, subdivision of a service, or group of subdivisions or services, but the items of this cost or of these needs, whether in terms of activities performed or things purchased. Or, reversing the order of consideration, the cost and needs of any activity or class of activities may be determined in terms of services engaged in the performance of these activities, or in terms of things purchased in performing them.

Before turning to a consideration of the accounting and reporting system needed to develop information regarding ex-

of expenditures. It would not be in place to enter here upon a consideration of the technical accounting questions presented. All that is needed is to point out the desirability that all systems of government accounting and reporting should make these distinctions.

Many accountants would also probably urge that the distinguishing of expenditures according to character should be carried much farther than here indicated; that for example expenditures should be recorded and reported according to subdivisions under each of the three heads. Whatever may be the theoretical arguments in favor of doing this, expediency, in the opinion of the writer, dictates that this should not be attempted at the present time. The primary distinction here urged can be made with comparative ease: to attempt to push the distinction much farther gives rise to many questions in the practical operation of the system and would greatly complicate and render more difficult the work of government bookkeeping.

[4] For a practical illustration of expenditures of a service reported from these five viewpoints, see Appendix 1 [in W. F. Willoughby, *The Problem of a National Budget*].

penditures under the several heads mentioned, attention should be called, in passing, to the high value, from an administrative standpoint quite apart from their value for budgetary purposes, which may be made to attach to classifications of organization units and of activities of the character above described.

The results of the analysis and classification of organization units can be shown in a number of ways — by charts, by a process of successive indentations in the listing of the units, or by a scheme of primary and supporting sheets. Of these several methods the latter is much to be preferred. Its advantages are twofold. It brings coördinate units into immediate juxtaposition, and permits changes to be made in the presentation as changes occur in organization without requiring the whole classification to be made over. Under this method each class of coördinate units is shown on a separate sheet. For example, sheet number 1 would show the four branches of the government, the legislative, the judicial, the executive and the administrative. The first supporting sheet for the administrative branch would show the several departments composing that branch. Each of these departments would have a supporting sheet showing the coördinate bureaus or other services into which it is divided. Each of these bureaus in turn would have its supporting sheet showing its subdivisions — a process that would be continued until the final working unit is reached. Each such final unit would have a sheet of its own which would show in detail its organization and personnel. These sheets should not be bound together but should be filed loose in vertical cases as are the cards in the card catalog of a library. When so filed in their proper order they would furnish a complete outline of the organization of the government. It is evident that if this method of presentation is employed it is an easy matter to keep the outline constantly revised to date. If a new unit is created all that is required is that a new sheet should be prepared for it and inserted in its proper place, and the necessary entry made on the sheet that it supports. If a unit is abolished its sheet can be removed and the corresponding change be made on the sheet it supports. In like manner any change in organization can be recorded by simply making the changes required on the one or two sheets affected.

It is hardly necessary to point out the value that such a record has as an instrument of administration. It enables the administrator at once to learn how any subdivision of his service is organized and managed, no matter where that subdivision may be located, and to keep track of all changes in organization and personnel as they occur. It would take us too far from our subject to attempt to point out the many other valuable uses to which such a record could be put. It may be of interest to note that the preparation of an outline of organization of the national government of the United States constituted one of the first steps taken by the Commission on Economy and Efficiency, appointed by President Taft, for the devising of means by which the national government might be put upon a more economical and efficient basis.[5] It should be noted, furthermore, that the work, though apparently one of magnitude, is by no means so difficult as might at first sight appear. Moreover, it is one which, as stated, once made, can be kept up to date with slight effort.

Similarly, a classification of the activities of a government furnishes a tool of administration that is of great value, apart from its serving as the essential basis of a system of accounts that will show expenditures from the standpoints of activities and functions. It furnishes the most effective showing that can be made in brief compass of the nature of the work being done by a government. By indicating for each activity the service or services performing it, the basis is laid for a consideration of the whole problem of regrouping services, and redistributing activities among the services, so as to eliminate overlapping and duplication of organization and work and secure generally a better integration and coördination of the administrative work of the government.

CHARACTER OF EXPENDITURE DOCUMENTS NEEDED

THE classifications of expenditures under the several heads discussed having been established, it remains so to revise the accounting system of the government as to develop the information required in accordance with those classifications. Manifestly, data of these several kinds cannot be had unless the system of accounts of a government is devised with a view to their production. It is just at this point that most systems of government bookkeeping are defective. The careful recording of all financial transactions and the rendering of accounts and reports may be said to have two ends in view: (1) The establishment of fidelity on the part of all officers having to do with the administration of financial affairs; and (2) the development of the data regarding financial conditions and op-

---

[5] Message of the President of the United States on Economy and Efficiency in the Government Service. Appendix. Report to the President on the Organization of the Government of the United States as it existed July 1, 1911. House Doc. No. 458, 62d Congress, 2d Sess., 2 vols., 1912.

erations, such as have just been described. Unfortunately the accounting system of our national government, as of most, if not all, our states and of many of our minor political divisions, has been devised wholly with a view to the first end, namely, that of determining the fidelity of financial officers in the discharge of their duties. These systems thus fail to produce the information required for making due provisions for the expenditure needs of the government and for controlling the expenditure of funds granted.

Without here entering into any discussion of technical accounting practice, it may be stated that two steps are essential if the desired information is to be secured: (1) A uniform system of expenditure documents must be installed that will secure with respect to each expenditure information regarding its classification under each of the heads above described; (2) the system of accounts must be so designed as to facilitate the recording and summarization of this information.

The starting point in all accounting operations is the execution of a series of documents recording all essential facts regarding financial transactions. In the case of expenditures, these documents consist of requisitions for supplies or services, purchase orders, invoices, vouchers, pay-rolls, etc. Collectively these papers have received the designation of expenditure documents. From these papers are taken the data for entry in the accounts of expenditures. It follows, therefore, that all distinctions which it is desired to make in the accounts must find expression in some one or all of these documents. Concretely, therefore, the problem of securing information regarding expenditures in accordance with the five schemes of classification that we have described requires the formulation and adoption of a system of expenditure documents calling for the statement, in respect to each expenditure, of the fund chargeable, the organization unit on whose account it is made, the activity on account of which it is made, the character of the expenditure, and the object or thing purchased. With these facts entered upon these documents, it is but a matter of simple bookkeeping to record the figure showing the result of the transactions from the several desired points of view.

The use of these schemes of classification is much facilitated by the designation of each item in them by an appropriate numerical symbol and the employment of these symbols instead of the names of the items themselves in the execution of the expenditure documents. Thus, if the Division of Vital Statistics is the fourth division of the Bureau of the Census, which is the twelfth of the bureaus of the Department of Commerce, which is the ninth of the Administrative Departments, which last figures as the fourth of the four great branches of the government, it would receive the numerical symbol of 4–9–12–4. In like manner each of the groups of activities and specific activities, and each class, sub-class and item of objects of expenditure would have its proper numerical designation.

The advantages of this scheme of symbols are that it is susceptible of indefinite expansion, that it shows not only the particular item but the place of this item in the scheme of classification, and that it lessens greatly the work of filling out the expenditure documents. It is not necessary that officers of the government should familiarize themselves with the entire list of symbols. Each division, of course, knows its own symbol and those of its subordinate divisions. These can, if desired, be stamped or printed on the expenditure document forms used by it. The same is true with respect to the activities performed by it and, in large part, its objects of expenditure, since the expenditures of most services are for a relatively few of the total objects of government expenditure.

The use of these symbols also aids greatly in compiling from these documents data regarding expenditures. Thus, for instance, following the example given, it is known that all vouchers or other documents, the symbols of which appearing in the space for the designation of the organization unit have 4 as their first integer, represent the administrative branch of the government, all those having 2 as the first and 9 as the second integer, the Department of Commerce, etc. It is thus an easy matter to transcribe expenditures as recorded on expenditure documents according to organization units. In precisely the same manner total expenditures according to activities, character and object of expenditure can readily be obtained.

These various data, it is evident, can also be obtained in combination. Thus the total expenditure of an organization unit can be shown by subordinate organization units, by activities, by character, and by object of expenditure; or the total expenditure for a given class of activities can be shown by specific activities, by organization units, and by character, and object of expenditure.[6]

[6] The whole problem of the system of expenditure documents, the use of symbols and accounting and reporting methods generally required in order to produce the financial data desired has been worked out with great care by the Institute for Government Research. The procedure employed by it in its own accounting is set forth in detail in its *Accounting Manual.*

ORGANIZATION UNITS THE PRIMARY BASIS FOR BUDGET
CLASSIFICATION

THE foregoing, though it may seem to represent a long digression from the subject of our paper, is not so in fact. No satisfactory budgetary system can be established unless the proper basis for such a system is laid in the adoption of a scheme of expenditure documents and accounting practices calculated to produce the information which must be furnished by a budget if it is fully to serve its purpose as an information document. It is also an essential part of our purpose to discuss not only what character of budgetary system should be established, if it is desired to put the administration of the finances of a government upon a scientific basis, but how this system can actually be achieved.

We have pointed out that expenditure data may be compiled from any of the five points of view represented by the five schemes of classification that have been described. It becomes necessary, therefore, that a government shall make a decision regarding which of the five shall be adopted as the primary, and which as the subordinate, factors in the formulation of the estimates and report of expenditures which constitute the budget proper. Whichever scheme is adopted should be rigidly adhered to, for, unless it is, no consistent or logical exposition of financial operations and needs is presented from any one point of view. The violation of this fundamental principle constitutes one of the most serious defects of budgetary practice in almost all governments. Their budgets show expenditures and estimates, partly in terms of organization units, partly in terms of activities, partly in terms of character and partly in terms of objects of expenditure. It is thus exceedingly difficult, if not impossible, to summarize the data from any one viewpoint, and to appreciate the full purport of the figures in terms either of administration, responsibility, or general policy.

In reaching a decision regarding the principle of presentation that should be employed in formulating a budget, there can scarcely be any question that the choice of the primary factor of classification should fall upon the unit of organization. The budget, in a word, should have as its primary purpose to show expenditures and estimates according to the units by which they were made, or for whose use the funds estimated for are intended. The primary showing will thus be that of the actual and estimated cost of maintaining and operating each unit and class of units of organization of the government.

A number of reasons unite to make this choice desirable. In the first place, it is important to emphasize in every possible way the factor of personal responsibility. In the actual organization and conduct of the affairs of government, individuals are in charge of particular divisions or subdivisions of the government and not in charge of the performance of particular categories of work, except in so far as such particular categories are intrusted to particular organization units. As a result, individual responsibility consists in expending money and estimating the needs of such subdivisions of organization. In actual preparation of estimates, the individuals constituting the direct personnel make estimates of the needs of the services under their direction and forward them to the official next in authority above them. Here they are scrutinized, criticized, revised and aggregated, and again forwarded to the person next in rank — this process being continued until the final aggregation is secured. If a man's estimates are broken up and scattered in different parts of a budget it is bound to lead to confusion and make it difficult for the legislator to reach the proper man or proper administrative report for further information. Only by keeping accounts and making reports according to organization units is it possible to determine the efficiency with which the individual services are being run. Only as the heads of services know that their services are going to be considered on the basis of the work for which they are individually responsible will there exist a real incentive to efficiency and economy. This being the necessary basis for accounting and reporting, it is of prime importance that the budget and appropriations should be in conformity with it.

It is, moreover, desirable that the budget and the appropriation acts based upon it should present in outline as complete a picture as possible of the organization of the government. They should reveal at a glance just what departments, bureaus and subdivisions are being maintained, their relations to each other, and the personnel required by each. If a budget is properly prepared it will constitute an invaluable document revealing the structure of the government. Without such a knowledge it is impossible to give intelligent consideration to the national finances.

The argument in favor of the employment of the unit of organization as the basis for the presentation of budget data does not ignore the desirability of furnishing information regarding expenditures from the other points of view. The later information may appear as sub-items under the totals for the organization units, thus furnishing detailed information regarding the purposes, character, and object of expenditure as incurred or estimated for. The expenditures of the government as a whole will be collated from each of these several viewpoints in the analyses which, as has been stated, should accompany the budget proper. In these analyses, the total expenditures of the government, actual and estimated, will be shown classified by activities, by character, and by objects, with organization units appearing as the subsidiary items. Information will thus be furnished regarding the total expenditures of the government for any given activity or class of activities, such as public defense, education, or public health, or for any given object or class of objects, such as salaries and wages, or munitions of war, itemized according to the division of the government responsible for them.

METHOD OF PRESENTATION OF BUDGETARY DATA

Two kinds of information are required regarding the financial operations of a government — general and particular. For the formulation of general policies, information regarding total expenditures according to a few grand divisions is required. On the other hand, to ensure that money voted will be applied in an effective manner, and to maintain a proper supervision and control over actual expenditures, information regarding the details of expenditures by particular units, or for particular activities or objects, is needed. A budget, which is essentially an information document, should present both classes of information in the clearest manner possible.

Both of these objects can be obtained if the principle of presentation adopted is that of proceeding from the general to the particular, and the means employed for putting this principle into application is that of primary and supporting tables. Under this scheme, the first table will be that showing the total expenditures of the government for the last completed year, the total of appropriations for the year in progress, and the total of the estimates for the year to be provided for. This table will be supported by a second table showing the items entering into these totals by the four great branches of the government, the legislative, the judicial, the executive and the administrative, and their primary divisions, such as the administrative departments in the case of the administrative branch. This table in turn will be supported by a series of tables in which the totals for each division shown are further itemized by their primary divisions, a process which can be continued until a series of tables is reached giving the expenditures, appropriations and estimates for the final units of organization.

This scheme of presentation has a number of notable advantages. In the first place, it makes it possible for the legislator, or any one interested in the administration of the national finances, to confine his attention to grand totals, or to push his inquiries as far into details as he may desire. Secondly, and more important still, it brings into immediate juxtaposition figures which should be shown side by side in order that they may be compared. Thus, for example, the total expenditures of the several administrative departments, or the total expenditures for the primary bureaus of a department will be shown in compact tables showing nothing but these totals. If the department having charge of public health matters maintains and operates a score or more of hospitals, the total expenditures of each of these hospitals and of all combined will be shown in one place so that they can be compared. If, on the other hand, a question is raised regarding the expenditure of a particular hospital, all that is necessary is to turn to the supporting table giving the details of the expenditures of that particular institution.

It is hardly necessary to dilate upon the advantages of this method of presenting budgetary data, for it must be evident how completely and clearly it meets the various demands for information regarding governmental expenditures. One point further may, however, be mentioned. In a government of law, no expenditure is legal unless made in pursuance of statutory authority. In the supporting tables giving the details of expenditure, it is desirable, therefore, that provision should be made for an additional column in which reference is made to the statute, or order issued in pursuance of statute, authorizing the establishment and operation of the unit involved, the undertaking of the work, or the making of the particular expenditure recorded. Finally, it may be stated that this whole question of the manner of compiling and presenting budgetary data has been considered thus fully, not only on account of its intrinsic importance, but because most nations have signally failed to formulate their budgets in such a manner that the figures contained in them may be readily used for the purposes of formulating national policies or exercising a proper control in respect to the manner in which the affairs of government are actually administered.

QUESTIONS AND PROBLEMS FOR DISCUSSION

1. Compare the methods of administering the finances of Great Britain, France, Germany, and the United States.
2. What is a public budget?

3. What advantages are there in the use of the budget in government finance?
4. What operations are involved in the administration of the financial affairs of a government?
5. What factors should be considered in estimating the revenue and expenditure needs of a government?
6. What supporting documents should accompany the budget proper?
7. Discuss the nature and importance of the problem of expenditure classification in budget making?
8. Draw up a hypothetical budget for a local government.

SUGGESTIONS FOR RESEARCH

1. The fiscal functions of the Federal Reserve Banks.
2. The budgetary practice of some particular state government or of some particular municipal government.
3. A model budgetary plan for state governments in the United States.
4. A model budgetary plan for municipal governments in the United States.
5. The importance of proper budgetary procedure in municipal finance.

BIBLIOGRAPHICAL NOTE

Works covering the general field of financial administration are legion. Some of the outstanding studies which present valuable material on this subject are: W. F. Willoughby, *Principles of Public Administration,* (Washington, D. C., 1927), Chap. XXVIII; W. W. Willoughby, W. F. Willoughby and S. M. Lindsay, *The System of Financial Administration of Great Britain,* (New York, 1917); Henry Higgs, *The Financial System of the United Kingdom,* (London, 1914); and Gaston Jèze, *Cours élémentaire de science des finances et de législation financière française,* (Paris, 1912).

For a discussion of the fiscal functions of the Federal Reserve banks, see J. M. Chapman, *Fiscal Functions of the Federal Reserve Banks,* (New York, 1923); and M. S. Wildman, "The Assumption of Treasury Functions by the Federal Reserve Banks," *Annals of the American Academy of Political and Social Science,* Vol. XCIX, (January, 1922).

An excellent treatment of public budgeting is given in W. F. Willoughby, *Principles of Public Administration,* (Washington, D. C., 1927), Chaps. XXIX-XXXIII; also his *The National Budget System,* (Baltimore, 1927). Other important works on this subject are: A. E. Buck, *Public Budgeting,* (New York, 1929); his *Municipal Finance,* (New York, 1930), Chaps. III, IV; and his "Development of the Budget Idea in the United States," *Annals of the American Academy of Political and Social Science,* Vol. CXIII, (March, 1924), pp. 31-39; F. A. Cleveland and A. E. Buck, *The*

Budget and Responsible Government, (New York, 1920); W. F. Willoughby, *The Movement for Budgetary Reform in the States,* (Washington, D. C., 1918); C. G. Dawes, *The First Year of the Budget of the United States,* (New York, 1923); Henri Bonjour, *Le budget du Reich,* (Paris, 1931); Gaston Jèze, *Traité de science des finances,* (Paris, 1910), Vol. I; and R. Stourm, *The Budget,* (New York, 1917).

CHAPTER XXIX

FINANCIAL ADMINISTRATION: SELECTED PROBLEMS

1. WHEN IS THE BUDGET BALANCED?

THE question of the proper treatment of capital outlays in relation to the problem of balancing the Federal budget is discussed below.*

THOSE who claim that the surplus or the deficit should be computed on a basis that excludes capital investments or outlays point to the huge expenditures in this category in recent years. For example, in the year ended June 30, 1931, the Government expended $437 million for public works; net advances on account of the agricultural marketing fund were $191 million; and a substantial amount was made available to other private borrowers. Capital items in 1932 expenditures included the $500 million subscription to the capital stock of the Reconstruction Finance Corporation and $125 million for capital stock of the Federal Land Banks, in addition to outlays for public works and advances on account of the agricultural marketing fund and private loans.

The view that expenditures for public works should not be included in the budget proper, and that a separate public works budget should be set up rests largely on the fact that this procedure is followed by business concerns and by a number of states, especially with respect to outlays for highways. Further, when all expenditures for public works are treated as charges against current receipts, increased public works as a means of alleviating unemployment in a period of depression augment the current deficit, and, as the latter increases, public works may be restricted because of the emphasis placed upon balancing the budget. This consequence would not follow under a system providing for a separate budget, and charging only interest and amortization charges against current receipts. If this system were followed, it is claimed that the budget proper would reflect a truer picture of governmental costs.

* From *Federal Finances, 1923–1932*, (National Industrial Conference Board, Inc., New York, 1933), pp. 113-116.

Regardless of the merits of this point of view, it may be doubted that many of the public works projects financed by the Government are similar in character to those financed by private business on the basis of gradual amortization over a period of years. Outlays for public buildings and road construction are not self-liquidating in character. In the case of post offices no part of the original cost constitutes a charge against postal revenues. This being the case, the justification for special treatment is greatly lessened. The entire cost would eventually be charged against receipts, with no compensating income serving as an offset. Perhaps the principal advantage of a separate public works budget would be the fact that a more even spreading of the cost would be achieved. An increased volume of public works in a period of depression, financed out of funds borrowed for specific projects, would not inflate the deficit, except to the extent that interest and amortization charges would increase.

Separate treatment is more justifiable in the case of self-liquidating secured loans made by agencies such as the Reconstruction Finance Corporation. This has been recognized in the manner of treating the advances made by the Government to this agency. When the obligations of the Corporation are purchased, the funds are advanced from the general fund and the amounts involved are not reflected in the deficit. They are reflected in the public debt, however, for the withdrawal of funds by the Corporation necessitates additional borrowings in order to replenish the general fund. There was probably less reason for treating the $500 million capital stock subscription as other than a charge against ordinary receipts, for the reason that any losses that may be incurred would logically fall upon the capital stock. Separate treatment was not accorded the capital stock subscription, and it was reflected in the 1932 deficit. It would appear that it would have been entirely logical, however, to consider this huge investment as an extrabudget item, on the theory that any losses that might eventually be incurred should be chargeable against receipts when the losses could be definitely ascertained.

The $125 million subscription to the capital stock of the Federal Land Banks was accounted for in the same manner as the subscription to the capital stock of the Reconstruction Finance Corporation. It resulted in an increase in the deficit by the amount of the subscription. This purchase may be liquidated in time, if the experience subsequent to the establishment of the Federal Land Banks may be taken as a guide. If so, it will later be a factor tending to reduce the deficit or increase the surplus for the years in which the liquidation takes place. The same applies, of course, to the liquidation of the investment in the capital stock of the Reconstruction Finance Corporation.

The secured loans to farmers and others are practically in the same category as the loans made through the Reconstruction Finance Corporation. If they are self-liquidating, separate treatment from an accounting standpoint might be justified. The amounts involved, however, are comparatively small, and the effect on the current accounts of the Government does not compare with that of the Reconstruction Finance Corporation loans.

The advances on account of the Agricultural Marketing Fund were also treated as charges against current receipts. The loans to the stabilization corporations and co-operative associations were theoretically repayable in every instance. They did not, however, fully meet the requirements of self-liquidating loans, especially in the case of the advances to stabilization corporations. Nevertheless, it would have been entirely logical to charge the amounts advanced into a separate account and to charge the losses as realized against current receipts. This procedure would have harmonized more closely with that followed by private concerns in treating similar losses. This justification, however, should not be over-emphasized, for methods followed in corporation accounting are not necessarily applicable to the accounts of the Federal Government.

The question as to what constitutes a balanced budget ultimately resolves itself into an accounting problem. As such, consideration should be given to the nature of the items entering into receipts as well as the varied character of expenditures. Receipts under present practice include the proceeds of the liquidation of assets and receipts on trust fund account, in addition to current income. If it is not proper to regard capital outlays as a charge against receipts, then the proceeds of the liquidation of assets should certainly not be included in receipts. Since the expenditures for capital purposes ordinarily exceed the proceeds from the liquidation of assets, exclusive of those specifically applied to debt retirement, the surplus tends to be smaller or the deficit larger, than it would be if computed on the basis of current income and expenditures. If, however, the proceeds from the liquidation of assets should exceed capital outlays, the result might be somewhat incongruous, for a balanced budget would be possible, even though current income were less than current expenditures.

It must be admitted that the deficits and the surpluses as officially announced may be misleading, unless one is thoroughly familiar with the manner in which they are derived. Whether a change in methods of accounting would be of any particular value, however, is an open question. It seems certain that a statement that would show current costs of operation and current income would represent a worthwhile departure. Such a statement for the years 1921 to 1930 has recently been prepared by a private investigator.[1] Needless to add, the surpluses for the years in question, as determined on a current basis, were considerably greater than those computed on the basis used by the Government.

2. THE CONTROL OF PUBLIC EXPENDITURES

AT the close of Chapter III it was pointed out that the general administrative, as distinct from the philosophical, problems of the control of public expenditures would be discussed in PART IV, FINANCIAL ADMINISTRATION. A discussion of these general administrative problems is now presented.*

THE great problem of governmental cost involves two quite separate constituent problems. One is the determination of that cost, which is, of course, the problem of expenditures. The other is the equitable distribution of that cost among all who should contribute toward it. Assuming that the first of these constituent problems could be satisfactorily solved by setting up an adequate and workable scheme of controlling governmental costs, the second, namely the equitable distribution of tax burdens, would still require attention. Nothing that can be done in the control or reduction of governmental costs will remove the obligation to strive for an equitable distribution of such taxes as must be paid. The National Tax Association's emphasis on tax reform and tax revision, on model plans and model tax laws, its efforts toward uniformity, the elimination of interstate conflicts and the improvement of tax administration, will be as important and as necessary as ever. These matters must be dealt with as long as taxes are paid.

We may grant without debate that the problem of controlling

---

* Adapted from H. L. Lutz, "The Control of Public Expenditures," *Proceedings of the National Tax Association*, (1931), pp. 155-171.

[1] See W. F. Willoughby, *Financial Condition and Operations of the National Government*, The Brookings Institution, 1931.

public expenditures is the primary element in the larger problems of governmental costs and their burden. The expenditure side of the budget determines the weight and burden of taxation. The reduction of taxes can only be accomplished by a control and reduction of expenditures. An increase of national wealth and income might occur at a rate sufficiently rapid to produce a relative lessening of tax burdens without any attempt at expenditure control. Our national history provides instances of this happy relationship; God willing, such periods of abundance may come again. But the best guesses which our most scientific guessers are able to make indicate that for some time the contrary relationship has prevailed between public expenditures and the national wealth and income. Whatever may be the fact as to this relationship, there can be no question, in view of the rapid absolute increases of public expenditures in recent years, that this aspect of the subject demands and deserves all of the intelligence and effort that can be brought to bear upon it. It is entirely appropriate, therefore, that there be a stock-taking at this time, and that we consult together over the problem of expenditure control, in order to see just what is involved in this control, to learn what progress has been made toward the goal, and to set up conditions and concepts which may be of service in this undertaking.

We must rule out, at the beginning, the pessimist, the cynic, and all others who may hold that no control of expenditures is possible. If, with these, we admit defeat before we begin to fight, our whole undertaking is worse than useless. If there is one thing that man must learn to do, it is to control his earthly destiny. Many people believe that another war like the last one will destroy civilization. If this be even approximately correct, we must control international affairs in such wise as to prevent another war. Others have said that our capitalistic society cannot survive many more crashes like the last one. If this be only a partial truth, it behooves the capitalistic régime to learn how to control its processes in order to avoid another November, 1929. The statement has often been made that taxpayers cannot endure many more decades in which taxes are to rise as rapidly as they have during the last twenty years. If this should prove to be an exaggeration, it is probably close enough to the truth to demand of all thoughtful persons their utmost toward the formulation of a workable plan for controlling public expenditures.

The idea of *controlling* public expenditure is comparatively new, since the weight of this expenditure has only recently become such as to command serious attention. The earlier text writers on public finance spoke of "laws of expenditure increase," which indicated that they thought of this tendency as something certain and immutable. In the good old days, when the tax collector took only the people's loose change, any one who advocated expenditure control would no doubt have been classed with those experts who believed in perpetual motion, squaring the circle, and bootstrap levitation. At best, the subject was suitable only for a professorial lecture topic. Many persons . . . will recall the thrill produced by the news, some thirty years ago, that the federal appropriations had finally passed one billion dollars. The general reaction was one of chestiness, of pride and added personal importance, at the thought of being a citizen of a billion-dollar country. More than one editor expanded this thought at length. I need not emphasize how completely this viewpoint has changed, now that the federal *deficit* is more than the total expenditure of that earlier day. The man who can really show how to set a bottom to the hole into which taxes are being poured, who can lead the way into the promised land of lighter taxes, will rate along with Moses.

In approaching this subject, we must dismiss the idea that expenditure control involves, everywhere, a recession in the volume of governmental services. Neither the taxpayers nor any other group are going to give up roads, or education, or charities or other services just to save some public money. As the facts in particular cases are better known, the people may be persuaded, or they may be compelled, to decide against some of the extravagances in expenditure, where a clear case can be made. The success of expenditure control cannot depend, however, on the sporadic savings resulting from an evangelistic conviction of the sin of extravagance, although this kind of evangelism is worth while preaching. In the main, the success of expenditure control rests on getting the same flow of services for less money.

I realize that this sounds suspiciously like "efficiency and economy," the famous "gold-brick" twins of many a hard-fought campaign. The old efficiency and economy song-and-dance turn has been put on many times by candidates and by investigating commissions. It was a good act, it made good head lines, and it often got quite a "hand" from the gallery. Unfortunately it was too often recognized to be simply a song and dance. We are invited now to consider this matter anew. The taxation thumbscrews provide a strong incentive to listen to those who believe in expenditure control, and we are ready to be shown that the old song-and-dance tune can be elevated into a national anthem.

It is my purpose, in opening this discussion, to indicate the scope and character of the problem of expenditure control and some of the elements or factors which are involved. . . My remarks are confined and applied largely to the field of local expenditure, for two reasons. First, the field of local government is now the scene of our largest expenditures, in terms of aggregates, which means that the great weight of taxation is produced by the activities of the local units. Second, I feel somewhat more at home in dealing with local conditions as a result of recent activities and opportunities for seeing the situation at first-hand. Much of what I may say is no doubt capable of application, with little modification, to state or even to federal conditions.

A rational and workable program of expenditure control involves three main elements or parts. These are :

(1). A setting or environment for governmental functioning which will permit of economical operation.

(2). A technique of expenditure control.

(3). A popular attitude of approving and favoring the methods and results.

All of these elements are essential ingredients of the plan. Much of the difficulty with the old "efficiency and economy" slogan was in the fact that, however serious may have been the intention, there was an altogether inadequate conception, in the minds of those pledging or recommending efficiency and economy, regarding the scope of the program that was needed if effective results were to be secured. An individual or even a party pledge to introduce and practice efficiency and economy was valuable only as an indication of good intention, since there was usually no discernment of the far-reaching improvements of setting and technique that were required in order to make greater efficiency and economy possible. This will be apparent as the discussion proceeds.

I shall outline briefly some of the main suggestions to be offered under each of the above headings. Of the three, the first and second are much easier of accomplishment than the third. All who have had to do with the electorate know that it is very much easier to perfect a plan than to secure popular approval. In this particular case, however, the rising tax burden is working steadily on the side of a reasonable plan of expenditure control, and it may in the end secure the votes which neither the beauty of the plan nor the persuasiveness of its advocates could command.

(1). THE SETTING

My thought here can best be set out by indicating some of the ways in which the present governmental environment is inimical to economy. I must repeat that I refer primarily to the conditions of local government.

The first fact which appears, in an examination of the organization and structure of local governments, is the extraordinary quantity of local governmental machinery that exists. There are counties, municipalities, school districts and a vast number of special districts for different purposes, piled one on top of another, in duplicating and overlapping layers. Produced in the older sections by accident and tradition, and in the newer sections by the rectangular survey, these small units have everywhere become endowed with a corporate existence and with varying powers as governmental corporate bodies. The condition, in the older states, dates back to the horse-and-buggy age, when the poor roads, the limited means of travel and the absence of regular, dependable means of communication compelled the establishment of many small governmental agencies for the convenience and need of the citizen. Aside from a few instances of the creation of metropolitan districts and a few cases of county-municipal consolidation, the local governmental plan remains exactly as it was in the days of Washington and Jefferson, except that the subsequent changes have been in the direction of adding to, rather than of diminishing the confusion. Such attention as has been given to the subject of governmental reorganization has been devoted exclusively to the state governments and, within very narrow limits, to the federal government. An examination of all of the state reorganization plans from Governor Lowden's initial undertaking in Illinois in 1917 to that of the Abell Committee in New Jersey in 1930 indicates an almost total absence of any realization of a problem of local governmental reorganization, and a naïve belief that the state government could be adequately reorganized without regard to the local counterpart.

A second defect in the present setting of local government is the absence of concentrated financial responsibility. This condition is a direct outgrowth of the multiplication of agencies. Each separate unit, whether county, municipality, school district or special district, is busy with its own little part of the general task of supplying a flow of services to the citizens. Each has its authority to levy taxes, to plan expenditures, to borrow money. None is ordinarily obliged to know or to consider what the others are doing, or what the aggregate charge upon the citizens is to be. The governing body of each unit or district could probably make out a case for spending what it plans to spend, since the subdivision of local functions corresponds to the chaotic subdivision of authorities. The theory of local self-government is that the citizens will keep an eye on their local officials and not let them spend too much. When the entire list of the spending agencies that have the power to levy upon any particular citizen or his property is considered, the individual's watch-dog function becomes hopelessly complicated. The taxpayers are guilty, as charged, of being negligent and indifferent toward the activities of their government. In extenuation, it should be said that there is not one government, but in some cases upwards of a dozen of these "governments" that must be watched. A cat can do a good job of watching one mouse hole, but when the mice have ten other ways out, pussy is likely to have a busy time getting her dinner. If a taxpayer in New Jersey or New York should set out to watch diligently all of the governmental agencies that are spending his money, he would have precious little time left to earn the taxes levied against him.

Urging the thousands of small local units to be efficient and economical is like advising the "water boy" to carry water in a sieve. The situation was hopelessly "stacked" against the old-time efficiency and economy advocate, because the effective practice of these admirable civic virtues was entirely out of the question without a thoroughgoing change in the whole governmental structure.

I will give one illustration of this condition which is provided by the situation in New Jersey. The five northeastern counties, across the Hudson from Manhattan, have a combined area of about 700 square miles, and a total population of about 2,500,000. This area, which is the equivalent of a rectangle 20 miles wide and 35 miles long, has five county governments, 140 municipal governments, 137 school districts, and a considerable number of other special districts. Hudson County, in this area, with 42.5 square miles, is cut up into 12 municipalities, some of which are only a few blocks wide. This means that each little municipality has its own police and fire departments, its own street and road department, and all of the other paraphernalia and equipment of a real city. Each is struggling with crime control, fire prevention, health and sanitation, poor relief, street and road planning, property assessment, tax collection, and all of the other activities that have devolved upon the municipality. There is a tremendous overmanning in many departments and the taxpayers are paying the bill. We have estimated that the 12 municipalities of Hudson County could save over one million dollars annually by establishing a county unit fire department on the standards of manning set up by the National Board of Fire Underwriters. Hudson County is approximately the size of the city of Pittsburgh.

This leads me to a third defect in the environment or setting, which is a bad allocation of functions. The distribution of responsibility for performing the several governmental functions has never had a rational basis in this country. Whether a given service is to be performed by central or by local authority has been largely a matter of accident or tradition. The original scope of state functions was small, and the centralizing tendencies of a generation ago resulted in some transfers of authority from local to state jurisdiction, but these were for the most part accidental, and not an outcome of any general and mature consideration of needs. As a result of the great population growth and changes of the past half-century, the cities find themselves today obligated to perform some services which could be given more satisfactorily and at lower cost, by other agencies. The occasional instance of the formation of metropolitan districts represents, thus far, the sole response that has come to this pressure for functional reallocation. Even these districts have been restricted to one, or to a very few functions, thereby leaving untouched the general question of relieving the local taxpayer of the excess cost involved in an improper placement of responsibility.

The agitation of this subject in New Jersey has led to a proposal for the organization of regional governments to which certain responsibilities shall be given. The proposed New Jersey regions would hardly be larger in extent than some counties in other states, but the difficulty encountered in setting up these glorified counties is that no provision has been made for the elimination of some part of the sub-structure of local government, which means that the full advantage of such a change is not likely to be realized.

A fourth environmental defect is the indifference now frequently displayed regarding the quality of the personnel in the public service. On the average, not far from half of the total state and local expenditure goes into wages and salaries. Despite the vogue which has been given by the teachings of some economists, or near economists, to the doctrine of high wages during a depression, regardless of the connection of the wages paid with the value of the product of labor, the governmental service could give private employment "cards and spades" in this game. Aside from some conspicuous exceptions, the governmental attitude, during good times and bad, had been one of notorious indifference to the quality of its personnel and to the value of the product in relation to the wages paid.

I appreciate fully the political aspects of this situation, and I realize the difficulties involved in improving the "government stroke," in view of the dangerous solidarity of the public employee vote. Nevertheless, I venture to suggest to the taxpayers who are providing the public wage fund that something might be done to improve the quality of the personnel, even if the prospects of changing the tempo of the government stroke appear to be but slight.

In order to make my point clear, I need only call attention to the wide gap which now exists between the concept of personnel administration as applied in private employment and the civil service, which marks the highest achievement of the public employment policy. Some civil service leaders are aware of this gap, and their own standards for the improvement of the public personnel service are far above those which are set by the existing legislation. When we consider the number of public employees who learn their job after getting on the payroll, the time seems ripe for the introduction of training schools or training courses for the larger groups of these employees.

The training-school idea is already given limited application. In some places assessors are offered such training, although the ridiculous and obsolete notion that the assessor is an official and not an employee has militated against general acceptance of the need for special training. Similarly, training for police and firemen, for inspectors and financial officers has been developed here and there. A broad opportunity exists for the establishment of training schools for public employees, under the coöperative guidance of state and municipal authorities, with provision for coördinating the results of this training with the procedure of certification under the civil service. Normal schools for teachers have long been an accepted feature of the improvement of teacher personnel. Why not a similar arrangement for other large and expensive classes of public servants? The cost of such a school would be saved many times over in the improvement that would result in personnel qualifications.

A final defect or condition in the current environment which I shall mention here is a certain belligerent attitude on the subject of home rule. Like many other manifestations of belligerency, this one rests usually on a misconception. The extreme advocate of home rule insists upon keeping within municipal control all of the functions placed there by accident or tradition, despite the evidence and the logic which would demonstrate the need of change. The criticisms that I have been making of the present chaotic system of local government obviously point toward some fundamental rearrangements of the pattern and structure. It is equally obvious that these changes would displace some local officials and quite possibly some local employees, since it is perfectly certain that there are now more, in both of these categories, than are required for efficient and economical administration. My experience is that the bulk of the opposition to the necessary changes, and the most heated invocations of the rights of home rule, come from those who foresee loss of authority or complete displacement.

Under these circumstances, an attitude of opposition is only human and natural. It all depends on whose ox is being gored. The perpetuation of the present disorder of local governmental organization, amounting to a calamity, means that the tax-payers' ox is now taking the punishment, and the reorganization of local government that must be effected if we are to provide a setting for the operation of an expenditure control technique is simply an application of the old hedonistic maxim of the greatest good to the greatest number.

In any reallocation of functions, some responsibilities will of course remain in the local jurisdiction, whether that be small or large. This local sphere, redefined and redetermined, will be the proper field for the exercise of home rule, and the proper field for the purely local expenditures. The unreasoning opposition which is frequently encountered against any and all changes in the traditional alignment does not ordinarily arise with the people, for the proportion of the registered vote which turns out in most local elections indicates the popular attitude toward home rule. The issue lies between those who must pay the cost of an antiquated system and those who stand to benefit most directly from its continuance.

The conception of the proper setting or environment for an economical administration of local government which I have been outlining here may be summarized as follows. There must be, first, a far more simple structure and organization of that government, a structure which will reduce the number of agencies responsible for supplying services over any given area, preferably to a single governmental unit. This simplification must be brought about in some cases by consolidation of munici-palities or districts, and in other cases by disorganization of the surplus units, with a transfer of their functions to some other better qualified administrative authority. Secondly, there must be a definite establishment of the financial responsibility where it will be known and felt, both by those who hold this responsibility and by those who must pay the bill. Thirdly, there must be a clear relationship between the functional services to be performed and the resources with which to carry on. So important is this balance that we must learn to think and to appraise results in terms of functions or services, rather than in terms of cities, towns or school districts. Fourthly, an improvement in the quality of the public personnel through better methods of training and selection is sorely needed. Finally, there must be an acceptance of the necessary flexibility, which will enable such functional adjustments as may be required to be made without encountering at every turn the blind and prejudiced opposition of the home-rule supporter, who, in nine cases out of ten, is primarily concerned with saving some unnecessary local office or job from the scrap heap.

In view of this statement of the conditions essential to the practice and observance of economy, it is small wonder that the efficiency and economy pledges and recommendations of the past have been so heavily discounted. My earlier characterization of these terms as the "gold brick" twins may have appeared unnecessarily flippant, but in view of the utter lack of discernment commonly displayed as to the depth and extent of the changes required before it is possible to be ready to economize and to be efficient, one must be harsh in order to be just.

For example, suppose that a candidate for mayor or councilman or county freeholder or township committeeman, or in fact any other local office should give the most solemn pledges of efficiency and economy in his administration, and suppose further that these pledges came from the heart. Under the conditions which exist practically universally the cards are stacked against this official, regardless of his intentions. The city must enlarge its water supply, for example, which may mean tapping a new source one hundred miles away. This becomes a tremendous burden for one city, but if all of the cities in a given region were to be supplied through one large trunk water line, the cost for each may be materially reduced. The mayor may pledge a reduction of crime, but he finds that he must increase the police force in order to get rid of the criminals which his neighbor cities are pushing over into his own boundaries, and as fast as he increases his force for the purpose of passing the criminals along, the other cities provide larger forces to send them back again. Crime control in the metropolitan sections of New Jersey is the old game of push-ball, and the city which will hire the most policemen will have, for the time, the fewest criminals, but its neighbors will have more. Competitive armament is not confined to the international sphere.

Again, the township committeeman agrees to be economical in road expenditure. His little district has only a few miles of road, but he must have a road gang, a steam roller, a tar cooker and other equipment. The equipment required for each system of township roads could easily maintain three or four times the mileage of a township road district. It is very much like a man with a 25-acre farm trying to operate with a sample of every piece of farm equipment sold by the International Harvester Company.

Because of these underlying essentials, I have no hesitation in declaring that economical administration, in any real and lasting sense, is simply out of the question until there are some fundamental readjustments in the environment which will permit the application of economical and business-like methods.

(2). THE TECHNIQUE OF EXPENDITURE CONTROL

I PASS now to some of the positive means of expenditure control. I have emphasized that these instruments cannot function properly and adequately in a poor or unfavorable environment or setting. It would be as reasonable to expect an automobile engine to operate as smoothly with sand as with oil in its bearings. The connection which I wish to establish will be made clear as I proceed, and in so doing I shall distinguish the instruments of control, the standards of control and the policy of control.

The Instruments of Expenditure Control. Among the more important instruments of expenditure control I would list the budget, an adequate system of accounting and auditing, a reasonable restriction of borrowing, and some device for assuring the taxpayer an opportunity of stating his case and adjusting any differences of viewpoint between himself and the tax-levying official.

These instruments of control are familiar, since they are in fairly general use. Under the adverse environmental conditions which so commonly prevail, however, they are operating on a low basis of efficiency. The states which have local budget acts have simply required every spending agency subject to the law to make a budget, which means that each one sets down what it intends to spend. Nothing has been done to eliminate the duplication of spending agencies, to assign functions according to the proper administrative agencies, nor to concentrate financial responsibility so that it cannot be evaded or avoided. Under these circumstances local budgets, even if properly prepared, merely give a certain orderliness to the expenditure process, without affecting seriously its total or its upward tendency.

I would dismiss, as suitable instruments of control, such crude devices as tax-rate limits and expenditure limits. As between a tax-rate limit and a debt limit, the latter is preferable on every count. Since it is obvious that both cannot be applied at the same time, I prefer the strict control of local borrowing to any rigid interference with tax rates, which is likely to be about as effective as the method of concealment employed by the ostrich. It is true that the experiments thus far recorded in tax rate and expenditure limitation have been unaccompanied by recognition of the inherent wastefulness of the existing local structure, and that nothing was done about these fundamental defects. If such defects as I have indicated are corrected, however, effective expenditure control can be realized without the introduction of these methods of restriction, while they would prove quite inadequate in the absence of the underlying reforms.

The objective of debt restriction is to compel observance of the sound principles of public credit, and to avoid the debt "joyrides" which have been taken at the expense of the taxpayer. One of the most ghastly tragedies of local financing has been the use of long-term loans "to keep the tax rate down," and "to make posterity pay." An enthusiastic application of these slogans in New Jersey, under debt-restrictive legislation which had lost such teeth as it may have had originally, resulted in increasing the local debt, less sinking funds, from $199,940,000 in 1918 to $875,000,000 in 1929. This meant an advance in the per-capita debt from $65.94 in 1918 to $216.51 in 1929. In 1918 the local debt was 6.6 per cent of the net taxable valuation, while in 1929 it was 14 per cent.

It is beyond my purpose to indicate here all of the features of model budget accounting, or debt-control legislation. I wish to suggest, however, two essential features of proper debt control. These are, first, the introduction of improvement planning and budgeting, and second, the payment in the current expense budget of an advance installment toward the cost of any improvement to be financed by borrowing.

Improvement budgeting will compel an orderly advance consideration of the projects contemplated and an equally careful consideration of the means of financing them. This attention will be given in advance, at the time when the improvement budgets are being set up and submitted to the people. There should also be a statement of the effect of the tax rate to be produced by these improvement proposals, and a projection of the effects on the tax rate through the period required for the financing. The ease with which bond ordinances may be enacted in many states encourages laxity in planning and in counting the cost. Each project is put through separately, and no one ever gets a complete picture of the combined results of the series of such ordinances. The possibilities of temporary financing and of delaying the inauguration of substantial redemption payments in the process of converting the temporary paper into long-term bonds have made credit so easy, and apparently so cheap, that municipalities have had no compunction about buying expensive improvements on long terms when they should have used shorter terms, and in some cases when they should have paid cash or have declined to buy them at all. The advance payment brings home to the taxpayer immediately the consequences of an improvement expenditure. It prevents one administration from taking the credit of making improvements without increasing taxes, while compelling the next one to assume the blame for increasing taxes to redeem the debt. An advance payment toward improvement costs is simply an application to the public business of the accepted rule of private installment credit, which is that there must be a down payment when the goods are taken.

I must dismiss also, as reliable control devices, the "strong man" theory and the slogan that "the way to reduce is to reduce." There are times when the strong man and his blunt slogan are welcome antidotes to excessive expenditure, but strong men are not dependably forthcoming. They are historical accidents, averaging one or less to each grave crisis. Expenditure control requires steady, consistent attention from the rank and file of administrators and the instruments to be used must be as nearly foolproof as they can be made.

Some states have apparently applied the slogan, "The way to reduce is to reduce," by ordering flat percentage cuts in salaries. All questions of salary deflation aside, I submit that a reduction of expenditures by any system of horizontal cuts is likely to be poor economy in the end. There is no easy, lazy man's way out of the present difficulty. The way to reduce to a level of true economy is to eliminate the sources of waste which now compel government to be uneconomical.

Standards of Control. The absence of standards of expenditure control is the weakest point of existing theory and practice, and the introduction of such standards would therefore present the greatest constructive opportunity for the future.

It is perfectly apparent that much of the pulling and hauling that passes for expenditure criticism today is predestined to futility for the reason that the spending official and his critic lack a common basis for their argument. The taxpayer or the taxpayers' association says that taxes are too high and must be reduced. The official who must manage a department or make up the entire budget insists that he needs as much as is asked for in order to operate his department or his municipality. From his standpoint the expenditure is not too great, and while he may admit that taxes are high, he can see nothing to be done about it. Clearly, the taxpayer who is seeking lower taxes and the officials who are supporting the budget estimates are not joined in the debate. They have no common meeting ground of difference since they are talking about different things. They cannot establish a rational basis for discussing their differences without some sort of yardstick by which the service to be given may be measured. Lacking such a yard-stick, the contention that expenditures for any department or *in toto* are too high, too low or just right has no recognizable meaning. The result is usually the calling of hard names and general bitterness. The taxpayer calls the official a "tax spender," a favorite form of reference in some circles to all of those who must manage the public affairs, while the official counters with "tax slacker," or "tax dodger," or some epithet of similar import. Both sweetness and light are lacking from such a controversy, which is about as far as many of the sporadic attempts at expenditure criticism have gone.

In order to end this kind of fruitless controversy and to provide a basis of criticism which will assure that the taxpayer and the budget-maker are talking about the same thing, it is necessary to establish standards of service and cost for the various activities which must be operated. The standard of service is a statement of exactly how much service is required to be given by any department or division. The units of measurement will vary, but however these are to be expressed, the budget-maker is quite as much at sea in any intelligent defense of his proposals as is his critic unless they are set up. The standard of cost is a statement of what it will cost to provide the volume of service called for by the standard of service.

The mere mention of these terms and of their significance reveals the extent to which they are now lacking. Occasionally one finds a governing body which determines its highway program by a survey of traffic needs and conditions, but there is no general application of the principle. Generally speaking, budget estimates are made by considering what was actually spent in prior years and in the current year to the date when the estimates were prepared. The appropriation for the future usually has an allowance for one good reason or another, but budgeting without the use of independent standards to determine the amount really required is like building a coral reef. The inevitable tendency of such a process is upward. Budget-making is in consequence more nearly depression-proof than any other industry.

The game of golf affords an excellent illustration of my point, and one which, I am sure, will be more readily grasped . . . than any other that might be selected. On any golf course, it is possible to send a ball from the tee to the putting green on any hole up to 200 yards. Knowing this, the person who knew nothing else about the game might insist that every 150-yard hole, for example, should be played in one stroke, while the person who had a long and sad experience with rough, bunker and sand trap might insist on five or six strokes, even for the 150-yard holes. But the argument as to what constitutes perfect golf has been settled once for all by establishing a par for the course, which is nothing more than a standard of performance. The par or standard for 150-yard holes is three strokes, and no one is expected or required to do better than this standard. The course par sets a measure for every player from that famous citizen of Atlanta known as the emperor of golf to the worst dub who swings a mashie iron.

Present-day expenditure and budget criticism is exactly like deciding what is good golf on a course where the par is unknown. The taxpayer wants eagles, birdies, and holes in one, while the budget-maker may want a Civil War score, out in 61, back in 65. Both the budget-maker and his critic, the taxpayer or the taxpayers' association, need to apply the basic principle of golf to the determination of expenditures. They must set pars, or standards, for each department and for the whole budget. In suggesting this, I will direct the attention of the budget-makers to the fact that golf is usually supposed to have originated in Scotland.

It is apparent that these standards or pars cannot be determined simply with regard to what was spent the previous year. The whole idea of the standard is that there must be devised an independent measure of the amount of service required and of the cost of that service. Standards of performance and of cost have been familiar to private management since the epoch-making essays of F. W. Taylor on Scientific Management. Those who have been heretofore among the keenest advocates of standards for determining production volume and costs have been comparatively indifferent to the possibilities of the same device as a check upon budget-making. Instead of determining by referendum whether to add 50 policemen or firemen or janitors, the question should be determined by the principles of job analysis. How much work is to be done, and how much should one man do? The quotient gives the answer. No magic cross, made within the mystic square by a voter in the privacy of his voting booth can ever provide the correct answer to such questions.

In setting the standards of service and cost there is a real opportunity for a clash between the taxpayer and the official, but if the debate is centered upon what should constitute the standard, both contestants will be dealing with the same problem and with a common conception of it. The collision will be head on, and not a side swipe. These differences regarding the proper standards of service and costs can and must be ironed out, arbitrated or settled in some fashion. An arrangement is needed whereby the taxpayer may bring serious disagreements into the open, either by appealing to a state authority as in Indiana or to his fellow taxpayers under a referendum as in Utah.

My emphasis upon standards as the key to expenditure control provides another reason for opposing tax-rate limits. Such a limit may force every department to a hole in one standard, or it may actually permit some of them five or six strokes for three-par conditions, to apply my illustration. At best, the tax-rate limit must be regarded as crude and unscientific in comparison with control by standards.

It is apparent that such a program of expenditure control as I am here sketching will not be self-operative. Equally apparent is the fact that it could not be bodily introduced without much preliminary planning. Many of the states have uniform budget and accounting acts, but the actual observance of uniformity is not always perfect. The development of standards must rest upon the accumulation and digesting of a mass of information, much of which is not even gathered at present under existing procedure. We have proposed, for New Jersey, a division of standards and costs, in the department of municipal accounts, to assist in planning the information required and in computing acceptable standards.

Policy of Control. In other words, there must be a policy

of supervision and control, exercised by the state through the enactment of the necessary legislation for budgets, accounting and debt control, and also through the provision of adequate supervisory contacts with local agencies. The tax commissioners . . . recognize thoroughly how important is supervision of local assessments. Those . . . whose responsibility extends to accounting and auditing realize the need and importance of their oversight in this field. As a general theorem, I would propose that there should be a universal integration or dovetailing of local and central administration. This integration need not and should not destroy local initiative and responsibility, but rather encourage it, since the higher the level of local administrative performance, the less actual central interference is needed.

The shortsightedness of state reorganization schemes has never been more manifest than in this failure to provide for a proper integration with local administration. State and local affairs are treated as separate water-tight compartments between which no communication or vital contact is to be considered. Functional reallocation has been completely blocked off under these plans, and thus the door has been closed to any consideration of the local problems which are creating such tremendous burdens of taxation.

It is necessary to recognize the handicap which patronage and influence impose upon the budget-maker. He may be perfectly well aware that there are too many men in the police, fire, street or other departments, but he may also be incapable of doing anything about it for political or patronage reasons. I doubt if this handicap is ever really an absolute alibi. My suggestion relative to the improvement of personnel may provide a partial solution of this difficulty. For the rest, I can only say that the patronage system, in all its manifestations, is up to the taxpayers in the end. It is their money which is being used to bestow these favors. Their attitude hitherto toward this subject is one of the strongest reasons for the belief that the taxpayers are fully qualified members of that group into which the late Mr. Barnum said a new one is born every minute. They break their backs getting the money to pay their taxes, and they either ignore or actively support a system which pays out an unknown but doubtless a substantial part of the total to provide favors, concessions and advantages to the beneficiaries of patronage. In this they deserve as little sympathy as they now receive. It may be urged that the friends and relatives of surplus employees and of other beneficiaries of patronage will combine to embarrass any official who does his duty. Why, it may be asked, are the bonds of family and friendship supposed to be so much closer in the case of surplus employees, than in the case of the taxpayers? Where are the friends and relatives of the taxpayer in such a crisis? I suggest that a better name for a taxpayers' association would be "An association of the Friends and Relatives of the Taxpayer." Whenever the taxpayers as a group decide to stop paying the patronage bill, they can eliminate it or reduce it to negligible proportions. The other obstacles to efficient and economical government are equally within their control if they and their friends and relatives care to make the effort to remove them.

(3). A POPULAR ATTITUDE FAVORABLE TO THE NECESSARY REFORM

THE statement just made brings me naturally to the third and final element in my program of expenditure control. This is that the people must want it badly enough to bring it about. A few more turns of the tax thumbscrews may be required before the necessary solidarity of public opinion is developed.

This solidarity of popular approval is necessary, both with respect to the control of the cost of established and accepted governmental functions, and to the extension of these functions through a broadening of their scope or the addition of entirely new services. The expenditure control devices which I have outlined will serve to regulate the cost of such governmental services as are now on the list. They will not operate to determine the length of the list of the functions to be performed.

It is perfectly evident that the growth of the list of so-called governmental functions, and the transformation of particular services by introducing all manner of frills, are matters which rest eventually with the people themselves. No device can be suggested which will relieve the citizens from the two-fold duty here indicated; namely, the duty of supporting the efforts at effective control of expenditures for services already authorized, and the further duty of considering with due care every proposed extension of these services. Popular sanction must become positive and vital, instead of going by default.

I have no prescription for securing the needed popular sanction. I said at the outset that this is the really difficult part of the job. It means a drive against the civic and political illiteracy of the American people, which is another way of saying that it is, in the broad sense, an educational undertaking. This is peculiarly a matter for coördinated, group action, and I suggest that one of the conspicuous opportunities of the vital and intelligently guided taxpayers' association is in the promotion of the necessary public sentiment. In order to serve this purpose, any organization must establish its good faith by playing the game squarely. That is, it must demonstrate its interest in fundamental matters, and not simply operate as an agent to secure tax reductions for its members. I have no hesitation in saying that the reward of such disinterested effort is immensely worth while, even for those who may support such an organization from selfish motives. No one can explore the dark fastnesses of local finance without being impressed, even overwhelmed, by the evidence of waste inherent in the existing system, and by the opportunities for reducing local governmental costs through the application of intelligent common sense. In this movement I venture to say that the National Tax Association is deeply interested, and that it will coöperate with other agencies in every way within its power.

3. Effective State Control of Local Expenditures

The provisions of a concrete plan for state administration of local expenditures are set forth in the following article.*

It would not be possible to review here the complete list of criticisms which investigators are leveling at contemporary local government and all of its works. The list is sufficiently lengthy to fill the pages of fairly thick reports. The present discussion deals with a particular stricture, namely, that local governments have been conspicuously remiss in the matter of setting up certain administrative machinery and in observing certain standard routines and principles which experience has shown to be absolutely essential to the effective control of public expenditures.

The particular arrangements and procedures to which reference is made are perfectly familiar to all students of public administration. They include the making of budgets, and what is perhaps more important, the setting up of machinery for insuring effective budgetary control. They include such devices as centralized accounting, independent audits, and adequate financial reports at periodic intervals. For certain functions, they involve an application of the methods of cost accounting and the development standards against which the adequacy of services and the reasonableness of costs may be checked. Last, but not least, they involve the strict observance of certain elementary principles of sound finance. These prin-

---

* Adapted from Clarence Heer, "Effective State Control of Local Expenditures," *Proceedings of the National Tax Association*, (1931), pp. 418-425.

ciples include such axiomatic propositions as the following: that budgets be balanced, that tax levies be sufficient to meet interest and amortization charges on funded debt, that the terms of bonds be limited to the economic life of the improvement which they represent, that tax anticipation notes be not in excess of the probable future revenue collections and that provision be made for their automatic retirement, that public funds on deposit in banks be adequately safeguarded, and that financial officials be properly bonded.

It is a notorious fact that very few local governments make any extensive use of the technique of expenditure control which has just been outlined. This may be due to unwillingness. It is more probably due to inexperience and lack of knowledge on the part of local governing bodies and administrative officials. All states have enacted mandatory legislation designed to compel the local governments within their jurisdictions to observe certain sound financial principles and practices. In the absence of any practical method of enforcement, these enactments have, on the whole, not been taken very seriously by local officials and their letter as well as their spirit has frequently been violated. In view of this situation, there is a growing feeling that state control over local governmental finances should be made more effective. This feeling is being embodied in the demand that state legislatures should not only pass mandatory legislation requiring the adoption of approved systems of expenditure control and the observance of at least the fundamentals of sound financial practice, but that they should also provide for state administrative agencies whose function it shall be to aid and advise local officials in the installation of the prescribed systems and methods as well as to exercise such administrative supervision over local governmental finances as is necessary to secure obedience to legislative mandates.

For an exposition of the salient features of a well-rounded plan of state administrative control over local finances, I refer you to two reports on the organization and administration of state and county governments in North Carolina which were recently prepared by The Brookings Institution of Washington, D. C., at the request of Governor O. Max Gardner. The recommendations of the Brookings report imply the existence of statutes which make it mandatory on all local governments to adopt certain prescribed forms of financial organization and procedure and to observe certain specified minimums of sound financial practice. Their purpose is to provide administrative machinery which will make legislation of this kind effective.

The Brookings plan provides, in brief, for the creation of a State Department of Local Government Finance to be headed by a commissioner appointed by the Governor. The commissioner is to be advised on questions of policy by a Local Government Advisory Council consisting of seven members. One of these is to be the State Treasurer. The others are to be appointed by the Governor from the ranks of local government officials.

The proposed Department of Local Government Finance is intended to serve as more than a mere policeman. It is charged with the duty of advising and assisting county, city, town, and village officers in their financial and accounting work. It is expected to make investigations and studies directed toward the improvement of local fiscal administration, and it must pass on the qualifications of candidates for certain local offices. It has, however, important functions of a supervisory nature. The basic machinery through which this supervision is to be exercised is supplied by a provision which vests in the department the authority to devise, install, and enforce uniform systems of budgeting, uniform systems of centralized accounting and uniform systems of financial reporting. The supervising functions themselves may be summarized under four general heads, review of budgets, periodic inspections and audits, periodic financial reports, and supervision over indebtedness.

It is proposed that certified copies of all county and municipal budgets be filed with the Department of Local Government Finance immediately after their enactment and before the adoption and fixing of local tax rates. The department is empowered to examine these budgets for the purpose of determining whether all legal requirements relating to budget formulation have been met. If the department finds that a budget fails to keep appropriations within the limits of prospective revenues or fails to make due provision for meeting all legal liabilities and obligations, as for instance, sinking fund and interest requirements, it is authorized to revise the budget so as to provide for the meeting of these requirements. In making such revisions, it is empowered to reduce or eliminate items of appropriations so as to bring the total of appropriations within the available revenue. The budget as amended is to be returned to the governing body of the locality together with a notification to the local accountant or comptroller that he is to be governed by the revised budget in the validation of warrants.

The proposed Department of Local Government Finance is

charged with the duty of making periodic or special audits of
county and municipal accounts for which purpose it is to be
provided with a staff of auditors. Upon discovery of violations
of law, the Commissioner is required to serve notice on the
responsible local official to correct the condition promptly. If
this notice is disregarded, the Commissioner is directed to
request the Attorney General to institute legal proceedings
against the offending officer. As a further assurance that the
provisions of law governing local financial affairs be duly observed, it is recommended that the Governor be empowered to
remove from office any county or municipal financial officer
found guilty of malfeasance in office or of deliberate neglect
to comply with the provisions of law governing the manner of
discharge of his duties.

One of the duties of the State Department of Local Government Finance is to publish an annual report covering the
financial operations of all counties, cities, towns and villages.
For this purpose, local governments are to be required to file
with the department periodic reports on prescribed forms.

It is in the matter of supervision over local indebtedness that
the powers recommended for the new department are most extensive. The creation of all local indebtedness, including
short-term borrowing, is subject to the approval of the department. In addition, the department is vested with the duty
of marketing all county debt offerings and attending to the
payment of interest and to the redemption of principal of such
indebtedness. In order to enable it to discharge these
latter duties, it is given the power to supervise sinking-fund
operations and to amend local budgets where insufficient
provision has been made for interest and sinking-fund requirements.

The recommendations of the Brookings report have been
described in considerable detail, not because they are new, but
because they bring together in a single plan many individual
features of state administrative control which have been in
effect in one state or another for a fairly long time. The North
Carolina prototype of the proposed State Department of Local
Government Finance is the County Government Advisory Commission which was created in 1927. The last North Carolina
legislature substituted for this body a Local Government Finance Commission [with extensive powers and duties]. . .
In a number of states of the Union certain of the powers and
duties which have been recommended for the proposed State
Department of Local Government Finance are now being exercised by state tax commissions, state budget directors, state

comptrollers, state sinking-fund commissions and similar agencies and officials.

Uniform budgets for all or for specified classes of local governments are now mandatory in at least ten states of the Union. Several states, including Indiana, New York and Ohio, prescribe uniform municipal accounts. In others a central state agency is authorized to devise uniform accounting systems and to aid in their installation, although the adoption of such systems is not made mandatory. Uniform financial reports are required annually in at least six states. State administrative review of local budgets is now provided for under various conditions and limitations in half a dozen states, the best known example of such administrative review being the much-discussed "Indiana Plan." Provisions for the auditing of local government accounts by central state agencies are exceedingly common. In many states, however, such audits are confined to certain kinds of accounts or are made only at the request of local authorities or interested taxpayers. Fully a score of states attempt to exercise some degree of administrative supervision over local indebtedness, at least to the extent of requiring reports covering its nature and amount. In only a few states, however, is this supervision as extensive as that proposed in the Brookings report.

The machinery of state administrative control over local expenditure is only a means to an end and, if the people as a whole do not approve of that end or do not understand it, it is extremely unlikely that the machinery will function effectively. In this connection it is necessary to face the fact that the setting up of state agencies to supervise and control the financial affairs of local political units is regarded in some quarters with grave suspicion. In the minds of many, such agencies are conceived of as a special invention for the benefit of large taxpayers who, despairing of reducing their taxes through the regular channels provided for in a democracy, seek to attain their ends through the creation of a dictatorship. This conception might have some justification if state supervisory agencies are to be policy-forming as well as administrative bodies. As long, however, as their powers are limited to the administration and enforcement of specific legislative enactments it is difficult to see in what respect they conflict with democratic ideals.

State control over local expenditures is no new development in the United States. It is as old as local government itself. The trouble with most of the controls which it was attempted to exercise in the past was that they were purely legislative. It was attempted to control local expenditures through tax and debt limitations and through special local acts, the latter type of legislation often emasculating and defeating the former. If our unfortunate experience with tax and debt limitations teaches anything, it is that legislation alone is not sufficient. Effective state control of local expenditures requires not only appropriate legislation but also a central supervisory body to act as an advisor and enforcing agent.

4. TAX AND DEBT LIMITATION MEASURES

THE methods of state supervision of local finance which have been developed in a number of American commonwealths are described in the succeeding study.*

CAREFUL examination of typical state plans establishing state supervision over local financial procedures shows that they have developed into four general types. These are as follows:

(1). *Tax Limitations.*— The use of tax limits has been extensive throughout the country. The most common types are:

a. Restriction of the tax levies to a specific millage rate of the assessed valuation of the taxing district.

b. Provision that the amount raised by a tax levy for any year cannot exceed by more than a fixed percentage (usually 5 per cent) the amount raised by the levy of the year immediately preceding.

(2). *Debt Limitations.*— A majority of the states have placed limits, either by statute or by constitutional provision, upon the authority of local governments to incur debt. As with tax limits, debt limitations vary in scope according to the number and importance of the debt financing functions. Provision is usually made for administrative control over any one or all of the following:

a. Administrative supervision and statutory control over the power to incur local indebtedness. Under this form of control specific percentage limits based on the assessed valuation of taxable property in the district are most commonly found. The percentage limits may vary from 5 to 10 per cent, with frequent exemptions of special assessments, and debts incurred for emergency cases.

b. Control over the marketing of securities.

c. Control over the creation and administration of local sinking funds.

* From *Summary Report of the California Tax Research Bureau,* (Sacramento, 1932), pp. 145-159.

d. Control over the life of bonds and the payments of interest and principal on outstanding obligations.

(3). *Budgetary Control.*— This type of local fiscal supervision generally provides for review of local budgets by a state authority. It is found in two forms, one of which requires an automatic review of all budgets, the other requiring review only upon appeal. A number of states require budgetary review, together with tax and debt limitations.

(4). *Establishment of Financial Standards and Adequate Dissemination of Facts.*— In the more progressive states popular thought has come to the realization that if local governmental machinery is to be improved the state should take the lead. It has been recognized in these states that local officials have neither the time nor funds to set up new forms and procedures, and even where they do, uniformity of budgetary forms and accounts is not prevalent throughout the state. Assistance and constructive guidance on the part of the state would seem to constitute a step in the right direction.

The extent of this supervisory power over local governmental units varies from state to state; however, among the states studied the following functions suggest the nature and purpose of various proposals:

a. Provision that the state gather, analyze and publish statistical information dealing with local finance. This is of importance, since it tends to familiarize the taxpayers with local tax rates, bonded debt, budget items, etc.

b. Periodic audits of all local accounts at the expense of the local governmental unit.

c. Prescribing of adequate and modern accounting systems for local governments and assistance in installing same.

d. Preparation of appropriate budget forms and procedures and aid in their installation.[1]

e. Conduct of efficiency studies upon request of the local governments.

In those states which make such services available to their political subdivisions the chief purpose is to advance the standards of local financial administration. Fact gathering and dissemination thereof tends to keep the local taxpayer, as well as the local officials, abreast of the status of their local fiscal affairs. Where the state takes the initiative in prescribing budget forms and procedures and offers guidance in an advisory capacity to

---

[1] California has statutory provisions substantially similar to these (Cal. Pol. Code, Sec. 3714); however, no effectual results have been obtained from use of this grant of authority.

the local governmental units, the nature and scope of the improvements that accrue are manifest. Let us turn our attention to a brief résumé of several specific state plans for tax and debt limitation.

COLORADO TAX LIMITATION

THE plan of tax limitation in force in Colorado provides that the amount to be raised for any one year shall not exceed by more than 5 per cent the amount raised for the year immediately preceding. Where the taxing district believes that the maximum levy permitted by law (5 per cent increase) will not produce sufficient revenue, it may petition the State Tax Commission for an increase. If upon investigation the commission deems an increase necessary, it may allow same but not to exceed 5 mills. In the event the State Tax Commission refuses to grant the increase, or in case the excess levy of 5 mills is insufficient the question may be submitted to the voters of the taxing district. If three-fourths of the votes cast at such election favor the increased levy it may be made.

Experience has shown that over a period of years the petitions asking for increases are in a majority of cases granted. In practically all instances where the commission has refused to grant the petition for increase, the matter has been carried to the voters and their approval has been secured over the veto of the State Tax Commission.

THE INDIANA PLAN
History of the Plan

THE so-called Indiana Plan for tax and debt limitation has received widespread publicity and served as a model for similar legislation in other states. Originating in 1919, the Indiana Plan has undergone three distinct changes, the most recent of which became effective August 8, 1932, materially altering the scope and administration of the old plan. The original act of 1919 empowered the State Board of Tax Commissioners to review all local budgets. The Home Rule Act of 1920, however, removed this power of the state commission and put it in the hands of the county officials. Actual figures show that in 1920, the year the state commission lacked authority to review budgets, the local tax levies rose approximately 36 million dollars, or 47 per cent.[2] This brief experience with *local* supervision proved so ineffective that in 1921 an act was again

[2] *Annual Report of State Board of Tax Commissioners*, State of Indiana, 1928, p. 9.

passed which returned administrative supervision over tax levies and indebtedness to the State Board of Tax Commissioners.

Important Features

Among the striking features of the famous Indiana Plan which have remained intact from 1921 to August 1933, three points are of especial interest. In the first place, the state commission does not review all local budgets but only those where 10 taxpayers petition for such action. Secondly, the statute gives the commission what seems to be unlimited power of approval or disapproval. There are no rules of procedure to restrict the judgment of the commission, and its decisions are final. The third point is not directly connected with the administration of the plan itself, but rather a legal justification for its validity. Many have doubted the constitutionality of such highly centralized plans for state tax and expenditure control over local tax units. As far as the Indiana Plan is concerned, this matter was settled in 1920 when the Supreme Court of Indiana held that act valid as against the charge of unconstitutionality.[3]

The New Act

The new act passed August 8, 1932, strange as it may seem, reverts to a plan similar to the old Home Rule Act of 1920. The act not only returns the power of supervision and review to a county board but in addition provides specific millage limits on state and local tax levies. The right of appeal to the state commission is now granted only when the county board of tax adjustment shall fix a total aggregate rate in excess of that limited by law. Appeal may then be made by any 10 taxpayers of the taxing district and the decision of the state commission is final.

The following excerpt from the new statute[4] shows the administrative and legal detail of the new plan.

"Sec. 3. That the total of all tax levies on property within any municipal corporation for all municipal corporations for which the property therein is taxable shall not exceed the total rate of one dollar and fifty cents on each one hundred dollars of taxable property therein, except as hereinafter provided.

"Sec. 4. There shall be created in each county of the State of Indiana, a county board of tax adjustment to consist of the county

[3] *Forrey* vs. *Board of Commissioners of Madison County*, 189 Ind. 257, 126 N. E. 673 (1920).

[4] Indiana, S. B. No. 359, Chap. 10, August 8, 1932.

auditor, three members of the county council, to be selected by such council and three members to be appointed by the Judges of the Circuit Court of such county, such members other than the auditor, to serve for one year from the date of their selection, which shall be made on or before the first day of September in each year. The members of such board shall serve without pay. Such county board of tax adjustment of each county shall hold a meeting in the office of the county auditor on the third Monday of September of each year and at such meeting the county auditor shall inform such board of the tax levies fixed by the proper officers of each municipal corporation in such county for the ensuing year and board shall have the power to, and it shall be its duty to revise, change, and if necessary reduce the tax levy of any and for all of such municipal corporations so that the total levy on property within any municipal corporation for all municipal corporations for which the property therein is taxable, including said state levy, shall not exceed the total of one dollar and fifty cents for all such corporations; provided, however, that if such board by a vote of at least five members thereof shall determine that an emergency exists for a total levy in excess of said rate of one dollar and fifty cents, including said state tax levy, upon the property in any municipal corporation for all municipal corporations for which the property therein is taxable, then such board shall have the power to fix such a tax levy therein and apportion the same among the different municipal corporations for which the property in such taxing district is taxable as is necessary to meet such emergency, though the total rate so fixed shall exceed the rate of one dollar and fifty cents on each one hundred dollars;

"Provided also that if such county board of tax adjustment shall fix a total aggregate rate in excess of said one dollar and fifty cents for all the taxing districts or municipal corporations which the taxpayers of any taxing district shall be required to pay, then any ten taxpayers of such municipal corporation or taxing district who own property which will be subject to such rate in excess of said one dollar and fifty cents, including the state tax, may appeal therefrom to the state board of tax commissioners by filing within ten days thereafter a petition with the county auditor of the county in which such order is effective, setting forth their objections to such order and tax levy."

It will be seen from the above discussion of the Indiana Plan that the old plan of limitation and review has been completely reversed by the new act. Review of budgets has been transferred from the state commission to a county board, and specific millage limits on tax levies have been added. It is significant, however, that the state commission retains the authority to review upon appeal, budgets in excess of the prescribed limitations. The fact that the Indiana Plan has served as the model plan of limitations for more than ten years should make it and the recent amendments thereto a most valuable guide in any study of this subject.

NEW MEXICO LAWS OF LIMITATION AND BUDGET CONTROL

Tax Limits

State.— Tax levies for all state purposes can not legally exceed 5½ mills on the dollar of the assessed valuation of all taxable property in the state.

County.— The maximum rate of tax to be levied for all county purposes, excepting schools and highways, may not exceed 5 mills on the dollar of assessed value. A 2 mill limit is placed on levies for the construction and maintenance of state highways. The maximum rate of tax for all general county school purposes may not exceed 18 mills on the dollar.

City-Town-Village.— The maximum rate of tax to be levied for city, town or village purposes may not exceed 5 mills on the dollar. Likewise, the maximum rate of tax for special school district purposes may not exceed 5 mills on the dollar. The foregoing limitations do not apply to levies for the payment of the public debt or interest thereon.

Limits on Revenue Increases

No county, city, town or village in New Mexico can in any year levy a tax which will produce revenues in an amount more than 5 per cent in excess of the amount raised by tax levies during the year preceding.

Levies in excess of 5 per cent of the amount produced by the tax levies in the year preceding may be made with the approval of the State Tax Commission.

Debt Limitations

Under the New Mexico law it is illegal for any county, city, town or village to become indebted to an amount in the aggregate, including existing indebtedness, exceeding 4 per cent of the assessed value of taxable property within the taxing district.

Finally, the law provides that all bonds must be approved by the State Tax Commission as to the issuance, form and rate of interest on said bonds.

Budget Control

Budgetary control as exercised in New Mexico is somewhat comprehensive, including a special arrangement for the review of school budgets. The State Tax Commission is empowered to prescribe forms and procedures for local budget officers, to hold public hearings on budget estimates, and approve or disapprove in whole or in part, or to amend or change such budget estimates as submitted to it by the local governments.

The State Comptroller works in co-operation with the State Tax Commission and is charged with the duty of examining and auditing the receipts and payments and other matters connected with the budget estimates and to see that the provisions of the act are enforced in the counties of the state.

An Educational Budget Auditor, learned in accountancy, finance and educational administration, is appointed by the Governor. It is his duty to compile accurate information concerning school finance, to confer with the State Tax Commission as to forms and budgetary procedure and to supervise and control the preparation of all budgets and estimates of all public schools and state educational institutions.

During the month of April of each odd-numbered year each Board of County Commissioners appoints one resident taxpayer of each of the dominant political parties to serve as school budget commissioners. Together with the Educational Budget Auditor they fix the budget allowances for all public elementary and high schools.

OHIO TAX AND BOND LIMITATION ACTS

Most notable among Ohio's tax limitation enactments is the "Smith One Per Cent Law." This law arrived at economy by imposing a limitation on the taxes which could be raised by all tax districts in the state. The history of the Smith Law shows that its enactment, instead of decreasing taxes actually increased them. The main shortcoming of the new law was its failure adequately to provide specific bond limitations along with tax limits.

Experience with the Smith Law did not result in the abandonment of limitation but rather a strengthening of the old laws. In 1921 the "Griswold Law" was passed which provided definite limits on the amount of bonds that could be issued. Again in 1925 the Legislature passed the "Krueger Bill" which required that all bond issues must be accompanied by an extra levy of taxes outside of the present 15 mill limitation to pay the interest and principal thereon. This law was passed for the express purpose of alleviating conditions brought about under the Smith Law where tax districts found themselves appropriating over half of their 15 mill limit for current operations to sinking funds and interest levies on outstanding bonds.

The most recent legislation on tax and bond limitations was passed in 1927. It is very comprehensive and thorough as the following brief will indicate.

Tax Limitations

The Ohio limitation act provides that the aggregate amount of taxes that may be levied on any taxable property in the state shall not exceed in any one year 15 mills on each dollar of tax valuation.

In the event that the tax authority of any subdivision may declare the amount of taxes which may be raised within the 15 mill limit to be insufficient for the necessary requirements of the subdivision, the question of an excess tax levy must be submitted to the electors of the subdivision at the next election. If the majority of the electors voting thereon at the election favor the increased rate, the taxing authority may levy a tax within such subdivisions at the additional rate outside of the 15 mill limitation during the period and for the purpose stated in the resolution.

Bond Limitations

County.— The net indebtedness of any county *without a vote of the electors* is limited to 1 per cent of the first $100,000,000 or part thereof of the tax list of the county plus ½ of 1 per cent of each tax list in excess of $100,000,000. The total net indebtedness created or incurred by any county shall never exceed a sum equal to 3 per cent of the first $100,000,000 or part thereof of the tax list, plus 1½ per cent of the tax list in excess of $100,000,000.

Municipal Corporations.— The net indebtedness created or incurred by a municipal corporation in Ohio *without a vote of the electors* is limited to 1 per cent of all property in such municipal corporation as listed and assessed for taxation.

The net indebtedness created or incurred by a municipal corporation *shall never exceed* 5 per cent of the total assessed value of all taxable property.

School Districts.— No school district in Ohio can incur net indebtedness, without a vote of the people, in excess of 1/10 of 1 per cent of the total value of all property in the school district as assessed for taxation. In no case shall the net indebtedness of a school district exceed 6 per cent of the total assessed value of the district. It is further provided that bonds shall not be submitted to popular vote in an amount which will make the net indebtedness after the issuance of the bonds exceed 4 per cent of the assessed value of the property within the district unless the State Tax Commission consents thereto.

Local Budget Control

Under Chapter 12, Section 5625–19 of the Code of Ohio, there is created in each county of the state, a county budget commission. This body consists of three members: the county auditor, the county treasurer, and the prosecuting attorney.

This budget commission is empowered to examine the respective county budgets, and ascertain that the following levies are properly authorized, and if so authorized, approve them without modification:

(1) All levies outside of the 15 mill limitation;
(2) All levies for debt charges not provided for by levies outside of the 15 mill limitation;
(3) Tax levies for the equalization fund of the county schools;
(4) The minimum board of education levy for current expenses.

Furthermore, if any debt charge is omitted from the budget, the local budget commission must include it therein. The budget commission shall also so adjust the estimated amount required from the general property tax for each fund, as shown by such budgets, as to bring the levies required therefor within the limitation specified, but no levy shall be reduced below a minimum fixed by law.

The law provides that at least two copies of the budget shall be filed in a public place for public inspection not less than 10 days before its adoption. In addition the taxing authority must hold at least one public hearing on the budget of which the public shall be fully notified.

The taxing authority of any subdivision which is dissatisfied with the actions of the county budget commission, may through its fiscal official appeal to the State Tax Commission. The State Tax Commission must consider the matters presented to the budget commission, and has the power to modify any action of the local commission, with reference to the budget, the estimate of revenues, and balances or the fixing of tax rates. The findings of the State Tax Commission shall be substituted for the findings of the county budget commission. In no case is the State Tax Commission authorized to place any levy outside of the 15 mill limitation, nor to reduce any revenue below the minimum fixed by law.

THE OREGON PLAN

THE so-called Oregon Plan of tax limitations and budgetary control enacted in 1919 provided for a tax supervising and conservation commission in counties having a population of 100,000 or over. This commission exercised advisory jurisdiction only in the matters of local budgets and tax levies. This law was repealed in 1921 on the enactment of the present statute which is reviewed hereafter.

In 1923 a legislative act attempted to extend the provisions of the tax supervising and conservation commission act to all of the counties in the state regardless of the number of inhabitants. This act, however, was held invalid by the Oregon Supreme Court on account of having a defective title.

Of interest is the fact that a tax and debt control constitutional amendment, applicable to all counties in the state, has been framed and will be presented to the coming session of the State Legislature.

The new amendment would extend the general provisions of the present law, applying in Multnomah County alone, to all other counties. It would strengthen the powers of the county board somewhat and also extend them, in a recommendatory way, to cover all propositions for the voting of special taxes and the incurring of indebtedness.

Oregon Tax Supervising and Conservation Act

Under the present act passed in 1921 the Tax Supervising and Conservation Commission of Multnomah County was established. The commission consists of three local resident taxpayers appointed by the Governor for a period of three years. The commissioners serve wholly without compensation but may employ and fix the salaries of such clerks and other assistants as they deem necessary.[5] Such clerks and assistants

---

[5] Under the Oregon Plan where the tax supervising commission is a county body no elaborate plan of organization is necessary. The Multnomah County Commission organized by appointing one of their number chairman. The detailed administration is carried out by an executive secretary appointed by the commission. The detailed personnel, with salaries, follows:

One executive secretary	$4,500
One accountant	2,400
One stenographer	1,500
Temporary help	200
Total	$8,600

are paid out of the general fund of the county, but the sum expended for any one year can not exceed $10,000.

The commission must review and approve the budgets of all tax levying districts within the county and pass on all tax levies. It is the duty of the commission to compile accurate statistical information as to tax rates and bonded indebtedness of the several municipal corporations within their respective counties. The commission is also empowered to recommend and install uniform accounting systems and adequate budget procedures, and to inquire into the management, books of account and systems employed by each of the taxing districts.

Comments based on the 1931 Annual Report of the Tax Supervising and Conservation Commission of Multnomah County disclose some interesting facts and figures on the operations of that body.

The year just completed, 1931, is the eleventh year of the commission's work and the 1932 budgets are the eleventh series of annual budgets which the commission has scrutinized and certified. The requested appropriations for 1932 were reduced $278,044.05, while the requested tax levies were reduced $414,944.72. These reductions added to the accumulated reductions for the 10 prior years that the commission has been in existence make an aggregate reduction in the 11 budgets from 1922 to 1932 inclusive, of $3,026,968.39 in appropriations and $4,497,730.32 in tax levies.

The following excerpts from the commission's report throw considerable light on their methods of operation in the revision of local budgets. The detailed thought and sound judgment evidently reflected in these opinions indicate that the Multnomah County Commission is doing its job in a comprehensive manner.

With regard to the Portland police department budget the commission makes the following comments:

"The installation of the police radio and the increase of three stenographers in the Bureau of Police should release approximately 40 officers for active duty. This Commission is of the opinion that this justifies a reduction of 20 patrolmen in the Police Bureau and in order to make such a reduction without depriving any man of his position, vacancies in the position of patrolmen are not to be filled until there is a reduction in personnel of 20 men. The estimated saving for the fiscal year 1932 is $5000 in addition to the regular turnover allowance and this amount is to be considered as an estimate only."

Proposed improvement programs in the city budget are rejected for the following reasons:

"The construction of the proposed swimming tank is postponed for the time being which also permits a reduction in personnel. The item of paving in Mt. Tabor Park is reduced from $7000 to $3500, which sum is sufficient to pave the upper end of the drive in said Park, which is the only part seriously in need of repair at the present time. The item of $5700 for surfacing the garden road in Washington Park is rejected for the year 1932."

It will be noted from these excerpts that the Multnomah County commission has power not only to modify and revise budgets but to exercise its discretion on matters of policy as well. Unlike various other commissions, the Multnomah commission is not merely a check on local budget makers to see that they do not exceed specific legal limits, and having no authority if the tax district stays within the law. This plan is flexible and allows supposedly capable men to use some judgment in matters of fiscal activities and policies of the taxing districts within the county.

It should be pointed out that the commission does not have jurisdiction over bonded indebtedness, nor over special levies voted by the people.

ANALYSIS OF VARIOUS STATE PLANS OF TAX AND DEBT
LIMITATIONS

ALTHOUGH concerned with the same purpose, that of curtailing taxes and decreasing public indebtedness, the methods and procedure for bringing about this desirable condition vary somewhat from state to state. Like most questions of government there are arguments for and against each plan, as compared with the others, and the ultimate conclusion must depend upon the balancing of the good against the bad.

The preceding presentation of five selected representative state plans for state supervision over local financial affairs sets forth the methods of procedure, practical operation and some experiences of the more important adventures in this field of government.

Some general aspects of the plans reviewed above in reference to specific tax and debt limits are briefly set forth as follows:

Two of the states, Oregon and Colorado, provide no specific millage limits on tax rates or bonded debt.

Ohio specifically limits both the tax levy and bonded debt, while in New Mexico, revenues are limited to a 5 per cent increase over the preceding year, and specific limits are prescribed for local indebtedness.

The Indiana Plan, as revised in August of this year, provides definite tax limits but makes no mention of specific limits on the bonded debt.

It is significant to note that all five state plans prescribe budgetary review of one form or another.

Three of the states, Indiana, Ohio and Oregon, establish local county boards or commissions for such review, and the other two, Colorado and New Mexico, place the power of review in the State Tax Commission.

In the three states prescribing review by county boards or commissions it is mandatory that all local budgets be scrutinized, while in the two states that provide for state review it has proven impossible to inspect all budgets, and it is only upon appeal that the state commission reviews them.

The New Mexico Plan for the review of school budgets is unique in that it establishes a county board of review for school budgets only.

Additional powers and functions exercised by the reviewing bodies are worthy of comment in this summary report. In all five states reviewed the supervising body is granted certain perfunctory functions, among which are included authority to prescribe uniform budgeting procedures, to recommend and assist in installing adequate accounting systems and to compile, analyze and disseminate information dealing with local fiscal affairs.

Another aspect of the problem of state supervision over local finances has to do with the question of final jurisdiction.

Under the revised Indiana Plan and the Oregon Plan no appeal from the reviewing body is open to the taxing district through a vote.

In Colorado the refusal of the State Tax Commission to grant the increase applied for, within the 5-mill limitation, may be overruled by a three-fourths vote of the people, and submission to popular vote may likewise be invoked if the budgeted increase exceeds the 5-mill increase in tax rate to which the state commission is legally restricted.

The New Mexico law provides no appeal from the decision of the State Tax Commission.

In Ohio likewise no special election is prescribed to alter the decisions of the reviewing boards. Appeal may be made to the State Tax Commission, but it is limited in that it can not place any levy outside of the 15-mill limitation. Certain specified levies in excess of the limitation must be submitted to the people.

CONCLUSIONS

THE following enumeration aims to set forth the conclusions of the bureau on the problem of tax limitations. It is hoped that they will prove of assistance to the Legislature during its deliberation on the question.

Briefly, the conclusions reached in this study are as follows:

(1). In view of the trend of local tax burdens and the weight of those burdens upon all taxpayers of the State, as developed in this report, it would appear that measures for prompt and adequate relief are in order.

(2). The remedy is not easily found. However, as a result of this study, it is evident that an efficient plan for tax and debt limitations, accompanied by measures which would encourage uniformity and adequate methods of accounting and budgeting in our local governments would materially help to correct present conditions.

(3). Experience in other states has shown that the effective plan of limitations is the simple plan. In evolving a plan, simplicity of organization and administration should be the keynote, consistent, however, with the ultimate efficacy of the plan.

(4). Investigation of other state plans indicates that the successful plan must include provision for both tax and debt limitations. Experience has shown that one without the other is worthless. In addition to these two measures, many states provide for review of local budgets.

(5). The extent of review to be exercised by any board is open to an honest difference of opinion. A majority of states have found that the successful plan of limitations must encompass jurisdiction over all local taxing districts. This would include counties, municipalities and school districts.

Of additional import is the factor relating to the nature of supervision. Of the two most common procedures, (a) a review of all budgets, (b) review only upon appeal, the latter would seem more practical in a state so large as California. It is manifest that no body, even if it were to function continuously, could give adequate consideration to the review of each and every budget of the multitudinous political subdivisions in this State.

(6). On the question of the nature of the reviewing board other states have developed plans in two separate directions, while some states have adopted a combination of the two. Plan

One prescribes review by a centralized state authority, in a majority of cases, the state tax commission, or a similar state tax body. Plan Two provides review by local county boards, in some cases elective county officials comprising the board and in others the members being appointed.

The recent amendment to the familiar Indiana Plan established local county boards and left the final power of review in the hands of the state board. This change in the Indiana Plan is significant, since before the revision the plan represented a strong centralized review by the state. It should be mentioned, however, that this review was made only upon appeal.

A plan of combining local county boards with a state board, final authority being placed in the state board, might prove feasible, since it would then be possible to review all local budgets without danger of misadministration. Furthermore, this plan would meet the arguments arising from the strong home rule sentiment in this state.

Under any plan it would seem essential that the final supervising and guiding authority rest in the hands of a state board.

(7). Economy in administration of a plan of limitations and review could be attained through following in the footsteps of most other states. The common practice is to compose the state board of review of members of official state tax bodies. Such members serve without pay, and with the assistance of small technical staffs are enabled to accomplish satisfactorily the desired results.

(8). Reduction of governmental expenditures, elimination of superfluous functions, reduction in the hundreds of overlapping tax districts, and general consolidation of local governmental units as well as functions, must all be made a part of the program for a return to a sane and sound local governmental finance. No plan of limitations or state supervision, good or bad, can be expected to prove an immediate panacea for all of our tax evils.

(9). With a full understanding of the magnitude of this problem the members of the bureau do not hesitate to commend for consideration by the Legislature certain specific principles that should not be disregarded in building a program for tax limitations. Two factors are of primary importance in laying the foundation : First, the specific limitation on governmental expenditures as is provided in the Colorado and New Mexico plans ; and Second, uniform accounting throughout the local political subdivisions.

(10). The foregoing conclusions, resulting from an impartial study of the subject as a whole, are set forth by the members of the bureau as pertinent factors, a knowledge of which is of paramount importance to a thorough understanding of the vital problem of tax limitation.

5. THE PLANNING OF GOVERNMENT ORGANIZATION AND EXPENDITURES TO PROMOTE BUSINESS STABILITY

DEFINITE suggestions for overcoming the administrative difficulties of a program of long-range planning of public expenditures are listed and discussed below.*

A CENTRALIZATION of control for each major function or group of functions. There should be a grouping into departments of all educational activities and institutions, all charitable and correctional institutions, all public works, in each case under a single administrative head.

A permanent body of technically equipped specialists in control of planning and operating.

A single agency charged with responsibility for considering the financial needs of all departments and activities present and prospective.

A budget system in all of its implications. This presupposes elimination of such restrictions as special funds, the ear-marking of certain revenues for certain purposes, and statutory salaries. It also assumes collection of all revenues into one pool available for any expenditure according to plan.

A central administrative authority with power to initiate and act.

It hardly needs to be said that such a set-up will make long-range planning and a stabilizing policy of government expenditures not only possible but inevitable. Let us see how.

Each department (be it a state department of roads or of charities and corrections or a city department of bridges or of fire) will consider the needs of its physical plant for years to come and plan, design, and estimate its construction well ahead. Each time when appropriations are up it will forward its whole program to the budget agency.

The budget agency will assemble the proposals coming from all departments and will advise with the department heads and the administrative head of the state or city as to the wisest

---

* Adapted from E. O. Griffenhagen, "The Planning of Government Organization and Expenditures to Promote Business Stability — with Particular Reference to States and Cities" and reprinted from *The Proceedings of the Academy of Political Science*, New York, 'Stabilizing Business,' Vol. XII, No. 3, July, 1927, pp. 757-764.

allotment of revenues and resources in view of the relative importance of the various projects and of business conditions present and prospective. The statistical work of the national and state departments of commerce will have been perfected to the point where a clear picture of existing business conditions and a definite indication of the trend will be available for the financial and administrative officers.

The suggestions of the budget agency, when approved by the executive, will be transmitted to the appropriating body and left to its tender mercies. But as the idea of the budget becomes better understood, there is less and less tendency on the part of the legislative bodies to make any material changes in the plans thus submitted.

A few words should be said with regard to the method of authorizing the capital expenditures that the administration is to be permitted to defer until in its judgment the time is right to make them. In this connection two suggestions have been made : one, that the future issuance and sale of bonds be authorized : the other, that a reserve be set up, presumably in cash to be earmarked and laid aside. Without going into a detailed discussion of the advantages and disadvantages of the bond issue as against the pay-as-you-go plan, it may be said that there is no reason why a clause cannot be attached to the appropriation made in any one year, providing that the expenditures under such appropriation need not be made until the executive finds it desirable in his discretion to make them. Or, if this is not considered sufficient, the legislature can attach a provision that the expenditure should not be made until the executive, acting on the advice of a specified agency, finds that business conditions and the indications of a probable approach of a period of depression make such expenditures desirable.

Under conditions which provide for a pooling of all resources and revenues of the state or city, any appropriation of this kind remaining unexpended for a time will be represented merely by an appropriation incumbrance on whatever current assets there may be rather than a physical segregation of assets into a special fund.

The conclusions to be drawn from this analysis of the requirements that must be met to put a public body into a position where it may plan and control its expenditures with relation to business conditions, is that the *same* simplification and directness in government organization and procedure are needed as are required to bring about effectiveness in public administration in general.

It is possible to paint a very discouraging picture of the ex-

isting weaknesses in our government structure and procedure
and of the long road that must be traveled to provide these
prerequisites of good administration, but when we consider
how far we have gone in the last twenty years toward these
very objectives, we need not feel any discouragement whatsoever. Most cities have simplified their departmental organization (although the problem of consolidating government
agencies in metropolitan areas is only now being seriously attacked). Many states have been reorganizing along functional
lines as suggested in these remarks. Practically every state
and city has a budget system in some form. The idea of the
short ballot and the elimination of constitutional restrictions
is meeting with favor. The progress of the civil service idea
is making for permanent and competent technical staffs in the
government service.

Mention should also be made of the great improvement that
has taken place in recent years in treasury administration which
has a distinct bearing on the main subject of this discussion.
The old system of holding cash in treasury vaults has largely
been abandoned and the sums so tied up have been restored
through the banks to the channels of trade.

Moreover the tendency in most governmental bodies is
towards centralization of treasury transactions, but a great deal
yet remains to be accomplished. In the selection of depositary
banks and the allocations of cash to active bank accounts, time
deposits, and deposits subjected to withdrawal on notice, and
in the stabilization of state deposits, the treasury can assist in
the stabilization of business conditions. If deposits are distributed because of political expediency and if sudden ill-timed
withdrawals of large sums are made from small country banks
havoc can be wrought with local business. On the other hand,
it is possible to work out allocations of deposits to banks that
will assist them in meeting seasonal demands.

6. Tax Delinquency

Some conclusions and the recommendations given in the
preliminary report of the Committee of the National Tax
Association on tax delinquency show the problem studied
to be a part of the larger one of public expenditure control
and local government organization. These conclusions
and recommendations are here reproduced.*

* Adapted from the "Preliminary Report of the Committee of the National
Tax Association on Tax Delinquency," *Proceedings of the National Tax Association*, (1932), pp. 314, 315, 324-329.

THE deeper and possibly most important causes of delinquency, at least of long-term delinquency, are found in excessive public expenditures and in forms of local government organization and distribution of state and local functions which are archaic and uneconomical. In consequence, the full solution of the problem of delinquency involves both a revised tax system and a reorganization of local governments.

Most short-term tax delinquency, that is deferred payment of taxes, appears to be due to a faulty collecting practice. The statutory penalties are so light or the enforcement of the law so lax that taxpayers delay payment of their taxes in order to meet the demands of more exacting creditors. The laxity of enforcement is largely a product of a system of popularly elected collectors. When taxpayers have once enjoyed leniency and as a result owe an accumulation of back taxes, it is especially difficult to get the legislature to tighten up on the procedure or to forego the waiving of penalties. Thus delinquency is encouraged by shifting the cost thereof to the backs of those who pay with promptness and regularity.

Long-term delinquency is of course an evidence of distress on the part of the taxpayer, which may be due to adverse economic conditions or a tax burden so severe as to invite a voluntary or involuntary surrender of the property.

There is reason to believe that most taxpayers will pay their taxes as diligently as they meet their other obligations when the taxes are not beyond their tax-paying ability, when they are satisfied that there is no partiality, when collecting procedure is prompt and certain, and when the costs of government are not so obviously inflated. There will always be some people who display an unreasoning resentment against any taxes; but most people are willing to pay their just share of the cost of a necessary public service that is wisely and prudently administered.

Governments are, or should be, armed with all the powers they need to collect the taxes which they impose. The powers should be exercised vigorously and impartially. If they were always so exercised it is believed that much of the delinquency would disappear. Where it did not disappear or greatly decline it would be reasonably certain that there were serious economic and fiscal maladjustments which needed attention. In fact, the full solution of the problem of delinquency undoubtedly involves both a revised tax system and a reorganization of local government itself.

* * *

It seems to this committee that, in the interest of economy, justice, and a higher respect for government on the part of the citizens, as well as for the purpose of making possible the orderly conduct of government through prompt receipt of revenue, the procedure for the collection of taxes should be made as simple, regular, and undeviating as possible. It is unfair to those taxpayers who pay promptly and without coercion to be compelled to pay for the delinquency of others. It is unfair to those who are negligent to be encouraged in their negligence or to those in adverse circumstances to be falsely reassured by lenient practice. Taxes are to most people onerous; they are frequently burdensome. They would be less onerous and less burdensome if it were universally recognized that they were being collected at the lowest possible cost and that no one was receiving favored treatment, and if the time of collection, while reasonably adjusted to fit the income flow of the taxpayer, were nevertheless fixed and certain.

Barring extreme circumstances such as loss of income through crop failure or similar causes, kindness is rarely done to a negligent or distressed taxpayer by permitting his taxes to accumulate. The practice only intensifies his difficulties, and at the same time creates embarrassing problems for the government. The taxes must eventually be paid, and if the taxpayer is solvent he should obtain credit from other sources than the government. If he is really insolvent, the government should know the fact, and failure to sell his property will not save him from foreclosure to meet his obligations.

There are of course times when a solvent taxpayer is temporarily without liquid assets and would be willing to pay a high rate of interest to get his tax payment deferred. Ordinarily other avenues of credit should be open to him, but to meet all possibilities the government should probably permit some extension in the payment of the tax on real estate. The extension might apply to the tax on both real and personal property if the land value were sufficient to justify it. Under conditions prevailing in many states, the extension should not exceed one year. If the taxpayer cannot raise the amount of the tax within a year, there should be an easy method of transferring the property. In other states, however, economic conditions including natural hazards affecting the flow of income may necessitate a redemption period longer than one year. In any event, the period should not be unduly long, and it should be reasonably adjusted to factors affecting the flow of income so that the limitation on redemption may not impose unreasonable hardships on taxpayers subjected to hazards likely to occur from time to time. This need not interfere with the central purpose of our recommendation, namely, that procedure leading to ultimate loss of title because of tax delinquency should be clearly defined, with specific time limits definitely enforced.

The procedure in collecting property taxes should not be any more severe than in the case of collecting income taxes. Due consideration should be given to differences between income taxes and property taxes in their relation to hazards affecting income. There are indeed considerations which require special grant of time for payment of property taxes, as where there is temporarily no income. But neither the taxing jurisdiction nor the taxpayer should be led into a practice of substituting tax liens for tax payments. It is true that in the case of landowners, the land stands as security, but so does it if the credit is obtained from other sources. The taxing authority should not pursue an indefinite and lax policy of tax collection that would lead the taxpayer to take it for granted that the government will in effect act as a credit agency to carry him over a period of temporary inability to pay his taxes or to serve his convenience when he may want to use his funds or credit for some purpose other than the payment of taxes due.

The attention which this report devotes to the means for securing a prompt and certain collection procedure should lead no one to infer that the committee has been interested solely or even chiefly in the problem of securing the revenues of the public bodies concerned and has assumed a hard-boiled attitude toward the unfortunate taxpayer. The reverse is the truth. In the opinion of the committee, the most serious aspect of the whole problem of tax delinquency is the danger of wholesale confiscation of private property as the result of bad tax laws improperly administered. . . Loosely-drawn tax laws and laxity and procrastination in collection are, in the long run, no kindness to the taxpayer. Both taxpayer and government should profit from a better collecting procedure.

It therefore seems to this committee that the cause of good government would be served and benefit would accrue to all groups of taxpayers if a procedure could be adopted that would cut through the maze of tradition, historic safeguards, and legal technicalities that now confuse and delay tax collections and that would provide a single course that is short and clear and certain. The committee is fully aware that the formulation of a model plan of tax collection is an ambitious undertaking and that the plan which it presents herewith can presume to be nothing more than a preliminary and tentative sketch, the purpose of which will be accomplished if it furnishes a focus for discussion and conference and so serves as the first step toward ultimate reform in this troublesome phase of state and local taxation.

The plan which the committee presents is based upon certain basic principles, of which the following should be especially emphasized:

The whole business of tax payment should be promptly brought to definite termination, by payment or foreclosure and transfer of clear title, rather than allowed to drag on by sale of liens, certificates, deeds, etc., with long and indefinite periods for redemption. The sale should be sale of the property itself and not sale of a tax certificate or lien.

The law should specifically state that there shall be no extensions.

Collection should be concentrated in the county, city, or corresponding jurisdiction.

The collecting officer should be appointed, not elected. The fee system should be abolished.

A local bank or some other local agency should be appointed as local receiver where required by convenience of the taxpayers.

Tax bills should be sent to every taxpayer.

A tax bill should be prepared for each piece of real estate and one for the personal property of each owner. Where convenient, the bills of each taxpayer should then be combined.

The taxes of all jurisdictions should be combined in one bill.

Taxes and special assessments on real estate should be a lien on the particular parcels of real estate. Seizure of personal property to satisfy real estate taxes should not be permitted.

Personal property taxes should be a debt and represent a claim against any property, real or personal, of the taxpayer, subject to limits of jurisdiction.

Payment of taxes in installments should be permitted (either semi-annual or quarterly). The committee recognizes that there is danger of loss in case of personal property, which may be sold, removed from the jurisdiction, or destroyed, and is prepared to modify this recommendation by limiting the installment privileges to real estate only or to personal property the owners of which also own real estate.

The following procedure is proposed as a concrete illustration of the plan recommended without implying that these

particular dates need be adopted. The assumption is that the
fiscal year of the state and all subordinate jurisdictions begins
on July 1.

(1). The assessment of property and the preliminary draft
of the budget should be completed and a tentative tax rate
fixed prior to May 1. Public hearings should be held on the
proposed budget during the first three weeks of May.

(2). The final budget should be adopted and the tax levy
fixed not later than the first of June.

(3). The work of preparing tax bills should be commenced
immediately thereafter, and tax bills should be sent out to all
taxpayers as soon as possible and not later than July 1. All
taxes of all jurisdictions on each parcel of real property and on
personal property should be consolidated into a single bill and
payable at a single office. The tax collector in a rural county
should be appointed by the county manager or other chief
financial officer of the county if there is one, otherwise by the
county board. The tax collector in an urban county should
be appointed jointly by the city and county managers, finance
officers, or boards. In no case should the office be filled by
popular election. The collector should be required to furnish
a security company bond. This should both protect the government from loss and limit the appointment of collectors to
men capable of furnishing such bond. A personal bond should
never be accepted on account of the reluctance of officials to
proceed against such a bondsman.

(4). The full tax, if the amount is less than $10.00, or the
first installment thereof if the amount exceeds $10.00 and in-
stallment paying is permitted, shall become delinquent if un-
paid before August 1, and on August 1 a penalty equal to 5
per cent of the amount due shall be added. Provided: the
minimum penalty shall be $1.00.

(5). Those permitted to pay their taxes by installment shall
be subject to no interest if they pay each installment before the
end of the installment period — that is, in the case of quarterly
payments, before August 1, November 1, February 1, May 1.
If a taxpayer defaults in meeting any installment, the 5 per cent
penalty, computed on the total portion of the tax then due,
shall be added. In addition to the penalty, interest shall be
computed on the tax (exclusive of the penalty) at 1 per cent
per month or fraction thereof. Any time after August 1 the
tax collector shall have the right to seize and sell tangible
personal property sufficient to cover the full tax if the real
estate value is being dissipated by logging operations, the
removal of buildings, or otherwise.

(6). Prior to August 1, which date is one year after the first installment shall have become due, there shall be prepared a list of the real estate delinquent for taxes and application made to the court for permission to foreclose as in the case of a mortgage. Moreover, letters of notification announcing a foreclosure sale on October 1 shall be prepared for mailing to all those with recorded equities in parcels of land against which there are delinquent taxes.

On August 1 these letters of notification shall be sent out by registered mail. For three successive weeks prior to October 1, the list of delinquent lands shall be published in a paper of wide circulation in the county or city in which the property is located, the last publication being at least five days before the sale date. The advertisement shall give the location, the legal description, the ownership, and the minimum bid that can be accepted. The cost of the advertising and notification shall be included in the costs. If any registered letter is not delivered, a personal summons shall be served and the charge thereof included among the costs.

(7). On October 1 a foreclosure sale shall be begun and continued from day to day. All parcels shall be offered except those for which the required notification has not been completed. No bid will be received in an amount less than the total of all taxes due (including those of the current year), interest, penalties, and costs. In case installment paying is permitted, the taxes of the current year shall include only the installment due, and the penalty and interest on account of current year's taxes shall be based on installment due. If all delinquent taxes, together with the interest, penalties, and costs, amount to less than 25 per cent of the assessed value of the property, the owner shall be given the option of having offered such portion of his property as he desires, provided that if no bid is received for such portion sufficient to cover the entire tax claim the whole property shall be offered. The purchaser at the tax foreclosure sale shall receive a deed similar to that which would be obtained if property were acquired at any other mortgage foreclosure sale, except that in this case the former owner or mortgagee shall have six months to redeem or bring suit for error. Any sum paid by a purchaser over and above the amount of the delinquent taxes (including those of the current year), plus interest, penalties, and costs shall be returned to the owner. Mortgagees, having been notified, must be present or represented at the sale, to protect their interests. Any political jurisdiction having an equity in the tax claim shall have the same right to bid as an individual. If no bid is received equal to the minimum, there should be a procedure whereby title to the property passes to some political jurisdiction, presumably the one economically most suitable to hold such property (not necessarily the one with the largest tax lien). Other jurisdictions should receive suitable reimbursement for their tax claims. The committee is not yet prepared to suggest the best procedure. The chief point is that the whole matter be definitely settled with clear title transferred to state, county, or municipality.

The foreclosure sale shall be conducted by the proper county or city officials without additional compensation.

Delinquent properties which cannot be foreclosed at the October sale for the reason that it has been impossible to notify all those having an equity therein shall be sold at the next regular sale after notification has been achieved. Tax foreclosure sales shall be held regularly on October 1 and April 1.

The procedure described above may be clarified by the following hypothetical example:

Prior to May 1, 1932 — Property assessed at $10,000.
June 1, 1932 — Tax rate fixed at 1 per cent.
On or before July 1, 1932 — Tax bill mailed. Tax $100.

Assuming that the tax, payable in quarterly installments, becomes delinquent and the property is sold October 1, 1933, the computation to determine the minimum bid is as follows:

1932 tax	$100.00
Penalty (added August 1, 1932)	5.00
Interest on $100 August 1, 1932 to October 1, 1933 at 12 per cent	14.00
Costs of advertising, notification, and sale (assumed)	2.00
Total 1932 tax charge	$121.00
1933 tax (first quarterly installment)	$25.00
Penalty (added August 1, 1933)	1.25
Interest on $25 August 1, 1933 to October 1, 1933 at 12 per cent	0.50
Minimum bid to satisfy tax claim	$147.75

(8). Within thirty days after a property has been sold at a tax foreclosure sale, all those having recorded equities therein shall be notified again. Any such holder of an equity may within six months after notification redeem the property by paying the purchase price plus interest at 12 per cent per annum to the time of redemption, or start a suit for setting aside the sale because of error. If at the end of six months after such notification the property has not been redeemed and no suit has been started or sustained, the deed received by the purchaser shall convey absolute and irrevocable title. When the state or city has acquired property through this procedure, it may dispose of it as any other public property or use it for its own purposes.

It is recognized that the plan here outlined may in some situations appear too severe. In particular it may be felt that the time allowed before loss of the taxpayers' property is too short, as in case of a period of depression such as the present [1932]. Where such opinion prevails, the period could be extended. Such extension, however, should be in the time allowed for redemption, rather than in the time before foreclosure.

The committee's plan, it should be noted, is intended for normal conditions. Its immediate introduction in a time of depression such as the present [1932] would require considerable adjustment in the direction of leniency in case of delinquency of long standing and heavy accumulation.

7. ASSESSMENT OF REAL PROPERTY IN THE UNITED STATES

AN important aspect of tax administration is the assessment of real property. Professor M. S. Kendrick's able treatment of this problem follows.*

WHAT can be done to improve the assessment of real property in the United States? How can the few bright spots [1] be made general instead of the product of an unusual combination of local circumstances? Perhaps the best approach to the problem raised by these questions is through an examination of the assessor, his selection, qualifications, tenure of office, equipment, and his task. The answer must lie in the assessor or in his task or in both. These will be examined with reference to the *general* system of assessment.

The assessor in a county, township, or town holds office usually by election. No special technical qualifications are required for his selection. With but one promising exception,

* Adapted from M. S. Kendrick, *Taxation Issues*, (Harper and Bros., New York, 1933), Chap. III, pp. 59-78.
[1] Duluth and Cleveland are indicated as bright spots in Nelson, R. W., and Mitchell, George W., *Assessment of Real Estate in Iowa and Other Mid-Western States*, Univ. of Iowa, Iowa City, Iowa, p. 134.

that of the state of Kentucky, where the candidate must pass a written examination submitted to him by the tax commission before his name may appear on the ballot, anyone who has the routine qualifications of age, citizenship, and occasionally ownership of real estate may stand for the office of assessor. The result of choosing experts by popular election is an old story in government and the assessor is no exception to the rule. The task of assessing requires certain technical qualifications for its effective performance, but getting elected requires certain personal vote-getting qualifications which commonly are complicated by party affiliations. Since the average voter is unable to distinguish between the technical qualifications of the candidates, but is abundantly able to distinguish between their personal and party qualifications, as they appear to him, the choice is made on the basis of personality and party. Unfortunately, a pleasant smile is of small assistance in assessing land. Nor is adherence to the correct political faith of more help in this task.

In those states where assessors are appointed, there is opportunity to distinguish between the technical qualifications of the candidates if the appointing agency is familiar with the task of assessing and its requirements. However, as a rule, the appointing officials, county supervisors, judges, etc., are not sufficiently informed regarding problems of assessment to distinguish intelligently between the qualifications of the various possibilities for appointment. Again, considerations of personality and party dominate in the selection.

The assessor holds his office for a limited period, usually for two or four years and sometimes for only one year. If he wishes to be reëlected or to be reappointed, he must keep his political fences in repair. Thus his task of learning by experience to assess property is all the while complicated by the other task of keeping himself personally and politically agreeable. If he manages to learn and at the same time keeps himself in favor, all is well. But in too many instances the political favor is retained at the expense of the learning, or the learning is not accompanied by sufficient political favor to continue in office. The result in either case is bad.

Tax maps, statistical records of sales, building-construction details, those indispensable aids to expert assessment wherever it is found, are missing in most assessment offices. Their absence is explained partly by ignorance of their value on the part of local governing bodies, who, therefore, have made no provision for such aids in the assessor's office. However, this neglect of the elementary requirements for good assessment is probably mostly to be explained by the absence of a well-qualified man with security of tenure in the position of assessor. Such a man, if secure in his position, would accumulate records of sales, construction, insurance, as the tools of his profession as the lawyer or the doctor accumulates a professional library. For without these aids he can neither work efficiently nor justify the work he has done.

Another difficulty besets good assessment in about one-third of the states. This is the township or town unit of assessment. A township or a town is not large enough to employ a full-time assessor and to pay him a good salary. In such a unit the assessor occupies a part-time low-paid position. Under such conditions of employment it may be stated as a general rule that it is not possible to obtain expert service. No one could afford to qualify himself to be a competent assessor for so meager a reward. Consequently, in these states assessing is and must be done by amateurs as a side line to other occupations.

The effects of a combination of the evils of election, township unit of assessment, short term of office, and lack of proper qualifications on the assessment situation is illustrated by the following appealing outburst from the tax commissioner of South Dakota: [2]

"Under the present system of assessment, a fair and equitable system is impossible. The assessment machinery is crude and inadequate. Every township, city, and village in this state has its own assessor. For the most part assessors are elected each spring just prior to the time the assessment is to be made. The law prescribes as the only qualification of the assessor that he must be a voter and owner of real property. Whether he can read and write does not seem to be of any importance. The assessor's work lasts but a few weeks and in most cases they are poorly paid. Under the present system there is no method of training these men for the work they are to do. A majority of them have not the necessary qualifications for valuing and appraising property, neither have they any clear idea of their legal duties. The tax commissioner is presumed to supervise the assessment of property in the state. It is impossible, however, to supervise and instruct 1800 men who are elected only a few days before their active work of assessment commences."

Such is the pitiful inadequacy of the whole framework of custom and law in which assessors are chosen and do their work. Selected without peculiar qualifications, provided with no aids for his task, the assessor muddles through as best he

2 Eighth Biennial Report, 1926.

can. The difficulty and significance of his work ought, in truth, to make him comparable to a judge in respect to selection, qualifications, and equipment with which to work. The one must decide what is the law; the other what is the value. It may be that the assessors in the United States decide annually between property-owners a total of "cases" involving a greater value consideration than the total of civil cases which are decided by the judges. At least this is true: the assessors decide each year the distribution of approximately five billion dollars of general property taxes.

The remedies for bad assessing, so far as they concern the assessment unit and the assessor, his selection, qualifications, tenure, and statistical records or other equipment, are easy to devise. They are suggested by the situation which has already been described.

The unit of assessment should be large enough to employ a full-time well-paid assessor. Otherwise the position cannot be made attractive to the trained expert who should occupy it. Fortunately, the matter of a sufficiently large unit is solved in most states. About two-thirds of the states have county assessors. No doubt some counties are too small and poor to employ a really well-paid assessor, but probably most of them could.

The assessor should be appointed by the state tax commission under civil service regulations. He should be under the supervision of that body and his tenure of office should be during proper performance of duty.

A state tax commission — constituted as it should be — is composed of experts in the field of tax administration. But whether its members reach the full stature of this requirement or not, such a body could judge the qualifications of candidates for assessor better than the voters or the supervisors, judges or other county officials. A state tax commission is in the business of tax administration. It has a unique opportunity to accumulate data on it, to compare performance here with performance there. If charged with the appointment of assessors, the supervision of assessment, and finally the removal of assessors for poor performance, all of this extraordinary power to determine and apply standards of good administration could be used.

Tenure during proper performance of duty means that the assessor who would continue in office must do his work well. Thus the emphasis is placed where it belongs — on the work. Moreover, there is every reason for continuing the good assessor in office rather than subjecting him to periodical hazards of election or appointment. Whatever mechanical aids further the proper assessment of real property, that knowledge of local values which the skilled assessor accumulates over a period of years is of capital importance. A good assessor becomes in time a better assessor. He should be continued in office in order that his district realize the benefit from this growth of his knowledge of assessment.[3]

The matter of records and other aids to assessing is mostly a question of a properly qualified assessor secure in his tenure of office, for such an assessor would accumulate records. Nevertheless, provision should be made for the keeping of assessment data and a tax map for each tax district should be mandatory.

The need of a tax map for purposes other than assessment is illustrated by a situation related by one of the writer's students. The sheriff collects taxes in this student's home county, which is in a Southern state. One year he paid the state tax commission more in taxes than the state account indicated as due from that county. The commission, after protesting the overpayment, sent a man to investigate. He found that the sheriff had collected $9000 of state and local taxes from persons who owned real property that had not been assessed. Comparison of the state assessment list with the sheriff's list disclosed the discrepancy in the state list and thus the reason for the apparent overpayment. In this instance an honest man did the collecting. But a tax map with all taxable properties indicated thereon would make the possibility of "graft" by this means remote.

THUS far the problem of assessment has been analyzed in relation to the assessor, his selection, qualifications, tenure, equipment with which to work, and the unit in which he functions. The deeper problem of his task remains for consideration. He is required to assess real property on the basis of its capital value. What difficulties are inherent in this basis of assessment? Is there any way out of them?

Perhaps the first observation of the assessor on beginning the duties of his office is that, although he is supposed to assess real property on the basis of its value as determined in a fair and open sale, the number of sales relative to the total number

[3] The committee of the National Tax Association to prepare a plan of a model system of state and local taxation recommended the county unit of assessment and favored the appointment of assessors. This committee recommended that the power of removing assessors for negligence or malfeasance in office should be lodged in the State Tax Commission. *Proceedings of the National Tax Association,* pp. 462, 463, 1919.

of pieces of real estate is few. Nor can all of these sales be
trusted to indicate a true sales value. A sale for cash may be
at a lower figure than one for credit. This is particularly
true in rural sections of a poor area. For a sale with a mortgage left on the farm might result in the owner having to take
the farm back to satisfy his mortgage claim. But a sale for
cash finally closes the transaction. A sale to a person familiar
with the property and its possibilities may well be at a different
figure from one to a person uninformed on these matters.
For example, Professor G. P. Scoville of Cornell University
has over a period of years obtained owners' estimates of the
value of their farms in the town of Newfane, New York.[4] He
finds that when a farm in this area is sold to a person of little
or no farm experience, the price paid averages 29 per cent
more than the owner said his farm was worth; but that when
it is sold to a hired man, a tenant, or an owner of a farm,
only 1 per cent more is paid than the owner's estimate of the
value of his farm.

Assuming that an assessor has analyzed sales in his tax district
and thus has a basis for estimating the value of a small percentage of the properties included therein, he has the problem
of assessing the vastly larger percentage which was not sold.
A possible method is to use the previous assessment as a base
and then to change the assessment of these properties to correspond to changes in the assessed value of the properties which
were sold. But this procedure assumes both the accuracy of
the previous assessment and the representative character of the
sales. The evidence of studies of assessment condemns the first
assumption; the statistical requirements for a representative
sample condemn the second.

In the end the assessor must use another method if he
really assesses the property in his district and does not merely
copy the assessment roll. This method is determined by the
nature of the market price of a durable good. It is the present
worth of all future incomes expected from this good. This
present worth is a summation of these expected incomes discounted at a rate of interest on account of their distance in time
from the present. In order to determine the present worth
or rather the present market worth of an item of real property,
the assessor is obliged to compute an estimate from the use
of all relevant material. This process of determining the value
of a house and lot or a farm is a most difficult task. Whatever
care is used, opportunities for error abound.

Perhaps the first of these follows from the nature of capital

4 Unpublished data.

value itself. Capital value is nothing but the market expectation of future incomes to be realized. These expected incomes are then discounted into a present worth. In the nature of things, capital value can be this and nothing else. The buyer of a farm, of a house and lot, of a factory, can have no conceivable reason for expending present dollars to buy these properties, except that over a period of years the incomes to be realized adjusted to a present basis are expected to equal the dollars of outlay required for the purchase.

The argument that some purchases are made for speculative ends does not answer this contention — it merely removes it a step. Such a purchaser expects that the future incomes will be realized, only he does not expect to realize them himself. Instead of waiting for them to materialize he prefers to sell the right to them to some one else.

The expectation which justifies a present capital value, like any other expectation, may be realized or it may not. If the expectation of the assessor finally materializes and thus justifies the capital-value assessment that for many years has been placed on the property, it may be said that although the owner has paid taxes on the basis of an expectation, he has finally realized the expectation and thus has lost nothing. But suppose a property is taxed on a capital value which is based on incomes expected but destined never to be realized. In this instance an injustice is done. The property is taxed for something which never will have any existence.

This type of inequality is present in various degrees everywhere in the assessment of real estate. No matter what kind of property is assessed, some estimates of value — future incomes discounted — will be incorrect and others will be correct. Merest contemplation of the uncertainties of the future indicates that many expectations are bound to go wrong and thus fail to justify present estimates based on them. Errors here — even significant ones — are unavoidable. They follow from the nature of the problem of capitalizing real property.

The capital value basis of assessment not only makes for inequalities in the assessment of real properties of the same kind but it makes for even more serious inequalities between real properties that differ in kind.[5]

5 Commonly, inequalities of this type are said to arise from the application of a uniform rule of taxation to properties which are not homogeneous. Thus in proposals for reform, the emphasis is on variation of the rate of taxation — classification of real property — rather than on assessment.

The problem may be approached from either point of view. But a classification adequate for purposes of the problem must be based ultimately on the income return, or lack of it, of the properties classified. This must ultimately be

Significant among inequalities of this type is that between good and poor farm land. In commenting on the tendency to undervalue good land relatively to poor, or to overvalue poor land relatively to good, Dr. G. F. Warren of Cornell University has remarked: "Agricultural surveys in nearly all the states in the Union show that in prosperous regions, labor incomes, hired men's wages, school-teachers' wages, taxes, tenants' profits, are higher than in poor regions, and that *land prices have not discounted the entire extra productive ability of the land."* [6] Survey records of farming operations in New York offer excellent illustrations of the second division of this generalization, the one relevant for consideration here. For example, a comparison of data from survey records of 2593 farms in 21 poor regions, with data from survey records of 2713 farms in 23 good regions of this state over a ten-year period, 1907 to 1917, showed that an average return of 5.3 per cent was received on capital invested in poor land and one of 7.5 per cent on capital invested in good land.[7] Clearly, the price of the poor land should be lowered or the price of the good land should be raised to equalize the returns from investment in these lands. A more striking illustration is afforded by survey data collected by Professor G. P. Scoville of Cornell University in an exhaustive study of farm income and costs in a fruit region. In a comparison by soil types of the returns from fruit-growing, he found that if a fruit-grower had to choose between paying $286 an acre for 127 acres of good fruit soil or $158 an acre for 109 acres of poor fruit soil, he should buy the good soil and should continue to buy it, whatever the reduction in the price of the poor soil. For in order to make opportunities equal on these soils, the buyer of the poor soil should receive his 109 acres free, and in addition should be given $10,000 in 5-per-cent bonds.[8]

Under a capital value basis of assessment, this overvaluation of poor land relative to good results in its overassessment and

the basis of any accurate assessment of capital value, for capital value is nothing but future incomes discounted into a present worth. The assessment rather than the classification approach also finds justification in the practical reason that it is much more flexible. A classification schedule fixed in the law would be changed but slowly, whatever changes appeared in the underlying economic situation. But assessment is or can be made to be a continuous process.

[6] Warren, G. F., Stencil 3468. Dept. of Agr. Economics and Farm Management, Cornell Univ., Ithaca, N. Y. The italics are added by the writer.

[7] Warren, G. F., Stencil 3467. Dept. of Agr. Economics and Farm Management, Cornell Univ., Ithaca, N. Y.

[8] Scoville, G. P., "The Apple Situation in New York," *Cornell Univ. Ext. Bul.* 172, 1928, p. 10.

therefore in its overtaxation relative to good land.[9] On the basis of present information, it is not possible to establish quantitatively the size of this error. Nevertheless, the proportion of good to poor land in the United States is such that any significant variation between the assessment of these lands means that a large sum of real estate taxes is misplaced.

Another important type of inequality is found in the assessment of real properties of the same present value whose incomes differ in time of receipt. In a discussion of forest taxation, Professor Fred R. Fairchild of Yale University has pointed out that the general property tax absorbs a larger proportion of the capital value of a property with a deferred income than it does of the capital value of a property which yields income currently.[10] He used two properties in his illustration of this fact, one yielding $500 a year in perpetuity, and the other nothing for fourteen years and then $1000 a year in perpetuity. At 5-per-cent interest each of these properties is worth $10,000. Assuming that each is assessed at $10,000, a property tax rate of 1 per cent would absorb 20 per cent of the capital value of the first property and approximately 34 per cent of the capital value of the second property.

This discrimination against properties the incomes of which are deferred is not limited to forest lands. It applies to every orchard not in bearing, to every building constructed ahead of the time of its full use, to every railroad line built for heavier than present traffic, and to some hydro-electric projects. Certainly as between real properties with deferred and real properties with current incomes, the inequalities in the capital value basis of assessment are serious even if the expected incomes on which the assessment is based be fully realized in the future.

Studies of taxation in Arkansas, Missouri, and Virginia suggest another type of inequality in the capital-value basis of assessment, that between rural and urban real estate in respect to the ratio between capitalized income and capital value.

In the Arkansas study it was found that, although the ratio of assessed valuation to estimated valuation is lower for rural than for urban properties, it becomes considerably higher for rural properties than for urban when assessed valuation is compared with capitalized earnings.[11]

[9] Except in the rare instance where the difference is equalized by state aid or shared revenues.

[10] *Bulletin of the National Tax Association,* June, 1926.

[11] Brannen, C. O., "The Farm Tax Problem in Arkansas," *Agr. Exp. Sta. Bul.* 223, p. 26.

In the Missouri study, rural real estate in four Missouri counties is compared over a five-year period with urban real estate in respect to the percentage which the capitalized net rent is of the owner's estimated value.[12] In all years except one this percentage was higher for rural real estate. The five-year average indicated that for each $1000 of owner's estimated value in the country, $457 was justified by the capitalization of net rent, but that for each $1000 of such estimated value in the city, $842 was justified by the capitalization of net rent.

In the Virginia study, it was found that although the percentage of net rent absorbed by taxes was higher for rural than for urban properties, the percentage which taxes were of the value of real estate was less for farm than for city properties.[13] Thus taxes that absorbed 16 per cent of the net rent of city properties were 1.02 per cent of the value of these properties. But taxes that absorbed 20 per cent of the net rent of rural properties were only 0.78 per cent of their value.

Legally, $1000 of real estate valuation is $1000, whether urban or rural, and is assessed as such. However, these Arkansas, Missouri, and Virginia studies suggest that from the point of view of economics $1000 of real estate value in the country may be something other than $1000 of real estate value in the city. If so, the assessment of real estate on a capital-value basis introduces inequality in taxation between urban and rural real estate.

Sometimes the capital-value basis of assessment is productive of another type of inequality than those mentioned. This happens when the capital value represents in part the present worth of a series of income of a non-monetary nature.[14] The writer is informed that certain land belonging to members of a closely knit religious sect in Illinois is valued at $75 an acre more than is land in the same region of equal accessibility to market and of equal productivity. The difference is explained by the capitalization of the non-monetary income from living

[12] Brannen, C. O., and Gromer, S. D., "Taxation of Farms in Missouri," *Agr. Exp. Sta. Bul.* 93, p. 12.

[13] Ballinger, Roy A., and Coombs, Whitney, "Taxes on Farm and Urban Real Estate in Virginia," *Agr. Exp. Sta. Bul.* 268, p. 17.

[14] It may be argued that farm lands are overvalued because of the inclusion of non-monetary elements of sunshine, fresh air, and space, and that, therefore, this is not another type of inequality. The writer, who has lived in the country, finds it difficult to accept this argument. Besides, where sunshine, fresh air, and space are in plenty, it is improbable that they are valued highly. The writer is inclined to believe that the explanation of such overvaluation of rural, relative to urban, real estate as may exist is that rural real estate is farther from the center of the price system, and therefore its price is less subject to the capitalization process.

in this religious brotherhood. Evidently these people are happier or they feel greater assurance of happiness to come by living in a group of their kind. At least, they prefer to, and their demand for their own type of community life is such that they are willing to pay $75 an acre for the privilege. Under capital-value assessment, in effect they are assessed for this privilege and therefore taxed for it.

IF the capital-value basis of assessment is inherently a seriously defective basis for the assessment of real property, what should be done about it? What is the way out? In the writer's mind, only one exit even borders on completeness. This is assessment on the basis of the net rental of the property. By net rental is meant the current annual net market rental. If the property is not leased, this becomes an estimated net rental. It should be clearly understood, too, that by net rental net income is not meant. The concept here expressed is a rental concept, actual or estimated, not a net-income one.

The assessment of real property on the basis of net rental would be much more equitable than on its present basis of capital value — so far as the test of equitable assessment is cor- respondence with the standard of assessment. This is because net rental is much easier to obtain than capital value. Many more properties, both rural and urban, are leased than are sold. Thus a large amount of data would be available for the assessor to use originally or for estimates of the net rental of properties not leased. Moreover, aside from the amount of comparative information available, the problem of estimating the net rental of an item of real property for one year is clearly much simpler and therefore less liable to error than that of estimating its market value. It is easier to foresee income for one year than it is to forecast income for a period of, say, twenty years.

But assessment on the basis of net rental is supported by reasons much weightier than that of correspondence with the assessment standard. Net rental assessment eliminates at once several fundamental types of inequality in the assessment of real property, so far as it is humanly possible to eliminate them.

Thus, in the case of two real properties, of which the ex- pected incomes of one are destined to be realized, those of the other destined to failure, assessment of both properties on a net rental basis equalizes them in both the present and the future. Each is taxed only on what it is worth annually to use. As the annual worth of the one mounts, it is taxed more. As the annual worth of the other declines, it is taxed less.

The overassessment and therefore the overtaxation of poor land relative to good, of real property the income of which is deferred in comparison with real property yielding income, and the possible overassessment and overtaxation of rural real estate relative to urban real estate are all eliminated by the reduction to the present inherent in the net rental concept.

The problem presented by the religious community whose members pay more for their land in order to live in a group, and who, therefore, are taxed more for it, would be mostly solved by assessment on a net rental basis. For it is improbable that the annual rental of any farm within this group would diverge as much from the annual rental of land outside as does its capital value. Payment of a higher than the market rental for the use of real estate not only is a constant reminder of overpayment, but has its own correction in the inability of the average tenant to continue to pay a rental higher than the market for the use of his land. Commonly, such a tenant has little surplus money and must pay his rent from current gains realized in the use of the property rented. The situation of one who buys may be similar if he goes heavily in debt. But if he has sufficient funds to pay for his land outright, he may choose to capitalize non-pecuniary values attaching to it, and thus to pay a higher price than its earnings justify. And he may continue to hold his acres permanently on these terms.

But, a consideration of the merits of assessment on the basis of net rental should not lead to the omission of certain serious problems which this method of assessment raises. No problem in economics or public finance is ever finally solved. A changed adjustment may well bring improvement, but inevitably with this change new problems arise. So it is with the problem of assessment. A change from assessment on the basis of capital value to assessment on the basis of net rental throws into relief certain problems not so evident under a system of capital value assessment.

Perhaps most obvious of these problems is that of the vacant lot for which no rental is being received, because it is useless for gardening and is not yet needed as a building site. Similar to this is the problem of the young forest plantation, and that of the orchard not in bearing. No net rental can be commanded by the orchard or the plantation because no annual income is being received. Like the vacant lot, both are instances of expectation, not of realization, of income. Under the general property tax, the values expected in the future cast their brightness in the present and there is a present worth, a capital value to tax. But under a net rental basis of assessment there can be no assessment, for there is no net rental.

Is the vacant lot, the orchard not in bearing, the growing forest, to remain untaxed until the period of annual income arrives and a tax can be levied on the basis of net rental? In the writer's mind, the answer is "Yes," whatever view of the basis of the property tax is taken. If the general property tax is thought to have its ultimate justification in the principle of ability to pay, then clearly no ability to pay has appeared until net income is realized. Taxes are paid in dollars. Their continuing payment requires a source from which dollars come. Such a source is not found in the unreal substance of hope and expectation, however generously this faith in the future is discounted in the present. If the general property tax is envisioned as ultimately payment for the benefits to property from government services, the answer to the question of current payment is still "Yes." For by no possibility can it be known that any benefit has been received until a net income is realized. However much is spent, this much is a dead loss from the point of view of benefit unless net income is received. Emergence of net income is the acid test of the benefit theory of property taxation as well as of the ability to pay theory.

But suppose no net income is ever to be received, must the property remain untaxed? Clearly, yes. So far as return from the property is concerned, the owner has no ability to pay. Nor has he through his ownership of the property received any benefits from government services. The property yields nothing of net income.

The objection may be made that such a program of taxation would encourage the speculative holding of land. The vacant lot would be vacant longer because of the removal of the heavy burden of annually recurring taxes. The prospective subdivision would remain bare of apartment houses longer. The owner of a tract of forest land near a city would be glad to have his acres tax exempt while waiting for the value of his land to rise. Without introducing an argument on the question whether taxes have anything to do with holding land out of use, it may be said that if such is recognized to be a problem, it can easily be remedied by introducing a steep transfer tax on the profits realized from the sale of land on which no annual taxes have been paid. Thus any speculator who deliberately held his land out of use for purposes of reaping a profit on it would find his incentive to make this profit lessened by the tax in as great a degree as seemed desirable.

Probably the percentage of property without a market rental would be small in most tax districts and therefore the exemption from taxation of such properties would raise no serious problems of revenue. But in some tax districts, especially in poor farming regions, the problem of revenue raised by the exemption of property yielding no market rental would be serious. At present such property is taxed because it has a capital value. In many instances it is taxed and the taxes continue to be paid after abandonment — at least this is true in the poor hill regions of New York State. But a shift of the assessment basis to net rental would disclose that many such properties have no net rental and that those which have yield such a small rental that the total of taxes collected from them is less than would be collected with the assessment based on capital value.

Another problem arises out of this one. Because the general property tax is the chief source of local revenues and thus is levied on an expenditure basis, the removal of any properties from the tax list or the lightening of their tax payments automatically throws the tax load borne by them on other properties. In a poor area, the adoption of net rental assessment might well result in a crushing load of taxation being put on those properties which yield a net rental.

What can be done about the problem of revenue? One suggestion is that units of local government in such an area be consolidated into a unit of efficient size. There is merit in this proposal. Many units of local government are so small that they should be classed as luxuries rather than as political necessities. Certainly a poor area cannot afford to indulge in the extravagant inefficiency of too small units of local government. Where such a consolidation, whatever its efficiency from the point of view of administration, results merely in a union of poverty, then the question whether settlement and therefore government, should continue in this area or whether it should be abandoned, planted to trees, or else used for some other purpose, should be faced frankly.

Be it noted that this question, hard as it is to answer, is not peculiar to assessment on the basis of net rental with its corollary of no assessment where there is no rental. The present capital-value basis of assessment merely avoids this issue by being productive of greater revenue — it does not answer it. But the costs of maintaining government in such a section go on just the same. The money to pay taxes levied on a capital-value assessment must come from somewhere. Even if it is obtained by working in town, from funds sent by children away from home, or by paring living expenditures to the veriest minimum, it is still a cost from a social point of view which cannot be disregarded. Government is being kept up in a region unable to support one and it is being kept up by certain persons. The real questions are: Should it be kept up at all; and if so, who should pay for it, those who pay for it now, or society as represented by the state?

Another problem is the effect of the basis of assessment on the continuance of farming operations on submarginal land. The capital-value basis of assessment, by overtaxing poor land, operates to encourage abandonment of such land. The net rental basis, by exempting it from taxation, operates to prolong or to arrest the process of abandonment. From the point of view of hastening an inevitable and painful process, should not the capital-value of assessment be used as a weapon to this end? Clearly the end should be hastened. The matter for questioning is the means.

There are two serious arguments against overtaxing property in order to compel its abandonment. One is that it is not a very effective way to deal with a complicated social problem. Submarginal lands in poor hill regions of New York State have been subjected to the surgery of the capital-value basis of assessment, but a vast total of these lands awaits abandonment in spite of the fact that the process of abandonment has been going on for many years. The other and more important objection is purely on the ground of ethics. It is extremely doubtful whether the state should deliberately perform an injustice in order to accomplish an end, however desirable. Certainly one of the reasons for the existence of the state is the establishment of justice. For the state by its own acts to deny this, even for desirable ends, is a contradiction in terms. Moreover, once the principle that the end justifies the means is adopted, there is no stopping-place.

By refusing to perform an injustice in order to accomplish a worthy end, the state is by no means precluded from using other means. Studies could be made of the possibilities of such areas for purposes other than farming. Facts from these studies could be widely disseminated. Also the state itself might buy the land and initiate the undertaking. By election in 1931, the voters of New York State gave a mandate to the legislature to issue bonds for $20,000,000 to be spent over a period of years in reforesting these poor lands. At least this is true — there are better and more humane means of evacuating such areas for general farming purposes than the clumsy and cruel process of overtaxation.

8. What Should a Permanent State Tax Commission Do?

In the following discussion Professor Lutz sets forth succinctly his opinions concerning the proper objectives of a permanent state tax commission.*

Before undertaking to say what a state tax commission should do, it would be well, perhaps, to say what it is and why it is. The state tax commission is the administrative organization that has appeared in a number of states for the supervision and direction of the state and local revenue system. It is the final product of a long process of evolution in American tax administration, during the course of which were produced local and district boards of equalization, the state board of equalization, and the state board of assessment. Not all of the states have state tax commissions, for the course of evolution has been delayed or sidetracked by various factors in the field of public administration as in other fields. Some of the mountain states, for example, embedded in their constitutions a provision for state boards of equalization composed of elective state officials acting in an *ex officio* capacity, while in California the movement was diverted by the constitutional changes of 1910, whereby a revenue system was introduced which appeared, at the time, to render a state tax commission unnecessary.

STATE TAX COMMISSION A GOOD ADMINISTRATIVE DEVICE

The principal reason why a competent state tax commission is a good administrative device for any state is that no revenue system, however fool-proof it may appear, is really self-executing. As long as taxes must be paid, it will be necessary to provide some sort of administrative organization to see that they are properly and equitably exacted. It is not so important that the head and center of this administrative organization be called a "state tax commission" or by any other specific name or title, as it is that its powers and duties should be properly determined and that it be provided with the necessary facilities for the discharge of these duties. By any other name a rose would smell as sweet, and its thorns would be as sharp.

The first of the modern state tax commissions appeared in Indiana in 1891. At the present time they are to be found

* From H. L. Lutz, "What Should a Permanent State Tax Commission Do?", *The Tax Digest*, Vol. VI, No. 3, pp. 80-83.

in more than thirty states. Not all of these states have observed in the same degree the conditions which will be outlined below for the attainment of the best results in tax administration but sufficent progress has been made here and there to indicate what may reasonably be expected if a state should really set out to secure a highly competent and highly intelligent administration of its financial system. The outline of a tax commission's powers and duties which is given here does not exactly conform to the situation in any one state. It is, rather, a composite picture, based for the greater part on actual results, but extending beyond existing practices at certain points — the points at which the writer believes still greater achievements to be possible for the tax commission which will approach its task with adequate vision and courage.

COMMISSION SHOULD SUPERVISE STATE AND LOCAL REVENUE SYSTEM

THE most important duty of the state tax commission is the administration and supervision of the state and local revenue system. No matter how we feel about it, the agencies of government must be provided with the necessary funds, and the first obligation of the administrative authorities is to see that these funds are obtained through a vigorous and impartial application of the tax laws. If these laws are inequitable, the tax commission may and should exert great influence in securing improvements through the study and recommendations referred to below. It is not, however, the agency to modify the laws, and its first duty is the enforcement of such tax laws as may be provided. This duty does not end with the administration of the revenue laws that may be provided for state purposes, even in the event that a state has undertaken to apply a system of separation of the sources of state and local revenues. The citizens of the state have a right to the assurance that they are being taxed, for local as well as for state purposes, with due regard to the equitable application of the tax laws. Every state, whether it has adopted separation of sources or not, is under the obligation to give them this assurance, and the only way by which this obligation can be adequately discharged is through a supervision and control of the process of local assessment. Supervision of the local assessment procedure should include: (1) power to instruct and direct the assessors as to their duties under the law; (2) power to review and equalize the assessments, and to this end to develop an adequate technique for the purpose of checking and testing the quality of the assessments; (3) power to suspend or remove recalcitrant or incompetent assessors.

It is often urged that this line of argument runs counter to the doctrine of "home rule" or "local self-government," or whatever we may call the idea that counties, or cities, or townships, or other local units should be in a large degree autonomous, *i.e.,* free from higher administrative control. Perhaps it does; but in reply it may be said that the doctrine of home rule does not really afford the escape from administrative dominion that some of its advocates believe it to do. It merely transfers the center of power from the state to some arbitrarily determined local unit within which the citizen remains subject to as much administrative domination as before. The assumption of the home rule doctrine is that there is some ideally perfect or proper local governmental unit, which is better for the purpose of administrative control than the state. Usually this is the city, but there is no *a priori* case in favor of the city. Cities are divided into wards, and the wards into voting precincts. Why subject one ward or voting precinct to the control of another? Why not permit home rule of the wards or precincts? Indeed, why not permit each block of the city to govern itself? There is no logical stopping place to "home rule" short of complete individual freedom, which means anarchy, or a denial of all governmental powers. The truth is that all grades of municipal corporations are matters of convenience, and may be set up, changed, or abolished as best suits the convenience of the state. While it may prove convenient to delegate certain tax powers and responsibilities to local subdivisions, it is nothing less than a shirking of responsibility for the state to decline to exercise a certain administrative and supervisory control over the operation of the entire tax system. Such supervision and control becomes the first and most important task of the state tax commission.

Various other duties are related to this primary obligation. The commission should naturally be in charge of the administration of all taxes. It would be responsible for the assessment of railroad and other public utility property, or for the administration of such other taxes as might be imposed on these classes of concerns in lieu of property taxes. The same would be true of the taxes imposed on banks, insurance companies, franchises, and similar exactions, and of those levied on transfers of property at death. In general it may be said that the state tax commission is the logical administrative authority for the control and direction of the entire taxing system, and that it would require a strong case to justify the transfer of responsibility for the assessment and collection of a tax to some other state official or agency.

It follows from this that the tax commission should not be burdened with other duties that are foreign to the field of taxation. This is short-sighted economy, for it simply means a diversion and distribution of the energies of the tax commission with a resultant loss of power all along the line. The efficient and equitable administration of the entire taxing system of almost any one of the American states is a task of sufficient magnitude to demand the full strength and energy of any commission of three or five men, and the state which attempts to economize by loading up its tax commission with various miscellaneous and unrelated duties is simply inviting disaster in the field of tax administration.

RESEARCH IS A FUNCTION OF COMMISSION

A SECOND important function of the state tax commission is that of research. It should conduct a continuous study of the effect of the state and local taxation system and of various other matters pertaining to the operation of governmental agencies. A vigorous commission of men equipped with the proper intelligence and resources could conduct fruitful research not merely into the operation of the tax system, but as well into public expenditures, which are the cause of taxation. Most state tax commissions have done but little on the side of public expenditures, and the taxpayers' associations that have appeared in a number of states are undertaking to supply this deficiency. Had the conditions which have been outlined in this paper been operative in California in recent years, there would have been little occasion for San Francisco and other cities to spend large sums in hiring an independent appraisal of real property as a means of checking up on the work of the local assessor. The state tax commission has the obligation to do this, year by year, and it should have the power to compel compliance with its instructions and findings.

RECOMMENDATIONS FOR IMPROVEMENT OF FISCAL SYSTEM

A THIRD function of the state tax commission is to formulate recommendations for the improvement of the fiscal system. While the Governor and the Legislature are primarily responsible for the determination of the public policy of the state in matters of taxation as in other fields, neither the Governor nor the Legislature can be expected to have as intimate knowledge of the needs of the tax situation as the tax commission, and their recommendations should have a careful hearing when taxation problems are being considered.

EDUCATING AND INFORMING THE PEOPLE

A FINAL responsibility of the commission is that of educating and informing the people in matters of taxation. This will be done in part through the publication of an annual or biennial report in which the tax system and tax problems should be discussed in a scientific but readable style, and in which such statistics as are compiled are interpreted so that they may be seen in their proper significance. The character of the report issued by any public officer is a fair measure of the calibre of the man and a fair index of the adequacy of his equipment for the proper administration of the office. Some officials of intelligence and vision are badly handicapped by niggardly provision of staff and equipment, while others of low intelligence are surrounded by equipment which they cannot direct effectively. Given adequate facilities, the report of stewardship becomes a fair test of capacity.

The tax commission's educational work does not stop, however, with the preparation of a periodical report. By means of bulletins, press releases, addresses, conferences and other methods of establishing contact with the taxpayers the educational work will go on. Since the commission will have better means than any other agency in the state for acquiring correct information regarding the tax system and the tax problems, it should be more active than any other agency in disseminating a correct knowledge and understanding of this system.

PERSONNEL AND EQUIPMENT OF A STATE TAX COMMISSION

A WORD should be said regarding the personnel and equipment of a state tax commission. The writer favors a commission of not more than three men, with the terms of office so arranged that there will not ordinarily be more than one new man on the commission at any time. One great disadvantage of a single tax commissioner is the loss of cumulated experience when changes are made. Members of the tax commission should be appointed by the Governor and should be removable by him for cause.

The most important thing about the tax commissioners is the question of their qualifications. The one and only basis of appointment should be fitness for the position. The tax commission should never be considered a political haven, and party services or party obligations should never be permitted to influence these appointments. As much will be claimed by many persons for the particular department of government in which they happen to be interested. But the administration of taxes calls for peculiar qualities of impartiality and fairness. Taxes must be paid by the just and the unjust, by party friend and party foe, by Republicans and Democrats and Socialists alike. The man who accepts appointment as a tax commissioner on a basis of partisanship can hardly avoid some sense of obligation to the interests that secured his appointment, and thus the door is insensibly opened to serious abuse and discriminations.

QUALITIES OF A GOOD TAX COMMISSIONER

AMONG the qualities that indicate fitness for such a position, the first would evidently be knowledge of the taxation system and of the principles of taxation in general. High general intelligence will go far to make up for deficiencies in technical knowledge, and will assure a speedy acquisition of the latter under the pressure of necessity. In addition, certain moral qualifications are indispensable. The tax commissioner must be unimpeachably honest and utterly fearless. He should be judicial in temperament, and strongly endowed with common sense. This may read like a picture of the ideal man, but it would be difficult to exaggerate the importance of these qualities in the men to whom is entrusted the task of determining finally the burden of taxes to be imposed on the several citizens of the state. Whatever shortcomings we may tolerate in ourselves or our friends or some of our public officials, we cannot be too scrupulous about the high quality of the men who are to wield the tremendous power of taxation.

It may be said that such a standard as this is an argument against a tax commission. But those who think thus should recall that the power of taxation is being exercised, and will continue to be exercised, whether we improve its administration or not. The question is whether to let Tom, Dick, or Harry continue in control or to select some of the highest grade men in the community and give them greater powers and responsibilities in this field.

How shall such persons be secured? The most important conditions are adequate compensation and stable tenure of office. A high salary does not eliminate the unfit, but it does make possible the attraction of enough properly qualified persons to serve the state without resorting to the incompetent, since the latter are willing to hold office at a low salary if more cannot be obtained. But a high salary alone is not sufficient. There must be a fairly long tenure of office, and no prejudice against reappointment, if satisfactory service has been rendered. By a long tenure is meant at least six years, and it would not be improper to consider terms of eight or ten years for state tax commissioners. As long as the Governor has the power of removal for cause the clearly incompetent incumbents can be weeded out, and since the office is never to be regarded as one of the plums of political victory, such exercise of the executive authority should occur only to preserve or improve the quality of the commission.

In addition to adequate compensation, stable tenure, and freedom from the distracting influences of partisan strife, the tax commission requires adequate support in the way of office staff and equipment. Stingy appropriations for such purposes mean saving at the spigot, and wasting at the bung. The tax commission must have the facilities for collecting, analyzing, and digesting the information necessary to a proper administration of the tax system, or its appointment will have been in vain.

It is not contended that the establishment of a state tax commission under the conditions that are here presented will make taxpaying a painless process. It will not cause the people to welcome the tax-gatherer with flowers, nor to commemorate his deeds with a memorial statue. It can fairly be said, however, that the intelligent and impartial administration of the tax system of any state by a high grade tax commission will measurably promote the equitable distribution of the tax burden, and the man who materially contributes to this great end needs no other monument.

QUESTIONS AND PROBLEMS FOR DISCUSSION

1. What is meant by the statement that the question of a balanced budget is ultimately an accounting problem?
2. What is needed in order to establish a technique of expenditure control?
3. Why is it difficult to create an environment which will permit of the efficient and economical functioning of government?
4. What are the advantages and disadvantages of state limitations upon local indebtedness?
5. What may be done to lessen the evils resulting from tax delinquency? Is the problem largely one of financial administration?
6. "Poor assessment of property is due in part to the existence of too many small political units." Explain.
7. City A chooses a council by popular election. The council in

turn appoints a city assessor. What is your opinion of this method of selecting an assessor? Can you suggest a better method?

8. An assessor by order of the city council in City A places a very low valuation on the industrial and business properties in his district in order to encourage their development. Can such a practice be justified?

SUGGESTIONS FOR RESEARCH

1. Centralization of the assessment and collection of taxes.
2. The work of a state tax commission in some particular state.
3. An evaluation of methods of controlling local expenditures.
4. A study of the efforts to control state and local expenditures in some particular state.
5. The problem of tax delinquency.

BIBLIOGRAPHICAL NOTE

Many excellent discussions of control of public expenditures in various commonwealths of the United States appear in the *Proceedings of the National Tax Association,* (1931). Here one will find a mine of information on the developments of this phase of fiscal administration. The following articles are recommended: A. J. Maxwell, "North Carolina's Plan of Consolidation, Retrenchment and Control of Expenditures"; R. A. Vandegrift, "Control of State Expenditures through Budgeting and Budgetary Procedure"; R. F. Asplund, "Local Expenditure Control through Uniform Budgets and Accounts"; C. M. Brown, "The Function of Taxpayers' Association in Expenditure Control"; Harry Miesse, "The Function of an Association of Taxpayers in Connection with the Control of Public Expenses"; and M. L. Wallerstein, "Viewpoint of the Local Official toward Expenditure Control." A discussion of the general aspects of the problem is Mark Graves, "State Expenditure Control," *Proceedings of the National Tax Association,* (1932), pp. 144-150. A useful study which presents a discussion of "restraints upon budget distribution" in seven selected cities of the United States is Mabel L. Walker, *Municipal Finance,* (Baltimore, 1930), Chap. VII. For a discussion of federal budgetary practice during the early years of President Franklin D. Roosevelt's administration, see J. Wilmer Sundelson, "Emergency Budget of the United States," *American Economic Review,* Vol. XXIV, pp. 53-66.

Various aspects of the problem of control of local indebtedness are dealt with in Horace Secrist, "Constitutional Restrictions on Municipal Debt," *Journal of Political Economy,* Vol. XXII, pp. 368-383; L. W. Lancaster, *State Supervision of Municipal Indebtedness,* (Philadelphia, 1923); F. L. Spangler, "Operation of Debt and Tax Rate Limits in the State of New York," *New York State Tax Commission,* Special Report No. 5, (Albany, 1932); and H. L. Lutz, *Public Finance,* (New York, 1929), pp. 684-689. As a part of his treatment of restriction of local debt, Professor Lutz offers suggestive provisions of a model local debt statute.

Relating to the assessment of farm property for taxation, L. B. Krueger gives a lucid discussion of "The Classification of Farm Lands for Assessment Purposes in Wisconsin," *Journal of Land and Public Utility Economics,* (May, 1932). P. H. Cornick deals with the "Assessment of Property for Taxation" in municipalities, in A. E. Buck, *Municipal Finance,* (New York, 1930), Chap. XI. Two additional studies which present valuable material on the assessment of property are J. E. Brindley and G. S. M. Zorbaugh, "The Tax System of Iowa," *Iowa State College Extension Bulletin,* No. 150, (Ames, Iowa, 1929); and R. W. Nelson and G. W. Mitchell, *Assessment of Real Estate in Iowa and Other Mid-Western States,* (University of Iowa Study, Iowa City, 1931). S. E. Leland lists devices for more effective administration of taxation of intangible property in *The Classified Property Tax in the United States,* (Boston, 1928), p. 146. A comprehensive study of "state control over the assessment of property" is H. L. Lutz, *The State Tax Commission,* (Cambridge, 1918).

A useful survey of the methods of property tax collection in the United States is M. S. Kendrick, "The Collection of General Property Taxes in Towns, Townships and Counties in the United States," *National Tax Association Bulletin,* Vol. XIV, (October, 1928), pp. 8-14. Definite suggestions for the correction of the existing evils of modern tax assessment and collection are offered by John A. Zangerle in his "Modern Tax Assessing and Collecting Administration," *Bulletin of the National Tax Association,* Vol. XI, June 1926, pp. 275-281.

A critical treatment of the general problem of property assessment and tax collection is given in J. P. Jensen, *Property Taxation in the United States,* (Chicago, 1931), Chaps. XIII-XIX.

For discussions of the problems of tax delinquency, see C. H. Chatters, "How Cities Collect Delinquent Taxes : A Summary of Actual Methods and Suggested Procedure," *Minnesota Municipalities,* Dec. 1932 ; M. H. Hunter, "Legal Provisions Affecting Real Estate Tax Delinquency, Tax Sales, and Redemption," *University of Illinois Bulletin,* Vol. XXX, No. 42, June 27, 1933 ; F. R. Fairchild, "The Problem of Tax Delinquency," *American Economic Review,* Vol. XXIV, No. 1, Supplement, pp. 140-150 ; Herbert D. Simpson, "Tax Delinquency, Economic Aspects," *Illinois Law Review,* June, 1933 ; and papers in the *Proceedings of the National Tax Association,* 1933.

INDEX

A

Ability, income as a measure of, 462-465
vs. benefit, 190-192
Adams, H. C., on theory of public credit, 691-693
Adams, T. S., on double taxation, 639-645
on separation of state and local revenues, 645-651
on tax-exempt securities, 795-800
Administration, financial, 847-952
Administrative charges, 109, 135-141
Assessment of real property, 931-945
Assessor, duties and qualifications of, 931-935

B

Banks, taxation of, 547-554
Bastable, C. F., cited, 38-39, 178 note, 220
on theory of public credit, 684-687
Benefit theory of taxation, 190
Benefits and burdens of public expenditures, 14-26
Bielschowsky, Georg, on business fluctuations and public works, 44-67
Blakey, R. G., on bonds and taxes in war finance, 716-736
on simplification of Federal income tax, 432-450
on Revenue Act of 1932, 416 note
Bonds in war finance, 716-726
tax-exempt, 795-800
Borrowing, when legitimate, 710
vs. pay-as-you-go in highway finance, 625-627
Bowley, A. L., cited, 45, 50-51, 57
Brown, H. G., on burdens of war finance, 733-737
on currency depreciation and war finance, 726-732
on increment taxation, 362-367
Budget, contents of, 863-865
essentials of, 860-863
expenditure data needed, 865-873
nature and functions of, 859-877
when balanced, 880-883
Bullock, C. J., translation of Wagner's socio-political theory, 178-181

Burden

Burden of public expenditures, 14-26
of state income tax, 428-429
of taxation, in various countries, 22
of taxation, its distribution, 181-194
Burnstan, A. R., on special assessments, 151-172
Business cycles and public expenditures, 44-84
Business corporations, taxation of, 443-445, 451, 488-491, 531-547
enterprises, taxation of, 523-531
Bye, R. T., on increment tax, 360-362

C

California tax research bureau, on tax and debt limitation measures, 906-921
Canning, J. B., on income concept for taxation purposes, 450-459
Canons of taxation, 227-231
Capital gains, taxation of, 434-440, 460-462, 488
Capital levy and changes in price level, 608-611
and war debt, 825-844
Capital outlays, borrowing for, 711-715
Carver, T. N., on minimum sacrifice theory of taxation, 214-227
on single tax, 330-332
Cassel, Gustav, cited, 47
Character of public expenditures and economic effects, 39-44
Clarification of terms relating to shifting and incidence, 234-246
Clark, J. M., cited, 73
Classification of public revenues, 103-112
Classified property tax, 300, 303
status in United States, 303-327
Colorado plan of tax and debt limitation, 908
Colwyn committee report, Snavely's discussion of, 468-487
Commodities, taxation of, 573-593
incidence of taxes on, 261-266
Control of public expenditures, 883-906
Conversion of public debts, 823-825
Corporations, taxation of, 443-445, 451, 488-491
taxes, development and forms of, 531-547
Costs of war, incidence, 740-766